McGRAW-HILL YEARBOOK OF
Science &
Technology

2001

McGRAW-HILL YEARBOOK OF
Science &
Technology

2001

**Comprehensive coverage of recent events and research as compiled by
the staff of the McGraw-Hill Encyclopedia of Science & Technology**

McGraw-Hill
New York   San Francisco   Washington, D.C.   Auckland   Bogotá   Caracas   Lisbon   London   Madrid
Mexico City   Milan   Montreal   New Delhi   San Juan   Singapore   Sydney   Tokyo   Toronto

Library of Congress Cataloging in Publication data

McGraw-Hill yearbook of science and technology.
1962–   . New York, McGraw-Hill Book Co.

———— v. illus. 26 cm.
Vols. for 1962–   compiled by the staff of the
McGraw-Hill encyclopedia of science and technology.
    1. Science—Yearbooks.   2. Technology—
Yearbooks.   1. McGraw-Hill encyclopedia of
science and technology.
Q1.M13   505.8   62-12028

ISBN 0-07-135867-6
ISSN 0076-2016

McGraw-Hill

A Division of The McGraw·Hill Companies

1 2 3 4 5 6 7 8 9 0   DOW/DOW   0 6 5 4 3 2 1 0

This book was printed on acid-free paper.

*It was set in Garamond Book and Neue Helvetica Black Condensed by
TechBooks, Fairfax, Virginia. The art was prepared by TechBooks.
The book was printed and bound by R. R. Donnelley & Sons Company,
The Lakeside Press.*

Contents

Roger Kasunic, Director of Editing, Design, and Production

Joe Faulk, Editing Manager

Frank Kotowski, Jr., Senior Editing Supervisor

Ron Lane, Art Director

Thomas G. Kowalczyk, Production Manager

Dr. Milton B. Adesnik. *Department of Cell Biology, New York University School of Medicine, New York.* CELL BIOLOGY.

Prof. Eugene A. Avallone. *Consulting Engineer; Professor Emeritus of Mechanical Engineering, City College of the City University of New York.* MECHANICAL AND POWER ENGINEERING.

A. E. Bailey. *Formerly, Superintendent of Electrical Science, National Physical Laboratory, London, England.* ELECTRICITY AND ELECTROMAGNETISM.

Prof. William P. Banks. *Chairman, Department of Psychology, Pomona College, Claremont, California.* PHYSIOLOGICAL AND EXPERIMENTAL PSYCHOLOGY.

Prof. Gregory C. Beroza. *Department of Geophysics, Stanford University, California.* GEOPHYSICS.

Dr. Eugene W. Bierly. *American Geophysical Union, Washington, D.C.* METEOROLOGY AND CLIMATOLOGY.

Prof. Carrol Bingham. *Department of Physics, University of Tennessee, Knoxville.* NUCLEAR AND ELEMENTARY PARTICLE PHYSICS.

Dr. Chaim Braun. *Altos Management Consultants Inc., Los Altos, California.* NUCLEAR ENGINEERING.

Dr. Melbourne Briscoe. *Ocean, Atmosphere, and Space and Technology, Office of Naval Research, Arlington, Virginia.* OCEANOGRAPHY.

Robert D. Briskman. *President, CD Radio, Inc., Washington, D.C.* TELECOMMUNICATIONS.

Dr. John F. Clark. *Director, Graduate Studies, and Professor, Space Systems, Spaceport Graduate Center, Florida Institute of Technology, Satellite Beach.* SPACE TECHNOLOGY.

Prof. David L. Cowan. *Chairman, Department of Physics and Astronomy, University of Missouri, Columbia.* CLASSICAL MECHANICS AND HEAT.

Prof. Ron Darby. *Department of Chemical Engineering, Texas A&M University, College Station.* CHEMICAL ENGINEERING.

Prof. Turgay Ertekin. *Chairman, Department of Petroleum and Natural Gas Engineering, Pennsylvania State University, University Park.* PETROLEUM ENGINEERING.

Prof. Altan M. Ferendeci. *Department of Electrical and Computer Engineering and Computer Science, University of Cincinnati, Ohio.* PHYSICAL ELECTRONICS.

Barry A. J. Fisher. *Director, Scientific Services Bureau, Los Angeles County Sheriff's Department, Los Angeles, California.* FORESIC SCIENCE AND TECHNOLOGY.

Peter A. Gale. *Chief Naval Architect, John J. McMullen Associates, Inc., Arlington, Virginia.* NAVAL ARCHITECTURE AND MARINE ENGINEERING.

Dr. John Gordon. *School of Forestry and the Environment, Yale University, New Haven, Connecticut.* FORESTRY.

Dr. Richard L. Greenspan. *The Charles Stark Draper Laboratory, Cambridge, Massachusetts.* NAVIGATION.

Prof. Terry Harrison. *Department of Anthropology, Paleoanthropology Laboratory, New York University, New York.* ANTHROPOLOGY AND ARCHEOLOGY.

Dr. Ralph E. Hoffman. *Associate Professor, Yale Psychiatric Institute, Yale University School of Medicine, New Haven, Connecticut.* PSYCHIATRY.

Dr. S. C. Jong. *Senior Staff Scientist and Program Director, Mycology and Protistology Program, American Type Culture Collection, Manassas, Virginia.* MYCOLOGY.

Dr. Peter M. Kareiva. *Department of Zoology, University of Washington, Seattle.* ECOLOGY AND CONSERVATION.

Prof. Gabriel Karpouzian. *Aerospace Engineering Department, U.S. Naval Academy, Annapolis, Maryland.* AEROSPACE ENGINEERING AND PROPULSION.

Prof. Robert E. Knowlton. *Department of Biological Sciences, George Washington University, Washington, DC.* INVERTEBRATE ZOOLOGY.

Prof. Konrad B. Krauskopf. *School of Earth Sciences, Stanford University, California.* GEOCHEMISTRY.

Dr. Thomas Lessie. *University of Massachusetts, Amherst.* MICROBIOLOGY.

Prof. Trevor Letcher. *University of Natal, School of Pure and Applied Chemistry, Durban, South Africa.* THERMODYNAMICS.

Dr. Philip V. Lopresti. *Retired; formerly, Engineering Research Center, AT&T Bell Laboratories, Princeton, New Jersey.* ELECTRONIC CIRCUITS.

Prof. Scott M. McLennan. *Department of Geosciences, State University of New York at Stony Brook.* GEOLOGY (PHYSICAL, HISTORICAL, AND SEDIMENTARY).

Dr. Ramon A. Mata-Toledo. *Associate Professor of Computer Science, James Madison University, Harrisonburg, Virginia.* COMPUTERS.

Dr. Henry F. Mayland. *Soil Scientist, Northwest Irrigation and Soils Research Laboratory, USDA-ARS, Kimberly, Idaho.* SOILS.

Prof. Arnold I. Miller. *Department of Geology, University of Cincinnati, Ohio.* INVERTEBRATE PALEONTOLOGY.

Dr. Orlando J. Miller. *Center for Molecular Medicine and Genetics, Wayne State University School of Medicine, Detroit, Michigan.* GENETICS AND EVOLUTION.

Prof. Jay M. Pasachoff. *Director, Hopkins Observatory, Williams College, Williamstown, Massachusetts.* ASTRONOMY.

Prof. David J. Pegg. *Department of Physics, University of Tennessee, Knoxville.* ATOMIC, MOLECULAR, AND NUCLEAR PHYSICS.

Dr. William C. Peters. *Professor Emeritus, Mining and Geological Engineering, University of Arizona, Tucson.* MINING ENGINEERING.

Prof. Allan D. Pierce. *Professor and Chairman, Department of Aerospace and Mechanical Engineering, Boston University, Massachusetts.* ACOUSTICS.

Prof. Arthur N. Popper. *Department of Biology, University of Maryland, College Park.* NEUROSCIENCE.

Dr. Kenneth P. H. Pritzker. *Pathologist-in-Chief and Director, Head, Connective Tissue Research Group, and Professor, Laboratory Medicine and Pathobiology, University of Toronto, Mount Sinai Hospital, Toronto, Ontario, Canada.* MEDICINE AND PATHOLOGY.

Dr. Donald R. Prothero. *Associate Professor of Geology, Occidental College, Los Angeles, California.* VERTEBRATE PALEONTOLOGY.

Prof. Krishna Rajan. *Materials Engineering Department, Rensselaer Polytechnic Institute, Troy, New York.* MATERIALS SCIENCE AND ENGINEERING AND METALLURGICAL ENGINEERING.

Dr. A. P. Russell. *Professor and Head, Department of Biological Sciences, University of Calgary, Alberta, Canada.* ANIMAL SYSTEMATICS.

Dr. Andrew P. Sage. *Founding Dean Emeritus and First American Bank Professor, University Professor, School of Information Technology and Engineering, George Mason University, Fairfax, Virginia.* CONTROL AND INFORMATION SYSTEMS.

Dr. Stanley Seltzer. *Chemistry Department, Brookhaven National Laboratory, Upton, New York.* ORGANIC CHEMISTRY.

Dr. Stephen E. Scheckler. *Associate Professor of Biology and Geological Sciences and Curator of Paleobiology, Department of Biology, Virginia Polytechnic Institute and State University, Blacksburg.* PALEOBOTANY.

Prof. Arthur A. Spector. *Department of Biochemistry, University of Iowa, Iowa City.* BIOCHEMISTRY.

Dr. Norman Sutin. *Chemistry Department, Brookhaven National Laboratory, Upton, New York.* INORGANIC CHEMISTRY.

Dr. Arthur A. Teixeira. *Professor of Food Engineering, Agricultural and Biological Engineering Department, Institute of Food and Agricultural Sciences, University of Florida, Gainesville.* FOOD ENGINEERING.

Dr. Shirley Turner. *U.S. Department of Commerce, National Institute of Standards and Technology, Gaithersburg, Maryland.* MINERALOGY.

Dr. Calvin H. Ward. *Department of Environmental Science and Engineering, Rice University, Houston, Texas.* ENVIRONMENTAL SCIENCE AND ENGINEERING.

Dr. Ralph E. Weston, Jr. *Department of Chemistry, Brookhaven National Laboratory, Upton, New York.* PHYSICAL CHEMISTRY.

Prof. Frank M. White. *Department of Mechanical Engineering, University of Rhode Island, Kingston.* FLUID MECHANICS.

Prof. Thomas A. Wikle. *Head, Department of Geography, Oklahoma State University, Stillwater.* PHYSICAL GEOGRAPHY.

Prof. W. A. Williams. *Department of Agronomy and Range Science, University of California, Davis.* AGRICULTURE.

The 2001 *McGraw-Hill Yearbook of Science & Technology* provides the reader with a wide overview of important recent developments in science, technology, and engineering, as selected by our distinguished board of consulting editors. At the same time, it satisfies the reader's need to stay informed about important trends in research and development that will fundamentally influence future understanding and practical applications of knowledge in fields ranging from astronomy to zoology. Readers of the *McGraw-Hill Encyclopedia of Science & Technology* will find the *Yearbook* to be a valuable companion publication, enhancing the timeliness and depth of the *Encyclopedia*.

Each contribution to the *Yearbook* is a concise yet authoritative article authored by one or more specialists in the field. We are pleased that noted researchers have been supporting the *Yearbook* since its first edition in 1962 by taking time to share their knowledge with our readers. The topics are selected by our consulting editors in conjunction with our editorial staff based on present significance and potential applications. McGraw-Hill strives to make each article as readily understandable as possible for the nonspecialist reader through careful editing and the extensive use of graphics, much of which is prepared specially for the *Yearbook*.

Librarians, students, teachers, the scientific community, journalists and writers, and the general public continue to find in the *McGraw-Hill Yearbook of Science & Technology* the information they need in order to follow the rapid pace of advances in science and technology and to understand the developments in these fields that will shape the world of the twenty-first century.

Mark D. Licker

PUBLISHER

Acoela

Acoelomates are triploblastic animals that lack an internal body cavity. Included in this group are the Acoela (acoel flatworms), which represent the earliest extant bilaterian metazoans holding a key position between the radially symmetrical animals and the more complex bilateral animals.

Bilateria include organisms characterized by bilateral symmetry, in contrast to the Radiata, which have radial symmetry. The essential feature of bilateral symmetry is that a section along the sagittal plane divides the body into right and left halves which are mirror images of each other (**Fig. 1**). Bilateria also have differentiated dorsal and ventral surfaces, and anterior and posterior ends. The ventral surface becomes locomotory, and the anterior end differentiates into a head, where the sensory equipment is concentrated. This allows the organism to adopt a unidirectional locomotion, in contrast to the nondirectional locomotion of the Radiata.

Another characteristic feature of Bilateria is their triploblastic level of organization, that is, the presence of a third embryonic layer, the mesoderm. For this reason, bilaterians are also called triploblasts.

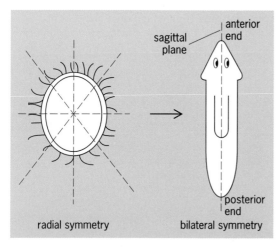

Fig. 1. Bilateral symmetry, in which only a section along the sagittal plane divides the body into two symmetrically identical halves.

Radiata are diploblasts, having only two embryonic germ layers. The internal cell layer (endoderm) forms the digestive cavity, while the external layer (ectoderm) gives rise to the epidermis and to nerve cells. The mesoderm, which lies between the other two, differentiates into many of the internal organs and the lining of the coelom, a fluid-filled compartment of variable size. The mesoderm has been correlated with an increase in size and complexity. Moreover, Bilateria exist in three grades of increasing structural complexity: the acoelomate, the pseudocoelomate, and the coelomate. Acoelomates, such as flatworms, are the simplest ones, lacking an internal cavity. Pseudocoelomates possess spaces between the digestive tract and body wall that are lined by extracellular matrix. Coelomates, such as annelids, arthropods, or vertebrates, contain a coelom lined with a mesodermal epithelium.

Another issue is the geologically sudden appearance of the triploblastic body plan in the fossil record. The Radiata appeared about 580 million years ago; no bilaterian animals are in the fossil record until the beginning of the Cambrian, approximately 540 million year ago. All bilaterian phyla appear during a relatively short time interval of probably less than 20 million years. This event is known as the Cambrian explosion. More than 90% of the extant metazoan phyla are triploblastic; only two phyla are diploblastic.

How this transition from radially to bilaterally symmetrical animals took place, and the ancestry of Bilateria, remains a major mystery of natural history. Decades of anatomical and embryological studies have led to two competing hypotheses. In the diploblast-acoel theory, a simple, acoelomate organism is proposed as the ancestor of all bilaterians, which would derive, growing in complexity, into the pseudocoelomates and, later, into fully coelomate ones. In the diploblast-coelomate theory, this key position is occupied by a developed, coelomate organism, with the acoelomate and pseudocoelomate phyla having lost the coelom by secondary simplification. *See* INVERTEBRATE EVOLUTION.

Molecular systematics. With the advent of molecular data 20 years ago, the phylogenic studies of metazoans entered a new stage. A considerable amount of evolutionary information is embedded in the genomic sequences of extant species. Among other molecules, 18S ribosomal deoxyribonucleic acid (rDNA) emerged as most ideal for phylogenetic studies. The 18S rDNA molecule is universal, it is slow-evolving, and it has different variable regions which bear evolutionary information at different taxonomic levels, allowing studies of both recent and ancient divergences. These advantages make 18S rDNA one of the most commonly used genes in phylogenetic studies. In a short space of time, analyses of ribosomal sequences have already thrown light onto some key events of animal evolution. One example refers to the phylum Platyhelminthes, or flatworms, which includes the free-living planarians and parasites such as tapeworms and liver flukes. Their simple features have led many researchers to support them as the most primitive bilaterians. Analyses of 18S rDNA showed that their actual position is within the protostomes in a clade now known as the lophotrochozoans, which includes annelids, mollusks, and nemertines (**Fig. 2**).

Molecular phylogenetics encounters many problems, especially with very ancient events. A common pitfall is the "long-branch attraction artifact." Some organisms, called fast-clock organisms, have an increased substitution or evolutionary rate. Thus, their sequences have accumulated many more mutations than the other taxa. Such sequences may share similarity due to chance rather than shared history, resulting in artifactual association of taxa. Fast-clock organisms appear in the inferred tree with very long branches. These long branches often give misleading results: they artifactually group together and tend to emerge in a very basal position in the tree, looking older than they actually are.

Long-branch attraction can be tackled in several ways. One way is to use more complex methods for inferring phylogenies, such as maximum likelihood. Another option is to use in the analysis only species with normal evolutionary rate, avoiding any with an increased substitution rate. The latter method was used to infer the real position of the phylum Nematoda, which contains many fast-clock species for the 18S rDNA. Due to the long-branch attraction, they appeared as the ancestor of bilaterians in the inferred tree. When only species with a normal evolutionary rate were used in the analyses, they clustered with the arthropods as members of the clade Ecdysozoa, composed of several phyla of molting animals.

Phylogenetic analysis. Although most of the platyhelminths clustered within the protostomes, one of the orders, the Acoela, never grouped in 18S-based molecular phylogenies with the rest of the platyhelminths. Acoels appeared, instead, in a very basal position as the likeliest sister group of the bilaterians. Nevertheless, this position was not reliable, because the acoels sequenced were fast-clock organisms. Trying to avoid the long-branch attraction artifact, 18 different species of acoels were sequenced in order to find among them non-fast-clock ones. They were all aligned together with the 18S of representatives of all metazoan phyla. Their evolutionary rate was tested, and one species (*Paratomella rubra*) appeared to have a regular evolutionary rate, similar to the rest of the metazoans. Using only this species, and once the data had been tested to show it was really phylogenetically informative, a thorough analysis was performed using maximum likelihood. The results showed, with a statistical support of 100%, that their basal position was real and not an artifact. Hence, acoels do not belong to the Platyhelminthes and represent the earliest extant bilaterian metazoan, occupying a key position between diploblasts and triploblasts (Fig. 2*b*).

This new evolutionary scenario needs to be made congruent with morphological and embryological data. Acoels are small, marine, and anatomically extremely simple: they lack an extracellular matrix, protonephridia, and a permanent gut lumen, all common features in the other platyhelminths and triploblasts. Their nervous system is also very simple, and they have a special network of ciliary roots of epidermal cells. Another key difference is their embryonic cleavage, that is, the way their cells

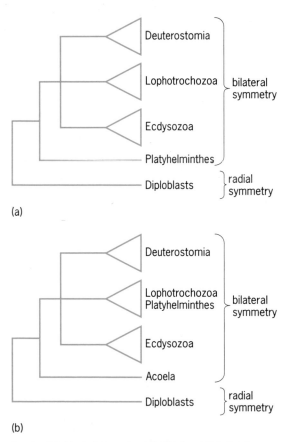

Fig. 2. Classical and new hypotheses regarding the first bilaterian taxa. (*a*) Acoelomate platyhelminths are the sister group of all the other Bilateria. (*b*) Platyhelminths appear within the lophotrochozoans. Acoels are not grouped with the rest of the flatworms. Acoels represent the extant descendants of one of the first organisms with bilateral symmetry, occupying a pivotal position between diploblast and triploblast organisms.

divide during the early stages of development. Acoels exhibit duet spiral cleavage in contrast to the typical quartern pattern that characterizes many protostomes and the rest of the flatworms. Moreover, all spiralian embryos have both endomesoderm and ectomesoderm. Acoel embryos generate only endomesoderm.

All these morphological and embryological features suggest that acoels and the rest of Platyhelminthes may be unrelated lineages. In fact, some authors had already proposed that the phylum Platyhelminthes may be artifactual. Morphology corroborates the molecular results in which acoels branch in an intermediate position between diploblast and triploblast phyla. This means acoels appeared before the other bilaterian taxa, probably before the Cambrian explosion, suggesting that during the pre-Cambrian period different bilaterian lineages may have already originated. Probably most of them became extinct. Acoels may then represent the extant descendants of one of the first bilateral-triploblastic organisms. This new position of acoels makes them highly interesting. Their study may help explain events surrounding the Cambrian explosion, such as the evolution of the developmental systems required to produce so many different lineages in such a brief episode or the nature of the first bilaterians. For example, even if acoels are not the direct ancestor, acoel features may be considered primitive among the Bilateria. This would suggest that the real ancestor was also an acoelomate, simple organism, supporting the diploblast-acoel theory.

For background information *see* CAMBRIAN; PLATYHELMINTHES in the McGraw-Hill Encyclopedia of Science & Technology.   Iñaki Ruiz-Trillo

Bibliography. M. Aguinaldo et al., Evidence for a clade of nematodes, arthropods and other moulting animals, *Nature*, 387:489–493, 1997; S. Bengston and Z. Yue, Fossilized metazoan embryos from the earliest Cambrian, *Science*, 277:1645-1648, 1997; S. Carranza, J. Baguñà, and M. Riutort, Are the Platyhelminthes a monophyletic primitive group? An assessment using 18S rDNA sequences, *Mol. Biol. Evol.*, 14(5):485–497, 1997; I. Ruiz-Trillo et al., Acoel flatworms: Earliest extant bilaterian metazoans, not members of Platyhelminthes, *Science*, 283:1919–1923, 1999.

Acoustic equivalent source methods

Inverse source methods are applied to solve acoustic boundary-value problems, and can be used to help design quiet machinery. An inverse source method is a type of boundary method for the solution of boundary-value problems.

The acoustic part of the pressure in the region outside a sound source satisfies a partial differential equation. In general, many functions can be found which satisfy the equation, and additional information is required to specialize the solution to the particular physical problem of interest. If time is one of the independent variables, the function itself must be specified at some initial time, leading to an initial value problem. Otherwise, the function may be specified on the boundary of the domain, leading to a boundary value problem. Initial value problems can be used to represent a wider variety of physical problems, but because they are more difficult to solve, only transient phenomena, such as impacts, are modeled in this fashion. More often, practical noise problems in machine design are modeled as time-harmonic, thus assuming that the sound source is vibrating in a steady-state condition and the pressure field is a linear superposition of deterministic discrete frequency waves. In this form, frequency is the independent variable rather than time, and the acoustic field can be determined by solving a boundary value problem. Boundary conditions for the acoustic pressure, or a related acoustic quantity, are specified as a function of frequency on a boundary completely enclosing the sound source. The solution of the problem is a function that (1) satisfies the partial differential equation everywhere in the solution domain, and (2) satisfies the specified boundary condition. Because all the frequencies making up the pressure field are independent of each other, the problem can be solved one frequency at a time, with the results superposed to give an overall solution.

Boundary methods. Boundary methods are used to solve boundary value problems. They are uniquely well suited to acoustic boundary value problems because only the boundary of the solution domain, that is, the volume of fluid where the pressure field is to be computed, needs to be discretized. Other, more familiar methods, including finite difference and finite element methods, require the entire solution domain to be discretized, which quickly becomes prohibitive when the solution domain dwarfs the sound source. The basic idea of all boundary methods is to assume a solution in the form of a series summation of basis functions, each of which satisfies the partial differential equation everywhere in the solution domain. This ensures that the composite function will automatically satisfy the partial differential equation, so that it is not necessary to discretize the solution domain, only the boundary surface (hence the name "boundary method"). The basis functions are weighted by undetermined coefficients, which are determined in the solution process such that the numerical solution approximately satisfies the specified boundary condition.

In the special case of acoustic boundary-value problems, the approximate solution for the acoustic pressure $p(\mathbf{x}, \omega)$ at the field point $\mathbf{x}$ (approximate quantities are denoted by an overbar) takes the form

$$\bar{p}(\mathbf{x}, \omega) = \sum_{n=1}^{N} s_n P_n (\mathbf{x}, \omega)$$

where the $P_n(\mathbf{x}, \omega)$ are functions satisfying the governing partial differential equation and the problem is typically formulated in the frequency domain. The undetermined coefficients s_n are determined in the solution process such that the boundary condition is approximately satisfied.

In most acoustic problems, the boundary condition is specified in terms of the normal component of the surface velocity of any surfaces in contact with the acoustic medium. There are a number of reasons why the boundary conditions are not specified in terms of the primary acoustic variable: pressure. First, surface vibrations are relatively insensitive to interference from the acoustic fields of nearby objects as long as the structural impedance is high, which cannot be said of the surface pressures. Also, the normal surface velocity can be accurately measured without significantly changing the vibration of the radiating structure. Finally, the surface velocity of a vibrating structure can be computed numerically using the finite element method for a wide range of practical problems, whereas no such method exists for computing the surface pressure.

Inverse source methods. The boundary method becomes an inverse source method when the functions $P_n(\mathbf{x}, \omega)$ are chosen as the acoustic fields of discrete sources. The general idea for using this type of source comes from the Kirchhoff-Helmholtz equation, which is an exact solution of the boundary-value problem in the form of an integral equation. The acoustic fields of simple and dipole sources distributed over the boundary surface of the radiating structure are superposed in the Kirchhoff-Helmholtz equation to give the solution of the boundary-value problem. These functions satisfy the governing partial differential equation everywhere in the solution domain, that is, everywhere outside the boundary surface. If viewed from the context of boundary methods, the acoustic fields of the simple and dipole sources are the basis functions, and the normal component of the surface velocity and the surface pressure are the exact solutions for their weighting functions, respectively. Thus, most researchers have tried to imitate the Kirchhoff-Helmholtz equation, using simple or dipole sources distributed over the boundary surface as basis functions with approximate representations of the surface pressure and normal surface velocity as weighting functions.

The basic difficulty with this idea is that the acoustic pressure fields of simple and dipole sources are weakly singular and strongly singular functions, respectively. Mathematically, this means that the pressure field of a simple source goes to infinity as $1/R$ as the distance between the source and field points R goes to zero, and that of a dipole source goes to infinity as $1/R^2$. The acoustical particle velocity is obtained by taking the gradient of the acoustic pressure field, resulting in strongly singular functions for simple sources and hypersingular functions (which depend on $1/R^3$ near the source point) for dipole sources. To enforce the boundary condition for the normal surface velocity, the acoustic particle velocity due to the distributions of simple and dipole sources is evaluated. When the field point is not near the boundary surface, the surface integrals can be easily evaluated using gaussian integration techniques; but when the field point approaches the boundary surface, the evaluation of the surface integrals becomes increasingly difficult due to the singularity in the acoustic field of the sources. It is difficult to express a finite-valued function as an integral over such singular functions.

Researchers have tried to alleviate this difficulty using a variety of schemes. One possibility is to move the source distributions off the boundary surface (into the volume enclosed by the boundary surface), so that the basis functions are no longer singular. When the sources are on the boundary surface, it can be shown that an exact solution for the weighting function of the surface integral always exists in the limit as the number of basis functions goes to infinity. However, when the sources are moved off the boundary surface, it may not be possible to exactly represent the acoustic field of the vibrating structure, no matter how many sources are used to reproduce the field. The numerical solution derived from these basis functions is then typically unstable, such that a small change in the solution for the undetermined coefficients causes a very large change in the numerical solution. The integral equation associated with the numerical solution is then classified as a first-kind integral equation, which is generally ill-posed, in contrast to the Kirchhoff-Helmholtz equation, which is well-posed. Thus, moving the sources off the boundary surface gives satisfactory results when the surface is relatively simple in shape, but is unsuitable for surfaces with edges and corners where the numerical procedure yields increasingly unstable solutions. This leads to the conclusion that it is generally better to place the sources on the boundary surface and perform the singular integrations. The real art in implementing an inverse source method is in the way that the singular integrals are evaluated. Fortunately, over time, methods have been developed to handle the integrals leading to much greater solution accuracy.

Design of quiet machinery. Inverse source methods have been applied to the design of quiet machinery. The basic idea is to encorporate the inverse source method into a design loop. The steps in a single design evaluation include (1) computing structural vibrations (most often, using finite element methods), (2) evaluating the acoustic radiation as a function of frequency with the structural vibrations as input, (3) predicting the overall cost function for the design, and (4) appropriately adjusting the design variables to reduce the cost function. The main challenges of this endeavor are defining the boundary conditions and forcing function for the structural analysis and performing sensitivity analyses to determine how to adjust the design parameters.

The end product of the design process is called a weak radiator, with vibrational modes which radiate sound inefficiently. Weak radiators are found to have surface velocity patterns with nearly balanced areas of positive and negative phase, causing the fluid to slosh back and forth between adjacent areas with out-of-phase motion. The sloshing motion reduces the residual compression of the fluid, and confines the acoustic field largely to the structure's nearfield. Several recent efforts at noise control by design have employed this concept, all using various types of material tailoring to achieve a weak radiator mode. A fully integrated, structural-acoustic optimization computer code has been developed to predict and subsequently minimize noise generated by a vibrating thin-shell structure. Weak radiator technology is applicable as long as the characteristic dimension of the structure is much smaller than the acoustic wavelength at the frequencies of interest.

Demonstration problem. To demonstrate how acoustic equivalent source methods are used in the design of quiet structures, the sound radiation from a thin plate driven into vibration by an electromechanical shaker and mounted on a box frame (**Fig. 1**) will be considered. In its initial configuration, the radiation from the structure is regarded as a source of unwanted noise. The goal of the example is to reduce the box's radiated sound power by placing lumped masses on the driven plate. The sizes and locations for the masses are taken to be the design variables, and the radiated sound power over a frequency band encompassing a single resonance is taken to be the objective function (the quantity to be minimized). Although this problem is somewhat contrived, it serves to demonstrate the principles that would be applied to more realistic problems.

To validate the numerical predictions, the results were replicated experimentally. The plate is bonded along its rim to a stiff aluminum frame using epoxy cement. The bonding helps to approximate a clamped boundary condition at the edges of the thin plate. The frame is bolted to an aluminum bottom plate which also holds the shaker. The shaker consists of an ordinary 133-mm (5.25-in.) loudspeaker which provides low mechanical impedance. It is connected to the plate's center via a plastic dome and an aluminum push rod.

There are two sets of masses, an optimized set of four masses and a baseline set of five masses having the same total mass as the optimal set. The fifth mass of the baseline set is placed at the center of the plate. The point masses are made from tungsten alloy for compactness and are attached to the plate with beeswax. The radiated sound power is determined by means of sound intensity measurements in 1/3-octave bands with center frequencies from 63 Hz to 630 Hz. The shaker is driven with banded white noise, while the input (voice coil) current is monitored to determine the excitation force.

In view of the considerable simplifications made in the structural and acoustical analysis, there is good agreement between the measured and computed 1/3-octave spectra for both the optimized (four-mass) and the baseline (five-mass) configurations (**Fig. 2**). Toward the upper end of the considered frequency

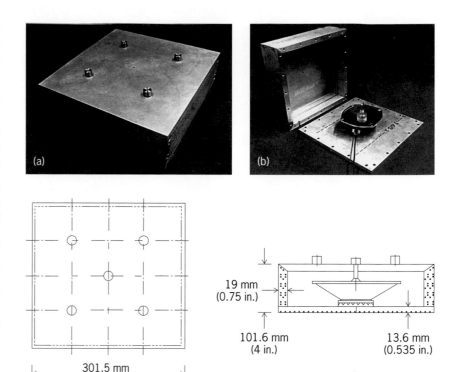

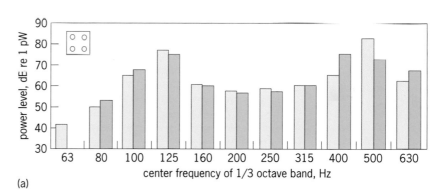

Fig. 1. Thin plate mounted on a box frame, used in the numerical analysis and experiment. (a) Structure with the box closed, showing the location and relative size of the masses used to achieve the sound reduction. (b) Structure with the box open, showing the loudspeaker (shaker). (c) Top view, showing location of the masses in baseline (five-mass) configuration. (d) Side view.

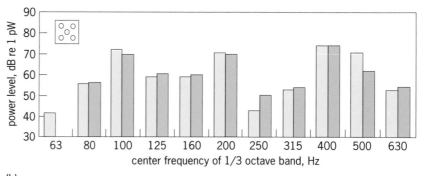

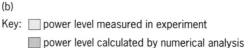

Key: ☐ power level measured in experiment

☐ power level calculated by numerical analysis

Fig. 2. Experimental and numerical third-band octave spectra for (a) optimized (four-mass) and (b) baseline (five-mass) configurations.

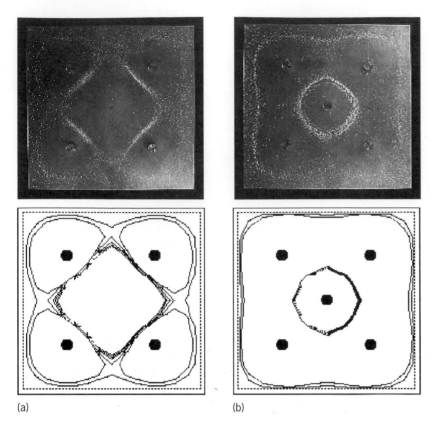

(a)   (b)

Fig. 3. Mode shapes of the second symmetric resonance: (*a*) optimized (four-mass) configuration; (*b*) baseline (five-mass) configuration. The experimental resonance frequencies are 209 and 192 Hz for the four- and five-mass configurations, respectively. Photographs show nodal lines as concentrations of powder that has been placed on the plate. In contour plots, the nodal lines are indicated by the contour lines, closely arranged around zero displacement in a symmetrical fashion.

range, the discrepancies become larger due to limitations in the Rayleigh-Ritz model used to predict the structural vibrations. Both spectra encompass the first three symmetric plate resonances, that is, the (1,1), (1,3/3,1), and (1,5/5,1) modes. However, as a consequence of the minimization of the sound radiated by the second mode in the 200-Hz band, the corresponding resonance does not appear in the sound power spectrum of the four-mass configuration.

The second-mode shapes for the two configurations (**Fig. 3**) illustrate how the vibration behavior of the plate is influenced by the point masses. Photographs and contour plots not only confirm the good agreement between theory and experiment but also reveal how the volume velocity cancellation is achieved. The mode shape of the five-mass configuration, similar to the one of a bare plate, exhibits deep valleys around the center crest which dominate the net volume displacement. These valleys are much less pronounced for the optimized configuration, in which case they balance the volume displacement of the center crest exactly.

Presently, acoustic equivalent source methods are used primarily to evaluate the performance of competing designs. Eventually, gains in computer speed will reduce the time for each design iteration to practical levels, so that the procedure can be fully automated, leading to designs meeting the frequently conflicting requirements of high strength, low weight, and minimum radiated noise.

For background information *see* DIFFERENTIAL EQUATION; INTEGRAL EQUATION; MECHANICAL VIBRATION; NUMERICAL ANALYSIS; OPTIMIZATION; VIBRATION in the McGraw-Hill Encyclopedia of Science & Technology.   Gary H. Koopmann; John B. Fahnline

Bibliography. E. W. Constans, G. H. Koopmann, and A. D. Belegundu, The use of modal tailoring to minimize the radiated sound power of vibrating shells: Theory and experiment, *J. Sound Vibrat.*, 217(2): 335–350, 1998; G. H. Koopmann and J. B. Fahnline, *Designing Quiet Structures*, Academic Press, London, 1997.

Advanced materials

The progress of humankind has been directly and indirectly dependent on materials. Periods of development in the archeological record, such as the Stone, Iron, and Bronze ages, reflect this. Since about 1970 there has been an unprecedented expansion in the number of new materials that have entered every aspect of human lives. The revolution in materials shows every sign of continuing, probably at an increased pace of development.

Applications. Advanced materials, perhaps better called advanced materials for engineering applications, are needed in hostile environments, including high pressure and temperature, where the materials should not be adversely affected by the surroundings; and in sensitive environments, where the materials should not adversely affect their surroundings, as in living systems. Testaments to the acute need for new materials are the expanding fields of electronics, operations in outer space, and medical science, to name a few.

Thermodynamics. The science of materials aids in the fundamental understanding of the chemistry and physics involved in their use. The engineering builds on this knowledge to design materials to meet specifications, parameters within which the materials must perform. A knowledge of the thermodynamic properties is an essential element in the characterization of any new material. The significance of the thermodynamics is manifested in several aspects: thermodynamic stability, which defines resistance to oxidation and decomposition; the sequence of reaction formation, including the rate-determining reaction and the resulting phases of the materials; the heats of formation and reaction; the free energies that equal either the amount of work the material can produce or the work needed to produce the material; and finally, information on molecular motion, disorder, and structural transitions in solids.

A complete thermodynamic characterization must include a determination of the thermophysical properties such as the heat capacity, from which can be derived the enthalpy, entropy, free energies, and structural information; the thermochemical properties such as the enthalpies and free energies of formation; and the thermodynamic stability of the material. The advantage of measuring the heat capacity as the primary determination over a wide range of temperature is that the heat capacity sees all the sources of the energy that contribute to the total energy budget of the substance. Appropriate integrations of the heat capacity yield values for the enthalpies, entropies, and free energies from which a host of subsequent information can be derived. In addition, any irregularities in the heat capacity–against–temperature plot may reveal structural or more subtle modifications occurring in the solid, and the associated differences in the enthalpy and in entropy help define the origin of the change. Also derived is information about the vibrational frequency distribution of the atoms and molecules, as well as magnetic ordering and electronic phenomena. While the traditional use of thermodynamic quantities has been mainly for equilibrium situations, the applications that encompass nonequilibrium phases and structures are increasing and constitute one area of great expansion anticipated for future development. Examples of materials to which these applications have been directed include the amorphous polymer-glass melts, the metal glasses, the metal alloys with dendritic coring, and thin-film superlattices.

Transition-metal silicides (ceramics). These materials are a well-defined family of compounds (M_aSi_b) formed by the reaction of silicon with the metal element M within groups 3 to 11 of the periodic table, namely those groups headed by the elements scandium across to copper to include titanium (Ti), vanadium (V), copper (Cu), yttrium (Y), molybdenum (Mo), tungsten (W), and platinum (Pt). At least 39 pairs of elements are possible, and it is not unexpected that every element within these groups will form a stable silicide even at room temperature. In general, however, where the stable compound does form, the stability remains to significantly elevated temperatures. Moreover, the high degree of stability, excellent resistance to oxidation, low electrical resistivity, and great tensile strength at elevated temperatures of these compounds lead to their use in high-temperature furnaces as coatings and heating elements, in interconnect technology, in semiconductors, and as ceramic reinforcements within metal matrices.

The scarcity of thermodynamic and other information is compounded by the fact that pure silicides are difficult to synthesize. They form a range of stoichiometric compounds, and each compound may in turn form polymorphic structures. For example, in the tungsten-silicon family, for which the phase diagram is fairly well known, two stable stoichiometric compounds exist as W_5Si_3 and WSi_2, written here in the sequence of increasing atomic percent of silicon in the compound, which also corresponds to decreasing melting point of the solids from about 2150°C to 2000°C (3900°F to 3630°F) respectively. For the molybdenum-silicon system, whose phase diagram is also fairly well known, three stable compounds exist as Mo_3Si, Mo_5Si_3, and $MoSi_2$, with decreasing melting points of the solids from about 2000°C to 1900°C (3630°F to 3450°F). It is not surprising that these high fusion temperatures, which are accompanied by extraordinary thermodynamic stability to resist decomposition and oxidation, have led to substantial recent research into obtaining accurate thermodynamic values of the pure forms of the materials. These compounds are proving to be superior for use in high-temperature construction materials, the computer and communications industry, and high-temperature aerospace applications.

Recently completed measurements of the heat capacity for pure tungsten disilicide, WSi_2, actually $WSi_{2.06}$, from the temperature of about 6 K to 341 K (−267°C to 68°C or −449°F to 154°F) produced very accurate results within about 0.2% over most of the temperature range, and provide the first such thermodynamic measurements below room temperature. The graph of the heat capacity plotted against temperature is smooth, continuous, and without any sign of anomalous behavior. This curve confirms that the tungsten disilicide, whose structure is tetragonal at room temperature, retains this configuration over this entire temperature range. In addition, these accurate results have allowed the calculation of accurate values of enthalpy, entropy, and free energy from absolute zero up to 341 K (68°C or 154°F) which, when combined with the measurments of the thermodynamic quantities determined previously above room temperature, provide a complete picture of the properties to 1200 K (1473°C or 1700°F). Analysis of the heat capacities reveals that the vibrations of the atoms within the crystal are normal, which allows for modeling and prediction of fairly accurate values of the thermodynamic properties of other members of the family where experimental measurements are lacking. In addition, the analysis shows that a significant contribution to the total heat capacity arises from the conduction of the electrons through the solid lattice and that this contribution equals that for pure metallic tungsten. The ability to model and thereby predict accurately the behavior of other members of the family is especially important where synthesis of the materials is difficult or expensive.

Thermodynamic knowledge of molybdenum disilicide, $MoSi_2$, another important member of the family, has been significantly advanced thanks to recent measurements by adiabatic calorimetry; and careful characterization showed the sample to be $MoSi_{2.067\pm0.002}$. The results show that its tetragonal structure at room temperature is retained from 2200 K (2473°C or 3500°F) down to absolute zero. Its heat capacity values and associated thermodynamic quantities are now known over this same temperature range.

Transition-metal chalcogenides. The transition-metal dichalcogenides exhibit some remarkable properties that also place them at the center of the revolution in advanced materials. They are suitable for engineering use in hostile environments of extreme temperature and pressure, but because of decomposition, not to the same degree of elevated temperature as the disilicides. This well-defined family of dichalcogenides has a general formulation MX_2, where M is a transition-metal element and X is a chalcogenide, specifically sulfur, selenium, or tellurium. The transition metal lies in groups 4 to 6 of the periodic table, including titanium, zirconium (Zr), molybdenum, tantalum (Ta), and tungsten. The 21 pairs of elements in this family are known to produce at least 26 stable compounds at $T = 300$ K ($27°$C or $80°$F). Virtually all members of the family crystallize into layered compounds made up of a sheet of metal atoms sandwiched between two sheets of chalcogens.

Within a layer, the bonds are strong, but between adjacent layers they are extremely weak. This feature gives rise to facile basic cleavage as one layer slides easily over an adjacent layer, to marked anisotropy in many of the physical properties, and to intercalation by foreign atoms. This intercalation results in the formation of new materials and in the enhancement of various properties that promotes their use in specific applications. These dichalcogenides are used as semiconductors, components of batteries, catalysts, and solid lubricants. Their attractiveness as semiconducting materials for use in photoelectrochemical energy conversion derives from their having a low susceptibility to photodecomposition because their band gaps are not in the region of maximum solar energy efficiency. The preparation of highly pure samples is not without difficulties. They are often prepared by vapor transport from the elements within a high-temperature furnace in a nonreactive environment. Great care must be exercised to remove surface oxides and avoid washing with agents that intercalate readily into the layered structure. Thermodynamic information has just begun to be determined for some members of this family.

The heat capacity measurements from 6 K to 326 K ($-267°$C to $53°$C, or $-449°$F to $127°$F) for the pure tungsten ditelluride, WTe_2, are the first reported results for the material, and they have allowed calculation of all the thermodynamic quantities from absolute zero to about 335 K ($62°$C or $143°$F). The continuous smooth curve of heat capacity plotted against temperature reveals that the substance retains its orthorhombic crystal structure from room temperature down to near absolute zero. This orthorhombic structure shows a distorted octahedral coordination around the tungsten atoms, which are displaced from the centers of the octahedra to form chains that extend through the crystal as buckled layers. The asymmetry or displacement of the tungsten atoms results in stronger metallic bonding and promotes conduction within the tungsten ditelluride as does the electronic band structure. The net effect is for greater electrical conductivity for the tungsten ditelluride than for any other chalcogenide whose properties are known.

The thermal stability of the three known tungsten dichalcogenides is substantially lower and the reactivity greater than that of the disilicides, which narrows the spectrum of application for the dichalcogenides, especially as a solid lubricant. Decomposition occurs in WS_2, WSe_2, and WTe_2 at 1423 K ($1150°$C or $2102°$F), 1073 K ($800°$C or $1472°$F), and as low as 673 K ($400°$C or $752°$F) respectively, with greatest stability in an inert atmosphere, less stability in vacuum, and least stability in a reactive environment. Fortunately their minimum coefficient of friction occurs in vacuum, and all are fairly stable against moisture.

For background information *see* CHEMICAL THERMODYNAMICS; CRYSTAL STRUCTURE; HEAT CAPACITY; INTERCALATION COMPOUNDS; POLYMORPHISM (CRYSTALLOGRAPHY); SILICON; SPECIFIC HEAT OF SOLIDS; THERMODYNAMIC PRINCIPLES in the McGraw-Hill Encyclopedia of Science & Technology.   Ron D. Weir

Bibliography. T. M. Letcher (ed.), *Chemical Thermodynamics: Chemistry for the 21st Century*, Blackwell, 1999; T. B. Massalski et al., *Binary Alloy Phase Diagrams*, ASM International, 1986; C. N. R. Rao, *Chemistry of Advanced Materials*, Blackwell, 1993.

Air pollution

Air pollution refers to changes in atmospheric composition by the addition of gases or particles with adverse impacts on human health, plant growth, and weather and climate; that is, there is a decline in air quality due to anthropogenic alterations in atmospheric composition. Air quality refers to the relative concentration of gases which constitute the air, and the physicochemical processes that occur within and among gases, with emphasis on the atmospheric composition in relation to its effects on plants and animals. Principal constituents which affect air quality comprise various gases, water vapor, particulate matter, and aerosols, which may be of natural (volcanic activity) or of anthropogenic origin (industrial emissions, dust emitted by soil disturbance, and so on). Air quality impacts plants and animals through its effects on net primary productivity (NPP) as determined by the difference between photosynthesis and respiration, and on the global mean temperature as determined by the radiation balance. The atmospheric composition affects the global mean temperature through altering the radiation balance of the Earth.

Carbon. There are five principal global carbon (C) pools: (1) the oceanic pool with 38,000 Pg C (1 petagram $= 10^{15}$ g $=$ 1 billion metric tons); (2) the geologic pool with 5000 Pg C, constituting 4000 Pg of coal, 500 Pg of oil, and 500 Pg of gas; (3) the soil pool with 1550 Pg of soil organic carbon (SOC) and 750 Pg of soil inorganic carbon (SIC), both to 1 m (3.3 ft) depth; (4) the atmospheric pool with 720 Pg C; and (5) the biotic pool with 560 Pg C (**Fig. 1**). As the third largest global pool, the soil pool plays an important role in the global carbon cycle. The soil carbon pool interacts with all other pools, but especially with the atmospheric and the biotic carbon pools. The atmospheric carbon pool has been steadily increasing since the onset of the industrial revolution. The atmospheric concentration of carbon dioxide (CO_2) was about 280 parts per million (ppm), or 0.028%, around 1850, and it is now about 370 ppm, or 0.037%. The present rate of carbon dioxide released to the atmosphere is 3.3 Pg per year. The atmospheric pool is increasing at the expense of the soil, biotic, and geologic carbon pools, primarily due to anthropogenic activities.

Principal global sources of carbon are fossil fuel combustion, tropical deforestation, biomass burning, soil cultivation, and cement manufacture (**Table 1**). The current rate of tropical deforestation is estimated at 12–14 million hectares (Mha) per year. Deforestation was responsible for 12–17% of the total carbon dioxide emission in 1980–1990. Soil cultivation, plowing, and other disturbances of the surface soil are sources of atmospheric carbon dioxide. The known sinks comprise atmosphere, ocean, biota, and cropland/pasture. While the increase in the atmospheric carbon pool is known, the nature and capacity of other sinks are not well established.

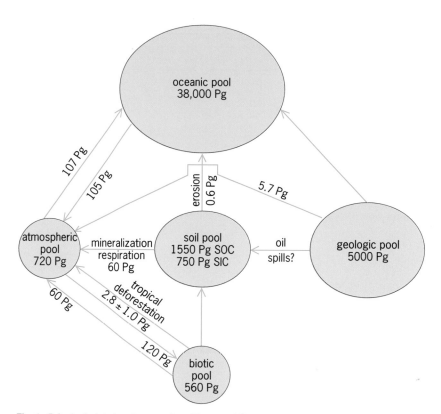

Fig. 1. Principal global carbon pools, with annual fluxes among them indicated by arrows.

TABLE 1. Sources and sinks of atmospheric carbon dioxide*

Sources	Pg/yr	Sinks	Pg/yr
Fossil fuel combustion and cement manufacture	5.7	Atmosphere	3.3
Tropical deforestation	2.1	Oceans	2.0
		Temperate and boreal forests	1.7
Biomass burning	0.7	Tropical forests and cropland	1.5
Total	8.5	Total	8.5

*From R. Lal, Soil management and restoration for C sequestration to mitigate the accelerated greenhouse effect, *Prog. Environ. Sci.*, 1:307–326, 1999; and W. H. Schlesinger, An overview of the global carbon cycle, in R. Lal et al. (eds.), *Soils and the Global Change*, pp. 9–25, CRC, Boca Raton, Fl.

TABLE 2. Concentration of stable atmospheric gases*

Gas	Concentration, ppmv
Nitrogen	780,840
Oxygen	209,460
Argon	9,340
Neon	18.18
Helium	5.24
Krypton	1.14
Hydrogen	0.50
Xenon	0.09

*T. Godish, *Air Quality*, 3d ed., Lewis Publishers, Boca Raton, FL, 1997.

Atmospheric pool. The atmosphere comprises a mixture of gases. The concentration of some gases is relatively stable (**Table 2**), while that of others is changing due to anthropogenic factors. Important gases that maintain a relatively stable concentration include nitrogen (N_2; 78.08%), oxygen (O_2; 20.95%), and argon (Ar; 0.93%). These three gases constitute 99.96% of the atmosphere. In addition, there are several gases whose concentration is small (trace) and changes mostly due to anthropogenic factors. Important among these are carbon dioxide (370 ppmv), methane (CH_4; 1.72 ppmv), and nitrous oxide (N_2O; 0.11 ppmv), which are called the greenhouse gases. Other greenhouse gases include water (H_2O) vapor, carbon monoxide (CO), nitrogen oxide (NO), nitrogen dioxide (NO_2), and ozone (O_3) [**Table 3**]. These greenhouse gases absorb heat from the incoming solar radiation but do not allow long-wave radiation to reflect back into space. The relative effectiveness of these gases to restrict long-wave radiation escaping back into space differs among gases, and is called radiative forcing. The contribution of a particular greenhouse gas to radiative forcing is measured as the change in average net radiation in watts per square meter ($W \cdot m^{-2}$) at the top of the troposphere that is caused by that gas. The radiative forcing depends on the wavelength at which the gas absorbs the radiation, the strength of absorption per molecule, and the concentration of the gas. The commonly used term is the global warming potential. The global warming potential of a greenhouse gas is the ratio of global warming or radiative forcing from

TABLE 3. Concentration of variable atmospheric gases*

Gas	Concentration, ppmv
Water vapor	0.1–30,000
Carbon dioxide	370
Methane	1.74
Nitrous oxide	0.33
Carbon monoxide	0.11
Ozone	0.02
Ammonia	0.004
Nitrogen dioxide	0.001
Sulfur dioxide	0.001
Nitric oxide	0.0005
Hydrogen sulfide	0.00005

*IPCC, *Climate Change 1995: Impacts, Adaptations and Mitigation of Climate Change: Scientific-Technical Analyses*, Cambridge University Press, 1996; and T. Godish, *Air Quality*, 3d ed., Lewis Publishers, Boca Raton, FL, 1997.

1 kilogram of a greenhouse gas to 1 kilogram of carbon dioxide over 100 years. Using global warming potential provides a way to calculate the contribution of each greenhouse gas to the annual increase in radiative forcing. The global warming potential can be expressed per mole or per kilogram (**Table 4**).

Greenhouse gases can be divided into two groups: natural and synthetic. Three important natural gases are carbon dioxide, methane (CH_4), and nitrous oxide (N_2O).

Carbon dioxide. The concentration of carbon dioxide in the atmosphere has been steadily increasing, from about 280 ppmv around 1850 to 370 ppmv in 2000, and is currently increasing at the rate of 0.5% per year (1.5 ppmv/yr). If this trend continues, carbon dioxide concentration is projected to be 600 ppmv during the twenty-first century. Principal sources of carbon dioxide include fossil fuel combustion, cement manufacture, biomass burning, decomposition of biomass, and the soil organic carbon pool. The known sinks for carbon dioxide include the atmosphere, ocean, tropical and temperate forests, and croplands. However, there are numerous uncertainties about the sinks. Whereas the adverse effects of increasing concentration of carbon dioxide on potential increase in global mean temperature are widely recognized, a positive effect may be an increase in the photosynthetic rate and the net primary productivity. Increase in atmospheric carbon dioxide may also lead to improving the water and nitrogen use efficiency of plants. These effects, if substantial, may be highly beneficial to agriculture and forestry.

Methane. The preindustrial concentration of methane at 0.7 ppmv has steadily increased to the present value of 1.74 ppmv. The current rate of increase is about 0.8% per year (13 ppbv/yr). There are natural and anthropogenic sources of methane. Natural sources comprise wetlands, termites, ocean water, and fresh water. Important among anthropogenic sources are coal mines, rice paddies, enteric fermentation, animal waste, domestic sewage, landfill, and biomass burning. There are three known sinks of methane: (1) oxidation in the atmosphere, (2) increase in the atmospheric concentration, and (3) uptake (oxidation) by soil. There are numerous uncertainties in sources and sinks of methane.

Nitrous oxide. The present atmospheric concentration of nitrous oxide is 0.33 ppmv, and it is increasing at the rate of 0.25% per year (0.8 ppmv/yr). The increase is primarily due to production and evolution of natural and fertilizer-derived nitrous oxide from the soil surface, biomass burning, and biotic processes in forest soils. The sources for nitrous oxide remain undetermined, but soil is a major source. The effect of nitrogenous fertilizer use on nitrous oxide emissions is particularly important (**Fig. 2**). Natural forests are a principal reservoir of carbon and nitrogen. Deforestation leads to release of both to the atmosphere.

The synthetic gases include chlorofluorocarbons (CFCs), hydrochlorofluorocarbons (HCFCs), and hydrofluorocarbons (HFCs). Both hydrochlorofluorocarbons and hydrofluorocarbons have a residence time of 10–130 years, and have low concentrations. In terms of their global warming potential, however, these synthetic gases are extremely effective (Table 4).

Soil carbon pool. The soil carbon pool comprises soil organic carbon and soil inorganic carbon. The soil organic carbon pool is estimated at about 1550 Pg to 1 m (3.3 ft) depth (**Table 5**). Soils with the large pool include Histosols (25.2%), Inceptisols (17.2%), Oxisols (9.6%), Alfisols (8.7%), Aridisols (7.1%), Entisols (6.8%), and Ultisols (6.5%). N. H. Batjes (1996) estimated the soil organic carbon pool

TABLE 4. Characteristics of greenhouse gases*

Parameter	Natural gases			Industrial gases	
	CO_2	CH_4	N_2O	CFC-12	HCFC-22
Preindustrial concentration (ppmv)	280	0.70	0.275	0	0
Concentration in 1999	370	1.74	0.33	503	105
Rate of increase in 1990s (%/yr)	0.4	0.8	0.25	4	7
Atmospheric life (years)	50–200	10	130–150	130	10–40
Global warming potantial $(mol)^{-1}$	1	21	206	12,400	15,800
Global warming potantial $(kg)^{-1}$	1	58	310	3970	5750

*IPCC, *Climate Change 1995: Impacts, Adaptations and Mitigation of Climate Change: Scientific-Technical Analyses*, Cambridge University Press, 1996; and Enquete Commission, *Climate Change: A Threat to Global Development*, Economics Verlag, Bonn, 1992.

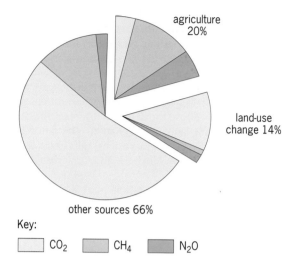

Key:

☐ CO_2 ☐ CH_4 ☐ N_2O

Fig. 2. Contribution of agricultural activities and land-use change to global radiative forcing in the 1990s. (*After IPCC, Climate Change 1995..., Cambridge University Press, 1996*)

at 1462–1548 Pg to 1 m depth and 2376–2456 Pg to 2 m (6.6 ft) depth (**Table 6**). Estimates of the soil inorganic carbon pool are even more tentative: this pool is estimated at about 750 Pg to 1 m depth.

Thus, the total carbon pool (soil organic and inorganic carbon) to 1 m depth is 2157–2296 Pg. With the atmospheric carbon pool estimated at 720 Pg, the soil carbon pool to 1 m deep is 3.0–3.2 times the atmospheric pool. The increase in the atmospheric carbon pool since the industrial revolution (about 1850) from 280 ppmv to 370 ppmv in 2000 is partly due to loss of the soil organic carbon pool. The soil organic carbon pool is a dynamic entity and depends on the gains and losses. The gains of soil organic carbon are due to addition of the litter, crop residue, and root biomass. The losses are due to mineralization, erosion, and leaching. The mobilization of 1 Pg of soil carbon is equivalent to carbon dioxide enrichment of 0.47 microliter per liter. Conversion of natural to agri-

cultural ecosystems involves deforestation, biomass burning, and plowing. These practices exacerbate the loss of the soil organic carbon pool to the atmosphere; this loss is exacerbated by soil degradative processes such as erosion, compaction, salinization, and pollution. Soil degradative processes also reduce the amount of carbon returned to the soil. *See* CARBON SEQUESTRATION.

Carbon emission. Important processes that govern the emission of carbon from soil to the atmosphere (**Fig. 3**) include the following:

1. *Oxidation*. This process, causing mineralization by aerobic organisms, is temperature-dependent. It leads to simplification of complex organic substances into simple inorganic compounds with attendant release of carbon dioxide to the atmosphere. The rate of mineralization is approximately doubled by every 10°C (18°F) rise in temperature. D. S. Jenkinson and A. Ayanaba (1977) observed that the rate of mineralization of crop residue in Ibadan, Nigeria, was four times that in Rothamsted, England. The rate of mineralization increases by land-use conversion from natural to agricultural ecosystems.

2. *Methanogenesis*. The emission of methane to the atmosphere occurs due to anaerobic decomposition of soil organic matter. Methanogenesis occurs in natural wetlands, poorly drained agricultural lands, rice paddies, and organic soils.

3. *Leaching*. The dissolved organic (polysaccharides, sugars, carbohydrates) and inorganic carbon (carbonates and bicarbonates) can be transported to the lower soil horizons or leached out of the soil. The magnitude of the loss depends on the climatic conditions, and it is usually greater in warm humid climates than in cool dry climates. The fate of leached carbon, once it enters aquatic ecosystems, is not well understood.

4. *Soil erosion*. Soil erosion by water and wind exacerbates the greenhouse effect. Soil erosion is a selective process and involves preferential removal of soil organic carbon, soil inorganic carbon, and clay

TABLE 5. Soil organic carbon pool for different depths in world soils*

Order	Depth, cm				Land area, 10^6 ha
	0–25	0–50	0–100	% of total	
Histosols	26 Pg	54 Pg	390 Pg	(25.2)	161
Inceptisols	162	215	267	(17.2)	946
Oxisols	88	128	150	(9.6)	1012
Alfisols	73	100	136	(8.7)	1330
Aridisols	57	95	110	(7.1)	1556
Entisols	37	52	106	(6.8)	2168
Ultisols	74	96	101	(6.5)	1175
Spodosols	39	53	98	(6.3)	348
Mollisols	41	52	72	(4.6)	925
Andisols	38	61	69	(4.4)	106
Vertisols	17	21	38	(2.4)	320
Gellisols	—	—	—	—	1120
Miscellaneous	?	?	18	(1.2)	1870
Total	652 Pg	927 Pg	1555 Pg	(100)	13,037

*After H. Eswaran, Global soil carbon resources, in R. Lal et al. (eds.), *Soil and Global Change*, CRC Publishers, Boca Raton, FL, 1995.

TABLE 6. Global estimates of soil C pool*

Pool	Depth	
	0–100 cm	0–200 cm
Soil organic carbon	1462–1548 Pg	2376–2456 Pg
Soil inorganic carbon	695–748 Pg	—
Total	2157–2296 Pg	

*From N. H. Batjes, The carbon and nitrogen in the soils of the world, *Eur. J. Soil Sci.*, 47:151–163, 1996.

fractions. The soil organic carbon content of eroded sediment varies depending on the antecedent soil properties, climate land use, and soil management practices. The enrichment ratio, the ratio of the soil organic carbon in eroded sediment to that in the original field soil, may be 1:5 for water erosion and 1:20 for wind erosion.

Soil erosion is a three-stage process: detachment, transport, and deposition. The soil carbon pool is impacted by all three processes. Soil detachment, by impacting raindrops with or without interaction with the overland flow and by the saltating sand particles blown by wind, leads to exposure of the soil organic carbon hitherto encapsulated and protected from microbial decomposition. The exposed soil organic carbon is easily mineralized. A large fraction of the soil displaced by erosional processes is redistributed over the landscape, especially in the microdepressions (Fig. 2). The soil organic carbon redistributed with the soil can also be readily mineralized. Some of the soil transported by wind and water is deposited in aquatic ecosystems and protected sites. The soil organic carbon deposited or buried in aquatic ecosystems may be sequestered and taken out of circulation. R. Lal (1995) calculated the global carbon budget of eroded sediments and estimated that water erosion worldwide leads to emission of 1.14 Pg C per year, of which erosion by water and wind in drylands leads to emission of 0.2–0.3 Pg C per year. These estimates of emissions are above the deposition/transfer/burial of carbon in the aquatic ecosystem. The latter is estimated at 0.57 Pg C per year by Lal (1995) and 1 Tg C per year by M. Meybeck and C. Vörösmarty (1999).

Biotic pool. The biotic carbon pool is the smallest of the five global carbon pools. World forests (**Table 7**) cover about 4.23 billion hectares, or 29% of the total land area. Forests comprise 422 Pg of biomass carbon, or 75.5% of the total biotic carbon pool of 558.8 Pg (Table 7). The net primary productivity of forest ecosystems is 25.5 Pg C per year, or 42.3% of the global net primary productivity. Arable land, with an area of about 11%, contributes 12.1 Pg C per year as net primary productivity, or 20% of the global net primary productivity.

The biotic carbon pool is decreasing, especially due to tropical deforestation. Deforestation has contributed significantly to increase in the atmospheric carbon pool. M. Williams (1994) estimated the change in land use in different ecosystems since the dawn of settled agriculture. The forest cover decreased by 7.5×10^6 km² (1 km² = 100 ha), woodland by 1.8×10^6 km², shrubland by 1.4×10^6 km², grassland by 6.6×10^6 km², and desert by 0.3×10^6 km² (**Table 8**). Most of these lands have been converted to agricultural uses, constituting the present area of about 15×10^6 km². Land-use conversion may have contributed a considerable amount of carbon to the atmosphere.   R. Lal

Agriculture. In pristine environments there are compounds that could be considered pollutants, from wildfire, volcanoes, native plants, and the ocean. The same and newer, synthetic compounds constitute the air pollution of industrialized societies. The distinction between pristine and industrial areas is disappearing, with pollutants now distributed globally.

The major phytotoxic air pollutants are ozone (O_3), fluoride (F), and sulfur dioxide (SO_2). Oxides of nitrogen (NO_x) are important precursors of ozone production and cause nitrogen fertilization that may affect biodiversity. High concentrations of nitrogen oxides may also damage vegetation. Particulate matter is a mixture of condensed products of gas-phase reactions, sea salt, and products of abrasion. Particles are not usually harmful to vegetation. Nitrogen, sulfur, and fluorine may be converted to and deposited as particles.

Effects on crops. Air pollutant exposure and damage may be chronic, long-term exposure to low concentrations or acute, short-term exposure to high concentrations. Chronic damage reflects toxic derangement of metabolism, whereas acute symptoms reflect tissue damage or necrosis (cell death).

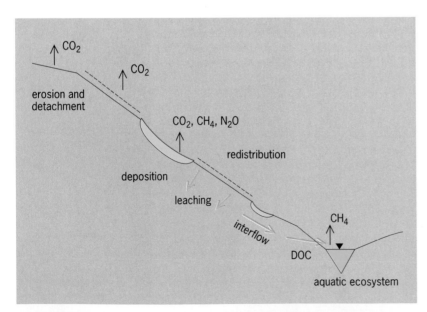

Fig. 3. Schematic of the erosional impacts on emission of greenhouse gases to the atmosphere.

TABLE 7. Land area under different biomes and the biotic carbon pool*

Biome	Land area, 10^9 ha	Biotic C pool, Pg	Net primary productivity, Pg C/yr
Tropical wet and moist forest	1.04	156.0	8.3
Tropical dry forest	0.77	49.7	4.8
Temperate forest	0.92	73.3	6.0
Boreal forest	1.50	143.0	6.4
Tropical woodland and savanna	2.46	48.8	11.1
Temperate steppe	1.51	43.8	4.9
Desert	1.82	5.9	1.4
Tundra	1.10	9.0	1.4
Wetland	0.29	7.8	3.8
Arable land	1.59	21.5	12.1
Rock and ice	1.52	0.0	0.0
Total	14.52	558.8	60.2

* Modified from R. A. Houghton and D. L. Skole, Carbon, in B. L. Turner et al. (eds.), *The Earth as Transformed by Human Action*, Cambridge University Press, 1990.

The symptoms of exposure to these air pollutants are similar to other factors such as nutrient deficiency and pathogen infection. Accurate diagnosis of air pollution exposure requires experience and may be facilitated by reference to photographic example. Visible symptoms are independent of reductions in growth and yield.

The major pollutants enter the plant as gaseous forms through the stomata (leaf pores). Some damage to the leaf-protecting waxy cuticle may occur without entry. Particulate- and soil-deposited forms are less damaging.

Sulfur dioxide. Sulfur dioxide was the first air pollutant recognized to harm vegetation. Sulfur is an essential nutrient for plant growth, and sulfur dioxide may substitute for the normal uptake of sulfur by roots as sulfate. Sulfur dioxide from coal and oil burning previously damaged crops and native vegetation in localized areas. However, in recent times, emission controls in developed countries have led to sulfur deficiencies in areas of previous sulfur dioxide damage. In developing countries, sulfur dioxide still impacts large areas of vegetation.

Visible symptoms include interveinal chlorosis (bleaching), silvering and pigmentation changes, and

TABLE 8. Estimates of change in land use in different ecosystems*

Ecosystem	Land use, 10^6 km^2	
	Preagriculture	Present
Forests	46.8	39.3
Woodlands	9.7	7.9
Shrubland	16.2	14.8
Grassland	34.0	27.4
Tundra	7.4	7.4
Desert	15.9	15.6
Arable	0	17.6

* Adapted from M. Williams, Forests and tree cover, in W. B. Meyer and B. L. Turner II (eds.), *Changes in Land Use and Land Cover: A Global Perspective*, Cambridge University Press, 1994.

ultimately necrosis (cell death), sometimes with an ivory coloration. In conifers a reddish tip dieback may be observed. Older leaves exhibit accelerated senescence and abscission (leaf loss).

Sulfur dioxide is converted to toxic sulfite and bisulfite in the wetted leaf interior. Oxidation of these to sulfate may both detoxify them and contribute to their mode of damage. Sulfur dioxide acts by tissue acidification as well as by reductive and oxidative reactions.

Ozone. Ozone is the single most damaging air pollutant for crops and native vegetation, due to its moderate toxicity and widespread distribution. It accounts for more damage to plants than all other air pollutants combined.

Visual symptoms are highly variable, even on the same plant. Leaf surfaces may initially appear oily or wetted, with some mesophyll swelling and epidermal deformation. Chlorosis, bronze dots that may coalesce on the upper leaf surface, called oxidant stipple, and tissue necrosis may follow. Recently fully expanded leaves are most sensitive. Younger and older leaves are often resistant. Newly developing leaves may exhibit enhanced photosynthetic capacity.

Ozone acts on tissues by inhibiting ion transport at the plasmalemma (cell membrane) which interferes with osmotic and metabolic regulation, by altering carbohydrate metabolism, and disrupting transport of sugars from leaves to roots and reproductive structures. Reduced root development may further inhibit shoot growth and photosynthesis by limiting supplies of water and nutrients from the soil.

Fluoride. Fluoride is the most phytotoxic of the common air pollutants. Its low impact on vegetation is attributed to its localized distribution and to the success of emission reduction technologies. Damaging exposures still occur when emissions are concentrated by unusual meteorology, and in developing countries with less effective emissions controls.

Foliar damage is mostly due to uptake through the stomata of the many gaseous forms of fluoride.

Uptake is rapid compared to other pollutants because of great solubility in the intercellular fluids. Particulate fluoride may be deposited to leaf surfaces. Deposition to vegetation is of particular consequence in forage species due to the debilitating nature of fluorosis (an abnormal condition caused by excessive intake of fluorides) in grazing animals.

Visible symptoms include tip, marginal, and finally interveinal chlorosis (an iron deficiency anemia) followed by necrosis. An early symptom is a wetted or oily appearance. Necrotic areas may appear tan or ivory colored. In some species the symptomatic areas are sharply demarcated by a dark band of necrotic tissue.

Fluoride is a potent inhibitor of many enzymes that catalyze metabolic reactions. It moves in the leaf in the transpiration stream to sites of evaporation, accounting for the pattern of symptoms. It is not redistributed throughout the plant.

Amelioration. Management options are minimal. Rate of growth correlates with sensitivity to ozone. Selection of slow-growing species may be useful. Stomatal uptake is the primary means of entry. Suboptimal growth conditions such as low light, nutrient deficiency, or water deficit cause stomatal closure, which excludes the pollutant. However, these conditions reduce potential productivity, and limit recovery during periods of low exposure. Increasing relative humidity increases stomatal opening, pollutant uptake, and damage. In contrast to ozone, resistance to sulfur dioxide is increased by adequate nitrogen and potassium nutrition, particularly if nitrogen is provided as nitrate and not as ammonium which further acidifies the tissue.

Crop protection chemicals have been tested as protectants, principally against ozone. Commercial applications and definitive demonstration of efficacy have proved elusive. The fungicide benomyl (methyl-l-butylcarbamoyl-2-benzimidazole carbamate) delays senescence and confers some resistance to ozone. The fungicidal properties do not seem to account for this protection. The antioxidant ethylene diurea (N-[2-(2-oxo-l-imidazolidynyl)ethyl]-N'-phenylurea) also confers considerable resistance to ozone, though the optimal dose, mode of action, and potential phytotoxicity remain subjects of research.

The primary means of achieving protection against these air pollutants is through genetics. Natural populations exhibit gradients of resistance along gradients of pollutant concentration, demonstrating natural selection. Crop plants selected for high yields in ozone-affected areas demonstrate inadvertent selection for resistance to air pollutants. In most cases the biochemical basis of such resistance is not known.

A new approach to modify genetic resistance involves biotechnology. Insertion of genes for antioxidant and other detoxifying systems may eventually lead to increased resistance. Many early efforts led to increased expression of target systems, but the proper targeting of the inserted material (for example, to chloroplasts, mitochondria, or nucleus) remains challenging to such efforts. Recent results suggest that appropriate targeting has considerable potential for increasing plant resistance to air pollutants.

Uptake of pollutants. Crops or native vegetation dominate the ground surface in rural areas. Urban shade trees and parklands may be significant in cities. The abundant leaf area removes pollutants from the air. Species with large stomatal conductance, for example, maize and cotton, may remove regionally significant amounts of compounds such as ozone. Shelter belts of tall trees may be effective in sheltering local areas, though this effect depends on local circulation patterns. Vegetation may also be effective in removing particles, including blowing dust, from the air. The pollutant molecules removed from the atmosphere are those that cause the symptoms described above.

Biogenic hydrocarbon emissions. A key precursor of ozone production is volatile organic compounds. In some areas, reducing emissions of gasoline and solvents has led to reduction in ozone concentrations. In other areas, vegetation is a dominant source of biogenic hydrocarbons (for example, the pleasant terpenes of a pine forest). In these areas, more stringent controls on the other precursors, such as nitrogen oxides, may be required. In some cities, selection of low-emission shade tree species may contribute to control of volatile organic compounds.

For background information *see* ACID RAIN; AGRICULTURE; AIR POLLUTION; ATMOSPHERE; ATMOSPHERIC CHEMISTRY; ATMOSPHERIC OZONE; CARBON; GAS AND ATMOSPHERE ANALYSIS; GREENHOUSE EFFECT; METHANE; NATURAL GAS; SOIL in the McGraw Encyclopedia of Science & Technology.　　David A. Grantz

Bibliography. N. H. Batjes, The carbon and nitrogen in the soils of the world, *Eur. J. Soil Sci.*, 47:151–163, 1996; H. Eswaran, E. Van den Berg, and P. Reich, Organic carbon in soils of the world, *Soil Sci. Soc. Amer. J.*, 57:192–194, 1993; D. A. Grantz et al., Study demonstrates ozone uptake by SJV crops, *Calif. Agr.*, 48:9–12, 1994; D. A. Grantz and S. Yang, Effect of O_3 on hydraulic architecture in Pima cotton: Biomass allocation and water transport capacity of roots and shoots, *Plant Phys.*, 112:1649–1657, 1996; D. S. Jenkinson and A. Ayanaba, Decomposition of 14C labeled plant material under tropical conditions, *Soil Sci. Soc. Amer. J.*, 41:912–915, 1977; E. J. Pell, C. D. Schlagnhaufer, and R. N. Arteca, O_3-induced oxidative stress: Mechanisms of action and reaction, *Physiologia Plantarum*, 100:264–273, 1997; C. Rosenzweig and D. Hillel, *Climate Change and the Global Harvest: Potential Impacts of the Greenhouse Effect on Agriculture*, Oxford University Press, New York, 1998; W. H. Schlesinger, An overview of the carbon cycle, in R. Lal et al. (eds.), *Soils and Global Change*, CRC, Boca Raton, FL, 1995; R. F. Stallard, Terrestrial sedimentation and the C cycle: Coupling weathering and erosion to carbon burial, *Global Biogeochem. Cycles*, 12:231–237, 1998.

Air quality

The World Health Organization has estimated that approximately 2.7 million deaths are attributable to air pollution each year. Among the air pollutants of greatest concern are ozone (O_3), suspended particulate matter (SPM), nitrogen dioxide (NO_2), sulfur dioxide (SO_2), carbon monoxide (CO), lead (Pb), and other toxins. Ozone is one of the most prevalent air pollutants in large cities, and suspended particulate matter has great impact worldwide. The sources and formation of these two air pollutants are described below. A review of the distribution and concentration of air pollutants worldwide is available from the World Health Organization (see **table**).

Ozone. Ozone is a reactive gas that has been associated with increased respiratory illness and decreased lung function, particularly in children. National Ambient Air Quality Standards (NAAQS) in the United States require that ozone concentrations, averaged over 1 h, be less than 0.12 part per million. This concentration standard is exceeded in most large cities in the United States and around the world. In 1997 the U.S. Environmental Protection Agency proposed, based on recent health studies, that the NAAQS for ozone be made more stringent. Meeting existing, as well as proposed, air-quality standards for ozone concentrations will require substantial reductions in emissions. Understanding which emissions need to be reduced is complex because ozone is not emitted directly. It is the product of atmospheric reactions, and therefore developing an effective strategy for controlling ozone requires a sound understanding of the complex atmospheric chemistry that leads to its formation.

Ozone is produced in the atmosphere by the reaction of atomic oxygen (O) with molecular oxygen (O_2), as shown in reaction (1). M is a third body,

$$O + O_2 + M \rightarrow O_3 + M \qquad (1)$$

such as molecular nitrogen (N_2) or O_2, that removes the energy of the reaction and stabilizes the O_3.

In the upper atmosphere (above 20 km or 12 mi, in the stratosphere), atomic oxygen is produced by the photodissociation of molecular oxygen. The ozone formed in the stratosphere absorbs solar ultraviolet radiation, heating the atmosphere and protecting the biosphere from harmful radiation. In the lower atmosphere, near ground level, exposure to ozone is a health concern. In the lower atmosphere, the atomic oxygen responsible for forming ozone is produced by the photodissociation of nitrogen dioxide, as shown in reaction (2). The nitric oxide

$$NO_2 + h\nu \rightarrow NO + O \qquad (2)$$

(NO) thus formed reacts rapidly with O_3, reforming NO_2 and molecular oxygen by reaction (3). During

$$NO + O_3 \rightarrow NO_2 + O_2 \qquad (3)$$

daylight hours, this three-reaction cycle (1–3) produces a steady-state concentration of ground-level ozone that depends on the ratio of the concentrations of NO and NO_2, as shown in Eq. (4). $[NO_2]$

$$O_3 = k[NO_2]/[NO] \qquad (4)$$

and [NO] are the concentrations of nitrogen dioxide and nitric oxide, respectively, and k is a temperature-dependent constant.

Air quality in megacities*

City	SO_2	SPM	Pb	CO	NO_2	O_3	Year in which data were collected
Athens	L	ND	ND	L	S	L	1995
Bangkok	L	S	L	ND	L	ND	1995
Beijing	S	S	ND	ND	ND	ND	1994
Bucharest	L	M-H	S	ND	M-H	ND	1995
Calcutta	L	S	ND	ND	L	ND	1995
Caracas	L	M-H	S	ND	M-H	ND	1995
Delhi	L	S	ND	ND	M-H	ND	1995
Johannesburg	L	L	S	L	L	L	1994
London	L	L	L	L	M-H	L	1995
Los Angeles	L	M-H	L	L	L	M-H	1995
Mexico City	L	S	ND	ND	M-H	S	1993
Santiago	L	S	ND	L	M-H	L	1995
Sofia	L	S	L	ND	S	ND	1995
Shanghai	M-H	S	ND	ND	ND	ND	1994
Sydney	ND	L	L	L	L	L	1995
Tokyo	L	M-H	L	L	M-H	L	1995
Xian	M-H	S	ND	ND	ND	ND	1994

*Data are from the World Health Organization.
L = low pollution; WHO guidelines are normally met.
M-H = moderate to heavy pollution; WHO guidelines are exceeded by up to a factor of 2.
S = serious problem; WHO guidelines are exceeded by more than a factor of 2.
ND = no data.

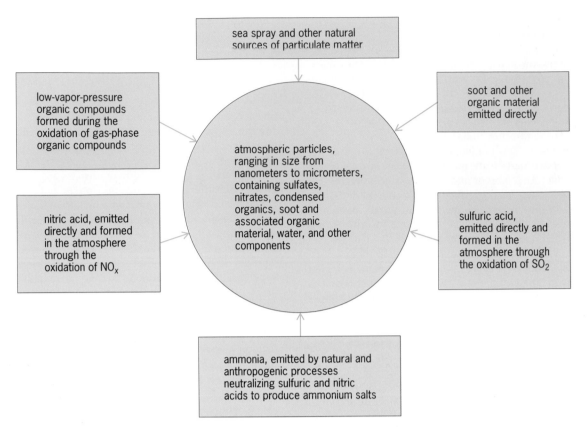

Processes important in the formation of fine particulate matter.

Any atmospheric reaction that influences the concentrations of NO and NO_2 will impact ozone concentrations. The reactions of hydrocarbons are particularly important in this regard. The main class of reactions that are of concern are those of the peroxy radicals, as shown in reaction (5). RO_2 is a peroxy radical and RO is an alkoxy radical.

$$RO_2 + NO \rightarrow NO_2 + RO \qquad (5)$$

Nitric oxide reacts with peroxy radicals, produced during the oxidation of hydrocarbons, to form NO_2 and an alkoxy radical. This class of reactions converts NO into NO_2, which increases the steady-state concentration of ground-level ozone, as indicated by Eq. (4).

Reactions (1)–(3) and (5) describe the main features of ozone formation in the lower atmosphere. However, the chemistry that leads to the formation of the peroxy radicals and the chemistry that determines the fate of oxides of nitrogen (NO_x) in the atmosphere are coupled and can lead to nonlinear relationships between ozone concentrations and the emissions of its hydrocarbon and NO_x precursors.

For example, increasing the concentration of reactive hydrocarbons generally results in more ozone formation by increasing the rate at which alkoxy radicals are produced. But increasing the concentrations of oxides of nitrogen (NO_x) can result in either higher or lower ozone concentrations, depend-

ing on whether the NO_x acts to scavenge reactive radicals from the atmosphere or participates in key classes of hydrocarbon reactions. This complex interplay between nitrogen oxides and hydrocarbons in the formation of ozone makes developing strategies for reducing ozone concentrations difficult. In some regions, controls on hydrocarbons will be the most effective strategy for reducing ozone; while in other regions, controls on the emissions of oxides of nitrogen may be more effective. In many parts of the United States, both hydrocarbon and nitrogen oxide emission reductions are used to reduce ambient ozone concentrations.

Particulate matter. Fine particles, suspended in the atmosphere, are the primary cause of morbidity and mortality associated with air pollution worldwide. Substantial statistical evidence indicates that exposure to high concentrations of fine particulate matter (diameters of less than 2 micrometers) reduces lung function and increases the incidence of respiratory ailments and mortality. Fine particles in the atmosphere are not homogeneous, however. They vary substantially in size and composition. Particles in the atmosphere range in size from a few nanometers to more than a micrometer. They contain both inorganic and organic materials, including metals, acids, organic compounds, soot, and biological materials. It is not yet clear which particle sizes or which components of the complex mix of chemical species present in particles are responsible for their health impacts. Substantial research is under way to resolve these uncertainties.

Particles are injected into the atmosphere by a variety of natural and anthropogenic processes, including the entrainment of dust and sea spray by wind, the eruption of volcanoes, and the combustion of fuels. Particles are also formed in the atmosphere as the result of the atmospheric oxidation of sulfur, NO_x, and hydrocarbon emissions. These complex processes interact in the formation of fine particulate matter (see **illus.**).

Given the diverse array of chemical components and physical sizes associated with atmospheric particulate matter, and given the uncertainty associated with the causal agents responsible for the health impacts of fine particles, developing effective control strategies for fine particles will be difficult.

Other air pollutants. Although ozone and fine particulate matter are only two of many air pollutants that are of concern worldwide, they illustrate characteristics shared by many air pollutants. They, or their precursors, are emitted by a variety of natural and anthropogenic sources; their concentrations in the atmosphere are governed by a complex set of chemical and physical processes, and they have known health effects, but the mechanisms of the health impacts may not be known with certainty. Research will continue to shed light on the atmospheric chemical and physical processes influencing air quality, as well as the relationships between outdoor air quality and indoor air quality.

For background information *see* AIR POLLUTION; ATMOSPHERIC CHEMISTRY; ATMOSPHERIC OZONE; CARBON; HYDROCARBON; NITROGEN OXIDES; OZONE; PHOTOCHEMISTRY; SULFUR in the McGraw-Hill Encyclopedia of Science & Technology.   D. T. Allen

Bibliography. B. J. Finlayson-Pitts and J. N. Pitts, *Chemistry of the Upper and Lower Atmosphere*, Academic Press, San Diego, 1999; National Research Council, *Research Priorities for Airborne Particulate Matter: I, Immediate Priorities and a Long-Range Research Portfolio*, National Academy Press, Washington, DC, 1998; J. H. Seinfeld and S. N. Pandis, *Atmospheric Chemistry and Physics*, Wiley Interscience, New York, 1998.

Angiosperms

The angiosperms, or flowering plants, are geologically a very young group. They first appeared in the fossil record in the earliest Cretaceous about 140 million years ago, almost 300 million years after the first occurrence of terrestrial plants. Despite this late appearance, angiosperms have developed a bewildering diversity exceeding by far that of any other plant group. In the present flora, angiosperms comprise between 250,000 and 300,000 living species. Timing of angiosperm origin and early diversification is still controversial, but new findings of exquisitely preserved Cretaceous flowers have greatly extended our knowledge of early angiosperms. It is clear from the fossil record that extensive extinctions have taken place in several angiosperm lineages, and that the total angiosperm diversity is much higher than what is seen today.

Reconstructing angiosperm phylogeny. Reconstructing the evolutionary pathway of early angiosperms is not yet completed. Progress has been impeded by a poor fossil record and an apparent wide evolutionary gap between angiosperms and other seed plants, which has induced problems in resolving phylogenetic patterns and testing phylogenetic models against the geological record.

Recent developments in molecular and morphological based systematics and powerful programs for analyzing large data sets in a phylogenetic context have greatly improved the potential for more stable results (**Fig. 1**). Furthermore, the discovery of three-dimensionally preserved flowers, fruits, seeds, and stamens from Cretaceous strata has provided a new source for studying reproductive structures in early angiosperms (**Fig. 2**).

The new phylogenetic analyses no longer support the traditional division of angiosperms into two distinct lineages, dicots and monocots. Instead they identify two major monophyletic groups, higher dicots (eudicots) and monocots, embedded in a grade of basal dicots often referred to as the magnoliids (Fig. 1). Eudicots are distinguished from the magnoliids and monocots by their pollen, which has three apertures or an aperture configuration derived from this basic type. Most magnoliids and monocots have pollen with a single aperture. The new

Fig. 1. Hypothesis for relationships among angiosperms based on molecular analyses. (*Simplified after Y.-L. Qui et al., The earliest angiosperms: Evidence from mitochondrial, plastid and nuclear genomes, Nature, 402:404–407, 1999*)

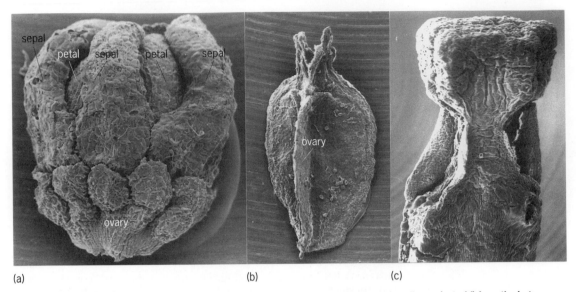

Fig. 2. Fossil floral structures from the Cretaceous. (a) *Scandianthus costatus*, a eudicot flower (asterid) from the Late Cretaceous of southern Sweden, showing differentiated perianth with sepals and petals borne on top of the ribbed ovary. (b) Magnoliid flower (Chloranthaceae) from the Early Cretaceous of Portugal, showing simple perianth-like structures at top of the ovary. (c) Stamen of magnoliid flower from the Early Cretaceous of Portugal, showing extensive sterile tissue between and above the small lateral pollen sacs.

analyses also split the paleoherbs, a group of herbaceous magnoliids and monocots that in previous analyses were resolved as a monophyletic clade.

In many earlier classifications, *Magnolia* was a basal taxon, and its large flowers with many parts were thought to be primitive in angiosperms. The fossil record, however, indicates that the ancestral flowers may have been smaller and simpler. This is in line with the new phylogenetic analyses that identify a basal grade of magnoliids referred to as ANITA (from its constituents Amborellaceae, Nymphaeales, Illiciales, Trimeniaceae, and Austrobaileyaceae), which includes several taxa with small, simple flowers.

Timing of diversification. Phylogenetic analyses indicate that angiosperms may have originated well before their first appearance in the geological record. Currently, however, there are no unequivocal records of angiosperms older than Cretaceous, and angiosperms clearly had their first major phase of diversification in the Early Cretaceous. Pre-Cretaceous records have invariably revealed problems with the determinations or dating.

The earliest angiosperm fossils are dispersed pollen occurring sporadically in pollen and spore assemblages of Valanginian–early Hauterivian age, about 140–135 million years old. In these assemblages, angiosperms constitute less than 1% of the total spore and pollen diversity, but the rise of angiosperms to ecological dominance was dramatic and rapid. By the Barremian-Aptian, only about 10 million years after their first appearance, angiosperms were already diverse and of almost worldwide distribution. About 30 million years later by the Albian-Cenomanian, they had attained a dominant position in the world's vegetation extending into the polar regions of both hemispheres.

Leaves, pollen, and wood. For a long time, dispersed pollen and leaves were the major source for studying Cretaceous angiosperms. Together they have yielded important information on general patterns of diversification, and have documented a distinct increase in diversity and complexity through the Cretaceous. These organs rarely provide enough characters for detailed systematic studies, but pollen in particular has been useful in establishing first occurrences of major clades.

There are very few records of wood and leaves from the earliest phases of angiosperm history. Dispersed pollen as well as the new reproductive fossils indicate that angiosperms were diverse and at least locally abundant early in the Cretaceous; that the lack of leaves and wood may be due to lack of large trees; and that early angiosperms were perhaps smaller plants (small trees, shrubs, or herbs) producing little wood and delicate leaves with low fossilization potential.

Fossil flowers. Until recently, angiosperm reproductive organs, such as flower, fruits, seeds, and isolated stamens, were also extremely rare. However, during the past 20 years a number of rich floras with angiosperm reproductive organs have been discovered from Cretaceous strata in Europe, North America, and Asia.

The first Cretaceous flora with abundant angiosperm reproductive organs was discovered in 1979 in southern Sweden. The fossils occur in Late Cretaceous (Santonian/Campanian, about 80 million years old) sediments, and could be extracted from the sediments by sieving in water. They are small, charcoalified flowers, fruits, and seeds, often with their three-dimensional form retained (Fig. 2a). Following this discovery, intensive search for similar sediments and fossils resulted in the finding of numerous floras from other parts of the world. Most significant are a number of floras from the Early Cretaceous of Portugal and North America. The Portuguese floras are Barremian or Aptian, perhaps 120–125 million years old. The North America floras are slightly younger and embrace a longer time interval.

Systematic position. The Early Cretaceous floras from Portugal are extremely rich in angiosperms. Currently about 140–150 taxa of flowers, fruits, and seeds have been identified. A survey of pollen in flowers, in dispersed stamens, and on fruit surfaces shows that about 85% of pollen taxa have a single aperture, indicating affinity to magnoliids and perhaps some basal monocots. Only 15% of the taxa have three equatorial apertures characteristic of eudicots. This ratio of basal angiosperms to eudicots strongly contrasts with that of Late Cretaceous and Tertiary floras, where eudicots are clearly dominant and basal angiosperms typically constitute less than 5% of the taxa. Also, in the present floras basal angiosperms constitute a minor fraction of the angiosperm diversity.

Most of the Early Cretaceous angiosperms from Portugal cannot be assigned to any existing family or order, and many of them clearly belong to extinct lineages. The Chloranthaceae are currently the only extant family that has been documented among these fossils (Fig. 2b). The Chloranthaceae is thought to be close to the base of the angiosperm tree, and its early occurrence in angiosperm history has also been suggested by dispersed pollen. Other fossil taxa from Portugal show close similarity to extant members of the ANITA grade, particularly to the Amborellaceae, Nymphaeales, and Illiciales, but exhibit a suite of characters unknown in the extant taxa. There are also fossils exhibiting monocot affinity as well as fossils showing a mixture of monocot and magnoliid features, but so far no extant monocot taxon has been identified from the Early Cretaceous. Eudicot fossils from the Early Cretaceous floras of Portugal are all of simple structure and organization, and share features with taxa resolved at the base of eudicots.

All Early Cretaceous angiosperm reproductive organs from Portugal are very small, ranging in length up to about 4 mm. Flowers are either unisexual or bisexual, often with few parts (Fig. 2b). They are simple, naked or with a simple perianth. In these small and simple flowers, the androecium often constitutes the most prominent part. Stamens often have massive sterile tissue (connective) between and above the minute pollen sacs (Fig. 2c). Filaments are usually poorly developed and anthers always attached basally. Dehiscence is by laterally hinged valves that open like doors or by longitudinal slits. The gynoecium consists of one to many free carpels. The number of seeds per carpel is always low, and many fruiting structures are one-seeded.

Subsequent evolution. Mid-Cretaceous angiosperm fossils, about 115–95 million years old, show an increased complexity in pollen features, leaf architecture, and floral structure. Eudicot angiosperms become more frequent, and the number of taxa assignable to modern taxa is higher, both among eudicots and magnoliids. Magnoliids are still the predominant element, and the flowers continually are relatively simple. In these slightly younger floras, there are also several larger floral structures, and these floras include the earliest records of Magnoliaceae.

In the Late Cretaceous, angiosperms pass through another major radiation phase. During this period, eudicots expanded dramatically; and more specialized flowers, including forms with well-differentiated calyx and corolla, floral tubes, and nectaries, occurred for the first time. By the end of the Cretaceous, all major eudicot groups were established as well as several distinct monocot lineages. A further major radiation event took place in the Tertiary. At this time, more specialized groups such as the grasses and orchids proliferated.

Coevolutionary relationships. The major radiation phases of angiosperms may be related to interaction with other organisms as well as changing physical conditions. Interaction with pollinators is believed to be an important factor in angiosperm diversification. The Early Cretaceous fossils include both wind-pollinated and insect-pollinated forms. In the early corolla-less insect-pollinated flowers, stamens probably played the major role in attraction of pollinators. Stamens were bulky with massive sterile tissue extended apically. Reward for pollinators was most likely pollen. Early Cretaceous insect pollinators were unspecialized, probably small flies, beetles, and micropterygid moths.

While attraction and reward in the earliest insect-pollinated flowers were mainly by the androecium, Late Cretaceous flowers show an array of specializations. Most important is the evolution of petals from stamens. This probably took place in the earliest Late Cretaceous about 95 million years ago. Petals are less expensive to produce and are, from an architectural point of view, more flexible than stamens. Late Cretaceous flowers also exhibit the first nectaries and extensive synorganization of parts. Petals, nectaries, and fusion of parts are important variables in establishing more efficient pollination, and during the Late Cretaceous a variety of flowers adapted for more specialized pollinators occur along with new insect taxa adapted for foraging pollen and nectar. The major radiation of specialized insect pollinators, however, does not occur until the Tertiary. During the Tertiary, there is also a marked radiation in pollinating vertebrates such as bats and birds.

In contrast to previous views, angiosperms may also have entered a coevolutionary relationship with fruit- and seed-eating animals early in their history. A survey of fruit types in the Early Cretaceous angiosperms indicates that one-fourth of the fruits were fleshy, either berries or drupes, and may have been animal-dispersed. There are also fruits with spiny surfaces indicating animal dispersal. Possible dispersers are small reptiles, birds, and tuberculates, small extinct mammals with an inferred ecology equivalent to that of modern rodents.

For background information *see* CRETACEOUS; FLOWER; FOSSIL; MAGNOLIOPHYTA; PALEOBOTANY; PLANT EVOLUTION; PLANT KINGDOM in the McGraw-Hill Encyclopedia of Science & Technology.

Else Marie Friis; Kaj Raunsgaard Pedersen; Peter R. Crane

Bibliography. C. B. Beck (ed.), *Origin and Early Evolution of Angiosperms*, Columbia University Press, New York, 1976; P. K. Endress and E. M. Friis (eds.), *Early Evolution of Flowers*, Springer-Verlag, New York, 1999; E. M. Friis, W. G. Chaloner, and P. R. Crane (eds.), *The Origins of Angiosperms and Their Biological Consequences*, Cambridge University Press, Cambridge, 1987; E. M. Friis, K. R. Pedersen, and P. R. Crane, Early angiosperm diversification: The diversity of pollen associated with angiosperm reproductive structures in Early Cretaceous floras from Portugal, *Ann. Missouri Bot. Garden*, 86:259–296, 1999; N. F. Hughes, *The Enigma of Angiosperm Origins*, Cambridge University Press, Cambridge, 1994; Y.-L. Qui et al., The earliest angiosperms: Evidence from mitochondrial, plastid and nuclear genomes, *Nature*, 402:404–407, 1999.

Apoptosis

Cell death is a fundamental concept in biology and medicine, and it is characteristic of many diseases. Cell death can take place through the mechanisms of apoptosis or necrosis. While necrotic cell death has been known for a long time, not until the 1970s was apoptotic cell death clearly recognized. Apoptosis requires energy, and it can be regulated by the cell itself. Necrosis is passive cell death, and it is usually caused by an outside factor, such as loss of blood supply. In necrosis, a large group of cells die simultaneously in the same area, and the process is often associated with inflammation and damage to the surrounding tissues. In apoptosis, individual cells die and the fragmented cell is removed by surrounding healthy housekeeping cells, the macrophages, making the process neat; no harm is done to the surrounding tissues. *See* CANCER; CELL CYCLE (CANCER).

Characteristics. Apoptotic cell death generally takes 12–24 h. It is divided into three phases: initiation, effector, and degradation. In the initiation phase, the apoptotic stimulus is introduced to the cell; depending on the strength and the nature of the stimulus, this phase may take several hours. In the effector phase, the apoptotic stimulus is modulated in the cell; this phase is still reversible (the cell can be salvaged). In the degradation phase, the cell is inevitably doomed to die; degradation of cellular proteins and fragmentation of nucleic acids in the cell (see **illus.**) characterize this phase, which normally takes 1–2 h.

Through apoptosis the organism can regulate the number of cells in a given tissue or destroy any unwanted or damaged cells without harming adjacent tissues. Apoptosis is already present at the embryonic stage, where it participates in the formation of different organs and tissues. Human digits, for instance, are formed because cells between the digit anlages die through apoptosis during embryonic development. Thus, apoptosis is the sculptor, which by deleting unnecessary cells gives rise to the appearance of organisms.

Apoptosis participates in the development of the human immune system. The immune system consists of white cells which attack and destroy foreign elements introduced into the human body. Early in development, the defense system is nonselective and consists of white blood cells which are not able to distinguish foreign molecules from self-derived molecules. When the defense system matures, white cells that cannot make the distinction are destroyed in the thymus through apoptosis. In adult tissues, a restricted loss of such a self-tolerance may sometimes take place (that is, harmful, self-directed white cells develop and fail to undergo apoptosis); the individual then suffers from an autoimmune disease. In such a disease, these white blood cells attack some of the host's own tissue components and induce apoptosis. Apoptosis thus functions to protect the host by participating in the development of the immune system, but it may also contribute to the development of an autoimmune disease.

Activation and inhibition. Apoptosis can be triggered by several factors, including irradiation, heat, several chemical drugs, and toxic compounds. Some of these factors may cause genetic alterations. If such alterations occur, the cells are often capable of correcting such damage; but if this fails, an apoptotic cell death program is stimulated. Apoptosis can also be induced through stimulation or inhibition of certain types of cell surface receptor molecules. A receptor serves as a sensor of the outside milieu of the cell. Hormone-dependent cells, such as breast or prostate cells, have hormonal receptors on their

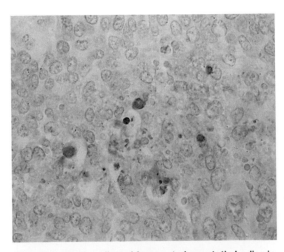

Several apoptotic cells and fragmented apoptotic bodies in cancer cells (in the center area of the figure). They are located by the TUNEL method, which detects apoptotically fragmented nucleic acids in tissue sections.

surface; the well-being of these cells depends on a constant stimulation of the receptors. If the receptors are blocked, the cells suffer an apoptotic death. For example, when receptors fail to respond to certain growth-promoting molecules (such as interleukins), apoptosis is initiated. Some cells, such as white blood cells, harbor ligand molecules, which are able to stimulate receptors that induce apoptosis.

Inside the cell, two families of proteins, the bcl-2's and the caspases, regulate apoptosis. The bcl-2 family proteins operate in the effector phase of apoptosis and may either promote or inhibit apoptosis. A balance between individual bcl-2 family proteins determines whether the cell will live or die. Caspases are enzymes which operate at the degradation phase of apoptosis. Their activation leads to degradation of cellular proteins and fragmentation of cellular nucleic acids. Recently, other groups of proteins involved in apoptosis have been discovered. Inhibitor of apoptosis proteins (IAPs) are capable of inhibiting caspases. There are also proteins, Fas-associated death-domain-like IL-1 beta converting enzyme inhibitory proteins (FLIPs), which inhibit receptor-mediated apoptosis early in the signaling cascade. See TUMOR SUPPRESSOR GENE.

Pathology. Apoptosis takes part in the development of several diseases. These include viral and other infections, autoimmune diseases, many neurodegenerative diseases such as Alzheimer's and Parkinson's diseases, and several metabolic and endocrinologic diseases. In these diseases, apoptosis is usually increased, leading to a loss of cells. In Alzheimer's disease, loss of nerve cells in the brain leads to loss of brain matter and deterioration of the intellectual function. Alzheimer's disease is characterized by a gradual accumulation of an aberrant protein in the neuronal cells called amyloid. Genes which produce this protein also influence apoptosis, and it has been suggested that dysregulation of apoptosis would play a primary role in causing the neuronal loss seen in Alzheimer's disease.

Apoptosis is also operating in vascular diseases such as ischemic heart disease. This disease is characterized by formation of plaques in the vessel walls, eventually leading to obstruction of the blood flow. A great amount of apoptosis has been shown in cells within such plaques. It has been suggested that apoptosis may contribute to the softening of plaques through deletion of cells capable of synthesizing hard collagenous tissue; this softening makes plaques more prone to rupture. A plaque rupture precipitates the formation of an obstructive clot in the blood vessel which leads to an acute heart infarct. When this happens, a part of the heart muscle nourished by the obstructed vessel is destroyed by necrosis. However, some cells at the marginal zone of the infarcted heart muscle undergo apoptosis. By different treatment modalities at an early stage of an acute heart infarct, one may diminish the size of the damaged tissue and save cells from death because at an early stage of apoptosis cells can still be revived and brought

back to normal. Apoptosis also plays a role in the further development of ischemic heart disease. As a consequence of heart infarct, some people develop heart failure; one reason is that the remaining heart cells, which are under continuous strain, slowly undergo apoptosis. This apoptosis gradually leads to a decrease in the number of functioning muscle cells in the wall of the heart and development of a failing heart.

Decreased apoptosis may also cause disease. For example, some types of lymphomas arise due to deranged apoptotic machinery and overproduction of a protein, which lengthens cell survival. In many other types of cancer, apoptosis is increased. The apoptotic rate in different cancer types may vary, but usually about 1–2% of cancer cells show apoptosis. Cancers arise, in part, because even though cell death in cancer tissues is high the rate of cell division is higher. One method to treat cancer would be to increase the proportion of apoptotic cells. In fact, treatments directed at increasing apoptosis are already in use. Both irradiation of tumors and cancer chemotherapy lead to apoptosis of cancer cells, and thus the tumors grow more slowly. In hormone-dependent tumors (such as breast cancer), cancer cells are deprived of hormonal stimulus by antiestrogenic treatment, resulting in their apoptosis. Unfortunately, cancer cell populations are heterogeneous, and such treatment destroys only a part of them. The remaining cells are usually resistant to the treatment and must be dealt with in some other way. More selective treatment modalities, including transfection of viral vectors expressing apoptotic genes, are under development. It is plausible that through increased knowledge of apoptosis a cure for some types of cancer will become possible in the near future. In addition, researchers will be able to develop better treatments for other diseases where apoptosis plays a role.

For background information see ALZHEIMER'S DISEASE; CANCER (MEDICINE); CELL BIOLOGY; DEVELOPMENTAL BIOLOGY; GENETICS; ONCOGENE; TUMOR in the McGraw-Hill Encyclopedia of Science & Technology.   Ylermi Soini

Bibliography. J. M. Adams and S. Cory, The Bcl-2 protein family: Arbitrers of cell survival, Science, 281: 1322–1326, 1998; A. Haunstetter and S. Izumo, Apoptosis: Basic mechanisms and implications for cardiovascular disease, Circ. Res., 82:1111–1129, 1998; J. Jenkins and E. P. Reddy, Reviews: Apoptosis, Oncogene, 17:3203–3399, 1998; Y. Soini, P. Pääkkö, and V.-P. Lehto, Histopathological evaluation of apoptosis in cancer, Amer. J. Pathol., 153:1041–1053, 1998; N. A. Thornberry and Y. Lazebnik, Caspases: Enemies within, Science, 281:1312–1316, 1998.

Arctic Oscillation

The Arctic Oscillation (AO) is a unifying description of how atmospheric pressure in the northern hemisphere varies. Recent changes in the Artic

Oscillation index appear related to changes in the marine and terrestrial environments of the Arctic. To understand this relation is akin to understanding the phenomenon of the El Niño Southern Oscillation (ENSO).

The AO index (**illus.** *b*) is an indicator of sea-level atmospheric pressure temporal variability for the Northern Hemisphere above 20°N. The Arctic Oscillation spatial pattern (illus. *a*) has a dominant low-pressure region roughly centered over the Arctic Ocean, and positive lobes over the North Pacific and North Atlantic. The pressure pattern near the top of the atmosphere correlated with the AO index is very similar to the surface pattern. Thus, a positive AO index implies a strengthening of the counterclock-

wise (cyclonic) polar vortex (spinning ring of air) throughout the atmosphere. The asymmetries in the pressure pattern mean cool winds sweep east-southeast across eastern Canada, and changes in the North Atlantic storm tracks that bring rain and mild temperatures to northern Europe.

Rising AO index. The AO index has been quite variable but has displayed a rising trend since the mid-1960s. The particularly large increase in the AO index after the late 1980s agrees with the pressure decrease observed over the Arctic by others. The AO index time series is similar to the pattern of the North Atlantic Oscillation (NAO) that expresses the north-south pressure difference over the North Atlantic (the NAO index is the sea-level pressure difference between Portugal and Iceland). The North Atlantic Oscillation has been seen as a key climate indicator, particularly for the Atlantic Ocean and the Eurasian continent. The NAO can be viewed as a regional expression of the hemispheric-scale Arctic Oscillation. In fact, research shows that the AO index is more strongly coupled to surface air temperature variations over the Eurasian continent than is the North Atlantic Oscillation. The spatial distribution of the Arctic Oscillation-correlated temperature change is consistent with the observed increases in Arctic air temperatures, including the strong increase over the Russian Arctic.

Changes in Arctic region. The rise in the AO index has occurred during the same period in which major changes in the Arctic Ocean and the high-latitude terrestrial environment have been seen. The sea ice cover has decreased in extent and thickness in recent decades. Based on satellite remote sensing data, investigators found a 3% decrease in Northern Hemisphere sea ice extent over the last 20 years. Even more significant in terms of total ice volume, scientists using ice draft measurements by submarines found that the average sea ice thickness has decreased 42% (from 3.1 m to 1.8 m, or 10 ft to 6 ft) over the past 30 years.

Oceanographic expeditions in the 1990s revealed changes in the circulation, salinity, and temperature of the Arctic Ocean. They indicate that the boundary between the Atlantic-derived and Pacific-derived upper ocean water types has moved. Earlier it was approximately aligned with the Lomonosov Ridge, but now it lies nearly parallel with the Alpha and Mendeleyev ridges. The salinity in the upper 250 m (820 ft) has increased dramatically in a wedge extending from the Lomonosov Ridge to a front roughly aligned with the Alpha and Mendeleyev ridges. The temperature has increased in the warm core of Atlantic water over the Lomonosov Ridge, with the maximum temperature over 1°C (1.8°F) greater than at any time in the observed past. A less intense warm core has become apparent over the Mendeleyev Ridge, and there is a general warming in the Makarov Basin centered near 200 m (656 ft) depth. The position of the increased temperature over sloping topography suggests that the warm water serves as a tracer

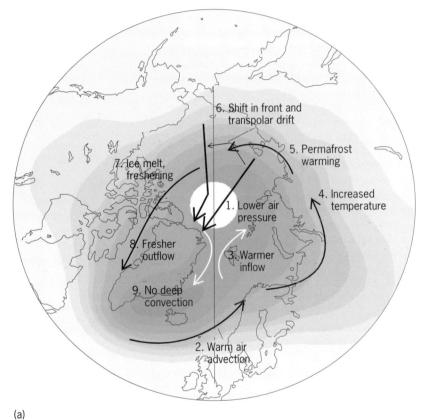

(a)

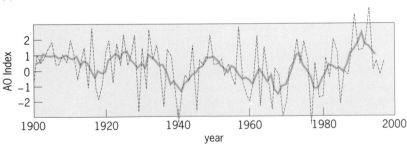

(b)

Contours of the Arctic Oscillation pattern of surface pressure variation (top panel) and the time series of the AO index (bottom panel, 5-year running average, of whole-year averages). A positive AO, as shown strongly in the last 10–15 years, is characterized by lower-than-normal air pressure over the Arctic Ocean and a counterclockwise spin-up of westerly winds (polar vortex). This causes the changes indicated in the Arctic environment.

that is carried by the bathymetrically steered flow of Atlantic water into the basin, and that the warming is due to changes in the Atlantic water inflow temperature. As part of these changes, the cold, salt-stratified halocline layer that isolates the surface from the warm Atlantic water is growing thinner and has disappeared altogether in some regions of the eastern Arctic. The near-surface region of the Beaufort Sea has become fresher and warmer than in the past. This appears to be related in part to a reduction in the ice coverage and thickness; the summer of 1998 was characterized by record retreat of the ice edge in that region.

Pressure and temperature. There have been changes in the atmosphere and terrestrial environment as well. The annual mean atmospheric surface pressure over the Arctic has been decreasing and has been below the 1970–1995 mean in every year since 1988. Also, the air temperature has been increasing since the mid-1970s, especially over the Russian Arctic. Changes in air temperature have been attended by reductions in spring snow cover since the mid-1980s. Other studies point to increased plant growth and increased fire frequency. The increased temperatures may be responsible for increased permafrost temperatures in the discontinuous permafrost zone of Alaska in the 1990s. Permafrost warming and thawing have been observed over large areas of the Russian Arctic.

Relation to AO. The changes in the Arctic Ocean appear related to the rising AO index. The Arctic Oscillation pattern includes a northward component in the average winds across the Atlantic sector, carrying warm air over the Greenland-Norwegian Sea, Scandinavia, and northern Russia. The increase in warm-air advection results in the observed increase in surface air temperature in the Greenland Norwegian Sea and northern Russia. The warming over the Norwegian Sea reduces the heat loss from the Atlantic water before it enters the Arctic Ocean, and leads to the warmer Atlantic water observed in the Arctic Ocean. The warmer air temperatures also lead to increasing permafrost temperatures and drying conditions on land.

Polar vortex. As the AO index increases and atmospheric pressure decreases over the Arctic, the strength of the polar vortex increases. This adds counterclockwise wind stress to the sea ice and the ocean circulation and, owing to the effects of the Earth's rotation, results in reduced ice convergence. This in turn results in more open water, greater radiative heat absorption, and increased summer melt as observed in the Beaufort Sea. The increased cyclonic forcing may also be responsible for rerouting of Siberian runoff to the east along the Siberian shore. This fresh water is thought to mix with Atlantic water to form cold halocline (region of strong vertical salinity gradient) water of intermediate salinity. Thus deflection of the runoff to the east, away from the source regions of the cold halocline, may be the cause of the shrinking cold halocline. The increased cyclonic vorticity added to the Arctic Ocean may also increase the flow of ice and relatively fresh surface water out through Fram Strait, increasing stratification in the Greenland Sea. This would contribute to the weakened deep convection there in recent years.

A central scientific and societal question is whether the recent rise of the AO index and consequent changes at high latitudes is part of an oscillation or a precursor of more permanent change. The Arctic Oscillation and an analogous annular mode in the Southern Hemisphere called the Antarctic Oscillation (AAO) are fundamental modes of atmospheric variability. As such, the Arctic Oscillation varies over a wide range of frequencies, and is quite noisy (see illus.). In the 1990s the 5-year average of the index is high, but the variability in individual years is nearly as great as the change in the 5-year average. In 1995 the index was even negative. Over the 1990s the index averaged about plus one standard deviation with a variation of about one standard deviation. With such a noisy signal there is no way to know for certain if the rising trend of the last 20 or 30 years will continue. However, the implications of the observed upward trend for global change are important. Simulations of anthropogenic (caused or produced by humans) climate change suggest that the indices of the Arctic Oscillation and the Antarctic Oscillation show strong positive trends in simulations of greenhouse warming. The changes seen in the last two decades are actually more abrupt than the models predict. Therefore, even if the present trend is merely transient rather than a precursor of change, it and the associated response in the ocean and on land give an idea of what to expect should global warming occur.

Outlook. The responses of the ice, ocean, and land that have already been seen suggest how climatically critical high-latitude feedbacks may evolve. For example, the cyclonic forcing of the Arctic Ocean due to a rising Arctic Oscillation will tend to cause ice divergence and more open water and thin ice. This will decrease the fraction of sunlight reflected from the surface (albedo) and allow more of the Sun's energy to melt even more ice. If the cyclonic circulation of a rising Arctic Oscillation also results in diversion of Siberian river water eastward along the shelves and consequent elimination of the cold halocline, the ocean heat flux to the ice will increase, further depleting the ice cover and albedo. Any of the factors increasing the amount of ice melt will increase the stratification, and a cyclonic circulation may carry more fresh water either through Fram Strait or through the Canadian islands, where it can shut down deep convection in the Greenland or Labrador seas. In both cases this would link the changes in the Arctic to changes in the global thermohaline circulation.

In the global climate system, the high latitudes are the regions providing a net loss of energy to space. This is due in part to the high albedo of the snow and ice covers, which reflect solar radiation. Therefore, the feedback mechanisms set in motion by the

Arctic Oscillation that affect the albedo, make the coupling of the rising Arctic Oscillation to the Arctic environment important to the heat balance of the Earth.

For background information *see* CLIMATE MODIFICATION; CLIMATE PREDICTION; EIGENFUNCTION; EL NINO; MARINE SEDIMENTS; SUN; UPPER-ATMOSPHERE DYNAMICS in the McGraw-Hill Encyclopedia of Science & Technology.   James Morison

Bibliography. J. H. Morison, K. Aagaard, and M. Steele, Recent Environmental Changes in the Arctic: A Review, *Arctic* (Arctic Seas: Currents of Change Special Issue), December 2000; D. A. Rothrock, Y. Yu, and G. A. Maykut, Thinning of the arctic sea-ice cover, *Geophys. Res. Lett.*, 26(23):3469–3472, 1999; D. T. Shindell et al., Simulation of recent northern winter climate trends by greenhouse-gas forcing, *Nature*, 399:452–455, 1999; W. J. Thompson and J. W. Wallace, The Arctic Oscillation signature in the wintertime geopotential height and temperature fields, *Geophys. Res. Lett.*, 25:1297–1300, 1998.

Astronomical catalogs

In 1781 the French astronomer Charles Messier published his catalog of star clusters and nebulae. Officially, the principal catalog of these objects is the *New General Catalogue of Clusters and Nebulae*, drawn up by J. L. E. Dreyer in 1888, but the Messier numbers are much more widely used by amateur astronomers. For example, the Andromeda Nebula is much more widely known as M31 than as NGC 224. Recently, the Caldwell catalog has been compiled to list notable objects that are absent from the Messier catalog.

Messier catalog. Messier's original catalog contained 103 entries. It has been slightly extended since, mainly from notes left by Messier and by his colleague Pierre Mechain, and is generally terminated at M109. NGC 205, one of the smaller companions of the Andromeda Spiral, is sometimes listed as M110, but this entry is not generally accepted.

Messier himself was not interested in nebulae. He was a comet hunter who was frequently misled by dim, misty patches in the sky, which had to be checked and eliminated; indeed, many clusters and nebulae look remarkably like faint comets, particularly in a small telescope such as was used by Messier. Messier therefore decided to list clusters and nebulae as "objects to avoid." Ironically, he never discovered a particularly interesting comet, but his catalog has remained popular. There are many Messier clubs, mainly among amateur observers, whose members compete to see how many of the Messier objects can be observed during the course of a single night.

However, the Messier catalog is unbalanced. In particular, Messier omitted some very prominent clusters and nebulae because there was no danger of mistaking them for comets; notable omissions include the Sword Handle in Perseus, the Hyades in Taurus, and the Helix planetary nebula in Aquarius. Also, he carried out all his observing from France, so that far-southern objects were inaccessible to him and do not appear in the catalog.

Caldwell catalog. Because of the omissions in the Messier catalog, in 1995 Patrick Moore decided to compile a new catalog for the use of amateur observers, based on the same principles as Messier's catalog but not containing any of the objects listed by him. It contains the same number of entries, 109, and all the objects are easy to locate with small telescopes. The compilation is named the Caldwell catalog (see **table**) and uses C as a prefix, after the compiler's hyphenated surname, Caldwell-Moore.

Arrangement of entries. There is no systematic order in Messier's list, but for the Caldwell catalog it seemed convenient to arrange the objects in order of declination, beginning in the far north (C1, NGC 188 in Cepheus) and ending in the far south (C109, NGC 3195 in Chamaeleon). This arrangement allows the observer to readily determine which objects are within range. For example, an observer sited at latitude +51° in southern England can see down to approximately declination −35°. This means that C67 in Fornax, declination −30°17′, is available; C68 in Corona Australis, declination −36°57′, is probably not. To observe the remaining Caldwell objects, it is necessary to travel farther south.

Limiting magnitude. The limiting magnitude was the next major consideration. The faintest object in Messier's list is M76, the Little Dumbbell, a planetary nebula in Perseus, whose official integrated magnitude is 12.2. There seemed no point in going much below this, and only one Caldwell object, C2 (NGC 40, a planetary nebula in Cepheus), is fainter than magnitude 12 (bearing in mind that integrated magnitudes for extended objects are somewhat arbitrary). The only other objects in the Caldwell catalog with official integrated magnitudes below 11 are C24 (NGC 1275, a Seyfert galaxy also known as the radio source Perseus A) and C35 (NGC 4889, the brightest galaxy in the Coma cluster).

Prominent objects. Some of the Caldwell objects are visible with the unaided eye, and many are within the range of binoculars. There seemed no reason to exclude some very prominent clusters and nebulae, such as the Hyades (C41; not listed in the NGC), the Sword Handle (C14), the Helix Nebula in Aquarius (C63), the Sculptor galaxy (C65), and the Tau Canis Majoris cluster (C64). In the Northern Hemisphere, selection was limited by the policy of excluding any objects given by Messier, but in the far south there was no such constraint, and most of the brightest nebular objects could be included, such as the Centaurus radio galaxy, NGC 5128 (C77), which is the radio source Centaurus A; the globular clusters Omega Centauri and 47 Tucanae (C80 and 106, respectively); the Omicron Velorum cluster (C85); the Theta Carinae cluster (C102); the Tarantula

The Caldwell catalog

C	NGC or IC*	Constellation	Type	Right ascension (2000)	Declination (2000)	Apparent visual magnitude	Size, arcminutes	Notes
1	188	Cepheus	Open cluster	00ʰ 44.4ᵐ	+85° 20′	8.1	14	
2	40	Cepheus	Planetary nebula	00ʰ 13.0ᵐ	+72° 32′	12.4	0.6	
3	4236	Draco	Sb galaxy	12ʰ 16.7ᵐ	+69° 28′	9.7	19 × 7	
4	7023	Cepheus	Nebula	21ʰ 01.8ᵐ	+68° 12′	—	18 × 18	Bright reflection nebula
5	IC 342	Camelopardalis	SBc galaxy	03ʰ 46.8ᵐ	+68° 06′	9.2	18 × 17	
6	6543	Draco	Planetary nebula	17ʰ 58.6ᵐ	+66° 38′	8.1	0.3/5.8	Cat's Eye Nebula
7	2403	Camelopardalis	Sc galaxy	07ʰ 36.9ᵐ	+65° 36′	8.4	18 × 10	
8	559	Cassiopeia	Open cluster	01ʰ 29.5ᵐ	+63° 18′	9.5	4	
9	Sh2-155	Cepheus	Bright nebula	22ʰ 56.8ᵐ	+62° 37′	—	50 × 10	Cave Nebula
10	663	Cassiopeia	Open cluster	01ʰ 46.0ᵐ	+61° 15′	7.1	16	
11	7635	Cassiopeia	Bright nebula	23ʰ 20.7ᵐ	+61° 12′	—	15 × 8	Bubble Nebula
12	6946	Cepheus	Sc galaxy	20ʰ 34.8ᵐ	+60° 09′	8.9	11 × 10	
13	457	Cassiopeia	Open cluster	01ʰ 19.1ᵐ	+58° 20′	6.4	13	Phi Cassiopeiae Cluster
14	869/884	Perseus	Double cluster	02ʰ 20.0ᵐ	+57° 08′	4.3	30 and 30	Sword Handle region
15	6826	Cygnus	Planetary-nebula	19ʰ 44.8ᵐ	+50° 31′	8.8	0.5/2.3	Blinking Nebula
16	7243	Lacerta	Open cluster	22ʰ 15.3ᵐ	+49° 53′	6.4	21	
17	147	Cassiopeia	dE4 galaxy	00ʰ 33.2ᵐ	+48° 30′	9.3	13 × 8	
18	185	Cassiopeia	dE0 galaxy	00ʰ 39.0ᵐ	+48° 20′	9.2	12 × 10	
19	IC 5146	Cygnus	Bright nebula	21ʰ 53.5ᵐ	+47° 16′	—	12 × 12	Cocoon Nebula
20	7000	Cygnus	Bright nebula	20ʰ 58.8ᵐ	+44° 20′	6.0	120 × 100	North America Nebula
21	4449	Canes Venatici	Irregular galaxy	12ʰ 28.2ᵐ	+44° 06′	9.4	5 × 4	
22	7662	Andromeda	Planetary nebula	23ʰ 25.9ᵐ	+42° 33′	8.3	0.3/2.2	
23	891	Andromeda	Sb galaxy	02ʰ 22.6ᵐ	+42° 21′	9.9	14 × 3	
24	1275	Perseus	Seyfert galaxy	03ʰ 19.8ᵐ	+41° 31′	11.6	2.6 × 2	Perseus A radio source
25	2419	Lynx	Globular cluster	07ʰ 38.1ᵐ	+38° 53′	10.4	4.1	
26	4244	Canes Venatici	S galaxy	12ʰ 17.5ᵐ	+37° 49′	10.2	16 × 2.5	
27	6888	Cygnus	Bright nebula	20ʰ 12.0ᵐ	+38° 21′	—	20 × 10	Crescent Nebula
28	752	Andromeda	Open cluster	01ʰ 57.8ᵐ	+37° 41′	5.7	50	
29	5005	Canes Venatici	Sb galaxy	13ʰ 10.9ᵐ	+37° 03′	9.8	5.4 × 2	
30	7331	Pegasus	Sb galaxy	22ʰ 37.1ᵐ	+34° 25′	9.5	11 × 4	
31	IC 405	Auriga	Bright nebula	05ʰ 16.2ᵐ	+34° 16′	9.5	30 × 19	Flaming Star Nebula
32	4631	Canes Venatici	Sc galaxy	12ʰ 42.1ᵐ	+32° 32′	9.3	15 × 3	
33	6992/5	Cygnus	SN remnant	20ʰ 56.4ᵐ	+31° 43′	8	60 × 8	Eastern Veil Nebula
34	6960	Cygnus	SN remnant	20ʰ 45.7ᵐ	+30° 43′	—	70 × 6	Western Veil Nebula
35	4889	Coma Berenices	E4 galaxy	13ʰ 00.1ᵐ	+27° 59′	11.4	3 × 2	Brightest galaxy in Coma Cluster
36	4559	Coma Berenices	Sc galaxy	12ʰ 36.0ᵐ	+27° 58′	9.8	10 × 5	
37	6885	Vulpecula	Open cluster	20ʰ 12.0ᵐ	+26° 29′	5.9	7	
38	4565	Coma Berenices	Sb galaxy	12ʰ 36.3ᵐ	+25° 59′	9.6	16 × 3	
39	2392	Gemini	Planetary nebula	07ʰ 29.2ᵐ	+20° 55′	9.2	0.2/0.7	Eskimo Nebula
40	3626	Leo	Sb galaxy	11ʰ 20.1ᵐ	+18° 21′	10.9	3 × 2	
41	—	Taurus	Open cluster	04ʰ 27ᵐ	+16°	0.5	330	Hyades
42	7006	Delphinus	Globular cluster	21ʰ 01.5ᵐ	+16° 11′	10.6	2.8	Very distant globular cluster
43	7814	Pegasus	Sb galaxy	00ʰ 03.3ᵐ	+16° 09′	10.5	6 × 2	
44	7479	Pegasus	SBb galaxy	23ʰ 04.9ᵐ	+12° 19′	11.0	4 × 3	
45	5248	Boötes	Sc galaxy	13ʰ 37.5ᵐ	+08° 53′	10.2	6 × 4	
46	2261	Monoceros	Bright nebula	06ʰ 39.2ᵐ	+08° 44′	10.3	2 × 1	Hubble's Variable Nebula
47	6934	Delphinus	Globular cluster	20ʰ 34.2ᵐ	+07° 24′	8.9	5.9	
48	2775	Cancer	Sa galaxy	09ʰ 10.3ᵐ	+07° 02′	10.3	4.5 × 3	
49	2237-9	Monoceros	Bright nebula	06ʰ 32.3ᵐ	+05° 03′	5.5	80 × 60	Rosette Nebula
50	2244	Monoceros	Open cluster	06ʰ 32.4ᵐ	+04° 52′	4.8	24	
51	IC 1613	Cetus	Irregular galaxy	01ʰ 04.8ᵐ	+02° 07′	9.3	12 × 11	
52	4697	Virgo	E4 galaxy	12ʰ 48.6ᵐ	−05° 48′	9.3	6 × 4	
53	3115	Sextans	E6 galaxy	10ʰ 05.2ᵐ	−07° 43′	9.1	8 × 3	Spindle Galaxy
54	2506	Monoceros	Open cluster	08ʰ 00.2ᵐ	−10° 47′	7.6	7	
55	7009	Aquarius	Planetary nebula	21ʰ 04.2ᵐ	−11° 22′	8.0	0.4/1.6	Saturn Nebula
56	246	Cetus	Planetary nebula	00ʰ 47.0ᵐ	−11° 53′	10.9	3.8	
57	6822	Sagittarius	Irregular galaxy	19ʰ 44.9ᵐ	−14° 48′	8.8	10 × 9	Barnard's Galaxy
58	2360	Canis Major	Open cluster	07ʰ 17.8ᵐ	−15° 37′	7.2	13	
59	3242	Hydra	Planetary nebula	10ʰ 24.8ᵐ	−18° 38′	7.8	0.3/21	Ghost of Jupiter
60	4038	Corvus	Sc galaxy	12ʰ 01.9ᵐ	−18° 52′	10.7	2.6 × 2	
61	4039	Corvus	Sp galaxy	12ʰ 01.9ᵐ	−18° 53′	10.7	3 × 2	
62	247	Cetus	S galaxy	00ʰ 47.1ᵐ	−20° 46′	9.1	20 × 7	
63	7293	Aquarius	Planetary nebula	22ʰ 29.6ᵐ	−20° 48′	7.3	13	Helix Nebula
64	2362	Canis Major	Open cluster	07ʰ 18.8ᵐ	−24° 57′	4.1	8	Tau Canis Majoris Cluster
65	253	Sculptor	Scp galaxy	00ʰ 47.6ᵐ	−25° 17′	7.1	25 × 7	Sculptor Galaxy
66	5694	Hydra	Globular cluster	14ʰ 39.6ᵐ	−26° 32′	10.2	3.6	
67	1097	Fornax	SBb galaxy	02ʰ 46.3ᵐ	−30° 17′	9.2	9 × 7	
68	6729	Corona Australis	Bright nebula	19ʰ 01.9ᵐ	−36° 57′	9.7	1.0	R Coronae Australis Nebula
69	6302	Scorpius	Planetary nebula	17ʰ 13.7ᵐ	−37° 06′	9.6	0.8	Bug Nebula

The Caldwell catalog (*cont.*)

C	NGC or IC*	Constellation	Type	Right ascension (2000)	Declination (2000)	Apparent visual magnitude	Size, arcminutes	Notes
70	300	Sculptor	Sd galaxy	00^h 54.9^m	−37° 41′	8.7	20 × 13	
71	2477	Puppis	Open cluster	07^h 52.3^m	−38° 33′	5.8	27	
72	55	Sculptor	SB galaxy	00^h 14.9^m	−39° 11′	7.9	32 × 6	Brightest galaxy in Sculptor Cluster
73	1851	Columba	Globular cluster	05^h 14.1^m	−40° 03′	7.3	11	
74	3132	Vela	Planetary nebula	10^h 07.7^m	−40° 26′	9.4	0.8	
75	6124	Scorpius	Open cluster	16^h 25.6^m	−40° 40′	5.8	29	
76	6231	Scorpius	Open cluster	16^h 54.0^m	−41° 48′	2.6	15	
77	5128	Centaurus	Peculiar radio galaxy	13^h 25.5^m	−43° 01′	7.0	18 × 14	Centaurus A radio source
78	6541	Corona Australis	Globular cluster	18^h 08.0^m	−43° 42′	6.6	13	
79	3201	Vela	Globular cluster	10^h 17.6^m	−46° 25′	6.7	18	
80	5139	Centaurus	Globular cluster	13^h 26.8^m	−47° 29′	3.6	36	Omega Centauri
81	6352	Ara	Globular cluster	17^h 25.5^m	−48° 25′	8.1	7	
82	6193	Ara	Open cluster	16^h 41.3^m	−48° 46′	5.2	15	
83	4945	Centaurus	SBc galaxy	13^h 05.4^m	−49° 28′	8.7	20 × 4	
84	5286	Centaurus	Globular cluster	13^h 46.4^m	−51° 22′	7.6	9	
85	IC 2391	Vela	Open cluster	08^h 40.2^m	−53° 04′	2.5	50	O Velorum Cluster
86	6397	Ara	Globular cluster	17^h 40.7^m	−53° 40′	5.6	26	
87	1261	Horologium	Globular cluster	03^h 12.3^m	−55° 13′	8.4	7	
88	5823	Circinus	Open cluster	15^h 05.7^m	−55° 36′	7.9	10	
89	6087	Norma	Open cluster	16^h 18.9^m	−57° 54′	5.4	12	S Normae Cluster
90	2867	Carina	Planetary nebula	09^h 21.4^m	−58° 19′	9.7	0.2	
91	3532	Carina	Open cluster	11^h 06.4^m	−58° 40′	3.0	55	
92	3372	Carina	Bright nebula	10^h 43.8^m	−59° 52′	—	120 × 120	Eta Carinae Nebula
93	6752	Pavo	Globular cluster	19^h 10.9^m	−59° 59′	5.4	20	
94	4755	Crux	Open cluster	12^h 53.6^m	−60° 20′	4.2	10	Jewel Box Cluster
95	6025	Triangulum Aus.	Open cluster	16^h 03.7^m	−60° 30′	5.1	12	
96	2516	Carina	Open cluster	07^h 58.3^m	−60° 52′	3.8	30	
97	3766	Centaurus	Open cluster	11^h 36.1^m	−61° 37′	5.3	12	
98	4609	Crux	Open cluster	12^h 42.3^m	−62° 58′	6.9	5	
99	—	Crux	Dark nebula	12^h 53^m	−63°	—	400 × 300	Coal Sack
100	IC 2944	Centaurus	Open cluster	11^h 36.6^m	−63° 02′	4.5	15	Gamma Centauri Cluster
101	6744	Pavo	SBb galaxy	19^h 09.8^m	−63° 51′	8.3	16 × 10	
102	IC 2602	Carina	Open cluster	10^h 43.2^m	−64° 24′	1.9	50	Theta Carinae Cluster
103	2070	Dorado	Bright nebula	05^h 38.7^m	−69° 06′	8.3	40 × 25	Tarantula Nebula
104	362	Tucana	Globular cluster	01^h 03.2^m	−70° 51′	6.6	13	
105	4833	Musca	Globular cluster	12^h 59.6^m	−70° 53′	7.3	14	
106	104	Tucana	Globular cluster	00^h 24.1^m	−72° 05′	4.0	31	47 Tucanae
107	6101	Apus	Globular cluster	16^h 25.8^m	−72° 12′	9.3	11	
108	4372	Musca	Globular cluster	12^h 25.8^m	−72° 40′	7.8	19	
109	3195	Chamaeleon	Planetary nebula	10^h 09.5^m	−80° 52′	8.4	0.6	

* Unless otherwise noted, the entries in this column are the numbers in the *New General Catalogue* (NGC). Entries with the prefix IC appear in one of the two supplementary *Index Catalogues*.

Nebula (C103); and Kappa Crucis, the Jewel Box cluster (C94). Also included is the Coal Sack, the great dark nebula in the Southern Cross (C99). In fact, the southernmost Messier object is M7, the bright open cluster in Scorpius (declination −34°48′). Had the southernmost objects been visible from France, Messier would certainly have included some of them, since his motive was to avoid wasting time during comet searches. (The Caldwell catalog may be useful in the same way for comet hunters in the Southern Hemisphere. Its unbalanced nature may even be advantageous in some respects.)

Observability of objects. All of the objects in the Caldwell catalog are available to telescopes of modest aperture, and a 15-cm (6-in.) reflector should be adequate for them all, though some of the dimmest planetary nebulae will be elusive. Any observer who has managed to observe all the Messier objects should be able to do the same for the Caldwell entries.

Some Caldwell clubs have been formed, based on experiences with Messier clubs, but it is most unlikely that anyone will be able to observe all the Caldwell objects in a single night; even from locations such as Singapore, practically on the Equator, the near-polar objects will be very low at opposite horizons.

Variety of objects. As with Messier's catalog, the Caldwell catalog contains a wide variety of objects (see **illus.**): open and globular clusters, diffuse nebulae, planetary nebulae, galaxies, and even supernova remnants. The observer who works systematically through the list will become familiar with the various types, and this activity can also lead to useful scientific research—for example, hunting for supernovae in external galaxies. Once all the Caldwell objects have been identified and checked, the observer will have a vastly improved knowledge of the sky.

For background information *see* ASTRONOMICAL CATALOGS; COAL SACK; GALAXY, EXTERNAL; HYADES;

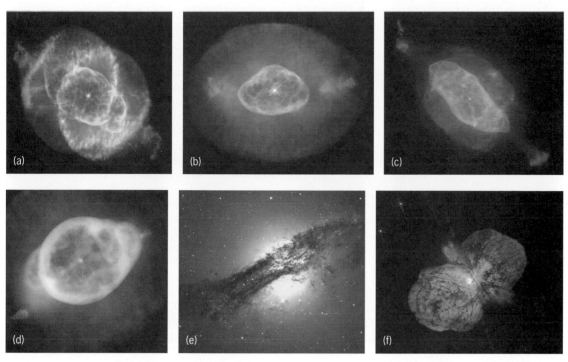

Some objects in the Caldwell catalog. (*a*) Cat's Eye Nebula, C6 (*P. Harrington, K. Borkowski, B. Balick, NASA*). (*b*) Blinking Nebula, C15 (*B. Balick et al., NASA*). (*c*) Saturn Nebula, C55 (*B. Balick et al., NASA*). (*d*) Ghost of Jupiter, C59 (*B. Balick et al., NASA*). (*e*) Centaurus A radio galaxy, taken during the commissioning of the FORS2 spectrograph at the Very Large Telescope, January 31, 2000 (*European Southern Observatory*). (*f*) Eta Carinae Nebula, C92 (*J. Morse, K. Davidson, NASA*). All images except *e* are from the Hubble Space Telescope.

MESSIER CATALOG; NEBULA; PLANETARY NEBULA; STAR CLUSTERS in the McGraw-Hill Encyclopedia of Science & Technology.   Patrick Moore

Bibliography. P. Moore, *Astronomy Data Book*, Institute of Physics Publishing, 2000; P. Moore, The Caldwell catalog, *Sky Telesc.*, 90(6):38–43, December 1995; D. Ratledge, *Observing the Caldwell Objects*, Springer-Verlag, 2000.

Asymmetrical digital subscriber line (ADSL)

Asymmetrical digital subscriber line is a high-throughput transmission system built upon the conventional telephone subscriber loop infrastructure originally designed for the "plain old telephone service" (POTS). Via a telephone subscriber loop, ADSL connects a user to a central office. The transmission throughput of ADSL is asymmetrical. In the downstream direction (from a central office to a user), the transmission throughput of ADSL is between 1 and 8 Mbps (megabits per second), while in the upstream direction (from a user to a central office) it is between 100 and 800 kbps (kilobits per second).

The transmission throughput of ADSL is about 10–100 times faster than a voice-band modem. Both ADSL and the voice-band modem connect a user to a central office using the telephone subscriber loop. But the similarity ends at the interface of a central office. The information carried by a voice-band modem goes through the traditional telephone switch that samples the telephone loop at 8 kHz.

Therefore the voice-band modem is limited by the maximum throughput of a telephone-switch–POTS interface at 64 kbps. However, a special ADSL circuit, called an ATU-C (ADSL terminal unit–central office), needs to be installed in a central office to communicate to its peer, an ATU-R (ADSL terminal unit–residence), at a user premise. The ATU-C is usually installed in one of the many shelves of a typical telephone equipment rack. The combination of many ATU-C units and associated backbone network interface and power supply circuits as well as management and maintenance software forms a digital subscriber line access multiplexer (DSLAM) within a telephone equipment rack. An ATU-R can be a standalone unit or in the form of a network interface card (NIC) to be plugged into a personal computer (PC). Both the ATU-C and the ATU-R are constructed with complex digital signal processing (DSP) circuits.

Subscriber loop transmission environment. A twisted-pair telephone cable with a plastic covering external to a metallic electrical sheathing can have thousands of twisted pairs organized into many binder groups. Functionally, an individual subscriber loop can be divided into portions consisting of the feeder cable, linking a central office to a concentrated customer area; the distribution cable, connecting the feeder cable to potential customer sites; and the drop wire, interconnecting the distribution cable and a customer premise (**Fig. 1**).

Because loop plant construction usually occurs ahead of customer service requests, distribution cables are usually made available to all potential

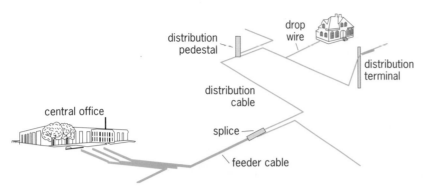

Fig. 1. General structure of a telephone loop plant.

customer sites. The unused distribution cables result in bridged taps. Extending the central office serving distances for the voice channel is accomplished through a procedure of installing load coils. Load coils are typically installed for cables with a total length (including bridged taps) exceeding 15,000 ft (4600 m). ADSL and other digital subscriber line systems are compatible with loops with bridged taps, but not with loading coils.

Due to capacitive and inductive coupling, there is crosstalk between each twisted pair, even though pairs are well insulated at zero frequency (that is, for direct currents). Crosstalk noise can be further divided into near-end crosstalk (NEXT) and far-end crosstalk (FEXT) noises. NEXT is defined as the crosstalk effect between a receiving path and a transmitting path of digital subscriber line transceivers at the same end of two different subscriber loops. A near-end receiver i will experience NEXT noise from the near-end transmitter j if they share the same frequency spectrum (**Fig. 2a**). Self-NEXT is defined as NEXT caused by other transceivers of the same type. Foreign-NEXT is defined as NEXT caused by other transceivers of different types.

FEXT is defined as the crosstalk effect between a receiving path and a transmitting path of digital subscriber line transceivers at opposite ends of two different subscriber loops. A near-end receiver i would experience FEXT noise from the far-end transmitter j if they share the same frequency spectrum (Fig. 2b). Self-FEXT and foreign-FEXT are similarly defined. For ADSL, the dominant noise component is different at different frequency regions. It is a combination of self-FEXT, foreign-NEXT, and background noises.

System deployment architecture. A basic ADSL system consists of ADSL transceivers on customer premises (ATU-Rs), nonloaded telephone subscriber loops, ADSL line cards (ATU-Cs), a DSLAM, and a backbone network router or an ATM switch (**Fig. 3**). The router is used mainly to implement the initial bridged Ethernet protocol. ATU-Rs, ATU-Cs, and telephone subscriber loops form the basic ADSL access network. The DSLAM concentrates ADSL traffic and provides a connection to the backbone broadband network. The DSLAM could also host backbone network interface and POTS splitter cards. Sometimes service provisioning and maintenance tools can also be built into the DSLAM chassis. Traditionally, a POTS splitter is required at a subscriber's premises to separate the low-frequency voice band from the high-frequency ADSL signal, minimizing interferences between them, as shown for the case of subscriber 1. Alternatively, microfilters can be used in conjunction with every POTS loop for the same purpose while avoiding the service company professional installation of the POTS splitter.

Figure 4 shows the same general network architecture with more details of the interconnection of ADSL access and the service provider's network. In this view, multiple central offices with ADSL access are connected with dedicated asynchronous transfer mode (ATM) trunks, and an ISP or a CPN is connected to the ADSL hub central office through a public ATM or frame relay network. This centralized approach makes administration relatively manageable. A telephone company providing ADSL access service is called a network access provider (NAP). An ISP or a CPN is called a network service provider (NSP).

Most network access providers initially offer the bridged Ethernet-over-ATM protocol across ADSL and central offices to internet service provider (ISP) or corporate private network (CPN) transmission links. The ADSL modem (ATU-R) in a user home encapsulates Ethernet frames into ATM AAL5 cells and transports these cells over the ADSL loop to the central office. Initially, the ATM quality of service associated with the ATU-R is unspecified bit rate (UBR, a traffic type that is suitable for data, or Internet access, application) only. Internet protocol (IP) addressing is the responsibility of the network service provider. Both static and dynamic (via the Dynamic Host Configuration Protocol, or DHCP) IP address assignment can be supported. For this initial scenario, an ADSL user can access only a single ISP or CPN destination based on a decision made at installation time.

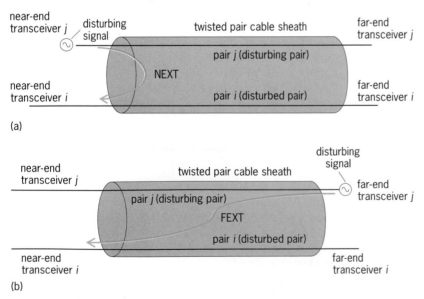

Fig. 2. Principles of crosstalk. (a) Near-end crosstalk (NEXT). (b) Far-end crosstalk (FEXT).

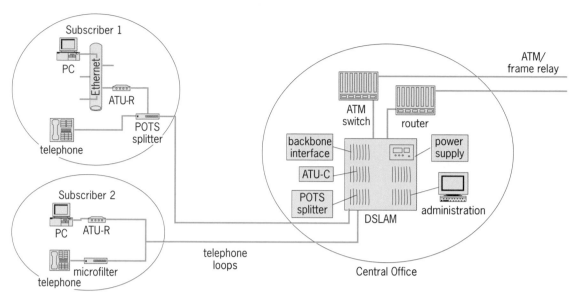

Fig. 3. ADSL system components.

The gateway router aggregates end users' data packets and passes them to the appropriate network service provider. The ISP or CPN connection is an ATM or frame relay permanent virtual connection (PVC) provisioned by a network access provider. Most network access providers plan to implement point-to-point protocol (PPP, which establishes a virtual computer network connection from one point to another) over ATM in the near future. PPP connectivity will allow an ISP or CPN to utilize existing authentication, authorization, and accounting systems established for voice-band modem dial-up services. PPP will also allow customers to connect to multiple destinations from a single ADSL line.

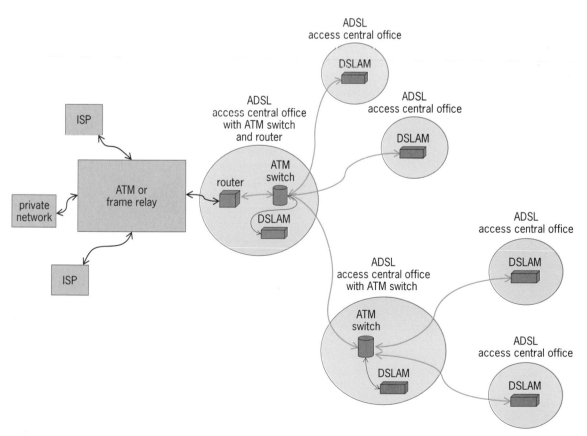

Fig. 4. Interconnection of the regional broadband network.

Further in the future, the ability to reach multiple destinations concurrently via a single ADSL line (from one or more personal computers) will likewise be supported.

Other DSL systems. Since there are many different versions of digital subscriber line systems, the term xDSL is used, where x stands for any version. Five DSL systems are closely related to standardization. The first standardized DSL system was called simply DSL and is the physical layer of the ISDN (integrated services digital network) Basic Rate Access Channel. This physical layer is characterized by a transmission throughput of 160 kbps based on a 2B1Q (2 bit per quaternary) line code for covering a loop distance of 18,000 ft (5500 m). The second DSL system, specified by a technical report from the ANSI (American National Standards Institute) T1E1.4 standards group, is the high-bit-rate digital subscriber line (HDSL). Deployed in a pair, the HDSL is promoted as the repeaterless T1 technology. HDSL is characterized by a transmission throughput of 800 kbps on each telephone subscriber loop using the 2B1Q line code for coverage of a 12,000-ft (3700-m) loop length. The third standardized system is ADSL. The fourth system being developed is the very high speed digital subscriber line (VDSL). It is characterized by downstream transmission throughputs (from a central office to a telephone subscriber) of 13, 26, or 52 Mbps. Both discrete multitone (DMT) and carrierless AM/PM (CAP) line codes have been considered. Concurrently, the standardization of the HDSL2 or single-pair HDSL (SHDSL) is also under way. HDSL2 is designed to deliver a T1 transmission throughput over a single twisted-pair telephone loop over a 12,000-ft (3700-m) loop distance.

A few other DSL systems are promoted by individual companies and industry groups. ISDN digital subscriber line (IDSL) is a variant application of the ISDN Basic Rate Access Channel physical layer technology. Instead of connecting to two 64-kbps B channels and one 16-kbps D channel, the whole transmission throughput of an IDSL, 160 kbps, is linked to a backbone data network with or without traffic concentration. Symmetrical digital subscriber line (SDSL) is a single-pair application of the basic HDSL technology. Depending on the serving distance, the transmission throughput of an SDSL can be lower or higher than the original design objective of 800 kbps. Rate-adaptive digital subscriber line (RADSL) is characterized by the CAP line code with transmission capabilities similar to those of the DMT-line-code-based standardized ADSL. The transmission throughputs of RADSL vary from a few hundred kilobits per second to a few megabits per second in the downstream direction.

For background information *see* CROSSTALK; DATA COMMUNICATIONS; INTEGRATED SERVICES DIGITAL NETWORK (ISDN); TELEPHONE SERVICE in the McGraw-Hill Encyclopedia of Science & Technology.

Walter Y. Chen

Bibliography. W. Y. Chen, *DSL: Simulation Techniques and Standard Development for Digital Subscriber Lines*, Macmillan, 1998; W. Goralski, *ADSL, Computer Communications*, 1998; T. Starr, J. Cioffi, and P. Silverman, *Understanding Digital Subscriber Line Technology*, Prentice Hall, 1999.

Asymmetry

Despite being bilaterally symmetric from an external viewpoint, vertebrates exhibit a significant degree of internal asymmetry, particularly regarding the formation and location of internal organs. While some of the internal organs are paired, such as the kidneys and gonads, the majority are unpaired and localized in a conserved position within the body. For example, the heart, spleen, and stomach are located on the left side of the body, while the bulk of the liver is on the right side. Even organs which appear paired, such as the lungs, are actually asymmetric; for example, in humans the right lung consists of three lobes, while the left lung has two. The organization of the internal organs allows for their efficient packing within the body cavity; it is also important for their functional development.

Placement alterations. The normal pattern of the internal organ placement is referred to as *situs solitus*. Alterations in this organization result in laterality defects which occur in the form of isomerisms, heterotaxia, or complete mirror-image inversions (*situs inversus*) of the internal organs. Isomerisms occur at the level of an individual organ and refer to changes in the normal asymmetry or aberrant bilateral symmetry of the particular organ. The more common isomerisms in humans are those involving the lungs or the atria of the heart. Heterotaxia refers to the reversed polarity of one or more individual organs with respect to the left-right axis. Except for complete *situs inversus*, individuals with disruptions in the normal left-right pattern of organ morphogenesis and position usually have severe consequences. Patterning the left-right axis of the vertebrate embryo, therefore, is a critical aspect of embryogenesis since this patterning is ultimately what ensures the correct placement and localization of the internal organs.

During development, the left-right axis is the last of the three main axes to be established, and it is defined with respect to the already formed anterior-posterior (head to toe) and dorsal-ventral (back to front) embryonic axes. Formation of these embryonic axes has been studied in several vertebrate model systems, including mice, chick, *Xenopus*, and zebrafish. Researchers have recently unveiled that the formation of the left-right axis is dependent upon a complex signaling cascade of gene expression that is initiated at a point during embryogenesis at which the embryo is bilaterally symmetrical. This left-right signaling cascade is responsible for the disruption of bilateral symmetry (the initial definition of the left and right sides of the embryo), propagation of this information along the left and right sides of the embryo, and ultimately converting this information into the pattern of organ development seen in the mature organism. The direction of organ looping during embryogenesis and the final placement of the internal organs within the body cavity are highly conserved among all vertebrates. Studies in different animal model systems have shown that, overall, the mechanism responsible for patterning the left-right axis is conserved at the molecular level with only a few notable differences among species.

Axis development. The initiation of left-right axial development has been studied in several model systems. In the mouse, an embryonic structure known as the node is critical for appropriate development of the left-right axis. The mammalian node is the equivalent of Hensen's node in the chick and Spemann's organizer in *Xenopus*, and it acts as an organizer region in the early embryo. Cells of the node give rise to many important structures of the early embryo, including the notochord, definitive endoderm, and floorplate in the ventral midline of the neural tube. Regarding left-right development, the monociliated cells located at the ventral surface of the node are particularly important. The uniform motion of these monocilia generates a regional leftward movement of extraembryonic fluid, known as nodal flow, which is believed to alter the distribution of one or more secreted signaling molecules in the vicinity of the node. Insight for this hypothesis arises from the study of several mouse mutants. Mutations in the *KIF3A* and *KIF3B* genes, which encode components of the molecular motors responsible for the motion of these monocilia, cause laterality defects. An almost completely penetrant *situs inversus* phenotype is observed in the inversus viscerum (*iv*) mutant mouse strain. The monocilia on the node in *iv/iv* mice are immotile; a mutation in an axonemal-type dynein heavy-chain molecule, leftright dynein, has been identified as the cause for this phenotype. These data indicate that the monociliated cells of the node may initiate left-right axis development in the mouse through the establishment of a left-right molecular asymmetry.

Cilia have not yet been detected on the cells of Hensen's node in the chick. However, asymmetric gene expression in the node has been observed at the point during chick embryogenesis that temporally corresponds to the period during which the nodal flow is thought to be important in mammalian embryos. The first gene demonstrated to be asymmetrically expressed in Hensen's node encoded the secreted signaling molecule sonic hedgehog (SHH). Sonic hedgehog is initially expressed bilaterally, but in response to an activin-like signal, it becomes restricted to the left side of the node. In fact, activin receptor IIa is observed only on the right of the node in the early chick embryo. Fibroblast growth factor 8 (FGF-8) is also expressed asymmetrically on the right side of the chick node. Neither SHH nor FGF-8 has been reported to be asymmetrically expressed in the nodes of other vertebrate species.

Propagation of asymmetry. Once molecular asymmetries have been established, it is necessary to pass this information along as embryogenesis proceeds. This point of the left-right signaling cascade appears to be finely regulated by members of the TGF-β family of extracellular signaling molecules. Asymmetric gene expression on both the left and right sides of the embryo is observed in the lateral plate mesoderm of all vertebrate species, with *nodal* being one of the first molecules to be asymmetrically expressed in the left lateral plate mesoderm. In the chick, the expression of *nodal* is indirectly induced by SHH on the left and inhibited by FGF-8 on the right. *Caronte* (*Car*), a member of the Cerberus/Dan family of extracellular antagonists, is believed to function as the intermediate between SHH expression in the node and *nodal* expression in the lateral plate mesoderm. *Car* is expressed in a small patch of paraxial mesoderm cells adjacent to the SHH-expressing cells of the node. Similarly to *nodal*, *Car* expression is induced by SHH, and ectopic expression of *Car* on the right side of the embryo induces ectopic expression of *nodal*. *Car* is believed to act by antagonizing the repressive effects of the bilaterally expressed bone morphogenetic proteins (BMPs) on *nodal* expression on the left side of the embryo. Bone morphogenetic proteins are also members of the TGF-β family of signaling molecules. Once turned on, *nodal* expression is, at least in part, autoregulated.

Two additional members of the TGF-β family, *lefty-1* and *lefty-2*, are also asymmetrically expressed on the left side of the embryo and involved in this phase of left-right development. *Lefty-1* is expressed in a small group of cells in the left perinodal region and in the left half of the floor plate. *Lefty-2*, which is a downstream transcriptional target of the Nodal signaling pathway, is expressed in the left lateral plate mesoderm. *Lefty-2* competes with Nodal for receptor binding. Therefore, *lefty-2* appears to act in a negative feedback loop to inhibit Nodal signaling, and potentially spatially refines the domain of Nodal signaling along the anterior-posterior axis of the embryo.

Experiments which disrupt the structure of the midline of the embryo or alter the expression of the molecules normally expressed within it, including *lefty-1*, affect development of the left-right axis and have led to the proposal that the midline has the capacity to function as a barrier. Thus, once the left and right sides of the embryo are established, the midline or molecules expressed within the midline prevent the transfer of information from the left side of the embryo to the right, and vice versa, thereby maintaining the integrity of the left-right signaling cascade.

Organ asymmetry. Once a left-right signaling cascade has been established, it must function to direct the asymmetric development of organs and their appropriate placement within the body cavity. Three transcription factors have been identified in the chick which are asymmetrically expressed in the lateral plate mesoderm and are presumed to regulate downstream transcriptional events in this developmental process. They are the homeodomain proteins,

Pitx2 and Nkx-3.2, which are expressed in the left lateral plate mesoderm, and the snail-related zinc finger protein cSnR, which is expressed in the right lateral plate mesoderm. In the chick, Pitx2 and Nkx-3.2 are induced by Nodal and repressed by FGF-8, while cSnR is repressed by Nodal and induced by FGF-8. To date, Pitx2 is the only transcription factor that is asymmetrically expressed on the left side of the embryo in all vertebrates. Interestingly, Pitx2 is also expressed asymmetrically in several of the organs which themselves exhibit left-right differences in their development. Mice which are null for the Pitx2 locus exhibit several defects which can be attributed to disruption of the left-right patterning cascade, including a delay in early embryonic rotation, right pulmonary isomerism, and failure of the ventral body wall to close. (Mutations in the human Pitx2 locus cause the autosomal dominant disorder known as Reiger syndrome.) Interfering with the translation of cSnR transcripts by incubating chick embryos with antisense ribonucleic acid (RNA) also results in laterality defects at the level of organ development. A specific role in patterning the left-right axis has not been demonstrated for Nkx-3.2, which unexpectedly is expressed in the right lateral plate mesoderm in the mouse.

Several additional transcription factors and structural proteins that are expressed asymmetrically within particular organs have been identified. Presumably these factors are downstream targets of the left-right patterning cascade. What remains to be revealed is how the events that promote asymmetric organ morphogenesis are coordinated with those responsible for positioning the organ in its conserved location within the body cavity during this final phase of patterning that occurs along the left-right axis of the embryo.

For background information *see* DEVELOPMENTAL BIOLOGY; SYMMORPHOSIS in the McGraw-Hill Encyclopedia of Science & Technology.

Aimee K. Ryan; Juan Carlos Izpisua Belmonte

Atherosclerosis

Atherosclerosis, or hardening of the arteries, is an inflammatory process that may cause a number of diseases. The diseases stem from the loss of normal function of the blood vessels caused by the presence of the atheromatous mass or plaque that progressively encroaches on the lumen of the artery. The ensuing loss of function results in the inability to provide an adequate flow of blood to a particular downstream organ, a circumstance called ischemia. The discomfort associated with intermittent and recurrent ischemia of the heart is called angina pectoris, or simply angina.

Endothelium. In the first half of the twentieth century atherosclerosis was considered a component of aging, but then it became clear that this view was erroneous. The process is a specific, fully orchestrated response to injury of the inner lining of the artery, the endothelium. This tissue is composed of a single layer of specialized endothelial cells that form an uninterrupted circuit so that in health and homeostasis the circulating blood never contacts any surface other than the endothelium. Endothelial cells normally exhibit a nonstick surface. They modulate their environment to maintain both the fluidity of the blood and a general state of vasodilation. When injured, they promote clotting of the blood and vasoconstriction (**Fig. 1**). This makes sense: When an external blood vessel is cut, an automatic and immediate mechanism is needed to stem the flow and prevent exsanguinating hemorrhage. The rapidity with which the endothelium can switch from an anticoagulant to a procoagulant state implies an underlying plasticity and specific genetic programs for specific milieux.

Assuming the clotting mechanism does its part following endothelial injury, the next phase at the site of injury is inflammation. The white cells of the blood (neutrophils, lymphocytes, and monocytes) home in on the molecular gradients created by the injured tissue and leave the vascular space to clean up the locale.

Atherogenesis. Atherogenesis, or the development of atherosclerosis, parallels the gross events described above. Injurious agents are referred to as risk factors for atherosclerosis and its complications (see **table**). Additional factors of less certain responsibility include obesity, sedentary lifestyle, elevated homocysteine, lipoprotein(a), polymorphisms in angiotensinogen, adhesion molecules and coagulation proteins, elevated fibrinogen, herpes viruses, *Chlamydia pneumoniae* infection, and Type A personality. Others will be identified in the future. All modify the vessel wall and presumably work through the common final pathway of inflammation.

Injury. The innermost layer of the arterial wall is the endothelium of the intima. The underlying middle layer is the media, composed primarily of smooth muscle cells. The outermost (lowest) layer, the adventitia has a few, small, nourishing blood vessels, the vasa vasorum (**Fig. 2**). Monocytes collide with the vessel wall and then roll along its surface by a process in which a receptor-ligand pair interact. The ligand on the monocyte is shed, allowing the cell to slip along the surface. A second ligation occurs, and the process is replicated until the cell reenters the bloodstream. In this phenomenon, the monocyte is allowed to search for signals of tissue

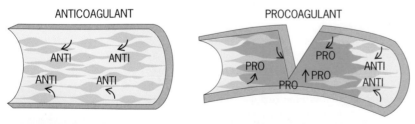

Fig. 1. Normal anticoagulant and abnormal procoagulant states of the vascular endothelium.

Risk factors for atherosclerosis		
Factor	Description	Mechanism of action
Family history	Presence of coronary atherosclerosis in a first-degree relative before the age of 55	Remains uncertain; a polygenic problem that may include mutations that cause hypercoagulability, abnormal responses to pressors, and others
Hyperlipidemia	Elevation, in particular, of low-density lipoprotein cholesterol (LDL-C) in response to hypercaloric diets with high proportions of saturated fats, and to certain genetic abnormalities	Oxidized LDL-C, the equivalent of circulating rancid fat, injures endothelium and induces the inflammatory state; lymphocytes and monocytes are attracted and take up residence in the arterial wall
Hypertension	Sustained blood pressure ≥ 135/85 mmHg	Physical injury of the endothelium due to abnormal stresses; unexplained genetic factors are operative as well
Diabetes mellitus	Abnormal glucose homeostasis due to a lack of insulin (type I) or an insensitivity to insulin (type II) that elevates blood glucose levels	Nonenzymatic formation of advanced glycation end products (AGE) that are adducts of proteins and glucose; modified proteins induce vascular inflammation; other mechanisms
Smoking	Inhalation of cigarette smoke	Tobacco glycoproteins, nicotine, and other small molecules induce stickiness of endothelial cells, white cells, and platelets, and cause inflammation
Age	Age > 45 in males, > 55 in females	Duration of the endothelial inflammation
Gender	Male	Remains uncertain; presumed hormonal

inflammation through intimate endothelial contact. Several changes occur when the endothelium is injured by any of the risk factors. The monocytes stop rolling, flatten out over the surface, and dive into the potential spaces between endothelial cells to take up residence just below the endothelial layer. In a sense, this is an evolutionary error. There is no need for the monocyte to be there, there is no threatening injury, there is only exposure to a circulating toxin that may be a product of another evolutionary curiosity—that is, consciousness and the ability of humans to invent efficient tools and produce excess food. At the molecular level, the injury induces the synthesis and surface expression by the endothelium of a neoreceptor, vascular cell adhesion molecule 1 (VCAM-1), that binds to a ligand on the rolling monocyte and communicates the message to stop rolling and activate (Fig. 2).

In the next phase of atherogenesis, the monocytes become trapped forever by chemoattractant molecules synthesized locally, such as monocyte chemoattractant protein (MCP). If oxidized low-density lipoprotein particles are in the circulation, the activated monocytes, now called macrophages ("big eaters"), ingest them, but they are indigestible and cause the cells to swell. The engorged macrophages cause little bumps in the surface of the intima and form the precursor lesion of the future atherosclerotic plaque, the fatty streak.

Plaque. To stabilize and strengthen the growing "scar," smooth muscle cells are recruited across a porous, elastic membrane that separates the intima from the media. There they divide for a time, secrete

extracellular matrix, and contribute to the growing bulk of the plaque and the resultant narrowing of the arterial diameter. It may be decades before the process narrows the internal diameter enough, about 65–75%, for symptoms of the ensuing ischemia to become manifest. The advanced lesion and its inherent disorder and instability are depicted in **Fig. 3**. In the center of a lesion, there is a lipid core that consists of extracellular, fatty debris from burst macrophages. Overlying the core is a fibrous cap consisting of displaced smooth muscle cells and fibroblasts. The

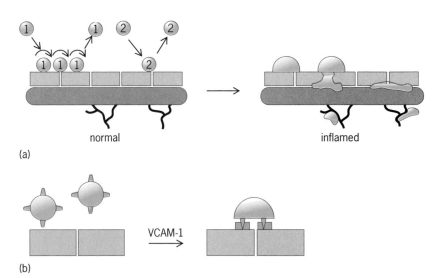

(a)

(b)

Fig. 2. Inflammation and the first stages of atherosclerosis. (*a*) Injury of the endothelium resulting in a modification of the interaction between monocytes and endothelial cells. (*b*) Molecular basis for the adhesion of the monocyte to the endothelial cell in *a*.

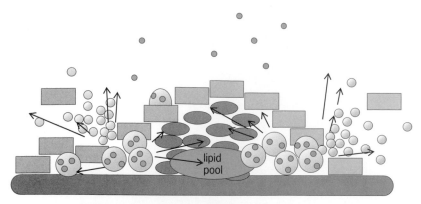

Fig. 3. Advanced lesion of atherosclerosis. Note the breaks in the endothelial surface with frank loss of endothelial cells and adhesion of clumps of platelets.

edges of the cap are attenuated, and the thinned area overlies, in the so-called shoulder regions, collections of lipid-laden macrophages. The arrows depict enzymes secreted by the macrophages and smooth muscle cells, neutral proteinases and metalloproteinases, that digest the extracellular matrix and weaken it. On the surface, now sticky, are clumps of aggregated platelets, small white clots that can further inflame or embolize downstream. Endothelial cells may float off the surface, a consequence both of the Bernoulli forces imparted by the wing-shaped plaque in a flowing column of blood, and of the digestion of the underlying matrix by activated macrophages and smooth muscle cells.

The consequences of the plaque are quite variable, and the causes of the variability are uncertain. Some plaques may never become clinical; that is, they may never induce a symptom such as angina. Some will impinge sufficiently on the lumen that flow reserve will be exhausted and the downstream organ will experience ischemia; if the organ is the heart, the symptom is angina. A more severe level of dysfunction is due to gross plaque instability. A crack or rupture develops, usually in the shoulder regions of plaques with large lipid cores, few smooth muscle cells, large collections of activated macrophages, and thin fibrous caps. The blood interprets this rupture as an external wound and forms a clot. If the rupture is in the coronary arteries of the heart, and if the clot is large but not totally occlusive, a condition called unstable angina arises characterized by prolonged angina with the patient at rest. If the rupture is in the carotid arteries leading to the brain, a transient ischemic attack (TIA) occurs with brief loss of neural function due to ischemia of a particular brain area. If a totally occlusive clot forms at the site of plaque rupture and nothing is done to remove that clot, either naturally or iatrogenically (secondarily), the watershed territory of the clotted artery will die, leading to a heart attack if in the coronaries, a stroke if in the carotids or basilar arteries.

Many experts believe that atherosclerosis is entirely preventable and can be eradicated by a combination of diet, exercise, designer drugs, and novel gene therapies.

For background information *see* ARTERIOSCLEROSIS; BLOOD; CHOLESTEROL; CIRCULATION; INFLAMMATION in the McGraw-Hill Encyclopedia of Science & Technology.   Richard I. Levin

Bibliography. J. L. Breslow, Mouse models of atherosclerosis, *Science*, 272:685–688, May 3, 1996; M. J. Davies, Stability and Instability: Two Faces of Coronary Atherosclerosis: The Paul Dudley White Lecture 1995, *Circulation*, 94:2013–2020, 1996; G. H. Gibbons and V. J. Dzau, Molecular therapies for vascular diseases, *Science*, 272:689–693, May 3, 1996; P. Libby, Molecular bases of the acute coronary syndromes, *Circulation*, 91:2844–2850, 1995; R. Ross, Atherosclerosis—an inflammatory disease, *N. Engl. J. Med.*, 340:115–126, 1999.

Attention

Acts of attention direct the limited neurological resources of humans to a number of stimuli, thoughts, and behaviors at any one time. Humans cannot process every stimulus that reaches the senses simultaneously, nor can they think about a great number of different problems and interests at the same time. Attention is not a single thing, for the brain has a large number of attentional processes, each performing specific tasks. In the past decade, the greatest body of work has concerned attentional selection in the visual system.

Serial and parallel processing. You, the reader, are familiar with attending to vision rather than to another sense—say, the support of your chair. You are attending to one object or location in space (the page in front of you) as you read these words. Even within the visual modality, however, attention has many aspects. You could attend to one feature of the words—say, the color of the letters, rather than their shape—but you don't. While selection is necessary (try reading two sentences at the same time), it is not absolute. It is obvious to you that attention to the words that you are reading does not make the rest of the world completely vanish. This suggests that there are some aspects of the visual input that can be processed in parallel (at many or all locations at the same time), while other aspects must be processed in series (one object or location at a time). One of the goals of research has been to determine when stimuli are handled by parallel processing and when serial processing is needed.

Treisman's feature integration theory proposed that a limited set of basic features such as color, size, and orientation could be processed in parallel. In this model, serial deployment of attention is required to "bind" the features together into a recognizable object. Thus, parallel processes might reveal that an object had the features red, curved, green, vertical, and horizontal. Only the deployment of attention would allow the observer to determine how these features fit together. This object could be a "T" with a curved red top and a green stem, or an "L" with a curved green upright and a red horizontal limb, or any of other possible combinations of these features. Other models have proposed different solutions to the problem of binding features to objects. Some of these propose parallel processing of multiple objects all the way to the level of object identification.

Behavioral methods. Much of the data in this area comes from behavioral studies in which an observer looks at a display and makes some response. Aspects of the underlying mechanisms can be inferred from the pattern of responses. For example, consider a visual search task in which subjects are asked to decide whether a target is present among some variable number of distractor items. Suppose that the target is vertical and all the distractors are horizontal. The amount of time (the reaction time) required to say "yes," a target is present, or "no," it is not, will be independent of the number of horizontal items. This suggests that the property of orientation can be processed in parallel. Similar results would be obtained with other basic features (such as red among green, moving among stationary, shiny among matte). However, if the target is the number 2 and the distractors are 5's, reaction time will increase linearly with the number of items. This is consistent with deployment of serial attention from item to item until the 2 is found. Unfortunately, it is also consistent with a variety of parallel models in which all items are processed at once but where increased numbers of distractors make that parallel processing less efficient. Much research has been devoted to the effort to distinguish between these possibilities. Suppose that the subject is looking for the tilted 2 among tilted and upright 5's. Now the parallel-processed, orientation feature information can be used to guide attention, limiting attentional deployment to the tilted items and not wasting time on the uprights.

In recent years, researchers have begun to determine how and where attentional functions are implemented in the physical brain. Information comes from many methods. Electrophysiological studies have recorded from single neurons (brain cells) of animals trained to do attentional tasks. Clues about normal attentional function can be obtained from studies of the damaged brain. These lesion studies can involve surgical lesions in animals or accidental lesions (from stroke or injury) in human patients. For example, damage to specific areas (such as the parietal lobe) on one side of the brain can lead to "neglect" of the opposite side of the world or of the body. Thus, patients with damage on the right side of the brain might fail to notice people to their left. They might leave the food on the left half of the plate or even forget to dress the left half of the body.

In the last few years, functional neuroimaging studies have allowed a noninvasive look into the biological processes underlying attention in healthy humans. Positron emission tomography (PET) and functional magnetic resonance imaging (fMRI) rely on the fact that blood flow and blood oxygenation levels increase locally in the vicinity of active neurons. Positron emission tomography measures blood flow by marking the blood with mildly radioactive particles. With functional magnetic resonance imaging, a strong magnetic field is used to differentiate between oxygenated and deoxygenated hemoglobin in the blood. These methods have shown activity in the healthy human brain in areas predicted from earlier electrophysiology and lesion studies. Together, they show that attention does not have a single control center, but is mediated by a distributed network of brain structures. There may be different brain areas responsible for different aspects of attention, such as engaging, disengaging, and moving attention. A contrasting view proposes that what is really happening is shifting of biases for competition between different demands for attentional resources.

Sensory areas. Attention can influence how the brain processes visual information. For example, in 1985 researchers showed how attention could change the activity in individual cells in V4 (a visual area of the brain's cerebral cortex known to process form and color information). Monkeys were trained to maintain fixation while performing a peripheral match-to-sample task on stimuli in a cued location. A cell in V4 will respond to stimuli over some region of the visual field (the cell's receptive field). When the monkey attended to one of two stimuli that fell within its receptive field, the cell would respond as if only the attended stimulus was in its receptive field, effectively filtering out any other items that were also present.

Other electrophysiological studies have tested how attention affects the sort of stimuli that a cell prefers. Cells can be "sharpened" by attention. For example, an orientation-selective neuron typically responds best to vertical lines and less well to slightly tilted lines. Attentional sharpening would mean that the response to the tilted stimuli would drop off more sharply, focusing the response more precisely on the optimal stimulus. Others cells might be "shifted" by attention. If the monkey needs to find the lines tilted a bit to the right, some cells that were responding to other orientations might come to respond best to the attended orientation. However, recent studies have argued that instead of producing a shift, attention simply enhances response to all orientations with the greatest effect at the optimal orientation.

Positron emission tomography and functional magnetic resonance imaging experiments show effects of attention at many stages in visual processing. The earliest stages of processing in the primary visual cortex show effects of spatial attention. If a subject attends to a target in a particular location, a corresponding part of primary visual cortex shows increased activity. The later visual areas that are selective for motion, color, faces, places, and shape are all modulated by attention. Thus, if a subject attends to faces, activity in the face area increases. If the subject attends to motion, other areas become active. Furthermore, if a subject attends to the motion of a moving face, both motion and face areas would show enhanced activity. This suggest that all attributes of an attended object are processed in parallel.

Other methods, such as event related potentials (ERPs) and magnetoencephalography (MEG), can be used to answer questions about the time course of attention. Event related potentials and magnetoencephalography have poor spatial resolution but much higher temporal resolution than functional magnetic resonance imaging or positron emission tomography. For example, recent investigations of event related potentials seemed to catch the serial deployment of attention from one item to the next. Finally, transcranial magnetic stimulation (TMS) uses brief bursts of radio-frequency pulses to temporarily disrupt the electrical signals in small regions of the brain. In one study, transcranial magnetic stimulation to the posterior parietal cortex disrupted visual search tasks for conjunction targets, but not for feature targets. These methods provide more ways to tease apart the different attentional demands of different tasks.

For background information *see* BRAIN; COGNITION; HEMISPHERIC LATERALITY; INFORMATION PROCESSING; MEDICAL IMAGING; PERCEPTION in the McGraw-Hill Encyclopedia of Science & Technology.

Jeremy M. Wolfe; Kathy M. O'Craven

Bibliography. M. S. Gazzaniga, *The New Cognitive Neurosciences*, 2d ed., MIT Press, Cambridge, 1999; Humphreys, Duncan, and Treisman, *Attention, Space, and Action: Studies in Cognitive Neuroscience*, Oxford University Press, 1999; R. Parasuraman, *The Attentive Brain*, MIT Press, Cambridge, 1998; H. E. Pashler, *Attention*, Psychology Press, Hove, East Sussex, 1998; H. Pashler, *The Psychology of Attention*, MIT Press, Cambridge, 1997.

Autonomous aircraft

At 7:29 a.m. local time on August 20, 1998, the aerosonde *Laima* lifted out of the cartop launch cradle on Bell Island, Newfoundland (**Fig. 1**). After 26 h 45 min it landed in a meadow on South Uist island off the Scottish coast, and so became the first crewless aircraft—and at only 13 kg (28.6 lb) gross weight and 2.9 m (9.6 ft) wingspan, by far the smallest aircraft—ever to have crossed the Atlantic Ocean. The flight consumed about 4 kg (9 lb) or 6 liters (1.5 gallons) of aviation gasoline and covered a distance of 3270 km (2031 mi). The purpose of the flight was to demonstrate the capabilities of autonomous miniaturized robotic aircraft for long-range scientific sensing missions.

This historic event was made possible by Global Positioning System (GPS) technology. Only a few years ago, reliable navigation over the oceans required heavy and costly hardware—LORAN, Omega, or perhaps an inertial navigation system. But the advent of the GPS afforded worldwide precision navigation with inexpensive equipment weighing less than 100 g (0.22 lb) and consuming less than 1 watt of power. Long-range accurate navigation consequently became possible for aircraft of miniature size and of relatively low cost.

Remote atmospheric sensing. There is particular interest in using these small aircraft to improve weather forecasting. Numerical weather forecasting depends critically on data from balloons carrying radiosonde instruments, which measure pressure, temperature, humidity, and wind during the rise from the surface to high altitude. About 1000 radiosondes are flown around the world every day from sites on land. At sea they can be launched from ships or dropped from crewed aircraft by parachute, but the costs are too high for routine operations. Soundings over the oceans are therefore few and far between, and with only satellite data to fill most of the gaps, weather forecasters are chronically handicapped. Miniature sounding aircraft, or aerosondes (**Fig. 2**), promise to remedy this problem by making ocean soundings affordable on a wide scale.

Trial flights. By mid-1998, around 30 prototype aerosondes had logged more than 800 flight hours, mainly in offshore trials around the Pacific. Conditions ranged from frontal rain and icing off the British Columbia coast to wilting humidity and fierce thunderstorms in tropical Australia and the South China Sea. The flights demonstrated the ability of these miniature aircraft to collect sounding data in severe weather; to deploy with relative ease (especially when researchers went to the field with aircraft boxed up as part of their airline luggage); and to stay in the air for a long time, with two flights over 30 h and several more exceeding 24 h. But since the flights all remained within about 200 km (125 mi) of the launch point, transoceanic capabilities had yet to be demonstrated.

Atlantic crossing. *Laima* needed a tailwind of about 10 m/s (20 knots) to cross the Atlantic with some fuel reserve after a flight of over 3000 km (2000 mi). Flight planning for aerosondes is based on the most current weather predictions, updated every 12 h, which are then input to a flight simulation program. Based on these predictions for Atlantic winds, the transatlantic itinerary was calculated just prior to launch. *Laima* was on its own for most of the crossing since on-board low-Earth-orbit communications capability was not yet implemented. Hence, except

Fig. 1. Aerosonde *Laima* lifting out of the cartop launch cradle on Bell Island, Newfoundland, at 7:29 a.m. on August 20, 1998. (*Photo by Ron Bennett*)

for takeoff and landing, the flight was autonomous with no ground-to-vehicle communications. The ground stations were in contact with the vehicle for about 45 km (27 mi) at each end of the flight. Within radio range, *Laima* could be monitored and controlled from a piloting console, with telemetry downlinked at 5 Hz, GPS position and groundspeed transmitted at 2 Hz, and airspeeds, altitudes, flight plans, and so on uplinked as necessary. For takeoff and landing, *Laima* was flown manually with a standard model-aircraft console.

Course tracking. During the flight, aerosonde course tracking is implemented by two nested feedback loops (**Fig. 3**). The inner loop controls the yaw rate with aileron and rudder action; it runs at 5 Hz. The outer loop sends commands to the yaw-rate controller to keep the aerosonde on track; it runs at 2 Hz. Position and velocity are about 0.5 s out of date when output by the GPS, and this time lag could compromise fine-tracking performance. To compensate, the GPS report is projected forward to the current time, using an estimate for the average groundspeed in the interval following the GPS time stamp. The GPS receiver and a yaw-rate gyro are the only sensors in the control loop. Thus the aerosonde does not know which way it is pointing—only which way it is moving. Likewise it does not know which way is up; it simply regulates altitude with a 5-Hz loop to the elevators and air speed with a 5-Hz loop to the throttle.

Safety. GPS made the aerosonde safe. Safety, and authorization for all of the field trials including the Atlantic demonstration, have rested on the aerosonde's being able to stay rigorously on track. In fact, the aircraft itself would have enforced that condition by cutting the engine had it wandered beyond a specified distance off course (usually set at 2 km or 1.2 mi), or had the GPS stopped updating. However, for the transatlantic crossing, *Laima* stayed strictly on course and schedule, arriving within a few minutes of the estimate from flight planning. The flight data were logged en route, and when downloaded from the flight computer memory, confirmed that the winds had been very close to the National Weather Service forecast all the way across the Atlantic, and every waypoint had been reached within minutes of the estimate.

Landing guidance. The control required for tracking (Fig. 3) is quite simple and effective throughout the flight envelope. This includes automatic takeoff and landing which, while not used in the Atlantic exercise, have been demonstrated in flight test. Landing guidance is based on a differential GPS (DGPS) technique, which is implemented using basic C/A code receivers with uplinked corrections from the ground station. This requires a protocol between the aircraft and ground station to keep tracking the same set of GPS satellites even though the selection of satellites that each has in view is changing. The position of the ground station antenna is first measured in runway coordinates. The ground station then corrects its GPS solution to the measured

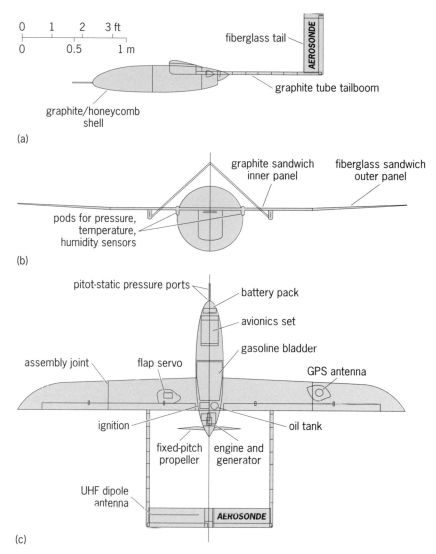

Fig. 2. Diagram of an aerosonde. (*a*) Side view. (*b*) Front view. (*c*) Top view. (*Aerosonde Robotic Aircraft Ltd.*)

runway-relative position, and then uplinks position and velocity corrections to the aircraft at 2 Hz. Typically the accuracy is about 3 m (10 ft). The technique is not as precise as phase-space DGPS, but it has the advantage of using only standard C/A GPS at each end.

Wind estimation. One more role for GPS is in estimating wind speed, a vital function for not only weather reconnaissance but also flight guidance. An aerosonde uses a windfinding-by-maneuver technique, which produces wind estimates typically accurate to about 0.5 m/s (1.0 knot), whenever the aircraft turns through more than about 90°. On long transects the aircraft is programmed to do periodic S-turns around track.

Prospects. The Atlantic crossing, together with various field trials around the Pacific, has shown the way toward application of miniature autonomous aircraft over the oceans. First-generation aerosondes like *Laima* will expand operations, but work is under way on a second generation of similar size but

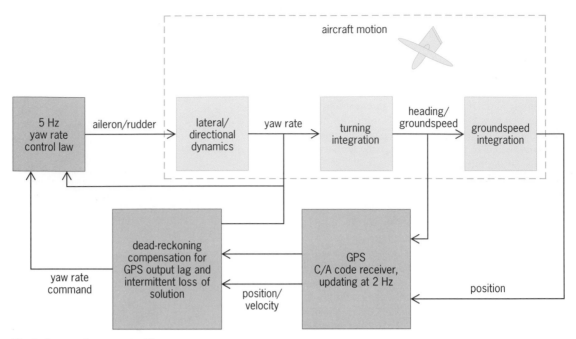

Fig. 3. Aerosonde course tracking.

offering about twice the range and endurance. Refinements of current systems and aircraft configuration, design of a mission-specific engine, and addition of low-Earth-orbit satellite communications capabilities will allow these vehicles to operate dependably over the oceans and other remote areas, opening new capabilities in remote atmospheric sensing.

For background information *see* DRONE; GUIDANCE SYSTEMS; SATELLITE NAVIGATION SYSTEMS; WEATHER OBSERVATIONS; WIND MEASUREMENT in the McGraw-Hill Encyclopedia of Science & Technology.

Tad McGeer; Juris Vagners

Bibliography. G. J. Holland, T. McGeer, and H. H. Youngren, Autonomous aerosondes for economical atmospheric soundings anywhere on the globe, *Bull. Amer. Meteorol. Soc.*, 73(12):1987–1999, December 1992; T. McGeer and J. Vagners, Historic crossing: An unmanned aircraft's Atlantic flight, *GPS World*, 10(2):24–30, February 1999; T. McGeer and J. Vagners, Wide-scale use of long-range miniature aerosondes over the world's oceans, *Proceedings of the AUVSI 26th Annual Symposium*, Association for Unmanned Vehicle Systems International, Baltimore, July 1999.

Background extinction

The fossil record of marine animal species reveals that over the last 550 million years the average species lived for only about 4 million years. Thus most species that ever lived on Earth are now extinct. Paleontologists have long recognized that extinction has not been a continuous process. Rather, it has alternated between mass extinction, geologically short intervals of time when substantial proportions of the global biota were eliminated, and background extinction, intervals of lower extinction intensity between mass extinctions. In studying extinction, paleontologists and other earth scientists have concentrated their efforts on a few of the major mass extinctions, such as the one that eliminated the dinosaurs 65 million years ago. However, recent studies indicate that mass extinction accounts for only a small proportion of all species extinctions recorded in the fossil record. Furthermore, background extinction occurs in pulses over a wide range of spatial and temporal scales that merges on the high end with mass extinction. This new view of extinction from the fossil record has important implications for the history of life, including the driving processes behind significant biotic transitions and evolutionary trends; and in understanding the modern biodiversity crisis and the response of Earth's biota to future global change.

Kill curve. A recent analysis of the stratigraphic ranges of marine animal genera from the last 550 million years indicates that extinction events have a distribution similar to floods and earthquakes. That is, extinction events occur episodically, and extinction intensity varies over a wide range of magnitudes. The average waiting time between events of a given magnitude is positively correlated with extinction intensity but is also subject to considerable random variation. The relationship between extinction magnitude and waiting time describes a "kill curve" (**Fig. 1**). Small extinction events are relatively common over geologic time, and larger events occur less often. Thus, on average a 5% species extinction occurs once every million years, a 30% species extinction occurs once every 10 million years, and the most severe mass extinctions, such as the end Cretaceous event, that eliminate at least 65% of species occur once every 100 million years. Extinction

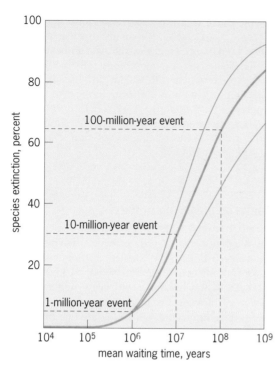

Fig. 1. Kill curve for marine species over the last 550 million years. The lighter lines indicate the uncertainty in placement of the kill curve (heavy line). (*After D. M. Raup, Extinction models, in D. Jablonski, D. H. Erwin, and J. H. Lipps (eds.), Evolutionary Paleobiology, pp. 419–433, University of Chicago Press, 1996*)

tion is not yet good enough in the Paleozoic to resolve events at a finer scale than this. Most of these extinctions are linked to stratigraphic and sedimentologic evidence of geologically rapid environmental change. For example, in some cases rising sea level led to incursions of cold or anoxic water into shallow seas that eliminated many marine benthic organisms. In other cases changes in ocean currents increased the flux of fine-grained sediments and nutrients to the shallow seas, destroying carbonate environments, thus eliminating many species. In all cases, extinction pulses led to a reorganization of marine communities; a significant proportion of species were eliminated and were often replaced quickly by new or immigrant species.

Evolutionary consequences. Background extinction may have played a previously unrecognized role in shaping the history of life. Major biotic transitions in the composition of Earth's biota appear as relatively smooth protracted events at a global scale. However, when viewed regionally such transitions appear more episodic. For example, the replacement of straight-necked turtles by those that can flex the neck and retract the head into the shell took place over tens of millions of years through the Cretaceous and Tertiary periods. Further study has shown that this replacement took place at different times on different continents and was preceded by extinction of the incumbent straight-necked turtle group. Much of this replacement was driven by background extinction. Likewise, long-term evolutionary trends in morphology within taxonomic groups may have been driven by preferential extinction of species with similar morphologic traits. For example, latest Cambrian

magnitude in the kill curve is continuous from low to high intensities; thus the cutoff between mass and background extinction is arbitrary. Another important implication of the kill curve is that most species became extinct in events outside mass extinctions. In the last 550 million years approximately 40% of species were eliminated in events of 5% or less species extinction, and approximately 55–60% were eliminated in events of 10% or less species extinction. Only 4% of all species that have ever lived became extinct in the most severe mass extinction events. Finally, the kill curve implies a record of extinction intensity characterized by pulses of extinction (**Fig. 2**) that occur with a frequency and magnitude currently beyond the ability to resolve at a global scale. Regional studies of the fossil record can achieve a level of temporal resolution much higher than what is possible at the global level and therefore can test some aspects of the kill curve, especially those concerning the smaller extinction pulses.

Regional studies of fossil record. Regional studies of diversity and extinction in the fossil record confirm that extinction is pulsed over a wide range of spatial and temporal scales. Some of the best information comes from studies of ancient shallow marine ecosystems that existed in North America during the Paleozoic Era from about 550 to 250 million years ago. These studies show that extinction events were common in the shallow seas at this time, occurring about every 3–9 million years; stratigraphic resolu-

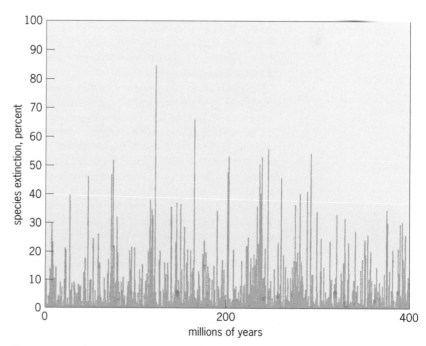

Fig. 2. A 400-million-year simulation of extinction intensity based on the kill curve in Fig. 1. According to the kill curve, background extinction is pulsed over a wide range of magnitudes. (*After D. M. Raup, Extinction models, in D. Jablonski, D. H. Erwin, and J. H. Lipps (eds.), Evolutionary Paleobiology, pp. 419–433, University of Chicago Press, 1996*)

through Silurian gastropods show a trend toward species with high spires and low apical angles. This long-term trend was driven largely by preferential elimination of species with low spires and high apical angles at a Middle Ordovician extinction event. This process, called species selection or species sorting, is directly analogous to classical Darwinian natural selection and may be a significant source of large-scale evolutionary trends throughout the history of life.

Modern extinction and future global change. The study of background extinction also has important implications for the modern biodiversity crisis and future global change, although extrapolations from the fossil record to the modern world must be done with caution. The fossil record is biased toward preserving the abundant and widespread species, and the temporal resolution of events is no better than 1000 to 10,000 years in the best cases. Nevertheless, the fossil record provides the only opportunity to observe the state of an ecosystem before, during, and after an extinction event; thus its study can provide information about modern extinctions and their consequences. Knowing patterns of extinction selectivity associated with background extinction may help in assessing extinction risk in the modern ecosystems and thus aid conservation efforts. For example, most species eliminated during background times were rare and endemic, and species with similar characteristics are the ones most at risk in modern ecosystems. Background extinction is also an important source of information for predicting the consequences of global change. Global change research suggests that Earth's temperature is rising and will soon reach levels perhaps never seen in historical times. Studying background extinction events that occurred under conditions similar to these inferred climate changes will aid in predicting the response of the global biota, such as which species go extinct and which survive.

The study of background extinction is just now beginning in earnest, and much remains to be learned about its role in evolution. In particular, the link between environmental change and extinction needs to be studied in much greater detail. It is important to know whether there is a single underlying driving mechanism for background extinction, such as climate or tectonics, and whether it ultimately is possible to predict magnitude and selectivity of background extinction given a certain environmental perturbation. It also remains to be determined how background extinction intensity varies through time and space in order to know whether the kill curve is an accurate description of extinction over time.

For background information *see* CRETACEOUS; ECOSYSTEM; EXTINCTION (BIOLOGY); MACROEVOLUTION; PALEOZOIC in the McGraw-Hill Encyclopedia of Science & Technology.   Mark E. Patzkowsky

Bibliography. A. I. Miller, Biotic transitions in global marine diversity, *Science*, 281:1157–1160, 1998; D. M. Raup, Extinction models, *in* D. Jablonski, D. H. Erwin, and J. H. Lipps (eds.), *Evolutionary Paleobiology*, pp. 419–433, University of Chicago Press, 1996; D. M. Raup, Large-body impact and extinction in the Phanerozoic, *Paleobiology*, 18:80–89, 1992; M. L. Rosenzweig and R. D. McCord, Incumbent replacement: Evidence for long-term evolutionary progress, *Paleobiology*, 17:202–213, 1991; P. J. Wagner, Contrasting the underlying patterns of active trends in morphologic evolution, *Evolution*, 50:990–1007, 1996.

Bacterial magnetic minerals

Certain bacteria can grow well-formed mineral crystals. Magnetotactic bacteria provide a striking example of such biologically controlled mineralization, as a result of which minerals are deposited within the cells of the organism and grow under a high degree of biological control. Magnetotactic bacteria produce intracellular, nanometer-scale magnetic iron oxide or sulfide minerals that are enclosed by membranes; the ensemble of the crystal and the surrounding membrane is called a magnetosome. Each crystal comprises a single magnetic domain. These nanomagnets form chains in the cell (**Fig. 1**) and are arranged to produce the largest possible magnetic dipole moment, which orients the bacteria parallel to Earth's geomagnetic field lines. Since these field lines are inclined to the surface of the Earth (except at the Equator), this magnetic sensing mechanism helps the bacteria find and maintain an optimal position in aquatic environments, which can be a great aid where vertical concentration gradients of oxygen and nutrients occur.

Studies of the sizes, habits, compositions, and microstructural characteristics of iron oxides and sulfides within magnetotactic bacteria are important because they shed light on biogenic mineral-forming processes. The results can also be used to define criteria for identifying bacterial crystals in geological samples. Magnetotactic bacteria seem to be ubiquitous in marine and fresh-water environments, and on a geological scale they may play a significant role

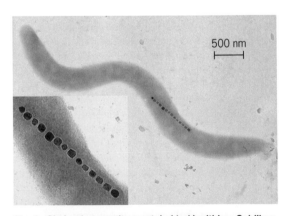

Fig. 1. Chain of magnetite crystals (dark) within a *Spirillum* bacterium. The inset shows an enlargement.

in the formation of magnetic iron minerals. However, the importance of the contribution of bacterial minerals to the magnetic remanence (magnetic flux density) of sediments and rocks is not known. Since single-domain magnetic particles have numerous practical applications, an understanding of the crystallographic and magnetic properties of magnetosomes is also a potential bonus for materials science.

Study of nanoscale magnetic crystals. Mineral inclusions in magnetotactic bacteria can best be studied using analytical transmission electron microscopy (ATEM), which allows the simultaneous characterization of crystal morphology, structure, and composition at high spatial resolution. Energy-dispersive x-ray spectrometry and electron energy-loss spectroscopy coupled with energy-loss imaging are used for studying the compositions of individual particles. Electron holography, an advanced ATEM method that represents the cutting edge in the study of fine-grained crystalline materials, reveals the magnetic microstructures of bacterial crystals, providing quantitative information about the domain structures, magnetic moments, and magnetic interactions between particles.

The bulk magnetic properties of samples that contain bacterial magnetic crystals can be studied in varying magnetic fields and at various temperatures. Magnetization and Curie-temperature measurements can be used to identify the magnetic mineral species, their characteristic grain sizes, and the relative and absolute amounts of magnetic material in a sample.

Mineral species. Most magnetotactic bacteria that have been described contain magnetite (Fe_3O_4) crystals. Magnetite has an inverse spinel structure in which Fe^{3+} cations occupy one-eighth of the tetrahedral positions, and Fe^{2+} and Fe^{3+} fill one-half of the octahedral sites within a cubic close-packed oxygen array. Owing to the two types of positions, the magnetic moments of the antiparallel-oriented, unpaired spins of the iron ions do not cancel, resulting in a net magnetic moment and a ferrimagnetic structure.

Some marine magnetotactic microorganisms produce intracellular iron sulfides. The identities of these minerals have been uncertain. Greigite (Fe_3S_4), the ferrimagnetic thiospinel, was identified in the first studies that reported iron sulfides from magnetotactic bacteria. Pyrite (FeS_2) and pyrrhotite ($Fe_{1-x}S$) were subsequently reported; however, recent studies indicate that these two minerals were likely misidentified. According to current knowledge, greigite is the main iron sulfide in these bacteria, and nonmagnetic mackinawite (FeS) also occurs. An additional phase, cubic FeS, was tentatively identified.

Mackinawite crystals were observed to convert to greigite over time. It seems likely that all greigite crystals formed from nonmagnetic precursors. An intriguing aspect of the mackinawite-to-greigite conversion is that the precursor crystals are aligned such that when they convert to magnetic greigite

the easy axis of magnetization will be parallel to the chain direction, thereby maximizing the magnetic dipole moment of the bacterium. In marine sediments, mackinawite converts to greigite and then to pyrite. This inorganically driven reaction sequence is similar to the transitions in bacteria, except that in bacteria the pathway is truncated at greigite. Such truncation may be under biological control and is beneficial to the cell since it precludes making nonmagnetic pyrite.

Crystal morphologies. The sizes and habits of the intracellular crystals are controlled by the bacterium and are species-specific. It is likely that the organic membrane that surrounds each crystal provides a template on which the crystal forms. However, the biological control mechanism over crystal growth is unknown.

Magnetite-producing strains typically contain crystals that have specific and, in some cases, even unique habits. Many species produce euhedral crystals that can include equidimensional cuboctahedral shapes (combinations of an octahedron and a cube), or grains that can be described as combinations of an octahedron, a dodecahedron, and a cube. Other strains contain elongated crystals that look like rectangles in the two-dimensional projections that are provided by electron micrographs. Perhaps the most remarkable morphologies are those that are unknown from inorganically formed minerals: bullet- or arrowhead-shaped crystals. Certain bacteria contain hundreds of such crystals within a single cell.

Sulfide-producing bacteria apparently exert less control. In contrast to magnetite, the morphologies of greigite crystals do not seem to be strictly regulated by the bacterium. Euhedral cuboctahedral as well as subhedral or anhedral, rectangular, bullet-shaped, and barrellike crystals can occur within the same cell (**Fig. 2**).

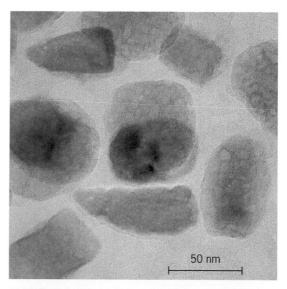

Fig. 2. Barrel- and bullet-shaped crystals of greigite from a multicellular magnetotactic prokaryote.

Fig. 3. High-resolution transmission electron microscope image of a twinned magnetite crystal in *Magnetospirillum magnetotacticum*, strain MS-1. An irregular twin plane is indicated by a Moiré effect, shown by the heavy horizontal lines in the middle of the figure, where two crystals overlap.

Size distributions of magnetite crystals from several strains show that even though the distribution curves overlap, the mean sizes are species-specific. These size distributions are commonly highly asymmetric, with sharp cut-offs toward larger sizes. The crystals do not grow further once they reach their species-specific sizes. The size and shape distributions of bacterial crystals were compared with those of synthetic magnetite grains of similar size, and the biogenic and synthetic distributions appear to be statistically distinguishable.

Microstructures. Although several studies reported that structural perfection is typical of bacterial magnetite, recent investigations show that magnetite from biologically controlled mineralization can contain structural irregularities in the form of twins. On the basis of an analysis of crystals from five strains, it was found that the only deviation from ideal structure is this occurrence of spinel-law twins. The frequency of twinning varies from strain to strain, and up to 40% of the magnetosomes can be twinned. Sparse multiple twins also occur. The contact surface between twinned individuals is commonly irregular (**Fig. 3**). In the twinned crystals, both individuals are roughly equally developed, suggesting that they nucleated more or less simultaneously and that twinning is a growth phenomenon. Since spinel-law twins are common in nonbiogenic magnetite, these

microstructural features are not unique to crystals from biologically controlled mineralization.

No twinned greigite has been reported from bacteria, but other types of defects are abundant. Greigite crystals typically show nonuniform, blotchy contrast in the transmission electron microscope and contain planar defects that may be remnants of the precursor structure. Likely all bacterial greigite formed by solid-state transformation from mackinawite or cubic FeS, and the irregular contrast effects result from the strains associated with defects that occur because of incomplete reaction. Some crystals contain bands of distinct contrast parallel to (222), and these grains seem to be in the process of transforming from a precursor to greigite. The two structures are oriented with respect to one another such that the cubic close-packed sulfur substructure is continuous across the interfaces.

Compositions. Magnetite magnetosomes are chemically remarkably pure. Except for a small amount of titanium in an uncultured bacterium, no metals other than iron were found in magnetite from magnetotactic bacteria. When *Magnetospirillum magnetotacticum*, the most studied magnetotactic species, was grown in culture in the presence of other transition metals, the iron in magnetite could not be replaced by other ions.

Both precursor nonmagnetic sulfides and greigite can contain up to 10 atomic percent copper, depending on the sampling locality and independent of the type of bacteria. The copper contents of some mackinawite crystals may hinder their complete conversion to greigite.

Magnetic microstructures. Magnetotactic bacteria provide a natural laboratory for advanced materials science studies. An understanding of the magnetic fields associated with chains of bacterial magnetic particles significantly extends the knowledge of small-particle magnetism. Such knowledge of both biogenic and nonbiogenic iron minerals has potential applications in fields such as electronics, catalysis, and magnetic recording.

Electron holography was used to study magnetite particles in two bacterial strains. This method produces images in which the magnetic field lines around the crystals are made visible. The magnetosomes then look like small bar magnets, with denser field lines within the crystals and fringing out between them (**Fig. 4**). The magnetic moments of individual magnetosomes were measured and found to be the same as calculated for magnetite spheres of the same size. Even those small crystals that would normally be superparamagnetic (that is, too small to have a permanent magnetic dipole moment at the time scale of the observation) turned out to be single-domain particles because of the magnetostatic interactions between magnetosomes within a chain.

Biomarkers. The 1996 report of the possible presence of former life on Mars stimulated intense interest in chemical and mineralogical ways of detecting past life in rocks. Iron minerals from biologically

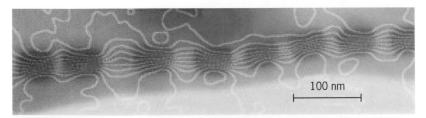

Fig. 4. Magnetic fields associated with magnetosomes from strain MV-1. The irregular lines show the magnetic field; individual magnetosomes are dark. The component of the magnetic induction in the plane of the sample, integrated in the incident beam direction, is proportional to the density of the contours.

controlled mineralization are of great interest as potential biomarkers. The morphological similarity of nanometer-scale magnetite and iron sulfides in the Martian meteorite ALH84001 to the same minerals produced by terrestrial magnetotactic bacteria was cited as part of the evidence for ancient life on Mars. Claims that magnetite and greigite particles recovered from modern and ancient sediments are of biological origin have been based on comparisons to similar grains produced by contemporary bacteria. Microstructural features and compositions are not unique to bacterial crystals. It seems that peculiar morphologies, such as bulletlike habits, and particularly the narrow size distributions of these iron minerals plus their occurrence in chains of crystals may be the best criteria for identifying bacterial magnetic minerals in sediments and rocks.

Paleomagnetic significance. Bacterially produced magnetic minerals can affect the paleomagnetic signal of sedimentary rocks. Thus, a knowledge of the mineralogy and magnetic properties of biogenic iron minerals is important for understanding the magnetic behavior of many types of sediments. Even though magnetotactic bacteria are ubiquitous, and in some aquatic environments they can have a dominating role, it is uncertain whether their contribution to the magnetic remanence of sediments is significant. Bulk magnetic methods show a strong single-domain-type remanence in places where magnetotactic bacteria live, such as within a horizon in the water or the sediment in which the dissolved oxygen content approaches or reaches zero (called the oxic-anoxic transition zone). Below this zone the magnetic remanence decreases; there are indications that magnetite magnetosomes within dead bacteria are dissolved in the sediment as a result of diagenetic redox changes. Bulk magnetic methods are very useful for identifying single-domain, likely biogenic magnetic minerals in sediments. Future studies should determine the depth profile of the contribution of single-domain bacterial crystals to the magnetic remanence of sediments.

For background information *see* BACTERIA; CRYSTAL GROWTH; DIPOLE; IRON; MAGNETISM; MAGNETITE; MICROPALEONTOLOGY; PALEOMAGNETISM; SPINEL; X-RAY SPECTROMETRY in the McGraw-Hill Encyclopedia of Science & Technology.

Mihály Pósfai; Peter R. Buseck

Bibliography. D. A. Bazylinski and B. M. Moskowitz, Microbial biomineralization of magnetic iron minerals, in J. F. Banfield and K. H. Nealson (eds.), *Geomicrobiology: Interactions Between Microbes and Minerals,* pp. 181–223, Mineralogical Society of America, Washington, DC, 1997; R. P. Blakemore, Magnetotactic bacteria, *Annu. Rev. Microbiol.,* 36:217–238, 1982; B. Devouard et al., Magnetite from magnetotactic bacteria: Size distributions and twinning, *Amer. Mineral.,* 83:1387–1398, 1998; R. E. Dunin-Borkowski et al., Magnetic microstructure of magnetotactic bacteria by electron holography, *Science,* 282:1868–1870, 1998; R. B. Frankel and R. P. Blakemore (eds.), *Iron Biominerals,* Plenum Press, New York, 1991; J. L. Kirschvink and S.-B. Chang, Ultrafine-grained magnetite in deep-sea sediments: Possible bacterial magnetofossils, *Geology,* 12:559–562, 1984; M. Pósfai et al., Reaction sequence of iron sulfide minerals in bacteria and their use as biomarkers, *Science,* 280:880–883, 1998.

Balloon

The first crewless circumnavigation of the globe was achieved by one of the 280 balloons flown around the Southern Hemisphere by the U.S. National Center for Atmospheric Research (NCAR) during 1966 as part of its GHOST project. Many of the lighter-than-air craft involved in this experiment, and the later EOLE and TWERLE crewless balloon projects, are known to have achieved multiple orbits. The record is probably held by a balloon designated GHOST 79R that was tracked making eight complete circumnavigations.

The first crewed round-the-world balloon flight was completed on March 20, 1999, with the *Breitling Orbiter 3,* an R-650 Roziere-type balloon piloted by Bertrand Piccard of Switzerland and Brian Jones of Great Britain. The balloon was launched from Chateau-d'Oex in Switzerland on March 1, 1999 (**Fig. 1**), and landed in Egypt on March 21. The round-the-world flight had been completed when the balloon crossed longitude 9°27′W while over

Fig. 1. *Breitling Orbiter 3* over the Swiss Alps, shortly after launch.

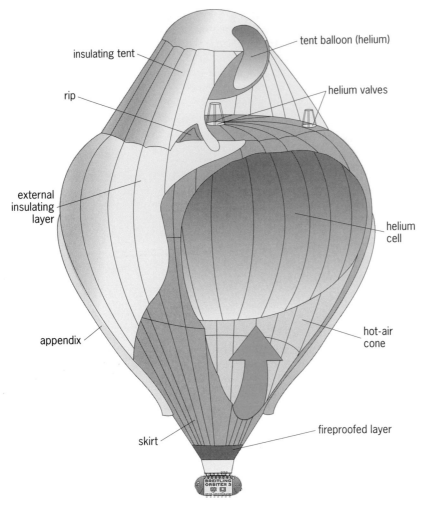

Fig. 2. Cutaway view of *Breitling Orbiter 3*.

Labels: insulating tent, tent balloon (helium), rip, helium valves, external insulating layer, helium cell, appendix, hot-air cone, skirt, fireproofed layer

to replace the missing solar heating. Even allowing for the weight of the liquefied gas and the 32 titanium fuel cylinders carried by the around-the-world balloon, a helium heating system is many times more efficient than ballasting.

Envelope. The envelope of *Breitling Orbiter 3* (**Fig. 2**) comprised an inner gas-holding cell and an outer skin of metallized Mylar. The gas cell, with a capacity of 650,000 ft³ (18,400 m³) of helium, was manufactured from nylon fabric to which had been laminated a thin double barrier film of polyurethane. During construction, panels of the gas cell were sewn together to ensure that the system was strong enough to withstand severe wind turbulence while in flight. During sewing, the cell had to be punctured by several hundred thousand needle holes, but leakage was prevented by heat-welding an impervious tape over the perforations.

Mylar has good tensile strength but tears easily. It was chosen to form the outer skin because of its light weight, and its propensity for tearing was reduced by gluing a flexible nylon scrim between two Mylar sheets to form a sandwich that could withstand handling and sewing.

The Mylar was coated with a fine layer of aluminum to help reflect ultraviolet radiation from the Sun during daylight hours and, conversely, to reduce the amount of artificial heat that was radiated away at night. The silvering, together with the insulating effects of the air gap between the inner and outer skins, plus a very large air gap on top of the gas cell produced by separating the two skins by use of a smaller helium-filled balloon (top tent), all assisted in improving total flight duration by maintaining the helium at a temperature close to that of the ambient air surrounding the balloon. Allowing the temperature of the helium to rise above ambient would have caused the lifting gas to expand, and at the ceiling this would lead to the helium venting freely from the two permanently open appendices (filler tubes), which would reduce duration. The ceiling is the height at which, due to lowering of atmospheric pressure, the helium inside the balloon has expanded to fill the gas cell. The balloon will float at this altitude until such time as the all-up weight is diminished, when it will rise to a new ceiling.

The outer skin below the gas cell was formed by a cone of silvered Mylar that entrained warmth produced at night by the heater. This cone was fitted with eight electric fans. During daylight hours the fans sucked cold ambient air into the space below the gas cell, again to help stabilize the temperature of the helium. Electric power for the fans was provided by solar panels hung around the equator of the envelope, which ensured that the fans did not operate at night when the heater was in use.

Gondola. Suspended beneath the balloon envelope was a gondola that provided a home for the crew. Measured externally, it was 5 m (16.4 ft) in length with a diameter of 2.25 m (7.4 ft). Manufactured from Kevlar and carbon fiber, it was tubular except that it was fitted with twin external box keels that would

Mauritania in West Africa, but the pilots continued their flight for another night to a more hospitable landing terrain in the Egyptian desert. The balloon and its crew achieved world records for the distance (40,814 km or 25,631 mi), duration (477 h 47 m), and shortest time around the world (370 h 24 m) of a free balloon flight.

Roziere principle. The Roziere principle, named after the French aeronaut Pilâtre de Rozier and rediscovered by balloon builder Don Cameron in 1977, made the flight possible. Roziere balloons, like conventional gas balloons, derive their lift from helium enclosed in a gas-tight cell. However, at night or when the balloon is flying below clouds, the lack of sunlight causes the helium to cool and become inefficient. Conventional gas balloons compensate for this problem by dropping sand ballast to maintain altitude, then vent gas when sunlight returns to offset the weight of discarded sand. This procedure is highly inefficient and limits flights over long distances because the ballast to be discarded during a 24-hour cycle can be as much as 15% of the all-up weight of the craft (the weight that must be lifted at launch). In contrast, a Roziere balloon pilot simply uses a small burner powered by liquid petroleum gas

fill rapidly with water to aid stability if a sea landing became necessary. It was designed to maintain life for two people for a period up to 4 weeks at altitudes exceeding 12,200 m (40,000 ft), where the temperature can reach $-50°C$ ($-58°F$) and the air density is only 20% of that at sea level.

A zero pressure loss system was chosen to pressurize the gondola, rather than an engine (which is employed in aircraft). When the gondola was sealed, the atmospheric pressure at the moment of hatch closure had to be maintained internally, necessitating perfect sealing. This required that the trapped atmosphere have its oxygen level replenished and carbon dioxide removed.

Oxygen was supplied from flasks which stored the gas in liquid form. The amount added to the gondola atmosphere automatically replaced that consumed by the crew members as measured by electronic instrumentation. Filters containing granules of lithium hydroxide removed carbon dioxide from the atmosphere. Carbon filters removed some of the foul odors from the enclosed craft.

Fresh food was eaten during the first few days of flight. After that, Piccard and Jones relied upon powdered food that was reconstituted using hot water, heated in a specially constructed kettle, plus long-life bread and spreads.

The electrical equipment was powered by lead acid batteries recharged by solar panels. Lithium–sulfur dioxide batteries provided an emergency alternative to the solar recharging system.

Communications and navigation. Radio and navigation aids were essential to the success of the flight. A Control Center established at Geneva Airport in Switzerland monitored the progress of the balloon, keeping in touch via the Inmarsat satellite system. The majority of communications utilized Inmarsat C, a relatively slow data transmission system that is reminiscent of Telex. Messages were composed at the Control Center using simple word-processing techniques that avoided the complications of embedded formatting. Sent by land line from Geneva to the British Telecom land station at Goonhilly in Cornwall, England, messages traveled to one of four geostationary equatorial satellites which retransmitted them to the gondola where they were read and stored on a laptop computer. Messages from the gondola, which were either typed onto the computer by a crew member or, in the case of position reports, produced automatically by (triplicated) Global Positioning System equipment connected to the onboard Inmarsat equipment, were received on a fax machine in the Control Center.

The position reports from Geneva were passed to the air-traffic control center (ATCC) that was responsible for the block of airspace through which the balloon was traveling. An ATCC equipped with a secondary surveillance radar system could pinpoint the exact location and height of the balloon from the transmissions emitted by *Breitling*'s radar transponder. But when the balloon crossed oceans and some less-developed countries, no ATCC was close enough to interrogate the on-board transponder, and then the satellite date reporting system became vital.

Twice while *Breitling Orbiter 3* was crossing the Pacific, its location was so close to the Equator and below the position of the communications satellite in space that the balloon envelope shielded the antennas on the gondola from the Inmarsat system. On these occasions the crew used high-frequency (HF; short-wave) radio equipment fitted to the gondola to transmit their position directly to the appropriate ATCC, which then advised the Control Center in Geneva.

Inmarsat M (voice satellite communications) and very high frequency (VHF; airband) radio completed the communications equipment carried inside the gondola. The VHF system was used over relatively short distances to allow the pilots to speak with other aircraft or local air-traffic services, including those controlling an airfield.

As well as transmitting position reports and valuable data such as fuel usage and outside air temperatures back to the control center, a primary use of the satellite communications system was to pass meteorological information. When the balloon was launched from Switzerland, a 5-day weather forecast was provided, which enabled the pilots to plan navigational strategies in advance for only the first quarter of the flight. Team meteorologists plotted the expected trajectory for the balloon using a computer program that had originally been written to track fallout from a nuclear accident.

Balloons have no motive power and no mechanical means of being steered. They move with the wind, only in the direction of the wind, and at the speed of the wind. They even lack the sailboat's ability to tack against the wind. Consequently, the role of the meteorologist on the ground is vital in predicting and controlling the route of the craft and its speed. Fortunately, air currents often vary in force and direction at different altitudes, and the primary role of the meteorologist is to interpret the available data and then advise the pilots on the most appropriate height to fly in order to achieve the best heading and speed.

Adding to the routing complications are the twin problems of politics and bureaucracy. Before any around-the-world flight commences, diplomatic clearance must be sought for overflight of all countries through whose airspace the flight may pass. While this was generally given, some countries failed to respond in advance. Shortly before launch a flight plan is filed providing air-traffic control with the anticipated position of the aircraft at specific times. Pilots of fixed-wing aircraft have little difficulty in meeting these objectives, but the balloon pilots enjoyed no such certainty. Their flight plans had to be renegotiated with ATCCs in different countries on an irregular basis at the behest of the wind, and these matters often required the intervention of the Control Center staff at a diplomatic level.

For background information *see* AIR NAVIGATION; AIR-TRAFFIC CONTROL; BALLOON; COMMUNICATIONS

SATELLITE; SATELLITE NAVIGATION SYSTEMS in the McGraw-Hill Encyclopedia of Science & Technology.

Alan Noble

Bibliography. D. Cameron, *Ballooning Handbook*, Pelham Books (Penguin Books), London, 1980, reprinted 1990; Major C. Davey and D. Cameron, *Zanussi, Transatlantic Balloon*, Sports Sponsorship Promotions, Jersey, Channel Islands, 1982; B. Piccard and B. Jones, *Around the World in 20 Days*, John Wiley, 1999.

Basalt

Basalt is a hard, black volcanic rock that constitutes the most abundant rock type at the surface of the Earth. Layers of basaltic lava floor the ocean basins and form the largest terrestrial volcanoes. Gases emanating from vast outpouring of basalt onto the continents could have contributed to the demise of the dinosaurs. Basalt is a rock type not confined to Earth: A large fraction of the meteorites that strike the Earth are basaltic. The circular impact basins (mare) on the Moon are filled with basalt. Olympus Mons, the most massive volcano in the solar system, is thought to be the product of sustained eruption of basalt from the Martian interior. As a material that emanates from depths that are inaccessible by direct sampling, basalt has provided scientists with an invaluable probe to elucidate the nature of the Earth's interior.

Global distribution. The dominant driving force for plate tectonics is solid-state convection in the Earth's mantle, which is the region extending from the base of the crust, at 10–70 km (6–40 mi), to a depth of about 2900 km (1800 mi). Nearly all eruption of basalt is confined to narrow zones corresponding to the margins of the tectonic plates, where basalt is produced by melting of the mantle rock known as peridotite.

Basalt that forms the ocean basins (termed mid-ocean ridge basalt, or MORB) is extruded at constructive plate boundaries, corresponding to zones of convective upwelling in the underlying mantle. The surface expression of this type of plate boundary is a 40,000-km-long (65,000-mi) chain of undersea ridges, which accounts for the largest amount of basalt production on Earth, averaging about 20 km^3 (5 mi^3) per year. Basalt is also produced along destructive plate margins, known as subduction zones, corresponding to regions of mantle downwelling where the oceanic crust produced at the ridge sinks into the mantle beneath the adjoining plate. Subduction zones are characterized by arcuate chains of volcanoes (termed island arcs, although they sometimes occur on continental margins), such as those comprising Japan, the Aleutians, and the Marianas (all members of the circum-Pacific "Ring of Fire").

Although more silica-rich volcanic rocks (such as andesite) occur in subduction zone volcanoes, about half of the material erupted is basalt (termed island arc basalt, or IAB), amounting to an average production rate of about 2.5 km^3 (0.6 mi^3) per year. A relatively limited amount of basalt is also associated with eruptions that occur in areas far removed from the plate margins (termed ocean island basalt, or OIB). Although isolated in occurrence, such loci of eruptive activity can last millions of years, and as such have been termed hot spots. Hot spots are the result of long-lived upwellings or plumes of anomalously hot material within the Earth's mantle. A hot spot beneath the central Pacific ocean basin has existed for 70 million years, and is responsible for the eruption of basalt that formed the Hawaiian-Emperor chain of islands. Such intense basalt outpourings are highly localized and globally sparse, accounting for less than 1 km^3 (0.2 mi^3) of basalt per year.

Chemistry. Although basalt occurs in a wide range of geological settings, its overall composition is surprisingly uniform, on average containing about 50% (by weight) of silica (SiO_2), 10% each of iron, magnesium, and calcium, 15% aluminum, and 2% each of titanium and sodium. Despite uniformity in its major chemical constituents, subtle differences do exist in the abundances of elements that are present at trace levels (in the parts per million range) and in the relative amounts of certain naturally occurring isotopes. Such differences are strongly correlated with the specific tectonic setting in which the basalt is erupted, and as such provide information bearing on the nature of the underlying mantle.

The trace-element and isotopic composition of mid-ocean ridge basalt is globally quite uniform, and reflects derivation from a mantle source that has lost part of its inventory of "incompatible elements." Such elements are usually characterized by their large ionic radius or high charge and are not easily incorporated into the structures of the common rock-forming minerals. As a consequence, incompatible elements are readily partitioned into a melt or fluid phase relative to the residual solid. Because the continental crust is more or less complementary to MORB in terms of being enriched in incompatible elements, the global depletion of the MORB mantle source is usually attributed to transfer of these elements to the continents. The nature of this transfer process is not well understood, but it is generally held that continental growth occurs at subduction zones and that incompatible elements are transferred during subduction of the oceanic crust.

Recycling of oceanic crust through subduction zones. Although the source for MORB appears to have lost a certain fraction of its incompatible elements, reinjection of MORB back into the mantle, in the form of subducted oceanic crust, offers an opportunity to at least partially recycle this inventory (**Fig. 1**). It would appear that the mantle source for MORB contains very little of this recycled material, but the effects of recycling are indeed imprinted on the mantle source of island arc and ocean island basalt.

Subduction of oceanic crust into the mantle has been well documented using two different types of seismic imaging techniques. First, as the oceanic crust descends into the mantle, it undergoes structural changes (buckling, phase transitions) resulting in the release of energy in the form of earthquakes. A map of the distribution of source points for these earthquakes (known as hypocenters) defines the path of the descending crust so long as its behavior is brittle. More recently, a technique known as seismic tomography has been developed to map the variation in seismic velocity at depth. Seismic velocities are typically a few percent faster through the subducted oceanic crust relative to the ambient mantle, owing to differences in both composition and mineralogy. Particularly detailed images across subduction zones in the western Pacific have clearly documented subduction of the oceanic crust to depths of 600 km (372 mi) or more.

Element transfer in subduction zones. Subsequent to its formation at the ridge, oceanic crust is exposed to the hydrosphere for millions of years prior to being subducted. As a result of this exposure, substantial chemical and isotopic modification of the upper portions of the oceanic crust can occur. Most significant of these modifications are hydration; addition of elements that are enriched in seawater (for example, boron); and shifting of the isotopic composition of such elements as strontium, boron, and oxygen from primary basalt values to that of seawater. In addition, the bulk composition of the oceanic crust may also be altered if it acquires a veneer of pelagic sediment. When this package of modified material is subducted, dehydration reactions occur as the oceanic crust heats and densifies. The fluid produced at this stage effectively strips the oceanic crust of much of its incompatible element inventory, including that which was acquired during contact with the hydrosphere, and transfers it to the overlying mantle and crust. This unique signature is readily apparent in the composition of island arc basalts, which are the melting product of the mantle overlying the dehydrating oceanic crust. For example, comparison of the abundances of an element acquired during modification, such as boron, relative to an element that is unaffected by seawater exchange, such as niobium, reveals that the boron/niobium ratio in IABs is up to 100 times higher than in MORBs (**Fig. 2**).

Role of subducted crust in formation of island basalts. The trace-element composition of basalts erupted above hot spots (OIBs) is complementary to that found in IABs in that elements that are most easily mobilized during the dehydration process are actually depleted in OIBs. For example, the abundance of boron relative to niobium in ocean island basalts is about 10 times lower than in MORB and up to 1000 times lower than in IABs (Fig. 2). However, similar to some IABs, the oxygen isotopic composition of minerals found in some OIBs overlaps that found in the upper portions of modified oceanic crust. These sorts of observations have led to the notion that the mantle source region for hot spot basalts contains some amount of oceanic crust that has been modi-

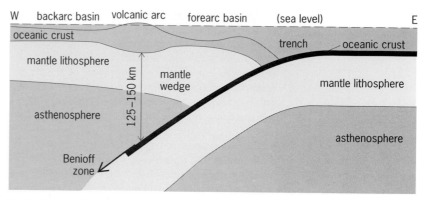

Fig. 1. Cross section through a typical subduction zone.

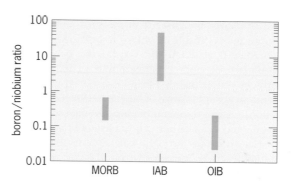

Fig. 2. Range of boron/niobium ratios for basalts erupted at the mid-ocean ridges (MORB), island arcs (IAB), and oceanic islands (OIB). (Data from J. G. Ryan et al., 1996, and T. Ishikawa and E. Nakamura, 1994)

fied by interaction with the hydrosphere (to produce the distinctive oxygen isotopic composition) and is subject to devolatilization during subduction (resulting in the depletion of fluid-mobile elements).

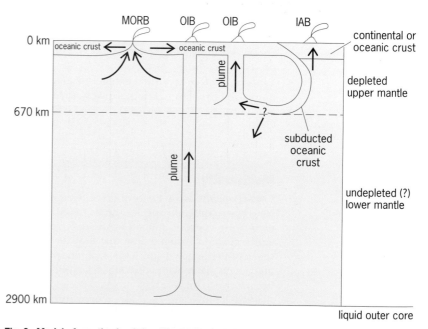

Fig. 3. Model of mantle circulation illustrating the distribution of source regions for MORB, IAB, and OIB. (After A. W. Hofmann, 1997)

Depths that basalts sample. By combining observations from both geophysics and geochemistry, there is a much better understanding of which regions of the inaccessible earth are sampled by basalts (**Fig. 3**). Estimates of the total volume of mantle material that has been depleted to form the continental crust suggest that the source for MORB probably reaches as deep as the lower mantle (below 670 km or 410 mi). In contrast, the mantle source for island arc basalts is likely to be much more shallow, corresponding to the depth interval over which fluid is lost from the oceanic crust during subduction (less than 200 km or 125 mi). The source for ocean island basalts bears the signature of oceanic crust that has been processed through subduction zones. Because of differences in composition, the subducted oceanic crust is denser than the surrounding peridotite and is capable of sinking to unknown depths. Whether it sinks all the way to the core-mantle boundary depends on whether it penetrates the upper-to-lower mantle transition zone, which represents an abrupt change in mantle density or composition. Seismic tomographic images suggest that the subducted crust either can be deflected at 670 km or can penetrate through. It thus seems that a minimum depth of origin for OIB is 670 km, and some sources could even be deeper.

For background information *see* BASALT; EARTH CRUST; EARTH INTERIOR; HOT SPOTS (GEOLOGY); LAVA; METEORITE; MID-OCEANIC RIDGE; PERIDOTITE; SEISMOLOGY; SUBDUCTION ZONES; VOLCANO in the McGraw-Hill Encyclopedia of Science & Technology.

James Brenan

Bibliography. M. G. Best, *Igneous and Metamorphic Petrology*, Blackwell Science, 1995; A. W. Hofmann, Mantle geochemistry: The message from oceanic volcanism, *Nature*, 385:219–229, 1997; T. Ishikawa and E. Nakamura, Origin of the slab component in arc lavas from across-arc variation of B and Pb isotopes, *Science*, 370:205–208, 1994; J. G. Ryan et al., The boron systematics of intraplate lavas: Implications for crust and mantle evolution, *Geochimica et Cosmochimica Acta*, 60:415–422, 1996; R. Van der Hilst et al., Tomographic imaging of subducted lithosphere below northwest Pacific island arcs, *Nature*, 353:37–43, 1991.

Biodiversity

Conserving the biodiversity of a region requires mapping where different species can be found and then identifying conservation sites that are large enough and arranged in such a way that long-term persistence of the targeted species is maximized. Increasingly, such planning entails looking beyond political boundaries to include regions whose boundaries are defined ecologically, such as a mountain range and the adjoining coastal plain. Mathematical models and other quantitative approaches are key elements in the toolkits of modern conservation planners and managers, both in investigating the extinction risks faced by different species and in identifying suites of sites that can protect as much of a region's biodiversity as possible.

One approach, population viability analysis, typically takes a single-species perspective, using data on a species' population dynamics, demography, and life-history traits to evaluate extinction risk. Such analyses can offer insight into the relative contributions of a species' different life stages (such as seed, seedling, and adult plant) to the rate of population growth, and can provide a framework for ranking competing management options in terms of their impacts on a species' risk of extinction.

Mathematics plays a central role in such analyses. For example, when the demographic details of a population's size- or stage-structure are known, researchers can construct a transition matrix from field-collected data by specifying the fecundity and probabilities of growth and survival for each size or stage class. These matrices are then used to quantify the population's growth rate and assess the sensitivity of that growth rate to changes in different matrix entries. Data for loggerhead sea turtles (*Caretta caretta*) were analyzed in this way, and helped identify mortality of juvenile turtles (primarily from shrimp trawling) as a key factor responsible for the species' decline.

Mathematics and population viability analyses can also be used to estimate extinction risks, using repeated censuses of the same population year after year. Two key factors that determine extinction risk are population size and the extent of population fluctuation from year to year (see **illus.**). By asking how population size influences extinction risk, many such analyses gauge how big a nature reserve must be. For example, using a particular kind of stochastic population model, called a diffusion approximation, researchers evaluated extinction risks

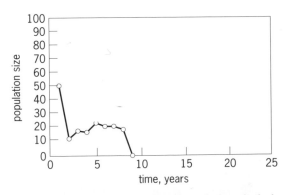

Time series of counts for two populations of a hypothetical species. Even though both populations start out under the same conditions and have identical parameters controlling the changes in their sizes, one population goes extinct quickly while the other persists. Using analytical solutions or computer simulations, population viability analyses try to use existing data on changes in population size to quantify the chance that a real population will go extinct within a given time frame. These data were generated using a stochastic process-error formulation of the Ricker model of population dynamics.

Erratum

The illustration in the article Biodiversity on page 48 of the McGraw-Hill Yearbook of Science & Technology 2001 was printed incorrectly. We are providing the correct version of the illustration below. We regret any inconvenience.

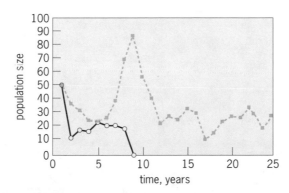

Time series of counts for two populations of a hypothetical species. Even though both populations start out under the same conditions and have identical parameters controlling the changes in their sizes, one population goes extinct quickly while the other persists. Using analytical solutions or computer simulations, population viability analyses try to use existing data on changes in population size to quantify the chance that a real population will go extinct within a given time frame. These data were generated using a stochastic process-error formulation of the Ricker model of population dynamics.

for the whooping crane (*Grus americana*), California condor (*Gymnogyps californianus*), grizzly bear (*Ursus arctos horribilis*), and several other endangered species.

Quantification of dispersal rates and patterns is yet another area in which mathematics connects with conservation planning through population viability analyses. For many species, population dynamics are so variable or local population sizes are so small that extirpation from individual sites is likely. For such species, dispersal among sites, which can allow small populations to avoid extinction or provide colonists to reoccupy empty sites, is the key to long-term persistence. However, dispersal parameters are generally much harder to estimate than changes in local population status, and ecologists often use simple approximations such as an exponential decay with distance to characterize dispersal in viability analyses. In contrast, when the details of an animal's movement characteristics are well known, individual behavior models that incorporate movement details in computer simulations are sometimes used. Understanding the essential contribution of dispersal among sites to persistence of the northern spotted owl (*Strix occidentalis caurina*) proved crucial to conservation decisions affecting that species.

Reserve siting approaches to conservation planning constitute an important complement to population viability analyses. By utilizing lists of species found in different areas, reserve siting approaches aim to identify sets of sites that, taken together, would protect a region's biodiversity.

Because financial constraints and concerns over the welfare of people living or working in an area preclude setting aside all sites for conservation, planners turn to a variety of quantitative approaches to identify suites of sites that achieve a particular conservation goal. Such goals are typically framed in terms of the identity of particular species that must be protected (because they are rallying points for conservation efforts or play a crucial ecological role), the fraction of a region's biodiversity to be protected, and the number of populations of each species to protect. Then, given constraints on the total amount of land that can be protected or the financial resources available for the reserve system, computer algorithms are used to select sets of sites that best meet the conservation goals.

A variety of different reserve siting algorithms have been developed over the years, and they have recently been compared in terms of their ability to design adequate reserve systems, given constraints on resources and other factors. Some algorithms focus on protecting species-rich sites first, whereas others emphasize sites harboring rare species. Key conceptual issues in such approaches include the notion of site complementarity (that is, picking sites that are very different from one another to maximize the array of species protected), site irreplaceability (emphasizing how sites differ in their uniqueness and threat), and site suitability (recognizing that

sites harboring similar species may differ in their potential to facilitate persistence of those species due to human impacts and other factors). The relative importance of these issues changes among regions, meaning that any generally applicable quantitative approach to conservation planning must be robust to the unique demands of individual planning regions.

Approaches to reserve design that effectively link the population dynamics and reserve siting perspectives appear essential in an era of growing interest in large-scale conservation planning. This interface, including attempts to develop shorcuts for categorizing species according to extinction risk when data are scarce, is an area of active research for ecologists and conservation biologists.   William F. Fagan

Bibliography. S. Andelman et al., Tools for conservation planning: General principles for reserve network design in an uncertain world, *Bioscience*, 2000; D. T. Crouse, L. B. Crowder, and H. Caswell, A stage-based population model for loggerhead sea turtles and implications for conservation, *Ecology*, 68:1412–1423, 1987; B. Dennis, P. L. Munholland, and J. M. Scott, Estimation of growth and extinction parameters for endangered species, *Ecol. Monog.*, 61:115–143, 1991; W. F. Fagan, E. Meir, and J. Moore, Variation thresholds for extinction and their implications for conservation strategies, *Amer. Natural.*, 154:510–520, 1999; R. L. Pressey, H. P. Possingham, and J. R. Day, Effectiveness of alternative heuristic algorithms for identifying indicative minimum requirements for conservation reserves, *Biol. Conserv.*, 80:207–219, 1997.

Biofilm

In most environments, microbes of all types are not found as individual cells swimming freely through liquid (planktonic cells), but are a part of surface-attached communities called biofilms. For instance, the water of a brook running through a rocky streambed is crystal clear, meaning that there are relatively few bacteria suspended in the water. However, attempting to cross this stream is an effort, because the submerged rocks are slippery due largely to the thick microbial mats that form on their surface. Another example is fish tanks: the "dirt" accumulating on the glass walls of the aquarium are microbial biofilms. Furthermore, microbial biofilms can be formed by pathogens (disease-causing bacteria) in a wide variety of environments: *Vibrio cholerae* in marine systems, *Mycobacterium avium* and *Escherichia coli* in fresh-water environments, and *Pseudomonas aeruginosa*, *Staphylococcus aureus*, and *Streptococcus mutans* in the human body. Historically, the study of microbes has focused on free-swimming cells. However, over the past two decades microbiologists have begun to shift their focus to the study of microbial biofilms.

Community formation. The bacterium *P. aeruginosa* has a rotating tail, known as a flagellum,

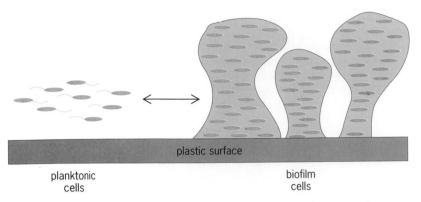

Fig. 1. Schematic of the bacterium *Pseudomonas aeruginosa* as either planktonic or biofilm-grown cells.

to propel it through liquid toward surfaces suitable for biofilm formation (**Fig. 1**). When these bacteria attach to a surface, they form a very complex series of mushroom-shaped structures. Each mushroom-shaped microcolony is composed of hundreds or thousands of bacteria stuck to the surface or to each other. The bacterial colonies are surrounded by carbohydrates, or long sugar chains, that the bacteria have produced. These carbohydrates are thought to give the bacteria some protection from environmental insults and to help the bacterial colony superstructures retain some measure of stability. Each mushroomlike structure is separated from its neighbor, allowing the nutrients required for growth to efficiently reach all the bacteria.

Several theories have been proposed as to why microbes form surface-attached communities, although these ideas have been very difficult to prove. For example, many fungi and bacteria produce antibiotics, probably in an effort to reduce local competition from other microorganisms. Biofilm-grown cells are notoriously resistant to antibiotics, and the resistance afforded by biofilm growth might help organisms normally sensitive to these antibiotics avoid death. Similarly, bacteria in a biofilm may be less susceptible to attack by bacteriophages and exposure to ultraviolet light. There may also be safety in numbers from eukaryotic organisms that graze on bacteria as a source of food. The availability of nutrients in the environment is often a signal that triggers biofilm formation. Anchoring to a surface allows microbes to remain fixed in a favorable environment instead of potentially being swept to a less hospitable location. There is also evidence that biofilms composed of multiple organisms in proximity may utilize nutrients more efficiently than individual organisms. Finally, microbes in a biofilm have increased rates of genetic exchange. The uptake of foreign deoxyribonucleic acid (DNA) may be used by some organisms as a source of genetic diversity to help adapt to a changing environment, or as a food source.

A picture of how microbes form communities on a surface is beginning to emerge. Signals from the environment, such as the availability of food and oxygen, are important factors in determining whether microbes will initiate the formation of a biofilm (although the exact nature of the signals is not yet known). Studies suggest that many microbes form biofilms in environments where all the raw materials required for growth are abundant. Bacteria also have a set of uncharacterized proteins, probably located on the surface of the cell, involved in sensing these environmental signals and triggering the induction of genes whose expression is required for biofilm formation. Other surface proteins, including the propellerlike flagella and protein rods, known as pili, are important for getting the bacteria to the surface and attaching them there. Once the microbes are attached, they can alter their physiology to adapt to this new lifestyle and develop their distinctive colony structure (Fig. 1). The formation of these structures does not occur accidentally; bacteria have an active system for ensuring their proper development that utilizes extracellular molecules known as homoserine lactones. Bacteria produce homoserine lactones at a low and steady rate. Bacteria sense the accumulation of homoserine lactones in the environment and use the concentration of these molecules as an indirect means to determine their population in a process known as quorum sensing. Presumably, once a quorum of bacteria is reached, the developmental pathway leading to formation of the characteristic biofilm structures can proceed. Interestingly, it appears that bacteria also have a means to detach from the surface and return to their free-swimming mode of life. It is believed that for many organisms this event is triggered when the cells starve and need to forage for a fresh source of nutrients. While the events for the formation and disassembly of the biofilm can be sketched out in a rudimentary form, a great deal of work remains to be done to understand all of the intricacies.

Negative impacts. The ability to form biofilms seems to be a behavior shared by a wide variety of microbes, including bacteria and fungi. Therefore, the establishment of these surface communities represents a fundamental aspect of the biology of microbes that has apparently been conserved across a vast range of species over evolutionary time. Furthermore, the formation of biofilms can have a profoundly negative impact in medical, industrial, and natural settings. For example, modern medicine uses implants and artificial materials to improve patient care. Plastic catheter tubes allow the routine and continuous delivery of drugs, antibiotics, and nutrients. Contact lenses correct vision without the need for glasses. Artificial hips help keep senior citizens active and mobile. Unfortunately, these implant surfaces also serve as ideal sites for colonization by bacteria and the formation of biofilms. Formation of the biofilm may damage the surface to which the microbes are attached. Of even greater concern is the phenomenon of increased antibiotic resistance of microbes growing in a biofilm. For reasons that are not yet understood, microbes growing on a surface can be up to 1000 times more resistant to antibiotics than the same organisms growing as individual, planktonic cells. Because the biofilms are so recalcitrant to antibiotic therapy, the only recourse for treatment often involves removal of the contaminated implant (resulting in additional trauma to the patient). In the case of the artificial heart, one of the main hurdles in their routine use is a 100% microbial contamination rate that often leads to the failure or clogging of valves. Among the most common organisms causing implant-based infections are *Pseudomonas*, *Staphylococcus*, and *Enterococcus*. These biofilm-associated infections result in increased hospital stays that cost more than a billion dollars per year.

Benefits. Biofilms may play a beneficial role in some circumstances. Some bacteria, such as *P. fluorescens*, can colonize the roots of vegetable crops such as tomatoes, potatoes, and cucumbers and protect these plants from disease-causing fungi in the soil. This biofilm-mediated protection is known as biological control, and could one day replace or supplement traditional chemical pesticides typically used in agriculture. Biofilms are also important players in the removal of contaminants from wastewater in modern sewage treatment plants. Fixed bacterial communities can degrade a wide array of chemical (pesticides) and organic (fecal matter) contaminants in a process known as bioremediation.

Confocal scanning laser microscopy. New microscopy techniques have been applied to the study of microbial communities. Traditional microscopy involves the drying or chemical treatment of samples before they are examined under the microscope. Another common method is the use of visible light to visualize samples that have been treated with a variety of dyes. These approaches sometimes alter the structure or properties of the sample, can result in out-of-focus images, and can give misleading information. The advent of confocal scanning laser microscopy allows visualization of the biofilms in their native state (**Fig. 2**). Confocal scanning laser microscopy utilizes a laser to excite fluorescent probes that tag the bacteria. Excitation of the tag results in the emission of light that can be acquired by an electronic camera attached to the microscope. The microscope is focused on one layer of the sample and

configured to eliminate any out-of-focus light that could blur the image. Eliminating unfocused light is accomplished by acquiring only the light that is emitted perpendicularly to the detector. The focal plane (the area in the sample where the microscope is focused) can be moved through the biofilm, and each optical cross section can be stacked with the aid of a computer to recreate the three-dimensional structure of the biofilm.

The genes. To truly understand the mechanisms involved in the development of microbial communities and to develop rational means to modulate their formation, the genes that control biofilm formation must be studied. For this task, the field of bacterial genetics is available. The approach is simple: (1) make a large collection of bacterial strains with random mutations on their chromosome, (2) look among these strains for ones that do not make biofilms, (3) then identify the genes disrupted in these strains. Presumably, these are the genes that are important for biofilm formation. One requirement for using a genetic approach is having an easy means to test for biofilm formation. The primary tool used is a plastic 96-well dish (**Fig. 3a**) where the bacteria can grow and form a biofilm. The biofilm is detected using a dye, crystal violet, that stains the bacteria but not the plastic. The biofilm is seen as a dark ring that forms on the walls of the wells (Fig. 3b). Mutant bacteria do not form such a ring.

The polymerase chain reaction (PCR) is used to identify the DNA sequence of the gene disrupted in each mutant. Each mutant contains a known DNA element called a transposon which disrupts the normal function of the gene into which the element is inserted. Polymerase chain reaction allows the specific amplification of the bacterial DNA directly adjacent to the transposon in order to obtain a partial sequence of the gene disrupted in the non-biofilm-forming mutant strain. The emerging fields of genomics (the study of the entire DNA sequence of an organism) and bioinformatics (using computers to study biological systems) allow determination of whether the function of the disrupted gene is known. Studies have revealed an important general principle: many of the genes required for biofilm formation have no known biochemical function. This tells

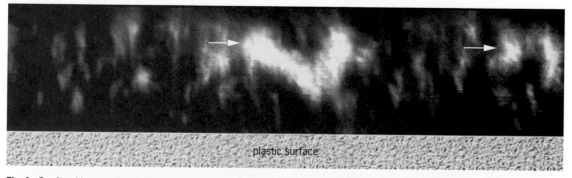

Fig. 2. Confocal image of a biofilm of *Vibrio cholerae*. This side view of the biofilm was reconstructed from 13 images taken at 1-micrometer increments. From top to bottom, the biofilm is approximately 15 μm thick (a bacterium is about 1 $\times$ 2 μm). The characteristic mushroom shapes of the bacterial microcolonies (indicated by the arrow) are evident.

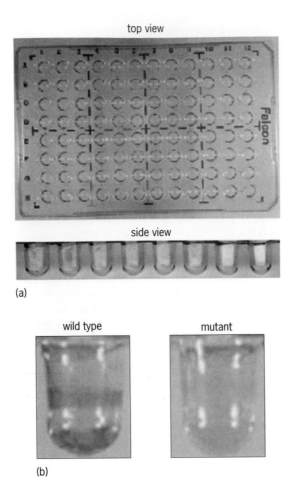

top view

side view

(a)

wild type   mutant

(b)

Fig. 3. Testing for biofilm formation. (*a*) 96-well dish. (*b*) Wild type leaves a dark ring; mutant bacteria do not form a ring.

based studies, and microscopy, scientists are poised to greatly increase the understanding of how microbes live attached to a surface.

For background information *see* ANTIBIOTIC RESISTANCE; BACTERIAL GENETICS; BIOFILM; FUNGI; MEDICAL BACTERIOLOGY in the McGraw-Hill Encyclopedia of Science & Technology.   George O'Toole

Bibliography. J. W. Costerton et al., Microbial biofilms, *Annu. Rev. Microbiol.*, 49:711–745, 1995; D. G. Davies et al., The involvement of cell-to-cell signals in the development of a bacterial biofilm, *Science*, 280(5361):295–298, 1998; M. Givskov et al., Eukaryotic interference with homoserine lactone-mediated prokaryotic signalling, *J. Bacteriol.*, 178(22):6618–6622, 1996; A. T. Henrici, Studies of freshwater bacteria, I. A direct microscopic technique, *J. Bacteriol.*, pp. 277–287, 1933; P. E. Kolenbrander and J. London, Adhere today, here tomorrow: Oral bacterial adherence, *J. Bacteriol.*, 175(11):3247–3252, 1993; J. R. Lawrence et al., Optical sectioning of microbial biofilms, *J. Bacteriol.*, 173(20):6558–6567, 1991; G. A. O'Toole et al., Genetic approaches to the study of biofilms, *Meth. Enzymol.*, 310:91–109, 1999; G. A. O'Toole, H. Kaplan, and R. Kolter, Biofilm formation as microbial development, *Annu. Rev. Microbiol.*, 54:49–79, 2000; G. A. O'Toole and R. Kolter, Flagellar and twitching motility are necessary for *Pseudomonas aeruginosa* biofilm development, *Mol. Microbiol.*, 30(2):295–304, 1998; L. S. Thomashow and D. M. Weller, Current concepts in the use of introduced bacteria for biological disease control: Mechanisms and antifungal metabolites., in G. Stacey and N. Keen (eds.), *Plant Microbe Interactions*, Chapman and Hall, New York, 1995.

researchers that they are looking at an aspect of the bacterial lifestyle that is poorly understood or has not been studied in any detail at the level of the gene.

Future research. While understanding the biology of biofilm formation is an important endeavor, long-term goals also include devising new strategies for controlling biofilm formation. Implant-based infections are an increasing problem in clinical settings. Recent studies also implicate biofilm formation in infectious diseases, including the infections associated with cystic fibrosis. Biofilms can also lead to the clogging of pipelines and contamination in industrial processes. Another current area of study is the search for new means to control the formation of biofilms. One class of recently discovered compounds that can interfere with the formation of biofilms is the furanones. Furanones, which are analogs of homoserine lactones, were originally isolated from a particular marine alga that was unusually free of microbial biofilms (most algae are covered with bacteria). The furanones appear to interfere with the development of the typical biofilm structure and apparently render these organisms more susceptible to treatment with natural biocides. Using bacterial genetics in conjunction with the newest molecular techniques, genome-

Bioluminescence

Bioluminescence, which is the ability of an organism to emit visible light, is a common attribute of marine creatures. The phenomenon is relatively rare on land, where fireflies are the best-known example. In the oceans it is ubiquitous, and is found at all depths. The most common sources in the marine environment are bacteria, dinoflagellates, jellyfish, crustaceans, cephalopods, and fish. Among cephalopods, which include squids, cuttlefish, and octopods, the expression of bioluminescence is extremely diverse. Out of 100 genera of squids and cuttlefish, 63 have been found to include bioluminescent species, but in octopods only 3 out of 43 genera do.

Evolution. Bioluminescence is produced when an enzyme, known as luciferase, catalyzes the oxidation of a substrate, known as luciferin, by molecular oxygen. Luciferase and luciferin are generic designations for any enzyme or substrate involved in a bioluminescent reaction. Based on the number of different chemistries and the variety of expressions of bioluminescence in different organisms, it appears that the ability to produce light arose independently many different times in many different groups of animals.

This remarkable degree of convergent evolution is a clear indication of the selective advantages afforded by light production.

The prevalence of bioluminescence in the open ocean is believed to be a consequence of selection pressures imposed by the struggle to survive in an environment that lacks hiding places. There are no trees or bushes to hide behind in the vast expanses of the open ocean, constituting most of the living space on Earth. However, survival frequently depends on the ability to hide from predators. During evolutionary history, as the oceans filled up with ever swifter and more ferocious predators, many prey that could not outswim them found refuge in the dark depths. Among these were many that depended on vision and visual signals to attract mates, to lure prey, and to avoid predators. As these vision-dependent animals colonized the twilight depths of the ocean, natural selection favored those with enhanced visual sensitivity and amplified visual signals.

Bioluminescence is one way to enhance a visual signal in an environment with little light. For example, the ink used by a squid or an octopus to distract or confuse a predator has little or no visual impact in dark depths. However, releasing bioluminescent chemicals directly into the water serves as a highly effective distraction, and is a common trick of many deep-ocean dwellers, including some shrimp, jellyfish, squid, and fish. Similarly, visual signals such as lures used to attract prey or body parts displayed to attract a mate, are made visible by bioluminescence. Many animals also have bioluminescent headlamps that they can use to help them see in the dark. Bioluminescence can also function as camouflage. In the depths between 200 and 1000 m (660 and 3300 ft), sunlight filtering down through surface waters creates a dim background light when viewed from below. Against this background, the silhouette of an opaque animal is an easy target for an upward-looking visual predator. Many fish, squid, and shrimp camouflage their silhouettes by producing downward-directed bioluminescence that exactly matches the color, intensity, and angular distribution of the background light field.

Light organs. Light organs in cephalopods run the gamut from simple patches of light-producing tissue to elaborate light organs known as photophores that contain complex optical elements such as lenses, filters, irises, reflectors, and shutters. Although there is little direct evidence for the functions served by these light organs, their anatomical locations often provide some hint as to their purpose. For example, in many otherwise transparent squid, photophores may occur beneath pigmented structures such as the eyes or liver, and it is thought that luminescence serves to eliminate the shadows that these opaque organs would cast. Similarly, many opaque squid have photophores arrayed over most of the underside of their bodies, and these too can provide camouflage. Light organs are also found on arms and tentacles, perhaps serving as sexual signals or lures to attract prey.

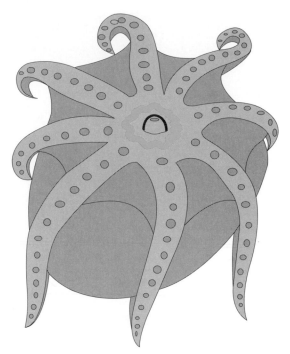

Fig. 1. Location of bioluminescence (indicated in color) in the octopus *Japetella diaphana*. (*Redrawn from P. J. Herring, Luminescent organs, in E. R. Trueman and M. R. Clarke, eds., The Mollusca, vol. II, Academic Press, New York*)

Differences in light organ distribution between males and females, which are usually taken as evidence that they function in sexual signaling, are rare in squid and cuttlefish. However, in two of the three genera of octopods with luminescent species, the bolitaenids *Japetella* and *Eledonella*, light organs take the unusual form of a ring around the mouths of breeding females (**Fig. 1**). The fact that these light organs occur only in breeding females and actually disappear following spawning provides sound evidence that they function in sexual signaling.

The only other confirmed case of bioluminescence among octopods is in the deep-sea cirrate (finned) octopus *Stauroteuthis syrtensis* (**Fig. 2**). Although this octopus was first described in 1879, it was not until 1999, when a live specimen was collected using a midwater submersible, that it was discovered to be bioluminescent. When this specimen, which was collected from 755 m (2490 ft) in the Gulf of Maine, was placed in a shipboard aquarium, researchers were surprised to note that its "suckers" did not stick to anything, and moreover that these suckers were capable of emitting blue light (**Fig. 3**).

An investigation of the anatomy and ultrastructure of the suckers-photophores revealed that although these organs still had suckerlike traits, light-producing cells replaced many of the muscles that are prominent features of normal suckers. In effect, they appear to be light organs that have evolved from suckers. Because there is no fossil record of bioluminescence, the evolutionary history of

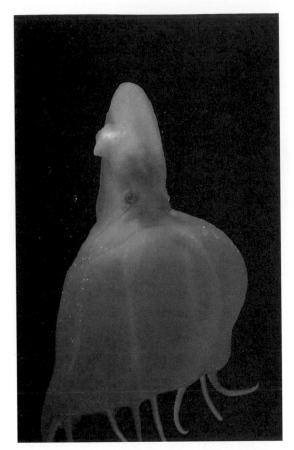

Fig. 2. Deep-sea finned octopus *Stauroteuthis syrtensis*. (*Photo by E. Widder/Harbor Branch Oceanog.* © 1999)

light-producing structures is difficult to deduce. Therefore, such light organs, which retain some indication of their previous function, offer valuable insight into that evolutionary history. In this case it is postulated that the change from sucker to light organ may have occurred during colonization of the deep open ocean by a creature that was originally a shallow-water bottom dweller. Once the suckers were no longer useful for clinging to the bottom, their only remaining value may have been for communication. Shallow-water species of octopus display their suckers for (nonbioluminescent) sexual signaling. In the dim depths such displays would lose visual impact unless amplified. One way to enhance visibility would be to evolve highly reflective suckers, which is in fact a notable characteristic of these suckers-photophores. If the suckers were then to develop a bioluminescent capacity, the effect would be further amplified, resulting in an immediate selective advantage for the light emitter.

Many bioluminescent animals exhibit multiple uses of light emission, which is undoubtedly a consequence of multiple selection pressures. For example, in many cases animals that use bioluminescence for attracting mates or finding food also emit light defensively. Since captured specimens of *S. syrtensis* were observed to emit light when disturbed, it may

be assumed that under such circumstances bioluminescence functions defensively, serving either to startle a predator or to attract larger secondary predators that may prey on the primary predator. An additional function for bioluminescence in these octopods may be as an attractant for their primary prey items, which are copepods. These tiny crustaceans, which are like the insects of the sea, seem an odd food choice for such a large, slow-moving animal. However, if the light organs act as a lure, attracting the copepods like moths to a flame, then perhaps this strange diet makes sense. When seen from submersibles, the posture of this octopus, with arms spread out in an umbrella or bell-shaped attitude, seems consistent with the idea that it uses its light organs as lures. Additionally, the blue light emitted by the suckers-photophores is a good match for the color that travels farthest through seawater, and therefore should be highly visible to potential prey. Once the copepods are attracted to the light, they may become enmeshed in a mucous web, which the octopus secretes from glands near the mouth.

Since there are only the three confirmed cases of bioluminescence in octopods (in the cirrate

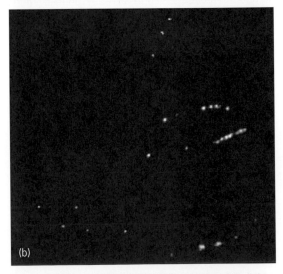

Fig. 3. Suckers as light organs. (*a*) Seen under white light, the suckers-photophores of the octopus *Stauroteuthis syrtensis* appear highly reflective. (*b*) In the dark these same structures emit blue light. (*Photos by E. Widder/ Harbor Branch Oceanog.* © 1999)

S. syrtensis and the incirrates *Japetella* and *Eledonella*), it is interesting that they occur in such dissimilar suborders (the Cirrata and Incirrata) with two such different forms of expression. While the cirrates have fins and cirri (two thin armlike projections associated with each sucker), the incirrates have neither. The primary similarity between these disparate octopods appears to be their pelagic existence. Because morphology alone is not an adequate indicator of bioluminescence potential, it is necessary to observe light emission from putative light organs. Such observations require access to healthy specimens. Unfortunately, most deep-sea octopods are collected with nets and are usually brought up dead. Perhaps, with greater access to the deep oceans with submersibles, unmanned vehicles, and long-term observatories, new instances of bioluminescence in octopods will be discovered.

For background information *see* BIOLUMINESCENCE; CEPHALOPODA; DEEP-SEA FAUNA; OCTOPUS; ORGANIC EVOLUTION in the McGraw-Hill Encyclopedia of Science & Technology.   Edith A. Widder

Bibliography. S. Johnsen et al., Bioluminescence in the deep-sea cirrate octopod *Stauroteuthis syrtensis* Verrill (Mollusca: Cephalopoda), *Biol. Bull.*, 197:26–39, 1999; S. Johnsen, E. J. Balser, and E. A. Widder, Light-emitting suckers in an octopus, *Nature*, 398:113–114, 1999; B. H. Robison and R. E. Young, Bioluminescence in pelagic octopods, *Pacif. Sci.*, 35:39–44, 1981.

Biomining

Biomining uses microorganisms to recover metals of value, such as gold, silver, and copper, from sulfide minerals. A technically and commercially proven process, biomining is acknowledged by the global mining industry as being cost-effective, simple to use, robust, less environmentally polluting than smelting or mineral roasting practices, and highly suitable for remote and inaccessible regions of the world.

Centuries of gold and silver mining have depleted many of the high-grade and easy-to-process deposits of precious metals. In remaining ore deposits the gold and silver are diluted by large amounts of nonvaluable rock (low-grade ores), or the precious metals occur in minerals that are not amenable to low-cost extractive processes (refractory ores). Bioheap leaching is a simple and cost-effective process that applies biomining technology to recover gold and silver from low-grade, refractory ores.

Microorganisms. Biomining microorganisms are unique and robust. They obtain energy for reproduction and growth by oxidizing ferrous iron (Fe^{2+}), elemental sulfur (S^0), and certain other sulfur substances. These organisms require oxygen (O_2) and carbon dioxide (CO_2), obtained from air, and some nitrogen and phosphorus. The biomining organisms need a sulfuric acid (H_2SO_4) environment of pH 2.5 down to a minimum of about pH 0.5. None of the biomining microorganisms causes disease in plants, animals, or humans.

There are three distinct groups of biomining organisms: (1) mesophilic bacteria that live and reproduce at about 50–110°F (10–45°C); (2) moderately thermophilic (heat-loving) bacteria that function at about 110–140°F (45–60°C); and (3) extremely thermophilic archaea, which grow in the 140–195°F (60–90°C) temperature range; the archaea are not bacteria, but are life-forms representing one of the earliest living inhabitants on Earth.

Mesophilic bacteria. Well-studied mesophilic biomining bacteria are *Thiobacillus ferrooxidans* (rod-shaped) and *Leptospirillum ferrooxidans* (curved-rod-shaped); both are 0.5 micrometer in diameter by 1.0–2.0 μm long. To obtain sufficient energy for growth and reproduction, these bacteria oxidize prodigious amounts of ferrous iron. *Thiobacillus thiooxidans*, which oxidize elemental sulfur to sulfuric acid, are also mesophilic bacteria of commercial importance. *Thiobacillus* and *Leptospirillum* species are found worldwide and are especially abundant in and around acid springs, volcanic regions, locales with sulfur mineralization, biomining operations, and some soils.

Thermophilic bacteria. Moderately thermophilic bacteria are less studied than mesophilic bacteria, and many are yet to be named. *Sulfobacillus* species obtain oxygen and carbon dioxide from the atmosphere to oxidize ferrous iron; some also oxidize elemental sulfur. Moderately thermophilic bacteria are 1 μm in diameter by 5–10 μm long and rod-shaped. The moderately thermophilic bacteria are found in the same types of natural environments as the mesophilic bacteria, becoming more abundant as the temperature increases.

Thermophilic archaea. The most studied extremely thermophilic archaea are *Sulfolobus acidocaldarius*, *Acidianus brierleyi*, and *Metallosphaera sedula*. There are many others which are yet to be named. These organisms are 1–2 μm in diameter and spherical in shape. Archaea have no rigid wall surrounding the microbial cell like the other biomining bacteria, but have a membrane covered with an amorphous layer. Archaea grow using ferrous iron and various sulfur substances and obtain oxygen and carbon dioxide from air. The archaea dwell in the harshest conditions on Earth—very hot acid springs, volcanic zones, hot coal waste piles, deep oceans where sulfur gases vent, and hot biomining operations. They grow and reproduce in sulfuric acid environments approaching boiling temperatures with high dissolved metal content and low amounts of oxygen, carbon dioxide, ammonium, and phosphate.

Metal recovery process. The biomining microorganisms oxidize ferrous iron in a sulfuric acid and water (H_2O) environment to ferric iron (Fe^{3+}) [reaction (1)]. Ferric iron is a strong oxidant that

$$4Fe^{2+} + O_2 + 2H_2SO_4 \rightarrow 4Fe^{3+} + 2SO_4^{2-} + 2H_2O \quad (1)$$

attacks sulfide minerals, causing the minerals to

Fig. 1. Sulfidic-refractory gold bioheap with plastic pipes to provide air for biomining microorganisms. (*Newmont Mining Corporation*)

dissolve in the sulfuric acid–containing water. The dissolved chemical constituents depend on which sulfide mineral is being chemically attacked by the ferric iron. For example, if pyrite (FeS_2) is oxidized by ferric iron, the constituents dissolved in the sulfuric acid-water mixture are ferrous iron, sulfate (SO_4^{2-}), and a great deal of acid (H^+) [reaction (2)].

$$FeS_2 + 14Fe^{3+} + 8H_2O \longrightarrow$$
$$15Fe^{2+} + 2SO_4^{2-} + 16H^+ \quad (2)$$

Chemical oxidation of sulfide minerals having other metals present in the crystal structure causes these metals to dissolve in the acid water. For example, ferric iron oxidation of arsenopyrite (FeAsS) re-

Fig. 2. Top surface of sulfidic-refractory gold bioheap showing drip irrigation with water, sulfuric acid, and biomining microorganisms. (*Newmont Mining Corporation*)

sults in dissolved arsenic, sulfate, and ferrous iron. All chemical oxidation reactions of sulfide minerals by ferric iron have one result in common—ferrous iron, a vital food source for the microorganisms. Some biomining organisms scavenge elemental sulfur, often produced from the chemical oxidation of some sulfide minerals by ferric iron, oxidizing it to sulfuric acid. This produces the desired acid environment for the microorganisms and keeps iron and other metals dissolved in the water. Some scientists believe that the biomining organisms directly attack the solid sulfide minerals, breaking the mineral's crystal structure, then oxidize the sulfide constituent of the mineral to release the metals. Biomining microorganisms oxidize sulfide-sulfur (S^{2-}-S) when it is dissolved in acidic water. It is uncertain whether the organisms directly attack the solid mineral.

The chemical oxidation of the sulfide minerals by ferric iron, the oxidation of elemental sulfur to sulfuric acid by the microorganisms, and rapid microbial reoxidation of the ferrous iron become a nonending cyclical process that continues until there are no more sulfide minerals to be oxidized by the ferric iron. With depletion of sulfide minerals, the microorganisms oxidize all of the iron and sulfur until there is no food source left. Then the organisms slowly die of starvation.

Precious metals ores. The use of biomining technology to improve gold and silver recovery is applicable only to ores with microscopic (micrometer or less in size) particles of gold or silver buried in sulfide minerals, such as pyrite and arsenopyrite. These types of precious metal ores, called sulfidic-refractory ores, represent a substantial amount of the gold and silver reserves remaining in the world. The conventional extraction process, which involves mixing precious metal–containing ores with water and a little sodium cyanide to dissolve the gold and silver, results in poor recovery of the metals. The cyanide, which normally dissolves the precious metals, is unable to contact the precious metal particles embedded in the sulfide mineral.

Biomining substantially improves gold and silver recovery from sulfidic-refractory ores. A mixture of sulfuric acid, water, and iron is added to these ores. The biomining microorganisms oxidize the ferrous iron, and the resulting ferric iron oxidizes the sulfide minerals in which the gold and silver are buried. As the sulfide mineral dissolves, the gold and silver are exposed. The treated ore is neutralized and mixed with water and small amounts of sodium cyanide or other chemicals that dissolve the precious metals. The dissolved gold and silver are separated from the ore, and the precious metals are reclaimed as pure products.

Engineering biomining technology. A plastic liner is placed on slightly sloping, smooth ground, and plastic pipes with small holes are placed on the liner. The pipes are connected to a fan, which supplies them with air. Sulfidic-refractory precious metal ore is crushed to 3/8 in. (9.5 mm) in size or larger and stacked to depths of 20–33 ft (6–9 m) on the plastic liner with piping (**Fig. 1**). A little sulfuric acid and biomining microorganisms can be blended with the ore as it is stacked. The heaps of ore are irrigated with water containing enough sulfuric acid to achieve a pH of 2.5 or less, some dissolved iron, and biomining bacteria (**Fig. 2**). The acid water trickles through the heap, is collected at the base of the heap, and is recycled to the top of the heap. Air from the pipes flows upward. An ideal environment for the microorganisms is created, and their numbers increase exponentially until every drop of water contains a million microbes and the surfaces of the ore particles have a film of microorganisms. The ferric iron, produced by the microorganisms, oxidizes the sulfide minerals, and the temperature, in what is now called a bioheap, increases because sulfide mineral oxidation releases heat. As the temperature rises above 110°F (45°C) in parts of the bioheap, the mesophilic bacteria begin to die, and the moderately thermophilic bacteria colonize that portion of the bioheap. If sufficient sulfide is present in the ore, the temperature in parts of the bioheap may climb to 140°F (60°C). Archaea may now colonize those areas of the bioheap. Some 30–180 days after the ore is stacked, the sulfide minerals are depleted and the precious metals exposed. The treated ore is removed from the plastic liner, the ore pH is increased, usually with lime, and the ore is mixed with water and a little sodium cyanide or other gold- and silver-dissolving agent to extract the precious metals.

For background information *see* ARCHAEBACTERIA; BACTERIA; BIOLEACHING; COPPER METALLURGY; GOLD METALLURGY; HYDROMETALLURGY; LEACHING; ORE AND MINERAL DEPOSITS; SILVER METALLURGY; SOLUTION MINING; SULFUR in the McGraw-Hill Encyclopedia of Science & Technology.   Corale L. Brierly

Bibliography. J. A. Brierley, 2000-Ore leaching by microbes, in J. Lederberg (ed.), *Encyclopedia of Microbiology*, vol. 3, 2d ed., Academic Press, New York, 1992; D. E. Rawlings (ed.), *Biomining Theory, Microbes and Industrial Processes*, Springer-Verlag, Berlin, 1997.

Bioprospecting

Bioprospecting is the search for new pharmaceutical, nutritional, or agricultural products from natural sources, including plants, animals, or microorganisms. Most commonly, it refers to the search for new medicines from plants or microbes. Plants have always been an important source of medicines, and approximately 25% of prescription pharmaceuticals contain a plant-derived ingredient. Examples of plant-derived drugs include the antihypertensive reserpine from *Rauvolfia serpentina*; vincristine and vinblastine, used to treat childhood leukemia and Hodgkin's disease, and derived from *Catharanthus roseus*; and taxol, derived from *Taxus brevifolia* and used to treat ovarian cancer.

While these compounds are used directly from plants without chemical modification, other compounds are extracted and chemically modified or synthetically produced but modeled after a known natural chemical structure. Salicylic acid, which is found in members of the rose and willow families, is a mildly effective pain reliever. However, its synthetic derivative acetylsalicylic acid, which is sold as aspirin, is more effective as a pain killer and causes less gastric upset than the naturally occurring compound. Quinine, a potent antimalarial derived from the bark of the South American *Cinchona calisaya*, is no longer commonly used because of potential adverse side effects. However, most modern antimalarials have chemical structures similar to quinine and would undoubtedly not have been discovered if the structure of quinine was not known.

Drug discovery efforts in the middle of the twentieth century were dominated by efforts to generate new products through synthesis. It was not until the mid-1980s that a resurgence of interest in plants led to significant efforts to systematically collect and evaluate large numbers of plants for new drugs. Only a very small percentage of the world's plant species have been evaluated for potential use in treating the many pathogenic diseases, physiological and genetic disorders, and other maladies that plague humans. As forests are cleared and plant species face an ever-increasing threat of extinction, there is great urgency to study their potential health benefits.

Screening. In order for compounds to be therapeutically useful, they must be both novel (not previously discovered) and bioactive. Novel compounds are not common and their discovery depends on evaluating large numbers of compounds. Modern bioprospecting efforts are dependent on high throughput screens, involving automated in vitro (performed in test tubes or otherwise miniaturized) bioassay programs that evaluate large numbers of crude plant extracts in a time-efficient manner. Bioassays are experiments to determine if chemicals or extracts can interfere with growth or function of the pathogens that cause disease, or with enzymes that are necessary for their growth and replication. Technological advances in microbiology that have allowed automation of bioassays and computerized tracking of results have increased pharmaceutical researchers' capacity to evaluate thousands of plant samples per week. This ability to study very large numbers of plant species represents a huge technological advance in natural products chemistry and greatly increases the rate of discovery of novel, bioactive compounds.

Botanists that collect plants for these screening programs may use several strategies to choose plant species for evaluation. Large-scale collecting programs may attempt to randomly sample biological diversity, may be driven by observations of ecological interaction, or may rely on information about how indigenous people have traditionally used plants as medicine in particular regions. Many large-scale programs are efforts to randomly sample the diversity of plant species that grow in a particular region, assuming that a survey of the taxonomic diversity will be representative of the chemical diversity that exists in nature. These programs use information about the taxonomy of plants to guide collecting and ensure that diversity is evenly sampled. Many of the large modern pharmaceutical bioprospecting programs rely on this strategy because programs driven by ecology or ethnobotany seldom yield large numbers of collections for screening. Observations on the ecology of individual species may also be used to select species for screening under the assumption that ecological interactions may provide clues about the chemistry of species. Species may be selected because they are comparatively free of insect damage or, alternatively, because they are fed upon by insects known to sequester compounds of interest. Thus, the larvae of butterflies of the family Ithomiidae are known to collect and store pyrrolyzidine alkaloids, often very bioactive compounds, so plants upon which they feed may be targeted for collecting.

Another method for selecting plants for screening is to survey plants that have a history of medicinal use in the area. Aspirin, codeine, digoxin, ephedrine, morphine, quinine, reserpine, and many others owe their discovery to recognition of their traditional use. Ethnobotanists assert that a history of traditional use may increase the likelihood of discovering bioactive compounds; experience has shown that plants with specific traditional uses often yield compounds with pharmaceutical utility against the same ailments. Another advantage of the ethnobotanical approach is that plants used as herbal medicines are more likely to yield compounds that are safe for human use. Presumably they would not be tolerated as herbal remedies if the active compounds were excessively toxic.

Compound isolation. Once species are selected, samples of plants are collected and sorted into individual plant parts, recognizing that chemical composition differs in leaves, stems, flowers, and fruits; each part is best sampled separately. Individual samples are collected and usually dried in cotton bags prior to shipping to a destination where analysis begins. After samples are transported to a laboratory, they are ground to a fine powder, then soaked in a solvent, and the solid material is removed by filtering. The resulting extract is concentrated by removing the solvent with a rotary evaporator to yield a crude plant extract that is usually a thick, dark-green paste. Crude plant extracts may be tested in a variety of in vitro bioassays to identify those samples with promising bioactivity. Once samples show activity, efforts begin to isolate the individual chemical compounds and identify those that show promise as candidates for drug development. These compounds are isolated by fractionating crude extracts and tracking biological activity by repeating the bioassays. This bioassay-guided fractionation eventually leads to pure compounds, and study of their chemical structure identifies those with novel structure and previously unknown activity.

Once compounds have been isolated, their structure has been determined, and they have been found to be of continuing interest, studies are conducted to understand their mechanism of action, toxicity, and bioavailability. Compounds approved for further development are evaluated in three phases of trials with human subjects that test toxicity, test efficacy, and look for undesired side effects before a new drug application may be submitted to the Food and Drug Administration (FDA). The whole process of new drug approval, from original collection of plant material to approval by the FDA, may take 10–15 years, and has been estimated to cost an average of more than $300 million.

Modern bioprospecting programs not only are efficient means of discovering new pharmaceuticals that may positively impact human health, but also help document the economic importance of plants as raw materials for medicine and agriculture. Modern programs also strive to promote the conservation of natural resources and equitably share the benefits that arise from commercial development of new products.

For background information *see* ALKALOID; ASPIRIN; BIOASSAY; BOTANY; PHARMACEUTICAL CHEMISTRY; PHARMACEUTICAL TESTING; PHARMACOLOGY; QUININE in the McGraw-Hill Encyclopedia of Science & Technology.   James Miller

Bibliography. M. J. Balick and P. A. Cox, *Plants, People, and Culture: The Science of Ethnobotany*, Scientific American Library, 1996; F. Grifo and J. Rosenthal (eds.), *Biodiversity and Human Health*, Island Press, 1997; K. T. Kate and S. A. Laird, *The Commercial Use of Biodiversity*, Earthscan, 1999.

Boiling

The boiling process is used in numerous technological applications and is of particular economic importance in the power generation industry. The primary purpose of early industrial applications of boiling was to generate steam for transportation and power. Today's power industry still takes advantage of the high heat transfer rates typical of boiling to extract energy from solar, fossil, and nuclear fuels. Boiling is essential to all closed-loop power and refrigeration cycles. It is a crucial aspect of technologies such as modern chemical and distillation processes and thermal management of microelectronics systems. Designers of energy generation and propulsion systems for spacecraft must deal with the complexities and safety issues of handling low-boiling-point cryogenic fluids in the absence of gravity. The study of liquid-vapor flows in the microgravity environment, where buoyancy no longer plays a dominant role and bubbles do not rise, has proven to be a challenge. Despite the growing importance and the familiarity of boiling, the fundamental physical processes associated with the various regimes of boiling, bubble formation, and dynamics are still not completely understood.

Boiling regimes and boiling curve. Boiling is a phase-change process whereby a heated surface causes adjacent liquid to form vapor and vapor bubbles. It can be divided into two categories: pool boiling and flow boiling. In pool boiling, fluid motion is induced solely by buoyancy forces (natural convection); whereas in flow boiling, an additional forced flow is imposed to induce fluid motion (natural plus forced convection). The following discussion is restricted to pool boiling, since flow boiling is intimately connected with the separate topic of two-phase flow.

A discussion of the regimes and applications of pool boiling is best presented in the context of a typical boiling curve as in **Fig. 1**, representing the interdependence of the wall heat flux and the wall superheat for a saturated liquid heated from a horizontal wire or flat surface. The wall superheat is defined as the temperature difference between the heated surface and the saturation temperature of the liquid at a given system pressure. The boiling curve can be categorized broadly into four separate regimes: natural convection or nonboiling, nucleate boiling, transition boiling, and film boiling.

Natural convection. As the curve is traversed from left to right (that is, as well superheat is increased), the first regime encountered is natural convection. Phase change does not take place in this regime. Motion of the liquid is due to rising of hot, light liquid and sinking of the relatively colder, denser liquid. As the wall heat flux and wall superheat increase, the onset of nucleate boiling is encountered, which separates the natural convection and the nucleate boiling regimes.

Nucleate boiling. At the onset of nucleate boiling, phase change takes place with the formation of vapor bubbles. Small cavities on the heater surface act as nucleation sites for the vapor bubbles. Thus nucleate boiling is strongly influenced by very complex conditions affecting vapor bubble formation at the heater surface such as the wettability of the fluid with the surface, solid-liquid-vapor phase contact line motion, and the surface roughness. Heat transfer is mainly through direct contact between the heated surface and the liquid and through the latent heat of vapor formation. The heater surface stays relatively cool since vapor bubble formation and rise promotes a replenishing flow of cooler liquid downward toward the wall. Nucleate boiling is the most efficient mode of heat transfer since high heat fluxes are possible at relatively low surface temperatures. Vapor bubble production increases with wall heat flux and wall superheat up to a local maximum point called the critical heat flux. Much attention has been focused on boiling enhancement in the nucleate boiling regime using either passive or active techniques. Passive techniques include heater surface modification using specially designed microcavities, microfins, and porous coatings. Active techniques focus on enhancement of vapor bubble motion through vibration and acoustical means or through electrohydrodynamic forces. One objective of these enhancement techniques is the design of more compact heat exchangers by achieving increased wall heat flux and decreased wall superheat.

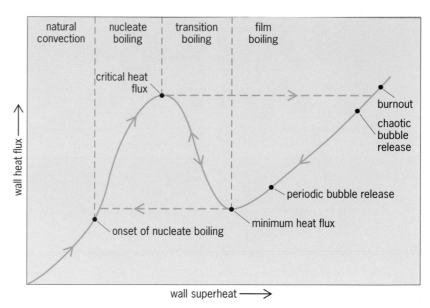

Fig. 1. Boiling curve and boiling regimes.

Beyond the critical heat flux point, it is crucial to distinguish how the surface is being heated. If, as in most cases, the wall heat flux is the independently controlled variable, then the boiling process quickly traverses the transition regime and enters the film boiling regime as denoted by the broken line to the right of the critical heat flux point in Fig. 1. This is the situation with electrically heated surfaces or in nuclear reactor applications. The result is an abrupt and often dangerous increase in the heater surface temperature. However, if the wall temperature is independently controlled, the boiling process enters the transition regime. Heater surface temperature control could be achieved by quenching or condensing of another fluid at various pressures on the opposing side of the heater.

Transition boiling. The transition boiling regime is a combination of nucleate and film boiling on different portions of the heater surface. It is characterized by the formation of vapor bubbles from the heater surface as in nucleate boiling, but also increasingly by the presence of large patches of vapor separating the heater surface from the liquid. These large vapor patches act as thermal insulators, reducing the effectiveness of the heat transfer process. Thus in transition boiling, the wall heat flux decreases (if temperature is controlled) to a local minimum point called the minimum heat flux or Leidenfrost point. Transition boiling is the most complex and least understood mode of boiling due to experimental difficulty in accessing this regime. There is some debate as to whether a hysteresis occurs in the transition curve in experiments performed in the direction of increasing temperature and those performed in the direction of decreasing temperature.

Film boiling. The film boiling regime is characterized by a continuous vapor layer completely

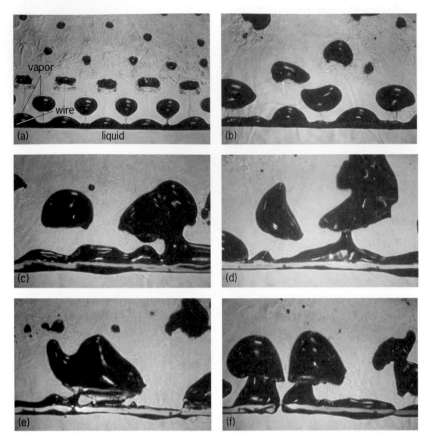

Fig. 2. Periodic and chaotic bubble release during film boiling. A 501-μm-diameter, electrically heated Nichrome wire is immersed in gas-saturated FC-72 at atmospheric pressure. (*a*, *b*) Periodic bubble release at low heat flux (37 and 61 W/cm^2). Density gradients are visible in the wake of the condensing bubbles. (*c*, *d*) Chaotic bubble release at high heat flux (90 and 99 W/cm^2). The glow of the wire indicates an increased surface temperature. (*e*, *f*) Consecutive frames (0.067-s interval) at the moment of burnout (107 W/cm^2). The melting point of Nichrome is approximately 1400°C (2550°F). (*From Y. S. Hong et al., Ordered and chaotic bubble release, J. Heat Transfer, 119:207, 1997*)

separating the heater and the liquid. The heater wall temperature is now high enough to cause vaporization of the liquid by conduction and convection (and radiation at higher wall temperatures) of heat through the vapor to the liquid-vapor interface. The liquid does not come into contact with the wall, and thus surface roughness and solid-liquid-vapor phase issues such as wettability and contact line motion do not play a role in film boiling. A balance is maintained between vapor generation due to vaporization at the liquid-vapor interface and vapor removal due to the break off and rise of vapor bubbles from the liquid-vapor interface.

Since the vapor layer nearly completely insulates the liquid from the heater, it is an inefficient mode of boiling heat transfer. Most serious, though, are the high wall temperatures associated with film boiling that can quickly lead to failure of the heater surface. The burnout point in Fig. 1 is reached when the wall temperatures meet the melting temperature of the heater material. The situation is particularly dangerous when the melting temperature of the material corresponds to a heat flux less than the critical heat flux. In this case, if the critical heat flux is exceeded in a heat-flux-controlled process, burnout will be

imminent. This has severe implications in nuclear applications where a loss of coolant accident could suddenly result in high wall superheat film boiling and subsequent compromise of reactor fuel and shielding.

Normally, it is desirable to operate in the nucleate boiling regime for maximum efficiency. However, in processes where the heat flux is controlled, the potential for a dangerous jump from the critical heat flux to film boiling and possibly burnout needs to be considered. Film boiling is also commonly encountered in metallurgy during quenching and in space technology, where regenerative cooling of rocket nozzles and combustion chambers is commonly used. Due to its independence from the complex effects of surface roughness, nucleation, and wettability, film boiling is the most amenable to analytic and numerical as well as experimental investigations.

Film boiling has been investigated from an electrically heated wire. At low surface heat flux the vapor film coating the wire breaks down in a Rayleigh-Taylor instability. Taylor-type bubbles are periodically released from the vapor layer in a regular array (**Fig. 2***a, b*). As one set of bubbles is released, an adjoining set of bubbles is just beginning to form from the vapor layer in preparation for release. The Taylor wavelength separating departing bubbles increases with heat flux. At high heat flux the regular Taylor array of bubbles breaks down into a more chaotic bubble release pattern (Fig. 2*c, d*) due to the increased vapor generation rate. The larger bubbles take on a more mushroomlike shape with lateral merging of adjacent bubbles. (The regions of periodic and chaotic bubble release are indicated on the boiling curve in Fig. 1.) At a slightly higher heat flux the temperature of the wire would exceed its melting point, resulting in burnout (Fig. 2*e, f*).

Reducing wall heat flux and wall superheat from the film boiling regime leads to the minimum heat flux point. The progress at this point depends again on how the surface is heated. With temperature control, boiling will enter the transition regime until the critical heat flux point is reached, whereupon further reduction in either wall heat flux or wall superheat takes the boiling process down the nucleate boiling slope and into natural convection. Conversely, with heat flux control, it will rapidly traverse from the minimum heat flux through the transition regime along the broken line to the left of the minimum heat flux point and enter either the natural convection or nucleate boiling regime, depending on the location of the onset of nucleate boiling point. Thus, a hysteresis effect is observed if the complete boiling curve is traversed with a heat-flux-controlled method.

A great variety of factors not previously mentioned can greatly influence the boiling process, including subcooling, surfactants, variable levels of gravity, heater geometry and orientation, and the presence of dissolved gases or additional species (boiling of mixtures).

For background information *see* BOILING POINT; CHAOS; CONVECTION (HEAT); HEAT TRANSFER; HYSTERESIS; SURFACE TENSION in the McGraw-Hill Encyclopedia of Science & Technology.   Damir Juric

Bibliography. V. P. Carey, *Liquid-Vapor Phase Change Phenomena*, Hemisphere, Washington, DC, 1992; J. G. Collier and J. R. Thome, *Convective Boiling and Condensation*, Oxford University Press, New York, 1994; Y.-Y. Hsu and R. W. Graham, *Transport Processes in Boiling and Two-Phase Systems*, American Nuclear Society, La Grange Park, IL, 1986; S. G. Kandlikar, M. Shoji, and V. K. Dhir, *Handbook of Phase Change: Boiling and Condensation*, Taylor and Francis, Philadelphia, 1999; L. S. Tong and Y. S. Tang, *Boiling Heat Transfer and Two-Phase Flow*, Taylor and Francis, Washington, DC, 1997.

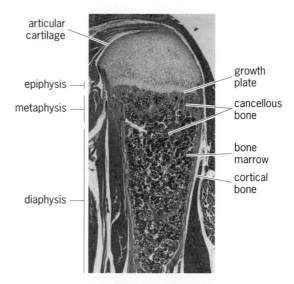

Fig. 1. Longitudinal section through the femur of a 7-day-old mouse. Bones grow in length by means of endochondral ossification in which cancellous (trabecular) bone formation takes place at the lower end of the epiphyseal growth plate after hypertrophic chondrocytes undergo apoptosis. Bone trabeculae are removed in the metaphysis by osteoclasts to create a space for bone marrow cells. Failure to remove bone results in filling of the marrow cavity with bone (osteopetrosis), which can be accompanied by anemia.

Bone

Bones provide structural support for ambulatory activities and protection for vital organs, such as the brain and heart. They also respond to changing concentrations of circulating hormones and locally released cytokines and growth factors, and along with cells in other organs regulate the blood concentration of calcium, an element essential for many critical functions, such as cell division and heart contraction. This regulatory activity takes precedence over the support function because bones can be weakened to the point of fracture following excessive removal of bone by osteoclasts (large multinucleated cells, associated with bone resorption) in response to estrogen or vitamin D deficiency. During embryonic development, the size, shape, position, and number of bones are determined by the activities of genes that are expressed at specific times by distinct groups of cells. Some of these genes also regulate the formation and activity of cells that remodel bones after they are formed.

Limb development. Vertebrate limbs develop from outgrowths of ectodermal cells and underlying mesenchymal cells that differentiate into chondrocytes (cartilage cells) that rapidly sculpt the shape and ultimately the position of future bones by separating into discrete bone-shaped masses. Some central chondrocytes become hypertrophic and form a nidus (center) of future bone formation after the matrix around them is calcified. This nidus is invaded by blood vessels from outside the rudimentary bones and expands toward both ends of developing long bones, and a medullary cavity consisting of bone and bone marrow is formed. The cartilaginous nidus persists as the epiphyseal growth plate at the ends of long bones, and regulates bone length in a process known as endochondral ossification that continues after birth until growth plates close following adolescence (**Fig. 1**). In this process, osteoclasts resorb much of the calcified cartilage, and osteoblasts (bone-forming cells) lay down bone matrix on surviving strips of unresorbed cartilage to form plates of cancellous (spongy) bone. Many of these plates are resorbed subsequently by osteoclasts to maintain a medullary cavity for normal hematopoiesis (process of blood formation). Failure of osteoclast formation or function results in osteopetrosis, a potentially lethal disorder, characterized by persistence of cancellous bone in the medullary cavity and anemia.

Limb development requires the coordinated expression of genes in the condensed mesoderm and ectoderm involving positive and negative regulatory feedback loops (**Fig. 2**). For example, fibroblast growth factor (FGF) 10 is expressed in the prospective limb mesoderm and initiates limb bud development. Ectopic application of FGF10 to the chick embryonic flank induces the expression of FGF8 in the adjacent ectoderm and of sonic hedgehog (Shh) in the mesoderm, resulting in the development of an additional complete limb. Sonic hedgehog initiates expression of FGF4 in the ectoderm and of bone morphogenetic protein (BMP) 2 in the mesoderm, and regulates anterior-posterior positioning and distal limb growth. Ectopic expression of FGF4 in the ectoderm causes polydactyly (presence of more than five digits on hand or foot); while mutations in *Twist*, a gene that may be an upstream regulator of fibroblast growth factor receptors, cause multiple skeletal abnormalities in the human Saethre-Chotzen syndrome. The *Hox* genes are members of a highly conserved set of transcription factors that determine limb position and number. Overexpression of *Hoxb-8* in a more anterior position than normal results in duplication of a forelimb, while knockout of *Hoxb-5* in mice causes a forward shift of the shoulder girdle, a defect similar to the human Sprengel anomaly. Knockout of *Hoxd* and *Hoxa* genes causes

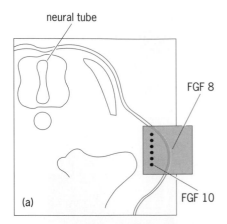

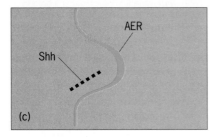

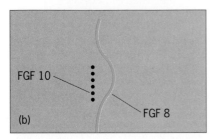

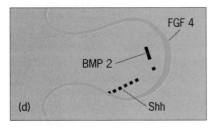

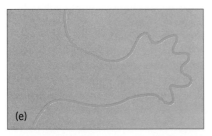

Fig. 2. Schematic diagram of limb development. (*a*) At an early stage in embryonic development, fibroblast growth factor (FGF) 10 is expressed in lateral mesodermal cells at the site where limb development will take place. (*b*) It induces FGF8 expression in overlying ectodermal cells that will give rise to the apical ectodermal ridge. (*c*) Secretion of sonic hedgehog (Shh) by posterior mesenchymal cells regulates anterior-posterior patterning and (*d*) induces expression of bone morphogenic protein (BMP) 2. (*e*) By this stage, the limb is a self-organizing structure that is able to form the bones of the arms and hands because transplantation of limb buds to ectopic sites on the flank results in full limb development.

loss of digits in mice, while increased number and fusion of digits (synpolydactyly) in humans is due to gain of function of *Hoxd-13*. Finally, mice with knockout of *noggin*, a gene involved in brain and nerve development, have multiple skeletal defects, including short vertebrae, ribs, and limbs. Most strikingly, they lack joints, their limbs being nearly continuous segments of bone coverd by cartilage, a phenotype similar to the effect of ectopic overexpression of BMP2 or -4 in developing chick limbs. Thus, Noggin appears to be a negative regulator of bone morphogenetic proteins in limb development. It also antagonizes bone morphogenetic protein–induced chondrocyte apoptosis, a form of cell death that helps remove cartilage to mediate joint formation.

Chondrocytes secrete several collagen types, including II, IX, X, and XI, into the matrix around them, and mutations in collagen genes can cause embryonic or neonatal death, dwarfism, and osteoarthritis. Type II collagen expression is regulated by the transcrition factor, Sox9, mutation of which causes multiple bone defects and sex determination abnormalities in humans with campomelic dysplasia (abnormal skeletal development characterized by bowing or curvature of the affected bone). Achondroplasia (a condition characterized by the failure of cartilage to convert to bone), the phenotype of the classical circus dwarf, results from mutation of the FGF receptor 3 gene. Although fibroblast growth factors mediate the signaling that drives limb bud development, the FGFR3 mutation in achondroplasia constitutively activates tyrosine kinase signaling by the receptor, suggesting that FGFR3 acts as a negative regulator of chondrocytes in long-bone growth, presumably by promoting proliferation at the expense of differentiation.

Short-limbed dwarfism and delayed endochondral ossification are skeletal abnormalities observed in Jansen-type metaphyseal chondrodysplasia, a disorder due to an activating mutation in the parathryroid hormone–related protein (PTHrP) receptor. PTHrP regulation of chondrocyte differentiation involves Indian hedgehog and bone morphogenetic proteins in a paracrine and autocrine signaling feedback loop between perichondrial and prehypertrophic chondrocytes that delays maturation of prehypertrophic to hypertrophic chondrocytes and prevents their premature death. Interestingly, PTHrP also stimulates osteoclastic bone resorption, and its aberrant expression by breast and lung cancers frequently causes hypercalcemia as well as bone fractures at sites to which tumor cells have spread and caused bone lysis.

Bone remodeling. The integrity of bone in the adult skeleton is maintained by bone remodeling in which trenches of wornout bone are resorbed from bone surfaces by osteoclasts. These trenches are filled subsequently with new bone laid down by osteoblasts in a process similar to the repair of wornout sections of roadways, which involves interactions between stromal and hematopoietic cells. The number of trenches (bone remodeling units) on bone surfaces increases in many of the common disorders that affect the skeleton, such as postmenopausal osteoporosis, hyperparathyroidism, Paget's disease, rheumatoid arthritis, and metastatic cancers (tumors that have spread to bone). In these disorders, there is frequently an imbalance between the amount of bone removed by osteoclasts and that replaced by osteoblasts such that the bones become weakened and fracture risk increases.

Osteoclasts are multinucleated cells that form by fusion of precursors in the mononuclear-phagocyte lineage of hematopoietic cells (**Fig. 3**). Their formation requires the expression of two major factors by marrow stromal cells that appear to be in the osteoblast lineage: RANKL [receptor activator of nuclear factor kappa B (NFκB) ligand] and macrophage-colony stimulating factor (M-CSF). Most of the hormones [such as parathyroid hormone (PTH), parathyroid hormone–related protein, vitamin D3] and cytokines [interleukin 1 (IL-1), interleukin 6 (IL-6), tumor necrosis factor (TNF)] and inflammatory mediators that are produced in increased amounts in common bone disorders stimulate increased bone remodeling indirectly. They do this by promoting stromal cell production of RANKL and M-CSF following binding to their receptors on these cells. RANKL binds to its receptor, RANK, in osteoclast precursors and activates NFκB, a set of gene transcription factors that regulate not only osteoclast formation but also the expression of interleukin 1, tumor necrosis factor, and interleukin 6 by macrophages, which leads to more RANKL production by stromal cells. Thus, a vicious cycle of increased osteoclastogenesis can be initiated by a variety of stimuli, including estrogen deficiency and inflammation in bone, that are associated with increased cytokine production and bone loss.

These cytokines can also cause decreased production of osteoprotegrin (OPG), a member of the tumor necrosis factor superfamily of receptors that acts as a decoy receptor for RANKL to inhibit osteoclast formation. Recent studies suggest that in normal and disease states osteoclast numbers and activity are determined by the relative amounts of RANKL and osteoprotegrin produced in the bone microenvironment. Knockout mice lacking expression of RANKL, RANK, or the p50 and p52 subunits of NFκB do not form osteoclasts and develop osteopetrosis, while osteoprotegrin knockout mice develop osteoporosis because of unregulated osteoclastic bone resorption. Expression of other transcription factors, including PU.1 and c-fos, is also necessary for osteoclast formation, but the genes that they or NFκB regulate in osteoclast precursors to promote osteoclast formation have not been identified.

Once formed, osteoclasts resorb bone matrix by forming a specialized ruffled area of their cell membrane next to the bone where they secrete proteases that break down matrix and acid that removes calcium and other elements. Expression of c-src, cathepsin-K, the microphthalmia transcription factor (MITF), and TNF receptor associated factor 6

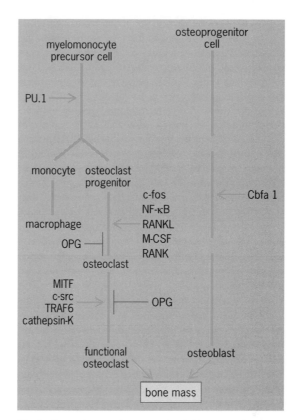

Fig. 3. Known factors that are essential for formation or activation of osteoclasts and osteoblasts. Myelomonocytic precursors give rise to osteoclasts and macrophages under the influence of genes transcribed by the transcription factor, PU.1. Osteoclast progenitors differentiate into osteoclasts in the presence of RANKL and M-CSF released by stromal cells in the osteoblast lineage, but they must express c-fos, NFκB, and RANK to do this. Osteoprotegrin (OPG) can prevent osteoclast formation and limit osteoclast survival by binding to RANKL and thus preventing its interaction with RANK. To date, only core binding transcription factor 1 (Cbfa1) has been identified as an essential gene for osteoblast differentiation. The relative activities of osteoclasts and osteoblasts determine bone mass.

(TRAF6) [involved in signaling downstream from RANKL and interleukin 1] is required for this resorptive activity in which RANKL appears to play a role in part by preventing osteoclast apoptosis.

Only a few genes essential for osteoblast formation or function have been identified to date. A necessary role for core binding transcription factor 1 (Cbfa1) in osteoblast formation was found unexpectedly in Cbfa1 knockout mice. They have a normally patterned skeleton composed of cartilage, but no osteoblasts or bone. Most bones in Cbfa1 heterozygous mice appear normal, but the animals have cranial bone defects and no clavicles, like humans with craniocleidodysostosis. Cbfa1 is expressed initially in mesenchymal condensations of the developing skeleton, but later only in cells of the osteoblast lineage in which BMP7 and vitamin D$_3$ regulate it. It binds to an osteoblast-specific *cis*-acting element in the promoter for osteocalcin, and its forced expression in nonosteoblastic stromal cells induces them to become osteoblasts. Osteocalcin is expressed almost uniquely by osteoblasts, but surprisingly it appears to act as a negative regulator of their function, because bones in osteocalcin knockout mice are denser than normal. A similar phenotype was observed unexpectedly in 5-lipoxygenase knockout mice. This enzyme promotes the formation of the arachidonic acid metabolites, leukotrienes, that mediate bone resorption in inflammatory bone disease, but it is not known how they or osteocalcin negatively regulate osteoblasts. Although many osteoblast-stimulating factors (such as bone morphogenetic proteins, fibroblast growth factors, insulin growth factors, transforming growth factor beta, and parathyroid hormone) have been identified, none has been shown yet to have an essential role as a positive regulator of osteoblast activity. In general, however, bone mass is likely to be determined by the relative contributions of positive and negative regulators of osteoblast and osteoclast activity.

The amount of matrix laid down by osteoblasts in each bone-remodeling unit is similar to that removed by osteoclasts before the age of 50 years. In disorders in which bone turnover is increased (such as estrogen deficiency, hyperparathyroidism, or Paget's disease), the number of bone remodeling units increases, and the activity and life-spans of osteoclasts relative to osteoblasts determine if the net effect is more or less bone. For example, after ovariectomy or the menopause, osteoclast generation, activity, and life-span are increased in response to increased production of the cytokines, IL-1, IL-6, and TNF, but bone formation is increased to a lesser extent, resulting in osteoporosis and increased fracture risk. In contrast, new bone formation exceeds the aggressive resorption seen typically in Paget's disease, but the thickened bone is disordered and weak and fracture risk is actually increased.

Treatment of estrogen-deficient or Pagetic patients with antiresorptive drugs prevents bone loss and reduces fracture risk, but to date there are no drugs available on the market that can restore osteoporotic bone to normal. Better understanding of the regulation of bone modeling and remodeling at the molecular level will lead to the development of more specific therapeutic modalities to prevent or treat congenital and acquired disorders of bone.

For background information *see* BONE; CARTILAGE; COLLAGEN; CYTOKINE; EMBRYOLOGY; OSTEOPOROSIS; PARATHYROID HORMONE; SKELETAL SYSTEM; SKELETAL SYSTEM DISORDERS; VITAMIN D in the McGraw-Hill Encyclopedia of Science & Technology.

Lianping Xing; Brendan F. Boyce

Bibliography. J. W. Innis and D. Mortlok, Limb development: Molecular dysmorphology is at hand, *Clin. Genet.*, 53:337–348, 1998; G. Karsenty, Genetics of skeletogenesis, *Dev. Genet.*, 22:301–313, 1998; S. Mundlos and B. Olsen, Heritable diseases of the skeleton: Part I. Molecular insights into skeletal development—transcription factors and signaling pathways, *FASEB J.*, 11:125–132, 1997; S. Mundlos and B. Olsen, Heritable diseases of the skeleton: Part II. Molecular insights into skeletal development—matrix components and their homeostasis, *FASEB J.*, 11:227–233, 1997; G. Panganiban et al., The origin and evaluation of animal appendages, *Proc. Nat. Acad. Sci. USA*, 94:5162–5166, 1997; S. T. Takahashi et al., Modulation of osteoclast differentiation and function by the new members of the tumor necrosis factor receptor and ligand families, *Endocrine Rev.*, 20(3):345–357, 1999.

Bose-Einstein condensation

The de Broglie wavelength associated with the center-of-mass motion of free atoms is usually so short that the atoms move like classical particles. However, if a gas is cooled to such a low temperature that the wavelength becomes comparable to the distance between atoms, quantum-mechanical features become important. If the total spin of the atom is an integer, the gas can undergo the quantum-mechanical phase transition known as Bose-Einstein condensation.

Bose-Einstein condensation has been observed in gases of lithium, sodium, and rubidium. In June 1998 hydrogen was added to the list. Because hydrogen is the simplest and best understood atom, the condensate's behavior is of particular interest. Furthermore, the physical properties of the condensate—its temperature, size, and dynamical time scale—are quite different from those of the alkali metal atoms, and the techniques for creating the condensate are novel.

The search to find Bose-Einstein condensation in an atomic gas actually began in atomic hydrogen almost a quarter of a century earlier. By 1976 it was understood that if the electronic spins could be completely polarized so that the atoms could not form molecules, the system would remain a gas at temperatures down to absolute zero. Even if other atoms could somehow be coaxed into a long-lived gaseous state at very low temperatures, they would require temperatures much lower than hydrogen in order to condense. Hydrogen was clearly the system of choice for pursuing Bose-Einstein condensation.

Spin-polarized hydrogen was first stabilized by Isaac Silvera and Jook Walraven in 1980. Many noteworthy scientific advances on the behavior of hydrogen followed, including the creation of doubly polarized atomic hydrogen in which both the electron and proton spins are completely aligned; a cryogenic hydrogen maser; and the observation of universal quantum reflection—a phenomenon at extremely low temperatures in which the sticking probability for an atom hitting a surface goes to zero as the square root of the temperature. These early experiments relied on liquid-helium-coated walls to help contain the hydrogen. Unfortunately, these walls catalyzed the conversion of hydrogen into molecules and precluded achieving Bose-Einstein condensation.

In 1986 Harald Hess, working in the group of Thomas Greytak and Daniel Kleppner, proposed confining the atoms without walls using magnetic trapping. He also devised a method for cooling the trapped atoms, based on evaporation, which allowed the atoms to reach temperatures much colder than their surroundings. Both of these developments were crucial to achieving Bose-Einstein condensation in hydrogen. Furthermore, the evaporative cooling technique also played the crucial role in the first demonstrations of Bose-Einstein condensation in alkali metal vapors by other groups in 1995. The alkalis were precooled by laser techniques, but the final cooling was done by the evaporative technique.

Evaporative cooling. The first step in achieving Bose-Einstein condensation in hydrogen is to precool the gas by collisions with liquid-helium-coated surfaces and then to load the atoms into a magnetic trap. Once in the trap, the atoms settle into thermal equilibrium at about 40 mK and lose thermal contact with the walls of the apparatus. Then they are evaporatively cooled by allowing the hottest atoms to escape from the trap and allowing the remaining atoms to reequilibrate at a lower temperature. Initially this was done by slowly lowering the magnetic field at one end of the long trapping region so that the atoms with the highest energies could spill out. By 1991 hydrogen had been cooled to 100 μK, just a factor of three above the Bose-Einstein condensation transition temperature at the gas density of 10^{14} atoms per cubic centimeter. But lower temperatures were difficult to obtain because the efficiency of the evaporative cooling was decreasing rapidly at that temperature. In addition, a more accurate method for probing the temperature and density of the trapped gas had to be devised.

To tackle the cooling problem, an alternative evaporation method which had been developed for the alkali metal atom experiments was employed. A radio-frequency magnetic field flips the spins of trapped atoms wherever the field satisfies the condition for resonance at the applied frequency. Atoms whose spins are flipped experience a repulsive potential and are expelled. By applying a radio-frequency field whose frequency is resonant with the highest magnetic field in the trap and then slowly lowering the frequency, successively lower-energy atoms are expelled while the remaining atoms cool. With this method, all the atoms on an energy surface in the trap are affected, not just those that happen to be at one end of the trap. This method ultimately cooled hydrogen to the temperatures needed for Bose-Einstein condensation.

Two-photon spectroscopy. Two-photon spectroscopy of the 1S-2S transition in hydrogen was employed as a probe of the gas (**Fig. 1**). A laser beam at 243 nanometers is reflected upon itself to create a flux of counterpropagating photons in the center of the trap. If an atom absorbs two photons traveling in the same direction, the resonant frequency will be higher than the natural frequency by a recoil shift of 6.7 MHz. This is because additional energy must be supplied to the atom due to its increased kinetic energy. The shape of the recoil-shifted line gives the distribution of atomic momenta along the

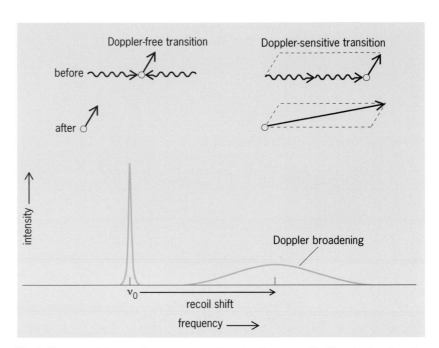

Fig. 1. Features of the two-photon spectrum in a standing wave. The Doppler-free line at the natural frequency, ν_0, is much taller and narrower than indicated in this sketch. Insets show momenta of photons (wavy arrows) and atom (straight arrows) before and after transition.

axis. Above the transition temperature, this is the familiar Doppler shape which provides an absolute measure of the sample temperature. However, if an atom absorbs two photons propagating in opposite directions, the transition is Doppler-free and the resonance is very narrow (in principle about 1 Hz, but currently limited by jitter in the laser frequency to about 2 kHz). The proximity of other hydrogen atoms causes a small decrease in an atom's resonant frequency which is proportional to the density (about -20 kHz at a density of 10^{14} atoms per cubic centimeter). Thus the shift in the position of the Doppler-free component gives the density of the gas.

Detection of two-photon excitation. The two-photon excitation in hydrogen is too weak to measure by absorption. Instead, the photoexcitation is detected indirectly when the excited atom emits a Lyman-alpha photon (**Fig. 2**). The emission is triggered by applying an electric field that Stark-mixes the long-lived 2S state with the short-lived 2P state. The number of Lyman-alpha photons detected is measured as the frequency of the laser is swept relative to the natural frequency of an isolated atom (**Fig. 3**). Just above the transition temperature the Doppler-sensitive part of the spectrum indicates a temperature of 40 μK, and the slight shift of the Doppler-free line to the red indicates the density of the gas to be about 2×10^{14} atoms per cubic centimeter. When the temperature is lowered a bit more, Bose-Einstein condensation is achieved, and the spectrum changes so as to demonstrate three of its features: condensation in real space, condensation in momentum space, and a characteristic phase-transition line.

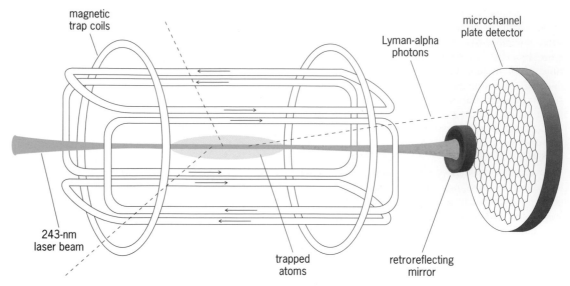

Fig. 2. Apparatus used to achieve Bose-Einstein condensation in hydrogen and to study the properties of the condensate by laser spectroscopy.

Features of spectrum. If an ideal Bose gas were to be cooled below the transition temperature, a significant fraction of the atoms would fall into the ground state of the system—for a harmonic trap such as those used here, the lowest-energy eigenstate of a three-dimensional harmonic oscillator. Real atoms interact through short-range repulsive forces, and as a result they are spread out over a region larger than the ground state of the trap, but still much narrower than the thermal cloud of uncondensed atoms. Thus the density of hydrogen at the center of the trap is much larger than the density of the uncondensed atoms.

Just below the transition, a new feature appears to the left of the sharp line in the spectrum (Fig. 3).

It is due to the atoms in the condensate. Comparison of the largest shift in this feature to the shift of the Doppler-free normal line indicates that the maximum density in the condensate is about 25 times that in the thermal cloud. A comparison of the areas under the two features gives a condensate fraction of about 5%. Using the known geometry of the trap, this percentage can be translated into a condensate population of about 10^9 atoms. In the world of atomic Bose-Einstein condensation, this number is enormous, more than ten times larger than previously achieved.

The condensate atoms have very low momenta compared to those in the thermal cloud. Thus they contribute a narrow feature to the Doppler-sensitive part of the spectrum (Fig. 3). Because this feature is broadened by the density shift (in a manner similar to that shown in the condensate contribution to the Doppler-free part of the spectrum), it cannot be used to measure the precise momentum distribution in the condensate.

Measurement of normal density. For a Bose gas at a fixed temperature, the density of atoms in the thermal cloud, in number of atoms per cubic centimeter, can never exceed a value given by $n_c(T) = 5.0 \times 10^{20} T^{3/2}$, where T is the temperature in kelvins. As more atoms are added to the gas, they fall into the condensate, leaving the density of the normal component fixed at the critical value. The density of the normal component was measured directly as the gas moved along the transition line; the $T^{3/2}$ behavior of the critical density was verified.

Applications. The fundamental reason it took so long to achieve Bose-Einstein condensation in hydrogen is that hydrogen has an extremely small scattering cross section, which makes evaporation difficult. However, for some purposes this disadvantage turns out to be an advantage, for it permits the creation of much larger samples than is otherwise possible.

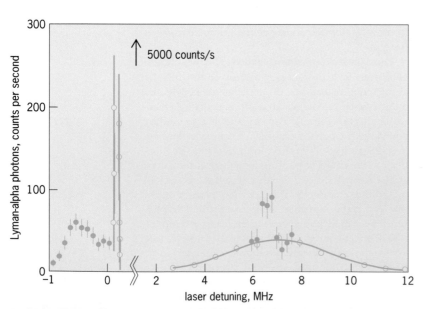

Fig. 3. Typical two-photon spectrum in ultracold atomic hydrogen. Open circles indicate the spectrum just above the transition temperature. Solid circles indicate additional features which appear only below the transition.

Consequently, the system is potentially attractive as the source for a high-intensity atom laser. Furthermore, ultracold hydrogen has many new applications in spectroscopy, including the creation of an optical clock operating on the 1S-2S transition.

For background information *see* ATOMIC CLOCK; ATOMIC STRUCTURE AND SPECTRA; BOSE-EINSTEIN STATISTICS; HYDROGEN; LASER SPECTROSCOPY; QUANTUM MECHANICS in the McGraw-Hill Encyclopedia of Science & Technology.

Thomas J. Greytak; Daniel Kleppner

Bibliography. K. Burnett, M. Edwards, and C. W. Clark, The theory of Bose-Einstein condensation of dilute gases, *Phys. Today*, 52(12):37–42, December 1999; D. G. Fried et al., Bose-Einstein condensation of atomic hydrogen, *Phys. Rev. Lett.*, 81:3811–3814, 1998; W. Ketterle, Experimental studies of Bose-Einstein condensation, *Phys. Today*, 52(12):30–35, December 1999.

Bryozoa (paleoecology)

The understanding of how Earth's biota has changed through time is based almost exclusively on times of appearance and disappearance of morphological types, commonly recorded as geological ranges of groups of organisms. A firm understanding of many large-scale patterns in the evolutionary history of life has been obtained. These insights include (1) the recognition that the oceans during the past 500 million years have been characterized by a sequence of three major faunas (Cambrian, Paleozoic, and Modern faunas); (2) the quantitative characterization of the severity of multiple extinction events; (3) the discovery that evolutionary innovations most commonly originate near shore rather than on outer shelves or deep ocean waters; (4) the recognition of patterns of increased exploitation of food resources through extension of feeding levels above and below the sediment-water interface; and (5) the diversification of predators and of organisms that can more rapidly exploit potential food within the sediment of the sea floor.

Taxonomic richness. Despite the important information on evolutionary and ecological history that total number or relative number of taxa can provide, there is no guarantee that taxonomic data by themselves can provide a sufficient basis for understanding the history of ecosystems. Different insights can be obtained from numbers of taxa (taxonomic richness), measures of abundance, and measures or approximations of energy flow and capture within ecosystems. Other than counts of individual organisms, direct information on abundance and energy consumption is difficult to obtain from the fossil record. However, skeletal mass can be used as a proxy for both abundance and energy capture by various marine organisms, and is especially useful for clonal organisms.

The correspondence between various measures of taxonomic richness and skeletal mass was tested in a recent study of two groups of marine bryozoans. Bryozoans are benthic marine organisms that are exclusively colonial and consist of small units called zooids. Fossil and living bryozoans with rigid skeletal parts superficially resemble diminutive colonial corals; others that are completely flexible (and virtually unknown as fossils) are commonly mistaken for marine plants.

Cyclostomes and cheilostomes. Two distantly related branches (clades) of skeletalized bryozoans have existed during the past 120 million years. These two clades, the cyclostome bryozoans and the cheilostome bryozoans, differ from one another in the construction of their zooids and in their patterns of reproduction. Cyclostome bryozoans originated during the Paleozoic Era, but they became common and diverse only after the Early Jurassic (206–202 million years ago). Cheilostome bryozoans originated during the Late Jurassic and began to diversify during the mid-Cretaceous (121–112 million years ago). The two clades have exploited similar environments and microenvironments, and they have evolved a virtually identical range of growth habits, although a few representatives of each clade have growth habits that have not been exploited by the other. In respect to their ecologies, the two clades are very similar.

Cyclostomes and cheilostomes increased in worldwide generic richness until the end of the Cretaceous, after which both suffered appreciable extinction during the end Cretaceous (41% extinction, cyclostomes; 30%, cheilostomes) and again by the end of the Danian Stage (the first 5 million years of the Cenozoic Era; 25% and 17% extinction, respectively). After that, the cheilostomes resumed their vigorous diversification while the cyclostomes never recovered (**illus.** *a*). The different diversification histories of the two clades resulted in a continuous decline in proportion of cyclostome to cheilostome genera in the worldwide marine fauna (illus. *b*).

More detailed information on local ecosystems through time can be obtained by scrutinizing lists of species occurring within individual exposures of sediments. Interestingly, the pattern of species richness of cyclostomes relative to cheilostomes is remarkably similar to that of global generic richness (illus. *c*). Although the average of within-fauna species richness of both groups declined from the Late Cretaceous into the earliest Paleogene, this did not interrupt the trend in decreasing proportion of cyclostomes within the bryozoan faunas which, with the exception of a slight mid-Cenozoic reversal, has continued from the time of initial diversification of the cheilostomes to the present.

Both measures of taxonomic richness summarized above imply that the cheilostomes were more resilient than the cyclostomes immediately following the end-Cretaceous extinction, because the trends of declining proportions of cyclostomes were uninterrupted by the major extinction event that marks the boundary between two geological eras (Mesozoic and Cenozoic). However, the ecological effect was quite different.

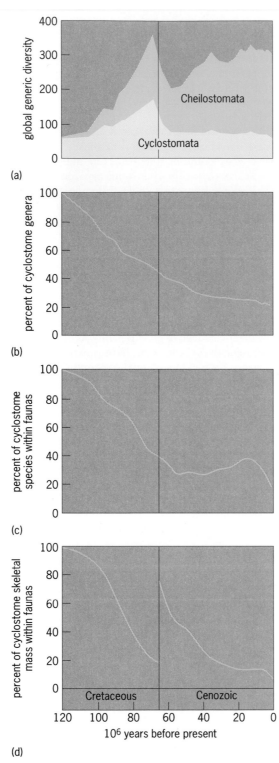

(a)

(b)

(c)

(d)

Measures of diversity and abundance of cyclostome and cheilostome bryozoans from mid-Cretaceous to the present. (a) Total global generic diversity per geological stage. (b) Proportion of total global generic diversity constituted by cyclostomes. (c) Moving average curve plotting percentage of cyclostome species within bryozoan faunas, based on 335 local assemblages. The curve for the Cretaceous was determined and plotted independently of the Cenozoic curve, yet the two curves meet at the Cretaceous-Cenozoic boundary. (d) Moving average curve plotting percentage of cyclostome skeletal mass within bryozoan faunas, based on 70 local assemblages. Curves for the Cretaceous and Cenozoic were determined and plotted independently.

Skeletal mass. From middle through Late Cretaceous, the within-fauna skeletal mass of cyclostomes declined even more steeply relative to skeletal mass of cheilostomes than either of the measures of taxonomic richness. But the proportion of bryozoan skeletal mass constituted by cyclostomes jumped abruptly, from about 21% in the Maastrichtian to about 74% throughout the 5-million-year-long Danian Age (illus. *d*). Data are less abundant and less clear for the next few million years, but it appears that the decline in the skeletal mass of cyclostomes relative to cheilostomes was very slow. It may have taken up to 25 million years following the end of the Cretaceous before the skeletal mass of cyclostomes relative to cheilostomes declined sufficiently to equal, and then decline below, the global proportion of genera and local proportions of species.

All three measures reported above are based on faunas from continental shelves and epicontinental seas of similar depths. Also, all measures are based on faunas derived from all over the world, but largely from Europe and eastern North America. The difference between the patterns of taxonomic richness and abundance cannot be explained by differences in ecological or geographical setting of the data on which the patterns are based.

Decoupling. The decoupling of taxonomic richness and skeletal mass proportions between the two groups following the end-Cretaceous extinction was unexpected. In practical terms, it means that organisms can become ecologically successful for very long periods of time, with no parallel increase in taxonomic richness. And, conversely, conspicuous increase in taxonomic richness can occur within a group while it is swamped ecologically.

The reasons for such a profound decoupling of evolution and ecology are not clear. It has been demonstrated that encrusting cheilostomes are competitively superior to encrusting cheilostomes, competitive superiority of erect cheilostomes over erect cyclostomes has been inferred, and the history of overall generic diversity of cyclostomes and cheilostomes is consistent with dynamic competitive interaction between members of the two groups. A different cause for the early Cenozoic ecological success of cyclostomes must be determined.

Cyclostomes are a less energy-intensive group of organisms than are cheilostomes. Cyclostomes generate slower feeding-current velocities, feed on smaller food particles, have smaller zooids, and grow more slowly than do cheilostomes. In these respects, they are more similar to members of the Paleozoic fauna than to organisms characteristic of the Modern fauna. Paleozoic seas apparently were lower in nutrients than are present seas, and the displacement of the Paleozoic fauna by the Modern fauna involves change from organisms that have a lower energy budget to those that have a higher energy budget.

Several lines of evidence, such as decrease in production of fossils of planktonic algae, suggest that there was an abrupt decline in marine productivity at the end-Cretaceous extinction, followed by an extended interval variously measured at 500,000 to 2 million years during which there was anomalously low marine productivity. The early Cenozoic ecological success of cyclostome relative to cheilostome bryozoans may be related to this temporary worldwide return to lower levels of productivity, conditions in which the less nutrient-demanding cyclostomes could thrive while the cheilostomes were relatively starved. This hypothesis relates two observed patterns (decline in oceanic productivity and ecological success of cyclostomes) to known differences in attributes of cyclostomes and cheilostomes. Adequately testing the hypothesis requires more detailed information on biology of living bryozoans and from the rock record.

One lesson to be learned from the several-million-year reversal in relative abundance of cyclostomes and cheilostomes is that mass extinctions can have effects on the global ecosystem that are long-term and that are not visible in lists of taxa. While the causes of the reversal in ecological success of cyclostomes and cheilostomes following the end-Cretaceous extinction cannot yet be confidently identified, it appears that the ecological effect lasted millions of years beyond the causes.

For background information *see* BRYOZOA; CHEILOSTOMATA; CTENOSTOMATA; EXTINCTION (BIOLOGY); FOSSIL in the McGraw-Hill Encyclopedia of Science & Technology.   Frank K. McKinney

Bibliography. F. K. McKinney, A faster-paced world? Contrasts in biovolume and life-process rates in cyclostome (Class Stenolaemata) and cheilostome (Class Gymnolaemata) bryozoans, *Paleobiology*, 19: 335–351, 1993; F. K. McKinney et al., Decoupled temporal patterns of evolution and ecology in two post-Paleozoic clades, *Science*, 281:807–809, 1998; J. J. Sepkoski, Jr., Biodiversity: Past, present, and future, *J. Paleontol.*, 71:533–539, 1997; J. J. Sepkoski, Jr., F. K. McKinney, and S. Lidgard, Competitive displacement between post-Paleozoic cyclostome and cheilostome bryozoans, *Paleobiology*, 26: 7–18, 2000.

Cancer

Wnt proteins are a widely conserved family of secreted signaling molecules that regulate many processes during animal development; but the Wnt pathway when misregulated can also contribute to several types of cancer. The genomes of animals as diverse as nematodes and humans contain multiple related Wnt genes (5 in the nematode and perhaps as many as 18 in humans) that act throughout development to control cell fate decisions, asymmetric cell division, embryonic axis specification, and other processes. Extensive genetic analyses of Wnt signaling, particularly in the fruit fly (*Drosophila melanogaster*), have led to the isolation of several additional genes that comprise a widely conserved signal transduction pathway that functions in the reception and response to Wnt signals.

The first member of the Wnt family, *Wnt-1*, was isolated in mice as a proto-oncogene capable of inducing the formation of mammary tumors when its expression is ectopically activated by integration of a mouse mammary tumor virus. More recently, studies of human colorectal cancers have indicated that mutations in downstream components that cause inappropriate activation of the pathway can contribute to tumor formation.

β-**Catenin.** Genetic and biochemical data suggest that the principal response of a cell to Wnt signaling is to increase the steady-state levels of β-catenin. β-Catenin is a multifunctional protein that, in addition to its function in Wnt signal transduction, plays an essential role in intercellular adhesion. β-Catenin is present at low levels in the cytoplasm of resting cells, and it is this pool of cytoplasmic β-catenin that is the target of Wnt signaling. β-Catenin levels are normally kept low in the cytoplasm by the action of a group of proteins collectively called the destruction complex (**illus.** *a*). In the absence of Wnt signaling, this complex targets β-catenin for degradation by cellular proteases. In response to the binding of Wnt ligand to its cell surface receptor, the degradation of β-catenin is blocked (illus. *b*). β-Catenin levels rise as newly sythesized protein accumulates in the cytosol. β-Catenin then translocates to the nucleus where, together with a deoxyribonucleic acid (DNA) binding protein of the TCF/LEF family, it activates the transcription of target genes. In the context of a developing embryo, these targets could include genes required to specify the differentiation of the cell into a particular tissue, or to induce the cell to

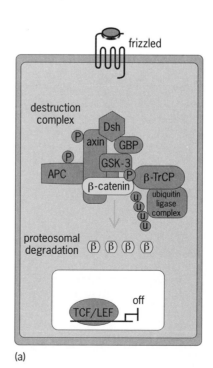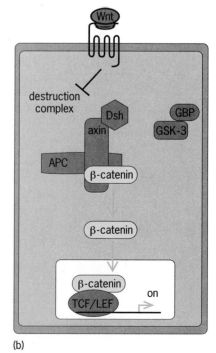

(a)   (b)

Regulation of β-catenin in the (a) absence and (b) presence of Wnt ligand may involve regulation of the composition of the destruction complex. Binding of Wnt ligand to its receptor inhibits the degradation of β-catenin, possibly by inducing the dissociation of GSK-3 from the destruction complex.

migrate to a new location in the embryo. Of interest to researchers studying the link between the Wnt pathway and cancer, β-catenin and TCF/LEF have recently been shown to increase the transcription of two genes, *c-myc* and *cyclin D1*, which function to stimulate cell proliferation, thus suggesting a mechanism by which an inappropriately active Wnt pathway could contribute to oncogenesis.

Destruction complex. Four proteins have been identified that are required for the degradation of β-catenin in the absence of Wnt signaling: GSK-3, axin, adenomatous polyposis coli (APC), and β-TrCP. The key step in maintaining low levels of cytoplasmic β-catenin is performed by GSK-3 (glycogen synthase kinase 3). GSK-3 phosphorylates one or more of four conserved serine and threonine residues near the amino terminus of β-catenin. Phosphorylation of these amino acids is essential for β-catenin downregulation. Mutations in the fruit fly homolog of GSK-3 result in the ectopic accumulation of β-catenin in cells not receiving the Wnt signal, leading to dramatic patterning defects in the fly embryo. Similarly, mutations in β-catenin that remove or alter these phosphorylation sites render β-catenin insensitive to regulation by GSK-3, also resulting in abnormally high levels of β-catenin and constitutive activation of Wnt-responsive target genes.

Axin and APC are required to facilitate the phosphorylation of β-catenin by GSK-3. GSK-3 binds β-catenin poorly. It is currently thought that APC and axin serve as scaffolds to which both GSK-3 and β-catenin bind. APC and axin are both large proteins, each containing multiple distinct protein-protein interaction domains, allowing them to interact simultaneously with several components of the pathway, including each other, GSK-3, and β-catenin. Thus, the formation of a complex containing axin, APC, GSK-3, and β-catenin brings GSK-3 into proximity with β-catenin, enhancing its ability to phosphorylate β-catenin and target it for degradation. Also, GSK-3 can phosphorylate both APC and axin, which increases the ability of these proteins to bind to β-catenin.

The recognition of this phosphorylated form of β-catenin as a target for degradation requires the β-TrCP protein, a component of the SCF ubiquitin ligase complex. β-TrCP contains two special protein-protein interaction motifs. One, the WD40 repeat domain, specifically interacts with phosphorylated β-catenin. The other domain, called the F-box, recruits the SCF ubiquitin ligase complex. This complex attaches multiple molecules of a small protein called ubiquitin to β-catenin. Ubiquitin-tagged β-catenin is then targeted to the proteosome, a multiprotein complex that degrades unwanted cellular proteins. As with GSK-3, mutations in the fly homolog of β-TrCP result in ectopic β-catenin accumulation, since the phosphorylated form of β-catenin is not ubiquitinated and delivered to the proteosome.

Activation of β-catenin. Two proteins are known to be required to rescue β-catenin from the destruction complex, Disheveled (Dsh) and GSK-3 binding protein (GBP). Disheveled appears to function directly downstream of the Wnt receptor, and is required for transducing the Wnt signal. Disheveled, too, has multiple protein-protein interaction domains, and is capable of binding some of the components of the destruction complex, including axin. GBP is a small protein, also known as Frat1, that can bind to both Disheveled and GSK-3. Expression in frog embryos stabilizes β-catenin and results in the activation of Wnt-responsive genes, implicating GBP as a positive regulator of Wnt signaling.

Two mechanisms have been proposed to explain how Wnt signaling, acting through Disheveled and GBP, functions to stabilize β-catenin. First, interaction of these proteins with GSK-3 may directly inhibit the kinase activity of GSK-3. Consistent with this idea, treatment of mammalian or *Drosophila* tissue culture cells with soluble Wnt protein causes a decrease in the activity of GSK-3 present in cell extracts. Similarly, overexpression of *XWnt-8*, a Wnt gene from the frog (*Xenopus laevis*), in embryos also leads to a decrease in the activity of GSK-3. Further, expression of Disheveled or GBP in *Drosophila* tissue culture cells also causes a substantial drop in the ability of GSK-3 to phosphorylate a peptide substrate. These experiments suggest a direct role for Disheveled and GBP in inhibiting the enzymatic activity of GSK-3.

Another mechanism by which Disheveled and GBP could block or reduce GSK-3-dependent phosphorylation of β-catenin is by disrupting the formation of the destruction complex. One study has shown that expression of the Wnt-3a gene in cultured cells can cause a reduction in the phosphorylation of axin, which reduces its affinity for β-catenin. Also, expression of Wnt-1 has been shown to destabilize the destruction complex. GSK-3 can bind either to axin or to GBP, but not simultaneously. A fragment of GBP capable of binding to GSK-3 has been shown to block the interaction of GSK-3 with axin, as well as its phosphorylation of axin and β-catenin. One function of Disheveled may be to recruit GBP to the destruction complex, where it can bind GSK-3, disrupting its association with axin and thereby blocking phosphorylation of β-catenin.

β-Catenin in cancer development. Ectopic stabilization of β-catenin is clearly linked to development of several forms of cancer. For example, mutations in the APC gene are associated with 80% of human colon cancers, and many of these mutations result in truncated forms of the APC protein that lack key stretches of amino acids that are important for binding to β-catenin. Also, mice with a mutated form of APC lacking the β-catenin binding region develop many small intestinal tumors, a phenotype known as multiple intestinal neoplasia. In cell lines derived from human colorectal tumors carrying such APC mutations, β-catenin has been shown to be present at abnormally high levels. Expression of full-length APC in these cells is sufficient to reduce β-catenin levels.

Many of the colon cancer cell lines that express wild-type APC carry mutations in β-catenin in the conserved serine/threonine residues required for phosphorylation by GSK-3. Since these mutated forms of β-catenin cannot be phosphorylated, and thus targeted for degradation, expression of exogenous APC in these cell lines has no effect on β-catenin protein levels. In addition to activated β-catenin being oncogenic in the colon, mutations in the GSK-3 phosphorylation sites of β-catenin have been observed in a subset of hepatocellular cancers, melanomas, and uterine and ovarian tumors. Further underscoring the oncogenic activity of a misregulated Wnt pathway, the human homolog of GBP, Frat1, was initially isolated as a proto-oncogene activated by proviral insertion that contributes to the progression of T-cell lymphomas in the mouse.

Given the link between ectopic activation of β-catenin and oncogenesis, it is reasonable to expect that mutations in other components of the pathway, such as axin and GSK-3, will be found to contribute to development of cancer. It will be important to understand more clearly the mechanism by which activated β-catenin promotes cancer. Cells have many guards against uncontrolled proliferation, and development of cancer usually requires eluding multiple blocks. Whether ectopic β-catenin is sufficient on its own to cause oncogenesis or whether mutations in additional genes are required remains a key question.

For background information *see* ONCOGENES; ONCOLOGY in the McGraw-Hill Encyclopedia of Science & Technology.   Chris Thorpe; Randall T. Moon

Bibliography. F. Fagotto et al., Domains of Axin involved in protein-protein interactions, Wnt pathway inhibition, and intracellular localization, *J. Cell Biol.*, 145:741–756, 1999; T.-C. He et al., Indentification of *c-MYC* as a target of the APC pathway, *Science*, 281:1509–1512, 1998; L. Li et al., Axin and Frat1 interact with Dvl and GSK, bridging Dvl to GSK in Wnt-mediated regulation of LEF-1, *EMBO*, 18:4233–4240, 1999; C. Liu et al., β-Trcp couples β-catenin phosphorylation-degradation and regulates *Xenopus* axis formation, *Proc. Nat. Acad. Sci. USA*, 96:6273–6278, 1999; P. Polakis, The oncogenic activation of β-catenin, *Curr. Opin. Genet. Dev.*, 9:15–21, 1999; K. Willert, S. Shibamoto, and R. Nusse, Wnt-induced dephosphorylation of Axin releases β-catenin from the Axin complex, *Genes Dev.*, 13:1768–1773.

Carbon dioxide reduction

The twin problems of global warming, caused by an increase in atmospheric carbon dioxide (CO_2) concentrations, and limited fossil fuel resources have stimulated research in the utilization of carbon dioxide. These problems would be partially alleviated by the development of artificial photochemical systems that could economically fix carbon dioxide into fuels or useful chemicals. Since the mid-1980s, intensive efforts have been directed toward the photochemical production of carbon monoxide (CO) and formic acid (HCOOH) from carbon dioxide. These systems have several common elements: they contain photosensitizers (such as metalloporphyrins, or ruthenium or rhenium complexes with bipyridine), electron mediators or catalysts, and sacrificial electron donors (such as tertiary amines or ascorbic acid). Progress along these lines has resulted in advances in understanding of the interaction of carbon dioxide with metal complexes, and the factors controlling the efficient storage of solar energy in the form of reduced carbon compounds.

Strategy. Natural photosynthesis by chlorophyll molecules involves the generation of carbohydrates and oxygen from the abundant raw materials carbon dioxide and water (H_2O) using sunlight as the driving force. Photosynthesis is balanced by the oxidation of the reduced carbon compounds back to carbon dioxide and water through combustion, decay, and respiration. Life on Earth is sustained by maintaining this balance between the production and removal of atmospheric carbon dioxide. However, widespread use of fossil fuels has upset this balance and led to the emission of 6 gigatons of carbon per year as carbon dioxide. This has raised levels of carbon dioxide in the atmosphere from about 280 ppm in preindustrial times to 360 ppm in the 1990s. Because of the high infrared absorbance and long atmospheric lifetime of carbon dioxide, global warming through the greenhouse effect is taking place.

The stability of carbon dioxide makes its economical utilization as a feedstock for fuels or chemicals a formidable challenge. The electrode potentials, E° (versus a normal hydrogen electrode, NHE, at $pH = 7$), for the reduction of carbon dioxide to formic acid, carbon monoxide, and methanol (CH_3OH) are shown in reactions (1)–(3). The fact that the

$$CO_2 + 2H^+ + 2e^- \rightarrow HCOOH \qquad E^\circ = -0.61\ V \quad (1)$$

$$CO_2 + 2H^+ + 2e^- \rightarrow CO + H_2O \qquad E^\circ = -0.53\ V \quad (2)$$

$$CO_2 + 6H^+ + 6e^- \rightarrow CH_3OH + H_2O \quad E^\circ = -0.38\ V \quad (3)$$

proton-assisted, multielectron routes to these products require much less energy than the one-electron process to $CO_2^{-\cdot}$ ($E^\circ = -1.9\ V$) suggests that it might be a considerable advantage to employ multielectron transfer routes using transition-metal complexes.

Transition-metal complexes consist of a central atom or ion surrounded by a set (typically two to six) of other atoms, ions, or small molecules, the last being called ligands. Transition-metal complexes have often been used as photochemical and thermal catalysts because they can absorb a significant portion of the solar spectrum, have long-lived excited states, can promote multielectron transfer, and can activate small molecules through binding. In transition-metal complexes, a central metal has octahedral, tetrahedral, square planar, square-pyramidal, or trigonal-pyramidal symmetry depending on the surrounding ligands. Reduced metal centers such

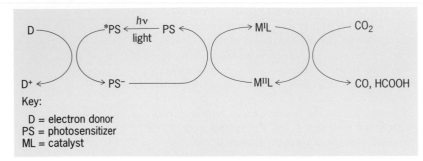

Fig. 1. Photochemical carbon dioxide reduction.

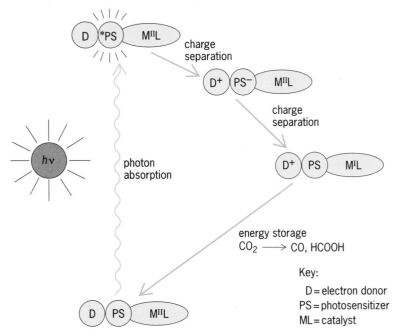

Fig. 2. Artificial photosynthesis.

as M^IL, in which the oxidation number of the central metal (M) is plus one (I) and the ligand (L) has four-coordinating atoms, typically have one or more vacant coordination sites. These sites can be used to bind and activate carbon dioxide (or other small molecules). The oxidative addition of carbon dioxide to M^IL to form a metallocarboxylate, $M^{III}L(CO_2^{2-})$, stabilizes the carbon dioxide moiety through a two-electron transfer. The $M^{III}L(CO_2^{2-})$ can then react with H^+ to form $M^{III}L$, CO, and OH^-. An example of this behavior is presented below.

Because the carbon dioxide reduction process is thermodynamically uphill, economical carbon dioxide fixation is possible only if renewable energy, such as solar energy, is used as the energy source. Solar energy can be harnessed to drive carbon dioxide conversion by (1) artificial photosynthesis using homogeneous and heterogeneous systems; (2) electrochemical reduction using solar electric power; and (3) hydrogenation of carbon dioxide using solar-produced hydrogen. Progress has been made in artificial photosynthesis driven by photon absorption, charge separation through electron transfer react-

ions, and energy storage in dark reactions, similar to the processes occurring in natural photosynthetic systems.

Photocatalytic reduction. The systems that have been used for photochemical carbon dioxide reduction studies can be divided into six groups: (1) $Ru(bpy)_3^{2+}$ [Ru = ruthenium; bpy = 2,2'-bipyridine] as both the photosensitizer and the catalyst; (2) $Ru(bpy)_3^{2+}$ as the photosensitizer and another metal complex as the catalyst; (3) $ReX(CO)_3(bpy)$ [Re = rhenium; X = halide or phosphine-type ligand] or a similar complex as both the photosensitizer and the catalyst; (4) $Ru(bpy)_3^{2+}$ or a $Ru(bpy)_3^{2+}$-type complex as the photosensitizer in microheterogeneous systems; (5) a metalloporphyrin as both the photosensitizer and the catalyst; and (6) organic photosensitizers with transition-metal complexes as catalysts.

Photochemical carbon dioxide reduction is normally carried out in aqueous solutions or organic solvents under 1-atmosphere carbon dioxide at room temperature. Therefore the concentration of dissolved carbon dioxide in the solution is quite low (for example, $0.28 M$ in acetonitrile and $0.03 M$ in water). These systems produce formate and carbon monoxide as products; however, the formate-to-carbon monoxide ratio varies from system to system. The total quantum yield reaches up to 40% assuming that one photon produces one molecule of product. With a ruthenium-bipyridine-type complex and ruthenium or osmium (Os) colloids, methane is produced with a low quantum yield. Mechanisms (**Figs. 1** and **2**) are generally believed to involve (1) light absorption by a photosensitizer to produce an excited state; (2) quenching of the excited state by an electron donor to produce a reduced complex; (3) electron transfer from the reduced complex to a catalyst; and (4) activation of carbon dioxide by the reduced catalyst. Metallocarboxylates (and metallocarboxylic acids) are postulated intermediates in photochemical and electrochemical carbon dioxide reduction and the water-gas-shift reaction.

However, in many cases the actual species invoked to interact with carbon dioxide have not been detected in the catalytic systems. Metallocarboxylates are typically prepared by insertion of CO into the M-OH bond, reaction of OH^- with M-CO, or direct carboxylation of reduced metal complexes. Several binding modes, including η^1-C-coordination and η^2-side-on coordination, have been characterized by x-ray diffraction studies, but the M-O-C-O (η^1-end-on) arrangement has never been observed (**Fig. 3**).

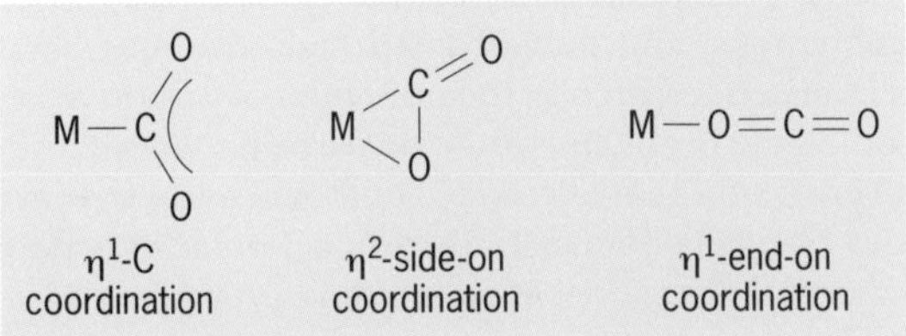

Fig. 3. Coordination geometry of M-CO₂ adducts.

Cobalt (Co) and nickel (Ni) tetraazamacrocyclic complexes [CoHMD^{2+} and Ni(cyclam)$^{2+}$, in which HMD and cyclam are more saturated ligands than a porphyrin, $\bar{P}$, as shown in **Fig. 4**] have been used as catalysts to produce carbon monoxide in photochemical and electrochemical carbon dioxide reduction. The square-planar CO^{I}HMD^{+} complex has been found to add nucleophilically to CO_2 to yield the square-pyramidal, five-coordinate η^1 adduct, [CoHMD(η^1-CO$_2$)]$^+$, containing a bent OCO moiety bonded to cobalt through carbon [reaction (4)]. The CO_2 adduct is thermochromic, be-

$$Co^IHMD^+ + CO_2 \leftrightarrow [CoHMD(CO_2)]^+ \qquad (4)$$

ing purple at room temperature and yellow at low temperature. Temperature-dependent visible and infrared spectra of the CO_2 adduct indicate that a solvent molecule ($\bar{S}$) binds from the opposite side of CO_2 to form the six-coordinate [$\bar{S}$-CoHMD(CO$_2$)]$^+$ (octahedral) species at the expense of the five-coordinate [CoHMD(η^1-CO$_2$)]$^+$ [reaction (5)].

$$[CoHMD(CO_2)]^+ + \bar{S} \leftrightarrow [\bar{S}\text{-}CoHMD(CO_2)]^+ \qquad (5)$$

$$(\bar{S} = \text{solvent})$$

X-ray absorption edge and Fourier transform infrared spectroscopy studies confirm that significant charge-transfer occurs from Co(I) to the bound CO_2 in both the five- and the six-coordinate species. The electron density of the five-coordinate [CoHMD(η^1-CO$_2$)]$^+$ is the same as that of [Co^{II}HMD]$^{2+}$, consistent with theoretical predictions. The six-coordinate species exhibits significant charge transfer and can be interpreted as a Co(III) carboxylate, [$\bar{S}$-Co^{III} HMD(CO$_2^{2-}$)]$^+$. This is the first unambiguous evidence that active metal complexes, such as Co^{I}HMD$^+$, can promote two-electron transfer to the bound CO_2 and thereby facilitate its reduction.

The cobalt macrocycle mediates electron transfer in the photoreduction of carbon dioxide with p-terphenyl (TP) as a photosensitizer and a tertiary amine as a sacrificial electron donor in a 5:1 acetonitrile/methanol mixture. The kinetics and mechanism of this system have been studied by continuous- and flash-photolysis techniques. Transient spectra provide evidence for the sequential formation of the TP radical anion, the CoHMD$^+$ complex, the [CoHMD(CO$_2$)]$^+$ adduct, and the [($\bar{S}$-Co^{III}HMD (CO$_2^{2-}$)]$^+$ complex in the catalytic system. This study provides clear evidence that (1) a photon captured by TP promotes the one-electron reduction of Co^{II}HMD^{2+} to Co^{I}HMD$^+$; (2) Co^{I}HMD$^+$ reacts with CO_2 to form [CoHMD(CO$_2$)]$^+$; and (3) the cobalt center provides two electrons to the CO_2 moiety to produce a [$\bar{S}$-Co^{III}HMD(CO$_2^{2-}$)]$^+$ species, which can react with a proton to produce [$\bar{S}$-Co^{III}HMD (COOH)]$^{2+}$. The reversible intramolecular two-electron-transfer process, sensitive to temperature, solvent, and pressure changes, could be of fundamental importance in processes involving the reduc-

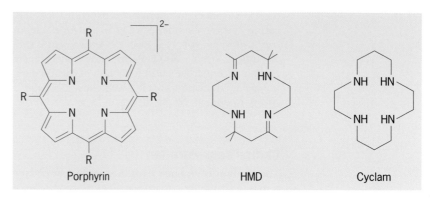

Fig. 4. Structures of porphyrin, HMD, and cyclam. For porphyrin, R $=$ C$_6$H$_5$, 3-F-C$_6$H$_5$, 3-CF$_3$-C$_6$H$_4$, and C$_6$F$_5$.

tion of carbon dioxide. The rate-determining step in the photocatalytic system appears to be a C-O bond-breaking step of [$\bar{S}$-Co^{III}HMD(COOH)]$^{2+}$.

Catalytic photoreduction of carbon dioxide to carbon monoxide and formate has also been carried out by visible-light irradiation of acetonitrile solutions containing cobalt and iron porphyrins (Fe$\bar{P}$) as catalysts and as photosensitizers, and triethylamine as a reductive quencher. In contrast to Co^{I}HMD$^+$, both [Co$^0\bar{P}$]$^{2-}$ and [Fe$^0\bar{P}$]$^{2-}$ react rapidly with carbon dioxide and reduce it to carbon monoxide and formate (HCOO$^-$). The two-electron interconversion of [M$^0\bar{P}$]$^{2-}$ and M$^{II}\bar{P}$ is important here. Further, [M$^0\bar{P}$]$^{2-}$ does not react with the carbon monoxide produced, thus avoiding poisoning of the catalyst. In the case of [Fe$^0\bar{P}$]$^{2-}$, the formation of an equilibrium mixture of Fe$^{II}\bar{P}$(CO) and Fe^{II}P was observed after the addition of carbon dioxide to a solution containing [Fe$^0\bar{P}$]$^{2-}$. Fe$^{II}\bar{P}$(CO) loses CO upon two-electron reduction of the metal center and reforms the catalyst, [Fe$^0\bar{P}$]$^{2-}$.

None of the approaches described above can be used for the commercialization of carbon dioxide reduction. All the systems require a sacrificial reagent. The stability of the systems is limited, the catalytic activities are too low, and the overall costs are too high for commercialization. Hopefully, the insight obtained from a fundamental understanding of the reactions occurring in the above systems will provide the knowledge for the future design of practical systems. One formidable challenge is the replacement of the "sacrificial" electron donors by species that will lead to useful (or benign) chemicals in their own right.

For background information *see* CARBON DIOXIDE; CATALYSIS; COORDINATION CHEMISTRY; ELECTRON-TRANSFER REACTION; FOSSIL FUEL; GREENHOUSE EFFECT; LIGAND; PHOTOCHEMISTRY; PHOTOSYNTHESIS; SOLAR ENERGY; TRANSITION ELEMENTS in the McGraw-Hill Encyclopedia of Science & Technology.

Etsuko Fujita

Bibliography. E. Fujita, Photochemical carbon dioxide reduction with metal complexes, *Coord. Chem. Rev.*, 185-186:373–384, 1999; E. Fujita, L. R. Furenlid, and M. W. Renner, Direct XANES evidence for charge transfer in Co-CO$_2$ complexes, *J. Amer. Chem. Soc.*, 119:4549–4550, 1997; T. Inui et al.

(eds.), Advances in chemical conversions for mitigating carbon dioxide, *Studies in Surface Science and Catalysis*, vol. 114, Elsevier, Amsterdam, 1998; N. Sutin, C. Creutz, and E. Fujita, Photo-induced generation of dihydrogen and reduction of carbon dioxide using transition metal complexes, *Comments Inorg. Chem.*, 19:67–92, 1997.

Carbon sequestration

The amount of organic carbon stored in an ecosystem is dependent on many variables. Carbon sequestration in soils is affected by pool size, tillage, fertilizer, and grazing, among other factors.

Pool Size

Some atmospheric gases absorb heat, much as greenhouse glass does, and restrict the absorbed heat from reflecting to outer space. These gases can be natural compounds, for example, water vapor and carbon dioxide (CO_2), or synthetic (such as chlorofluorocarbons). Concentrations of carbon dioxide, one of the greenhouse gases, are increasing steadily because of fossil-fuel burning, land-use changes, and other causes. Climatologists are concerned because carbon dioxide can affect the atmosphere's capacity to trap solar heat, possibly increasing global temperatures. The relationship of the large reservoir of soil organic carbon (SOC) and atmospheric carbon dioxide is important.

Soil organic carbon is the largest terrestrial carbon pool, globally containing perhaps 1550 petagrams (3.4×10^{15} lb) C, while terrestrial vegetation contains about 600 Pg (1.3×10^{15} lb) C. (A petagram is equal to 10^{15} grams, 1000 million metric tons, or 1.1 billion tons.) Combined, the SOC pool and vegetation carbon pool are about three times larger than the atmospheric carbon dioxide carbon pool. Net annual increase in the atmospheric carbon dioxide carbon pool is about 3.3 Pg C yr^{-1}, and a small percent change in the carbon stored or released from terrestrial carbon pools can affect annual net changes in atmospheric carbon dioxide.

Green plants capture carbon from the atmosphere by photosynthesis to form carbon compounds in plants, such as sugars and carbohydrates. Plant carbon enters the SOC pool as plant litter, root material, and root exudates; or if consumed by animals, it enters as animal excreta. Litter-sized plant material at the soil surface is abraded into smaller sizes or broken by livestock hooves, and is called light fraction or particulate organic matter (POM). Soil microbes, fungus, and animalia (that is, earthworms and other soil animals) utilize plant carbon and root exudates for energy while also releasing essential nutrients. Microbial exudates, fungal hyphae, earthworm casts, amorphous iron and aluminum, mineral cations and anions, and complex organomineral compounds that resist microbial attack help bind clay mineral to the particulate organic matter to form soil aggregates. Soil aggregates and complex organic carbon compounds form and break down continuously in soil to provide SOC pools wherein carbon is sequestered, and then are sensitive to human influence. A SOC fraction that can be dated using carbon-14 (^{14}C) isotopes to determine its mean residence time (MRT) is nonhydrolyzable SOC (that is, insoluble in hot, strong hydrochloric acid). This fraction provides information about the size and mean residence time of old resistant SOC. When the size and age of this fraction are large, carbon sequestration in soil is also large. Physical or chemical protection provided by aggregates and complex organomineral compounds slows microbial degradation and can result in recalcitrant SOC that can remain in the soil for hundreds or even thousands of years. Although other processes cause SOC losses, soil erosion breaks down soil aggregates and exposes SOC to oxidation and microbial degradation, causing up to one-third of all the carbon dioxide emissions that result from United States cropland production.

If amounts of carbon entering the soil exceed that lost to the atmosphere, SOC increases, and if not, it decreases because the soil organisms and roots are continually respiring carbon back to the atmosphere as carbon dioxide. Leaching of dissolved SOC can occur during soil erosion, sedimentation, and deposition and moves carbon deeper in the soil profile, possibly into ground water, or by interflow back to the soil surface. Dissolved SOC contains soluble compounds such as sugars, carbohydrates, amino acids, and perhaps proteins that can be utilized by microbes. A SOC pool that is quite sensitive to human activities but relatively small (3–8% of the total SOC) is the soil microbial biomass (SMB). Plant carbon is used as a source of energy for SMB. Energy flux through SMB determines whether the system is building or depleting the SOC pool and if the rate of substrate depletion (decomposition) is equal to the rate of substrate addition (input of litter, roots, and other plant materials) on an annual basis. Energy flux through the SMB drives decomposition of organic residues and SOC. If decomposition exceeds carbon inputs, SOC declines. Soil microbial biomass is generally in a resting state with periodic flushes of activity and growth. Much of the yearly throughput of energy (plant carbon) is used for population maintenance. However, where there are no or limited inputs of carbon, the SMB utilizes available supplies of SOC, and the size of the SMB pool itself also decreases.

Understanding the importance of SOC and its sensitivity to change under human influence is important because natural resource management and agricultural sustainability require maintaining high soil quality. Increases in SOC content are directly linked to increased soil nutrient and water-holding capacity and to agronomic productivity. Soil quality, air quality, and water quality are strongly associated with SOC. The hidden value of SOC lies in its ability to regulate the environment, especially to mitigate the greenhouse effect. If SOC is maintained and increased in soils, it results in a scenario that includes increased soil productivity, improved soil quality, and mitigation of the greenhouse effect.

Ronald F. Follett

Intensive Tillage

The increase in atmospheric carbon dioxide, a greenhouse gas, has heightened interest in carbon storage in agricultural production systems. Agricultural soils play an important role in carbon sequestration (storage) and global warming. Intensive tillage has caused a 30–50% decrease in soil carbon or soil organic matter since the United States' soils were brought into cultivation around 1870. Understanding tillage processes and mechanisms leading to carbon loss is directly linked to soil productivity, soil quality, and environmental issues. The dynamics of soil carbon can have an indirect effect on climate change through net absorption or release of carbon dioxide from soil to the atmosphere in the carbon cycle.

Crop production with different tillage methods and soil management are important factors for sustainable agriculture. Moldboard plow tillage has shown a number of detrimental effects on soil physical, chemical, and biological properties and processes that adversely affect agroecosystems and the environment. Soil erosion, organic matter losses, and structural degradation are major issues that have brought renewed interest in less intense tillage and conservation agriculture. Conservation tillage, particularly no-till or direct seeding, is of interest because of its potential to reduce negative effects of plow tillage and better sequester carbon.

Tillage affects the turnover and loss of soil carbon in agricultural systems. In 1993, major short-term gaseous losses of carbon were shown to occur immediately after tillage that partially explains the long-term carbon loss from tilled soils. Gas exchange was measured using a large, portable chamber to determine carbon dioxide loss from various types of tillage. Moldboard plow tillage was the most intensive and caused more carbon dioxide loss than less intensive tillage methods. No-till or no soil disturbance lost the least amount of carbon dioxide, suggesting minimal environmental impact. Plowing decreases soil carbon content of the surface layer by accelerating microbial decomposition and soil aggregate breakdown. Untilled soils generally contain particulate organic matter, which impacts aggregate formation and stability.

In 1995, the role of tillage was reviewed in enhanced biological oxidation of soil organic matter. Intensive tillage incorporates crop residues and maximizes residue and soil contact. The release of carbon dioxide from the tilled soil and simultaneous entry of oxygen enhances the biological oxidation. Stirring the soil in tillage is analogous to stirring the coals in a fire. Stirring enables carbon dioxide to escape but also enables oxygen to enter the soil. This interaction of soil and residue mixing enhances aerobic microbial decomposition of the incorporated residue to decrease soil organic carbon.

In 1997, short-term carbon losses were reported after four conservation tillage tools that released 31% of the carbon dioxide of the moldboard plow. The moldboard plow lost 13.8 times as much carbon dioxide as the soil not tilled, while conservation tillage tools averaged about 4.3 times as much carbon dioxide loss. Moldboard plowing had two major effects: (1) to loosen and invert the soil to allow rapid carbon dioxide loss and oxygen entry, and (2) to incorporate and mix residues for enhanced microbial attack. The smaller carbon dioxide loss from conservation tillage tools was significant and suggests progress in equipment development and policy implications for enhanced soil carbon management. Conservation tillage reduces the extent, frequency, and magnitude of mechanical disturbance caused by the moldboard plow and reduces the air-filled macropores to slow the rate of carbon oxidation. Any effort to decrease tillage intensity and leave crop residues on the surface should result in soil carbon sequestration.

Concern for soil quality and greenhouse gas emissions requires new knowledge to minimize agriculture's impact on the environment. In 1998, different strip tillage tools and moldboard plows were compared to quantify short-term, tillage-induced carbon dioxide loss relative to tillage intensity. Less intensive strip tillage reduced soil carbon dioxide losses. Again, no-till had the lowest carbon dioxide loss and moldboard plow had the highest immediately after tillage. Forms of strip tillage had an initial flush related to tillage intensity intermediate between these extremes. The cumulative carbon dioxide losses for 24 h were directly related to the soil volume disturbed by the tillage tool. Reducing the volume of soil disturbed by tillage should enhance soil and air quality by increasing the soil carbon content, and suggests that soil and environmental benefits of strip tillage be considered in soil management decisions.

Soil carbon management is vital for agricultural production because of its role in maintaining soil fertility, physical properties, and biological activity required for food production. Minimizing agriculture's impact on the global increase of carbon dioxide requires that high soil carbon levels are sequestered and maintained. Intensive tillage and certain crop rotations have contributed to significant soil carbon loss and the greenhouse effect throughout the United States. Evidence shows that carbon dioxide released immediately after moldboard plowing suggests little carbon sequestration with intensive tillage. Conservation tillage methods that leave most of the crop residue on the surface with limited soil contact yield better carbon sequestration and enhanced environmental quality. Soil carbon sequestration and aggressive tillage are not compatible.

D.C. Reicosky

Fertilization and Grasslands

Soils contain an estimated 1.5×10^{18} g (3.4×10^{15} lb) of carbon, or twice as much as the atmosphere and three times the level stored in terrestrial vegetation. Carbon released from agricultural soils has been a significant source of increase in atmospheric carbon dioxide concentration over the last century. Along with being a source of carbon for the atmosphere, soils can act as a sink of atmospheric carbon dioxide by sequestering carbon in the organic matter, and thus attenuate the increase in atmospheric carbon dioxide. In addition to its influence on global warming, soil carbon plays a key role in determining long-term soil fertility necessary to sustain profitable agricultural production.

Fertilization, primarily with nitrogen (N), along with crop rotation and tillage practices, affects soil carbon levels. Long-term field experiments provide a unique opportunity to study the effects of fertility management on soil carbon levels and the potential for carbon sequestration in soils. Results from many long-term studies conducted primarily on cereal crops show a general tendency of increase in soil carbon as nitrogen inputs increase.

Grasslands occupy twice as much area as cultivated land in the world today. However, few long-term experiments have focused on measuring changes in soil carbon levels of grasslands under different fertilization practices. The Park Grass experiment is an invaluable experiment which has been maintained for more than 120 years in Rothamsted, U.K. In this experiment, two sources of nitrogen fertilizer were applied at different rates with and without liming. Increased nitrogen fertilization had no effect on soil carbon levels except when ammonium-based fertilizer used in the absence of liming resulted in a decreased soil pH and lower organic matter decomposition rates. The acidifying nature of ammonium-based fertilizers also resulted in increased soil carbon levels after 79 years of nitrogen fertilization of the Palace Leas meadow hay plots at the Cockle Park Experimental Farm in England.

The increase in soil carbon due to nitrogen fertilization is often attributed to increased plant biomass production, and thereby increased crop residues or root growth. Soil carbon concentration was not related to the wide range of aboveground net productivity of a grass sward resulting from contrasted long-term fertilization treatments in a study conducted over 35 years in eastern Canada. Soil carbon concentration, however, was negatively correlated to soil pH (**Fig. 1**). In all three long-term experiments cited above, increased fertilization did not result in increased soil carbon concentration. Low soil pH, however, resulted in higher soil carbon concentration.

Increases in soil carbon storage related to increased plant biomass production due to nitrogen fertilization were observed in two long-term studies conducted in the Canadian Prairies. Soil carbon concentration increased from 50.3 g C/kg with no nitrogen applied, to 64.1 g C/kg with 112 kg N/ha applied annually to a grass sward for 27 years. Soil carbon concentration was positively related to the rate of applied nitrogen, but as was observed in other long-term experiments, soil carbon concentration was also negatively related to soil pH. In Minnesota, nitro-

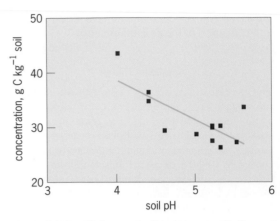

Fig. 1. Relationship between soil carbon concentration and soil pH after 35 years of fertilization of grasses with different rates of nitrogen, phosphorus, and potassium in eastern Canada.

gen inputs to grasslands for 12 years also increased soil carbon storage, but the increase depended on the type of grassland. Increases in soil carbon storage with nitrogen fertilization can also be observed when grasses are reestablished on crop land previously depleted in carbon.

Soil carbon concentration measured after many years of fertilization reflects the direct effects of fertilization on biomass production, but also the indirect effects operating through soil properties such as soil pH. In most long-term field experiments like those described above, it is difficult to partition the interacting, and potentially conflicting, effects of nitrogen addition on soil carbon.

The potential to increase soil carbon sequestration of grasslands through fertilization appears to vary with soil and site characteristics. Grassland soils generally contain larger amounts of carbon than soils that are used for annual crop production. This high soil carbon concentration of grasslands might explain the lack of response to increased fertilization in some situations. With high initial soil carbon concentrations, the relative change in soil carbon might be so small as to be masked by natural variation, or saturation of the soil carbon retention potential might have been reached. In cases where initial soil carbon contents are depleted and plant biomass production is significantly enhanced by fertilization, increases in carbon storage can be observed with nitrogen fertilization.

Although fertilization can increase the soil carbon sequestration of grasslands in some situations, this positive impact of fertilizers on the balance of greenhouse gases must be weighed against their possible effects on the production of other gases such as nitrous oxide (N_2O) and the energy cost of fertilizer manufacturing.   Gilles Bélanger; Denis A. Angers

Effects of Grazing

Grazing lands, including native ecosystems and improved pastures, represent the largest most diverse land resource in the world, occupying about twice the area devoted to cultivated agriculture. In the United States, lands grazed by domestic livestock or wildlife make up approximately 55% of the total land surface, about 400 million ha (990 million acres), and are estimated to contain 40 billion metric tons (44 billion tons) of carbon in the top 2 m (6.6 ft) of surface soil. The large reservoir of carbon stored in grazing lands is an important but often overlooked component of terrestrial carbon. With atmospheric carbon dioxide projected to increase in the coming decades, an understanding is needed not only of the potential for grazing-land ecosystems to sequester carbon but also of how grazing management strategies might affect this potential.

In ecosystems dominated by grasses, only about 10% of total system carbon is in the above-ground plant biomass, with the majority of plant carbon below ground in the root system (50–90%). About 90% of the carbon in grassland ecosystems is stored in soil organic matter, the largest and most stable pool of carbon in terrestrial ecosystems (**Fig. 2**). The potential to increase the amount of carbon sequestered in the soil of a particular grazed ecosystem depends on the overall health of the landscape. A site that is in good condition, with a stable productive plant community and minimal erosional soil losses, will likely have a lower potential for increased carbon storage than sites that are in fair or poor condition. Management of these degraded landscapes to improve the health and composition of the plant community and minimize erosion results in increased carbon sequestered in the soil-plant system. Although reliable estimates of the potentials for increased carbon sequestration in grazed ecosystems are limited by the scarcity of available data, current estimates place the potential for increased carbon sequestration as the result of improved United States grassland management at 11×10^{12} g C/yr (24 billion lb C/yr).

Changes in the amount and distribution of carbon stored in the soil occur in response to grazing management, but the effects of grazing on soil carbon are not clearly defined for all systems. While some studies have found a decrease in soil carbon with grazing, others, particularly studies on improved pastures, have reported increases. The inconsistent response of below-ground carbon to grazing management practices is the result of differences in grazing strategies, plant community, soil properties, and climate. Differences in the depth of sampling also affect the perceived response of soil carbon content to grazing management. Often only the surface 15–30 cm (6–12 in.) of the soil is sampled because the majority of roots and soil organic matter are found in this portion of the soil profile. However, as much as 40% of soil carbon can be found below 30 cm, so the carbon content of the entire soil profile should be measured in order to distinguish between actual losses or gains of carbon in the surface soil, and vertical redistribution of existing carbon within the soil profile.

A number of studies have reported that the effect of grazing on soil carbon content varies with graz-

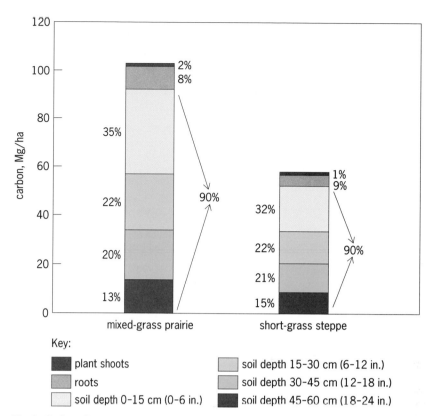

Fig. 2. Carbon distribution in two semiarid grasslands of the northern Great Plains, to a depth of 60 cm (24 in.) in the soil profile.

ing intensity. Grazing at a light-to-moderate stocking rate, and with a management strategy appropriate for the plant community and climatic conditions, promotes a healthy plant-soil system by stimulating carbon cycling of above-ground plant litter into the soil, maintaining a desirable plant species composition, and stimulating early-season photosynthesis. Grazing at stocking rates sufficiently heavy to change the plant species composition may actually result in increased carbon sequestration in the surface soil because of differences in rooting patterns of different plant species (**Fig. 3**). However, grazing intensities that cause dramatic changes in plant community composition are generally undesirable because of lower forage production, decreases in cattle weight gains, and a less diverse plant community which is undesirable for wildlife and community stability. Entirely excluding grazing generally results in an excessive buildup of plant litter on the soil surface, increased weedy species and decreased grasses, and a disruption of carbon cycling between the plants and soil, which can result in a significantly lower carbon content of the soil profile (Fig. 3).

Because grazing lands represent such a large pool of carbon, preservation of existing reserves by sound management practices is critical. The consequences of poor management are the loss of a stable productive plant community and an increased potential for loss of soil carbon by wind and water erosion. Increasing carbon storage in grazing lands can be accomplished with grazing management practices

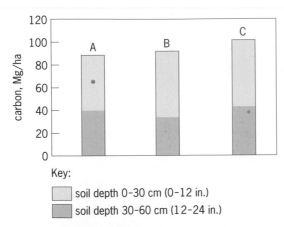

Key:
■ soil depth 0-30 cm (0-12 in.)
■ soil depth 30-60 cm (12-24 in.)

Fig. 3. Comparison of carbon content of the soil profile (0–60 cm or 0–24 in.) with different grazing intensities on a mixed-grass native prairie in Wyoming. A, exclosure not grazed for > 40 years, B, 12 years of continuous season-long grazing at a light stocking rate (21 steer-days/ha), and C, 12 years of continuous season-long grazing at a heavy stocking rate (59 steer-days/ha). Soil carbon content of the surface 30 cm (12 in.) of the soil profile is significantly lower (0.05 probability level) when grazing was excluded (*) than when the pastures were grazed at either the light or heavy stocking rate. Prolonged heavy grazing increased the production of warm-season short grasses and decreased production of cool-season midgrasses and browse shrubs.

that enhance and maintain a plant community appropriate to the local climate and soil. Most grassland ecosystems evolved under grazing by large herbivores, and removing livestock entirely may, over the long term, decrease the level of carbon sequestered in the soil and reduce the productivity and sustainability of the system.

For background information *see* AGRICULTURAL SOIL AND CROP PRACTICES; CARBON; FERTILIZER; GREENHOUSE EFFECT; SOIL; SOIL CHEMISTRY; SOIL ECOLOGY in the McGraw-Hill Encyclopedia of Science & Technology.

Jean D. Reeder; Gerald E. Schuman

Bibliography. G Bélanger et al., Long-term fertilization effects on soil carbon under permanent swards, *Can. J. Soil Sci.*, 79:99–102, 1999; R. F. Follett, Dynamics and pools of organic carbon in grazing land soils, in R. F. Follett, J. M. Kimble, and R. Lal (eds.), *Carbon Sequestration Potential of U. S. Grazingland*, CRC Press, Boca Raton, FL, 2000; R. F. Follett et al., Carbon isotope ratios of Great Plains soils and in wheat fallow systems, *Soil Sci. Soc. Amer. J.*, 61:1068–1077, 1997; A. B. Frank et al., Soil carbon and nitrogen of Northern Great Plains grasslands as influenced by long-term grazing, *J. Range Manag.*, 48:470–474, 1995; R. Lal et al., *The Potential of U.S. Cropland To Sequester Carbon and Mitigate the Greenhouse Effect*, Sleeping Bear Press, Ann Arbor, MI, 1998; S. S. Mahli et al., Increasing organic C and N in soil under bromegrass with long-term N fertilization, *Nutrient Cycling Agrosys.*, 49:255–260, 1997; E. A. Paul et al. (eds.), *Soil Organic Matter in Temperate Ecosystems*, CRC Press, Boca Raton, FL, 1997; K. Paustian, H. P. Collins, and E. A. Paul, Management controls on soil carbon, in E. A. Paul et al. (eds.), *Soil Organic Matter and Temperate Ecosystems: Long-Term Experiments in North America*, CRC Press, Boca Raton, FL, 1997; D. C. Reicosky, Strip tillage methods: Impact on soil and air quality, *Proc. ASSI Nat. Soils Conf.*, Brisbane, Australia, 1998; D. C. Reicosky, Tillage-induced CO_2 emissions from soil, *Nutrient Cycling Agrosys.*, 49: 273–285, 1997; D. C. Reicosky et al., Soil organic matter changes resulting from tillage and biomass production, *J. Soil Water Conserv.*, 15(3):253–261, 1995; D. C. Reicosky and M. J. Lindstrom, Fall tillage methods: Effect on short-term carbon dioxide flux from soil, *Agron. J.*, 85(6):1237–1243, 1993; G. E. Schuman, J. E. Herrick, and H. H. Janzen, Soil carbon dynamics of rangelands, in R. F. Follett, J. M. Kimble, and R. Lal (eds.), *Carbon Sequestration Potential of U.S. Grazingland*, CRC Press, Boca Raton, FL, 2000; G. E. Schuman et al., Impact of grazing management on the carbon and nitrogen balance of a mixed-grass rangelend, *Ecol. Appl.*, 9: 65071, 1999; D. A. Wedin and D. Tilman, Influence of nitrogen loading and species composition on the carbon balance of grasslands, *Science*, 274:1720–1723, 1996.

Cartographic animation

Defined as a graphic art that occurs in time, animation is a dynamic visual statement that evolves through change in the display. Early examples of cartographic animation on film and video could not be easily duplicated, transported, or displayed, thus severely limiting their distribution and use. The making of these early animations also was time-consuming and expensive. Computer technology, particularly storage devices such as the CD-ROM and advanced forms of data communications such as the World Wide Web, spurred new interest in this method of mapping during the 1990s. However, animation is still not widely used in cartography, has not been integrated in software for Geographic Information Systems (GIS), and faces a number of conceptual and methodological hurdles.

Development. Although the beginnings of cartographic animation are related to the development of film in the early part of the 1900s, it is reasonable to assume that animated maps are as old as maps themselves. Because movement is part of the environment, its depiction was likely a part of illustrations of prehistoric humans. The drawings on cave walls from 10,000–20,000 years ago have received much attention. Drawn with charcoal, these pictures of animals and other objects have survived because of their protected environment. Illustrations that were done on a less permanent and protected medium have been lost. Drawn with a stick in the sand, an early cartographic animation may have depicted the movement of animals or a fast-moving river.

Maps turned to stone, so to speak, approximately 4500 years ago, beginning with clay in Mesopotamia and then switching to paper some time later. In many ways, maps are still emerging from a stone age and a corresponding "paper thinking" that is tied to a static form of map display. The static map on paper has had a profound effect on the way the world is represented and the way it is thought about. Even cartographic animations are influenced by traditional paper maps in the graphic design of the individual frames and their normal presentation as a noninteractive sequence of maps.

Film influenced the presentation of maps as early as the 1930s. A Disney animation from 1940 depicted the invasion of Poland by Germany. Arrows, representing the movement of the German army, are shown moving toward Warsaw and quickly encircling the city. Shown as a part of a newsreel before the feature film, these early animations were an effective means of both education and propaganda.

The film metaphor is still an important part of cartographic animation. Many of the current cartographic animations are implemented as digital movies in either the MPEG or QuickTime™ formats. While some digital video formats allow the user to access individual frames, they provide very little control over which frames make up the animation and how they are shown. Current cartographic animations include little more than play/stop/forward/reverse controls that are associated with video cassette recorders (VCRs). The film/video metaphor is still tied to a certain way of thinking about cartographic animation that has been described by the German word *ablauf* (an uninterrupted progression from beginning to end). This limited view of carto graphic animation is changing, as are the types and uses of cartographic animation.

Types. A distinction is now made between temporal and nontemporal cartographic animation. Temporal animations show change over time, such as the diffusion of a farming method like irrigation. These animations show change through maps as a time lapse. An example of a nontemporal animation is the fly-through. Here, a series of oblique views of a landscape are displayed in quick succession to provide the appearance of flying through the terrain. The fly-through is usually constructed by draping a satellite image or an air photograph over a digital elevation model (DEM). A DEM encodes the terrain as a grid of elevation values.

In making the distinction between temporal and nontemporal animation, D. Dransch differentiates between geo-objects and animation-objects. In temporal animation, there is a change in the geo-objects relative to time. In nontemporal animation, there is a change in the animation-objects relative to factors such as a change in the position of the "camera" or light source. However, time is a part of all animations. According to Dransch, *realen Zeit* (real time) is depicted as a time lapse in a temporal animation, and *Präsentationszeit* (presentation time) is the time used to show the animation, whether the animation depicts temporal phenomena or not.

Many types of nontemporal cartographic animations have been proposed. A cartographic zoom, for example, shows a series of maps at increasing or decreasing map scales. This form of animation has been the most difficult to automate because it involves all aspects of the cartographic generalization process, especially the selection and simplification of features. A normal zoom is also possible that does not involve feature selection and simplification.

Other forms of nontemporal animation depict different ways of classifying data. A classification animation shows different methods of data classification, such as equal interval, quantile, standard deviation, and natural breaks. A generalization animation depicts maps with a single method of data classification, but multiple classes. The purpose of these animations is to provide a less misleading view of the data than simply relying on one form of data classification.

A spatial trend animation depicts a trend in space over time. An example is an animation of the percentage of population in different age groups within a city (for example, 0–4, 5–9, 10–14, etc. years of age). Older populations tend to live closer to the center of the city, and younger populations are at the periphery. This type of spatial trend animation for the city of Omaha shows older populations on the right side, closer to the older parts of the city along the Missouri River, and younger populations on the left corresponding to the western suburbs.

A set of dynamic variables have been proposed that can be used in nontemporal animation. Reordering, for example, involves presenting a temporal animation in a different order. In depicting earthquake activity the frames could be ordered by the number of deaths so that the more severe earthquake activity relative to human population is shown first. Changing the pace of the animation has also been proposed to highlight certain attributes. Using the earthquake example, the duration of each scene in the animation could be made proportional to the magnitude of the earthquake or the number of deaths.

Interaction. In addition to developing new forms of cartographic animation, new methods have emerged for adding interaction to animation creation and display. A program that both automated the production of the individual frames of a cartographic animation and brought interaction to its display was MacChoro II. Limited to the display of choropleth maps that use shadings to depict values over areas, the program used dialogs to control the selection of variables and data classification methods. The individual maps were then constructed and stored in memory at a speed of approximately one map per second (late 1980s technology). Following this, a pop-up control palette could be used to change the speed and direction (forward/backward) of the animation. Alternative methods of viewing cartographic animations through the World Wide Web have been developed using JavaScript.

These methods of animation are closely linked with cartographic visualization—an analytical form of cartography that is broadly defined as helping individuals, or groups of individuals, think spatially. This view of cartography is in contrast to the traditional view of maps as a form of presentation. The distinction between maps for analysis and maps for presentation is not clearly defined. Map use is by definition an inquisitive process that incorporates varying levels of analysis. Every map can be used for analysis, even maps on paper that are supposedly designed for presentation. Although a cartographic animation is a presentation viewable in time, it, like any other map presentation, only has meaning if it is used for analysis.

Outlook. Cartographic animation is an important technique to further our understanding of the spatial environment. It demonstrates that individual maps are only "a snapshot in time." When examining a static map, one should ask what trends would be evident if the time element were viewed as animation. The individual map is also a snapshot in reference to other data sets. What nontemporal trends would be evident if the map were viewed along with other related spatial data? Finally, the individual map is a snapshot in the choice of representational forms that were used to depict the data. A cartographic animation can provide a more meaningful view of the data through the use of different symbols or different forms of data classification.

Cartographic animation has been limited both by the difficulty of construction and distribution, and by a continued fixation of the individual, static map. Viewing static maps without interaction or animation is of limited value, particularly in the process of searching for spatio-temporal patterns. Computer technology is making it possible not only to create different types of cartographic animations but also to distribute these animations to a wider audience.

For background information *see* CARTOGRAPHY; COMPUTER GRAPHICS; MAP DESIGN; MAP PROJECTION; MAP REPRODUCTION in the McGraw-Hill Encyclopedia of Science & Technology.   Michael P. Peterson

Bibliography. D. DiBiase, Stretching space and splicing time: From cartographic animation to interactive visualization, *Cartog. Geog. Inform. Sys.*, 19(4):215–227, 1992; D. Dransch, *Computer Animation in der Kartographie: Theorie und Praxis*, Springer-Verlag, Berlin, 1997; M. P. Peterson, Active legends for interactive cartographic animation, *Int. J. Geog. Inform. Sci.*, 13(4):375–383, 1999; M. P. Peterson, Interactive cartographic animation, *Cartog. Geog. Inform. Sys.*, 20:40–44, 1993.

Catalytic antibodies

Catalytic antibodies are large proteins that are naturally produced by the immune system and have the capability of initiating diverse chemical reactions similarly to enzymes. They are elicited against small molecules that are bound to carrier proteins and contain a specific binding site. In their native form, they are constructed of two pairs of polypeptide chains that differ in length and are connected to each other

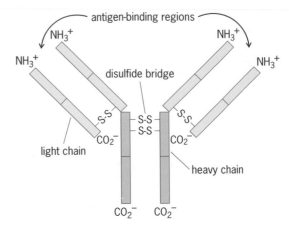

Fig. 1. Schematic structure of an antibody molecule. The protein consists of two heavy chains and two light chains.

by disulfide bridges. Various antibody molecules share a common structure (**Fig. 1**), but they differ in the N-terminal regions of antibody light and heavy chains which are responsible for antigen recognition. These regions vary greatly in the sequence and number of their constituent amino acids and therefore provide an enormous diversity of antigen-binding domains.

In principle, catalysis is achieved by lowering the free energy of activation for a chemical reaction. Therefore, the catalyst has to bind the transition state more tightly then either the reactant or the product. If an antibody could be elicited against a transition state, it would have the potential to catalyze this chemical reaction.

Catalytic antibodies are produced according to standard monoclonal technology. Stable transition-state analogs (haptens) are synthesized and coupled to two carrier proteins. One such conjugate is used for mouse immunization, and the second for screening purposes. The carrier proteins trigger strong immune responses, and specific antibodies which bind only to the hapten are selected and screened for catalysis.

Catalytic antibodies were first reported in 1986 independently by Richard Lerner and Peter Schultz. Both used antibodies that were elicited against tetrahedral phosphonate as transition-state analog to catalyze hydrolysis reactions of aryl esters and carbonates (**Fig. 2**).

Since then, several hundred different examples of catalytic antibodies have been reported from various research groups, including highly enantioselective, disfavored, and nonenzymatic reactions. However, the transition-state analog immunization strategy produced antibodies that were highly specific for their substrates, and therefore only a very limited number of compounds could be used for antibody reactions.

A major breakthrough has been achieved with the development of a new immunization concept. Instead of immunizing against transition-state analogs, immunization is done with a highly reactive compound in order to create a chemical reaction during the binding of the antigen to the antibody. The same reaction becomes part of the mechanism of the catalytic event. In other words, the antibodies are elicited against a chemical reaction. This strategy is termed reactive immunization.

1,3-Diketone was used as a trap for an amino lysine residue in an antibody active site (**Fig. 3**). Two antibodies which contained the desired lysine were found to mimic type I aldolases very efficiently. Type I aldolases are enzymes that catalyze reversible aldol reactions

$$R{-}CH{=}O + R'CH_2C{=}OR'' \rightleftharpoons$$
$$R{-}CHOH{-}CHR'{-}C{=}OR''$$

through the intermediacy of enamine formation with an enzyme amino group. For the first time, a catalytic antibody was capable of accepting a very broad range of substrates. Furthermore, in most cases the antibody's reactions were highly enantio selective and could be performed easily on a preparative scale. The synthetic advantages of these unique antibodies were clearly demonstrated, and include organic enantioselective synthesis of natural products and preparation of both enantiomers of a variety of aldol products. The surprising success of this aldolase catalyst made it the first commercially available catalytic antibody.

Synthetic achievements. The early skepticism of the synthetic capability of catalytic antibodies has rapidly diffused. The first large-scale reaction with a catalytic antibody was reported in 1994, in which the synthesis of 1.4 g of enantiomerically pure enol ether was achieved. Just a year later, the first total synthesis of a natural product using a catalytic antibody was reported. Aldolase antibody 38C2 has accomplished several important achievements in organic synthetic chemistry. It started with enantioselective synthesis of the important synthetic block, the Wieland-Miescher ketone, and followed with the enantioselective total synthesis of 10 different brevicomins (sex pheromones of the bark beetle). A total synthesis of the sex pheromone frontalin was reported shortly after.

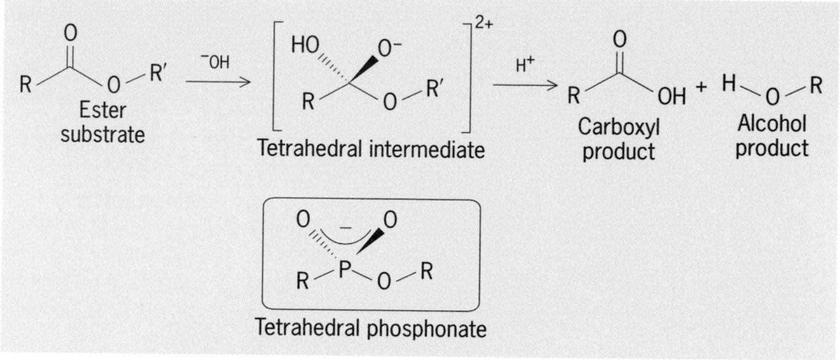

Fig. 2. Early highlights of the first antibody-catalyzed reaction of ester hydrolysis. Stable tetrahedral phosphonate was used as the transition-state analog.

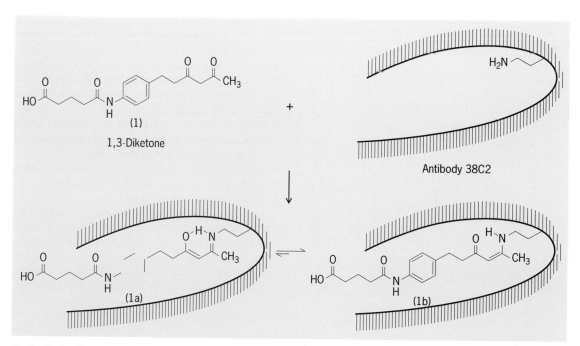

Fig. 3. Mechanism of trapping the essential ε-amino group of a lysine residue in the antibody's binding pocket by using the 1,3-diketone hapten.

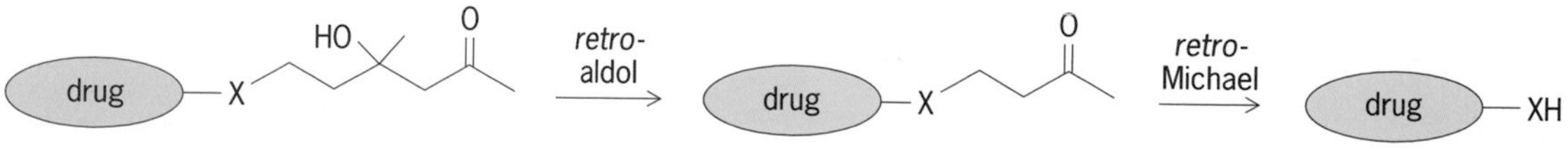

Fig. 4. Prodrug activation via a tandem retro-aldol-retro-Michael reaction. X stands for heteroatoms N, O, or S (nitrogen, oxygen, or sulfur).

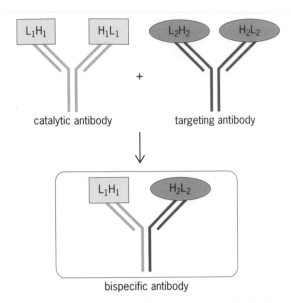

Fig. 5. **Generation of bispecific antibody originating from a catalytic antibody and a targeting antibody.**

The most stimulating achievement in the synthesis of a natural product by an antibody catalyst has been accomplished by the total synthesis of Epothilone, in which an important chiral synthon was prepared using antibody 38C2 to resolve 18 g of racemic mixture to 9 g of enantiomerically pure compound. Furthermore, the antibody was shown to perform aldol addition reactions very efficiently with unprotected hydroxyacetone as a donor. This is remarkable in

that no other catalyst, chemical or biological, is capable of using hydroxyacetone as a donor substrate for the aldol reaction. The advantage of this reaction was elegantly demonstrated in the short total synthesis of the biologically important sugar 1-deoxy-L-xylulose.

Medical potential. The intriguing concept of using catalytic antibodies as therapeutic agents became more appealing when it was shown that most of the amino acids in a mouse antibody molecule could be replaced with human sequences and thereby make the antibody molecule compatible for in vivo treatment in humans. This strategy has been exploited within the application of prodrug activation by a catalytic antibody.

In principle, a catalytic antibody can be designed to modify a prodrug into an active drug. Several groups reported prodrug activation by antibody catalysis. All of them used phosphonate hapten as tetrahedral transition-state analog for the hydrolytic reaction which released the free drug.

The aldolase antibody 38C2 has a major advantage regarding prodrug activation. Since it has the capability to accept a broad variety of substrates, the antibody may potentially activate any prodrug. A general prodrug chemistry was developed to take advantage of the broad scope and mechanism of catalytic antibody 38C2. The drug masking/activation concept was based on a sequential retro-aldol-retro-Michael reaction catalyzed by antibody 38C2 (**Fig. 4**).

This reaction is not known to be catalyzed by any other enzyme and has a very low background; that is, the reaction is very slow in the absence of the catalyst. This chemistry was applied to the anticancer drugs doxorubicin and camptothecin. Weakly or nontoxic concentrations of their corresponding prodrugs can be activated by therapeutically relevant concentrations of antibody 38C2 to kill colon and prostate cancer cell lines. To further test the therapeutic relevance of this model system, it was shown that antibody 38C2 remained catalytically active over weeks after intravenous injection into mice. Based on these findings, it is possible that the system described here has the potential to become a key tool in selective chemotherapy.

The development of strategies that provide for selective chemotherapy presents significant multidisciplinary challenges. Selective chemotherapy might, in the case of cancer, be based on the enzymatic activation of a prodrug at the tumor site. The enzymatic activity must be directed to the site with a targeting molecule, usually an antibody, that recognizes a cell surface molecule selectively expressed at the tumor site. Since a single molecule of enzyme catalyzes the activation of many molecules of prodrug, a localized and high drug concentration may be maintained at the tumor site. This concept of antibody-directed enzyme prodrug therapy (ADEPT) holds promise as a general and selective chemotherapeutic strategy if several criteria can be met.

A number of antigens that are expressed on the surface of tumor cells or in their supporting blood

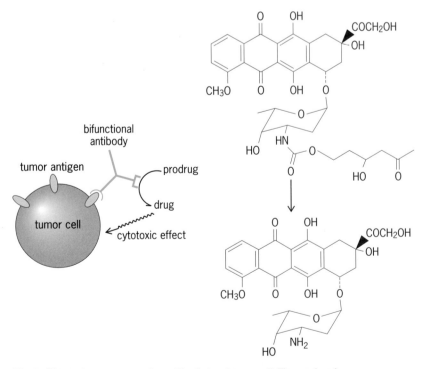

Fig. 6. **Chemotherapy targeted specifically to a tumor cell. The prodrug is Prodoxorubicin, which is transformed to the active drug doxorubicin by the catalytic arm of the bifunctional antibody. The other arm binds to an antigen on a tumor cell.**

vessels (vasculature) have been shown to be effective targets for antibody-mediated cancer therapy. Thus, for the most part, the targeting antibody component of this strategy is not limiting. By contrast, the requirements of the enzyme component and complementary prodrug chemistries for ADEPT are difficult to achieve. First of all, selective prodrug activation requires the catalysis of a reaction that must not be accomplished by endogenous enzymes in the blood or normal tissue of the patient. Enzymes of nonhuman origin that meet these needs are, however, likely to be highly immunogenic, a fact that makes repeated administration impossible. Finally, the chemistry used to convert a drug into a prodrug should be versatile enough to allow for the modification of many drug classes while not interfering with the operation of the enzyme so that a single enzyme could be used for the activation of a multiplicity of prodrugs.

Outlook. The limitations of the ADEPT complex encourage scientists to suggest that the enzyme component for ADEPT might be replaced by a catalytic antibody. The potential of catalytic antibodies for ADEPT are indeed compelling; both catalysis of reactions not catalyzed by human enzymes and minimal immunogenicity through antibody humanization are feasible. Combining these features, the ADEPT conjugate translates into a bispecific antibody consisting of targeting and catalytic arms (**Fig. 5**). Two parent antibodies are combined in a manner such that each antibody contributes one light chain and one heavy chain. The bispecific construct contains two different binding regions. One originates from the targeting antibody and can bind specifically to antigens which are expressed on tumor cells, and the other originates from a catalytic antibody and is used to activate a prodrug.

A bispecific antibody could be used for selective chemotherapy (**Fig. 6**). This possible future treatment can consist of two steps. First, a dose of the bispecific antibody can be administered, and the targeting arm can locate and attach to specific antigens on tumor cell surface. Excess of the antibody can be cleared after a limited time from the patient's blood, preventing nonspecific prodrug activation. Second, several doses of prodrug can be administered on suitable time gaps. The prodrug can reach the tumor site through the blood circulation and can be activated by the catalytic arm very close to the tumor cell. The damage to noncancer cells should be therefore minimized, and the free drug can specifically target cancer cells.

Catalytic antibodies are useful synthetic tools in enantioselective synthesis and also play an important role in performing organic reactions with unprotected chemical functionalities. However, the most promising use for them is probably in the medicinal field. The previously described strategy of targeting cancer with selective chemotherapy is highly encouraging.

For background information *see* ANTIBODY; ANTIGEN-ANTIBODY REACTION; CATALYSIS; CATALYTIC ANTIBODY; CHEMOTHERAPY; ENZYME; IMMUNITY; MONOCLONAL ANTIBODIES; ORGANIC SYNTHESIS; PHEROMONE; PROTEIN; REACTIVE INTERMEDIATES; STEREOCHEMISTRY in the McGraw-Hill Encyclopedia of Science & Technology.

Richard A. Lerner; Doron Shabat

Bibliography. T. Hoffmann et al., Aldolase antibodies of remarkable scope. *J. Amer. Chem. Soc.*, 120: 2768-2779, 1998; B. List et al., A catalytic enantioselective route to hydroxy-substituted quaternary carbon centers: Resolution of tertiary aldols with a catalytic antibody, *J. Amer. Chem. Soc.*, 121:7283-7291, 1999; B. List et al., Enantioselective total synthesis of some brevicomins using aldolase antibody 38C2, *Chem. Eur. J.*, 4(5):881-885, 1998; H. Miyashita et al., Prodrug activation via catalytic antibodies, *Proc. Nat. Acad. Sci. USA*, 90(11):5337-5340, 1993; S. J. Pollack, J. W. Jacobs, and P. G. Schultz, Selective chemical catalysis by an antibody, *Science*, 234:1570-1573, 1986; J. L. Reymond, J. L. Reber, and R. A. Lerner, Antibody-catalyzed, enantioselective synthesis on the gram scale, *Angew. Chem.*, 106:485-486, 1994; P. G. Schultz and R. A. Lerner, From molecular diversity to catalysis: Lessons from the immune system, *Science*, 269(5232):1835-1842, 1995; D. Shabat et al., A short enantioselective synthesis of 1-deoxy-L-xylulose by antibody catalysis, *Tetrahedron Lett.*, 40:1437-1440, 1999; S. C. Sinha and E. Keinan, a-Multistriatin: The first total synthesis of a natural product via antibody catalysis, *Isr. J. Chem.*, 36:185-193, 1996; D. Shabat et al., Multiple event activation of a generic prodrug trigger by antibody catalysis, *Proc. Nat. Acad. Sci. USA*, 96:6925-6930, 1999; S. C. Sinha, C. F. Barbas III, and R. A. Lerner, The antibody catalysis route to the total synthesis of epothilones, *Proc. Nat. Acad. Sci. USA*, 95:14603-14608, 1998; A. Tramontano, K. D. Janda, and R. A. Lerner, Catalytic antibodies, *Science*, 234:1566-1570, 1986; J. Wagner, R. A. Lerner, and C. F. Barbas III, Efficient aldolase catalytic antibodies that use the enamine mechanism of natural enzymes, *Science*, 270(5243):1797-1800, 1995; Toward antibody-directed "abzyme" prodrug therapy, ADEPT: Carbamate prodrug activation by a catalytic antibody and its in vitro application to human tumor cell killing, *Proc. Nat. Acad. Sci. USA*, 93(2):799-803, 1996; G. Zhong et al., Antibody-catalyzed enantioselective Robinson annulation, *J. Amer. Chem. Soc.*, 119(34):8131-8132, 1997.

Cell cycle (cancer)

Cell division requires regulation and coordination of many events in the cell cycle. The cell cycle has four phases (see **illus.**). Mitosis or cell division occurs in the M phase. This is followed by the gap 1 (G1) phase. Late in G1, cells commit to enter deoxyribonucleic acid (DNA) replication in the S phase. The S phase is followed by the gap 2 (G2) phase, which leads to the next M phase. Progression through the cell cycle is regulated by cyclin-dependent

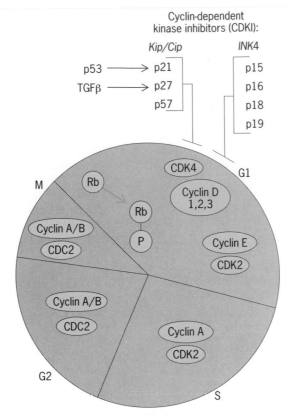

Cyclin, cyclin-dependent kinase (CDK), and cyclin-dependent kinase inhibitor (CDKI) interaction during the cell cycle progression. The CDKs are negatively regulated by CDKIs. The CDKIs are regulated by growth factors such as transforming growth factor beta (TGFβ) and other proteins such as the p53 suppressor gene product.

kinase (CDK) proteins whose activity is regulated by phosphorylation, activation by cyclins, and inhibition by cyclin-dependent kinase inhibitors (CDKI). The cyclin-dependent kinases control check points are biochemical pathways that coordinate the exact timing of cell cycle transitions. Passage from G1 to S is regulated by cyclins D1, 2, and 3, cyclin E, and cyclin A associated kinases. The activities of G1 cyclin-dependent kinases are in turn influenced by growth factors, cell-cell contact, and growth inhibitory signals. The B-type cyclins and associated kinases regulate the G2-M transition phases.

Cyclin-dependent kinase inhibitors. The cyclin-dependent kinase inhibitor proteins fall into two families based on their structural and functional properties. The INK4 family includes p16/INK4A (p16), p15/INK4B (p15), p18/INK4C (p18), and p19/INK4D (p19). Each member of the INK4 family has four ankyrin repeats and forms complexes with CDK4 or CDK6 (or both) cyclins and the D-type cyclins. The INK4 proteins have functional activities that are dependent on the presence of a normal retinoblastoma (Rb) protein. Maximal expression of the INK4 proteins occurs during the middle of the S phase in proliferating cells. Both p15 and p16 show a high frequency of gene deletions, and p16 gene mutations are found in various human tumors and cell lines, suggesting that these genes may function as tumor suppressors.

The second group of cyclin-dependent kinase inhibitors, the Cip/Kip family, includes p21/WAF1/CIP1 (p21), p27/kip1 (p27), and p57/kip2 (p57). These proteins inhibit kinase activities of the preactivated G1 cyclins, including cyclin E–CDK2 and cyclin D–CDK4/6. The Cip/Kip proteins interact with various cyclin-dependent kinase complexes, as well as with cyclins A, E, and D and cyclin-dependent kinases. Overexpression of the Kip proteins leads to cell cycle arrest. Kip proteins have a nuclear localization signal at their carboxyl-terminal domain. Unlike INK4 family, which inhibits CDK4/6 only, the Cip/Kip inhibitors can also target CDK2 in complexes.

Proteins and cancer. A growing body of knowledge indicates that cyclins, cyclin-dependent kinases, cyclin-dependent kinase inhibitors, and other critical cell cycle proteins such as retinoblastoma and p53 are targets for genetic change in the development of cancers or that they may be disrupted during tumor development. For example, cyclins D1, E, and A are overexpressed in some human cancers. Overexpression of D-type cyclins may lead to tumor development in experimental systems, and increased expression of cyclin E proteins in some tumors is associated with a poor prognosis. *See* CANCER.

The retinoblastoma gene was identified from germ line mutations that predisposed children with the mutant gene to develop retinoblastoma, an uncommon cancer of the retina. The retinoblastoma protein is a regulator of gene transcription in all cells of adults. The retinoblastoma protein plays an important role in cell cycle progression from the G1 to the S phase, when retinoblastoma becomes phosphorylated. Experimental animals without retinoblastoma gene expression develop various types of tumors, including tumors of the pituitary gland, which are hormone-producing tumors located at the base of the brain. Along with mutations of the retinoblastoma gene, functional inactivation of retinoblastoma also occurs in a variety of tumors. Osteosarcoma, a malignant bone tumor, is associated with inactivation of retinoblastoma function. Small-cell carcinoma of the lung is commonly associated with decreased retinoblastoma protein expression.

p53. p53 is a nuclear phosphoprotein which was originally discovered in extracts of transformed cells using antiserum from animals with tumors induced by Simian virus 40. Transforming p53 complementary deoxyribonucleic acid (cDNA) clones were found to be mutant forms of p53. The p53 gene is the most frequently mutated gene in human cancers, and it has a critical role in the cell cycle when cells sustain DNA damage. After DNA damage, p53 orchestrates cell arrest in G1, and attempts are made to repair the damaged DNA before cell replication. Although p53 is normally a short-lived protein, it is stabilized and accumulates in cells undergoing DNA damage or in those responding to certain forms of stress. Because p53 is so important for DNA repair, mutation of this gene is frequently associated with development of various cancers. The cyclin-dependent kinase inhibitor p21 is a downstream effector of p53. *See* TUMOR SUPPRESSOR GENE.

Cyclins. Cyclin D1 and other D-type cyclins probably play important roles in tumor progression. In esophageal, hepatic, and head and neck cancers, there is a correlation between cyclin D1 amplification and cycle D1 protein overexpression. Aberrant overexpression of cyclin D1 is also seen in other cancers, including carcinomas of the colon and thyroid, as well as melanomas, and sarcomas. In experimental systems, mice with a targeted deletion or knockout of the cyclin D1 gene have developmental defects in breast duct tissues, indicating that cyclin D1 plays an important role in the maturation of breast tissue.

Alterations in cyclin E and cyclin A genes in human cancers appear to be uncommon to date. However, cyclin E protein is aberrantly overexpressed in some cancers, including those of the breast, stomach, colon, and endometrium, and in some white blood cell malignancies.

Some cyclin-dependent kinase inhibitors are tumor suppressor gene candidates. Although mutations of the p27 gene are uncommon in human cancers, the levels of p27 protein are decreased in many cancers. Studies with experimental animals show that knockout of the p27 and p18 genes in transgenic mice leads to hyperplasia and tumor development in several organs.

p27. Many investigators have examined the role of p27 as a prognostic factor in human cancers, so more information is available about this cyclin-dependent kinase inhibitor than any of the others. Many putative functions are attributed to p27. Extensive studies have been performed to elucidate the role of p27 as a cyclin-dependent kinase inhibitor in normal and neoplastic cells. Some studies suggest that p27 may have a role as a tumor suppressor gene. Loss of p27 protein expression may result in tumor development or progression; however, this loss of expression does not appear to result from gene mutations. A number of studies have shown that p27 has a role in regulating differentiation in some tissues. p27 protein levels increase in cells treated with cyclic adenosine monophosphate (AMP), lovastatin, rapamycin, and tamoxifen. This increase is probably related to the G1 block produced by these agents. Cells undergoing differentiation also have increased levels of p27 protein. Some studies have shown that p27 levels are regulated by alterations of protein stability; thus the half-life of p27 is much longer in quiescent cells than in proliferating cells.

Ubiquitination is the principal mechanism regulating p27 protein degradation. Ubiquitin is a small protein of 7000 molecular weight that is covalently linked to a target protein. The ubiquitin-target protein complex is specified by the ubiquitinating enzymes E1, E2, and E3. The ubiquitin-activating enzymes (E1s) are the first enzymes involved in protein ubiquitination. E2s are designated as ubiquitin-conjugating enzymes and form a thioester bond between the internal systemic residue and the car-boxy terminus of a molecule of ubiquitin. E2 transfers the ubiquitin to ε-amino groups of lysine in the target protein. The ubiquitin ligases (E3s) are not as well characterized. They act as substrate recognition factors. The proteasome, which is a multimeric protein complex, recognizes the covalent adduction between ubiquitin and the target protein such as p27, which leads to degradation of the target protein with recycling of ubiquitin.

In the past few years, numerous studies have examined the diagnostic and prognostic significance of p27 expression in various tumors. Almost all studies report decreased p27 expression in more aggressive tumors. p27 expression is reported to be an independent prognostic factor and a potentially useful diagnostic tool in a broad spectrum of tumors. Various studies have shown that p27 has an important role as a prognostic factor in breast carcinoma. p27 can predict reduced disease-free survival. Lower p27 expression and lymph node status are independent prognostic factors. In addition to breast cancers, various other types of tumors, including those in the colon, prostate, esophagus, stomach, lung, ovary, and uterus, as well as melanoma skin cancers, have shown a relationship between lower p27 expression and tumor behavior and patient prognosis. Studies of other types of cancers, including tumors of lymph nodes (lymphomas) and some cancers affecting the white blood cells (leukemias), have shown that the amount of p27 expression may help predict patient prognosis.

p16. The p16 gene is a tumor suppressor gene. Deletion or mutation of this gene leads to tumor development or tumor progression. The p16 protein has shown prognostic utility in some human cancers. Various groups have used immunohistochemical staining with p16 antibody to predict tumor behavior. In various types of lung cancer, loss of p16 protein expression has been associated with adverse prognosis. Separate groups of investigators have shown independently that loss of p16 correlated with progression and was an independent predictor of poor overall survival in some types of lung cancer.

Studies with melanoma skin cancers have shown that loss of p16 expression is associated with decreased overall survival. p16 has also been associated with tumor progression in pituitary tumors, which are endocrine tumors that do not commonly metastasize or spread outside the brain. A normal pituitary often expresses abundant p16, while many pituitary tumors exhibit decreased p16 expression. Analysis of the p16 DNA molecule has shown that increased levels of methylation of the p16 gene are responsible for the loss of expression.

Other members of the cyclin-dependent kinase inhibitor family regulate tumor development and progression. For example, p57 is expressed in newly differentiated cells and in many adult tissues. Recent studies have shown that in the adrenal cortex, a gland that produces steroid hormone, there is loss of p57 expression in benign and malignant tumors compared to normal adrenal cortex, implicating p57 in adrenal tumor development and progression.

The importance of cyclins, cyclin-dependent kinases, and cyclin-dependent kinase inhibitors in the development of human cancers is becoming more appreciated. The cyclin-dependent kinase inhibitor proteins, such as p27 and p16, appear to have critical roles as independent prognostic factors for many human cancers. Future advances will include the discovery of new members of the cyclin-dependent kinase and cyclin-dependent kinase inhibitor families and elucidation of their roles in cancer development and progression.

For background information *see* CANCER (MEDICINE); CELL BIOLOGY; CELL CYCLE; CELL DIVISION; GENETICS; ONCOLOGY in the McGraw-Hill Encyclopedia of Science & Technology.

Ricardo V. Lloyd; Lori A. Erickson

Bibliography. R. V. Lloyd et al., p27^{kip1}: A multifunctional cyclin-dependent kinase inhibitor with prognostic significance in human cancers, *Amer. J. Pathol.*, 154:313–323, 1999; C. J. Sherr, Cancer cell cycles, *Science*, 274:1672–1677, 1996; J. Tsihlias, L. Kapusta, and J. Slingerland, The prognostic significance of altered cyclin-dependent kinase inhibitors in human cancer, *Annu. Rev. Med.*, 50:401–423, 1999; K. H. Zavitz and S. L. Zipursky, Controlling cell proliferation in differentiating tissues: Genetic analysis of negative regulators of G1 → S-phase progression, *Curr. Opin. Cell Biol.*, 9:773–781, 1997.

Cell motility

Most cells in adult tissues, such as muscle or liver, are fixed in place by cell junctions. However, certain white blood cells (leukocytes) are motile and able to migrate through the walls of blood vessels into the surrounding tissues, where they actively seek out and destroy bacteria. In response to infection, waves of neutrophils and macrophages arrive at a site of bacterial growth and start to engulf the bacterial population. This action, part of the innate or nonspecific immune response, is thought to protect humans from at least 98% of the pathogens they encounter, and there is little doubt that the migratory capacity of these leukocytes is of fundamental importance to human survival. Cell migration is not confined to these specialized bacteria-destroying leukocytes. A wound that damages the skin or other tissue will elicit the migration of connective tissue cells known as fibroblasts. These cells repopulate the lesioned area and begin to lay down the connective tissue that will form a scar. Finally, during early development many cell types show migratory activity, some being capable of long journeys through the embryonic mass to reach their final destination. Thus, motility is a fundamental property of cells, and is retained in a cryptic form even in static adult tissues.

Dynamics. Cell motility is most frequently analyzed on tissue cells that have been isolated from biopsies. Once purified, these cells will attach to and spread upon suitably prepared glass or plastic surfaces and begin migration. Such cells tend to retain certain characteristics of their origin: nerve cells will produce long extensions reminiscent of dendrites or axons, and epithelial cells will move as sheets of linked cells. But there are fundamental similarities in their locomotion which suggest that all tissue cells share a common motile machinery. This concept is demonstrated best by the observation that isolated cultured cells will display short surface protrusions called filopodia (or microspikes), which are extensions about 0.1–0.2 micrometer in diameter and up to 20 μm in length, supported by a core of bundled actin filaments (microfilaments). These filopodia appear to support thin veils or sheets of membrane-enclosed cytoplasm (lamellipodia) containing a meshwork of microfilaments. The underside of the cell is decorated with punctate densities, the focal adhesions (or focal contacts) rich in actin filaments, that act as anchorage points of the cell to the underlying substratum (**Fig. 1**).

The translocation of cells such as a migrating fibroblast is now known to be dependent on the combined activities of filopodia, lamellipodia, and focal adhesions. Forward movement can be divided into steps: cell protrusion of filopodia and lamellipodia at the leading edge, adhesion of the protruding front to the substratum via focal adhesions, contraction of the cytoplasm, and finally release from contact sites at the tail of the cell. A number of molecular events need to be integrated in order to allow a cell to move across a substratum, and it seems that this coordination is largely mediated by the actin-filament cytoskeleton (microfilaments) within cells. Extension of filopodia and lamellipodia entails the assembly of actin filaments from monomeric precursors that move into the region of the advancing cell margin. There they are added to the ends of actin filaments at or very close to the plasma membrane. Contact of the cell margin with the substratum induces microfilaments to collect into bundles at that point, cooperating in the accumulation of the membrane-spanning integrin proteins that have binding sites for extracellular matrix components as well as for microfilaments. Together, the aggregates of integrin and microfilament bundles recruit several structural and signaling cytoplasmic proteins to form focal adhesions. Behind the leading edge, a

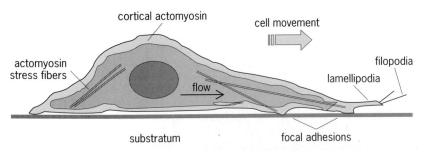

Fig. 1. Role of actomyosin in cell migration. This motile cell shows actin filament structures regulated by Rho proteins. Rho stimulates actomyosin-based contractility within the cortex of the cell and in the stress fibers, allowing the cell to move forward toward the leading edge containing the filopodia and lamellipodia.

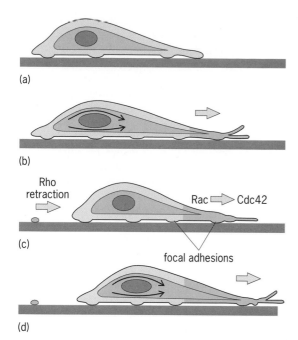

Fig. 2. Migration of cells over a substratum. (*a*) Extension of the leading edge. (*b*) Contact to matrix at focal adhesions. (*c*) Contraction of the cytoplasm (Rac regulates the formation of lamellipodia and membrane ruffles, while Cdc42 is required for filopodium extension). (*d*) Release from contact sites at the rear. Each step is dependent upon one or more cyclical biochemical processes in which Rho proteins are critical.

cortical meshwork of microfilaments contracts through the action of nonmuscle myosin II. This contraction generates a pulling of the cell body toward the newly formed focal adhesions and also squeezes the cytoplasm, thus generating a hydrostatic pressure that drives cytoplasmic constituents toward the front of the cell. Finally, at the very rear of the moving cell, integrin-based adhesions to the substratum are lost as a consequence of microfilament bundle contractions mediated again by myosin II (Fig. 1 and **Fig. 2**).

Molecular switches. In the last decade the regulation of the complex behavior of the actin cytoskeleton has been at least partially determined. The integration of actin dynamics largely resides with a group of proteins belonging to the Ras superfamily of small guanosine triphosphatases (GTPases) and known as the Rho family. Rho was first identified in 1985 as a sequence encoding a small guanosine triphosphate (GTP)–binding protein related to Ras. Other members of the family have subsequently been reported, although only three members, Cdc42, Rac, and Rho itself, have been characterized extensively to date. Rac and Cdc42 regulate lamellipodia and filopodia, while Rho regulates stress fiber formation and cell contraction. In general, Rho proteins can bind guanosine diphosphate (GDP) and guanosine triphosphate, and hydrolyze guanosine triphosphate to yield bound guanosine diphosphate and free phosphate. They also bind to proteins in the cytoplasm known as guanine nucleotide dissociation inhibitors (GDIs), which are thought to sequester them in an

inactive form. The exchange of guanosine diphosphate for guanosine triphosphate is catalyzed in cells by nucleotide exchange factors (GEFs), and well over 30 GEFs for Rho guanosine triphosphatases have been identified so far. Rho proteins are active when bound to guanosine triphosphate, and their activity is terminated by its hydrolysis, which results in the formation of inactive guanosine diphosphate-bound protein. While the Rho proteins do have a relatively high rate of spontaneous guanosine triphosphate hydrolysis when compared to Ras, the intrinsic hydrolysis rate is also stimulated by guanosine triphosphatase–activating proteins (GAPs). All these proteins work together to form a molecular switching system in which the guanosine triphosphate-bound form of the guanosine triphosphatase is active in signaling to the actin cytoskeleton, the specificity of which will depend upon the downstream targets of individual members of the Rho family.

Actin cytoskeleton. Most cultured fibroblasts and epithelial cells contain stress fibers, large bundles of microfilaments associated with myosin II and other proteins that terminate at focal adhesions. In addition, most cells possess a more delicate tracery of bundled microfilaments also associated with myosin II. Leukocytes or other cell types that are normally motile in vivo do not possess stress fibers; instead they contain groups of bundled microfilaments which terminate at smaller adhesion structures called focal complexes. An increase in the level of active Rho stimulates the accumulation of stress fibers; Rho is required for the formation of stress fibers induced by integrin engagement with extracellular matrix. Many observations on Rho function are consistent with its ability to stimulate the formation of actomyosin-based stress fibers and to regulate their contractility. In macrophages, microinjection of activated Rho rapidly stimulates cell contraction, and since macrophages do not possess stress fibers, the

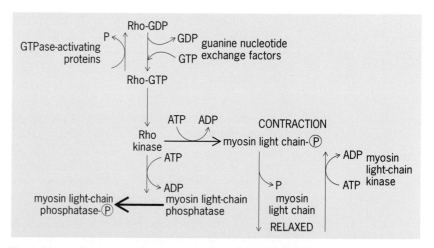

Fig. 3. Role of Rho in regulation of actomyosin contractility. The schematic shows the critical effects of Rho kinase (ROK), the major downstream target of active Rho. By simultaneously phosphorylating the regulatory myosin light chain and the enzyme myosin light-chain phosphatase, contractility is promoted and sustained.

finer actin cables must also be Rho-sensitive. In neuronal cells, Rho also stimulates cell contraction and mediates the retraction of long dendritic-like processes.

It seems likely that Rho interacts with several different target (or effector) proteins in the cell to allow the coordinated assembly of actin, the formation of stress fibers, and microfilament bundle contractility mediated by myosin II. The best-studied Rho targets are two related serine/threonine kinases, ROKα and ROKβ (also known as Rho kinase or p160Rock). Both kinases regulate actomyosin-based contractility by modulating intracellular levels of phosphorylated myosin II. Myosin II is a hexameric protein composed of two heavy chains, two essential light chains, and two regulatory light chains. The heavy chain consists of a globular head domain which contains the adenosine triphosphate and actin-binding sites necessary for motor activity, a neck region that binds the light chains, a long intermediate domain that forms the coiled-coil responsible for heavy-chain dimerization, and a C-terminal nonhelical tailpiece. The motor activity of smooth muscle and nonmuscle myosin II is regulated primarily by phosphorylation of the regulatory light chains, which stimulates the actin-activated adenosine triphosphatase activity of myosin II. Phosphorylation of the regulatory light chains is balanced by two enzymatic activities: myosin light-chain kinase and myosin phosphatase. Rho kinase phosphorylates the myosin-binding subunit of the myosin light-chain phosphatase, which inhibits the activity of the phosphatase. Downregulation of myosin phosphatase activity allows for the maintenance of phosphorylated regulatory light chains, which in turn supports the actin-stimulated myosin adenosine triphosphatase activity leading to actomyosin contraction. In addition, Rho kinase directly phosphorylates the regulatory light chains, an action that would clearly augment contraction (**Fig. 3**).   Gareth Jones

Bibliography. D. Bray, *Cell Movements*, Garland, New York, 1992; L. Kjoller and A. Hall, Signaling to Rho GTPases, *Exp. Cell Res.*, 253:166–179, 1999; J. M. Lackie, G. A. Dunn, and G. E. Jones, Cell behaviour: Control and mechanism of motility, *Biochemical Society Symposium 65*, Princeton University Press, 1999; A. J. Ridley, Stress fibres take shape, *Nat. Cell Biol.*, 1:E64–E66, 1999.

Chemical bond

Atoms in a molecule are held together by covalent chemical bonds that rely on the interaction of the outermost, or valence, electrons of each atom. Even though one refers to electrons, one should think rather of the electron density distribution, otherwise known as the electronic orbitals. The overlapping of atomic electronic orbitals determines the chemical, thermal, and mechanical stability of a covalent bond. The mechanical stability of a molecule represents a very fundamental question in chemistry. Thanks to

recent advances in nanomanipulation techniques, it is now possible to address the mechanical strength of an individual covalent bond.

Force spectroscopy. The atomic force microscope has become a widely used instrument for material characterization in the nanoscopic regime (10^{-9} m). Initially, atomic force microscope studies were aimed at visualization of surface morphology and molecular structure. More recently, the spectrum of atomic force microscope application has broadened substantially due to the discovery of new capabilities. The atomic force microscope has been applied to the study of molecular mechanics of single polymer chains. In a typical experiment, the polymer sample is left to adsorb on a flat solid surface which is attached to a piezoelectric positioner, capable of precise nanometer displacement. Individual polymer segments of random length are picked up (by adsorption or by specific attachment) by the atomic force microscope tip and stretched (**Fig. 1**) up to some micrometers in length. The deflection of the cantilever arm of the microscope that is detected upon

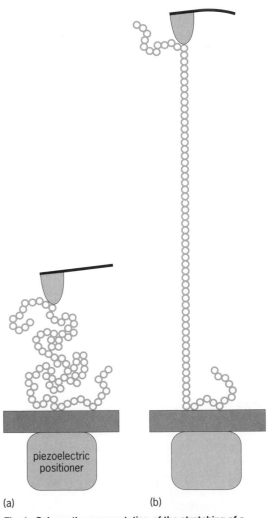

(a)   (b)

Fig. 1. Schematic representation of the stretching of a single polysaccharide chain attached between an atomic force microscope tip and a surface mounted on a piezoelectric positioner. (*a*) Before stretching. (*b*) After stretching.

stretching of the molecule can be converted into units of force if the spring constant of the cantilever is known. Force-extension curves that are recorded during stretching and relaxation of a single polymer chain have revealed a wealth of fingerprintlike features, such as entropic elasticity, conformational transition, and supramolecular rearrangements.

Polymer elasticity. Several molecular factors contribute to the elasticity of a single polymer chain (**Fig. 2**). The entropy of the polymer chain is the most ubiquitous. At equilibrium, an ideal polymer chain adopts a loose coil conformation with its two extremities separated by a minimum distance, R. That configuration corresponds to a maximum degree of freedom (that is, entropy) for the polymer chain. When stretched, the single polymer chain loses some degrees of freedom, and this loss generates an entropic restoring elastic force. This entropic restoring force ranges from zero to a few tenths of piconewtons. Attractive (nonideality effect) or repulsive (excluded volume effect) interaction within the polymer chain can modulate the magnitude of the entropic restoring force. At higher forces (>300 pN), covalent bond deformation starts to play an important role in the polymer elasticity. The stretching of a covalent bond is analogous to the elongation of a hookean spring, where the restoring force is the product of the elongation and a spring constant. Similarly, bond angle deformation contributes to the elastic properties of the polymer chain. The rupture of an intramolecular covalent bond may be observed in the highest force range (>1000 pN). Very peculiar elastic features often characterize polysaccharides. Upon stretching, dextran or amylose undergoes a pronounced conformational transition during which the sugar rings switch into a more extended arrangement. These transitions are fully reversible on the time scale of the experiment and therefore also contribute significantly to the chain elasticity, but only in very narrow windows of force.

Covalent bond rupture. In order to be able to measure the rupture force of a single covalent attachment, a protocol was developed to allow a symmetric covalent attachment of an amylose polysaccharide between the surface and atomic force microsope tip. Both the surface and the atomic force microscope tip had been amino-functionalized beforehand, using an aminosilane. The amino-reactive amylose, activated via carbodiimide chemistry, was first coupled to the surface. Then the tip was slowly brought into contact for a short time with this amylose-coated surface, allowing the amino-reactive amylose to react with the tip. In approximately 30% of the tip contacts with the surface, an individual polymer was attached in between. In the other cases, either multiple bonds occurred or no bonds at all. Tip and substrate were gradually separated while the force was recorded (**Fig. 3**).

Upon stretching, amylose undergoes a pronounced transition during which the ring switches from a chair to a boat configuration (Fig. 2). This results in a characteristic plateau at 275 pN with an

extension of 0.05 nm per sugar ring unit (C in Fig. 3). Thus, this transition may be used as a molecular strain gauge that may be built into an experiment to report the force that is acting at any point of the molecular

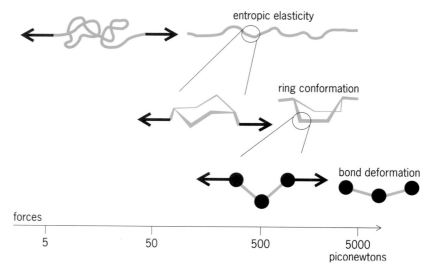

Fig. 2. Elastic regime of an amylose chain. At first, the stretching generates a restoring force that is entropic in nature. Then, chair-boat transition of the sugar ring unit is observed (~275 pN). In the highest force range, bond deformation (>300 pN) and bond rupture (>1000 pN) may be observed.

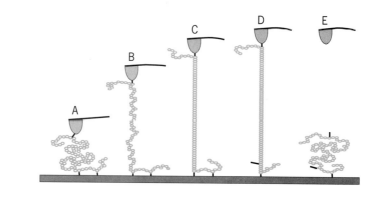

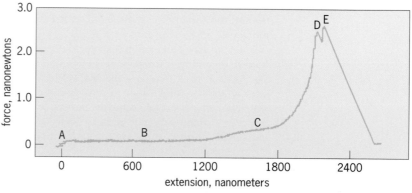

Fig. 3. Force-versus-extension curve of an amylose polymer covalently bound between an atomic force microscope tip and a glass surface. The force is measured through the deflection of the cantilever, whereas the extension is performed with a piezopositioner. At A the tip is left to react with the amylose-coated surface. In the initial stage of the stretching (B), the entropy of the single amylose chain generates a low restoring force. At C, the chair-boat conformation change (275 pN) of the amylose sugar rings is observed; then follows the bond deformation. The first peak (D) is due to the breaking of the first covalent attachment. Breaking of the last covalent attachment occurs at E. The number of covalent attachments found in different experiment is variable, and their breaking may occur either at the surface or at the tip.

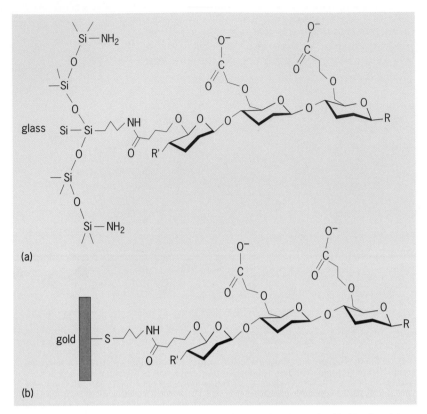

Fig. 4. Schematics of the covalent attachment of the amylose by carbodiimide chemistry to (*a*) glass or (*b*) gold surfaces, which were both functionalized with amino groups.

bridge. More importantly, this transition was used to identify those experiments in which only a single polymer is attached between tip and substrate. If two or more polymers are stretched simultaneously, the plateau forces add up and either shift the plateau to higher forces or spread it out. Both cases can easily be distinguished from the plateau of a single polysaccharide. In a typical amylose rupture experiment, the plateau was analyzed by repeatedly stretching and relaxing the polymer through the conformation transition. After confirming that a single molecule was bound, the force was gradually increased until the molecular bridge ruptured.

The rupture of these single molecule bridges occurred in multiple irreversible steps (D and E in Fig. 3). One peak precedes the final rupture event, after which the force drops to zero. Because only a single polymer is stretched and the molecular bridge between tip and substrate remains intact after the individual rupture events, these multiple bond rup-

tures reflect the stepwise detachment of the polysaccharide from the surfaces. Given the manner in which a polymer interacts with a surface, it is to be expected that the polysaccharide is bound to the surface in loops and trains. With increasing force, the bonds of the loops to the surface break one by one, while the polymer backbone stays intact. After each detachment, the force drops abruptly because the previously unstretched section can take up the slack and therefore increase the length of the stretched polymer bridge. A quantitative analysis (150 experiments) of the bond rupture gives a mean rupture force of 2.0 ± 0.3 nanonewtons at loading rates of 10 nN/s.

This finding—that it is the attachment that ruptures and not the polymer backbone—indicates that the measured bond rupture must be attributed to some of the bonds that are part of the attachment and not part of the polysaccharide. For example, in the covalent attachment of amylose by carbodiimide to glass (**Fig. 4a**), four bonds (involving silicon, oxygen, carbon, and nitrogen) are unique to the attachment: the Si-O, Si-C, C-C, and C-N bonds. The C-O bond is found in the attachment as well as in the amylose backbone. At first, it seems difficult to determine which of these four bonds is breaking. As a first approximation, one can correlate the strength of a covalent bond with the ratio of the dissociation energy and the bond length. Considering the enthalpy for dissociation and the bond length (see **table**), the Si-C bond is the most likely candidate for rupture in the covalent bond rupture experiment.

Researchers compared the bond strength of the Si-C bond to the strength of the attachment of the polymer via sulfur to gold (S-Au). The experimental setup was identical to the previous experiments except that the substrate was an evaporated gold surface (Fig. 4b), which was activated with an aminothiol. The attachment to the tip was unaltered. This replacement resulted in a reduction of the bond rupture force to values of 1.4 ± 0.3 nN. Whereas in the symmetric silicon oxide experiment the measured rupture force could be attributed to the Si-C bond, the S-Au rupture experiments leave room for speculation. Whether this measured value of 1.4 nN represents the rupture of the S-Au bond or the extraction of the S-bonded gold atoms from the metal surface remains unclear for the moment.

Outlook. Nanomanipulation techniques such as atomic force microscopy offer new prospects for

Enthalpy of dissociation and length for different bonds			
Type of bond	Enthalpy of dissociation (ΔH_d), kJ/mole	Bond length (L), nm	$\Delta H_d/L$, nN
Si-C	318	0.185	2.9
Si-O	452	0.166	4.5
C-C	346	0.154	3.7
C-O	356	0.143	4.1
C-N	305	0.147	3.4

studying the mechanical stability of a chemical bond. Material scientists now have the ability to probe the strength of an individual bond forming a supramolecular structure. Probably the most important feature of such an experiment is that mechanical activation of chemical bonds, here in the simplest form as bond rupture, can now be investigated on an individual basis.

For background information *see* CHEMICAL BONDING; INTERMOLECULAR FORCES; POLYMER; SCANNING TUNNELING MICROSCOPE; STRUCTURAL CHEMISTRY in the McGraw-Hill Encyclopedia of Science & Technology.   Michel Grandbois; Hermann Gaub

Bibliography. M. Grandbois et al., How strong is a covalent bond?, *Science*, 283:1727–1730, 1999; P. E. Marszalek et al., Polysaccharide elasticity governed by chair-boat transitions of the glucopyranose ring, *Nature*, 396:661–664, 1998; M. Rief et al., Single molecule force spectroscopy on polysaccharides by atomic force microscopy, *Science*, 275:1295–1297, 1997; S. B. Smith, L. Finzi, and C. Bustamante, Direct mechanical measurements of the elasticity of single DNA molecules by using magnetic beads, *Science*, 258:1122–1126, 1992.

Chemical microreactors

Chemical microreactors are characterized by the extremely small dimensions of the reaction devices and related unit operation elements. In comparison to macroscale devices, large temperature and concentration gradients are feasible in microreactors, resulting in correspondingly high heat and mass transfer rates. Since the boundary conditions concerning flow, temperature, pressure, and other parameters can be precisely adjusted, and since the thermal mass of such microsystems is small, an exact setting of the residence time in the reaction volume is easily obtained. This leads to a novel approach for process control. Usually a number of microreactors are operated in parallel, with all devoted to either different or identical reactions. In the first case, microreactors may be regarded as devices generating information like miniaturized analytical laboratories; in the second case, they work as production units for chemical substances which achieve the required throughput by parallel operation. The unique characteristics of microreactors open up novel approaches for utilizing a wide variety of reaction pathways, for improving safety aspects, for a faster transfer of laboratory results into production, and, evidently, for cost-saving innovations in many fields of modern chemistry and biotechnology.

Technology. Processes have been developed for the fabrication of three-dimensional microdevices. These fabrication methods have their basis in the production technologies for integrated microelectronic circuits as well as in advanced precision mechanical techniques which, in general, make it possible to utilize a wide variety of materials. As a result, microsystems are feasible for nearly all types of fluid handling, including chemical and biochemical reactions where nearly all requirements for resistance against corrosion can be met, as well as those for operation at high temperature or under biocompatible conditions.

Such microsystems for chemical and biochemical reactions, including fluid handling and unit operations of chemical engineering, as well as the corresponding analytical systems, are more or less precisely called microreactors. They are characterized by small effective dimensions and the possibility of making a large number of devices at comparatively low cost. As a consequence, one has the ability to work with many microreactors. For billions of years, these simple characteristics—small dimensions and large numbers—have been applied by nature. For example, the living cell can produce a vast number of compounds in great quantities with extremely high flexibility.

Microreactors can be characterized by two fundamentally different tasks: they may serve to produce either information or chemicals. Consequently, they may be regarded as miniaturized chemical laboratories, many of which solve different analytical tasks and deliver information connected with the structure of molecules. Since information is not connected with a specific size, as in microelectronics, miniaturization is a strategy of success which saves space, energy, time, and costs while allowing performance to be improved by integration of functional units. Microreactors operated in parallel, but all with different analytical tasks, are becoming an absolutely essential tool for high-throughput screening and combinatorial material science. Examples are the development of drugs and agrochemicals as well as catalysts or polymers.

Microreactors can be used to produce chemicals in small as well as in large quantities just by operating a variable number of microreactors with the same reaction in parallel. A general answer whether the application of microreactors is favorable or not cannot be given, since there are always various prerequisites regarding the reaction as well as the amount of chemicals to be produced. However, some general conclusions can be drawn which will be summarized below.

Since the driving forces for heat and mass transfer are determined by the gradients of temperature and concentration, respectively, the small dimensions of microreactors result in extremely high transfer rates per unit volume. In addition, defined boundary conditions can be adjusted in microreaction systems so that reaction pathways can be precisely selected for specific chemical reactions. This makes it possible to minimize adverse effects resulting, for instance, from incomplete mixing, hot spots, or a wide variation of process conditions in the reaction volume (such as exists in a large stirred tank). The small mass of the microsystems, in addition, makes it possible to change the temperature of the educts and products extremely fast and to quench unfavorable secondary reactions very effectively. Accordingly, microreactors generate higher yields and selectivities, or more generally, achieve technological and economic progress through process intensification. A precise adjustment of process conditions, short response times, and defined residence times result in a major advantage of microreactors in process control.

The obvious advantages in process control, the tiny amounts of substances in the reaction volumes, and the flame resistor effect, resulting from the small dimensions of microreaction systems, lead to a completely new situation concerning safety aspects. Besides explosions and other causes of damage connected with large amounts of materials, microreactors open the way to the inherent safety of chemical production processes. In addition, transport and storage risks can be reduced by microreactors since, in principle, microreactor plants could be operated economically in a much smaller size than macroscopic plants (that is, microreactors make possible a distributed production on site and on demand). Such favorable safety prerequisites are also of major interest concerning the utilization of novel reaction pathways which offer economical advantages that were not used in the past because of safety reasons.

Applications. Although the discussion about the potential of microreaction technology started during the mid-1980s, a major interest of chemical industry in this new technology began only during the mid-1990s. The breakthrough in this connection resulted first from the implementation of the international conferences on microreaction technology organized by the Institute of Microtechnology Mainz (IMM), DECHEMA, the American Institute of Chemical Engineers (AIChE), and the Battelle Institute, and second from the availability of microreactor components manufactured by means of modern microfabrication methods (**Fig. 1**).

Researchers of DuPont reported about their work to produce, in particular, hazardous gases by means of integrated microreaction systems made of silicon. Chemists of BASF used a microreactor fabricated by IMM as a tool for process optimization and demonstrated that yield and selectivity of a two-phase liquid-liquid reaction for the synthesis of a vitamin precursor could be enhanced considerably. Chemical engineers of Merck, in Darmstadt, Germany, used micromixers developed by IMM to change a batch

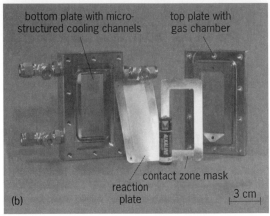

Fig. 2. Microreaction systems for the direct fluorination of aromatics. (*a*) Micro bubble column. (*b*) Falling film reactor.

process for fine chemicals into a continuous process with higher yield and much smaller process times. At the Pacific Northwest National Laboratory of the Battelle Institute, a number of research projects have been carried out dealing, for instance, with hydrogen production through reforming of hydrocarbons and methanol. The IMM has presented a large number of microreactor components as well as integrated microreaction systems which are applied by industry and research institutes for a wide variety of chemical reactions dealing with oxidation of ethene and propene, fluorination of aromatics (**Fig. 2**), synthesis of hydrogen cyanide, and reforming processes.

A common feature of most microreactors developed for medium- or large-scale synthesis of materials may be characterized by the fact that continuous processes will replace standard batch processes comprising large vessels and stirred tanks and other devices of macroscopical chemical engineering. As a result, the productivity per unit volume of a chemical plant will increase dramatically, since the advantages of continuous processes and of process intensification through miniaturization will be combined.

Besides microreactors for synthesis, miniaturized devices for analytical chemistry have been developed (**Fig. 3**). By far the major part of this development work deals with biotechnology where miniaturized systems for the polymerase chain reaction, fluidic

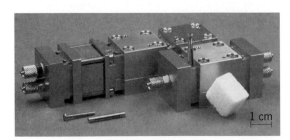

Fig. 1. Assembly of several standardized housings for different microreactor components.

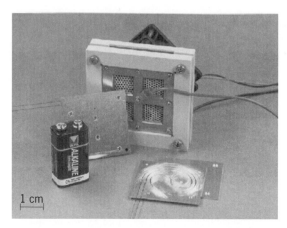

Fig. 3. Frame module with resistive heaters, cooling fan, and column support.

Fig. 4. Components of a membrane module for product enrichment in microreactors.

chips for DNA sequencing, biosensors using hybridization, and many other devices were realized. Other microanalytical devices deal with fluorescence correlation spectroscopy, electrochemical systems with interdigital microelectrodes, polarization measurements, membrane modules (**Fig. 4**), and various microchromatographic and microelectrophoretic channel systems. Since high-throughput screening and methods of combinatorial chemistry are increasingly important for drug development and material science, it is to be expected that microreaction systems for the production of information will have a fast-growing market.

Outlook. The progress in microreaction technology achieved in the last few years clearly demonstrates that a revolutionary development process has started in chemical engineering, analytical chemistry, biotechnology, pharmacy, and other fields of chemistry. A large number of industrial companies are investing considerably in microreaction technology, and industrial experts even dare to make the prognosis that, within the first 10 years of the twenty-first century, 50% of all fine chemicals will be produced by means of microreactors. The application potential of microreactors in drug development and production of so-called personal pharmaceuticals is even bigger than in the field of fine chemicals. The question is not whether a race will start, but which companies will be the winners or losers. The pressure to transfer the results of research much more rapidly into production and to penetrate the market continuously with innovative products will increase, and one suitable tool to meet this requirement is microreaction technology.

For background information *see* ANALYTICAL CHEMISTRY; CHEMICAL CONVERSION; CHEMICAL ENGINEERING; CHEMICAL REACTOR; COMBINATORIAL CHEMISTRY; ORGANIC SYNTHESIS; PROCESS ENGINEERING in the McGraw-Hill Encyclopedia of Science & Technology.   Wolfgang Ehrfeld; Stefan Kiesewalter

Bibliography. W. Ehrfeld (ed.), *Microreaction Technology: Proceedings of the 1st International Conference on Microreaction Technology*, Frankfurt, Springer-Verlag, 1997; W. Ehrfeld, I. H. Rinard, and R. S. Wegeng (eds.), *Process Miniaturization: 2d International Conference on Microreaction Technology*, March 9–12, 1998, New Orleans, Topical Conference Preprints, American Institute of Chemical Engineers, 1998; W. Ehrfeld (ed.), *3d International Conference on Microreaction Technology*, April 18–21, 1999, Frankfurt, Topical Conference Preprints, Springer-Verlag, 2000; W. Ehrfeld, V. Hessel, and V. Haverkamp, Microreactors, *Ullmann's Encyclopedia of Industrial Chemistry*, 6th ed., 1999.

Chemical process safety

During the 1950s and 1960s a new generation of larger chemical plants were built. These plants operated at higher temperatures and pressures. An unforeseen result was an increase in fires, explosions, and other serious incidents. The fatal accident rate (the number of fatal accidents in 10^8 working hours or in a group of 1000 people in a working lifetime) reached a high point in the mid-1960s in a very large chemical company (see **illus.**). The industry realized that safety required a stronger technical basis. This led to the growth of process safety as a distinct branch of chemical engineering. It is often called loss prevention, especially in Europe. The illustration also shows the results achieved by this chemical company as it applied process safety. Many other chemical companies had similar experiences, although some have not yet achieved full benefits from process safety.

Process safety differs from traditional safety in the following ways:

1. Process safety is more concerned with those accidents that arise from the technology employed.

2. Process safety emphasizes foreseeing hazards and taking action before accidents occur.

3. Process safety emphasizes a systematic rather than a trial-and-error approach, particularly systematic methods of identifying hazards and of estimating the probability that they will occur and their consequences.

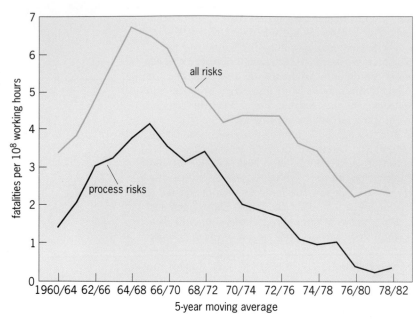

Fatal accident rate expressed as a 5-year moving average for the period 1960–1982 for a very large chemical company.

4. Process safety is concerned with accidents that cause damage to the plant and loss of profit but do not injure anyone, as well as with those that do cause injury.

5. Traditional practices and standards are looked at more critically.

6. The emphasis has shifted from blaming the operator after an accident to asking what designers and managers might have done to prevent it.

Risk assessment. In developing process safety, the chemical industry soon realized that everything could not be done at once and that it needed a systematic and defensible method of deciding priorities. The answer was quantitative risk assessment (QRA): estimates of the risk to life for employees and members of the public were used as a criterion. Risks above an agreed level were reduced as a matter of priority; those below the level were left alone. For example, a writer suggested that the same criteria used for fixing the height of storm dikes in the Netherlands be used to decide whether the risks from the Dutch chemical industry were tolerable.

A more recent development provides for two levels of risk. Risks above the upper level are considered intolerable. Below the lower level, the risks are negligible. In between the two levels, the risk should be reduced if the benefits outweigh the costs, using cost-benefit analysis. If risks cannot be reduced, the plant should not be built, or not be operated if it has been built. An example is the Shoreham Nuclear Power Plant in the United States. When it was first being built, it was not considered a high risk. However, due to its proximity to large human populations, it later was deemed a high risk. Although the plant was completed at a total cost exceeding $4 billion, it never went into full operation. In fact, the plant has been shut down completely.

Quantitative risk assessment has been accepted more readily in some countries than in others. In the United Kingdom, for example, it has long been accepted by law that it is impossible to remove every hazard and that companies should weigh the size of a risk versus the cost of reducing it in money, time, and trouble. If there is a gross disproportion between them, a risk being insignificant compared with the cost, the company does not have to reduce it. In many countries there is no similar tradition, and companies for a long time were reluctant to admit that they were not doing everything possible to remove every hazard, however small in consequences or unlikely to occur.

Identification of hazards. The biggest source of error in quality risk assessment is failing to recognize all the hazards or all the ways in which they can occur. Time may be wasted quantifying with ever greater accuracy the risks that have been identified, while bigger risks go unseen.

The most widely used method of identifying hazards is the hazard and operability (Hazop) study. For example, a team of people examine one by one all the pipelines in a plant and ask, if the flow rate, temperature, pressure, or composition could depart from the design, could this be hazardous and, if so, how could this be prevented. It is no longer a matter of course to build a plant, see what happens, and then remove or control any unforeseen hazards. Plant designers try to foresee potential hazards.

Inherently safer design. For a long time the chemical industry reacted to hazards by keeping them under control. Unfortunately, control measures may fail. Having once identified hazards, they should be removed, if possible. There are various approaches to removing hazards, such as: Use so little hazardous material that is does not matter if it all leaks out (intensification or minimization). Use a safer material instead (substitution). Use the hazardous material in the least hazardous form (attenuation or moderation). Simplify the design so that there is less equipment to fail and fewer opportunities for error.

For example, the chemical that leaked at Bhopal in India in 1984 and killed over 2000 people was an intermediate, not a product or raw material. It was convenient to store it but not essential to do so. Afterward, many companies substantially reduced their stocks of hazardous intermediates, often eliminating them altogether by using the intermediates as soon as they were made. Instead of, say, 50 tons in a tank, there were only a few pounds in a pipeline.

Quantitative risk assessment is a second-best option. It should first be seen if the hazard can be avoided. If a hazard cannot be removed, it needs to be controlled, usually by defense-in-depth. If one line of defense fails, there are others to fall back on. If flammable liquids or gases are handled, some or all of the following approaches should be used: Prevent leaks and other equipment failures by good design, construction, maintenance, and operation. Install automatic detectors so that leaks are detected promptly and people not required to deal with the leak can leave the area. Install remotely operated emergency isolation valves in places where leaks are most likely to occur or where a large quantity can leak out. Remove all known sources of ignition. Minimize damage by installing fire protection; passive equipment such as fire insulation is usually better than active equipment such as water spray turned on by automatic equipment (which, however, is better than active equipment turned on by people). Provide fire-fighting equipment.

It is essential to carry out regular audits, tests, and inspections to make sure that protective equipment is in working order and that procedures have not lapsed.

Accident investigation. Many people—from the chemists who chose the process, through the designers, down to the last link in the chain, the operator who closed the wrong valve—have an opportunity to prevent a chemical accident. The traditional safety officer looked only for the last link. Today many companies pay more attention to the preceding links. There are various ways of reducing the probability of an incident (the risk) and also the size of the consequences (the hazard). For example, use less hazardous raw materials. Reduce the amount of raw materials in process and storage. Include more protective equipment in the design. Provide the operators with more adequate training and instruction. It is possible that previous incidents were often overlooked because the effects fortunately were only trivial. The emphasis has shifted from blaming the operator to removing opportunities for errors.

Details of an accident and the recommendations made are often published or circulated privately to other chemical companies. Unfortunately, they are being published less often than 20 years ago because, with reduced manpower, people have less time to prepare reports for publication.

Preparing a good report is not enough. All too often, the report is read, filed, and forgotten. After few years the accidents happen again. Organizations have no memory. Only people have memories, and after a few years they move on taking their memories with them. The following are some actions that companies might take to improve the corporate memory: Include in every instruction, code, and standard a note on the reasons for it and accounts of accidents that would not have occurred if the instructions had been followed. Never remove equipment before knowing why it was installed; never abandon a procedure before knowing why it was adopted. Describe old accidents as well as recent ones in safety bulletins and discuss them at safety meetings. Carry out regular audits to check that the recommendations made after accidents are being followed, in

design as well as operations; all people carrying out routine tasks tend to cut corners after a while. Include important accidents of the past in the training of undergraduates and company employees; giving the message once is not enough, especially if the message is one that the audience would rather not hear. Devise better retrieval systems to find, more easily than at present, details of past accidents, in various companies, and the recommendations made afterward.

Other procedures. Whenever possible, chemical plants are made safer by good design and safe processes. Otherwise, procedures have to be depended on. All too often, managers and supervisors eventually lose interest in maintaining particular procedures. A continual management effort is needed to make sure that procedures are followed and that everyone understands the reasons for them.

In addition to procedures already mentioned, particular attention should be paid to preparation for maintenance and the control of modifications. Many people have been killed or injured because they opened up equipment for repair and found that it had not been isolated from sources of danger or freed from hazardous material; or they opened up the wrong piece of equipment. Sometimes procedures were poor; sometimes they were not followed.

Many changes to plant or process design, or just to company organization, had unforeseen side effects. No changes should take place until they have been authorized by a competent, professionally qualified person, who should first carry out a systematic study of the proposed change.

Outlook. Fatal accidents are now rare in most chemical companies, and most accidents are due to nonchemical causes such as transport. Thus, such events are of little use as a continuing measure of safety. The lost-time accident, the most widely used measure, shows that the chemical industry is far safer than many industries that have fewer inherent hazards. Process safety distinguishes hazards—what can happen; and risks—the probability that they will happen. The chemical industry has many hazards but low risks.

For background information see CHEMICAL ENGINEERING; CHEMICAL PROCESS INDUSTRY; HEALTH PHYSICS; INDUSTRIAL FACILITIES; INDUSTRIAL HEALTH AND SAFETY; RISK ANALYSIS in the McGraw-Hill Encyclopedia of Science & Technology.

Trevor A. Kletz

Bibliography. T. A. Kletz, *An Engineer's View of Human Error*, 3d ed., Institution of Chemical Engineers, Rugby, U.K., 2000; T. A. Kletz, *What Went Wrong? Case Histories of Process Plant Disasters*, 4th ed., Gulf Publishing, Houston, 1998; F. P. Lees, *Loss Prevention in the Process Industries*, 2d ed., Butterworth-Heinemann, Oxford, 1996; R. E. Sanders, *Chemical Process Safety: Learning from Case Histories*, Butterworth-Heinemann, Boston, 1999.

Chemical separation

Most industrial chemical processes involve a separation stage. This may involve a preliminary purification stage before the reaction process, or a final stage involving the separation of the desired product. Two well-known processes are distillation and crystallization.

Distillation and crystallization. The distillation process is based on the relative volatilities (that is, vapor pressures) of the components. It involves the heating of the feed material (which is to be separated) in a boiler. The heated vapors enter a column and partially condense on the many plates or trays. These plates have a large surface area to facilitate the equilibrium between the vapor and the liquid. The vapor in the column is richer in the more volatile (lighter) component. As the vapor travels up the column, this process of enrichment is enhanced. The final stage of the distillation process is the complete condensation of this vapor as it leaves the column. This is done by cooling the vapor to a temperature well below its boiling point. The result is a separation of a light component or components (the condensate) from heavy components left in the boiler. The overall separation achieved depends not only on the relative vapor pressures of the components but also on the number of trays in the column. In spite of the high energy demands of the distillation process, 90% of all separation processes in the chemical and petrochemical industries worldwide are distillation processes.

In the crystallization process, separation is based on the relative solubilities of the components. The separation of sea salt from water is usually done by crystallization through the evaporation of the water either by heating or by using solar energy.

Thermodynamics offers a proper understanding of all separation processes. Not only is it useful in quantifying the separation of components, but thermodynamic relationships are also vital in the design of industrial separation plants.

Basic theory. When an equilibrium exists between phases (solids, liquids, or gases), the chemical potential, μ_i, for species i in each phase may be expressed by Eq. (1). For a vapor-liquid equilibrium process

$$\mu_i(\text{solid}) = \mu_i(\text{liquid}) = \mu_i(\text{gas}) \qquad (1)$$

(distillation) this equality results in Eq. (2), the re-

$$y_i/x_i = \gamma_i P_i^0/P_{(\text{total})} \qquad (2)$$

lationship between the vapor composition (y_i) and the liquid composition (x_i) at a temperature T. Here, γ_i is the activity coefficient of species i, P_i^0 is the vapor pressure of pure i at T, and $P_{(\text{total})}$ is the total vapor pressure of the system. It is this ratio that defines the separating efficiency and is known as the distribution coefficient. Other relationships can be derived for other phase separation processes (such as crystallization), and in every case the results will be based on Eq. (1).

Separation processes. Industrial separation processes involve all the possible phase pairs apart from solid-solid, which is kinetically too slow for useful applications (**Table 1**).

Supercritical fluid extraction. The process of supercritical fluid extraction is a relatively new separation technique. Interest in it is based on the high solubility of some solids in the supercritical solvent, the high degree of selectivity, the ease of separating the required product, and the ease with which the solvent can be recovered. To understand the process requires an understanding of the critical point.

The liquid-vapor phase line (as opposed to the solid-vapor and solid-liquid phase lines) for pressure and temperature discontinues at a certain point (**Fig. 1**), known as the critical point. At temperatures above the critical temperature (T_c), it is not possible to liquefy the gas by pressure alone. In other words, it is impossible to produce a liquid meniscus from the gas phase by pressure alone. At conditions above the critical temperature and pressure (P_c), the gas is known as a supercritical fluid (Fig. 1).

For an understanding of the general process, it is best to look at the most important supercritical fluid extraction process, the decaffeination of coffee using carbon dioxide. Carbon dioxide fluid, at a pressure of 200 atm (20 megapascals) and a temperature of 50°C (122°F) [in excess of P_c (CO_2) = 73 atm and T_c (CO_2) = 31°C (88°F)], is pumped through the extraction cell containing the ground coffee in a mesh basket. The supercritical carbon dioxide has the unique capacity for dissolving only the caffeine and not the compounds that give coffee its taste and flavor. The carbon dioxide fluid, now containing dissolved caffeine, leaves the cell, and its pressure is reduced to below its critical value. As a result, the fluid vaporizes to a gas and the solid caffeine precipitates as it is not soluble in gaseous carbon dioxide. The coffee without caffeine is recovered and the carbon dioxide compressed and recycled. Apart from the simplicity of the process and the fact that it is done at a low temperature (it apparently does not affect the coffee taste or flavor), its main advantage is that the solvent is a natural substance and if any residue is left in the coffee it will be harmless. This is not true for some other decaffeination processes which use organic solvents such as methylene chloride.

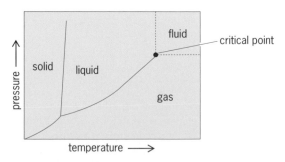

Fig. 1. Typical pressure-temperature (P-T) phase diagram showing the critical point discontinuity.

TABLE 1. Some important separation processes

Phase pair	Process	Industrial separation
Gas-liquid	Distillation	(i) Gasoline, paraffin and diesel fuel separated from oil (ii) Acetic acid from water
	Gas adsorption	Ammonia gas and air separated by passing the gas mixture through water
	Gas desorption	Ammonia and water mixture separated by passing air through the solution
	Pervaporation	Alcohols removed from esters and aroma compounds in aroma production
Gas-gas	Membrane	Methane gas or hydrogen gas separated from carbon dioxide
Gas-solid	Sublimation	Removal of water from heat-sensitive foodstuff by freeze drying; the food is cooled below 0°C and vacuum is applied, resulting in the sublimation of water
	Desorption	Drying of clay or wood by exposure to air
	Adsorption	Drying of wet air by passing over silica gel
Liquid-liquid	Solvent extraction	A mixture of acetone and water can be separated by adding carbon tetrachloride (CCl_4); phase separation takes place and the acetone is found in the CCl_4-rich layer
	Reverse osmosis	Seawater and brackish water purified by removal of salts
Liquid-solid	Supercritical fluid extraction	Separation of caffeine from coffee; the caffeine in the ground coffee beans readily dissolves in supercritical carbon dioxide
	Zone refining	Purification of benzene or metals to produce ultrapure compounds
	Fractional crystallization	Salts from seawater are usually separated on a basis of solubility

Carbon dioxide is the most popular solvent used in supercritical fluid extraction. This is largely due to its relatively low critical pressure and temperature, and the ease with which the supercritical state can be achieved. It is extensively used in the perfume industry, where high temperatures would destroy the chemicals. It is used, for example, in separating oxygenated compounds (such as geranyl acetate), valuable as perfumes, from lemon oil, which consists largely of terpenes of low value, such as limonene.

Water has received much attention as a possible solvent for supercritical fluid extraction. Its critical properties are, however, too high for convenience [$P_c = 218$ atm (22.1 MPa) and $T_c = 374°C$ (705°F)], but it does have the interesting property of dissolving nonpolar liquids such as hexane. This is not possible at ambient temperature and pressure.

Membrane separation processes. An important new technology uses membranes to effect separation. The membrane is usually a thin plastic film (0.1–5 micrometers) on a thick porous and inert support layer (100–500 μm) [**Fig. 2**]. The driving force pushing the permeate across the membrane is invariably a pressure difference between the feed mixture and the permeate. The membranes are made of synthetic polymers such as polyvinyl alcohol, for separating water and alcohol liquids; polyurethane, for separating aromatic liquids from cycloalkane liquids; poly-imides, for separating gases such as oxygen and nitrogen; and cellulose acetate, for separating pure water from seawater.

When the feed and the permeate are both gases, the process is known as gas separation. The pressure difference is usually between 10 and 100 atm (1 and 10 MPa), with the pressure of the permeate

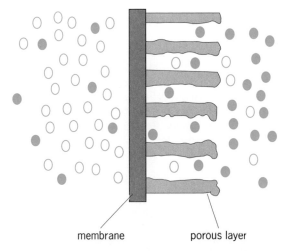

membrane   porous layer

Fig. 2. General description of the membrane separation process. Molecules A (white) and B (black) are separated by a membrane supported on a porous layer and driven by a flux, which is usually pressure.

TABLE 2. Examples of separations based on membrane processes

Membrane	Mixture	Preferentially selective for	Process
	Gas separation		
Polyimide	O_2/N_2	O_2	Oxygen enrichment
Polyethersulfone	CH_4/CO_2	CO_2	CO_2 recovery
Cellulose acetate	H_2/CO_2 or H_2/N_2	H_2	Hydrogen recovery
	Reverse osmosis		
Cellulose acetate, aromatic polyamides	Seawater	Water	Desalination
	Sugar solutions	Water	Concentration of food ingredients
	Fruit juices	Water	Concentration of food ingredients
	Pervaporation		
Polyvinylalcohol	Water+alcohol	Water	Dehydration
Polyoctylmethylsiloxanes	Water+alcohol	Alcohol	Dealcoholization
Polyoctylmethylsiloxanes	Aroma compounds in water	Aroma compounds	Aroma production

being about 1 atm (0.1 MPa). When the feed and permeate are liquids, the process is reverse osmosis, and it is best known for desalination of dilute aqueous solutions such as seawater, brackish water, and industrial wastewater. The pressure applied on the feed side is usually 80–100 atm (8–10 MPa), while the permeate is kept at ambient pressure. If the feed is a liquid under its own saturation pressure and the permeate is a gas or vapor kept at a low pressure (5–20×10^{-3} atm or 0.5–2 kPa) by a suitable vacuum pump, the process is known as pervaporation. The permeate is recovered in a cooling trap.

Perhaps the main advantage of the membrane technique is that it is possible to tailor-make a membrane for a particular separation. Its limitations include chemical breakdown of the membrane with time and its slowness. The mechanism of the process is complex and involves properties such as the relative solubilities and relative diffusion coefficients of the feed chemicals in the membrane (**Table 2**).

For background information *see* ADSORPTION OPERATIONS; CHEMICAL EQUILIBRIUM; CRYSTALLIZATION; DISTILLATION; MEMBRANE SEPARATIONS; SALINE WATER RECLAMATION; SUPERCRITICAL FLUID; VAPOR PRESSURE in the McGraw-Hill Encyclopedia of Science & Technology.   Trevor M. Letcher

Bibliography. J. Gmehling et al., Status and results of group contribution methods, *Pure Appl. Chem.*, 65:919–926, 1993; J. L. Humphrey, Separation processess playing a critical role, *Chem. Eng. Prog.*, 91: 31–41, 1995; K. E. Porter, Why research is needed in distillation, *Chem. Eng. Res. Des.*, 73:357–362, 1995.

Cloning (genetics)

The word "clone" is derived from the Greek *klon*, meaning twig; it has been known for millennia that one can copy or reproduce certain plants by simply planting a piece of the plant. The sexual processes of meiosis and fertilization are not involved in this method of reproduction, so a broad definition of cloning is asexual reproduction. This mode of genetic copying is the routine agricultural procedure for producing potatoes, asparagus, and manioc, just to name a few examples. Another method of cloning is the production of offspring by nuclear transfer from a somatic cell. Mammals can be cloned by this method as demonstrated by the sheep Dolly, which was produced asexually by researchers in the 1990s; this sheep is a genetic copy of a previous animal.

Genetic identity. Genetically identical mammals occur naturally in the form of identical twins, triplets, and so on. While infrequent in cattle or humans, identical multiplets occur in every armadillo pregnancy. Such identical multiplets are a "gold standard" for cloning; clones produced by nuclear transplantation will be less identical to each other than identical twins.

Mammalian identical multiplets also can be produced deliberately by dividing early-stage embryos into two, three, or more pieces. This was first done with two-cell to eight-cell embryos of sheep, cattle, pigs, and horses. Subsequently, a simple microsurgical procedure was developed for dividing embryos of 50–500 cells into two or more parts; this procedure has been used to produce thousands of sets of identical twin or (rarely) triplet and quadruplet cattle. The commercial principle here is that potentially twice as many calves are produced from valuable embryos by dividing them in half to make two embryos from one. Identical multiplets, whether born naturally or derived from microsurgical procedures, sometimes look quite different from each other. For example, identical twins rarely have identical patterns of coat color spotting.

While the fidelity of genetic identity is maximized by subdividing embryos, the subdivision approach has two limitations that nuclear transplantation does not have. First, an embryo that was produced sexually is being copied, so its adult phenotype is unknown. Second, while identical twins can be produced very successfully, success rates decline precipitously when aiming for three or more identical multiplets.

Nuclear transplantation. The egg, whether in women, cows, mice, elephants, chickens, frogs, or mosquitoes, is the largest cell in the body. Its importance is illustrated by the tens of thousands of nurse cells that nourish and protect the mammalian egg. Conceptually, the egg is a factory that will develop into an embryo upon fertilization, and then a fetus. This factory comes with a haploid (half) set of genetic instructions, the maternal genetic contribution. Normally, the complementary paternal half of the blueprint comes from the sperm. Upon fertilization, the resulting one-cell embryo has a complete diploid set of genetic instructions that ultimately will specify the characteristics of the resulting individual, such as its sex, hair color, size, some aspects of personality, and resistance to certain diseases. Before the one-cell embryo divides to two cells, the genetic instructions are duplicated so each cell gets a complete set. This duplication process is repeated with each cell division. Thus, every cell in the body has the same set of genetic instructions as every other cell, with a few exceptions, such as sperm and eggs.

To make a clone by nuclear transplantation (see **illus.**), the egg's genetic instructions are removed. Then, instead of fertilizing the egg with a haploid sperm, the egg is provided with a complete, diploid nucleus. Thus, the resulting animal will have the same genetic composition as the animal from which the donor, diploid nucleus originated; it will be a clone, or genetic copy.

The first successful cloning of mammals by nuclear transplantation was published in 1986. The diploid nuclei came from sheep embryos with fewer than 100 cells. Thus, as with splitting embryos, copies of embryos, not adult animals, were being made. This research then progressed to using nuclei of cells of fetuses, newborns, and finally of adult mammary tissue to produce Dolly. To date, nuclei from a dozen adult tissues have been used successfully, including cells from muscle and skin.

Characteristics of clones. Although clones are very similar to each other and their parent, they are not identical because characteristics of individuals (phenotypes) are determined partly by genetics, partly by environment, and partly by chance. This is why identical twins, although very similar, are far from identical. Cloning by nuclear transplantation adds additional variation from five major sources on top of that expected between identical twins.

First, unless the eggs to which nuclei will be transferred are from the same maternal line as the donor nucleus, mitochondrial genetics will vary from clone to clone. Mitochondria are small structures in the cell that produce chemical energy for muscle movement, cell division, duplication of deoxyribonucleic acid (DNA), and so on. Humans inherit mitochondria, which have their own genetic instructions, from mothers via the egg. Mitochondrial genes represent

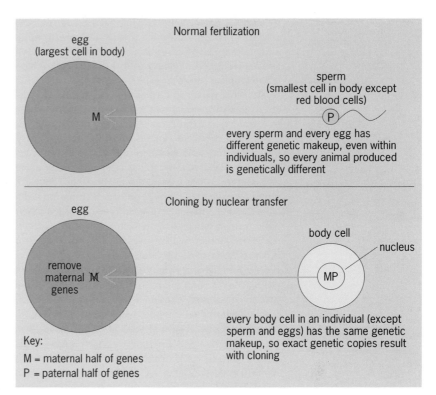

Comparison of fertilization and cloning by nuclear transfer.

less than 1/10,000 of the genetic composition of an individual, but these genes have very important functions. While clones will have the same nuclear genetic instructions, mitochondrial genetics may differ.

A second difference among clones will be due to mutations of nuclear genes. Mutations are chemical changes in genetic instructions caused by radiation, chemical reactions such as oxidation, and errors from duplicating DNA. To illustrate the latter problem, there are about 3 billion building blocks (bases) in each mammalian haploid set of genetic instructions. Thus, each time a diploid cell divides, 6 billion pieces must be assembled. If there was only one mistake in a billion, there would be six mistakes with every cell division. Nature employs many mechanisms to minimize copying errors, including proofreading enzymes, antioxidants, and DNA repair enzymes. Even so, some mutations occur, making clones imperfect genetic copies.

The third source of variation is gestation in different uteri. All cloning procedures start with early embryos, and these must be placed into a female reproductive tract for gestation and birth. Nutrition and environment differ among females during pregnancy and at birth, as does the amount and quality of milk produced. All of these factors will affect the characteristics of individual clones differently.

A fourth source of variation is the length of telomeres, the ends of the chromosomes, which contain the genetic material in the nucleus. Telomeres tend to shorten with each cell division (except in cells that form sperm and eggs). Thus, cloning from an adult cell means that embryos start out with older, shorter telomeres. This could be a problem with some cloning procedures.

The fifth reason for dissimilarities among clones stems from abnormalities in cloned pregnancies due to problems with the placenta, the sac of membranes containing the fetus during gestation in the uterus. The placenta provides nutrients to the fetus and removes waste products. If it is not functioning properly, abnormalities may result in abortion. Newborn clones sometimes have problems originating from an abnormal placenta; a common complication is oversized newborns, resulting in difficult birth. If the cloned individual survives the first few days after birth, problems thereafter are minimal. The clones themselves have normal gestations and offspring when they become pregnant, proving that these problems are not genetic.

Applications. An obvious application of cloning is to make genetic copies of valuable animals—a prize ram or a high-producing dairy cow. Even though genetic copy does not equal phenotypic copy, clones would be fairly similar to the valuable animal, and usually superior to most individuals resulting from conventional reproduction.

A futuristic application is to make tissues for transplantation to humans. For example, tissues such as the liver or pancreas likely can be made from embryonic cells without going through the production of the other parts of a baby, such as a head or a heart. If one started with a cell nucleus from the proposed recipient and a human egg, the new tissue would have the same genetics as the recipient, thus eliminating rejection upon transplantation.

Another application, the one closest to commercialization, is to make transgenic animals that produce valuable pharmaceutical products in their milk, blood, urine, or body tissues. For example, the protein-synthesizing cells in the mammary gland might be harnessed to make a human blood clotting factor in milk, in addition to regular milk proteins. The required genetic changes can be made by adding DNA to cells in vitro; such cells then become the genetic parent of an animal by nuclear transfer into an egg, so the resulting animal will have the genetic modifications in every cell in the body. When this animal matures and lactates, the valuable pharmaceutical can be extracted from the milk and sold. This likely would be a much less expensive source of blood clotting factors for hemophiliacs than the current procedure of extracting these factors from huge quantities of human blood. An important fringe benefit is safety, since milk from cows, goats, or sheep would not have human pathogens such as hepatitis virus.

A final application of cloning is research. Cloning is leading to truly novel insights about cell function. This information may lead to developing new treatments or preventive methods for diseases, including certain cancers; decreasing birth defects; making prosthetics; and circumventing aging and infertility.

Ethical issues. Cloning, like any other tool, can be used for good or evil. It is imperative to prevent abuse of the technology and minimize untoward and unexpected outcomes. Institutional animal care and use committees by law must approve research protocols in order to prevent or minimize experimental animal suffering. For any human experiments or applications, institutional ethics boards must be fully engaged in approval of protocols and procedures. Repressing research on cloning is not a workable option, as it drives research to institutions that may have less oversight.

For background information *see* GENE; GENETIC ENGINEERING in the McGraw-Hill Encyclopedia of Science & Technology.   George E. Seidel, Jr.

Bibliography. G. E. Seidel, Jr., Production of identical sets of mammals: Cloning?, *J. Exp. Zool.*, 228: 347–354, 1983; S. Willadsen, Nuclear transplantation in sheep embryos, *Nature*, 320:63–65, 1988; I. Wilmut et al., Viable offspring from fetal and adult mammalian cells, *Nature*, 320:63–65, 1997.

Coelacanths

A group of lobe-finned fishes, distantly related to tetrapods, that spans some 375 million years of geological time from the first known fossil in the Middle Devonian to the living fish *Latimeria chalumnae*. There is, however, a gap of some 70 million years in the fossil record between the most recent known fossil and the living fish. Indeed, coelacanths had long been thought to have become extinct with the dinosaurs at the end of the Cretaceous. Great excitement therefore ensued when the first living coelacanth was found off East London, South Africa, in 1938. Much debate followed concerning the status of the living species: for example, where does *Latimeria* live, how has it survived, and how many are there now are still issues. Recently a new population of the species has been discovered in the western Pacific Ocean, throwing many previously held theories into disarray.

A living fossil. Living fossils are generally considered to be taxa that have survived for abnormal lengths of geological time but have changed very little, morphologically or physiologically, from their older fossil ancestors. The term was coined by Darwin for those rare living species that preserve the biology of otherwise extinct groups. Typically such species are geographically restricted, while the older fossils may have been distributed worldwide. They are thought to be ecologically marginal and to exist in small population numbers. They persist against all the odds, their morphological conservatism unexplained. When first discovered, the species *L. chalumnae* appeared to fit all the criteria for such a living fossil. Although it has to be emphasized that there are no grounds for believing that the species itself has been in existence for more than a few million years, the species certainly preserves unchanged the structural characteristics of its Devonian coelacanth forebears. *See* LIVING FOSSILS.

First living specimen. The discovery of the first living coelacanth off South Africa in December 1938 was a zoological landmark. It was caught in a trawl in relatively shallow water. No other specimens were found for 14 years, until December 1952 when a second was caught, off the Comoro Islands to the northwest of Madagascar. With this, the true home of the living coelacanth seemed to have been found as, in subsequent years, at least 300 specimens have been caught there, all by local fishermen using baited hooks at depths between 100 and 500 m (330 and 1640 ft). It eventually emerged that the distribution of the fish was restricted to just two of the four Comoro Islands: Grande Comore and Anjouan. Since the fish were caught only at night, the belief developed that they normally lived at deeper depths, coming toward the surface at night after their prey of fish and squid. As the catches predominantly came in the months of the southern summer, other migrations were hypothesized, perhaps to account for the single specimen caught off South Africa. However, this seemed to be contradicted by the observation that coelacanths were physiologically incapable of long periods of sustained swimming effort. Examination of the statistics then began to show that the catch records merely reflected the behavior of the fishermen rather than the fish. Almost all the coelacanths caught were landed by fishermen seeking a different, more commercially attractive fish, *Ruvettus pretiosus*. The possibility remained, therefore, that *L. chalumnae* would be found elsewhere. Meanwhile, there seemed to be a strong correlation between the catches and the underwater topography, *Latimeria* being caught only on or near submarine lava flows so recent that there has been no time for a fringing coral reef system to develop.

Next, undersea explorations showed that in fact the Comoroan coelacanths spend a lot of time in underwater caves in the lava slopes of these volcanic islands, perhaps migrating deeper at night to feed. Studies show that the fishes live in ecologically impoverished environments lacking large shark predators. But these underwater surveys also seemed to show very small population sizes, and the fish appeared threatened with extinction, especially if the local fishing pressure continued.

None of this explained the fact that a specimen had been found off South Africa. In 1992 a fish (a pregnant female) was caught in a trawl off Quelimane, Mozambique, and another was taken, also in a trawl, off the southwest coast of Madagascar in 1995. These occurrences had to be explained as strays from the Comoroan population that had been carried south down the Malagasy Channel by the strong Mozambique Current. This seemed to be confirmed by deoxyribonucleic acid (DNA) analysis of the Mozambique specimen. If so, the Comoroan population was normally restricted, by ecological preference and by

behavior, to a very small localized island setting with a special geological structure.

Specimen from Indonesia. In July 1998 all was changed by the discovery of a living coelacanth in Indonesia. In fact, in the summer of 1997 researchers spotted what seemed to be a coelacanth being taken from Bersehati Market at Manado on the northwest tip of Sulawesi (formerly Celebes). A year later, they obtained a second specimen and confirmed their discovery. A third specimen was caught later. Some researchers consider the Indonesian form to be a separate species from *L. chalumnae*. The researchers' specimen had been caught in a deep trawl set for sharks off the tiny island of Manado Lau, which is of very recent volcanic origin, suggesting that it had been living in an environment similar to that of the Comoroan fishes.

By these discoveries, the known range of living coelacanths has been extended by some 6000 km (3730 mi). From the beginning, ichthyologists had wondered whether the discovery of the living coelacanth and its apparent rarity might in part reflect the absence of fishing industries at 100–200 m (330–660 ft) or more anywhere in the tropical Indo-Pacific, and indeed a paucity of research survey work. The recent Indonesian discoveries confirm this and throw a whole new light on the biology of the living coelacanth, suggesting that it is a very widespread species, although probably locally very patchily distributed according to the availability of suitable volcanic substrates that it needs for some still unknown aspect of its ecology. Individual fishes may undertake significantly long oceanic migrations, aided by currents, perhaps at particular seasons of life-cycle stages. The size of the entire population may not be small; it may for the moment be unknowable. The species might even extend into the Central Pacific Ocean.

Living fossils often appear, from an anthropocentric standpoint, ecologically maladjusted animals and plants hanging on "by their fingernails" in changing environments in which they are barely able to survive, while their sister species have already succumbed to the inevitability of extinction. Their survival is attributed either to success at some very specialized behavior or to extreme generalism. In fact, the living coelacanth may be a quite successful species, as well adapted—if to some quite specialized environment—as any other. Survival of the coelacanth lineage may well reflect the constancy of a particular environment over geological time.

In order to discover the full range of coelacanth distribution, it will be necessary to survey the range of recent volcanic islands across the Indian and Pacific oceans. Meanwhile, there are many features of coelacanth biology that are still unknown. Coelacanths have a curious jointed structure in their head, apparently associated with feeding, but no coelacanth has ever been observed taking its prey and using this joint. On the snout there is a sensory organ, the rostral organ, the function of which is not fully explained. While coelacanths (from at least the

Pennsylvanian to the present) are known to be ovoviviparous, mating and birth have not been observed. No coelacanth has been observed in the open ocean. None have been looked for deeper than about 500 m (1640 ft).

Discoveries in Indonesia have deepened the fascination of scientists and nonscientists alike. While progress may be frustratingly slow and the results often contradictory, the future holds out the prospect of further dramatic developments. *See* ANIMAL EVOLUTION.   Keith S. Thomson

Bibliography. M. V. Erdmann, R. L. Caldwell, and M. K. Moosa, Indonesian "king of the sea" discovered, *Nature*, 395:335, 1998; H. Fricke and R. Plante, Habitat requirements of the living coelacanth *Latimeria chalumnae* at Grande Comore, Indian Ocean, *Naturwissenschaft*, 75:149–151, 1998; U. Schllewen et al., Which home for the coelacanth, *Nature*, 363:405, 1993; J. L. B. Smith, A living fish of Mesozoic type, *Nature*, 143:455–456, 1939; J. L. B. Smith, The second coelacanth, *Nature*, 238:58–59, 1953; K. S. Thomson, The capture and study of two coelacanths off the Comoro Islands, *Nat. Geog. Soc. Res. Rep.*, 13:615–622, 1981; K. S. Thomson, The coelacanth: Act three, *Amer. Sci.*, 87:213–215, 1999.

Complex organic compounds

The question of how life on Earth arose has been a challenging one for many years. Charles Darwin suggested in 1888 that life originated "in some warm little pond, with all sorts of ammonia and phosphoric salts . . . present." Variations on this idea held sway for much of the next century. J. B. S. Haldane suggested in the late 1920s that since cells were basically a series of chemical reactions encased in an oily film, the early Hadean ocean, possessing both in large quantities, would have spontaneously given rise to life. A. I. Oparin expanded on this idea, postulating chemical reactions occurring within micelles of long-chain fatty acids that persisted in that protected environment until they evolved into true cells. Oparin also contributed the valuable concept that these early organisms were heterotrophs; that is, they could utilize molecules that already existed in their environment rather than having to synthesize them through some primitive but already complex photosynthetic mechanism. These theories gained great credibility with the report of the Urey-Miller experiments of the early 1950s. By assuming a simulated reducing atmosphere, as the Earth was thought to have possessed, it was possible to produce a variety of amino acids and other important prebiotic organic molecules in good yield. *See* MOLECULAR FOSSILS.

Unfortunately, several difficulties arose. The model of the early atmosphere was challenged and replaced by a new one containing less methane and ammonia, and more carbon dioxide and carbon monoxide. Under these conditions the Miller-type experiments do not produce the same yields or diversity of prebiotic compounds. There is also the problem of dilution and of chance in the origin of life. In simple terms, organic molecules would have been available only in low concentrations, and the probability of reactions would have been smaller. Furthermore, if the molecules are concentrated in Darwin's "warm shallow pool," then the "primordial soup" is not terribly selective and a complex series of interlocking reactions must then occur completely by chance. The standard argument is that, given enough time, molecules that are able to catalyze their own formation, or co-catalyze the formation of others, will come to dominate the solution.

This is possible, but recent analysis of carbon isotopes in rocks from Greenland indicates that life probably originated roughly 3.8 billion years ago. This was still a time when the Earth was under intense bombardment by meteors and other debris from the early solar system. There was little time for life to arise and gain complexity without being exterminated more than once. This would suggest that by whatever mechanism life arose, the time between prebiotic reactions and stable metabolism was shortened.

Of the several suggestions that have been made to get around this problem, one of the more popular recently has been the suggestion by Wächtershäuser that instead of a low-temperature origin near the Earth's surface, life arose through reactions of prebiotic compounds on iron-sulfur mineral surfaces at deep-sea vents. Acceptance of this view has been helped by the existence of extremophiles, which are bacteria that survive under extremes of heat, pressure, and salinity. Analysis of their genetic code indicates that they are the most primitive organisms known, or the oldest branch on the evolutionary tree. This has been taken to suggest that the ancestor, or ur-bacterium, was an organism adapted to just these conditions. The iron-sulfur vent origin is appealing in that it gives an explanation for the prevalence of iron-sulfur clusters and chemistry in many primitive organisms, and gives a ready source of energy to drive several thermodynamically unfavorable reactions. However, while various synthetic reactions do occur more readily under hydrothermal conditions, destructive reactions are more prevalent and would inhibit the accumulation of organic complexes synthesized under such conditions. Furthermore, modern extremophiles maintain their integrity through fairly sophisticated chaperone proteins and rapid replacement of degraded proteins, an option not available to the proto-organism. An alternative explanation for the extremophile nature of the oldest organisms would be that after life arose under more mild conditions, an early diversification of organisms resulted in extremophiles, which were then the only survivors of some catastrophic event.

It should be noted that when the first organism is discussed, what is actually envisioned is a self-replicating, self-templating, chemical system. This sequence of reactions would be capable of consumption of prebiotic molecules, use of energy, and self-directed replication. The ancestor, or even the proto-organisms of the ribonucleic acid (RNA) world, are already tens, if not hundreds, of millions of years further evolved than the "organisms" discussed here. What is sought is that first set of chemical reactions that crossed the border between abiotic organic chemistry and a recognizable self-sustaining biochemistry.

Formation of basic compounds. Most of the basic prebiotic organic compounds needed to form life were probably available from the environment. The actual atmospheric composition, surface temperature, or prebiotic molecules are not known, so only educated guesses can be made. For example, while the atmosphere itself may have been different from the reducing one postulated by Miller and others in the 1950s, the atmosphere might have been influenced to a considerable degree by volcanic activity. Outgassing from volcanoes would have produced localized versions of the conditions required for the Miller reactions to occur, including the requisite spark in the form of lightning which is common in volcanic clouds. Deep-sea vents, probably demonstrating a chemistry similar to the one postulated by Wächtershäuser, would have contributed sulfur-containing organics, as would the atmospheric reactions when hydrogen sulfide was one of the products of the outgassing. Thioorganics, particularly thioesters, have been suggested to be a stage of prebiotic chemistry before even RNA became commonplace. They have also been implicated in reactions with inorganic phosphate ions in solution to form pyrophosphate (P_2O_7), to form a chemistry similar to the adenosine diphosphate/adenosine triphosphate (ADP/ATP) energy cycle employed by modern organisms. Organics would also have been provided by cometary impacts, which would have provided cyanide derivatives as well, and by the hydrogeothermal cracking of complex hydrocarbons from carbonaceous meteorites. Therefore, it is assumed that appropriate prebiotic monomers were present, and attention can focus on how they formed into proto-living systems.

It is accepted that many biomolecules were not present in their modern form at that time. RNA, the simpler cousin to deoxyribonucleic acid (DNA), is a complex molecule with each unit of its chain built up from three components: a sugar (ribose), an organic component (nucleic acid), and an inorganic component (phosphate). The phosphates are coupled to each other to form the backbone of the RNA chain. Variants of this motif form both information-carrying molecules (RNA) and energy-carrying molecules (ADP/ATP). Unfortunately, this is a high-energy and difficult process. Ribose is unstable at elevated temperatures and hydrolyzes quickly, such that formation of RNA from monomers in modern cells involves a large, complex protein known as a polymerase, which obviously would have been unavailable in prebiotic time. Therefore, it has been suggested that the early RNA would instead have been a protein nucleic acid (PNA), with an amino acid chain replacing both the phosphate and sugar portions of RNA. These molecules have been investigated as antisense agents for medicinal use, and have been found to form more stable Watson-Crick base pairs than DNA or RNA; this would have been a useful trait in the early days when concentrations of monomers were low. It is commonly assumed that these molecules formed spontaneously until by chance one acquired the ability to catalyze the formation of itself. Autocatalysis or co-catalysis would give a slight advantage to molecules capable of it, allowing them to reproduce more readily and rapidly to become the dominant species in the solution.

Mineral surfaces. Even with the ease of synthesis of the correct organic precursors, it is still difficult to reproduce this hypothetical chemistry. RNA has been shown to autocatalyze, but only in the case of carefully designed sequences. It has been suggested by several researchers, notably A. G. Cairns-Smith, that there must have been an earlier stage when some other material performed the functions of modern-day enzymes. In his genetic takeover model, the free-floating, autocatalytic proto-life did not arise from an undifferentiated primordial soup, but by using the surface of clay minerals as a reactive scaffold to perform many metabolic functions, including ordered replication and catalysis. Once the supported reactions gained sufficient complexity to template and catalyze their own formation, they diffused into solution, and the role of the clay vanished from the biochemical record.

This is not an unreasonable model, since clays fulfill many requirements of an early component of metabolism. They have a layered silicate structure, with two-dimensional surfaces separated by water layers, ordered in nature, possessing catalytic sites, and easily incorporating metals from the environment. They provide a semicrystalline ordered surface, which would have allowed prebiotic organics to adsorb in ordered patterns and to react in repeatable fashion. The primary difficulty is that clays are primarily hydrophilic in nature, thereby attracting polar molecules and repelling organics. Therefore it is doubted that they would bind the organic precursors well, which would inhibit accumulation of sufficient material to evolve into a complex metabolism. Some evidence to the contrary is the observation that one clay, montmorillonite, has been shown to catalyze the formation of small polypeptides under mild environmental conditions. It has not, however, been shown to form longer chains.

Organophilic siliceous minerals. Recent research has led to the conclusion that a more organophilic surface, capable of a finer local modification than that demonstrated by the clay-type minerals, is the probable scaffold upon which the first proto-organisms formed. Either naturally occurring zeolites or more probably feldspar-type minerals are viewed

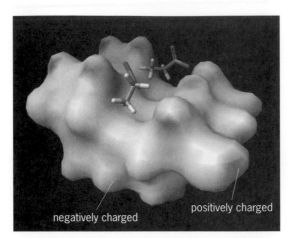

Fig. 1. Two amino acids lying in a channel on a mineral surface. The surface is solvent-accessible, and is locally positively charged, negatively charged, or neutral. The charged portions will attract polar atoms such as oxygen or nitrogen, while the neutral majority will not bind such atoms, preferring to bind nonpolar hydrocarbon groups instead. The combination of the regularly spaced charged sites in the channel helps to orient the amino acids. The positively charged amino group of one acid is oriented toward the negatively charged carboxylate group of the other. Elimination of water will allow the formation of a peptide bond, which extends a growing protein chain.

as the likely candidates. Both complexes will hereafter be referred to as silicaceous minerals. Such minerals are organophilic, possess channel structures to act as vessels for reaction and to control local molecular geometries, have the requisite catalytic sites, and easily incorporate water, metals, and organic molecules into the channels in their structures. Acidic sites on a mineral surface may serve as an anchor

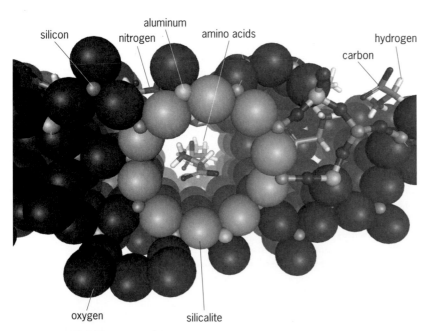

Fig. 2. A 10-ring channel of silicalite with several glycine amino acids encapsulated within. The aluminum atoms substitute for silicon in the structure, causing a local charge deficiency which is compensated through the conversion of a neighboring bridging oxygen (Si-O-Al) bond into a bridging hydroxyl (Si-(OH)-Al). These hydroxyl sites are catalytic acidic sites.

for an amino acid or nucleic acid, from which a polymeric chain may extend while being held near appropriate reaction sites (**Fig. 1**). The channel structure would then serve to concentrate the reactants in a small area so as to increase the likelihood of reaction, protect them from environmental degradation, and assist in orienting them so as to facilitate reaction. Zeolites were initially employed as a model, since they are a commonly used industrial catalyst for the reasons mentioned above, a large body of literature is therefore available, and they allow a simpler model system to be constructed. The zeolite known as silicalite was used; it possesses channels made up of a ring of 12 oxygen atoms connecting adjacent silicon atoms (**Fig. 2**). Monte Carlo–type simulations showed that approximately 28 glycine residues, or 8 larger molecules, such as adenine, could easily be incorporated per unit cell. Furthermore, the structure of the zeolite channel helped to confine the amino acids to the center by restricting their lateral motion, helping to arrange them correctly for polymerization. The polypeptide chain would grow to a certain size dependent upon the channel dimensions and would gradually diffuse outward where it could interact with other molecules in solution or along the silica surface. It could also remain tethered as in Fig. 2, where a nucleic acid, adenine, has coordinated to an acid site on the surface of the channel and thereby serves as an anchor for a growing PNA chain.

In practice, it is more likely that larger grooves and pits in feldspars would provide the requisite mineral surface because of their much greater abundance in the natural world. These surface features would provide the same catalytic and protective function that the zeolite model does while providing a greater surface area on which to react, thereby increasing the concentration of primitive biopolymers. A protected groove or channel within a feldspar, derivatized with acidic and metal-ion functional groups, would provide the same function as the modern cell wall. A channel system, open at one end, would therefore serve as the primitive model of a cell. Organic precursors would diffuse in from the outside, and systems that were not quite autocatalytic would react on the mineral surface in an ordered manner with these. The channel would provide both the catalytic sites, and a protective environment. Haldane's "oily sea" would accumulate on the outside surfaces of such silicaceous minerals; and daily hot/cold cycles, plus mild agitation from the Hadean ocean, would serve to incorporate molecules that floated free from the channels into micelles. Therefore proto-cells made up of fatty acid micelles and encapsulated semiliving chemical reactions would not arise by a fortuitous combination of free-floating chemicals, but through incorporation of well-defined metabolisms. The advantage of this system lies in the structure and catalytic properties of the silicaceous substrate, which facilitates the origin and evolution of complex systems more readily than the undifferentiated "primordial soup." The substrate would either facilitate the rate of reactions or allow several disparate paths to emerge simultaneously. By adaptation and chemical evolution, one set of reactions will rapidly displace the less efficient alternatives and will become the root of all subsequent organisms.

Outlook. There is some skepticism as to the origin of the prebiotic molecules from the environment and, to a certain extent, as to which specific set of reactions (PNA, thioesters, pure-inorganic templating) actually gave rise to life on Earth. However, the evidence supports an externally catalyzed system under environmentally fairly mild conditions, as the first stage on the path to an independent biochemistry. One speculative addendum is that should the low-temperature, mineral-templated, prebiotic synthesis be correct, then it is possible that certain exotic environments, such as Jupiter's upper atmosphere or the hydrocarbon-covered surface of Saturn's moon, Titan, may also serve as incubators for proto-life. Although the technical challenges of verifying this hypothesis at either site are daunting, it would give much credence to the commonly held view that life is stubborn and ubiquitous, the almost inevitable product of a chemical system reaching sufficient complexity to self-organize.

For background information *see* ADENOSINE DIPHOSPHATE (ADP); ADENOSINE TRIPHOSPHATE (ATP); AMINO ACIDS; ATMOSPHERE, EVOLUTION OF; BACTERIA; BIOSPHERE; DEOXYRIBONUCLEIC ACID; ENZYME; HYDROTHERMAL VENT; MINERAL; NUCLEIC ACID; ORGANIC CHEMISTRY; ORGANIC EVOLUTION; ORGANIC SYNTHESIS; PREBIOTIC ORGANIC SYNTHESIS; PROTEIN; ZEOLITE in the McGraw-Hill Encyclopedia of Science & Technology.   Fred Arnold

Bibliography. A. G. Cairns-Smith, *Seven Clues to the Origin of Life: A Scientific Detective Story*, Cambridge University Press, 1991; F. Dyson, *Origin of Life*, Cambridge University Press, 1999; A. I. Oparin, *Genesis and Evolutionary Development of Life*, Academic Press, 1968; A. I. Oparin, *Origin of Life*, Dover, 1953.

Composite structures

Fiber steering is an emerging design concept for advanced fiber-reinforced composite materials and structures. Steered-fiber architecture has the potential to offer significant weight savings over conventional composite materials by improving tailoring of local fiber orientation to the specific internal load path of a structure. Increased complexity in fabrication of steered-fiber composites can now be handled easily by existing automated manufacturing techniques.

Background. Historically, research in composite manufacturing technology has focused on performance rather than cost considerations. This trend changed during the 1990s with new strict cost guidelines on emerging civil and military platforms, such as the Joint Strike Fighter. Industry has responded to the low-cost-composites challenge by developing innovative manufacturing techniques, including producing unitized parts with automated processes. The most significant technology promising reduced-cost fabrication is the fiber placement process, which allows large, complex-shaped composite structures to be produced faster, approximately 40% cheaper, and with greater quality than traditional approaches. Fiber placement has been used to manufacture military hardware such as the inlet duct of the Joint Strike Fighter and the landing gear pod fairing of the C-17 transport, as well as lighter aircraft for civil aviation.

Fiber placement. Fiber placement technology is a modern, automated method of manufacturing complex composite structures cost-effectively. Fiber placement is a unique process combining the differential material payout capability of filament winding and the compaction and cut-restart capabilities of automatic tape laying. In the fiber placement process, narrow (about 0.3 cm or 0.125 in.) strips or tows of resin-impregnated fiber are drawn under tension across a tool geometry by a computer-controlled head. This head is capable of delivering up to approximately 30 adjacent tows simultaneously, allowing for high production rates. The narrow tows provide precise control over fiber orientation, and since each tow can be controlled independently thickness tapers of complex geometry are readily produced. Fiber adds and cuts (the starts and stops of individual tows) are controlled through a computer-aided design (CAD) interface. The feed rate of each tow is also individually controlled, allowing the longer-path outside tows of a steered radius to feed faster than the shorter-path inside tows (**Fig. 1**). The ability to support differential tow feed rates combined with the ability to drop individual tows provides the opportunity to place fibers along a relatively tight radius with no degradation in component quality.

Fiber steering is made possible by local compaction during placement and because the impregnated tow has enough tack to overcome any sliding forces. When tows are steered through a radius, the fibers on the outside of the radius are placed in tension and the fibers on the inside of the radius are placed in compression; but since fibers are inextensible the fibers along the inside radius can buckle

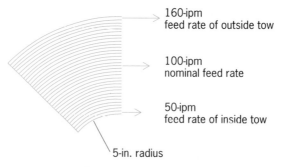

Fig. 1. Steered 45° band, illustrating the difference in feed rate across the band.

if steering is severe. Industry quality-assurance programs have demonstrated that using fiber placement technology, carbon-epoxy fiber path geometry can be tailored to a maximum steering radius of 50 cm (20 in.) with no loss in specimen quality. Tighter steering radii are possible if the extent of the steering is not severe, for example if the arc radius extends less than 45°. In contrast, tape laying equipment [another automated process utilizing single bands of material approximately 15 cm (6 in.) in width] is restricted to maximum steering radii in excess of 66 m (20 ft), or almost no steering. Manual methods of composite fabrication preclude any steering at all.

Typical fiber-placed parts might generate 2–15% material scrap, compared with 50–100% for conventional hand layup. The reduced material scrap rate directly equates to acquisition cost savings due to reduced material usage. Furthermore, the large unitized structures that can be fabricated equate to life-cycle cost savings due to reduced nonrecurring costs, touch labor, and part tracking. Finally, the automated process leads to increased accuracy (thus improved quality) and to reduced costs due to fewer processing errors and scrapped parts.

A key advantage of fiber placement that has been largely overlooked is the capability of fiber steering. Fiber steering offers potential weight savings by overcoming the restriction of discrete linear fiber orientations commonly associated with traditional composites. This is best explained by examining the differences in the design processes for conventional composites and for fiber-placed composites. With conventional hand-layup composites, one starts with tape or fabric plies of linear fiber orientation, and assembles these into desired stacks of laminate families (combinations of various orientations in a preferential stacking sequence). A ply boundary is discrete, and fiber orientation is fixed within that boundary. Thus, for a given component there are two predominant design conditions to consider: the overall laminate thickness required, and the proper combination and stacking of various ply or lamina orientations. To change either thickness or orientation requires a

discontinuity in one or more plies. In other words, these requirements necessitate a ply termination at a boundary between adjacent regions of differing orientation. Ply terminations to produce a change in orientation unnecessarily increase the overall number of plies, which results in an increased manufacturing cost. This limitation is magnified by current analytical techniques that focus on laminate optimization and not ply optimization, thus producing design concepts that are not optimized for manufacturability or production cost. The fiber placement process, however, allows tailoring of the composite structure within a ply level by placing composite tows along curvilinear paths. Fiber orientation is free to vary within a discrete ply boundary. This capability offers the potential for optimized structural configurations by tailoring fiber paths within a ply to load paths of the component. This capability was precluded with hand layup due to the prohibitive cost of the required touch labor. There is now the potential to produce reduced-weight fiber-steered components with no increase in manufacturing cost.

Steering mechanics. Steered concepts can have each layer independently steered, or can be linked such that the laminate or 0° axis is steered and a more conventional laminate family analysis is performed (though the thickness layers are restricted to orientations of 0°, 45°, −45°, and 90° with respect to some curvilinear laminate axis). There is some logic to the latter approach, as primary loading takes the form of axial, transverse, and shear components that are best handled by the four primary fiber axes identified. A steered-fiber composite can orient the primary local laminate axis to follow the path of the principal loads, and the laminate family (percentage of fiber reinforcement in each of the principal material directions) can be optimized based upon the magnitude of local load components.

Fiber-placed and fiber-steered composite materials exhibit specific fiber architecture flaws that can affect the mechanical performance of the final component. These flaws include gaps and overlaps of adjacent tows (**Fig. 2**). It is logical to expect that if

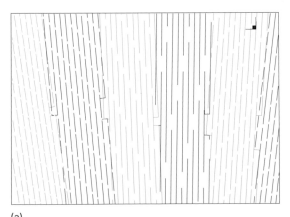
(a)

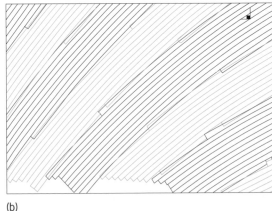
(b)

Fig. 2. Linked fiber steering in (a) ±90° and (b) 45° layers, showing increased overlaps and gaps.

a local gap or overlap can affect mechanical performance, then repeating patterns of these flaws can have a magnified effect. This interaction behavior is documented in conventional laminates with out-of-plane waves and in woven or braided textile composites.

Development. Preliminary investigations have been performed to assess the potential weight savings of fiber-steering technology. These preliminary studies utilized simple to complex geometry and combined load cases. Results from these studies indicate weight savings of up to 30% for simple idealized structures due merely to the effect of steered fibers. More realistic studies on representative aircraft structures such as an advanced military aircraft wing illustrate less dramatic but still significant weight reduction. Weight savings of 7–10% are expected for real-world structures when manufacturability and structural stability are considered as design constraints. Since this weight savings comes at no increased cost to manufacture, the potential advantage is quite appealing. These preliminary analyses, however, assume that the steered-fiber composite behaves in the same manner as traditional fiber composites.

Ongoing research will provide significant advancements in understanding the mechanical performance of fiber-steered composite materials, enabling improved design and analysis of the fiber placement process, particularly with respect to steering. This information will allow future engineers to readily incorporate steered fiber structures into a variety of consumer products.

For background information, *see* COMPOSITE MATERIAL; MANUFACTURED FIBER in the McGraw-Hill Encyclopedia of Science & Technology.   Rick Hale

Bibliography. Boeing Company, *Fiber Steering for Reduced Weight Affordable Composite Structure*, Contract N00140-95-2-J044 awarded by the Office of Naval Research Center of Excellence for Composites Manufacturing Technology, April 1997 to April 1998; V. P. McConnell, Fiber-placed C-17 landing gear pod fairings reduce price and parts, *High Perform. Composites*, 6(4):48–50, July/August 1998; B. McIlroy, Boeing Company, *Fiber Placement Benchmark and Technology Roadmap Guidelines*, final report, Air Force Research Laboratory contract F33615-95-2-5563, July 1999; E. H. Phillips, *Premier 1* readied for first flight, *Aviat. Week Space Technol.*, 149(9):39, August 31, 1998; A. L. Velocci, R & D unit pressed to save $1 billion, *Aviat. Week Space Technol.*, 148(19):75–76, May 11, 1998.

Computational aeroacoustics

Airplanes, helicopters, and high-speed road vehicles all produce annoying sounds or noise. Industrial processes and machinery produce noise, as do home appliances such as vacuum cleaners and fans. Some sounds such as music are pleasing to the ear, but most unwanted sounds cause annoyance to humans; the level of annoyance depends on the loudness, the du-

ration, and the frequency content of the sound. Some sounds have dominant tones, such as the "singing" of high-voltage power lines in strong winds, and others are broadband, such as the noise of a jet-engine take-off.

The science of aerodynamically generated sound is called aeroacoustics. The theoretical framework for this branch of acoustics was pioneered by James Lighthill in the 1950s. Aeroacoustics includes a study of how particular sounds are produced; how they are propagated through air, water, or other media, including propagation in ducts carrying fluid flows; how they interact with obstacles, barriers, or wave-bearing surfaces; how they radiate away; how they can be managed or controlled; and how they are measured or predicted.

Mathematical models. Computational aeroacoustics is a study of the problems of aeroacoustics using computational techniques. The first step involves the formulation of a suitable mathematical model. This could be in a form of the wave equation or a more complex set of equations describing the flow problem and its associated acoustics. For example, to find how the radiation pattern of the noise from road vehicles on an expressway is affected by the design of barriers built along the road, the mathematical model of the acoustic wave equation is sufficient. Of course, good descriptions of the noise sources associated with the road vehicles, and realistic boundary conditions to represent the barriers, need to be used. However, more complex mathematical

Fig. 1. Sound radiation pattern from an engine inlet. Noise sources specified at the fan face set up the spinning modes within the inlet duct. The noise radiation pattern is visualized on two hypothetical surfaces placed near the inlet duct. (*Courtesy of Lyle Long*)

models are needed in many problems of aeroacoustics. Such a problem is determining the impact of different inlet-nacelle designs on the noise of a ducted fan in an aircraft engine. The mean flow around the engine nacelle needs to be solved first. A compressible mean flow solver, such as commonly employed in computational fluid dynamics, can be used. The sound propagation can be described next, using linearized (or nonlinear) disturbance equations. Again, a representation of the sources of the fan noise, and suitable duct-wall boundary conditions, are needed (**Fig. 1**).

Other noise problems require many more details of the unsteady flow phenomena. The noise of helicopter blades, the noise of high-lift airframe configurations, and the noise of high-speed jet exhaust are common examples.

A mathematical representation needs to be chosen depending on the specific objectives of the study. In this way the flow features most central to the noise problem are retained, while other details are removed. For example, in the noise due to high-speed jet exhaust, the large-scale turbulent eddies of the jet are believed to be central to the generation of the peak noise. A mathematical model which retains the large scales of jet turbulence, such as the large-eddy simulation, would then suffice for predicting the peak noise. Recently, it has also become possible to base aeroacoustic predictions on first principles, by a direct calculation resolving all scales of fluid motion (**Fig. 2**). Such a direct numerical simulation can be used to study the noise-generation

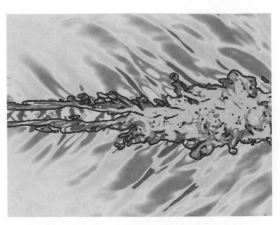

Fig. 2. Direct computation of noise radiation from a high-speed turbulent jet. A supersonic jet at Mach number of 1.92 and Reynolds number of 2000 is computed with 2.2×10^7 grid points using high-order compact schemes. The contours of vorticity in the middle of the figure show the breakdown of the jet shear layers into turbulence. The radiated sound is shown via contours of dilatation, or the rate of expansion of the local fluid volume. (*Courtesy of Jonathan Freund*)

processes from a fundamental viewpoint, and can be exploited in research on approximate-hybrid methods for more practical use. *See* DIRECT NUMERICAL SIMULATION; TURBULENCE MODELING.

Discretization. Once a mathematical model (the governing equations and boundary conditions) for the problem of interest has been identified, the next step is a careful discretization of the mathematical model which can be solved on a computer.

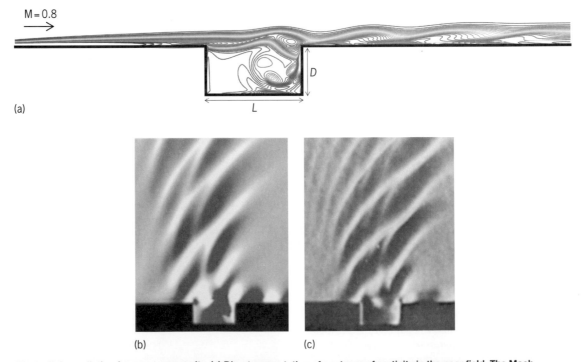

Fig. 3. Noise radiation from an open cavity. (*a*) Direct computation of contours of vorticity in the near field. The Mach number is 0.8; $L/D = 2$; and Re_θ, the Reynolds number based on the momentum thickness of the laminar incoming boundary layer, is 57. The ratio L/θ, where θ is the momentum thickness, is equal to 53. There are two primary resonant frequencies f detected at Strouhal number $St = fL/U = 0.61$ (dominant) and $St = 0.36$. (*b*) False Schlieren image of the direct numerical simulation (contours of the steamwise gradient of density) of the sound radiated by the flow over the open cavity. (*c*) Experimental Schlieren image. (*Courtesy of Tim Colonius*)

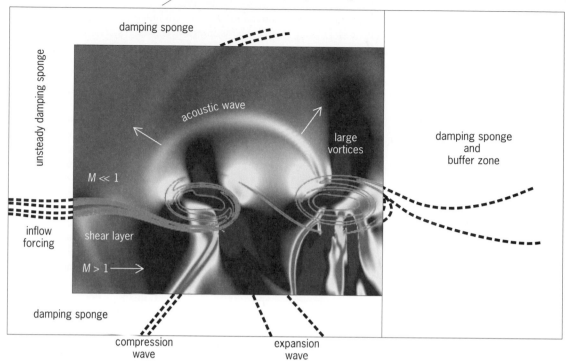

Fig. 4. Model problem of screech noise generation. The interaction of shear-layer vortices with the shock-cell structure in a jet, modeled here as a compression wave and its reflection as an expansion wave, generates strong acoustic waves when the amplitude of the shear-layer disturbances is sufficiently large. The radiated sound waves can be seen as the two cylindrical waves in the visualization of dilatation above the shear layer. The unsteady flow and the radiated sound are calculated via direct numerical simulation. The methods used to specify boundary conditions (damping sponge, unsteady damping sponge, and damping sponge and buffer zone) are indicated. (*Courtesy of Ted Manning*)

The discretization may involve the use of finite differences, the finite element method, or some hybrid technique. In the simplest cases this amounts to obtaining a numerical solution of the acoustic wave equation, but in most aeroacoustics problems a much more complex unsteady flow problem needs to be solved. Depending on the complexity of the mathematical model, the numerical solutions can be obtained on a personal computer or may require the use of a high-performance computational platform.

Numerical and modeling challenges. Even for the loudest noise sources, such as the launch of the space shuttle, the energy radiated away as sound is modest. A sound wave with a pressure disturbance of 0.1% of the ambient mean pressure corresponds approximately to a noise level of 130 decibels and would cause pain in human eardrums. Persistent exposure to such noise can cause permanent hearing impairment.

The noise levels encountered in aviation or in the industrial environment are usually much lower. Stringent regulations mandating acceptable noise levels exist in different industries. Numerical prediction of sound fields relevant to technological applications requires that the methods used have the ability to accurately track sound waves of modest-to-low amplitude.

Often the sound waves need to be propagated over distances which are large compared to the wave-length of the sound wave, and in many circumstances the overall sound field is the result of constructive and destructive interference between the waves originating from different regions. Since human hearing typically extends over the frequency range of 20 Hz–20 kHz, a rather broad range of frequencies needs to be predicted to allow an assessment of the annoyance due to the noise.

Error minimization. Predicting noise levels and radiation patterns requires that the numerical methods used accurately preserve the phase and amplitude of the sound waves over the expected range of frequencies. In a more technical language, the dispersion and dissipation errors associated with the numerical schemes need to minimized. Numerical tests on a range of benchmark test problems have shown that low-order and upwinded schemes, popular in industrial uses of computational fluid dynamics, are inappropriate for computational aeroacoustics. Special numerical schemes [such as compact or Pade schemes, and dispersion relation–preserving (DRP) schemes] which minimize dispersion and dissipation errors over a wide range of scales perform much better. Typically schemes with high accuracy (fourth-order or higher) which are further optimized to better represent the wave phenomena are good candidates for use in computational aeroacoustics.

Similar numerical requirements also arise in simulations of other wave phenomena such as elastic

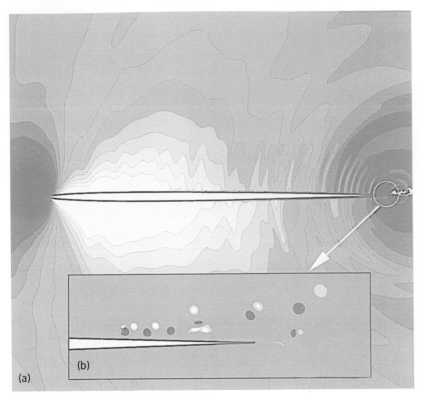

Fig. 5. Composite visualization of acoustic scattering from the trailing edge of an airfoil due to vortical disturbances passing over it. Two-dimensional Euler equations were solved on a multiblock mesh chosen to resolve the very small vortices shed by a very small vertical plate placed one plate length above the upper surface of the airfoil at 98% chord. The free-stream Mach number is 0.2. The vortices shed by the plate convect over the trailing edge of the airfoil and scatter acoustic waves. (*a*) Complete airfoil with gray-scale contours of the density. The nondimensional density contours vary between 0.999 and 1.001. The light regions have lower density, the dark regions have higher density. (*b*) Magnified view of the region near the trailing edge. Gray-scale contours of vorticity are shown. Dark regions are positive vorticity, light regions are negative vorticity. (*Courtesy of Bart Singer*)

waves in solids (computational solid mechanics) and electromagnetic wave scattering (computational electromagnetics), in magnetohy-drodynamics, and in direct numerical simulation of turbulence.

Boundary conditions. Additional numerical challenges in computational aeroacoustics arise from the requirement of accurate and robust boundary conditions. The physical domain of the simulation is chosen to adequately capture the expected flow and acoustic phenomena. However, it is essential to ensure that the physical disturbances which reach the computational boundary continue to evolve in a way which mimics the processes which would have occurred had the domain been much larger. In other words, numerical boundary conditions are required to replicate or simulate the physical behavior of acoustic and nonacoustic disturbances at a fictitious boundary.

Computational boundaries need to behave as nonreflecting or anechoic for acoustic disturbances propagating out of the domain, and allow other nonacoustic flow disturbances such as vortices and entropy nonuniformities to convect out silently, that is, without the generation of spurious reflected waves. **Figures 3** and **4** illustrate the numerical challenges faced in specifying boundary conditions for compu-

tational aeroacoustics. In some problems, specific incoming disturbances need to be imposed, while maintaining the nonreflection of outgoing disturbances. Numerical challenges also arise in treating complex geometrical shapes while maintaining tight control over dispersion and dissipation errors, in treating surfaces with sharp edges and corners, and in treating nonlinear acoustic waves which steepen to form shock waves.

Disparities in low-speed flow. A further challenge is faced in studies of the noise produced by low-speed or low-Mach-number flows, typical of hydroacoustics or underwater noise. In this case, there is also a large length-scale disparity between the sound waves and the characteristic length scale of the unsteady flow generating the noise. For instance, the aeolian tones of a high-voltage electricity cable (2.5 cm or 1 in. in diameter) when exposed to a cross-wind (of 20 m/s or 45 mi/h) are associated with the unsteady forces on the cable due to vortex shedding. The frequency of these tones is low (approximately 160 Hz for the case considered here), giving a dominant acoustic wavelength much larger than the cable diameter (80 times in the present case). Numerically resolving both the unsteady flow and the sound it generates becomes very challenging (**Fig. 5**).

Hybrid methods. The situation can be helped by use of hybrid methods designed specially for low-Mach-number flows. Several variants of hybrid methods are possible with the common theme of separating the overall problem into two parts. First the unsteady flow is simulated in a limited region. Then some form of aeroacoustic theory is exploited to relate the unsteady flow data to the sound radiated by the flow. It is also possible to carry out this second step with a numerical solution which uses data from the unsteady flow calculation. Sound is regarded in these hybrid approaches as a small by-product of the unsteady flow. It is also assumed that the sound produced by the flow does not affect the flow itself. This assumption is sometimes questionable.

Acoustic feedback. Processes such as edge tones in jets, supersonic jet screech, cavity resonances, and combustion instability are examples of situations with acoustic feedback. The approach of direct computation of aerodynamic noise avoids a priori assumptions since the sound and the unsteady flow are treated as different parts of the same overall flow. But the amplitude disparity between the nonacoustic flow disturbances and the radiated sound demands a very exacting peformance from the numerical algorithms (Figs. 2, 3, and 4).

Progress and prospects. Despite these formidable challenges, significant progress has been made in the numerical algorithms for computational aeroacoustics and in the application of computational aeroacoustics to study model noise problems motivated by technological applications. Research continues in both areas. Better numerical boundary conditions, and more robust numerical schemes which minimize dispersion and dissipation errors would be useful. Applying the computational aeroacoustics methods to problems of practical interest also requires further development of hybrid methods. Ideally, it should be possible to compute the details of the unsteady flow with high fidelity only in the noise-producing region and blend this solution with a lower-fidelity calculation of the rest of the flow. Similarly, it is desirable to estimate the noise radiated by the processes not captured in a calculation so that the predictions made by computational aeroacoustics can be extrapolated. Hybrid schemes which effectively combine aeroacoustic theory with numerical simulations are also needed. But ultimately the research in computational aeroacoustics aims toward a better understanding of the noise-generation mechanisms and methods to suppress or control the unwanted noise.

For background information *see* ACOUSTIC NOISE; AIRCRAFT NOISE; COMPUTATIONAL FLUID DYNAMICS; KÁRMÁN VORTEX STREET; SOUND; TURBULENT FLOW in the McGraw-Hill Encyclopedia of Science & Technology.   Sanjiva K. Lele

Bibliography. S. K. Lele, Direct Numerical Simulations of Compressible Turbulent Flows: Fundamentals and Applications, *Invited Lectures at the 2d ERCOFTAC Summer School on Transition and Turbulence Modeling*, ed. by H. Alfredsson et al., Kluwer Academic, 1999; C. K. W. Tam, Computational aeroacoustics: Issues and methods, *AIAA J.*, 33: 1788–1796, 1995.

Computational fluid dynamics

In the past three decades, there has been enormous progress in the development of computational methods for the study of fluid flow over flight vehicles. Computational simulations, combined with experimental testing, afford a cost-effective means of evaluating numerous geometrical modifications required for developing flight vehicles. Computational analysis of the aerodynamic performance of a flight vehicle requires a multistep process. First, a geometric description of the configuration is obtained in discretized form; second, a grid is generated around the object, which provides a set of points on which the flowfield solution is calculated by solving the appropriate governing equations of fluid dynamics. Enormous amounts of flowfield solution data for pressure, temperature, and velocity variables are then processed to obtain the aerodynamic quantities of interest, namely, the lift, drag, moment coefficients, and other parameters required to assess the flight vehicle's performance. This article briefly describes the current state of the art in geometry modeling, mesh generation, numerical algorithms, and turbulence modeling as it relates to the Euler/Navier-Stokes simulations of whole-body transport and fighter aircraft.

Geometry modeling. In the aerospace industry, the geometric description of the aircraft configuration in discretized form is created using a computer-aided design (CAD) system. Geometry processing involves

defining an accurate numerical description of all solid components by using the CAD data.

Surface mesh generation. Surface grid generation involves determining the desired distribution of grid points on the surface of the body (based on the expected flow characteristics) by using the mathematically accurate description of the geometry. However, generation of a satisfactory surface grid from CAD data is a difficult task because these data in general contain gaps, overlaps, and a variety of geometry output formats. The main approach to address this problem has been to cover the irregular patches from the CAD data with a regular set of patches which are then converted to nonuniform rational B-splines (NURBS) or rational Bezier curves.

Bezier curves are free-form curves described by higher-order polynomials, which can be manipulated by control points. Designers know the shapes of the curves they want, but do not know the coefficients of the polynomials. Various schemes are used to provide a physical (intuitive) link between the shape and the coefficients. A general Bezier curve of degree n blends $n + 1$ control points, each of which affects the entire curve between the start and end points. B-spline curves blend together control points, also called knots. The effect of each of the control points lies within a local region that can be controlled independently. Therefore, B-spline curves are better suited for representing long curves. Bezier curves are a special form of B-spline curves.

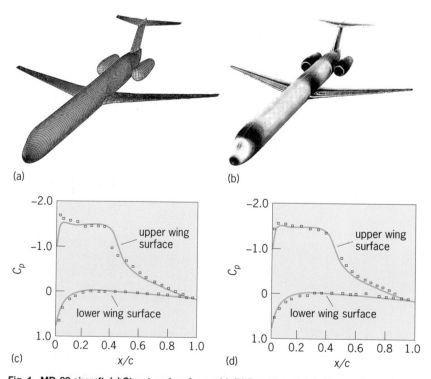

(a)   (b)

(c)   (d)

Fig. 1. MD-80 aircraft. (*a*) Structured surface grid. (*b*) Pressure distribution on the surface. The graphs permit comparison of computed and experimental surface pressure at two wing-span locations: (*c*) 42% semispan and (*d*) 79% semispan. Curves show Navier-Stokes computations, and nearby data points show experimental data. (*After R. K. Agarwal, Computational fluid dynamics of whole-body aircraft, Annu. Rev. Fluid Mech., 31:125–169, 1999*)

Surface grids are then generated on the NURBS carpet composed of interfacing NURBS patches. Surface grids can be structured or unstructured. A structured grid (**Fig. 1***a*) covers the entire body by establishing an appropriate mapping from physical to computational space for the desired point distribution on the surface, while the unstructured grid (**Fig. 2***a*) covers the entire body by establishing an ordering of nodes and background mesh for the desired surface point distribution.

(a)

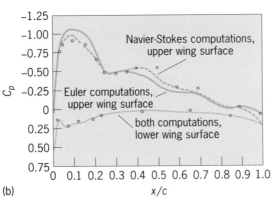

(b)

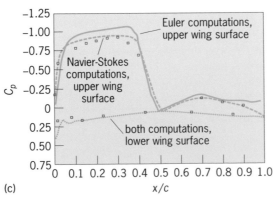

(c)

Fig. 2. F-15 aircraft. (*a*) Unstructured surface grid. The graphs permit comparison of computed and experimental surface pressure at two wing-span locations: (*b*) 59% semispan and (*c*) 86% semispan. Curves show Euler computations with ULTRA and Navier-Stokes computations with NASTD; nearby data points show experimental data. (*After R. K. Agarwal, Computational fluid dynamics of whole-body aircraft, Annu. Rev. Fluid Mech., 31:125–169, 1999*)

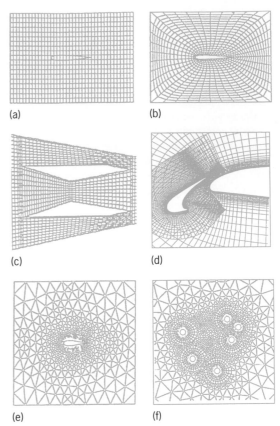

Fig. 3. Types of meshes. (*a*) Cartesian mesh. (*b*) Body-fitted single-block structured mesh. (*c*) Body-fitted multiblock structured mesh. (*d*) Chimera mesh. (*e*) Unstructured mesh. (*f*) Hybrid structured-unstructured mesh. (*After R. K. Agarwal, Computational fluid dynamics of whole-body aircraft, Annu. Rev. Fluid Mech., 31:125–169, 1999*)

Volume grid generation. Once the surface grid is generated on the body of the aircraft, a surface mesh is created on a chosen simple shape (such as the surface of a sphere, an ellipsoid, or a parallelepiped) at the outer or farfield boundary of the computational domain. With surface mesh created at the aircraft surface and at the outer computational boundary, the three-dimensional volume mesh is then generated by using algebraic or partial differential equation–based grid generation techniques for structured grids and Delaunay or advancing-front-based techniques for unstructured grids.

Under the broad categories of structured and unstructured grids, a variety of grid generation strategies have been developed for volume grid generation about complex three-dimensional configurations. They can be categorized (**Fig. 3**) as cartesian mesh, single-block body-fitted structured mesh, multiblock body-fitted structured mesh, overlapping or chimera structured mesh, unstructured mesh, and hybrid structured-unstructured mesh. All six types of meshes offer some advantages and some disadvantages as they relate to issues such as implementation of boundary conditions on the body surface, grid adaptation, automatization of the grid

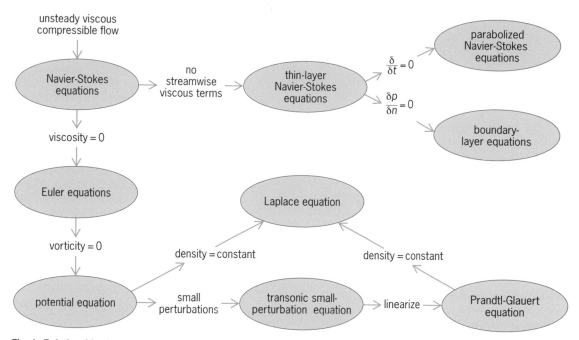

Fig. 4. Relationships between the equations of fluid dynamics for mathematical models of various complexities. (*After R. K. Agarwal, Computational fluid dynamics of whole-body aircraft, Annu. Rev. Fluid Mech., 31:125–169, 1999*)

generation process, and the time required to generate the grid, especially for a complete aircraft configuration. For example, the cartesian mesh (Fig. 3a) is the simplest and most straightforward way of gridding a computational domain; however, the accurate implementation of boundary conditions on the body surface requires careful consideration because of the staircasing effect of the cartesian grid on the surface, which results in a lack of smoothness in the implementation of boundary conditions. Body-fitted single-block (Fig. 3b) or multiblock grids (Fig. 3c) are excellent for implementation of boundary conditions; however, the grid generation process is extremely time-consuming because of the difficulty in achieving automation. Furthermore, the grid adaptation in three dimensions has been extremely difficult. The overlapping or chimera grids (Fig. 3d) offer considerable flexibility and, in addition, can address multiple moving-body problems which occur, for example, when a bomb or missile is ejected from a fighter aircraft (store separation). However, the automation of the grid-generation process and, to some degree, grid adaptation remain the major issues with the chimera approach for complex three-dimensional configurations. In recent years, unstructured grids (Fig. 3e) have shown the most promise in terms of dealing with geometric complexity, grid adaptation, and automation of the grid generation process. However, the difficulties remain in generation of high-quality grids for turbulent flow simulations requiring high-aspect-ratio cells near the body surface.

Numerical algorithms. For flowfield solutions, the mathematical models vary in complexity from simple Laplace equations to unsteady compressible Navier-Stokes equations (**Fig. 4**). Physically the most complete model describing the continuum behavior of an unsteady, compressible, viscous, heat-conducting fluid is the unsteady compressible Navier-Stokes equations, but they are mathematically the most difficult to solve. A mathematically simpler set of equations can be obtained by invoking some physical assumptions such as viscosity $= 0$, vorticity $= 0$, constant density, pressure gradient normal to the solid surface $(\delta p/\delta n) = 0$, or unsteadiness $(\delta/\delta t) = 0$. The simpler sets of equations, which are designated by special names, can be employed to analyze flow fields where an invoked assumption remains valid in order to capture the relevant physics of the problem.

During the late 1960s, panel methods were developed for calculating the inviscid subsonic flow about complex aerodynamic shapes by solving the Laplace equation. Also, boundary-layer solution techniques were developed to allow for viscous effects, primarily for attached flows. During the early 1970s, a major breakthrough was achieved for solving the mixed elliptic-hyperbolic transonic small-disturbance equation which was later extended to the solution of the transonic full-potential equation. Transonic full-potential codes are now routinely used in transport aircraft design and have proven to be an effective tool (sometimes combined with boundary-layer codes) for predicting the aerodynamic performance of a variety of flight vehicles in the transonic range.

Since the 1980s, driven by the availability of advanced computing platforms, most of the progress in the development of numerical algorithms has been for the solution of the Euler and Navier-Stokes equations. The design of algorithms for these equations has been very challenging because these algorithms must be capable of capturing a variety of complex flow features, such as shock waves and contact discontinuities, vortex shedding from sharp edges, shock and boundary-layer interactions, flow separation, and unsteady effects under maneuvering conditions or owing to store separation, which are associated with transonic viscous flow over a whole-body transport or fighter aircraft. Good numerical algorithms should be able to capture these diverse features without introducing significant numerical errors that can contaminate the solution. Accurate and stable central-difference algorithms with artificial viscosity (dissipation), characteristic-based upwind schemes, and total-variation-diminishing (TVD) schemes have been developed for conservation laws that take the form of hyperbolic partial differential equations and successfully applied to the solution of the compressible Euler and Navier-Stokes equations. Strong discontinuities (shocks) are captured by these schemes with small oscillations and minimal dispersive and dissipative errors. Several of these schemes are employed in many production-level proprietary or commercial computational fluid dynamics codes currently in use in the aerospace industry.

For cost-effective calculations with quick turnaround, a numerical method must converge rapidly. For this purpose, a number of techniques have been devised. The techniques that have provided the major improvements in convergence are known as the multigrid methods. The multigrid technique is a general strategy for solving continuous problems by cycling between coarser and finer levels of discretization. The basis of the method is to eliminate error components on a given grid whose wavelengths are comparable to the node spacing in the grid. By cycling between coarse and fine grids, both the high- and low-frequency components of error are reduced efficiently. Explicit multigrid schemes have proved to be very effective for steady-state calculations, while implicit multigrid methods have been shown to improve efficiency in unsteady-flow calculations.

Turbulence modeling. Despite over a century of research, turbulence remains an intractable problem in fluid dynamics. Although the basic physics of turbulence can be described by the Navier-Stokes equations, limitations in computer capacity make it impossible for now and in the foreseeable future to solve directly these equations for complex three-dimensional flows. At present, in simulation of whole aircraft flowfields, the turbulence effects are accounted for by phenomenological modeling of turbulence. The time-averaged form of the Navier-Stokes equations, known as the Reynolds-averaged Navier-Stokes (RANS) equations, is solved. Time averaging introduces the turbulent stresses in the Reynolds-averaged Navier-Stokes equations which are calculated by multiplying an eddy-viscosity coefficient with the strain-rate tensor. The phenomenological description of eddy viscosity is what is known

as turbulence modeling. There is no universal turbulence model which works for all flow situations. Turbulence models are generally developed by validating them against the experimental data for simple flow situations. They are then employed for calculation of complex flowfields. This approach introduces an element of unreliability into the prediction of complex flows. A variety of turbulence models of varying complexity have been developed. *See* TURBULENCE MODELING.

Whole-aircraft simulations. Whole-aircraft simulations of two aircraft will be discussed.

MD-80 aircraft. Figure 1 shows the Reynolds-averaged Navier-Stokes calculations for the complete MD-80 aircraft at a cruise Mach number of 0.76, Reynolds number of 6.39×10^6, and angle of attack of $4.2°$ on a $160 \times 46 \times 54$ mesh. Computations show a small separation bubble on the upper surface of the wing. The difference between the computed and experimental pressure distributions at 42% semispan is due to the separation bubble. It is attributed to the inadequacy of the Baldwin-Lomax turbulence model; there is enough grid resolution in the calculations. The computations show excellent agreement with the experimental data in the attached (nonseparated) flow regions over the wing. Although not shown here, the Reynolds-averaged Navier-Stokes predictions, obtained with a Baldwin-Lomax turbulence model, show good agreement with the experimental data at angle of attack of $2°$ at all spanwise locations. The flow is attached over the entire wing at this angle of attack.

F-15 aircraft. Figure 2 shows the Euler and Navier-Stokes computations for a complete F-15 aircraft at a Mach number of 0.9 and angle of attack of $4.84°$ obtained with the Euler code ULTRA on a $161 \times 31 \times 54$ structured mesh and an unstructured-grid Navier-Stokes code, NASTD. The unstructured grid in the computations contained a single zone with 44,272 nodes and 235,363 tetrahedra, with 6404 nodes and 12,669 faces on the surface. The Navier-Stokes solution shows excellent agreement with the experimental data. In the outboard regions of the wing (for example, the 86% semispan location shown in Fig. 2c), a strong shock develops on the wing surface.

For background information *see* COMPUTATIONAL FLUID DYNAMICS; COMPUTER-AIDED DESIGN AND MANUFACTURING; DIFFERENTIAL EQUATION; EULER'S MOMENTUM THEOREM; FLUID FLOW; FLUID-FLOW PRINCIPLES; NAVIER-STOKES EQUATIONS; TURBULENT FLOW in the McGraw-Hill Encyclopedia of Science & Technology.   Ramesh Agarwal

Bibliography. R. K. Agarwal, Computational fluid dynamics of whole-body aircraft, *Annu. Rev. Fluid Mech.*, 31:125–69, 1999; D. A. Caughey, Convergence acceleration methods, in R. W. Johnson (ed.), *The Handbook of Fluid Dynamics*, CRC Press, Boca Raton, FL, 1998; P. L. Roe, Characteristic-based schemes for the Euler equations, *Annu. Rev. Fluid Mech.*, 18:337–365,1986; D. C. Wilcox, *Turbulence Modeling for CFD*, 2d ed., DCW Industries, La Canada, CA, 1998.

Consciousness

Consciousness has become an important subject of scientific research, due in part to the emergence of B. J. Baars' global workspace theory of consciousness. One direction of this research involves designing and building "conscious" software agents that implement global workspace theory. Such implementations serve to flesh out the theory and to provide testable hypotheses for cognitive scientists and cognitive neuroscientists.

Global workspace theory. Global workspace theory postulates that human cognition is implemented by a multitude of relatively small, special-purpose mental processes, almost always unconscious. Coalitions of such processes find their way into a global workspace and from there into the contents of consciousness. From this limited-capacity workspace, the information contained in the coalition is broadcast globally to all unconscious processes in the system, thereby becoming conscious. This broadcast serves to recruit other processes to join in responding to the current novel situation or in solving the current problem. In problem solving, almost anything can prove relevant. The conscious broadcast allows the relevant processes to self-select and to respond, thereby solving the relevancy problem via a brute force approach. Thus, consciousness enables humans to deal with novel or problematic situations that cannot be handled efficiently, or at all, by habituated unconscious processes.

Though comprehensive, global workspace theory is quite abstract, as a psychological theory should be. It offers general principles, functional accounts, and broad architectural sketches. Questions of architectural detail, that is, of just how functional components fit together and who talks to whom, are sometimes left open. The same is true of almost all questions of mechanisms, that is, of how these components do what they are shown to do. As a good theory should, this one raises as many questions as it answers. Providing a more detailed and discriminated architecture, and computational mechanisms with which to implement it, can be expected to suggest answers to many of these questions about human cognition.

Consciousness. With this expectation in mind, conscious software agents designed within the constraints of global workspace theory have been introduced. A software agent is a particular kind of computer program. It "lives" in a computational environment such as an operating system or a network, and both senses and acts on that environment. These software agents act under their own volition motivated by built-in drives and goals. The architecture and mechanisms of these agents serve to flesh out global workspace theory, and promise to provide a fertile source of hypotheses for cognitive scientists and cognitive neuroscientists.

Rather than modeling some limited aspect of cognition, conscious software agents attempt to implement a fairly full range of cognitive functions. These include perception, several memories, emotion, consciousness, action selection, deliberation, several types of learning, and metacognition. The architecture of the agents is constrained not only by global workspace theory but also by what is known of human cognition. The mechanisms are, for the most part, inspired by various computational devices from the "new artificial intelligence." These include P. Maes' behavior nets, P. Kanerva's sparse distributed memory, and J. V. Jackson's pandemonium theory. This architecture, together with its mechanisms, constitutes a computational, conceptual model of consciousness and cognition.

Codelets. In conscious software agents, codelets play the role of cognitive processes in global workspace theory. Codelets are small, special-purpose pieces of computer code that act independently, watchfully waiting for an appropriate situation in which they can jump into action. Perceptual codelets help understand incoming sensory data; emotion codelets form quick judgments as to how well things are going; attention codelets bring novel or problematic situations to consciousness, and so on. Codelets initiate and control almost all the internal and external actions taken by these agents, just as processes do in humans.

Coalitions of codelets constitute many of the agent's higher-level features. In particular, global workspace theory stresses the importance of contexts, perceptual contexts, conceptual contexts, goal contexts, and cultural contexts. These contexts, most being unconscious, both compete and cooperate in influencing the contents of consciousness. Each context consists of a coalition of processes. Goal contexts are implemented in the conscious software agent architecture as behaviors in a behavior net. Each behavior (goal context), once executed (becoming dominant), is carried out by a coalition of codelets (processes). The behavior and its coalition of codelets are identified. Conceptual contexts are also implemented as nodes in a net identified with an underlying collection of codelets that serve to recognize or comprehend instances of that particular concept. All this is to say that these agents have built in the required architecture and mechanisms for consciousness, as global workspace theory prescribes them.

New agents. Presently, two such conscious software agents are being designed and built. Cmattie, a conscious clerical software agent, handles seminar announcements for an academic department in a university. "She" corresponds with seminar organizers in natural language, maintains her mailing list, warns organizers of missing information, time conflicts, and so on. Her design is essentially finished, and the coding is in the debugging stage. IDA, a conscious information and decision-making software agent, is being designed for the U.S. Navy. IDA is to find new billets for sailors completing a tour of duty, including deliberating about suitability and negotiating with the sailor in natural language. She is to replace a human who now does this job. This same technology should allow the work of many other types of human information and decision-making agents to be automated. These may well include travel agents, loan officers, insurance agents, telephone operators, and many others. The technology provides artificial intelligence and computer science with a tool that goes beyond the now classical expert system.

Since these software agents have built-in architecture and mechanisms for consciousness, they may actually turn out to be sentient. This issue is the subject of current research aimed at locating consciousness in nervous systems. Success at finding criteria for sentience would help solve the problem for humans and animals. Struggling with these provocative questions about artificial sentience may add, in yet another way, to knowledge of human consciousness.

For background information *see* COGNITION; CONSCIOUSNESS; SOFTWARE in the McGraw-Hill Encyclopedia of Science & Technology.   Stan Franklin

Bibliography. B. J. Baars, *In the Theater of Consciousness*, Oxford University Press, Oxford, 1997; S. Franklin, *Artificial Minds*, MIT Press, Cambridge, MA, 1995; S. Franklin and A. Graesser, Is it an agent, or just a program?: A taxonomy for autonomous agents, *Intelligent Agents III*, Springer-Verlag, Berlin, 1997; S. Franklin and A. Graesser, A software agent model of consciousness, *Consciousness and Cognition*, 8:285–301, 1999; J. V. Jackson, Idea for a Mind, *SIGGART Newsl.*, no. 181, July, 23–26, 1987; P. Kanerva, *Sparse Distributed Memory*, MIT Press, Cambridge, MA, 1988; P. Maes, How to do the right thing, *Connection Sci.*, 1:3, 1990.

Crystalline plasma

A plasma is matter in an ionized state. The assumption is often made that such matter is necessarily in a fluid state, and this is the case most often observed. However, cold, highly correlated ion plasmas confined in a vacuum by magnetic and electric fields have recently been observed to crystallize into lattice patterns that depend on the sizes and shapes of the plasmas. These studies are relevant to the understanding of dense astrophysical objects, such as neutron stars and white dwarfs, in which plasmas having similar properties are believed to exist.

One-component plasmas. The one-component plasma (OCP) is an idealized theoretical model of matter consisting of a single species of charged particles embedded in a uniform, neutralizing background of opposite charge. It is the simplest system in which crystallization of an ion plasma occurs. The thermodynamic properties of an infinite homogeneous OCP are determined by a dimensionless parameter $\Gamma = q^2(4\pi\varepsilon_0 akT)^{-1}$, which is a measure of the ratio of the electrostatic potential energy of neighboring particles [about $q^2/(4\pi\varepsilon_0 a)$] to the kinetic energy per particle (about kT). Here, q is the charge of the particles, ε_0 is the permittivity of the vacuum, k is the Boltzmann constant, and T is the temperature. The Wigner-Seitz radius a is a measure of the average interparticle spacing and is defined in terms of the density n by $4\pi a^3/3 = n^{-1}$; that is, the average number of particles in a sphere of radius a is equal to 1. When Γ is much less than 1, the OCP is said to be uncorrelated; when Γ is greater than or approximately equal to 1, it is said to be strongly coupled or strongly correlated. When Γ is greater than a value Γ_{crit} equal to about 170, the OCP is predicted to crystallize, forming a body-centered cubic (bcc) lattice.

These results hold for an infinite OCP. For finite-sized systems, the spatial arrangement of the particles may be something other than a bcc lattice. Numerical simulations of as many as tens of thousands of particles have shown that solidified, finite OCPs have layered structures. In the case of a sphere, for example, an approximate two-dimensional hexagonal lattice forms at the outer surface. A series of concentric spherical layers of particles forms inside the sphere. For a sufficiently large number of layers, the spatial arrangement of the particles near the center should form a bcc lattice, as for the infinite OCP. This number may be about 30, according to theoretical estimates. Numerical simulations have not yet verified this transition from a layered structure in the outer regions to a bcc lattice in the central region directly, since the number of particles required is around 10^5, which is too large for current computers to handle. Other geometries have also been investigated theoretically, for example, one in which the particles are confined to a cylindrical region that is unbounded along the axis of the cylinder. In this case, the structure consists of a series of coaxial cylinders.

Astrophysical applications. In some dense astrophysical bodies, the electrons form a degenerate Fermi gas. That is, the electrons have the maximum density allowed by the Pauli exclusion principle, which prevents two electrons from occupying the same quantum state. At sufficiently high pressures, the Pauli principle, not Coulomb repulsion, limits the density of the electrons. Under these conditions, the electrons form a uniformly charged background, in which the fully stripped ions move. The ions, being much more massive than the electrons, remain nondegenerate even at pressures much higher than those needed to force the electrons into a degenerate state. If there is only a single ion species, the system resembles an OCP.

A neutron star is a gravitationally collapsed stellar object with a mass on the order of that of the Sun but with a radius of only about 10 km (6 mi). The core consists of degenerate neutrons. The crust of a neutron star is believed to consist mainly of iron nuclei embedded in degenerate electrons. When the density is high enough and the temperature low enough, the iron nuclei are predicted to freeze into a solid. It is not known whether this is a bcc crystal, as for the idealized OCP, or a disordered solid.

A white dwarf is a star that no longer generates energy by thermonuclear reactions and is stabilized against gravitational collapse by the pressure of degenerate electrons. The interiors of white dwarfs are believed to consist of a mixture of carbon and oxygen nuclei embedded in a degenerate electron gas. Thus, rather than being a one-component plasma, the core is a binary ionic plasma with some other minor ionic components. At high enough densities and low enough temperatures, such a mixture should crystallize. Knowledge of the details of the crystallization process is needed to estimate the age of a white dwarf from its observed luminosity. For example, if the carbon and oxygen nuclei separate into different regions of the core before crystallizing, heat is released that slows the cooling process.

Estimates of the age of the universe are based on the Hubble constant, which is a measure of the rate of expansion of the universe. Hubble-constant measurements have varied, indicating an age of the universe between about 10 and 20 billion years, though recently they have been converging on a value of about 12 billion years. The estimated ages of the oldest white dwarfs are from about 9 to 15 billion years. Of course, the age of the universe must be greater than that of any star, so both the Hubble-constant measurements and the estimates of white dwarf ages need to be refined to make sure that they are not in contradiction.

Experiments. Crystallization of plasmas has been observed in ion traps, which are devices that confine charged particles by various configurations of electric and magnetic fields. A collection of a single species of ions in a trap is similar to a finite OCP, where the trap fields take the place of the uniform, neutralizing background. In order to lower the temperatures enough for crystallization to occur, laser cooling has been used. Laser cooling is a method of reducing the temperature of atoms or ions by the use of resonant light pressure. In its simplest form, called Doppler cooling, the frequency of a laser is tuned slightly below the frequency of a strong atomic resonance. Ions with velocities directed against the laser beam scatter light at a higher rate than those moving with the beam, and lose kinetic energy.

A radio-frequency or Paul ion trap confines charged particles with the use of spatially nonuniform, alternating electric fields. Crystallization of ions has been observed in such traps, notably at the Max Planck Institute for Quantum Optics in Germany, at the University of Aarhus in Denmark, and at the U.S. National Institute of Standards and Technology (NIST). However, while layered structures have been observed, the plasmas were not large enough to allow the observation of the infinite OCP structure.

Recent work at NIST has resulted in the production of crystallized ion plasmas in Penning traps that are large enough in all three dimensions for the bcc lattice structure expected for the infinite OCP to be observed. A Penning trap uses a static, uniform magnetic field superimposed on a quadrupolar electrostatic potential to confine charged particles in all three dimensions. A collection of a single type of

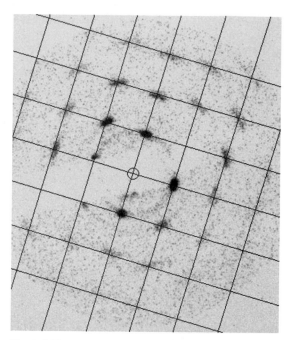

Fig. 1. Diffraction pattern of a beryllium ion plasma, showing the square grid pattern characteristic of a bcc lattice irradiated along a fourfold symmetry axis. The open circle marks the position of the undeflected beam. The grid spacing corresponds to an angular deviation of 2.54×10^{-2} rad. The ion density is 3.83×10^8 cm^{-3}. (Reprinted from W. M. Itano et al., Bragg diffraction from crystallized ion plasmas, Science, 279:686–689, January 30, 1998)

ion in a Penning trap has properties equivalent to an OCP, aside from an overall rotation about an axis parallel to the magnetic field direction.

Diffraction of collimated radiation (radiation whose particles are nearly parallel) by the ordered atoms of a crystal is called Bragg scattering. The incident beam is scattered in a discrete set of directions, from which the lattice structure of the crystal can be inferred. Ordinarily, x-rays are used for Bragg scattering; but for ion plasmas confined in Penning traps, it is convenient to use the same laser radiation used to cool the ions. **Figure 1** shows a diffraction pattern observed in the forward-scattered 313-nanometer laser radiation that has passed through an approximately spherical plasma of about 5×10^5 trapped beryllium-9 (^{9}Be$^+$) ions. The square array of spots is the signature of a cubic lattice irradiated along one of the fourfold symmetry axes. Precise measurements of the plasma density and the scattering angles show that the pattern is due to a bcc lattice and not to a simple cubic (sc) or a face-centered cubic (fcc) lattice. A diffracted beam is expected at each intersection of the grid lines overlaid on the image. Some spots are obscured by a beamstop. In order to obtain this image, it was necessary to synchronize the detection with the 126-kHz overall rotation frequency of the plasma. For spherical plasmas having approximately 200,000 ions or more, the diffraction patterns were consistent with bcc ordering. It is also possible to study the spatial ordering by direct optical imaging of the individual ions.

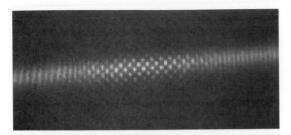

Fig. 2. Image of a $^9Be^+$ ion plasma, illuminated by a laser beam perpendicular to the magnetic field, showing the presence of a bcc crystal in the central region. The horizontal extent of the image is 0.5 mm. (*After T. B. Mitchell et al., Direct observations of the structural phases of crystallized ion plasmas, Phys. Plasmas, 6:1751–1758, May 1999*)

Figure 2 shows a view in a direction parallel to the magnetic field of the fluorescence from a narrow laser beam directed through a plasma. A bcc crystal is observed in the central region. Other lattice types, including fcc and hexagonal-close-packed (hcp), are observed in very flat plasmas.

Future experiments might include a measurement of the melting temperature of the trapped-ion crystals and of the details of the spatial structure changes during the melting transition. Another area for experimental study is the crystallization of a binary ionic mixture, for example, $^9Be^+$ with aluminum-27 ($^{27}Al^{3+}$). These ions have nearly the same charge-to-mass ratio and hence will tend to remain mixed rather than undergoing centrifugal separation. It is not known how such a mixture will crystallize—in particular, whether like ions will group together or will remain mixed with the others in a kind of alloy. The results of such a study might yield some insights into the structure of the interiors of white dwarfs.

For background information *see* CRYSTAL STRUCTURE; CRYSTALLOGRAPHY; PLASMA (PHYSICS); SUN; X-RAY CRYSTALLOGRAPHY; X-RAY DIFFRACTION; WHITE DWARF STAR in the McGraw-Hill Encyclopedia of Science & Technology.   Wayne M. Itano

Bibliography. W. M. Itano et al., Bragg diffraction from crystallized ion plasmas, *Science*, 279:686–689, January 30, 1998; T. B. Mitchell et al., Direct observations of the structural phases of crystallized ion plasmas, *Phys. Plasmas*, 6:1751–1758, May 1999; T. M. O'Neil, Trapped plasmas with a single sign of charge, *Phys. Today*, 52(2):24–30, February 1999; H. M. Van Horn, Dense astrophysical plasmas, *Science*, 252:384–389, April 19, 1991.

Deoxyribonucleic acid (DNA) microarrays

The Human Genome Project, the effort to decode the entire deoxyribonucleic acid sequence of humans, is showing how much of the makeup of cells remains to be elucidated. DNA is the blueprint of life and encodes all of the genes which are expressed from the genome in the form of messenger ribonucleic acid (mRNA). The mRNA is translated by cellular machinery into proteins. Determining the sequence of the entire genome allows a comprehensive analysis of all genes, and hence proteins, that make up cells, tissues, and the entire organism. There is now access to the complete genome sequence of over a dozen bacterial genomes and the complete sequence of small genome eukaryotes such as yeast (*Saccharomyces cerevisiae*, 6200 genes encoded in about 12 million base pairs), worm (*Caenorhabditis elegans*, 18,000 genes encoded in about 80 million base pairs), and fruit fly (about 200 million base pairs). By late 2001, highly accurate sequencing of the human genome (about 3 billion base pairs encoding an estimated 100,000 genes) will be available due to recent increases in sequence production from government-funded laboratories. The mouse genome, generally considered one of the best models for human diseases, will be sequenced before 2005.

This avalanche of sequencing information will provide a comprehensive view of genes. However, the sequence data from the smaller-genome yeast and worm are quite humbling. Even with the vast amount of prior gene information and two decades of highly focused molecular biology experimentation, it is possible to guess the function of only a third of all the 6200 genes identified in yeast. The rest are a complete mystery. Therefore, there are vast frontiers of biology not yet explored by modern tools. The problem will be more severe as the much larger human genome is completed and the sequence of approximately 100,000 genes is determined. The era of individual gene cloning, which has dominated human genetics, is coming to an end, and a new era of discovering functions for all of the genes identified is beginning. In the efforts to identify the function of each of these 100,000 genes in the human genome, tools that allow the sampling of many genes in individual assays are needed. Two key technological advances since 1995, oligonucleotide and complementary DNA (cDNA) microarrays, allow testing to determine which genes are turned on in a given cell and to what level.

Gene expression. The set of genes that are turned on in a cell and the timing of the activation of the genes are key events in determining the cell type. The cell responds to its local environment frequently by sending messages to the cell nucleus to change which genes are turned on or off. This process is extremely important in all developmental processes and in the responses of cells to changes in the environment. Because of this, a major clue to a gene's function is in what cell type it is found and when it is turned on. Since their inception in 1995, gene expression microarrays are providing unprecedented analysis of gene expression levels—a critical measurement in the diagnosis, prognosis, and management of cancer and other diseases. The application of DNA microarray technologies will provide vast quantities of data regarding how genes are used to build tissues and how genes are affected in disease processes.

Fabrication. Expressed sequence tags (ESTs) provide a sneak peak to that portion of the genome which is used to make mRNA (and ultimately proteins). Due to the large commercial and public efforts to sequence these genes in bulk, a piece of almost every gene has already been sampled and a small piece of sequence exists. The complete genome sequence is needed to position all of these genes throughout the genome, but their current existence makes the fabrication of large-scale gene expression microarrays possible today.

DNA microarrays are fabricated using physical reagents from the genome project. As tens of thousands of genes from the human genome have been cloned in the form of expressed sequence tags, they can be organized into nonredundant sets. Each clone represents one gene in the genome. The clones are organized into sets of 96 well plates for automated handling. Each gene is individually amplified by polymerase chain reaction (PCR) which generates a probe for the gene from 300 to 2000 bases long. The PCR product, which is an exact replica of the gene, is placed onto glass microscope slides using a fast robotic arrayer. The process proceeds by fountain-pen-like tips dipping into the 96 well plates and then touching gently onto coated glass slides. One-thousandth of a milliliter is deposited on each slide in a spot that is about 0.1 mm wide. The robotics are sufficiently precise that additional spots can be placed just 0.1–0.2 mm apart. This precise array allows the positioning of up to 20,000 genes on each slide in an area of about 4 cm², such that each gene is at a known exact position. The printed DNA is permanently attached to the glass slide.

An alternate means of fabricating DNA arrays is performed by actually building short 24-nucleotide DNA sequences (oligonucleotides) on the surface of a silicon wafer. The process of fabrication of these arrays has been commercialized. The approach utilizes light-directed synthesis of the oligonucleotides borrowed from technology in widespread use in microelectronics. Briefly, a mask shields some of the surface of the array from light and exposes other regions; each region can be as small as 20 by 20 micrometers. The regions that are exposed de-protect a molecule that allows the oligonucleotide chain to grow. The whole surface is flooded with one of the four building blocks of DNA (guanosine, cytosine, thymidine, adenine). The new base attaches only where the light de-protected the surface. This process allows combinatorial surface chemistry so that an array with about 400,000 facets can be built up in any one cycle. This allows any set of 400,000 different oligonucleotides, each up to length 24 bases, to be synthesized in only 96 chemical steps. Even though these oligonucleotides are much shorter than full-length genes, they can hybridized with great specificity.

Experimentation. DNA and RNA have the powerful property that they will bind to complementary sequences at very high specificity. Thus, it is a straightforward process to develop a probe for any gene sequence once the sequence is known. Each of the many arrayed genes is a probe for the abundance of that gene from a given tissue or cell type. Microarray experiments are performed by extracting mRNA (that portion of the genome that is actively transcribed and will make proteins) from the cells of interest. This population of mRNAs are labeled with a fluorescent tag, such that all of the molecules are evenly labeled. Typically there are 10,000–20,000 genes that are turned on or expressed in any given human cell. This complex mixture of labeled mRNAs is dissolved in a high-salt solution and applied over the gene expression microarray. The amount of each gene in the mRNA sample is obtained by measuring the amount of fluorescence at each gene on the array. This is highly specific as each labeled mRNA binds only to the arrayed gene which it matches. As up to 20,000 genes can be on the array, the expression level of all 20,000 genes is determined simultaneously.

Applications. DNA microarrays are being used to address a wide array of problems in biology in many different species. Large-scale arrays which contain virtually all genes from the yeast *S. cerevisiae* and the worm *C. elegans* have been fabricated. In addition, large-scale arrays of more than 10,000 genes have been fabricated for mouse and humans. Yeast is an excellent model organism as it is unicellular, is grown and genetically manipulated easily in the laboratory, and contains much of the same cellular circuitry as humans and mouse. Genome-wide experiments as yeast progress through the cell cycle and divide (mitosis), undergo meiosis, and respond to starvation are revealing numerous genes that participate in these processes. These experiments are indicating potential roles for genes whose sequence alone does not indicate the likely gene function. Many other cellular states will be tested in simple eukaryotes to suggest functions for novel genes in human cell lines.

Another area of active investigation is the use of large-scale cDNA microarrays to distinguish different types of cells or tissues. One area that will be fruitful for this research is cancer diagnosis and prognosis. Many patients with the same cancer diagnosis receive the same treatment, even though only a portion of the cancers will respond to the treatment. There is great hope that analysis of the set of genes turned on or off in a given cancer will provide a much more refined view of the cancer. This information may allow therapy that is tailored to each cancer and may lead to a much more effective use of currently available chemotherapy and biological agents. In addition, large-scale gene expression analysis is providing researchers a significantly more comprehensive view of the cancer cell. Thus, new pathways active in the cancer cells will be identified that will point the way to new therapeutic agents. DNA microarrays will be applied to the study of many disease states, greatly enhancing understanding of the disease process. DNA microarray technology will be a major tool for sorting out the function of genes as they are identified through large-scale sequencing.

For background information *see* DEOXYRIBONU-CLEIC ACID (DNA); GENE; GENE AMPLIFICATION; YEAST in the McGraw-Hill Encyclopedia of Science & Technology.   Stanley Nelson

Bibliography. J. L. DeRisi, V. R. Iyer, and P. O. Brown, Exploring the metabolic and genetic control of gene expression on a genomic scale, *Science*, 278:680–686, 1997; T. R. Golub et al., Molecular classification of cancer: Class discovery and class prediction by gene expression monitoring, *Science*, 286: 531–537, 1996; D. J. Lockhart et al., Expression monitoring by hybridization to high-density oligonucleotide arrays, *Nat. Biotech.*, 14:1675–1680, 1996; M. Schena et al., Quantitative monitoring of gene expression patterns with a complementary DNA microarray, *Science*, 270:467–470, 1995.

Developmental sequences

The diversity of animal species is overwhelming, and an important goal of biology is to make sense of this diversity by arranging animals into groups. Classification can be done by grouping like with like, for example, by looking for similarities and differences in anatomical structure or gene sequences. This is a phenetic approach, with all similarities weighed equally regardless of their history. Alternatively, animals can be arranged into an evolutionary (phylogenetic) family tree by grouping species according to their ancestry. This approach depends on theories about the time at which a particular trait arose in evolutionary history.

Most studies of animal classification and evolution are based on adult animals (including fossils that are assumed to be adults). However, scientists are increasingly turning to earlier stages of development, especially embryos, as potential data sources. This is partly because the genes which control embryonic development are being identified, and partly because new computer techniques make it easier to analyze complex sets of developmental data.

Developmental characters. Development, or ontogeny, describes the changes, in one life-span, extending from fertilized egg to sexually mature adult. In early (embryonic) stages, cells are arranged into miniature models of the body's organs. In later (postembryonic) stages, these organ primordia undergo differentiation and growth. Developmental data are dynamic in that they change during the lifetime of the individual. This can make the data difficult to analyze because one has to compare different characters in different species at different stages of development as well as the same character at different stages.

In recent years, most phylogenetic studies of development have been concerned with postembryonic stages, and have involved the measurement of continuous variables such as changes in size and shape. These measurements are plotted as trajectories on a graph and provide information about growth and shape change (allometry).

Developmental data can also take the form of discrete (discontinuous) characters called developmental events. These are seen particularly during embryonic development, when the development of numerous organ primordia leads to a rapid succession of structural changes. Examples of developmental events in the vertebrates include an increase in the number of body segments, the appearance of a thickening in the surface layer of the embryo to form the lens primordium, and the bending of the heart tube into an S-shape. Most developmental events that have been studied are structural. In principle, though, it is possible to look at other types of events such as the activation of gene transcription.

The distinction between continuous processes, such as growth, and developmental events is not rigid. If embryonic development were rerun in slow motion, one would see that events happen gradually. In practice, however, events take place in such rapid succession in the embryo, and in such large numbers, that they can be treated as discrete characters.

Time scale. If developmental events are to be used in classification or evolutionary studies, the time element must be expressed in the data. This is relatively straightforward when measuring growth or shape changes in postembryonic development. In these cases the data can be plotted against an external reference such as body size or age. An external time scale is essential in these cases because the rate of change is being measured. However, external time scales do not provide sufficient resolution for ordering developmental events in the embryonic period because too many things are happening too quickly. However, this rapid succession of events is most prevalent in the early embryonic stages and slows down once the basic body plan has been established.

A further problem occurs when there is variation in the rate of maturation among members of a species. For example, in humans the bones of the body ossify at different ages in different individuals. Therefore, a comparison of ossification sequences would be more informative than using chronological age as an index of time. Another example to which this principle may be applied is the sequence of fusion of cranial sutures in mammalian skulls. The skull is composed of many skeletal components that have specific spatial relationships to one another and that must be integrated throughout the postnatal growth process. For these reasons, the time element in developmental data is often expressed by ordering the events as a developmental sequence (**Fig. 1**). The time scale is internal to the data and is relativistic, because the timing of each event is described relative to the timing of other events in the sequence.

Heterochrony and uncoupling. One reason why embryology has tended to be excluded from phylogenetic studies is that embryos are often assumed to be highly resistant to evolutionary change. Thus, it is often thought that developmental sequences are

African clawed toad (*Xenopus laevis*)

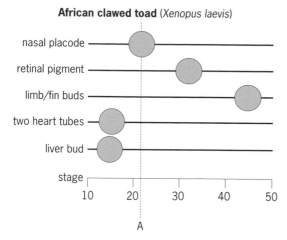

Fig. 1. "Abacus" model of developmental sequences and stages. Selected developmental events are shown as beads. The position of the bead along its horizontal line shows the stage at which the event first takes place. There is no external reference to time. A developmental stage can be defined by dropping a vertical line (the broken line at A) and noting the events which it covers. Note that developmental stages are clusters of developmental events happening at the same time, and are purely arbitrary.

invariant in a given group of animals. In fact, heterochrony (evolutionary shifts in developmental timing) are an important feature of the embryonic period, indicating that natural selection can modify embryonic development. Heterochrony also demonstrates that the timing of developmental characters is not necessarily tightly coupled; there may be the potential for them to shift their timing independently of one another. For example, frogs develop their limbs very late (around the time of metamorphosis), whereas in marsupials the limbs develop at a very early embryonic stage. The evolutionary analysis of developmental sequences depends on this property of uncoupling (dissociation) because, by looking for heterochronic shifts in different species, one can uncover evidence of evolutionary change.

Analytical techniques. Developmental sequences in different species can be compared by looking at their gross similarity, for example, by doing a simple calculation called a correlation coefficient. More sophisticated methods have recently been developed that allow information on evolutionary relationships to be extracted from the data. First, the position of each character in the sequence, relative to other characters, is determined. This can be done by drawing up a table called an event-pair matrix. Each character in the matrix is coded according to whether it appears before, at the same time as, or after the other character in the pair. Next, the event-pair matrices of different species are compared using specialist software which allows theories of evolutionary kinship to be tested. The technique represents an important advance in the effort to extract an evolutionary signal from developmental data.

Problems. The "abacus" diagrams (Fig. 1 and **Fig. 2**) tend to give the impression that developmental characters can shift their place in the se-

quence as easily as beads sliding along a rod; but characters do not necessarily show this freedom, for several reasons. Characters appearing early in the sequence may have different properties from late characters. They may, for example, be more resistant to the action of natural selection. Changing early events might disrupt all subsequent stages, leading to a state whereby the offspring are not viable. Furthermore, some characters may be coupled, so that they shift in concert with others. Finally, some characters may form part of a dependent sequence, in which one character in a pair always has to develop first. For example, retinal pigmentation cannot develop before the retina has formed.

A further issue is the ontogenetic criterion. To put it simply, this is the theory that the generalized features seen in an embryo are primitive, whereas the more specialized characters, found only in certain species and often developing at late stages, are of more recent evolutionary origin. There have been lively debates about the validity of this idea. However, these arguments are not important if one is simply looking for patterns in the data so as to group animals according to their similarities and differences. In these cases, and indeed for most practical purposes, developmental data are not used to make revised family trees, but are plotted onto existing trees based on nondevelopmental data. This makes it pos-

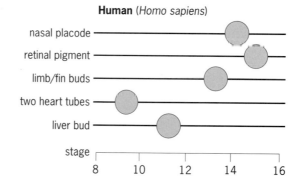

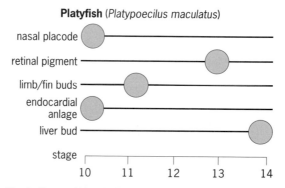

Fig. 2. Comparison of selected developmental sequences in two species. Heterochrony is reflected in differences in the relative positions of the beads in the two species. For example, development of the platyfish liver bud is shifted to the right relative to several other characters in the human sequence; that liver bud therefore develops relatively late. The model is purely relativistic in that the observer need look only at the positions of the beads relative to each other.

sible to evolve new theories about the patterns of change in development down the generations.

A major goal for future work will be to see how developmental sequences based on molecular data can be mapped onto those based on structural data. This could be a big step toward the long-awaited synthesis of developmental biology, evolutionary biology, and classification.

For background information *see* ANIMAL EVOLUTION; ANIMAL GROWTH; CHROMOSOME; DEVELOPMENTAL BIOLOGY; EMBRYOLOGY; FATE MAPS (EMBRYOLOGY) in the McGraw-Hill Encyclopedia of Science & Technology.   Michael K. Richardson

Bibliography. S. J. Gould, *Ontogeny and Phylogeny*, Belknap Press, Cambridge, MA, 1977; C. J. Humphries (ed.), *Ontogeny and Systematics*, British Museum (Natural History), London, 1988; C. L. Nunn and K. K. Smith, Statistical analyses of developmental sequences: The craniofacial region in marsupial and placental mammals, *Amer. Nat.*, 152:82–101, 1998; M. K. Richardson, Heterochrony and the phylotypic period, *Dev. Biol.*, 172:412–421, 1995.

Diamond

Diamond was first described in India about 4000 years ago. Discoveries of diamond were made in Brazil in 1720, in South Africa in 1867, and in Russia, China, the United States, Canada, and Finland during the twentieth century. Diamond is one of the naturally occurring minerals that crystallize from the element carbon (C); the others are lonsdaleite and graphite. Diamond is covalently bonded such that each carbon atom is tetrahedrally coordinated to every other carbon atom. This leads to its special properties, for example, its extraordinary optical properties, unparalleled hardness (10 on the Mohs scale), and a thermal conductance that is six times greater than copper. Diamond crystallizes in the cubic system with octahedral habit and perfect cleavage. Colors may vary from pale yellow (due to nitrogen substitution of carbon), to brown (deformed), green (radiation damage), blue (boron substitution), pink (unknown cause), and gun-metal gray (graphite inclusions). Pink and violet stones are very rare. Varieties include ballas (spherical and fibrous), framesite (loosely aggregated), carbonado (robustly aggregated), and stewardite (magnetic). Diamond evaluations are based on color [D is exceptionally white (clear), through to Z which is tinted in colors], mineral inclusions (FL is flawless, through to VVS, VS, S, and I; where V is very, S is small, and I is inclusion), and weight (measured in carats, 1 ct = 0.2 g). The largest single crystal of diamond is the Cullinan Diamond (3106 ct) from South Africa, and the largest (3167 ct) polycrystalline stone is the Sergio Diamond, a carbonado from Brazil. Diamond is classified spectroscopically into type I (nitrogen-bearing), and type II (nitrogen-free). In about 98% of the former, nitrogen atoms are repositioned in the crystal structure on annealing at high temperatures (~1000°C) over long periods of time, and the diamond becomes a type Ia; in rapidly cooled synthetic diamond, and in rare, naturally occurring diamond, nitrogen is randomly dispersed and these are type Ib.

Synthesis. Diamond was first synthesized in Sweden in 1953 and in the United States in 1954. Standard procedures of industrial synthesis employ a solvent-catalyst of iron, cobalt, chromium, titanium, and aluminum in which amorphous carbon is transformed to millimeter-size diamond at pressures of approximately 5 gigapascals and temperatures of 1500–1600°C. Large diamonds (up 25 ct) are expensive to produce, and growth is aided by nucleation on diamond seeds. Carbon vapor deposition (CVD) films of diamond, nanometers in thickness, are synthetically precipitated on hot (~1000°C) silicon carbide and metal substrates from critically constrained mixtures in the system C—H—O at plasma temperatures (>2000°C), and under vacuum. Other noncommercial methods are by ballistic shock techniques and by hydrothermal crystallization on diamond seeds.

Occurrence and formation. Diamond is mined from kimberlite (named after the diamond mining town of Kimberley in South Africa) and a closely related rock known as lamproite. Both rocks are characterized by unusually rich magnesium oxide content, potassium content greater than sodium, and high volatile (CO_2 and H_2O) content. These rocks are volcanic, and their intrusion into the crust was rapid and highly explosive, leaving craters tens to hundreds of meters in diameter clustered into fields (10–50 km) and provinces (100–1000 km) of a hundred or more volcanoes. It is only those intrusions injected into cratons (old, cold, and stable continental crust) that are likely to contain diamonds, and of these, less than 1% are likely to be economically viable with 4–5 parts per million (ppm) of diamond. About 500 metric tons of diamond have been mined since 1900.

A minor population of microdiamond (<1 mm) may crystallize directly from kimberlitic and lamproitic magmas, but the majority of macrodiamonds were formed in the lithosphere of the upper mantle at depths of 180–200 km. These depths are estimated from the experimental transformation of graphite to diamond, and from temperatures and pressures of coexisting mineral inclusions in diamond whose characteristic chemistries can be directly related to depths of origin. Some diamonds formed in the transition zone (410–660 km), and others are from the lower mantle (deeper than 660 km). The mineral inclusions (garnet, pyroxene, and sulfides) can be dated by radiogenic techniques. Most diamonds are older than 3 billion years before present (Ga), with a few at 2 Ga, and rare occurrences at 1.5 Ga. These ages are supported by experiments on the periods of time required to mobilize substituted nitrogen in diamond to the aggregated state; extrapolations give 2–4 Ga. This ancient mineral has been modeled as having formed by the breakdown of methane (CH_4) into carbon (diamond) and hydrogen, by oxidation of CH_4, by the reduction of CO_2, or a combination of the three reactions. The carbon is primordial and dates back to condensation of the solar system at 4.55 Ga.

The ages [53 million years (Ma) to 1.1 billion years before present] of kimberlites and lamproites are significantly younger than the diamonds in these volcanic rocks. Intrusions were globally synchronous with major eruptive events at 1 Ga (Africa, Australia, Brazil, Greenland, Siberia); 450–500 Ma (China, Finland, South Africa, Zimbabwe); 370–410 Ma (Siberia, United States); 200 Ma (Botswana, Canada, Swaziland, Tanzania); 80–120 Ma (in all of the locations listed); and 53 Ma (Canada and Tanzania). The depths of origin of diamond, rapid intrusion, global synchroneity, and the primordial nature of carbon collectively suggest that volcanism was driven and that eruption was assisted by thermal plumes that originated at the core-mantle boundary at depths of 2900 km.

Diamond also formed in continent-continent subduction zones. During assembly of the Eurasian supercontinent between 200 and 500 Ma, microdiamonds (<1–100 micrometers) crystallized under mantle conditions (deeper than 120 km) from mixtures of recycled and primordial carbon in Norway, Kazakhstan, and China. Continental crust is difficult to subduct because it is buoyant, and this contrast in density between the crust and the mantle may have assisted the transport of diamond to the surface in a process referred to as syntectonic exhumation. A significant feature of these diamonds is their enclosure in garnet and zircon; these minerals may have acted as preservation capsules that inhibited the transformation of diamond to graphite, but enclosure also points to the possible presence of hydrogen bonds, a departure from ideal covalence, and metastable crystallization.

Diamond of extraterrestrial origin. The first report of diamond in a meteorite was in 1888 near Nova-Urei in Siberia. Diamonds are ubiquitous in this class of meteorite now known as ureilites. The high temperatures and high pressures required to form diamond were created by shock metamorphism on the asteroidal parent body. Meteorites hitting the Earth also produce diamond, and in some cases hexagonal lonsdaleite forms in the plasma sheets of molten rock that were created on impact. The known sites are Meteor Crater (Arizona), Ries (Germany), Popigai (Siberia), and at the Cretaceous-Tertiary boundary, where anomalies of high iridium are linked to a large meteorite impact and associated events that may have led to the demise of the dinosaurs.

Carbon is the fourth most abundant element in the solar system, and the existence of carbon stars has long been known; however, the speciation of carbon in the interstellar media was controversial. In 1987, in an unrelated search, the puzzling source of rare gas (xenon in particular) anomalies in chondritic meteorites that had been recognized for over a decade

was finally isolated in nanometer-size diamonds. But even more extraordinary is that the anomalies are of presolar origin, a conclusion that was reached in part from theory, nucleosynthetic reactions for the origin of the elements, experiments, and direct stellar observations. Other carbon-bearing minerals (silicon carbide, SiC; tungsten carbide, WC; molybdenum carbide, MoC; graphite) coexist with diamond in these meteorites, and these too are of presolar origin, possibly as old as 8 Ga. As carbon stars evolve, the carbon:oxygen ratio increases from the burning of hydrogen and helium and the synthesis of carbon by the high-energy interaction of three helium atoms [3 (2 protons + 2 neutrons) → ^{12}C]. The product may be diamond, but diamond is also considered to have formed by a process analogous to carbon vapor deposition in the circumstellar atmospheres that developed after supernovae explosions. Diamond concentrations in meteorites reach an astounding 1600 ppm. Because the bulk composition of the Earth is chondritic, and given the intensity of early (3.8–4.2 Ga) meteoritic bombardment, it is reasonable to conclude that a significant proportion of carbon in the planet was deposited as presolar diamond.

For background information *see* CARBON; CARBON-NITROGEN-OXYGEN CYCLES; DIAMOND; LITHOSPHERE in the McGraw-Hill Encyclopedia of Science & Technology.   Stephen E. Haggerty

Bibliography. E. Anders and E. Zinner, Interstellar grains in primitive meteorites: Diamond, silicon carbide, and graphite, *Meteoritics*, 28:490–514, 1993; R. C. Coleman and X. Wang (eds.), *Ultrahigh Pressure Metamorphism*, Cambridge University Press, Cambridge, 1995; S. E. Haggerty, A diamond trilogy: Superplumes, supercontinents, and supernovae, *Science*, 285:852–860, 1999; G. E. Harlow (ed.), *The Nature of Diamonds*, Cambridge University Press–American Museum of Natural History, Cambridge, 1998.

Digital imaging (forensics)

Images are used in forensic applications to document the condition of crime scenes and evidentiary items in the laboratory. In some cases the images themselves are the evidence, such as bank surveillance film. Digital imaging technologies are extending, and in many cases improving upon, the capabilities of traditional silver-based film techniques through processing and analysis techniques that can enhance the images and extract additional information from them.

Image capture. Digital images utilized in forensic applications are captured in a number of ways. The quickest method is direct capture using a digital camera. Digital cameras are utilized in a number of law enforcement and forensic applications to document minor traffic accidents, victim wounds in nonfatal assaults, gang member tattoos, and so on. In some laboratories, digital cameras attached to microscopes are used to document trace evidence such as hairs and fibers.

Rarely, however, are digital cameras used to document major investigations or to generate images that will be subject to detailed forensic analysis. This is due to current limitations on digital camera technology. Traditional film is preferred in forensic applications because it can offer better resolution and a greater dynamic range (more colors and brightness variations) than most digital cameras.

High-quality color film offers a resolution of approximately 75 line pairs per millimeter, or 150 pixels per millimeter, and has a dynamic range capable of recording 2 to 27 levels of brightness and color (or 27 bits per pixel). The resolution offered by charge-coupled devices (CCDs) in digital cameras available today can approach 150 pixels per millimeter, but their dynamic range is typically restricted to 2 to 24 levels of brightness and color (24 bits per pixel, or 8 bits for each color).

Of greater importance to law enforcement, in order to keep the cost of digital cameras down, the detectors included in these cameras are typically only one-third to one-half the size of a frame of 35-mm film. A reduction in the size of the detector means that in order to retain a comparable resolution, a smaller field of view must be imaged in a single exposure and more exposures taken to cover the same area. Such an approach is to be avoided when the images must later be enlarged to life size for forensic comparison, such as in the case of photographs of tire-tread and footwear impressions.

In many forensic applications, images first captured on film are converted to digital format through the use of film or print scanners. Both devices scan across the original, using either a linear-array or an area-array CCD imager. By scanning across an image rather than simply projecting the entire image onto a fixed imager, it is possible to achieve higher resolutions and record finer detail in the image. Film scanners that can achieve an optical resolution of 1200 pixels per inch or greater and flatbed (print) scanners that can achieve an optical resolution of

500 pixels per inch or greater are used in many forensic applications.

Another source of digital images used in forensic applications is video tapes. Since video signals are recorded electronically in an analog format, the conversion to digital format is accomplished by means of a frame grabber that converts each line of image data. Video signals in the United States follow the RS-170 standard, in which each frame contains approximately 486 visible lines of data. In order to maintain the proper width:height aspect ratio of 4:3, a digitized video image that is 486 lines (or pixels) high is sampled 648 times to create a digitized video image size of 486 pixels high by 648 pixels wide. Some frame grabbers permit a user to sample each video line more than 648 times. In order to maintain the proper aspect ratio in such cases, additional vertical lines must be added to the digital image, either through duplication of entire lines or through interpolation between alternate lines.

A related factor that complicates the processing of video images is that each video frame actually consists of two interlaced fields scanned sequentially at a rate of 60 fields per second. By interlacing these fields, each line is scanned approximately 1/60th of a second before or after the lines immediately above and below it, which provides relatively continuous motion. However, when time-lapse video systems are in use, this can result in extreme discontinuities between subsequent fields, as when an object or person moves across the field of view in the one second or more that it may take to record sequential fields. In such cases, a technique known as de-interlacing is used to eliminate one field while maintaining the image height of 486 lines or pixels. This is accomplished through either duplication of every other line or through interpolation between alternate lines.

Image enhancement. Digital image processing provides a means of enhancing images using operations based on both traditional photography and electronic signal processing. In most forensic applications, image processing is utilized to enhance the visibility of specific details in an image. **Figure 1***a*

(a)   (b)   (c)

Fig. 1. Partial view of a minivan. (*a***) Original video image. (***b***) Image after histogram equalization. (***c***) Image that results from averaging four separate fields.**

depicts a portion of a single field taken from a surveillance video tape. A detailed examination of the scratches and dents on the side of the unknown minivan depicted in this image was desired for comparison with a minivan owned by a suspect. In order to make these details visible, the brightness and contrast of this image were adjusted uniformly across the image through the process of histogram equalization. Histogram equalization improves the overall appearance of an image by reassigning the brightness values of all of the pixels so that they are uniformly distributed from black to white. The result is shown in Fig. 1b.

Whereas histogram equalization acts on an entire image, other commonly used enhancement operations adjust the relative brightness and contrast of adjacent pixels based on an analysis of pixels in their neighborhood. Edge sharpening and unsharp mask are two such techniques.

In some cases, enhancement involves reducing or eliminating the noise signature present in an image. Noise is a particularly prominent factor in video imagery and can arise at the detector or in the camera or recorder electronics. A great deal of video noise is generated randomly, leading to minor fluctuations in the brightness of individual pixels. This results in an image with a somewhat speckled appearance, as in Fig. 1b.

One way to reduce the speckling associated with noise, without reducing the effective resolution of the image, is to average multiple images on a pixel-by-pixel basis. Figure 1c shows the result of averaging four images of the minivan in Fig. 1a and then applying histogram equalization. This reveals that many of the dark and light spots that appear to be present on the side of the minivan in Fig. 1b are actually artifacts associated with random noise, so that those remaining in Fig. 1c can be attributed to physical features on the minivan.

In some cases the noise present in an image is repeating. A useful technique that may be applied is based on Fourier analysis. The fast Fourier transform (FFT) is used to reduce nonrandom, repeating noise or other background patterns within an image. A typical example involves the presence of a fingerprint on fabric. The thread pattern of the fabric can make it difficult to see ridge detail in the print necessary to make an identification. Since the threads are regularly spaced and oriented, the digital image of that fabric will contain regular brightness variations that can be identified and removed through the use of the fast Fourier transform.

In video imagery, nonrandom noise may be generated by the system itself. **Figure 2a** provides an example in which repeating noise has superimposed a pattern of diagonal and vertical banding upon an image of a robber's shirt. Figure 2b shows the resulting image when a fast Fourier transform has been utilized to remove that part of the image associated with the repeating noise. Although the resolution of the image is insufficient to permit the specific details of the shirt to be observed, the general outline

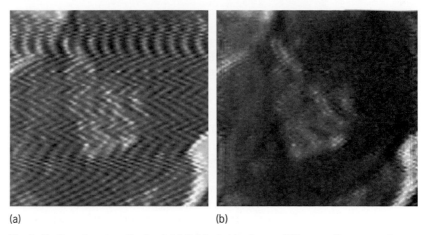

(a)   (b)

Fig. 2. Portion of a suspect's chest. (a) Original video image. (b) Image after processing using a fast Fourier transform.

of the bright pattern on the dark shirt may now be compared with that on the shirt of the suspect.

Image analysis. Digital imaging simplifies the application of a number of analytical tools in forensic analysis. Among these are photogrammetric applications which permit the determination of a suspect's height or of distances involved in a traffic accident. Such technologies also permit the creation of three-dimensional views from two-dimensional images, as well as a means of conducting virtual tours through these scenes.

In addition, a major benefit of digital imaging involves the ability to conduct automated searches and comparisons of fingerprints, bullets, shell casings, mug shots, and other evidence. The automated systems are used to identify candidates for further examination. Each system utilizes a rating system through which the best potential matches can be selected and examined by trained personnel who make the final determination of whether a match is present.

For background information *see* CHARGE-COUPLED DEVICES; FOURIER SERIES AND TRANSFORMS; IMAGE PROCESSING; PHOTOCOPYING PROCESSES; PHOTOGRAMMETRY; PHOTOGRAPHY; PRINTING in the McGraw-Hill Encyclopedia of Science & Technology.

Richard W. Vorder Bruegge

Bibliography. H. L. Blitzer, Assessing forensic imaging options, *Security J.*, 9:35–41, 1997; D. Capel et al., An automatic method for the removal of unwanted, non-periodic patterns from forensic images, in K. Higgins (ed.), Investigation and Forensic Science Technologies, *Proc. SPIE*, 3576:274–284, 1999; J. C. Russ, *The Image Processing Handbook*, 2d ed., CRC Press, Boca Raton, 1994; Scientific Working Group on Imaging Technologies, Definitions and Guidelines for the Use of Imaging Technologies in the Criminal Justice System, *Forensic Sci. Commun.*, vol. 1, no. 3, 1999; Scientific Working Group on Imaging Technologies, Guidelines for Field Applications of Imaging Technologies, *Forensic Sci. Commun.*, vol. 2, no. 1, 2000; R. W. Vorder Bruegge, Noise reduction of video imagery through simple averaging, in K. Higgins (ed.), Investigation and Forensic Science Technologies, *Proc. SPIE*, 3576: 185–194, 1999; P. Warrick, Identification of blood prints on fabric using amido black and digital enhancement, *J. Forensic Ident.*, 50(1):20–32, 2000.

Direct numerical simulation

Free-surface and multiphase flows are relevant to a variety of industrial and natural processes. At relatively small spatial scales, droplet impacts with solid surfaces are important for spray cooling, ink-jet printers, film coating, spray painting, erosion in steam turbines, and soil erosion due to rainfall. In fuel sprays the disintegration of liquid jets is attained via primary breakup of the fluid column and secondary breakup of the generated droplets. To optimize the injection systems and the subsequent combustion, it is crucial to determine the drop size distribution function. The interaction of a large number of droplets is relevant to boiling water–steam flows in pipes and to rain formation. At greater scales the wind is responsible for the wave formation and breaking on the ocean surface. Finding the flow around an advancing ship is a difficult free-surface problem whose solution would bring large rewards in design and optimization. All these processes are quite complex in themselves, but it is also necessary to couple the fluid dynamics description to other effects such as the chemistry of combustion or solid mechanics, for example, to determine the stress tensor in the hull of a fast ship moving in rough seas. Experimental techniques have shown the intrinsic beauty of drop impact, formation, and coalescence to such an extent that these processes are widely used in commercial advertisements.

Dealing with interfaces. The basic equation for the evolution of the flow for both analytical and numerical studies is the Navier-Stokes equation or one of its limiting simplified versions obtained by neglecting viscosity (perfect fluid flow) or inertia (Stokes flow). In three-dimensional space, an interface between two phases can be considered as a surface of discontinuity of density, viscosity, and pressure.

Moreover, the phenomenon of surface tension makes the interface behave as a stretched membrane (keeping, for instance, small droplets and bubbles approximately spherical). Discontinuities in physical variables, surface stresses, and changes in interface topology, which occur, for example, when two colliding droplets coalesce, represent singularities that considerably increase the difficulty of numerical resolution. For some cases of liquid-gas flow, the pressure in the gas can be considered as a constant (for instance, atmospheric pressure), and liquid dynamics is then studied as a free-surface flow. In all other cases, it is necessary to solve the problem of interfacial or multiphase flow.

Numerical techniques. When the simplified perfect or Stokes flows are studied, the boundary integral method allows relatively inexpensive and accurate solutions to be found. The interface is "drawn" as a series of lines between control points or markers. The velocity field is computed as a simple integral over the lines, and then the markers are moved with the local velocity field. However, for the full Navier-Stokes equation for multiphase flows, it is necessary to adopt more conventional methods, which are also used for the single-phase flow calculations and in other fields of mechanics, such as in finite-element, finite-volume, and finite-difference calculations. In these methods the velocity field must be found on an entire network of points defining a grid. The physical computational domain is thus divided into cells, which can be fixed in a regular or an unstructured grid or may move and deform (**Fig. 1**). In the last case the interface is a boundary between two subdomains of the grid. The solution of the Navier-Stokes equation is the velocity field at the computational grid points.

When surface markers are used, the interface can be advanced by moving the markers in the velocity field. In another description, a function C is defined, with a value equal to 1 in a cell full of one fluid, and to 0 in an empty cell. An intermediate value indicates a mixed cell crossed by the interface. This method is referred to as volume-of-fluid. In the level-set method, the function C instead varies slowly and smoothly, and the interface is localized as the set of

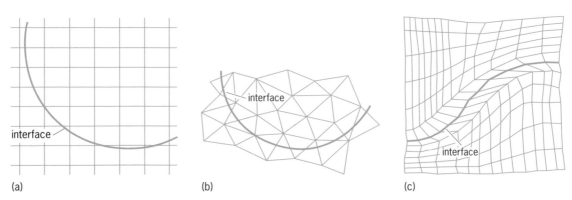

(a)   (b)   (c)

Fig. 1. Interfaces across (*a*) a fixed regular grid and (*b*) a fixed unstructured grid, and (*c*) a moving grid following the fluid-interface motion.

points x corresponding to $C(x) = 0$, C being negative in one fluid and positive in the other. From the knowledge of C and of its spatial variations, the interface can be reconstructed and evolved in time. In either case, from the knowledge of the interface, it is possible to calculate the surface curvature and appropriate averaged values of density and viscosity for mixed cells to be entered in the Navier-Stokes equation.

Personal computers and workstations currently have clock rates of several hundred megahertz, and random-access memories (RAM) of a few hundred megabytes. With these features a three-dimensional computational grid can contain 64^3–128^3 cells. For the largest grids a simulation requires several days of central processing unit time. Considering that the smallest scale of resolution requires about 10 grid points, at most a dozen droplets in each direction can be followed (a few thousand overall, for a dense flow), and the flow is usually laminar or in the transition regime. Even if the speed and memory capability of central processing units continue to increase while their prices drop, the use of parallel computers for large-scale simulations will still be unavoidable. Typically a three-dimensional rectangular domain is divided into subdomains of comparable size, each of which resides in a different processor. The exchange of information across these subdomains, that is, the values of physical variables near the boundaries, is performed with dedicated software, such as message-passing libraries.

Fluid flows are often characterized by localized regions of high vorticity, for example near the interface, and others where the flow is more uniform, frequently extending to most of the domain. The fine-grid resolution required in the convoluted regions is unnecessary in the more uniform part. The use of adaptive grid refinement, which amounts to local zooming to resolve complex fluid motion, allows considerable memory and computation savings.

Results. In many problems, it appears at first that viscosity is either very large (in small-scale flows in biology, for instance) or negligible (in many large-scale processes). This allows simulations by the powerful boundary integral methods. However, in the last several years a general trend has been to move from the solution of special cases (perfect or Stokes flow) by boundary integral methods to the direct numerical simulation of the full viscous case. Three types of simulations seem particularly challenging: droplet

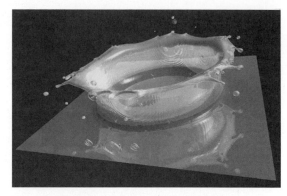

Fig. 2. Liquid droplet splashing on a liquid layer. (*Courtesy of Denis Gueyffier*)

splashing and collision, jet atomization, and bubbly columns, in increasing order of difficulty.

Droplet splashing and collision. Several simulations of this problem have already been performed. A droplet is launched at finite velocity against a wall covered with a thin film of liquid. The formation of the "milk crown" (**Fig. 2**), or fingers expanding above a ringlike lamella, is observed. However, the simulations show a crown only if the droplet surface or the layer surface is strongly perturbed before impact. A very likely explanation is that there is insufficient grid resolution around the time and place of the first contact of the droplet with the film. Very small, naturally occurring perturbations are probably violently amplified at this point. Another difficulty with splashing is that very thin layers of fluid are sometimes created, which cannot be followed with the volume-of-fluid methods when they become thinner than the grid spacing. The layers then break numerically, and the solution is qualitatively modified.

The situation with droplets collision is very similar. Frontal collisions at high speed also generate thin sheets and milk crowns. Adaptive grid refinement would help here. Currently simulations with 256^3 cells are possible using the largest supercomputers and symmetries. A factor of 10 in computer power and adaptive gridding would be necessary to attain realistic simulations. A further factor of 4 is necessary to perform the calculation in the nonsymmetric case, such as oblique impacts or collisions, which have the largest interest for applications. Using the rule that computer power increases by a factor of 5 every five years (a factor of 2 every two years would give similar results) yields the results in the **table**, which

Computational requirements for various interfacial flows				
Type of flow	Size of grid needed	Adaptive gridding	Mixed method	Year
Frontal droplet collision or splashing	512^3	Without	No	2000
Oblique droplet collision or splashing	512^3	With	No	2005
Jets, moderate-speed	$256^2 \times 2048$	With	No	2005
Jets, high-speed	$2048^2 \times 8096$	With	Yes	2035
Bubbly columns and pipes	$256^2 \times 20{,}000$	Without	Yes	2015

Fig. 3. Side view of a section of a turbulent liquid jet in air. Interface between liquid and gas is depicted, with light face facing the gas and dark face facing the liquid. The liquid has a Reynolds number of 2700 and a Weber number of 184,000, which are too large to allow resolution of the smallest droplets. However, while underresolved, this simulation is very informative on the process of droplet formation by growth of surface waves and filaments. (*Courtesy of Bruno Lafaurie and the Renault Group*)

indicates the year in which a simulation would probably be possible. Beyond computer power, another difficulty is the writing of parallel, adaptive codes with interfaces. The predictions in the table take into account the development time for such codes (three to five years).

Jet atomization. This problem involves mainly a Reynolds number, $Re = UD/\nu$, and a Weber number, $We = \rho U^2 D/\sigma$, where U is the jet velocity, D the diameter, ν the liquid viscosity, ρ the liquid density, and σ the surface tension. A small hydrocarbon or liquid oxygen jet as used in current experiments has $We \sim 10,000$ and $Re \sim 1000$. Jets can be done on 128^3 boxes for a fraction of their length. In many cases the simulations are done with grids which are too sparse to resolve the smallest droplets, which become smaller than the grid cell. Such a simulation can follow the largest scales of the flow, but it is a drastic approximation for the smallest droplets. Such underresolved simulations are of necessity a common feature of direct numerical simulations (**Fig. 3**), even in single-phase flow. It may be decades before computer power increases sufficiently to move from underresolved to well-resolved simulations. Many applications require scaling up both the Weber and Reynolds numbers by a factor of 10, and the geometry to the full length of the jet; hence the result in the table. A mixed method, able to follow small objects in a lagrangian way (in which droplets are treated as moving points of vanishing size) in the far region of the jet, where the grid would inevitably be coarser, is also necessary.

Bubbly columns. Estimates for these structures are more approximate. They have already been simu-

lated in some detail, but the scale of the droplets relative to the pipe diameter is still too large. Mixed methods seem unavoidable, and very long pipes are necessary. A preliminary estimate was carried out for a pipe with a length-to-diameter ratio of 64, but a ratio of 40 is deemed necessary for fully established turbulent flow.

In summary, direct numerical simulation must overcome three challenges: an algorithmic challenge, to perform adaptive calculations on parallel computers; a computer-power challenge, to deal with increasing grid sizes; and a modeling challenge, to take into account the necessary physics of thin sheets and the mixing of conventional with lagrangian methods. Following past trends, the rapid development of this field is likely to bring some spectacular results in the next few years, while harder problems and routine engineering use will wait for more powerful computers.

For background information *see* COMPUTATIONAL FLUID DYNAMICS; CREEPING FLOW; FLUID-FLOW PRINCIPLES; NAVIER-STOKES EQUATIONS; REYNOLDS NUMBER; SURFACE TENSION; TURBULENT FLOW in the McGraw-Hill Encyclopedia of Science & Technology.

Ruben Scardovelli; Stephane Zaleski

Bibliography. J. Eggers, Nonlinear dynamics and breakup of free-surface flows, *Rev. Mod. Phys.*, 69(3): 865–929, July 1997; R. Scardovelli and S. Zaleski, Direct numerical simulation of free-surface and interfacial flow, *Annu. Rev. Fluid Mech.*, 31:567–603, 1999; M. Sussman et al., An adaptive level set approach for incompressible two-phase flow, *J. Comput. Phys.*, 148:81–124, 1999.

Drug efflux pumps

Following the introduction of antibiotics into clinical usage in the 1940s, it soon became apparent that some bacteria were able to resist the killing action of the antibiotics. Bacteria resist or evade the toxic effects of antibiotics in a number of ways, one of which involves the energy-dependent efflux or pumping of antibiotics out of the bacterial cell. This mechanism was first identified in the early 1980s for tetracycline, and examples involving other antibiotics have since been reported. These original efflux pumps accommodated, and therefore provided resistance to, a single antibiotic or class of antibiotic. More recently, efflux pumps able to accommodate a variety of structurally unrelated antibiotics (and nonantibiotic molecules as well) have been described (**Fig. 1**). These pumps contribute significantly to the phenomenon of multiple antibiotic resistance in bacteria, a problem that severely complicates antibacterial chemotherapy. Multidrug efflux pumps are grouped into four families based upon amino acid sequence homology: the major facilitator superfamily (MFS), the ATP-binding cassette (ABC) family, the resistance-nodulation-division (RND) family, and the small multidrug resistance (SMR) protein family. Recently, a fifth family, referred to as the multidrug and toxic compound extrusion (MATE) family, has been identified.

Major facilitator superfamily. The MFS is an extremely large family that includes transporters of amino acids, sugars, as well as single and multiple antibiotics. The multidrug transporter members of the MFS group are integral cytoplasmic membrane proteins, about 400–500 amino acids in length, composed of two subgroups characterized by 12 or 14 membrane-spanning segments (**Fig. 2**). Antibiotic export (efflux) occurs via a drug-proton antiport mechanism whereby export of an antibiotic or drug molecule is directly coupled to import of a proton (H^+), with both processes catalyzed by the MFS exporter. Thus, the proton gradient (also called the proton motive force) which is maintained across the cytoplasmic membrane of most bacteria provides the impetus or energy for export of drug molecules. Although there are many examples of MFS transporters that accommodate single antibiotics, most MFS-type multidrug efflux systems accommodate very few (sometimes no) antibiotics and tend, rather, to export a limited range of nonantibiotics such as antiseptics and disinfectants, dyes (such as ethidium bromide), detergents, and uncouplers [protonophores that dissipate the proton gradient across the cytoplasmic membrane and thus inhibit proton motive force–dependent processes, such as carbonyl cyanide *m*-chlorophenylhydrazone (CCCP)] (see **table**). Still, the NorA and PmrA MFS multidrug efflux pumps of *Staphylococcus aureus and Streptococcus pneumoniae*, respectively, play a significant role in the resistance of these organisms to an important class of antibiotics, the fluoroquinolones (such as ciprofloxacin) [see table].

Multidrug efflux systems of the MFS type tend to occur in gram-positive bacteria (which stain with a dye, crystal violet, and possess a single lipid bilayer membrane, the cytoplasmic membrane, bounding the bacterial cell) with only a few examples reported in gram-negative bacteria (which do not stain with crystal violet and possess two bilayer membranes external to the cell, the cytoplasmic membrane and a second, outer membrane). Some of the MFS-type multidrug transporters which have been described in gram-negative bacteria appear to function with auxiliary proteins located in the periplasm (the region between the cytoplasmic and outer membranes) and the outer membrane. Thus, the MFS transporter is apparently physically linked to an outer membrane, presumed channel-forming protein (sometimes called outer membrane efflux protein [OEP]) by a periplasmic linker or membrane fusion protein (MFP) [**Fig. 3**]. This organization serves to facilitate expulsion of drugs from the cell interior to the exterior in one step. Still, the MFS transporter, LfrA, of *Mycobacterium smegmatis*, an organism which does not possess an outer membrane per se but which does have a second membranelike structure exterior to the cytoplasmic membrane, appears not to utilize auxiliary proteins. In this instance, drugs are presumably exported across the

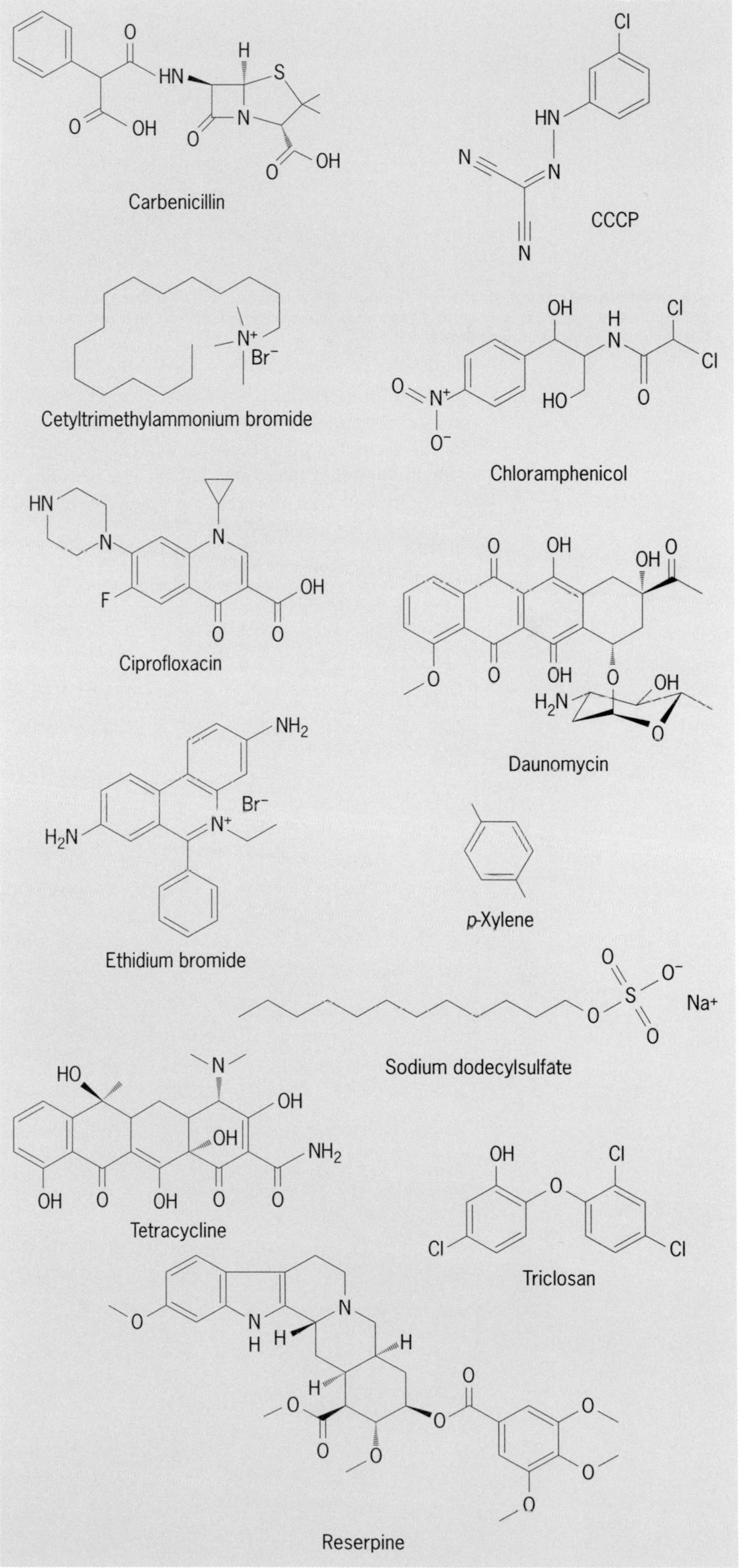

Fig. 1. Chemical structures of some substrates and an inhibitor (reserpine) of bacterial multidrug efflux systems.

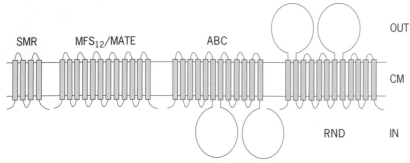

Fig. 2. Membrane topology of the five families of bacterial multidrug efflux pumps, highlighting the membrane-spanning segments (shaded) and loop regions internal and external to the cytoplasmic membrane (CM).

cytoplasmic membrane and then diffuse across the outer membranelike structure via channels much like the porins of gram-negative bacteria (Fig. 3).

Small multidrug resistance family. The smallest of the multidrug transporters, members of the SMR family, are typically about 100 amino acids in length and span the cytoplasmic membrane four times (Fig. 2). It has been suggested that the proteins function as oligomers, probably homotrimers, such that the functional pump actually contains three Smr proteins and 12 membrane spanning segments. Members of the SMR family export a limited range of compounds, many of which are components of disinfectants (such as benzalkonium chloride or cetyltrimethylammonium bromide), and do not export or facilitate resistance to antibiotics (see table; Fig. 1). Found in both gram-positive (for example, Smr, *Sta. aureus*) and gram-negative (EmrE, *Escherichia coli*) bacteria, this family of transporters utilizes the proton-motive force to facilitate drug efflux (see table; Fig. 3).

Resistance-nodulation-division family. Members of the RND family of exporters are limited to gram-negative bacteria and play roles in multidrug export, as well as export of heavy metals [such as cobalt

Multidrug transporter class	Multidrug transporter	Bacterium	Disease or infections caused	Transporter substrates
Examples of bacterial multidrug efflux pumps				
Gram-positive				
MFS$_{14}$	QacA	*Staphylococcus aureus*	Food poisoning, skin, and wound	Antiseptics, disinfectants, dyes
MFS$_{12}$	NorA	*Staphylococcus aureus*	Food poisoning, skin, and wound	Antibiotics, antiseptics, disinfectants, dyes
MFS$_{12}$	PmrA	*Streptococcus pneumoniae*	Pneumonia	Antibiotics, dyes
SMR	Smr	*Staphylococcus aureus*	Food poisoning, skin, and wound	Dyes, antiseptics, disinfectants
ABC	LmrA	*Lactobacillus lactis*	None	Lipophilic cations, dyes, anticancer drugs
Gram-negative				
MFS$_{14}$	LfrA	*Mycobacterium smegmatis* (model system for *M. tuberculosis*)	Tuberculosis	Antiseptics, disinfectants, dyes, antibiotics
MFS$_{14}$/MFP/OEP	EmrA-EmrB-TolC	*Escherichia coli*	Diarrheal	Uncouplers, metabolic inhibitors
MFS$_{14}$/MFP/OEP	VceA-VceB[a]	*Vibrio cholerae*	Cholera	Uncouplers, dyes, detergents
SMR	EmrE	*Escherichia coli*	Diarrheal	Lipophilic cations
RND/MFP/OEP	MexA-MexB-OprM	*Pseudomonas aeruginosa*	Respiratory and urinary tracts, wound	Antibiotics, dyes, detergents, organic solvents, disinfectants
RND/MFP/OEP	CeoA-CeoB-OpcM	*Burkholderia cepacia*	Respiratory tract	Antibiotics
RND/MFP/OEP	AcrA-AcrB-TolC	*Escherichia coli*	Diarrheal	Antibiotics, dyes, detergents, organic solvents, disinfectants
RND/MFP/OEP	AcrA-AcrB	*Salmonella typhimurium*	Food poisoning and gastrointestinal	Antibiotics, dyes, detergents
RND/MFP/OEP	AcrA-AcrB	*Hemophilus influenzae*	Meningitis and pneumonia	Antibiotics, dyes, detergents
RND/MFP/OEP	MtrC-MtrD-MtrE	*Neisseria gonorrhoeae*	Urogenital and rectal	Antibiotics, dyes, detergents, lipids, antimicrobial peptides
RND/MFP/OEP	SmeA-SmeB-SmeC	*Stenotrophomonas maltophilia*	Respiratory tract	Antibiotics
MATE	NorM	*Vibrio parahaemolyticus*	Food poisoning	Antibiotics, dyes, lipophilic cations

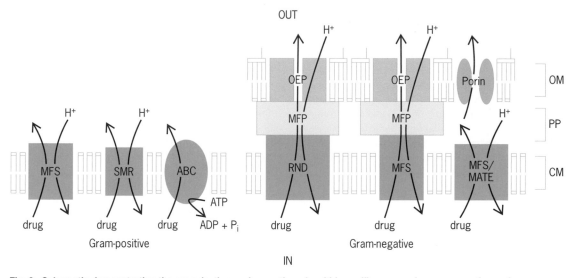

Fig. 3. Schematic demonstrating the organization and operation of multidrug efflux pumps in gram-negative and gram-positive bacteria. OM, outer membrane; PP, periplasmic space; CM, cytoplasmic membrane.

(Co^{2+}), zinc (Zn^{2+}), cadmium (Cd^{2+}), and nickel (Ni^{2+})] and nodulation factors (produced by *Rhizobium* species which nodulate legumes). Individual RND-type multidrug transporters export the broadest range of compounds of any known multidrug efflux system, including a variety of antibiotics (for example, ciprofloxacin, chloramphenicol, carbenicillin, and tetracycline), dyes (such as ethidium bromide), detergents (such as sodium dodecylsulfate), disinfectants (such as triclosan), organic solvents (such as *p*-xylene), toxic lipids, and metabolic inhibitors (Fig. 1). Thus, they play an important role in clinical resistance to a large number of antibiotics and disinfectants in those organisms in which they occur. From the perspective of bioremediation, the ability of these transporters to export organic solvents provides a means of bacterial resistance to these toxic environmental pollutants, a feature that may facilitate the development of microbes capable of detoxifying such pollutants. Transporters of the RND type are integral cytoplasmic membrane proteins composed of 12 membrane spanning segments and two large periplasmic loops between MSS1 and 2 and between MSS7 and 8 (Fig. 2). These transporters tend to be large (greater than 1000 amino acids), and they operate with an outer membrane efflux protein and a periplasmic membrane fusion protein (Fig. 3).

ATP-binding cassette family. Unlike the other multidrug efflux families, members of the ABC family of efflux pumps utilize the hydrolysis of adenosine triphosphate (ATP) to provide the energy for drug efflux rather than the proton-motive force (Fig. 3). There are innumerable examples of ABC-type transporters in bacteria, yeast, protozoa, plants, and animals, involved for the most part in transport of nutrients into or export of proteins out of the cell. ATP-binding cassette–type multidrug transporters are comparatively rare, with the best-studied examples, P-glycoprotein and multidrug resistance-associated protein (MRP) 1, occurring in mammalian cells, where they play a role in the resistance of tumors to anticancer drugs. ATP-binding cassette–type multidrug transporters are extremely rare in bacteria, with only a single example, the LmrA exporter of *Lactococcus lactis* (a nonpathogen), described to date. The prototypic ABC-type multidrug transporter is an integral cytoplasmic membrane protein comprising 12 membrane spanning segments and two large cytoplasmic loops (between MSS6 and 7, and after MSS12) [Fig. 2]; the latter are involved in the binding and hydrolysis of ATP (Fig. 3). Although LmrA, like its P-glycoprotein counterpart, accommodates a range of substrates, these are limited to nonantibiotics such as dyes (such as ethidium bromide) and anticancer agents (such as daunomycin) [Fig. 1]. Like its P-glycoprotein homolog, LmrA appears to capture its drug substrates from within the lipid bilayer of the cytoplasmic membrane and not from the aqueous phase bordering the membrane.

Multidrug and toxic compound extrusion family. The newest family of multidrug efflux proteins, members of MATE are also cytoplasmic membrane proteins of 12 membrane spanning segments that utilize the energy of the proton motive force to facilitate drug expulsion (for example, a drug-proton antiport mechanism) [Figs. 2 and 3]. The prototypic MATE protein, NorM, was first proposed to be an MFS transporter, although more detailed phylogenic analysis confirmed that it was a representative of a novel though poorly characterized family. Described only in gram-negative bacteria to date, MATE transporters appear to function without auxiliary proteins and, thus, deliver substrates to the periplasm, where they likely leave the cell via diffusion through so-called porin channels in the outer membrane (Fig. 3). NorM substrates include antibiotics (for example, ciprofloxacin) as well as dyes (such as ethidium bromide) [Fig. 1].

Clinical significance. Multidrug efflux systems of the RND and MFS families contribute to clinically relevant antibiotic resistance in a number of important human pathogens (see table). Widely distributed among gram-negative pathogens and affording resistance to many antibiotics, the tripartite RND-MFP-OEP exporters are by far the most important of the multidrug efflux systems. Moreover, many organisms possess multiple examples of these pumps, such that the opportunity for export of and resistance to most known antibiotics is available in these bacteria. Multidrug efflux systems can be expressed constitutively, whereby they contribute to the intrinsic multidrug resistance of the organism. In many instances, however, expression of the efflux systems in clinical strains results from mutational deregulation of the efflux genes, providing for high-level expression of the efflux pump components. This can occur for constitutively expressed systems, in which case mutation increases efflux gene expression, or for systems which are normally quiescent, in which case mutation turns on efflux gene expression. Those multidrug efflux pumps which fail to accommodate antibiotics but do export and provide resistance to disinfectants and antiseptics (such as SMR and some MFS transporters) are important, too, as they compromise the use of such agents in hospitals and the food industry. RND-MFP-OEP efflux systems that accommodate both disinfectants and antibiotics are of particular concern, given the widespread use of disinfectants in the home. The use of triclosan and pine oils as antibacterial agents in many home products, for example, risks selecting for bacteria hyperproducing RND-MFP-OEP-type multidrug efflux systems, which will provide resistance not only to triclosan or pine oil but also to many clinically relevant antibiotics. The potential therapeutic use of efflux pump inhibitors is currently being studied, with several inhibitors (such as reserpine, which acts against MFS multidrug transporters) able to enhance the antibiotic susceptibility of pump-producing strains of bacteria (Fig. 1).

Natural function. The broad substrate specificity of bacterial multidrug efflux systems flies in the face of the biological norm of substrate-specific transporters which have traditionally recognized and transported or exported a single substrate. While the molecular basis of this broad substrate specificity remains to be elucidated, it is clear that it is a reflection of the natural function of these efflux systems in bacteria. Antibiotic efflux per se is unlikely to be the intended role, but rather to be a product of the inherent flexibility of these transporters in relation to substrate recognition. The P-glycoproteins have been implicated as possible membrane vacuums (cleaners), which clear the cytoplasmic membrane of hydrophobic molecules that will tend to partition into such structures naturally and could, if allowed to accumulate, adversely affect membrane function. Substrates of the RND-type multidrug transporters, though structurally diverse, are somewhat hydrophobic and probably capable of partitioning into biological membranes. Thus, these transporters may play a similar membrane-cleaning role. Alternatively, certain multidrug efflux systems are proposed to export the by-products of metabolism (waste products) associated with bacterial growth. These are likely to be many and necessitate flexibility in substrate recognition by the export machinery. Still, it is likely that some multidrug efflux pumps play a protective role in the bacterial cell. For example, the AcrAB-TolC multidrug efflux system of *E. coli* exports and likely protects the bacterium from bile acids present within the digestive secretions of the human gut, an environment in which the organism is commonly found. Similarly, the MtrCDE efflux system of *Neisseria gonorrhoeae* provides resistance to toxic fatty acids which occur in the mucous lining of the rectum, a possible site of infection by this organism. Given the structural variability of bile acids and fecal lipids, both of these pumps would have to be flexible in terms of substrate recognition.

For background information *see* ANTIBIOTIC; BACTERIA; BACTERIAL PHYSIOLOGY AND METABOLISM; CELL MEMBRANES; DRUG RESISTANCE; GENE in the McGraw-Hill Encyclopedia of Science & Technology.

R. Keith Poole

Bibliography. P. N. Markham et al., Multiple novel inhibitors of the NorA multidrug transporter of *Staphylococcus aureus, Antimicrob. Agents Chemother.*, 43:2404–2408, 1999; M. C. Moken, L. M. McMurry, and S. B. Levy, Selection of multiple-antibiotic-resistant (Mar) mutants of *Escherichia coli* by using the disinfectant pine oil: Roles of the *mar* and *acrAB* loci, *Antimicrob. Agents Chemother.*, 41:2770–2772, 1997; H. Nikaido, Multiple antibiotic resistance and efflux, *Curr. Opin. Microbiol.*, 1:516–523, 1998; J. L. Ramos et al., Efflux pumps involved in toluene tolerance in *Pseudomonas putida* DOT-T1E, *J. Bacteriol.*, 180:3323–3329, 1998.

Earth mantle

At the high pressures and temperatures found in the Earth's mantle, rock responds to stress by slow, creeping flow. The mantle, although solid, is a dynamic system. Convection is driven by density variations primarily caused by temperature variations and possibly also by compositional variations. Hot, relatively low-density material wells up to the surface, and cold, higher-density material plunges into the interior. This phenomenon influences the Earth's surface processes and drives the motion of the tectonic plates.

A long-standing question in mantle convection concerns the nature of this flow and whether the mantle has a uniform bulk composition or is stratified at some depth. All the evidence regarding the structure and dynamics of the mantle is obtained indirectly by observations made at the surface. The most important source of information comprises observations of seismic velocity variations, which are affected by temperature and composition. Over the past several decades, the accumulation of more and better data from global seismic networks has made it possible for seismologists to generate clearer views of the structure of the mantle on global and regional scales. Additional information comes from other types of observations, including measurements of the composition of volcanic rocks derived from the Earth, the fluxes of noble gases from the mantle, the surface heat flow, the heat production of mantle materials, and the Earth's shape and gravity field (which are related to internal density variations). Forward modeling of convection on computers and by laboratory analogs provides additional insight into the processes occurring in the mantle.

Seismic velocity variations. The velocity of seismic waves traveling through the Earth varies with the composition, temperature, and phase of the material that the wave is traveling through. The overall radial structure of the Earth is well known from these seismic velocities. The crust and mantle are composed primarily of solid oxide crystals, while the core is composed of iron alloy and is molten from the core-mantle boundary to a depth of 5150 km (3193 mi) [see **illus.**]. Several internal interfaces have been identified within the mantle. One such interface is the mantle transition zone at a depth of 670 km (415 mi). At shallower depths, the mantle consists largely of the oxide crystals olivine, pyroxene, and garnet; below this depth, pressures and temperatures are such that perovskites dominate.

Mapping out the regions in which seismic velocity diverges from its average value at a given depth provides a means for inferring the structure caused by mantle convection and for searching for compositional layering in the mantle. Seismological observations of compressional-wave (P) velocity and shear-wave (S) velocity typically show anomalously fast velocities associated with subducted slabs. These high velocities are likely due to colder temperatures in the slabs, which were cooled at the surface of the Earth before plunging into the interior. As slabs reach the mantle transition zone, the slabs appear to deform, thicken, and bend. Seismic images show that deformed subducted slabs penetrate through the mantle transition zone and into the deep mantle to at least 1700 km (1054 mi) depth. Seismic signals from the slabs break up in the lowermost 1000 km (620 mi) of the mantle, suggesting that slabs may not extend all the way to the core-mantle boundary.

At very great depths, there is evidence that lateral variations in composition play a role in seismic velocity. The lowermost mantle exhibits large-amplitude lateral variations in S- and P-wave speed, indicating a mix of different compositions and variations in temperature. In some regions, S-wave speed is not positively correlated with P-wave speed as would be expected if the velocity variations were due to temperature alone. Regions of anomalous composition also appear to scatter high-frequency seismic waves in the lower mantle.

After very large earthquakes, such as the magnitude-8.4 Bolivia earthquake of 1994, long-period oscillations are recorded which are sensitive to long-wavelength structure in the Earth. The peri-

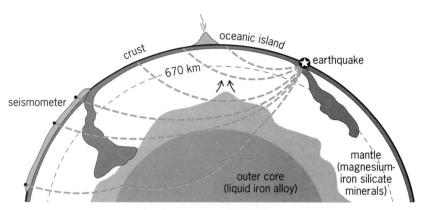

Schematic cross section of the Earth. Note the subducted slab and possible layering in the mantle. Seismic waves from earthquakes travel through the Earth and are recorded by seismometers, revealing the structure of the interior of the planet.

ods of free oscillations in the Earth depend on the seismic velocity and the Earth's density as a function of depth. Comparing density and seismic velocity data obtained from free oscillations to models that assume a uniform composition for the mantle suggests that the lower mantle is slightly (up to 2%) more dense than it would be if it had the same composition as the upper mantle. The free-oscillation data indicate that material that is intrinsically dense but hot and therefore somewhat buoyant may be welling up beneath Africa and the Pacific.

Heat production and surface heat flow. Mantle convection cools the interior of the Earth. Heat generated by radioactive decay of potassium, uranium, and thorium, and heat left from the formation and early differentiation of the Earth, are lost by cooling of the plates at the surface. Heat currently flows out of the Earth at a rate of 44 terawatts. Some of this (6 TW) is generated by radioactive decay within the crust. The remainder is provided by a combination of heat generation within the mantle and core (which is then transferred out of the Earth by mantle convection), or by cooling of the planet.

The exact proportions of current heat generation to cooling are not known and vary over time, but an approximate heat "budget" can be estimated. It is thought that the Earth contains heat-producing elements in approximately the same proportions as the class of meteorites known as chondrites. A chondritic Earth would have a total heat production and loss of 31 TW, with the remaining 13 TW provided by cooling at an average rate of 65°C (117°F) per billion years. The rate of cooling is expected to have been higher in the Archean, and 3 billion years ago heat production was approximately twice as high as the current rate.

Heat-producing elements. The concentration of heat-producing elements in the upper mantle is estimated from the composition of mid-ocean ridge basalts (MORB), which form by partial melting and melt extraction at the spreading centers between divergent tectonic plates. As diverging plate boundaries migrate randomly over the Earth's surface, the MORB source provides a reasonable approximation of average upper mantle. The source region of MORB is quite uniform in composition, and is depleted in heat production by a factor of 5 to 10 relative to the value that would be expected in the mantle of a chondritic Earth. Thus if the entire mantle has the same composition as the MORB source, it would currently produce only 2–6 TW, comparable to the amount currently produced in the much smaller volume of crust. The remainder of the current heat flow from the Earth would have to originate from cooling of the planet, at an exceptionally high rate of $175°C$ ($315°F$) per billion years. Extrapolating this rate of heat loss back to the early Earth would produce mantle temperatures that are not compatible with the composition of magmas produced during the Archean. Thus the heat flow data for the Earth predict that there is an additional reservoir that contains a higher concentration of heat-producing elements than the MORB source region.

Outgassing of noble gases. The process of melting that creates MORB and oceanic island basalts also outgasses noble gases such as helium and argon into the atmosphere. Like the heat budget, the argon budget can be used to infer the composition of the mantle. The isotope argon-40 is produced as a product of radioactive decay of potassium-40. Only about half of the radiogenic argon that must have been produced in the Earth resides in the atmosphere; the rest remains stored in the interior of the planet, most likely within the mantle, although some may reside in the crust. If the composition of the mantle is like that of the MORB source region, it would not be able to account for the missing argon. However, a layer deep within the mantle could hold the extra radiogenic argon through billions of years of Earth's history.

Computer and analog models of convection. Further insight into the dynamical processes within the mantle arises from numerical simulations of thermochemical convection on the computer and from analog models in the laboratory. Advances in computer power, especially the advent of parallel computers, are beginning to make it possible to realistically simulate these processes. Numerical simulations of thermochemical convection have been carried out to try to understand how intrinsically dense but hot material would behave in the deep mantle. These models indicate that intrinsically dense material would tend to pile up under mantle upwellings and be deflected downward beneath subducted slabs. The intrinsic high density is balanced to some extent by the reduction in density due to high temperatures in the deep mantle. Thus any compositional interface in the deep mantle is likely to exhibit substantial topography. Some recent data indicate a large zone of anomalously slow seismic velocity beneath Africa; this has been interpreted as a large mantle upwelling which may be associated with ongoing volcanic activity in the Afar rift. Anomalously hot mantle beneath Africa would explain the elevated topography of this continent. Ongoing seismic experiments and numerical and laboratory models will make it possible to produce more accurate images of the deep mantle structure within the next few years.

For background information *see* EARTH; EARTH, CONVECTION IN; EARTH, HEAT FLOW IN; MID-OCEANIC RIDGE; SEISMOLOGY; SUBDUCTION ZONES in the McGraw-Hill Encyclopedia of Science & Technology.

Louise Kellogg

Bibliography. A. W. Hofmann, Mantle geochemistry: The message from oceanic volcanism, *Nature*, 385: 219–229, 1997; R. Jeanloz and T. Lay, The core-mantle boundary, *Sci. Amer.*, 268:48–55, May 1993; L. H. Kellogg, B. H. Hager, and R. Van der Hilst, Compositional stratification in the deep mantle, *Science*, 283:1881–1884, 1999; R. D. Van der Hilst, S. Widiyantoro, and E. R. Engdahl, Evidence for deep mantle circulation from global tomography, *Nature*, 386:578–584, 1997.

Earth oscillations

After a large earthquake, the Earth oscillates with natural, resonant frequencies like the tones of a bell. This phenomenon was theoretically predicted in the nineteenth century and was actually discovered after the 1960 magnitude-9.5 Chilean earthquake, the largest tremor of the twentieth century. These so-called free oscillations are now commonly observed after earthquakes of about magnitude 6.5 and larger because of improved seismometers with high sensitivity.

Just as each bell has its own particular tone, the Earth has particular free-oscillation periods. After different earthquakes, the same periods (modes) of oscillations are generated, although amplitudes vary from earthquake to earthquake and from seismic station to seismic station. During the last 20 years, these oscillation periods and their amplitudes have been studied in detail and have given great insight into the interior structure of the Earth.

Discovery of background oscillations. Until 1997, all observable free oscillations were assumed to be generated by earthquakes or by so-called slow earthquakes. Slow earthquakes are mysterious seismic events that are thought to release energy gradually, without the sudden rupturing of faults. Whether the oscillations are caused by typical earthquakes or slow earthquakes, their occurrence should be transient; such oscillations should decay within a few days after excitation, because of energy loss due to the inelastic properties of the Earth.

However, it was shown in 1997 and repeatedly thereafter, by using different seismic instruments, that the Earth is oscillating continuously, regardless of earthquake occurrence. Observed free oscillations are the type of modes called fundamental spheroidal modes, for frequencies between 2 and 7 millihertz (mHz). Spheroidal modes of free oscillations contain vertical as well as horizontal motions, but detection of oscillations has been done exclusively from vertical seismometers.

Fundamental modes contain most of their energy close to the surface, although fundamental-mode oscillations at 2 mHz shake more than 1000 km (600 mi) down into the Earth, moving approximately the outer one-sixth of the Earth. These continuous oscillations are called background oscillations and contain only fundamental modes. Overtone modes which have energy at greater depths have not been observed in the data, suggesting that the source of excitation is close to the surface of the Earth.

Background oscillations were detected by conventional Fourier analysis of seismic records. This was initially demonstrated by selecting seismically quiet days, meaning days with no earthquakes larger than magnitude 5.5, and examining spectral peaks of fundamental spheroidal modes in data. Although fundamental spheroidal mode peaks for frequencies below 7 mHz should not be excited on such seismically quiet days, spectral peaks persisted. It was shown later that the spectral peaks exist continuously, regardless of earthquake occurrence (**Fig. 1**). The manner in which the background oscillations were discovered is surprising in that all it required was conventional Fourier analysis for ordinary broadband seismometer records.

The amplitudes of observed modes are about 0.4 nanogal (1 ngal = 10^{-11} m/s^2) and are approximately constant in acceleration (Fig. 1). At a frequency of 3 mHz, these observed amplitudes are equivalent to about 10^{-6} cm in displacement; the ground goes up and down by this amount in about 300 seconds.

The observed spectral amplitudes are approximately constant as long as there are no earthquakes larger than magnitude 6. When a large earthquake occurs, amplitudes of oscillations increase linearly with size of earthquakes, overwhelming the amplitudes of background oscillations. But in the absence of such large earthquakes, the amplitudes of background oscillations are constant and persistent.

It was shown in 1999 that these amplitudes contain seasonal variations with two maximum peaks in a year, one in December–February and the other in June–August. The peak-to-peak amplitude variation is approximately 8 (+/− 4%).

Cause of oscillations. The cause of the oscillations is hard to determine because, like a bell, the Earth vibrates much the same regardless of what sets it going. The three-dimensional patterns of oscillations depend mainly on the shape of the Earth, its composition, and its thermal state—not on what excites them. So, free oscillations reveal the interior structure of the Earth but do not reveal very much about the source of oscillations. Three possible sources are (1) cumulative effects of small earthquakes, (2) slow earthquakes, and (3) atmospheric pressure variations.

Cumulative effects of small earthquakes. Since the Earth is a tectonically active planet, it seems natural to consider the effects from many small earthquakes to be the cause of these continuous oscillations. However, an order of magnitude estimated by this effect to

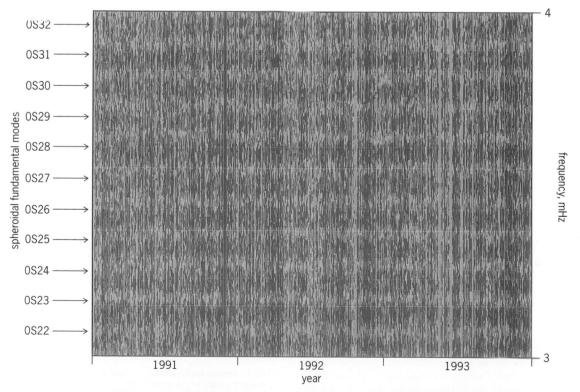

Fig. 1. Three years of acceleration spectral amplitude at Canberra, Australia. Frequency range is between 3 and 4 mHz. Continuous background oscillations are clearly seen as horizontal stripes. These stripes are exactly at the frequencies of spheroidal fundamental modes from 0S22 to 0S32.

be at the level of excitation was shown to be too small. A more detailed argument goes as follows: The statistics on the number of small earthquakes follows the Gutenberg-Richter law quite well. This empirical law says that for a reduction of magnitude by one, the number of earthquake increases tenfold. However, energy emitted by an earthquake reduces by a factor of 30 for a reduction of magnitude by one. In total, the energy emitted by earthquakes becomes about one-third for a reduction of magnitude by one. Even if all the energy from the small earthquakes is summed up for the excitation of oscillations, it would not reach a sufficient level to explain the observed amplitudes of continuous oscillations.

Constancy of amplitudes for days without earthquakes larger than magnitude 6 also argues against this hypothesis. Even if there are no earthquakes larger than magnitude 6, there are variations of earthquakes below magnitude 6. The amplitudes of background oscillations are constant and do not seem to be affected by such variations. This observation suggests strongly that these oscillations are controlled by some other mechanism.

Slow earthquakes. Earthquakes are not the only tectonic motions in the Earth. There are perhaps much larger aseismic tectonic motions in the Earth; examples include slow and silent earthquakes, the creeping motions of tectonic plates, and magmatic processes under active volcanoes. Among those possibilities, slow earthquakes are considered to be a serious candidate. Although these earthquakes are not well known, there are some reports from oceanic fracture zones, a little-studied remote part of the Earth. Some of these slow earthquakes may be large enough to excite background oscillations. But quantitative tests have not been possible, and it is uncertain whether or not they can explain various characteristics of the observed amplitude behaviors in background oscillations.

Atmospheric pressure variations. The atmosphere is a serious candidate for the excitation of background oscillations. This mechanism is considered to work in the following way: The atmosphere in the frequency band between 2 and 7 mHz is turbulent, and there are vigorous motions in the atmosphere which cause pressure fluctuations at the surface of the Earth. When the pressure rises, the atmosphere presses down on the ground or sea beneath it. When the pressure drops, the surface rebounds. The Earth is then like a bell being constantly hit by atmospheric pressure changes (**Fig. 2**). While this effect may be small locally, the atmosphere applies this process on the solid Earth everywhere, constantly in time. Integrated effects from the whole Earth have been shown to be sufficiently large to excite background oscillations.

This hypothesis is favored not only because the atmosphere seems to have sufficient energy to explain the observed amplitudes of background oscillations but also because seasonal variation is reported in the background oscillations. Amplitudes of the background oscillations become higher in June–August and in December–February. The variation of amplitude is about 8% from peak to peak throughout a year and is proportional to variations of atmospheric pressure. The real cause of this pattern may be the occurrence of winter in some parts of the world, either in the Northern Hemisphere or in the Southern Hemisphere, since the average atmospheric pressure variation in each hemisphere is known to have a maximum in winter and a minimum in summer.

Other hypotheses that attribute the cause to some processes in the ocean are also being considered for the excitation of the background oscillations. It remains to be seen whether ocean processes have sufficient energy in the frequency band between 2 and 7 mHz, and whether they can maintain constancy of amplitudes and show seasonal variations. Currently, the most favored hypothesis is the atmospheric excitation, but it seems likely that processes in the solid Earth are not the cause of the background oscillations because solid Earth processes do not usually have seasonal variations.

Application in planetary seismology. If the atmospheric excitation hypothesis turns out to be true, other planets with atmospheres may be oscillating by the same mechanism. This could provide a new approach for studying the interior of these planets. It may be an important approach since a planet such as Mars is thought to have very low tectonic activity and probably has few quakes. If so, even if a seismic instrument is installed on Mars's surface, waiting for quakes to be recorded, researchers may never get a sufficient amount of quake data to study the planet's interior. However, if the whole planet is oscillating by the atmospheric excitation mechanism, researchers can observe free oscillations of Mars. Resonant oscillation periods could then give information on the

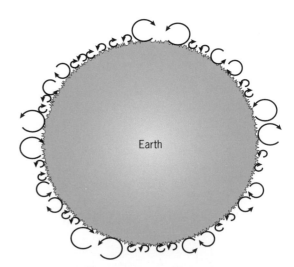

Fig. 2. Atmospheric excitation hypothesis. Atmospheric pressure fluctuations exert force on the solid Earth, which leads to ringing of the Earth with its natural resonant frequencies.

interior structure of Mars. This approach may work for Mars as well as for Venus, although the technical challenge of installing seismometers on these planets may be enormous.

For background information *see* EARTHQUAKE; FOURIER SERIES AND TRANSFORMS; OSCILLATION; PLATE TECTONICS; SEISMOGRAPHIC INSTRUMENTATION; SEISMOLOGY; TONE (MUSIC AND ACOUSTICS) in the McGraw-Hill Encyclopedia of Science & Technology.   Toshiro Tanimoto

Bibliography. N. Kobayashi and K. Nishida, Continuous excitation of planetary free oscillations by atmospheric disturbances, *Nature*, 395:357–360, 1998; N. Suda, K. Nawa, and Y. Fukao, Earth's background free oscillations, *Science*, 279:2089–2091, 1998; T. Tanimoto et al., Earth's continuous oscillations observed on seismically quiet days. *Geophys. Res. Lett.*, 25:1553–1556, 1998; T. Tanimoto and J. Um, Cause of continuous oscillations of the Earth, *J. Geophys. Res.*, 104:28723–28739, 1999.

Earthquake

Since the early 1900s there have been documented cases of humans influencing the occurrence of earthquakes by gold and coal mining, fluid injection and withdrawal, and reservoir impoundment. Famous examples include the magnitude-5 earthquakes in the Denver, CO, area in the 1960s, which were caused by the injection of hazardous waste; and two earthquakes associated with reservoir loading, the magnitude-6.5 earthquake in Koyna, India, in 1967 and the magnitude-5.3 earthquake at Aswan Dam on the Nile River in Egypt in 1981. The Koyna earthquake killed 200 people. Near Reading, PA, a magnitude-4.6 earthquake in 1994 caused more than $2 million in damage; this earthquake, in a setting where tectonic activity rarely produces earthquakes, was caused by quarry unloading. Human-induced earthquakes are best detected in regions where the Earth's strain rates are quite low and therefore the earthquakes stand out in contrast to the very low expected number of events. Scientists develop mathematical models of stresses in the earth generated by human activity and correlate the stresses with the location and time of the subsequent earthquakes.

The scenario of earthquakes themselves triggering or delaying subsequent earthquakes is also recognized as a scientific and societal problem. Earthquakes rarely occur as lone events but generally occur in sequences. The usual situation is for a larger earthquake called a mainshock to be followed by a series of smaller earthquakes called aftershocks in the same geographical region. Aftershocks can occur up to many years after the primary event, and a connection between mainshocks and aftershocks was recognized more than 100 years ago. Although there still is not an exact model for the physical relationship between mainshocks and aftershocks, scientists

now calculate the probabilities of aftershock occurrence by examining temporal and spatial earthquake patterns in earthquake-prone regions around the world. The public is then informed about the likelihood of an aftershock in a specific magnitude range during a specific time period. In the future, as the understanding of earthquake mechanics evolves, the probability estimates may encompass more specifics, such as which faults are likely or unlikely to produce damaging aftershocks.

Some of the progress in understanding the physical relationship between mainshocks and aftershocks is based on theories of earthquake stress triggering that are similar to those developed for human-earthquake interactions. Earthquake-earthquake interactions are more complicated to grasp, as neither the cause nor the effect is well understood. Studies of mainshock-aftershock interactions and interearthquake stress triggering can be divided into two categories: earthquakes that occur far (many fault lengths) apart, and earthquakes that occur in proximity (less than one fault length). Geophysical information collected from a large earthquake in 1992 has provided significant clues for both categories.

Cases of apparent distant earthquake triggering have been reported anecdotally in the scientific literature for many decades, but it was not until the 1990s, with the advent of digital broadband seismographic instruments, that scientists were able to carefully evaluate and analyze the physical relationships between distant events. The digital broadband seismometers record wide ranges of frequency and amplitude in seismic signals and are thereby better able to detect the effects of near and distant earthquakes than the older analog, narrow-frequency-band instruments. In 1992 the magnitude-7.3 Landers earthquake in the Mojave Desert of southern California was reported to be the cause of smaller earthquakes hundreds of kilometers away. Seismologists were able to discern that some of these distant earthquakes occurred during the passage of the seismic waves from the Landers earthquake, and therefore the dynamic stresses carried by the Landers seismic waves triggered the subsequent distant earthquakes.

For earthquakes that occur in proximity, there is also speculation about the impact of stress triggering. The Landers earthquake, which was the cause of distant seismicity, was also triggered internally by its own seismic waves. The earthquake started on one fault, and then the stress waves generated by that propagation jumped to at least four more faults. This triggering occurred quickly, and the entire multifault earthquake was over in less than a minute.

Three hours after the Landers earthquake, a magnitude-6.7 aftershock, the Big Bear earthquake, occurred just a few kilometers to the southwest. Over this interval the seismic waves had long passed out of the region, so it was proposed that the static (permanent) stress changes generated by the final slip on the Landers faults helped set off the Big Bear earthquake. The calculations assumed that the earth between the Landers and Big Bear earthquakes behaved elastically during the 3-hour period and that faults obey a simple model of Coulomb failure, a basic theory of friction that has been in use for more than 200 years.

According to Coulomb failure, a fault will fail (slip) and produce an earthquake when its strength is exceeded. If τ_{slip} is the shear stress in the direction of fault slip, σ_n is the stress normal (perpendicular) to the fault, p is pore pressure on the fault, μ is the coefficient of friction, and C is cohesion, then the fault can fail when the Coulomb failure stress (CFS) [Eq. (1)] is greater than zero. In general, the absolute

$$\tau_{\text{slip}} + \mu(\sigma_n + p) - C \qquad (1)$$

values of τ_{slip}, σ_n, p, and C are unknown for the earth, but it is possible to do a simpler calculation of the change in CFS on the fault, due to a human activity or an earthquake on another fault.

The change in Coulomb failure stress, ΔCFS, is shown in Eq. (2), where Δ indicates change. ΔCFS

$$\Delta\text{CFS} = \Delta\tau_{\text{slip}} + \mu(\Delta\sigma_n + \Delta_p) \qquad (2)$$

is the combined effect of the shear and normal stress changes, friction, and pore-pressure changes. If ΔCFS is positive, the first event encouraged (or triggered) the second event. If the change in Coulomb stress, ΔCFS, is negative, the first event discouraged (or delayed) the second event. When ΔCFS > 0, the first event (human activity or earthquake) has increased the stress on the fault plane and advanced it toward failure. $\Delta\tau_{\text{slip}}$ is the resulting change in shear stress resolved in the slip direction on the fault. If $\Delta\tau_{\text{slip}} < 0$, the stress change acts in the opposite direction from fault slip. If $\Delta\tau_{\text{slip}} > 0$, the shear stress change acts in the direction of fault slip. $\Delta\sigma_n$ is the resulting change in normal stress. If $\Delta\sigma_n < 0$, the two sides of the fault are relatively clamped. If $\Delta\sigma_n > 0$, the two sides of the fault are relatively pulled apart.

The idea of earthquakes triggering other earthquakes can also be applied in the opposite direction whereby a large earthquake may delay subsequent events. This would be expressed as ΔCFS < 0. The best demonstration is seen in the San Francisco Bay area of central California where a magnitude-7.8 earthquake in 1906 seems to have seismically quieted this densely populated area for more than 70 years. In the 70 years preceding the great earthquake, 18 earthquakes of magnitude ≥ 6 occurred in the San Francisco Bay region; but in the 70 years following 1906, only 3 earthquakes of magnitude ≥ 6 occurred. Scientists evaluated the slip that occurred along the San Andreas Fault during the 1906 earthquake and calculated the stress effect on other faults in the region. They found that the 1906 earthquake had a stress effect that acted in the opposite direction from the usual tectonic loading in this area. The result was that the 1906 earthquake delayed earthquakes that might have otherwise occurred,

and placed these faults into a "stress shadow" for many decades. As time passes, tectonic loading will erase a stress shadow so that presently many San Francisco Bay area faults have already or are about to come out of the stress shadow and are prime for more earthquake activity.

Earthquake stress triggering and stress shadow calculations may be used to adjust aftershock forecasts. At present, most probability estimates of aftershock occurrence do not include the stress-change effects from nearby earthquakes, but in the future this practice may be modified. In some regions, such as the San Francisco Bay area, the occurrence of large earthquakes has clearly been impacted by the stress changes of a previous great event. This relationship was also seen in southern California after a great earthquake in 1857. Some have proposed that aftershock probabilities following slightly smaller (magnitude-6–7) mainshocks should also be modified to reflect the stress-change effects, particularly for faults near Kobe, Japan, and Istanbul, Turkey.

For background information *see* EARTHQUAKE; FAULT AND FAULT STRUCTURES; SEISMOGRAPHIC INSTRUMENTATION; SEISMOLOGY in the McGraw-Hill Encyclopedia of Science & Technology.

Ruth A. Harris

Bibliography. R. A. Harris, Stress triggers, stress shadows, and implications for seismic hazard: Introduction to the Special Issue, *J. Geophys. Res.*, 103: 24347–24358, 1998; A. McGarr and D. Simpson, A broad look at induced and triggered seismicity, in S. Lasocki and S. Gibowicz (eds.), *Rockbursts and Seismicity in Mines*, Balkema, Rotterdam, 1997; P. A. Reasenberg, Foreshock occurrence before large earthquakes, *J. Geophys. Res.*, 104:4755–4768, 1999; P. A. Reasenberg and L. M. Jones, Earthquake aftershocks: Update, *Science*, 265:1251–1252, 1994; R. S. Stein, The role of stress transfer in earthquake occurrence, *Nature*, 402:605–609, 1999.

Ecological and human health

Procedures for establishing environmentally acceptable end points for environmental cleanups include consideration of local, regional, or state background levels, waste or material-specific criteria or guidelines, risk-based generic state or federal limits, and site-specific target levels. Risk factors typically considered in developing any environmental cleanup standard or criterion have included land use and exposure to human, animal, or plant populations. However, there is evidence suggesting that a contaminant present in the subsurface or in sediments may not necessarily pose a risk to human health or the environment. Sorption is an important physical-chemical process governing the behavior of organic and inorganic contaminants and, thus, their bioavailability.

Human health risk assessment. Risk assessment is the basis for both policy and technical decisions in determining priorities for site management. The assessment of human health risks follows a widely accepted model developed by the National Academy of Sciences (NAS) in 1983 and reiterated in 1994 in *Science and Judgment in Risk Assessment.* The elements of the model are (1) hazard identification, (2) dose response assessment, (3) exposure assessment, and (4) risk characterization. An example of the traditional procedure for incorporating human health risk assessment into the regulatory process is given by the Safe Drinking Water Act (SDWA), passed in 1974 and amended in 1986 and 1996. The act gives the Environmental Protection Agency (EPA) the authority to set drinking water standards. Initially, the EPA identifies health risks and contaminant occurrence, then establishes priorities for regulation, health research, and occurrence data collection. After reviewing health effects studies, best available control technology, treatment techniques, and related issues including cost, the EPA sets enforceable maximum contaminant levels (MCLs). In 1997 the Office of the EPA Administrator issued a guidance memorandum on the subject of cumulative, or integrated, human health risk assessment. Whereas early human health risk assessments tended to be based on individual contaminants, sources, pathways, or adverse impacts, it was suggested that multiple sources, effects, pathways, stressors, and populations be incorporated into cumulative human health risk analyses.

Ecological risks and assessment end points. Ecological risk assessment is distinctive from human health risk assessment in its emphasis on three areas. (1) Ecological risk assessment may consider risks beyond those to individuals of a single species and may examine populations, communities, or ecosystems. (2) No single set of ecological values to be protected can generally be applied; instead, these values are selected from a number of possibilities based on scientific and policy considerations. (3) Ecological risk assessments consider nonchemical as well as chemical stressors such as loss of habitat. Ecological risk assessment includes preparation of a conceptual model that identifies the environmental values to be protected, that is, assessment end points. The difficulties in assessing ecological risks may be reflected in the fact that in 1994 the EPA noted that no office had set a quantitative threshold representing an unacceptable risk to nonhuman organisms. Interactions among animal and plant communities and their physical environment had generally not been considered in ecological risk assessments. In 1998 the EPA published proposed guidelines for ecological risk assessment, and recommendations were solicited for specific ecological risk-related topics including assessment end points.

Applying risk evaluations. As an example of current efforts to more accurately quantify risks, the EPA is developing sediment quality criteria pursuant to the Clean Water Act. Sediment quality criteria are important to both human health and ecology. In addition to effects on bottom-dwelling organisms, some sediment-associated contaminants may pose a direct risk to wildlife and human health through consumption of contaminated organisms such as clams and lobsters, or an indirect risk through the transfer of contaminants up the food chain into edible fish. The EPA expects that remediation programs will not use the criteria as mandatory cleanup levels, but as a means to identify potential contamination problems and to provide focus and continuity in remediation efforts. However, states may adopt the sediment quality criteria as state water-quality standards or criteria.

Bioavailability. Bioavailability, or the ability of organisms to access contaminants, is emerging as a potentially more accurate risk-based approach than that currently in use. Site-specific values can prevent the systematic overestimation of the toxic effects of chemicals bound to soils and sediments. Furthermore, some remedial technologies have failed to remove all of the contamination from soils and sediments. For example, a number of "pump and treat" ground-water remediation systems have not achieved cleanup goals. The difficulty in removing all of the contamination has been attributed to physical-chemical factors such as physical heterogeneity, sorption of contaminants to subsurface materials, and the presence of nonaqueous-phase liquids (NAPLs). It has been suggested that the residual contamination may not pose a risk to human health or the environment and, thus, an "environmentally acceptable end point" could be defined. This end point would be a nonzero, risk-based, and site-specific value measuring contaminant bioavailability instead of presence alone.

The bioavailability of organic compounds to plants has received a great deal of attention from the agricultural chemical industry concerned with the application of certain pesticides. Certain soils require a greater pesticide application rate since a portion of the chemical becomes unavailable in the soil. Although organic contaminants have received a great deal of attention, bioavailability of metals is an equally important issue. It is reasonable to believe that the soil properties governing or affecting bioavailability of contaminants to plants also pertain to mammals, other animals, and microorganisms. In fact, the availability to these organisms could be greater because ingestion of soil particles exposes the contaminants to an aqueous environment that may include stomach acids, biosurfactants, and enzymes produced by the organism. Enhanced bioavailability of some organic compounds in stomach fluids has been shown to occur. Consequently, the EPA recommends consideration of ingestion of sorbed contaminants in the preparation of risk assessments. According to the EPA, "The availability of chemicals adsorbed on ingested soils affects the amount of contaminant exposure. When evaluating the ingestion of contaminated soils, an oral absorption factor should be used to account for the differing availability between the contaminant in the soil matrix and the contaminant in an experimentally administered medium such as solvent or food."

Contaminant properties, soil characteristics, receptors, modes of uptake, and duration of uptake all determine bioavailability. Bioavailability of organic compounds to living organisms generally depends on the physical accessibility of the molecules. Remote or sequestered molecules may not be available for biodegradation by microorganisms or uptake by animals or plants. Yet, what is considered sequestered for one organism may be available for another. The principal factor governing contaminant bioavailability at any instant is its concentration or chemical potential in the aqueous phase in contact with the receptor membrane.

Sorption and bioavailability. Sorption includes adsorption on mineral surfaces, partitioning into natural organic matter present in many soils and sediments, condensation in the pores of particles, or partitioning into NAPLs in the system. Desorption refers to the release of sorbed contaminants from the solid surface into water in contact with the contaminated solid. Microbiologists, toxicologists, and other biologists concerned with bioavailability have typically considered sorption as a reversible, rapid process wherein sorption occurs, and desorption simply the reverse. However, there are now data indicating that the sorption process is not reversible and that desorption is complex and is not simply the opposite of adsorption; that is, a fraction of desorption is from a different, or rearranged, solid environment. This is similar to the rearrangement of an enzyme after interacting with a substrate. This phenomenon is known as irreversible desorption or hysteresis. Its effects are shown in **Fig. 1**, which demonstrates that, after an initial rapid decline, contaminants frequently desorb at nonzero concentrations for long periods of time. It is the impacts of long-term, nonzero aqueous concentrations which must be addressed.

Several important factors contribute to nonlinear, irreversible desorption. In the field, soils and sediments usually contain a complex mixture of chemicals that may substantially alter partitioning to the pore water phase. Hysteresis causes a fraction of

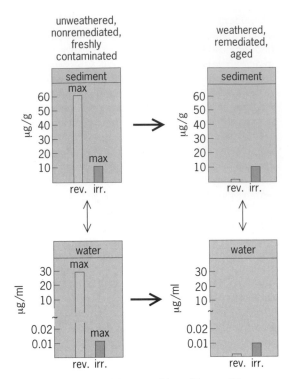

Fig. 2. Comparison of the reversible and irreversible compartment for freshly contaminated and weathered sediment.

the contaminants to be released reversibly and the remaining fraction to be released in a different nonreversible manner, implying multiple, complex mechanisms. Sorptive and desorptive behavior may be influenced by aging, weathering, and biodegradation in field soils, depleting the more soluble components and leaving behind less soluble components that are unavailable or slowly available to the water phase (**Fig. 2**). Biologically produced acids and enzymes may also affect soil structure and sorptive behavior. The term "irreversible" does not imply permanent immobilization, but merely that desorption of contaminants may not be the opposite of adsorption. However, in some cases the time span before the contaminant is desorbed may be years or even decades. Evidence that the residual contaminant fraction in some soils and sediments may be irreversibly sorbed and unavailable to leach to water or to be taken up by organisms has considerable importance in risk assessment.

When comparing predicted concentrations using the reversible and irreversible sorption models, it is necessary to consider the time scale. Figure 2 illustrates the effects of aging on contaminated sediments. Freshly contaminated soils have a high concentration of pollutants, as predicted by the reversible model. However, with aging, the irreversible model accounts for the observed decline in availability to a fixed value. The "weathered" section of Fig. 2 depicts the two model compartments with time. According to the reversible compartment, concentrations would be reduced to negligible levels, while the irreversible compartment predicts a

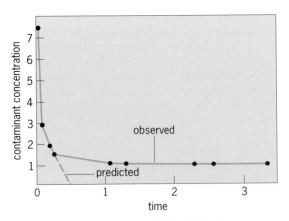

Fig. 1. Representative graph depicting the initial rapid decline of contaminant concentration followed by long-term stabilization at nonzero concentration.

continued, small, but ever-present level of contamination. Therefore, the irreversible model shows that although available concentrations may be less than expected initially, the contaminant will persist in the environment for a longer period of time.

Traditional linear, reversible, mathematical models that are used to predict sorptive behavior accurately predict the activity of approximately 80% of the contamination. When remedial strategies include removal of contaminated water in contact with contaminated solids, nonlinear or irreversible desorption often results in residual contamination that is difficult to remove. However, it is often this residual 15–20% that has the greatest impact on risk assessment and cleanup levels. Models such as the Equilibrium Partitioning Model (used to develop sediment quality criteria for organic compounds) use an equilibrium partitioning approach that does not consider sorption irreversibility. Thus, a new model is needed to more accurately predict desorption in the field and determine the associated risk of different end points. Because bioavailability and toxicity are frequently associated with contaminants in the aqueous phase, incorporating irreversibility into sorption-desorption models is essential to providing more reliable estimates of contaminant concentrations in water that is in contact with contaminated solids. As a better understanding of the mechanisms involved in the sorption-desorption process is achieved, estimates of risk will come closer to predicting actual risk.

Outlook for risk evaluation. Traditionally, the required cleanup levels for a contaminated site have been determined by federal- or state-mandated standards or criteria designed to protect human health and the environment. Establishing more reliable risk relationships and assessment end points will involve research into the bioavailability and trophic transfer of contaminants in soils and sediments. At present, the EPA's sediment quality criteria methodology for organic compounds does not consider sorption irreversibility; thus, it may be an incomplete model of contaminant bioavailability. Research is currently focused on developing new tools to measure and predict availability in order to develop more realistic risk assessments. New information will assist in determining the classes of compounds and conditions warranting sediment criteria protective of human health.

The recent National Sediment Inventory concluded that potential risk to aquatic life, human health, and wildlife from sediment contamination was widespread and present in every state in the United States. Research in the twenty-first century will seek to reveal the fundamental toxicological, ecological, and chemical processes that control bioavailability of individual chemicals and mixtures in the environment. Some of the problems that must be addressed are determining which environmental phases control the bioavailability of inorganic and organic stressors; incorporating data into reliable predictive modeling tools; and ensuring that contaminants sequestered today remain that way forever.

For background information *see* ADSORPTION; DESORPTION; ECOLOGY, APPLIED; ENVIRONMENTAL ENGINEERING; ENVIRONMENTAL TOXICOLOGY; GROUNDWATER HYDROLOGY; HAZARDOUS WASTE; HYSTERESIS; POPULATION ECOLOGY; RISK ANALYSIS; SOIL in the McGraw-Hill Encyclopedia of Science & Technology.

Laine Vignona; Ellen Moore; Amy T. Kan; Mason Tomson

Bibliography. W. C. Anderson, R. C. Loehr, and B. P. Smith, *Environmental Availability in Soils: Chlorinated Organics, Explosives, Metals*, American Academy of Environmental Engineers, 1999; A. T. Kan et al., *Environmental Science and Technology*, 32:892–902, 1998; D. G. Linz and D. V. Nakles, *Environmentally Acceptable Endpoints in Soil: Risk-Based Approach to Contaminated Site Management Based on Availability of Chemicals in Soil*, American Academy of Environmental Engineers, 1997; T. H. Weidemeier et al., *Natural Attenuation of Fuels and Chlorinated Solvents in the Subsurface*, John Wiley, 1999.

Electric utility restructuring

Over the last two decades, public policy in the United States has shifted toward restructuring in the electric utility industry. Many have believed that restructuring is a good idea that could result in benefits for customers.

Inappropriately, some refer to this on going process as deregulation. While some deregulation of the generation or supply side of the utility industry is occurring, massive new regulation of other aspects of electric power is in process. Regulation is being imposed on electric power transmission to an unprecedented degree, with regulators setting standards for system reliability, enforcement of reliability criteria, appointment of members of boards of directors, and divestiture of assets.

The result is that the traditional vertically integrated electric utility in the United States, with a specified price for total service, will take on the form of one that is horizontally integrated, with many prices for each level of service, in order to better compete under restructured conditions. Generally speaking, utilities would unbundle their operations into generation, transmission, and distribution portions, and price each service independently to compete in the market. In many cases, each of these operations would become a separate company with generation or power supply unregulated and the transmission and distribution companies continuing to be regulated.

Along with the unbundling of the traditional system components, a large number of mergers or acquisitions of utilities are taking place. These often involve systems in diverse geographic locations. In some cases, generation assets in one region of the

United States are being sold to companies located in other regions, and at considerably higher than book value. In other cases, they involve electric companies merging with gas suppliers.

Electric utility restructuring is also occurring in many other countries. This restructuring consists of three basic types of changes: privatization (sale of government-owned assets), introduction of new competitive procedures (generally competitive bidding to provide power), and new regulatory procedures. These changes in other countries provide the opportunity for a review of results prior to setting United States policy.

Effects of restructuring. Restructuring will enhance customer choice and will impact both the costs (particularly in the introduction of stranded costs) and the reliability of electric power.

Increased customer choice. The main benefit of restructuring is the improved ability of individual customers to choose their energy supplier. Many will want lower market rates, but some will want higher quality of service or a different mix in order to maximize value from existing cost levels. For example, many industrial production technologies are developing that require extremely reliable electricity supply, and these customers may be willing to pay more for this higher reliability. Some others may require improved power quality (that is, greater reliability regarding frequency, voltage transients, and so forth) commensurate with the evolving process applications at their facility. A major concern is the ability to design and operate a single system which will be able to deliver different levels of service reliability. Engineers agree that distribution systems can be designed to provide different reliability to different customers; this is not feasible with the transmission system.

Impact on costs. While some studies have been made to determine the costs and benefits involved, these have not evaluated the impact of the changed requirement for electric power system facilities and the impact on operations. While prices for any class of customer are a matter of commercial policy, the overall cost of electricity to the public will depend on the cost for producing it, transmitting it, and distributing it—matters for which engineering expertise is required and needed additional study has yet to be made. Among the factors contributing to increased costs are the following:

1. Increased transmission facilities are required to provide for future uncertainties of generator locations and power sources, and for the large increase in transactions.

2. Major rearrangement of the transmission networks is needed to limit the effects of transactions in one region on the transmission facilities in other regions.

3. New technologies will have to be developed to facilitate the new operating procedures. These will include new communication systems, new power electronic devices, and new control mechanisms. Costs for these could be significant.

4. New metering capability must be installed. With the very large numbers of real-time transactions that may occur in a restructured industry, both at the wholesale and retail level, metering will be essential to record all the necessary traffic. Costs for the metering and communications facilities and systems required will be huge.

5. There will be increased costs for production of electricity. Past procedures have called for the production of electricity based on marginal production costs. This procedure minimized total production costs. Payments for power exchanges were based on these marginal production costs. Revised procedures call for dispatching based on bid price and for payment to all bidders based on the highest bid price accepted. Deviations from the marginal cost dispatching of generating units will unavoidably increase generation costs. Many new procedures for competitively dispatching generating units have been proposed with varying opportunities for generation owners to profit from the process. The basic fact remains that uncoordinated dispatching will increase total costs, and this must be balanced against the cost reduction pressures of competition.

6. A large number of middlemen will be involved, such as marketers and brokers. They will have to profit from their businesses, adding to electricity costs.

7. Power plants will be purchased at above book value, increasing the cost recovery required.

8. "Risk management" must be purchased. A form of insurance, risk management consists of two parts: physical delivery risk and price risk. Risk management will add to the cost of electricity since present regulatory procedures now provide it. Physical delivery risk will depend on how reliable the supplier is. In the deregulated environment, power will be delivered differently to the site, in some cases creating higher risk. Customers will need to decide whether they are willing to accept a higher-risk delivery for a lower cost or whether playing it safe is worth the higher cost.

The hope is that competition will lead to improved performance sufficient to overcome these cost increases. A majority of utility executives believe, however, that restructuring to provide customer choice will increase overall costs.

Stranded costs. These are special costs resulting from restructuring. This major impediment to restructuring, in its most simply defined form, is the difference between the value of regulated assets and obligations under monopoly prices and the value of these assets and obligations in a competitive utility market. The three primary sources of stranded cost categories normally include (1) uneconomic utility generating assets, which may include nuclear and other nonnuclear facilities; (2) power contracts purchased above market that utilities were obliged to make by regulatory rules; and (3) regulatory assets and liabilities.

One of the most significant groups of assets described as stranded costs from a dollar-value perspective are uneconomic generation units.

Investments in these generating units were based on long-term analyses where higher capital costs were justified by long-term savings in fuel and operating costs. Recent developments in combustion turbine technology coupled with low natural gas prices have made some generating units noncompetitive with the new sources of power. In addition, utilities have been obliged to enter into purchase power contracts to buy power from nonutility generators meeting certain conditions established by previously enacted legislation to promote energy or environmental benefits. As an example, in New York State, until recently, there had been legislation requiring utilities to buy power from nonutility generators under 80 megawatts at 6 cents per kilowatt-hour. This price is much greater than the price that utilities can pay to purchase wholesale power from other sources.

The last item defined as stranded costs is generation-related regulatory assets and liabilities, that is, those accounting transactions that would normally be recovered when incurred in a free market, but because of regulatory decision have to be recovered over several years in order to limit rate fluctuations. Stranded costs can be very large and vary widely among different locations. They affect not only investor-owned utilities but publicly owned systems and cooperatives as well.

A major question yet to be resolved is, "Who will pay for these stranded costs: consumers, shareholders, or tax payers?" But the most important question is, "How can these stranded costs be identified, analyzed, mitigated, and recovered prior to restructuring?" The general view seems to be that legitimate and verifiable stranded costs should be recovered by the utility entities involved. Doing otherwise would represent an unreasonable and unfair burden on many systems and would significantly distort the transition to industry competition.

These stranded costs are sometimes called a competition transition charge (CTC). In California, this charge, which is to be added to the bill, is estimated initially at 17% of the total price of electricity.

Impact on reliability. The reliability of electric power systems has two characteristics: adequacy and security. Adequacy is the ability of the system to provide sufficient generation, transmission, and distribution capacity under steady-state conditions. Security is the ability of the system to withstand perturbations caused by failure of equipment. In the past the integrated system that provided service had the overall responsibility for reliability. As a result of the Federal Energy Regulatory Commission (FERC) Orders 888 and 889, the responsibility for reliability has been spread among many organizations. Both planning and operation have been made considerably more complicated. All else being equal, lower reliability is the expected result.

Major questions exist about future adequacy of supply. In the past, systems were required to provide adequate generation capacity. Proposals exist that the generation capacity provided should be deter-mined by market forces. Many believe needed capacity will not be provided in time. Recent experience has shown that some suppliers take on the responsibility to supply power without the capacity to do so, counting on subsequent power purchases in the open market. This practice caused significant problems in the summer of 1998.

The functioning of the bulk supply system is not understood by many of the new organizations involved. The use of transmission systems to reduce the investment required in generating capacity by pooling reserves, as well as to transfer energy, is no longer generally recognized. Competitors no longer fully exchange information on their transmission systems. In some cases, the past obligation of a utility to provide service to new customers is being discontinued.

The reliable operation of transmission systems requires the provision of many ancillary services. These include generator spinning reserves, operating reserves, automatic generator dispatch, frequency control, reactive supply, and voltage control. In the past the single integrated system, working in close cooperation with its neighbors, ensured that the necessary ancillary services were provided. With restructuring, these services are being provided by many suppliers and often through competitive bidding. The coordination of these diverse supplies of ancillary services adds another complication and reliability risk.

All of these changes lead in the direction of lower reliability. There is general agreement that coordinated institutional and technical solutions need to be developed if reliability is to be maintained, including the provision of increased reserves to provide for increased uncertainties.

The future. Because of concerns about abuse of market power and reliability, the U.S. government and some state commissions are proposing the formation of impartial independent system operators (ISOs), power exchanges (PXs), and reliability councils. The ISO will have reliability responsibilities for the entire bulk supplying system under rules established by the reliability councils. The ISO differs from previous voluntary electric utility power pool arrangements. Under the guidance of federal and state regulators, an ISO can take over from an integrated utility the responsibility for system control, generator unit commitment, dispatch, and system operation subfunctions. Some believe the ISOs are an interim arrangement and will be replaced by new companies called regional transmission organizations (RTOs) which will own and operate the regional transmission systems.

The responsibility of a power exchange is to obtain power supply and demand bids (amount of power and price) to ensure that supply meets the demands of all customers. A power exchange will establish prices between sellers and buyers on a 24-hour advance basis as well as spot prices of energy and capacity. The power exchange makes the spot market for customer loads and generation supply for whoever chooses to participate, certainly not all customers, and finds the lowest market clearing price in each hour. It gives the bids to the ISO, which can then determine and ensure that the implemented bids can meet operational requirements. Major questions exist, however, about the incentives to be given to the ISO to operate efficiently and reliably.

A transmission system will never be infinite, and thus competition always will be limited to some extent. The challenge will be to achieve effective competition in generation with reasonable transmission facilities. Incentives are needed to assure that transmission improvements are made to reduce constraints when this is in the public interest.

Procedures recently have been initiated with Federal Energy Regulatory Commission approval for technical methods to determine the available transmission capacity (ATC) and provide this information to potential users of the transmission system. OASIS (Open Access Same Time Information System) has also been initiated for making information available online about the transmission capacity available for additional transaction. Efforts are continuing to eliminate problems currently existing from the use of OASIS.

While some states are proceeding with restructuring changes, some are proceeding very cautiously, wanting to review results of others. Generally, states with high electricity costs are proceeding quickly, and those with low costs are proceeding cautiously. Many believe restructuring results in a considerable transfer of wealth from low-cost areas to higher-cost areas. Additional technical study and review remains a dominant requirement.

Other important and growing effects of restructuring have been the significant reduction in cooperative research in the electric power industry and the reduction in power system education programs nationally. These are the results of the belief that technical skills have become less important than commercial skills in the electric power business.

For background information *see* ELECTRIC POWER GENERATION; ELECTRIC POWER SYSTEMS in the McGraw-Hill Encyclopedia of Science & Technology.

J. A. Casazza

Bibliography. J. A. Casazza, *The Development of Electric Power Transmission: The Role Played by Technology, Institutions, and People*, Institute of Electrical and Electronics Engineers, 1993; G. C. Loehr, Ten myths about electric deregulation, *Public Utilities Fortnightly*, April 15, 1998; G. C. Loehr and J. A. Casazza (eds.), *The Evolution of Electric Power Transmission Under Deregulation: Selected Readings*, Institute of Electrical and Electronics Engineers, 2000.

Electronic mail

The purpose of automatic electronic mail (e-mail) reading is to provide people with access to their e-mail over the telephone. Text-to-speech (TTS) synthesis is the core technology for providing such a service. However e-mail is one of the most challenging types of document for a text-to-speech system to handle: In e-mail, plain text is often interspersed with other types of material—tables, itemized lists, signature blocks, or ASCII graphics (artwork drawn with keyboard characters). These structured elements need to be detected, and proper auditory rendering policies need to be designed for each type of material. In addition, e-mail texts may contain various types of embedded messages, such as forwarded material and quotations, that should be detected and set off auditorily in order to aid the listener in navigating the document. Finally, e-mail text is rife with nonstandard words, including trade names (WinNT) and electronic addresses (brsnyder@netcom.com), which are typically not correctly treated by a text-to-speech system. All these problems need to be addressed for automatic e-mail reading to be comprehensible.

E-mail reading is useful in situations where the user cannot get to a terminal but can get to a telephone, and would like to access his or her electronic mailbox. In such situations, the user employs some sort of interactive voice response system (or else a touch-tone-driven menu system) to navigate through the mailbox, and uses e-mail reading to render the contents of the messages into an audible format. The technology is also useful for visually impaired users who depend upon speech synthesis as their normal mode of interaction with their desktop computer.

Document structure analysis. The first phase of analysis is the detection and markup of significant portions of the input e-mail. One approach is to assume that the input text is blocked into regions, where a region is defined to be a block of contiguous lines separated from other regions by either (1) one or more blank lines or (2) a clearly defined separator, such as a delimiter of a forwarded message. Each region is assumed to be of a single uniform type. For example, a region may be tagged as plain text (PTEXT) or as a table (TABLE), but not both. This uniformity assumption, while not absolutely correct, is nonetheless correct often enough to be useful. If this assumption were not made, the computational expense of analyzing the input text would be significantly increased, since every block of contiguous lines would have to be considered a potential region.

In some cases the detection of a region is straightforward. For example, it is relatively easy to detect e-mail headers since they are readily identifiable by the existence of certain line-initial tags, such as "From:", "To:", and "Subject:" (**Fig. 1**). Detection of other region types requires more sophisticated analysis. Distinction is made among eight basic text-region types: plain text (PTEXT), artwork (GRAPHIC), quoted regions (QUOTED), itemized lists (ITEM), signatures (SIG), headlines (HEADL), addresses (ADDRESS), and tables (TABLE).

The initial detection of these regions starts with the following intuition: For many types of regions,

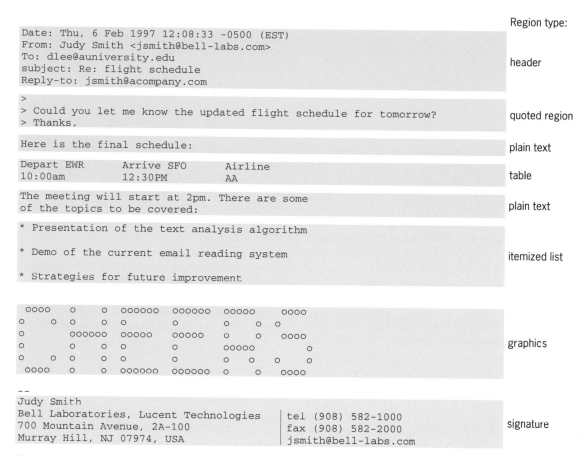

Fig. 1. E-mail message, illustrating some of the region types.

it is not necessary to see the text clearly in order to decide that the region is of a particular type. If a page were being viewed from a distance, so that it was impossible to read what was on the page, still it would be possible to clearly detect tables, many signatures, addresses, headlines, and graphics by the mere appearance of the text. Each of these region types has a fairly reliable distribution of real text material and white space. For example, headlines tend to be short regions of text where the material is centered on the page. Tables and many signatures tend to have the text arranged in columns with the columns separated by a fair amount of white space. Addresses tend to consist of a series of short lines. Finally, graphics tend to have a lot of white space and only sparsely distributed printed material. Plain text, quoted text, and itemized list elements are more difficult to detect by such coarse means, and more special-purpose techniques are needed in these cases. For example, quoted regions are frequently marked with one of a handful of distinguished characters (often ">") at the beginning of each line.

The basic intuition outlined above is implemented as follows. First, each character in the input is deterministically mapped to one of a set of predefined character classes. The character classes currently used include SPACE, DIGIT, ALPHABETIC, >, and : (common indicators of quoted messages), and

PUNCTUATION. Second, the individual character-class-encoded lines of each block are matched against a set of eight statistical models, one for each text region type. These models are trained on 5590 lines of hand-tagged netnews text. Applied to each line, the models give a measure, for each text region type, of how strongly the given line matches that particular type. Of course, what is desired is a unique classification for each line, and a uniform classification for the block. The third phase of the analysis accomplishes this by applying grammatical restrictions, such as the restriction that all elements of a block must be of the same type. Also implemented are some length restrictions. For example, address fields are rarely shorter than two lines; and signature fields are rarely longer than ten lines.

Two types of blocks then receive further treatment: quoted regions are recursively subjected to the classification and parsing algorithm just described; and potential signature blocks undergo a finer-grained analysis.

The signature block analysis starts with a two-dimensional geometrical analysis that attempts to find connected components. For example, the signature block in **Fig. 2** consists of two connected components, corresponding to the two columns. The geometrical analysis yields a set of reading blocks corresponding to the discovered connected components. In general, it is assumed that when reading

```
Charles Davies                    Email:  ced@research.bell-labs.com
Lucent Technologies Bell Labs     WWW: http://www.bell-labs.com/noname/mcs/
600 Mountain Avenue, 2D-500       Voice: 908 582-1234
Murray Hill, NJ 07974            Fax: 908 582-4321
```

Fig. 2. E-mail signature block with two connected components.

the text in the signature, elements that are part of the same reading block belong more naturally together than elements in different reading blocks. But within a reading block there may be several functional blocks. For example, in Fig. 2 the right-hand reading block contains an e-mail address, some World Wide Web (WWW) contact information, a phone number, and a fax number. Each of these constitutes a separate functional block. Functional blocks are detected using language analysis of the text material within each reading block. If the signature-block analysis algorithms detect certain required components—e-mail addresses, web addresses, phone or fax numbers, names or postal addresses—then the algorithms proceed with the complete analysis and mark the signature region as "verified." Otherwise they mark the region as unverified and return it to the parsing phase.

Device-independent rendering. The function of the device-independent rendering phase is to "normalize" various elements in the marked-up document to improve the final rendering into speech. Among the functions that this phase performs are to detect and mark separator lines, such as the "—" commonly found at the beginning of signature fields; expand "[Rr]e:" in the "Subject:" line into "regarding"; detect various conventions for marking emphasis; expand emoticons (smileys) into words; decide whether capitalized words should be read as words (LOS ANGELES, UNESCO) or as sequences of letters (CIA, WABC); expand electronic addresses, pathnames, and URLs appropriately; and expand nonconventional words such as WinNT into appropriate renderings.

Emphasis marking. Conventions for marking emphasis include capitalization, and delimiting the word with asterisks (*require*). Emphatic words are marked with the tag <emph>.

Rendering of capitalized words. A simple but effective algorithm to determine whether or not to read a capitalized word as a word or as a sequence of letters is: (1) If the capitalized sequence is longer than five letters, read it as a word. (2) If the capitalized sequence is five letters or shorter, check the word against a dictionary of known words of five letters or shorter. If it is in this dictionary, read it as a word. Otherwise read it as a sequence of letters.

Naturally, such disambiguation cannot always reliably be done in a context-independent fashion: It is impossible to tell whether "ADA" should be read as a word (that is, the name Ada) or as a sequence of letters (that is, as an abbreviation for the American Dental Association) without consider-

ing the context in which the word occurs. More sophisticated disambiguation methods are being developed.

Audio rendering. Audio rendering is the phase in which the e-mail preprocessor performs its final formatting of the input text, and passes it off to a text-to-speech system for conversion into speech. The marked-up and normalized text is rendered by converting it into text interspersed with controls for the text-to-speech system. The most important function of the controls in this application is to change the voice used by the synthesizer as a means of indicating the document structure. Thus, when the system renders an embedded quotation, for example, it changes to a different voice, staying in that voice until the end of the quotation, at which point it reverts to the previously used voice. (The user is also explicitly informed that the system has entered a new level of structure. For example, by default a top-level quoted message will result in the system informing the user that "this is a level 1 quoted message.") For some types of text element, little more is done than inform the user that there is a region of that type present. For a graphic region, for example, the listener is informed that "there is a region of non-text of type ascii-graphic here."

Status. Current commercial products for e-mail reading offer only limited capability in terms of structure and content analysis. Research in this area is still in its early stages. Certain types of text, such as headers, signature blocks, and quoted regions, can now be reliably identified. However, there are still many challenges, including how to reliably identify complex structures such as tables and itemized lists and, once identified, how to render them properly in audible form.

For background information *see* ELECTRONIC MAIL; VOICE RESPONSE in the McGraw-Hill Encyclopedia of Science & Technology.

Jianying Hu; Richard Sproat; Hao Chen

Bibliography. H. Chen, J. Hu, and R. Sproat, Integrating geometrical and linguistic analysis for E-mail signature block parsing, *ACM Trans. Inform. Sys.*, 17(4):343–366, October 1999; R. Sproat (ed.), *Multilingual Text-to-Speech Synthesis: The Bell Labs Approach*, Kluwer, Boston, 1997; R. Sproat, H. Chen, and J. Hu, EMU: An E-mail preprocessor for text-to-speech, *IEEE Workshop on Multimedia Signal Processing*, Redondo Beach, CA, December 1998; D. Yarowsky, *Three Machine Learning Algorithms for Lexical Ambiguity Resolution*, Ph.D. thesis, University of Pennsylvania, 1996.

Electronic security

Electronic transmission systems are evolving with the expansion of broadcast satellite, cable, wireless [cellular, local area networks, and LMDS (local multipoint distribution service)], and satellite radio. While the systems are designed for transport of different types of media, convergence is changing this aspect of the systems. More importantly, these systems share the common feature of being multiple-access systems. These transmission systems allow new applications ranging from very small amounts of information directed at a single user to incredibly large amounts of information directed at a large but selective group of individuals. With these capabilities comes the responsibility to provide security, protecting the property of the content providers and service providers as well as maintaining the privacy demanded by the individual subscribers or users. The conditional access of information involves the three A's: auditing (identifying what has been accessed by whom), authorization (addressing the information only to those entitled to receive it), and authentication (guaranteeing the identity of all the parties involved). This article addresses the threats to modern electronic transmission systems as well as the mechanisms used to prevent these threats. While each system has its unique problems, the generic issues associated with most of the systems will be treated here.

Threats. Attacks on electronic transmission systems come in various forms, the difficulty in implementing them depending both on the nature of the transmission system and on the techniques used to defend it.

A theft-of-service attack typically results from the use of cloned customer equipment. In this attack the perpetrator masquerades as a legitimate user to steal service. Typically this is detected only when legitimate subscribers report spurious charges on their monthly bills or, as is now common in the case of cellular phones, multiple users request service at similar times from different locations.

Invasion of privacy is another threat to electronic transmission systems. In this attack the pirate listens to transmissions and records data for use at a later time. The captured information might be used for something as mundane as obtaining access to a pay-per-view broadcast, or for stealing more valuable items such as credit card numbers or access control messages.

A more difficult attack involves masquerading as a service provider to gain access to subscribers' equipment. This type of attack has several possible scenarios, one being the downloading of software to subscribers ostensibly to update their equipment. This "update" might actually be a virus that captures credit card numbers from a personal computer, or prevents the normal reception or playback of information—often referred to as a denial-of-service attack.

Basic cryptography. Common to all of the systems attacked in the above scenarios is the transmission of digitally encoded data, making it possible to readily take advantage of cryptographic techniques for protection (**Fig. 1**).

Symmetric key encryption is one means for providing privacy. With symmetric key algorithms, both sides of the transmission must possess the same key. On the transmitting side the encryptor uses the key along with the algorithm to encipher the information, theoretically making it impossible for an attacker to use; and at the receiver a decryptor uses the key to decipher the information, returning it to cleartext. Two types of symmetric key algorithms exist: block and stream ciphers. Each type has different properties and advantages, depending on the system. The strength of both block and stream

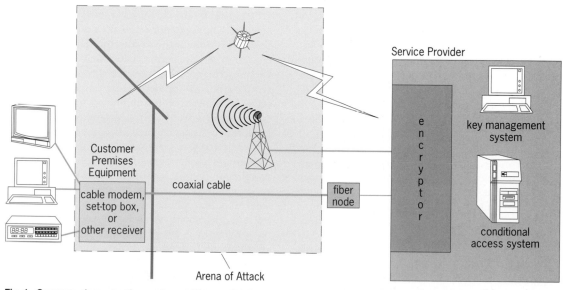

Fig. 1. Common elements of a cryptographic security system and the arena for attack.

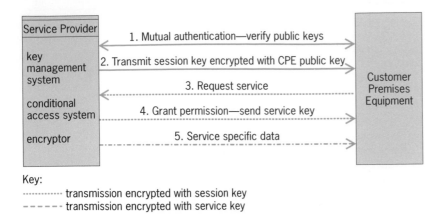

Key:
.... transmission encrypted with session key
- - - - - transmission encrypted with service key

Fig. 2. **Typical security initialization scenario.**

ciphers is typically rated by the length of the key used with the cipher, although when choosing the algorithm it is important to understand how well the algorithm has been analyzed and understand the weaknesses found with it if any. The most common symmetric key algorithm is the Data Encryption Standard (DES), which was developed in the 1970s and uses a key that is 56 bits in length. Today most systems are being built with triple DES, using a key length of 168 bits. The National Institute of Standards will eventually determine the replacement for DES, to be called Advanced Encryption Standard (AES).

A major problem with symmetric key algorithms is supplying both sides with the key. Whitfield Diffie and Martin Hellman first described public key cryptography in 1976. Public key cryptography uses a set of complementary keys, one public and the other private, to create a shared secret at both ends. This allows the end points of the transmission system to pass information securely without the need to secure the channel first or share symmetric keys through some out-of-band method. The two most common public key methods are Diffie-Hellman and RSA (named for its inventors Ronald Rivest, Adi Shamir, and Leonard Adelman), both based on mathematical problems which are easy to compute in one direction but difficult (or computationally impossible) to compute in the reverse direction. These algorithms tend to be slow and can be vulnerable to cryptanalysis, and hence they are typically used only to transmit small amounts of essential information such as keys used with symmetric key algorithms.

An additional feature of public key cryptography is that it can be used to authenticate messages verifying both its contents and the identity of the sender. In this case the sender "signs" the message with her private key and transmits the result along with the message to the receiver. The receiver can then decrypt or verify the message with the sender's public key. If the check is correct, the receiver knows the message was not modified between the sender and receiver and that the message originated at the sender.

One last function used in cryptography is the hash function. Hash functions create a cryptographic checksum or message digest similar to a cyclic redundancy check but using one-way functions. These functions, such as SHA-1 or MD5, are easy to compute, but it is extremely difficult to find a similar message that results in the same hash value when processed by the algorithm. These functions are typically used to authenticate long messages and may be used with a key to provide authentication of the source as well as message authentication.

Security systems. Typical electronic transmission security systems include an access control system, a key management system, and an encryption system. The encryption system encrypts and decrypts information using the chosen symmetric key algorithm, while the key management system generates keys, controls the use of the keys, and ensures that all parties requiring use of the keys have them available. In addition, the key management system performs the public key operations to guarantee that both sides of the transmission know to whom they are talking and that messages received are from the parties indicated.

A typical initiation scenario involving the threats previously listed is illustrated in **Fig. 2.** In the first step, the customer premise equipment requests service. In this step the customer sends its public key up to the service provider. The public key is either located in a public key database to see that it is legitimate, or when it is created it is signed by a manufacturer's private key. The equipment's public key can then be verified at the service provider by doing a signature verification using the equipment manufacturer's public key.

In the second step, the service provider sends down a session key used for encryption of control messages encrypted with the customer's public key and signed by its own private key. The customer can verify the public key and then decrypt the session key with its private key. From this point on, the messages are encrypted and potentially authenticated using symmetric key algorithms.

Step 3 allows the customer to subscribe to various services. The customer sends up a request, and the service provider authenticates the request and then checks its access control database to determine if the subscriber should have access to the particular service (this may be dependent on past payments, physical location, or any number of restrictions). In step 4, after approving the customer, the service provider's key management system sends the key for the requested service down to the customer. Step 5 concerns what happens to the key at the customer equipment. If this is a pay-per-view event, the equipment must be designed in a manner to prevent the subscriber from obtaining the key and selling or giving it to others so that they can receive service without paying for it. Preventing access to the key is a very difficult process, with new attacks constantly being developed.

Securing transmission systems is a very active field with new threats and attacks occurring almost daily, with subtle nuisances seemingly being designed to enhance security often opening the hole the attacker needs to compromise the system. This article describes only the very basics of securing a system.

For background information *see* COMPUTER SECURITY; CRYPTOGRAPHY in the McGraw-Hill Encyclopedia of Science & Technology.   Daniel Heer

Bibliography. C. Kaufman, R. Perlman, and M. Speciner, *Network Security: Private Communication in a Public World*, Prentice Hall, 1995; R. Rance, Cable modem security, *Cable Modems: Current Technologies and Applications*, pp. 369–390, IEEE Press, 1999; B. Schneier, *Applied Cryptography*, 2d ed., John Wiley, 1996.

Environmental pollution

Animal and plant life on Earth has evolved over hundreds of millions of years, together with the chemicals that make up the biosphere of air, soil, seas, lakes, rivers, and sediments. These environmental components have remained reasonably constant over the millions of years of human evolution, and this is reflected in the limited human tolerance of the environment. This delicate balance has been compromised over the past 50 years of industrial activity by the presence of a new class of chemicals, many of which are halogenated organic compounds. These include dichlorodiphenyltrichloroethane (DDT), polychlorinated biphenyls (PCBs), and dioxins. One of the dioxins is reputed to be the most toxic chemical known to humans (**Fig. 1**).

Toxic compounds. To exacerbate the issue, many of these compounds are not readily degraded by the natural processes of atmospheric oxidation, photochemical decomposition by the Sun's radiation, or the activity of bacteria in the soil or sediments. These chemicals persist in the environment, sometimes for decades. The capacity of the environment to dilute, degrade, and render inert many of these "new" compounds is not infinite. Perhaps in a few more million years bacteria capable of degrading these halogenated compounds will have developed, but for the present the concern is to restrict the presence of these compounds.

Many pollutants are a result of the advancing industrialization and the development of new materials, pesticides, herbicides, and plastics. An example is the compound DDT, which was developed in the first half of the twentieth century as a pesticide. Another example is the formation of PCBs and dioxins as unwanted by-products in the manufacture of chlorinated plastics. Although the concentrations of these toxic compounds in the air, water, and soil are very low, the compounds do migrate from one region of the biosphere to another and can appear in unexpected places and in unsuspectedly high concentrations. At these concentrations the deleterious effect on animals and humans is very noticeable.

There is a need to understand these pathways from one region to another and also a need to predict the concentrations of new pollutants in the various com-

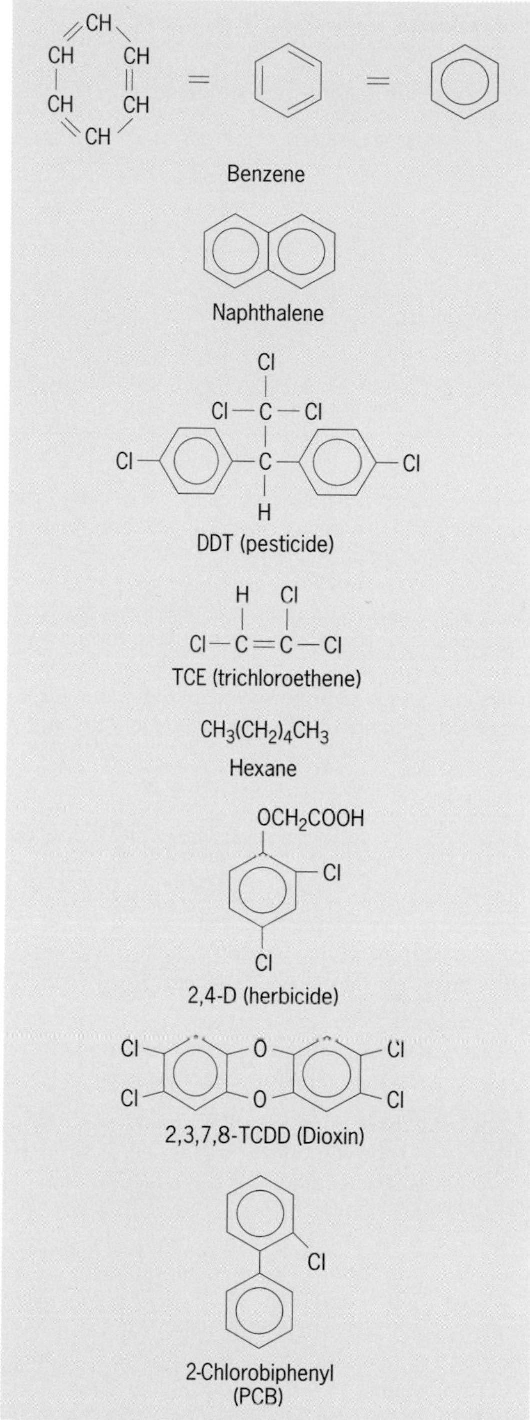

Fig. 1. Formulas and structures of well-known pollutants.

partments of the biosphere even before they are allowed to escape from the factories producing them. Thermodynamics offers a way of understanding and predicting how these polluting chemicals are distributed in the environment.

Thermodynamic approach. The fundamental concept is that the chemical potential (μ) of any chemical species (i), present at equilibrium in two or more phases (such as air, water, or aquatic biota) may be expressed by Eq. (1). This implies that their

$$\mu_i \text{ (air)} = \mu_i \text{ (water)} = \mu_i \text{ (aquatic biota)} = \ldots \quad (1)$$

Values of important properties of some toxic species at 298 K (25°C or 80°F)

Solute (i)	Molar mass (M_i), g mol^{-1}	Henry's law constant (H_i), Pa m^3 mol^{-1}	Air-water partition coefficient $(K_{AW,i})$	Vapor pressure (p_i^0), pascals	Solubility in water $[c_i^*$ (water)], mol m^{-3}	Octanol-water partition coefficient $(K_{OW,i})$	Log $K_{OW,i}$
Benzene	78.1	557	0.22	12,700	22.8	134.9	2.13
Naphthalene	128.2	42	0.017	36.4	0.87	2 239	3.35
DDT (pesticide)	354.5	2.36	9.5×10^{-4}	2×10^{-5}	8.7×10^{-6}	1.549×10^6	6.19
TCE	131.4	117.9	0.47	9 870	8.37	195	2.29
Hexane	86.2	1.833×10^5	73.9	20,200	0.11	12,882	4.11
2,4-D (herbicide)	221	1.39×10^{-5}	5.6×10^{-9}	5.6×10^{-5}	4.0	646	2.81
2,3,7,8-TCDD (dioxin)	322	1.7	6.9×10^{-4}	1×10^{-7}	6.0×10^{-8}	6.3×10^6	6.80
2-Chlorobiphenyl (PCB)	188.7	296	0.12	2.04	6.9×10^{-3}	3.47×10^4	4.54

fugacities (f) are equal, as in Eq. (2). The relationship

$$f_i \text{ (air)} = f_i \text{ (water)} = f_i \text{ (aquatic biota)} = \ldots \quad (2)$$

ships of thermodynamics define these fugacity values. For a species, i (which is sparingly soluble in water) in equilibrium between air and water, the fugacities are given by Eq. (3), where c_i (air) and c_i

$$c_i \text{ (air) } RT = c_i \text{ (water) } H_i \quad (3)$$

(water) are the concentrations of species i, R is the gas constant (8.314 J mol^{-1} K^{-1}), T is the temperature (for example, 298 K), and H_i is the Henry's law constant for the solubility of i in water. The ratio of the equilibrium concentration c_i (air) to c_i (water) is the air-water partition coefficient, $K_{AW,i}$, given by Eq. (4) [see **table**].

$$K_{AW,i} = c_i \text{ (air)}/c_i \text{ (water)} = H_i/RT \quad (4)$$

Applying these equations illustrates the enormous disparity in relative concentrations seen with these compounds. For example, if the concentrations of hexane and of 2,4-D in water are both 1 part per billion (1 g in 10^9 g of water), then the equilibrium concentrations of these compounds in air are 7.4×10^{-2} g m^{-3} and 5.6×10^{-12} g m^{-3} respectively, a difference of ten orders of magnitude. It can also be shown that the equilibrium atmospheric concentration of hexane is 73.9 times its concentration in water. Furthermore, the concentration of 2,4-D in water is 7.2×10^4 times the concentration in air. This illustrates the enormous changes that take place when a compound migrates under equilibrium conditions from one phase to another.

Another property that is very important in describing and predicting pollution concentrations is the octanol-water partition coefficient, $K_{OW,i}$. When octanol (C$_8$H$_{17}$OH) is mixed with water at 298 K (25°C or 80°F), phase separation takes place and the upper layer (less dense) is composed of 73 mol % of octanol and 27 mol % of water. The lower layer is composed of almost pure water (**Fig. 2**). The partition coefficient $K_{OW,i}$ is defined as the ratio of the concentrations of species i that partitions be-

tween these two layers when a small amount of i is added to the system, as in Eq. (5).

$$K_{OW,i} = \frac{c_i \text{ (octanol-rich)}}{c_i \text{ (water-rich)}} \quad (5)$$

The property $K_{OW,i}$ is related to the partitioning of the species i between the lipid (or organic, that is, fat) material of animals (and plants) and water. Octanol (C$_8$H$_{17}$O) is used here as a model substance as it behaves in a similar way to lipid material and the ratio of its atoms (carbon, hydrogen, and oxygen) is similar to that found in lipid material. The toxic compounds discussed here are all very much more soluble in organic substances (such as fat and lipid material) than in water. They are known as hydrophobic (water-hating) compounds. The property $K_{OW,i}$ is a measure of the hydrophobic ($K_{OW,i} > 1$) or hydrophilic ($K_{OW,i} < 1$) nature of the substance i.

The partition coefficient, $K_{BW,i}$ of i between the biota (animal or plant lipid material) and water is another important property which is useful when discussing contamination. It is given by Eq. (6), where c_i

$$K_{BW,i} = f_B K_{OW,i} = c_i \text{ (biota)}/c_i \text{ (water)} \quad (6)$$

(biota) and c_i (water) are the equilibrium concentrations of i. The term f_B is the mass fraction of biota (animal or plant) which is lipid. For fish (aquatic biota), f_B is about 0.05 (5%). With this information it is

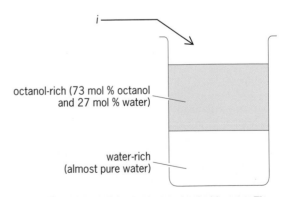

Fig. 2. **Phase separation of octanol mixed with water. The partition coefficient $K_{OW,i} = c_i$ (octanol-rich)/c_i (water-rich).**

possible to determine the effect of the partitioning of a toxic compound between fish and water. In the following example, if the concentration of DDT in the water of a lake is 2 parts per billion (2 mg per 1000 kg of water) and for DDT, $K_{OW} = 1.549 \times 10^6$, then for DDT, $K_{BW} = 7.7 \times 10^4$ and c_i (fish) = 155 parts per million (155 mg per kilogram of fish). The equilibrium concentration of DDT in the fish is thus 77,000 times greater than the concentration of DDT in the water. Experimental evidence has shown that the results from this very simple approach are usually very close to the chemically analyzed value.

The same approach can be made to the other environmental compartments, such as soil and sediments, and the fate of a pollutant entering into a complex environment (assuming equilibrium conditions) can readily be calculated. It is necessary to make assumptions on the relative size of each compartment, and a typical assumption is based on compartment sizes in air ($6 \times 10^9 \, m^3$), water ($6 \times 10^6 \, m^3$), soil ($4.5 \times 10^4 \, m^3$), sediments ($2 \times 10^4 \, m^3$), suspended sediments ($35 \, m^3$), aquatic biota [fish] ($7 \, m^3$), and terrestrial biota ($3 \times 10^3 \, m^3$). Using this information together with the concentration of the toxic compound in water [c_i (water)] and the octanol-water partition coefficient ($K_{OW,i}$), it is possible to determine the amount of substance i in any part of the biosphere assuming equilibrium conditions hold. This latter constraint is usually not a problem as most toxic compounds have a long residence time, of years rather than days, in each compartment. More advanced models take into account the amounts of pollutant flowing into and out of each compartment, and with these values and a steady state approximation, calculations on pollutant concentrations can be made.

Biomagnification. There is a further magnification effect which takes place up the food chain. It is found that large fish and eagles that eat small fish contain pollutant concentrations which are significantly higher than the equilibrium amounts noted above. As a first approximation, it might seem reasonable to assume that, if equilibrium conditions prevail, the concentration of DDT (as an example) should be the same in the predators' bodies as it is in the bodies of the hunted. Chemical analysis, however, shows that for chemical species with a log $K_{OW,i}$ value between 5 and 7, biomagnification of the order of ten times the equilibrium value takes place. These toxic compounds happen also to be large molecules. One explanation for the biomagnification is that the pollutant molecules, on entering the predator's gut, cross the membrane boundary and dissolve in the lipid layers. Once there, these molecules, on account of their size and their hydrophobic nature, do not readily leave, and concentrations in the lipid layers tend to increase. This type of biomagnification has received much public attention, but as already seen it is indeed many orders of magnitude smaller than the equilibrium effect across phase boundaries.

For background information *see* AIR POLLUTION; CHEMICAL EQUILIBRIUM; CHEMICAL THERMODYNAMICS; ENVIRONMENT; ENVIRONMENTAL TOXICOLOGY; FUGACITY; INSECTICIDE; PESTICIDE; POLYCHLORINATED BIPHENYLS in the McGraw-Hill Encyclopedia of Science & Technology.   Trevor M. Letcher

Bibliography. S. Banerjee, S. H. Yalkowsky, and S. C. Valvani, Water solubility and octanol/water partition coefficients of organics: Limitations of the solubility-partition coefficient correlation, *Environ. Sci. Technol.*, 14:1227–1229, 1980; D. Mackay and S. Paterson, Evaluating the multimedia fate of organic chemicals: A level III fugacity model, *Environ. Sci. Technol.*, 25:427–436, 1991; D. Mackay and S. Paterson, Model describing the rates of transfer processes of organic chemicals between atmosphere and water, *Environ. Sci. Technol.*, 20:810–816, 1986.

Enzyme

Proteolysis of extracellular matrix proteins is a crucial phenomenon in connective tissue remodeling during developmental tissue growth and morphogenesis, angiogenesis, and tissue repair. In addition, excessive extracellular matrix degradation plays an important role in the pathogenesis of rheumatoid arthritis, osteoarthritis, autoimmune blistering skin disorders, periodontitis, tumor invasion and metastasis (and so forth). Tumor invasion is a multistage process in which cellular motility is associated with controlled proteolysis, and which involves interactions among tumor cells, stromal cells, and the extracellular matrix. During the process of invasion, malignantly transformed cells detach from the primary tumor, migrate, and cross structural barriers, including basement membranes and surrounding stromal collagenous extracellular matrix, to metastasize (spread) to a distant site (**Fig. 1**). The capacity to degrade extracellular matrix proteins of the basement membrane and the stroma is essential for tumor cell invasion. The degradation is achieved by proteinases derived from tumor and stromal cells. Recent studies have indicated that proteinases belonging to a family of matrix metalloproteinases (MMPs) play an important role in various stages of tumor cell invasion and metastasis.

Matrix metalloproteinases. Matrix metalloproteinases are a family of at least 19 structurally related zinc-dependent neutral endopeptidases (enzymes that act on centrally located peptide bonds of a protein molecule) collectively capable of degrading essentially all components of extracellular matrix. According to their substrate specificities and structures, they are divided into collagenases, stromelysins, gelatinases, and membrane-type MMPs which, in contrast to other MMPs, are not secreted but remain attached to the cell membrane by a short transmembrane domain. Substrate specificities of different MMPs toward extracellular matrix proteins are not clear in vivo, but as assessed by in vitro assays different MMPs are thought to have roles in different stages of tumor cell invasion. For example, stromelysins (stromelysin-1, MMP-3; stromelysin-2, MMP-10; metalloelastase, MMP-12; matrilysin,

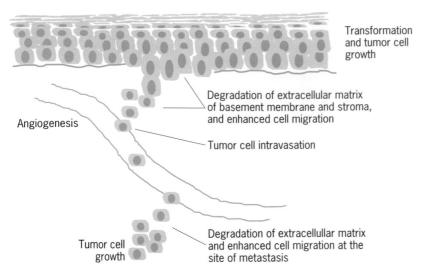

Fig. 1. Schematic presentation of steps during tumor cell invasion and metastasis. A role for MMPs as effectors of each step has been proposed.

MMP-7) and gelatinases (gelatinase-A, MMP-2; gelatinase-B, MMP-9) have a capability to degrade various components of basement-membrane extracellular matrix, whereas collagenases (collagenase-1, MMP-1; collagenase-2, MMP-8; collagenase-3, MMP-13) mainly degrade fibrillar collagens and are thus expected to have role in the degradation of stromal extracellular matrix. Importantly, collagenase-3 (MMP-13) is capable of degrading almost all components of the extracellular matrix, which, together with its prominent expression in invasive tumor

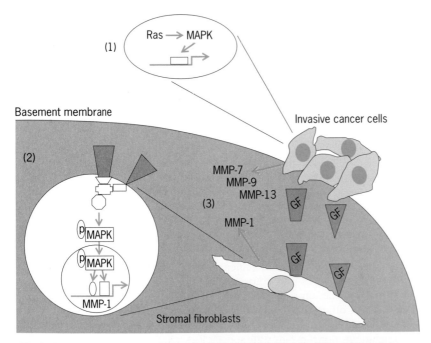

Fig. 2. Proposed mechanism of the concerted action of tumor and stromal cells in tumor invasion. (1) Transformation of epithelial cells (for example, by mutation of Ras) results in increased expression of MMPs and soluble growth factors and cytokines (GF). (2) Tumor-cell-derived soluble factors (GF) trigger activation of intracellular signaling pathways in the fibroblasts, resulting in increased expression of MMPs (such as MMP-1). (3) Concerted degradation of extracellular matrix by tumor-cell- and stromal-cell-derived MMPs at the site of tumor invasion.

cells, makes it a candidate for tumor-invasion-promoting MMP.

Until recently, the role of MMPs in tumor invasion was mainly based on the observations of enhanced expression of them in tumor samples and studies showing that expression of especially collagenase-1 in the tumor correlated to a poor prognosis of various cancers. In addition, a vast amount of evidence has been provided showing that MMP activity is required for in vitro invasion, extracellular matrix degradation, angiogenesis (development of blood vessels), and increased motility of the epithelial cells. Interestingly, MMPs have also been shown to regulate cell growth at the site of metastasis and to promote carcinogenesis. Recent studies using MMP knock-out mice has provided experimental in vivo evidence that MMP activity truly plays an important role in the tumor invasion and metastasis. Mice lacking MMP-7 showed a reduction in intestinal tumorigenesis, and MMP-2-deficient mice show reduced angiogenesis and tumor progression. MMP-11 knock-out mice showed reduced tumorigenesis in response to chemical mutagenesis.

Cancer. Different MMPs are thought to have roles in the stages of cancer progression and invasion. Beside differences in their capability to degrade distinct extracellular matrix components, MMPs show tissue-restricted expression in both physiological and pathological conditions. Although many MMPs are found to be highly expressed by malignant epithelial cancer cells in vitro and in vivo, MMPs expressed by paratumoral cells, such as stromal fibroblasts, endothelial cells, and inflammatory cells, are thought to play a crucial role in the extracellular matrix turnover during cancer cell invasion and therefore to fundamentally contribute to tumor invasion.

MMP-1 is an example whose expression is detected in the stromal compartment of the tumor. Increased expression of MMP-1 has been observed in lung carcinomas, squamous cell carcinomas of the head and neck, and colorectal tumors. In all these tumors the most abundant expression of MMP-1 was observed in the stromal cells (fibroblasts), but significant expression of MMP-1 has also been observed in the stromal or intratumoral endothelial cells. In addition, expression of MMP-1 was observed in head and neck squamous cell carcinoma cells, located at the invading margin of the tumor, providing a mechanism for the highly concerted degradation of extracellular matrix at the site of tumor invasion. In contrast to MMP-1, expression of MMP-13 is predominantly confined to tumor cells at the invading margin, although in a subset of tumors, significant expression of MMP-13 was also observed in stromal fibroblasts. In addition to collagenases, gelatinase-A and -B matrilysin, and membrane-type MMPs are abundantly expressed in various malignant tumors. The role of distinct MMPs at the site of tumor invasion is not clear. It is more probable that proteolytic activity and promotion of tumor invasion is achieved not merely by the activity of a single MMP but also by cooperation among distinct MMPs. This view has been formed from observations that different MMPs activate each other, and that they may bind to the cell membrane of both tumor and stromal cells through interactions with membrane-type MMPs and certain cell surface receptors; and it has been pointed out that cascades involving MMP activation and localization may be required to ensure cooperation between tumor and stromal cells to enhance proteolytic activity in vivo.

The expression of MMPs at the site of tumor invasion is regulated by many factors. Transformation of epithelial cells (such as mutation of Ras) is accompanied by activation of intracellular signaling molecules that activate expression of MMPs in epithelial cells. In addition, a large amount of growth factors and cytokines are secreted by inflammatory cells, as well as by tumor or stromal cells in the tumor, and these factors are presumed to play important role in the crosstalk between cell types to regulate MMP expression in a paracrine manner (**Fig. 2**). Also, the ability of MMPs to degrade and inactivate interleukin-1-beta (IL-1β), and cleave the tumor necrosis factor-alpha (TNF-α) precursor to a biologically active form, indicates that MMPs may also regulate the availability and activity of inflammatory cytokines at the site of tumor invasion and thus modulate transcriptional and immunological responses.

Transcriptional regulation. MMP gene expression is primarily regulated at the transcriptional level, but there is also evidence about modulation of mRNA stability in response to growth factors and cytokines. The promoter regions of inducible MMP genes (MMP-1, MMP-3, MMP-7, MMP-9, MMP-10, MMP-12, MMP-13) show remarkable conservation of regulatory elements, and binding sites for AP-1 and ETS families of transcription factors are found from each of these promoters. Furthermore, it has been shown that AP-1 and ETS transcription factors mediate induction of MMP gene expression in response to growth factors, cytokines, and other environmental factors, such as contact to ECM. Furthermore, direct link between AP-1 activity, MMP expression, and tumor progression has been demonstrated by studies showing that AP-1 transcription factor c-Fos is required for expression of mouse collagenase-3 expression and malignant progression of skin tumors by using c-Fos knock-out mouse model (1, 4). Overexpression of ETS-related transcription factor E1A-F induces invasive phenotype in breast carcinoma cells. In vivo, expression of ETS-1 co-localizes together with MMP-1 expression to paratumoral fibroblasts of several types of tumors, and ETS-1 is also expressed in endothelial cells during tumor vascularization.

In addition, members of the ETS family of transcription factors bind to a conserved PEA3 element that is also found in the promoters of all inducible MMPs. Overexpression of certain ETS factors (ETS-1, ETS-2, and PEA3) activate MMP-1 expression, and furthermore, overexpression of ETS-related transcription factor E1A-F induces carcinogenesis.

Paracrine growth factors and cytokines expressed in the tumor area are thought to play a crucial role in the concerted regulation of metalloproteinase expression in the tumor. Binding of these factors to their corresponding cell surface receptors triggers intracellular signaling that in turn regulates MMP gene expression by a mechanism involving regulation of transcription factor expression and activity by phosphorylation (Fig. 2). Mitogen-activated protein kinases (MAPKs) are a large kinase network in which upstream kinases activate downstream kinases that, in response to phosphorylation, translocate to the nucleus and activate transcription factors. Three MAP kinase pathways (ERK, JNK, and p38) have been characterized in detail. MAPKs have been shown to determine AP-1 (activator protein-1, a transcription factor) and ETS dependent gene regulation. Recent studies have shown that MAP kinases also mediate regulation of MMP gene expression in response to a variety of stimuli.

Even though increased MAP kinase activity has been observed in human tumor tissues and recent studies have shown that increased MAP kinase activity may transform cells and increase malignant behavior of cells by changes of the cell shape, migration capacity, and expression of invasion related genes such as MMPs, the role of distinct MAP kinases in the regulation of tumor invasion is not yet clear.

The vast amount of data generated in the 1990s indicates that expression of MMPs in the tumor enhances metastatic capacity (malignancy of the tumor). This suggests that every level of regulation of MMP expression and proteolytic activity should be considered as a target for therapeutic intervention in the treatment of cancer. In the future, it is essential to challenge the findings obtained from in vitro studies by developing in vivo human and animal models in order to reveal targets for intervention that would specifically prevent tumor invasion and malignancy without disturbing physiological functions and roles of MMPs in humans.

For background information *see* CANCER (MEDICINE); CELLULAR ADHESION; ENZYME; GENE; MOLECULAR BIOLOGY; ONCOLOGY in the McGraw-Hill Encyclopedia of Science & Technology.

Jukka Westermarck

Bibliography. P. Basset et al., Matrix metalloproteinases as stromal effectors of human carcinoma progression: Therapeutical implications, *Matrix Biol.*, 15:535–541, 1997; U. Benbow and C. Brinckerhoff, The AP-1 site and MMP gene regulation: What is all the fuss about?, *Matrix Biol.*, 15:519–526, 1997; L. Blavier et al., Tissue inhibitors of matrix metalloproteinases in cancer, *Ann. N.Y. Acad. Sci.*, 878:108–19, 1999; T. S. Lewis, P. S. Shapiro, and N. G. Ahn, Signal transduction through MAP kinase cascades, *Adv. Cancer Res.*, 74:49–139, 1998; M. D. Sternlicht et al., The stromal proteinase MMP3/stromelysin-1 promotes mammary carcinogenesis, *Cell*, 98:137–146, 1999; J. Westermarck and V. M. Kähäri, Regulation of matrix metalloproteinase expression in tumor invasion, *Faseb. J.*, 13:781–792, 1999.

Evolution

The first 3 billion years of evolution saw the origin of life itself, the diversification of bacterial lineages, the origin and diversification of eukaryotes, and the appearance of many lineages of multicelled life, including animals. This time span culminated in the Cambrian explosion of complex metazoan organisms, but the fuse to the explosion was lit well before the start of the Cambrian (about 540 million years ago). Coupled with these events were major geologic events, such as the origin of the Earth's atmosphere and the appearance of tectonic plates, that profoundly influenced the history of life.

Earliest eukaryotes. Until fairly recently, the oldest known eukaryote fossils were single-celled, more or less spherical forms of uncertain affinities but probably representing stages of algal life cycles, known as acritarchs. The oldest definite acritarchs date back 1.6–1.8 billion years. This is corroborated by biomarkers, complex molecules in petroleum and other buried organic matter that are distinctive for particular taxa. Eukaryotic biomarkers have been documented from rocks in Australia 1.69 billion years old. The recent discovery of relatively large ribbon-like fossils in 2.1-billion-year-old rocks pushed the age of the oldest eukaryotes farther back, coinciding with the transition from an anaerobic reducing atmosphere to an oxygenated atmosphere.

New evidence may push the origin of eukaryotes even farther back in time. In 1999, researchers announced the results of their analysis of organic biomarkers from 2.7-billion-year-old rocks of northwestern Australia. These biomarkers included both methylhopanes, which are characteristic of cyanobacteria, and steranes, which are derivatives of sterol lipids, key components of eukaryote cell membranes but supposedly absent in prokaryotes. This result may prove troublesome for current thinking on the origin of eukaryotes. Based on several lines of geochemical evidence, it is fairly well established that approximately 2 billion years ago the Earth's atmosphere switched from anaerobic and reducing to a minimally aerobic state, at 1% of present oxygen levels (the Pasteur point, considered the minimum level to sustain any aerobic respiration). Eukaryote origins were associated with the appearance of an oxygen atmosphere; the nucleus, for instance, may have evolved as protection for fragile deoxyribonucleic acid (DNA) against oxidization. Eukaryotes also cannot fix molecular nitrogen, and thus were thought to have evolved at a time when nitrogen was available in forms such as nitrate (NO_3^-) , which is chemically unlikely to have been the case in an anoxic atmosphere. If eukaryotes arose 700 million years before the development of a minimally aerobic atmosphere and abundant nitrogenous compounds, the story becomes less clear. However, at least some archaean prokaryotes have flexible cell membranes and have been suspected of having membrane sterols. On various lines of evidence, archaeans are suspected to be the closest relatives of eukaryotes, and there is a possibility that the fossil steranes in question belonged to archaeans, or to an otherwise unknown microbial group perhaps related to archaeans, eukaryotes, or both. Though extremely significant, these 2.7-billion-year-old biomarkers should be studied further, in part by careful characterization of the lipids of a wide range of archaeans.

Eukaryote evolution. A number of fossil discoveries have begun to fill in the record of eukaryote diversification, in particular the diversification of multicellular eukaryotes. Although the fossil record is still incomplete, well-supported examples of red, green, brown, and golden algae are now known from rocks as old as 1 billion years, including spectacular and diverse biotas from the Doushantuo Formation of China (580 million years old) and the Svanbergfjellet Formation of Spitsbergen (700–750 million years old). A sparse but growing amount of evidence has accumulated for the existence of various heterotrophic protist lineages in the Precambrian, including shelled amebas and plausible ciliates from rocks as old as 850 million years. The growing fossil evidence supports the conclusion from molecular phylogeny that eukaryotes underwent a major radiation roughly 1 billion years ago. When thinking about the origin of animals, it is important to remember that the Animalia did not evolve in an ecological vacuum. Rather, they appeared in a world that was rich in unicellular and multicellular protists inhabiting various ecological niches.

Ediacaran organisms. The Ediacaran biota is a group of soft-bodied organisms preserved as impressions in certain rocks. They are known from about 30 localities worldwide, including some recently discovered sites in Nevada. Thick mats of microbes growing on sediment surfaces are now thought to have been crucial for preserving these soft organisms as fossils. Trace fossils suggest that many organisms were adapted to graze on these mats or to "mine" the organic-rich sediment underneath them.

Ediacaran organisms were commonly regarded as a taxonomically distinct group from the Animalia, separated from the animals of the Cambrian by a sizable time gap. The emerging consensus in recent years, however, has been that the Ediacaran organisms included many enigmatic forms, some of which could well have been members of extinct kingdom-level taxa, but that they also included some true animals. In addition to trace fossils made by bilaterian animals, fossil sponges, cnidarians, arthropod relatives, and probable mollusks have been found. The time gap between Ediacaran and Cambrian biotas has also been erased: recent new and refined radiometric dates have shown that most Ediacaran biotas existed between 543 and 555 million years ago, with the oldest estimated to be about 600 million years old. Ediacaran biotas are now known to have lived right up to the base of the Cambrian. In fact, Ediacaran-type fossils have been documented from Cambrian sediments in Australia, western North America, and northern Norway. Furthermore, a small number of shelly fossils have been found in conjunction with soft-bodied Ediacaran-type organisms. Sites in Namibia and Nevada have yielded low-diversity assemblages of mineralized fossils, typically tubular, cone-shaped, or cup-shaped, and mineralized sponge spicules were documented from Ediacaran-age rocks in Mongolia in 1997. Although a great deal of ecological change and evolutionary radiation did take place in marine ecosystems around the start of the Cambrian, the contrast between the Ediacaran biotas and the life of the Cambrian no longer seems so sharp; the two overlapped in time, and several higher taxa cross the boundary between them.

Ironically, considering the controversy over their taxonomic identity, the Ediacaran organisms probably do not include the oldest animals. A phosphorite deposit that is 580 ± 20 million years old, the Doushantuo Formation of China, has yielded a number of fossilized animal embryos, preserved by replacement with phosphate, and preserved so well that individual cells are clearly visible. Embryos of sponges, arthropods, and worms are known from the Doushantuo Formation, and more taxa are likely to be found in the future, suggesting that the origin of the Animalia lies even farther back in time. Meanwhile, trace fossils made by large (centimeter-scale) mobile animals have been found in rocks from central India claimed to be about 1.1 billion years old. However, although the fossils themselves are almost certainly genuine, the age of these rocks has been questioned, and exactly what they mean for early animal evolution is not yet clear. In the absence of well-dated, unambiguous evidence for large animals before about 600 million years at the earliest, some scientists have concluded that the earliest animals were microscopic in size, and thus unlikely to be preserved in typical ways. It is hoped that fossil finds and molecular clock estimates will eventually converge on single, well-supported estimates for the dates of the origins and early radiations of the Animalia.

Animal phylogeny. Molecular sequence data have been widely used for nearly a decade to reconstruct the big picture of animal phylogeny: the relationships among animal phyla and classes. The past few years have seen some revisions of formerly accepted animal phylogenies. Older hypotheses grouped arthropods close to annelids; these two groups, along with mollusks and a few minor phyla, constituted the superphylum Protostomia; lophophorates (such as brachiopods and bryozoans) were commonly placed near the deuterostomes (echinoderms, chordates, and related phyla). This approach has largely been replaced by a grouping of the annelids, mollusks, lophophorates, and a few other phyla in a large clade, the Lophotrochozoa. Arthropods now seem to be closer to nematodes, priapulid worms, and a few other phyla in the clade Ecdysozoa (molting animals, which periodically shed a chitinous cuticle). According to another reconstruction, the traditional phylum Platyhelminthes (flatworms) is not monophyletic. Rather, whereas most flatworms belong within the Lophotrochozoa, the Acoela, a group characterized by extremely simple morphology and the lack of a gut cavity, belong at the base of the bilaterian animal clade. Acoels, which differ from other flatworms in several anatomical and developmental respects, may be the closest living relatives of the ancestral bilaterian animals.

While molecular data have provided new information on relationships, the data have also been a source for controversial estimates of the age of the Animalia. In 1997, researchers announced that the Animalia originated as early as 1200 million years ago, based on "molecular clock" estimates of lineage divergence times. This raised a storm of controversy, since the estimated molecular clock dates of divergence of various animal phyla are typically several hundred million years older than the dates of their appearance in the fossil record. Different genes gave different dates, with a broad scatter; for example, estimates of the divergence time between Echinodermata and Chordata range from 786 million years (based on adenosine triphosphatase 6) to 1312 million years (based on β-hemoglobin), averaging about 1000 million years. However, this work has been repeated several times in the past few years, and while precise dates differ, the results continue to suggest a very early age for the diversification of metazoans, several hundred million years older than the fossil record can show unambiguously. The emerging consensus seems to be that the animal phyla do have a history that extends well past their appearance as fossils. Just how long that history was remains controversial, with some authors arguing for a compromise date of about 750 million years for the origin of the Animalia.

Radiation of animal phyla. Reconstructing the pattern and timing of animal diversification remains an important area of investigation, but research has also intensified on the possible causative factors for animal diversification. What caused animals to arise? Why did modern animal taxa radiate rapidly in the Cambrian Period? Why was there a sizable time lag between the origin of animals and their diversification into recognizable phyla? Hypothesized answers have traditionally been either extrinsic, focusing on external environmental factors such as changes in climate, ocean chemistry, and ecosystems; or intrinsic, focusing on factors within organisms, such as cell-cell interactions and the appearance of new genes.

Among intrinsic factors, the homeotic genes of animals, which regulate the formation of the basic body plan during development, continue to be studied intensively for their role in the evolution of animal body plans, especially the *Hox* gene cluster which regulates anteroposterior patterning. *Hox* genes are present in both cnidarians and bilaterians; the common ancestor of the bilaterians is inferred to have had a cluster of at least six *Hox* genes. *Hox* genes, and homeotic genes in particular, are highly conserved in function; for example, the homeotic gene *Pax6* in mice governs eye formation, and its homolog in fruit flies has the same function, even though the structures of vertebrate and insect eyes are radically different. Despite perhaps 750 million years or more since the phylogenetic split between the lines leading to vertebrates and insects, the same "genetic toolkit" has been conserved. This also implies that the common ancestor of bilaterian animals had some kind of photoreceptors whose patterning was controlled by the ancestral gene to *Pax6*. Similar examples have been discovered for homeotic genes in divergent taxa controlling the formation of appendages, muscles, hearts, and anteroposterior patterning. Various *Hox* genes apparently were duplicated during animal evolution; in fact, the entire *Hox* cluster was duplicated several times in the line leading to vertebrates, which have four *Hox* clusters. Furthermore, the patterns of expression, regulation, and interaction among *Hox* genes also changed during animal evolution, giving rise to the apparent paradox of diverse animal body plans built using very similar toolkits.

In the most widespread type of bilaterian animal development, the zygote develops into a primary larva, typically consisting of a few thousand cells. The size and growth potential of such larvae are limited, and most such larvae have "set-aside cells," tissue rudiments which are capable of indefinite division and which give rise to the larger adult animal. The evolution of set-aside cells in a common ancestor of bilaterians, and the evolution of the regulatory gene networks that govern pattern formation in the set-aside cells and generate the adult body plan were crucial events in animal evolution. Before the appearance of set-aside cells, bilaterians were small (and thus unlikely to be fossilized). After the evolution of set-aside cells and regulatory genes, including homeotic genes, changes in gene expression and regulation could have occurred relatively rapidly. This scenario accounts for the probable missing fossil record of the earliest bilaterians, and suggests a decoupling of bilaterial origins and early cladogenesis from their later, rapid diversification.

Many potential extrinsic factors affecting the rise of animals are known, and these could have served as triggers, releasing the evolutionary potential created by homeotic gene evolution and other intrinsic factors. A global rise in oxygen levels was one possible factor. Global episodes of glaciation, the last of which occurred just before the rise of the Ediacaran biotas, may also have played some role, although it is not clear exactly what they would have done. Ecosystems themselves became more complex in the Cambrian. Predation, epibiosis (organisms living on top of each other), active filter feeding, and deep burrowing and certain other behaviors were all rare in Ediacaran ecosystems but widespread in the Cambrian. Increased ecological complexity may have been a self-stoking process. For instance, the rise of predation may have caused natural selection for complex skeletons and behaviors as antipredator defenses, which in turn may have selected for more sophisticated predatory adaptations. Also, because both biomineralized metazoans and mineralized algae radiated during the same time interval, it seems likely that an environmental change favored or selectively drove the evolution of biomineralization in algae and animals alike; biomineralization in turn could have stimulated further diversification by the ecological feedback process mentioned. Rising temperatures in the wake of the end of the last Precambrian glaciation may have contributed to the origin of biomineralization; changes in seawater chemistry are also possible.

For background information *see* ANIMAL EVOLUTION; CAMBRIAN; CLASSIFICATION, BIOLOGICAL; EDIACARAN FAUNA; FOSSIL; ORGANIC EVOLUTION; PRECAMBRIAN; SPECIATION in the McGraw-Hill Encyclopedia of Science & Technology.   Ben Waggoner

Bibliography. J. J. Brocks et al., Archean molecular fossils and the early rise of eukaryotes, *Science*, 285:1033–1036, 1999; J. G. Gehling, Microbial mats in terminal Proterozoic siliciclastics: Ediacaran death masks, *Palaios*, 14:40–57, 1999; A. H. Knoll and S. B. Carroll, Early animal evolution: Emerging views from comparative biology and geology, *Science*, 284: 2129–2137, 1999; G. M. Narbonne, The Ediacara biota: A terminal Neoproterozoic experiment in the evolution of life, *GSA Today*, 8(2):1–6, 1998; K. J. Peterson, R. A. Cameron, and E. H. Davidson, Set-aside cells in maximal indirect development: Evolutionary and developmental significance, *Bioessays*, 19:623–31, 1997; I. Ruiz-Trillo et al., Acoel flatworms: Earliest extant bilaterian metazoans, not members of platyhelminthes, *Science*, 283:1919–1923, 1999; A. B. Smith, Dating the origin of metazoan body plans, *Evol. Dev.*, 1:138–142; J. W. Valentine, D. Jablonski, and D. H. Erwin, Fossils, molecules, and embryos: New perspectives on the Cambrian explosion, *Development*, 126:851–850.

Evolutionary computation

Evolutionary computation is a rapidly growing interdisciplinary science area that is concerned with modeling aspects of natural evolution in order to solve real-world problems. Living organisms, as well as those long extinct, demonstrate optimized complex behavior at all levels: cells, organs, individuals, and populations. Charles Darwin wrote of "organs of extreme perfection" when describing the ability of evolution to craft ingenious solutions to complex problems such as vision. Evolution is the great unifying principle of biology, but it extends beyond biology and can be used as an engineering principle where individuals in a population of candidate solutions to some particular problem undergo random variation (mutation and recombination) and face competition and selection based on their appropriateness for the task at hand.

Process. The common use of an evolutionary algorithm requires four elements: (1) an evaluation (fitness) function that describes the quality of any candidate solution in quantitative terms, (2) a representation or data structure that the computer uses to store solutions, (3) a random variation operator (or operators) that transform "parents" into "offspring," and (4) a means for selecting which solutions will survive to the next generation and which will be eliminated. In addition, the process must be initialized with a population of candidate solutions to the task at hand. This is often accomplished by seeding the first population with completely random solutions; however, if domain-specific knowledge is available regarding which solutions may be better than others, these hints can be used to bias the initial population and may accelerate the evolutionary optimization procedure.

An evolutionary algorithm (**Fig. 1**) is executed over a series of generations of random variation and selection. The variation to the existing solutions can come in the form of single-parent or multiparent operators. Alternative choices offer different sampling distributions from the space of all possible solutions. Each of the individuals in the population is scored with respect to how well the individual accomplishes the task at hand (fitness), and selection is used to eliminate some subset of the population or to amplify the percentage of above-average solutions. The algorithm terminates when some extrinsic criterion has been satisfied, such as prescribed maximum number of generations, or a suitable error tolerance. Over time, by eliminating poor solutions and extending the evolutionary search around those that appear better, the population can discover superior solutions to complex problems.

Origins. Although this idea of using evolutionary computation to solve problems is currently under-going a renaissance that promises to have a significant impact on computing, its origins date back to the 1950s and 1960s. Some of the first experiments performed on John von Neumann's computer involved what would now be called artificial life. A program written for this machine by Nils Barricelli in 1953 simulated an environment, separated by cells in a grid. Numbers resided in each cell and migrated to neighboring cells based on a set of rules. When two numbers collided in the same cell, they competed for survival. Even with very simple rules for propagating throughout the environment, certain numeric patterns would evolve and could persist only when other patterns were also present. These first experiments already demonstrated something akin to symbiosis.

The idea of simulating evolution on a computer arose as many as eight to ten times independently from 1953 to 1969 in diverse fields of study. Evolutionary algorithms were proposed in 1957 and again in the mid-1960s to simulate biological processes with the aim of understanding adaptation in nature. Another proposal (1960) was to use Darwin's ideas to generate artificial intelligence by evolving models that would predict future events in an environment. The use of evolutionary algorithms was also proposed (1962) for function optimization, and this led to work on the prospects of evolving neural networks. And in 1964, principles of evolution were used to search for improved designs for physical devices in fluid-mechanics problems (such as a supersonic flashing nozzle). The multiple simultaneous beginnings of evolutionary computation attest to the compelling nature of the idea of simulating the fundamental processes of evolution in fast time.

Putting evolution to work. As a stochastic search technique, an evolutionary algorithm is a means for generating useful solutions rather than perfect solutions. For example, a traveling salesperson problem comprising 1000 cities involved finding the minimum tour length required to cover each city once and only once and return to the starting position. The initial best solution required over 50,000 units to accomplish this tour, while the best found solution, after examination of 4×10^7 possible solutions, had a distance of just over 2000 units (**Fig. 2a**). This solution was not the best possible solution for this problem, but it was within about 5–7% of the expected minimum length for all 1000-city traveling salesperson problems. Moreover, the improvement in the quality of the solution was quite rapid in the initial phases of the evolutionary search (Fig. 2b). The size of the search space was over 10^{1200} (1 followed by 1200 zeros), indicating that the evolutionary algorithm had searched only a small fraction of all possible solutions while finding one of very high quality. Real-world applications of the traveling-salesperson problem include scheduling, the optimization of distribution networks, and computer chip layout and design.

Adaptability of technique. In comparison to traditional problem-solving techniques, evolutionary algorithms are often much faster and more adaptable to changes

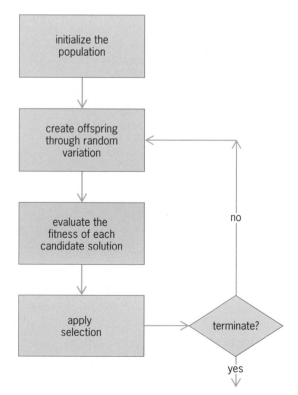

Fig. 1. Typical flowchart for an evolutionary algorithm.

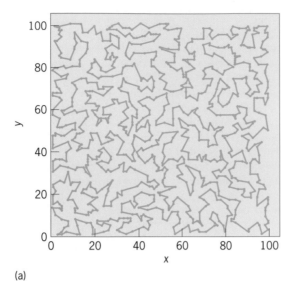

(a)

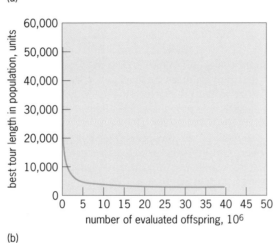

(b)

Fig. 2. Traveling salesperson problem comprising 1000 cities. (*a*) Best-evolved solution after examination of 4×10^7 possible solutions. (*b*) Rate of evolutionary optimization. (*After D. B. Fogel, Applying evolutionary programming to selected traveling salesman problems, Cybernet. Sys., 24:27–36, 1993*)

in the environment because whatever knowledge has been learned about how to solve a problem is contained in the collection of individual solutions that has survived up to that point. In contrast with, say, dynamic programming, an evolutionary algorithm need not be restarted when facing new data. This feature promises to have a significant potential in future problem solving. As the spread of data and processing speeds continue to increase, it will be necessary to make decisions ever more quickly. The evolutionary approach of bootstrapping off the current basis set of knowledge may eventually become the standard approach to real-world, real-time problem solving.

Contrast with conventional approaches. The utility and applicability of evolutionary algorithms requires a shift in thinking that may require some time to overtake conventional engineering. The typical approach to problem solving is to think in terms of reducing complex situations into simpler elements (building blocks) and then working to optimize each of these components. The hope is that when brought back together, these optimized components will serve to make the best design. But it is well known that outstanding individuals do not necessarily make a great team. Evolution works in an entirely different manner. Only the entire cohesive functional unit is measured by selection. Owing to the complex effects of genetic interactions, where a single genetic change can affect myriad behaviorial traits (a relationship known as pleiotropy), evolution tinkers with the underlying genetics and simultaneously generates a diverse array of new behaviors. Selection then culls out the least appropriate designs.

Choice of evolutionary algorithms. Even though there have been some attempts to analyze evolutionary algorithms as a parallel to human engineering, focusing mainly on recombination as a mechanism for bringing together "good ideas," there is no reason to expect that the evolutionary model of learning is the model that is used by engineers. Moreover, there is little reason to expect that it will be possible to improve evolutionary algorithms by capturing idealized models of genetic operators that occur in nature. The effects of those operators may be wholly different in the natural setting. A flapping wing will have different effects on a seagull in contrast to a jet aircraft. Airplanes can be designed to have increased biological fidelity by gluing feathers to their wings, but in the end all that will be accomplished is to increase their drag. What is termed the phenotypic effect, the manner of behavioral response to the environmental demands, is all that selection can assess. By consequence, in evolutionary algorithms, variation operators must be tailored to the task at hand in order to gain the most benefit and achieve the greatest efficiency.

This notion has been written down in formal mathematics in the "no free lunch theorem." Within some overarching assumptions, all algorithms perform exactly the same on average when applied across all possible functions. The consequence of this result is that if an evolutionary algorithm is good for a certain class of problem, then it is not good (worse than a random search) on some other class. There is no single best construction for an evolutionary search (or any other search algorithm). Much of the early theory that supported using binary representations, one-point crossover, and proportional selection has now been shown to be either incorrect or of no practical value. What remains is a significant challenge for the future: Analyzing classes of optimization problems and determining useful means for identifying which types of evolutionary algorithms are appropriate in each case. This is a wide-open area of investigation and it promises to be quite difficult.

Prospects. Computing power has now caught up with the concept of evolving solutions to complex problems. Current real-world applications include supply chain optimization, screening for new drug leads, electronic circuit design, scheduling logistic and transportation services, and gaming.

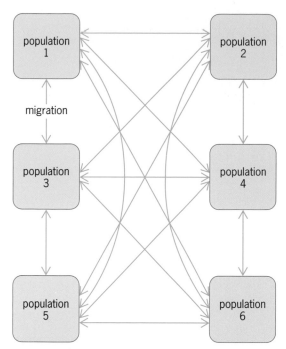

Fig. 3. Arrangement for distributing an evolutionary algorithm across multiple processors. Each processor holds its own population that undergoes random variation and selection. Occasionally, solutions will migrate from one population to another and begin competing for survival in their new environment.

The processing speed of modern desktop machines is rated at about 10^9 floating-point operations per second (flops). But evolution is an inherently parallel process in which potential solutions can often be evaluated simultaneously rather than sequentially. In these cases, a parallel distributed computing architecture can offer a tremendous speedup, since many more trials can be conducted per unit of time. An evolutionary algorithm can be implemented with multiple populations on independent processors, with occasional migration being applied to introduce solutions from different populations (**Fig. 3**). In this manner, the parallel nature of evolution can be captured and many more trials can be conducted per unit of time. The best manner in which to set up such a distributed network of populations is problem-dependent and is an open question for research.

Experiments are being conducted with distributed architectures that comprise 1000 350-MHz computers. This computing power is roughly what can be expected for desktop machines around 2010. The products that will emerge from these massively parallel designs remain a matter of speculation; some foresee the use of evolutionary algorithms to design surrogate artificial brains that will supplant human cognition. Whether or not this conjecture becomes reality, with the price of desktop computers continuing to fall, the parallel approach to supercomputing is increasingly attractive and appears to be perfectly suited to evolutionary problem solving.

For background information *see* ALGORITHM; CONCURRENT PROCESSING; DISTRIBUTED SYSTEMS (COM-PUTERS); GENETIC ALGORITHMS; MULTIPROCESSING; OPTIMIZATION; ORGANIC EVOLUTION; SUPERCOMPUTER in the McGraw-Hill Encyclopedia of Science & Technology.   David B. Fogel

Bibliography. T. Bäck, *Evolutionary Algorithms in Theory and Practice*, Oxford University Press, New York, 1997; D. B. Fogel (ed.), *Evolutionary Computation: The Fossil Record*, IEEE Press, Piscataway, NJ, 1998; Z. Michalewicz and D. B. Fogel, *How To Solve It: Modern Heuristics*, Springer-Verlag, Berlin, 2000.

Fluid coating

Fluid coating is the operation of depositing a liquid film on a solid, due to a relative motion between them (**Fig. 1**). It occurs in many situations of everyday life as well as in numerous industrial processes. Examples include a water drop sliding on a window and leaving behind a trail; an object or a person coming out wet from a bath; or the emptying of a solid full of liquid (such as a glass containing water or a porous medium filled with oil), leaving some liquid inside the solid. In all these cases, an important practical question is the thickness of the film adhering to the solid. It may be desirable to control the thickness for coating purposes, or conversely to avoid a film altogether to keep the solid dry. To achieve this control, it is important to understand the parameters affecting the existence of such a film, and the laws of deposition.

Before addressing a dynamic problem, it is often worth describing the statics. The very general situation in which a solid, a liquid, and a vapor meet together occurs, for example, in the case of a drop deposited on a solid with air all around. The different surface energies involved in such a situation (between the solid and the liquid, the liquid and the

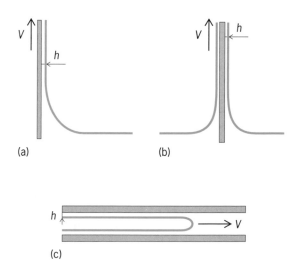

Fig. 1. Different kinds of fluid coating, according to the geometry. (*a*) Plate coating. (*b*) Fiber coating. (*c*) Film deposition in a tube. In each case, the macroscopic film coating the solid comes from a relative motion between the liquid and the solid, and the film thickness *h* can be tuned by the coating velocity *V*.

vapor, and the solid and the vapor) impose an equilibrium condition at the contact line where the three phases coexist. Since each surface tension tries to draw the contact line so as to reduce the corresponding interface, the balance of the tensions, which defines the equilibrium, fixes a contact angle close to this line. For a drop, it is the angle with which the liquid-vapor interface meets the solid. A liquid totally wets a solid if it joins it with a zero contact angle. If that is not the case (contact angle larger than zero), the corresponding situation is referred to as partial wetting.

Total wetting can occur by itself (for example, oils on most solids) or be realized by adding wetting agents to the liquid (the most common ones being surfactants, for example, soaps in water). Drawing a solid out of such a liquid always produces a film deposition. Of course, this deposition is favored by the wetting situation, since a film would spontaneously spread from the bath onto the solid, even at rest. But such wetting films are microscopic, which is not generally the case in fluid coating (at least, for sufficiently large coating velocities): the trail of a drop is visible. The thickness of the coating film can be determined with the help of a canonical law of hydrodynamics: Because of its viscosity, a liquid in the close vicinity of a solid moves at the same velocity as the solid. This principle is the basis of fluid coating and the cause of entrainment, and calculating the film thickness requires identifying the extent of this vicinity. Different answers exist, depending on the velocity of deposition.

Low-velocity coatings. The case of low velocities was understood in the 1940s by the Russian physicists Lev Landau, Benjamin Levich, and Boris Derjaguin. The Landau-Levich-Derjaguin (LLD) picture is as follows: Drawing a solid out of a bath implies a deformation of the free surface (Fig. 1a), which the surface tension of the liquid opposes. The film thickness thus results from a balance between the effects of viscosity (which causes a macroscopic entrainment of liquid by the solid) and surface tension of the liquid, which resists to this deformation (and thus to the film entrainment). A dimensionless number called the capillary number compares the intensity of these antagonistic effects (defined as $Ca = \eta V/\gamma$, with η and γ the liquid viscosity and surface tension, and V the deposition velocity). In the limit of low velocities, the film thickness, h, should be a function of this unique parameter (this function was found by Landau, Levich, and Derjaguin to obey a simple power law: $h \sim Ca^{2/3}$), whatever the geometry of the coating. This is indeed the case, and the geometry of the situation enters only through the length that normalizes the film thickness: For plate coating, this length is the capillary length (a millimetric length that corresponds physically to the size of the static meniscus, formed when a wetting liquid meets a vertical plate), or the capillary radius for a wire or a capillary tube.

Coating at higher velocities. The hydrodynamics of fluid coating becomes more complicated at higher velocities. Then, inertia must be taken into

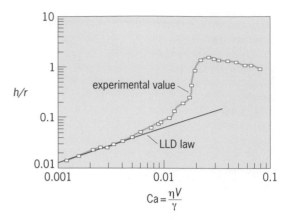

Fig. 2. Different regimes of fluid coating, according to the coating speed. These experimental data correspond to fiber coating. The film thickness h normalized by the fiber radius r is plotted as a function of the capillary number Ca. Experimental values are compared with the Landau-Levich-Derjaguin (LLD) law for low-velocity flow.

account—in the above example, the inertia of the fluid set in motion by the solid in the bath. When the moving fluid comes out from the bath, in the tiny zone where the film thickness fixes, its inertia must be compared with the capillary force (which was found to limit the film thickness). A negligible inertia defines the LLD frame. If the inertia is not negligible, it should act to make the film thicker than predicted by the LLD picture, since it tends to pull the liquid out of the bath. It was shown experimentally in fiber (or wire) coating that this is indeed the case. The film thickness displays critical behavior as a function of velocity: Above a threshold in velocity (typically of order 1 m/s or 3 ft/s), a simple doubling of the velocity causes the film thickness to increase about tenfold (**Fig. 2**).

At still larger velocities, the film thickness stops increasing with the coating speed and even slowly decreases with it (Fig. 2). This regime concerns most industrial coating processes, where the coating speed can be of order 10–30 m/s (30–100 ft/s). At such high speeds, the contact time of a piece of solid in the bath becomes very short (it is simply $t = L/V$, with L the bath length). Thus, the problem now is to understand how much liquid this piece of solid can put in motion inside the bath—a classical question, called the viscous boundary layer problem and solved in the early twentieth century by Ludwig Prandtl. Balancing inertia with the viscous force gives the answer: The thickness of the layer moved by the solid (and thus coming out with it) increases as the square root of the contact time (it scales as $\sqrt{\eta t/\rho}$, with ρ the liquid density). Hence, the film thickness in this regime indeed slowly decreases with the coating speed (as $1/\sqrt{V}$, since t varies as $1/V$). This law expresses a balance between the viscosity (which is, of course, still responsible for the coating) and inertia—but now, the inertia of the bath, which is globally at rest and thus resists the motion. The action of the liquid tension, which was predominant at low velocity (the LLD frame), has become negligible in this high-speed regime.

Complex fluid coatings. Most liquids used in coating processes are complex fluids: emulsions (which are fine dispersions of oil in water) or water-containing surfactants. In the cases where inertial effects are dominant (high-speed regimes), the above description remains valid because the parameters fixing the coating are bulk parameters (viscosity and density). The situation is much more interesting at smaller velocities, where surface effects are important. For example, a soap bubble is drawn from soapy water with a well-defined thickness, but a solid is not necessary to make it. (Likewise, bubbles form at the liquid-air interface in a glass of beer.) Hence, a liquid-vapor interface has the same ability as a solid to entrain matter, providing that surfactants are present at this interface. This is due to the fact that in such a process the surfactants at the surface are not homogeneous in concentration, but diluted by the motion: A gradient of surfactant concentration exists there, and thus a gradient of surface tension, which induces a force that is able to entrain liquid below the surface. If a solid is drawn out of a bath containing surfactants, the film thickness can be expected to be about twice as large as is predicted by the LLD theory for pure liquids, because two interfaces (solid-liquid and liquid-vapor) are now responsible for the coating, instead of one. This is indeed what the experiments show (although more sophisticated arguments involving, for example, the kinetics of adsorption of the surfactant must be taken into account for a complete quantitative understanding of the data).

Coating threshold velocity. A solid slowly drawn out of a liquid which only partially wets it can come out dry, as is commonly observed. For example, a drop moving on a water lily leaves the leaf dry after passing on it. At rest, the liquid meets the solid with a nonzero contact angle. This angle decreases when the solid is moved, but it can remain nonzero thanks to the action of the liquid surface tension which opposes the deformation of the meniscus. Above a threshold in velocity (typically of the order of 1 cm/s or 0.4 in./s), viscous forces dominate capillary ones: A film is deposited and the LLD regime is recovered. The critical velocity of deposition is not yet fully understood, but it depends on both the static contact angle and the liquid viscosity.

Self-running droplets. In some cases, the coating may form by itself, instead of being forced to form by an external motion. The so-called running droplets discovered separately by Colin Bain and Thierry Ondarçuhu are a remarkable example (**Fig. 3a**). These drops contain molecular species which have a double property: first, they are likely to react with the solid; second, the solvent ceases to wet the solid once it is coated with these molecules. Depositing such a drop on a solid generally produces a spontaneous motion (self-running droplets). If the chemical reaction with the solid starts for some reason on one side of the drop, then the two sides sit on different solids: one on the bare solid, the other on the solid coated with the reactive species. This asymmetry provokes the motion, until the reservoir of reactives is exhausted or the whole solid is coated.

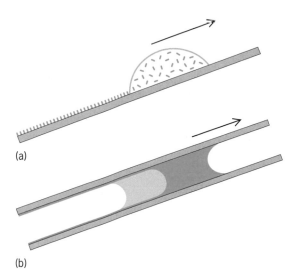

Fig. 3. Self-running droplets. (a) Bain-Ondarçuhu device. (b) Bico bi-drop.

These drops realize a dry coating of the surface, but other possibilities exist if a wet coating is desired. For example, the so-called bi-drops discovered by José Bico, which juxtapose two (wetting) drops inside a tube, also produce a self-motion, again because of the asymmetry of the device (Fig. 3b). Each drop can leave a film behind, so that a great variety of coatings (including double coatings) can be realized. The coatings can also be used to achieve better transport properties: The film left behind by the first drop can lubricate the way for the second one. Liquids of very high viscosities can be self-transported by such a device.

In all these cases, it is in a sense the coating which makes the motion (instead of the motion, the coating, as is usually the case). The driving forces are capillary in essence, so that these droplets can creep upward, as in capillary rise. Research on self-running drops is active and promising, in particular in the context of microfluidics. More sophisticated devices may be possible, where the coating can be addressed and tuned.

For background information *see* BOUNDARY-LAYER FLOW; SURFACE COATING; SURFACE TENSION; SURFACTANT; VISCOSITY in the McGraw-Hill Encyclopedia of Science & Technology.   David Quéré

Bibliography. B. V. Derjaguin and S. M. Levi, *Film Coating Theory*, 1964; S. F. Kistler and P. M. Schweizer (eds.), *Liquid Film Coating*, 1997; D. Quéré, Fluid coating on a fiber, *Annu. Rev. Fluid Mech.*, 31:347–384, 1999; K. J. Ruschak, Coating flows, *Annu. Rev. Fluid Mech.*, 17:65–89, 1985.

Food science

Foods are physicochemical systems in which a number of phases and chemical compounds can coexist in a metastable condition (that is, far from true thermodynamic equilibrium), and in the presence of microbes, whose metabolism may cause significant modifications of the chemical composition and physical properties of the hosting product. For this reason, food science not only deals with protection from external chemical, physical, and microbial injuries (for example, through the use of suitable additives or packaging), but also investigates the intrinsic causes of food instability, such as phase separations of dispersed systems, phase transitions (which mainly concern food polymers, such as starch, gluten and other proteins, and fats), enzymatic reactions (often related to the "endogenous" microbial agents), and preparation procedures (such as cooking, extruding, and freezing), all of which can profoundly modify the nutritional and sensory properties of the product.

Foods as metastable systems. The main sensory and nutritional properties of a food are often strictly related to its metastability. For example, mayonnaise becomes unacceptable when from the metastable emulsion state it collapses into a thermodynamically stable state with the separation of lipid and aqueous bulk phases. Wine, even when carefully shelved in a suitable cellar, cannot keep its optimum flavor and taste indefinitely, since sooner or later it undergoes sedimentation of suspended particles, redox shifts, and enzymatic spoiling reactions.

Strictly speaking, the metastable state of foods should be described quantitatively in terms of the Gibbs function, G, that is, as a condition of relative G minimum, but because of energy wells, it does not decay toward the true equilibrium state. However, this approach is rather difficult in systems with many compounds and phases. It is possible instead to describe food metastability in terms of poor molecular mobility that cannot overcome frictional hindrances and sustain the structural or chemical rearrangements required to attain a more stable state. Rheological characterization of foods (the study of their deformation and flow), which in the past was aimed mainly at a quantitative representation of sensory properties, such as chewability, firmness, and crispness, has found a new *raison d'être* for food scientists and technologists, who are now inclined to approach foods much in the same way that polymer scientists approach synthetic macromolecules.

Many foods show behavior very similar to that of polymer solutions, the properties of which can be related to the gap between the actual temperature of the system and its glass transition temperature, T_g. The glass transition corresponds to a large change (four or more orders of magnitude) of the viscosity that occurs in a relatively narrow temperature range. The midvalue of this range, T_g, can be referred to as a reference threshold between an upper temperature region, where molecular mobility can sustain chemical and physical transformations, and a lower temperature region, where any displacement of polymer molecules is supposed to be severely reduced, since the relevant relaxation time scale becomes much longer (years or centuries) than the time lapse of the experiment.

It should be stressed that for $T < T_g$ roto-vibrational degrees of freedom are still accessible for some segments of polymer chains or their side branches, as well as for nonpolymer compounds, such as H_2O, which still can be mobile and produce some effects. Among all the ingredients of foods, water is indeed the last to be immobilized on cooling and the first to reattain its degrees of freedom on thawing. The relatively large mobility of water molecules even at subzero temperatures can induce collapse phenomena and degradation of tissues and supramolecular structures (mainly because of formation of ice crystals) and can affect the final structure of a product that undergoes a freeze-thaw cycle. The control of the behavior of water molecules is therefore of paramount importance and represents the main goal of the so-called cryostabilization of foods.

This role of water can be easily highlighted in simple foods, which can be treated as water-polymer pseudo binaries and described with a state diagram that shows how the glass transition temperature, T_g, depends on the water content of the system. The state diagrams of a polymer-water binary is the representation of the macroscopic phases, including the glassy ones, formed as a consequence of heating, cooling, or dehydration (**Fig. 1**). It cannot be considered a picture of equilibrium states of the system, although, for practical scopes, it can be used much in the same way as a simple eutectic phase diagram, where the eutectic invariant is replaced by the point (T_g', C_g').

At this point the maximal freeze-concentrated liquid solution (with composition C_g') turns directly into a glassy state, since any ice segregation is hindered by the large viscosity of the medium. The point (T_g', C_g') belongs to the locus $T_g(C)$ that spans the whole concentration range with an upper limit at the glass transition temperature of the pure polymer and a lower limit at the glass transition temperature of water (about $-140°C$). The knowledge of the state diagram is of help when planning dehydration treatments, extrusion processes, and freeze-thawing cycles for frozen foods and food ingredients.

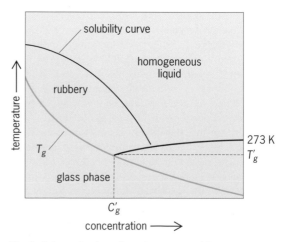

Fig. 1. Schematic view of a polymer-water binary.

Although such an approach has been proved adequate in describing simple aqueous binaries of sugars, polysaccharides (such as amylose and amylopectin), and proteins (such as gelatin, glyadin, glutenin, and vital gluten), its application to real food systems is not straightforward. Many, if not all, ingredients of a given food would simultaneously compete for the available water, thus modifying its interactions and directly affect interphase processes, like moisture migration toward regions where the thermodynamic activity of water, a_W, is lower.

This competition has to be viewed in the broad perspective of the nonspecific interactions between food ingredients: a perspective that is not always taken into account by food technologists. Based on well-known reaction pathways of the organic chemistry, a number of specific interactions have been so far proposed to explain transformations in foods. The most important of these is the Maillard reaction involving proteins and reducing sugars and producing brownish compounds that are responsible for undesirable colors and off-flavors of some dairy products.

Foods as dispersed systems. Dispersed systems include foams, emulsions, suspensions, and gels. Many foods are multiple dispersed systems in that particles spread in the dispersion medium can themselves be dispersed systems. This situation includes the classical oil-in-water and water-in-oil emulsions; but it can also occur when water is the only solvent shared by different polymer solutes, such as proteins and starch and nonstarch polysaccharides (each being reasonably soluble in aqueous media), and water-in-water emulsions are formed. Such behavior can be explained by taking into account that the molecules of these biopolymers are surrounded by a shell of solvent molecules that prevents them from approaching each other too closely. In other words, the aqueous mixtures of these polymers are characterized by a large excluded volume (for example, more than 4% for protein-polysaccharide mixtures). The repulsive and attractive forces between different macromolecules underlie two opposite phenomena: polymer incompatibility and the formation of molecular complexes or aggregates. As an example, unfolded proteins tend to aggregate and become thermodynamically incompatible with other polymers (including native globular proteins).

The thermodynamic incompatibility between macromolecules, such as a polysaccharide and a protein, can be represented quantitatively in a phase diagram. A binodal curve separates an upper two-phase region from a lower single-phase region (**Fig. 2**). The two phases coexisting above the binodal curve are separated aqueous solutions enriched in protein and polysaccharide, respectively. These two liquid phases form a water-in-water emulsion with low interfacial tension, low density and viscosity of the interfacial (depletion) layer between the phases, high deformation of dispersed particles in flow, and different polymer concentrations in the phases. Addition of one polymer to a solution of another makes both of them behave as if the solution was more concentrated.

Addition of a polysaccharide reduces the protein concentration required for its multilayer adsorption at the interface of oil-in-water emulsions. Multilayer formation can be regarded as an encapsulation of dispersed lipid particles and a transition from the single oil/water to the double oil/water/water emulsion. A lipid continuous phase can be formed due to phase inversion. Interfacial layers can adsorb lipids and form a continuous lipid phase between the aqueous phases of a water/water emulsion. This corresponds to the formation of a honeycomblike structure of lipids which can encapsulate up to 80% water. This type of low-fat spread is a composite formed by small spherical granules of aqueous gel bound together by a thin lipid film. These effects are of practical use for food innovations. Some examples are worth mentioning.

Filling a lipid phase with aqueous droplets or gel particles reduces fat content. Filling it with aqueous droplets and gas bubbles equalizes the density of the phases. Filling a lipid phase with dry proteins allows the control of the composition and masks the flavor of foods. Under shearing conditions the low adhesion of aqueous particles to each other and lipids results in a "ball-bearing" effect that can mimic the behavior and properties of fat globules. The freezing of water leads to an increase in the total concentration of aqueous phases and to their gelation. The increase of the concentration of polymers tightens the structure during processes that reduce the excluded volume, like aggregation, gelation, and crystallization of the polymer components. Gels formed from polymer blends (with composition below the binodal curve of the phase diagram) show a decreased gel point and an increased elastic modulus. The opposite holds for two-phase systems: the higher the volume fraction of dispersed particles, the lower the modulus of elasticity of the gels. This reflects a low adhesion between the filler and the matrix (similar to low-fat spreads). The gel network can be thermally broken into macromolecular aggregates and free macromolecules. The properties of a gel surface

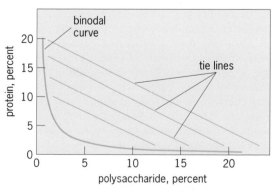

Fig. 2. Isothermal section of the phase diagram for an aqueous mixture of two thermodynamically incompatible polymers (for example, casein) and a polysaccharide (for example, amylopectin).

depend on the medium where gel is formed (gelatin gels formed in oil medium are not wetted with water, but are perfectly wetted with oil).

It should be mentioned that incompatible biopolymers form interpenetrating networks. This is possible because gelation implies aggregation of macromolecules and leads to a decrease in their excluded volume. Formation of mixed gels is due to the better miscibility of a given polymer within the gel network of another one.

Fractal approach. The results of various experimental approaches coupled with some general models drawn mainly from polymer science allow reasonable descriptions of many phenomena that occur in foods, including those related to their multiphase nature (foams, suspensions, emulsions, interdispersed gels, and so on), as well as quantitative evaluations of many properties and exhaustive pictures of structures, like the layered amorphous and crystal phases in starch granules. There is, however, a gap between molecular and mesoscopic descriptions allowed by direct experimental investigations. One therefore has to make assumptions and induce conclusions based on the findings related to macroscopic or molecular features. For example, it is impossible to have direct evidence of the heterogeneity of a flour dough, where thermodynamically incompatible polymers, such as gluten and starch polysaccharides, are present together with some lipid. This system is too thick to be separated by ultracentrifugation and too opaque to be investigated with some light-scattering experiment. A phase split can be evidenced when the water content of the dough is increased at least twofold. But this leaves unexplained the real partition of minor dough components, such as pentosans (nonstarch polysaccharides naturally present in many cereal flours) and added hydrocolloids (xanthans, guar gum, and so on), and their interactions with gluten proteins or amylose and amylopectin in a real dough, which can be responsible for the substantial differences observed in the structure and properties of the bread produced.

As a result, the present knowledge of foods is rather poor at the mesoscopic level where most of the processes underlying or sustaining the formation of food structure and functionality take place. In the absence of some innovative technique, fractal geometry, which has proven intriguingly powerful in describing natural structures, percolation transport processes, growth of crystal phases, clustering of particles and shape of macroscopic bodies, like snow flakes, cauliflower, powder aggregates, and cocoa butter fat crystal phases, may facilitate progress. The trajectories produced in viscous fluids, too, like those observed in many foods prepared from mixed doughs or thickened emulsions, can be described by fractal geometry. A relationship must still be found beween fractal structure and fractal functionality, the limit of the fractal domain being the size of the dispersed particles. Finally, it seems that fractal geometry coupled with thermodynamics of irreversible processes may be useful in predicting and describing dissipative structures, which may be reasonable models for transformations in food systems.

For background information *see* CHEMICAL THERMODYNAMICS; FOOD ENGINEERING; FOOD SCIENCE; POLYMER in the McGraw-Hill Encyclopedia of Science & Technology.　　　　Alberto Schiraldi

Bibliography. B. Binks (ed.), *Modern Aspects of Food Emulsions*, Royal Society of Chemistry, 1998; V. Ya. Grinberg and V. B. Tolstoguzov, *Food Hydrocolloids*, 11:145, 1997; Y. H. Roos (ed.), *Phase Transitions in Foods*, Academic Press, London, 1995; Y. H. Roos and M. Karel, in J. M. V. Blanshard and P. J. Lillford (eds.), *The Glassy State in Foods*, page 207, Nottingham University Press, Loughborough, England, 1993; A. Schiraldi, in *A Chemistry for the 21st Century, Chem. Thermodyn*, vol. 251, 1999; L. Slade and H. Levine, *C. R. C. Crit. Rev. Food Sci. Nutr.*, 30:115, 1991; V. B. Tolstoguzov, *Food Hydrocolloids*, 11:181, 1997; V. Tolstoguzov, *J. Therm. Anal. Cal.*, 2000.

Fungal diversity

True fungi are an extremely diverse group of organisms that have tubular bodies (hyphae) with cross walls (septa) and reproduce by means of spores. Their mode of nutrition is heterotrophic. Hyphae secrete external enzymes that break down organic matter, and the resulting products are absorbed. It is estimated that there are 1.5 million species of fungi, of which only 5% are known.

Fungi in nature. Fungi cause disease of animals and plants, huge losses in food spoilage, and unwanted biodegradation. The fruiting bodies of aboveground mushrooms and underground truffles also provide a food source for animals, including humans (**Fig. 1**). The most important role of fungi is their ability to cycle nutrients. Fungi can break down simple carbohydrates, and also can degrade complex carbohydrates (such as cellulose) in plant material. White rot fungi are the principal organisms capable of degrading lignin which, along with cellulose, is a major component of wood. Without fungi the Earth would be filled with unwanted dead wood. Fungi also degrade wood and other organic matter in streams, lakes, and seas.

Symbiotic and mutualistic relationships. Fungi form symbiotic relationships with animals and plants. Termites and leaf cutting ants develop mushroom gardens within their chambers. They carefully tend the gardens, which they replenish with fresh leaves and woody material. From the gardens, a diet of hyphae and spores provides the insects with energy for life. Rumen fungi in the gastrointestinal tract of herbivores break down complex carbohydrates, and the products are utilized by the animals for energy. Plants with mycorrhizal associations grow better than those without. Mycorrhizae form associations with plant roots and gain nutrients through the plant's photosynthetic capabilities. In return, the fungi provide an extensive network of minute roots, capable of absorbing nutrients from soils far more efficiently than the plant roots themselves. Endophytes are fungi that live within plant tissues without causing external symptoms, gaining their nutrients from the plant by preventing grazing by insects and herbivores. Others increase the ability of the plant to survive drought. Some become pathogens when plants are stressed. Some turn into saprobes following plant death; such endophytes have the advantage of being the first fungi on the scene.

Biotechnology. Fungi have long been used by humans as a food source and in the production of alcoholic beverages. Initially, edible fungi were gathered and eaten; but as methods were developed, mushrooms were grown commercially. In China it is now possible to cultivate more than 50 species of edible fungi, mostly on dead woody grass, but few of these reach the supermarkets in western countries. Fungi are also used to produce many Asian foods such as Indonesian ket-jap and tempeh. The fungi convert soybeans to the edible products. Fungi have also been used to make quorn, a high-protein food produced when a fungus is grown on glucose syrups and ammonia. Yeasts are single-celled forms of filamentous fungi, used in the production of alcohol, breads, and yeast extracts. Fungi are also used in biocontrol of insects, weeds, and pathogenic fungi, and their potential to degrade lignin-like pollutants makes them target organisms for bioremediation.

Medical uses. Penicillin is produced by *Penicillium chrysogenum*, the blue mold fungus often found growing on rotting oranges (**Fig. 2**). Production of penicillin became feasible with the discovery of a commercial strain, and this led to the successful search for other antibiotics from fungi and other microorganisms. In 1995 the antibiotics augmentin and ceftriaxone, the immunosuppressant ciclosporin, and the cholesterol-lowering drugs lovastatin, pravastatin, and simvastatin were in the top 20 products in terms of pharmaceutical sales. These are all derived from fungal natural products. The search for new drugs from fungi is continuing by major drug companies.

Fungi are also used in Chinese medicine. *Ganoderma* species are proclaimed to cure numerous diseases. The caps are ground and consumed. Different species have different colored caps, and the medical claims vary for each color. *Cordyceps sinensis* is parasitic on dead caterpillars. The fungus invades the caterpillar, eventually killing it and digesting it from inside. It produces a long cigar-shaped process from one end of the insect, which contains the reproductive spores. The insect and fungus are used in Chinese medicine concoctions for curing various diseases. Cordyceps tea and whiskies are also produced and are proclaimed to strengthen the body and to be aphrodisiacs.

Measuring fungal diversity. With only 5% of the 1.5 million fungi on the Earth presently known, there appears to be a potentially huge untapped resource for biotechnological exploitation. Fungi can

Fig. 1. A variety of edible and medicinal mushrooms.

also be monitored to establish the effects of disturbance and global warming. Most fungi are less than 1 mm in diameter and can be observed only with the aid of a microscope. They do, however, lend themselves to measurement, as some are conspicuous, others can be easily separated with the aid of a microscope, and others can be grown and identified on artificial media.

Rapid biodiversity assessment. Fungi are also amenable to rapid biodiversity assessment. This assessment is founded on the approach that certain areas of ecological research, biodiversity assessment, conservation planning, resource management, and environmental monitoring can be carried out without knowing the scientific names of species. Fungi are excellent organisms to work with both in the field and in the laboratory. Unlike animals, they do not require complicated trapping methods, but the collection must be planned at the optimum time, usually after a wet spell. A variety of macrofungi, microfungi, and microhabitats are selected to avoid bias.

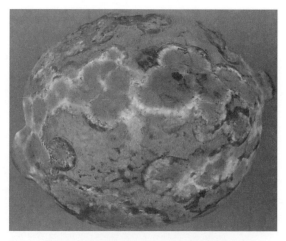

Fig. 2. Blue mold fungus growing on a rotting orange.

Macrofungi can be assessed directly in the field, with checking where necessary in the laboratory. Microfungi can be separated under the microscope, while fungi are isolated from microhabitats onto artificial media and then can be separated by their characters. The use of fungi in future environmental impact assessment is a real option.

For background information *see* FUNGI; MYCORRHIZAE in the McGraw-Hill Encyclopedia of Science & Technology.   Kevin D. Hyde

Bibliography. K. D. Hyde, *Biodiversity of Tropical Microfungi*, Hong Kong University Press, 1997; K. D. Hyde, Can we rapidly measure fungal diversity?, *Mycologist*, 11:176–178, 1997; B. Kendrick, *The Fifth Kingdom*, Mycologue Publications, 1992; S. B. Pointing and K. D. Hyde, *Bioexploitation of Fungi*, Fungal Diversity Research Series 2, Hong Kong, 2000.

Fungi

Mycorrhizal fungi are ecologically significant because they form symbiotic relationships in and on the roots of host plants. The host plant provides the fungus with a soluble carbon source, and the fungus provides the host plant with an increased capacity to absorb water and nutrients from the soil. Thus, both partners benefit from this relationship. It has been found that the majority of plants do have mycorrhizal fungi associated with them; some of these associations are very specific while others are very broad.

Mycorrhizal fungi are classified into four major types: ectomycorrhizal, arbuscular mycorrhizal, ericaceous mycorrhizal, and orchid mycorrhizal. (see **illus.** and **table**) Ectomycorrhizal fungi are characterized by the presence of a Hartig net and a fungal sheath, and the absence of fungal hyphae in the plant root cells. The Hartig net is a complex network of fungal hyphae that penetrates between the root cells but does not penetrate into the root cells. Nutrient exchange between the fungus and the host plant occurs at the Hartig net. The fungal sheath is a compact layer of fungal hyphae, with varying thickness depending on the specific fungus, that surrounds the young root surface of the host plant. The fungal sheath prevents direct contact between the root and the soil. The fungal sheath serves as a nutrient reservoir and also provides protection from pathogenic microorganisms for the host plant.

Arbuscular mycorrhizal fungi are characterized by the presence of fungal hyphae within the root cells, the absence of a Hartig net, and the presence of fungal hyphae on the root surface but not as a fungal sheath. The arbuscules are branched hyphae found inside the root cells, and this is the area of nutrient exchange between the fungus and the host plant.

Ericaceous mycorrhizal fungi form symbiotic associations with plants in the Ericaceae family. They are divided into three subgroups which are characterized by the presence or absence of a Hartig net, a fungal sheath, and fungal hyphae within the root cells.

Orchid mycorrhizal fungi are characterized by the absence of a Hartig net and a fungal sheath and the presence of hyphal coils in the root cells. This type of fungus–host plant relationship is actually more parasitic than symbiotic in the early stages of plant growth because as a seedling the orchid is totally dependent on the fungus for growth.

Numerous studies have shown the important benefits of the fungus–host plant relationship for the plant in terms of water and nutrient uptake.

Plant host, fungi, and important characteristics of major types of mycorrhiza*

Mycorrhizal type	Hosts involved	Fungi involved	Characteristic structures	Characteristic functions
Ectomycorrhizal	Mostly gymnosperms Some angiosperms Restricted to woody plants	Mostly basidiomycetes Some ascomycetes Few zygomycetes	Hartig net Mantle Rhizomorphs	Nutrient uptake Mineralization of organic matter Soil aggregation
Arbuscular	Bryophytes Pteridophytes Some gymnosperms Many angiosperms	Zygomycetes (Glomales)	Arbuscules Vesicles Auxiliary cells	Nutrient uptake Soil aggregation
Ericaceous	Ericales Monotropaceae	Ascomycetes Basidiomycetes	Some with hyphae in cell, some with mantle and net	Mineralization of organic matter Transfer between plants
Orchidaceous	Orchidaceae	Basidiomycetes	Hyphal coils	Supply carbon and vitamins to embryo
Ectendomycorrhizal	Mostly gymnosperms	Ascomycetes	Hartig net with some cell penetration Thin mantle	Nutrient uptake Mineralization of organic matter

*From D. M. Sylvia et al. (eds.), *Principles and Applications of Soil Microbiology*, Prentice Hall, 1998.

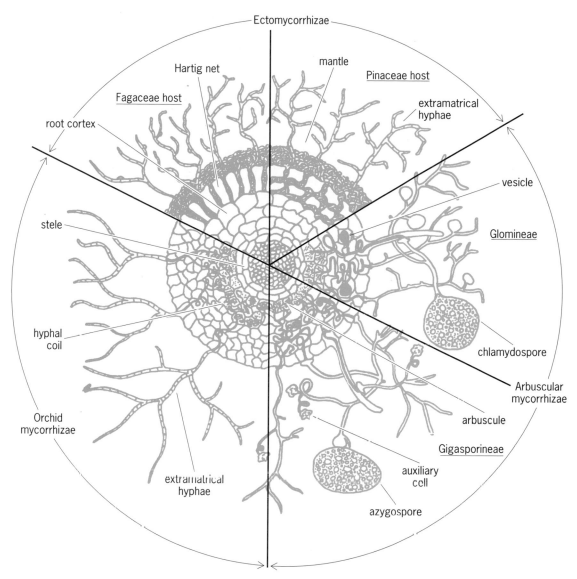

Cross section of several types of mycorrhizal fungi. (*Modified from original drawing by V. Furlan; used with permission*)

Mycorrhizae greatly increase the total volume of soil which is now available for nutrient and water uptake, by increasing the root surface area for absorption of water and nutrients. Because the fungal hyphae can penetrate areas of the soil not available to the plant roots, it can access water and nutrients, especially phosphorus, that would otherwise be unavailable to the plant. This is especially noticeable in a stressed environment. In arid climates or nutrient-deficient soils, this capability often makes the difference between plant survival or death.

The uptake of nutrients by the mycorrhizal fungi is affected by the same conditions that affect uptake by the root, such as temperature and oxygen. Nutrients known to be absorbed by mycorrhizal fungi include phosphorus, nitrogen, potassium, copper, zinc, and sulfur. These nutrients often exist in low concentrations or have low mobility in the soil. The most dramatic example of increased mineral uptake by mycorrhizal fungi is with phosphorus. In a phosphorus-deficient soil, uninfected plants grow quite poorly.

However, if the plant is infected with mycorrhizal fungi, there is good, healthy, normal plant growth despite low concentrations of soil phosphorus. Sometimes phosphorus is present in a soil but not in a form available to the plant, or it is adsorbed to the soil particles. The sources of phosphate available to the mycorrhizal fungi are inorganic orthophosphate and phytate. The mycorrhizal fungi are capable of utilizing or degrading organic matter to obtain phosphorus which is unavailable to plant roots; one example is the organic phosphorus source, phytate. After the mycorrhizal fungus has decomposed the phytate, phosphorus is absorbed, and is translocated by cytoplasmic streaming to the plant root. In the mycelial strands a large portion of the phosphorus exists as polyphosphate, which can be stored and later translocated to the root via cytoplasmic streaming.

Increased nitrogen uptake, especially in the form of ammonium, has also been observed with mycorrhizae. Mycorrhizal fungi are able to utilize insoluble organic nitrogen compounds found in humus. Once nitrogen is taken up by mycorrhizae, it is converted to glutamine in the fungal hyphae and is then transferred to the host plant. Nitrogen and phosphorus metabolism are closely interrelated, and the increase in nitrogen uptake in mycorrhizal plants may actually be an indirect effect of the increased phosphorus uptake.

Carbon flows from plant leaves to roots in the form of sucrose produced via photosynthesis, and it is then transferred to the mycorrhizal fungus. In arbuscular mycorrhizal fungi, the plant carbon is converted to glycolipids by the fungus, which allows for the accumulation of carbon by the fungus. In ectomycorrhizal fungi, the plant carbon is converted by the fungus to carbohydrates that the plant cannot utilize and is stored in the fungal sheath. This provides the fungus with a carbon concentration gradient in its favor. Studies have found trehalose, mannitol, and glycogen present in ectomycorrhizal roots but absent in uninfected roots. Mannitol and trehalose are known to be utilized by ectomycorrhizal roots but not by uninfected roots. Sucrose from the host plant is translocated to the roots, where the ectomycorrhizal fungus converts it to glucose and fructose. These two types of carbohydrates are then transferred to the fungal sheath, where the glucose is converted to glycogen and trehalose and the fructose is converted to mannitol. Studies have shown that the majority of the carbon received from the host plant by the fungus is used as an energy source for nutrient uptake instead of for fungal growth. If most of the carbon was used for fungal growth, the fungus would not be able to continue in its role of nutrient uptake in this symbiotic relationship with the plant.

Studies have also shown that plants with mycorrhizal fungi associated with their roots have an extra form of protection against toxins in the soil, root pathogens in the soil, and pH and temperature extremes. Because the fungal sheath prevents direct contact between the soil and the root, it allows the plant to survive in soil conditions which may be harmful to the plant alone.

Mycorrhizal fungi play a large role in helping to maintain a balance within an ecosystem. Because the fungal hyphae extend throughout the soil, they help to improve the soil structure by increasing aeration and moisture infiltration. They are also involved with various nutrient cycles, including carbon, phosphorus, and nitrogen. Mycorrhizal fungi provide a direct link between soil nutrients and plants by providing the host plant with nutrients otherwise not available. These fungi also have an effect on the decomposition of organic matter in soils. This may be due to the competition between the mycorrhizal fungi and the decomposers for limiting nutrients such as nitrogen. Some ectomycorrhizal fungi have been shown to obtain energy and nutrients by degrading organic materials in soil, thereby living independently of a host plant.

Some fungi, especially the ectomycorrhizal and ericaceous mycorrhizal fungi, may not be as dependent on the host plant as previously thought. Mycorrhizal fungi do possess a wide variety of enzymes which would account for their ability to utilize other carbon sources. Mycorrhizal fungi long have been studied for their ecological benefits to the plant. Because many plants cannot survive without this relationship with the fungus, most emphasis was put toward how to improve the plant's growth. More recently the emphasis has been moving toward the capabilities of the fungus itself. Mycorrhizal fungi have been studied for applications in phytoremediation of toxic organic chemicals, heavy metals, and radionuclides in contaminated soils.

For background information *see* ERICALES; FOREST ECOSYSTEM; FUNGAL BIOTECHNOLOGY; FUNGAL ECOLOGY; FUNGI; MYCORRHIZAE; RHIZOSPHERE; ROOT (BOTANY) in the McGraw-Hill Encyclopedia of Science & Technology.

Paula Donnelly Nellessen; James A. Entry

Bibliography. M. F. Allen, *The Ecology of Mycorrhizae*, Cambridge University Press, Cambridge, 1991; J. L. Harley, The significance of mycorrhiza, *Mycol. Res.*, 92:129–139, 1989; S. E. Smith and D. J. Read, *Mycorrhizal Symbiosis*, Academic Press, San Diego, 1997; D. M. Sylvia, Mycorrhizal symbioses, in D. M. Sylvia et al. (eds.), *Principles and Applications of Soil Microbiology*, Prentice Hall, Upper Saddle River, NJ, 1998.

Fungi (medicine)

Many medicines in use today are derived from compounds originally produced by fungi. A number of modern drugs are the purified form of chemicals present in traditional medicines, but only a few macrofungi, such as *Cordyceps sinesis*, which grows on caterpillars of the moth *Hepilis fabricius*, have been used in traditional medicines. However, since the 1940s the pharmaceutical industry has relied upon microfungi as sources of new medicines. Of the current top-selling prescription medicines, pravastatin, simvastatin, and lovastatin (all used to lower plasma lipoprotein levels) are derived from a molecule, mevinolin, produced by *Aspergillus terreus*. Three other top-selling medicines derived from fungi include the antibacterial antibiotics amoxicillin (a semisynthetic penicillin which is sold in combination with another compound) and ceftriaxone (a cephalosporin), and the immunosuppressive agent cyclosporin.

Secondary metabolites (natural products). Fungi growing in natural environments utilize surrounding nutrients and extract energy for conversion into biomass using primary metabolism. So-called secondary metabolites are often produced during growth and, more especially, as growth slows during nutrient depletion. The role of these metabolites in the producing organism is not entirely clear, but it is argued that fungi have evolved the ability to biosynthesize secondary metabolites due to the selectional advantages they obtain as a result of the functions of the compounds. As many systems in cells are common across the evolutionary scale, enzymes, proteins, and various biological systems in microbial cells may be similar to those in the human cell. Thus, fungal secondary metabolites or natural products may be very useful as medicines, while others, such as mycotoxins, can be extremely toxic.

High-throughput screening. An important route of new drug discovery for most large pharmaceutical companies is high-throughput screening. This consists of the rapid and often automated testing of libraries of compounds and natural product extracts against a biological system involved in a disease condition. The latter may be a whole cell system or a cloned and purified enzyme or receptor.

Fungi to be used in screening are usually isolated from a variety of substrates, including soil and plant material. Once purified, a fungal isolate can be stored indefinitely in a stable form at ultralow temperature (less than $-135°C$). However, for reasons that are not understood at present, the ability of some isolates to produce secondary metabolites may deteriorate upon storage.

The cultures are grown in small-scale liquid- or solid-phase culture to produce biomass for screening, with each culture usually being grown in a variety of media. It is well established that different media can stimulate the production of different secondary metabolites and, as such, growth of isolates on a number of media helps maximize the chemical diversity obtained from each isolate. The cultures and their growth medium often contain intra- and extracellular enzymes that may cause interference in screens; therefore, cultures are treated prior to screening to eliminate high-molecular-weight compounds. This is usually achieved through extracting the culture and growth medium with a solvent, which will preferentially extract lower-molecular-weight compounds.

Most companies screening natural product extracts store these extracts as libraries held at low temperatures, which consist of master copies of extracts from which daughter copies can be generated as required for screening. Extracts are commonly stored in microtiter plates (as 96, 384, or 1536 well layouts) as they can be handled easily by automated laboratory systems and robots.

Compounds that are selected as hits through screening rarely become drugs in their own right due to a lack of potency, selectivity, bioavailability, or stability. These lead compounds usually become the starting points for chemical development programs, which seek to optimize the biological activity and pharmacokinetic properties of the molecule.

Fungal biodiversity. Although thousands of known fungal secondary metabolites have been isolated after screening hundreds of thousands of isolates, these might represent less than 1% of the 1.5 million fungi estimated to exist. Past experience with fungi and other groups of microorganisms such as the actinomycetes and bacteria has shown that biological

diversity reflects an underlying molecular diversity. The untapped pool of fungal diversity is enormous and, undoubtedly, large numbers of fungi remain to be discovered, especially in underexplored habitats. Attempts have been made to isolate fungi from extreme environments (for example, with extreme salinity, temperature, or pH) where they may have evolved unusual metabolisms to adapt.

Combinatorial biology. As only a small percentage of the fungi in the environment have been isolated and cultivated in the laboratory, an enormous wealth of bioactive compounds remain to be discovered and tested for their medicinal properties. It is thought that many fungi will be difficult to cultivate. Combinatorial biological approaches have now been developed to isolate genetic material from unknown fungi that are difficult to cultivate, and to clone this deoxyribonucleic acid (DNA) into cultivable strains. These surrogate hosts can then be grown in the laboratory to allow for the cloning, screening, and production of enzymes and biosynthetic pathways leading to novel small-molecule natural products. This approach is based on observations that genes required for the production of secondary metabolites are often found in clusters, and that these suites of genes could be removed intact and transferred between organisms, perhaps in a manner analogous to the horizontal transfer of genetic material between organisms that occurs in nature. The application of combinatorial biology approaches to drug discovery is, however, at an early stage.

Combinatorial biosynthesis. Combinatorial biosynthesis techniques have been used to generate chemical diversity within a fungus that may be producing compounds of interest through modifications of its genetic makeup. The genes required for the production of secondary metabolites are often found in clusters, and the deletion, shuffling, and blocking of gene domains has enabled the production of novel chemical structures.

The ongoing sequencing of the human and microbial genomes will allow the possibility of treating previously untreatable diseases and the identification of new targets for screening. Advances in robotics, automation, and information technologies provide an opportunity for screening on a larger scale than ever before. There is no doubt that fungi will continue to be a major source of diverse chemical structures for screening for new medicines.

For background information *see* ANTIBIOTIC; FUNGI; MEDICAL MYCOLOGY; MYCOLOGY in the McGraw-Hill Encyclopedia of Science & Technology.

Howard G. Wildman

Bibliography. L. H. Caporale, Chemical ecology: A view from the pharmaceutical industry, *Proc. Nat. Acad. Sci USA*, 92:75–82, 1995; M. M. Dreyfuss and I. H. Chapella, Potential of fungi in the discovery of novel, low-molecular weight pharmaceuticals, in V. C. Gullo (ed.), *The Discovery of Natural Products with Therapeutic Potential*, Butterworth-Heinemann, London, 1994; K. ten Kate and S. A. Laird, *The Commercial Use of Biodiversity* Earthscan Publications, 1999.

Gas solubility

Chemical thermodynamics is the study of the relationship between heat and other forms of energy involved in chemical and physical processes. It is concerned with properties of materials such as equilibrium, solubility, and phase changes, as these properties are important in understanding energy transformations. Gas solubility is a particularly interesting property as it relates to important aspects of life on Earth.

The solubility of gases in liquids has been of interest since 1803, when William Henry showed that the solubility of a gas in water was directly proportional to the partial pressure of the gas in equilibrium with the liquid. Every time a person takes a breath, the body is involved in a series of processes involving gas solubilities in various bodily fluids: in the mucosa coating the alveoli of the lungs, through cell membranes to the blood, complexation in the hemoglobin of red blood cells, back to the bloodstream, through more cell walls and into the interior of cells, before reversing this series until gas of a different composition is exhaled.

Applications. Gas solubilities are of interest in various industrial processes, limnology, and oceanography. An early application had to do with preventing the bends that divers experienced. For every 10 m (33 ft) that a diver descends under the water, the pressure increases by about 1 atm. So, at a depth of 10 m using Henry's law, the atmospheric gases that dissolve in the blood and bodily tissues are at twice the concentration that they are out of the water. If the diver rises too quickly from being submerged, these higher concentrations of gases are not eliminated and appear as bubbles, particularly in joints ("bending" them becomes excruciatingly painful). Knowledge of this pressure effect, and how long it takes to adjust to the amount of gas dissolved at each depth, led to the development of dive tables giving allowable times to surface from submersion for a particular length of time at a given depth. The solubility of helium in water and blood is extremely low. Thus, helium-oxygen mixtures became the breathing gas of choice for submersibles that go to great ocean depths.

Joel Hildebrand's discovery that certain fluorocarbons (such as perfluoro-n-heptane) had an exceptional solubility for oxygen led to the development of artificial bloods. The familiar examples of soda pop and champagne illustrate William Henry's experiment on the effect of pressure on gas solubility.

From a theoretical standpoint the solubility of gases in liquids is an excellent vehicle for investigating the nature of both pure fluids and solutions. Since gases are available in a large variety of shapes, sizes, and polarities, they are excellent probes of the liquid state. For example, helium (He), neon (Ne), argon (Ar), krypton (Kr), xenon (Xe), methane (CH_4), carbon tetrafluoride (CF_4), and sulfur hexafluoride (SF_6) are a series of spherical nonpolar molecules which gradually increase in size and polarizability. The latter has to do with the distortability of the electron clouds which surround a molecule, and is related to the strength of the attractive forces between two molecules. Some molecules are strongly polar, indicating a separation of electrical charge within the molecule. A series of polar gas molecules of increasing polarity are fluoromethane (CH_3F), chloromethane (CH_3Cl), and bromomethane (CH_3Br). Generally, the rule for solubility is that like dissolves like. That is, the more similar in size, shape, and polarity the solvent and the solute are, the greater the solubility. The wide variety in these characteristics of gas solute molecules lets them be used to study the nature of liquids and solutions. Some gases such as ammonia (NH_3), carbon dioxide (CO_2), hydrochloric acid (HCl), and chlorine (Cl_2) chemically interact with water and show extraordinary solubilities.

Values. The Ostwald coefficient of solubility, L, is a measure of the ratio of the volume of gas V_g that dissolves in a given volume of liquid V_l at a particular pressure, that is, $L = V_g/V_l$. Another measure of gas solubility is the mole fraction, x_2, which is defined as the number of moles of gas, n_2, dissolved in the number of moles of solvent, n_1, plus n_2 at a given partial pressure of gas and a given temperature. That is, $x_2(T, P) = n_2/(n_1 + n_2)$. The parenthetical T and P emphasize that x_2 depends on both temperature and pressure. The **table** presents some representative gas solubilities in pure water at 298.15 K (25°C or 77°F) and 1 atm (101.325 kilopascals) partial pressure of gas. For the least soluble gas, CF_4, five volumes of the gas dissolve in 1000 volumes of water; while for the very soluble gas NH_3, 313 volumes of gas dissolve in one volume of water. Another way of viewing this is that four molecules of CF_4 dissolve in 1,000,000 molecules of water; for NH_3 it is two molecules dissolving in 11 molecules of water. Thus, these solubilities differ by a factor of about 50,000. The solubility of a gas in a liquid depends on the strength of the intermolecular forces between the molecules—in effect, the stronger these attractions, the greater the solubility. Also, the more alike the gas and the liquid are with respect to size, shape, and polarity, the greater the solubility.

Measurement. Most gas solubility measurements reported in the literature are of the order of 1–2% in precision. However, the results reported by B. B. Benson and his coworkers, and by R. Battino and his coworkers (using a modified Benson apparatus),

Solubility of some representative gases in water*					
Gas	$10^5 x_2$	L	Gas	$10^5 x_2$	L
CF_4	0.382	0.00517	C_2H_6	3.40	0.0453
He	0.708	0.00946	Xe	7.95	0.105
N_2	1.18	0.0159	CO_2	61.5	0.828
O_2	2.30	0.0312	H_2S	185	2.51
Ar	2.53	0.0341	SO_2	2460	35.1
CH_4	2.55	0.0340	NH_3	18,760	313

*At 298.15 K (25°C or 77°F). x_2 is the mole fraction at 1 atm (101.325 kPa) partial pressure of gas. L is the Ostwald coefficient.

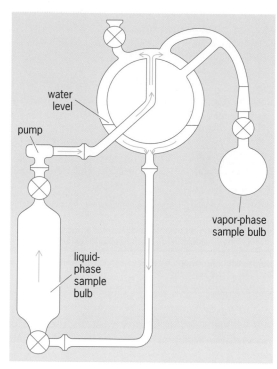

Equilibration portion of apparatus for measuring gas solubility. (*After B. B. Benson, D. Krause, and M. A. Peterson, The solubility and isotopic fractionation of gases in dilute aqueous solutions, J. Soln. Chem. 28:655–690, 1979*)

generally attain precisions that are better than 0.1%, and range down to 0.01%.

Many different methods are used to determine the solubility of gases in liquids. Before a gas can be dissolved in a liquid, the liquid must first be degassed; that is, a sufficient amount of the dissolved gases must be removed so they will not interfere with the measurements. Many methods have been used for this purpose.

The equilibration portion of the apparatus of Benson, D. Krause, and M. A. Peterson is shown in the **illustration** (this apparatus and procedure are effectively the same as used by Battino and coworkers.) The equilibration apparatus is kept in a thermostat controlled to ±0.002 K for the duration of the measurements. Degassed water fills the apparatus to the indicated water level. The gas to be dissolved is added and the apparatus is sealed. A magnetically driven pump pushes the water up the central tube, where it gently flows over the surface of the inner sphere, dissolving the gas. It takes 17–48 h to attain equilibrium. When equilibrium is reached, the liquid-phase and vapor-phase sample bulbs are sealed. The volumes of these bulbs are known as a function of temperature to better than $\pm0.01\%$. Separately, the gas in each bulb is extracted in the dry state, and its pressure ($\pm0.01\%$), volume ($\pm0.01\%$), and temperature (±0.002 K) are determined. From these three measurements, and using corrections for nonideality of the gas, the amount of gas in both bulbs is determined to about $\pm0.01\%$. The solubility can then be calculated.

The solubility of oxygen in water has been recom-mended as a standard for calibrating gas solubility apparatuses since it can be determined by both physical and chemical methods. The best measurements on this system have been made by T. R. Rettich, Battino, and E. Wilhelm. The recommended values at 298.15 K are $10^5 x_2$ (1 atm partial presure of gas) = 2.2996, and $10^2 L = 3.1152$.

Heat effects. Although the heat (actually enthalpy) changes on solution for a gas dissolving in water are reasonably large per mole of gas dissolved, the heat effects that can be measured by direct calorimetry are quite small due to the very low solubility of gases. However, two groups have managed to obtain quite precise values. The temperature dependence of solubility yields the enthalpy change on solution. An excellent measure of the quality of gas solubility measurements is how well the derived heats agree with the direct calorimetric measurements. Remarkably, the results of the two methods—direct and indirect—agree within their respective experimental errors. This is also a validation of the laws of thermodynamics, since the connection between direct and indirect methods is via thermodynamic equations.

For background information *see* CALORIMETRY; CHEMICAL THERMODYNAMICS; DECOMPRESSION ILL-NESS; DIVING; SOLUTION; THERMOCHEMISTRY in the McGraw-Hill Encyclopedia of Science & Technology.

Rubin Battino

Bibliography. R. Battino and H. L. Clever, The solubility of gases in liquids, *Chem. Rev.*, 66:395–463, 1966; IUPAC, *Solubility Data Series*, Pergamon Press, Oxford (and subsequent publishers), 1979 onward; G. L. Pollack, Why gases dissolve in liquids, *Science*, 251:1323–1330, 1991; E. Wilhelm, R. Battino, and R. J. Wilcock, Low-pressure solubility of gases in liquid water, *Chem. Rev.*, 77:219–262, 1977.

Geomicrobiology

Although scientists in a wide variety of disciplines have long studied interactions between microorganisms and minerals, the science of geomicrobiology has finally come into its own in recent years. Arguably the most interdisciplinary of all sciences, geomicrobiology enables scientists from fields such as chemistry, geochemistry, mineral physics, molecular biology, microbiology, and microbial ecology to collaborate on fundamental issues ranging from maintaining soil fertility to explaining the origin of life.

A number of recent discoveries have contributed to the surge in interest in the role played by biological processes in geological events. Recognition of the existence of microorganisms that tolerate extreme environmental conditions (extremophiles) and form complex communities powered by energy sources other than light has expanded the definition of the biosphere to include lithotrophic (rock-eating) microbes from kilometers below the Earth's surface; thermophilic (heat-loving) organisms from hot springs in Yellowstone National Park;

chemosynthetic-based food chains at deep-sea hydrothermal vents and in caves; acidophilic microbes from acid waters associated with ore deposits; and organisms tolerant of extreme cold at the Poles and in the deep ocean.

In addition to the realization that life thrives in a much wider range of environments, recent studies utilizing deoxyribonucleic acid (DNA) sequence analyses have demonstrated how much is to be learned regarding microbial diversity and phylogeny. The "tree of life" has been redrawn to include an entirely new kingdom, Archaea, and many new groups within the archaeal, as well as bacterial, and eukaryotic domains have been recognized. Notably, many archaea derive their energy by catalyzing inorganic reactions, and a significant fraction of the species found to date occupy geologically important niches (such as saline lakes, hydrothermal vents). Molecular biological methods pioneered in the 1980s are allowing breakthroughs in the ability to grow, isolate, and characterize the majority of microbial species that exist in the environment. It is now commonplace to identify microorganisms from natural samples containing hundreds or thousands of species by analysis of their genetic signatures. In the foreseeable future, it will be possible to decipher the essential biochemical character of uncultured organisms via comprehensive analyses of their genomic DNA.

Against this backdrop of a rather astounding array of interrelated interdisciplinary discoveries, the report of putative extraterrestrial microbial fossils in a Martian meteorite in 1997, ignited a firestorm of scientific controversy. The ultimate resolution of this question depends entirely upon a greater knowledge of geomicrobiology. The need to develop unambiguous "mineralogical biosignatures" with which to assess robotically retrieved samples from Mars in the future has lent fresh urgency to the drive to understand microbe-mineral interactions.

A thorough understanding of microbe-mineral interactions at the molecular level, and related questions of microbially maintained chemical microenvironments, constitute the groundwork which must be laid. While much is known regarding medically important interactions involved in pathogenicity or oral disease, understanding of interactions between mineral surfaces, microbes, and the extracellular polymers produced by organisms is in its infancy. This is a very active research area, and findings on this topic will be relevant to a wide array of environmental and technological problems as well as the evaluation of possible biosignatures in extraterrestrial materials.

Microbe-mineral interaction studies may be grouped into two categories, dissolution and precipitation. Consider the following list of processes affected by biogeochemically mediated mineral reactions: soil formation and plant nutrition; stability of architectural materials; geochemistry of ground water and movement of contaminants; generation of acid mine drainage; long-term stability of geological reposito-

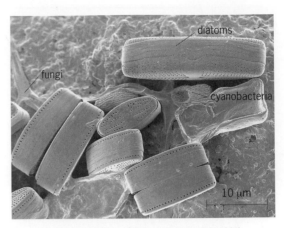

Fig. 1. Scanning electron micrograph of a microbial community of diatoms (d), cyanobacteria (c), and fungi (f) on the surface of a sandstone quartz grain. Organic by-products produced by these organisms contribute to etching of the surface.

ries for high-level radioactive waste; and effects of mineral weathering on climate on a geological time scale.

Soil scientists are concerned with pedogenesis, the process of soil formation, and recognize the central role of organisms in mineral weathering. Weathering of minerals in soils releases major nutrients such as potassium, phosphorus, iron, calcium, magnesium, and silicon as well as trace ions which are essential for microbial and plant growth. Engineers and architectural conservationists, concerned with the long-term stability of building materials, have contributed greatly to defining communities of organisms and the damage they cause to both natural and synthetic materials. Enhanced corrosion and weathering of these materials are associated with attached organisms due to the production of acidic, alkaline, or complexing compounds.

Microbial weathering of minerals in soils (**Fig. 1**) and structures at the Earth's surface is widely recognized, and it is now known that similar processes occur in subsurface environments. Recent surveys of deep aquifers (hundreds of meters) show relatively high microbial numbers (approximately 10^5 to 10^7 cells/cm^3). Microbial abundance and diversity are variable, but do not decrease systematically with depth. Most subsurface microorganisms occur attached to mineral surfaces where they can directly influence mineral surface chemistry, water-rock interaction, and ground-water geochemistry. Microbial redox processes in aquifers can directly affect the distribution of elements such as carbon, oxygen, nitrogen, iron, manganese, sulfur, arsenic, and uranium and the rate of mineral dissolution. A major feedback mechanism controlling atmospheric partial carbon dioxide (pCO_2) is the weathering of calcium-magnesium silicates and subsequent precipitation of calcium-magnesium carbonates. Since microorganisms affect biogeochemical weathering reactions and life may have been present for at least 3.8 billion years, it seems plausible that the biota could have moderated the carbon dioxide cycle, and could have therefore affected global climate.

Cost-effective strategies for dealing with multiple environmental problems are another potential benefit from geomicrobial research. For example, microbes are capable of existing at extremely acid pH values and metabolizing iron, sulfur, and other species from sulfide mineral surfaces (**Fig. 2**).

These organisms are principal causative agents of acid mine drainage. Understanding the ways in which microbial communities contribute to acid mine drainage generation will provide new insights for ways of remediating this widespread problem. Conversely, microbes can be utilized in cost-effective, low-pollution routes to extract metals from ores (biohydrometallurgy). Environmentally acceptable sequestration of nuclear waste materials over periods of time approaching geological scales constitutes another pressing environmental problem. Vitrification (encapsulation of radioactive materials in a glass matrix) and storage in underground repositories is the technique currently being pursued. In these environments, particularly over the long periods of time needed to safely ensure storage, ground water and its associated microorganisms may interact with the glass surfaces, releasing ions (possibly radioactive) to the environment. Bacteria colonizing mineral surfaces in aquifers preferentially etch surfaces and can solubilize glass. If and when water and subsurface microorganisms interact with vitrified radwaste, release of radioactive contaminants will occur. However, some microbes efficiently concentrate toxic metals (such as selenium and uranium; **Fig. 3**) and may limit radionuclide dispersion. In some cases, the ability of microbes to concentrate metals can be utilized to clean up contaminated soils, sediments, and water.

In addition to such applied problems as environmental pollution, geomicrobiology can contribute to more fundamental questions. The origin of life is a scientific mystery that is almost certainly explained in part by organic-mineral interactions under early Earth conditions. Plausible theories utilize min-

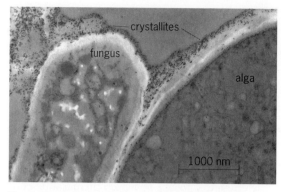

Fig. 3. Transmission electron micrograph of uranium uptake from solution by a lichen. The small black crystallites are an unidentified uranium mineral that has precipitated in extracellular polymers surrounding fungi and algae.

eral surfaces to concentrate organic molecules and polymerize DNA, RNA, and proteins and to protect sensitive products from photolytic degradation and hydrolysis. For example, polymerization of nucleotides and amino acids on clays under laboratory conditions has been achieved. The existence of iron-sulfur active centers in some of the most primitive proteins supports the recent concept that prebiotic reactions occurred on iron-sulfide mineral surfaces at deep-sea hydrothermal volcanic vents. For example, iron-sulfur enzymes (such as carbon monoxide dehydrogenase) are central to carbon fixation in methanogens. Methanogens possess one of the most primitive metabolisms and essentially require only hydrogen gas and carbon dioxide for energy (unlike photosynthesis, energy from sunlight is not required). Thus, subsurface environments in proximity to mineral surfaces may have played central roles in both creation and maintenance of early life on Earth.

The oldest rocks known on Earth display isotopic evidence of carbon fractionation (biological processes preferentially select the lighter isotope). Rocks 3.45 billion years old contain microfossils of what have been interpreted to be cyanobacteria. Possible eukaryotic fossils date back 2.7 billion years. Thus, it is clear that geobiological research is of paramount importance for it provides the framework to begin understanding the coevolution of the bio-, atmo-, hydro-, and lithospheres over geologic time.

For background and information *see* ARCHAEBACTERIA; BACTERIA; CLASSIFICATION, BIOLOGICAL; EUKARYOTAE; METHANOGENESIS (BACTERIA); MICROFOSSIL; MICROMETEOROLOGY; ORGANIC EVOLUTION; PROKARYOTAE in the McGraw-Hill Encyclopedia of Science & Technology.

William W. Barker; Jillian F. Banfield

Bibliography. J. K. Fredrickson and T. C. Onstott, Microbes deep inside the Earth, *Sci. Amer.*, 275(4):68–73, 1996; E. K. Gibson, Jr., et al., The case for relic life on Mars, *Sci. Amer.*, 277(6):58–65, 1997; M. T. Madigan and B. L. Marrs, Extremophiles, *Sci. Amer.*, 276(4):82–87, 1997.

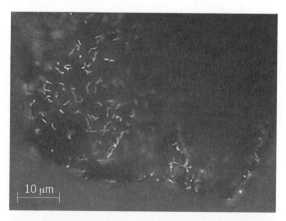

Fig. 2. Fluorescence micrograph of bacteria colonizing the surface of a pyrite grain from an acid mine drainage environment.

Giraffe

The giraffe is a ruminant mammal and the tallest animal in the world (average height for males is about 5 m or 16 ft). Giraffes include about 40 extinct species and the living okapi of the west African rainforest. In most species the neck was either short as in the okapi or long as in the extinct *Samotherium*. In no species was the neck as long as in the modern giraffe.

The long neck is the most characteristic feature of giraffes. These herbivores use the long neck to reach high tree foliage for which there is little competition. The long tongue is used to grasp leaves. In addition, the males use the long neck for fighting. Two males will club each other by swinging their necks; their necks intertwine, pushing from one side to the other. This is done to establish the giraffe's territorial position. The winner of the duel will gain females and form a harem.

Most mammals (including humans) have a stable count of seven neck bones (vertebrae). In the giraffe the seven neck bones are numbered as cervical 1 through 7, but it is the seventh cervical that carries the first rib. That seventh bone, however, is situated in the position of vertebral bone eight. The first thoracic, bone 8 carries the second rib, but it was supposed to carry the first. (Cervical bones in mammals are distinguished by the reduction of the ribs, and thoracic vertebrae by the presence of ribs.) The seventh bone is number eight counting down from the head due to the insertion of a new vertebra.

Most vertebrae have specific shapes. In a typical mammal such as the okapi (**Fig. 1**), the first two cervicals (the atlas and the axis) are unique in shape.

Cervicals 3 through 5 appear similar to one another and have clearly developed ventral tubercles (small rounded protrusions on the anterior surface of the bone). Dorsally, the cervicals appear wide due to large spaces between the bones (articulations). The typical mammalian sixth cervical bone has two large flanges (the ventral laminae) for the scalene muscles going down to the ribs, and the muscle longus capitis going up to the head. On the underside of the sixth vertebra, fibers of the muscle longus coli are shaped like the letter V toward the thorax and an upside-down V toward the atlas. The fibers (both V shaped) meet in the center of the sixth vertebra, where the opposite shapes form a diamond-shaped muscular center. The seventh bone of the neck is wide like the rest of the cervicals, but it has no ventral tubercles.

In most mammals the vertebral artery enters the transverse foramina of the cervicals with the sixth vertebra first and then moves up to the head by passing through each cervical above 6 (through the transverse foramina, which are formed on the sides of the cervicals by the shortened reptilian ribs). Thus, the seventh bone does not have a transverse foramen (an opening) for the vertebral artery. The eighth bone (the first thoracic) has a unique form which can be readily recognized in addition to the presence of the first rib. It has wide anterior articulations but narrow posterior articulations because all the subsequent thoracic vertebrae have only narrow articulations; the anterior articulations are set wide to join the wide-shaped seventh, and the posterior are set narrow to join the narrow-shaped second thoracic. In addition, the first thoracic forms a tall bony pillar to join the seventh cervical. Finally, the nerves going into the front limb form a brachial plexus which exits the spinal cord around the seventh vertebra; the center for the four major nerves is about the seventh with two major nerves exiting in front of seven and two in back of seven.

In the giraffe (**Fig. 2**), the bones, muscles, and nerves are identical to those of other mammals, but in position all structures are displaced down one vertebra. The shape of the seventh bone resembles a sixth vertebra. The shape of the seventh bone is in the position of the first thoracic and has the first rib on it; the first thoracic bone is in the position of the second thoracic and has the second rib on it. After this point the total number of thoracics and lumbars is normal (same as in the okapi). Thus, one thoracic has been lost in the giraffe after T2, and cervical 7 has taken its place.

Since the atlas and the axis of the giraffe are normal in form and position, an extra bone has been added between the third and the sixth cervical. The first thoracic occupies the position of the second thoracic and carries the second rib instead of the first. At that position, morphological blending takes place so that posterior to this area the giraffe possesses a normal morphology. Presently, it is not known which bone of the neck is the extra one, but most likely there is a duplication of C3.

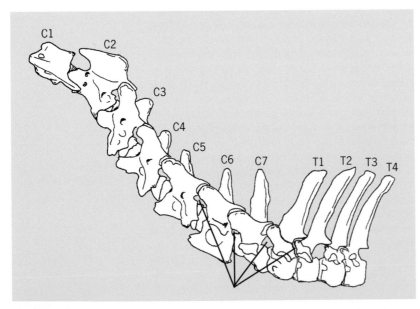

Fig. 1. Lateral view of the neck of the okapi (cervicals 1–7) and the first four thoracic vertebrae (thoracics 1–4). The first rib attaches on T1. Heavy lines show the major four roots of the nerves exiting about C7 (brachial plexus). For simplicity, the front limb and ribs are not shown.

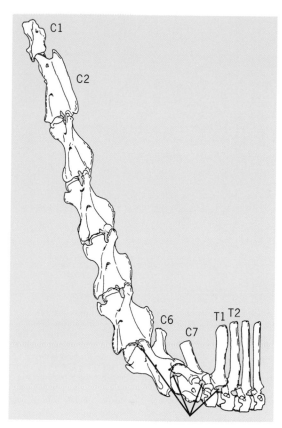

Fig. 2. Lateral view of the neck of the giraffe (cervicals 1–8) and the first four thoracic vertebrae. The first rib attaches on C7, and T1 carries the second rib. Unlabeled vertebrae indicate that it is not known which one is the extra. The blending of C7 into the thorax has eliminated one thoracic vertebra. Thus, vertebrae past T2 are not labeled. Heavy lines show the major four roots of the nerves exiting about C7 (brachial plexus). For simplicity, the front limb and ribs are not shown.

The individual cervical vertebrae of the giraffe are long, and the extra bone contributes to the long neck as well. The seventh vertebra makes the thorax slightly longer as well because C7 is long; thoracics are short.

It is not clear why such a vertebral shift has occurred in evolution. One explanation may be that the extra length contributed to a type of neck fighting different from that of the ancestral species, and to the ability to feed at a higher tree level.

The neck of the giraffe attaches to the thorax from a dorsal position instead of from the anterior. The change in the neck position has created the giraffe's characteristic silhouette. The shoulder joint protrudes more in the lateral view than in other mammals.

Giraffes have extremely elastic blood vessels and special valves in the veins of the neck to control blood flow to the head. This allows them to compensate for the sudden increase in blood pressure when they lower the head. A unique system of valves that prevents backflow solves the problem of fluctuating venous pressure. This helps to retain blood to feed the brain when the animal returns the head to an upright position.   Nikos Solounias

Bibliography. A. I. Dagg and J. Bristol Foster, *The Giraffe*, Van Nostrand Reinhold, New York, 1976; L. Sherr, *Tall Blondes*, Andrew McMeel, Kansas City, 1997; N. Solounias, The remarkable anatomy of the giraffe's neck, *J. Zool.*, 247:257–268, 1999.

Graptolites

Graptolites are common fossils in black shales of the Ordovician and Silurian periods (490–417 million years ago). Many species are globally distributed and have short time ranges, making them ideal for dating and correlating sedimentary rocks, with a precision, reliability, and wide applicability matched only by groups such as ammonites and conodonts.

Characteristics. Graptolites were colonial, filter-feeding animals, ranging in colony size from a few millimeters to about 200 mm in maximum dimension, with rare species reaching a meter or more. The main group, order Graptoloidea, was a major component of the macrozooplankton, and is thought to have derived from sessile ancestors (order Dendroidea). Colonies comprise linear arrays of zooids produced by asexual apical budding and connected by a stolon system, housed in thecae composed of collagenlike material. From the mode of secretion and composition of the skeleton, graptolites are thought to be most closely related to modern pterobranchs and are classed in the Hemichordata. Given that so much is known of their stratigraphic distribution, it is surprising that so little is known of their paleobiology. In particular, the extent to which the colony functioned as a single coordinated organism, rather than as a collection of individuals, is very uncertain. However, some interesting details are emerging.

Details of growth, morphology, histology, and composition are derived from the rare examples preserved in full relief in limestone or chert that can be dissolved away to reveal the skeleton. Ultrastructural studies of the skeletal wall of these specimens have revealed the mode of secretion and construction of the skeleton. Some biological inferences can be made from comparison with living relatives such as *Rhabdopleura*, and some by analogy with modern unrelated organisms (locomotion and function of the colony).

Graptolites are unusual among colonial organisms in the regularity of the skeletons (**Fig. 1a**). Phylogenetic studies show that a relatively restricted range of rhabdosome types was repeatedly reoccupied. Even the morphologically complex and specialized phyllograptid form (Fig. 1d) was occupied by two, and possibly three, distinct lineages. This implies strong functional control on form, developmental constraints, or inherited genetic (bauplan) programming. Most workers have looked for functional explanations of rhabdosome design, particularly in relation to hydrodynamic and feeding efficiency, buoyancy, and stability in the water. Certainly, the planktic graptoloids have skeletons with much more

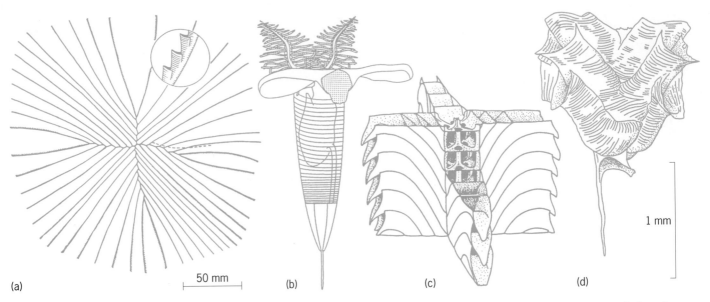

Fig. 1. Graptolite characteristics. (*a*) Large branching graptolite *Goniograptus alternans*, with enlargement of a branch fragment showing thecae which housed the zooids (*based on specimen figured by R. B. Rickards and A. Chapman, Mem. Mus. Victoria, 52:1–135, Fig. 29, 1991*). (*b*) Proposed rhabdopleuran-like zooid for graptolites, with winglike extensions of the cephalic shield for locomotion; total height is approximately 2 mm (*from M. J. Melchin and M. E. DeMont, Possible propulsion modes in Graptoloidea: A new model for graptolite locomotion, Paleobiology, 21:110–120, Fig. 1, 1995*). (*c, d*), Complex skeleton of *Phyllograptus* consisting of four rows of thecae (boxlike tubes), joined along their dorsal margins. Cutaway section (*c*) and isolated growth stage (*d*) show the complex growth patterns and coordination required for development of the skeleton.

symmetry and regularity in development than the sessile dendroids. Developmental and inherited constraints have been little explored, however, and may restrict the available morphospace within which functional selection can operate.

Rhabdosome development. For Ordovician many-branched graptolites, two basic instructions for rhabdosome development are (1) the approximately simultaneous distal addition of new thecae to each branch in the colony at the same rate and (2) periodic bifurcation of branches. A regularity and symmetry can be imparted to the skeleton by two additional instructions: (3) all branches must grow in approximately the same plane and (4) growth paths of branches, and frequency of bifurcations, must be such that neighboring stipes do not too closely approach each other.

Close matching between computer-generated rhabdosomes and known fossil forms suggests that apparently complex branching patterns can be generated by a few simple instructions such as might be inherited as part of a developmental body plan, and does not require a high degree of genetic programming in the colony. Among the dichograptids, the growth mechanism at branching nodes, where one thecal zooid produces two daughter thecae, is inherited from the ancestral sessile dendroids, and is employed for all stipe division in the colony. This explains why branches only bifurcate and never trifurcate. Three or more branches arising from a single parent theca was possible only after an alternative mode of branching had evolved (in other graptolite families) in the Late Ordovician.

By analogy with pterobranchs, growth of a single theca has been estimated to take from 1.2 to 12 days, and a sicula (the initial "theca" of the colony) 10 to 33 days. A large colony might thus take months, even years, to mature.

Colony coordination. Tightly coordinated growth of thecae seems essential to form the complex proximal structure of diplograptids and the internal structure of *Phyllograptus* (Fig. 1*c* and *d*). Developmental abnormalities in a range of taxa suggest that a feedback mechanism (physical-chemical feedback) operated to some extent, and failure of a theca or stipe to develop resulted in realignment of subsequent thecal growth or rhabdosome symmetry so that the colony continued to function effectively, rather than lose functionality. Feedback mechanisms were also likely to control branch spacing and frequency of branching in many-branched forms such as *Rhabdinopora* and *Clonograptus*. Morphological growth gradients in thecal size or shape are common and have been inferred to imply growth hormone gradients within the rhabdosome, providing a mechanism for developmental coordination.

Little is known of sexual reproduction in graptolites. Thecal dimorphism in dendroids, taken to indicate sexual dimorphism, is apparently lost in graptoloids. However, asexual colony regeneration has been demonstrated.

Automotility and feeding. Most branching species have discoidal skeletons. Vertical migration through the water column by passive buoyancy control has long been suggested as an aid for feeding (the fishing net analogy), and a passive floating habit was favored for graptolites with long slender branches, and long spines and attached disks, interpreted as

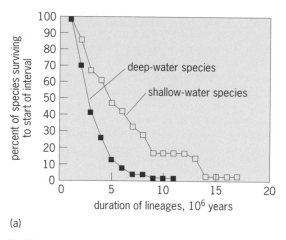

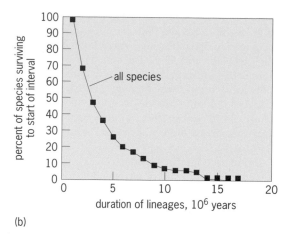

(a)   (b)

Fig. 2. Survivorship curves for Ordovician graptolites. (*a*) Deep-water species and shallow-water species, showing greater longevity for the latter. (*b*) All species, showing the relatively short-lineage life-spans of graptolites.

drag or floatation structures. However, automotility of the graptolite colony has been supported by analogy with comparable living macrozooplankton. Researchers explored possible locomotory mechanisms and concluded that only active swimming is likely for the graptolites, using putative winglike extensions of the cephalic shield (Fig. 1*b*) by analogy with such modern groups as pteropods, or by modified lophophores. Automotility would confer obvious advantages, such as allowing the colony to seek better feeding or living environments, and responding to negative stimuli.

The feeding intensity of colonies, as inferred from the spacing of thecae along stipes, together with the number, attitude, and width of stipes, ranges from very high in scandent biserial forms to very low in multiramous horizontal forms. Low-intensity forms are common in the deep-water biotope, whereas high-intensity forms prevail in the shallow, wind-mixed zone.

These functional interpretations carry a (usually unstated) corollary: there must have been some mechanism, such as niche partitioning or water mass separation, to avoid direct competition between the more efficient adult astogenetic stages and earlier, less efficient stages of the same species. Perhaps this is another argument for automotility.

Life habitat. Some species of Ordovician graptolites are found only in deep-water shales and never in sediments of the continental shelf. They are inferred to have lived at a depth in the water column below the shelf-slope break (meso-bathypelagic zone), about 1–200 m (3–660 ft) or deeper. A second main group of species is found in both deep- and shallow-water sediments, and is inferred to have lived in the near-surface, epipelagic zone (0–50 m or 0–165 ft) which extends across both depositional environments. The shallow-water biotope has a ready analog in the epipelagic zone of high productivity in modern oceans.

By analogy with the oxygen minimum zone in modern oceans, the deep-water habitat is believed to be a nutrient-rich zone of high productivity depleted

in oxygen by microbial activity, capable of supporting relatively high biomass, including macroplankton adapted to low oxygen levels.

From their distribution in sediments, it is inferred that graptolites were most abundant and diverse in the region of the ancient continental slope and outer shelf; they become rarer and less diverse toward the shoreline and, possibly, toward the open oceans. The graptolite biotopes are likely to be best developed along the ancient continental margin where upwelling currents supply nutrient salts and support high primary productivity. The graptolite habitat was thus confined by both vertical and lateral zonation within the oceans.

Species longevity. The deep-water graptolite biotope was likely to have been a relatively unstable one, dependent on ocean circulation and stratification patterns, and linked to a warm global climate. During the Ordovician, when strong global climatic oscillations occurred, it is envisaged as a high-risk, high-reward life environment for the plankton. It is not surprising, therefore, to find that the mean life-span of deep-water species (2.35 million years ago) is significantly less than that of shallow-water species (4.24 million years ago), based on a sample of 88 mainly Early Ordovician species. Survivorship curves of the two groups (**Fig. 2a**) similarly show the shorter life expectancy of deep-water species. This accords with the pattern found in modern planktic foraminifera. The drastic changes in ocean circulation and stratification patterns at the end of the Ordovician, associated with a global glaciation, led to the near extinction of the entire Graptoloidea; only two or three lineages survived to give rise to the Silurian radiation of the group.

For background information *see* GRAPTOLITHINA; ORDOVICIAN; SILURIAN in the McGraw-Hill Encyclopedia of Science & Technology.   Roger A. Cooper

Bibliography. R. A. Cooper, R. A. Fortey, and K. Lindholm, Latitudinal and depth zonation of early Ordovician graptolites, *Lethaia*, 24:199–218, 1991; P. R. Crowther, Fine Structure of the Graptolite Periderm, *Spec. Pap. Palaeontol.*, no. 26, 1981; S. C.

Finney and W. B. N. Berry, New perspectives on graptolite distributions and their use as indicators of platform margin dynamics, *Geology*, 25:919–922, 1997; M. J. Melchin and M. E. DeMont, Possible propulsion modes in Graptoloidea: A new model for graptolite locomotion, *Paleobiology*, 21:110–120, 1995; S. Rigby, Feeding strategies of graptolites, *Palaeontology*, 34:797–815, 1991; S. Rigby and N. P. Dilly, Growth rates of pterobranchs and the life span of graptolites, *Paleobiology*, 19(4):459–475, 1993; C. J. Underwood, The position of graptolites within Lower Paleozoic planktic ecosystems, *Lethaia*, 26: 189–202, 1993; A. Urbanek and J. Uchmanski, Morphogenesis of uniaxiate graptoloid colonies—a mathematical model, *Paleobiology*, 16(1):49–61, 1991.

Gravitational constant

Isaac Newton, from celestial observations, deduced the force law that describes the gravitational interaction $F = GmM/r^2$, where F is the attractive force between two point masses, m and M, separated by a distance r, and the gravitational constant G scales the equation to physical reality.

The value of G, accepted in 1998 to be $6.673(10) \times 10^{-11}$ m^3/kg s^2, is under intense scrutiny. Not only is G the least precisely known physical constant, but knowledge of its value is improving very slowly. The accepted value represents less than a tenfold improvement over the accuracy claimed by Henry Cavendish in the first laboratory measurement of G, performed in 1798. The gravitational constant is very hard to measure for several reasons. The gravitational force is very weak in comparison to other forces, such as the electromagnetic force. For example, the ratio of the gravitational to the electrostatic attraction between a proton and an electron is 10^{-40}. The relative strength of the electrostatic force is demonstrated each time that a charged piece of lint resists the gravitational pull of the entire Earth by sticking to clothing. Additionally, the gravitational force cannot be shielded. A hollow container of metal will shield everything within it from electric forces but not from gravity. This means that gravity experiments are much more sensitive to stray signals than other experiments.

Torsion experiments. Cavendish's experiment pioneered an experimental approach that has been the mainstay of G measurements ever since. This was the use of a fiber support to permit the measurement of small forces perpendicular to the relatively huge attraction of the Earth. Thin fibers can be used because they are very easy to twist, yet can still support substantial loads along their lengths. Torsion fibers have been used in balances (torques are balanced) and in "time-of-swing" measurements (the frequency of oscillation of a fiber system is examined). These two basic approaches are illustrated in **Fig. 1**.

A torsion balance allows the comparison of two torques—the first induced by the gravitational ac-

tion of a source mass system on the hanging bob, and the second resulting from the twisting of the fiber. The source mass pulls on the bob, twisting the fiber, but the material in the fiber resists this twisting, as in Hooke's law. The change in the equilibrium angle of the bob, $\Delta\theta$, occurring because of a change in the position of the source mass, is directly proportional to G. The resistance of the fiber to twisting (the fiber torsion constant) would be calibrated by measuring the natural frequency of oscillation of the fiber-bob system, f_0. Once a fiber is twisted and released, it continues to twist, first causing the bob to rotate clockwise and then counterclockwise (where the axis of the "clock" is aligned with the fiber). The resonant frequency of the system is a measure of how often the bob rotation changes direction. If the fiber were harder to twist, it would change direction more

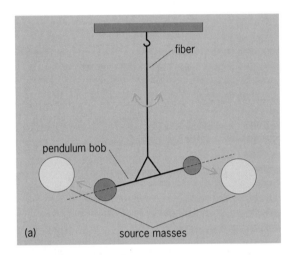

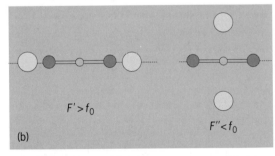

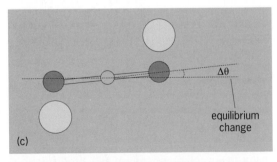

Fig. 1. Two torsion experiment setups. (*a*) In both systems, the torsion bob and the source masses lie in a single horizontal plane, perpendicular to the fiber. The broken line represents the equilibrium position of the bob. (*b*) Top view of the time-of-swing orientation. (*c*) Top view of the torsion balance orientation.

quickly, and the frequency would increase. Thus the frequency of the twisting indicates the strength of the fiber.

In a time-of-swing experiment the orientation of the source masses introduces an additional gravitational torque to the restoring torque of the fiber. In the orientation of Fig. 1b, left side, the gravitational torque assists the fiber in returning the bob to the equilibrium position, effectively making the fiber harder to twist, and increasing the resonant frequency of the system. In the orientation of Fig. 1b, right side, however, the source masses make it easier to twist the bob, lowering the resonant frequency. The change in the frequency is related to G. A time-of-swing determination of G made in 1982 forms the basis of the current accepted value of G.

Recent concerns about G. Two events in 1995 raised a warning flag about determining G from only one type of experiment. Kazuaki Kuroda identified a systematic error in time-of-swing experiments and some torsion balance experiments. He realized that fibers have a frequency-dependent torsion constant. This meant that in the time-of-swing experiments some of the change in frequency of the system was not due to the gravitational effects of the source masses, but to a change inherent in the fiber support. And in torsion balance measurements, calibration of the torsion constant by observation of the resonance frequency of the system was not completely valid because the two different positions of the source masses change the resonant frequency, possibly changing the frequency-dependent torsion constant of the fiber support. In 1995, also, German scientists released the results of a long-running torsion experiment that used a mercury bath instead of a fiber to support a bob. Incredibly, the results disagreed with the accepted value by 40 times the estimated experimental error. The apparent strength of the research served to increase the uncertainty surrounding the value of the constant. As of early 2000, no fault had been found in this experiment.

Alternative measurements of G. Since Kuroda's observations and the German result, several determinations of G have been developed that are geared toward exploring alternative measurement methods. One is an experiment in which the gravity field of a source mass affects the hanging angle of a simple pendulum. In another experiment, a balance is used to measure the weight change of a mass as a function of the position of a source mass made of 13.5 tons (12.2 metric tons) of mercury.

A unique and conceptually simple measurement used a completely unsupported test mass to sense the gravitational field of the source mass. It was designed around a free-fall absolute gravimeter (**Fig. 2**). Gravimeters are devices that measure the acceleration due to the attraction of the Earth, g (roughly 9.8 m/s^2 or 32 ft/s^2). A free-fall gravimeter measures the acceleration of a test mirror dropped in vacuum. The mirror defines one arm of an interferometer, with a second mirror used as a position reference. Thus, interferometer fringes can be used to deter-

mine the falling mirror's change in position (typically 0.2 m; 8 in.) as a function of time during the drop (0.2 s). A mathematical algorithm using a least squares fit of a parabola to the position-time data allows the extraction of g. In the last 30 years, free-fall gravimeters have achieved incredible levels of accuracy and precision. A gravimeter can measure a change in g of $1 \times 10^{-8} \text{ m/s}^2$ ($32.8 \times 10^{-9} \text{ ft/s}^2$). This is equivalent to a 3-mm shift in the gravimeter's distance from the center of the Earth.

Gravimeters can measure G by measuring the change in g resulting from a known change in the mass distribution attracting the falling mass. If the distribution of mass in the Earth itself were well known, then g could easily be related to G. Unfortunately, this distribution is not well known—so much so that in Cavendish's time his G measurement was known as a measurement of the density of the Earth. For this reason, a smaller but well-known mass must be used to connect g and G. This idea was behind the first laboratory measurement of G using a free-fall meter.

In this experiment a carefully designed 500-kg (1102-lb) tungsten mass was used to change the acceleration of the falling gravimeter mirror. Tungsten was used because of its high density (18 times more dense than water) and low magnetism. The source mass changed g by only $4 \times 10^{-7} \text{ m/s}^2$ ($4.1 \times 10^{-8} \text{ ft/s}^2$). This is equivalent to changing the time it took the test mass to complete its fall by 4 billionths of a second (4 nanoseconds). The tungsten was placed first above the falling mirror (where it pulled upward on it), and then below the mirror (where it pulled downward), as shown in Fig. 2. When the mass was high, g decreased; when it was low, g increased. The change in g was directly proportional to G.

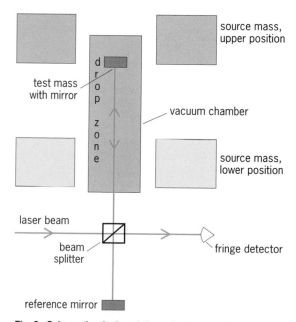

Fig. 2. Schematic of a free-fall gravimeter used to calculate the gravitational constant.

Outlook. Many new experiments are in progress or being planned. Some continue to use the torsion methodology while addressing the frequency dependence of the fiber. Experimenters are developing a cryogenic torsion balance that will operate at the very low temperature of 2 K ($-271°$C; $-456°$F) for this reason. Another torsion balance uses a broad band of material rather than a fiber to support the bob, and yet another uses a superconducting magnetic support. Farther in the future a more radically different experiment has been proposed in which two masses, simultaneously in orbit around the Earth, will affect each other's path.

It is hoped that these continuing efforts to improve the understanding of G will succeed to the point at which G will be as well known as the other fundamental constants. Then G might be used to indicate the validity of theories unifying all the known forces.

For background information *see* ACCELEROMETER; EARTH, GRAVITY FIELD OF; GRAND UNIFICATION THEORIES; GRAVITATION; GRAVITY; GRAVITY METER; HOOKE'S LAW; INTERFEROMETRY; PENDULUM; TORSION in the McGraw-Hill Encyclopedia of Science & Technology.   Joshua Schwarz

Bibliography. The gravitational constant: Theory and experiment 200 years after Cavendish, *Meas. Sci. Technol.*, 10(6):421–530, June 1999; D. Halliday, R. Resnick, and J. Walker, *Fundamentals of Physics*, 5th ed., Wiley, New York, 1996; D. Kestenbaum, Gravity measurements close in on big G, *Science*, 282:2180–2181, 1998; J. Schwarz et al., A free fall determination of the Newtonian constant of gravity, *Science*, 282:2230–2234, 1998.

Gravitational radiation

Gravitational waves are an implicit outcome of the special theory of relativity, and were explicitly put forward in Einstein's theory of general relativity in the early twentieth century. Einstein showed that the acceleration of masses generates time-dependent gravitational fields that propagate at the speed of light, carrying energy away from their source. Evidence of their existence, however, has been elusive. Even indirect evidence did not come until many decades after their prediction, with the 1974 discovery and subsequent observations by Russell A. Hulse and Joseph H. Taylor of the first binary pulsar ever found. By precisely monitoring the orbital period of the binary star system, they were able to confirm that it was speeding up at just the rate predicted by the general-relativistic emission of gravitational waves. Efforts at direct detection of gravitational waves have been made since the 1960s, pioneered by Joseph Weber's resonant-mass detectors, essentially giant "tuning forks" which would ring if sufficiently excited by a passing wave. Since then, these detectors have been greatly improved, and new concepts developed—laser interferometry on the ground, Doppler tracking in space—but so far with no detection.

A new generation of detectors based on suspended-mass interferometry has undergone a quarter-century of worldwide development and now promises the requisite sensitivity for observing gravitational waves. Major projects in the United States and Europe are under construction, with the first sensitive searches due to begin in the early years of the twenty-first century. These instruments are all based on long L-shaped laser interferometers, designed to take advantage of the field pattern of a passing gravitational wave. Such a wave produces a strain in space itself, transverse to the propagation direction. It is useful to imagine a ring of particles of radius L in flat space-time, that is, in the absence of gravity (**Fig. 1**). As a gravitational wave passes through, it will distort the ring into an ellipse, stretching it to a semimajor axis of $L + \delta L$ and a semiminor axis of $L - \delta L$ during the first half-cycle of the wave, with the pattern rotated by $90°$ during the second half-cycle, so that the ellipse is elongated in the orthogonal direction. The waves come in two independent polarization states, denoted the plus and cross polarizations; the strain patterns for the two states are rotated $45°$ from each other.

The concept of the laser interferometric detector is to measure this distortion by comparing the light travel time in two perpendicular directions. A laser beam may be sent along the x direction of Fig. 1. At the center of the ring is placed a beam splitter, which reflects half the laser light to travel along the y direction, and transmits the other half. Each beam propagates to the edge of the ring, where the particles are actually mirrors which reflect the beams back on themselves, such that the two beams recombine at the beam splitter. The mirrors and beam splitter are freely suspended as pendula, so that they act as gravitational test particles. In the absence of a gravitational wave (or at a time when its amplitude is zero), the imaginary ring of particles is a perfect circle, and the two beams take exactly the same time interval to make the round trip from the beam splitter. The phase of the beam originally transmitted through the beam splitter is now inverted by $180°$ when it reflects off the beam splitter, so that it interferes destructively at the output port of the

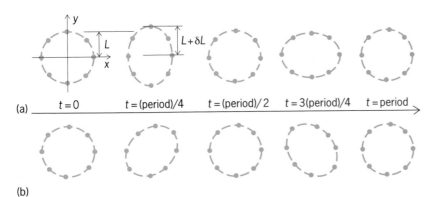

(a) $t = 0$ $t = $(period)/4 $t = $(period)/2 $t = 3$(period)/4 $t = $period

(b)

Fig. 1. Effect of a gravitational wave, passing in a direction perpendicular to the plane of the paper, on a ring of test particles. (*a*) Plus polarization. (*b*) Cross polarization.

beam splitter with the beam from the orthogonal arm; therefore a photodetector placed at this port sees no light, all of it having been diverted by constructive interference back to its source. With a gravitational wave present, the travel time down and back one arm is longer than that of the other, and the beams are no longer perfectly out of phase at the output. Thus some light appears at the output photodetector, indicating the presence of a gravitational wave.

The challenge of actually making such a measurement lies in the scale of the distance changes involved. The strain nature of the wave implies that the magnitude of the distortion δL is in fact proportional to L, the length of each interferometer arm. This fact provides the motivation for making the arms as long as possible. In the United States LIGO (Laser Interferometer Gravitational-Wave Observatory) project, for example, each arm is 4 km (2.5 mi) long (**Fig. 2**). Nonetheless, considering that plausible astrophysical sources typically lead to strains of only 10^{-21}, the resulting displacement δL which must be measured is only of order 10^{-18} m, a thousand times smaller than the width of a nucleus.

Refinements. Many refinements have been made to this basic concept to obtain the required sensitivity. One of these is to increase the interaction time of the light with the gravitational wave beyond the round-trip time, which is 27 microseconds in the LIGO. The longer the interaction time—up to one-half the gravitational wave period—the longer the resulting time delay and thus optical phase shift that produces the light intensity change at the photodetector. The interaction time is increased by folding the optical beams within the arms, typically by means of optical cavities. In the LIGO, each 4-km-long (2.5-mi) arm contains a resonant optical cavity in which each photon, on average, makes about 50 round trips before recombining with photons from the other arm of the beam splitter, so that the interaction time is increased to about 1 millisecond. The interference is measured with a photodetector, which is sensitive enough to detect phase shifts to a few times 10^{-10} of an interference fringe, such as might be produced by a passing gravitational wave.

Another special technique increases the effective light power in the interferometer by making the entire interferometer a resonant optical cavity. As mentioned above, in the unstrained interferometer the input laser light is actually returned toward the light source. Unavoidable optical losses and imperfections mean that not all the input light is returned, but at most a few percent of the light is lost, a benefit of the very high quality, low-loss optics used. This makes it possible to achieve a significant gain by placing a mirror between the laser and the beam splitter. By properly choosing the position and transmission of this mirror, the system can be arranged so that no light is reflected toward the laser, and light is instead optimally built up in the interferometer. This technique should increase the effective light power by perhaps a factor of 50.

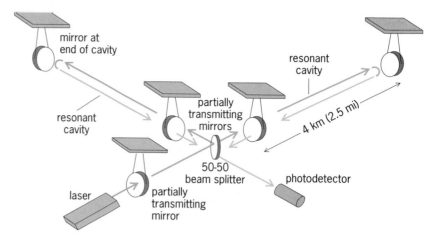

Fig. 2. Experimental setup of the LIGO (Laser Interferometer Gravitational-Wave Observatory) project. The interferometric gravitational-wave detector is an equal-arm Michelson laser interferometer whose hanging mirrors serve as gravitational test masses. Beam paths and all optics are enclosed in a high-vacuum system. Each 4-km (2.5-mi) arm contains a resonant optical cavity, and the partially transmitting mirror between the laser and the beam splitter increases the effective power.

Noise reduction. A significant technological challenge has been to study and control the various types of noise that compete with the exceedingly small strain signals. Random forces on the mirrors arise, for example, from ground motion or—more fundamentally—from brownian motion driven by thermal excitations. Such forces produce mirror motions which are independent of the length of the interferometer arms, in contrast to the displacements due to gravitational waves, which grow linearly with the arm length. Thus, overcoming such random-force noise is the principal reason for making the arms as long as practical. Isolation from motions of the ground is provided by cascaded stages of vibration isolation, each stage similar in concept to the suspension in a car. Each mirror is suspended from such a cascade as a pendulum, roughly 1 m (3 ft) long, that provides further vibration isolation and also serves to reduce the influence of thermal noise.

Quantum sensitivity limits. Even in the absence of random force noise on the mirrors, there are limits to the smallest optical phase change that can be measured. One such limit arises from the fact that the laser light is made up of a stream photons that does not "flow" at a perfectly constant rate, but varies statistically according to a Poisson distribution. Now the photon number and phase are conjugate variables obeying a Heisenberg uncertainty relation, and so a variation in the photon number implies a certain variation in the optical phase and, ultimately, an uncertainty in the interferometer strain; the result is that the uncertainty in the phase or strain varies inversely as the square root of the light power. Pushing down this limit is the reason for increasing the effective light power as described. In order to reach this limit of quantum-mechanical origin, however, many practical issues must be dealt with, such as laser frequency, amplitude, and beam direction fluctuations, and light scattered from the optical elements. A key aspect to achieving the sensitivity limit due to

Fig. 3. Aerial photograph of the LIGO (Laser Interferometer Gravitational-Wave Observatory) detector at Hanford, WA. A nearly identical facility is located in Livingston, LA. The lasers and optics are contained in the white buildings; the 4-km-long (2.5-mi) vacuum tubes are covered by the arched concrete enclosure.

photon statistics is the unprecedented degree of (short-term) laser stability attained through a complex system of laser sensors and feedback control.

Signal detection. The new generation of detectors will provide a 100- to 1000-fold improvement over previous searches, in both sensitivity and bandwidth (range of gravitational wave frequencies). Nevertheless, it is not expected that a gravitational wave signal will obviously stand out among the noise present in the data stream. It will be critical to eliminate false signals associated with local transient noise events. A powerful method is to require coincidence between multiple detectors: A gravitational wave signal must show up in all detectors within a time window determined by their separations. For this reason, the LIGO project is building two widely separated detectors, one in Hanford, WA (**Fig. 3**), and the other in Livingston, LA, which will also be operated in coincidence with the other detectors around the world.

It is often stated that gravitational wave astrophysics promises to open a new window on the universe. The current knowledge of the universe comes predominantly from electromagnetic astronomy—from radio to gamma-ray telescopes. Compared to these, gravitational wave detectors are sensitive to very different phenomena. Electromagnetic observations study things, such as stellar atmospheres and interstellar gas and dust, to which gravitational wave detectors are insensitive. Gravitational wave detectors will search for waves from the final inspiral and coalescence of binary neutron stars and black holes, the rapidly spinning cores of supernovae, and the first fraction of a second of the universe's expansion; electromagnetic telescopes have little or no sensitivity to these phenomena. These differences produce both uncertainty and great expectations for the results from the new searches for gravitational waves.

For background information *see* BROWNIAN MOVEMENT; CAVITY RESONATOR; GRAVITATION; GRAVITATIONAL RADIATION; GRAVITATIONAL RADIATION DETECTOR; INTERFEROMETRY; UNCERTAINTY PRINCIPLE; VIBRATION ISOLATION in the McGraw-Hill Encyclopedia of Science & Technology.   Peter Fritschel

Bibliography. A. Abramovici et al., LIGO: The Laser Interferometer Gravitational-Wave Observatory, *Science*, 256:325–333, April 17, 1992; B. Barish and R. Weiss, LIGO and the detection of gravitational Waves, *Phys. Today*, 52(10):44–50, October 1999; K. S. Thorne, *Black Holes and Time Warps: Einstein's Outrageous Legacy*, W.W. Norton, 1995; K. S. Thorne, in S. Hawking and W. Israel (eds.), *300 Years of Gravitation*, Cambridge University Press, Cambridge, 1987.

Green fluorescent protein

Green fluorescent protein (GFP) is produced by the bioluminescent jellyfish *Aequorea victoria*. The gene for it has been isolated, and the protein has been extensively characterized biochemically and found useful in biological research. After synthesis of GFP, three of the amino acids undergo a self-catalyzed reaction that produces an internal fluorophore (fluorescent molecule). The protein does not require a specific cellular environment to become fluorescent and can be artificially expressed in cell types as diverse as bacterial, plant, and animal cells. It can be attached to other proteins of interest using recombinant DNA techniques, making it possible to easily trace the synthesis, location, and movement of these proteins in single living cells using conventional fluorescence microscopy.

Previously, such experiments in living cells required purifying the protein of interest, chemically coupling it in vitro with a fluorescent molecule, and then adding it back to the cell. Following the intracellular location of a protein by light microscopy was technically difficult or impossible unless the protein was one of the small minority taken up by endocytosis or phagocytosis. Such experiments required difficult indirect biochemical techniques, or immunofluorescent stainings of fixed cells—in which only a single "snapshot" per sample of the process being studied was obtained.

Tracking and quantitation. Green fluorescent protein technology, by allowing observations over time of processes in living cells, has begun to provide new biological insights. It can be attached to a protein marker for specific organelles (such as mitochondria or the Golgi apparatus), allowing the organelle's location and morphology to be followed over time. Changes in organelle structure in response to drug treatments, or natural processes such as differentiation or mitosis can be studied.

Green fluorescent protein tagging also makes it possible to follow the trafficking of proteins between different parts of the cell or between different organelles. Moreover, the exact levels of the tagged

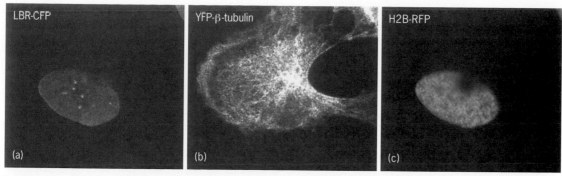

Labeling of multiple organelles in the same cell with spectrally distinguishable GFP variants. (*a*) Lamin-binding receptor (a protein found in the nuclear envelope) tagged with CFP. (*b*) Microtubules containing tubulin tagged with YFP. (*c*) Histone 2b (a protein that binds to DNA in the nucleus) tagged with RFP. (*Jan Ellenberg, EMBL*)

protein in different organelles can be quantitated, since the intensity of light emission from GFP is directly proportional to the number of molecules. It is possible to quantitate the absolute number of GFP molecules in an organelle of interest.

A laser scanning confocal microscope, which scans a laser over the sample, can be used for imaging GFP within cells or within small organisms, and unlike conventional microscopes it can map the location of GFP in three dimensions. Green fluorescent protein, like other fluorophores, can be photobleached (rendered nonfluorescent) when exposed to intense light. The laser in a confocal microscope provides an ideal tool for selective bleaching of GFP in a particular region of an organelle or of an entire organelle. Recovery by diffusion of GFP into the bleached area or by transport from other organelles can be monitored, providing important information about the mobility of the protein not previously available. This technique, known as fluorescence recovery after photobleaching (FRAP), has been utilized to show that resident proteins of the Golgi apparatus are freely mobile (rather than anchored to fixed positions), and to track movement of proteins between organelles.

Other uses. Green fluorescent protein can also be placed under the control of promoters [regulatory deoxyribonucleic acid (DNA) sequences] that allow its selective expression only in specific cell types (for example, neurons). This has proved highly useful in studies of developmental biology for examining the differentiation and migration of a wide variety of cell types in development, particularly in small relatively transparent organisms such as *Drosophila* embryos, nematodes, and zebrafish. It is also possible to do genetic studies of the promoter sequences themselves (for example, by examining the effects on GFP expression of changes of the DNA seqence at different regions of the promoters) to better determine which specific DNA sequences within the promoter contribute to its capacity to regulate expression of a linked gene.

Cells expressing GFP-tagged proteins can be separated from nonexpressing cells or cells expressing different levels of GFP using devices called cell sorters. Cells are sent one at a time past a laser beam set at a frequency that excites fluorescent molecules. The cells can then be scored for fluorescence and deposited into distinct pools. One application is identification of transfected cells after foreign DNA coding for a gene of interest and also for GFP is introduced. The GFP identifies the transfected cells, and the cell sorter can then provide a pure population of them.

Biological role. The original function of the GFP in the jellyfish was to convert the blue light emitted by a calcium-regulated protein called aequorin into green light. When the animal is disturbed (for example, when it is touched lightly), calcium stores inside some of its cells are released, causing excitation of the aequorin. The excitation energy is then transferred to GFP (probably by a quantum-mechanical process) and released as a brief green glow. The biological significance of this process is still not known. The protein when expressed alone (in the absence of aequorin) is fluorescent and emits green light when excited with ultraviolet light (and to some extent when excited with blue light).

Spectral variants. New improved variants of the protein have been devised that are brighter than the original and show a preference for blue light (which is nontoxic to cells) rather than ultraviolet (which can rapidly kill cells being observed). Also, variants have been engineered which excite and emit at different wavelengths, allowing tagging and following two or more different proteins in the same cell. Two fluorescent proteins, a cyan-emitting variety (CFP) and a yellow-green-emitting variety (YFP), have proved particularly useful in double-label experiments since they can be visualized separately in a fluorescence microscope. Recently, a related red fluorescent protein (RFP) has been identified from other coelenterates, so it is now possible to tag three different proteins in the same cell or in a cell population (see **illus.**).

For background information *see* CELL (BIOLOGY); CYTOSKELETON; FLUORESCENCE; FLUORESCENCE MICROSCOPE; IMMUNOFLUORESCENCE in the McGraw-Hill Encyclopedia of Science & Technology.

John Presley

Bibliography. J. Ellenberg, J. Lippincott-Schwartz, and J. F. Presley, Dual-color imaging with GFP variants, *Trends Cell Biol.*, 9:52–56, 1999; J. F. Presley et al., ER-to-Golgi transport visualized in living cells, *Nature*, 389:81–85, 1997; K. F. Sullivan and S. A. Kay, *Green Fluorescent Proteins*, Academic Press, New York, 1999.

Ground-water cleanup

Contaminants can migrate through ground water from leaking underground storage tanks, landfills, and tailings ponds to wells or surface water bodies.

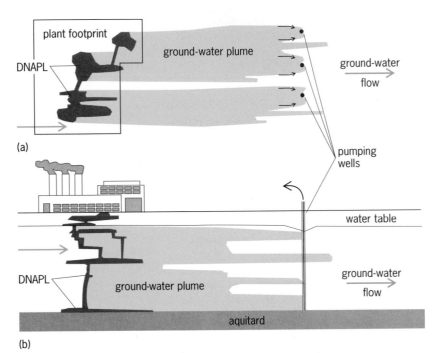

Fig. 1. Ground-water cleanup using pump-and-treat. (*a*) Plan view. (*b*) Section view.

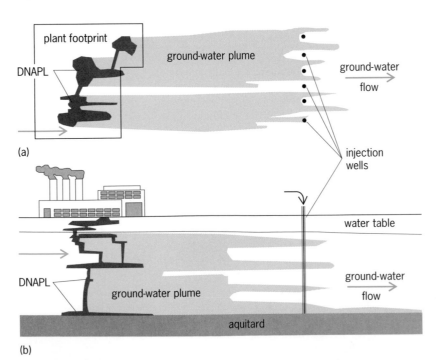

Fig. 2. Ground-water cleanup using wells to inject solutions and bacteria in situ. (*a*) Plan view. (*b*) Section view.

Cleanup usually includes the removal of sources of contamination and contaminated ground-water using wells followed by treatment. This approach is termed pump-and-treat. It led to perpetual remediation at many contaminated sites, often because many sources of contamination cannot be effectively removed. This is especially true when nonaqueous-phase liquids (NAPLs) such as gasoline (lighter than water, LNAPLs) and chlorinated solvents (denser than water, DNAPLs) remain in the subsurface, acting as ongoing sources of ground-water contamination. DNAPLs are particularly troublesome because the dense liquid can migrate deep below the water table. With the source remaining, pump-and-treat could operate in perpetuity, protecting potential receptors by cutting off the contaminant plume, but presenting ongoing costs. So, alternate remedial strategies were sought. Two additional approaches have emerged.

One approach recognizes that aquifers have natural attenuation capacity that in some cases may protect potential receptors. This so-called monitored natural attenuation has been most successfully applied to ground water contaminated by petroleum hydrocarbons which are biodegraded during migration.

The second approach is in situ treatment of contaminated ground water. The key is to concentrate remedial actions in small areas of the aquifer with the goal of treating the contaminants as they flow through. The in situ treatment zone is termed a permeable barrier or reactive barrier. As in most pump-and-treat cleanups, this in situ treatment cuts off contaminant plumes rather than remediating the whole plume.

Delivery systems for in situ treatment. Figures 1–4 illustrate some typical in situ ground-water cleanup systems. The hypothetical site is an operating plant with DNAPL contamination in the underlying sand aquifer. An aquitard of much lower permeability provides a hydrogeological bottom to the flow system. In **Fig. 1** showing a pump-and-treat system, three ground-water extraction wells capture almost all of the contaminant plume.

In some cases, in situ treatment can be accomplished with a minimum of engineering by using "fences" of wells closely spaced across a contaminant plume (**Fig. 2**). The wells can be used to remove volatile organics by bubbling air into the wells or to deliver microorganisms or oxygen to promote in situ biodegradation. Some down-gradient distance will be required before additions become sufficiently mixed with contaminants to promote the desired attenuation reaction.

Figure 3 illustrates a typical reactive barrier installed across the entire plume and "keyed" into the underlying aquitard, ensuring that all contaminated ground water enters the barrier. Where the treatment zone is expensive and impermeable barriers or "funnels" (such as sheet piling and slurry walls) are much cheaper, an alternative delivery system, termed a funnel-and-gate, may be more economic (**Fig. 4**). This system often has faster ground-water flow through the treatment zone, requiring a longer gate to provide adequate residence time to treat ground-water contaminants.

Various optimized funnel-and-gate setups can be used to meet site-specific requirements at minimum cost. For example, a funnel keyed into the underlying aquitard can direct contaminated ground water through a shallow, "hanging" gate. This has cost and installation advantages over a deeper, keyed gate. A hanging reactive barrier or hanging funnel-and-gate are particularly cost-effective for shallow contamination, for example, when LNAPL is the source of ground-water contamination. While both of these setups are cheaper than a keyed system (Fig. 3 or 4), the hydrogeological design must ensure that the plume does not plunge under the treatment system. All these delivery systems have been demonstrated at least to pilot scale in the field.

In situ treatment techniques. The most mature in situ treatment technique is the use of granular iron (Fe^0) to dechlorinate solvent molecules such as tetrachloroethylene and trichloroethylene. Products of the nonbiological reaction are chloride ion and innocuous methane or ethene. This technology is simple and robust and has been used successfully at over 30 sites in North America and Europe.

Other ground-water contaminants are being addressed at pilot or full scale. Metals and inorganics such as Cr(VI), U(VI), and Tc(VII) are treated by using Fe^0 or organic matter addition to promote sulfate reduction and metal precipitation as sulfide; and also by sorption onto various barrier media. Acid-generating capacity of mine-tailings waters was eliminated by using organic matter addition to promote sulfate reduction and Fe(II) precipitation. Petroleum hydrocarbons are cleaned up by aerobic biodegradation with oxygen (and nutrients) provided by solid oxygen releasing compound installed in wells in fences, and by gases, such as oxygen and ammonia, via sparging or diffusion through plastic tubing in gates; and also by sparging (volatilization) in fences of wells. DNAPL residual sources are being oxidized using permanganate and other strong chemical oxidants. Denitrification is promoted by solid organic matter addition in barriers and by dissolved organic matter addition via wells in a fence. Phosphate is handled by sorption and precipitation. MTBE, a gasoline additive, is cleaned up by injection of a specific bacterial culture via wells and addition of oxygen in other wells in a remedial fence.

Challenges for in situ treatment. To be cost-effective, installation and operational costs must be minimized. Simple designs and lower-cost installation procedures must be attained. Treatment approaches should be robust and passive to minimize operational costs.

All in situ treatments have been done at depths of less than 80 ft (24 m) in granular subsurface material. Cost-effective techniques for deeper contamination and for fractured rock aquifers are needed. Interesting developments include injecting Fe^0 and bimetals as fine grains or even colloids into fractures to intercept chlorinated solvent plumes in fractured rock aquifers.

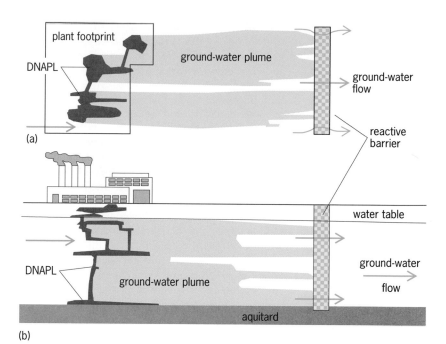

Fig. 3. Reactive barrier used to cut off a ground-water plume. (*a*) Plan view. (*b*) Section view.

Some multiple contaminants are treatable with a single system. For example, an Fe^0 reactive barrier has been effective in cutting off both trichloroethylene and Cr(VI) plumes. Other multiple contaminants require sequential treatment. A two-stage, pilot-scale in situ treatment gate was reasonably successful in treating a mixture of chlorinated solvents and aromatic petroleum hydrocarbons (such as benzene and toluene) at Alameda Point, CA. More development is needed if complex contaminants are to be cleaned up using in situ techniques.

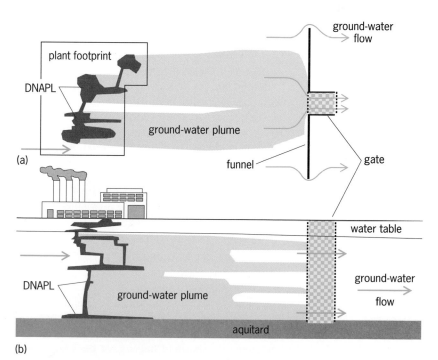

Fig. 4. Funnel-and-gate used to cut off a ground-water plume. (*a*) Plan view. (*b*) Section view.

At Alameda Point, contaminants had a very uneven distribution as they entered the in situ treatment gate. Concentrations of both cis-1,2-dichloroethene and vinyl chloride varied from less than 1 to greater than 100 mg/L when measured in depth-discrete sampling points. The highest concentrations were not adequately treated by an Fe^0 reactive barrier. Similar challenges posed by a high contaminant concentration should be anticipated whenever in situ treatment is placed near a source. The Alameda experience also highlights the need to assess influent concentrations in some detail and to adequately design in situ treatment. The experimenters had used depth-averaged contaminant concentrations derived from sampling fully screened wells in treatability tests that were the basis for designing the thickness of Fe^0 in the gate. These samples did not identify discrete zones of much higher concentration. Also at the site, a semipassive system of mixing influent ground water to obtain a more homogeneous influent concentration distribution would have been useful.

Outlook. Ground-water cleanup needs to be based on realistic objectives, recognizing the limited potential for complete remediation. In some cases, natural attenuation processes in ground water provide adequate cleanup. Where active ground-water cleanup is required, pump-and-treat remains the standard approach. It can usually be designed and installed quickly and its performance anticipated from over 30 years' experience. The development of in situ treatment techniques is expanding the toolkit for ground-water cleanup. Clearly, both hydraulic capture and treatment of contaminants must be verified over the long term. As these techniques mature, lower-cost ground-water cleanup within site-specific limitations should be realized.

For background information see BIODEGRADATION; GROUND-WATER HYDROLOGY; HAZARDOUS WASTE; MINING; SURFACE WATER; TERRESTRIAL WATER; WATER CONSERVATION; WATER POLLUTION; WATER SUPPLY ENGINEERING; WELL in the McGraw-Hill Encyclopedia of Science & Technology.　　Jim Barker

Bibliography. D. W. Blowes et al., Treatment of dissolved metals using permeable reactive barriers, in M. Herbert and K. Kovar (eds.), *Groundwater Quality: Remediation and Protection*, IAHS Publ. 250, 1998; S. Fiorenza, C. L. Oubre, and C. H. Ward (eds.), *Sequenced Reactive Barriers for Groundwater Remediation*, Lewis Publications, Boca Raton, FL, 1999; D. M. Mackay and J. A. Cherry, Groundwater contamination: Pump-and-treat remediation, *Environ. Sci. Technol.*, 23(6):630–636, 1989.

Guidance systems

Both the U.S. Navy and the U.S. Army have considerable stockpiles of unguided munitions, such as the Navy's MK64 and the Army's MK483 155-mm (6.1-in.) spinning rounds. These rounds are relatively ineffective in the field because of their large miss distances, which result from a combination of gun pointing errors, shot-to-shot velocity variations, and aerodynamic disturbances that cause the flight path to deviate from the expected trajectory. As a consequence, the hit probability for a single projectile is very low. In fact, the single-shot hit probability for these unguided rounds is so low that over 350 rounds are required to achieve a hit probability of 90%.

The availability of highly accurate navigation information at any time and at any place using Global Positioning System (GPS) technology and the emergence of micromechanical inertial navigation instruments in the 1990s enabled the development of a new generation of precision-guided projectiles (**Fig. 1**). The projectile is initialized with the coordinates of the target. After firing, the navigation system provides the current position and velocity of the projectile to an on-board guidance computer that commands control surfaces (canards) to alter the airflow around the projectile in a way that will reduce the predicted miss distance.

ERGM Demonstration Program. The Extended Range Guided Munition (ERGM) Demonstration Program funded the first demonstration of this concept. The program culminated in three flight tests in November 1996 and April 1997 that demonstrated extended range and improved accuracy over conventional Navy 5-in. (127-mm) projectiles. The extended range was achieved by means of rocket-assisted flight. The improved accuracy resulted from the navigation system, which integrated the GPS and the inertial navigation system (INS), and an on-board flight control computer. In addition to the GPS receiver and the micromechanical inertial sensor assembly (MMISA), the system included a shock-hardened reference oscillator, the guidance and navigation electronics, and the power conversion electronics, all packaged in an 8-lb (3.6-kg) cylindrical volume 8.4 in. (213 mm) long with a diameter of 4 in. (102 mm).

The ERGM Demonstration Program developed the GPS/Micromechanical Inertial Measurement Units (MMIMU) that were integrated into demonstration rounds. These rounds were test-fired at facilities at the Yuma Army Proving Grounds. The demonstration round was a modified rocket-assisted projectile airframe from the Navy's Semi-Active Laser Guided Projectile (SALGP) Program. The round was approximately 60 in. (1.5 m) in length and weighed 101 lb (45.8 kg; **Fig. 2**). A customized propellant charge was used to fire the projectile from a Navy MK54 gun at an acceleration of approximately 6500 g (where g is the acceleration of gravity, 9.8 m/s² or 32.2 ft/s²) as it exited the gun barrel. This is approximately 40% of the nominal g-level for firing Navy and Army projectiles.

The three flight tests conducted at Yuma Proving Ground were characterized by a 110-s flight time line with impact approximately 18 nautical miles (33 km) downrange. The flight tests showed that the micromechanical sensors and electronics survived the high-g firing environment and functioned during flight. The GPS receiver demonstrated an ability to reacquire the GPS satellites approximately 15 s following gun firing. The attitude determination algorithms demonstrated the ability to quickly establish estimates of local level (the orientation of the horizontal plane) following launch, which is necessary prior to integrated INS/GPS navigation and execution of canard deflection commands.

CMATD program. The successful ERGM tests were followed by further development to reduce the size, weight, and cost of the guidance system so that it could be retrofitted into the existing inventory of projectiles. This work was conducted for the Competent Munitions Advanced Technology Demonstration (CMATD) program. The goal was to prove the feasibility of developing an INS/GPS-based guidance, navigation, and control system that could be used with the current inventory of Navy 5-in. (127-mm) rounds and Army 155-mm (6.1-in.) rounds. That system would significantly reduce the miss distance of the projectile, thereby improving the probability of aim-point hit to over 90% with a single projectile.

Inertial sensor technology employed in the INS/GPS guidance, navigation, and control system uses the same micromechanical gyroscopes and accelerometers that are currently in preproduction for automobile skid control applications. Its role as the production base of a large commercial market should enable the micromechanical inertial sensor assembly to serve as the inexpensive guidance system for tactical weaponry.

Another critical requirement for the INS/GPS guidance system developed under the CMATD effort is that it can be easily incorporated into existing Navy and Army projectiles without modification to the projectile body. The only method for accomplishing this objective is with a fuze replacement, which screws into the front of the projectile in place of the current NATO Standard Fuze (**Fig. 3** and **Fig. 4**). Under this program a miniature INS/GPS guidance system that occupies approximately 8 in.^{3} (131 cm^3) has been developed using a micromechanical inertial sensor assembly implemented as six laminated multichip modules and a GPS receiver built from two such modules. The CMATD flight computer combines the GPS pseudo-range and delta-range measurements with micromechanical inertial sensor measurements to produce a 50-Hz navigation solution (that is, one that is updated 50 times per second), and uses the navigation data with a prespecified aim-point location to generate guidance commands, also at a 50-Hz data rate. An autopilot algorithm computes commands for the canard actuator subsystem to steer the projectile to the desired aim-point.

This program has successfully demonstrated closed-loop guidance of a 5-in. (127-mm) MK64 projectile. This was the first demonstration of GPS/INS navigation and closed-loop guidance of a spinning projectile after gun launch and represents a milestone in the development of an inexpensive guidance system for Navy guided projectiles. It is anticipated that volume production costs of based on microelectromechanical systems (MEMS), like those employed in CMATD projectiles, will be an

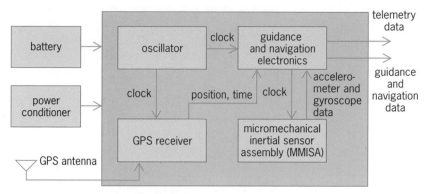

Fig. 1. Concept of integrated navigation system for precision-guided projectiles, with inputs from the Global Positioning System (GPS) and inertial sensors.

order of magnitude lower than those of fiber-optic instruments.

The system was flown twice in 1999, and the final test of CMATD program was conducted at the Yuma Army Proving Ground in February 2000. The system survived the launch shock, actively despun the nose section and stabilized the round, determined which way was down based on inertial sensor output, reacquired the GPS, and implemented closed-loop guidance. System operation was verified through a telemetry downlink.

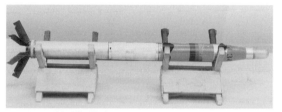

Fig. 2. Extended Range Guided Munition (ERGM) demonstration projectile.

Fig. 3. CMATD projectile with prototype fuze-replacement guidance, navigation, and control system.

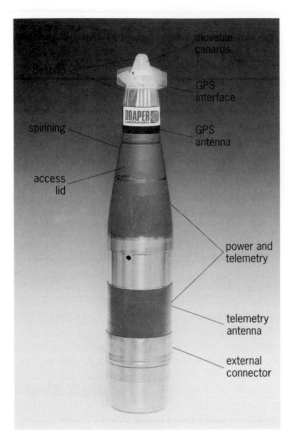

movable canards

despin

GPS interface

spinning

GPS antenna

access lid

power and telemetry

telemetry antenna

external connector

Fig. 4. CMATD projectile with prototype fuze-replacement guidance, navigation, and control system.

Further reductions in size and power consumption of the navigation system are being realized as microelectronics technology advances allow the GPS and processor functions to shrink. The processor and GPS now consume the most power in the avionics implementation, and so the integration of these functions will also dramatically reduce the battery requirements.

Production systems. The Navy has initiated a development program, the Extended Range EX-171 MOD 0, for a 5-in. (127-mm) projectile launched from a naval vessel to destroy targets at ranges of up to 63 nmi (117 km). An upgrade is planned for the MEMS inertial system of this weapon in order to lower the cost of the guidance assembly.

The Army is developing the XM-982 Guided Munition, which is a 155-mm (6.1-in.) projectile using a similar MEMS-based inertial system. Both of these programs went into production in 2000.

The Army also has under development the Precision Guided Mortar Munition using an inertial MEMS guidance unit for applications in mortar-launched 120-mm (4.7-in.) projectiles.

For background information *see* ARMY ARMAMENT; GUIDANCE SYSTEMS; INERTIAL GUIDANCE SYSTEM; NAVAL ARMAMENT; SATELLITE NAVIGATION SYSTEMS in the McGraw-Hill Encyclopedia of Science & Technology.   James L. Sitomer

Bibliography. N. Barbour et al., Micromechanical Instrument and Systems Development at Draper Laboratory, *AIAA Guidance, Navigation and Control Conference on Integrated Navigation Systems*, San Diego, CA, July 29-31, 1996; J. Dowdle and K. Flueckiger, An Integrated GPS/Micromechanical IMU for Navy 5″ Projectiles, *Proceedings of the 52d Annual Meeting of the Institute of Navigation*, Cambridge, MA, June 19-21, 1996; A. Kourepenis et al., Performance of MEMS Inertial Sensors, *Joint Services Data Exchange for Guidance, Navigation and Control*, Anaheim, CA, November 16-20, 1998; *Microelectromechanical Systems: A DoD Dual Use Technology Industrial Assessment*, Final Report, Department of Defense, December 1995.

Hair loss

Alopecia or hair loss is a common problem that involves numerous potential etiologic factors. Nearly every patient consulting a physician because of hair loss should receive a diagnosis.

Assessment. The correct diagnosis is usually made following a good case history and meticulous examination. The physician will consider:

1. Is the hair coming out by the roots or is it breaking off?
2. Are there symptoms such as itching or burning? Are there associated redness, scaling, and pustules?
3. Is the hair loss diffuse or patchy? Is it patterned?
4. Did the hair loss begin 3-4 months after a traumatic event (death in the family, major illness, general anesthesia, delivery, crash diet, febrile illness)? Was the patient given a new drug a few months before the onset?

In the physical examination, the physician will:

1. Look at the back of the head. Look at the density and the quality of the hair. This area is often used as a "control."
2. Look at the crown and vertex. Can the scalp easily be seen through the hair?
3. Look for a pattern, either patchy or diffuse.
4. In a bald spot, look for follicular openings and exclamation hairs (!).
5. Look for erythema, scaling, and atrophy.
6. Do a pull test by grabbing approximately 60 hairs from the proximal end and pulling them firmly but gently. A normal pull test will release 0-2 hairs if the patient has not washed the hair within 48 h. A positive pull test is 6 or more hairs. The test could be falsely negative if the patient just washed the hair that same day.

Most cases involve hair coming out by the roots— alopecia areata, telogen effluvium, anagen effluvium, androgenetic alopecia. If the hair is breaking, a differential diagnosis should be considered; possibilities include hair cosmetics, tinea capitis, tichotillomania, traction alopecia, and structural hair shaft abnormalities. Improper use of hair care cosmetics is seldom encountered, as most products are safe. In such cases, stopping the offending agent is usually sufficient. Hair shaft abnormalities are uncommon and should be referred to a dermatologist.

Once it has been established that the hair is coming out by the roots, scarring alopecia must be ruled out. These conditions are trichologic emergencies. If not treated, patients can lose significant amounts of hair that will not regrow, since the follicles are destroyed in the inflammatory process. If there is atrophy, erythema, scales, or pustules with no visible follicular openings, the diagnosis is likely a scarring alopecia. A biopsy is often necessary to make a final diagnosis, and treatment should be undertaken promptly. These conditions are uncommon, and referral to a dermatologist is required.

The last step is to identify the pattern. The diffuse pattern may be telogen effluvium or anagen effluvium. Patterned hair loss may be alopecia areata, traction alopecia, trichotillomania, or androgenetic alopecia. According to the pattern, a differential diagnosis should be considered.

Alopecia areata. Alopecia areata is considered an autoimmune disorder and affects 1–2% of the population. The exact pathophysiology is unknown. It usually presents with one or many oval, slightly erythematous (red), asymptomatic patches of alopecia. There is often a spontaneous regrowth. Alopecia areata can be diffuse in 5% of cases and mimic androgenetic alopecia or telogen effluvium. Ten percent of cases may proceed to alopecia totalis, affecting the entire scalp. One percent may go on to alopecia universalis, affecting all hair-bearing areas. The condition is chronic, and patients will likely have more than one episode. Nail changes, mostly pitting, are often associated with alopecia areata.

Alopecia areata is unpredictable in its clinical presentation and response to treatment. Patients with onset before puberty, with atopy, with a longstanding hair loss, or with an ophiasis pattern (hair loss in the occipital or temporal regions of the scalp) usually have a poorer prognosis.

Many autoimmune disorders have been associated with alopecia areata, but they run a separate course. The most commonly associated disorders include atopy, thyroid diseases, and vitiligo (a skin disease characterized by areas of complete loss of pigment). The risk of a concurrent autoimmune disorder is low, and no further testing is necessary, unless clinically indicated, to rule this out.

Because the condition is benign and episodes may resolve spontaneously, treatment is not mandatory. An early aggressive treatment will not change the future outcome. Therapeutic options depend on the extent of hair loss and the age of the patient.

A good treatment for localized alopecia areata is intralesional corticosteroids. Triamcinolone acetonide (5 mg/cc on the scalp, 2.5 mg/cc for eyebrows and beard) every 4 weeks is recommended (maximum 20 mg per visit). Injections of 0.1 ml through a 30-gauge needle are spread over affected areas. Other options include potent topical steroids daily, topical minoxidil 5% solution twice a day, and daily short-contact anthralin. The exact mechanism of action of minoxidil is still unknown. It is believed that minoxidil has a direct mitogenic effect on epidermal cells and prolongs their survival time. Local vasodilation does not seem to play a role in hair growth.

For extensive disease, topical immunotherapy shows a 50–60% success rate. A physician or nurse familiar with the treatment applies the topical allergen weekly onto the scalp.

The lowest concentration that gives a mild allergic contact dermatitis is used. Side effects include contact dermatitis, cervical lymphadenopathy, and pigment changes. No major side effect has been reported with topical immunotherapy, but there are still questions regarding its long-term safety. Other options for extensive conditions include daily short-contact anthralin, minoxidil 5% solution twice a day, and psoralen with ultraviolet A radiation (PUVA).

Trichotillomania. Trichotillomania is an artificial alopecia secondary to manipulation of the hair. Any hair-bearing area can be affected. The condition is more common in children and adult women. Patients often deny pulling their hair. Clinically, the alopecic patches have unusual shapes and sizes, and show broken hairs. There is no inflammation or epidermal change. If the diagnosis is difficult clinically, a scalp biopsy can be helpful.

Trichotillomania is an obsessive-compulsive disorder. The underlying emotional problem is often less severe in children, and the condition resumes in most cases. Management varies from patient to patient, but a few guidelines can be used. First, the diagnosis should be discussed with the patient, and the patient should be seen periodically.

Stressful events must be searched for and dealt with. If the condition persists or has been present for more than a year, the underlying psychological problem may be more serious, and psychological support is recommended if the patient agrees to it. Hair regrows when the compulsive behavior is controlled. In rare chronic cases, the hair follicles are damaged, and the alopecia is permanent.

Traction alopecia. Traction alopecia results from prolonged, tightly pulled hair styles. It occurs most frequently in the temporal areas. Hair regrows spontaneously once grooming habits are modified. Repetitive damage to the follicles can result in permanent alopecia.

Tinea capitis. Tinea capitis is seen more commonly in children, with a higher incidence in the African-American population. The most common agent in the United States is *Trichophyton tonsurans*. Tinea capitis rarely leads to permanent hair loss. The diagnosis is suggested by erythema, scaling, and crusting locally on the scalp. Other family members should be examined. The Wood's lamp examination is often negative since *T. tonsurans* does not fluoresce. The diagnosis is confirmed with microscopic examination of a potassium hydroxide scraping or a mycologic culture. The condition is treated with systemic antifungal agents. The use of Nizoral shampoo by the patient and family members is recommended. Personal objects in contact with hair should not be shared.

Telogen effluvium. Telogen effluvium is due to increased shedding occurring after a metabolic disturbance. Different causes can be associated with this type of hair loss, including childbirth, high fever, chronic illness, major surgery, hyper- or hypothyroidism, crash diets, drugs, and severe psychological stress.

Normally, 90% of the hair follicles are in anagen phase and 10% are in telogen phase. When an unusual event occurs, the anagen hairs go prematurely into telogen phase. The telogen phase lasts 2–4 months and then shedding occurs. The condition is more common in women. The diagnosis is made from the history of diffuse shedding and a positive pull test. Without evidence of underlying conditions, only ferritin and thyroid-stimulating hormone should be ordered. Ferritin level should be above 40 micrograms per liter to ensure normal hair growth. No treatment is needed once the cause is eliminated. In some instances, the process can be chronic and last a few years. A cause is seldom found in chronic cases. Minoxidil 5% solution can speed the regrowth in both acute and chronic telogen effluvium. Although there is usually complete regrowth following telogen effluvium, it can sometimes unmask androgenetic alopecia.

Anagen effluvium. Anagen effluvium is an acute hair loss that usually follows chemotherapy or radiotherapy. It occurs shortly after the treatment. The hair usually regrows. This condition may also be secondary to ingestion of heavy metals (thallium, mercury, arsenic, copper). Because 90% of the hair follicles are in anagen (growth phase of the hair cycle), the hair loss is extensive and occurs shortly after the precipitating event (days to a few weeks). If the insult is removed, regrowth is usually rapid since the normal cycle, which was interrupted, may resume. If the hair loss is secondary to radiotherapy, there may be radiation injury to the hair follicle, and the alopecia can be permanent. Minoxidil 5% solution can help regrowth.

Androgenetic alopecia. Androgenetic alopecia is the most common cause of hair loss. Fifty percent of men by age 50 and 40% of women by menopause have some degree of androgenetic alopecia. This type of hair loss involves both genetic and hormonal factors. Hair loss is gradual, with miniaturization of genetically programmed hair follicles. Androgenetic alopecia presents differently in men and women. In women, it is more diffuse and located centroparietally. The frontal hairline is usually intact. In men, hair loss occurs in the fronto-temporal regions or the vertex.

If there is any sign of virilization in women (such as severe acne, hirsutism, menstrual irregularities, and infertility) or if the androgenetic alopecia is a stage III, laboratory studies including serum levels of testosterone, dihydroepiandrosterone sulfate, prolactin, and thyroid-stimulating hormone should be ordered. Referral to an endocrinologist or gynecologist may be appropriate.

There is still no cure for androgenetic alopecia, and emphasis should be placed on prevention, not hair regrowth when a medical therapy is given. In women, the only proven medication with an indication for androgenetic alopecia is minoxidil 5% solution. Its mechanism of action is still unclear. It stabilizes the condition in 50% of patients. Fifty percent show minimal regrowth and 13% moderate regrowth. Discontinuation of therapy results in loss of hair; thus it must be continued for as long as the problem is important to the patient. The 5% solution has greater efficacy than the 2%. The solution must be applied with a dropper directly onto the scalp. The patient should make five parts, put five drops in each part, and slightly spread the solution with the fingers. Seven percent of patients may experience some irritation (burning, itching, redness), and 5% may develop increased hair on the face. Pregnant or lactating women should not use minoxidil. Accidental ingestion of minoxidil could lead to serious adverse effects since each milliliter of the 5% solution contains 50 mg of minoxidil. The use of a systemic antiandrogen such as spironolactone (Aldactone), cyproterone acetate (Androcur), or flutamide (Eulexin) may have some benefit in reducing the amount of hair thinning. Finasteride has not been approved for women of childbearing age, and it is not effective in postmenopausal women.

For men, treatment options include finasteride (Propecia) 1 mg daily and minoxidil 5% solution twice a day. Finasteride is a 5-alpha reductase inhibitor and thus inhibits the conversion of testosterone to dihydrotestosterone. Finasteride stabilizes the condition and prevents further hair loss in approximately 80% of patients. Fifty to sixty percent of patients have mild to moderate regrowth. It is a safe treatment. Side effects include impotence, decreased libido, and decreased semen volume in less than 2% for each side effect. Side effects are totally reversible upon discontinuation of the drug, and they usually resolve spontaneously even if the treatment is continued. Minoxidil stabilizes the condition in 30% of men, and a mild regrowth is seen in approximately 10%. Both treatments must be continued for sustained benefit.

Therapeutic efficacy is evaluated through patient satisfaction and comparison of the current status with a baseline photograph.

For patients who want to add density to their hair or who have an advanced stage of androgenetic alopecia, hair transplantation is usually the best option for both men and women. It involves the transplantation of permanent hairs from the back of the scalp to balding areas. The advent of mini- and micrografting has revolutionized hair transplantation, and the procedure results in a very natural appearance.

For background information *see* CHEMOTHERAPY; HAIR; SKIN in the McGraw-Hill Encyclopedia of Science & Technology.   Chantal Bolduc; Jerry Shapiro

Bibliography. A. K. Gupta et al., Tinea capitis: An overview with emphasis on management, *Ped. Dermatol.*, 16(3):171–189, 1999; R. Paus and G. Cotsarelis, The biology of hair follicles, *N. Engl. J. Med.*, 341(7):491–497, 1999; J. Shapiro and V. H. Price, Hair regrowth: Therapeutic agents, *Dermatol. Clinics*, 16(2):341–356, 1998; L. C. Sperling, Evaluation of hair loss, *Curr. Prob. Dermatol.*, VIII(3):97–136, 1996.

High-pressure food processing

Japanese food processors were the first to commercially preserve foods by high pressure. In 1990, these food products included commercially sterile (shelf-stable) jam, yogurt, and pourable salad dressing in 125-g (4.4-oz), hermetically sealed plastic cups. These products had a pH below 4.5 (acid food) to inhibit spore germination, and were treated with pressures in the range of 400 megapascals (60,000 lb/in.^{2}). This treatment was sufficient to inactivate vegetative forms of yeasts, molds, and bacteria when the product was held at pressure for up to 20 min at room temperature. Because high isostatic pressure does not break covalent bonds, the flavors, colors, and nutritive contents of these foods were not changed by the process.

Increased use of high isostatic pressure (above 150 MPa or 22,500 lb/in.^{2}) depends on the development of high-pressure equipment designed specifically for food processing. This equipment is under intensive development. Some design criteria for high-pressure food processors are rapid cycling of the pressure vessel to allow rapid product throughput; a pressure vessel life of up to 1 million cycles; safety and compatibility of operation in a food processing environment; high up-time and minimum maintenance; a design operating pressure of 680 MPa (100,000 lb/in.^{2}); stainless steel food product and package contact surfaces; and use of pure water as the hydrostatic contact fluid.

History. Work by Bert Hite and his associates at the West Virginia Agricultural Experiment Station from 1899 through 1929 showed that high hydrostatic pressure could be used to inactivate most vegetative microbes. Spore-forming bacteria were found to be pressure-resistant. Thus, low-acid foods such as milk and snap beans could be pasteurized but not preserved for storage at room temperature. Fruits and foods with a pH below 4.5 could be rendered commercially sterile for storage at room temperature, since the hydrogen ion concentration at or below pH 4.5 is sufficient to inhibit the germination and outgrowth of spores.

The food pathogen *Clostridium botulinum* and spore-forming food spoilage bacteria are particularly pressure-resistant. Hite's work described the incentives and disincentives of food preservation by high isostatic pressure. Hite was able to treat foods at pressures over 680 MPa (100,000 lb/in.^{2}).

The effect of high hydrostatic pressure on biological systems was studied extensively from 1920 onward. In 1970 A.M. Zimmerman presented an excellent summary of these studies, and papers by G. W. Gould and A. J. H. Sale on the inactivation of bacterial spores brought attention to high-pressure food preservation. Studies were aided by the use of high-isostatic-pressure equipment, under development since the 1930s, for the pressing of metal powders and ceramics into high-strength parts such as gas turbine blades. These isostatic presses were designed to operate at pressures up to 680 MPa (100,000 lb/in.^{2}) and could be built to an operating volume of several hundred liters.

Workers in the Food Science Department at the University of Delaware in 1982 used a small isostatic press to treat a number of food products and food microbial pathogens at pressures up to 340 MPa (50,000 lb/in.^{2}). This work showed that isostatic presses could be used routinely to pasteurize low-acid foods and commercially sterilize a variety of acid products. In 1989 R. Hayashi in Japan started similar work independently on high-pressure preservation of foods using isostatic pressing technology. Hayashi formed a consortium of food manufacturers in Japan. Their pooled research efforts resulted in the marketing of pressure-preserved acid foods such as yogurt, fruit preserves, and pourable salad dressings in the early 1990s.

The first high-pressure-preserved product to be marketed in the United States was guacamole prepared from ripe avocados. High-pressure treatment extended the refrigerated shelf-life of this low-acid food from 7 days to over 30 days. High pressure was found to inactivate the enzyme system responsible for product darkening upon exposure to air. Currently the product is packed in plastic bags holding several pounds for food service or 454 g (16 oz) for national retail sales. Guacamole has been well received. Additional products under development for the United States and European markets include orange juice, shucked oysters, and processed meat products. High-pressure-treated ham, milk, and orange juice are sold in selected European countries.

High isostatic pressure. Food products are lost through the action of microbes and enzymes; chemical deterioration; contamination by parasites, insects, and rodents; and mechanical damage in handling and transport. Foods packaged in hermetically sealed containers can be pressure-treated to eliminate most vegetative forms of microbes as well as parasites and insects. Vacuum packaging in a high-oxygen-barrier package can reduce oxidation. Packaging can prevent mechanical damage and loss to insects and rodents. High-pressure treatment of packaged foods can extend the refrigerated shelf-life of low-acid foods such as guacamole from 1 to over 4 weeks. Acid foods can be made shelf-stable. A pH below 4.5 inhibits the germination and outgrowth of spores. Spores are highly resistant to inactivation by high pressure.

Protein denaturation appears to be the mechanism by which high pressure inactivates vegetative microbes and enzymes. High pressure can change the character of high-protein foods such as meat, eggs, and milk. The effect of high pressure on the rate and degree of irreversible protein denaturation depends on the composition and structure of each protein, pH, pressure applied, temperature, and type and concentration of solutes in the liquid surrounding the protein.

As the pressure is increased, microbes in the food experience an instant decrease in the volume of the liquid surrounding them. At some threshold pressure the least pressure-resistant protein in a microbe starts to denature. If this protein is critical to reproduction or the control of water or ion transport across the cell membrane of the microbe, inactivation can occur. Electron photomicrographs of pressure-treated microbes show collapsed cell walls, indicating a loss of cell turgor. Enzyme inactivation and loss of protein functionality by high-pressure treatment proceeds by disruption of hydrogen, ionic, and hydrophobic bonds. The effect is similar to the loss of protein functionality by heating.

Water activity (as determined by measuring the vapor pressure of the water in the system) is critical to the rate of inactivation of proteins by pressure. For this reason, bacterial spores are extremely pressure-resistant since they contain very little free water. However, pressures of 100–150 MPa (15,000–22,500 lb/in.^{2}) have been found to induce germination of bacterial spores. Once germination has started, the spore becomes susceptible to inactivation by pressures of 500–700 MPa (74,000–103,000 lb/in.^{2}). Combinations of pressure and temperatures to 110°C (230°F) have been found to inactivate spores. Pressure cycling has also been found to help inactivate spores. Pressure inactivation of at least 10^{12} spores of *C. botulinum* in a low-acid food would be required to match an equivalent accepted heat sterilization treatment.

Commercial equipment. Batch treatment is the simplest form of high-pressure processing. Packaged foods are loaded in a canister and placed in a pressure vessel capable of withstanding up to 1 million cycles of compression and decompression to 680 MPa (100,000 lb/in.^{2}). The vessel is sealed and brought to processing pressure with water delivered by an intensifier. The compressibility of water at 22°C (72°F) is 7% at 200 MPa (29,000 lb/in.^{2}), 11.5% at 400 MPa (58,000 lb/in.^{2}), and 15% at 600 MPa (88,000 lb/in.^{2}). Pumping work to compress water is the main energy requirement for high-pressure food processing. A 100-liter (26-gallon) vessel requires the compression of over 15 liters (4 gallons) of water to bring its pressure to 680 MPa (100,000 lb/in.^{2}). Several hundred horsepower are needed to compress this water in 20 s. Large, reliable intensifiers are needed to provide the short compression times used in rapid-cycling high-pressure food processing equipment.

High-horsepower intensifiers, adapted from the high-pressure water jet cutting industry, are filling this need. An intensifier uses a high volume of low-pressure oil acting on a large-diameter piston to drive a small-diameter water compression piston. Piston diameter ratios may be 20 to 1, with 20 volumes of oil at 34 MPa (5000 lb/in.^{2}) generating one volume of water at 680 MPa (100,000 lb/in.^{2}). High-pressure vessels are being developed to cycle up to 15 times per hour with a 3-min pressure hold. After decompression (10 s) the products are discharged from the pressure vessel, placed in cartons, and sent to market.

Liquid foods can be treated in semicontinuous equipment by pumping them into a pressure vessel fitted with a free piston. When the vessel is filled, the inlet port is closed, and high-pressure water is pumped into the vessel behind the free piston to compress the food. After the desired hold period, the water pressure is released and the treated food is discharged through a sterile port to a sterile hold tank. The treated product can be packaged under aseptic conditions for distribution. Semicontinuous equipment uses 100% of the pressure-vessel volume, and the equipment can cycle over 15 times per hour with a 3-min hold. Controls provide for automatic operation and recording of critical control point data such as pressure, hold time, and temperature. Units are designed to be cleaned in place.

The cost to treat foods by high pressure is related to equipment and operating costs and the yearly throughput of the equipment. Equipment and operating costs include the equipment itself, energy, labor, maintenance, repairs, and the cost of money. Throughput per year depends on pressure-vessel volume, treatment cycles per hour, hours of operation per year, and the weight of food processed per cycle. This last factor is a function of the volumetric efficiency of the package-vessel system. Volumetric efficiency in batch systems can range from 30% for small round canisters to 80% for products treated in large bags or pouches. Cost per pound can be minimized by maximizing volumetric efficiency, minimizing process cycle time and pressure, driving two or three vessels from one intensifier, and operating the process line in multiple shifts for as many days as possible throughout the year. For example, a pair of 100-liter (26-gallon) pressure vessels operating two 10-h shifts for 250 days per year, treating a product with a 60% volumetric efficiency, at 12 cycles per hour, can deliver 7.2×10^6 kg (15.84×10^6 lb) of unit density product per year. A $0.05 cost per pound for treatment would require equipment and operating costs to be below $792,000 per year, based on the current rate of equipment development.

Outlook. Equipment design research is focused on providing high-cycle-rate, reliable, safe, and cost-effective high-pressure batch and semicontinuous food processors. These units will be compatible with existing food preparation and processing systems, and will be installed on the food process line alongside batch and continuous heat sterilizers, freezers, blanchers, and drying equipment.

Food process research will continue to focus on process conditions to inactivate spores and enzymes related to food spoilage. Efforts will be directed to reduce process hold times and pressures to reduce equipment and process costs. The combination of mild heat (50°C; 122°F) with pressure is expected to reduce process times and pressures.

High-pressure processed foods distributed under refrigeration are regulated as refrigerated foods. While high-pressure treatment does not change the chemistry of the food, treated foods cannot be labeled as fresh. High-pressure-treated juices can be labeled as pasteurized where applicable. The treatment used must be shown to inactivate at least 10^6 microbes per gram of the pathogens normally associated with the product. Treated acid foods stored at room temperature are regulated as naturally acid or directly acidified foods, depending on their formulation and composition. The treatment used must be shown to inactivate at least 10^6 microbes per gram of the pathogens normally associated with the product. For example, *Escherichia coli* O157:H7 could be the pathogen of concern in apple juice.

For background information *see* COLD STORAGE; FOOD ENGINEERING; FOOD MANUFACTURING; FOOD MICROBIOLOGY; FOOD PRESERVATION; PASTEURIZATION; STERILIZATION in the McGraw-Hill Encyclopedia of Science & Technology.   Daniel F. Farkas

Bibliography. F. J. Francis (ed.), *The Wiley Encyclopedia of Food Science and Technology*, 2d ed., John Wiley, New York, 1999; G. W. Gould and A. J. H. Sale, Initiation of germination of bacterial spores by hydrostatic pressure, *J. Gen. Microbiol.*, 60:335–346, 1970; R. Hayashi, Application of high pressure to food processing and preservation philosophy and development, in W. E. Spiess and H. Schubert (eds.), *Engineering and Food*, vol. 2, Elsevier, New York, 1989; A. M. Zimmerman (ed.), *High Pressure Effects on Cellular Processes*, Academic Press, New York, 1970.

Horizontal gene transfer

A key source of genetic variation is exchange of genetic material among individuals. Genetic exchange among closely related individuals is common in nature, and occurs in prokaryotes via conjugation and other processes, and in eukaryotes during sexual reproduction. When these same processes occur among individuals that are more distantly related and would not typically exchange genetic material, they are referred to as hybridization. But occasionally genetic material is exchanged among organisms that are very distantly related. This phenomenon, termed horizontal (or lateral) gene transfer, occurs relatively rarely, and was long presumed not to be important in evolution. However, as increasing amounts of information from deoxyribonucleic acid (DNA) sequences have become available, it has become clear that horizontal gene transfer is a significant part of evolution in nature.

Phylogenetic analysis. Evidence of gene transfer can be found by way of comparative study of molecular phylogenies, which rely on the fact that when a mutation occurs in an individual's germ line its descendants can inherit the resulting variant sequence. Thus the descendants of the individual that underwent mutation can be recognized by their possession of a particular sequence variant. Over time, many mutations occur in any phylogenetic lineage; molecular phylogenetic analysis uses computer modeling to estimate the evolutionary relationships by reconstructing the history of mutation within the lineage. Because molecular phylogenetic analysis of gene sequences relies on the comparison of the same (homologous) gene from many individuals, each such phylogeny is really the phylogeny of a particular gene. If molecular phylogenies are determined for two or more genes from the same group of organisms, one would expect these genes to have the same phylogenetic history (except, of course, for studies within a single species). In most cases, this is what is observed; phylogenetic analyses of multiple genes produce congruent phylogenies. However, there are several known cases where different genes seem to have different evolutionary histories, and it is among these that evidence of horizontal gene transfer is to be sought.

Incongruence among gene phylogenies does not necessarily indicate gene transfer. In some cases the sequences do not contain enough information for reliable phylogenetic analysis. In other cases the analyses are flawed because the analytical method used makes assumptions that are inappropriate for the data, or because nonhomologous genes have been included in the study. But in cases where these possibilities can be excluded, the best explanation for incongruent gene phylogenies is horizontal gene transfer. Ideally one would know the true phylogeny of the organisms in question. If this were the case, then identification of which conflicting gene phylogenies did not match that phylogeny would be possible. Because the true organismal phylogeny is rarely known, most studies look for a group of gene phylogenies that agree, and assume that these represent the organismal phylogeny. The discordant gene or genes are then assumed to have undergone gene transfer. If the putative transferred gene closely resembles the homolog from an unrelated organism, the hypothesis of gene transfer is strongly supported.

Codon usage patterns. Although phylogenetic analysis provides a powerful way to study horizontal gene transfer, there is the disadvantage that it requires examining several genes from a number of organisms. This can be difficult, particularly if some of the organisms involved have not been well studied with molecular methods. Another way to identify genes that have undergone horizontal transfer is to find regions of the genome that seem to be out of place; that is, they have characteristics that are atypical of the genome in which they reside. This approach provides information that complements that from phylogenetic analysis, and has the advantage that it is possible to examine every gene within a genome and assign to the gene a likelihood that it has undergone recent transfer. From this information it is possible to make an estimate of the frequency with which horizontal gene transfer has occurred.

To make these calculations, one examines the patterns of base composition and codon usage within the genome. These patterns are quite variable, and are generally characteristic of an organism, although some variation is found within genomes as well. Base composition refers to the relative quantities of each nucleotide in the DNA. There is a typical or background base composition for each major region of a genome, probably because of biases in the mutation-repair mechanisms and variation in the nucleotide precursor pools within the cell. The base composition is often different in genes than in intergenic regions, which are under weaker selective pressures and consequently are more free to adopt the background base composition for the genome. Layered on top of base compositional patterns are patterns of codon usage (the relative frequency with which each of the 64 codons is used in protein-coding genes). The genetic code is degenerate (includes redundancy), with 64 codons to represent only 20 amino acids, and most amino acids can be encoded by more than one codon. These synonymous codons are not typically used with equal frequency. Rather, each organism has a distinctive pattern of codon usage. Because these patterns of base composition and codon usage, often referred to simply as codon usage, are characteristic of the genome, they can be used as markers for the origin of each gene. Genes that are native to the genome have the characteristic codon usage for that genome. Genes that have recently undergone horizontal gene transfer from another organism have the codon usage characteristic of the donor genome. However, once a transferred gene is resident in its new genome, when mutations occur, replacements reflect the codon usage biases characteristic of that genome. Thus, over time the codon usage of a transferred gene tends to change to resemble its new home, and consequently codon usage is useful only for detecting relatively recently transferred genes.

Many individual genes that have undergone horizontal gene transfer have now been identified in both prokaryotes and eukaryotes. Some of the most thoroughly documented cases of horizontal gene transfer involve the gene *rbcL*, which encodes the large subunit of ribulose-1,5-bisphosphate carboxylase/oxygenase (often called rubisco), a key enzyme in carbon fixation during photosynthesis by plant chloroplasts and their cyanobacterial relatives, as well as by photosynthetic proteobacteria. Rubisco genes have had a complex evolutionary history, and have undergone both gene duplication and horizontal gene transfer. Similar patterns have been identified in genes involved with adenosine triphosphate (ATP) synthesis, nitrogen fixation, and transfer ribonucleic acid (tRNA) synthesis, to name just a few. In a study of the relationship between prokaryotes and eukaryotes, researchers used molecular phylogenetic approaches to study the evolution of over 60 protein-coding genes and found a highly complex pattern that suggests substantial horizontal gene transfer. This has led researchers to further investigate hierarchical classification, particularly at higher taxonomic levels.

Hierarchical classification. Horizontal gene transfer could substantially affect the concept of organismal phylogeny. Because all life is thought to be descended from a common ancestor, the history of speciation provides the basis for a natural classification of all living things (see **illus.**).

While the general pattern of reproductive isolation and diversification is well established, horizontal gene transfer complicates the situation. Hierarchical classification assumes that genetic exchange is important only within species. However, if horizontal gene transfer has been important in evolution, the real pattern of relationships may be much more complex.

To understand the significance of horizontal gene transfer in the reconstruction of evolutionary history, it is important to consider the distinction between gene phylogeny and organismal phylogeny. Each organism has a genome which is composed of many genes. Each of these genes has its own evolutionary history, and molecular phylogenetic methods make it possible to reconstruct this history. If horizontal gene transfer never occurred, one would expect that every gene within the genome would have the same phylogeny, and this phylogeny would correspond to

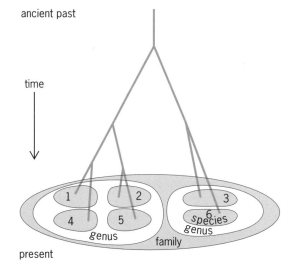

Hierarchical classification. The branching tree on the left represents the history of speciation within the group, with the present-day populations depicted at the tip of each branch, and their classification shown to the right. The hierarchical clustering of species reflects the history of speciation.

the organismal phylogeny. At the opposite extreme, if horizontal gene transfer were the dominant mode of inheritance, every gene would have a different evolutionary history, and it would be extremely difficult to reconstruct the evolutionary history of the organism. Certainly reality lies somewhere between these two extremes. It is also to be noted that even in the case of frequent gene transfer there is a true evolutionary history of the organisms; it is only the ability to accurately reconstruct this history that is in question.

Consequently, to determine the significance of horizontal gene transfer in evolution, it is necessary to examine genomes for evidence of shared evolutionary history among their genes. The degree to which individual genes within a genome have congruent histories provides a measure of the relative importance of horizontal gene transfer in evolution and, by extension, the feasibility of reconstructing organismal phylogeny. The genome of the radiation-resistant bacterium *Deinococcus radiodurans* R1 has been examined in this context. This extraordinary bacterium was first detected in studies of radiation sterilization; it is able to survive doses of radiation so high that they literally shred its two chromosomes and plasmids into hundreds of pieces. The ability to reconstruct its genome following this massive damage is probably originally an adaption to environmental stresses such as desiccation; and *D. radiodurans* is thought (on the basis of phylogenetic analysis of ribosomal RNA sequences) to be related to another very tough organism, *Thermus aquaticus*, a hot-spring bacterium. To test this organismal phylogeny, researchers compared the 175 currently known *T. aquaticus* genes to the entire genome of *D. radiodurans*, as well as to other completely sequenced genomes. Of these 175 genes, 143 were more similar to those of *D. radiodurans* than to those of any other organism. This indicates considerable congruence among these genomes, so horizontal gene transfer has not wiped out all evidence of organismal phylogeny in this case. It is significant, however, that all but one of these genes are encoded on one of the two *D. radiodurans* chromosomes. This suggests that the entire second chromosome of *D. radiodurans* has been acquired by horizontal gene transfer (a hypothesis that awaits further study). This work indicates that while organismal phylogeny remains a valid and important concept in evolutionary biology, the role of horizontal gene transfer in evolution should not be neglected.

Charles F. Delwiche

Prokaryotes. Lateral gene transfer among prokaryotes has long been known to occur, but the recent availability of complete genome sequences has brought its biological significance to the foreground. A number of mechanisms are known by which foreign DNA is naturally introduced into prokaryotic cells. Bacteriophages (bacterial viruses) can pick up genes from their hosts and readily transmit them across species boundaries (transduction). Many bacteria can mate across species boundaries (transconjugation), a property that bacterial geneticists often

exploit in the laboratory. And many bacteria are naturally competent; that is, they simply take up DNA from the environment as part of their lifestyle and occasionally integrate it into their genome (transformation). By no means does every piece of DNA that enters a bacterial cell become integrated into the genome and successfully transferred. Rather, prokaryotes seem to preferentially integrate DNA from their own species over DNA from other species, and to possess mechanisms to protect their genomes against intrusion by foreign DNA, but such protection is not 100% effective.

For example, DNA restriction enzymes preferentially degrade intruding genes, discerning between self and non-self DNA by virtue of chemical modifications introduced into DNA by the corresponding modification systems. Once in a while, intruding DNA escapes restriction and becomes integrated. Also, mismatch repair systems lead to degradation of the intruding strand in mismatch-containing heteroduplexes formed during transpecific recombination. In some species, mismatch repair is repressed when the SOS-response is in effect, a physiological state that signals life-threatening circumstances to the individual and promotes integration of genes from other species. In naturally competent bacteria, which take up DNA from the environment as part of day-to-day life, the genome contains numerous short species-specific uptake sequences that are recognized by specific receptors at the surface of the cell and are preferentially taken up. For example, in *Haemophilus influenzae*, which is naturally competent, the uptake sequence contains a 9-base pair core motif that occurs in 1465 copies in the genome, 160 times greater than the frequency expected by chance, facilitating species-specific DNA uptake. However, the uptake sequences can also occur by chance in DNA from other species, in which case they will then also be taken up.

Evidence. Current evidence for lateral gene transfer among prokaryotes is generally of two types. The first type comes from searches within individual genomes for genes that possess sequence attributes such as guanine plus cytosine (G + C) content or codon bias which significantly differ from the brunt of genes in the genome. Since G + C content and codon bias can differ markedly across species but tend to be uniform within species, genes that were acquired from donors with G + C content and codon bias bear these attributes as the imprint (signature) of their donor genome. If the imprint is sufficiently different from that of the recipient genome, the transferred genes can be identified in computer analyses as having been acquired from other species. Using such criteria, researchers found that about 10% of the *Escherichia coli* strain MG1655 genome consists of genes that were acquired in over 200 events of lateral gene transfer, which occurred subsequent to the divergence of the eubacteria *E. coli* and *Salmonella* some 100 million years ago. Overall, the study suggested that about 18% of *E. coli*'s genes might be relatively recent foreign acquisitions, and that the average rate of acquisition may be close to about

16 kilobases per million years. Yet, once a gene is introduced into a recipient genome, it starts to take on the G + C content and codon bias of the recipient, such that over time spans of millions of years it eventually becomes similar to the rest of the genome in these attributes and hence undetectable as an intruder. Thus, this approach can reveal only evolutionarily recent acquisitions.

The other kind of evidence comes from gene-for-gene and region-for-region database searching and sequence comparison across species. For example, in the analysis of the genome of *Thermotoga maritima*, researchers found that about 24% of the genes of that eubacterium shared their greatest similarity with archaebacterial homologs rather than with eubacterial homologs, suggesting that extensive genetic acquisition from archaebacterial donors had taken place in that organism's history. Furthermore, a great number of individual cases of lateral transfer have accumulated from studies of microbial physiology. One striking example entails a roughly 40-kilobase-long region in the genome of an α-proteobacterium that encodes enzymes involved in the process of oxidizing methanol to carbon dioxide (CO_2). The genes in that region had never previously been found among eubacteria, but they are highly conserved and ubiquitous among methanogenic archaebacteria, where they function in the process of reducing carbon dioxide to methane. In this case, it appears that the acquisition encompassed a unit of biochemical function that was physiologically useful for the α-proteobacterial recipient, but required that the encoded biochemical pathway run backward relative to its normal function in the methanogenic donor.

Integration. Intruding genes can thus occasionally overcome the mechanisms intended to keep them out of bacterial genomes, integrating into the chromosome and creating new combinations of genes to be passed on to progeny. Integration may be extremely rare in terms of events per individual per generation, but countless bacterial individuals have existed for countless generations since prokaryotes arose (over 3.8 billion years ago), so a very large number of rare events has certainly occurred. This means that selection for useful combinations of genes so introduced into prokaryotic genomes is likely to play an important role in determining which combinations become fixed subsequent to transfer. Some units of physiological function, such as some biochemical pathways and "pathogenicity islands," are organized as operons for gene clusters in prokaryotes, and it has long been believed that such modular units of function may be particularly well suited to undergo transfer and fixation.

Eukaryotes. The kind of lateral gene transfer that is most widely recognized in eukaryotes differs quite fundamentally from that observed in prokaryotes. Eukaryotes do not naturally mate with distantly related species (whereas prokaryotes do), but eukaryotes possess DNA-containing organelles (which prokaryotes do not). Mitochondria (and chloroplasts in the case of photosynthetic eukaryotes) were once free-living eubacteria, and they contain remnants of prokaryotic genomes that unequivocally attest to their prokaryotic heritage. But the genomes of chloroplasts and mitochondria are highly reduced, containing only about 1% of the DNA that free-living α-proteobacteria (the progenitors of mitochondria) and cyanobacteria (the progenitors of chloroplasts) do. Despite their paucity of DNA, both organelles contain a spectrum of proteins that is comparable to that of their free-living eubacterial cousins. Accordingly, a great many genes for organellar proteins have been transferred from organelles to the nucleus during the course of evolution. Many proteins encoded by such transferred genes have acquired a transit peptide so that they can be imported back into the organelle. When this occurs, the organellar copy of the gene becomes unnecessary and can be lost such that over time genetic material in eukaryotes steadily trickles out of the organelles and into the nucleus.

Endosymbiotic gene transfer. This type of intercellular gene transfer in the wake of the endosymbiotic origin of organelles (endosymbiotic gene transfer) is a special case of horizontal gene transfer that occurs in the well-established biological context of endosymbiosis and that is specific to eukaryotes. However, not all of the proteins that are encoded by genes which were transferred to the nucleus from organelles are directed to the organelle from which the gene was donated. The reason is that many cytosolic proteins in eukaryotes are encoded by genes that were acquired from organelles.

Just how many genes eukaryotes have acquired from organelles is currently an issue of debate. Analyses of the yeast genome have found that over half of its genes share more similarity to eubacterial than to archaebacterial homologs. This might reflect a major influx of genes from the ancestors of mitochondria, but other explanations are possible; and methodological problems relating to the ability to reconstruct ancient evolutionary events on the basis of individual gene sequences, which have limited resolving power, also figure into this issue.

Determining which and how many genes eukaryotes have acquired and from which source(s) is no simple matter, partly because this requires an explicit null hypothesis for the expected similarities of eukaryotic genes (so that the exceptional acquisitions can be identified). This in turn hinges upon the question of how eukaryotes are related to prokaryotes in the first place and whether any eukaryotes exist that never possessed mitochondria which might serve as a reference system for comparison.

Nuclear genes. Despite these vagaries, there are many well-documented cases of functional nuclear genes that have been acquired through transfer from organelles. Although the mechanisms of transfer are not known in detail, wholesale integrations of large chunks of organelle DNA into nuclear chromosomes does occur. For example, scientists found a 270-kilobase piece of the mitochondrial genome of the plant *Arabidopsis thaliana* that had been integrated into nuclear chromosome 2 in an evolutionarily recent transfer event. Such transfer events represent raw starting material for the establishment of functional organelle genes in nuclear chromosomes.

Implications for natural systematics. Since Darwin, the evolution of species through time has generally been viewed as a branching process like that of a tree. Yet Darwin was not aware of genes, nor was he primarily concerned with the evolution of microbes, and he was certainly not aware of lateral gene transfer. If there were no lateral gene transfer at all in nature, all genes would tend to paint the same picture of evolutionary history; that is, in phylogenetic analyses they would tend to give the same tree. But lateral transfer does occur, and many different genes give very different trees for the same sets of species (albeit sometimes due to ancient gene duplications or the pitfalls of phylogenetic inference rather than due to lateral transfer).

With increasing awareness of the prevalence of lateral transfer in nature, views on the evolution of organisms (prokaryotes in particular) may gradually shift from classical treelike models to more differentiated models that describe the phylogeny of organisms as the sum of the individual evolutionary histories of their genes. Yet such views run contrary to Darwin's vision of a natural system for classifying organisms, since organisms possessing genes that they have acquired from many different sources would belong in part to many different taxonomic groups at the same time. This does not pose a problem for the systematics of higher organisms where elaborate biological reproductive barriers exist and where Mayr's biological species concept applies. But for prokaryotes, which relatively freely exchange their genes on a geological time scale, a hierarchical classification system that depicts the phylogeny of organisms as reflected in their genomes may be unattainable. This does not mean that ribosomal RNA phylogenies depicting the relatedness of eubacteria, archaebacteria, and eukaryotes as found in textbooks of microbiology are fundamentally flawed. Yet it does mean that they should not be thought of as a tree of life, but perhaps as a tree of ribosomes.

For background information *see* BACTERIOPHAGE; GENE; ORGANIC EVOLUTION; PATHOGEN; PHYLOGENY; PLASMID; RECOMBINATION (GENETICS); TRANSDUCTION (BACTERIA); TRANSFORMATION (BACTERIA) in the McGraw-Hill Encyclopedia of Science & Technology.   William Martin

Bibliography. C. F. Delwiche, Tracing the thread of plastid diversity through the tapestry of life, *Amer. Natural.*, 154:S164–S177, 1999; W. F. Doolittle, Phylogenetic classification and the universal tree, *Science*, 284:2124–2128, 1999; J. G. Lawrence and H. Ochman, Molecular archaeology of the *Escherichia coli* genome, *Proc. Nat. Acad. Sci. USA*, 95:9413–9417, 1998; X. Lin et al., Sequence and analysis of chromosome 2 of the plant *Arabidopsis thaliana*, *Nature*, 402:761–768, 1999; M. G. Lorenz and W. Wackernagel, Bacterial gene transfer by natural genetic transformation in the environment, *Microbiol. Rev.*, 58:563–602, 1994; W. Martin, Mosaic bacterial chromosomes—a challenge en route to a tree of genomes, *BioEssays*, 21:99–104, 1999; W. Martin and R. G. Herrmann, Gene transfer from organelles to the nucleus: How much, what happens, and why?, *Plant Physiol.*, 118:9–17, 1998; K. E. Nelson et al., Evidence for lateral gene transfer between Archaea and Bacteria from genome sequence of *Thermotoga maritima*, *Nature*, 399:323–329, 1999; M. C. Rivera et al., Genomic evidence for two functionally distinct gene classes, *Proc. Nat. Acad. Sci. USA*, 95:6239–6244, 1998; A. J. Roger, Reconstructing early events in eukaryotic evolution, *Amer. Natural.*, 154:S146–S163, 1999; M. Syvanen and C. Kado (eds.), *Horizontal Gene Transfer*, Chapman Hall, London, 1998; J. A. Vorholt et al., Distribution of tetrahydromethanopterin-dependent enzymes in methylotrophic bacteria and phylogeny of methenyl tetrahydromethanopterin cyclohydrolases, *J. Bacteriol.*, 181:5750–5757, 1999; O. White et al., Genome sequence of the radioresistant bacterium *Deinococcus radiodurans* R1, *Science*, 286:1571–1577, 1999.

Human migration

Before 1492, marking the beginning of modern transoceanic journeys, humans had established themselves on all habitable continents. These migrations are thought to have originated in Africa and to have occurred during the last 100,000 years. Today, populations that still live in the land they inhabited before 1492 are referred to as aboriginal populations. Thus, Europeans (such as Basques and Germans) are aboriginals of Europe, Africans (such as San and Pygmies) are aboriginals of Africa, and Native Americans are aboriginals of America. Most of these populations have few historical records of their origins and, in any case, these do not go back beyond 5000 years.

To investigate prehistoric events, scientists have dealt mostly with vestiges of ancient cultures (archeology), fossil bones (physical anthropology), or language (linguistics), but more recently they have used the genetic variability in the deoxyribonucleic acid (DNA) of living individuals, which preserves a record of their past. In addition, modern techniques of DNA recovery from ancient bones and tissues can provide information on the variation present in ancient times, a field called molecular archeology. Indeed, the DNA analysis of a 40,000-year-old Neandertal bone has suggested that the Neandertals are not direct ancestors of humans.

Population analysis. Questions have traditionally been framed in terms of populations: Where and when did the common ancestor of all populations live? What was the route of migration of a population? When did they arrive in their homeland? Such questions assume that a population is a discrete entity that can be followed through time. If so, an individual's DNA will tend to be more similar to that of other individuals from the same population than to that of individuals from different populations. The level of genetic similarity (and dissimilarity) between populations can be arranged along a scale of time. Therefore, the more different two populations

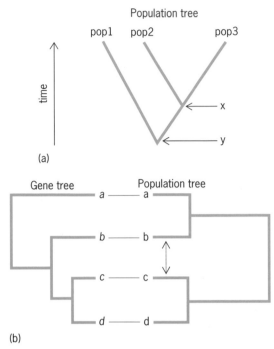

(a)

(b)

Fig. 1. Phylogenetic trees. (*a*) A representation of a hypothetical tree of three populations (pop1, pop2, and pop3). The most recent common ancestor of pop2 and pop3 is represented by the putative x population located in a recent past. The ancestor y represents the common ancestor of pop1, pop2, and pop3, which is more ancient than x. (*b*) This scheme shows a comparison between a hypothetical true tree of populations (a, b, c, d) and a tree obtained using DNA variability analyzed in the same populations. Several factors such as migration (broken line), gene duplication, and reverse and recurrent mutation can generate these differences.

are, the more ancient the common ancestor they share. However, populations are not isolated: there are migrations between them and they may fuse. Consequently, it may not be easy to draw conclusions about populations over long periods of time (**Fig. 1**).

Lineage analysis. The molecular analysis of DNA led to the development of an alternative approach. The classic DNA markers, or mendelian loci, are located on the autosomes, the chromosome pairs numbered 1 to 22; they are always inherited by the offspring from the mother and the father in equal contributions. However, two special segments of DNA show uniparental inheritance; that is, they come exclusively from the father or the mother. These segments are the Y chromosome which is transmitted only from fathers to sons, and the mitochondrial DNA (mtDNA) which is passed only from mothers to children. They provide examples of DNA lineages which can be followed over long periods of time. The histories of different lineages may be not identical because of chance or distinct male or female contributions to a present-day population. Habits such as polygyny (many wives for a man), and female transfer from other populations, are examples of factors leading to distinct histories of males and females found in the same population. Small regions of autosomes also provide lineages that can be followed through time. However, most work has concentrated

on mitochondrial DNA and the Y chromosome.

Native American origins. Native Americans were descendants of hunters who came from Asia by land a long time ago. This idea is now generally accepted by scientists. In its modern form, it proposes that the ancestors of Native Americans came through Beringia, a land bridge located where the Bering Strait is now between North America and Siberia, formed when the sea level was lowered during glacial times between 40,000 and 13,000 years ago (**Fig. 2**). The most likely pathway for further movement into the Americas was through an ice-free corridor which was open irregularly between 36,000 and 20,000 years ago and then completely open after 9,000 years ago when the glaciation ended.

There are currently three major questions concerning the pre-Columbian peopling of the Americas: (1) How many distinct groups of individuals made the journey from Asia to Americas? (2) How long ago: early (35,000 to 20,000 years ago) or late (after 14,000 years ago)? (3) Which populations in Asia share the most recent ancestors with the Native Americans?

One theory, based originally on linguistic data, proposes that ancestors of present-day Native Americans came from Siberia in three separate migrations (at different times) giving rise to distinct groups, namely Amerindians (from South, Central, and most of North America, such as Yanomami), Na-Dene (from North America, for example, Navajos), and Aleut-Eskimos (from the tip of North America) [Fig. 2]. The Amerindians are thought to be

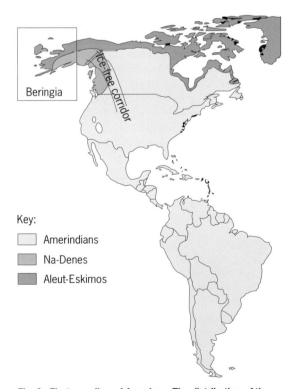

Fig. 2. First peopling of Americas. The distribution of the three major groups of Native Americans defined by linguistic affinities is shown. The ice-free corridor linking Beringia to the rest of Americas during some periods in the glacial period is also represented.

descendants of the first migrants, also called Paleo-Indians.

However, new genetic and anthropological data are challenging the Three Migrations theory. Recent findings of ancient bones (about 10,000 years old) in North and South America suggest a distinct migration of non-Mongoloid people, different in appearance from typical East Asians and present-day Native Americans. They could have become extinct, without leaving descendants. This hypothesis cannot readily be investigated by geneticists as they usually study only the DNA of living people, but it may in the future be studied by molecular archeologists. However, analysis of the Y chromosome and mitochondrial DNA lineages is being used to tell the paternal and maternal histories of the first peopling of the Americas.

The mitochondrial DNA analysis reveals that most present-day Native Americans belong to only four distinct lineages, which are also found (but are rare) in parts of Asia. Thus, these Native American mitochondrial DNAs can be traced back to only four mothers, who probably lived in Asia. Sources have been proposed in the region around Mongolia and south Siberia, while suggested times for entry into the Americas range between 30,000 and 15,000 years ago.

The Y-chromosomal analysis suggests that most males, about 90% in South America and 50–70% in North America, are descended from a single male who lived perhaps 5,000 to 30,000 years ago. In contrast to the four mitochondrial DNA lineages, this lineage is found almost exclusively in Native Americans, and the only other populations carrying it, in Siberia, display it in low frequency, perhaps due to back-migration. The lineage therefore probably arose in the Americas or Beringia. Other studies demonstrate that there are more distantly related Y chromosomes in populations from Siberia, namely the Kets from the Yenissey River Basin and the Altai from the Altai Mountains. Interestingly, Y chromosomes related to those of Native Americans are very uncommon in Asians such as Chinese and Japanese but are frequent in Europe. The implication of these studies is that a common Y chromosome ancestor existed a long time ago (greater than 30,000 years) in Eurasia who gave rise to most European Y chromosomes, to Kets and Altai in Siberia, and finally to Native American Y chromosomes. It would imply an ancient migration route to the Americas coming from Africa and passing through northern Eurasia, Siberia, and Beringia.

These recent analyses of mitochondrial DNA and the Y chromosome, despite tracing distinct parts of the history of Native Americans, suggest that all three major groups—Amerindians, Na-Dene, and Aleut-Eskimos—are too similar to have entered by separate migrations. Some additional migration movements may have brought other low-frequency mitochondrial DNAs and Y chromosomes to the continent, but the findings do not support a separate entry for each of the three Native American groups. The DNA analysis indicates that most of the Native Americans today are descended from the people coming in a first and major migration movement during the Pleistocene. Molecular dating methods are not yet accurate enough to distinguish between an early or a late Pleistocene entry, but this is an exciting area for future work.

For background information see ARCHEOLOGICAL CHEMISTRY; CYTOPLASMIC INHERITANCE; DEOXYRIBONUCLEIC ACID (DNA); FOSSIL HUMAN; MIGRATORY BEHAVIOR; PALEOINDIAN; POPULATION DISPERSION; POPULATION GENETICS in the McGraw-Hill Encyclopedia of Science & Technology.

Fabrício R. Santos; Chris Tyler-Smith

Bibliography. S. L. Bonatto and F. M. Salzano, Diversity and age of the four major mtDNA haplogroups, and their implications for the peopling of the New World, *Amer. J. Human Genet.*, 61:1413–1423, 1997; L. L. Cavalli-Sforza, P. Menozzi, and A. Piazza, *The History and Geography of Human Genes*, Princeton University Press, Princeton, NJ, 1994; T. M. Karafet et al., Ancestral Asian source(s) of new world Y-chromosome founder haplotypes, *Amer. J. Human Genet.*, 64:817–831, 1999; F. R. Santos et al., The central Siberian origin for native American Y chromosomes, *Amer. J. Human Genet.*, 64:619–628, 1999.

Hybrid control

As computers and their associated memory have become cheaper, faster, and easier to use, engineers have used them to expand the capabilities of control systems. Loosely speaking, such systems—which include both digital and analog devices working together to enhance the controller's functionality—are known as hybrid controllers. Most controllers built today are, to some extent, hybrids because digital implementation is usually cheaper and more reliable than analog. The computer in the controller can then be used easily to provide additional capability, such as better response to internal failures. However, the potential benefits of control systems combining the symbol manipulation and decision-making capability of the computer with precise tracking capability of analog controllers are much greater.

Automobile engine control unit. The current state of the art in hybrid control is well represented by a typical automobile engine control unit. Bosch's Motronic engine management system primarily controls ignition and fuel injection. The ignition map, basically a nonlinear function mapping engine speed and load into spark advance angle, is extremely complex in comparison to analog versions of the same controller. The complexity results from individually optimizing dozens of points on the map and then interpolating smoothly between them. This would not be feasible without the computer in the controller (see **illus.**).

The rest of the Motronic engine management system includes several such complex, optimized functions. It also includes two other functions that depend on the computer. First, the controller is adaptive. The controller continually monitors certain

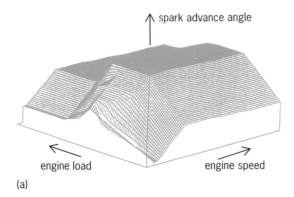

(a)

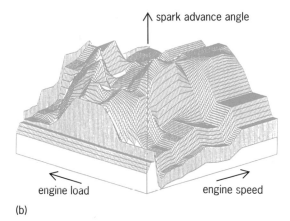

(b)

Ignition timing maps. (*a*) Mechanical advance system. (*b*) Electronically optimized system. (*After R. K. Jurgen, ed., Automotive Electronics Handbook, 2d ed., McGraw-Hill, 1999*)

controlled variables and changes the controller's parameters to maintain the overall system's performance despite changes in the engine's parameters. This also minimizes the need for adjustments during vehicle servicing. Second, the hybrid controller continuously monitors itself for component failures. When a failure is detected, it modifies its operation to protect other components that might be damaged by the failure, and adopts an emergency mode that allows the vehicle to still operate. The computer stores the diagnostic information and supplies it, on demand, to a repair person. Lastly, since the driver may be unaware of the problem, it provides a warning indication.

The engine management system has some decision-making capability. Another automotive example illustrates additional possibilities. The controller that deploys the airbags and seat belt pretensioners in a car is a decision-making feedback control system. The controller senses the vehicle's acceleration, either positive or negative. The analog signals from the sensors are then input to a digital system that must decide whether to deploy the seat belt pretensioners and the airbags and, if so, at what precise instants. The decision is, in principle, difficult. The vehicle is continually accelerated by the driver, by bumps in the road, by the wind, and occasionally by minor impacts. Deployment must not occur unless there is a real crash and, furthermore, it must

occur at the right instant. Future systems are expected to have enhanced decision-making capability. They are expected to classify the occupant and adapt the airbag and seat belt pretensioner to the occupants and the crash severity. Current systems also self-test, a very common feature of hybrid control systems.

Incorporating humanlike decision-making into an automatic control system creates very exciting possibilities. For example, there is a great deal of current research on various types of autonomous vehicles. These include pilotless reconnaissance and combat aircraft, driverless earthmoving equipment, and various mobile autonomous robots. With the Global Positioning System (GPS) providing very accurate location sensing; the computer optimizing routing, adjusting speed, and choosing the best lane; and the analog controller maintaining speed and heading, driverless passenger vehicles are nearly feasible. The lack of a good obstacle sensor, cost, and people's willingness to trust their lives to a decision-making machine are all that stand in the way of a true "auto" mobile. *See* AUTONOMOUS AIRCRAFT.

Design. The digital and analog parts of a hybrid control system have different requirements from those imposed on them in nonhybrid situations. Even though step inputs are common tests of control systems, it is generally undesirable for the inputs to a physical system to change suddenly by a large amount. For example, rapidly flooring the accelerator of a car will usually spin the wheels. Rapid changes in the parameters of an analog control system can have even worse effects and should be avoided.

Digital computers can respond almost instantly to a change in an input signal. Thus, they facilitate rapid changes. Hybrid control systems must be designed to prevent harmful jumps in signals and parameters. Alternatively, the controller can be designed to mitigate the effects of sudden changes. In either case the designer has a problem to solve.

A second design challenge results from the fact that digital computers normally act asynchronously. The exact instant at which the computer returns an answer does not matter. Analog systems operate in real time; they need a control signal at every instant. In a hybrid system the computer is constrained to respond no later than a rigid deadline imposed by the analog system. Because the computer is typically capable of many more operations per second than are needed for analog control, it is usually performing other operations, such as a self-test, in its spare time. The designer has to ensure that this does not interfere with the analog operation.

Ensuring that the controller works properly in all situations is an extremely important, and difficult, aspect of hybrid control system design. A software crash that freezes the computer is normally a nuisance; in a hybrid controller it can be a disaster. Testing and verification of the hybrid controller's operation is related to, but substantially more difficult than, the software verification problem.

Theory. Most of the theoretical work on hybrid control has been devoted to the problem of finding a single, unified description of an arbitrary hybrid system. Without such a framework it is impossible to answer many basic questions about control. For example, is the system stable? This single mathematical model must be a reasonably accurate description of an interesting class of real hybrid systems; otherwise it has only academic interest. The difficulty results from the completely different mathematics associated with the two main parts of any hybrid system.

Analog systems act continuously on continuously applied inputs; they are "time-driven." The driver must keep her foot on the accelerator pedal of her car; the car responds to any change in the pedal angle. The usual mathematical models of analog systems are differential equations or difference equations in which time is an independent variable. Digital systems are more naturally viewed as "event-driven;" they respond to discrete instantaneous inputs. The computer does nothing until the operator strikes the return key; it then executes a string of instructions, stops, and waits for the next command. The mathematical description of discrete-event (event-driven and discrete-state) systems is more like a language—if this event occurs then that event results. In many such systems and their models, time is simply ignored. When time is included, it is just an attribute of an event and not the driving independent variable.

Many mathematical models for hybrid systems have been proposed. There does not seem to be agreement on one such model. The most useful model seems to depend on the specific application. Two examples are given below. They were chosen because they are substantially less abstract that most.

One research project has concentrated on automobile engine control. Motivation includes the importance of the automobile to society and the importance of hybrid controllers to the automobile. An additional motivation is that the four-stroke single-cylinder internal combustion engine can be viewed as a discrete-event system in its own right, even without the hybrid controller. The onset of each stroke is an event. Torque generation, which depends on the stroke, is then a discrete-event system. The power train and air dynamics are described by differential equations; equivalently, they are analog systems. Naturally, the group of researchers involved in this project formulates a hybrid model for the internal combustion engine. They also pose several optimal control problems associated with this engine. A key to the solution of these problems is that they are able to "relax" the original hybrid model of the engine to a purely analog description. Finally, they map the relaxed solution back to the full hybrid engine model to obtain a suboptimal solution to the original problem.

Several aspects of the project illustrate the value of good mathematical modeling. The system specifications can be given at a high level of abstraction so that they are independent of implementation decisions. The rigorous mathematical framework ensures formal correctness of the control algorithms.

Another research project on hybrid control focuses on motion control systems, primarily in robotics. Controlling a movement in such a system requires both discrete event and analog elements. The discrete-event part is obvious—the robot moves until it touches the wall. The analog part is less obvious—it is necessary to describe and control the analog compliance that governs the interaction with the wall. A hybrid model is therefore created for movement description. This model leads to a motion description language, a basis for robot programming that facilitates specification of both the motion and its analog control. Theory such as this that simplifies the programming of hybrid controllers would greatly facilitate their development.

For background information *see* AUTOMOTIVE ENGINE; CONTROL SYSTEMS; DIGITAL CONTROL; ROBOTICS in the McGraw-Hill Encyclopedia of Science & Technology.   William S. Levine

Bibliography. P. Antsaklis et al. (eds.), *Hybrid Systems V*, Springer-Verlag, Berlin, 1999; R. L. Grossman et al. (eds.), *Hybrid Systems*, Springer-Verlag, Berlin, 1993; B. K. Mattes, Passenger safety and convenience, in R. K. Jurgen (ed.), *Automotive Electronics Handbook*, 2d ed., Chap. 23, McGraw-Hill, 1999; Robert Bosch GmbH, *Automotive Handbook*, 4th ed., p. 452, 1997.

Hypersonic flight

Hypersonic flight is considered flight at Mach 5 (five times the speed of sound) or greater. The aerodynamic flow and characteristics of a flight vehicle as it accelerates from Mach 4.99 to Mach 5.01 do not markedly change. In contrast, when it accelerates from Mach 0.99 (subsonic) to Mach 1.01 (supersonic), there is a dramatic change in the physics of the flow, including the generation of shock waves at supersonic speeds. Hypersonic flight may be regarded as that portion of the high-speed flight regime where certain physical phenomena become important that are not so important at lower speeds. At hypersonic speeds, shock waves lie very close to the surface of the vehicle, and there is a major thickening of that portion of the flow immediately adjacent to the surface that is affected by friction (the boundary layer), causing an interaction between the shocks and the boundary layer. Moreover, at high Mach numbers, the tremendous kinetic energy of the freestream flow ahead of the vehicle is dissipated through the shock waves and in the boundary layers, and it is converted into heat which creates high temperatures in the flow around the hypersonic vehicle—temperatures that are frequently high enough to chemically dissociate and ionize the gas in the flowfield. Under these conditions, extreme aerodynamic heating becomes a driving consideration in the design of a hypersonic vehicle. All of

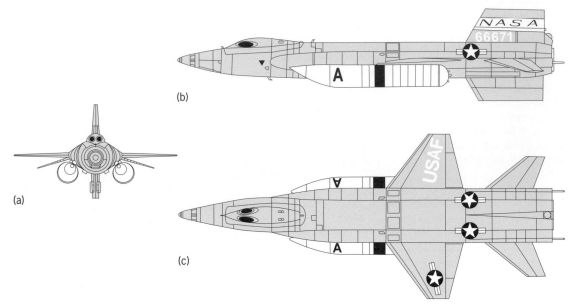

Fig. 1. X-15 hypersonic airplane. (*a*) Front view. (*b*) Side view. (*c*) Top view.

this and more comprise the aerodynamic characteristics of hypersonic flight, making it perhaps the most challenging flight regime to conquer. However, the quest to fly faster and higher historically has been a major driving force in the advancement of flight, and hypersonic flight is the next objective in this quest.

History. The first human-made vehicle to achieve hypersonic flight was the V-2/WAC Corporal two-stage rocket that was fired on February 24, 1949, and achieved a speed of over 5000 mi (8000 km) per hour in the atmosphere (about Mach 7). The first practical hypersonic vehicles were reentry nosecones of intercontinental ballistic missiles designed in the mid-1950s, which entered the Earth's atmosphere on their way down at about Mach 23. This speed was extended during the crewed space program, first to the Mach 26 entry of orbital space vehicles such as the Mercury and Gemini capsules during the 1960s, and then to Mach 36 for the Apollo lunar return module on its way back from the Moon. To date, the Apollo atmospheric entry Mach number of 36 is the highest speed achieved by a human-made vehicle, as well as that for a human being. These rocket and space vehicles provided the major impetus for the first era of hypersonic research and development, roughly between 1955 and 1972.

However, this era also included the first hypersonic airplane, the North American X-15 (**Fig. 1**). In the early 1950s, the National Advisory Committee for Aeronautics (NACA, now NASA) initiated a series of preliminary studies for an aircraft to fly beyond Mach 5. This fed into an industry-wide design competition for a hypersonic airplane, which was won in 1955 by the North American Aircraft Corporation. The X-15 was designed to be capable of flying at Mach 7 and at a maximum altitude of 264,000 ft (80,500 m). Three X-15 aircraft were built, all powered by a rocket engine. On June 23, 1961, with U.S. Air Force test pilot Major Robert White

at the controls, the X-15 achieved the first hypersonic airplane flight, reaching Mach 5.3. In so doing, Major White accomplished the first "mile per second" flight in an airplane, reaching a maximum velocity of 3603 mi (5798 km) per hour. The highest flight Mach number achieved with the X-15 was 6.72 in a flight on October 3, 1967, with Air Force Major Pete Knight at the controls. The last flight of the X-15 took place on October 24, 1968.

The second era of hypersonic flight is associated with the space shuttle (**Fig. 2**). Its first flight took place in April 1981. Designed to orbit the Earth, the space shuttle enters the Earth's atmosphere on its return at orbital velocity, about Mach 26. The space shuttle is part space vehicle, part airplane. The latter is in the sense that it executes an unpowered glide through the atmosphere, relying on aerodynamic lift to land safely at a predetermined location. The space shuttle will remain in operation at least through the first decade of the twenty-first century. It continues to be, by far, the most successful hypersonic "airplane."

Design. The nose and wing leading edges of the space shuttle are rather blunt and rounded. This may seem counterintuitive for a very high speed vehicle, which one might think should be very slender with a pointed nose and sharp leading edges. However, in 1952 Harvey Allen at the NACA Ames Aeronautical Laboratory introduced the concept that a hypersonic vehicle should be a blunt body in order to reduce the intense aerodynamic heating to the vehicle at hypersonic speeds. For such a blunt body, the bow shock wave is very strong and is located a small distance ahead of the nose. As a result, much of the heat generated by the shock goes into the airflow around the body, with less to go into the body, hence reducing the aerodynamic heating. Allen's blunt body concept has been incorporated in all operational hypersonic vehicles to date. Notable, in particular, is the extreme bluntness of the Apollo return capsule, which has

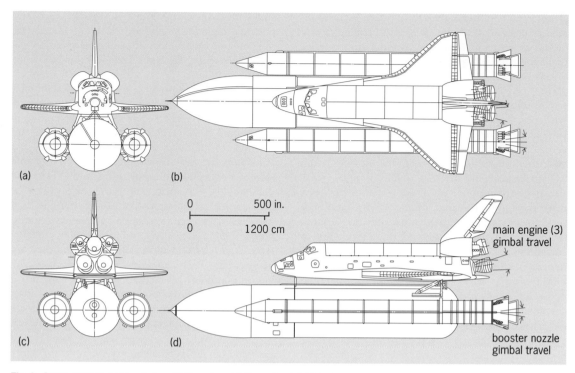

0   500 in.
0   1200 cm

main engine (3)
gimbal travel

booster nozzle
gimbal travel

Fig. 2. Space shuttle. (*a*) Front view. (*b*) Top view. (*c*) Rear view (*d*) Side view.

a nose radius of 16 ft (5 m). Even the X-15 has a rounded nose.

Recent concepts for new hypersonic flight vehicles are driven by a different design philosophy. Sustained hypersonic flight, even extended cruise, within the atmosphere has become a major focus. The vehicles include hypersonic air-breathing missiles in the Mach 8 range, single-stage-to-orbit vehicles incorporating air-breathing propulsion for a substantial portion of their boost phase, and several X-vehicles for the purpose of gaining some new flight data in the hypersonic regime. An example is the X-43 Hyper-X vehicle sponsored by NASA (**Fig. 3**). Instead of a blatantly blunt configuration, it has a rather streamlined configuration with a fairly sharp leading edge at the nose—a major departure from the previous hypersonic blunt body shapes. Hypersonic vehicles designed to fly efficiently within the atmosphere must have a much higher aerodynamic lift-to-drag ratio, which can be obtained only with more slender configurations. The nose and leading edges of these vehicles still have some, albeit small, bluntness in order to deal with aerodynamic heating; but on the scale of the overall size of the vehicle, such small bluntness is not readily apparent. In comparison to the rather bulky and blunt configuration of the space shuttle (Fig. 2), the Hyper-X clearly has a slender body. The intense heat transfer to the small-radius noses and leading edges is dealt with by the use of advanced high-temperature materials and sophisticated internal cooling devices.

Engine. The air-breathing powerplant for this new group of hypersonic flight vehicles is the supersonic combustion ramjet engine (SCRAMjet). Unlike more conventional jet engines and ramjets, where the incoming air is slowed to subsonic speeds be-

fore entering the combuster, in the SCRAMjet the flow through the entire engine remains supersonic. This poses challenging problems in the mixing of fuel and obtaining proper combustion within the engine. As of mid-2000, no vehicle powered by a SCRAMjet had flown, so this technology is unproven. However, a considerable amount of research and development on SCRAMjet engines has been carried out, and successful deployment appears to be just around the corner.

Indeed, the primary objective of NASA's Hyper-X is to demonstrate for the first time in free flight the successful operation of an airframe-integrated SCRAMjet-powered vehicle. Other objectives are to verify the computational predictions, analysis, and

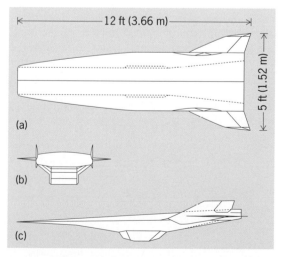

Fig. 3. X-43 Hyper-X hypersonic research vehicle. (*a*) Top view. (*b*) Front view. (*c*) Side view.

ground test methodologies for modern hypersonic vehicle design, and to investigate the scaling of this design concept of future operational air-breathing hypersonic cruise and space access vehicles. The first X-43 is scheduled for flight in or before the year 2001.

The temperature and pressure levels associated with the very high speed flow over a hypersonic vehicle and through a SCRAMjet engine are so severe that they are difficult and sometimes not possible to simulate in any ground test devices, such as hypersonic wind tunnels. To fill this void, extensive use of computational fluid dynamics has been made during the research, development, and design processes for modern hypersonic vehicles. Computational fluid dynamics deals with the computation of such flows on a high-speed digital computer. Indeed, hypersonic flight has been one of the major forces behind the rapid development of computational fluid dynamics, which today is a fundamental discipline in aerospace engineering, of equal importance as pure experiment and pure theory.

Hypersonic flight, attempted and achieved to some limited extent during the last half of the twentieth century, is poised for new advances with completely new vehicle concepts. It remains the final frontier of powered atmospheric flight.

For background information *see* AERODYNAMICS; AIRCRAFT DESIGN; COMPUTATIONAL FLUID DYNAMICS; HYPERSONIC FLIGHT; MACH NUMBER; RAMJET; SPACE SHUTTLE; SUPERSONIC FLIGHT in the McGraw-Hill Encyclopedia of Science & Technology.

John. D. Anderson, Jr.

Bibliography. J. D. Anderson, *Fundamentals of Aerodynamics*, 2d ed., McGraw-Hill, 1991; J. D. Anderson, *Hypersonic and High Temperature Gas Dynamics*, McGraw-Hill, 1989; J. D. Anderson, *Introduction to Flight*, 4th ed., McGraw-Hill, 2000; J. D. Anderson, *Modern Compressible Flow*, 2d ed., McGraw-Hill, 1990.

Information retrieval

As networking and storage technologies become faster and cheaper, people will amass more kinds of digital information than ever before. Much of this will be multimedia information such as faxes stored as bitmap images, voice-mail messages stored as audio files, and handwritten notes captured on a personal digital assistant and stored as pen stroke sequences. The problem of managing a database of such diverse media types requires fundamentally new techniques.

Traditionally, information retrieval is thought of as searching a given collection of textual documents using a textual query, where the goal is to find all documents in the collection that satisfy (that is, are relevant to) the query according to some measure. For simplicity, it can be assumed that the query consists of a collection of terms, and the goal is to find documents that contain these terms, either singly or in some logical combination. This is the way that most search engines on the World Wide Web currently operate. The query and the target documents typically arise from similar sources in that they are likely to have been entered by human operators typing on computer keyboards, with some amount of attention paid to minimizing mistakes. In this case, the problem of determining whether a given document matches the query is relatively straightforward.

Problems arise if the query and the database are derived from different media. For example, the query could be textual while the documents might be handwritten or perhaps voice recordings or some mixture of types. A significant fraction of the text present on some Web pages is actually encoded in image format. Nontextual media are not directly searchable for keywords unless they are first transcribed into a machine-readable format (for cxamplc, thc ASCII character code), either manually or via one of a number of recognition processes: automatic speech recognition in the case of speech, optical character recognition in the case of image text, and handwriting recognition in the case of electronic ink. These technologies, now widely available, accept input in the appropriate media type and output text.

This, however, introduces another serious problem: coping with recognition errors. Even the best of current systems can be error-prone, especially when presented with anything other than perfectly clean input. Humans excel at deciphering noisy or ambiguous communications, whereas computers are not nearly as adept. Accuracy rates for optical character recognition, for example, may exceed 98% in some cases (typeset pages in standard fonts), but this quickly drops off to the range of 85% for otherwise quite readable fax images. Certain types of degradation (for example, very dark or light photocopies) that offer little challenge for the human may result in no output at all when run through optical character recognition. The situation is worse with automatic speech recognition and handwriting recognition, as these problems seem inherently more difficult. Any attempt to search a database built using the output of such processes may miss intended matches because of the errors that arise (**Fig. 1**).

Searching noisy data. Manual correction of recognition results is a labor-intensive proposition. Assuming this approach is too expensive in most cases, and in the absence of a fundamental breakthrough in recognition technology, there is a need for retrieval

Domain	Intent	Input	Result	Error
Optical character recognition	Division,	Division, (2-D bitmap)	Division,'	→ ' (insertion)
Handwriting recognition	top	*tap* (pen strokes)	tap	o → a (substitution)
Speech recognition	fOnEm ("phoneme")	(audio signal)	fOnE ("phoney")	m → (deletion)
Keyboard entry	quick	q-u-i-k-c (keystrokes)	quikc	c k → k c (transposition)

Fig. 1. Examples of domains and recognition errors.

techniques that can tolerate errors. Approximate string matching is one such paradigm with important applications in domains ranging from information retrieval to molecular biology. A key principle in this field is the concept of edit distance, a measure for quantifying the similarity between two strings (that is, search terms) as well as for understanding the precise ways in which related strings may differ. In its most popular formulation, three basic operations are permitted: the deletion, insertion, and substitution of individual symbols. Each of these operations is assigned a cost, and the edit distance between two strings is then defined as the cost of the least expensive sequence of operations that transforms one string into the other.

This optimization problem can be solved using a well-known dynamic programming algorithm. The final distance is a measure of the similarity of the two strings, and the optimal sequence of editing operations highlights the actual differences. For example, the word "tap" can be transformed into "top" by performing the single character substitution 'a' → 'o'. In situations where this operation is determined to be a common error, it can be given a low cost and will thereby be detected and accounted for when performing retrieval.

In a particular domain, the manner in which strings are produced suggests a means for judging the similarity between strings. In the domain of scanned pages processed through optical character recognition, the two strings "baseball" and "baseba11" might be regarded as being quite similar, as 'l' (el) is frequently mistaken for '1' (one) in optical character recognition. However, in the domain of text typed on a keyboard, "baseball" and "baseba11" might be more similar, as the 'K' key is adjacent to the 'L' and it is easy for a typist's finger to slip from one to the other. These sorts of observations are encoded in the cost functions and captured during the edit distance computation.

Cross-domain information retrieval. The problem becomes more challenging when examining the interactions between different media and their associated error models. For example, to query via voice a database that was created from faxed documents, it is necessary to contend with errors from the automatic speech recognition process, a completely different class of errors from the optical character recognition process, and the issue of judging the similarity between spoken and printed keywords.

For instance, the strings "through" and "threw" differ significantly in their ASCII representations, so a substantial amount of editing would be required to transform one into the other. Their pronunciations in English, however, are identical. Hence, there should be a way to express the fact that while their textual edit distance is large, their phonetic edit distance is small.

There exist standard rules for mapping between domains (for example, transcribing text into phonemes reflecting the way it would be pronounced if spoken). However, an illustration of the problems that can arise is the recognition of an input word as

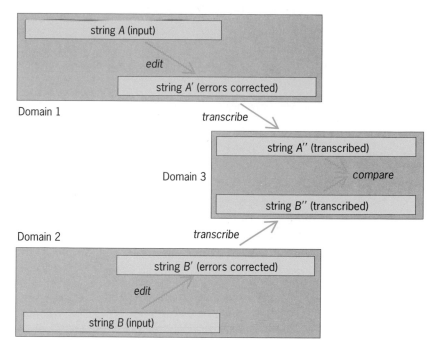

Fig. 2. Visualization of the cross-domain string matching problem.

"throu9h" by an optical character recognition process. Mistaking a 'g' for a '9' is a common error in some systems. There is, of course, no rule for suggesting how "ou9h" should be pronounced. Hence, there is no way to know that it would be close to "ew" once the optical character recognition error was accounted for.

Addressing this issue requires a significant extension to the approximate string matching paradigm. The cross-domain approximate string matching problem is, given a string A from one domain and another string B from a second, possibly different, domain, to compare the two strings by transcribing them into a common third domain using an appropriate set of rules. This optimization must at the same time take into account any errors that might have arisen in A and B as a result of the imperfect recognition processes that generated the two strings. In particular, the cost of the comparison is the least-cost way of (1) editing A into some other string A' and B into some other string B', (2) transcribing A' from the first domain and B' from the second domain into A'' and B'' in the third domain, respectively, and (3) matching A'' and B'' in the third domain (**Fig. 2**). This task can be solved efficiently using a dynamic programming approach that builds on traditional approximate string matching.

Figure 3 shows an optimal alignment generated when the algorithm mentioned above is run on two sample strings, one from the ASCII text domain and the other from the domain of spoken English (that is, phoneme sequences). The text input (top) is "crosis doman string mataching," which reflects several edits (typing or optical character recognition errors, perhaps) relative to the intended target, "cross domain string matching." The speech input (bottom), "kr > s dOmAnspriN laCiN," is expressed using a standard

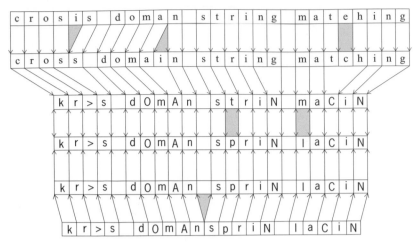

Fig. 3. Example of cross-domain approximate string matching.

phonetic alphabet and represents a pronunciation of the similar but not identical phrase "cross domain spring latching." There is an automatic speech recognition error resulting in a missed word boundary between "domain" and "spring."

The editing operations of the optimal sequence as determined by the algorithm are shaded in Fig. 3. After the first set of edits, both the text string and the phoneme string have been corrected to their intended targets. In the final editing stage, the two remaining differences ("string" versus "spring" and "matching" versus "latching") are detected. In this way, it becomes possible to perform retrieval across fundamentally different media types regardless of the recognition errors that might arise in practice.

For background information *see* CHARACTER RECOGNITION; IMAGE PROCESSING; SPEECH RECOGNITION; VOICE RESPONSE in the McGraw-Hill Encyclopedia of Science & Technology.

Daniel Lopresti; Gordon Wilfong

Bibliography. W. B. Frakes and R. Baeza-Yates, *Information Retrieval: Data Structures and Algorithms*, Prentice Hall, Englewood Cliffs, NJ, 1992; D. Lopresti and G. Wilfong, Cross-domain approximate string matching, in *Proceedings of the 6th International Symposium on String Processing and Information Retrieval*, Cancún, Mexico, September 1999, IEEE Computer Society Press; S. V. Rice, G. Nagy, and T. A. Nartker, *Optical Character Recognition: An Illustrated Guide to the Frontier*, Kluwer Academic, Boston, 1999; D. Sankoff and J. B. Kruskal (eds.), *Time Warps, String Edits, and Macromolecules: The Theory and Practice of Sequence Comparison*, Addison-Wesley, Reading, MA, 1983; J. P. H. van Santen et al. (eds.), *Progress in Speech Synthesis*, Springer-Verlag, New York, 1997.

Insulin

Insulin and insulin-like growth factors (IGF1 and IGF2) regulate a variety of metabolic and growth-related effects in target tissues, including stimulation of glucose transport, glycogen synthesis, lipogenesis, gene transcription, and deoxyribonucleic acid (DNA) synthesis. Moreover, the insulin/IGF signaling system promotes cell growth and survival and is essential for normal reproductive capacity. Insulin binds to the insulin receptor, whereas IGF1 binds to the related but distinct IGF1 receptor. These receptors are transmembrane protein kinases that catalyze phosphorylation of tyrosine residues on intracellular proteins. IGF2 provides cross-talk between these receptors as it activates IGF1 receptors and the a-isoform of the insulin receptor that predominates during fetal life (**Fig. 1**). Consequently, all three factors contribute to fetal growth and development. But insulin has special importance because it regulates carbohydrate and lipid metabolism throughout life; and when it becomes unavailable or fails to function, diabetes ensues.

Diabetes. Diabetes is associated with serious complications and mortality among millions of people worldwide. Overt hyperglycemia before and after meals is the hallmark of diabetes, which arises when insulin secretion is insufficient to control glucose metabolism. Diabetes frequently arises in children when a protracted autoimmune disease destroys the beta cells in the pancreatic islets of Langerhans. This form of the disorder is called type 1 diabetes. By contrast, adults usually develop diabetes as a consequence of impaired insulin action in liver, muscle, and adipose tissues, which is exacerbated by inadequate compensatory insulin secretion from pancreatic beta cells. The prevalence of this latter form, called type 2 diabetes, is increasing worldwide with serious complications and mortality.

Insulin resistance is an important factor in the pathogenesis of type 2 diabetes. It accompanies acute trauma, severe infection, pregnancy (gestational diabetes), or chronic obesity. However, insulin resistance does not cause overt hyperglycemia as long as the pancreatic beta cells compensate by hyperplasia (excessive formation of cells) and increased insulin secretion. Chronic obesity together with a sedentary lifestyle is strongly associated with type 2 diabetes, because it places a significant burden on the pancreatic beta cells, which fail to secrete sufficient insulin over long periods of time.

Efforts to treat type 2 diabetes are largely inadequate because the underlying causes of the disorder are unknown. The identification of common elements in the pathogenesis of diabetes might provide a common framework to understand diabetes and develop rational treatments. The discovery of insulin receptor subtrate (IRS) protein, and the role of IRS2 in insulin action and insulin secretion, holds promise for the future.

Insulin signaling. The receptors for insulin and IGF1 are protein tyrosine kinases, enzymes that catalyze the transfer of phosphate from adenosine triphosphate (ATP) to tyrosyl residues in cellular proteins. During insulin binding, the beta subunit of the insulin receptor phosphorylates several of its own tyrosine residues, which stabilizes the activated state of the receptor. The activated insulin receptor interacts with and phosphorylates tyrosine residues in other cellular proteins; similar events occur to the IGF1 receptor when it is occupied by IGF1. Proteins that are phosphorylated on tyrosine residues by these activated receptors are called insulin/IGF1 receptor substrates or IRS proteins.

IRS proteins undergo rapid tyrosine phosphorylation in response to insulin and IGF1. The mammalian IRS protein family contains at least four members: IRS1 and IRS2 are widely expressed; IRS3 is restricted to adipose tissue; and IRS4 is expressed in the thymus, brain, and kidney. Murine gene disruption reveals that *irs2* coordinates the effects of insulin and IGF1 upon peripheral carbohydrate metabolism and beta-cell function, whereas IRS1 mediates embryonic and postnatal somatic growth, IRS3 might be redundant in adipose tissue, and the physiological role of IRS4 is unclear.

Complementary studies in lower organisms implicate homologous signaling pathways in growth, energy homeostasis, longevity, and reproductive function. In *Caenorhabditis elegans*, the insulin/IGF1 receptor homolog DAF2 regulates reproduction, development, and longevity in response to environmental signals such as food. Mutations in these pathways induce developmental arrest at the dauer stage, reduce fertility, and extend life-span. Deletion of the IRS-protein homolog in *Drosophila* causes female sterility, reduced somatic growth, and abnormalities in lipid storage.

IRS proteins possess considerable potential to coordinate and regulate biological responses, because they contain multiple tyrosine phosphorylation sites that act as on/off switches to control insulin/IGF1 responses. Each tyrosine phosphorylation site is surrounded by a unique amino acid sequence that attracts and activates specific effector proteins [such as growth factor receptor–bound protein (Grb2), SHP2, and p85] (**Fig. 2**). Grb2 serves as an adapter

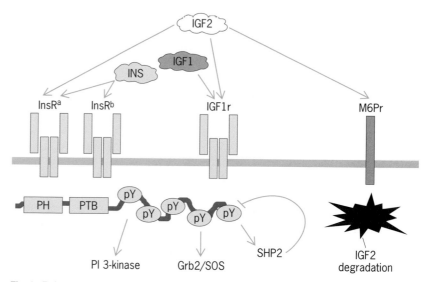

Fig. 1. Relation between the insulin family of receptors and the IRS proteins. The a- and b-isoforms of the insulin (INS) receptor (InsRᵃ, InsRᵇ) and the insulin-like growth factor receptor (IGFr) are tyrosine-specific protein kinases. Binding leads to a signal cascade that may activate phosphatidylinositol-3-kinase, Grb2/SOS, or SHP2. By contrast, insulin-like growth factor 2 (IGF2) binds preferentially to the mannose-6-phosphate receptor (M6Pr) which promotes IGF2 degradation; to promote growth, IGF2 binds to the InsRᵃ or IGF1r.

protein that couples IRS1 to the Erk1/2 mitogen-activated protein (MAP) kinase cascade; MAP kinases promote cell growth. Tyrosine phosphorylation sites in the carboxy (COOH) terminus bind and activate SHP2, a phosphotyrosine-specific phosphatase that contributes to the activation of MAP kinase or mediates the dephosphorylation and inactivation of IRS1. IRS proteins strongly bind p85, a regulatory subunit of the phosphatidylinositol-3-kinase, implementing activation. Phosphatidylinositol-3-kinase generates phospholipids that attract other enzymes to the plasma membrane. This step promotes the action

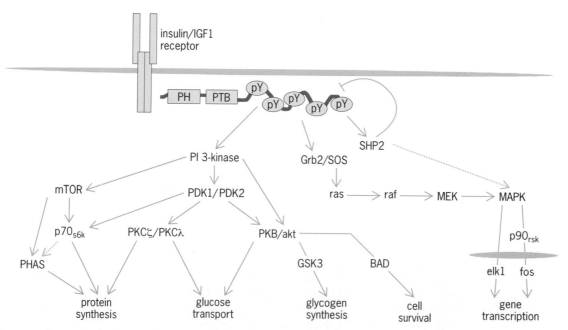

Fig. 2. Various pathways regulated by insulin and IGF1 through tyrosine phosphorylation of IRS proteins.

of insulin upon glucose transport, glycogen synthesis, protein synthesis, antilipolysis, and the control of hepatic gluconeogenesis via regulation of the expression of phosphoenolpyruvate carboxykinase. When IRS proteins fail to do their job and compensatory insulin secretion wanes, the liver produces more glucose than muscles can utilize, and adipose tissue releases fatty acid into the blood.

Insulin action. In efforts to dissect the components that are critical for normal glucose metabolism, many investigators examine the function of specific genes by altering their expression in mice. The elucidation of gene effect might unravel the complex pathophysiology of diabetes. Remarkably, the deletion of *irs2* from mouse chromosomes causes peripheral insulin resistance without diabetes after birth and during adolescence; however, young adults develop diabetes with defects in both insulin action and beta-cell insulin secretion. The result is remarkable, because it reveals the IRS2 signaling pathway to be essential for both peripheral insulin action and long-term beta-cell function. By contrast, the disruption of *irs1* causes peripheral insulin resistance without diabetes, because IRS2 continues to promote lifelong compensatory beta-cell hyperplasia and hyperinsulinemia. Recent evidence suggests that IGF1 receptor signaling plays an important role in beta-cell expansion, especially during the response to peripheral insulin resistance.

IRS2 is a common element in peripheral insulin action and beta-cell expansion and survival, and is essential for normal metabolic regulation. Scientists have searched without success so far for mutations in IRS2 that might contribute to diabetes in people. Reduced expressions of *irs2*, owing to mutations in the promoter region of the *irs2* gene, or mutations in transcription factors that regulate *irs2* expression are attractive candidates. By contrast, dysfunctional regulation of IRS2 might be a critical step in the progression to type 2 diabetes. Signaling pathways that are activated during chronic stress or obesity might disrupt IRS2 function. Obesity is well known to cause insulin resistance and beta-cell dysfunction in humans and in several animal models. However, the mechanism by which these metabolic intermediates interact with and inhibit the insulin signaling pathways is not well understood. Evidence is starting to point to an inhibitory block at the IRS proteins, possibly involving the phosphorylation of serine residues in IRS1 and IRS2 that inhibits insulin/IGF1 stimulated tyrosine phosphorylation and reduces normal signaling.

For background information *see* DIABETES; GROWTH FACTOR; INSULIN; PANCREAS; SIGNAL TRANSDUCTION in the McGraw-Hill Encyclopedia of Science & Technology.   Morris F. White

Bibliography. B. B. Kahn, Type 2 diabetes: When insulin secretion fails to compensate for insulin resistance, *Cell*, 92:593–596, 1998; S. Paradis et al., A PDK1 homolog is necessary and sufficient to transduce AGE-1 P13 kinase signals that regulate diapause in *Caenorhabditis elegans* [in Process Citation], *Genes Dev.*, 13(11):1438–1452, 1999; D. J. Withers et al., Disruption of IRS-2 causes type 2 diabetes in mice, *Nature*, 391(6670):900–904, 1998; D. J. Withers et al., Irs-2 coordinates Igf-1 receptor-mediated beta-cell development and peripheral insulin signalling, *Nat. Genet.*, 23(1):32–40, 1999; D. J. Withers and M. F. White, Insulin action and type 2 diabetes: Lessons from knockout mice, *Curr. Opin. Endocrinol. Diab.*, 6(2):141–145, 1999; L. Yenush and M. E. White, The IRS-signaling system during insulin and cytokine action, *BioEssays*, 19(5):491–500, 1997.

Interplanetary dust particles

Interplanetary dust particles (IDPs) are micrometer-sized objects that enter the Earth's atmosphere as part of the total solar system inventory of meteoroids. They have the lowest mass, only a few picograms to nanograms, of all meteoroids impinging on the atmosphere. Once freed from their parent bodies, they spiral in decaying orbits toward the Sun as a result of pressure effects by sunlight (Poynting-Robertson drag). In orbit they are also eroded by mutual collisions. These short-lived interplanetary dust particles spent about 10,000–100,000 years in space before falling into the Sun. When captured by the Earth's gravitational field, they enter the atmosphere at hypervelocity speeds of many kilometers per second. Between 120 and 80 km (75 and 50 mi) altitude the atmospheric density gradually increases enough for gentle deceleration of incoming dust by collisions with air molecules. Collected interplanetary dust particles have approximate orbital velocities between 11 and 20 $km \cdot s^{-1}$ (7 and 12 $mi \cdot s^{-1}$). During deceleration all interplanetary dust particles experience a brief (5–15 s) period of flash heating that causes the typically faster-moving cometary dust (Comet Halley's dust travels at 76 $km \cdot s^{-1}$ or 47 $mi \cdot s^{-1}$) to evaporate and become shooting stars. Interplanetary dust particles in the atmosphere are mostly asteroidal dust that entered at about 11 $km \cdot s^{-1}$ (7 $mi \cdot s^{-1}$) with approximately 20% from low-velocity comets. Flash-heating temperatures in 10-micrometer interplanetary dust particles are typically below 800°C (1472°F). When heated above about 1200°C (2192°F), due to a higher entry velocity or greater mass, they melt, forming cosmic spherules. In unmelted interplanetary dust particles the increased heating results in a loss of sulfur, recognizable modifications of the original minerals, and formation of characteristic iron oxide rims on particles. Unique stratospheric interplanetary dust particles are solid debris from solar system bodies other than those yielding the conventional meteorites and micrometeorites found in the Antarctic and Greenland ice sheets and deep-sea sediments. Interplanetary dust particles are important samples of comets and asteroids, including the icy, carbon-rich bodies in the outer asteroid belt. Information on the materials and processes that occurred in the solar system 4,560 million years ago could survive in the dust in these primitive small bodies but is mostly destroyed in conventional meteorites by parent body processes.

Collection. The atmosphere gently decelerates hypervelocity interplanetary dust particles to a few centimeters per second, after which they settle to the Earth's surface where they are lost to collection. Collection of interplanetary dust particles is relatively easy in the stratosphere using balloon-borne collectors above 30 km (19 mi) altitude. They are routinely collected in the lower stratosphere at approximately 18 km (11 mi) altitude using inertial-impact, flat-plate collectors mounted underneath the wings of high-flying aircraft. Collected interplanetary dust particles range from 2 to 60 μm, but a typical interplanetary dust particle is about 10 μm. The flux of 10-μm interplanetary dust particles is 1 particle per square meter per day, which makes efficient collection at the lower altitudes where their spatial density is $10^{-3}/m^3$ quite feasible. The evidence that unmelted interplanetary dust particles are extraterrestrial includes (1) high abundances of helium (He) and neon (Ne) and close-to-solar ^{3}He/^{4}He and ^{20}Ne/^{22}Ne isotope ratios from implantation by solar wind particles; (2) uniquely large deuterium (D) to hydrogen (H) [record: $\delta D(\%_0) = +50,000$] isotope ratios and ^{15}N/^{14}N [record: δ^{15}N$(\%_0) = +500$] isotope ratios measured by ion microprobes in carbonaceous materials from cold molecular clouds and the outer fringes of the solar system; and (3) solar flare tracks in silicate minerals such as enstatite, diopside, and magnesium-rich olivine (forsterite), and amorphous rims on these crystals, owing to the impact and deceleration of energetic nuclei in these minerals.

Classification. Unmelted interplanetary dust particles are first classified according to composition as chondritic and nonchondritic type, with subdivision in aggregates and fragments (**Fig. 1**). Chondritic IDPs have a composition similar to the chondritic meteorites which are the most primitive meteorites in the solar system. In chondritic interplanetary dust particles the relative abundances of C, O, Mg, Al, Si, Ca, Ti, Cr, Mn, Fe, and Ni are similar to those in the solar photosphere, and hence to the average solar system abundance. For a number of reasons, volatile element abundances such as sulfur and zinc in chondritic interplanetary dust particles can differ considerably from the solar values. Nonchondritic Fe-Ni sulfides (mostly pyrrhotite) and silicates (mostly olivine and pyroxenes) approximately 0.1 to 5 μm in size are embedded in the matrix of chondritic aggregates. The matrix contains three principal components: carbonaceous material, carbon-bearing ferromagnesiosilica, and ferromagnesiosilica ($\pm$Ca, Al) [**Fig. 2**]. These principal components resemble the (carbon-hydrogen-oxygen-nitrogen), "mixed carbon-silicate," and "silicate" dust analyzed by space probes in Comet Halley. Units with nanometer-sized Mg-Fe olivine and pyroxene, Fe-oxide, Fe-Ni-sulfides, and Fe-Ni metal crystals in an amorphous matrix are characteristic for the subset of iron-rich ferromagnesiosilica principal components. The magnesium-rich

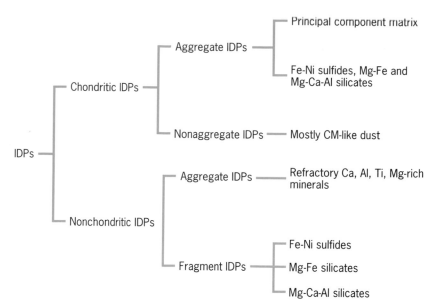

Fig. 1. Classification of interplanetary dust particles (IDPs) according to chemical composition, morphology, and mineralogy. Aggregate IDPs and fragments entered the atmosphere as individual IDPs and as parts of cluster IDPs, measuring 60–100 μm, that broke apart during collection. Chondritic cluster IDPs are assemblages of entities larger than ~10 μm and include chondritic aggregates, Fe-Ni sulfides, Mg-Fe silicate and Mg-Ca-Al silicate fragments, and rare refractory aggregates with distinctly nonchondritic element abundances. The chondritic nonaggregate IDPs resemble the matrix of CI and CM carbonaceous chondrite meteorites. [The carbonaceous (C) chondrites include four different petrographic classes that are each named after the first-described meteorite in each class. The most primitive class, CI, is named after the meteorite Ivuna, a hydrated meteorite that is characteristically free of chondrules. The CM class is named after the meteorite Mighei, a primitive meteorite with chondrules and a unique mineralogy of secondary minerals due to aqueous alteration.]

ferromagnesiosilica principal components typically consist of three large (up to 410 nm) associated grains, such as Mg-Fe olivine, Mg-Fe pyroxene, and amorphous calcium-bearing aluminosilica. Classification of chondritic interplanetary dust particles based on infrared spectroscopy reveals olivine-rich, pyroxene-rich, and phyllosilicate-rich groups. The

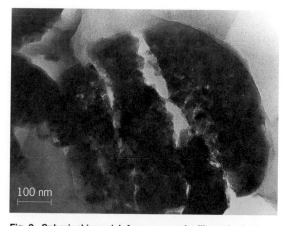

Fig. 2. Spherical iron-rich ferromagnesiosilica principal components with nanometer-sized crystals (black and gray specks) embedded in the amorphous matrix of a chondritic aggregate IDP viewed in the transmission electron microscope. The gray background is an epoxy wherein the IDP was embedded for cutting of 80-nm-thin transparent sections. During this process the samples suffer minor tearing apart.

Fig. 3. Scanning electron microscope image of a collected porous (or fluffy) chondritic aggregate IDP showing the matrix with smooth plates of Mg-Fe silicates. (*From F. J. M. Rietmeijer, interplanetary dust particles, in Planetary Materials, Reviews in Mineralogy, 1998; courtesy of the Mineralogical Society of America*)

first two groups are mostly porous aggregates (**Fig. 3**), and phyllosilicate-rich interplanetary dust particles are compact aggregates. This infrared classification does not consider the observations that all aggregate and cluster interplanetary dust particles are made out of the same building blocks and that they can contain all three of these minerals. It is more germane to classify the interplanetary dust particles using their building blocks instead of the mineralogy, including phyllosilicates that are secondary minerals that often form by the hydration of olivines and pyroxenes.

Mineral analyses. Analytical and transmission electron microscopes (ATEM) are used to characterize the grains that are typically a few nanometers to a few micrometers in size in aggregate interplanetary dust particles. The grain properties are size, composition, a crystalline or amorphous nature, defects such as solar flare tracks, and the oxidation states of carbon, sulfur, and iron such as Fe^0 (metal), Fe^{2+}, or Fe^{3+}. Synchrotron x-ray fluorescence can measure the minor and trace elements such as zinc and bromine, but the exact nature of their nonchondritic abundances is still uncertain. Aggregate interplanetary dust particles are often carbon-rich due to various unidentified hydrocarbons, polycyclic aromatic hydrocarbons, amorphous and poorly graphitized carbons, hexagonal diamond, and carbonates. Their identification relies on ATEM and Raman spectroscope analyses that determine the energy of the C-C and C-H bonds. Phyllosilicates such as serpentine and smectite, and salts such as Mg-Fe carbonates and Ca-Na sulfates, in interplanetary dust particles are evidence that water was available for hydrous alteration. Except for flash heating, there is little mineralogical evidence for other thermal episodes in the interplanetary dust particle. Recently ATEM analyses of aggregate interplanetary dust particles and vapor-condensed laboratory analogs indicate that the ferromagnesiosilica principal components were originally amorphous. It is not known if the minerals that are found in these principal components formed during flash heating or in the parent bodies.

Origins. The short-lived interplanetary dust is continuously replaced by dust ejected from active periodic comets from the Oort Cloud and Kuiper Belt. Dust is ejected during sublimation of ice at the nucleus surface during perihelion and becomes arranged in trails that move in the orbit of their parent comet. Dust is replenished by collisions among the moderately small bodies without visible cometary activity such as extinct and dormant comet nuclei and asteroids. The nonchondritic interplanetary dust particles could be fragments from earlier protoplanets that broke apart by collisions, and the fragments coaccreted with principal components into aggregates. The remarkably limited number of building blocks in chondritic aggregate and cluster interplanetary dust particles suggests that the accretion process repeated itself in a hierarchical manner. A combination of vapor condensation and thermal annealing including amorphization by energetic hydrogen and helium nuclei likely resulted in the formation of the ferromagnesiosilica principal components. There are many possibilities considering that the infrared reflectance spectra of chondritic aggregates and the iron-rich ferromagnesiosilica principal components resemble those of comets and interstellar dust and the icy, carbon-rich bodies in the outer asteroid belt.

Significance. Comets are believed to contain presolar dust from the solar nebula. It is possible that amorphous ferromagnesiosilica principal components could be the common presolar dust. The most likely sources of the collected interplanetary dust particles are energy-deficient small bodies that are not conducive to substantial postaccretion thermal and aqueous dust alteration. Because amorphous dust is more susceptible to alteration than mineral dust, mineralogical activity in the earliest icy protoplanets could be considerable, with important implications for the physical properties that are critical in defining comet nucleus sampling missions. Laboratory simulations of the physical processes that occur in comet nuclei during perihelion indicate that the temperatures could be sufficient for small-scale aqueous and thermal alteration.

Future studies. The ROSETTA mission to Comet 46P/Wirtanen in 2012 will determine the compositions and mass of the dust, using techniques that were also used on the Comet Halley missions. It will also acquire the first in situ atomic force microscope images of comet dust. The STARDUST mission will sample dust ejected from Comet P/Wild 2 during its 2003/2004 perihelion and will bring the samples to Earth. There are plans to drill a core sample in a comet nucleus and bring it to Earth. Both missions will provide the first comet nucleus samples for laboratory analyses and will allow comparison with the collected interplanetary dust particles.

For background information *see* ASTEROID; COMET; COSMIC SPHERULES; COSMOCHEMISTRY; ELEMENTS, COSMIC ABUNDANCE OF; HALLEY'S COMET;

INTERPLANETARY MATTER; METEORITE; MICRO-METEORITE; SOLAR SYSTEM; SPACE PROBE in the McGraw-Hill Encyclopedia of Science & Technology.

Frans J. M. Rietmeijer

Bibliography. D. E. Brownlee, Cosmic dust: Collection and research, *Annu. Rev. Earth Planet. Sci.*, 13:147–173, 1985; F. J. M. Rietmeijer, Interplanetary dust particles, in J. J. Papike (ed.), Planetary Materials, *Reviews in Mineralogy*, vol. 36, Chap. 2, pp. 1–95, 1998; S. A. Sandford, The collection and analysis of extraterrestrial dust particles, *Fundament. Cosmic Phys.*, 12:1–73, 1987.

Intraplate earthquakes

Intraplate (within the plate) earthquakes occur far removed from the plate boundaries. Although nearly two-thirds of the Earth's continental crust is stable interior crust, less than 10% of all earthquakes are intraplate earthquakes. The causes of intraplate earthquakes are poorly understood, but it is likely that they relate to the driving forces of plate tectonics. As the plates collide, separate, or slide past one another, some plates gain and other plates lose material at their edges, and the plate boundaries change over geologic time. Weakened former plate boundaries become part of the interiors of plates. Stresses originating at the edges of the plates or in the deeper crust may be localized (concentrated) by these weaker structures, causing intraplate earthquakes. Other, more localized possible causes of intraplate earthquakes include growing or shrinking glaciers, impoundment or drawdown of reservoirs, and upwelling of mantle plumes.

Characteristics. Intraplate earthquakes differ from interplate (between the plates) earthquakes, which occur at plate boundaries, in a number of ways. First, recurrence times of intraplate earthquakes are usually much longer than those of interplate earthquakes. Second, intraplate earthquake faults are rarely recognized at the surface. This is because the faults are generally buried under several kilometers of surface materials and the longer recurrence intervals allow any surface expression of faulting to be eroded. Third, intraplate earthquakes release more stress (force per unit area) than interplate earthquakes. The effects of intraplate earthquakes differ from those of interplate earthquakes in one very important aspect: the ground motion caused by intraplate earthquake seismic waves dissipates more slowly. The strong, coherent rocks that make up the interiors of plates transmit seismic energy more efficiently over longer distances than the less coherent, weaker rocks near plate boundaries.

The locations of intraplate earthquakes are not randomly distributed throughout the stable continental crust. Intraplate earthquakes, particularly those that are magnitude 6 or larger on the Richter scale, tend to occur in parts of continents that have undergone extension in the past. Extension occurs when tectonic forces stretch the crust of the Earth, causing the crust to become thinner and broken into fault-bounded blocks. Thinned extended crust within the continents is called a rift. Thinned extended crust along the edges of continents but not near a plate boundary is called a passive margin. Most of the earthquakes in and around the United States are in the west, along the plate-boundary faults and the wide zone of deformation associated with them (**Fig. 1**). Plate-boundary tectonics affects the United States from the Rocky Mountain front (between approximately 105° and 110°W) to the Pacific Ocean. The eastern two-thirds of the United States is stable continent. Thus, earthquakes located east of the Rocky Mountain front are intraplate earthquakes.

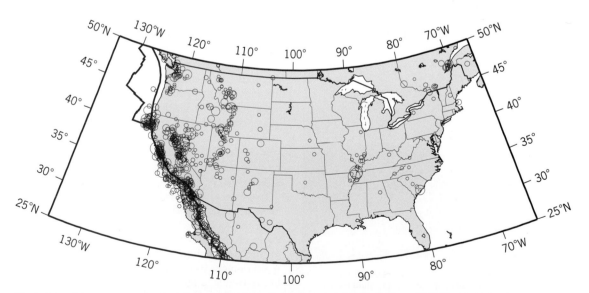

Fig. 1. Locations of magnitude 5 or greater earthquakes that occurred in and around the United States between 1701 and 1996 are shown as circles, whose size is proportional to the magnitude of the earthquake. The western plate boundary of the North American plate is shown by the heavy line near the west coast. The eastern plate boundary of the North American plate (not shown) is in the middle of the Atlantic Ocean. The three large circles near 90°W and about 36°N show the locations of the 1811–1812 New Madrid earthquakes, the largest intraplate earthquakes known to have occurred in the United States.

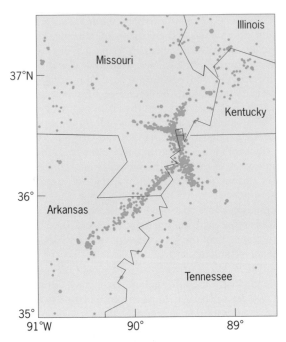

Fig. 2. Locations of earthquakes recorded in the New Madrid region since 1974 are shown as black dots, whose size is proportional to the magnitude of the earthquake. The earthquakes were recorded and located by the Cooperative New Madrid Seismic Network, operated by the University of Memphis Center for Earthquake Research and Information and St. Louis University.

Historic examples. During the winter of 1811–1812, three large intraplate earthquakes, each estimated to be approximately magnitude 8, occurred near the "boot heel" region of Missouri in the central United States. These earthquakes and thousands of aftershocks are known as the New Madrid earth-

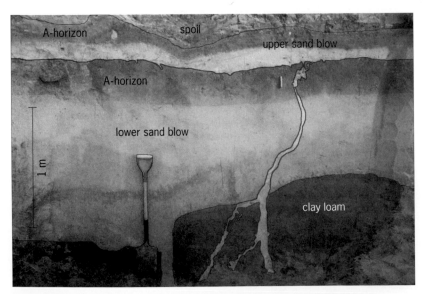

Fig. 3. Stacked sand blows in the walls of a drainage ditch in the New Madrid seismic zone. Sand was vented through cracks in the lower clay loam. Both of the sand blows were exposed at the ground surface long enough to form thick soil A-horizons, or accumulations of organic matter. The lower sand blow is probably from about the year 900; the upper sand blow is probably from the 1811–1812 New Madrid earthquakes. (*Courtesy of E. S. Schweig*)

quake sequence. Shaking from the mainshocks of this sequence was felt as far away as Montreal, Canada. Shaking from one of the mainshocks was strong enough to collapse scaffolding erected around the U.S. Capitol in Washington, DC. The New Madrid earthquakes altered the landscape tremendously. The course of the Mississippi River was changed as several waterfalls formed within the river and the land along the banks sank as much as 5 m (16 ft). Reelfoot Lake (3000 km²) formed in northwest Tennessee when the Reelfoot River access to the Mississippi River was blocked by uplifted land. Fortunately, few people lived in the central United States in the early 1800s. A repeat of even one of the large New Madrid earthquakes today would be devastating.

Another large intraplate earthquake, estimated to be approximately magnitude 7, occurred near Charleston, South Carolina, in 1886. At least 60 people died and the city suffered extensive damage. Shaking from the Charleston earthquake was felt as far away as northern New York and eastern Iowa. Plaster was shaken from walls in a building in Chicago, Illinois. Smaller earthquakes continue to occur in both the New Madrid and Charleston regions today.

Even though the numerous and widespread effects from both of these large intraplate earthquake sequences have been carefully and fully documented, no faults large enough to be the sources of the mainshocks have been clearly identified. The Charleston earthquake occurred in the passive margin along the east coast of the United States. The New Madrid earthquakes occurred in a buried rift that underlies part of Arkansas, Kentucky, Missouri, and Tennessee. But there is no surface expression of the faulting in either region.

Recurrence studies. A repeat of any of these earthquakes or the occurrence of a large intraplate earthquake in a previously inactive region poses enormous hazards. This has motivated scientific investigations to determine where and how often intraplate earthquakes occur and how big these earthquakes are expected to be. Scientists apply statistical methods using assumptions developed by studying the rate of earthquakes worldwide to estimate average recurrence intervals of large intraplate earthquakes in regions where repeat events have not occurred. For the New Madrid region, these statistical studies produce an estimated 500–600-year recurrence interval for an earthquake the size of those in 1811–1812.

Seismicity studies. The locations of the New Madrid and Charleston mainshock faults are inferred from the locations of the earthquakes recorded in those regions during the last several decades. The locations of earthquakes recorded in the New Madrid region since 1974 are concentrated along several linear trends (**Fig. 2**). A long southwest-northeast linear trend of earthquakes runs from northeast Arkansas to the Missouri-Tennessee border, where it terminates against a southeast-northwest linear trend of earthquakes. These two trends of earthquakes are assumed to represent faults, as are several of the smaller linear trends. For the most part, surface expressions of faulting along these trends of earthquakes are either absent or ambiguous. Over time, the Mississippi River and its tributaries have eroded uneven surfaces and covered the entire region with several kilometers of sediments. Thus, scientists must look below the surface to find evidence of faults.

Geophysical methods. Various methods of subsurface imaging and remote sensing have been used in intraplate regions to see below the surface. Seismic reflection and refraction methods image the rock layers in the subsurface using recordings of waves generated by explosive or vibrating sources. Other geophysical techniques, such as mapping the variations in the strength of the Earth's gravity or magnetic fields or differences in the electrical conductivity of rocks, can produce clear images of buried features such as rifts or large bodies of igneous rock. All of these methods have been used to look below the surface in the central and eastern United States. The long southwest-northeast linear trend of earthquakes in the New Madrid region coincides with the center of a buried rift. The terminus of this trend and the southeast-northwest linear trend of earthquakes coincide with a large, buried mass of igneous rock.

Paleoseismology. Paleoseismology is the study of prehistoric earthquakes, especially their size, location, and recurrence times, using the geologic record. Paleoseismologists collect detailed structural and stratigraphic information about near-surface rock layers and faults that are either naturally exposed at the surface (in an outcrop) or artificially exposed by shallow excavations. Fault movement during an earthquake can create offsets (abrupt changes in levels) in buried rock layers. In areas where sediments contain water, strong shaking during a large earthquake can transform the sediments into a liquid, a phenomenon called liquefaction. The differences in pressure between any buried liquefied and nonliquefied sediments force the liquefied sediments upward and onto the ground surface, forming a sand blow. Sand blows have the surface appearance and subsurface features of a volcano, but are composed of sand (**Fig. 3**). Various methods are used to estimate the ages of small pieces of organic materials (such as wood, charcoal, or shells) buried by sand blows. The ages of the buried materials provide estimates of the date of the earthquakes. The thickness of the overlying A-horizons, which are soils that develop after a sand blow was deposited, provides an estimate of the amount of time between the deposition of the upper and lower sand blows. The geographical distribution of liquefaction features of the same age can be used to estimate the epicenter and magnitude of the prehistoric earthquake that created the features. Evidence of liquefaction from about the year 900 in the New Madrid region covers an area nearly the same length as the liquefaction area documented from the 1811–1812 earthquake sequence. Paleoseismologists have also found evidence of liquefaction dating from about 1300 that covers a smaller area. They interpret these results to mean that a large New Madrid earthquake occurs about every 1000 or so years, and smaller but still damaging earthquakes occur more often.

Each type of study of intraplate earthquakes yields estimates of the sizes, locations, and recurrence intervals of large or damaging earthquakes. Unfortunately, there are large uncertainties associated with these estimates. Thus, many intraplate earthquake researchers currently are undertaking studies designed to reduce these uncertainties.

For background information *see* EARTHQUAKE; PALEOSEISMOLOGY; PLATE TECTONICS in the McGraw-Hill Encyclopedia of Science & Technology.

Kaye M. Shedlock

Bibliography. A. C. Johnston and E. S. Schweig, The enigma of the New Madrid earthquakes of 1811-1812, *Annu. Rev. Earth Planet. Sci.*, 24:339–384, 1996; J. P. McCalpin (ed.), *Paleoseismology*, Academic Press, 1996; R. S. Yeats, K. Sieh, and C. R. Allen, *The Geology of Earthquakes*, Oxford University Press, 1997.

Intraspecific variation

Individual organisms within a species vary morphologically (size, shape, color), physiologically, behaviorally, and demographically. Some humans are tall, some are short; some are blond, some are brunette. Some trees in a species grow tall with narrow, compact crowns; others are more stocky with dense, wide-radius crowns. Some dogs in a litter are more active and aggressive than some of the others. These variations are of genetic interest in terms of whether they are heritable. They are of ecological and evolutionary interest in terms of the environmental influences that shape them, both nongenetically in the present and genetically over an evolutionary time scale.

Background concepts. It is useful to generalize the patterns of intraspecific variation into several key concepts. Variation is a population phenomenon. Individual traits within a population vary according to some statistical frequency distribution. Thus in a human population, the heights of most individuals are near the population average, while progressively lower percentages of people are taller or shorter. Moreover, there is intrapopulation variation and interpopulation variation in the same species.

Taxonomic groups that have determinate growth (organisms that grow to relatively characteristic body size in an early stage of life and spend the remainder of their lives at a roughly constant adult size) are distinct from those with indeterminate growth. The latter tend to grow throughout their lives, even if at declining rates. Their growth rates, and ultimate sizes, may be strongly constrained by environmental factors, and they may never achieve the body size of conspecifics growing in more favorable environments. Animal groups that characteristically have indeterminate growth patterns are the ectothermic vertebrates, notably fishes and reptiles. Plants in general have indeterminate growth, being highly plastic in response to their physical environments.

Endothermic vertebrates, birds and mammals, and terrestrial arthropods with complex life histories typically have determinate growth patterns. However, their adult body sizes may vary slightly under such environmental pressures as nutritional deprivation and suboptimal physical environments. Traits of terrestrial arthropods other than body size are as profoundly influenced by their physical environments as are traits of ectothermic vertebrates.

Central theoretical questions. Variations in observable traits (morphological, behavioral, demographic) between individuals or populations are termed phenotypic variations. These variations may or may not be genetically determined. When they are genetically determined, the phenotypic variations are also genotypic variations. The statistical distribution of genes determining genotypic variations within a population is termed the allelic or gene frequency. The phenotypic distribution of a genetically determined trait in a population reflects the allelic frequencies of the genes that determine that trait. Much genetic variation is continuous (such as height, or weight at birth) as opposed to discrete (blue versus brown eye color). Quantitative genetics is used to describe this variation, and plant and animal breeding is based on selecting for particular extremes from distributions of continuous variation (even though the differences probably involve hundreds of gene loci, none of which are identified).

Two questions of particular ecological and evolutionary interest arise in connection with the genetic variation within a population. If it is assumed that one of the genotypes within a population is best adapted for survival and reproduction of offspring (is fittest), (1) why has selection not weeded out the other genotypes and left only the fittest one; or stated differently, what maintains variability in a population? (2) what factor or combination of environmental factors makes a given genotype optimal or fittest?

Finally, a great deal of research has striven to analyze the variations between populations of a given species. It must be determined if those differences are nongenetic and produced by contemporary environmental pressures, or if they are genotypic differences; and if so, what selective factors produced the evolutionary divergence? (Note that one basic definition of evolution is a change in gene frequency.)

Intrapopulation variation. Answers to the questions on intrapopulation variations have been sought in two ways. One is with a series of mathematical models of population genetics that make simplifying but reasonable assumptions about what population processes maintain allelic frequencies, and what causes them to change. The simplest models begin by assuming random interbreeding in large populations,

no genes that confer on their holders any adaptive advantage, no immigration of individuals from the outside, and no gene mutations. Under these admittedly oversimplified conditions, gene frequencies remain the same over time as individuals in a population periodically reproduce. This generalization is known as the Hardy-Weinberg Law.

Changes in allelic frequencies are predicted mathematically by models that represent small subsets of a population (demes) that do not interbreed with the whole. In these, chance combinations of alleles are maintained and gradually result in changes over time in gene frequencies—a process termed drift. Changes are predicted with more complex models that provide for gene mutations, alleles that confer superior fitness on some individuals, and introduction of individuals with different allelic frequencies. In general, population geneticists recognize that the entire question is extremely complex since most traits are determined by more than one gene, and many genes influence the nature of more than one trait, in some cases beneficially and in others detrimentally. The mathematics of models that accommodate this level of complexity becomes extremely difficult.

The question of what maintains variability in a population has also been addressed by deducing the fitness implications of observed phenotypic frequencies, and in some cases with experimental investigation. A much publicized example is the question of clutch size in birds. The eggs which a female lays at a single reproductive effort is termed the clutch. In many species, different females in a population lay clutches of different sizes, and one can think of the frequency distribution and mean size of clutches in a population. Most females lay clutches near the mean size, but some lay smaller and some lay larger clutches.

If fitness is determined by the largest number of offspring which a female produces, one might assume that the allelic frequency for clutch size would gradually shift to the genes influencing the largest clutches. Hence the question arises as to why the majority of females lay clutches near the population mean rather than the largest sizes. The British avian ecologist David Lack postulated that the fittest, and most frequent, clutch size is the largest number for which the adult birds can bring sufficient food to the hatchlings to assure their health and survival. This turns out to be the average clutch size. In the case of larger clutches, the adults are forced to make fewer trips per young per day to the nest in order to bring food to all young. As a result, the young grow more slowly, are not as strong, and survive less well; in total, fewer offspring go on to adulthood than in average-sized clutches.

The hypothesis has been looked on with favor by other avian ecologists, and was experimentally supported in one study that added eggs to nests and observed lower survival of the young. However, a recent study found lower survival in females laying large clutches, perhaps due to the stress of laying and of feeding a larger number of young. Variation in clutch size within a population is assumed to be maintained by gene mutation, ingress of other genotypes, and linkage of genes influencing clutch size to other genes determining alternative traits affecting fitness.

Interpopulation variation. There are clear differences in traits between populations of the same species. The genetic and evolutionary basis appears to fall along a spectrum of clearly nongenetic determination, commonly in species with indeterminate growth, at one end of the spectrum. At the other end are interpopulation differences that are probably adaptive with a genetic basis. Examples in between are uncertain in terms of their genetic basis.

Fish size is a classic example of variations between populations that are clearly environmentally determined, with no necessary assumption of genetic involvement. There are numerous cases in which fishes in a population with insufficient food sources grow slowly and never attain the sizes of conspecifics in richer environments or with lower population densities. A common fish-management practice is to encourage heavy fishing pressure to maintain low population densities, and high per capita levels of food supplies in order to encourage faster growth and size of the fish.

Another classic example of environmentally determined growth patterns and body shape is that of most tree species and many other species of plants. Trees that grow in the open some distance from each other, and are therefore unshaded, grow slowly in height and produce dense growths of lateral branches that grow to considerable lengths and form large, globular canopies. Trees of the same species growing closely together grow vertically at a faster rate, extend fewer and shorter lateral branches per unit of height, and shed (self-prune) the lower branches as they grow. The effect is small canopies near the apices of the trees.

The environmental factor producing these differences is light. The open-grown trees receive abundant light and do not need to grow rapidly to receive it. The closed-grown trees compete with each other for light and thus grow swiftly to avoid being shaded by their neighbors. In timber production, the closed-grown trees are valued for making the straightest boards with the fewest knots. Shaded house and garden plants stretch out in their growth to find light, and their long slender body forms are termed etiolated or leggy.

A number of organismal traits vary intraspecifically along gradients of physical environmental factors. The correlations, and in most the influences of the factors, are well established. But it remains to be determined with molecular genetic studies whether the populations along the gradients vary genetically and therefore have changed microevolutionarily, or whether the differences have simply been molded by the environment in species that can survive within these ranges of phenotypic variation.

Insects are common examples. Populations of species at low latitudes with long warm seasons may go through more life cycles or generations in a year than their conspecifics at high latitudes and short warm seasons. The Queensland fruit fly (*Dacus tryoni*) goes through eight generations in tropical, northeastern Australia, but only two in the temperate southeast. The result is very different levels of fitness measured on an annual time scale. Similar patterns have been shown for North American lizards.

One study examined the demographic performance of golden-mantled ground squirrel (*Spermophilus lateralis*) populations at different elevations in the Sierra Nevada of California. At the lower elevations the longer growing season allowed the young an extended period of growth before going into hibernation, and most females reproduced the year after their birth. At higher elevations, the short warm season allowed young animals less growth before being forced into hibernation. Most females did not breed until 2 or even 3 years of age, and they bore smaller litters.

A much publicized example is the latitudinal gradient in avian clutch size. Average clutch size of the European robin (*Erithacus rubecula*) is 6.3 in Scandinavia, 5.9 in Germany and France, 4.9 in Spain, and 4.2 in North Africa. David Lack has hypothesized that this is the result of longer daylengths at higher latitudes, providing the adults more time to feed more young adequately. But this does not satisfactorily explain the clutch-size gradient in precocial birds (such as ducks and pheasants) whose young forge for themselves within an hour or two after hatching and seek their own food. In addition, it does not explain similar, latitudinal gradients in the size of mammalian litters (number of young born at a single birth period).

Interpopulation variations are also produced by the selective action of biotic factors. A frequently cited example is the colors of British moths. Several species of moths in Britain were light-colored. Then, with the arrival of the industrial revolution and extensive use of coal for fuel, buildings and vegetation became coated with soot. Within a limited period of time, moths of these same species were predominantly dark-colored or even black. The prevailing interpretation is that once the backgrounds darkened, the light-colored moths became conspicuous and vulnerable to predation. Over time, predators gradually selected them out, shifting genotypic frequencies to a predominance of dark moths.

Another biotic example is the role of interspecific competition in causing character displacement, a shift in the nature of one or more traits. Individuals of species A may have a certain body form or size over much of its geographic range. But in parts of its range where it overlaps (is sympatric with) the range of one or more other species that use the same resources, individuals of species A may be of different size or have differently shaped appendages from their conspecifics in the nonoverlapping portion of the range. The change appears to enable the altered phenotypes to specialize their use on a subset of the resources and avoid or minimize competition with the other sympatric species using other subsets. The characters of species A have been displaced through selection, as may also have occurred in the sympatric species (organisms that occupy the same range as other species but maintain their identity by not interbreeding).

Character displacement has been observed in the bill shapes and plumages of Middle Eastern birds, shapes of appendages in worker castes of North American desert ants, and body sizes of Caribbean island lizards and North American coyotes.

For background information *see* BIOLOGICAL PRODUCTIVITY; ECOLOGICAL ENERGETICS; ECOLOGICAL METHODS; ECOSYSTEM; FOREST GENETICS; POPULATION DISPERSION; POPULATION ECOLOGY; POPULATION GENETICS in the McGraw-Hill Encyclopedia of Science & Technology.   Frederic H. Wagner

Bibliography. M. T. Bronson, Altitudinal variation in the life history of the golden-mantled ground squirrel (*Spermophilus lateralis*), *Ecology*, pp. 272–279, 1979; W. L. Brown, Jr., and E. O. Wilson, Character displacement, *Syst. Zool.*, pp. 49–64, 1956; J. D. Congdon and R. C. van Loben Sels, Relationships of reproductive traits and body size with attainment of sexual maturity and age in Blanding's turtles (*Emydoidea blandingi*), *J. Evol. Biol.*, pp. 547–557, 1993; D. W. Davidson, Size variability in the worker caste of a social insect (*Veromessor pergandei* Mayr) as a function of the competitive environment, *Amer. Nat.*, pp. 523–532, 1978; J. Harper, *Population Biology of Plants*, Academic Press, 1977; A. Hastings, *Population Biology/Concepts and Models*, Springer, 1997; M. T. Murphy, Evolution of clutch size in the Eastern Kingbird: Tests of alternative hypotheses, *Ecol. Monog.*, pp. 1–20, 2000; R. H. Peters, *The Ecological Implications of Body Size*, Cambridge University Press, 1983; J. Roughgarden, Niche width: Biogeographic patterns in *Anolis* lizard populations, *Amer. Nat.*, pp. 429–442, 1974; J. Sarukhan, M. Martinez-Ramos, and D. Pinero, The analysis of demographic variability at the individual level and its population consequences, in R. Dirzo and J. Sarukhan (eds.), *Perspectives on Plant Population Ecology*, Sinauer Associates, 1984.

Invertebrate evolution

The animal kingdom is composed of approximately 35 phyla, with each phylum representing a distinct body plan. Only a portion of one phylum (Chordata) includes vertebrates; the remainder are invertebrate animals. Traditional phylogeny is based on a number of morphological and developmental traits, or characters. The animal kingdom is probably derived from unicellular protozoanlike ancestors, most likely by the evolution of cytoplasmic separation to form multiple cells.

It is well accepted that most animal phyla were already present in Early Cambrian times, at least 540 million years ago, and some fossil animal embryos have been found in 570-million-year old deposits. Some recent and highly controversial fossil interpretations have suggested animal traces 1 billion years old, while some molecular studies have dated the origin of animal phyla at least as old. The 1-billion-year-old fossil animal traces are most likely misinterpreted, and molecular clock studies used to estimate divergence times are notoriously inaccurate.

The characters most often used to broadly outline invertebrate evolutionary relationships include the number of embryonic tissue layers, early embryonic cleavage patterns, body symmetry, the fate of the blastopore (the opening of the cavity of the gastrula of an embryo forming a primitive gut), the type and origin of the body cavity, and aspects of the digestive and excretory system. In phylogenetic studies, a group of organisms (taxon) is described as monophyletic if all members evolved from an immediate common ancestor and the taxon includes all the descendants of that ancestor. A group is paraphyletic if it *does not* include all descendants of an immediate common ancestor, and polyphyletic if members are derived from multiple common ancestors. One important criterion for a phylum is that its members be monophyletic.

Classic animal phylogeny. In classic animal phylogeny (**Fig. 1**), diploblastic animals (those with two embryonic tissue layers, ectoderm and endoderm) comprise a paraphyletic assemblage of ancient animals. Porifera, the earliest branching phylum, has an asymmetric body plan and is characterized by choanocytes, ciliated cells that move water through the animal. The diploblastic animals include several phyla (Cnidaria—jellyfish, corals and anemones; Ctenophora—comb jellies) with radial body symmetry and a radial embryonic cleavage pattern.

The evolution of a third embryonic tissue layer, the mesoderm, gave rise to the bilateral animals. In some classical phylogenies, the first group of bilaterians is considered to have been similar to flatworms, lacking a body cavity and having a mouth but no anus. Direct modern descendants would include Platyhelminthes (flatworms) and Nemertea (ribbon worms). As animals became larger and more complex, they required better organization, which led to the evolution of a body cavity and a flow-through gut with both a mouth and anus. A so-called false body cavity, or pseudocoelom, arose as a space between the mesoderm and endoderm, providing a place for organs. Approximately 10 phyla, notably Nematoda (roundworms) and Rotifera, are considered to have evolved from a pseudocoelomate ancestor and are collectively known as aschelminths.

A true body cavity, or eucoelom, arose as a space completely within the mesoderm. The eucoelomate ancestor led to two major groups of animals. In protostomes, the blastopore becomes the mouth, cleavage is spiral and determinate, and the eucoelom is thought to arise by a splitting of the mesoderm, or schizocoely. Protostomes include mollusks, annelids, and arthropods. Annelids and arthropods were considered to be a monophyletic group known as

Articulata because they are both segmented. In deuterostomes, the mouth arises from a secondary opening in the embryo, cleavage is radial and indeterminate, and the eucoelom develops as an outpocketing of the gut, or enterocoely. Deuterostomes include Echinodermata (urchins, starfish), Chordata (vertebrates, lancelets, tunicates), and Hemichordata (acorn worms). The lophophorates, a group of three phyla that are united by the presence of the lophophore, a distinctive feeding organ, have been considered as intermediate between protostomes and deuterostomes, or as basal deuterostomes because they have deuterostomelike embryonic cleavage patterns. The most recent and complete molecular clock analyses date the protostome/deuterostome split to a little more than 600 million years ago, a figure generally consistent with the fossil record.

Modern animal phylogeny. Three important developments in phylogenetic methods have occurred in recent years: electron microscopy, cladistics, and molecular studies. Electron microscopy is now widely used to study the ultrastructure of invertebrate morphology, helping to determine truly homologous structures. Cladistics is an approach to phylogeny that requires members of a taxon to have shared derived characters, or apomorphies. In molecular analyses, deoxyribonucleic acid (DNA) sequences from homologous genes of different taxa are aligned and analyzed to reveal evolutionary relationships. The combination of ultrastructural, cladistic, and molecular analyses have revealed many exciting new ideas about animal phylogeny (**Fig. 2**).

Ultrastructural studies suggested that body cavity type is not a reliable character in determining animal phylogeny, and these results have been confirmed with molecular studies, changing the view of the bilateral animals in a dramatic fashion. The lack of a body cavity and anus in flatworms is now considered a secondary loss. The pseudocoelom found in many "aschelminth" taxa is likely the result of partial loss or modification of a eucoelom; neither the pseudocoelomates nor acoelomates need be considered monophyletic groups. It also appears that early embryonic cleavage patterns have been misinterpreted, because lophophorates, once thought to be a monophyletic group associated with the deuterostomes, fall clearly among the protostomes in molecular studies.

Protostomes. The close association of arthropods and annelids to form Articulata based on the common character of segmentation is not supported by molecular analysis. Instead, the protostomes have been shown to be composed of two major groups, Ecdysozoa (molting animals) and Lophotrochozoa (nonmolting protostomes, including those with a trochophorelike larvae and those with a lophophore). Ecdysozoans do not exhibit spiral cleavage, while most of the lophotrochozoans do, so some authors use the name Spiralia for the nonmolting protostomes instead of Lophotrochozoa.

Ecdysozoa. Ecdysozoans are composed of two groups; the Panarthropoda, which include the phyla

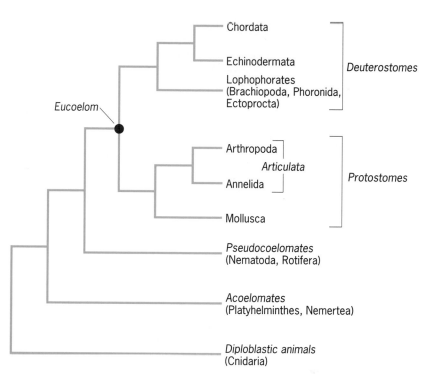

Fig. 1. In the old view, the type of body cavity played a prominent role in the major outline of animal evolution with three grades of bilateral animals: acoelomates, pseudocoelomates, and eucoelomates. Two major groups of eucoelomates were discerned: protostomes, with spiral cleavage and the mouth forming from the first embryonic opening; and deuterostomes, with radial cleavage and the mouth forming from a secondary embryonic opening. The three lophophorate phyla were considered to be deuterostomes. Within the protostomes, annelids and mollusks were usually placed together as Articulata because both are segmented. Only selected phyla are shown.

Arthropoda (insects, crustaceans), the arthropodlike Onychophora (velvet worms), and Tardigrada (water bears); and the Cycloneuralia, containing the former aschelminth groups Nematoda, Nematomorpha, Priapulida, Kinorhyncha, and Loricifera. Precise relationships within Ecdysozoa remain uncertain. In classical views of phylogeny, molting was considered to be a convergent character which evolved independently several times; while in the modern view, segmentation is considered a convergent character.

Lophotrochozoa. Lophotrochozoa appears to be composed of two clades or branches. The first includes Annelida (segmented worms) and Mollusca (clams, squid), the lophophorate phyla (Ectoprocta, Phoronida, Brachiopoda), Entoprocta (nodding heads), and Sipuculida (peanut worms). Cladistic and molecular studies have shown that some taxa previously associated with annelids but considered to be separate phyla (Echiura, Pogonophora) are now included within the annelids. The other group of lophotrochozoans are those associated with Platyhelminthes (flatworms) and include Rotifera, Gastrotricha, Gnathostomulida, and the recently described phylum Cycliophora. Acanthocephala, a group of large parasitic worms once considered to be an independent phylum, has been shown to be a subgroup of Rotifera, a phylum of microscopic free-living animals.

Deuterostomes. Deuterostomes are composed of four major clades. Molecular analysis demonstrates

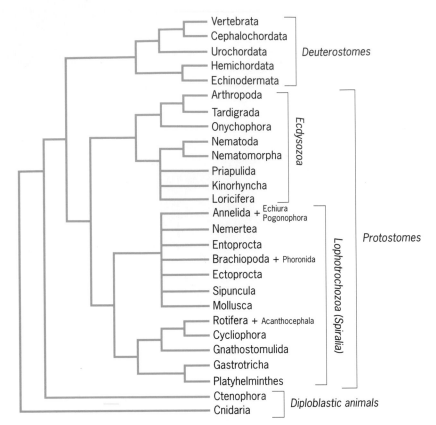

Fig. 2. In the new view, ultrastructure, cladistics, and molecular analysis have dramatically altered the interpretation of animal evolutionary relationships. The type of body cavity and the presence of segmentation are no longer considered important characters in defining the broad outline of animal phylogeny. Instead, it appears that there were three great radiations of bilateral animals: the molting protostomes (Ecdysozoa), the nonmolting protostomes (Lophotrochozoa), and the deuterostomes. The lophophorates appear to be nonmolting protostomes, rather than deuterostomes as in the old view. The acoelomate and pseudocoelomate phyla are intermingled with coelomate phyla among the protostomes. Parts of the tree where exact branching patterns are still uncertain are shown with straight lines of equal length. Taxa once considered to be independent phyla but now placed as subtaxa within other phyla are shown in a smaller font by a plus sign to the right of the phylum to which they belong.

that Chordata forms a monophyletic group with cephalochordates closely associated with the vertebrates, and urochordates as a more distantly related group. The other deuterostome lineage consists of Hemichordata and Echinodermata as sister taxa. Lophophorates are not associated with the deuterostomes.

Significance of new view. Under the old view of animal phylogeny, bilateral animal evolution was considered to consist of two major radiations, that of the protostomes and that of the deuterostomes. According to the new view, there were three great radiations of bilateral animals: deuterostomes, lophotrochozoans, and ecdysozoans. Invertebrate model organisms are often utilized to investigate aspects of biology that cannot easily be studied in humans or other vertebrates. Phylogeny indicates that biological mechanisms and systems found in one animal should be similar in another animal. The most studied invertebrate model organisms are the fruit fly *Drosophila melanogaster* (an arthropod) and the nematode *Caenorhabditis elegans*. Under the old view, these two invertebrates were considered to

be only distantly related, leading to the assumption that any biological mechanism discovered in both animals would likely be universal to all animals. Under the new view, they are both within the Ecdysozoa taxon, and it is likely that at least some aspects of their biology are related to molting and therefore not applicable to either deuterostomes or lophotrochozoans. The complete genome sequences of both *D. melanogaster* and *C. elegans* have recently been completed, but it is clear that there is a need for establishment of a new invertebrate model organism from the lophotrochozoans.

For background information *see* ANIMAL EVOLUTION; ANIMAL SYSTEMATICS; INVERTEBRATE EMBRYOLOGY; PHYLOGENY; TAXONOMIC CATEGORIES in the McGraw-Hill Encyclopedia of Science & Technology.

James R. Garey

Bibliography. A. M. A. Aguinaldo et al., Evidence for a clade of nematodes, arthropods and other moulting animals, *Nature*, 387:489–493, 1997; G. Balavoine and A. Adoutte, One or three Cambrian radiations?, *Science*, 280:397–398, 1998; J. R. Garey and A. Schmidt-Rhaesa, The essential role of "minor" phyla in molecular studies of animal evolution, *Amer. Zool.*, 38:907–917, 1998; J. Pechenik, *The Biology of the Invertebrates*, 4th ed., McGraw-Hill, New York, 2000.

Latest Paleocene thermal maximum

Superimposed on generally warm climates of the early Tertiary Period was an abrupt and extreme warming interval at the end of the Paleocene Epoch some 55 million years ago. This event, the latest Paleocene thermal maximum (LPTM), coincided with a mass extinction of deep-sea organisms and a sudden radiation of terrestrial mammalian orders, including primates. The LPTM also was characterized by a global carbon-isotope excursion that was caused by a massive injection of carbon into the ocean and atmosphere. All of these phenomena were likely related to the escape of large amounts of biogenic methane from gas hydrate deposits on the sea floor. Although many details surrounding the LPTM are poorly known, it is probably the best past analog for understanding long-term effects of future fossil fuel inputs to the atmosphere.

Abrupt ocean warming. Stable isotopes are central to understanding global warming and carbon cycling during the LPTM. Many elements, including oxygen and carbon, have multiple stable isotopes, each with the same number of protons but different number of neutrons. In the case of oxygen with 8 protons, there are two dominant stable isotopes, ^{16}O with 8 neutrons and ^{18}O with 10 neutrons. The abundance of stable isotopes in a substance can be determined accurately with a mass spectrometer. Measured stable isotopes typically are normalized to a standard and expressed in delta (δ) notation, whereby a heavy isotope is compared to a light isotope in units of per mille (‰). Positive and negative values in δ signify relative enrichments and depletions of the heavy isotope. For example, a substance with a negative $\delta^{18}O$ is depleted in ^{18}O (or enriched in ^{16}O) relative to a standard.

When calcium carbonate ($CaCO_3$) precipitates from water, the $\delta^{18}O$ of the mineral phase decreases with water temperature according to established equations. Many marine organisms make tests or shells of calcium carbonate that can be extracted from sediment or sedimentary rocks and subsequently analyzed for isotopic composition. By this procedure, ancient water temperatures can be estimated. Carbonate tests of single-celled foraminifera are particularly useful in these paleotemperature investigations. Their cosmopolitan distribution, small size, and easy identification allow numerous specimens of a single species to be collected from sediment deposited in many regions of the globe. Moreover, for at least 150 million years different species of foraminifera have inhabited different depth ranges in the ocean. The temperature profile of an ocean water column can be reconstructed through time by determining the $\delta^{18}O$ of planktic foraminifera that lived in surface waters and benthic foraminifera that lived on the sea floor from sequential samples of sediment in cores.

Records of $\delta^{18}O$ from foraminiferal tests show a change across the LPTM that is unique in the last 90 million years. Both planktic and benthic records contain a pronounced drop of about 1.5‰ over several centimeters followed by a gradual return to previous values. Using established isotope equations and quality age constraints, this change in the $\delta^{18}O$ of foraminiferal calcium carbonate indicates that ocean temperatures, shallow and deep, soared by 5–8°C (9–14.4°F) within 10,000 years and subsequently cooled over the next 100,000 years. The reconstruction of past temperatures on land or in the ocean by other techniques is more complicated. Nevertheless, current work using other approaches supports the general hypothesis that the entire ocean and atmosphere warmed abruptly by at least 5°C (9°F).

Benthic foraminiferal extinctions. Between 40 and 60% of benthic foraminiferal taxa in the deep ocean disappeared in the latest Paleocene. In many locations the last appearances of these benthic species occurred over several centimeters and without introduction of new species so that faunal diversity suddenly plummeted. This striking benthic foraminiferal extinction, unparalleled in the last 90 million years, happened globally and precisely over the 10,000 years of extreme bottom-water warming during the LPTM. However, the actual cause of the deep-ocean extinction appears to have been a simultaneous combination of three key factors: increased temperature, decreased dissolved oxygen (O_2), and enhanced calcium carbonate dissolution. In several marine sediment records, unusual laminated sediments and benthic faunal assemblages indicative of low O_2 conditions immediately follow the extinction. In these same records and many others, the total amount of calcium carbonate drops and foraminiferal tests are partly dissolved. The latter observation suggests that the pH of the deep ocean suddenly dropped during the LPTM.

Radiation of mammalian orders. Although the Age of Mammals begins at the Cretaceous/Tertiary boundary about 65 million years ago, the most significant change in mammal evolution occurred about 10 million years into the Tertiary. In both Europe and North America, vertebrate fossil assemblages of early Tertiary age are dominated by the extinct mammalian orders Champsosaurus and Plesiadapidae. These are overlain by entirely different vertebrate fossil assemblages that include the modern and cosmopolitan orders Primates, Perissodactyla (odd-toed hoofed mammals such as horses), and Artiodactyla (even-toed hoofed mammals such as camels). Paleontologists have recognized this major distinction between Paleocene and subsequent mammal orders for over a century. Only recently, however, has it become clear that modern mammal orders appeared suddenly and simultaneously across all continents of the Northern Hemisphere and precisely during the LPTM. This discovery again comes through stable isotopes.

Global carbon isotope excursion. Carbon with 6 protons has two stable isotopes, ^{12}C with 6 neutrons and ^{13}C with 7 neutrons. During chemical reactions such as photosynthesis or calcium carbonate precipitation, the two isotopes can be separated. The variety of natural compounds containing carbon can thus have a large range in their carbon isotopic composition, or $\delta^{13}C$.

The exogenic carbon cycle includes all carbon in the ocean, atmosphere, and biomass. Each of these major carbon reservoirs contains some mass of carbon with an average $\delta^{13}C$. Carbon transfers between these internal reservoirs through exchange reactions. For example, the atmosphere and biomass exchange carbon through photosynthesis and respiration. Carbon moves through the entire exogenic carbon cycle in less than 2000 years at present and presumably in the past. At present, the total mass of carbon in the exogenic carbon cycle is enormous, about 4.6×10^{13} tons (4.2×10^{13} metric tons).

Carbon is added to and removed from the exogenic carbon cycle through several well-known external inputs and outputs of different $\delta^{13}C$. In particular, rivers, weathering, and volcanoes add carbon to the ocean and atmosphere, whereas calcium carbonate and organic matter deposition remove carbon from the ocean and land. Much like a water tank, the mass and composition of the exogenic carbon cycle can change through time because of variations in external inputs and outputs.

At least 30 different $\delta^{13}C$ records show an extraordinary −3‰ anomaly across the LPTM. These records have been constructed from planktic and benthic foraminiferal tests and bulk calcium carbonate of all oceans, and terrestrial calcium carbonate and organic matter from multiple continents. The $\delta^{13}C$ anomaly immediately follows the $\delta^{18}O$ excursion and benthic foraminiferal extinction in marine records, and coincides with the appearance of modern mammal orders in terrestrial records.

The magnitude, timing, and global nature of the $\delta^{13}C$ excursion across the LPTM indicates that the entire exogenic carbon cycle suddenly and coincidentally became greatly enriched in ^{12}C. No conceivable mechanisms exist to rapidly and globally remove massive quantities of ^{13}C-rich carbon. Thus, the LPTM $\delta^{13}C$ anomaly reflects a rapid and prodigious injection of ^{12}C-rich carbon to the ocean and atmosphere. Simple calculations demonstrate that the rate of carbon addition must have approached that of current industrial inputs of fossil fuel to the atmosphere. An outstanding problem for the earth science community is understanding how such quantities of carbon could have been naturally released 55 million years ago.

Methane release from sea floor. Gas hydrates are crystalline substances composed of cages of water molecules that surround molecules of low-molecular-weight gas. The stability of these compounds depends on temperature as well as pressure and gas concentration. Gas hydrates will dissociate (melt) to constituent water and gas phases with a prescribed increase in temperature.

Gas hydrates naturally occur in the pore space of deep-sea sediment on many continental slopes because bacterial decay of organic matter produces large quantities of methane (CH_4) over time. Although gas hydrates are restricted to the upper few hundred meters of sediment because of increasing temperatures with depth, regions with gas hydrate can cover vast areas of the sea floor and store enormous quantities of carbon. For example, the crest of the Blake Ridge off the southeast coast of the United States probably contains about 3.9×10^{10} tons (3.5×10^{10} metric tons) of carbon as methane, an amount equivalent to about 7% of the entire terrestrial biosphere. Current estimates in the literature place the total mass of carbon in present-day marine gas hydrate deposits at 1.3×10^{13} tons ($1.1 \times$

10^{13} metric tons). Most of this gas is extremely enriched in ^{12}C (average $\delta^{13}C$ of $-60\%o$) because both original organic matter production and bacterial methane generation significantly fractionate the isotopes of carbon.

All of the phenomena discussed previously can be linked by a single hypothesis involving a sudden change in ocean circulation and rapid escape of about 2.2×10^{12} tons (2.0×10^{12} metric tons) of methane from gas hydrate reservoirs on continental slopes (see **illus.**). Similar to the present, vast quantities of ^{12}C-rich methane were stored as gas hydrate in sediment on continental slopes. These slopes were bathed in relatively cold water that formed and sank at high latitudes. However, long-term global warming during the late Paleocene pushed the ocean-atmosphere system past some critical threshold, causing warm surface waters to sink at low latitudes, and intermediate- to deep-ocean temperatures to rise. This warming propagated into the sediments, converting once solid gas hydrates into free gas bubbles. The resulting increase in pore pressure at depth led to sediment failure and the release of massive quantities of methane into the ocean. The gaseous methane reacted with dissolved O_2 to produce ^{12}C-enriched carbon dioxide that caused pronounced carbonate dissolution and then propagated into the atmosphere and biomass. Higher bottom-water temperature, lower dissolved O_2, and greater carbonate dissolution killed many of the benthic foraminifera. On land, higher pCO_2 and elevated temperatures quickly opened high-latitude migration routes for the widespread dispersal of mammals as Europe, North America, and Asia were connected near the Arctic Circle 55 million years ago. Global carbon and oxygen cycles gradually returned to equilibrium conditions following the LPTM, although marine and terrestrial ecosystems were forever changed.

There is at least one critical test of this extraordinary story. One should be able to drill locations on Paleocene continental slopes and find single sediment sections across the LPTM that contain remarkable negative $\delta^{18}O$ and $\delta^{13}C$ excursions and evidence for sediment failure, carbonate dissolution, dissolved oxygen deficiency, and benthic foraminiferal mass extinctions. The first of these sites was drilled recently and the predicted section was found.

For background information *see* BIOMASS; BIOSPHERE; CARBON; CARBONATE MINERALS; CRETACEOUS; EXTINCTION (BIOLOGY); FORAMINIFERIDA; HYDRATE; METHANE; PALEOCENE; PHOTOSYNTHESIS; RADIOISOTOPE; TERTIARY in the McGraw-Hill Encyclopedia of Science & Technology.   Gerald Dickens

Bibliography. G. Dickens, The blast in the past, *Nature*, 401:752–755, 1999; W. Clyde and P. Gingerich, Mammalian community response to the latest Palaeocene thermal maximum: An isotaphonomic study in the northern Bighorn Basin, Wyoming, *Geology*, 26:1011–1014, 1998; M. Katz et al., The source and fate of massive carbon input during the Latest Paleocene Thermal Maximum,

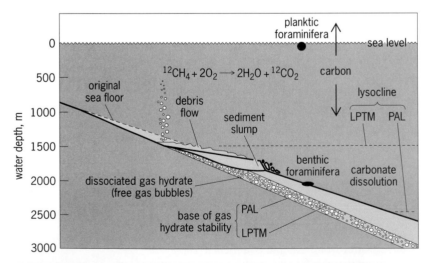

Release and fate of methane from gas hydrates during the Late Paleocene thermal maximum.

Science, 286:1531–1533, 1999; J. Kennett and L. Stott, Abrupt deep sea warming, paleoceanographic changes and benthic extinctions at the end of the Palaeocene, *Nature*, 353:319–322, 1991.

Lipoprotein

Cholesterol is an essential component of all animal cell membranes, especially the limiting plasma membrane. It must be made available in sufficient amount either by synthesis in situ or by acquisition from the diet. Yet, the accumulation of excess cholesterol in cells and tissues can be toxic. Thus, a highly regulated system has evolved for the synthesis and distribution of cholesterol within and between cells. This is particularly important in the brain, which by far has the highest concentration of cholesterol in the body. Indeed, the central nervous system has about 25% of the total body cholesterol of an adult animal.

Distribution. The protein components that combine with lipids to form lipoproteins are termed apolipoproteins or apoproteins. Apoprotein E (apoE) is an important component of the system that distributes cholesterol between cells. It is one of the apoproteins that forms lipoproteins responsible for the distribution of cholesterol, triglyceride, and phospholipids between the liver, intestine, and peripheral tissues. It is associated with three major subclasses of circulating lipoproteins: chylomicrons, very low density lipoprotein (VLDL), and high-density lipoprotein (HDL). Low-density lipoprotein (LDL), which carries the largest load of cholesterol as cholesteryl ester, is notably free of apoE. Dietary fat (triglycerides) and cholesterol are packaged by the intestine as chylomicrons (lipid droplets), and they are metabolized (see **illus.**) to form remnants that are taken up by the liver. Chylomicrons do not contain apoE when they are secreted by the intestine but acquire it rapidly from other lipoproteins as they circulate in the plasma. The acquisition of apoE is important because it acts as a ligand for the recognition and removal of the chylomicron remnants in the liver by one of the three liver cell surface molecules: low-density lipoprotein receptor, low-density lipoprotein receptor–related protein (LRP), or heparan sulfate proteoglycan. This transport system distributes fatty acids from the diet to muscle, including heart muscle, and to adipose tissue, and delivers dietary cholesterol to the liver. The removal of fat-rich chylomicrons from the blood is such a high priority (otherwise the blood would rapidly become creamy) that there is more than one pathway for the removal of their remnants by the liver.

Just as the chylomicron system distributes dietary fat to tissues, an analogous system delivers triglyceride (fatty acid) and cholesterol from the liver to the peripheral tissue, including muscle and adipose tissue. The liver produces very low density lipoprotein, which contains triglycerides and their constituent fatty acids. These are made from excess carbohydrate

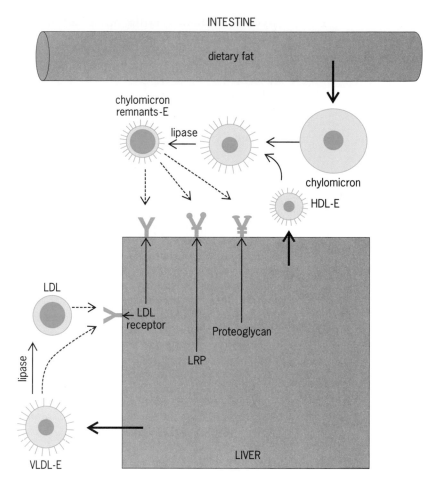

Lipoprotein formation and clearance in the liver. Dietary fat is formed into chylomicrons (rich in triglyceride but lacking apoE) by the intestine. ApoE is acquired by chylomicrons from other lipoproteins, such as high-density lipoprotein in the circulation (HDL-E). Lipoprotein lipase acts on chylomicrons as they circulate to produce chylomicron remnants with apoE. The latter are taken up by the liver after binding to one of three cell-surface molecules—low-density lipoprotein (LDL) receptor; LDL receptor–related protein (LRP); or heparan sulfate proteoglycan—perhaps acting cooperatively. Liver triglyceride is secreted as very low density lipoprotein containing apoE (VLDL-E). It may recycle to the liver via the LDL receptor or be converted by lipase action to low-density lipoprotein, which is in turn taken up by the LDL receptor. Lipase action on very low density lipoprotein results in the loss of apoE, so low-density lipoprotein lacks this apoprotein. Lipoproteins contain surface molecules (depicted as blue circle) which include protein, phospholipid, and free cholesterol. The core or center of the lipoprotein contains either cholesteryl ester (solid blue balls) or triglyceride (gray background in lipoprotein core). The proportion of cholesteryl ester and triglyceride changes as lipoprotein is processed by lipases. The apoE on lipoprotein surfaces is depicted as radial spikes.

(not derived from adipose tissue) or from fatty acids that are mobilized from adipose tissue, particularly during fasting. ApoE is an important component of very low density lipoprotein during its assembly in liver. Very low density lipoprotein is metabolized in the circulation to generate low-density lipoprotein, which contains little or no apoE. Some apoE secreted from the liver is associated with high-density lipoprotein or remains associated with the liver cell surface, where it is available to enrich and promote the uptake of incoming remnant particles. Low-density lipoprotein is cleared only by the LDL receptor, which recognizes the major apoprotein of low-density lipoprotein, apoprotein B100. The LDL receptor–related protein does not recognize this protein. Individuals with familial hypercholesterolemia (excessive cholesterol in the blood) lack normal LDL receptors, have very high blood cholesterol levels in the form of low-density lipoprotein, and develop premature and florid atherosclerosis.

ApoE. ApoE in humans has 299 amino acids and exists in the population in three major forms or isoforms that are genetically determined. These are designated apoE2, E3, or E4, which differ from one another by a single amino acid. ApoE2 has a cysteine at position 158, whereas the other two forms have arginine at this position. ApoE4 has arginine at position 112, whereas the other two forms have cysteine in this position. The apoE3 gene is most frequent in the population, and apoE2 gene is the least frequent. Each individual has two copies of the apoE gene encoding one of the apoE isoforms, so the circulating apoE may be of one isoform or a mixture of two isoforms. Most circulating apoproteins are made either in the liver or in the intestine. ApoE is a major exception to this generalization. It is made in many cells of the body, including some cells of the brain and peripheral nervous system, suggesting that it also has local functions in the organs and cells where it is produced. However, it is not made in the intestine.

ApoE3 and E4 are equivalent as ligands for the LDL receptor and lipoprotein receptor–related protein, whereas apoE2 is a less efficient ligand for lipoprotein receptor–related protein and much less for the LDL receptor. So people who have two copies of E2 (are genetically E2/E2) and who additionally have a tendency to overproduce very low density lipoprotein, have elevated plasma cholesterol in very low density lipoprotein. These individuals are said to have type III hyperlipoproteinemia (excessive lipoprotein in the blood) and generally have atherosclerotic vascular disease. Among the general population, those who express apoE4 have higher plasma cholesterol levels than those with apoE3, whereas those expressing apoE2 have lower cholesterol levels. The variation of apoE isoforms accounts for about 10% of the population variation in blood cholesterol levels and a similar variation in atherosclerosis. It is well known that there is a strong correlation between blood cholesterol level and the extent of atherosclerosis, which is the basis for most cardiovascular disease in the American population. But the effect of apoE on blood cholesterol levels is probably not its only influence on atherosclerosis. Atherosclerosis is a disease affecting the major blood vessels, such as the aorta, coronary arteries, or carotid arteries. Disease begins as fatty deposits at select sites of the blood vessels. These fatty deposits are the result of the accumulation in the artery wall of low-density lipoprotein, much of which is modified and taken up by infiltrating blood monocytes that become loaded with fat to form fatty macrophages or foam cells. Such fat-loaded macrophages produce apoE locally, as a function of the amount of cholesterol they have taken up. This locally produced apoE has an important influence on the fate of the ather-

osclerotic lesion. The local influence of apoE has been highlighted in mice engineered genetically to lack apoE. Such animals manifest not only marked hypercholesterolemia, reflecting the role of apoE in the clearance of very low density lipoprotein and chylomicron remnants, but also spontaneous atherosclerosis that is very similar to the disease seen in humans. In these animals, the restoration by bone marrow transplantation of macrophages producing apoE significantly reduces the atherosclerosis, but it has only modest influence on the blood cholesterol.

Alzheimer's disease. High levels of apoE are also made in the brain. The astrocytes, which are supporting cells of the brain rather than nerve cells, make apoE. ApoE probably plays a critical role in the redistribution of cholesterol and perhaps other lipids within the brain. Two observations have highlighted the importance of brain apoE. First, apoE has been implicated in the repair of injured nerves, probably by salvaging the membrane cholesterol of the damaged nerve and redistributing it to the growing end of the regenerating nerve fiber. Second, apoE4 is much more common in patients with Alzheimer's disease than it is in the general population. The presence of apoE4 is now an established risk factor for this disease. It is also a risk factor for a poor prognosis in head trauma incidents (such as boxing injury), strokes, and hemorrhages within the brain. These observations are compatible with a beneficial role for apoE3 and apoE2 but not apoE4 in the repair of injury to the nervous system. The precise mechanism of these effects is not clear. In neuronal culture, apoE3 (and apoE2) but not apoE4 promotes the growth of neural processes. ApoE3 accumulates in nerve cells much better than apoE4 does. Other mechanisms relate to the influence of apoE on plaque deposition. Alzheimer's disease is associated with the deposition of amyloid plaque in the extracellular spaces of the brain, especially the hippocampus and the cortex—areas associated with memory and higher cerebral function. A major constituent of this plaque is the small β-amyloid protein, which may be toxic to nerve cells. ApoE can form a complex with the β-amyloid protein and perhaps facilitate either its removal or its detoxification. ApoE3 (and probably apoE2) does this much more effectively than apoE4.

The precise role of apoE in the functioning of the nervous system and its repair remains unclear. Many functions have been proposed. An understanding of the differences that account for the apoE3 (and apoE2) protective role in the pathogenesis of Alzheimer's disease in contrast to that of apoE4 should illuminate the important function of apoE in the brain. As a first approximation, it may be inferred that in the brain, as elsewhere in the body, apoE promotes the redistribution of lipids needed for nerve cell repair, although other possible functions need to be considered.

For background information *see* ALZHEIMER'S DISEASE; ARTERIOSCLEROSIS; CHOLESTEROL; LIPID

METABOLISM; LIPOPROTEIN; METABOLIC DISORDERS in the McGraw-Hill Encyclopedia of Science & Technology.   Godfrey Getz

Bibliography. J. Jordan et al., Isoform specific effect of apolipoprotein E on cell survival and β amyloid-induced toxicity in rat hippocampal pyramid neuronal cultures, *J. Neurosci.*, 18:195–204, 1998; R. W. Mahley and Y. Huang, Apolipoprotein E from atherosclerosis to Alzheimer's disease and beyond, *Curr. Opin. Lipidol.*, 10:207–217, 1999; R. W. Mahley and Z.-S. Ji, Remnant lipoprotein metabolism: Key pathways involving cell surface heparan sulfate proteoglycans and apolipoprotein E, *J. Lipid Res.*, 40:1–16, 1999; A. D. Roses, Apolipoprotein E, a gene with complex biological interactions in the aging brain, *Neurobiol. Dis.*, 4:170–186, 1997.

Lithium batteries

Lithium batteries have become commercially important power sources because they can supply significantly more energy for a given volume or weight of cell in comparison with conventional cells, such as alkaline zinc or nickel-cadmium. The reason is that lithium is the lightest metal and has one of the highest electrode potentials. One kilogram of lithium can supply 3860 ampere-hours of electricity in comparison with 820 Ah for zinc or 260 Ah for lead. However, because lithium is such an active metal, it reacts with water. Therefore, lithium battery electrolytes must be based on nonaqueous solvents or polymers, manufacture must be carried out in specially constructed dry rooms, and safety precautions are necessary both for use and for disposal of lithium cells.

A lithium battery consists of an anode (negative electrode) or lithium source and a cathode (positive electrode) or lithium sink, separated by an ion-conducting electrolyte (**Fig. 1**). When the cell is discharged through a load, a complete chemical re-

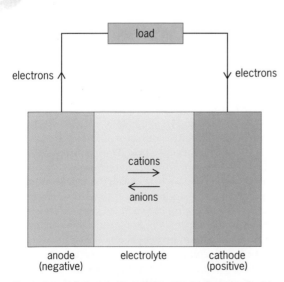

Fig. 1. Ion and electron flow during discharge of an electric cell.

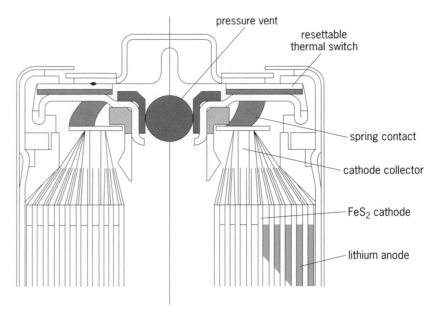

Fig. 2. Cross section of the upper part of a cylindrical, spiral wound, AA-size, Li-FeS$_2$ cell.

action takes place. Thus if the anode is lithium metal and the cathode consists of copper oxide, the reaction below applies. At the anode, lithium atoms

$$2\mathrm{Li}(s) + \mathrm{CuO}(s) \rightarrow \mathrm{Li_2O}(s) + \mathrm{Cu}(s)$$

on the metal surface are oxidized and enter the electrolyte solution as Li$^+$ ions, while electrons flow through the load to the cathode. Here copper oxide is reduced to copper, while the oxide ions form solid lithium oxide with Li$^+$ ions extracted from the electrolyte.

A wide variety of cathode materials are used in practical primary cells, including polycarbon fluorides; metal oxides, sulfides, and oxosalts; soluble reagents such as sulfur dioxide (SO$_2$); and liquid systems, such as thionyl chloride (SOCl$_2$) and sulfuryl chloride (SO$_2$Cl$_2$).

Despite its very high reactivity, lithium is found in practice to be very stable when in contact with suitable electrolyte solutions, so that self-discharge is minimal. The reason is that a fresh lithium surface reacts rapidly with components of the electrolyte solution to form a thin, adherent, electronically insulating film which passivates the electrode and stops further reaction. On drawing current from the cell, a well-designed passivating layer is rapidly disrupted and interferes little with the discharge process, but reforms whenever the discharge is interrupted.

The most common electrolyte solutions consist of a mixture of polar organic liquids, including ethers (such as dimethoxyethane), and cyclic and acyclic esters (such as propylene carbonate and dimethylcarbonate), containing a dissolved lithium salt, typically LiAsF$_6$ or LiPF$_6$. Optimization of the electrolyte solution is a critical part of battery development since a compromise must be found between good electrolyte performance—in particular, stability and low

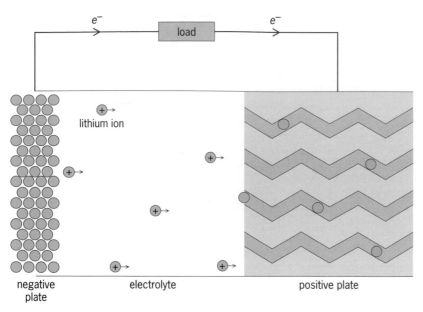

Fig. 3. Discharge of a lithium secondary cell.

electrical resistance—and the formation of the best possible passivating film.

Batteries are classed either as primary cells, which are thrown away once their reactants are consumed, or secondary cells, which may be recharged, usually many hundreds of times, before their performance becomes seriously degraded. Lithium primaries have been available commercially since the early 1970s, but successful secondary cells are much more recent.

Primary cells. Because of their high energy content and their excellent electrical characteristics such as high voltage, flat discharge, wide operating temperature range, and long shelf life, primary lithium cells have found wide application. Examples include portable consumer products such as electric watches, calculators, and remote controls; and medical applications including implantable cardiac pace-

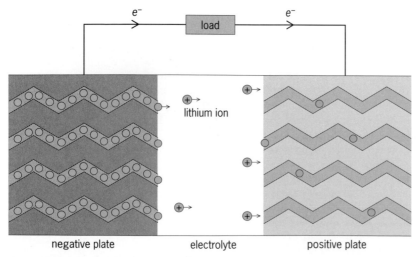

Fig. 4. Discharge of a lithium ion secondary cell.

makers and cardioverter defibrillators. Button and coin cells, together with standard cylindrical cells, are widely available. Thin-film or "paper" batteries are also manufactured, and have a total thickness of a few hundred micrometers.

The majority of lithium batteries have open circuit voltages in excess of 3 V. However, the cylindrical, spiral-wound, $Li-FeS_2$, AA-size cell (**Fig. 2**) discharges at around 1.5 V and thus can be used as a direct replacement for conventional zinc cells in high-drain consumer devices such as toys, cassette or CD (compact-disk) players, and cameras.

Secondary cells. The key discovery which led to the successful development of lithium secondary batteries was solid solution electrodes. In these electrodes a number of transition-metal oxides or sulfides and other materials were found to act as hosts for lithium and were able to reversibly incorporate or intercalate lithium atoms into vacant sites in their crystal lattices without substantial alteration of their structures. Initially, layered materials such as TiS_2 and MoS_2 were developed as cathodes or positive plates; more recently, CoO_2, NiO_2, and a number of MnO_2 phases have been utilized.

During the discharge of a lithium secondary cell (**Fig. 3**), lithium atoms at the surface of the lithium-metal negative plate ionize and enter the electrolyte solution. At the cathode they are reduced and inserted into the lattice structure. On recharging the cell, the whole process is reversed, with the lithium leaving the cathode, traversing the electrolyte, and being deposited or plated on the negative electrode.

While lithium can be plated with high efficiency, there are significant problems in producing practical secondary cells with lithium-metal negative plates because of the very high reactivity of the newly plated lithium with components of the electrolyte. This passivation phenomenon, which is responsible for the excellent shelf life of primary lithium cells, causes a number of undesirable effects in secondary cells. Two solutions to this problem have been found. (1) careful design of the electrolyte system to optimize the formation of the passivating layer, in particular by the use of polymer electrolytes, and (2) replacement of the lithium metal electrode by a second insertion host, usually based on graphitic carbon, and the fabrication of what is now generally referred to as a lithium ion cell.

When a lithium ion cell is fully charged (**Fig. 4**), most of the lithium is contained within the lattice structure of this negative host. During discharge, the lithium is transferred from here through the electrolyte to the positive host. Again the whole process is reversed on charging. The lithium is sometimes said to rock or swing between the high-energy negative host and the low-energy positive host. There is no metallic lithium present at any stage.

The main commercial impetus for the development of secondary lithium batteries has been the power requirements of the "3 C's"—cellular telephones, camcorders, and notebook computers.

These successful consumer products have energy demands which are too large to be satisfied by primary batteries. Lithium ion cells for these applications are generally formed using spiral-wound construction with positive and negative layers applied uniformly to both sides of aluminium and copper foils, respectively, using appropriate binders. A microporous polyethylene separator contains the mixed solvent-based liquid electrolytes. Cells have working voltages of around 3.6 V, an energy density of over 120 Wh kg^{-1}, and a cycle life of at least 500 deep discharges. Worldwide production is now approaching 500 million units per year.

Major government-backed programs in a number of countries are supporting projects to scale up this technology so that high-energy electric vehicle batteries may be manufactured. One of the most advanced lithium ion electric vehicle systems provides 35 kWh of energy, weighs 385 kg (850 lb), and consists of twelve modules each containing eight cylindrical lithium ion cells.

In lithium polymer batteries the liquid electrolyte is replaced by an ion-conducting polymer electrolyte. A modular battery using such an electrolyte and weighing 256 kg (565 lb) gives a range of 240–320 km (150–200 mi) between charges for a typical small automobile.

Status and prospects. Primary lithium cells are now regarded as a mature technology. Further improvements in performance and reduction in manufacturing costs are aimed at competing with alkaline zinc cells for consumer applications. There is also, however, a very wide range of specialized applications for such cells, including consumer products with built-in batteries, commercial monitoring and control systems, computer memory backup, and military and space systems. The 1995 *Galileo* probe, which investigated the atmosphere of Jupiter, was powered by three batteries each consisting of 13 lithium–sulfur dioxide cells. In the final hour of a 6-year mission and following deceleration forces of 360 g (where g is the acceleration of gravity at the Earth's surface), these batteries provided 18 Ah of electrical power.

Intensive work can be expected to produce very safe consumer cells with higher energy densities and improved electrical characteristics. The most challenging area is undoubtedly the production of reliable long-life electric vehicle batteries at reasonable cost.

For background information *see* BATTERY; INTERCALATION COMPOUNDS; PRIMARY BATTERY; SOLID-STATE BATTERY; STORAGE BATTERY in the McGraw-Hill Encyclopedia of Science & Technology.

Colin A. Vincent

Bibliography. D. Linden, *Handbook of Batteries*, 2d ed., McGraw-Hill, New York, 1995; G. Pistoia, *Lithium Batteries*, Elsevier Amsterdam, 1994; C. A. Vincent and B. Scrosati, *Modern Batteries*, 2d ed., Arnold, London, 1997; M. Wakihara and O. Yamamoto (eds.), *Lithium Ion Batteries*, Wiley-VCH, Weinheim, 1998.

Liver regeneration

The liver provides a critical interface between body and food. Digestion facilitates absorption of nutrients and other substances into the blood. Unfortunately, some of these substances are potentially toxic and cannot be incorporated into cellular components or excreted from the organism without chemical modification. Blood from the intestine goes to the liver through the hepatic portal vein, carrying with it all absorbed food components. Toxic chemicals might be found in this mix, such as plant alkaloids (for example, mushroom toxins), drugs, or chemicals formed during food processing. Hepatic architecture is based on inflow and outflow of blood from the microanatomical units making up the whole organ, and known as lobules or acini, each about 4–5 mm in diameter. Areas around the points of entry of blood into each lobule are called periportal, whereas areas around the outflow of blood from each lobule are called pericentral.

A family of enzymes with broad affinity for a variety of substances (including plant alkaloids, modified food components, and drugs), collectively called cytochrome P450, is expressed in the hepatocytes (liver cells) of pericentral areas. The net result of the action of cytochrome P450 (and other associated enzymes of the pericentral areas of the liver) is to effectively detoxify dangerous xenobiotics (chemicals or substances foreign to the body). In some instances, however, depending on the chemical, the process does not work as expected, either because there is no cytochrome P450 enzyme that can react with the ingested xenobiotic, or because the product of the chemical reaction becomes a reactive electrophile, more toxic than the original ingested chemical. When this enzymatic or chemical mishap occurs on a massive scale, the pericentral portions of the liver tissue die.

Liver regeneration is the process that has evolved to counter this series of events; it allows the liver to restore its mass after such catastrophic toxic events. This phenomenon occurs often in nature. In humans, necrosis of the pericentral areas of the liver lobules occurs most often after massive toxic exposure to drugs (such as acetaminophen).

Hepatocytes are the main cellular and functional elements of the liver, carrying out most of its specialized functions. Hepatocytes normally are quiescent, with minimal proliferative activity, until regeneration is triggered. At that point, they undergo rapid changes and enter into the cell cycle. Other cell types include stellate cells, typically surrounding hepatocytes and responsible for synthesis of matrix, some growth factors, and storage of vitamin A; sinusoidal endothelial cells, differing from their counterparts in other areas of the body by the presence of large fenestrations; Kupffer cells, specialized tissue macrophages residing in the sinusoids; and biliary epithelial cells, lining ductules which collect bile synthesized by hepatocytes.

Though liver regeneration is most often stimulated

after massive exposure to toxins, the most frequently used experimental model for studying it is two-thirds partial hepatectomy (removing a portion of the liver) in rodents. Rat liver has five lobes completely independent of each other in terms of circulation. Removal of three of the lobes is performed by a simple surgical procedure, leaving behind roughly one-third of the original tissue. The residual two lobes increase in size until total liver mass is restored. Typically, this process lasts about 5–8 days in all mammals and birds.

Events after partial hepatectomy. A cascade of events, mostly manifested through altered hepatic gene expression, follows removal of two-thirds of the liver. It is triggered by changes in cytokines and growth factors, leading to activation of specific transcription factors.

Within minutes after partial hepatectomy, hepatocyte plasma membrane becomes hyperpolarized. There is rapid rise in activity of urokinase, an enzyme triggering an enzymatic cascade leading to activation of plasminogen to plasmin, which leads to activation of metalloproteinase 9 (MMP9) within 1–3 h after the procedure. MMP9 is associated with matrix remodeling. There is also rapid decline of beta-catenin, simultaneous with the rise of protein APC (Adenomatous Polyposis Coli), associated with triggering beta-catenin degradation.

A massive change in gene expression occurs (within 60–120 min after partial hepatectomy) which is seen as a rise in more than 80 messenger ribonucleic acid (mRNA) species, encoding a variety of new proteins not present in normal quiescent hepatocytes. These mRNA products include cell-cycle-related proteins, such as Ras, Myc, Fos, and p53. Rat hepatocytes enter deoxyribonucleic acid (DNA) synthesis within 12–14 h after partial hepatectomy and reach maximum DNA synthesis rates at approximately 24 h. Periportal hepatocytes enter into DNA synthesis first, followed by midzonal and pericentral hepatocytes, the latter reaching peak DNA synthesis at 48 h. The other cellular elements of the liver enter into DNA synthesis after the hepatocytes. Stellate cells and Kupffer cells reach DNA synthesis peaks at 48 h, whereas sinusoidal endothelial cells have a broader curve of DNA synthesis activity, peaking around 3–4 days after partial hepatectomy. The time course of proliferation of the different cellular elements during regeneration suggests that multiplying hepatocytes trigger growth of the other cellular elements. Indeed, proliferating hepatocytes produce transforming growth factor alpha (TGFα), fibroblast growth factor 1 (FGF1), and vascular endothelial growth factor (VEGF) which are mitogenic to hepatocytes themselves (TGFα and FGF1) as well as to sinusoidal endothelial cells (TGFα, FGF1, VEGF).

At day 3 after partial hepatectomy, newly synthesized hepatocytes are arranged in small clumps without endothelial cells. Endothelial cells progressively enter the clumps of new hepatocytes, and eventually (by day 5–6) hepatocytes become rearranged in typical one- or two-cell plates lined on both sides by si-

nusoidal endothelial cells. Other than accumulation of microvesicular fat and some changes in gap junctions of the bile canaliculi, hepatocyte morphology during regeneration is normal. Hepatocyte function remains remarkably unaffected during the proliferative cycle, with minimal changes noticed in plasma concentrations of proteins synthesized exclusively by hepatocytes (such as albumin and coagulation factors).

Recent studies have focused on changes in transcription factors during the early stages of hepatocyte proliferation. Within hours after partial hepatectomy, there is activation of transcription factors such as mitogen activated protein kinase (MAPK), signal transducers and activator of transcription 3 (STAT3), and nuclear factor kappa B (NFκB), as well as enhanced activity of Jun kinase and associated increase in transcription factor AP1 (dimer composed of members of Jun and Fos family of proteins). All of these transcription factors have been associated with complex gene expression changes in hepatocytes in vivo and in vitro, and are considered as related to the generation of the mitogenic signal leading to hepatocyte proliferation.

Factors involved in regeneration. There are several outside stimuli currently believed to contribute to triggering liver regeneration or to be essential components of the complex mitogenic signal.

Hepatocyte growth factor. Hepatocyte growth factor (HGF) is a potent inducer of proliferation and motility in hepatocyte cultures. It rises rapidly (within 1–2 h) in plasma after partial hepatectomy. Elevated expression of HGF in stellate cells of liver (and similar cells in lung and spleen) is noticed within 5–6 h after partial hepatectomy, reaching a peak at 24 h. These data suggest that the source of the increased concentration of HGF in plasma is preexisting stores. A candidate reservoir leading to rapid increase in HGF in the ambient environment of hepatocytes is hepatic biomatrix, known to contain large amounts of HGF bound as inactive precursor. Increased urokinase activity and the associated matrix remodeling after partial hepatectomy may be a source for plasma HGF. Urokinase also causes HGF activation, further linking the enhanced urokinase activity after partial hepatectomy with both release and activation of HGF at the earliest stages of regeneration.

Consistent with the above findings, active and precursor forms of HGF decrease after partial hepatectomy as they are consumed from preexisting stores. Significant increase in both forms of HGF is seen at 6–24 h as stellate cells synthesize new HGF. The HGF receptor protein Met undergoes tyrosine phosphorylation at 30–60 min after partial hepatectomy, demonstrating that HGF is actually exercising effects at that early period of time. HGF receptor can activate STAT3, STAT5, MAPK, NFκB, and AP1 in hepatocyte cultures. Neutralization of HGF by antibodies abrogates hepatocyte proliferation for at least 72 h. Infusion of small amounts of HGF leads to proliferation of periportal hepatocytes. This is enhanced by tumor necrosis factor and matrix degradation by collagenase. Infusion of large amounts of HGF leads to dramatic enlargement of liver size in normal mice. Mice deficient in HGF or its receptor Met die in utero due to abnormalities in development of liver, placenta, and skeletal muscle.

Tumor necrosis factor. Tumor necrosis factor (TNF) is produced in the liver by Kupffer cells. It has been shown to induce apoptotic or proliferative signals in many cell types, dependent on intracellular concentrations of reactive oxygen species (ROS). The anti-apoptotic and mitogenic effects of TNF are mediated by activation of transcription factor NFκB, which is present as an inactive complex with protein IκB. In the presence of elevated ROS, IκB is inactivated by ubiquitination and destruction by proteasomes. Overexpression of IκB in transgenic mice is associated with massive apoptosis of hepatocytes after partial hepatectomy. Antibodies against TNF decrease liver regeneration and prevent activation of Jun kinase. Mice with homozygous deletions of the TNF receptor 1 have suppressed and delayed liver regeneration, with markedly deficient activation of NFκB. TNF itself is not mitogenic for hepatocytes in culture or in whole animals, but it potentiates the effects of complete mitogens such as hepatocyte growth factor and transforming growth factor alpha. TNF concentration increases in plasma after partial hepatectomy. The above studies suggest that TNF is associated with priming hepatocytes to become responsive to mitogenic stimuli during the early stages of liver regeneration.

Interleukin 6. This cytokine stimulates synthesis of acute-phase proteins by hepatocytes. It is not mitogenic in hepatocytes in vivo or in vitro, though it is a mitogen for biliary epithelial cells. Mice deficient in interleukin 6 (IL6) have delayed liver regeneration and enhanced morbidity after partial hepatectomy, associated with marked reduction of activation of STAT3. Hepatocyte hyperplasia is seen in livers of transgenic mice with overexpression in hepatocytes of both IL6 and its soluble receptor. IL6 also rises in plasma after partial hepatectomy.

Epidermal growth factor. Epidermal growth factor (EGF) is a potent mitogen for hepatocytes in culture. It is available to liver continually through exocrine glands in the duodenum, or from the salivary glands. EGF receptor tyrosine phosphorylation reaches peak levels at 60 min after partial hepatectomy, similar to that of hepatocyte growth factor. Infusion of EGF in normal mice leads to DNA synthesis in periportal hepatocytes. EGF levels do not rise in the plasma after partial hepatectomy. Male mice subjected to removal of salivary glands (major site of EGF production in male mice) have deficient regeneration.

Norepinephrine. This sympathetic neurotransmitter, though not a mitogen for hepatocytes in culture, enhances the mitogenic effects of epidermal growth factor and hepatocyte growth factor, acting through its own alpha-1 adrenergic receptor. It also decreases the mitoinhibition induced by transforming growth factor beta 1. Thus, in mutually balanced concentrations of epidermal growth factor and transforming growth factor beta 1 such that they abolish one another's effects, addition of norepinephrine leads to hepatocyte DNA synthesis. Blockade of the alpha-1 receptor prior to partial hepatectomy leads to a decreased regenerative response. Norepinephrine levels rise in the plasma after partial hepatectomy. Norepinephrine stimulates production of epidermal growth factor in exocrine glands of the duodenum and hepatocyte growth factor from human fibroblasts. Though not a mitogen itself, norepinephrine apparently plays a vital role in liver regeneration by coordinating production of mitogenic growth factors and function of their receptors.

Transforming growth factor alpha. Even though transforming growth factor alpha (TGFα) acts through the same receptor as epidermal growth factor, their effects often differ in intensity and scope. TGFα is produced by proliferating hepatocytes after partial hepatectomy, reaching peak levels at 24 h. TGFα is also mitogenic for hepatocytes in culture, raising the possibility of an autocrine mitogenic loop between TGFα and hepatocytes after partial hepatectomy. Mice deficient in TGFα do not have any obvious defects in liver regeneration, but this may be due to the multiple ligands capable of activating the epidermal growth factor receptor besides TGFα.

Transforming growth factor beta 1. This cytokine inhibits hepatic proliferation in culture, and delays regeneration when it is infused immediately prior to partial hepatectomy. Yet it is produced in large amounts after partial hepatectomy peaking at 24–72 h. Mice with overexpression of transforming growth factor beta 1 (TGFβ1) in hepatocytes have almost normal regeneration after partial hepatectomy. Regenerating hepatocytes appear in culture resistant to the mitoinhibitory effects of TGFβ1. Receptors mediating TGFβ1 effects decrease after partial hepatectomy. Progression of regeneration from periportal to pericentral areas is associated with removal of immunoreactive TGFβ1 from hepatocyte cytoplasm. While all these findings appear inconsistent, it should be remembered that the primary effect of TGFβ1 appears to be related to stimulation of new matrix synthesis, probably a key process toward the terminal stages of the regenerative process. In addition, TGFβ1 has motogenic effects on hepatocytes, likely to be of importance with cellular movements aimed at accommodating new cells and reorganizing hepatic histology.

Conclusions. Liver regeneration is a complex process probably triggered by multiple signals. Elimination of any signal delays hepatic regeneration but does not abolish it. Many of the above-mentioned signals activate the same transcription factors. This redundancy may explain the inability to completely abolish the regenerative response by eliminating any single cytokine. As part of this redundancy in signaling, interleukin 6, tumor necrosis factor, and hepatocyte growth factor rise in the plasma, as does norepinephrine and transforming growth factor beta 1. The combined presence of all these molecules is probably the reason why hepatic tissue or single hepatocytes transplanted to remote sites also enter regeneration, following partial hepatectomy of the orthotopic liver. While much has been learned about liver regeneration, much remains to be explained. Liver regeneration remains an excellent model of integration of complex changes in gene expression at the tissue and organ level.

For background information *see* CELL (BIOLOGY); CYTOKINE; GROWTH FACTOR; INTERLEUKIN; LIVER; REGENERATION (BIOLOGY) in the McGraw-Hill Encyclopedia of Science & Technology.

George K. Michalopoulos

Bibliography. N. Fausto, A. D. Laird, and E. M. Webber, Liver regeneration: 2. Role of growth factors and cytokines in hepatic regeneration, *FASEB J.*, 9(15):1527–1536, December 1995; G. K. Michalopoulos, Hepatocyte growth factor in liver growth and differentiation, in A. J. Strain and A. M. Diehl (eds.), *Liver Growth and Repair*, pp. 219–240, Chapman and Hall, 1998; G. K. Michalopoulos and M. DeFrances, Liver regeneration, *Science*, 276:60–71, 1997; R. Taub, L. E. Greenbaum, and Y. Peng, Transcriptional regulatory signals define cytokine-dependent and -independent pathways in liver regeneration, *Semin. Liver Dis.*, 19(2):117–127, 1999.

Loess

Thick, extensive deposits of windblown dust (loess) and interbedded buried soils, such as occur in north-central China and Tajikistan, are presently the subject of intense scientific attention. These sediments span at least the last 2 million years; they preserve the longest and most detailed record of Quaternary climatic changes yet found on land.

Covering some 440,000 km² (169,840 mi²), the Chinese loess forms a vast wedge of sediment, thickest (350 m or 1150 ft vertical extent) near the eastern edges of Mongolia and Tibet, approximately 150 m (492 ft) thick in the central area, and thinning out toward the southern and eastern cities of Xi'an and Beijing. It has long been thought that dust was blown (in cooler, drier climate stages) by winter monsoon winds from desert sources, such as the Gobi. The particle size of the loess becomes finer toward the southeast, suggesting transport from the northern and northwestern deserts. Geochemical "fingerprints," including strontium and neodymium isotopic compositions and rare-earth and trace-element concentrations, also suggest the deserts as key sources. However, in terms of magnetic properties, there is a mismatch between the loess and the deserts; the loess is significantly more magnetic than modern desert sand. The loess also has variable but often very high values of beryllium-10, possibly indicating a source area with moderate-to-high rainfall, such as the glaciated uplands of the Himalayas and Tibetan Plateau. A two-step transport path might account for these data. Winter surface winds blow from the western Himalayas to the northeast; this transport path could thus supply Himalayan dust to the deserts to the north and west of the Loess Plateau. In turn, dust is blown from the deserts to the Loess Plateau to the southeast, especially during the spring months of the winter monsoon.

Interbedded within the buff-colored loess are numerous buried soil layers (paleosols), traceable over hundreds of kilometers as near-horizontal, reddened layers. The soils formed at intervals when the climate became warmer and wetter so that successive loess surfaces became vegetated and subject to increased weathering and soil formation. More than 30 alternations between cool, dry periods (loess transported and then deposited) and warmer and wetter periods (soils and vegetation established) are evidenced by the thick, interbedded sequences exposed in the precipitous walls of erosional gullies (**Fig. 1**).

The basal age of the Chinese sequences has been defined paleomagnetically; all six major reversals of the Earth's magnetic field from the last 2.5 million years have been identified within the central Loess Plateau area. High-resolution paleomagnetic dating is significantly hindered, however, by magnetic overprinting—replacement of the depositional magnetic signal due to those soil-forming processes induced by climate change. Improvements in radiocarbon and, particularly, optically stimulated luminescence dating provide increasing potential for robust, detailed dating for the last 50,000 years. As more dates become available, the episodic nature of loess deposition is being revealed; notably, there appears to have been a major peak in deposition around 16,000 years ago—a few thousand years after the last glacial maximum.

Magnetic proxies of climate. Given the prospect of future changes in monsoonal activity and rainfall in

Fig. 1. Loess/paleosol sequence in the central Loess Plateau of China; the paler layers of loess are interbedded with the darker paleosol units.

this densely populated region, retrieval of quantitative paleoclimatic data from these natural archives is an important and timely task. The Chinese sequences carry a detailed magnetic record of climate change. The soils contain higher concentrations of strongly magnetic iron oxides (magnetite and maghemite), of distinctively ultrafine grain size (<0.05 micrometer); the less weathered loess layers contain much less of this material. These differences can be easily and rapidly quantified by measuring the magnetic susceptibility of the sediments; the soils have susceptibility values two to five times higher than the loess layers.

Studies of modern soils show that ultrafine-grained magnetite and maghemite are formed in situ in well-drained, moderately acidic soils (pH ~5.5–7) on iron (Fe)-bearing, weatherable parent materials. Measurements of modern soils across the Chinese Loess Plateau and other sites around the Northern Hemisphere temperate zone show that the amount of magnetic material formed is strongly and positively correlated with annual rainfall. New, ultrafine-grained magnetic materials can form when iron is supplied in its reduced (Fe^{2+}) form, through the action of iron-reducing bacteria. Upon thorough wetting, parts of the soil microenvironment become oxygen-poor.

The iron reducers then become active (using iron rather than oxygen in their metabolism) and releasing Fe^{2+} extracellularly, where it may, upon drying and reoxidation of the soil, react with Fe^{3+} oxides to form magnetite. It seems logical that such bacterial activity will be greater in soils that undergo more frequent wetting and drying cycles. These pathways of magnetite formation during soil development can thus account for the strong positive correlation between rainfall and soil-formed magnetic susceptibility.

Retrieving paleo-rainfall from magnetic susceptibility. For the Chinese sequences, with their well-drained, near-neutral soils, the numerical relationship between magnetic susceptibility and rainfall defined from modern soils can be used to calculate paleo-rainfall from the paleo-susceptibility values of the buried soils. This approach is valid if the susceptibility of the buried soils formed rapidly enough to reflect the rainfall at the time of soil formation. For the last glacial/interglacial cycle, significantly higher rainfall (more intense summer monsoons) occurred in the early Holocene and the last interglacial, especially in the presently semiarid western plateau. During the last glaciation, rainfall was reduced across the whole region (**Fig. 2**). F. Heller and colleagues

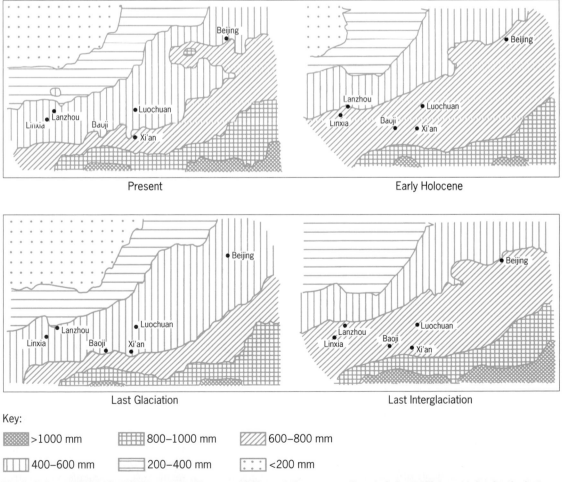

Present

Early Holocene

Last Glaciation

Last Interglaciation

Key:

>1000 mm   800–1000 mm   600–800 mm

400–600 mm   200–400 mm   <200 mm

Fig. 2. Paleo-rainfall estimates from magnetic susceptibility variations across the whole Loess Plateau region for the last glacial/interglacial cycle. (*After B. A. Maher and R. Thompson, eds., Quaternary Climates, Environments and Magnetism, Cambridge University Press, 1999*)

took a different approach; susceptibility fluxes (that is, susceptibility × sedimentation rate) were used on the basis that rates of soil, and magnetic mineral, formation are modified not just by rainfall but also by variations in the rate of deposition of loess. They estimated similar rainfall values (~600 mm/yr or 2 ft/yr) for the last 10,000 years and the last interglacial, zero rainfall for the last glacial stage (~20,000 years ago), and short intervals of very high rainfall (1200–1500 mm/yr or 4–5 ft/yr) at the glacial/interglacial transitions.

Multi-proxy climate studies. Other proxy climate indicators, retrievable with greater effort, from the loess/soil sequences include fossil snails, plant phytoliths (silicate exudates from plant roots), and loess particle size and carbonate content. H. Y. Lu and colleagues analyzed the relationship between temperature and rainfall and the distribution and abundance of modern phytoliths from across the Loess Plateau. Fossil phytoliths were extracted from a loess/soil sequence in the central Loess Plateau, and past climate conditions were calculated. This independent but time-consuming approach essentially validates the rapid magnetic proxy methods, although the phytoliths record climate variations at slightly higher resolution than do the magnetic properties (not unexpectedly, since soil formation processes require hundreds of years to reach equilibrium with the ambient climate).

Particle-size variations in the loess can record the strength of the winter monsoon winds, responsible for much of the dust transport to the Loess Plateau. Larger maximum grain sizes may indicate periods of increased wind strength (or increased proximity to dust sources), and smaller sizes may indicate periods of decreased winter monsoon intensity (or increased distance from dust sources). Carbonate content, in contrast, may reflect variations in summer monsoon moisture supply, causing dissolution of detrital carbonate and its reprecipitation in illuvial soil horizons. High-resolution studies of the loess/soil sections in the western Loess Plateau, where the sequences are thickest, indicate decoupling of the summer and winter monsoons during the last glacial cycle. For example, from about 50,000 to 30,000 years ago the summer monsoon was generally strong while the winter monsoon was weak; and from about 30,000 to 12,000 years ago the winter monsoon was strong and the summer monsoon weak. It is desirable to make detailed comparisons between the loess records and both deep-sea records (for example, the sequence of Heinrich layers in the North Atlantic) and ice-core records to identify the leads and lags and possible causal links between the climate system components. Some researchers seek to link individual climate events in the western Loess Plateau with events in the North Atlantic. However, accurate absolute dating of the loess sequences beyond the radiocarbon age limit is a prerequisite for such work. Developments in optically stimulated luminescence dating techniques probably offer most potential for improved accuracy in this regard.

Magnetic susceptibility/climate relationships. Thinner, less complete loess/soil sequences occur around the Earth. Several, including those in Alaska, Siberia, and Poland, show low susceptibility values associated with the soil units, and highs with the loess layers. This opposite pattern to the Asian sequences reflects two major factors: the presence of very strongly magnetic dust (much more magnetic than the Chinese loess), and a lack of magnetic mineral formation in the buried soils. Again, modern soil studies show that arid conditions can prevent formation of new magnetic material, while waterlogging and acidification of soils not only can inhibit magnetic mineral formation but also can destroy detrital magnetic minerals. Thus, it can be inferred that the climate at soil-forming intervals in these locations was not conducive to in situ magnetic mineral production.

For background information *see* ASIA; DATING METHODS; EOLIAN LAND FORMS; GLACIOLOGY; LOESS; MAGNETIC FIELD; MAGNETITE; MONSOON METEOROLOGY; PALEOMAGNETISM; PALEOSOL; PLAINS; RADIOCARBON DATING; SEDIMENTOLOGY; SOIL in the McGraw-Hill Encyclopedia of Science & Technology.

Barbara A. Maher

Bibliography. F. Heller and M. E. Evans, Loess magnetism, *Rev. Geophys.*, 33:211–240, 1995; H. Y. Lu et al., Seasonal climatic variation recorded by phytolith assemblages from the Baoji loess sequence in central China over the last 150 ka, *Past Global Changes Newsl.*, 6:4–5, 1998; B. A. Maher, Magnetic properties of modern soils and loessic paleosols: Implications for paleoclimate, *Palaeogeog. Palaeoclimatol. Palaeoecol.*, 137:25–54, 1998; B. A. Maher and R. Thompson, Palaeomonsoons I: The magnetic record of palaeoclimate in the terrestrial loess and palaeosol sequences, in B. A. Maher and R. Thompson (eds.), *Quaternary Climates, Environments and Magnetism*, pp. 81–125, Cambridge University Press, Cambridge, 1999; R. M. Taylor, B. A. Maher, and P. G. Self, Magnetite in soils: I. Synthesis of single domain and superparamagnetic magnetite, *Clay Miner.*, 22:411–422, 1987.

Macromolecules

Since the mid-1960s, miniaturization has been a dominant theme in technology, especially in the electronics industry. Simple extrapolation of the computers of the 1960s would have predicted that the powerful desktop computers of today would have to be as large as buildings. This miniaturization of electronic components is primarily the result of advances in lithography for the fabrication of integrated circuits. This process involves using electromagnetic radiation, such as light, to carve very small devices from large ones. However, it is generally believed that there are limitations to this top-down approach for construction of small devices, particularly with sizes in the nanometer range.

Another approach to the preparation of very small functional devices is from the bottom up, that is, using chemistry to create very large functional molecular structures. This goal can be approached with either of two chemical strategies. One involves the preparation of large single macromolecules using covalent bonds; the other involves assembling smaller molecules into large supramolecular structures using noncovalent bonds. These same strategies are used by nature for the preparation of very small functional structures—from cell membranes to receptors. Nature still surpasses humans with respect to the complexity of the functional structures produced, and remains an inspiration. However, the future is bright because humans are not restricted to preparing functional devices from a limited number of reactants, such as amino acids, or having them operate within the limited temperature ranges of living systems.

Some successful approaches used in the preparation of nanostructures are discussed below. Because nanostructures are large compared to atoms, the objects shown in the accompanying figures do not look like molecules in the traditional sense. However, these objects represent real molecules whose structures are accurately known and whose diverse properties can be controlled by organic synthesis.

Dendrimers. In preparing functional nanostructures using macromolecules, work on the dendrimers has been particularly exciting. Whereas most synthetic macromolecules, such as polyesters, possess a linear one-dimensional molecular structure, the dendrimers are three-dimensional macromolecules with a treelike architecture. Because of the development of clever synthetic methods, it has been possible to prepare dendrimers with specific domains containing functional entities such as metals (**Fig. 1**). The relationships of these specific domains to the other regions of the dendrimer give them special properties. As a consequence of their size, shape, and physical properties, the dendrimers hold considerable promise for the solution to a number of technological problems. Dendrimers have been explored as building blocks for nanostructures, magnetic resonance imaging (MRI) contrast agents, drug delivery systems, and catalysis.

Because their constituent parts are held together by covalent bonds, dendrimers are very robust. This property is an advantage for materials applications. However, the number of covalent bonds present in a single dendrimer is very large, and their formation can be a challenge to current synthetic technology.

Rotaxanes. The unusual relationship of components in interlocking molecules is particularly adaptable to molecular machines. For example, in rotaxane (**Fig. 2**), the "donut" can have two positions with respect to the "dumbell." The position of the donut can be controlled by the chemical state of components. Entities whose existence is due to mechanical bonds were once considered exotic and very rare. However, this situation has changed, as the syn-

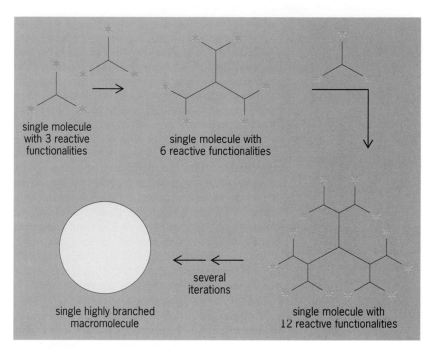

Fig. 1. Divergent synthesis of a dendrimer.

thetic chemistry for their preparation has developed. This unusual chemical approach to the preparation of nanostructures holds considerable promise for the development of functional devices.

Block copolymers. An important molecular approach to the preparation of designed nanostructures is the self-assembly of block copolymers (**Fig. 3**). Block copolymers are linear macromolecules consisting of domains or blocks derived from the same

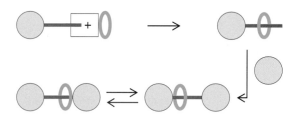

Fig. 2. Assembly of a two-state rotaxane using mechanical bonds.

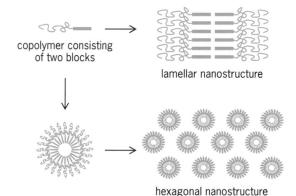

Fig. 3. Assembly of block copolymers into different nanostructures.

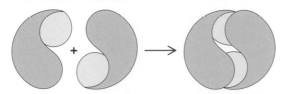

Fig. 4. Assembly of two half spheres to produce a spherical object with a cavity.

monomer. There is a tendency for chemically similar blocks in different macromolecules to self-associate in a process analogous to crystallization. Depending upon the chemical nature of the blocks and the conditions of association, these macromolecules can be induced to organize, producing nanoscale supramolecular structures. An advantage of this strategy is that the highly developed field of polymer chemistry supports both the preparation and characterization of the component macromolecules.

Molecular recognition. One of the more challenging approaches to the preparation of nanostructures from molecules is the use of molecular recognition. This strategy involves the preparation of molecules with the information for assembly into a designed supramolecular nanostructure encoded into the molecular structure. Although this approach is capable of producing very sophisticated functional nanostructures, it is difficult to implement. The molecular structures are relatively complex requiring significant organic synthesis, and the nanostructures are usually assembled using weak noncovalent bonds that are difficult to control. Nevertheless, important advances have been made in this field of research.

One approach for the creation of a well-defined cavity is the preparation of a half-spherical molecule with functional groups properly arranged for dimerization to produce a spherical assembly (**Fig. 4**). The size of the cavity and its functional abilities are controlled by the chemical nature of the constituent parts. There is interest in the preparation of designed cavities because of applications such as reaction catalysis, selective sensors, and molecular separations.

Outlook. One advantage of a molecular approach in preparing functional nanostructures is that the process is highly parallel; that is, a large number of structures are prepared in a single process. However, this field is still in its infancy. Most of the research efforts have been devoted to developing methods for the preparation of nanostructures that have little or no practical function. Although this synthetic work will continue to develop, there will be increasing efforts to incorporate function into these nanostructures.

For background information *see* COPOLYMER; DENDRITIC MACROMOLECULE; MACROCYCLIC COMPOUND; MOLECULAR RECOGNITION; NANOCHEMISTRY; NANOSTRUCTURE; NANOTECHNOLOGY; SUPRAMOLECULAR STRUCTURES in the McGraw-Hill Encyclopedia of Science & Technology.

Frank W. Fowler

Bibliography. Issue on molecular self-assembly, *Acc. Chem. Res.*, 32(5), 1999; Issue on nanoscale materials, *Acc. Chem. Res.*, 32(4):387–454, 1999; Issue on nanostructures, *Chem. Rev.*, 99(7):1641–1990, 1999.

Magnetic random access memories

In magnetic random access memories (MRAMs), submicrometer-size magnetic structures store digital information in their magnetic orientation. In the most common architecture, the stored information can be retrieved by sensing the electrical resistance difference that exists in the magnetic structures between the two possible magnetization directions, using an effect called giant magnetoresistance. As long as the bit is not rewritten, the information is maintained; hence MRAM is a nonvolatile memory. The most appealing characteristics of MRAM are its miniaturization to deep submicrometer memory bits, its unlimited read-write capability, and its fast access. MRAM circuits are expected to be available in consumer products by 2003.

Integrated magnetic bits. The magnetic elements representing the bits are specially designed components that store the information in their magnetization with two stable states and provide an electronic signal reflecting this magnetization state. The most attractive components are spin valves and magnetic tunnel junctions.

In its simplest form, a spin valve (**Fig. 1***a*) is a trilayer structure consisting of two magnetic layers spaced by a noble metal. All layers are 3–10 nanometers thick. The magnetic layers have well-defined magnetic orientations: either aligned or opposing. The surprising effect is that the resistance of the spin valve to a current parallel to the layer planes is lower when both orientations are aligned than when they are opposing. This effect is related to giant magnetoresistance, discovered in the late 1980s independently by A. Fert and P. Grünberg. The difference in resistance amounts to 5–10% at room temperature and enables the readout of the magnetic bit.

A similar magnetoresistance effect occurs in a magnetic tunnel junction (Fig. 1*b*), in which two magnetic layers are separated by an insulating barrier, 1–2 nm thick, typically aluminum oxide (Al_2O_3). Under a small electric bias, electronic current can tunnel through the barrier. The transport across this barrier depends on the magnetic orientation of both magnetic layers. The probability of an electron tunneling through is higher when the two magnetic orientations are parallel. The resistance difference for parallel versus opposed magnetic moments reaches 40% at room temperature. The current direction is perpendicular to the multilayer planes, and the absolute resistance is much higher than that of spin valves. Both characteristics are favorable for high-density integration. A drawback is the fragility of the thin oxide tunneling layer and the subnanometer tolerance on its thickness across the wafer. The electrical reliability of the tunnel junction is related to the ultrathin tunnel barrier and is still unexplored. In order to achieve reasonable resistance values for submicrometer devices, the aluminum oxide tunnel barriers are made as thin as 0.7–1.1 nm. The product of the resistance and the area of the device varies from 60 Ω-μm^2 for a 0.7-nm-thick barrier, to 160 Ω-μm^2 at 0.9 nm, to 800 Ω-μm^2 at 1.1 nm.

Physics of giant magnetoresistance. The magnetoresistance originates from the different physical properties of spin-up and spin-down electrons in a ferromagnetic metal. Spin-up refers to the majority of electrons whose spin is aligned to the macroscopic magnetic orientation of the film. In a ferromagnetic metal, the electron density and transport properties of the electrons are spin-dependent; for example, the electron scattering is larger for a minority-spin electron. The electrons in the spin valve pass across the interfaces of the multilayer several times. When the magnetizations of the layers are aligned, the majority-spin electron current finds a low overall resistance. When the magnetizations are opposed, both spin currents are minority spins in one of the layers, leading to an overall higher resistance.

Write and read in MRAM. The magnetization state of the spin valve or magnetic tunnel junction can be changed by magnetic fields which are locally generated by currents flowing in conductors close to the bits. In one particular organization (**Fig. 2**), the magnetic bits are arranged in a regular array. Conductors run along the columns and rows, and each can generate half of the magnetic field to switch a magnetic bit. Superposition of the two magnetic fields from orthogonal conductors will result in switching of that bit located at their crossing. When one bit is switched, the others are not disturbed. No external magnetic fields are used. This arrangement is particularly suited for tunnel-junction memories, where a transistor can be integrated into each bit to perform the bit-selective read action (**Fig. 3a**). The transistor serves as a switch to guide the current to the selected magnetic element, preventing the current from finding other stray paths through the array, which would dilute the measured signal from the interrogated bit.

Demonstration devices combining semiconductor switches and magnetic devices in a single memory cell are currently being proposed. The effort to actually integrate the small magnetic elements in arrays with the appropriate switching devices in standard semiconductor technologies is just beginning. The objective is to be fully compatible with standard and mature processing technologies in order to ensure that the new devices will be rapidly accepted for integration into existing types of products.

Architecture alternatives. Spin valves can be connected in series to form large strings (Fig. 3b). When one of the magnetic devices in the string is triggered by a magnetic pulse, it will produce a resistance change corresponding to the change in its memory state. This change in the resistance of the whole string, caused by the interrogated element, can be accurately measured by comparing the string's total

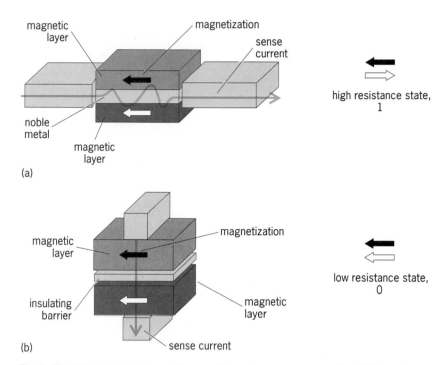

Fig. 1. Magnetic components used in magnetic random access memories. (*a*) Spin valve. (*b*) Magnetic tunnel junction.

resistance to the resistance of a reference string. In such an organization, there is no need to place switches next to each memory device; hence, the memory array can be integrated on top of any type of integrated circuitry. This three-dimensional stacking potential can result in an overall density advantage. However, the resistance change of a single resistor element will have a relatively very small effect in a long chain of resistors. The MRAM will therefore be subdivided into small blocks of memory, each consisting of a set of resistor strings, whose length is short enough to allow for reliable read signals. Prototype circuits have been produced using single magnetic films that

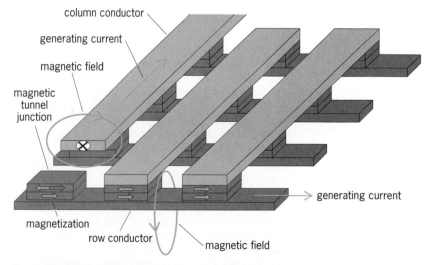

Fig. 2. Magnetic tunnel junctions in an array, integrated with conductors for local magnetic field generation.

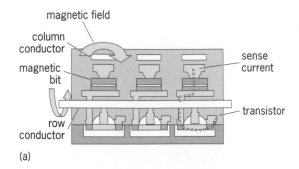

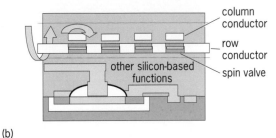

(a)

(b)

Fig. 3. Cross sections of MRAM alternatives employing (a) magnetic tunnel junctions integrated with transistors, and (b) spin valves separated from the underlying electronics.

show only 2% resistance changes. The next generation, using spin valves, will achieve higher density and speed.

Still other alternatives have been proposed for the structure of the magnetic element (**Fig. 4**). The principle of storing the information in the magnetization remains identical; only the readout mechanism is different in each case.

In one structure (Fig. 4a), the fringing fields from the magnetic storage element penetrate a small semiconductor Hall-effect element. The voltage across this Hall-effect device can be either positive or negative, depending on the magnetization orientation of the magnetic storage element.

In another design (Fig. 4b), a magnetic thin film with a perpendicular magnetization is patterned into a submicrometer cross. A current through the cross generates a Hall-like voltage (the anomalous Hall effect) across the structure. This voltage is dependent on the magnetic polarization of the film.

Challenges. High-speed bit storage and retrieval operations are a high priority in the design of computer memory. Read speed is affected by resistance-capacitance (*RC*) products that determine the time constants in the transients of the electrical signals in the circuits. Very high capacitance and resistance values in the circuit will cause slow read operations. For a certain design and a certain integration technology, the resistance and capacitance are more or less predetermined. Only larger signals from the memory cell can speed up the process. A magnetic tunnel junction, for instance, has a large resistance value, but fortunately the resistance change can be large enough to compensate for this.

The speed of writing, that is, of switching the magnetic elements, is largely dependent on the size of the element. When devices are reduced to deep submicrometer dimensions (say, below 0.1 μm), even the softer ferromagnetic materials become magnetically harder as domain-wall generation and movement become more difficult. For the same power, this effect will lengthen write times or even make writing impossible, since the current levels are then too low to generate sufficiently large fields. However, for the present and the coming two generations of devices, write times can be expected to remain in the nanosecond range, competitive with fast devices such as static and dynamic random access memories (SRAMs and DRAMs).

Spin-dependent transport. The general conclusions regarding the performance and miniaturization of the magnetoelectronic memory circuits lead to the desire for more "flexible" magnetic devices. Such devices would use materials whose magnetic properties could be controlled, for example, by modulation of a carrier concentration or by injection of spin-polarized current.

Recently there has been an increasing interest in III–V compound semiconductors in which a large number of magnetic impurities have been introduced. These materials, called diluted magnetic semiconductors or semimagnetic semiconductors, are compatible with conventional semiconductors and are paramagnetic above and ferromagnetic below a transition temperature. Since the magnetic and electronic properties of these materials are strongly intertwined, the modulation of magnetic properties by voltage, current, and light may be possible in dilute-magnetic-semiconductor/semiconductor heterostructures. Such materials can also play an important role in the design of electronic components where the use of spin-polarized electron currents is the goal.

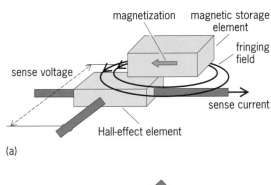

(a)

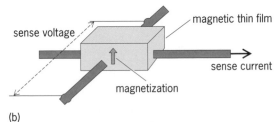

(b)

Fig. 4. Alternative magnetic bits. (a) Semiconductor Hall-effect component with magnetic stray-field element. (b) Magnetic element that displays the anomalous Hall effect.

For background information *see* COMPUTER STOR-
AGE TECHNOLOGY; ELECTRICAL CONDUCTIVITY OF
METALS; INTEGRATED CIRCUITS; MAGNETORESIST-
ANCE; TRANSISTOR; TUNNELING IN SOLIDS in the
McGraw-Hill Encyclopedia of Science & Technology.
                                            J. De Boeck

Bibliography. J. A. C. Bland and B. Heinrich (eds.),
Ultrathin Magnetic Structures, Springer-Verlag,
1994; J. De Boeck and G. Borghs, Magnetoelectron-
ics, *Phys. World*, 12(4):27–34, April 1999; H. Ohno,
Making non-magnetic semiconductors ferromagnetic, *Science*, 281:951–957, 1998; G. A. Prinz, Mag-
netoelectronics, *Science*, 282:1660–1663, 1998.

Marine engine

Diesel engines remain the dominant means of ship
propulsion. In recent years, they have shown continuing progress in areas of refined manufacturing,
higher power output per unit of engine volume
(power density) and per unit weight, reduced fuel
and lubricating oil consumption, improved tolerance
for fuels of low quality, simplified maintenance requirements, suppression of vibration, application of
electronic monitoring and control, and reduction of
exhaust emissions. There have been promising developments in the use of natural gas as a marine
fuel. There has been a dramatic consolidation in the
diesel-engine manufacturing industry, resulting from
the increasing sophistication (and cost) of the research, design processes, prototype testing, manufacturing methods, and after-service sales obligations
that have become part of the manufacturing process,
leaving fewer engine designs of increasing similarity
to be built worldwide by closely cooperating manufacturers.

Types of engines. The largest marine engines remain the two-stroke, low-speed, crosshead types,
directly connected to the propeller shafting. The
largest of these engines, installed in large container
ships, deliver almost 100,000 horsepower (75 megawatts) from 12 in-line cylinders, each almost 1 m
(3 ft) in bore, and are over 23 m (75 ft) long and
weigh more than 2000 tons. Engines of this type are
built in smaller sizes with fewer cylinders, suitable
for even modest-sized merchant ships. These engines
remain in favor because of their simplicity and their
ability to burn low-quality heavy fuels with relatively
modest maintenance requirements (for spare parts
and labor).

The more compact medium- and high-speed engines have also reflected a trend to higher power
density, with the largest medium-speed designs now
capable of over 2500 hp (1.9 MW) per cylinder.
These engines must be connected to propellers
through speed-reducing gearing or electric drive. Although geared drive remains more popular because
of its higher efficiency, advances in the field of solid-
state power electronics have led to wider use of
diesel-electric drive. A further evolution of electric
drive is the integrated power plant, in which multiple diesel-generator sets supply power to a common
electrical bus for distribution to ship's services as
well as for propulsion. The combined advantages of
the power density of medium- and high-speed engines and the flexibility in arrangement and operation of the integrated power plant have led to increasing use of this arrangement, particularly in passenger
ships.

In the high-speed engine sector, increases in
power density have allowed high-performance
engines with 20 or 24 cylinders to develop up to
10,000 hp (7.5 MW). These engines (see **illus.**)
can compete effectively with gas turbines for propulsion of high-speed ferries and smaller naval
combatants, usually in multiple-engine installations.
Although these engines require light-distillate fuels
(as do the gas turbines), and require far more maintenance than diesel engines of lower performance,
they are more efficient and simpler to maintain than
the gas turbines.

Higher cylinder pressures. These increases in power
density are directly traceable to improvements in
turbochargers which, by supplying air to the cylinders under ever-more elevated pressure, enable a
cylinder of given dimensions to be charged with a
greater mass of air. In turn, a greater mass of fuel
can be burned in that cylinder, developing correspondingly greater power. The parameter associated
with this more effective use of cylinder dimensions
(and therefore of engine dimensions) is the mean effective pressure (MEP). High-performance engines
today have mean effective pressures in excess of
25 bars (2.5 megapascals), and normal production
engines have 18–25 bars (1.8–2.5 MPa)—values only
contemplated a generation ago. In addition to higher

High-speed, high-performance engine, which utilizes two-stage turbocharging to achieve
high power and is therefore suitable for high-speed vessels. (*GEC ALSTOM Paxman
Diesels Ltd.*)

power density, turbocharging generally improves engine efficiency and reduces exhaust emissions. Except for some engines intended for special applications, all diesel engines in current production are turbocharged.

However, the high mean effective pressures of modern engines generally reflect more highly stressed engine components. To accommodate these stresses, engine designers and builders use computer-aided design and manufacturing processes, and stronger iron and steel alloys, and often employ such features as bore-cooled components, insert rings in cylinder liners, coated piston rings, and multiple-layered metallic bearings.

Maintenance. Diesel engines require regular maintenance, and a fairly extensive overhaul after 10,000–20,000 hours of service is common in most marine applications, although high-performance engines usually require overhaul at much shorter intervals. Engine designers increasingly incorporate such labor-saving features as built-in lifting gear, modularized components, hydraulically tensioned bolts, and purpose-built tools. Under pressure of owners and operators, ship designers and builders are increasingly aware of the need to provide adequate working space, permanently installed lifting gear, and carefully considered access routes to and from machinery spaces, workshops, and store rooms. Most marine engines are overhauled in place, but in some space-constrained installations the engines are designed to be removed for overhaul, a practice common with aircraft-derivative gas turbines. For large propulsion engines in most merchant ships, overhaul is a continual process, with each cylinder or pair of cylinders overhauled separately as its turn comes up, at convenient intervals while the ship is in port. Thus, there is an increasing trend to compensate for smaller crews by contracting this work to shoreside firms.

Vibration reduction. The reciprocating motion of diesel engine components and the development of torque in discrete power strokes has always rendered diesel engines prone to vibration. It is now feasible, using computer-aided design methods, to accurately predict not only the frequency and severity of vibration produced by the engines but also the responses of the ship structure and of the connected load, generally enabling vibration problems to be avoided by design. Design techniques have included detail changes to structure and to shafting arrangements, or the addition of balancing devices to the engine. For medium- and high-speed engines, vibration-isolating couplings are normally installed between the engines and their loads, while resilient mounting of these engines to their foundations is increasingly common.

Electronic control. Electronic monitoring and control of engine functions has become common, and is now often extended to incorporate sensors for wear and computer-tracked trend monitoring, enabling a degree of automated maintenance supervision. The timing of the key cycle events of fuel injection and of air and exhaust-valve operation, traditionally controlled mechanically with little or no flexibility by a gear- or chain-driven camshaft, can now be done by electronically controlled hydraulic operators. Such control offers an ability to adjust timing in service to optimize engine performance to suit changing circumstance, for example, for low fuel consumption at sea or for low exhaust emissions while maneuvering.

Reduction of exhaust emissions. This is arguably the biggest challenge currently faced by the diesel-engine community. Nitrogen oxides are the most difficult constituents to suppress. Methods include adjustment of engine parameters (increased compression ratios, higher air-to-fuel ratios, longer stroke-to-bore ratios, and shorter, more intensive fuel-injection periods), introduction of water during combustion, exhaust-gas recirculation, and treatment of the exhaust gas by catalytic converters. Some efforts to reduce exhaust emissions unfortunately increase fuel consumption, and the ability to adjust operating parameters to suit the circumstance, cited above, is obviously advantageous. The precision and response of electronic control is also helpful in reducing hydrocarbon emissions during maneuvering. The matter of sulfur dioxide emissions is principally an economic issue, as the sulfur is introduced in the fuel. High-sulfur fuels, less marketable ashore, have had a ready market among oceangoing ships. When these ships enter emission-regulated waters, the fuel supply is switched to a tank containing low-sulfur fuel.

Natural gas fuel. Natural gas is a clean-burning fuel, suitable for use in adapted diesel engines, with which there is a wealth of shoreside experience. A major issue is the means of storage of sufficient gas on board a vessel. When the gas is stored in high-pressure cylinders, the vessel's range is necessarily restricted. A number of ferries and other inshore vessels fueled with compressed gas are already in service, some for many years, and many more are likely to enter service in the near term. For oceangoing vessels, it is likely that the gas will be liquefied and stored at cryogenic temperatures. A depth of marine experience already exists in the large fleet of liquefied natural gas carriers. While these carriers transport the gas as cargo, they also use it as fuel. At present all of the liquefied natural gas carriers are steam ships, but the reasons for this are more economic and political than technical, and there is every likelihood that new liquefied natural gas carriers will be driven by diesel engines.

For background information *see* AIR POLLUTION; DIESEL ENGINE; LIQUEFIED NATURAL GAS (LNG); MARINE ENGINE; MERCHANT SHIP; TURBOCHARGER; VIBRATION ISOLATION in the McGraw-Hill Encyclopedia of Science & Technology.   Alan L. Rowen

Bibliography. *Marine Propulsion International*, DMG Business Media, Red Hill, Surrey, U.K., 1999; *MER (Marine Engineers' Review)*, Institute of Marine Engineers, London, 1999; *The Motor Ship*, Reed Business Information, Maidenhead, Berkshire, U.K., 1999; *Technology Review*, Wartsila NSD, Winterthur, Switzerland, 1999.

Marine reptiles

Adaptations that make tetrapods efficient, fast swimmers make it difficult for them to move on land. This can pose a problem for marine reptiles, which must return to land to lay eggs. Ichthyosaurs are known to have given birth to live offspring. Mosasaurs (now extinct, and related to snakes and lizards) are believed to have also given live birth because (1) their limbs are short and weak, (2) their bony ribs do not enclose the entire chest, and (3) their pelvis is wider than necessary for passage of an egg. The evidence was circumstantial until a recent discovery of the first mosasaur embryos. A skeleton of *Plioplatecarpus primaevus* (from the Pierre Shale of South Dakota) contains the bones of up to four tiny mosasaurs in the posterior pelvic area. The lack of pitting or corrosion on the tiny bones suggests that these are not stomach contents but embryos. The bone microstructure indicates that these are very immature embryos. The "bone" is calcified cartilage, not true bone.

Mosasaurs. Bone microstructure in mosasaurs is an important key to understanding their evolution and ecology. The microstructure of ribs for *Clidastes, Platecarpus,* and *Tylosaurus,* the three common North American genera, is sufficiently different that the genus can be identified from the microstructure alone. Thus, it may be possible to determine the genus of fragmentary specimens that lack the diagnostic bones. Furthermore, some of the differences in microstructure are characteristics of immature bone in primitive genera. The implication is that some genera retain juvenile characters as adults, a process called paedomorphosis. Thus, changes in developmental timing and rates of growth may have been a mechanism for the rapid diversification of mosasaurs in the Late Cretaceous. Moreover, the genera with the fewest juvenile traits as adults are the smaller, more primitive forms, whereas the genera with the most juvenile traits as adults are the larger, more derived forms. Retention of juvenile traits may have allowed mosasaurs to evolve to their huge sizes. The lizard ancestors to mosasaurs were less than a meter in length. An adult *Clidastes,* a fairly primitive genus, was about 4 m (13 ft) long, whereas *Tylosaurus,* a highly derived genus, was over 10 m (33 ft) long. Interestingly, *Tylosaurus* retains more juvenile characteristics than *Clidastes.*

Bone microstructure is also an indicator of ecology. An animal that lives in water is essentially weightless because of buoyancy. Without the influence of gravity, the spongy bone tends to have thin struts of bone enclosing the many open spaces. The denser outer bone is merely a thin covering. In contrast, Beluga whales and manatees, which live where stresses from waves influence bone growth, have thicker struts in spongy bone and thicker outer bone layers. Thus, some general features of the bone microstructure can indicate what portion of the water column was inhabited. *Clidastes* and *Tylosaurus* have porous bone, suggesting that they frequented deep water. *Platecarpus* has denser bone and probably lived in the upper portion of the water column. Interestingly, *Platecarpus* has a high incidence of bone damage due to "the bends," whereas *Clidastes* has none. If *Platecarpus* was indeed a shallow-water species, sudden deep dives, for example to escape a predator, could produce serious bone damage. *Clidastes,* however, living deeper in the water column, was better adapted physiologically to deal with the change in pressure between the surface water and deep water.

Ichthyosaurs. The earliest known ichthyosaurs, *Chensaurus* from the Early Triassic of China and *Utatsusaurus hataii* from Japan, had a very elongate bodies. Triassic ichthyosaurs are typically more elongate than the better-known post-Triassic forms. Instead of a crescent-shaped tail, Triassic ichthyosaurs had highly asymmetric tails with the dorsal lobe much smaller than the lower lobe, an inference that was confirmed by a new discovery from British Columbia: a skin impression of the tail of an Early Triassic ichthyosaur. Triassic ichthyosaurs were probably slower swimmers, capturing prey by using an ambush strategy rather than by a sustained chase. This contrasts with the picture of Jurassic and Cretaceous ichthyosaurs. The most commonly pictured species display remarkable similarities to living dolphins in their deep streamlined body, tall dorsal fin, and crescent-shaped tail. Because of these similarities in body shape, most Jurassic ichthyosaurs were thought to have been fast, efficient swimmers comparable to modern dolphins. New evidence suggests, however, that Jurassic ichthyosaurs employed a variety of swimming styles, some of which show similarities to Triassic forms. Some osteological features are indicators of the stiffness of the vertebral column: the shape of the vertebral centra, the anterior-posterior extent of single-headed ribs, the length of the ribs, and the relative height of neural spines. These features suggest that the German species *Suevoleviathan disinteger* and *Temnodontosaurus triginodon* had highly flexible trunks that undulated during swimming. At the other end of the spectrum, *Stenopterygius quadriscissus* and the British species *Ophthalmosaurus icenicus* had much more rigid torsos, with the propulsive force being generated almost exclusively by the oscillation of the tail fluke. Thus, Jurassic ichthyosaurs probably employed a range of predation strategies, from ambush to pursuit, depending on the flexibility of their vertebral column.

Ichthyosaurs show many adaptations for a completely aquatic life. They are so different from terrestrial reptiles that the question of their origin has been debated for many decades. It is now known that ichthyosaurs are diapsid reptiles, the group that includes dinosaurs, crocodiles, lizards, and snakes. The ability to give live birth suggests that ichthyosaurs are more closely related to lizards and snakes than to dinosaurs and crocodiles; some features of the palate and skull support this hypothesis. New specimens of the primitive ichthyosaur *Utatsusaurus,* however, suggest that ichthyosaurs diverged from the main line of diapsid evolution just before the dinosaur/crocodile and the lizard/snake lineages diverged from one another. This would imply that ichthyosaurs diverged from the main line of diapsid evolution toward the base of the diapsid family tree. A group of primitive, lizardlike reptiles, the Younginiformes, may be their closest terrestrial relatives. These relationships, however, are still being debated.

For background information *see* CRETACEOUS; DINOSAUR; ICHTHYOPTERYGIA; JURASSIC; MESOZOIC; REPTILIA; TRIASSIC in the McGraw-Hill Encyclopedia of Science & Technology.   Judy A. Massare

Bibliography. G. L. Bell, Jr., et al., The first direct evidence of live birth in Mosasauridae (Squamata): Exceptional preservation in the Cretaceous Pierre Shale of South Dakota [abstract], *J. Vert. Paleontol.*, 16:21A, 1996; E. Buchholtz, A.-M. Chomat, and J. A. Massare, Whales, tails, and ichthyosaurs: Axial locomotion in two planes [abstract], *J. Vert. Paleontol.*, 19:34A, 1999; M. W. Caldwell, Ichthyosauria: A preliminary phylogenetic analysis of diapsid affinities, *Neues Jahrb. Geol. Paläntol. Abh.*, 200:361–386, 1996; L. D. Martin and B. Rothschild, Paleopathology and diving mosasaurs, *Amer. Sci.*, 77:460–467, 1989; R. Motani, N. Minoura, and T. Ando, Ichthyosaurian relationships illuminated by new primitive skeletons from Japan, *Nature*, 393:255–257, 1998; R. Motani, H. You, and C. McGowan, Eel-like swimming in the earliest ichthyosaurs, *Nature*, 382:347–348, 1996; E. L. Nicholls and M. Manabe, The dorsal caudal fin of an early Triassic ichthyosaur—the tale of the tail, *Paludicola*, 2:190–205, 1999; A. Sheldon, Ecological implications of mosasaur bone microstructure, in J. M. Callaway and E. L. Nicholls (eds.) *Ancient Marine Reptiles*, pp. 333–534, Academic Press, New York, 1997; M. A. Sheldon and G. L. Bell, Jr., Paedomorphosis in Mosasauridae (Squamata): Evidence from fossil bone microstructure, *Paludicola*, 2:190–205, 1999; M. A. Sheldon, G. L. Bell, Jr., and J. P. Lamb, Jr., Histological characters in prenatal specimens of the mosasaur *Plioplatecarpus primaevus* [abstract], *J. Vert. Paleontol.*, 16:64A, 1996.

Mars's magnetic lineations

The question of whether the planet Mars ever had an internally generated magnetic field was answered recently. More than 16 United States and Russian missions were launched to explore the planet between 1962 and 1996 with different degrees of success. The early missions established that a magnetic field on Mars, if it existed at all, would be weak—less than 1/1000th of the Earth's field at the surface near the Equator.

From an orbiting or flyby spacecraft, only two kinds of measurements provide information about the interior of a planetary body: gravity and magnetic field measurements. With the exception of radar soundings of ice, all other remote sensing measurements from spacecraft provide information about the atmosphere or the surface to a depth not exceeding perhaps a few centimeters. The spacecraft trajectory is affected by gravity, which in turn reflects how mass is distributed in the body. However, the detection of a magnetic field of internal origin provides evidence that a dynamo is active in the interior. Planetary dynamos are driven by thermal convection of electrically conducting fluids in the core and lower mantle of the body. In the case of the Earth, the fluid is an iron-rich, molten magma. Rotation of a planet is believed to be an essential ingredient of the process, organizing the convection patterns into cells leading to the existence of a self-regenerating magnetic field.

Mars Global Surveyor arrived at Mars on September 11, 1997, and unlike previous missions, was injected into a highly elliptical orbit with very low periapsis altitudes (100–150 km; 62–93 mi). From this vantage point, it quickly established unambiguously that the planet does not currently have a magnetic field of internal origin. However, the craft made a surprising discovery: the existence of local, strongly magnetized regions close to the surface indicating that an Earth-like dynamo had existed in Mars's interior in the past and had magnetized its iron-rich crust. This dynamo is no longer active. What is observed today is the fossil or remanent magnetization of the ferromagnetic materials in the crust as it cooled below the Curie point (the temperature above which ferromagnetic materials lose their ability to retain a field) in the presence of the ancient planetary magnetic field. The *Global Surveyor* executed more than 1000 orbits with periapses below 200 km (114 mi) and was able to map the global distribution of crustal magnetization sources to a spatial resolution sufficient to make even more surprising discoveries.

A map showing the radial component of the magnetic field measured by the craft below 200 km (114 mi) along orbit tracks is shown in the **illustration**. Shown as circles are craters of 15 km (9 mi) diameter and larger. The strongly magnetized regions are found almost exclusively in the ancient, high, and heavily cratered terrain south of the dichotomy boundary (the imaginary line separating the young lowlands of the north from the ancient cratered highlands in the south). The giant impacts that formed the Hellas and Argyre basins some 3.9 billion years ago destroyed the crustal magnetization in these areas, allowing scientists to date the epoch of dynamo cessation to at least this time, and no magnetization is found associated with the giant volcanoes in Tharsis and Elysium. Hence, the magnetized regions represent the oldest surviving, unmodified crust of Mars hidden from observation until the arrival of the *Global Surveyor*. This remarkable picture is further enhanced by the discovery of long, linear, and parallel features of positive and negative radial magnetic field polarity extending thousands of kilometers and covering almost one-third of the southern hemisphere.

What geological processes could have generated these unique features? On the Earth, large-scale

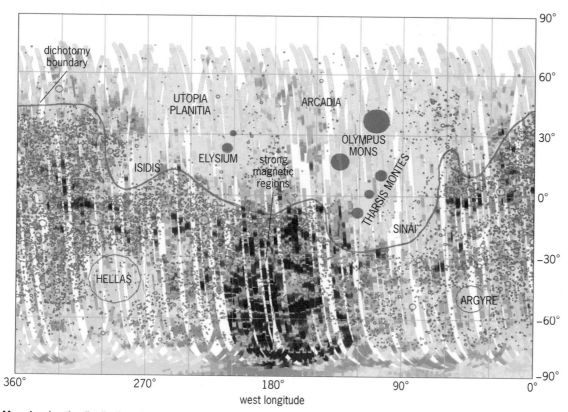

Map showing the distribution of crustal magnetic field sources and the distribution of craters greater than 15 km (9 mi) in diameter, as well as the dichotomy boundary. The spacecraft tracks below 200 km (114 mi) altitude have been projected onto the surface as light lines to illustrate the orbital coverage. Magnetic lineations in the southern hemisphere are seen as alternating darkened areas with linear features. The magnetic field intensity varies from −1500 to 1500 nanoteslas (1 nT = 1×10^{-5} gauss). (*NASA*)

magnetic lineations are generated by sea-floor spreading, plate tectonics, and poorly understood periodic (a few times in a million years) reversals of the magnetic field—new crust is generated at the mid-ocean ridges and is imprinted with the Earth's field polarity as it cools below the Curie point. It has been suggested that the same "sea-floor spreading" process operated on Mars while the dynamo was active in its ancient past. However, the intensity of magnetization required to explain the Martian lineations is more than 10 times larger than that of the most intense magnetic anomalies found in the Earth's crust. In addition, models developed to date require that the thickness of the magnetized layer be of the order of 30–40 km (19–25 mi), with a sharp magnetic contrast incompatible with slow cooling of the crust and magnetic reversals. An alternate scenario that does not require magnetic reversals and can produce sharp magnetic contrasts is that of a thin, uniform layer of crust magnetized by the strong early dynamo, which is later broken up along linear faults by tectonic stresses when the dynamo has ceased to operate. Some evidence to support this scenario can be found in the grabens and faults (for example, the Sirenum and Memnonia fossae), which are observable in photographs of this region and which appear to be aligned with the magnetic features. These faults are believed to have been created by tectonic

stresses associated with the rise of the Tharsis bulge primarily during the Hesperian age (Mars's geological ages are classified in three major epochs starting with the oldest: Noachian, Hesperian, and Amazonian). However, the faults are only a few tens of kilometers wide, while the separation between linear magnetic features of opposite radial polarity is measured in hundreds of kilometers. One is therefore led to the conclusion that, regardless of the model chosen, some form of "crustal spreading" process took place at Mars at an early age although it is not understood at present.

It is generally accepted that Mars started as a very hot object (from the dissipation of the kinetic energy of the impacting bodies), which cooled off and differentiated rapidly into a core, mantle, and crust. The dynamo shuts off when thermal convection in the core and lower mantle ceases to operate. Most models of Mars thermal history and evolution have difficulties shutting off the dynamo in less than 1 billion years and dissipating the initial heat by radiation from the crust unless some form of convection is invoked. A "sea-floor spreading" process associated with plate tectonics, as on the Earth, would provide an efficient mechanism for recycling the crust and getting rid of the excess heat in the mantle.

What are the implications of the absence of a magnetic field for the evolution of the Martian atmosphere and the loss of water from the planet? Mars is a low-gravity planet, and atmospheric atoms (hydrogen and oxygen), because of their thermal velocity, can reach large distances from the surface. Some of those atoms will be photoionized by solar ultraviolet radiation forming the Martian ionosphere; while others, because of the absence of a magnetic field forming a protective shield deflecting the solar wind, will reach regions on the dayside where they can interact directly with solar wind particles and become ionized by charge exchange with protons or by electron impacts. These newly created ions now respond to electrical and magnetic fields and are "picked up" by the solar wind, carried downstream, and lost from Mars. Since it is now known that the planetary dynamo ceased to operate almost 4 billion years ago, the amount of oxygen lost to space can be estimated. Assuming that this oxygen existed in the form of water on the planet, a loss estimate obtained is equivalent to a planetwide ocean 50 m (165 ft) deep. Although this is only a fraction of the amount of water believed to have been lost from Mars, it is clear that the early disappearance of the dynamo contributed significantly to the loss process.

The *Global Surveyor*'s magnetic field measurements and discoveries have revolutionized the understanding of the early history and thermal evolution of Mars. Although it is tempting to think of Mars and its geological evolution as Earth's look-alike, it is clear that the processes that took place there, as well as their time scale, were nothing like the Earth's. The sheer physical scale and intensity of Mars's magnetic lineations has triggered a critical reassessment of the understanding of the Earth's magnetic anomalies and the physicochemical process responsible for their formation. Because of its large remanent magnetization per unit volume, single-domain magnetite is usually invoked as a possible source for Mars's crustal magnetism. But it is difficult to imagine by the Earth's standards geological formations containing single-domain magnetite tens of kilometers thick and extending thousands of kilometers. Recent meteorite measurements in the laboratory show that coarse-grained hematite can exhibit significant remanent magnetization when exposed to Earth-like fields, providing a more viable mechanism for the formation of crustal magnetic sources at Mars where hematite formations have already been detected by the *Global Surveyor*. On the Earth, the presence of a strong geomagnetic background field introduces significant difficulties when trying to separate the induced from the remanent components of magnetization associated with magnetic anomalies. Mars is an ideal laboratory where nature has shut down the background field, and the "pure" remanent magnetization of the crust can be observed without concern for ambiguous interpretations. Future Mars missions will provide additional local data which can be correlated to the discoveries of *Mars Global Surveyor* to gain further insight into Mars's fascinating thermal history and perhaps the Earth's own.

For background information *see* GEOMAGNETISM; MAGNETIC FIELD; MARS; SPACE PROBE in the McGraw-Hill Encyclopedia of Science & Technology.

Mario H. Acuña

Bibliography. M. H. Acuña et al., Global distribution of crustal magnetization discovered by the *Mars Global Surveyor* MAG/ER experiment, *Science*, 284:790–793, 1999; M. H. Acuña et al., Magnetic field and plasma observations at Mars: Preliminary results of the *Mars Global Surveyor* mission, *Science*, 279:1676–1680, 1998; A. L. Albee et al., *Mars Global Surveyor* mission: Overview and status, *Science*, 279:1671–1672, 1998; J. E. P. Connerney et al., Magnetic lineations in the ancient crust of Mars, *Science*, 284:794–798, 1999; H. H. Kieffer et al. (eds.), *Mars*, University of Arizona Press, Tucson, 1992; J. H. Shirley and R. W. Fainbridge (eds.), *Encyclopedia of Planetary Sciences*, Chapman and Hall, London, 1997.

Memory

Understanding how the brain registers and retrieves information remains a formidable challenge. Since the acceptance of the neuron doctrine, neuroscientists have embraced the idea that memories are stored as modifications of neuronal connections. Following the remarkable studies of W. B. Scoville and B. Milner with the patient H.M., considerable attention has been devoted to the role of the hippocampus (a part of the limbic system located bilaterally in the temporal lobe of the brain) in information storage. Work with H.M. and other amnestic patients has revealed the existence of several distinct types of learning and memory. Successes of neurophysiologists in understanding the characteristics of synaptic transmission in invertebrate preparations has led to the search for simple models that could be used to identify the molecular and cellular mechanisms of learning and memory. Among these elementary forms of activity-dependent synaptic modifications are the phenomena of long-term potentiation and long-term depression. Several forms of learning and memory are also recognized in the temporal domain as the distinction between short-term memory (which is intact in H.M.) and long-term memory (absent in H.M.) is readily perceived. Finally, the concept of memory consolidation has been extensively developed. Thus, both molecular and behavioral approaches to the problem of learning and memory have converged to provide a rich and complex picture of the properties and mechanisms of memory systems.

Cellular and molecular mechanisms. Because of the simplicity of its nervous system, which consists of approximately 20,000 neurons, the marine mollusk *Aplysia* has been widely used for the study of the cellular and molecular mechanisms underlying learning and memory. One behavior that has been studied in detail is the gill withdrawal reflex: the animal withdraws its gill when its siphon is stimulated. If the stimulus is benign and appears repeatedly, the reflex becomes smaller and smaller; the animal is habituated. If the stimulus is strong or noxious, the response is enhanced; the animal becomes sensitized. The gill withdrawal reflex can also be conditioned if the siphon stimulus is appropriately coupled with a conditioning stimulus. These modifications of the gill withdraw reflex—habituation, sensitization, and conditioning—can last for a few minutes (short-term) or days and weeks (long-term).

Short-term sensitization. In short-term sensitization a noxious stimulus to a body part activates sensory neurons that excite facilitatory interneurons. These interneurons form axo-axonal synapses on the siphon sensory neurons and facilitate the responses of gill motor neurons by increasing neurotransmitter release. Short-term sensitization involves activation of second messengers [G-proteins, cAMP-dependent protein kinase (PKA), and so on], reduction in potassium (K^+) current, and increase in calcium (Ca^{2+}) influx.

Long-term sensitization. Long-term sensitization is induced by repeated noxious stimuli. Long-term and short-term sensitization share several properties; for example, both occur at the synapses between sensory neurons and motor neurons, both depend on PKA, and both involve presynaptic facilitation. However, long-term sensitization depends on novel protein synthesis, while short-term sensitization does not. Molecular studies indicate that long-term sensitization involves translocation of PKA to the nucleus of sensory neurons and activation of transcription factors, in particular the cAMP response element binding (CREB) protein. Other processes participating in long-term plasticity consist of morphological changes in synaptic connections. For example, long-term habituation is accompanied by pruning of synaptic connections, while increase in synapses is a consequence of long-term sensitization.

Long-term potentiation. Long-term potentiation was first described in 1973 in the hippocampus, a structure known to be critical for learning and memory. Because of its rapid onset, long duration, and synaptic specificity, long-term potentiation has been widely investigated as a cellular substrate for memory over the last few decades. Long-term potentiation requires postsynaptic depolarization and presynaptic neurotransmitter release. The associative nature of long-term potentiation is due to the unique properties of N-methyl-D-aspartate (NMDA) receptors that are blocked by magnesium in a voltage-dependent manner. It is generally agreed that long-term potentiation induction is a postsynaptic process that involves NMDA receptor activation and calcium influx. However, regarding the mechanisms of long-term potentiation expression, there has been a vigorous debate between facilitation of postsynaptic responses or increased presynaptic neurotransmitter release.

More recently, solid evidence has shifted the focus to the postsynaptic side: long-term potentiation expression is due to modifications in the distribution of α-amino-3-hydroxy-5-methyl-4-isoxazde propionic acid (AMPA) receptors and in the structure of synaptic contacts. Biochemically, two calcium-dependent enzymes have been widely implicated in long-term potentiation expression: a calcium-dependent protease (calpain) and a calcium/calmodulin-dependent protein kinase II (CaMKII). Activation of calpain modifies synaptic cytoskeletal proteins, cell adhesion molecules, and AMPA receptors, and thereby synaptic communication. Activation of CaMKII phosphorylates key synaptic proteins, including glutamate receptors, and thus could alter synaptic efficacy. Autophosphorylation of CaMKII, which maintains the enzyme in an active state, is believed to participate in long-term potentiation expression.

In addition, changes in lipid composition of synaptic membranes resulting from activation of calcium-dependent phospholipases have been proposed to also alter synaptic contact properties. Morphological studies have shown that long-term potentiation induction results in transient remodeling of postsynaptic membranes followed by a marked increase in split synapses—one axon terminal contacting two or more dendritic spines. Numerous extracellular matrix proteins and integrins have been implicated in long-term potentiation consolidation. It is hypothesized that stabilization of the modifications triggered during the induction phase of long-term potentiation is accomplished first by the disruption of the adhesive properties of synaptic contacts, followed by the activation of integrins (cell surface molecules). In this way, synaptic contacts undergo a cycle of destabilization resulting from intracellular as well as extracellular proteolysis of proteins contributing to the morphology of synaptic contacts, followed by restabilization of new synaptic structures implicating integrin activation and extracellular matrix components. Changes in gene expression have been reported after long-term potentiation induction; however, it has been difficult to establish links between gene induction and mechanisms underlying long-term potentiation expression and consolidation. An obvious question is how a cell-wide modification (gene regulation) could account for a local event (synaptic modulation).

Long-term depression. Long-term depression was discovered first in the cerebellum and more recently in other brain structures. Mechanisms underlying its induction and expression in the cerebellum are not yet fully understood. Long-term depression is difficult to induce in adult hippocampal slices, and can be reliably induced in some strains of rats but not others. Furthermore, the existence of long-term depression in adult hippocampus is affected by the behavioral history of the animal. In addition to long-term depression, long-term potentiation reversal has been discovered and proposed to participate in memory cell biology as a counter process of long-term potentiation.

Cellular models and behavior. Considerable discussion continues regarding whether any of the cellular or molecular mechanisms of synaptic plasticity take place in learning and memory. Some scientists argue that the important point is that the identification of these mechanisms has provided tools to solve the mystery of memory, and meanwhile to improve memory impairment associated with age or neurological diseases. Others argue that this is a prerequisite, and various approaches have thus been employed to link specific cellular mechanisms to specific types of learning and memory.

Pharmacological agents inhibiting or stimulating cellular processes underlying synaptic plasticity have been widely tested on various forms of learning and memory. Among these, NMDA receptor antagonists were first reported to inhibit learning and memory processes. More recent studies have indicated that under certain conditions, these agents, while blocking long-term potentiation, do not block learning and memory, thus casting doubts regarding long-term potentiation involvement in learning and memory. Allosteric modulators of AMPA receptors (the so-called ampakines) have been shown to facilitate both long-term potentiation formation and memory. Genetic modifications of key components of synaptic contacts to establish links between molecular processes and behavioral properties of learning and memory have also been widely used. A variety of gene knock-out mutants with alterations in AMPA or NMDA receptors, protein kinases, or cytoskeletal proteins exhibit various degrees of long-term potentiation and learning and memory impairment. Conversely, a recently described mutant that overexpresses a subtype of NMDA receptors displays improved long-term potentiation and increased learning abilities for certain tasks. Nevertheless, the correlation is far from perfect, which reflects more the complexity of the problem than the dissociation between these issues. It is also important to note that the links between long-term depression and learning are even more tenuous than for long-term potentiation except for long-term depression in the cerebellum where there is compelling (although not definitive) evidence that long-term depression plays a critical role in classical conditioning of skeletal motor responses.

For background information *see* INFORMATION PROCESSING (PSYCHOLOGY); LEARNING MECHANISMS; MEMORY; NEUROBIOLOGY; SYNAPTIC TRANSMISSION in the McGraw-Hill Encyclopedia of Science & Technology.   Michel Baudry; Xiaoning Bi

Bibliography. G. Lynch, Memory and the brain: Unexpected chemistries and a new pharmacology, *Neurobiol. Learning Memory*, 70:82–100, 1998; R. C. Malenka and R. A. Nicoll, Long-term potentiation—a decade of progress?, *Science*, 285:1870–1874, 1999; R. G. M. Morris et al., Selective impairment of learning and blockade of long-term potentiation by the *N*-methyl-D-aspartate receptor antagonist, AP-5, *Nature*, 319:774–776, 1986; A. J. Silva, A. M. Smith, and K. P. Giese, Gene targeting and the biology of learning and memory, *Annu. Rev. Genet.*, 31:527–546, 1997.

Metallocene catalysts

Metallocene catalysts are organometallic coordination compounds in which one or two cyclopentadienyl rings (with or without substituents) are bonded to a central transition-metal atom (**Fig. 1**). The nature and number of the rings and their substituents (S), the type of transition metal (M) and its substituents (R), the type of the bridge (B) if present, and the co-catalyst type determine the catalytic behavior of these organometallic compounds toward olefin polymerization.

The importance of these catalysts is revealed by the hundreds of patents issued in this field since 1980. In brief, the impact of metallocenes in the polyolefin manufacture industry can be attributed to the following factors: (1) *Enhanced polymer microstructure control*: Metallocenes can produce polymer with narrow distributions of molecular weight, chemical composition, stereoregularity, and long-chain branching. (2) *High catalytic activity*: Metallocenes have very high activities and therefore are adequate for the production of commodity polymers. (3) *Versatility*: Metallocenes can produce several different types of polymers with enhanced or entirely novel properties. (4) *Compatibility*: Metallocenes can be used in existing polymer manufacturing processes with minimal modifications.

D. S. Breslow and N. R. Newburg were among the first researchers to apply metallocenes for polymerization in the late 1950s. They used soluble bis(cyclopentadienyl)titanium derivatives and alkylaluminums for ethylene polymerization. Several other researchers (including G. Natta) followed their original work, using the same catalyst or modifications of that system. However, these catalysts had low activity and stability for the polymerization of ethylene and produced only low-molecular-weight polyethylene. Additionally, they were not active for propylene polymerization.

However, it was noted in the late 1970s that the activity of metallocene/alkylaluminum systems

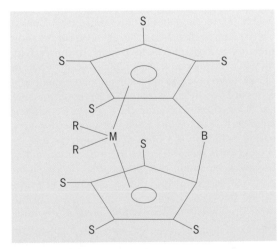

Fig. 1. Generic structure of a metallocene catalyst.

could be significantly increased by the controlled addition of water to the polymerization reactor. This enhanced activity was attributed to the reaction between water and alkylaluminum to form alkylaluminoxane. This single discovery led to the development of an entirely new class of catalysts that are today the most promising branch of Ziegler-Natta catalysis. All the major polyolefin-manufacturing companies are currently adapting their industrial reactors to the use of metallocene catalysts, and several grades of polyethylene and polypropylene made with these remarkable catalysts are already commercially available.

Role of aluminoxane. The type of aluminoxane has a marked influence on the efficiency of metallocenes. Methylaluminoxane (MAO) seems to be more effective than ethylaluminoxane and isobutylaluminoxane. More remarkably, the activity of the metallocene complex is directly proportional to the degree of oligomerization of the aluminoxane. Besides, for most homogeneous metallocenes, a large excess of aluminoxane is required for the polymerization to reach its optimum value. Aluminum/transition-metal ratios of 1000 are commonly reported in the literature. The exact structure of aluminoxanes is still a matter of controversy. They supposedly exist as a mixture of different cyclic or linear oligomers with the degree of oligomerization commonly varying from 6 to 20. Some recent experimental evidence suggests that MAO might have a three-dimensional open-cage structure.

Despite its marked influence in catalytic performance, the exact role of the aluminoxane is not known precisely. Experimental evidence seems to indicate that, besides acting as alkylation agents and impurity scavengers, aluminoxanes are involved in the formation of active sites and in the prevention of their deactivation by bimolecular processes.

It is now widely accepted that the active site of metallocene catalysts is cationic. The metallocene complex is therefore a cation associated with a stable anion. The hypothesis that the catalyst center is polar or ionic is further supported by the electronic effects observed in some metallocenes of the type $(X_2C_9H_5)_2ZrCl_2/MAO$, where X can be a chlorine atom, a hydrogen atom, a fluorine atom, a methyl (CH_3) group, or a methoxy (OCH_3) group. It was observed that, for ethylene polymerization, electron-withdrawing atoms such as fluorine significantly lowered the catalytic activity and molecular weight of the produced polymer, while electron donors such as CH_3 had little influence over the polymerization. For the case of polypropylene production, electron-withdrawing groups might reduce the stereochemical control of the catalyst. This has been related to changes in the degree of association of the metallocene and the MAO counterion or to the increase in the strength of the metal-carbon bond between metallocene and ligands.

Metallocene applications. Achiral cyclopentadienyl catalysts are commonly used to produce polyethylenes at high productivity with narrow distribution of molecular weight and chemical composition. The most commonly used catalysts for polyethylene production are achiral cyclopentadienyl derivatives of zirconium, titanium, and hafnium. Titanium and hafnium catalysts have a smaller activity and are generally less thermally stable than the equivalent zirconium catalyst.

The molecular weight of polymer made with metallocenes is generally very sensitive to temperature. Molecular weight averages decrease with increasing temperature, presumably due to an intensification of β-hydride elimination. Hydrogen is an efficient chain transfer agent when used with most metallocene catalysts. Only traces of hydrogen are necessary to significantly reduce the molecular weight of the polymer product, which has opened a viable route for the production of olefin oligomers and waxes.

One remarkable property of these catalysts is their ability to produce copolymers of ethylene and α-olefins (linear low-density polyethylene) with narrower chemical composition distribution than the ones produced with heterogeneous Ziegler-Natta catalysts (**Fig. 2**). From an application point of view, the low-crystallinity tail increases the amount of extractables and the high-crystallinity fraction leads to haze in films. Therefore, metallocene linear low-density polyethylene films can be more transparent and have less extractables than equivalent ones made with conventional Ziegler-Natta catalysts. These films are desirable, for instance, for food packaging applications. Additionally, metallocenes can produce copolymers with almost random incorporation of comonomers, which results in a maximum decrease in polymer crystallinity for a given amount of comonomer incorporation. This is an important feature for the production of impact polypropylene.

The versatility of metallocenes is well illustrated when examining the evolution of metallocene catalysts for propylene polymerization. The first stereospecific metallocenes, such as racemic Et[Ind]$_2$ZrCl$_2$ [ethylenebis(indenyl) zirconium dichloride], could only produce polymers with low

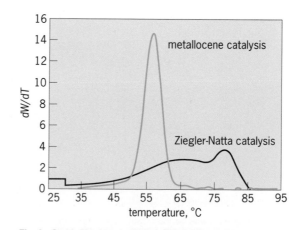

Fig. 2. Crystallization analysis fractionations of two commercial ethylene-α-olefin copolymers. The graph is a distribution of crystallinity as a function of temperature. The mass of polymer (dW) that crystallizes in the temperature interval (dT) is indicated by dW/dT.

molecular weight; and although they could polymerize propylene with a high degree of isotacticity, several regio-irregularities such as 2–1 and 1–3 insertions were detected in the chains. Consequently, these polypropylene resins had a melting temperature significantly lower than the ones made with heterogeneous Ziegler-Natta catalysts. By changing the ligand and bridge types around the central metal atom, catalysts for the production of polypropylene have evolved considerably, and today it is possible to synthesize polypropylene with high molecular weight and high melting temperature with catalysts such as racemic $Me_2Si[2\text{-}Me\text{-}Benz(e)Ind]_2ZrCl_2$ [dimethyl silylenebis(2-methylbenz[e] indenyl) zirconium dichloride].

By the appropriate selection of metallocenes, it is possible to produce polypropylene with different chain microstructures. Polypropylene with atactic, isotactic, isotactic-stereoblock, atactic-stereoblock, and hemiisotactic configurations has been produced with metallocene catalysts (**Fig. 3**). For the synthesis of stereospecific metallocenes for propylene polymerization, C_2 symmetric precursors are necessary to obtain a catalyst for isospecific polymerization; and C_s symmetric precursors, to produce a catalyst for syndiospecific polymerization. Asymmetric precursors can be used to synthesize metallocene catalysts that produce hemiisotactic and isotactic-stereoblock polypropylene (**Fig. 4**).

Polypropylene having the properties of a thermoplastic elastomer can be synthesized with the asymmetric metallocenes $Et(Me_4Cp)(Ind)TiCl_2/MAO$ and $Et(Me_4Cp)(Ind)TiEt_2/MAO$ [ethylene (tetramethylcyclopentadienyl)(indenyl) titanium dichloride/MAO and -titanium diethylene/MAO]. This is the first example of a thermoplastic elastomer consisting of only one monomer type. It is supposed that the active sites exist in two different states, one stereospecific

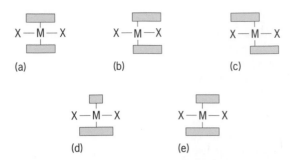

Fig. 4. Catalyst symmetry requirements for polypropylene (PP) synthesis. Complexes with C_1 symmetry have no symmetry operations by which the complex can be converted into itself. C_2 symmetry complexes have only one C_2 axis. C_s symmetry precursor complexes have only a mirror plane. (a) C_{2v}: attactic PP. (b) C_s (meso): attactic PP. (c) C_2 (racemic): isotactic PP. (d) C_s: syndiotactic PP. (e) C_1: no unequivocal prediction.

and the other nonstereospecific. Since they can change states during the lifetime of a polymer molecule, the chain has alternating blocks of atactic and isotactic polypropylene. The isotactic domains act as physical cross-links and give the polymer its elastomeric properties.

Metallocenes have also been used to polymerize styrene (notably syndiotactic polystyrene). Additionally, they can be used to a lesser extent to polymerize α-olefins and polar monomers, although generally activities are much lower. It is usually necessary to treat the polar comonomer with electron donors to shield their polar groups from the active sites during polymerization or to introduce spacer groups between the comonomer functionality and the terminal double bond.

MAO-free systems. MAO-free metallocenes are prepared by combining at least two components. The first is an alkylated metallocene, and the second is an ion-exchange compound such as tris(pentafluorophenyl)borane, comprising a cation and a noncoordinating anion. The cation reacts irreversibly with at least one of the first component's ligands. The anion must be capable of stabilizing the transition-metal cation complex and must be labile enough to be displaced by the polymerizing monomer. The relationship of the counterion to the bridged structure controls monomer insertion and isomerization.

Long-chain-branch formation. Although long-chain branch formation has been reported for polymerization with several biscyclopentadienyl complexes, the most suitable metallocenes for this formation appear to be based on monocyclopentadienyl complexes. The active center of these catalysts is based on group 4 transition metals that are covalently bonded to a monocyclopentadienyl ring and bridged with a heteroatom, forming a constrained cyclic structure with the titanium center. This geometry allows the titanium center to be more "open" to the addition of ethylene and higher α-olefins, but also for the addition of vinyl-terminated polymer chains. In other words, this configuration leads to higher comonomer reactivity ratios with long α-olefins.

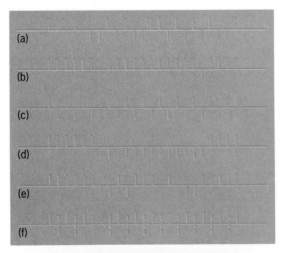

Fig. 3. Polypropylene configurations obtained with different metallocene catalysts: (a) atactic, Cp_2ZrCl_2; (b) isotactic, $Et(Ind)_2ZrCl_2$; (c) syndiotactic, $iPr(Flu)(Cp)HfCl_2$; (d) isotactic-stereoblock, $(NMCp)_2ZrCl_2$; (e) isotactic-atactic stereoblock, $Et(Me_4Cp)(Ind)TiCl_2$; (f) hemiisotactic, $iPr(Cp)(Ind)ZrCl_2$.

There is significant evidence showing that the mechanism of long-chain branch formation for metallocenes is terminal branching. In this mechanism, dead polymer chains containing terminal vinyl unsaturations are reinserted into another growing polymer chain, thus forming long-chain branches. Dead polymer chains containing a terminal vinyl unsaturation are formed by β-hydride elimination or transfer to ethylene. An important characteristic of these polymers is that they combine the good mechanical properties of polymers with narrow molecular weight distribution, with the good processability of polymers containing long-chain branches.

Supported metallocene catalysts. Metallocenes are generally supported on inert carriers, since most of the conventional Ziegler-Natta polyolefin industrial plants are designed to use heterogeneous catalysts. This considerably simplifies their use in already existing polymerization processes ("drop-in" technology).

Metallocenes can be effectively supported on several inorganic oxides. The most commonly used is SiO_2, but $MgCl_2$, Al_2O_3, MgF_2, CaF_2, and several zeolites have also been investigated. Polyolefin particles and natural polymers such as cellulose have also been used to support metallocene catalysts.

The type of support and the technique used for supporting the metallocene and MAO have a crucial influence on catalyst behavior. Several techniques for supporting metallocenes and MAO have been proposed, such as (but not restricted to) adsorption of MAO onto the support followed by addition of the metallocene; immobilization of the metallocene on the support, followed by contact with MAO in the polymerization reactor; and immobilization of the metallocene on the support, followed by treatment with MAO.

Aluminoxanes can be synthesized separately and then supported on the carrier, or they can be produced in situ by reaction of an alkylaluminum with the water adsorbed on the support. It has been observed by several groups that, when the support is treated with aluminoxanes or alkylaluminums prior to metallocene supporting, the behavior of the supported metallocene approximates more closely that of the equivalent soluble system.

Supported metallocenes usually require smaller aluminum/transition-metal ratios than the equivalent soluble systems, and some can be activated by common alkylaluminums in the absence of aluminoxanes. This reduced dependence on aluminum/transition-metal ratios has been related to a reduction in catalyst deactivation by bimolecular processes due to the immobility of the active sites on the surface of the support.

The catalytic activity of supported metallocenes is usually less than that of the equivalent soluble catalyst, probably due to deactivation of catalytic sites or inefficient production of active sites during the supporting process. Broadening of the distribution of molecular weight and chemical composition for supported catalysts can also occur under certain conditions. Although it is generally accepted that this might be caused by the formation of sites of different types due to support-metallocene interactions, some experimental and mathematical modeling results seem to indicate that mass-transfer resistance can play an important role as well.

Designing multiple-site-type catalysts. One way of using metallocene catalysts to produce polymers with broad distribution of molecular weight and chemical composition is the combination of different metallocenes on the same support, therefore engineering a multiple-site-type catalyst. If each site type has distinct ratios of chain transfer to propagation rates as well as different reactivity ratios, copolymers with "tailored" distribution of molecular weight and chemical composition can be synthesized by the planned selection of metallocene types and their relative proportions. Additionally, several mathematical models can predict polymer microstructure from the knowledge of the leading polymerization kinetic parameters.

At first sight, this approach seems to contradict one of the main advantages of metallocene catalysis, that is, the production of polymer with uniform molecular structure, since its main objective is to produce polymers with nonuniform microstructure, apparently similar to the molecular structure obtained with heterogeneous Ziegler-Natta catalysts. However, what must be realized is that the nonuniformity of polyolefins made with heterogeneous Ziegler-Natta catalysts arises from the intrinsic multiple-site-type nature of these catalysts, which is very difficult, if not impossible, to control with a high degree of confidence. Consequently, the selective combination of different metallocene types under appropriate polymerization conditions opens the door to a much improved control of the microstructure of these polyolefin chains.

For background information *see* CATALYSIS; COORDINATION COMPLEX; HETEROGENEOUS CATALYSIS; METALLOCENE; MOLECULAR WEIGHT; ORGANOMETALLIC COMPOUND; POLYMERIZATION; POLYOLEFIN RESINS in the McGraw-Hill Encyclopedia of Science & Technology.   João B. P. Soares/Archie E. Hamielec

Bibliography. V. K. Gupta, S. Satish, and I. S. Bhardwaj, Metallocene complexes of group 4 elements in the polymerization of monoolefins, *J.M.S. Rev. Macromol. Chem. Phys.*, C34:439–514, 1994; A. E. Hamielec and J. B. P. Soares, Metallocene catalysed polymerization: Industrial technology, in J. Karger-Kocsis (ed.), *Polypropylene: An A-Z Reference*, pp.446–453, Kluwer Academic, Dordrecht, 1999; A. E. Hamielec and J. B. P. Soares, Polymerization reaction engineering: Metallocene catalysis, *Prog. Polym. Sci.*, 21:651–706, 1996; W. Kaminsky, New polymers by metallocene catalysis, *Macromol. Chem. Phys.*, 197:3907–3945, 1996; N. Kashiwa and J. I. Imuta, Recent progress on olefin polymerization catalysts, *Catalysis Surv. Jap.*, 1:125–142, 1997; R. Po and N. Cardi, Synthesis of syndiotactic polystyrene: Reaction mechanisms and catalysis, *Prog.*

Polym. Sci., 21:47–88, 1996; S. S. Reddy and S. Sivaram, Homogeneous metallocene-methylaluminoxane catalyst systems for ethylene polymerization, *Prog. Polym. Sci.*, 20:309–367, 1995; J. B. P. Soares and A. E. Hamielec, Metallocene/aluminoxane catalysts for olefin polymerization: A review, *Polym. React. Eng.*, 3:131–200, 1995; J. B. P. Soares and A. Penlidis, Measurement, mathematical modelling and control of distributions of molecular weight, chemical composition and long chain branching of polyolefins made with metallocene catalysts, in J. Scheirs (ed.), *Preparation, Properties and Technology of Metallocene-Based Polyolefins*, pp. 237–267, John Wiley, 2000; K. Soga and T. Shiono, Ziegler-Natta catalysts for olefin polymerizations, *Prog. Polym. Sci.*, 22:1503–1546, 1997; N. Tomotsu and Ishihara, Novel catalysts for the syndiospecific polymerization of styrene, *Catalysis Surv. Jap.*, 1:89–110, 1997.

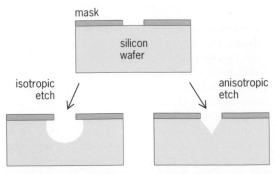

Fig. 1. Bulk micromachining of a silicon wafer.

Microscopic microphones

Microphones have advanced tremendously since Thomas Edison patented a device in 1877 based on the resistance of carbon granules. The most commonly used microphone today is the foil electret microphone, which was developed in the 1960s, and enabled microphones to be easily incorporated into a multitude of products. It appears that a new breakthrough in microphone technology may be imminent: the MEMS microphone. MEMS, an acronym for microelectromechanical systems, refers to any small mechanical device that can be fabricated on a silicon chip, often connected to some form of electrical system. A MEMS microphone can be very small (less than 1 mm) and can be incorporated directly onto an electronic chip.

MEMS technology. The MEMS concept developed from the semiconductor industry when it was realized that the processes used to fabricate integrated circuits on silicon chips could also be used to make mechanical structures. The standard integrated circuit techniques of epitaxy, doping, deposition, and lithography are referred to as silicon planar integrated-circuit technology. Two recent processes that that have become critical in the development of MEMS devices are bulk micromachining and surface micromachining. In bulk micromachining, relatively deep holes are carved into the silicon wafer, typically using a wet etch. For an etchant such as HNA (a combination of hydrofluoric, nitric, and acetic acids), the etch is isotropic; that is, silicon is removed in all directions. For chemicals such as potassium hydroxide (KOH), the etch preferentially removes materials along particular planes of the silicon's crystalline structure (**Fig. 1**). In surface micromachining, sacrificial layers are typically deposited onto the silicon wafer. The sacrificial layers become a type of mold around which mechanical structures can be formed. The sacrificial layers are then removed using etching techniques. The difference between the two techniques is that bulk micromachining removes some of the bulk silicon whereas surface micromachining typically adds a structure without removing a significant amount of the bulk silicon. MEMS devices are constructed using a number of sequential processing steps. It is critical to design the process properly so that a structure formed by one step is not destroyed by a later step.

The most ubiquitous MEMS device currently is the MEMS accelerometer, which is used in the deployment system of air bags in automobiles. The accelerometer, together with its associated electronics, measures 2 mm (0.08 in.) on a side and is one-tenth the size and one-tenth the cost of the older mechanical devices. In recent years, MEMS technology has been used to build microscopic microphones. In 1998, a working microphone in micromachined silicon technology, claimed to be the world's smallest, was announced, with integrated adaptive electronic amplifier circuits.

Microphone design. Sound can be sensed in a large number of ways, as witnessed by the variety of conventional microphones that are manufactured. In MEMS there is a wide variety of sound detection techniques. The majority of the designs use some form of membrane to detect sound. A small thin membrane is fabricated on the silicon chip. When a sound wave is incident on the membrane, the membrane moves back and forth with the sound wave. If the membrane is significantly smaller than a wavelength of the sound, it vibrates in almost perfect synchronicity with the sound wave. At higher frequencies, however, the motion of the membrane can be significantly diminished. There are a number of techniques (**Fig. 2**) by which the membrane motion can be sensed.

Capacitative or condenser microphone. This is the most popular means of detecting the membrane motion and works on the same principle as conventional condenser microphones. The membrane is configured to be one plate of a capacitor (Fig. 2*a*). The second plate is fixed to the main silicon wafer. As the membrane moves, the distance between the plates changes and the capacitance changes. If a fixed charge is stored on the capacitor (normally using a dc bias), the voltage across the capacitor varies as the membrane moves. The electret is a form of capacitative microphone, except that it uses a permanently polarized dielectric (typically Teflon). MEMS electret microphones have been fabricated by spinning Teflon onto silicon.

Piezoelectric microphone. A piezoelectric material is one that produces a voltage when it is squeezed. Therefore the fluctuating pressure of a sound wave makes a piezoelectric material respond with a fluctuating voltage (Fig. 2*b*). Until recently, piezoelectric materials were not commonly used for MEMS pressure transducers because these materials do not bond well to silicon. However, new techniques have allowed piezoelectric materials such as zinc oxide (ZnO) and lead zirconate (PZT) to be deposited on silicon. Current devices are very insensitive and typically do not have a uniform response over the audio bandwidth. However, the PZT-based devices appear to be practical for the use at ultrasonic frequencies.

Piezoresistive microphone. In this device a piezoresistive material (Edison's original carbon microphone also used a piezoresistive effect) is deposited on the edges of the membrane (Fig. 2*c*). As the membrane moves, the resistance changes. The piezoresistive elements are typically placed in a Wheatstone bridge. These devices have the advantages of low noise and low output impedance.

Channel FET microphone. In this device the membrane is used as the gate to a field-effect transistor (FET). The FET is located just below the membrane (Fig. 2*d*). As the membrane (and hence the gate) moves, the current between the source and drain is modulated. The advantage of this device is that its transduction mechanism is also an active amplifier and the device therefore has very low output impedance.

Optical microphone. The motion of the membrane can be detected optically. A light beam and one of a number of interferometers (such as Mach-Zender or Fabry-Perot) can be used to detect the motion of the membrane (Fig. 2*e*). The displacement can also be sensed by using the motion of the membrane to deflect a laser beam. Typical displacements for sound in air are 0.1 micrometer, and these can easily be detected by using laser light in the infrared region. Optical techniques have two advantages: they are typically wide-bandwidth, and they are relatively immune to electrical noise. However, they are very complicated, and hence costly, to fabricate.

Applications. Microphones that are currently being fabricated have membranes on the order of 1 mm wide and just a few micrometers thick. The sensitivities of MEMS microphones range from 100 μV to 1 mV/Pa compared to 10–100 mV/Pa for conventional microphones. As development proceeds, sensitivities can be expected to improve. However, the reduced sensitivity of a MEMS microphone can be offset by amplification, because it is possible to incorporate the MEMS device and electronics into the same package. The proximity alleviates problems associated with noise. This ability to miniaturize holds immense potential for the MEMS microphone. MEMS microphones have been sug-

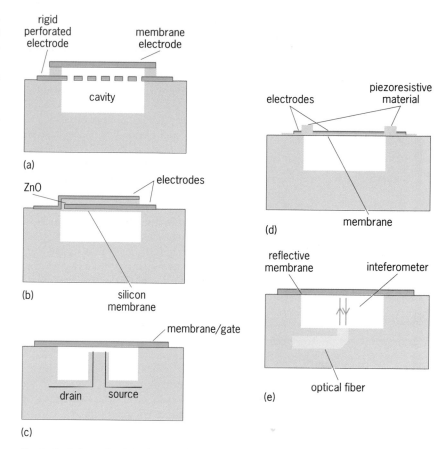

Fig. 2. **Techniques for detecting membrane motion in a MEMS microphone.** (*a*) Capacitative. (*b*) Piezoelectric. (*c*) Field-effect transistor. (*d*) Piezoresistive. (*e*) Optical.

gested as the next step in hearing aids, where the microphone and electronics could perhaps be camouflaged as an earring. MEMS microphones are the technology that would be used as the "ears" of proposed remote surveillance devices, such as a flying microbat. *See* AUTONOMOUS AIRCRAFT.

Arrays. One advantage of silicon-based technology is the ease with which structures can be replicated on a single device. Arrays of microphones have been constructed on a silicon chip. Among the numerous applications that are associated with these arrays, the most practical is the ability to "beamform," that is, to receive information from a specific direction. For example, using a MEMS microphone array in a cell phone would allow the speaker's voice to be picked up even in a very noisy background. With active beamforming, it would even be possible to track the speaker's mouth if it moves around.

Ultrasound. MEMS devices have also been constructed for higher-frequency applications. Ultrasound, in the range of 2–10 MHz, is widely used for medical imaging. The transducers in these devices are very complex arrays that can utilize the fabrication advantages associated with MEMS. The U.S. Navy is developing a MEMS hydrophone array to find underwater mines in the surf zone. The optical visibility in the surf is typically less than 1 m (3 ft), and divers often "find" mines by swimming into them.

MEMS-based acoustic arrays offer the opportunity to "see" with sound for ranges of 3–10 m (10–30 ft).

Speech recognition devices. It appears likely that within the near future appliances in the everyday world, such as the videocassette recorder (VCR), will be able to respond directly to vocal commands. The MEMS microphone appears to be the ideal component to be the ear of the device, as it can be fabricated directly onto the microchip that will be the device's "brain."

Competition. Although MEMS microphones can be manufactured in bulk, and hence cheaply and with high levels of reproducibility, they face intense competition. The foil electret microphone is small, can be fabricated very cheaply, and is well accepted. However, as integration becomes more important, MEMS microphones have a significant advantage: they can, in principle, be integrated on a silicon chip that contains all the electronics. The non-silicon-based production step associated with attaching the microphone to the chip is therefore removed. This is particularly important for microphone arrays, associated with very complicated wiring.

For background information *see* ELECTRET TRANSDUCER; INTEGRATED CIRCUITS; INTERFEROMETRY; MICROPHONE; PIEZOELECTRICITY; TRANSDUCER; TRANSISTOR; ULTRASONICS in the McGraw-Hill Encyclopedia of Science & Technology.

Robin Cleveland

Bibliography. J. J. Bernstein et al., Micromachine ferroelectric transducers for acoustic imaging, *Proc. Int. Conf. Solid-State Sensors and Actuators*, Chicago, 1:421–424, June 1997; M. Royer et al., ZnO on Si integrated acoustic sensor, *Sensors and Actuators*, 4: 357–362, 1983; P. R. Scheeper et al., A review of silicon microphones, *Sensors and Actuators A*, 44: 1–11, 1994; G. M. Sessler, Acoustic sensors, *Sensors and Actuators*, 25–27:323–330, 1991.

Microwave technology

The development of microwave heating was preceded by work with radio waves, which were experimentally produced by Heinrich Hertz at Karlsruhe Polytechnic in Germany between 1885 and 1889. Hertz measured the wavelength and velocity of these waves. His first oscillator operated between 500,000 and 1,500,000 Hz (cycles per second), and the waves were tested on animals. He concluded that the only effect of these waves was that owing to heat. This work led to the first example of high-frequency heating therapy on humans at a Paris hospital in 1895.

Magnetron. The magnetron is the major microwave energy generator used today in the food and other industries. It was invented by British scientists H. A. H. Boots and J. T. Randall at Birmingham University in England, based in part on information in Hertz's notes, and was mass-produced in the United States. It played a major role in radar in the defense of Britain during German air attacks in World War II. In the early postwar years the search for other applications for excess magnetron production capacity resulted in microwave oven development. The magnetron's low cost, long life, and high efficiency allow for a low cost per kilowatt-hour of operation. Early research on microwave heating of food was carried out at the Massachusetts Institute of Technology.

Allocated frequencies. By international treaty a number of specific microwave frequencies were allocated for industrial, scientific, and medical (ISM) use. These frequencies can be used license-free in every country around the world. The frequency allocations for electromagnetic heating and processing in the United States are:

$$678 \pm 0.015 \text{ MHz}$$
$$1356 \pm 0.007 \text{ MHz}$$
$$27.12 \pm 0.163 \text{ MHz}$$
$$40.68 \pm 0.02 \text{ MHz}$$
$$915 \pm 13 \text{ MHz}$$
$$2450 \pm 50 \text{ MHz}$$
$$5.8 \text{ GHz} \pm 75 \text{ MHz}$$
$$24.125 \text{ GHz} \pm 125 \text{ MHz}$$
$$61.25 \text{ GHz} \pm 250 \text{ MHz}$$
$$122.5 \text{ GHz} \pm 500 \text{ MHz}$$
$$245 \text{ GHz} \pm 1000 \text{ MHz}$$

The frequencies 2450 MHz and 915 MHz (896 MHz in some countries, including the United Kingdom) are used for a variety of applications, particularly the heating and cooking of food. The consumer microwave oven is the most notable example of a microwave device and is used worldwide.

Food processing. Only when a conveyorized microwave oven became available in the early 1960s could some early ideas about food processing become realities. One promising example was the microwave finish-drying of potato chips. The process was developed at a time when potato chip manufacturers were experiencing difficulties in procuring good chipping potatoes, with a low reducing-sugar content. The available potatoes at the time produced chips that were too dark to be salable. The microwave process made it possible to use such potatoes by first frying to the desired color, then microwave-drying to crispness without further color development. This process also made it possible to use cold-storage potatoes instead of potatoes stored at a high controlled temperature to prevent reducing-sugar development. At the height of this microwave process there were over 20 installations in the United States. In spite of the obvious benefits, the potato chip manufacturers opted to return to the traditional process. However, microwave techniques were developed in the 1990s that eliminate the frying step completely and produce a low-fat chip. Microwave systems utilizing 2000 kW are involved in which a split folded waveguide applicator is used. This early experience led to process development activity in such diverse areas as sausage manufacture, bread baking, drying short-goods pasta, vacuum-drying fruit juice concentrates, cooking bacon and chicken parts, tempering frozen food, blanching, pasteurization, and sterilization. A few of these processes resulted in pilot plant operations, while others were discontinued in spite of potential value.

Advantages of microwave energy. Microwave energy is compatible with other forms of thermal and radiated energies such as steam, hot air, infrared, and other microwave frequencies. Thus it is possible to heat internally by microwaves while affecting surface appearance with thermal energy sources. Microwaves penetrate deeply into food materials, and because of the generally high moisture content of food materials, microwave energy is absorbed and heat is generated. This feature of microwaves results in substantially shorter heating times and less moisture, nutrient, and quality changes. Other advantages are improved working conditions, easier cleanup, and less space required. Microwaves are also more efficient, resulting in further economies of energy usage. The 75-kW, 915-MHz magnetron used in most United States installations has a reputation of long-term reliability. It can also be refurbished at a significant cost saving. Further, it is easily replaced by plant maintenance personnel in 30 min or less so that there is little downtime. There are also systems operating at 2450 MHz in which 1.5-kW or higher magnetrons are used.

Very successful processes. There are a few very successful microwave food processes in use today: tempering of frozen foods; bacon cooking; pasteurization of fresh pasta, ready meals, and bread; and sterilization of ready meals.

Tempering is the application of microwave energy to raise the temperature of case lots of frozen meat, fish, and poultry to a few degrees below the freezing point of water, at which temperature the product can be easily further processed. For example, after tempering, beef is easily removed from its case and can be easily sliced, diced, chopped, or ground. Microwaves accomplish this task because food in the frozen state is very transparent to microwaves at 915 MHz and 2450 MHz, the main frequencies used in food processing. This deep penetration gives up energy uniformly so that process time is on the order of 10–15 min for 50-lb (23-kg) cases. The main advantage of microwave tempering is that it replaces the slow-tempering room system that required 2 to 3 days. Consequently there are never very large quantities in process, and adjustments are easily made. Thus, microwave processing has become well established in the food industry. Most tempering systems operate at 400–600 kW of microwave power. Processing cost is under $10 per ton ($11 per metric ton).

Microwave cooking of bacon is the second major application in the United States, and the primary user is the fast food industry. The equipment is similar to the tempering equipment in that it is a series of microwave cavities, but with a linked polymeric conveyor belt and a hold-down belt of the same material to keep the bacon from curling. The rendered fat is drained off and sold as an ingredient for use in prepared food products. Most of these systems are in the same range of power as tempering units, 400–600 kW, although one system in use is rated at 1000 kW. Since these systems are modular in nature, additional units can be added whenever necessary to increase production. Microwave-cooked bacon is currently in consumer market testing. If this product should become popular with consumers, much of the additional production required could be provided by add-on units.

A system for the microwave and steam cooking of cut-up chicken parts was placed in operation in 1966 and was in use for more than 10 years, producing a precooked breaded product for the restaurant trade. This process replaced a labor-intensive steam chest process. The advantage of the microwave process was in labor savings and higher yield. There also have been several installations of microwave equipment for cooking beef patties in Sweden, Japan, and elsewhere. This process is performed at 2450 MHz. Unlike the tempering and cooking equipment, which is based on a series of microwave cavities, the Swedish equipment has a unique system consisting of several antenna units above and below the conveyor belt with magnetrons mounted at the apex of a bell-shaped section of each antenna element.

Sterilization. There are several microwave systems in use for the sterilization of shelf-stable ready meals. In this process, compartmented polymeric trays are filled with two or three components. For example, rice and curried beef are lidded and processed in a continuous pressurized microwave system and cooled while under pressure. The current practice is to quarantine each day's production for 30 days before releasing it to the market. In that time, it is assumed that any microorganism load will be evident from expanded lids. Each of the known systems in use is 200 kW or more at 2450 MHz. There are no installations in the United States because the Food and Drug Administration (FDA) requires a temperature record of the process indicating that the coldest location in each container has reached a specific temperature and is held at that temperature for a suitable length of time. Studies have shown that in food processes involving heating, a number of time-temperature indicators have been developed in which chemical markers are formed as a result of thermally induced reactions of sugar and protein precursors. The destruction of spoilage bacteria spores has been shown to be correlated with marker formation. Since marker analysis takes far less time to carry out than microbiological methods, which require several days of incubation, lengthy quarantine is not required. It is probable that food manufacturers in the United States may now be encouraged to apply to the FDA for approval to use this process. Also, new fiber-optic temperature sensors have been developed for use in microwave ovens and can produce the time-temperature data needed for sterility assurance.

This process could lead to very significant competition with the food canning and frozen food industries because of the strong demand for convenience foods by the microwave oven user community. Studies with high-temperature short-time (HTST) thermal processing have been shown to produce very high quality shelf-stable food products in retort pouches. Since thermal death rate of bacteria increases exponentially with temperature, high temperatures allow for a much shorter process time. Hence, a microwave HTST process should be capable of equal or better quality, as well as being in microwavable trays that also function as serving dishes. The brief reheat time for shelf-stable ready meals suggests possible use of the meals in vending machines. Pending further research and development, microwave HTST sterilized ready meals, vegetables, and side dishes could revolutionize the food processing industry.

For background information *see* FOOD ENGINEERING; FOOD MANUFACTURING; MAGNETRON; MICROWAVE in the McGraw-Hill Encyclopedia of Science & Technology.   Robert V. Decareau

Bibliography. R. E. Edgar, The economics of microwave processing in the food industry, *Food Technol.*, 40(6):106–112, 1988; R. A. Lampi, G. L. Schulz, and J. W. Szczeblowski, New packaging of food service systems, in G. E. Livingston and C. M. Chang (eds.), *Food Service Systems*, Academic Press, New York, 1979; B. E. Proctor and S. A. Goldblith, Radar energy for rapid cooking and blanching and its effect on vitamin content, *Food Technol.*, 2(2):95–104, 1948.

Mining pollution

The coal, sand, gravel, and other minerals extracted from the earth by mining continue to help fuel the world economy and improve the standard of living. However, the decades of mineral extraction and processing around the globe have produced a massive amount of waste containing toxic metals and materials that pollute land and water and pose health threats to humans and wildlife.

Water pollution. Of particular concern are impacts on the watersheds, rivers, and lakes that provide drinking and irrigation water and support aquatic life. Potential sources of mining-related contamination include ground water that seeps into underground mines and must be pumped out and discharged to keep the mine works dry; water used to process mined materials; and rain that falls on mine waste or mill tailings (the small rocks and particles left over from the milling process) and subsequently transports contaminants to streams or other bodies of water.

In many mining operations, wastewater is treated by adding lime or other chemicals that raise the pH, causing the metals to precipitate. The metals can then be removed before the water is discharged.

Technology. Mining technology has evolved far beyond the pick and shovel. The modern industry uses satellite communications, automation, smart sensors, and robotics. Due to public demand for tighter environmental standards in the United States, the mining industry, government agencies, and private firms are pursuing more efficient, innovative methods for mineral extraction, waste treatment, and cleanup. The industry indicates that refinement of existing technologies and discovery of new mining, processing, and treatment methods will be necessary to ensure progress in mining production and protection of the environment.

In 1998 the U.S. Department of Energy (DOE) and the National Mining Association agreed to develop a technology roadmap for mining. The agreement establishes a government-industry research and development partnership charged with developing and deploying new technologies to improve the mining industry's environmental performance and competitiveness.

The pact's objective is to help address technology needs in exploration and characterization; extraction; processing; utilization; and environment, safety, and health. Technology advances in one of these areas may lead to positive results in other areas. For instance, improved characterization and extraction technologies contribute solutions to waste treatment and cleanup by allowing mining operations to more efficiently identify and remove minerals, resulting in less waste and disturbance to the environment.

Biological treatments. The initiative between the DOE and the mining industry is focused on the future. There are many innovative waste treatment and cleanup technologies already developed by private firms, government research institutions, and public-private partnerships. Some of these methods employ biological organisms to clean up water pumped from mines or used in processing before the water is discharged to streams.

Bacteria, for example, are showing promise for treating mine wastes and protecting watersheds. In particular, systems have been developed that utilize sulfate-reducing bacteria to curb the amount of metals and other contaminants in the mine wastewater discharged to the environment.

These "passive treatment" systems typically range from less than 1 acre to more than 5 acres (0.4 to 2 hectares), depending on the metal loading in the discharge water, and have been used at hard rock and coal mining sites. Essentially, the systems are composed of bacteria and a customized substrate. The substrate can be a mix of green wastes, manure, sawdust, limestone, or a variety of other materials assembled in anaerobic cells or containers, which range from tanks to excavations lined with protective material.

The bacteria, which live and grow in the substrate, require simple organic compounds and sulfate for metabolism, and produce sulfide and bicarbonate. As metal-laden wastewater is introduced into the cells, the sulfide joins with most metals to form metal sulfides, and the bicarbonate increases the alkalinity of the water, raising the solution pH. This causes precipitation of metal sulfides within the substrate and reduction of metals in the waste stream. Depending on the system design, the water either can be discharged or can be sent to a polishing system that further purifies the water.

The substrate, based on its composition and the level of usage, can remain effective for many years before being replaced. When replacement is necessary, the substrate is tested for toxicity and either is taken to a smelter for recycling or used as a growth medium for vegetation.

A passive treatment is currently operating at a lead mine in Missouri. The system covers 4 acres (1.6 hectares). Rising ground water must be pumped out of the mine continuously so that operations are uninterrupted. The water is pumped through the treatment system, which is designed to handle 1500 gallons (5680 liters) per minute. In this system, metals are reduced to meet Missouri's permissible limits. For example, analyses of total metal levels have shown a decrease from 4 parts per million to 0.005 ppm.

Attention also is being paid to fungi as an aid in reclamation of mined lands. Studies and actual applications have shown that some types of mycorrhizal fungi, which form symbiotic relationships with plants, have helped revegetate mine waste dumps, halting erosion and helping prevent runoff of water containing toxic metals. Essentially, a mycorrhizal fungus infects the roots of host plants and helps gather nutrients and water, improving the plant's ability to survive stressful conditions. In return, the fungus feeds on sugar produced by the plant. By combining the appropriate fungus and plant, it has been demonstrated that revegetation can occur more effectively in the harsh soil conditions presented by mine wastes.

Although fungus-related technology is not a new development, a new approach using vesicular-arbuscular mycorrhizal (VAM) fungi has been applied at mine waste sites in Colorado, Montana, Utah, and Wyoming. The fungi are incorporated into pellets, which are sown on mine dumps or tailings along with grass and other plant seeds. As the seeds sprout and grow, the roots come in contact with the pellets, and the fungi form a symbiotic relationship with the roots. This approach has made it possible to inoculate grass and plants with fungi directly in the field, increasing the survival and growth rates of the vegetation. *See* FUNGI.

It is possible that certain varieties of higher fungi can be used to actively remove mine waste, preventing metals from leaching into waterways. Selected fungal mycelium (the network of filaments that make up the organism's perennial body) can be applied to break down organic contaminants, such as petroleum hydrocarbons, organophosphate pesticides, and explosives, in soil and other substrates.

By physically, chemically, and biologically challenging the mycelium, the performance of the mycelium in contaminant cleanup can be improved in some cases. Fungi could also be conditioned or specially deployed to more efficiently extract and absorb metals from soil and wastewater. Elemental metals that potentially are toxic to the fungus are naturally accumulated by certain species (but are avoided by others) and are expelled through the fungal fruiting bodies, mushrooms. The mushrooms could be gathered for recovery or disposal of the accumulated metals.

Developers of passive and fungal treatment methods stress that these technologies are not miracle cures. There is no "cookie cutter" approach for using either technology, because each contaminated site has a variety of factors—including climate, waste composition, and regulatory issues—that must be evaluated and addressed before applying such treatments.

Ceramic materials. A number of research organizations in the United States are exploring the integration of mesoporous ceramics and functional monolayers for use in cleaning contaminated waterways and recovering precious metals.

Self-assembled monolayers on mesoporous supports (SAMMS) material integrates mesoporous ceramics technology with an innovative method for attaching monolayers (single layers of densely packed molecules) to the pore surfaces throughout the ceramic material. The molecules are custom-designed to seek out mercury, lead, chromium, and other toxic (or precious) metals. The coated SAMMS materials are useful in catalysis, separations, and controlled release applications.

SAMMS can be used effectively in water and non-aqueous solutions, and are produced in bead or powder form. Each grain of ceramic material (in this case, a type of silicate) is only 5–15 micrometers in diameter and contains a densely ordered array of cylindrical caverns or pores, giving the material a honeycomb appearance. The chemically tailored monolayers reside within the pores, with the molecules strongly binding at one end to the ceramic material. The free ends of the tethered molecules then are available for binding to a targeted metal species passing through the pore.

These pores provide a large surface area for selective trapping of metal ions in solution. In fact, a tablespoon of this material in powder form has surface area equivalent to a football field. Upon release in water, SAMMS quickly immobilize the targeted metal, reducing the concentration to far below drinking-water standards. The small pore size also precludes the metal from leaving and resolubilizing into a more toxic or mobile form.

Currently, development of SAMMS is focused on creating the most effective forms (dispersed powders, solid pellets, membranes, or filters) for use. Developers believe the best uses for SAMMS may be removal of mercury and arsenic from hazardous and radioactive wastes, and recovery of gold and other precious metals at mining operations.

For background information *see* FUNGI; LAND RECLAMATION; MINING in the McGraw-Hill Encyclopedia of Science & Technology.   Tim Ledbetter

Bibliography. A. Leeson and B. C. Alleman, Bioremediation of metals and inorganic compounds, *5th International In Situ and On-Site Bioremediation Symposium*, vol. 4, Battelle Press, Columbus, OH, 1999; L. F. Marrs, D. H. Marx, and C. E. Cordell, Establishment of vegetation on mined sites by management of mycorrhizae, *National Meeting of the American Society for Surface Mining and Reclamation*, Scottsdale, AZ, 1999.

Molecular fossils

Approximately 2.7 billion years ago, braided rivers transported mud and sand from the land of a small continent to the sea. The sand on the riverbanks and beaches contained pyrite crystals preserved in an atmosphere low in oxygen. The continent possessed no life form. However, the ocean teemed with single-celled organisms that floated close to the sur-

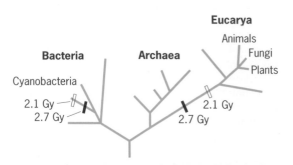

Fig. 2. Universal tree of life with three main branches, the domains Archaea, Bacteria, and Eucarya. The oldest known physical fossils of cyanobacteria and Eucarya are about 2.1 Gy old. The white bars indicate where these fossils belong in the tree. Molecular fossils reset the minimum age of the two groups back to 2.7 Gy (black bars). Nevertheless, the exact ages of the lowest branching points in the tree remain unknown.

face. In the shallows, microorganisms lived in mat-like communities on the sea floor and grew layer by layer closer to the sunlight, forming domelike, finely laminated structures. Some of these stromatolites attained a height of several meters. Later, this continent, called the Pilbara, would collide with other plates of continental crust to form the Australian mainland.

The Pilbara region today is the hottest part of Australia and covers about 500 km on 500 km in the country's northwest. Ironically, the Pilbara is a desert again, but now it is covered with pale-green Spinifex grass that beautifully contrasts with orange and red rock formations. These rocks are 3.5–2.5 billion years old, from a period called the Archean [**Fig. 1**; 1 billion years = 1 gigayear (Gy)]. Most rocks that formed during Archean times were deformed by tectonic events and heat destroyed their original composition and structure. The Archean sediments in the Pilbara, however, have escaped the worst effects of such metamorphism and are the best-preserved rocks of this age in the world. Microscopic fossils and stromatolites have been found in even the oldest sediments of the region, indicating that single-celled organisms must have existed throughout the Archean. Scientists hope to reveal how complex and evolved these organisms were, to which group they belonged, and how they lived. Unfortunately, their fossil remains are rarely more than minuscule black spheres of unknown origin and, as a result, early life remains a mystery.

However, dead organisms leave other, albeit invisible traces in rocks: relics of a chemical nature called molecular fossils. These molecules, extracted from rocks and fed into analytical instruments, are "fingerprints" that can help to distinguish between major groups of life. They open the possibility of exploring life in Archean oceans and lakes.

Three domains of life. All living things belong to one of three fundamental groups called domains: Bacteria, Archaea, and Eucarya (**Fig. 2**). Bacteria have a simple cell that is not divided into different compartments and is usually not much longer than 0.002 mm

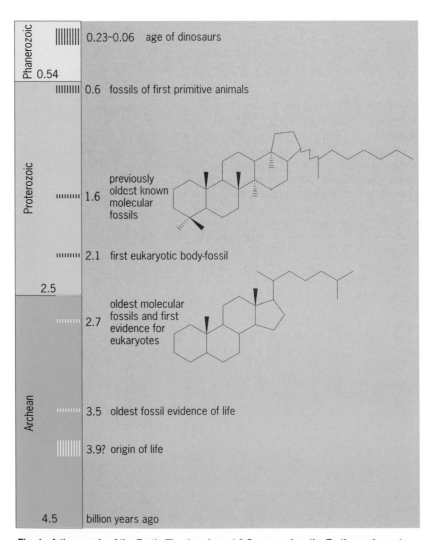

Fig. 1. A time scale of the Earth. The time from 4.6 Gy ago, when the Earth was born, to 2.5 Gy ago is called the Archean.

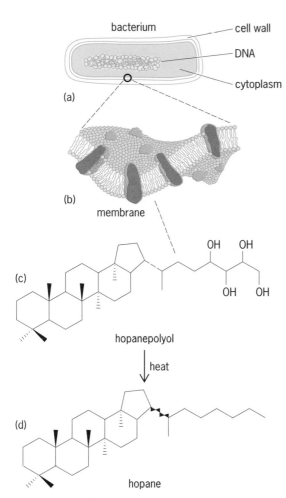

Fig. 3. The cytoplasm of (a) a bacterium is separated from the outside world by a double layer of lipid molecules, (b) the cell membrane. Membranes of many bacteria contain (c) hopanepolyols, molecules that serve as membrane rigidifier. Heat can turn these molecules under geological conditions into (d) hopanes, molecular fossils that can be extracted from ancient sediments and are indicative of the existence of bacteria.

energy in plants and algae; or lysosomes specialized in food digestion. Advanced eukaryotes utilize sexual reproduction and contain enormously complex multicellular units. All three domains of life produce distinctive molecular fossils.

Molecular fossils are organic chemical compounds. They are too small to be visible even under the best microscope and can be examined only by using analytical instruments such as mass spectrometers. When the remains of microorganisms are trapped in mud of an ocean floor, most parts of the cell will decay while more resistant components such as lipids that form cell membranes (Fig. 3b and c) may escape the recycling process. As more sediment accumulates over the top, pressure and temperature will eventually turn the mud into shale and the remaining biomolecules into more stable molecular fossils in a chemical process called diagenesis (Fig. 3c and d; Fig. 4b and c).

Sterols are molecular building blocks of eukaryotic membranes. Diagenesis transforms sterols into steranes, molecular fossils with structures similar to

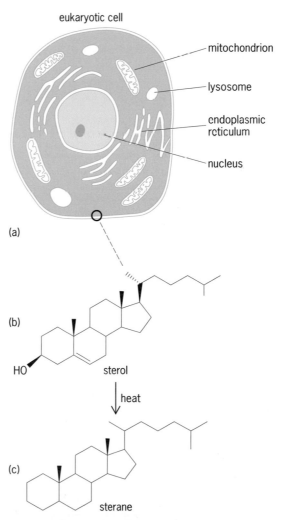

Fig. 4. Membranes of (a) eukaryotic cells contain (b) sterols as stabilizing molecular building blocks. Heat can turn sterols under geological conditions into (c) steranes, molecular fossils characteristic of eukaryotes.

(Fig. 3a). Bacteria more than 3 Gy ago probably did not look fundamentally different from Bacteria today, and are assigned to the deepest branch of the universal tree of life (Fig. 2). Archaea look similar to Bacteria at first glance, but their lifestyle and biochemistry are so fundamentally different that biologists assigned them to a second domain of life. Many Archaea prefer extreme conditions like boiling-hot water or high concentrations of salt. Bacteria and Archaea together are referred to as prokaryotes because their DNA code is freely floating in the cell and not stored in a nucleus as in the third domain of life, Eucarya or eukaryotes. Animals, plants, fungi, and protist (single-celled organisms such as amoebae and algae) are eukaryotes. Eukaryotic cells are huge with a volume three orders of magnitude (about 1000×) higher than that of Bacteria. They have a complex structure including many separate and specialized compartments called organelles (Fig. 4a). These organelles comprise mitochondria, the power plant of the cell; chloroplasts that convert sunlight into

their parent compounds (Fig. 4*b* and *c*). Thus, if steranes are found in rocks of a certain age, then eukaryotes must have existed at that point in time. Similarly, hopanes are derived from hopanepolyols (Fig. 3*c* and *d*), molecules that indicate the domain Bacteria. Other molecular fossils are more specific and distinguish, for example, between different groups of eukaryotes such as certain plants or sponges.

If host rock is buried at great depths with temperatures far exceeding 200°C (392°F), the carbon skeleton of molecules will crack until finally all organic matter is turned into gas and graphite. As all Archean rocks have suffered considerable temperatures, it became an accepted dogma that all molecular fossils of that age must have been destroyed. And indeed, molecular fossils older than 1.6 Gy have never been found before. Further, even if traces of these molecules were preserved in Archean rocks, it is extremely difficult to show that the molecules are as old as the rock and not younger contamination.

Crude oil is a liquid concentrate of molecular fossils and other organic molecules that were expelled from a source rock particularly rich in organic matter. Products made from crude oil such as diesel and grease might still contain molecular fossils, and the tiniest amount coming into contact with an Archean sample would feign positive results. More threatening, crude oil has the capacity to migrate many kilometers from its original source rock into other rock units. Therefore, it is difficult to determine if younger oil migrated into the Archean rock. It is important to understand that molecular fossils are very different from normal fossils and are not necessarily as old as their host rock.

Proving age. Exceptionally well-preserved black shales (2.7 Gy old) were collected at about 700 m (2300 ft) depth from a drill hole located in the center of the Pilbara desert in Western Australia. The rock was cleaned and crushed to powder, and the powder was extracted with organic solvents. Despite the minute amount of oil contained in the rock (about 30 parts per million), using advanced analytical techniques such as the metastable-reaction-monitoring mode of gas chromatography–mass spectrometry, it was possible to identify hundreds of different molecules. The composition clearly indicated that the oil had suffered high thermal stress, while other characteristics were symptomatic for oil of Precambrian age. Both are highly unusual attributes for potential contaminants. If crude oil expelled from younger Precambrian source rocks had migrated into the shale, all rocks in the vicinity would be tainted by the same contaminant. However, oil was found exclusively in black shales, while directly adjacent volcanic rocks were clear. Volcanic rocks are naturally void of indigenous molecular fossils. Moreover, ratios of molecular fossils—for example, eukaryotes versus bacteria—fluctuated within a few meters of black shale in the drill core. This is typical for genuine host rocks where the biocommunity originally contributing to the sediment changed over time. Such a fluctuation, however, is inconsistent with any sort of contamination.

Earliest ancestors. Three key discoveries were made.

1. Hopanes are abundant (Fig. 3*d*). While it was believed that Bacteria originated early in Earth's history, until now there has been no direct evidence. This finding confirms that tiny black spheres found in Archean sediments indeed might belong to this domain.

2. Very significant is the discovery of 2α-methylhopanes in remarkably high concentrations. These molecules are the fingerprint of the great liberators of the Earth, cyanobacteria (Fig. 2), blue-green bacteria that are capable of capturing sunlight to produce energy and release oxygen into the atmosphere as a by-product. Cyanobacteria paved the way for more complex forms of life that required oxygen to breathe. This oxygen also reacted with reduced iron upwelling from the deep ocean to form the biggest iron ore deposits in the world, the 2.5-Gy-old Hammersley Banded Iron Formation in the south of the Pilbara. The formation of iron ore was a great sink for oxygen, and it took another 500 million years until oxygen accumulated in higher concentrations in the atmosphere.

3. Sterane molecules (Fig. 4*c*) were found in a wide variety of different forms, similar to those in much younger sediments. Steranes are derived from well-known compounds such as cholesterol and other steroids, and are, as a complex mixture, evidence for the existence of the domain Eucarya in the late Archean. They represent the oldest remains of the ancestors of all plants, fungi, and humans, along with all other animals. This discovery pushed the origin of complex cells back by another 600 million years (by far the oldest physical fossils big enough to be of eukaryotic origin is *Grypania*, a spiral-shaped impression in 2.1-Gy-old rocks found in Michigan; Fig. 1). The evolution of the eukaryotic cell was one of the most complex processes in the history of life. However, it must have occurred in a relatively short period of time between 3.8 and 2.7 Gy ago (Fig 1). It is puzzling that it took so much longer until eukaryotes eventually became prominent in the fossil record 1.2–1.0 Gy ago. It is unknown just how complex late Archean eukaryotes were and how they survived in an environment still low in oxygen.

New window on early life. The discovery of almost 3-Gy-old molecular fossils is a revelation that has opened a new window on early life. This new tool can be used to study primordial organisms in different environments and to uncover nature in archaic oceans, ancient lakes, and braided rivers. Older molecules might even yet be unearthed, enabling a look at life further back in time. Molecular fossils of unknown organisms that disappeared billions of years ago might be found.

For background information *see* ARCHAEBACTERIA; ARCHEAN; BACTERIA; BANDED IRON FORMATION; CYTOPLASM; DIAGENESIS; EUCARYOTAE; FOSSIL; GAS

CHROMATOGRAPHY; MASS SPECTROMETRY; STROMA-
TOLITE in the McGraw-Hill Encyclopedia of Science
& Technology.   Jochen J. Brocks
   Bibliography.   J. J. Brocks et al., Archean molecu-
lar fossils and the early rise of eukaryotes, *Science*,
285:1033–1036, 1999; A. H. Knoll, A new molecular
window on early life, *Science*, 285:1025–1026, 1999;
K. E. Peters and J. M. Moldowan, *The Biomarker
Guide*, 1993; J. W. Schopf, in S. Bengtson (ed.), *Early
Life on Earth*, pp. 193–206, 1994.

Molecular simulation

Molecular simulation and computational quantum
chemistry are rapidly evolving tools which are having
an increasingly significant impact on the chemical,
pharmaceutical, materials, and related industries.
These tools provide a mechanism for predicting
entirely computationally many useful functional properties of systems of interest in these industries. Included are thermodynamic properties (such as
equations of state, phase equilibria, and critical constants), thermochemical properties (such as energies
of formation and reaction, and reaction pathways),
spectroscopic properties (such as dipole moments
and vibrational and other spectra), mechanical properties (such as stress-strain relationships and elastic
moduli), transport properties (such as viscosity, diffusion, and thermal conductivity), and morphological information (such as location and shape of binding sites on a biomolecule and crystal structure). This
list continues to grow as algorithmic and computer
hardware advances make it possible to access additional properties.

Definitions. The two main molecular simulation
techniques are molecular dynamics and Monte Carlo
simulation, both of which are rooted in classical
statistical mechanics. Given mathematical models for
the internal structure of each molecule (the intramolecular potential which describes the energy of
each conformation of the molecule) and the interaction between molecules (the intermolecular potential which describes the energy associated with
molecules being in a particular conformation relative to each other), classical statistical mechanics
provides a formalism for predicting properties of a
macroscopic collection of such molecules based on
statistically averaging over the possible microscopic
states of the system as it evolves under the rules of
classical mechanics. Thus, the building blocks are
molecules, the dynamics are described by classical
mechanics, and the key concept is statistical averaging. In molecular dynamics, the microscopic states
of the system are generated by solving the classical
equations of motion as a function of time (typically
over a period limited to tens of nanoseconds). Thus,
one can observe the relaxation of a system to equilibrium (provided the time for the relaxation falls within
the time accessible to molecular dynamics simulation), and so molecular dynamics permits the calculation of transport properties which at the macro-

scopic scale describe the relaxation of a system in
response to inhomogeneities. In Monte Carlo simulation, equilibrium configurations of systems are generated stochastically according to the probabilities rigorously known from classical statistical mechanics.
Thus, Monte Carlo simulation generates equilibrium
states directly (which has many advantages, including bypassing configurations which are not characteristic of equilibrium but which may be difficult
to escape dynamically) and so can be used to study
equilibrium configurations of systems which may be
expensive or impossible to access via molecular dynamics. The drawback of Monte Carlo simulation is
that it cannot yield the kind of dynamical response
information that leads directly to transport properties. Many hybrid methods exist that combine the
best features of molecular dynamics and Monte Carlo
simulation. Today, intra- and intermolecular forces
are determined by a combination of computational
quantum chemistry methods and fitting to available
experimental data, and the development of these
functions (also known as force fields) is a very active subfield of molecular simulation.

In computational quantum chemistry, the Schrödinger equation for the electronic degrees of freedom of a collection of atoms (nuclei and electrons)
is solved numerically to determine the minimum
energy configuration of the atoms. The strength of
computational quantum chemistry is that it makes
few, if any, assumptions (unlike molecular dynamics
and Monte Carlo simulation, in which a model must
be assumed for the intra- and intermolecular interactions). The problem is that the computational cost
is very high, limiting the methods to relatively small
system sizes on current computers. The success of
computational quantum chemistry methods resulted
in one of the pioneers in the field, John Pople, receiving the 1998 Nobel Prize in Chemistry. One of the
developments that has significantly sped up computational quantum chemistry calculations is density
functional theory, which solves equations for electron density rather than positions of individual electrons. The primary developer of density functional
theory, Walter Kohn, shared the 1998 Nobel prize
with Pople. In the course of finding the minimum
energy configuration of a collection of molecules,
computational quantum chemistry yields information about intra- and intermolecular interactions, and
so represents a route to these functions needed by
molecular dynamics and Monte Carlo simulation. In
fact, by combining molecular dynamics with the density functional theory form of computational quantum chemistry (so that the interactions needed by
molecular dynamics are provided by density functional theory calculations) one can perform so-called
ab initio molecular dynamics, the best-known version being Car-Parrinello. The Car-Parrinello and similar hybrid methods are presently restricted to fairly
small systems simulated over periods of 1–10 pico-
seconds, yet they offer a glimpse into the future of
molecular simulation and computational quantum
chemistry when improvements in hardware and

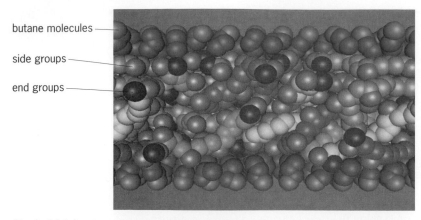

Fig. 1. A lubricant component, squalane (a 30-carbon alkane with a 24-carbon backbone and 6 methyl side groups), is confined to a nanoscale gap created by a surface to which butane molecules have been attached. The visualization depicts the carbons only. Molecules are shaded differently to distinguish them. The goal of such simulations is to understand the changes in lubrication properties induced by confinement to such narrow gaps.

algorithms will make ab initio hybrid methods the primary tool for predicting the properties of systems about which little or nothing is known experimentally.

The use of molecular simulation and computational quantum chemistry has become widespread, well beyond the research specialists, by the development of commercial versions of research codes, often with graphical interfaces that facilitate use of the methods. Companies which market such codes include Molecular Simulations Inc. (molecular simulation and computational quantum chemistry), Gaussian Inc. (computational quantum chemistry), Oxford Molecular (molecular simulation and computational quantum chemistry), and Schrödinger

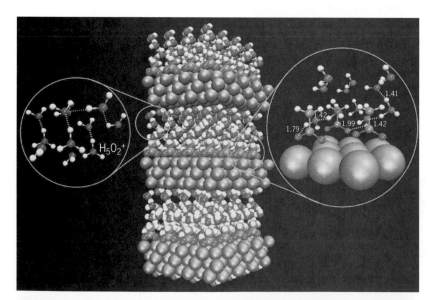

Fig. 2. Snapshot from an ab initio molecular dynamics simulation probing the effect of water on the dissociation of acetic acid over Pd(III). The change in binding energy of the acetate anion on Pd(III) in the liquid phase is measured in the simulation to be −142 kJ/mol, while the same quantity in the vapor phase (that is, in the absence of the aqueous solvent) is −212 kJ/mol. (*Simulation performed by, and image courtesy of, Matt Neurock, University of Virginia*)

Inc. (molecular simulation/computational quantum chemistry hybrid). This list is not exhaustive. In addition, many noncommercial ventures (located at national laboratories or universities) make available molecular simulation and computational quantum chemistry codes. Examples include the NWChem package from Pacific Northwest National Laboratory (molecular simulation and computational quantum chemistry) and the DL POLY code (molecular simulation) available from Daresbury Laboratory in the United Kingdom.

Capabilities and impact. Computational quantum chemistry and molecular simulation methods can be used to predict properties that once were only accessible experimentally, resulting in several significant applications in basic and industrial research. These applications include providing estimates of properties for systems for which little or no experimental data are available, which is especially useful in the early stages of chemical process design; yielding insight into the molecular basis for the behavior of particular systems, which is very useful in developing engineering correlations, design rules, or quantitative structure-property relations; and providing guidance for experimental studies by identifying the interesting systems or properties to be measured.

In the fields of chemical engineering and materials science, academic and industrial interest in molecular simulation and computational quantum chemistry has grown exponentially over the past decade. Two developments are making molecular simulation and computational quantum chemistry and practical tools for application to systems of industrial interest. One is the continuing exponential increase in computing power, often referred to as Moore's law, which states that the speed of computers is increasing by a factor of two every 18 months (equivalently, an order of magnitude every 5 years). The practical consequence of Moore's law is that today's desktop work stations and laptops have the computational power of a supercomputer of a decade ago, thus making it possible for an ordinary user to perform calculations that once would have been prohibitively expensive. The second development is the proliferation of efficient algorithms for calculating properties of practical interest. In molecular simulation, for example, the Gibbs ensemble Monte Carlo algorithm, introduced just over a decade ago, made it possible to predict the phase envelope of a fluid system directly from knowledge of the intermolecular forces, thus opening up the possibility of calculating many properties relevant to the engineering design separations processes (such as distillation). Algorithm advances (which can result in order-of-magnitude or more increases in efficiency), combined with the steady exponential increase in computational power, will continue to dramatically broaden the range of applicability of computational quantum chemistry and molecular simulation methods in the coming years. The expectations for molecular simulation and computational quantum chemistry are very high, and they have been identified as key technologies for the chemical industry to achieve its vision of completely automated product and process design in the year 2020.

Examples. A sampling of companies, and examples of the industrial problems which they have tackled using molecular simulation and computational quantum chemistry techniques, is provided in a National Science Foundation report (1997). Applications are diverse and include molecular design of zeolites for air separation, design and optimization of catalysts for homogeneous and heterogeneous catalysis, evaluation of the feasibility of methane adsorption, molecular modeling of polysaccharide rheology, molecular design of detergent enzymes, and molecular design of photocopying materials. Another report, expected to come out in 2000, will provide additional comparative information on the ways that European, Japanese, and American companies are applying these tools.

One area which is increasingly benefiting from molecular simulation methods is rheology. Nonequilibrium molecular dynamics methods have become very powerful tools for direct simulation of systems subject to flow fields, such as the shear flow field present in lubrication and the extensional flow fields present in polymer processing. The theory for deriving and validating methods for performing nonequilibrium molecular dynamics simulations has been perfected over the past 15 years. Recently, this technique has been used to predict the viscosity index of several typical lubricant components. The viscosity index is a key performance indicator for lubricants, measuring the degree to which the viscosity diminishes with increasing temperature. Nonequilibrium molecular dynamics methods are also being used to understand how nanoscale confinement, such as in the case of hard disk drive lubrication, affects the rheological properties of lubricants (**Fig. 1**). These studies also shed light on the lubrication of microelectromechanical systems.

Rational catalyst design is one example of the use of computational quantum chemistry and ab initio molecular dynamics. Density functional methods make it possible to study catalytic processes qualitatively, and in some cases quantitatively, with increasingly sophisticated questions becoming answerable. For example, **Figure 2**, based on ab initio molecular dynamics simulations, shows a snapshot from a simulation study of the effect of water on the dissociation of acetic acid over Pd(III). The protons remain solvated in the water layer (as $H_5O_2^+$ species), while acetate anions are bound to the surface. The solvent lowers the interaction energy significantly. The water solvent interacts with the naked negative charge of the anion, thus decreasing the anion's affinity for the surface.

The rapidly evolving capabilities of molecular simulation and computational quantum chemistry, and hybrids of these methods, suggest that they are beginning to fulfill their promise as equal and complementary partners with experiments in chemical and related industries.

For background information *see* CHEMICAL DYNAMICS; COMPUTATIONAL CHEMISTRY; MONTE CARLO METHOD; QUANTUM CHEMISTRY; SIMULATION; STOCHASTIC PROCESS in the McGraw-Hill Encyclopedia of Science & Technology.　　Peter T. Cummings

Bibliography. M. P. Allen and D. J. Tildesley, *Computer Simulation of Liquids*, Oxford University Press, Oxford, 1987; R. Car and M. Parrinello, Unified approach for molecular dynamics and density-functional theory, *Phys. Rev. Lett.*, 55:2471, 1985; P. T. Cummings et al., *Report: NSF Workshop on Future Directions for Molecular Modeling and Simulation: Fundamentals and Applications*, National Science Foundation, Arlington, VA, November 3–4, 1997; D. J. Evans and G. P. Morriss, *Statistical Mechanics of Nonequilibrium Liquids*, Academic Press, New York, 1990; A. Z. Panagiotopoulos, Direct determination of phase coexistence properties of fluids by Monte Carlo simulation in a new ensemble, *Mol. Phys.*, 61:813, 1987; A. Z. Panagiotopoulos et al., Phase equilibria by simulation in the Gibbs Ensemble: Alternative derivation, generation, and application to mixture and membrane equilibria, *Mol. Phys.*, 63:527, 1988; *Technology Vision 2020: The U.S. Chemical Industry*, a joint report by the American Chemical Society, American Institute of Chemical Engineers, Chemical Manufacturers Association, Council for Chemical Research and Synthetic Organic Chemical Manufacturers Association, published by the American Chemical Society, 1996; S. Sarman, D. J. Evans, and P. T. Cummings, Recent developments in non-equilibrium molecular dynamics, *Phys. Rep.*, 305:1–92, 1998.

Molecular wires

The developing field of molecular electronics has come to encompass many types of molecular electronic devices, including polymer-based light-emitting-diode (LED) displays, solar energy conversion devices, and a variety of chemical sensors. A characteristic feature of most molecular electronic devices is that they involve an intimate coupling of molecular materials with conventional solid-state electronic materials. A very promising subdiscipline within the field of molecular electronics involves the use of individual molecules or molecular aggregates in place of solid-state materials as active elements in circuits designed to accomplish logic functions. Such circuits are being considered as possible building blocks for futuristic molecule-based computing devices. A great attraction of such devices is the potential for miniaturizing computing devices, thereby increasing their power and enabling entirely new applications.

The manner in which molecules might be utilized in logic circuits and computing devices is still far from clear. Even so, it seems likely that a crucial component of any molecular electronic device will be that portion which transmits electrons to and from (or through) the device. Molecular fragments that can accomplish this function have been termed molecular wires, a name that invokes a similarity to the use of metal wires as current-carrying elements in conventional electronic circuits. The electronic structure of most molecules is very different from that of most metals; therefore it may not be appropriate to directly compare a molecule to a metal wire as a current-carrying device. Nonetheless, it is now established that individual molecules can serve as conduits to facilitate electron transport from one end of the molecule to the other. In this sense, it is appropriate to consider the current-carrying action of molecules as being analogous to that of a wire.

Structures. Many different chemical structures have been considered as molecular wire candidates from both a theoretical and experimental perspective. Some representative structures are shown below. There is general agreement that structures

Polyene

Polyphenylene

Poly(phenylethenyl)

Poly(phenylethynyl)

Poly(phenylbutadiynyl)

Poly(thiophene)

Poly(thiophene ethynyl)

Polycyclic aromatic hydrocarbons

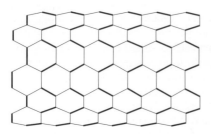

Nanotubes

that include extended electronic conjugation over long distances are the most likely candidates for promoting the type of long-range electronic coupling that is needed in a molecular wire. Inspection of the structures shown here reveals that all possess this type of extended electronic conjugation. Universal agreement on the exact relationship between molecular structure and the electrical/electronic properties of a molecular wire has not yet been achieved, although a general trend linking greater conductivity and stronger electronic coupling with a greater extent of electronic delocalization is evident. Work in progress promises many new insights on this point in the near future. Even so, there is general agreement that structures that include extended electronic conjugation over long distances are the most likely candidates for promoting the type of long-range electronic coupling that is needed in a molecular wire. Inspection of the structures shown here reveals that all possess this type of extended electronic conjugation.

Experimental configurations. Figure 1 illustrates four experimental configurations in which a molecular wire could serve as a conduit for electron transport. All four configurations have been used in experimental studies of molecular wires. In Fig. 1*a*, the wire serves to link two discrete molecules, one an electron donor and the other an electron acceptor. Such molecular structures have been termed bridged donor-acceptor (D-A) molecules, and they have been studied since the 1950s as models for charge separation in photosynthesis. The role of the molecular wire is to enhance the electronic coupling between the two entities on either end of the bridge.

Experiments using such molecules typically involve measurement of the rate of electron transfer from one side of the molecule to the other. Such measurements are most often made in a pulse-probe mode using fast lasers to study either a photoinduced charge separation event or a thermal charge recombination event. In some cases, a fast electron source (for example, an electron accelerator or van de Graaf generator) may be used to generate electrons which are captured on one side of the molecule and then transferred to the other. In any case, strong coupling results in rapid electron transfer, which in turn provides a measure of control over where the electron goes. A characteristic feature of such structures is that electron transport occurs across them one electron at a time. The structure cannot pass true steady-state current unless one continually supplies fresh electrons to one side and removes the excess electrons from the other. Also, studies on such molecules are almost always performed in solution, without connections being made to individual molecules.

In Fig. 1b, a molecular wire is poised across the gap between two small and closely spaced metal contacts. The fabrication of such structures is a challenge to modern microfabrication technology; however, small numbers of such structures have been made with gaps on the order of a few to tens of nanometers, which is close to the dimensions of some individual molecules (albeit large molecules). It is possible to measure steady-state currents across such structures, since both ends of the wire are connected to conventional metal contacts. A difficulty with such structures is that it is hard to be sure of the detailed structure within the gap, or of how many individual molecules are spanning the gap.

A configuration that has been widely used in research on molecular wires is illustrated in Fig. 1c. A metallic proximal probe (for example, an extremely sharp scanning tunneling microscopy tip) is brought into proximity to a metal substrate that has been modified with a monomolecular layer in which wire molecules are connected at one end to the metal surface. One can poise the tip above the wire and apply a bias voltage between the probe tip and the metal substrate, and then measure a current-voltage curve that should correspond to electron transport mediated by the wire. An advantage of this approach is that one can readily find and measure steady-state currents corresponding to individual wire molecules. A disadvantage is that little is known about the contact between the probe and the unattached end of the wire. Indeed, it is hard to be sure of the exact probe tip location in such a measurement, since one positions the tip while monitoring current, and more current can always be made to flow simply by pushing the tip closer to the substrate. Even so, this experimental configuration offers the best method to date for studying the properties of individual molecular wires.

There is some qualitative indication from studies of individual molecular wires in this configuration that extended electronic conjugation as a bridge does promote stronger coupling and higher conductivity. Uncertainties regarding the nature of the contact between the proximal probe (usually an STM tip) and the molecular wire have in most cases precluded a more quantitative treatment.

The configuration in Fig. 1d is a hybrid of the structure in Fig. 1a with a wire bridging between two molecules, and the structure in Fig. 1b with the wire bridging between two metal contacts. In this hybrid structure, the molecule on one side of the wire is replaced by a metal contact, while the other side remains attached to a molecular electron donor or acceptor. The metal contact is then configured as the electrode in an electrochemical cell. Wire-mediated electron transport between the electrode and the electron donor or acceptor occurs when an electrochemical potential suitable for oxidizing

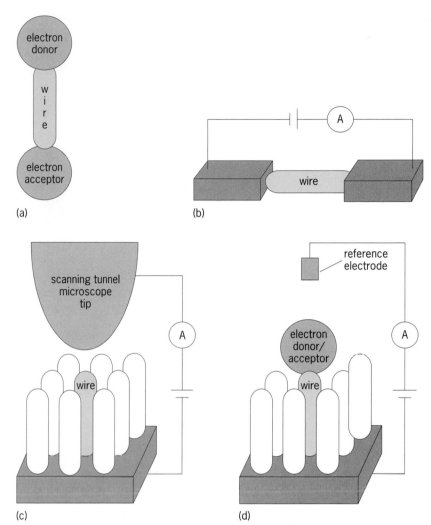

Fig. 1. Experimental configurations for studying the electronic properties of molecular wires. (a) Bridged donor-acceptor molecule. (b–d) Measurement of current (A).

or reducing the attached molecule is applied to the metal. An electric current corresponding to electron transport across the wire can be measured, and the time scale and potential dependence of the current may be interpreted in terms of the strength of wire-mediated electronic coupling between the metal and the molecule on the opposite end of the wire. As with bridging donor-acceptor molecules, steady-state electron transport occurs only if electrons are continually supplied to one end of the wire and removed from the other end. Even so, this configuration has the advantage that electron transport across the molecular wire can be measured as a current in a conventional electrical circuit. This should facilitate adoption of such structures into molecular electronic devices.

Applications. Though it is too early to envision many specific applications that might evolve out of research on molecular wires, some intriguing possibilities are emerging. One such possibility is illustrated in **Fig. 2**, which shows a length of deoxyribonucleic acid (DNA) attached to a metal electrode via an oligo(phenylethynyl) molecular wire linkage. This linkage can promote strong electronic coupling

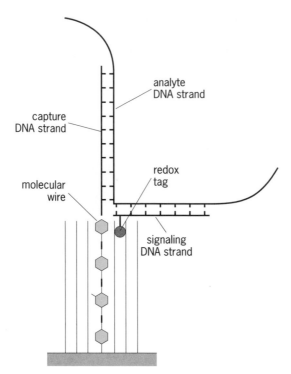

Fig. 2. Proposed electrochemical DNA hybridization sensor using a molecular wire to link a DNA chain to a metal electrode.

between the metal electrode and any electron donor (redox molecule) that might be near the wire. One could envision an analytical scheme whereby capture of a single strand of DNA from a sample onto the DNA-modified surface is followed by binding of another strand of DNA that includes a redox-active signaling agent. Electrochemical techniques could then be used to detect the presence of the captured DNA via the redox-active agent near the molecular wire. The molecular wire enables electron transfer between the redox-active agent and the electrode to occur on a time scale that would enable electronic hybridization detection. In the absence of the molecular wire bridge, the capture events could occur, but direct electron transfer between the electrode and the redox-active agent would be too slow to enable detection. This is just one of many possible schemes that might utilize molecular wires as active elements in functional molecular devices.

For background information *see* CIRCUIT (ELECTRONICS); DEOXYRIBONUCLEIC ACID (DNA); ELECTRON TRANSFER REACTION; LOGIC CIRCUIT; NANOCHEMISTRY; NANOSTRUCTURE; NANOTECHNOLOGY; PHOTOSYNTHESIS; SOLID-STATE CHEMISTRY in the McGraw-Hill Encyclopedia of Science & Technology.

Stephen E. Creager

Bibliography. S. E. Creager et al., Electron transfer at electrodes through conjugated "molecular wire" bridges, *J. Amer. Chem. Soc.*, 121:1059–1064, 1999; W. A. Reinerth et al., Molecular scale electronics: Syntheses and testing, *Nanotechnology*, 9:246–250, 1998; J. M. Tour, M. Kozaki, and J. M. Seminario, Molecular scale electronics: A synthetic/computational approach to digital computing, *J. Amer. Chem. Soc.*, 120:8486, 1998; E. K. Wilson, Instant DNA detection, *Chem. Eng. News*, p. 47, May 25, 1998.

Molten glass jets

A wide variety of products are manufactured by the glass industry, such as optical lenses, glass plates, windshields, preforms for drawing optical fibers used in telecommunications, fiberglass, and various consumer products. Glass is produced in melting furnaces or tanks, in which combustion of fossil fuels or electrical heating results in the melting of the raw materials or batch. The molten glass flows out of the melting tank through a glass delivery system for further processing. This transfer of molten glass may be driven by gravity, and as the molten glass is poured into molds or casts or other enclosures, the glass stream may "neck down" and form a gravity-driven viscous jet.

Molten glass jets are also encountered in the nuclear industry in the vitrification of nuclear wastes. A recent problem is the long-term disposition of surplus weapons-grade plutonium following the "can-in-canister" option. Surplus plutonium is mixed with ceramic materials or glass to make it unsuitable for use in weapons, and it is placed in small stainless steel cans. These cans are suspended on a stainless steel rack, and the resulting assembly is placed inside a larger stainless steel canister [approximately 600 mm (2 ft) in diameter and 3 m (10 ft) tall]. To provide a proliferation barrier, the larger canister is backfilled with molten glass containing high-level radioactive waste. The rigidified glass logs are placed in a geological repository for long-term storage. The canister filling operation is accomplished by a continuous pour of a thin stream (approximately 1–10 mm or 0.04–0.4 in.) of molten waste glass lasting 24 h.

Another example where molten glass jets are encountered may be found in the glass art industry. Hydrodynamic instabilities (small disturbances in a flow that grow in time) that may develop in the gravity-driven jet may result in novel glass structures upon cooling and rigidification. One such structure, referred to as a bird's nest, develops when the viscosity of a thin molten glass jet increases rapidly with rapid cooling, the bottom of the jet rigidifies and buckles over, and a random pile of glass fibers accumulates into a larger structure resembling a bird's nest (**Fig. 1**).

Basic flow phenomena. Molten glass can be treated as a viscous, incompressible fluid, with highly temperature-dependent fluid properties (in particular, viscosity). Above the glass transition temperature (T_g), molten glass may also be considered to be a newtonian fluid (a fluid in which the velocity is linearly related to the shear stress). Glass transition temperatures vary with the particular composition of the glass, but typically range 300–800°C (572–1472°F). At temperatures below T_g, the molten glass becomes extremely viscous and non-newtonian behavior is encountered. At the elevated temperatures typical of molten glass, significant heat transfer

Fig. 1. Bird's nest structure.

occurs due to a combination of thermal radiation, convection, and conduction. This heat transfer results in significant cooling of a molten glass jet as it falls, and consequently greatly affects the jet behavior through its temperature-dependent fluid properties. Putting aside the heat transfer phenomena, the behavior of molten glass jets bears many similarities to that of isothermal viscous jets of other liquids at ambient temperature levels. Thus, an understanding of molten glass jet phenomena begins with an understanding of viscous jet phenomena in low-temperature fluids.

Viscous jets. When viscous fluids fall under their own weight due to gravity, the straight fluid stream may become unstable upon impingement on a solid surface, resulting in meandering sinusoidal shapes. Such flows are known as buckling flows, drawing analogy to the buckling of a solid column under a load. The jet necks down continuously as it falls, rapidly near the inlet and more slowly as the distance from the inlet increases. When the jet impinges on a solid surface, the column of fluid may buckle under certain flow conditions, and begin to oscillate with a frequency ω. The parameters that determine whether buckling will occur, and the frequency and characteristics of the oscillatory fluid column if buckling does occur, are the jet fall height H; the jet diameter d; the gravitational acceleration g; the volumetric flow rate Q; and the fluid viscosity μ, density ρ, and surface tension σ; namely, $\omega = \omega(H,d,g,Q,\mu,\rho,\sigma)$. Various nondimensional groupings have been proposed to characterize the jet behavior over relatively narrow parameter ranges; however, no universal scaling has been found that applies throughout the entire range of these parameters. Several different buckling regimes have been observed, including a three-dimensional regime in which the pile topples over in random directions as coils of fluid are laid down at high frequencies (**Fig. 2a**), a two-dimensional regime in which the pile undergoes a periodic planar folding as additional coils of fluid are laid down (Fig. 2b), a stable regime

with constant pile height in which the base of the pile spreads out uniformly as the coils of fluid accumulate (Fig. 2c), and a second stable regime with constant pile height in which the jet experiences a two-dimensional or planar buckling as the fluid is laid down rather than the coiling exhibited in the previously described regimes (Fig. 2d)

Investigation of phenomena. A series of investigations to understand the strongly coupled fluid-flow and heat-transfer phenomena observed in axisymmetric molten glass jets was recently completed, motivated by the can-in-canister plutonium disposition problem described earlier. Predictions and measurements of the axial velocity and jet diameter variations along the length of the jet, the axial bulk mean temperature distribution, and the radial temperature distribution have been made for different processing conditions. A combination of numerical simulations using computational fluid dynamics software, analytical modeling, and experimentation have been employed in these investigations.

Experiments involving actual molten glass jets (high-temperature experiments), as well as surrogate glass jets using analogous fluids (room-temperature experiments), have been employed. Room-temperature experiments are particularly helpful in identifying the important characteristics of the glass pouring process and in providing data required to validate mathematical models. In order to imitate the behavior of highly viscous molten glass, 42/43 corn syrup and silicone oils were chosen as analogous fluids, since their density, viscosity, thermal conductivity, and specific heat approximately match those of borosilicate glasses. Of these properties, the most important to match is the viscosity; the viscosity of corn syrup, for example, over a temperature range of 0–40°C (32–104°F) can be matched with the viscosity of molten glass over a temperature range of 650–1050°C (1202–1922°F).

High-temperature effects. The flow of molten glass has many unusual properties, beginning with the very strong and highly nonlinear dependence of viscosity

Fig. 2. Buckling regimes of a silicone oil gravity jet. (*a*) Three-dimensional toppling. (*b*) Pile folding. (*c*) Stable pile. (*d*) Two-dimensional buckling.

on temperature. The viscosity of molten glass can increase by five orders of magnitude as it cools from 1000°C (1832°F) to below the glass transition temperature. (Surface tension effects have not yet been quantified for molten glass jets, and are usually assumed to be negligible.) Since glass is an amorphous, noncrystalline material, the glass transition temperature depends not only on the composition of the glass but also on its cooling history; strong hysteresis effects may be exhibited. There is also significant thermal radiation in a molten glass jet, both from its surface and within its volume, since at elevated temperatures molten glass is semitransparent in a spectral range of approximately 0–5 micrometers (becoming opaque at wavelengths beyond 5 μm). Analytical treatment of thermal radiation is further complicated by the specular glass-gas interface at the jet's surface.

Convective cooling also occurs at the jet surface to the surrounding ambient air, which may have very complicated and turbulent flow patterns due to the downward-acting viscous shear forces exerted by the jet on the air in proximity to very strong upward-acting buoyancy forces due to the rapid thermal expansion of the air as it is heated by the molten glass jet. Accurate measurements or numerical predictions of the convective heat transfer coefficient associated with this complicated airflow are not presently available, further complicating efforts to predict the cooling rate of a molten glass jet, and hence its temperature distribution, which is in turn needed to predict the jet's velocity profile.

As the jet travels downward from its inlet, the stream of molten glass is accelerated by the gravity force (in excess of viscous drag), and the jet diameter decreases. Near the inlet, this decrease in diameter is pronounced and is called the neck-down region. Due to the significant curvature in the neck-down region, the velocity field is two-dimensional, although it is one-dimensional away from the inlet. However, due to the buckling instabilities noted above, the jet flow may become three-dimensional and oscillatory at a critical height above a surface of impingement. This behavior is evident in **Fig. 3**, at the top of the glass pool, where

the jet initially begins to form a pile.

Piling instabilities. Multiple instabilities may be observed in the region where the glass jet forms a pool of molten glass in a canister-filling operation. At low flow rates, a small-diameter pile forms as coils of molten glass are laid down at a high oscillation frequency. The pile height grows rapidly since the compression of the pile due to its own weight and the force of the impinging jet is small compared to its extension from added coils. The pile itself then becomes unstable, toppling over and changing the spiral direction periodically. Significant entrainment of air accompanies the toppling of the molten glass pile, and large voids may be set in place as the glass cools and rigidifies. The presence of voids is undesirable in the can-in-canister disposition option from economic and operational perspectives, while voids are highly undesirable in optical components and are usually avoided in artware.

As the flow rate increases, the jet may undergo a transition to a two-dimensional folding regime, where glass accumulates in planar layers. The compression of the pile becomes balanced by its extension due to added layers of molten glass, resulting in a stable pile of fixed height with no toppling and little entrainment of air. With further increases in flow rate, the amplitude and frequency of the oscillations become smaller, and the pile height decreases due to increasing compression, until another transition is encountered resulting in a stable jet in stagnation flow.

The molten glass pool itself may exhibit instabilities in addition to those detailed above, as the weight of the accumulated glass causes the pool to form breaches in an irregular manner. In Fig. 3a, the glass pool has grown in a fairly axisymmetric manner, maintaining a roughly cylindrical shape. In Fig. 3b, the first breach has occurred, resulting in the flow of molten glass from the original pool to form a side lobe. Finally, in Fig. 3c, a second breach has occurred, and an additional side lobe has formed. This process continues throughout the glass pour, and can lead to large-scale, three-dimensional banded structures in glass casts.

For background information *see* FLUID FLOW; GLASS; RADIOACTIVE WASTE MANAGEMENT; VISCOSITY in the McGraw-Hill Encyclopedia of Science & Technology.   Kenneth S. Ball; Theodore L. Bergman

Bibliography. K. S. Ball and E. M. Taleff, Can-in-canister alternative for vitrification of surplus weapons plutonium: Overview of thermal issues, in K. L. Peddicord, L. N. Lazarev, and L. J. Jardine (eds.), *Nuclear Materials Safety Management*, pp. 291–296, Kluwer Academic, Boston, 1998; A. Bejan, Buckling flows: A new frontier in fluid mechanics, *Annu. Rev. Num. Fluid Mech. Heat Transfer*, 1:262–304, 1987; M. Song, K. S. Ball, and T. L. Bergman, A model for radiative cooling of a semitransparent molten glass jet, *ASME J. Heat Transfer*, 120:931–938, 1998; R. Viskanta, Review of three-dimensional mathematical modeling of glass melting, *J. Non-Cryst. Sol.*, 177:347–362, 1994.

Fig. 3. Photographs of a glass pour showing the formation of the glass pool and instabilities leading to large-scale banded structures. (*a*) Roughly cylindrical glass pool. (*b*) Formation of side lobe. (*c*) Formation of additional side lobe.

MOSFET sensors

Chemical sensors are used in a large variety of applications where manual chemical analysis is at a disadvantage. Chemical analysis may be difficult to perform, for example, because the sample is too small, because the measurement results are needed immediately to close a feedback loop, or because the measurements have to be performed in remote locations. One way to construct a chemical sensor is by measurement of a material property that reversibly changes upon exposure to the chemical species of interest. The property must be easily measurable (in practice, only optical and electrical material properties seem to meet this criterion), and it must change considerably when the material is exposed to the target species, but it must not depend on exposure to any other species or on temperature (that is, it must not be cross-sensitive). Practical sensors meet only a relevant subset of these criteria; that is, they can be used over only a certain range of temperatures or in a certain concentration range.

Work function of materials. The direct-current resistance is probably the electrical property that has been most studied for use in chemical sensors, tin oxide being the most studied material. The main attraction of this kind of sensor is that the measurement is extremely easy to perform and understand, but practical problems, including signal drift and cross sensitivity, pose a serious challenge. An alternative electrical property that can be used for the fabrication of a sensor is the work function of the material, that is, the work that is needed to move an electron from the bulk of a material to a position infinitely far away and in vaccum. In practice, this amount of work can be separated into two parts: (1) the energy the electron has when it is inside the bulk of the material, which is determined by the material structure and which will be called the bulk part of the work function; and (2) the work that is needed for the electron to pass the material-vacuum interface, which depends strongly on molecules that are adsorbed at this interface and which will be called the surface part of the work function.

Gas sensors. The easiest way to monitor changes in the work function of a material M is by using it as the (metal) gate contact of a metal-oxide-silicon field-effect transistor (MOSFET; **Fig. 1a**). Advantages of these structures include ease of miniaturization and the fact that they can be used to determine the work function of materials that have a very high resistance. The current that will flow when a potential is applied between the source and drain of the MOSFET depends on the gate voltage V_G between the source and a third contact, called the gate, made of a material M. When the bulk part of the work function of M changes, this will induce a change in $\Delta_M^{Cu}\phi$, the potential difference between M and the copper wire to which it is connected (Fig. 1b). The resulting change in the current between source and drain can be counterbalanced by a change in V_G, making the change in V_G at constant drain-source current a mea-

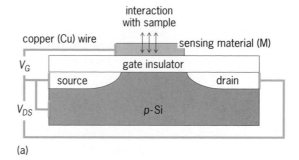

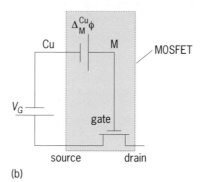

(a)

(b)

Fig. 1. MOSFET-based sensor. (a) Cross section.
(b) Illustration of the working principle. V_G is the externally adjustable gate voltage.

sure of the change in work function. Since a change in the surface part of the work function has exactly the same effect, an independent theory or experiment would be needed to determine which part of the work function has changed when a change in V_G is recorded. However, for the construction of a sensor this distinction is unimportant.

Gas sensors based on changes in the surface part of the work function of palladium upon exposure to hydrogen, so-called GasFETs, were first fabricated in 1981. Investigation of the catalytic activity of the palladium surface has enabled a detailed mechanism to be elucidated to explain the sensitivity to pure hydrogen as well as the cross sensitivity to other hydrogen-bearing gases. Applications in smoke detection and exhaust monitoring have been realized.

Sensors for redox-active solutes. Many substances can be recognized by their ability to be oxidized or reduced at an electrode that is kept at a certain potential with respect to a so-called reference electrode, which produces an electric current. In practical cases the reference electrode is often made from a silver wire that is coated with silver chloride (AgCl) and immersed in a saturated potassium chloride (KCl) solution. The reduced and oxidized forms of such a couple are referred to as a red/ox or redox couple, and the potential is called the electrode potential E. A simple way to determine the concentration of the reduced or oxidized species is by measuring the value of E at which oxidation and reduction rates are exactly equal so that the resulting current is zero.

In this classical electrochemical experiment (**Fig. 2**), the measured quantity is the voltage difference between an electrode that is covered with the sensing material and the reference electrode. While this measurement method functions very well in a large number of applications, it has some disadvantages, the most important of which is the fabrication of a good reference electrode: a glass tube filled with saturated potassium chloride contacting the sample solution by means of a porous frit while contacting the wire attached to it by means of solid silver chloride (AgCl) or calomel. While only a very small patch of sensing material is needed, it has proven to be extremely difficult to fabricate a miniature reference electrode that is stable over a longer period of time. Thus, a complete setup of this kind is relatively bulky.

There is a long history of FET-based devices that are sensitive to dissolved ions, beginning with the proton-sensitive ISFET (ion-sensitive FET) and followed by the CHEMFET, which can be made sensitive to a large range of different ions. The metal contact in these devices has been replaced by the sample solution. The sensor responds to a change in the ion concentration because the partition of ions at the interface of the sensor membrane with the sample solution induces a potential difference $\Delta_S^M \phi$ (Fig. 2), a phenomenon that cannot be observed in MOSFETs. These devices need a reference electrode for their proper operation.

In contrast, true MOSFETs can be used as chemical sensors for the determination of dissolved redox active species. When they are immersed in a solution, the basic working principle of the MOSFET does not change from that of the GasFET (Fig. 2), although it happens to be the bulk part of the work function that changes when the sensing material is oxidized or reduced. Because the redox active species in the electrolyte is able to influence the sensor signal without being part of the metal-oxide-silicon chain, these devices are called electrolyte-metal-oxide-silicon FETs or ^{E}MOSFETs. The classical electrochemical experiment, the ISFET, and the ^{E}MOSFET measure three different phenomena: The ISFET measures ion dissociation at the membrane-solution interface, the ^{E}MOSFET measures the state of oxidation of the

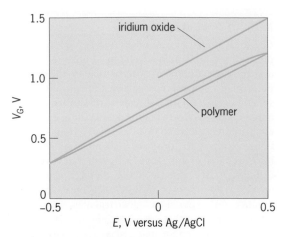

Fig. 3. Measured changes in gate voltage V_G as a function of applied electrode potential E for two sensing materials, iridium oxide, and polyvinylpyridine polymer containing electrochemically active osmium complexes. The electrode potential was measured with respect to a Ag/AgCl reference electrode.

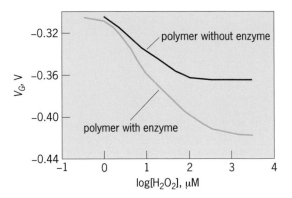

Fig. 4. Changes in gate voltage V_G as a function of the hydrogen peroxide (H_2O_2) concentration in a phosphate buffered solution (pH = 7.1). Gate material is the same polyvinylpyridine polymer as in Fig. 3, with and without the enzyme horse radish peroxidase. (*Data courtesy of Dam T. V. Anh*)

membrane, and the measurement of the electrode potential measures both.

The strong relation between the gate voltage V_G and the electrode potential E is an important advantage when it comes to the interpretation of the measured signal. When the proper gate material is used, changes in V_G and E are the same within a few percent. This behavior is apparent in **Fig. 3,** where measured changes in V_G are shown as a function of applied E for two different gate materials, iridium oxide and a commercially available polyvinylpyridine polymer containing osmium redox centers while both are being oxidized and reduced.

^{E}MOSFETs having a sensitivity toward oxygen as well as hydrogen peroxide have been demonstrated. In the hydrogen peroxide sensor (**Fig. 4**), the enzyme horse radish peroxidase (HRP) is built into the polyvinylpyridine polymer. The horse radish peroxidase selectively catalyzes the reduction of hydrogen peroxide and thus improves the sensor selectivity. Polymers of this kind have received much attention recently because of their ability to

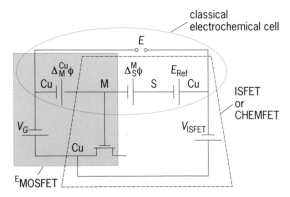

Fig. 2. Working principles of a conventional electrochemical cell, an ion-sensitive ISFET or CHEMFET, and the ^{E}MOSFET, sensitive to redox active species. The principles of each device are illustrated by the portion of the figure within the indicated boundary.

"electrically wire" enzymes to electrode surfaces; they show great promise for incorporation into MOSFET-based sensors. The polymer plays a large number of different roles here: It entraps the enzyme and facilitates the redox reaction while its changing work function is used as a sensor signal.

For background information *see* ELECTRODE PO-TENTIAL; ION-SELECTIVE MEMBRANES AND ELEC-TRODES; OXIDATION-REDUCTION; TRANSDUCER; TRANSISTOR; WORK FUNCTION (ELECTRONICS) in the McGraw-Hill Encyclopedia of Science & Technology.

Jan Hendrikse

Bibliography. R. W. Cattrall, *Chemical Sensors*, Oxford Chemistry Primers, no. 52, Oxford University Press, 1997; W. Göpel, J. Hesse, and J. N. Zemel (eds.), *Sensors: A Comprehensive Survey*, vols. 1–9, VCH, Weinheim, 1989–1995; R. F. Taylor, *Handbook of Chemical and Biological Sensors*, American International Distribution Corp., 1996; *Sensors and Actuators B* (Elsevier), exclusively devoted to chemical sensors; *Analytical Chemistry* (ACS); *Analytica Chimica Acta* (Elsevier); *Mikrochimica Acta* (Springer); *Proceedings of Transducers X*, Sendai, Japan, 1999; *Proceedings of Eurosensors XIII*, The Hague, Netherlands, 1999.

Multifunctional proteins

Proteins are polymers of amino acid building blocks that are joined by covalent peptide bonds (proteins are also known as polypeptides). They play critical roles in all organisms, from acting as channels through which metabolites enter cells to converting nutrients into energy or regulating production of other proteins. Until recently, each polypeptide prescribed by a genetic message was thought to have a single purpose or function. As more amino acid sequences of proteins were determined in various organisms, and as more experiments were done with specific proteins, the one-protein–one-function assumption was called into question because it underestimated the ingenuity at work in the cell. Geneticists and biochemists continue to discover that many proteins have more than one purpose.

Mechanisms of multifunctionality. Multifunctional or "moonlighting" proteins perform their distinct roles by several mechanisms. First, the specific location of the protein may determine which function it will perform. A protein with a particular function in the cytoplasm of the cell may serve a completely different purpose when it is imported into the cell nucleus or is exported outside the cell. The bacterial protein PutA, for example, has one role when it is bound to the cell membrane and another when it is in the cytoplasm. Second, different cell types may produce the same protein but use the protein for a function that is unique to the cell type. For example, neurophilin is involved with blood cell recruitment in endothelial cells and with the orientation of nerve fibers in neuronal cells. Some proteins have different roles depending on their state of oligomer-ization, that is, whether they are a monomer, dimer, trimer, or even a higher-order multimer. An example is the tetrameric glyceraldehyde-3-phosphate dehydrogenase, which catalyzes a step in intermediary metabolism but, when dissociated into a monomer, facilitates the repair of damaged deoxyribonucleic acid (DNA).

Another mechanism by which proteins can adapt their function is in response to the local concentration of a ligand (a molecule that binds to another molecule) whose production or use depends on the activity of the protein. In this case, the protein may assume the additional role of a regulator of its own production—adjusting its own concentration to the immediate need of the cell—or a regulator of the production of other proteins that have related functions. This regulation is accomplished by direct action of the protein on a gene or on the messenger ribonucleic acid (mRNA) copy of a gene. Aconitase is a protein that acts as a catalyst in the tricarboxylic acid cycle when iron is abundant. In contrast, aconitase is a regulator of the production of proteins needed for iron capture or storage when iron is depleted. In another vein, with more than one function a protein can amplify its effects through distinct actions in a reaction cascade. For example, in the blood-clotting cascade, thrombin catalyzes cleavage of fibrinogen to generate fibrin (which forms the fibers of blood clots), while it also cleaves cell surface receptors to initiate aggregation of blood cell platelets. Both functions therefore contribute to the end result of clot formation.

In one case, several members of a protein superfamily manifest multifunctional behavior when evaluated individually. The lens crystallins are a diverse family of water-soluble proteins that constitute up to 90% of the proteins found in the eye lens. These polypeptides together play a structural role by orienting themselves to facilitate refraction of light, an essential function in the complex mechanism of vision. Some of the individual proteins that act as crystallins inside the eye, however, exhibit other distinct functions when expressed elsewhere in the organism.

Lens crystallins can be divided into two general classes: the ubiquitous crystallins are typically found in all vertebrates, while a second class, includes representatives that are unique to each kind of organism. Within the ubiquitous vertebrate proteins, the α-crystallin subfamily contains members that are closely related or identical to small heat shock proteins, which act in a protective manner to help cells respond to stress. For example, αB-crystallin can act as a molecular chaperone that prevents heat-induced aggregation of other lens crystallins; this aggregation interferes with vision. Thus, this chaperone activity may be critical for adjusting the distribution of proteins so as to achieve optimal light refraction.

Several organism-specific lens crystallins exhibit enzymatic functions outside the eye. The δ-crystallin found in some bird and reptile lenses is identical to the metabolic enzyme argininosuccinate lyase.

Another enzyme of the glycolytic pathway, lactate dehydrogenase-B, is also present in bird and reptile eyes as ε-crystallin, while the enzyme α-enolase is identical to τ-crystallin in a variety of organisms. Although the chaperone function of αB-crystallin described above may provide a rationale for its recruitment as a refractory protein in the eye lens, the rationale for the enzyme activities of the aforementioned organism-specific crystallins is not known.

In the examples above, a single protein has more than one function, with the diversity of function being generated in one of several different ways. In these cases, the protein itself remains intact, even though it may change its activity. In an entirely different mechanism, a protein generates a new activity not by remaining intact but by breaking into pieces. Each piece then plays a role different from that of the parent protein.

An example is human tyrosyl-tRNA synthetase (TyrRS), a protein that catalyzes attachment of the amino acid tyrosine to a transfer RNA in preparation for protein synthesis at the ribosome. Human TyrRS contains a region that is highly similar to the protein endothelial monocyte activating protein II (EMAPII) [see **illus.**]. EMAPII is a cytokine, a protein that promotes the migration of white blood cells (leukocytes and monocytes) to regions of inflammation and that stimulates production of specialized molecules such as tumor necrosis factor and tissue factor at sites of tissue injury. Although TyrRS has a segment that is highly similar to EMAPII, it has none of the activities associated with the cytokine. However, upon cleavage of human TyrRS by an enzyme such as leukocyte elastase, the EMAPII-like piece is released and is then active as a cytokine with the same activities as EMAPII. Surprisingly, the portion of TyrRS that remains after removal of the EMAPII-like region also functions as a cytokine. This "mini-TyrRS" fragment retains the ability of the parental protein to catalyze attachment of tyrosine to transfer RNA, but also has an activity that mimics that of another cytokine, interleukin-8. Here again, the interleukin-8 activity is not evident in the full TyrRS but only when the protein is split into the two pieces.

Advantages of multifunctionality. The discovery of multifunctional proteins has led to the question of why a single polypeptide sequence might do double duty. What advantages might such doubling up contribute to the organism? One suggestion is that, by achieving more than one function from a single gene, the chromosome upon which genetic information is stored can be smaller. Therefore, less cellular energy needs to be expended to maintain and copy such information from one generation to the next. In the case of proteins that regulate their own production, the dual functions of catalysis and control serve a more obvious purpose. Once enough of the protein is produced, or if a substrate or ligand is in short supply, the internal feedback mechanism attenuates any further unnecessary production of the protein.

Interestingly, many multifunctional proteins are concerned with essential cell functions. This observation suggests that these essential functions do not operate in isolation from other cellular events. Some protein components of the ribosome, responsible for protein biosynthesis, have additional roles in DNA repair, RNA processing, and translational regulation. These multifunctional properties of single proteins thus enable connections between global cellular networks. For example, when TyrRS is split, cytokine signaling pathways are linked to protein synthesis. Thus, multifunctional properties may have been incorporated into single proteins as an essential element in building a communications network within and between cells.

For background information *see* AMINO ACIDS; PEPTIDE; PROTEIN in the McGraw-Hill Encyclopedia of Science & Technology.

Rebecca W. Alexander; Paul Schimmel

Bibliography. C. J. Jeffery, Moonlighting proteins, *TIBS*, 24:8–11, 1999; K. Wakasugi and P. Schimmel, Two distinct cytokines released from a human aminoacyl-tRNA synthetase, *Science*, 284:147–150, 1999; G. Wistow, Lens crystallins: Gene recruitment and evolutionary dynamism, *TIBS*, 18:301–306, 1993; I. Wool, Extraribosomal functions of ribosomal proteins, *TIBS*, 21:164–165, 1996.

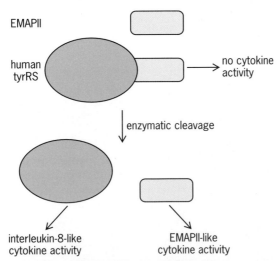

Human tyrosyl-tRNA synthetase, which attaches tyrosine to tRNA molecules for protein synthesis is cleaved into two polypeptides with different cytokine activities.

Nematoda

Caenorhabditis elegans is a small nematode worm. In the wild it lives in the soil and eats bacteria. Sydney Brenner chose *C. elegans* in the early 1960s as a "model organism" for biological research, particularly the genetic control of development and the nervous system. He was interested in a simple animal that was easy to grow, easy to observe, and easy to work with genetically. *Caenorhabditis elegans* grows quickly in the laboratory (it takes 3 days to proceed from a newly fertilized egg to a reproducing adult). This worm is transparent at all stages of development, so it has been possible to observe *C. elegans* from egg to adult in exquisite detail. One fascinating outcome of this study has been the realization that development in *C. elegans* is strongly determined; that is, each adult has very nearly the same number of cells, and in development these cells arise at the same time and in identical patterns. The complete cell lineage of *C. elegans*, from single-celled fertilized egg to 959-celled adult female, is known. Male adults have an additional set of muscle and nerve cells used in mating, making 1031 cells in all.

Structure. With so few cells, the structure of *C. elegans* might be expected to be very simple, but the nematode has a nervous system, a skin, a muscular system, a gut, and a secretory system, as well as a reproductive system. Each of these organs or tissues has very few cells (the gut, for example, has only 34 nuclei in the adult) but carries out all the functions expected of other, more complex animals. The adult nervous system at 282 cells (361 in males) can sense chemical and mechanical stimuli in the environment, coordinate sensory inputs, and control a wide range of complex behaviors. The extensive interconnections of the nervous system of *C. elegans* have been reconstructed from serial electron-microscope sections, and all junctions between nerve cells have been mapped.

Genetics. *Caenorhabditis elegans* is used as a genetic model. Researchers look for mutant nematodes that have specific defects in a phenomenon of interest. For example, an interest in the control of muscle activity has led to the isolation of "Unc" or uncoordinated mutants, which have defects in movement. Similarly, study of development using genetics has led to the isolation of nematodes that are defective in following the usual determined path of cell divisions: some steps are missing, or executed wrongly. These studies have led to deep understanding of the mechanisms that underlie development not only in *C. elegans* but also in humans and other animals.

One component of this understanding is the isolation of the genetic material that is affected in each mutant line of nematodes. Cloning the genes involved in developmental control or nervous system function can reveal how, in a molecular sense, the cell functions as part of an organism. The cloning of an individual gene can be an arduous and exacting process, taking many worker-years of research. The genome of *C. elegans* is small, about 100 million base pairs of deoxyribonucleic acid (DNA). In this DNA are encoded all the instructions for making the nematode and for carrying out its life processes. It was thus proposed, by John Sulston and Robert Waterston, that the entire genome of *C. elegans* should be sequenced. This would allow *C. elegans* biologists direct access to the sequence of all the genes and make analyses of how the nematode functions much easier. The *C. elegans* genome sequencing project was also conceived as a test run for sequencing the human genome—to determine whether biological science laboratories could scale up to do such huge projects and devise the technology to achieve them.

Beginning with only one automated sequencing machine and a team of four, the *C. elegans* genome project gathered pace, met goals with ease, and came in on target at the end of 1998. The people working on the international (U.K.-U.S.A.) project extends into the hundreds, and the centers that performed the work are now equipped with hundreds of sequencing machines, currently employed sequencing the human genome. The *C. elegans* genome was the first from a multicellular organism to be completed (several bacterial and the baker's yeast genomes had been completed earlier), and it is a milestone in biological research.

Genetic sequence. The sequenced genome is just over 98 million base pairs of DNA. The genome is organized as six chromosomes (I, II, III, IV, V, and X; the X chromosome is present in two copies in females and one in males). The sequence allows researchers to look at the whole, discerning long-range patterns in organization, as well as the local structure of the genome. All the chromosomes except the X chromosome have a similar structure, with the ends being rich in repetitive, noncoding sequences, and the centers being rich in coding DNA (genes). The repetitive DNA-rich ends are thought to be the birthplaces of new genes in evolution, as they contain many genes that are apparently unique to *C. elegans*. The X chromosome has genes distributed evenly along it.

There are about 19,100 genes that code for proteins, and another 1000 that code for ribonucleic acid (RNA) products. The analysis of the sequence was another major hurdle for researchers to overcome. Very powerful tools were developed for the *C. elegans* project that have proven to be useful for the analysis of other genomes as well, and are in use worldwide. These tools use information such as patterns in the sequence, the presence of particular motifs, and similarity between the genome sequence and other known sequences to predict where genes are to be found. The sheer number of genes discovered was a surprise, as initial estimates had suggested that there were likely to be only 6000–10,000 genes. Another surprise was the number of genes that were entirely novel; over half had no clear similarity to anything else known. Some of these apparently novel *C. elegans*-specific genes form families with tens or hundreds of members. They are obviously of importance to the nematode, and research is under way to discover just what they do. It is clear that the sequencing of the genome is only the beginning. With the genetic blueprint at hand, much more is possible in *C. elegans* research. A phase of post-genomic, or functional genomic, research is now under way, using genome data to elucidate patterns and processes in *C. elegans* biology at a resolution previously unattainable. Using DNA microdots in arrays on microscope slides, it is possible to measure, for every gene simultaneously, how much the gene is turned on or off by a particular challenge. In a similar way, maps of protein-protein interaction can be built for all 19,100 proteins predicted from the sequence. Individual genes can be targeted for mutation or interference so that the effects of their removal or downregulation can be studied. These techniques are permitting researchers to look at responses of

C. elegans to drugs also used on humans, and to identify potential targets and new leads for novel therapies. *Caenorhabditis elegans* mutants can be used to model human genetic diseases. Because many basic biological processes are common to humans and *C. elegans*, if a particular human gene is known to be involved in disease processes, its homolog from *C. elegans* can be isolated and studied with relative ease. A genome-wide analysis of particular pathways and events in the nematode can lead to basic insights into the function of all animals. An important advance that the genome sequence makes possible is the exhaustive testing of all possible genes for involvement in a particular phenomenon. If there are 20 different genes that could possibly act to give a particular pattern of development or behavior, they can all be tested, and their individual and collective effects measured.

Phylogenetic relations. As *C. elegans* is a nematode, a fair question is how relevant the knowledge of this tiny worm will be for humans and other animals. The nematodes are a diverse and abundant group of animals, and they play a major role in the ecological processes in soils and sea muds. They are also important as parasites of humans, domestic animals, and food crops. For example, *Ascaris lumbricoides* infects over a billion people worldwide, and the soya bean cyst nematode (*Heterodera glycines*) causes significant crop losses in many countries, including the United States. *Caenorhabditis elegans* is an excellent model for these nematode species, and many workers are using its simple biology to investigate new drugs and treatments for human, animal, and plant diseases caused by nematodes.

Nematodes are invertebrates, only distantly related to vertebrates. This deep phylogenetic separation (humans last shared a common ancestor with nematodes about 750 million years ago) makes the conservation of gene sequence and function all the more remarkable. The genome sequence also helps illuminate the relationship of nematodes to other animals such as insects, mollusks, and annelids. Nematodes were traditionally thought to be very primitive, and to have arisen before the major split of the animals into the protostomes (animals whose mouth develops from the first opening made during embryogenesis, including most invertebrate phyla such as Arthropoda and Annelida) and deuterostomes (animals whose mouth develops from a secondary opening, such as Echinodermata and the subphylum Vertebrata). Developmental and sequence data now suggest that nematodes are protostomes and more closely related to the insects than other major groups. By looking at the sequences of genes in the genome, comparing them to the homologous genes from vertebrates or insects, and reconstructing their evolution, it has been observed that many genes suggest a nematode-insect group rather than an insect-vertebrate affinity. The structure and arrangement of genes, particularly developmental control genes, on the chromosomes also supports a closer link between nematodes and insects than was previously considered.

The *C. elegans* research venture is not even 40 years old. The availability of the complete sequence and the development of a sophisticated array of tools and techniques have made the *C. elegans* research field a booming one. While much is clear, the huge numbers of genes with unknown function will provide many new insights in coming years. Of great interest will be genes unique to nematodes (these genes could be developed as drug or vaccine targets for disease control), or genes found in both nematodes and humans (thus probably universal) that have no known function. Analysis of *C. elegans* could reveal an underlying common biology, thus expediting the application of the human genome sequence project to alleviating disease.

For background information *see* ANNELIDA; DEVELOPMENTAL GENETICS; GENE; GENETIC MAPPING; MOLECULAR BIOLOGY; MUTATION; NEMATA; RHABDITIDA, TYLENCHIDA in the McGraw-Hill Encyclopedia of Science & Technology.   Mark Blaxter

Bibliography. M. L. Blaxter, *Caenorhabditis elegans* is a nematode, *Science*, 282:2041–2046, 1998; The *C. elegans* Genome Sequencing Consortium, Genome sequence of *Caenorhabditis elegans*: A platform for investigating biology, *Science*, 282:2012–2018, 1998; The *C. elegans* Genome Sequencing Consortium, How the worm was won, *Trends Genet.*, 15:51–58, 1999; D. Riddle et al. (eds.), *C. elegans II*, Cold Spring Harbor Laboratory Press, 1997.

Neurogenesis

There are multipotent stem cells in the adult brain that might not be very different from those found in other tissues capable of regeneration. Recent studies revealed that neurogenesis does occur in specific areas of the mature central nervous system in a variety of mammals, including humans. Proliferating cells provide regions such as the hippocampus and the olfactory bulb with new neurons throughout life (see **illus.**). Evidence from in vitro studies demonstrates that undifferentiated progenitors with characteristics of stem cells can be isolated from both neurogenic, hippocampus and subventricular zone regions, and nonneurogenic, spinal cord regions of the adult mammalian central nervous system. Stem cells are capable of proliferation, extended self-renewal, and generation of multilineage (neurons and glia) cell types. Stem cells can produce differentiated cell types while maintaining a pool of themselves. The maturation of stem cells involves a continuing loss of pluripotency and narrowing of commitment before more mature progenitors arise and migrate to regions where they fully differentiate. These studies suggest possible strategies for directed neuronal regeneration and structural repair.

Stem cell isolation. The first evidence for the existence of central nervous system stem cells with

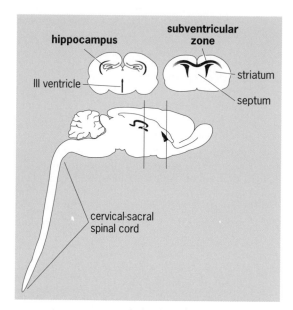

Schematic of the mammalian brain indicating the regions which exhibit persistent neurogenesis throughout life and from which growth factor expanded cells have been isolated. Neural stem cells have been isolated not only from neurogenic regions (such as the subventricular zone and hippocampus) but also from regions where neurogenesis has not been described in the adult, such as the periventricular region of the III and IV ventricles and the entire length of the spinal cord. Multipotent progenitors have also been isolated from other nonneurogenic regions such as septum and striatum.

regenerative possibilities came from culture studies. Specific growth factors such as epidermal growth factor (EGF) or fibroblast growth factor (FGF-2), as well as less defined culture supplements such as conditioned media, have been employed for the isolation and the in vitro propagation of cells with stem-like properties from the mammalian brain. Multipotent cells that respond to EGF or FGF-2 alone have been isolated from the adult subventricular zone. By clonal analysis, some of these cells were shown to bear characteristic stem cell features, such as the ability to self-renew, to expand their own population in vitro, and to differentiate spontaneously into neuronal and glial cell types. FGF-2 alone was also used to expand multipotent stem cells from the adult hippocampus and spinal cord. More recently, FGF-2 was used to propagate progenitors from the adult human subventricular zone. Data from different studies suggest that neural stem cells that differ in their growth requirements might exist. For example, proliferation of neural stem cells from the adult mouse spinal cord required combined exposure to EGF and FGF-2.

Withdrawal of mitogens and exposure to other factors such as serum, retinoic acid, FGF-2, brain-derived neurotrophic factor, or to neurotrophic factor-3, insulin, insulinlike growth factor-1, and other growth factors can influence stem cell fate or instruct cells to adopt neuronal and glial fates. It has been found that thyroid hormone in vitro promotes differentiation of FGF-2-responsive stem cells into oligodendrocytes; ciliary neurotrophic factor into astrocytes; and platelet-derived neurotrophic factor or low concentrations of FGF-2 into neurons. Bone morphogenic proteins also promote astrocytic differentiation from EGF-derived stem cells. Exposure to both activin and FGF-2 appeared to promote acquisition of a catecholaminergic phenotype by neuronal progeny of EGF-responsive neural stem cells. The role that intrinsic factors play in neural stem specification is not clear. Overall, evidence indicates that extrinsic cues can influence neural stem cell development; however, it is difficult to determine the degree of intrinsic heterogeneity among stem cells and the degree to which neural stem cells are irreversibly committed to a particular neuronal or glial progeny.

Influencing factors. The plasticity of growth factor-responsive central nervous system stem cells has also been suggested by in vivo studies. In the mammalian forebrain, neurogenesis continues throughout adult life in two regions: the dentate gyrus of the hippocampus, which continues to produce granule neurons; and the subventricular zone of the lateral ventricles, which generate new neurons that migrate through the rostral migratory stream to the olfactory bulb. The regulation of adult neurogenesis and the functional significance of these newly born neurons are the subject of several current studies. Interestingly, the external environment seems to affect the rate of neurogenesis. New neurons are added throughout adulthood in rodents, although there seems to be a decrease in neurogenesis in senescent animals. More cells are born in the dentate of the adult than survive over time, but the rate of survival is greatly increased by housing either young adult or aged animals in "enriched environments." Genetics (that is, strains of adult mice) also strongly influences neurogenesis in this region. The exact elements of the enriched environment that are critical for the survival effect are not known, but new findings suggest that learning of a specific task as well as voluntary exercise can significantly increase the number of dividing cells as well as the number that survive as neurons. These findings open an exciting opportunity to investigate the possibility that central nervous system stem cells might help replace neurons that have been lost through disease or trauma.

It has also been shown that growth factors that can induce proliferation in vitro (that is, EGF and FGF-2) can also influence proliferation and fate of cells in the subventricular zone and the subgranular zone, following their infusion into the lateral ventricles of the adult. Both factors increase proliferation in the subventricular zone, but have different effects on cell fate. While FGF-2 increases neurons reaching the olfactory bulb, EGF infusion abolishes neuron incorporation in the olfactory bulb. In contrast, EGF infusion augments the number of astrocytes and oligodendrocytes but not neurons in the subgranular zone. Other factors are being examined for their effects.

Neurogenesis in the adult hippocampus is also influenced by factors associated with stress and neural activity. Adrenal hormones and the excitatory neurotransmitter glutamate negatively regulate cell proliferation in the dentate gyrus. The inhibitory role of glucocorticoids and glutamate (excitatory neurotransmitter) in neurogenesis is best characterized by the increase in dentate gyrus cell division observed following adrenalectomy (removal of an adrenal gland) and blockade of the glutamate receptor, N-methyl-D-aspartate (NMDA), and the antagonism of this effect with increased corticosterone and NMDA activation. It is likely that the reduced proliferation in the dentate gyrus of animals exposed to stress may be partly explained by elevated levels of corticosterone. However, in apparent contrast, seizure activity induced by excitatory amino acids leads to a dramatic increase in cell proliferation in the dentate gyrus and the formation of more granule neurons. However, these newly formed neurons form aberrant connections not observed in ongoing neurogenesis. Thus, while normal neurogenesis can be enhanced and linked to functional activity, neurogenesis can be recruited abnormally, resulting in a correlation with aberrant neural function. Several studies demonstrate that a large and diverse group of growth factors and neurotransmitters can work together to regulate proliferation and differentiation in the developing and adult brain (see **table**).

Stem cell source. Regarding the cellular source of adult brain neurogenesis, a recent paper suggested that stem cells reside in the one-cell-thick ciliated ependymal layer that lines the central nervous system ventricles. However, two additional reports offer strong evidence that refutes that idea, and suggest that a subset of cells in the subventricular zone and not in the ependymal layer gave rise to self-renewing multipotent stem cells in culture. The subependymal zone location as the source for stem cells has received further support from another recent study: a virus that infects only nonependymal, glial fibrillary acid protein (GFAP) positive cells from the adult subventricular zone was found to label cells that gave rise to neuroblasts that migrated to the olfactory bulb and to self-renewing neurospheres in culture. Determining the exact localization and identity of adult central nervous system stem cells remains an important question in neurobiology.

During development, radial glia guide the migration of newborn neurons from the ventricular zone to their final destination. Postnatally, the radial glia scaffold is dismantled. Though some of the molecules that play a role in guiding migration in the developing brain persist in the adult brain in areas where neurogenesis continues, some differences may exist between mechanisms of migration in the adult and developing brain. In the adult, neuroblasts that arise from the subventricular zone migrate

---

Effects of growth factors and neurotransmitters on proliferation in the adult and developing central nervous system

Factor	Proliferation	Region	Age
Growth factors			
EGF	Increase	Dentate gyrus Subventricular zone Spinal cord	Adult
TGF-α	Increase	Dentate gyrus	Adult
FGF-2	Increase	Cerebellum Hippocampus	Postnatal
	Increase	Subventricular zone Spinal cord	Adult
Neurotransmitters			
Glutamate			
NMDAR agonist*	Decrease	Dentate gyrus	Adult
NMDAR antagonist	Increase	Dentate gyrus	Postnatal 2–5 and adult
Biogenic amines			
Decrease monoamines	Decrease	Subventricular zone	Postnatal 11
	Decrease	Brain (not specified)	Embryonic
Neuroleptics	Decrease	Subventricular zone	Postnatal 11
Decrease serotonin	Decrease	Superior colliculus Hippocampus	Embryonic 8–12
	Decrease	Dentate gyrus Subventricular zone	Adult
Cholinergic agonist	Decrease	Cortex	Embryonic Postnatal
Adrenergic antagonist	Decrease	Brain (not specified)	Postnatal
Opioids			
Met⁵-enkephalin	Decrease	Cerebellum	Postnatal 6
Opioid antagonist	Increase	Cerebellum Dentate gyrus Subventricular zone	Postnatal
Vasoactive intestinal peptide antagonist	Decrease	Prosencephalon	Embryonic 9

*NMDAR = N-methyl-D-aspartate receptor.

rostrally to the olfactory bulb, where they integrate as neurons. There is, however, no radial glia on which progenitors can migrate; neuroblasts migrate on top of each other in rows ensheathed by glial cells, representing a novel type of cell migration termed chain migration. Homotypic interactions direct the neural migration; the polysialylated neural cell adhesion molecule (PSA-NCAM) is a critical regulator of this cell-cell interaction. PSA-NCAM is also present in the dentate gyrus on the surface of the newborn adult progenitor cells as they migrate from the subgranular zone into the granular cell layer. After granule cells mature and cease migrating, they no longer express PSA-NCAM.

Therapeutic applications. The presence of neural stem cells in the adult central nervous system may open new avenues to replace cells lost due to injuries or various neurologic diseases. Stem cells amplified in vitro with growth factors have exhibited some degree of successful incorporation into intact and injured adult brain circuitries. Adult progenitor cells expanded in FGF-2 can generate region-specific neurons in areas that express neurogenic signals following transplantation into the adult brain. Recent studies have shown that central nervous system precursors which differentiated into dopaminergic neurons in vitro prior to transplantation into the striatum of an animal model of Parkinson's disease, could integrate and show some functional recovery. Thus, in vitro expanded stem cells can be used as a source of donor cells for transplantation for cell replacement therapy, directed at replacing a particular cell type lost to neurodegenerative disease. This approach also offers the opportunity to manipulate these cells genetically during the culture period to express therapeutic gene products and use them as vectors for gene therapy to replace substances lost after injury or disease. Finally, it has been shown that growth factor infusions in vivo can expand the endogenous population of stem cells and, in some instances, can coax migration into adjacent brain structures. Thus, these cells can represent an endogenous source of cells for replacement, by recruiting endogenous stem cells and induction of migration and differentiation toward specific phenotype in situ.

The prospects for using progenitor cell therapeutic strategies to repair the damaged central nervous system are promising, given the reports of widespread distribution and cross-species persistence of neural precursors, including the human central nervous system.   Lamya S. Shihabuddin; Fred H. Gage

Bibliography. H. A. Cameron et al., Regulation of neurogenesis by growth factors and neurotransmitters, *J. Neurobiol.*, 36:287–306, 1998; F. H. Gage et al., Multipotent progenitor cells in adult dentate gyrus, *J. Neurobiol.*, 36:249–266, 1998; R. McKay, Stem cells in the central nervous system, *Science*, 276:66–71, 1997; L. S. Shihabuddin et al., The search for neural progenitor cells: Prospects for the therapy of neurodegenerative disease, *Mol. Med. Today*, 5:474–480, 1999; S. Temple and A. Alvarez-Buylla,

Stem cells in the adult mammalian central nervous system, *Curr. Opin. Neurobiol.*, 9:135–141, 1999.

Nobel prizes

The Nobel prizes for 1999 included the following awards for scientific disciplines.

Chemistry. Ahmed H. Zewail received the prize for his development of femtochemistry. He is professor of chemistry and physics at the California Institute of Technology.

Femtochemistry utilizes ultrafast lasers to determine what takes place during a chemical reaction as it occurs in real time. Zewail's technique enables researchers to observe and study the exact moment when chemical bonds are made or broken. These molecular reactions can take place in femtoseconds (1 fs $= 10^{-15}$ second, or a millionth of a billionth of a second). Zewail's research utilizing lasers has brought about a dramatic increase in understanding the nature of chemical bonds. This methodology has had a wide-ranging impact, resulting in vastly increased knowledge of transition states in chemical reactions.

Femtochemistry uses ultrashort laser flashes to study molecules in "slow motion" during a chemical reaction. This enables scientists to "see" when chemical bonds are being made or broken. For a chemical reaction to occur, a so-called barrier has to be overcome. The energy required to overcome it is termed the activation energy. During the 1980s, Zewail performed experiments that allowed the observation of molecules in their transition state (which occurs during the precise moment when this barrier is reached). For example, the dissociation of iodocyanide (ICN) occurs in 200 fs, and Zewail and his team were able to observe the transition state as the carbon-iodine bond was broken. This technique now plays an integral part in elucidating and understanding how chemical reactions actually occur.

More recent experiments have been directed to the study of reaction intermediates, transient species that may be very short-lived but play a critical role in a complex reaction chain. Formerly, the existence of intermediates was shown only indirectly, and due to their brief time of existence, their structures were not known. However, by using the techniques of femtochemistry researchers were able to determine and confirm the actual structures. For example, the dissociation of tetrafluordiiodethane ($C_2I_2F_4$) into tetrafluorethylene (C_2F_4) and two iodine (I) atoms revealed that the two carbon-iodine bonds break apart one at a time. This important piece of the puzzle was needed to better understand reaction mechanisms. Femtochemistry is increasingly important in elucidating structures of short-lived intermediates in a reaction chain.

Zewail performed experiments to study various reactions. Zewail and coworkers also made important contributions in various fields such as organic chemistry (work involving the ring opening of cyclobutane), photochemistry (light-induced conversion of a molecule to another structure, known as photoisomerization), and biology (energy conversion in chlorophyll molecules during photosynthesis).

For background information *see* LASER PHOTOCHEMISTRY; ULTRAFAST MOLECULAR PROCESSES in the McGraw-Hill Encyclopedia of Science & Technology.

Physics. The physics prize was awarded to Gerardus 't Hooft and Martinus J. G. Veltman for elucidating the quantum structure of the electroweak interactions.

Particle physics deals with the fundamental constituents of matter and their interactions. The most successful description of the phenomena in this branch of physics is quantum field theory. Here, particles are represented by quantized fields, which are functions of space and time that include creation and annihilation operators for particles. The first such theory was quantum electrodynamics, which describes the electromagnetic interactions of electrons, positrons, and light at·low energies. Initial efforts to develop this theory in the 1920s ran into difficulty when attempts to perform calculations of physical quantities yielded results that were infinitely large. The problem was solved in the 1940s with the development of the method of renormalization by R. P. Feynman, J. Schwinger, S.-I. Tomonaga, and others, yielding some of the most precise predictions of physical quantities ever made.

A theme of modern physics has been the quest to find hidden unities underlying the action of apparently disparate forces in nature. The theory of electromagnetism is the result of the unification of electric and magnetic forces by J. C. Maxwell in the 1860s. In the 1960s, S. L. Glashow, A. Salam, S. Weinberg, and others formulated the electroweak theory, which unites electromagnetism and the weak interactions (which govern radioactive decay). However, this theory also gave infinitely large results, and many researchers were pessimistic about overcoming this difficulty. The force-mediating particles in electromagnetism are massless, noninteracting photons, but those in the electroweak interaction include the massive and interacting W and Z bosons, a circumstance that gives rise to serious mathematical complications. In mathematical terms, the electroweak theory is a nonabelian gauge theory, which is much more complex than an abelian theory such as quantum electrodynamics.

However, Veltman, optimistic that these obstacles could be overcome, developed a computer program for simplifying the complicated expressions that arise in quantum field theories. In 1969–1971, 't Hooft, his doctoral student at the University of Utrecht (Netherlands), developed methods of renormalizing nonabelian gauge theories; and with the help of Veltman's computer program, these results were verified and methods of calculation were worked out in detail.

Veltman's work has had great impact on the development of particle physics by showing that nonabelian theories such as the electroweak theory make sense, and by providing a method for performing precise calculations with these theories. Predictions of the values of quantities such as the properties of the W and Z bosons and the mass of the top quark have been confirmed by experimental measurements.

For background information *see* ELECTROWEAK INTERACTION; FUNDAMENTAL INTERACTIONS; GUAGE THEORY; WEAK NUCLEAR INTERACTIONS in the McGraw-Hill Encyclopedia of Science & Technology.

Physiology or medicine. Günter Blobel was awarded the Nobel prize for discovering that proteins carry signals that help direct the proteins' movement among the organelles of the cell. Blobel is a professor of cell biology at the Rockefeller University in New York.

In the 1970s, Blobel discovered that newly synthesized proteins, destined to be transported out of the cell, have an intrinsic signal that directs them to and across the membrane of the endoplasmic reticulum, one of the cell's organelles, and then on to specific other compartments of the cell. He suggested that the protein traverses the membrane of the endoplasmic reticulum through a channel. Subsequently, Blobel characterized in detail the molecular mechanisms underlying these processes.

Proteins are long, folded chainlike molecules made up of building blocks called amino acids. The signals that Blobel found are particular sequences of amino acids either at one end of a protein or within it. These signals are present in each newly synthesized protein to designate its compartment and membrane destination. Following targeting and translocation, the signal sequence is often removed by an enzyme (signal peptidase). Signal sequence–mediated targeting and protein translocation across the membrane can occur by two mechanisms: The signal sequence is first recognized by a soluble signal recognition factor, which in turn binds to a receptor in the target membrane. After its release from this targeting complex, the signal sequence binds to a receptor that opens a protein channel, allowing translocation across the membrane. After translocation, the channel closes. Another mechanism of protein trafficking is seen in transport into and out of the nucleus. Proteins dock on fibers that project from the nuclear pore complexes. These complexes contain a central tube that serves as a conduit for translocation of proteins.

Blobel's research led other scientists to develop laboratory procedures in which cells are altered slightly to make them churn out drugs such as insulin, human growth hormone, and a substance used during chemotherapy that helps in the production of bone marrow. In addition, this work has had a profound impact on modern cell biology research. When a cell divides, large amounts of proteins are synthesized and new organelles are formed. In order for the cell to function properly, the proteins have to be targeted to their specific locations. Blobel's research has substantially increased understanding of the molecular mechanisms governing these processes.

In the future the knowledge about protein trafficking may be applied to different parts of the cell which may contribute to the development of new drugs. The ability to alter cellular instructions in a specific way may also be applied to cell and gene therapy.

For background information *see* CELL MEMBRANES; CELL ORGANIZATION; ENDOPLASMIC RETICULUM in the McGraw-Hill Encyclopedia of Science & Technology.

Nonpoint source pollution

The subsurface migration of hazardous wastes from point sources has caught the public's attention with well-publicized case histories such as Love Canal and Woburn. In the United States there have been tremendous advances in the last 25 years related to point source pollution. For example, cleaning up the aquatic environment by controlling pollution from industries, and remediating the legacies associated with failed hazardous waste landfills are well-established practices in today's environmentally conscious society. Nonpoint source pollution, with all the implications of scale and variability (both spatial and temporal), can pose even greater environmental problems than those from point sources. Nonpoint source pollution occurs when rainfall, snowmelt, or irrigation water runs over land or through the ground, picks up pollutants, and deposits them into rivers, lakes, and coastal water or introduces them into ground water. Nonpoint source pollutants are spread over large areas, as opposed to point source pollutants that are located at a single site. Nonpoint source pollutants can be diffuse and intermittent and are influenced by changes in climate, geology, hy-

drology, land use, topography, and vegetation at regional scales. Obviously, nonpoint source pollution can be a much more difficult problem to control than point source pollution. The Environmental Protection Agency has identified nonpoint source pollution as the nation's largest water quality problem. Due in large part to nonpoint source pollution, approximately 40% of the surveyed rivers, lakes, and estuaries in the United States are not clean enough to meet basic uses such as fishing or swimming.

During the 1990s, significant headway was made in addressing nonpoint source pollution in the United States. Nonpoint sources are regulated under Section 319 of the 1972 Clean Water Act, by amendments approved by Congress in 1987 (Nonpoint Source Pollution Management Program). States are required to identify the major sources of nonpoint source pollution and draft plans (Best Management Programs, or BMPs) to rectify the problems. Also, the Coastal Nonpoint Pollution Program (for states and territories with approved Coastal Zone Management Programs), established in the 1990 Coastal Zone Act Reauthorization Amendments, has helped to reduce nonpoint source pollution impacts. The cost of remediation for nonpoint source pollution at the regional scales associated with, for example, modern agricultural and forestry practices can be staggering. Therefore, input reduction is the cheapest way to reduce nonpoint source pollution.

Types. Nonpoint source pollution is widespread because it can occur any time that activities disturb the land or water. Major sources are (1) air pollution fallout, (2) agriculture, (3) construction, (4) forestry, (5) mining, and (6) urban areas. Other sources include grazing, septic systems, recreational boating, urban runoff, physical changes to stream channels, and habitat degradation.

Acid rain is the result of air pollution fallout. Runoff from agriculture can result in, for example, agrochemicals and topsoil washing into streams or other water bodies, and agrochemicals leaching through

Relative importance of pollutant concentrations*							
Nonpoint source category	Suspended solids/sediments	Nutrients	Pesticides	Toxic metals	Salinity	Pathogens	Acids
Air pollution fallout	M	L-M	L-M	L-H	N	N-L	L-M
Agriculture							
Nonirrigated crop production	H	H	H	N-L	N	N-L	N
Irrigated crop production	L	H	M-H	N-L	H	N	N
Pasture and range	L-M	H	N	N	N-L	N-L	N
Construction	H	L	N	N-L	N	N	N
Forestry							
Growing	N	L	L	N	N	N-L	N
Harvesting	M-H	L-M	L	N	N	N	N
Urban storm runoff	M	L	L	H	M	H	N

*N = negligible; L = low; M = moderate; H = high.
SOURCE: After J. J. Peirce et al., *Environmental Pollution and Control*, 4th ed., Butterworth-Heinemann, Boston, 1998.

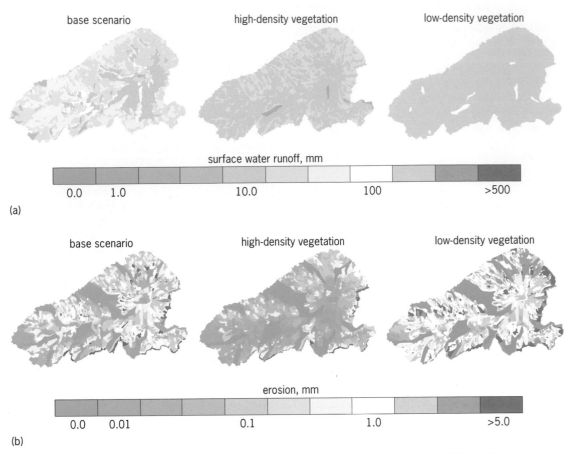

base scenario   high-density vegetation   low-density vegetation

surface water runoff, mm

0.0   1.0   10.0   100   >500

(a)

base scenario   high-density vegetation   low-density vegetation

erosion, mm

0.0   0.01   0.1   1.0   >5.0

(b)

Fig. 1. Impact of vegetation on (a) surface runoff and (b) nonpoint source erosion for Kaho'olawe. (*After E. Wahlstrom, K. Loague, and P. Kyriakidis, Hydrologic response: Kaho'olawe, Hawaii, J. Environ. Qual., 28:481–492, 1999*)

the near-surface vadose zone to ground water. Runoff in areas of construction can result in accelerated rates of erosion and high sediment loading into streams, rivers, lakes, and estuaries. Runoff from forested hillslopes, where the near surface has been disturbed by logging and timber operations, can result in sediment loading to streams, and slope instability and landslide-type events. Water seeping through large mined areas can result in acid drainage. Urban storm runoff (including water off buildings and streets) can transport oil, grease, trash, salts, and other pollutants into surface water bodies depending upon the type of sewerage (separate or combined). The different types of nonpoint source pollutants include acids, nutrients, pathogens, pesticides, toxic metals, salts, and suspended solids/sediments. The **table** summarizes the relative importance of pollutant concentrations for the different nonpoint source categories.

Nonpoint source pollution impacts from agriculture can be minimized, in part, by properly managing the use of agrochemicals and irrigation. Nonpoint source pollution impacts from forestry can be managed by minimizing detrimental timber harvesting, establishing restricted streamside areas, proper road construction, and efficient replanting. Nonpoint source pollution impacts from urban runoff can be minimized by reducing pollutant loads for both existing and new developments (residential, commercial, and industrial).

Assessing impacts. The information age has resulted in global awareness of complex environmental problems that do not respect political or physical boundaries, such as climatic change, ozone layer depletion, deforestation, desertification, and nonpoint source pollution. Scientists working on nonpoint source pollution problems are concerned with the public policy aspects of their efforts. The difficulties associated with the enormous amount of information required (such as climate, geology, hydrology, land use, topography, and vegetation) for the assessment of regional-scale nonpoint source pollution impacts can often be facilitated by remote sensing and geographic information system (GIS) technologies. The ability to simulate spatially and temporally variable environmental impacts via mathematical modeling is a necessity; simulation provides the ability to ask and answer "what if" questions that can be used to guide decision-making strategies.

In general, nonpoint source vulnerability assessments rest upon data that are extremely sparse and therefore contain considerable uncertainty. Uncertainty in simulated assessments is unavoidable and sometimes even undetectable in environmental modeling. Quantification of accuracy and uncertainty in environmental modeling establishes the extent to which simulated results are reliable predictions of observed truth. Uncertainty can be due to model errors (produced from oversimplification of process complexities) or data errors (resulting from errors in the input data or lack of information). Intrinsic model and data uncertainties have significant practical implications, either affirming or negating the use of predictive outputs from environmental models for guidance in a decision-making process. There are obvious questions: What reductions in uncertainty could be made in nonpoint source vulnerability assessments if the data used to drive the models were themselves less uncertain? How much additional information is required to realize the reductions in data uncertainty? How much would this supplemental information cost?

Kaho'olawe. Erosion resulting from surface runoff has historically been a major nonpoint source pollution problem for Kaho'olawe, the eighth largest (117 km²) island in the Hawaiian chain. Land-use practices (overgrazing and military activities) over the last 150 years have resulted in a dramatic loss of vegetation and (subsequently) soil across Kaho'olawe, causing substantial damage to the island's ecosystem. In 1999, near-surface hydrologic response simulations were reported that were designed to evaluate the impact of landscape remediation on Kaho'olawe. Based upon the event-based simulations in this report, landscape restoration via the introduction of vegetation, which is a strong control on runoff and erosion, was shown to be an effective means of significantly reducing erosion

across Kaho'olawe. **Figure 1**, abstracted from the report, shows the impact on runoff generation and erosion from the introduction or removal of vegetation across the entire island, as compared to the base (current) scenario. Large portions of the island that experienced significant erosion under the base scenario had erosion reduced by nearly an order of magnitude with the introduction of vegetation. The removal of all vegetation, however, shows that the rate of soil removal from the island would be significantly accelerated.

Tenerife. The nonpoint source ground-water contamination problem is especially important for insular systems. As in most insular systems, the ground-water resources on the Canary island of Tenerife are in the form of an easily impacted lens of fresh water floating on top of a saltwater body. Tenerife is the largest (2038 km²) island of the Canary Archipelago; it has a triangle-based pyramid shape with generally steep relief except in the coastal agricultural areas. Agriculture in Tenerife is dependent upon pesticides; therefore, precious ground-water resources are vulnerable to contamination from leaching pesticides. In 1999, researchers combined soil, climatic, and chemical data in a GIS framework with simple pesticide leaching indices to generate ground-water vulnerability assessments for all the agricultural areas across Tenerife for the most important agrochemicals currently in use. A major focus in the efforts was to characterize the uncertainty in the Tenerife ground-water vulnerability assessments resulting from data uncertainties. The vulnerability maps of

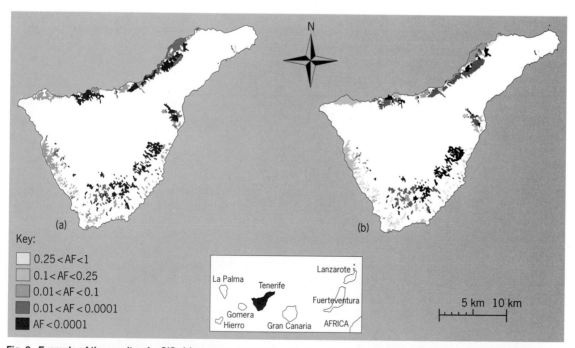

Key:

- ☐ 0.25 < AF < 1
- ☐ 0.1 < AF < 0.25
- ☐ 0.01 < AF < 0.1
- ☐ 0.01 < AF < 0.0001
- ■ AF < 0.0001

Fig. 2. Example of the results of a GIS-driven assessment of regional-scale nonpoint source ground-water vulnerability for Tenerife. (*a*) Estimates of pesticide (Ethoprophos) leaching, were made for the agricultural areas with the AF (attenuation factor) index. (*b*) Uncertainty (AF + S_{AF}) in the estimates of pesticide leaching are indicated, where S_{AF} is one standard deviation in the AF estimate. When the value of AF is 0.0 the leaching classification is "very unlikely," and when the value of AF is 1.0 the leaching classification is "very likely." (*Adapted from R. Diaz-Diaz and K. Loague, Regional-scale leaching assessments for Tenerife: Impact of data uncertainties, J. Environ. Qual., 29:835–847, 2000; R. Diaz-Diaz, K. Loague, and J. S. Notario, An assessment of agrochemical leaching potentials for Tenerife, J. Contam. Hydrol., 36:1–30, 1999)*

pesticide leaching that were produced identified locations where ground-water contamination was a potential problem, as well as areas of limited information (**Fig. 2**).

Regional-scale vulnerability maps of nonpoint source pollution and their associated uncertainty maps (of the type shown in Fig. 2) have tremendous potential, when used together, as management tools for identifying which pesticides are the least likely to result in ground-water contamination in the future, and for targeting the most efficient data collection strategies.

For background information *see* ACID RAIN; AIR POLLUTION; EROSION; GEOGRAPHIC INFORMATION SYSTEMS; HAZARDOUS WASTE in the McGraw-Hill Encyclopedia of Science & Technology.   Keith Loague

Bibliography. D. L. Corwin, P. J. Vaughan, and K. Loague, Modeling nonpoint source pollutants in the vadose zone with GIS, *Environ. Sci. Technol.*, 31:2157-2175, 1997; R. Diaz-Diaz and K. Loague, Regional-scale leaching assessments for Tenerife: Impact of data uncertainties, *J. Environ. Qual.*, 29:835-847, 2000; R. Diaz-Diaz, K. Loague, and J. S. Notario, An assessment of agrochemical leaching potentials for Tenerife, *J. Contam. Hydrol.*, 36:1-30, 1999; J. L. King and D. L. Corwin, Science, information, technology, and the changing character of public policy in non-point source pollution, in D. L. Corwin, K. Loague, and T. R. Ellsworth (eds.), Assessment of Non-Point Source Pollution in the Vadose Zone, *AGU Geophys. Monog.*, no. 108, pp. 309-322, 1999; K. Loague, D. L. Corwin, and T. R. Ellsworth, The challenge of predicting nonpoint source pollution, *Environ. Sci. Technol.*, 32:130A-133A, 1998; J. J. Peirce, R. F. Weiner, and P. A. Vesilind, *Environmental Pollution and Control*, 4th ed., Butterworth-Heinemann, Boston, 1998; E. Wahlstrom, K. Loague, and P. Kyriakidis, Hydrologic response: Kaho'olawe, Hawaii, *J. Environ. Qual.*, 28:481-492, 1999.

Notch signaling

Notch signaling is an evolutionarily conserved developmental pathway utilized during the differentiation of a plethora of tissue types, in organisms as diverse as nematodes and humans. Neurogenesis, hematopoiesis, apoptosis, formation of somites, and limb development are just a few of the cellular differentiation events which rely upon cell-to-cell communication mediated by the Notch signaling mechanism. The *Notch* gene, which was first discovered in the fruit fly, *Drosophila melanogaster*, and was named for the presence of "notches" in the wings of mutant animals, encodes a cell-surface receptor molecule. The fruit fly has only a single identified Notch-like gene in its genome, nematodes have two Notch-like genes, while at least four homologs have been identified in mammals. Given this diversification of Notch and its widespread use during development, it is not surprising that mutations in compo-

nents of the Notch system are associated with human diseases. The Notch mutation TAN-1 is a truncated form of human Notch1 that may be constitutively active and is associated with neoplastic lymphomas. Mutations in human Notch3 are associated with a disorder known as cerebral autosomal dominant arteriopathy with subcortical infarcts and leukoencephalopathy (CADASIL) which affects vascular integrity. Finally, mutations of a human activating ligand, Jagged1, are associated with the dominant disorder Alagille syndrome, resulting in childhood chronic liver disease and heart, eye, facial, and skeletal disorders.

Function. As one might expect with such a widely used signaling system, the pathway is highly regulated at many levels. Components of the Notch pathway fall into general categories common to many signaling pathways. These are activators (ligands), the receptor itself, effectors (CSL proteins, which are DNA-binding proteins), and transcriptional target genes.

The best-studied Notch signaling event is neurogenesis in flies. In this ectodermal differentiation process, proneural clusters of cells express transcription factors initiating the neuronal program. All cells of the cluster begin with equivalent potential and express both a ligand and the Notch receptor. As a result of a feedback mechanism, small differences in the expression levels of ligand and receptor are amplified and reinforced such that ultimately a single cell expresses ligand while the surrounding cells express the Notch receptor. The ligand-expressing cell will become the neuroblast, while those receiving the Notch signal delay differentiation. In the absence of Notch function, all cells of the proneural cluster follow the neuronal differentiation pathway, resulting in overspecification of neuronal tissue at the expense of other ectodermally derived structures. In the case just described, Notch is used in a lateral inhibition mechanism to limit the number of cells following the neuronal differentiation pathway. Mesodermal and endodermal tissues also require Notch-based decisions during development, and some of these decisions can utilize Notch in more inductive roles. However, for the most part, the mechanism of signal transduction is generally thought to be the same for both processes.

Notch-ligand interactions. In flies, the Notch molecule spans the cell membrane and has a large extracellular domain consisting of 36 epidermal growth factor (EGF)–like repeats and three cysteine-rich Notch/lin-12 repeats (see **illus.**). Intracellularly, Notch has six tandem CDC10/ankyrin repeats, a glutamine-rich stretch (called opa), and a PEST (proline, glutamate, serine, and threonine) sequence which may regulate stability of the molecule. Studies of known Notch mutations and a variety of expression investigations indicate that the function of the extracellular domain is to regulate the signal transducing intracellular domain. When one examines Notch-like molecules from other organisms,

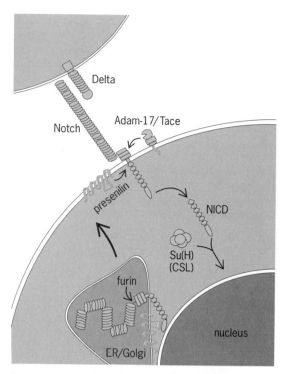

Regulation of Notch signaling begins in the ER/Golgi, where Notch is cleaved by a furin-like protease and associates with presenilin. At the plasma membrane, Notch can interact with ligand such as Delta. This interaction leads to an extracellular cleavage event mediated by an ADAM protease (TACE or TNF-α converting enzyme) and a transmembrane cleavage requiring presenilin. Following cleavage, the intracellular domain (NICD) is released and travels to the nucleus where, in conjunction with a CSL protein, it alters transcription within the cell.

differences in the number or arrangement of the extracellular EGF-like repeats is observed; but, with the exception of the opa region, the elements of fly Notch are found in other species as well. Thus, from studies of Notch in many diverse organisms, a common mechanism of Notch function is emerging.

Communication through the Notch receptor is thought to be limited to areas between adjacent cells or at least within a few cell diameters because the identified ligands for this receptor are, like the receptor itself, membrane-bound molecules. In general, two ligand types are identified: the Delta or Delta-like ligands, and the Serrate-like ligands (also known as Jagged in vertebrates). The ligands are structurally similar: each has an extracellular N-terminal domain consisting of a conserved DSL segment (named for the founding members Delta and Serrate in flies and *lag-2* in *Caenorhabditis elegans*), a varying number of EGF-like repeats, a transmembrane segment, and a small intracellular domain. Available evidence suggests that both Delta-like and Serrate-like Notch ligands activate Notch signaling. However, the interactions of the ligands and the receptor can be differentially modified by other gene products. In particular, the product of a gene called *fringe* appears capable of blocking many Serrate/Notch interactions with a lesser or no effect on Delta/Notch interac-

tions. Additionally, there is evidence for proteolytic processing of the ligands; and, at least for Delta, an extracellular, soluble fragment capable of activating Notch has been observed. Such processing likely provides additional levels through which ligands can be regulated. Thus, even in the presence of both ligand and receptor, the potential for signal initiation can be modulated by other gene products to control when and where Notch is activated.

Regulation. The Notch receptor is probably the most regulated of all of the molecules in the pathway studied to date. Notch is synthesized as a single polypeptide that is proteolytically processed by a furin-like protease as it is transported through the Golgi, ultimately becoming inserted into the cell membrane as a heterotypic molecule (see **illus.**). Activation of the Notch receptor is mediated by binding with ligand through the 11th and 12th EGF-like repeats of Notch and the N-terminal domains of Delta or Serrate. This binding results in an additional cleavage event in the Notch extracellular domain likely to be mediated by a metalloprotease enzyme related to tumor necrosis factor-alpha (a converting enzyme) or by ADAM-17.

The events following the extracellular cleavage of Notch remained mysterious for many years. Laboratories had reported that when forms of Notch lacking the extracellular domain were ectopically expressed, the Notch intracellular domain (NICD), which contains consensus nuclear localization signals, localized preferentially to the nucleus of the cell. This suggested that Notch, unlike many membrane-bound signaling receptors which utilize second messenger pathways, may directly affect transcription in the nucleus. This evidence was made even more tantalizing when it was found that a CSL transcription factor (named for *CBF1* in vertebrates, *Su(H)* in flies, and *lag-1* in *C. elegans*), which is the major effector gene of the Notch pathway, can be preferentially localized to the nucleus in tissue culture cells in the presence of the NICD. The problem was that in an intact animal the NICD could not be detected by antibody staining in the nucleus of cells known to be receiving a Notch signal. This problem was recently solved by attaching sensitive transcriptional activation domains to membrane-bound Notch molecules and demonstrating that, upon ligand binding, transcriptional activation is induced. Furthermore, in these experiments the amounts of NICD in the nucleus were at levels below that expected for antibody detection. Hence, not only does Notch appear to take a direct route to the nucleus where it alters gene transcription in conjunction with the CSL transcription factor, but the cell appears to be exquisitely sensitive to low levels of the NICD.

Once it was established that the NICD does access the nucleus of the cell, the mechanism of how the NICD is released from the membrane was addressed. Logically, the process has to involve a proteolytic cleavage. Initial clues to the identity of the protease came from studies in *C. elegans* where a gene called

SEL-12 was shown to be necessary to facilitate signaling of the Notch-like gene *LIN-12*. The interesting finding is that *SEL-12* is a *C. elegans* homolog to mammalian presenilin genes. Presenilins are best known for their role in processing the transmembrane β-amyloid precursor protein (APP). Dominant mutations in human Presenilin 1 and 2 are associated with Alzheimer's disease and the production of β-amyloid plaques composed primarily of aberrantly processed APP. APP processing is remarkably similar to that proposed for Notch. APP is processed by α, β, and γ secretases. The α and β secretases cleave APP extracellularly, and the γ-secretase cleaves APP on the transmembrane domain. It is not clear whether the presenilins represent the APP γ-secretase activities themselves or whether they act as requisite cofactors in the process. However, studies in a variety of systems have demonstrated that the presenilin genes are required for the release of the NICD. Furthermore, mice lacking the genes for presenilin 1 and 2 show phenotypes remarkably reminiscent of defects associated with loss of Notch activity. This conserved use of presenilins in both APP and Notch processing (and perhaps other essential cellular processes) has tempered initial hopes of treating Alzheimer's disease by simply inhibiting γ-secretase activity. Although such action would likely decrease the production of amyloid plaque material, the affects on Notch activity, which is widely used even in adults, would likely produce devastating results.

Interactions with other signaling pathways. The widespread use of Notch-based decisions during development suggests that Notch is tightly regulated. Indeed, there are components of this regulation which appear to function in tissue-specific events. For instance, the selection of sensory organ precursors in the fly requires Notch to differentiate between two potentially equivalent daughter cell types following each of two cell divisions. The product of a gene called *numb* is preferentially localized to one of the two daughters where it binds the NICD and inhibits the Notch signal. This causes the alternate daughter cell to receive the Notch signal and biases the cell fate choices of these cells. Interestingly, after each cell division, the Notch-based decision produces cell types of different competency, suggesting that the same Notch signal is differentially interpreted in each successive round. Since such signals can occur in subsequent cell generations, there must be mechanisms for rapid degradation of NICD signals to "reset" the system. In addition, Notch-based decisions have the potential to integrate signals from multiple pathways. For instance, it is clear that Notch activity is modulated by other signaling systems such as the EGF tyrosine kinase and Wingless (Wnt) signaling pathways. Some of these interactions may be direct since molecules such as disheveled (a wingless pathway component) and Disabled (a component of the Abl kinase signaling pathway) have been shown capable of directly interacting with the NICD. These regulatory interactions demonstrate that tissue-specific regulation and signal integration events are likely to influence Notch-based decisions. Such complex interactions help to explain how the straightforward signal cascade presented above can be used to influence the broad spectrum of tissue types known to rely on Notch-based signals.

The long evolutionary history of Notch has produced a diverse range of organisms and tissue types that utilize the system. It has also allowed for diversification of Notch function in different cellular contexts. For instance, many investigators have noted that mutations of *Su(H)*, the main CSL gene in flies, are phenotypically less severe than mutations of the Notch receptor. This implies that not all of Notch signaling is accounted for by the mechanism described above. Recent evidence suggests that Notch interacts with more than the Delta and Serrate ligands. There exist a set of dominant Notch mutations in flies called Abruptex mutations which affect the 24th through 29th EGF-like repeats of Notch. These repeats are not within the known Delta/Serrate binding region. The existence of these mutations combined with genetic interaction data suggests there may be other molecules capable of binding to the extracellular region of Notch. Evidence is accumulating that one such molecule may be wingless, a member of the Wnt signaling group. Thus, it is possible that the Notch and wingless pathways intersect through interaction both extracellularly by direct binding and intracellularly through disheveled, forming a regulatory network. An even more profound example involves the effects of Notch on the expression of C-Jun N-terminal kinase (JNK) signaling in fly embryos. Not only is this Notch interaction independent of *Su(H)*, but it does not appear to require proteolytic processing and release of the NICD. This implies that there may be several mechanisms through which Notch can affect intercellular signaling in developing animals.

It is clear that Notch is woven inextricably from developmental signaling and differentiation. Researchers will likely learn more diverse mechanisms of Notch action and discover more extensive interconnections with other signaling and regulatory pathways utilizing and controlling Notch signals in developing organisms.

For background information *see* ALZHEIMER'S DISEASE; CELL BIOLOGY; DEVELOPMENTAL BIOLOGY; DEVELOPMENTAL GENETICS; GENE in the McGraw-Hill Encyclopedia of Science & Technology.

Robert J. Fleming

Bibliography. S. Artavanis-Tsakonas, M. D. Rand, and R. J. Lake, Notch signaling: Cell fate control and signal integration in development, *Science*, 284: 770–776, 1999; Y.-M. Chan and Y. N. Jan, Presenilins, processing of β-amyloid precursor protein, and Notch signaling, *Neuron*, 23:201–204, 1999; P. Simpson (ed.), Special issue on Notch signaling, *Semin. Cell. Dev. Biol.*, 9:581–625, 1998; V. Zecchini, K. Brennan, and A. Martinez-Arias, An activity of Notch regulates JNK signalling and affects dorsal closure in *Drosophila, Curr. Biol.*, 9:460–469, 1999.

Nuclear hormone receptors

It has been estimated that approximately 100,000 genes are expressed in the human genome. The transcription of these genes into messenger ribonucleic acid (mRNA) and their subsequent translation into protein determines the identity and function of each cell in the human body. The balance between sickness and health requires that transcription of these genes be precisely regulated in response to both physiological and environmental changes. A variety of signaling strategies have evolved to coordinate the body's transcriptional response to such events. The nuclear hormone receptors represent perhaps the largest family of proteins that directly regulate transcription in response to hormones and other ligands (chemical entities which bind to the receptor).

Nuclear hormone receptors have been identified in many species ranging from *Caenorhabditis elegans* (worms) to humans. In insects, the process of metamorphosis is initiated by the binding of 20-hydroxyecdysone to its nuclear receptor. Similarly, the transformation of a tadpole into an adult frog is triggered by another member of the nuclear receptor superfamily, the thyroid hormone receptor. Nearly 50 distinct nuclear receptor genes have been identified in the human genome. These include receptors for the steroid hormones (glucocorticoids, mineralocorticoids, estrogens, progestins, and androgens), thyroid hormones, vitamin D, and retinoic acid. Many of these classical hormones were first described about a century ago. In the past decade, an even larger number of nuclear receptor proteins have been found for which no known hormone or ligand has been identified. These proteins have been termed orphan receptors, and their existence leads to the prediction that new hormones and signaling molecules will be identified in the future. Orphan receptors hold considerable promise as they provide the first clues toward the identification of novel regulatory molecules and new drug therapies.

Molecular view. Although each of the nuclear receptors mediates distinct biological effects, their activities at the molecular level are remarkably similar. Nuclear receptors contain two functional modules that characterize this family of proteins: the deoxyribonucleic acid (DNA)–binding domain and the ligand-binding domain (**Fig. 1**).

DNA-binding domain. In order to regulate gene transcription, nuclear receptors must first bind specific DNA sequences adjacent to their target genes. These sequences are referred to as hormone response elements (HREs). The DNA-binding domain is the portion of the receptor which binds to these sequences. As each receptor controls only a specific subset of all genes, the DNA-binding domain must discriminate between its hormone response elements and other closely related sequences. Structural analyses demonstrate that the DNA-binding domain of nuclear receptors folds into a three-dimensional structure containing three α-helical segments. The first of these helices makes direct contacts with nucleotides in the major groove of DNA, while the third helix contacts phosphate groups in the minor groove. These specific interactions help to determine the precise DNA sequence that each receptor recognizes. Some receptors bind to DNA by themselves (as monomers); however, the majority of receptors bind to DNA in association with a partner receptor (Fig. 1). The formation of such dimers adds another level of selectivity to the DNA-receptor interaction as each receptor subunit may recognize different DNA sequences. Moreover, the relative orientation of the two DNA-binding domains may vary from one dimer to another. This forces each dimer pair to recognize hormone response elements containing sequence gaps of different sizes in the center of the element. The combination of these features allows individual nuclear receptors to regulate a specific set of genes.

Ligand-binding domain. While the DNA-binding domain selects the target genes, it is the hormone- or ligand-binding domain that determines which hormones activate these genes. The ligand-binding domain contains a cavity or pocket that specifically recognizes the cognate ligand. When a hormonal ligand is bound within this pocket, the receptor undergoes a conformation change that reorients the position of the activation domain (Fig. 1). This reorientation switches the receptor into a transcriptionally active state. Thus, the ligand-binding domain senses the presence of specific ligands in the body, and in the presence of that ligand it allows the receptor to activate gene transcription. In addition to serving as the hormonal sensor, the ligand-binding domain contains a dimerization domain that determines which receptors can interact with each other.

Regulation of target genes. In the nucleus, DNA is wrapped around histone proteins in a structure

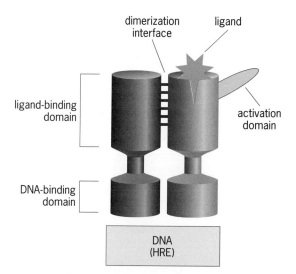

Fig. 1. Schematic illustration of a nuclear receptor dimer bound to DNA. The DNA-binding domains are shown contacting the hormone response element (HRE). The receptor at the right is shown bound to its ligand. In addition to binding ligand, the ligand-binding domain contains subdomains for transcriptional activation and dimerization.

known as chromatin. DNA that is in a more compact chromatin structure is less transcriptionally active. Indeed, one way in which nuclear receptors activate transcription is to modulate chromatin structure. Thus, in the absence of ligand, some receptors (such as the thyroid hormone and retinoic acid receptors) associate with a corepressor complex. This association is facilitated by a groove on the surface of the receptor that binds to coregulator proteins. Formation of receptor-corepressor complexes is critical as the corepressor complex contains an enzymatic activity that removes acetyl groups from histones (**Fig. 2**, top). Since hypoacetylated chromatin is transcriptionally repressed, the recruitment of corepressors allows the receptor to specifically deacetylate the surrounding chromatin, thereby repressing transcription of its target genes.

Ligand binding to the receptor results in the reorientation of the activation domain so that it now sits in the coregulator groove. This displaces the corepressor from the receptor and results in a loss of transcriptional repression (Fig. 2, middle). Genes that

are in this state are neither repressed nor activated; that is, they are actively transcribing mRNA at low or basal levels. This basal rate of transcription is determined by RNA polymerase II, which functions as part of a complex of proteins that bind the TATA sequence within the promoters of these genes. Thus, one role of ligand is to relieve repression, thereby raising activity to basal levels. Note that many nuclear receptors are unable to recruit corepressors; genes regulated by these receptors are already in the basal state in the absence of ligand (Fig. 2, middle).

Remarkably, in addition to relieving repression, the hormonal ligands activate transcription above and beyond the basal state; the same ligand-induced conformation change that displaces corepressor also allows the receptor to associate with coactivator complexes (Fig. 2, bottom). One class of coactivator complex functions in a manner opposite to that of corepressors; specifically, it acetylates (Ac) histones leading to a more transcriptionally active chromatin structure. A second type of coactivator complex directly links the receptor to the RNA polymerase II

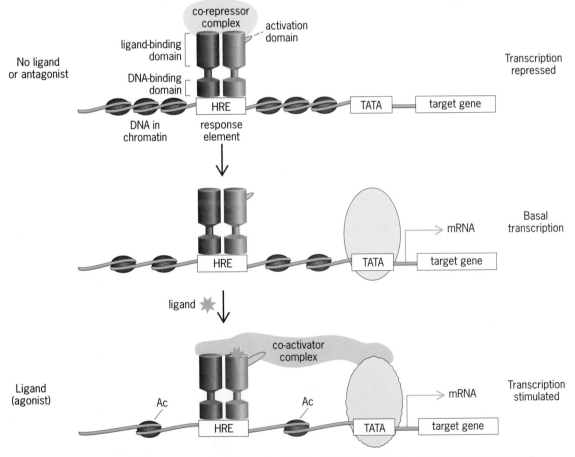

Fig. 2. Schematic illustration of the mechanism of transcriptional regulation by nuclear receptors. Nuclear receptor dimer binds to its HRE in the absence of ligand [or in the presence of an antagonist] (top). Receptors in this state interact with corepressor complexes that deacetylate histones. Hence, chromatin is compact and transcription is repressed. In the presence of ligand, corepressor is released and transcription can proceed at low or basal levels (middle). Note that many receptors do not recruit corepressors; hence in the absence of ligand their target genes are transcribed at basal levels (middle). When ligand is present, coactivators are recruited to the complex (bottom); chromatin is then acetylated (Ac), becomes less compact, and the rate of transcription is stimulated (bottom). In the case of the estrogen receptor, target genes are in the basal state in the absence of ligand. Estrogen agonists promote coactivator recruitment and transcriptional activation (bottom), whereas antagonists promote corepressor association and transcriptional repression (top).

complex. Taken together, the recruitment of these protein assemblies allows nuclear receptor ligands to simultaneously modify chromatin and increase RNA polymerase II–dependent transcription.

Estrogen, breast cancer, and osteoporosis. The estrogen receptor provides an interesting example of how receptors can be exploited to develop selective drug therapies.

Following menopause, estrogen production declines, causing changes in gene transcription that increases the risk of developing osteoporosis (bone loss), atherosclerosis, and hot flashes. These adverse effects can be delayed by the administration of ligands that activate the estrogen receptor (agonists). However, estrogens also promote the proliferation of breast cancer cells. Thus, for patients at risk for breast cancer, it may be more important to inhibit estrogen action. Indeed, synthetic drugs have been identified which bind to estrogen receptors but fail to activate the receptor. These drugs are known as antagonists because they function in a manner opposite to that of the natural hormone; they lead to the displacement of coactivators and the recruitment of corepressors. Thus, estrogen receptor antagonists are currently used for both the treatment and prevention of breast cancers.

If a given estrogen receptor ligand either activates or antagonizes the receptor, the physician must carefully evaluate whether an individual patient is more likely to benefit from estrogen receptor agonists or antagonists. However, the ligand does not modulate receptor activity by itself; transcriptional activity is determined by the type of coregulator protein that associates with the ligand-bound receptor (Fig. 2). An important advance in understanding nuclear receptors has been the realization that these receptors interact with a variety of coactivators and corepressor proteins. Thus, an ideal drug for the estrogen receptor may be one that recruits a coactivator in bone cells and a corepressor in breast cancer cells. Several drugs have been identified (tamoxifen, raloxifene) which can inhibit estrogen action in breast cancer while promoting its positive effects on osteoporosis.

Another level of flexibility in the estrogen response has emerged with the identification of a second receptor. Estrogen receptor β binds to similar DNA sequences as estrogen receptor α, but it is found in different tissues and can bind different synthetic ligands. Preliminary results suggest that the positive cardiovascular effects of estrogens result from activation of estrogen receptor β, not estrogen receptor α. In the future, it is likely that highly selective drugs will be identified based on their ability to recruit tissue-specific coregulators or interact with either estrogen receptor α or β.

Obesity and diabetes. A major health problem in industrialized societies, obesity is associated with an increased risk for the development of diabetes, heart disease, stroke, and other disorders. The identification of the orphan receptor peroxisome proliferator activated receptor gamma (PPARγ) as a factor

required for fat cell formation led to the exciting suggestion that a yet-to-be discovered ligand may control this process. Indeed, a fatty-acid derivative known as 15-deoxy-$\Delta^{12,14}$-prostaglandin J_2 promotes fat cell formation by binding to and activating PPARγ. These findings raise the possibility that synthetic PPARγ antagonists might potentially to be developed as antiobesity agents.

Non-insulin-dependent diabetes mellitus is a major clinical problem associated with disorders of lipid metabolism. The underlying problem is the inability of patients to metabolize glucose in response to insulin. Several decades of research by the pharmaceutical industry led to the identification of thiazolidinedione drugs that effectively reverse this underlying problem. Thus, much interest was generated by the discovery that thiazolidinediones function as PPARγ agonists, as this finding allows future antidiabetic drugs to be identified by rapid automated assays that directly search for PPARγ ligands. In just 5 years, several promising drug candidates have been identified that are 50-fold more potent than existing antidiabetic drugs.

Orphan receptors. Other orphan receptors have been identified that may play critical roles in cholesterol homeostasis, Parkinson's disease, vision, and other processes. However, the biological function of many other orphan receptors remains to be elucidated. Thus, these proteins will continue to provide tools for the identification of novel transcriptional regulatory pathways and important drug therapies.

For background information *see* CELL NUCLEUS; DIABETES; DEOXYRIBONUCLEIC ACID; ESTROGEN; GENE; NUCLEIC ACID; NUCLEOPROTEIN; NUCLEOSOME in the McGraw-Hill Encyclopedia of Science & Technology.

Barry Marc Forman

Bibliography. L. P. Freedman, *Molecular Biology of Steroid and Nuclear Hormone Receptors*, Birkhauser Press, 1997; C. K. Glass and M. G. Rosenfeld, The coregulator exchange in transcriptional functions of nuclear receptors, *Genes Dev.*, 14(2):121–141, 2000; R. Kumar and E. B. Thompson, The structure of the nuclear hormone receptors, *Steroids*, 64(5):310–319, 1999; R. Sladek and V. Giguere, Orphan nuclear receptors: An emerging family of metabolic regulators, *Adv. Pharmacol.*, 47:23–87, 2000; C. L. Smith and B. W. O'Malley, Evolving concepts of selective estrogen receptor action: From basic science to clinical applications, *Trends Endocrinol. Metab.*, 10(8):299–300, 1999; T. M. Wilson et al., The PPARs: From orphan receptors to drug discovery, *J. Med. Chem.*, 43(4):527–550, 2000.

Nuclear reactor

Nearly all commercial nuclear reactors now in operation are based on a conventional design in which ordinary light water is the coolant. However, in recent years there has been increasing interest in alternative designs, including the modular high-temperature gas-cooled reactor and the lead-cooled reactor.

Modular High-Temperature Gas-Cooled Reactors

High-temperature gas-cooled reactors offer the potential of increasing the efficiency of conventional light-water reactors that use the steam cycle from 33% to close to 50%. They also provide high temperatures that can be used for process heat applications such as the generation of hydrogen for transportation and the desalinization of water.

Early development. High-temperature gas reactors have been used in the past with early prototype plants such as the 115 megawatt-thermal (MWth) plant at Peach Bottom, PA, that successfully operated from 1966 to 1974. A larger 849-MWth [330 megawatt-electric (MWe)] commercial plant at Fort St. Vrain, CO, was operated from 1973 to 1989. This plant experienced numerous technical difficulties with fundamental engineering issues not associated with the nuclear technology and was eventually shut down and decommissioned. General Atomics Corporation, the developer of the gas reactor technology in the United States, tried to deploy large high-temperature gas reactors, but utility support was lacking due to the early technical difficulties of the Fort St. Vrain plant.

In Europe, the nation with the most advanced high-temperature gas reactor program was Germany, which has been a leader in the development of fuel technology and reactor designs. The German AVR research gas reactor was a 40-MWth pebble bed plant that was capable of producing 15 MWe using the steam cycle. The AVR operated for over 22 years as a research facility before it was shut down in 1988. This facility and the Jülich Research Center developed the fundamental technology to design and build a 300-MWe pebble bed plant. The THTR plant used thorium pebble fuel and operated for 5 years until shutdown due to design difficulties with control rods penetrating the pebble bed and interior insulation of the helium ducts. Due to these difficulties and the political desire to move away from nuclear energy, the plant was shut down in 1990.

Rebirth. Despite these setbacks, there appears to be a rebirth of the gas reactor technology as several nations are developing this technology in smaller versions. In November 1998, Japan started operation of the High Temperature Engineering Test Reactor (HTTR), a 30-MWth research reactor. China is in the final stages of construction of a 10-MWth research reactor near Beijing. South Africa is in the licensing process to build and operate a commercial 115-MWe pebble bed reactor for use by their state-owned utility, ESKOM.

The rebirth is centered largely on the inherent or passive safety of high-temperature gas reactor technology and a belief that these plants can be competitive with combined-cycle natural gas plants. The high-temperature gas reactor permits higher thermal efficiencies and potentially can be operated with higher capacity factors, especially at plants that have

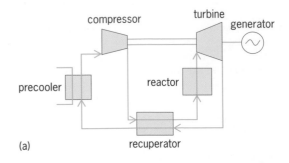

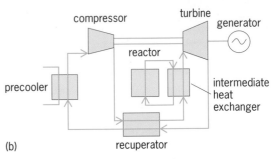

Fig. 1. Brayton helium-cycle plant options for high-temperature gas-cooled reactor. (*a*) Direct cycle. (*b*) Indirect cycle.

on-line refueling. In addition, these plants provide advantages in addressing concerns about nuclear proliferation since the fuel can be used at higher levels of fissile-material consumption, and since different fuel types such as thorium can be used that greatly reduce the risk of nuclear weapons materials diversion. These plants can also be used to consume excess plutonium from the nuclear weapons program. General Atomics, in a cooperative effort with Russian research institutes and the United States government, is designing a high-temperature gas reactor that uses plutonium as the fuel to rid Russia of its supply of excess plutonium, since the gas reactor is an efficient means of eliminating plutonium while producing electric power. Thus, there exists a development strategy aimed at taking advantage of the lessons learned from past operation and the technological developments in materials and component design.

Direct and indirect cycles. High-temperature gas reactors use helium as the working fluid in a Brayton cycle, which allows for higher cycle efficiencies (**Fig. 1**). The two chief options are the direct cycle, in which the helium gas coming from the reactor is sent directly into the turbine to drive a generator, and the indirect cycle, in which the reactor-side helium transfers its heat through an intermediate heat exchanger to either another helium loop or water or air to then drive the turbine-generator component of the plant system. The general design criteria (see **table**) call for inlet temperatures of approximately 500°C (930°F) with outlet temperatures in the range of 850–950°C (1560–1740°F). Pressures in the primary reactor circuit are about 7 megapascals (1000 lb/in.²).

Fuel. The reactor core contains fuel in microsphere form (**Fig. 2***a*). The fuel for gas reactors is

Typical high-temperature gas reactor operating conditions	
Parameter	Value
Core power	250–600 MWth
Core inlet temperature	475–510°C (890–950°F)
Core outlet temperature	850–950°C (1560–1740°F)
Helium flow rate in core	240 kg/s (530 lb/s)
Helium gas pressure in core	7.07 MPa (1025 lb/in.^{2})
Turbine inlet temperature	950–775°C (1740–1430°F)
Turbine outlet temperature	600–442°C (1110–828°F)
Thermal efficiency*	47–50%
Net electrical efficiency	44–47%
Capacity factors	84–92%

*For direct or indirect helium balance of plant.

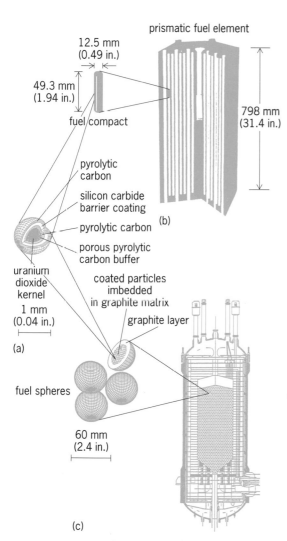

Fig. 2. Microsphere fuel for two reactor types. (a) Microsphere. (b) Prismatic fuel. (c) Pebble bed fuel.

moderately enriched in uranium-235 (8–20%) and is operated at low volumetric heat rates of 3.5–7 MW/m^3. Other fuel types can be used such as thorium or plutonium. The microsphere is 0.9 mm (0.035 in.) in diameter and is contained in a extremely hard silicon carbide shell that is designed to contain all fission products and is able to withstand the high

temperatures of operation and any conceivable accident condition. These microsphere containments in a graphite matrix, combined with the low power density of the core, provide high thermal capacity, thus avoiding fuel meltdown situations in case of accidents.

These microspheres constitute the basic safety feature of the plant. In the event of a major loss-of-cooling accident with no emergency cooling and no operator action, no fuel failure is expected to occur with a 500°C (900°F) margin of error, and clearly no fuel melting. This natural safety feature of the design is an important advantage for this technology since the cost of constructing expensive emergency core cooling systems can be avoided and the public's demand for melt-free designs can be met.

Prismatic and pebble bed designs. There are two variants on the gas reactor core design. In the prismatic reactor, the fuel microspheres are compacted into chalk-size sticks about 50 mm (2 in.) long in a graphite matrix (Fig. 2b). The other design uses pebble bed fuel, in which the same microspheres in a graphite matrix are shaped into a sphere about the size of a tennis or billiard ball (Fig. 2c).

The prismatic reactor allows for larger plant size, which is believed by some to be required, due to considerations of economies of scale, to make the plants competitive. The General Atomics–Russian design (**Fig. 3**) has a maximum thermal rating of 600 MWth with a 45% thermal efficiency. This maximum rating is established to maintain many of the inherent safety features and uses a direct helium cycle. The power plant consists of two large vessels, one housing the reactor and the second the entire balance of plant. The relatively large physical size of this reactor makes it less modular, although parts could be factory-assembled.

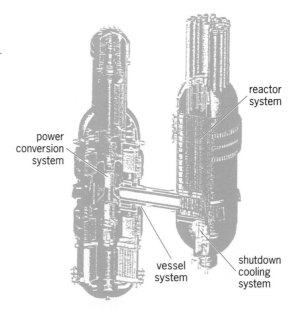

Fig. 3. General Atomics–Russian modular high-temperature gas-cooled reactor with prismatic core design.

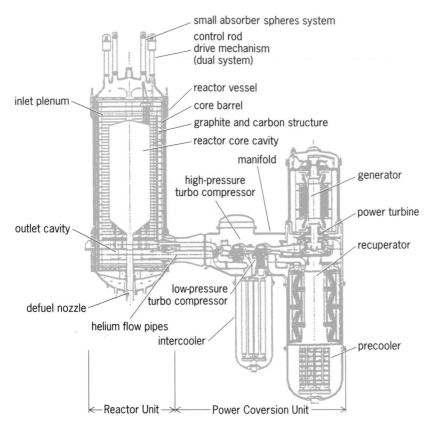

inlet plenum

small absorber spheres system

control rod
drive mechanism
(dual system)

reactor vessel

core barrel

graphite and carbon structure

reactor core cavity

manifold

high-pressure
turbo compressor

generator

power turbine

outlet cavity

recuperator

defuel nozzle

low-pressure
turbo compressor

helium flow pipes

intercooler

precooler

|← Reactor Unit →|← Power Coversion Unit →|

Fig. 4. ESKOM pebble-bed 250-MWth reactor.

The pebble bed reactors are smaller in size and hence modular. Their maximum power rating is 250 MWth (115 MWe). The ESKOM plant design (**Fig. 4**) also uses a direct cycle. It also has two major vessels with a connecting vessel housing compressors to improve accessibility for maintenance. This plant circulates the pebbles in a continuous closed system to allow for on-line refueling, with fresh pebbles being inserted and used pebbles being discharged and placed in interim storage at the plant for the life of the facility. This plant, since it is small and modular, can be built in about 2 years, with additional modules added to meet demand. This feature, which allows for factory manufacture, modules, and site assembly, takes advantage of economies of production rather than economies of scale to be cost-effective. If preliminary estimates are realized, this plant would be cheaper than a combined-cycle natural gas plant.

Massachusetts Institute of Technology's Nuclear Engineering Department students are working on a pebble bed plant that utilizes the indirect cycle with an intermediate heat exchanger to allow for easier plant maintenance and for process heat applications using exhaust heat. Studies indicate that the gas reactor cycle has superior proliferation resistance properties and that the waste from the reactor can be directly disposed in a geological repository without any special overpacks since the graphite (coal) pebbles are good waste forms.

In early 2000 the Japanese HTTR 30 was the only high-temperature gas-cooled reactor in operation.

This prismatic reactor will be used to research fuels and components for larger commercial reactors of the prismatic type. China's pebble bed research reactor is expected to go "critical" at the end of the year 2000. Both plants use an intermediate heat exchanger in which the helium in the primary system transfers its heat either to a separate helium system for process heat applications or to a steam cycle plant to make electricity.   Andrew C. Kadak

Lead-Cooled Reactors

Lead-cooled nuclear reactors use molten lead as the coolant of their fuel. The function of the coolant is to transport the energy released in the fission process away from the nuclear fuel rods in the reactor core. This energy is eventually used to make steam that drives a turbine generator that makes electricity. The other function of the coolant is to keep the fuel rods and their clad—the structural material that encapsulates the nuclear fuel—from overheating, which could result in the melting of the nuclear fuel and the release of fission products. Interest in lead-cooled reactors has increased in recent years due to the expectation that they might be simpler, safer, and more economically attractive than other types of nuclear power reactors.

Need for liquid-metal-cooled reactors. Interest in liquid-metal coolants for nuclear reactors dates back to the late 1940s. It stemmed from the desire to increase fuel utilization, or the amount of energy produced from a given initial quantity of mined fuel. The amount of economically recoverable uranium-235—the only fissile isotope found in nature—is limited. Fortunately, some isotopes, referred to as fertile isotopes, can be converted into fissile isotopes in a nuclear reactor. For example, uranium-238 can be converted into the isotope plutonium-239, which is fissile. The natural abundance of the fertile isotopes uranium-238 and thorium-232 is several hundred times larger than the abundance of uranium-235. If a reactor can be designed to breed, that is, to convert at least one fertile nucleus into a fissile nucleus per fissile nucleus it consumes, the available nuclear fuel resource base will be significantly increased. It is for this reason that designing reactors to breed was a long-term goal of the nuclear industry. Breeding could extend the useful life of nuclear fission energy to a range approaching renewable energy resources.

In order to make a reactor breed, it must be designed to have a good neutron economy. Neutron economy can be measured by the ratio of the number of fission neutrons released per neutron absorbed in the fuel. This ratio, denoted η, is higher for highly energetic or fast-moving neutrons than it is for low-energy (thermal) or slow-moving neutrons. Thus, reactors with fast neutrons, or simply fast reactors, can be designed to be good breeders. Thermal reactors, such as water-cooled reactors, have a poorer neutron economy; it is difficult to design them to breed. Commercial water-cooled reactors (nearly all of the presently operating commercial reactors) are far from breeding; they produce approximately one fissile nucleus per two fissile nuclei they consume, hence they have a low fuel utilization.

Most neutrons are highly energetic at the time of their release in the fission reaction. When a neutron collides with a nucleus of the coolant, part of the neutron kinetic energy is transferred to that nucleus, causing the neutron to slow down. The heavier the coolant nuclei, the less effective they are in slowing down the fission neutrons. For example, whereas a neutron colliding with a hydrogen nucleus (mass $\cong$ 1 atomic mass unit) loses, on the average, 50% of its kinetic energy, it loses an average of 8% in a collision with a sodium nucleus (mass $\cong$ 23 amu), or less than 1% upon collision with a lead nucleus (mass $\cong$ 207 amu). Consequently, whereas the average speed of the neutrons in water-cooled reactors is approximately four orders of magnitude lower than the average speed of the fission-borne neutrons, in sodium-cooled reactors this ratio is only about one order of magnitude. This higher average speed is referred to as a hard neutron spectrum, and is the defining characteristic of a fast reactor. Liquid-metal coolants enable designers to create a reactor with a harder spectrum, higher η, higher breeding capability, and thus greater fuel utilization.

Sodium-cooled reactors. After a few years of experimenting with different types of liquid metals, sodium was selected as a potential coolant for both the naval and civilian programs in the United States. Sodium was the liquid metal of choice due to its relatively low melting temperature (98°C or 208°F), good heat transfer properties, compatibility with steels (not being corrosive), and low cost. The first experimental liquid metal reactor, EBR-I, started operation in Idaho in 1951. It used a sodium-potassium alloy for the coolant. The *USS Seawolf*, the world's second nuclear-powered submarine, launched in 1955, used a sodium-cooled reactor. Several experimental and demonstration reactors cooled with sodium have been constructed and operated in the United States and other countries, including the former Soviet Union, England, France, and Japan. A sodium-cooled reactor is being constructed in the People's Republic of China.

Unfortunately, sodium is very chemically reactive with air and water. Consequently, special engineering measures must be taken in the design of sodium-cooled reactors to minimize the probability of sodium leaks and sodium fires. These measures increase the construction and operating costs of sodium-cooled reactors and hence increase the cost of the electrical energy they generate. As a result of these safety and economic considerations, the interest in sodium-cooled reactors has recently declined.

Lead reactor coolant. Lead and its alloys (such as lead-bismuth) are preferable to sodium in a number of ways: (1) They are chemically inert with air and water; (2) they offer a harder neutron spectrum and a better neutron economy; and (3) they have a significantly higher boiling temperature and can absorb approximately four times more heat before they start boiling. On the negative side, lead and its alloys are denser than sodium, require more pumping power, are less efficient in removing heat from the fuel, are biologically toxic, produce the radiotoxic isotope polonium-210, and are more expensive. None of these drawbacks, however, makes lead an unacceptable or unattractive reactor coolant. For example, a simple technology to safely cope with polonium-210 was developed in Russia. The main reason for preferring sodium over lead in the early days of reactor development was the compatibility with structural materials; lead and its alloys were found to be significantly more corrosive with the steels available at that time.

Russian Alpha submarine technology. In the early 1990s, following the end of the cold war, Russia revealed that it had successfully developed nuclear reactors for submarines that used a lead-bismuth alloy as the coolant. These lead-bismuth cooled reactors powered their Alpha-type submarines, which hold the world underwater speed record. The Russians constructed ten lead-bismuth cooled reactors and accumulated 80 reactor-years of operating experience.

Russia secretly invested 25 years of research and development to overcome the corrosion tendency of lead-bismuth coolant. The Russians developed new corrosion-resistant steels, characterized by relatively low nickel and high chromium content. They also found that by maintaining the lead-bismuth in a slightly oxidized state, it is possible to inhibit the corrosion process, and they developed the technology for doing so. A similar technology is expected to make lead an acceptable coolant. The main advantages of lead over lead-bismuth are lower cost, greater abundance, and lower production of polonium-210. Its primary disadvantage is a higher melting temperature (327°C or 621°F for lead versus 125°C or 257°F for lead-bismuth eutectic, which has 44.5 weight % lead).

Current status. In recent years Russian scientists and engineers have developed conceptual designs for a number of lead- and lead-bismuth-cooled reactors for commercial power plants, including the following:

(1) TES-M. This is a transportable 1-MWe nuclear power plant. It would be transported completely assembled from the factory to a remote site and supply power for 10–15 years without any refueling. The total weight of this power plant is 50 metric tons (55 short tons).

(2) ANGSTREM. This is a modular nuclear power plant designed to supply 6 MWe plus heat in order to provide for the power needs of a community of up to 5000 inhabitants. With a total weight of 220 metric tons (242 short tons), it can be transported to site on up to 12 railway platforms or transport vehicles and assembled on site within one month. It is designed to operate 6 years without refueling.

(3) CRUISE-50. This is a 50-MWe power plant to be factory-constructed on a floating barge and

transported to a coastal site. There, it is to be anchored and is to supply electricity for 6 years. After that time, it would be replaced by another barge-mounted CRUISE-50 plant and transported back to the factory for refueling.

(4) LBFR-75. This is a reactor module designed to repower old VVER-440 power plants in which the reactor has reached its end of life. These plants use a pressurized water reactor that supplies the heat to six steam generators. The Russians are proposing to dismantle the old steam generators and replace each one of them with an LBFR-75 module. Each module is to supply the same flow rate of steam of the same pressure and temperature as the original steam generator. This repowering is estimated to be significantly more economical than constructing a new pressurized-water reactor plant.

(5) LBFR-600. This is a preliminary design of a lead-bismuth-cooled reactor that is to be initially fueled with enriched uranium but refueled with natural uranium. The natural uranium utilization in such a reactor is expected to be an order of magnitude higher than in water-cooled reactors. The fuel is not to be recycled; that is, this reactor is to operate on the "once-through" fuel cycle.

(6) BRUS-300. Whereas all previous designs are to use lead-bismuth coolant, the BRUS reactors are to use lead coolant. The Russian government recently approved the construction of a 300-MWe demonstration reactor.

(7) BRUS-1200. This is a design for a large 1200-MWe central power plant as a scale-up of the BRUS-300 technology.

Research and development of lead and lead-bismuth reactor technology has recently started in a number of countries in addition to Russia. These include Italy, Switzerland, Spain, France, Germany, Japan, and the United States, where there is research activity at a number of universities and national laboratories, and in industry. Two novel United States design concepts are the core cartridge design and the encapsulated nuclear heat source (ENHS). Both are for a small reactor module that is intrinsically safe, proliferation-resistant, and easy to operate, and can run for at least 15 years without refueling.

Expected characteristics. Relative to water-cooled reactors, the backbone of the contemporary nuclear industry, lead-cooled and lead-bismuth-cooled reactors are expected to have the following advantages: (1) more reliance on physical phenomena than on engineered systems to assure a high level of safety, (2) a higher thermodynamic efficiency (more than 40% for lead-bismuth cooled reactors versus 33% for water-cooled reactors), (3) a higher uranium ore utilization (by up to a factor of 50), (4) a possible reduction in the cost of electric power, and (5) reduced volume of and long-term risks from the nuclear waste. Relative to sodium-cooled reactors, lead-cooled and lead-bismuth-cooled reactors are expected to be simpler, safer, and more economical.

For background information *see* BRAYTON CYCLE; NUCLEAR FUELS; NUCLEAR POWER; NUCLEAR REACTOR;

RADIOACTIVE WASTE MANAGEMENT in the McGraw-Hill Encyclopedia of Science & Technology.

Ehud Greenspan

Bibliography. ESKOM, *Pebble Bed Modular Reactor*, Executive Description, PB-000-79/1, Issue E, ESKOM, Johannesburg, South Africa; *Evaluation of the Gas Turbine Modular Helium Reactor*, Gas Reactor Associates, DOE-HTGR-90380, December 1993; E. Greenspan et al., The Encapsulated Nuclear Reactor Heat Source Concept, Pap. 8150, *Proceedings of the 8th International Conference on Nuclear Engineering* (ICONE-8), Baltimore, April 2–6, 2000; B. F. Gromov et al., Use of lead-bismuth coolant in nuclear reactors and accelerator-driven systems, *Nucl. Eng. Design*, 173:207–217, 1997; R. N. Hill et al., Development of small, fast reactor core designs using lead-based coolant, Pap. 339 in *Proceedings of Global '99: International Conference on Future Nuclear Systems*, Jackson Hole, WY, August 29–September 3, 1999.

Nuclear receptor

The regulation of lipid metabolism and glucose utilization is critical for the maintenance of cellular energy homeostasis. Cells have developed several means to respond to internal and external stimuli that would signify an imbalance in metabolic processes and energy utilization. These means include rapid responses such as phosphorylation events as well as latent effects on gene transcription. Ultimately, the result of altered gene expression is the synthesis of new signaling molecules and enzymes that are able to meet the physiological needs of the cell and the organism. Thus, important components of the cell must be a sensor of fatty acids and their metabolites, and an effector of nuclear transcriptional regulation. These roles may be fulfilled by one type of protein.

Peroxisome proliferator–activated receptors. Peroxisome proliferator–activated receptors (PPARs) are members of the nuclear hormone receptor superfamily of transcription factors, similar in both structure and function to the steroid, thyroid, and retinoid receptors. Peroxisome proliferator–activated receptors respond to specific ligands by altering gene expression in a cell-, developmental-, or sex-specific manner. Peroxisome proliferator–activated receptors were initially characterized as being activated by peroxisome proliferators, a large group of hypolipidemic (producing a decrease in the level of lipids in the blood) agents and pollutants. Subsequently, it was shown that PPARs respond to endogenous fatty acids and control a variety of target genes involved in lipid homeostasis. Further, PPARs were shown to play a key role in the response to antidiabetic drugs. The multifaceted responses of PPARs are actually carried out by three subtypes expressed in different tissues. Currently, the subfamily has been defined as PPARα, PPARβ (also called PPARδ and NUC1), and PPARγ, each with a possibility of different ligands,

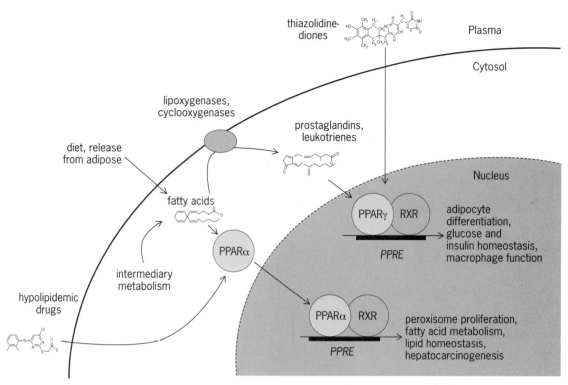

Basic mechanism of action of PPARα and PPAR-γ and effects on gene expression. Similar to other nuclear hormone receptors, PPAR acts as a ligand-activated transcription factor. Upon binding fatty acids or hypolipidemic drugs, PPARα and PPAR-γ both interact with RXR; this interaction regulates the expression of target genes. These genes are involved in the catabolism of fatty acids. Conversely, PPAR-γ is activated by prostaglandins, leukotrienes, and antidiabetic thiazolidinediones and affects the expression of genes involved in the storage of fatty acids.

target genes, and biological role (see **illus.**).

Ligands. Many peroxisome proliferators and fatty acids are PPAR activators. The xenobiotic peroxisome proliferators, such as the fibrate hypolipidemic drugs, are structurally similar to endogenous and dietary fatty acids and their metabolites, containing a carboxylic acid functional group and a hydrophobic tail. The term "activator" denotes a chemical with the ability to convert PPARs into a transcriptionally active complex, most often examined using transfection and reporter assays (incorporating DNA or a specific gene to be analyzed into a host genome). Until recently, there has been some debate as to whether peroxisome proliferators and fatty acids activate PPARs through a direct, physical interaction. However, most receptor activators have been demonstrated to bind to PPAR subtypes with reasonable affinity. For example, certain mono- and polyunsaturated fatty acids bind directly to PPARα and PPAR-γ at physiological concentrations. The eicosanoid 8(S)-hydroxyeicosatetraenoic acid is a PPARα ligand, while 15-deoxy-δ12,14-prostaglandin J2 (PGJ2) specifically associates with PPAR-γ. The chemotactic (referring to chemical stimuli that influences cellular migration) agent leukotriene B4 and the hypolipidemic drug Wy 14,643 are reasonably specific for the PPARα subtype. A great deal of interest in PPARs has been initiated by the discovery of highly specific PPAR-γ ligands among the class of antidiabetic agents termed thiazolidinediones (TZDs). Many thiazolidinediones, (including ciglitazone, pi-oglitazone, and BRL49653) are highly specific and potent activators of PPAR-γ.

Target genes. Similar to other steroid hormone receptors, PPARs are ligand-activated transcription factors that control gene expression by interacting with specific deoxyribonucleic acid (DNA) response elements (PPREs) located upstream of responsive genes. The peroxisome proliferator response element site is virtually identical for the three PPAR subtypes; this signifies that much of the differences in function of the PPARs are derived from tissue-specific expression as well as subtype-specific activators. The molecular sequence (motif) recognized by PPAR, contains two copies of a core consensus sequence (AGGTCA) with a one nucleotide spacer, termed a DR-1 site. A second nuclear receptor, retinoid-X-receptor (RXR), is required for PPARs to bind to DNA and regulate gene expression. There are several genes that contain this peroxisome proliferator response element motif, and they are often referred to as target genes (see **table**).

The ultimate response of a cell to PPAR activators is the sum total of the genes regulated in that cell. Both PPARα and PPAR-γ play key roles in regulating fatty acid metabolism, although in seemingly opposite directions (see table). The result of PPARα activation in hepatocytes and certain other tissues is an increase in the peroxisomal and mitochondrial oxidation of fatty acids. The array of genes regulated by PPAR-γ in adipocytes is indicative of fatty acid accumulation. This regulation of gene expression is concomitant with increased differentiation of

Summary of genes regulated by PPARα and PPARγ

PPARα-regulated genes in liver	Function	PPARγ-regulated genes in adipose	Function
Acyl-CoA oxidase	Fatty acid oxidation	aP2	Fatty acid uptake
Cytochrome P450 4A	Fatty acid oxidation	Lipoprotein lipase	Fatty acid uptake
Enoyl-CoA hydratase	Fatty acid oxidation	Fatty acid transporter protein	Fatty acid uptake
Peroxisomal thiolase	Fatty acid oxidation	Acyl-CoA synthetase	Fatty acid esterification
Acyl-CoA binding protein	Fatty acid transport	Phosphoenolpyruvate carboxy kinase	Glyceroneogenesis
Carnitine acyltransferase	Fatty acid transport	Malic enzyme	Lipogenesis
Fatty acid binding protein	Fatty acid transport		
Acyl-CoA synthetase	Fatty acid esterification		
Lipoprotein lipase	Fatty acid uptake		
Apolipoprotein AI	Lipid export		
c-myc	Growth regulation		
ZFP-37	Growth regulation		

immature adipocytes into mature fat-storing cells. The key genes regulated by PPARγ that are associated with diabetes have not been conclusively demonstrated, but may involve adipocyte-secreted cytokines and hormones such as tumor necrosis factor alpha (TNFα) and leptin.

The genes regulated by PPARγ in adipocytes are similar to those in the macrophage and include lipoprotein lipase and CD36. Treatment of macrophages with PPARγ synthetic agonists inhibits the production of several cytokines such as interleukin 1-β and TNFα, and may result in an anti-inflammatory response. Another link between PPARγ and inflammation is the fact that 15-deoxy PGJ2, a product of the cyclooxygenase pathway, and nonsteroidal anti-inflammatory drugs (NSAIDS) are activators of PPARγ.

Function. The potency of various chemicals to activate PPARs is subtype-specific. The expression of PPARα, β, and γ varies widely from tissue to tissue. In numerous cell types from ectodermal, mesodermal, or endodermal origin, PPARs are coexpressed, although their concentration relative to each other varies widely. Peroxisome proliferator–activated receptor α is highly expressed in hepatocytes (liver cells), cardiomyocytes (heart cells), enterocytes (intestinal cells), and the proximal tubule cells of kidney. Peroxisome proliferator–activated receptor β is expressed ubiquitously and often at higher levels than PPARα and γ. Peroxisome proliferator-activated receptor γ is expressed predominantly in adipose tissue, colon epithelium, and macrophages and exists as two distinct forms, γ1 and γ2, which arise by differential transcription start sites and alternative splicing. The distinct tissue distribution suggests that the PPAR subtypes play different biological roles. In fact, it is widely believed that of the different subtypes, PPARα predominates in hepatic lipid metabolism and PPARγ plays a pivotal role in adipogenesis and immune responses. There is also evidence to support the role of PPARs in cell growth and differentiation.

Peroxisome proliferator–activated receptors, in particular PPARγ, have been clearly established to be involved in differentiation of several cell types. The wide variety of cells that can be induced to differentiate with peroxisome proliferators, fatty acids, thiazolidinediones, and other PPAR ligands suggest that this subfamily of proteins are master regulators of differentiation. This classification is reserved for genes that specify the fate of a particular cell, such as transcription factors capable of activating the program of differentiation. Peroxisome proliferator-activated receptors have been shown to induce differentiation of adipocytes, oligodendrocytes, myoblasts, keratinocytes, and monocytes (macrophages). Ectopic expression of PPARγ in fibroblasts regulated development of the adipose lineage in response to endogenous lipid activators. That is, expression and activation of PPARγ is sufficient to result in a phenotypic change in fibroblasts. Also, ligand activation of PPARγ is sufficient to induce growth arrest in fibroblasts, a key step in committing a cell to differentiate.

In contrast to PPARγ, PPARα may play a larger role in cellular proliferation than in differentiation. Activators of PPARα have long been known to be rodent liver tumor promoters, and it is generally held that altered gene expression is the key. Support for this theory includes the induction of growth regulatory genes (such as c-myc; c-Ha-ras, fos, jun, and egr-1; and ZFP-37) by peroxisome proliferators. The most convincing data regarding a PPAR–cell proliferation-tumor promotion connection comes from the PPARα-null mouse model system. Remarkably, the mice that lack PPARα do not display the typical pleiotropic response when challenged with the peroxisome proliferators, such as hepatomegaly, peroxisome proliferation, and transcriptional activation of target genes. These mice display abnormal lipid homeostasis, including fatty acid metabolism. Importantly, in PPARα null mice fed a peroxisome proliferator in the diet, no increase in hepatic cell proliferation or hepatocellular neoplasms was noted whereas all of the wildtype mice developed tumors.

The biological role of PPARβ has not been clearly established. Although it is expressed in many cell types, there has been no report of a specific, high-affinity activator to examine its role relative to PPARα and PPARγ. Recent work performed with a PPARβ-null mouse model system may shed some light on the function of this protein.

For background information *see* GENE; LIPID; LIPID METABOLISM; NUCLEIC ACID in the McGraw-Hill Encyclopedia of Science & Technology.

John P. Vanden Heuvel

Bibliography. H. Keller et al., Peroxisome proliferator-activated receptors and lipid metabolism, *Ann. N. Y. Acad. Sci.*, 684:157–173, 1993; T. Lemberger, B. Desvergne, and W. Wahli, Peroxisome proliferator–activated receptors: A nuclear receptor signaling pathway in lipid physiology, *Ann. Rev. Cell. Dev. Biol.*, 12:335–363, 1996; L. Gelman, J. C. Fruchart, and J. Auwerx, An update on the mechanisms of action of the peroxisome proliferator-activated receptors (PPARs) and their roles in inflammation and cancer, *Cell Mol. Life Sci.*, 55:932–943, 1999; J. P. Vanden Heuvel, Peroxisome proliferator-activated receptors: A critical link among fatty acids, gene expression and carcinogenesis, *J. Nutrit.*, 129: 575S–580S, 1999.

Ocean physical-biological models

For more than a century, physical oceanographers—those who study the physics of the ocean—have been expanding their ability to interpret oceanic observations. The first crucial step is the application of dynamical equations, the fundamental equations of fluid mechanics. The task of developing dynamical models, written out as equations, is not yet complete. There remain unresolved issues such as turbulence, mixing, and friction, and the appropriate way in which to represent them. Nonetheless, the fundamental equations are well accepted and, in many different case studies, well understood. With especially rapid progress in recent years, oceanographers have developed computer models of ocean currents, just as meteorologists have developed numerical models of winds in the atmosphere.

Beginning with somewhat simplified models applied to small segments of the sea and building on experience, oceanographers have learned how to put the ocean into these models. Researchers focused on fundamental problems of ocean dynamics, including the representation of wind forcing, mixing, and bottom friction; the influence of stratification and bottom topography; and the application of boundary conditions. This work advanced rapidly in the 1980s with the advance in computers, and today there is substantial confidence in a variety of types of models to the point where operational oceanography is being practiced at several different locations. Data assimilation, using observations to adjust models, is another approach borrowed from meteorology that is gaining wide currency in ocean modeling. Physical oceanographers have also benefited from instrumentation developments that have enhanced their ability to describe ocean currents and water properties.

Modelers are also interested in the plants and animals in the sea. Most marine organisms have planktonic stages, meaning they are freely drifting, but some do exhibit directed swimming behavior, for example, larval, juvenile, and adult fish. The groups receiving the most attention are phytoplankton, zooplankton, meroplankton, and larval fish (icthyoplankton). There has been some modeling with mature fish, but behavioral models of adult fish are still limited. Phytoplankton are the primary producers in the sea. While they have much in common in their dependence on light and nutrient requirements, there is also substantial variability, with latitude, depth, regime (for example, coastal versus open ocean), and season. Zooplankton (technically, holozooplankton, which spend their entire lives in the water column) are the "insects" of the sea with complex life histories; they are the most numerous multicellular animals in the ocean. Meroplankton are the planktonic stages of a range of invertebrates, for example, crabs and bivalves, which have complex life histories but are primarily coastal organisms that settle on the shore or sea floor as adults. Larval fish can swim and so swimming behavior is a potential issue for modeling, but for the most part behavior can be ignored for the very young and small (length less than tens of millimeters) fish.

Unfortunately, in biology there are no fundamental equations underlying the processes that regulate life—at least none that achieve consensus. Still, for life in the ocean, some basic empirical formulations can be used to describe different processes for the organisms. The two basic types of biological equations are those that define the biological state of

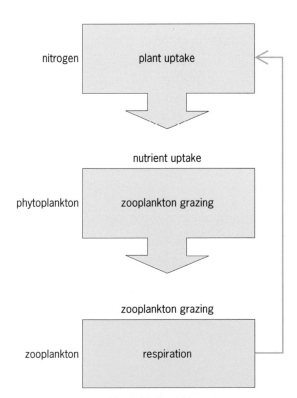

Fig. 1. In this box model, nutrient uptake leads to growth of phytoplankton, zooplankton grazing leads to loss of phytoplankton, and growth of zooplankton and respiration leads to a reinjection of nutrients.

an individual organism; and those that define population parameters, for example, the number of organisms at different ages, or interactions between populations. Metabolic rate processes, an example of individual relationships, can be defined for many organisms, and parameters set for selected species. Standard formulations from population biology can be applied to determine the growth of populations. Detailed models of ocean biology have been developed that combine the individual and population levels explicitly. There are also simplified models that integrate these two notions into bulk models. One popular class of such models considers all quantities in terms of carbon (or nitrogen) and includes nutrients, phytoplankton, and zooplankton, but only in terms of their weight as carbon (or nitrogen). Such bulk models must give up much detail, but for certain modeling problems they have provided significant insights (**Fig. 1**).

Temperature and circulation are the two most important aspects of the ocean to organisms. Because so many of the ocean's crucial biota are planktonic—at the mercy of the motions in the sea—satisfactory biological models must incorporate oceanic transport and mixing. That is, ocean physics and biology must be linked. Such linked models might be called biophysical models. The most detailed examples of biophysical modeling insert the biological model directly into the physical model. Biological quantities are calculated like physical quantities, such as salinity, or temperature (of course, the equations governing the biological quantities differ from those governing, say, salinity). In many cases, however, the calculations of physical and biological quantities can be decoupled by simply taking the output from the physical model and using the calculated physical fields to drive the biology. In general, there is very little impact of the biology on the physics, so the information flow is from the physical property fields to the biological quantities. There are some numerical advantages to this decoupling. That is, once the physical fields are fully described, there is no need to carry out repeated runs of the physical model, even though there may be reasons to explore multiple runs of the linked biophysical model. The primary effects of the physical fields on the biology comes from their determining the local physical conditions, for example, temperature and salinity, which may influence biological rate processes; and from the influence of the circulation on the movement of the organisms. The majority of linked models to date have considered the effect of the horizontal circulation, for two reasons: (1) Even models that produce quite reasonable horizontal velocity fields have quite noisy and sometimes unrealistic vertical velocities. (2) For many organisms, little is known about movement in the vertical. Horizontal swimming behavior is ignored for the organisms discussed here since their

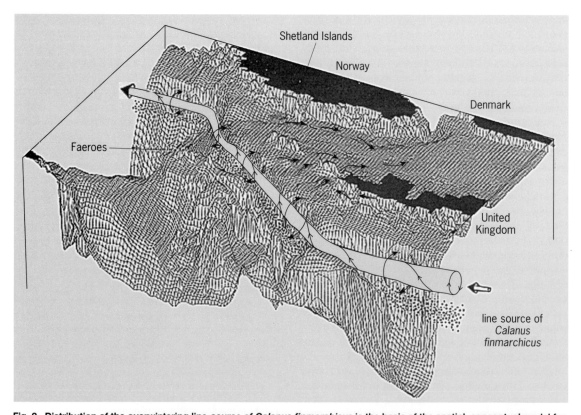

Fig. 2. Distribution of the overwintering line-source of *Calanus finmarchicus* is the basis of the spatial, conceptual model for their life cycle in the northeast Atlantic. These copepods, just millimeters in length, are caught up in ocean currents covering thousands of kilometers, and move from the deep waters off the shelf to shelves of the North Sea and the Norwegian continental shelf. (*From J. O. Backhaus et al., An hypothesis concerning the space-time succession of Calanus finmarchicus in the northern North Sea, ICES J. Mar. Sci., 51:169–180, 1994*)

swimming speeds are generally very small relative to the horizontal currents. The same cannot be said in the vertical. Large vertical velocities in the ocean are of order millimeters per second or less, approximately the swimming speeds of many planktonic animals. Even phytoplankton, which do not swim, can change their buoyancy sufficiently to influence their vertical position.

Biophysical models applied to the development of phytoplankton growth in the ocean have been able to reproduce the fundamental features of the seasonal cycles of plant growth. Research is ongoing to enhance the sophistication of these models and to embed them in circulation models to include the influence of horizontal transport. Such developments point to the problem at the heart of much biophysical modeling—the simple models, even when they appear to work, are clearly too simplified. They miss fundamental features of the ocean; for example, they have only a few species when it is known that there may be many more. Yet it is not possible to include the full ocean ecosystem since too little is known to implement such a model. Some researchers doubt that such a full ocean ecosystem program is possible in principle, given the limitations in the ability to observe all the species or processes in the ocean.

At higher trophic levels, work is under way to model zooplankton in the sea. Some models treat food as a defined input, while others explicitly model the food supply, as well as the response to available food. The complexity of the models varies substantially, ranging from models that are spatially uniform to large-scale spatially explicit models covering ocean basins. European investigators are working on one of the dominant zooplankton in the North Atlantic, *Calanus finmarchicus*. They are hypothesizing that the life cycle of this copepod is coupled with the circulation in the northwest Atlantic (**Fig. 2**). In the winter these organisms enter a resting stage and are hypothesized to lie at depth off the shelf. In the spring they rise to the surface and are carried by currents along the shelf and into the North Sea. In the late fall the next generation of copepods is ready to enter their resting period, and are carried by fall currents offshore and then into a deep subsurface current which carries them back along the shelf, thereby completing the cycle. Investigators are working with coupled life history and circulation models to test this idea.

One long-term goal of fisheries oceanography has been to relate changes in the ocean environment to successful reproduction (recruitment) of fish. In the Gulf of Alaska, researchers have shown that circulation in the Shelikov Strait is an important factor in determining the survival of walleye pollack larvae. Larvae are placed in a sophisticated circulation model which either carries the larvae into favorable or unfavorable regions for survival. This model has proven to be so successful that it is now used as a tool for fisheries management of this stock. Similar studies on shelves around the world—on Georges Bank and the Scotian Shelf, off Australia, off Europe, and elsewhere—are beginning to yield results that will likely become operational in coming years.

For background information *see* BIOPHYSICS; COPEPODA; MARINE BIOLOGY; MARINE ECOLOGY; OCEAN CIRCULATION; OCEANOGRAPHY; PHYTOPLANKTON; SEAWATER; ZOOPLANKTON in the McGraw-Hill Encyclopedia of Science & Technology.

Brad deYoung; Thomas M. Powell

Bibliography. J. O. Backhaus et al., An hypothesis concerning the space-time succession of *Calanus finmarchicus* in the northern North Sea, *ICES J. Mar. Sci.*, 51:169–180, 1994; E. E. Hofmann and C. M. Lascara, Overview of interdisciplinary modelling for marine ecosystems, in *The Sea*, vol. 10, ed. by K. H. Brink and A. R. Robinson, John Wiley, New York, 1998; Special Volume for Fisheries Oceanography Coordinated Investigations, *Fisheries Oceanography*, vol. 5, suppl. 1, 1996.

Open source software

Open source software is not a specific program or company so much as a philosophy of creating and distributing intellectual property. While a group called the Open Source Initiative has published an explicit definition, the term is generally regarded as the practice of writing software in such a way that others are encouraged to freely redistribute it. Moreover, the most popular form of open source explicitly prohibits making changes to such code without also making the changes freely available.

Unix. Open source software distribution traces its history to the roots of Unix. Early versions of Unix source code were made available at low cost to universities, and enhancements and modifications were freely passed around among researchers and students. A major set of enhancements, named the Berkeley Software Distribution (BSD), became commonly used (many updated forms of it are still in use).

The Berkeley Software Distribution code was freely passed around and made no restrictions on subsequent use. Believing that free software was a social good, Computer Programmer Richard Stallman created the Free Software Foundation in 1984, which sought to create a free Unix clone called GNU (GNU's Not Unix). Stallman's distribution scheme differed from Berkeley Software Distribution in that users of GNU software could not make proprietary changes. Any modifications or enhancements to GNU software must be freely distributable. The document that described Stallman's scheme is the GNU Public License, usually referred to as the GPL but also known widely as "copyleft" (as opposed to "copyright").

The GNU Project succeeded in replicating many of the basic Unix tools, most importantly a free C language compiler to allow programmers to create their own free software using open source software tools. However, GNU efforts to re-create an entire operating system were moving much slower.

Linux. In 1991, Linus Torvalds created Linux, and open source software caught widespread public attention. Torvalds started with an operating system kernel which he put on the Internet, encouraging others to download, use, and enhance the original work. By using the GPL, Torvalds was able to assure other programmers that the changes they offered for Linux could never be made proprietary, and as a result Linux became the center of an entire community of developers and enthusiasts.

Less than a decade after first releasing it, Torvalds has seen Linux develop into the heart of a major operating system, with the kernel and most of its surrounding utilities and applications distributed as open source software. Linux use worldwide is well into the tens of millions, though exact counts are extremely difficult because of the number of copies obtained though Internet downloads of freely copied media.

Advantages. The freedom of the GPL, combined with the community approach popularized by Torvalds, had led to the development of open source software of many kinds. The best-known open source applications gained popularity for their heavy use in the infrastructure of the Internet: the Apache web server, the Sendmail mail-forwarding server, and the Perl programming language. Beyond this are hundreds of projects working to produce open source software of all kinds: games, databases, office productivity suites, programming tools, even accounting systems and educational programs.

Another attraction of open source software has been its great adaptability. Because any programmer has access to the source code and can freely adapt it, Linux has been ported to almost every computer hardware platform available. While it started on the Intel-based "PC" platform on which it is still most popular, Linux is widely used on reduced instruction set computing (RISC) systems such as the Alpha and SPARC processors. Network Berkeley Software Distribution (NetBSD) is also widely ported to different architectures.

While open source software is often referred to as free software (and in fact, the GNU Project prefers that term), latitude in the English language causes problems with that use. The double meaning of "free," as in "free of cost" and "free of restrictions," has caused some confusion. Open source software is free of restrictions, but it is not necessarily free of cost. Any person or company is allowed by the GPL to resell open source software for any amount they wish, so long as they do not prohibit purchasers from freely redistributing the open source components.

Future directions. A whole industry has developed to package open source software and documentation, combining Linux or Berkeley Software Distribution cores with applications of all kinds, sometimes taking up six full CD-ROMs or more of free applications. The best known of these packagers is Red Hat Software, but the field is increasingly competitive as established companies apply their existing distribution and marketing expertise to the field of open source software.

As part of the community spirit under which Linux and other open source software are produced, many resources exist to simplify the task of getting Linux help. To accompany a growing number of commercial support organizations, user groups around the world hold meetings and often hold "installfests" to assist newcomers in their introductions to Linux. The need for installfests, however, is decreasing as Linux distributions are increasingly easier to install and maintain. Originally written by programmers for programmers, open source software has become friendlier, gaining easy-to-use graphic interfaces such as K Desktop Environment (KDE) and GNU Network Object Model Environment (GNOME). New initiatives, such as the Eazel project, promise to make open source operating systems even easier.

To the programmer, open source distribution together with the community development model offers many advantages. The existence of large numbers of coders who can study each other's code allows for easier spotting of software bugs (what one person fails to catch, another will). This model has been proven through the development of increasingly stable and secure open source operating systems, often surpassing the efforts of commercial vendors. Detractors argue that since would-be crackers have access to the source code of open source operating systems, they can break in more easily. However, such openness also allows for problems to be discovered more easily and responded to faster than with commercial vendors.

At a technical level, Linux is adapting for use on both larger and smaller systems. Future versions of the Linux kernel will be tunable to maximize performance from multiprocessor systems. A number of clustering technologies promise to allow open source systems to scale into enterprise-level systems: Project Avalon, a cluster of 140 Linux-based systems, is one of the world's fastest supercomputers.

But not everything is being directed at the big equipment. A number of projects and companies are working to produce slimmed-down versions of Linux suitable for use in "embedded" systems—small palm-type computers as well as mass-production appliances.

In many ways, Linux and other open source software are making their mark on the computing landscape. Thousands of community software projects and millions of open source–based systems used worldwide are proving that some of the most valuable parts of the computer are free.

For background information see COMPUTER PROGRAMMING; PROGRAMMING LANGUAGES; SOFTWARE; SOFTWARE ENGINEERING; SYSTEMS INTEGRATION in the McGraw-Hill Encyclopedia of Science & Technology.   Evan Leibovitch

Bibliography. *Open Sources: Voices from the Open Source Revolution*, O'Reilly & Associates, 1999; E. Raymond, *The Cathedral and the Bazaar*, O'Reilly & Associates, 1999; R. Young, *Under the Radar*, Coriolis Groupm, 1999.

Pain

Pain is an intensely unpleasant sensory and emotional awareness that signals threat or damage to the body or that is experienced as bodily injury. Pain is acute if it accompanies an injury or a disease of limited duration. Acute pain disappears with healing. Pain is chronic when it lasts beyond the healing of damaged tissue, is associated with a chronic disease, or persists indefinitely with no apparent cause. Acute pain sometimes provides a protective function, but chronic pain serves no apparent purpose.

Nociception. Acute pain arises when injury-sensitive nerve endings, called nociceptors, fire in response to tissue injury and send signals to the spinal cord and brain. When provoked, a nociceptor generates a volley of signals called nociception. These tissue damage signal volleys travel along the peripheral nerves and enter the central nervous system at the spinal cord.

The concept of a nerve ending that responds to injury (the nociceptor) is perhaps the most basic building block in understanding pain. Nociceptors respond primarily to injury-induced chemical changes in their environments, although some react to direct mechanical stimulation such as crushing or extreme temperatures. Nociceptors inhabit skin, muscle, joints, blood vessels, visceral organs, and other tissues. In the skin and in muscle, they respond readily to obvious harm such as burning and tearing, but they are insensitive when skin or muscle stretches. In contrast, in the visceral organs nociceptors are insensitive to cutting or burning but respond readily to stretching and tension.

The readiness of a nociceptor to fire, thereby provoking reflexes and sending signals of tissue damage to the brain, increases when certain chemicals such as prostaglandins are present in its environment or if something has stimulated it repeatedly. This readiness to fire is called sensitization. Inflammation, a process of chemical change in tissue that occurs during injury or disease, can sensitize nociceptors and thereby increase pain. Nociceptors in inflamed tissues typically send noxious signals in response to minor, harmless stimulation. Aspirin and other medications in its class can help control pain by blocking the formation of the prostaglandins that sensitize nerve endings in inflamed tissue.

Pain perception. Nociception, although often the mechanism of pain, is not the same thing as pain. Pain is a conscious experience that occurs only in the brain. However, even when a person is anesthetized and unconscious, nociceptive signaling in the nervous system can exert powerful effects. The neural signals of tissue damage that occur during surgery often cause muscle reflexes such as twitching and protective reflexes in the nerves that control micro-circulation of blood. Because the spinal cord controls these reflexes, consciousness is unnecessary for reflex activity. In ordinary life, such reflexes are helpful during injury because they cause the muscles around an injury to stiffen and form a splint, and they minimize blood loss by closing down small vessels. However, such reflexes can have harmful effects in the surgical patient. When muscle spasm after surgery causes a stiff chest, it can impede normal breathing and lead to pulmonary disease.

The injury signals that eventually reach higher levels in the central nervous system may or may not lead to direct awareness of pain. Messages from the spinal cord reach several destinations, some of which determine the psychological character of the pain. Some pathways lead to brain structures involved in sensory awareness, but others lead to areas that control attention or produce emotional arousal. One pathway for nociceptive signaling reaches the hypothalamus, which strongly influences the emotional brain and orchestrates the powerful stress reaction that the brain produces during a crisis. Another delivers injury signals to the thalamus, which sends neurons to various structures involved in emotion as well as to the somatosensory cortex where awareness of sensation occurs.

Functional imaging studies of brain activity in conscious people experiencing pain show that emotional as well as sensory parts of the brain become active. In addition to detecting injury and feeling unpleasant emotion, the injured person thinks about the cause of the pain, the immediate consequences of the injury or disease, and the long-range implications of the pain. The anguish of pain often depends upon the meaning that the pain has for the person experiencing it.

Chronic pain. Like acute pain, chronic pain is not only a discomfort but also a stressor. Persisting pain typically causes fatigue, prevents restorative sleep, limits physical functioning, and interferes with mental concentration. Over time, some people with chronic pain, such as low back pain, become disabled because pain severely interferes with their ability to work productively and function effectively. Chronic pain is a major source of distress and disability for millions of people.

Chronic pain has many causes. For some patients, continuous noxious signaling originates not with nociceptors but with injured or diseased nerves. Physicians call pain due to nerve damage neuropathic or neurogenic pain. Nerve injury can sometimes cause abnormal patterns of firing activity that mislead the spinal cord and brain, so that the person falsely locates the pain in the area of the body that the injured nerve would normally serve. Causes of such pain include damage to a nerve from direct physical injury (a wound), chemical toxicity (a damaging drug or chemical), mechanical pressure such as a ruptured disc in the spine pressing upon a nerve root, and some nerve conditions caused by diabetes, alcoholism, or other diseases. Physicians suspect that a patient's pain stems from nerve injury if the pain comes from a numb area of the body or has electric shock or burninglike qualities. Neuropathic pain is harder to relieve than pain coming from nociceptors.

Central pain. It is possible to have chronic pain without either nociception or neuropathy. This condition is called central pain. Persons who have lost a limb, for example, typically experience a phantom representation of that limb, and some feel continuous pain in the phantom. Having pain in an arm or leg at the time of amputation increases the likelihood of pain in the phantom limb. From moment to moment, the brain records immediate awareness of body areas, erasing the last impression in order to write the next. Amputation of a limb prevents the overwriting of the immediate impression with a new awareness of that limb. Consequently, when a person loses a painful limb suddenly, the last awareness of that limb remains indefinitely in the brain. For example, the worker who had a painful pebble in his boot just before the accident that severed his leg will experience that painful pebble hurting his phantom foot for the rest of his life. To date, no satisfactory cure exists for phantom limb pain.

Another kind of central pain occurs after events that injure the central nervous system in specific ways. Stroke and spinal cord injuries are the most common sources of such pain. The pain typically has a steady aching or burning quality, worsening occasionally. Stimuli that are not normally painful, such as light touch or cold, can sometimes exacerbate pain originating in brain structures.

Chronic pain serves no useful protective function. Why pain should persist indefinitely is a puzzle because the brain has the capability to gate or block noxious signaling in the central nervous system. Tissue injury signaling activates sites in the midbrain and brainstem that control descending pathways. These pathways gate the transmission of injury messages at the spinal cord. In this way, the brain spontaneously regulates the amount of injury signaling that reaches higher brain centers. Opioid drugs such as morphine activate such gates, both at the level of the spinal cord itself and in the brainstem. Such drugs resemble chemical messenger substances that the brain produces and employs to control the gating mechanisms.

Psychological processes originating in higher brain areas also affect these gating mechanisms. The spontaneous actions of the gating mechanism can produce dramatic effects. In certain emergencies such as combat, severely injured persons sometimes feel no pain whatsoever. Moreover, in some ritual ceremonies celebrants regularly undergo significant mutilation or injury and appear to experience no pain.

Pain is a complex phenomenon. It normally originates with activation of nociceptors or damage to peripheral nerves, but under certain conditions the brain can produce pain in the absence of bodily injury. Neurotransmitters such as serotonin and substance P have roles in mediating pain. These endogenous substances exert effects in nociception and may enhance drug potency. Analgesic drugs such as morphine and methadone are useful agents in the treatment of pain.

For background information *see* ANALGESIC; ENDORPHINS; NERVOUS SYSTEM (VERTEBRATE); PAIN in the McGraw-Hill Encyclopedia of Science & Technology.   C. Richard Chapman

Bibliography. C. R. Chapman and J. Gavrin, Suffering: The contributions of persistent pain, *Lancet*, 353(9171):2233–2237, 1999; C. R. Chapman and M. Stillman, Pathological pain, in L. Kruger (ed.), *Pain and Touch*, 2d ed., Academic Press, New York, 1996; R. Kugelmann, Complaining about chronic pain, *Social Sci. Med.* 49(12):1663–1677, 1999; W. D. Willis and K. N. Westlund, Neuroanatomy of the pain system and of the pathways that modulate pain, *J. Clin. Neurophysiol.*, 14(1):2–31, 1997.

Paleopathology

With the growth of interest during the past decade in the place of dinosaurs in the history of life on Earth, scientists have begun to reconsider different aspects of dinosaur daily life (such as mating patterns, diet, and social behavior). Creatures once believed to be clumsy, heavy, and stupid, turn out to be fast, highly socialized animals. The dramatic increase in knowledge about dinosaurs has enabled a more complete understanding of these animals and the environment in which they thrived.

Although separated by millions of years, dinosaurs share an important aspect of their life with humans: disease susceptibility. Diseases, as well as human biology and behavior, are the result of millions of years of evolutionary history, beginning with the earliest forms of life. Characteristics allowing recognition of present-day diseases are also identifiable in dinosaurs, going back more than 150 million years.

Dinosaurs. Dinosaurs, like all other living creatures, were susceptible to disease. Gout (a form of hyperacute arthritis in which the metabolic byproduct uric acid is deposited in tissues) was recognized in tyrannosaurids. Osteoarthritis, although rare in dinosaurs, was found in *Iguanodon*. Diffuse idiopathic skeletal hyperostosis (ossified tendons) appeared in hadrosaurs and pachycephalosaurs. Evidence for infectious diseases was found in *Camptosaurus, Allosaurus, Hypsilophodon*, and *Dilophosaurus*. However, the existence of neoplasms (cancer) among dinosaurs is by far the most intriguing issue.

Neoplastic conditions. Neoplasm refers to a mass of localized tissue growth whose cellular proliferation is no longer responsive to normal growth-regulating mechanisms. Neoplasms that are localized and incapable of distant dissemination are considered benign. Neoplasms that are capable of destroying surrounding normal tissues and can disseminate via blood or lymphatic vessels to establish growth at new sites (metastases) are considered malignant and are called cancer.

Three different types of neoplasm have been confirmed in the Tertiary Period, which witnessed dinosaur supremacy. Hemangiomas (vascular tumors) and metastatic carcinoma have been confirmed in dinosaurs. Osteomas (benign bone tumors) have been documented in mosasaurs, which were lizard contemporaries of dinosaurs and which lived in the seas. While osteomas were recognized very early in the study of mosasaurs, the search for neoplasm in dinosaurs is characterized by several false starts.

When dinosaur paleopathology was in its infancy, publication of untested opinions sometimes occurred. In the 1910s a dramatic form of bone fusion in *Diplodocus* (a long-necked and long-tailed giant herbivore sauropod from the Late Jurassic period of North America) was identified. Superficial examination of the cut surface of fused vertebrae revealed several large (by human standards, but not by dinosaur scale) vascular spaces. However, these fused dinosaur vertebrae were not compared to documented cases of hemangioma. Missing that step led to a mistaken impression, which was only corrected half a century later. As hemangiomas do not cause bone fusion, collaboration of medical and paleontologic expertise could have avoided the error. Comparison with human skeletons revealed that the bone fusion was identical to a disease known as diffuse idiopathic skeletal hyperostosis, implying ligamentous ossification. This phenomenon proved later to be common in sauropods. While a false start clouded the neoplasm story, it actually stimulated scientific investigation and provided a subsequent window on dinosaur behavior: the suggestion that the fusion was actually a sexual modification for mating. Another misdiagnosed case relates to an *Allosaurus* (a large carnivore from the Late Jurassic of North America) humerus. The bone was thought to have a chondrosarcoma, a malignant transformation of cartilage. Subsequent examination of that pathologic humerus revealed new bone formation and disorganized internal architecture that was quite different from what is seen with cancer. The *Allosaurus* humerus was actually a healed fracture that was infected. Such osteomyelitis, or bone infection, is well described in dinosaurs. While relatively rare, there are scores of examples.

Hemangiomas, benign tumors of blood vessel derivation, were recently identified in a dinosaur vertebra (Morrison Formation, Upper Jurassic). Macroscopic and radiologic examination of the cut surface reveals sharply defined abnormal areas, completely enclosed by normal bone. The abnormal bone consists of unidirectional thickened bone trabecular

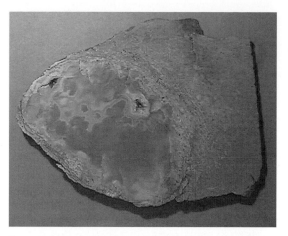

Cross section of a dinosaur bone containing a mass. The mass dissolved the bone, leaving a hole which was filled in by crystal salts.

struts, separated by wide zones of radiolucent matrix, without evidence of bone expansion. Microscopic examination reveals two varieties of spongy bone surrounding large cavities. The macroscopic, radiologic, and microscopic appearance of this Jurassic bone pathology corresponds to that of hemangioma. Hemangiomas are common in modern humans, found in isolated vertebra (usually lower thoracic or upper lumbar) of 6–12% of people today.

Metastatic cancer was found in a dinosaur bone from the Upper Jurassic Morrison Formation in western Colorado. Its original diagnosis was osteosarcoma. The perimineralized bone contains an ovoid agate filling in an 11.5×7.5 cm hole (see **illus.**). The appearance is that of a lytic zone that seems to have resulted from an expansile mass. The lytic lesion is slightly ellipsoid in shape, penetrated by irregular, minimally remodeled trabeculae. Surrounding cortical bone is invaded, leaving only a thin residual cortical shell at the outermost margins. There is a zone of transition between normal bone and the tumorous space, characterized by a pattern of bone destruction, which ranges in thickness from 1 mm to 2 cm. A widened zone of transition, irregular trabeculae, and a residual cortical shell are characteristics of metastatic cancer.

Osteomas, benign bone tumors (small, ivorylike bone growths, usually dome-shaped, common on skulls but also on long bones), were recognized about a century ago on a mosasaur vertebra. This extremely elongated (some up to 15 m or 50 ft in length) marine lizardlike form, with a fin on the end of the tail, modest-sized flippers for maneuvering, and an extremely large skull equipped with very large conical teeth, was among the top carnivores of the Late Cretaceous and Jurassic seas.

Disease occurrence. Throughout life history, diseases such as cancer manifested themselves in a relatively low incidence. The dramatic increase in frequency of cancer in the twentieth century is incompletely explained. The complex nature of contemporary environments together with changes in human demography complicates identification of potential carcinogens or promoting factors. In question is whether the investigation of cancer in dinosaurs could provide useful insights for tackling this human malady. Identifying the frequency of cancer in past living creatures requires that cancer be recognized. Evidence that tumors existed in dinosaurs is derived from the fact that dinosaur bones are large and therefore, relatively well preserved over long periods of time. Tumors in soft tissues and tumors in species with smaller bones may not be recognized in past eras because of insufficient remains. Although the vertebrate paleontologic record is predominantly limited to bone, frequent involvement of bone by metastatic cancer means that the question can be explored. However, only one-third of metastatic cancer is identifiable by just looking at the bone surface. Fortunately, x-rays provide the opportunity to see the metastatic cancer, without destroying the bones. Preliminary x-ray study suggests that not all dinosaurs developed neoplasms, or at least that some families did so at much higher frequencies than others. Examination of frequencies and family specificity of cancer in dinosaurs may provide insights to etiologic agents and predisposing environmental factors.

Many aspects of the life of dinosaurs may be discovered by studying their diseases. Developmental disorders provide insight into bone growth and adaptation to huge body mass; infections (secondary to injury) provide insight to interspecies and intraspecies behaviors (mating pattern, hunting techniques, and so on); and metabolic disorders (such as gout) open a small window to dinosaur physiology. The long history of tumors may reveal something about the interaction between a species and the diseases it encounters. When humans affect the environment, the changes such as increased frequency of cancer can be adverse to the existence of a species. It should be noted that other natural phenomena changing the environment rapidly can also result in tumors.

For background information see CANCER (MEDICINE); DINOSAUR; FOSSIL; MESOZOIC; PALEONTOLOGY in the McGraw-Hill Encyclopedia of Science & Technology.   Israel Hershkovitz; Bruce M. Rothschild

Bibliography. B. M. Rothschild et al., Mesozoic neoplasia: Origins of haemangioma in the Jurassic age, *The Lancet*, 351:1862, 1998; B. M. Rothschild and L. Martin, *Paleopathology: Disease in the Fossil Record*, CRC Press, London, 1993; B. M. Rothschild, B. J. Witzke, and I. Hershkovitz, Metastatic cancer in the Jurassic, *The Lancet*, 354:398, 1999.

Paleosols

Paleosols, or ancient soils, are now widely recognized in ancient sedimentary and volcanic rocks, and along major geological unconformities as old as 3500 million years. They provide information, independent from the fossil record of organisms, for terrestrial environments, plant evolution, atmospheric composition, and global change in the past.

Early life on land. Much early debate on whether Precambrian weathering profiles should be called paleosols concerned evidence for life in them. Life need not be a definitive criterion for a soil or paleosol, as is shown by common usage of soil to describe lunar and Martian surfaces. In any case, the isotopic composition of carbon within Precambrian paleosols reveals not only life but a variety of life. Unusual excesses of the light carbon isotope (^{12}C) compared with the heavy stable carbon isotope (^{13}C) in organic carbon of a paleosol 2765 million years old from Mount Roe, Western Australia, are evidence of methanotrophic microbes and of atmospheric methane at that time. Another paleosol, from Schagen in South Africa, some 2560 million years old, has a heavy mix of carbon isotopes like those of saline desert soils. Isotopic values of carbon normal for soil biota are also found in Precambrian paleosols, including some as old as 2450 million years near Elliot Lake, Ontario. It is also remarkable, given this isotopic evidence for a variety of microbial life on land, that Precambrian paleosols have remained relatively clear of organic matter like most Phanerozoic paleosols. Some kind of decomposer microbial community must also have lived within Precambrian paleosols.

Atmospheric oxidation. Many Precambrian paleosols are deeply and thoroughly weathered, with clayey alteration around corestones reaching 10 m (30 ft) or more down into crystalline bedrock. They provide direct evidence for weathering by hydrolysis, presumably in dilute solutions of carbonic acid from a carbon dioxide greenhouse. Despite this evidence for long-term weathering of stable, well-drained landscapes, paleosols at geological unconformities older than about 2000 million years have remained gray-colored and little oxidized because of the scarcity of oxygen in the atmosphere at that time. Although biological reduction of these soils could have played a role in keeping them unoxidized, this has not prevented comparable well-drained Phanerozoic paleosols from being highly oxidized, and pigmented with red hematite. Red oxidized paleosols appear in the rock record by 2000 million years, though geochemical modeling of their oxygen consumption indicates less atmospheric oxygen at that time than during the past 800 million years. Mass balance modeling of the global carbon cycle over the past 500 million years, supported by carbon isotopic data from sediments and paleosols, has shown considerable fluctuation in atmospheric oxygen and carbon dioxide abundance. Comparable variation also can be inferred for the Precambrian (**Fig. 1**).

Ordovician greenhouse. Mass balance models showing large fluctuations in atmospheric gas composition and former soil respiration of the last 500 million years can now be confirmed with isotopic data from Phanerozoic paleosols. The atmosphere is isotopically heavier with carbon in its carbon dioxide than biologically fractionated carbon dioxide respired by soils, which is preserved in soil carbonate. Isotopically heavy soil nodules are characteristic of greenhouse periods of high partial pressure of carbon dioxide, whereas isotopically light nodules form in periods of low carbon dioxide. In addition, former soil respiration can be gauged from the distance within the paleosol over which isotopically light soil carbon dioxide is mixed with isotopically heavy atmospheric carbon dioxide. Isotopic studies of Late Ordovician paleosols, some 440 million years old, have shown that they formed during a steamy greenhouse period (16–18 times present levels of atmospheric carbon dioxide). Furthermore, these paleosols had near-modern levels of soil respiration, which is surprising considering their lack of rooted or rhizomatous plants. Both paleosols and fossil spores in Ordovician rocks indicate primary producers on land no more complex than cyanobacteria, lichens, or liverworts. Late Ordovician paleosols and fluvial deposits contain burrows and trackways of millipedes. High respiration rates inferred from isotopic studies of Ordovician paleosols indicate an abundance of these and other consumers in soils. Late Ordovician communities on land were unusual in having a high ratio of consumption to production, and thus would have contributed to the atmospheric carbon dioxide greenhouse.

Land plants. A major biological innovation during the Early Silurian (435 million years ago) was the evolution of lignin, at first in slender vascular strands of early land plants, but by Middle Devonian time (380 million years ago) forming massive tree trunks. Lignin is physically durable and chemically resistant to decay, and so sequesters carbon from atmospheric carbon dioxide that fuels its photosynthetic production. Lignin also forms rigid plant endoskeletons, supporting enormous aboveground biomass, as well as copious underground supporting roots. The evolution of woody root traces can be seen from their progressively deeper and more profound bioturbation of paleosols of Silurian and Devonian age (**Fig. 2b** and *e*). Furthermore, the degree of weathering of essential mineral nutrients increased in paleosols over this span of time, as does the drawdown of atmospheric carbon dioxide evident from isotopic study of carbonate nodules in the same paleosols (Fig. 2*a* and *c*). The drawdown is already far advanced by Late Silurian time, well before the Middle Devonian appearance of trees and Late Devonian appearance of woody coals. Trees and coals were important carbon sinks during Carboniferous expansion of glaciation in the southern continents, but were preceded by the long-term atmospheric carbon dioxide consumption by soils and plants (Fig. 2*d*–*f*).

Life crisis. Abrupt global oxidation of carbon and green-house warming is now documented from car-

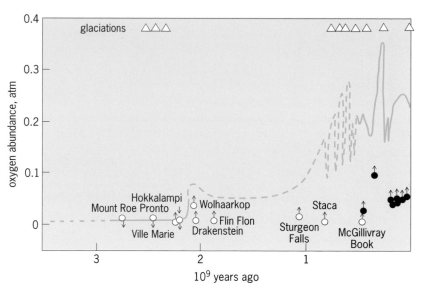

Fig. 1. Abundance of atmospheric oxygen through geological time, as inferred from the oxidation state and carbon isotopic composition of paleosols. Constraints on the curve come from redox chemistry of paleosols (open circles) and carbon isotopic composition of pedogenic goethites (solid circles). Also indicated are times of widespread glacial paleoclimate (triangles).

bon isotopic studies of paleosols and sediments across the Permian-Triassic boundary, some 250 million years ago, which was the most profound extinction event of geological time. A post-apocalyptic greenhouse also is reflected in earliest Triassic paleosols of Antarctica and Australia, which include deeply weathered soils (Ultisols) of kinds found now in warm climates of low latitudes and anomalous for paleolatitudes within the polar circle (**Fig. 3**). Extremely light carbon isotopic composition of organic matter in some of these paleosols is evidence that biogenic methane must have been a part of this earliest Triassic greenhouse. Antarctic and Australian south polar lowlands remained humid and had sedimentation rates that should have encouraged peat accumulation, yet no coals are found in Early Triassic rocks there or anywhere else in the world. Extinction of peat-forming plants at the end of the Permian is the best explanation for this global coal gap, just as extinctions of corals and bryozoans may explain the earliest Triassic reef gap in the marine fossil record.

Dinosaurs. The Jurassic Period of 146–208 million years ago was another time of greenhouse atmosphere. The carbon isotopic composition of pedogenic carbonate in formerly well-drained Jurassic paleosols is again heavy, and Jurassic paleosols of temperate (rather than frigid) paleoclimatic affinities are found at high paleolatitudes. Many of these red calcareous paleosols with large nests of termites and the bones of sauropod dinosaurs resemble soils of the semiarid seasonally dry tropics. Plant productivity of comparable modern soils is surprisingly low to support such biomass of insects and dinosaurs. Jurassic paleosols could thus have contributed to the atmospheric greenhouse by overconsumption of

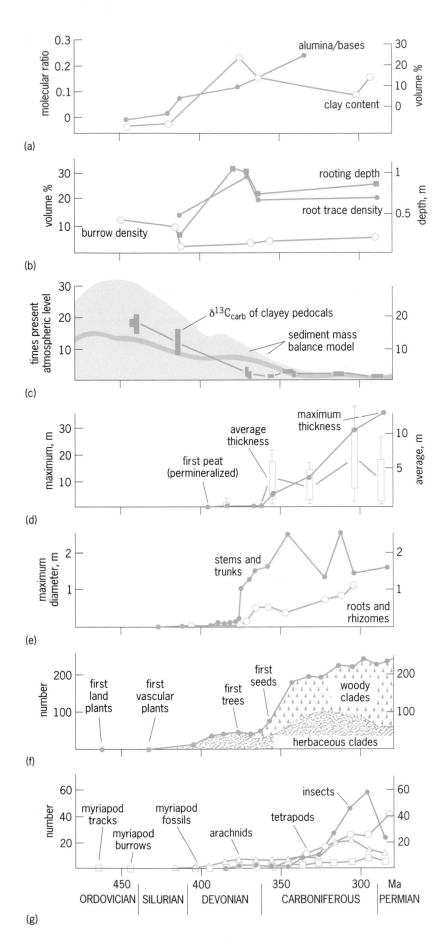

(a)

(b)

(c)

(d)

(e)

(f)

(g)

plant production comparable to human overgrazing of marginal rangelands today.

Angiosperms. By Late Cretaceous time, weedy angiosperms are common in weakly developed paleosols worldwide. They also dominated mangrove and fresh-water tropical swamp vegetation. These new kinds of plants, with their unprecedented ability to recover from disturbance, coevolved with a suite of ornithischian low-browsing dinosaurs. Organic matter content and soil structure of Late Cretaceous paleosols, together with the lighter isotopic composition of their carbonate, indicate decline from the peak greenhouse of the Early Cretaceous and Late Jurassic. This trend was abruptly reversed by a post-apocalyptic greenhouse following impact of a large asteroid in Yucatan and extinction of the dinosaurs at the end of the Cretaceous some 65 million years ago. This greenhouse was short-lived, perhaps no more than 50,000 years, judging from the perturbation in carbon isotopic composition of organic matter in paleosol sequences. Another short-lived (less then 100,000 years) greenhouse spike at the end of the Paleocene some 55 million years ago is reflected in unusually deep weathering of paleosols in Wyoming and elsewhere in the world. Yet another greenhouse spike in the middle Miocene some 16 million years ago is reflected in deeply weathered paleosols at high paleolatitudes in Oregon, Germany, Japan, and Australia. These transient perturbations are variously blamed on meteorite impacts, methane clathrate release, and flood basalt eruptions.

Grasses. During the past 40 million years of the Cenozoic, a long-term trend of paleoclimatic cooling and drying into the ice ages of the past 2.5 million years is matched in the fossil record of soils by a spread of the finely rooted, organic-rich, crumb-structured soils of grasslands (Mollisols) [**Fig. 4**]. Coarsely granular paleosols with a dominance of fine root traces first appear some 33 million years ago, at the Eocene-Oligocene boundary, and represent the appearance of dry rangelands with bunch grasses, rather than only woody shrubs that dominated Eocene and earlier arid lands. Grass pollen and fruits become only a little more common in the fossil record

Fig. 2. Early Paleozoic changes in weathering, atmosphere, and evolution of plants and animals in eastern North America. (*a*) Soil differentiation is indicated by clay content (volume %) and alumina/bases (molecular ratio) of the most weathered horizon of calcareous red paleosols. (*b*) Soil bioturbation is indicated by proportion of line transect in paleosols occupied by roots or burrows (%) and by measured rooting depth (cm). (*c*) Atmospheric CO$_2$ levels (relative to present atmospheric level, or PAL) are calculated from a mass balance model (curve) and estimated from carbon isotopic composition of pedogenic nodules (solid boxes). (*d*) Maximum coal seam thickness and average thickness of at least 10 consecutive seams (meters). (*e*) Diameter of fossil plant stems and roots (meters). (*f*) Diversity of fossil plants, including both woody and herbaceous forms (number of species). (*g*) Diversity of soil animals (number of families). (*Used with permission from G. J. Retallack, Early forest soils and their role in Devonian global change, Science, 276:583–585, 1997, and the American Association for the Advancement of Science*)

at this time, and despite extinctions of some archaic browsing lineages, mammals show only modest evolutionary adaptations to grasslands in tooth and limb structure.

The advent of sod grasslands in the early Miocene (some 20 million years ago) was restricted to dry regions, because all these finely rooted, crumb-structured paleosols have carbonate nodules at shallow levels within their profiles as in soils of regions receiving less than 400 mm mean annual precipitation. At this time there is a major evolutionary radiation of mammals, such as horses in North America, notoungulates in South America, and antelope in Asia, with high-crowned teeth adapted to gritty graze and with cursorial limbs for sprinting in open vegetation. By late Miocene time (some 7 million years ago) finely rooted and crumb-structured paleosols of sod grasslands are for the first time found with calcareous nodules as deep as a meter. These paleosols signal the advent of tall sod grasslands, and the heavy carbon isotopic composition of their nodules indicates that this also was a time of increasingly widespread use of the C4 photosynthetic system by grasses.

Alternations of grassland and woodland vegetation also can be documented on most continents through the glacial-interglacial paleoclimatic fluctuations of the Quaternary. Grassland soils could contribute to global cooling and drying in several ways. Their underground storage of carbon as organic matter is much more substantial than for desert scrub and woodlands of comparably dry climates. They also consume carbon dioxide as carbonic acid for weathering of silicate minerals within a crumb-structured soil that has a much higher internal surface area than soils of woodlands and deserts. The sod of grasslands also keeps the soil moister and the air above drier than soils of woody plants that actively desiccate the soil by root uptake and moisten the air with water vapor from transpiration of their leaves. Finally, grasslands have high albedo and are less absorptive of incoming solar radiation than dark and diffuse woody plants.

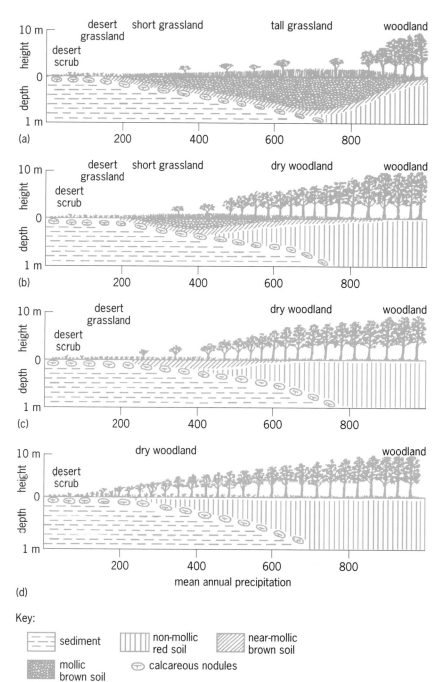

Key:

sediment   non-mollic red soil   near-mollic brown soil

mollic brown soil   calcareous nodules

Fig. 4. Scenario for climatic and geographic expansion of grassland soils and their characteristic crumb-structured horizons in the North American Great Plains during the Cenozoic. (*Used with permission from G. J. Retallack, Neogene expansion of the North American Prairie, Palaios,12:380–383, 1997, and the Society for Sedimentary Research*)

Fig. 3. This deeply weathered clayey paleosol (Ultisol) formed at a paleolatitude of at least 69°S during the Early Triassic in the Allan Hills, Antarctica. Such soils form today in warm climates, at latitudes no higher than 48°. The paleosol is thus evidence of high-latitude greenhouse paleoclimate.

There is a long fossil record of soils, with major events linked intimately with those of terrestrial ecosystems that they supported. Soils are an important part of terrestrial ecosystems. Paleosols now are revealing that this was also the case in the geological past.

For background information *see* CARBON; CRETACEOUS; LIGNIN; PALEOCLIMATOLOGY; PALEOSOL in the McGraw-Hill Encyclopedia of Science & Technology.   Gregory J. Retallack

Bibliography. G. J. Retallack, *A Colour Guide to Paleosols*, Wiley, Chichester, 1997; G. J. Retallack, *Soils of the Past*, Unwin Hyman, London, 1990; M. Thiry and R. Simon-Coinçon (eds.), *Palaeoweathering, Palaeosurfaces and Related Continental Deposits*, Blackwell, Oxford, 1999; M. Widdowson (ed.), *Paleosurfaces: Recognition, Reconstruction and Paleoenvironmental Information*, Geological Society, London, 1999.

Photogrammetry

Particle tracking velocimetry (PTV) is a well-known technique for the determination of velocity vectors of flow within an observation volume. However, for a long time it was rarely applied because of the intensive effort necessary to measure coordinates of a large number of flow marker particles in many images. With today's imaging hardware in combination with the methods of digital image processing and digital photogrammetry, however, new possibilities have arisen for the design of completely automatic particle tracking velocimetry systems.

A powerful three-dimensional (3-D) particle tracking velocimetry system has been developed in a collaboration of the Institute of Geodesy and Photogrammetry with the Institute of Hydromechanics and Water Resources Management at the Swiss Federal Institute of Technology (ETH) Zürich. This system is currently capable of determining three-dimensional coordinate sets of some 1000 particles in a flow field at a time resolution of 30 or 60 data sets per second and a sequence length of about 2000 time steps. The system is fully automatic after initialization by an operator. A laser-induced fluorescence (LIF) system at the same location generates three-dimensional flow tomography data sets and tracking structures of interest through time and space.

3-D PTV system. Particle streaks, the time-exposed images of particles made visible by continuous illumination or pulsed illumination, have long been used for velocity measurements. Digital image analysis techniques opened the way for an automated analysis of particle streak images. This technique, however, has some disadvantages. If applied to three-dimensional flows, it can bias the results toward small velocities. It is therefore preferable to use pulse illumination and multiple-exposure techniques, and track the positions of individual particles recorded on a photographic or video frame.

Hardware. Two-dimensional particle tracking techniques, based on one camera, have been used in the past. By adding a second or even third and fourth camera, particle positions can be tracked in three-dimensional space. However, a new problem arises: the establishment of correspondences between images of individual particles in the frames of the different cameras. Three-dimensional particle tracking therefore involves three steps: the establishment of particle image correspondences, the determination of particle coordinates in three-dimensional space at a given time, and the tracking of the paths of individual particles in time. Once links between consecutive positions of particles are established, the velocity vector u is estimated from $u = \Delta s / \Delta t$, where Δs is the vector of particle displacement during the time increment $\Delta t = f_c^{-1}$, f_c being the frame rate of the camera.

In the particle tracking velocimetry system at ETH Zürich mentioned above (**Fig. 1**), three or four off-the-shelf monochromatic charge-coupled-device (CCD) cameras are used with an image full-frame acquisition rate of 30 or 60 Hz. The volume of interest and the included particles in the medium are visualized by two halogen short-arc lamps with suitable reflectors. The optical axes of the cameras form angles close to $60°$. The camera set can move with the average speed of the water flow. The cameras are synchronized by one master camera. The 8-bit images are produced in progressive scan mode at a size of 640×480 pixels. A maximum of two cameras can be controlled by one microcomputer, and the images are stored on a hard disk in real time.

Calibration and data processing. Since the imaging rays are reflected twice due to different refractive indices in the optical path through water, glass, and air, a fairly complex "multimedia sensor model" had to

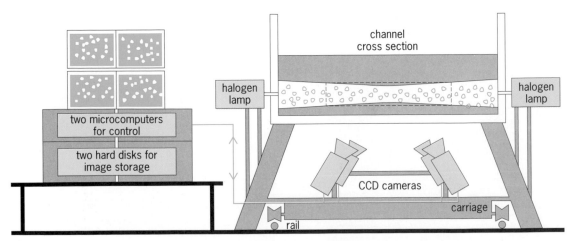

Fig. 1. Particle tracking velocimetry hardware installation for measuring flow velocities in a laboratory water channel.

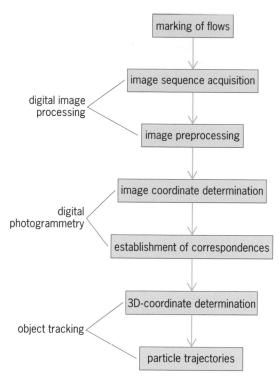

Fig. 2. **Task flow scheme of a three-dimensional particle tracking velocimetry system.**

be developed. The fidelity of this model is crucial for the achievement of accurate results in particle measurement and tracking.

Before data processing can commence, a thorough calibration of the system is necessary. For this purpose a calibration frame spanning the entire observation volume is placed into the object space and imaged by all cameras. For such a frame, a three-dimensional grid is used with an array of marked and well-defined points whose object-space coordinates are known and have been determined with high accuracy.

The processing of the calibration images is performed automatically after a user-supported preorientation of the cameras. After the calibration, the 16 parameters describing exterior and interior orientation, lens distortion, and affine transformation

for each camera are known and can be used for the spatial intersections in the particle positioning.

The calibration frame can also serve for checking the accuracy of the system. In the particle tracking velocimetry system at ETH Zürich, the standard deviation of particle image coordinates (σ_0) was found to be 1.1 μm, that is, about one-tenth of a sensor pixel, and the root-mean-square error of the three-dimensional object points (in a volume of 200 × 160 × 50 mm^3) was 0.021 mm in X, 0.034 mm in Y, and 0.044 mm in Z (depth). This corresponds to a relative lateral accuracy of about 1:7000. However, these numbers refer to an older system version, where the storage of images was on analog video tape, thus degrading the image quality. Modern digital storage devices will give significantly better results.

The chain of automatic data processing from the digitized images to the three-dimensional particle trajectories (**Fig. 2**) can be divided into image preprocessing, particle detection and determination of particle image coordinates, establishment of stereoscopic correspondences, three-dimensional coordinate determination, and tracking in object space.

The task of automatic particle identification and particle image coordinate determination in the digital images is trivial, since the particles appear as bright stains on a dark background (**Fig. 3**). After high-pass filtering of the images to remove nonuniformities of the background intensity level due to reflections and the nonuniform intensity profile of the light sheet, particle images can be segmented by a simple thresholding algorithm, and image coordinates can be determined with subpixel accuracy by using the gray-value-weighted center of gravity of the segmented blobs.

However, with the large number of particles employed (typically more than 1000 particles in the illuminated section), a problem occurs when particles optically block or overlap each other in one or more views. An efficient procedure has been developed to deblock particles in the images. Whenever a human observer is able to distinguish overlapping particles, the algorithm will succeed as well.

To compute three-dimensional particle coordinates, a spatial intersection has to be performed with

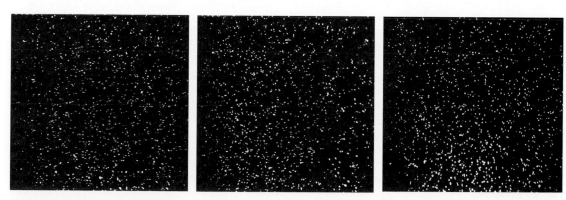

Fig. 3. **Particle cloud imaged with three cameras.**

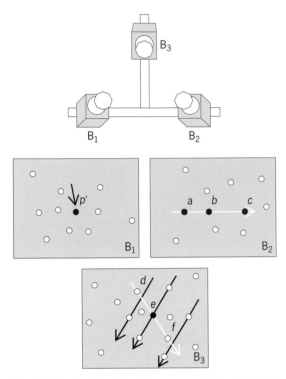

Fig. 4. Determination of particle correspondences in image space through the principle of intersection of epipolar lines. Point p' in image B_1 has three matching candidates, a, b, and c, in image B_2. Through the use of a third image, B_3, the ambiguity can be resolved such that now p', b, and e are corresponding image points.

corresponding image coordinates of a stereopair. However, the establishment of these stereoscopic correspondences poses some problems. The particle images do not show any characteristic features (such as color, size, or shape) which would allow the particles to be distinguished. The only criterion which can be applied is the geometric constraint of the epipolar line. Since the orientation parameters of the cameras are known from the calibration procedure, proceeding from a point p' in one image, an epipolar line in another image can be calculated, on which the corresponding point has to be found. In the strict mathematical formulation, this line is a straight line; in the more general case with convergent camera axes, nonnegligible lens distortion, and multimedia geometry, the epipolar line will be a slightly bent line. Through this epipolar line concept, together with the use of more than two (usually three or four) cameras, the problem of ambiguity in image correspondence (particle matching) can be solved (**Fig. 4**).

After the establishment of correspondences, the three-dimensional coordinates for the nonambiguous triplets or quadruplets can be determined by spatial intersection using a least-squares adjustment. Another benefit of the three- and four-camera system as compared with a two-camera system is the improvement of the accuracy of the coordinates of the points by a factor of approximately 1.3 laterally and 1.7 in depth.

The results are data sets with three-dimensional particle coordinates and the associated standard deviations. This information is passed to the tracking module to establish correspondences in time.

Particle tracking is performed in three-dimensional object space. It consists of establishing correct links between successive positions of individual particles. The two major problems in tracking are that particles are determined with (known) noise and that some of them are dropping out of the observation volume while others are appearing as new particles.

The criteria used to resolve ambiguities in track continuation are based on the assumptions that (1) particle paths are smooth (in mathematical terms, they can be described by regular functions, differentiable to any order desired); (2) acceleration magnitudes of particles are bounded (that is, they are never larger than a specified upper limit); and (3) acceleration change magnitudes are also bounded.

The particle tracking procedure gives velocities at randomly distributed locations inside an observation volume. For further analysis, it is often desirable to have information at all the points on a regular grid. For that purpose, an efficient interpolation scheme has been developed.

3-D laser-induced fluorescence. With this technique, it is possible to determine and track three-dimensional patterns in flows of liquids tagged by a fluorescent dye. The laser images are obtained as three-dimensional voxel (volume pixel) data sets (tomography) by rapidly sweeping a thin laser sheet through the observation volume with simultaneous imaging by a high-speed (500-Hz) solid-state camera. The observation volume is subdivided into small cuboids which are tracked through space and time using a newly developed method of three-dimensional adaptive least-squares matching. The method yields the shifts and deformations of liquid cuboids associated with these patterns and enables the determination of velocity vectors and their derivatives simultaneously and accurately at a large number of locations. This technique opens new possibilities in the research of turbulence and in particular in the mixing of passive scalars (materials that are carried by the flow and exposed to the flow mechanics) in turbulent flows.

For background information *see* CHARGE-COUPLED DEVICES; FLOW MEASUREMENT; FLUID FLOW; FLUID-FLOW PRINCIPLES; IMAGE PROCESSING; PHOTOGRAMMETRY; VELOCITY in the McGraw-Hill Encyclopedia of Science & Technology.   A. Gruen

Bibliography. Th. Dracos (ed.), *Three-Dimensional Velocity and Vorticity Measuring and Image Analysis Techniques*, Kluwer Academic, Dordrecht, 1996; Th. Dracos and A. Gruen, Videogrammetric methods in velocimetry, *Appl. Mech. Rev.*, 51(6): 387–413, June 1998; H.-G. Maas, A. Gruen, and D. Papantoniou, Particle tracking velocimetry in three-dimensional flows, Part A, *Exp. Fluids*, 15:133–146, 1993; H.-G. Maas, A. Stefanidis, and A. Gruen, From pixels to voxels: Tracking volume elements in sequences of 3-D digital images, *Int. Arch. Photogram. Remote Sens.*, 30(part 3/2):539–546, 1994.

Phototaxis

Both microorganisms and higher organisms display a variety of motile responses to light as an environmental signal. Such light-elicited motility responses are generally referred to as photomovement. The organisms use the photomovement to adapt to optimal physiological and growth conditions. Phototaxis refers to the movement of a motile organism toward (positive phototaxis) or away from (negative phototaxis) the source of light. Rigorously speaking, the positive and negative phototaxis refers to the organism's response with respect to the direction of light source. However, the term phototaxis often is used in reference to the light-elicited movement behavior of a population of organisms toward or away from the source of light, which may or may not be in response to the direction of light propagation. Phototaxis can result from different mechanisms of the light-elicited movement. For example, an individual ciliate cell may stop its swimming upon encountering a sudden increase in light intensity, and it then steers away from the higher to the lower light intensity area. This response is called step-up photophobic response, and results in a negative phototaxis, as the cell swims away from the high-intensity light. To define various light-elicited movements of organisms that may result in phototaxis, it is necessary to discuss various photomovement responses. The photomovements of specific ciliates and bacteria will be used as typical examples.

Photophobic response. The photophobic response of a motile organism refers to a transient alteration in swimming direction or velocity when the organism is exposed to a sudden change in light intensity. The most common photophobic response is a stop response, followed by a change in movement direction. A response elicited by a sudden increase in light intensity is a step-up photophobic response (**Fig. 1**).

This type of step-up photophobic response results in negative phototaxis, as a population of the cells swims away from the source of light. If the photophobic response of a cell results when the cell encounters a sudden decrease in light intensity, the step-down photophobic response occurs. In this case, the cell moves into the illuminated area. The step-down photophobic response results in positive phototaxis. However, the term phototaxis is more rigorously defined in terms of the organisms responding to or detecting the direction of light propagation rather than to the change in light intensity.

Positive phototaxis. A population of organisms may be placed in an environment that is half-shaded. Each organism is capable of detecting the direction of light, regardless of changes in light intensity, and orients itself such that it swims toward the source of light. This results in the organisms' staying within the brightly lit side. If a population of the organisms was observed after a time, more organisms would be in bright rather than dim light. This is positive phototaxis in which the organism responds to or determines the direction of light. In other words,

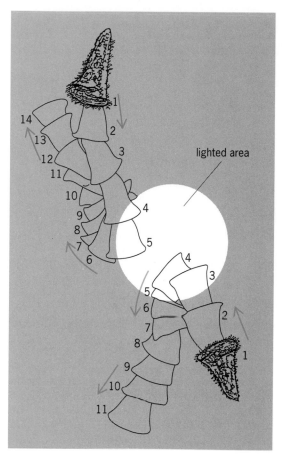

Fig. 1. Step-up photophobic response exhibited by *Stentor coeruleus.* The successive numbered positions correspond to a time period of about 0.16 s. As the organism encounters the boundary between the dark and illuminated areas, it stops for a fraction of a second and then steers away from the high-intensity area.

the phototactic response of an organism is an orientation response with respect to the direction of light propagation. To distinguish the orientation response from the more general term "phototaxis," the terms "phototactic response" or "phototactic orientation" are more appropriate.

Negative phototaxis. If the organism orients and moves away from the source of a light stimulus, that is, the organism moves parallel with the propagation of light, then the oriented movement is referred to as negative phototaxis, or more appropriately negative phototactic response. It is difficult to establish the true phototactic response when the organism also displays the photophobic response, which results in its moving toward or away from the source of a light stimulus. *Stentor coeruleus* displays the step-up photophobic response (Fig. 1), but also exhibits a negative phototactic response. (**Fig. 2**).

Photoaccumulation and photodispersal. Responses that result in organisms accumulating or dispersing from a region of higher light intensity are referred to as photoaccumulation and photodispersal, respectively. The photoaccumulation of organisms is a behavioral consequence of a step-down photophobic response or positive phototaxis. However,

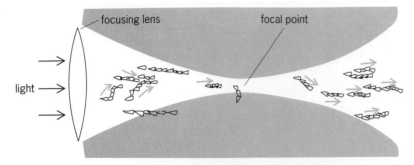

Fig. 2. The lens focuses the beam of light. The *Stentor* cells moving away from the light source continue to do so, in spite of the fact that the light intensity increases and decreases before and after the focal point of the lens, respectively.

the photodispersal results from a step-up photophobic response or negative phototaxis. Interestingly, the photomovement response of the high-salt-water bacterium *Halobacterium halobium* displays photodispersal upon exposure to a step-up increase in intensity in the blue wavelength region. Exposure to yellow-green wavelength light results in photoaccumulation. These contrasting photoresponses of the *H. halobium* cell arise from the two photoreceptor pigments: sensory rhodopsin, sR_{587}, and its photocycling intermediate, sR_{373}; the former mediates the photoaccumulation, and the latter elicits the photodispersal.

In addition to photophobic responses, phototactic orientations, and photoaccumulation and photodispersal—all of which contribute to phototaxis—certain organisms, especially photosynthetic cyanobacteria and purple bacteria, exhibit photokinesis. Positive photokinesis refers to the faster movement of the organism upon entering an illuminated area, and negative photokinesis refers to the slower movement relative to its velocity of movement in the dark or dim light. The positive photokinesis results in photodispersal, since the organisms end up spending less time in the illuminated area but more time in the dark or dim light. The photokinetic responses of photosynthetic bacteria reflect photosynthetic adenosine triphosphate (ATP) synthesis which accelerates the bacterial motor activity. Thus, the photoreceptor pigments for these responses are photosynthetic pigments (chlorophylls).

Photoreceptors. The diverse responses of organisms to light are mediated by a selected group of the pigment molecules. These "photoreceptors" include (a) retinals—for example, the sensory rhodopsins of *H. halobium* are proteins containing the covalently linked retinal known as Schiff's base; (b) tetrapyrroles, such as the pigment molecule of phytochromes for plant photomorphogenesis and chlorophylls for photokinesis in photosynthetic bacteria; and (c) flavins [riboflavin, flavin mononucleotide (FMN), and flavin adenine dinucleotide (FAD)], as the blue light receptor for phototropism in plants. Recently, *p*-coumaric acid was found to be in the photoactive yellow protein for the phototaxis of Eubacteria. To this list of the photoreceptor pigments, the pigments of *S. coeruleus* and *Blephar-*

isma japonicum, stentorin and blepharismin, respectively, have recently been added. Stentorin (**1**) and blepharismin (**2**) are structurally derivatives of hypericin (**3**). This latest class of hypericin-like photoreceptor molecules is unique among the photobiological light sensors.

(**1**)

(**2**)

(**3**)

Photosensory transduction. Stentorin and blepharismin are mainly localized in the pigment granules. In both *Stentor* and *Blepharisma* the pigment granules are about 500 nanometers in diameter, membrane-bound, and arranged in strings parallel to the ciliary rows, spread all over the cellular body. A honeycomb-like structure, made up of a folded membrane, has also been suggested to be contained in *Blepharisma* pigment granules. The photomovement responses of microorganisms such as ciliates involve a chain of chemical or physical events triggered by the light-excited photoreceptor molecule. The nature and efficiency of the photomovement initiation trigger is linked to the primary photochemical reactions of the photoreceptor molecules. The primary photochemical reactions of stentorin and blepharismin have been suggested to involve electron transfer coupled with proton transfer. Stentorin and blepharismin can mediate electron transfer processes in the excited state as an electron donor. It has been suggested that the primary photoreactions of stentorin (and blepharismin) lead to an intracellular pH change, following the electron transfer reactions of the photoreceptors. Such a transient pH change could serve as the initial signal for the subsequent signal transduction pathway involved in the photomovement of the ciliate cells.

The photomovement responses of *S. coeruleus* (Figs. 1 and 2) are controlled by ciliary strokes, and their stop-turn maneuver at the light-dark boundary results from the reversal of ciliary stroke direction (from clockwise to counterclockwise). Membrane potentials control the ciliary movement. As most organisms do, *Stentor* maintains a negative resting potential of about −50 to −55 mV across the cell membrane in the absence of light stimuli. Upon excitation of the cell with a step-up light illumination, a membrane-depolarizing action potential is generated as the result of an influx of calcium ions into the ciliate cell. The calcium influx appears to trigger the reversal of ciliary stroke for the stop-steer movement response of the ciliates. However, the biochemical mechanisms for the light-induced membrane potential change are not fully understood. However, it appears that G-protein and cyclic guanine monophosphate/guanine monophosphate (cGMP/GMP) play a signaling role in the phototactic and photophobic sensory signal transductions in *Stentor* and *Blepharisma*.

The light excitation of stentorin in the pigment granule is proposed to generate a transient intracellular pH change, which can serve as a cellular signal associated with the depolarizing receptor potential. Subsequently, the initiating signal appears to be amplified by a sudden trigger of Ca^{2+} ion influx into the cell. It has also been suggested that a heterotrimeric G-protein plays an important role as a signal transducer in *Stentor* as well as *Blepharisma*. Thus, these cells provide an analogy to the "visual" excitation system reminiscent of the rhodopsin-mediated vision process in higher animals. In both cases, G-protein activates a phosphodiesterase as an effector molecule, which leads to the lowering of cellular cGMP level. In the vertebrate visual system, the light-induced, rhodopsin-mediated lowering of the intracellular cGMP level transiently closes cGMP-gated cation channels. Thus, the working hypothesis for the photomovement responses of *Stentor* and *Blepharisma* involves the following sequence of events: light excitation of stentorin/blepharismin → G-protein → phosphodiesterase → cGMP lowering → Ca^{2+}-channel opening → ciliary stroke reversal.

For background information *see* CELL MOTILITY; ORGANIC PHOTOCHEMISTRY; PHOTOCHEMISTRY; PHOTORECEPTION; PHOTOSYNTHESIS; PLANT MOVEMENTS; TAXIS in the McGraw-Hill Encyclopedia of Science & Technology.   Pill-Soon Song

Bibliography. G. Checcucci et al., Chemical structure of blepharismin, the photosensor pigment for *Blepharisma japonicum, J. Amer. Chem. Soc.*, 119: 5762–5763, 1997; B. Diehn et al., Terminology of behavioral responses of motile microorganisms, *Photochem. Photobiol.*, 26:559–560, 1977; H.-W. Kuhlmann, Do phototactic ciliates make use of directional antennas to track the direction of light?, *Eur. J. Protistol.*, 34:244–253, 1998; P.-S. Song, Protozoan and related photoreceptors: Molecular aspects, *Annu. Rev. Biophys. Bioeng.*, 12:35–68, 1983; N. Tao et al., A new photoreceptor molecule from *Stentor coeruleus, J. Amer. Chem. Soc.*, 115: 2526–2528, 1993.

Phytoremediation

Selenium (Se) is intriguing in its nutritional and toxicological duality. Depending on its concentration and chemical form, selenium functions as an essential element for, or as a toxic compound to, humans, livestock, waterfowl, and certain bacteria. The range between the beneficial and harmful selenium concentrations is quite narrow. In areas of China, both severe nutritional selenium deficiencies and endemic selenium toxicity were identified in the population. Awareness of the environmental impact of selenium increased after evidence of selenium poisoning was observed in waterfowl frequenting Kesterson Reservoir in central California in 1983. As a result, research on selenium has focused on two contrasting issues: developing strategies to augment this trace element in selenium-deficient soils, and establishing methods to remediate selenium-contaminated ecosystems by reducing the element's accumulation in the soils and thus to manage its entry into the food chain.

Selenium pollution. This is a very serious problem in arid areas where soils formed from marine sedimentary rocks and seleniferous deposits. Irrigation of these soils can result in concentrations of selenium in drainage water that exceed criteria for the protection of fresh-water aquatic life. In the western United States, over 2.6 million acres (1 million hectares) of land have been identified as environmentally susceptible to irrigation-induced selenium contamination. Thus, much attention has been focused on developing cost-effective and environment-friendly approaches for the remediation of selenium-contaminated soils.

Practical remediation strategies for reducing selenium contamination were investigated during the 1990s by researchers from the U.S. Department of Agriculture–Agricultural Research Service (USDA-ARS) in central California. In conjunction with improving irrigation and drainage management practices in selenium-rich soils, they have explored the possible role of higher plants in managing or reducing high levels of naturally occurring soil selenium. This strategy is termed phytoremediation, which involves growing selenium-accumulating plant species

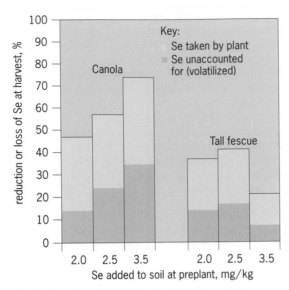

Fig. 1. Percent reduction of soil selenium levels and percent accumulation of selenium in canola and tall fescue used for phytoremediation.

that have substantial ability to absorb, accumulate, and volatilize selenium in contaminated soils. Once the plants have accumulated selenium, they are harvested, removed from the site, and either dispersed on low-selenium soils or used as a selenium-rich animal feed additive. This plant-based technology would lower selenium levels in the soil and thus reduce the migration of selenium into water systems and eventual entry into biological ecosystems.

The basic idea that plants can be used for environmental remediation is very old and cannot be

traced to any particular source. However, selecting plants to scavenge selenium from soils is a complicated process, since plants generally do not require selenium as an essential element for growth. Some plants are known selenium accumulators, possessing a unique pathway for absorbing a large quantity of selenium safely. Canola (*Brassica napus*) has been investigated for its ability to accumulate selenium. Sulfur, which has similar physical structure to selenium, is also taken up in large amounts by *Brassica* species (canola, Indian mustard). It has been demonstrated that these plants can effectively lower soil selenium concentrations in both greenhouse and field studies. Under ideal conditions, canola can lower soil selenium concentrations by up to 74% (**Fig. 1**) if the form of selenium available is selenate. Mass-balance calculations based on the quantity of selenium found in the soil at preplant and at harvest, and the amount of selenium residing in plant tissue, suggested that significant amounts, but not all of the lost soil selenium, was accounted for in plant tissues.

Phyto-utilization. Because not all selenium removed from the soil was accounted for in the plant tissue, processes other than plant uptake must have contributed to lowering soil selenium levels. One such process is biological selenium volatilization, whereby the release of nontoxic volatile selenium gases into the atmosphere may explain the disappearance of substantial amounts of selenium from the soil. Volatilization involves the transformation of inorganic selenium by both microorganisms and plants to volatile forms of selenium. Thus, canola was found to be an ideal candidate for phytoremediation of selenium because of the plant's ability to both extract and volatilize selenium at substantial

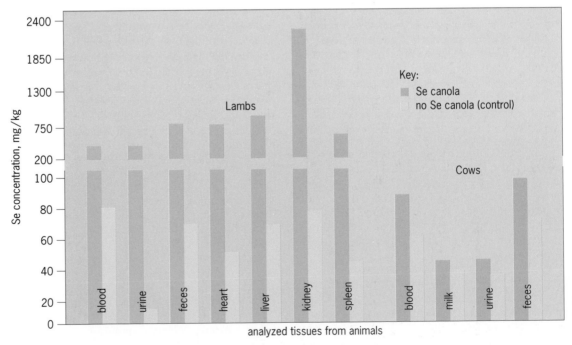

Fig. 2. Mean selenium concentrations in selected tissues, blood, urine, and milk in lambs and cows fed seleniferous and nonseleniferous canola.

rates. Moreover, it has been suggested that the seleniferous plant material used for phytoremediation of selenium, for example, *Brassica* species, may be carefully mixed with other animal feedstuffs (amount depends on tissue selenium concentration) and fed to animals in selenium-deficient areas. Hence, the term "phyto-utilization" was coined.

Selenium deficiencies probably cause greater problems than selenium toxicities in animals. Animal producers wishing to ensure adequate supplies of selenium to their livestock have a variety of techniques at their disposal, including giving selenium by injection or by mouth as a feed supplement. Generally, diets containing 0.1–0.3 mg Se kg^{-1} will provide an adequate and safe level in animal feed. Thus, it is important to reduce high selenium concentrations in harvested plant material to a safe level for animal consumption by blending the material with other forage that does not contain selenium. Using blended selenium-rich plant material as supplemental animal feed or as part of a daily ration may be a potential disposal option for plants used for phytoremediation of selenium.

Selenium absorption from selenium-enriched plant material varies among animals. In one study, lambs fed only freshly cut canola used in phytoremediation of selenium had higher selenium concentrations in selected tissues and blood (**Fig. 2**). In another study, as part of their daily ration cows were fed dried canola that was previously used for phytoremediation of selenium. Milk, blood, and urine were evaluated for the presence of selenium; the levels were higher in blood and urine but not significantly higher in milk. This was an important finding since increased levels of selenium in the milk would likely have produced a disagreeable aroma. These preliminary animal studies indicate that phyto-utilization may be a safe and successful disposal option for plants used in selenium phytoremediation.

Phytoremediation technology must integrate both phytoextraction and phyto-utilization. The long-term success of selenium phytoremediation as a cost-effective and environmentally friendly technology depends not only on governmental policies but also on user acceptance. Moreover, a grower who uses phytoremediation on soils laden with selenium will eventually need a disposal option for the crop.

For background information *see* ANIMAL FEEDS; PLANT MINERAL NUTRITION; SELENIUM; SOIL CHEMISTRY; TOXICOLOGY in the McGraw-Hill Encyclopedia of Science & Technology.   Gary Bañuelos

Bibliography. G. S. Bañuelos et al., Phytoremediation of selenium laden soils: A new technology, *J. Soil Water Conserv.*, 52:426–430, 1997; H. F. Mayland, Selenium in plant and animal nutrition, in W. T. Frankenberger, Jr., and S. Benson (eds.), *Selenium in the Environment*, 1994; N. Terry and A. Zayed, Phytoremediation of selenium, in W. T. Frankenberger, Jr., and R. A. Engberg (eds.), *Environmental Chemistry of Selenium*, Marcel Dekker, New York, 1998.

Precedence effect (hearing)

Almost all organisms live in reverberant environments in which a sound from a particular source is reflected from many surfaces (**Fig. 1**). Even outdoors the ground is a significant reflective surface. Thus, sounds from sources are combined with their reflections before reaching a listener's ears. Most of the time, interest focuses on the sound from the source, and not from reflective surfaces. An organism would not survive if it ran from, pursued, or tried to mate or communicate with a reflective sound instead of the sound coming from the source. Thus, from an evolutionary point of view, it is not surprising that humans are good at processing sounds in highly reflective environments. The ability to process sound from the source even when there are significant reflections is called the precedence effect. The term is derived from the observation that the sound from the source reaches a listener before that from any reflection (Fig. 1). The fact that humans process sounds from sources in reflective environments suggests that the first-arriving sound from the source takes precedence over those arriving later from reflections.

To understand how the auditory system processes sounds and their reflections, it is important to realize that the location of a sound source can be determined entirely by the sound produced by the source. This can be verified by closing one's eyes and listening to sounds in the surroundings. In most cases, it is possible to determine the spatial location of the

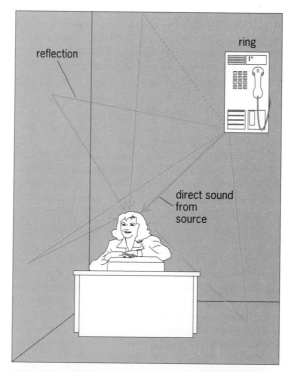

Fig. 1. Paths traveled by sound from a ringing telephone. Sound travels directly to the listener, but is also reflected from the many surfaces. These reflected sound paths are longer and, therefore, reflected sound reaches the listener after the sound traveling directly from the source.

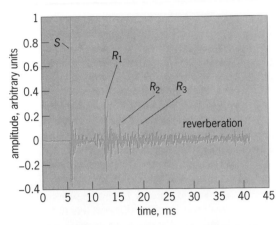

Fig. 2. Recording of sound in a classroom, displaying the sound from the source (S), the early reflections (R_1, R_2, and R_3), and reverberation arriving at the recording microphone. Reverberation decays over time as sound from the reflections dies out.

originating source based entirely on the acoustic information reaching one's ears. That is, perception of sound makes it possible to locate the sources of sound in the three-dimensional spatial world.

Reflections and reverberation. **Figure 2** displays the waveform of a sound recorded in a classroom. The sound was a brief click played from a loudspeaker located 1 m (3 ft) from the front wall. A recording microphone was located another meter into the room, and the figure displays the recorded sound. The early peaks, early reflections, are those from reflective surfaces near the recording microphone (such as the front wall). Later reflections rebound off the room surfaces several times and combine to produce a background sound, called reverberation, that slowly decays over time. The time it takes the reverberant level to decline by 60 decibels (dB) from the level of the originating sound is called reverberation time. Rooms with short reverberation times are less reflective than those with long reverberation times.

The study of precedence relates to the study of how early reflections perceptually interact with the sound from the source. Understanding precedence is of interest to both hearing scientists and architectural acousticians. Hearing scientists want to understand how the auditory nervous system processes sound and its reflections. Architectural acousticians want to build enclosed spaces that have some, but not too much, reflected sound. Some reflected sound helps establish an acoustic space in which it is easy and pleasant to listen to speech and music. If the reflective sounds are too strong relative to those coming from sources, both the intelligibility and the perceived pleasantness of sounds from the originating sources are compromised.

Perception of reflected sound. A reflective sound is an attenuated, time-delayed, spatially separated, and similar (correlated) version of the originating sound. If the reflected sound is perceived as separate from the sound coming from the source, the reflection forms an audible echo. Even when a reflection is not perceived as an echo, the sound from the source combined with that from reflections can be perceived as different from the originating sound. The reflected sound may alter the perceived quality (timbre) of the originating sound. The reflected sound may also make the spatial location of the originating sound source appear less focused (more diffuse) than when the originating source produced the sound in the absence of any reflections.

Characteristics of the effect. In cases of precedence, a reflected sound is not perceived as an echo, that is, separate from the originating sound. In this case there is fusion of the source and reflected sound so that a single sound is perceived. In addition, the perceived location of the sound from the source combined with reflected sounds is dominated by the location of the sound source (localization dominance). The ability to process changes in the location of the source sound is not significantly disrupted by reflections (localization discrimination suppression). That is, even when the perception of the sound from the source plus those from reflections is clearly different from that provided by the sound from the source alone, fusion, localization dominance, and localization discrimination suppression occur. These three characteristics define the precedence effect. Precedence allows humans to process the sound from a source and identify its spatial location with a high degree of accuracy, even in reflective environments.

Information suppression. In most acoustic environments, a brief sound must be separated from its reflections by at least 5–10 milliseconds in order for the reflection to be perceived as an echo and not be perceptually fused with the source. It is within this same time period that changes in the location of a reflection appear to have little effect on the perceived location of the source. For sounds of longer duration, it may take as long as 50 ms before the reflected sound is perceived as fully separated from the originating source sound. These effects are often explained by assuming that information about the location of a reflection is suppressed for several milliseconds following the presentation of the source sound. Several neural circuits in the brain appear to show this suppressive or inhibitory influence of the first-arriving neural signal on later-arriving signals. Thus, these circuits may be part of neural networks that make the precedence effect possible.

Buildup and breakdown of fusion. In the laboratory a simulation of a source and its reflection is often used to study precedence (**Fig. 3**). In a room designed to have very few natural reflections (an anechoic room), a brief sound (a click) is delivered from one loudspeaker and a few milliseconds later an identical click is delivered from a different loudspeaker. The lead click serves as a simulation of the sound source, and the lagging click, which originates from a different location, is a simulated reflection. Under these conditions, the two clicks are often fused into a single auditory percept at the location of

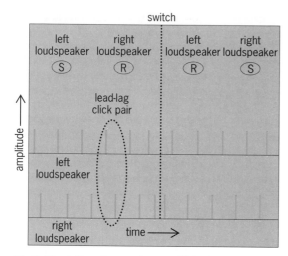

switch

left loudspeaker | right loudspeaker | left loudspeaker | right loudspeaker
Ⓢ | Ⓡ | Ⓡ | Ⓢ

lead-lag click pair

left loudspeaker

right loudspeaker   time ⟶

amplitude ⟶

Fig. 3. Simulation of a sound source (*S*; lead sound is on the left before the switch) and a reflection (*R*; lag sound is on the left after the switch). Lead-lag click pair can be repeated (time axis is not drawn to scale), and after several repetitions the locations of lead and lag sounds can be reversed.

the lead click (source), and changes in the perceived location of the lead click are not significantly altered by changes in the location of the lag click (reflection). Thus, this simulation allows scientists to study fusion, localization dominance, and localization discrimination suppression.

If the lead-lag click pair is repeated at a slow rate (Fig. 3), two interesting effects occur. First, fusion of the source and reflection becomes stronger as the number of repetitions increases up to about three to five repetitions. Thus, there is a buildup of fusion with repeated repetitions of the lead-lag click pair. In some special cases, fusion of the source and reflection disappears after a change is introduced after several presentations of the lead-lag click pair. For instance, after six presentations of the lead-lag click pair the lead and lag clicks form a strongly fused image perceived at the location of the source. If, between the sixth and seventh presentations, the lead and lag switch spatial locations (that is, the loudspeaker originally delivering the lead now delivers the lag and vice versa; Fig. 3), fusion no longer occurs. That is, immediately after the switch, listeners detect both the lead and lag clicks as two separate sound sources. This breakdown of fusion lasts for a few more lead-lag presentations after the switch until buildup of fusion once more occurs, at which time a single fused image is perceived at the new location of the source. Thus, prior experience with a sound source and its reflection clearly has a pronounced effect on fusion, as well as on localization dominance and localization discrimination suppression. The recent discovery of the buildup and breakdown of precedence suggests that precedence is a complicated phenomenon revealing an auditory system that responds dynamically to sounds and their reflections. The ability to adapt to changes in the acoustic environment may provide additional advantages for processing sounds and their reflections in

the complex acoustic world.

For background information *see* ANECHOIC CHAMBER; ARCHITECTURAL ACOUSTICS; HEARING (HUMAN); PHYSIOLOGICAL ACOUSTICS; REFLECTION OF SOUND; REVERBERATION in the McGraw-Hill Encyclopedia of Science & Technology.   William A. Yost

Bibliography. J. Blauert, *Spatial Hearing*, MIT Press, Cambridge, MA, 1997; R. Litovsky et al., The precedence effect: A review, *J. Acous. Soc. Amer.*, 106:1633–1654, 1999; W. A. Yost and R. H. Dye, Binaural psychophysics, *Seminars in Hearing: Binaural Issues in Clinical and Rehabilitative Audiology*, 18:321–344, 1997; P. M. Zuerk, The precedence effect, in W. A. Yost and G. Gourevitch (eds.), *Directional Hearing*, pp. 85–105, Springer-Verlag, New York, 1987.

Primate behavior

In primate societies, correctly assessing genetic similarities among organisms is fundamental to the interpretation of their behavior and other interactions occurring within these groups. Levels of similarity have traditionally been inferred from behavioral observations. While maternity is possible to assess based on observations of pregnancies and observations at parturition or during lactation, paternity has been more difficult to infer. Theories concerning the evolution and adaptiveness of some aspects of social behavior have proven challenging to evaluate because of the difficulty in reliably determining paternity in free-ranging populations of primates. Male reproductive output was usually inferred from rates of sexual activity, but most researchers now agree that this is not a good predictor of number of offspring sired. Matings may be discreet and difficult to observe, cuckoldry may occur, and some matings may not result in conception.

Genetic associations. Protein electrophoresis has been an important tool for determining genetic associations within animal populations. This technique essentially isolates different proteins according to charge and size. Variations in mobility of the same protein among individuals reflect underlying allele differences, and determine levels of similarity by the presence of shared alleles. However, these proteins tend to be monomorphic (usually only 10–15% of them are variable), and consequently they are not well separated by the procedure and have limited resolving power. For example, analyses of allozyme loci usually underestimate the levels of extrapair matings. More recently, advances in the field of molecular biology have resulted in techniques that allow assessment of genetic variability and similarity between individuals, populations, and species by scoring differences and associations directly from the deoxyribonucleic acid (DNA), and not from DNA-coded products. Among the most common procedures that have had an impact on primatological studies are the restriction fragment length polymorphism (RFLP), microsatellite, and mitochondrial DNA analyses. These terms refer to the specific kind of genetic marker being studied. Different markers target different parts of the organism's genome; because of differing evolutionary rates, and the manner of transmission from parents to offspring, these markers may be used to answer ecological and evolutionary questions. Other genetic markers have also been targeted for the study of natural populations, but the three described here are the markers of choice because they are accessible, highly variable, and easy to interpret.

Restriction fragment length polymorphism. In this procedure, also referred to as DNA fingerprinting, DNA strands are cut with a particular set of enzymes called restriction enzymes. These enzymes are able to recognize a specific sequence of nucleotides (usually four to six bases in length) and cut the DNA at a targeted location containing that sequence. This produces a large number of DNA fragments of different sizes, which are then separated using electrophoresis. Specific fragments are then identified using a series of probes that recognize a sequence of tandem repeats (which consist of repetitive units of about 10–100 nucleotides). Pedigree analysis reveals that these bands are inherited in a mendelian fashion (that is, one copy of the genome from each parent). In this way, paternity can be assessed since all the bands present in the offspring can be traced to either the mother or the father. This method has proven useful to determine paternity in primates. However, it is rather impractical in the study of natural populations for the following reasons: (1) It requires large amounts of genomic DNA (which are not easy to obtain from wild animals). (2) DNA from all individuals under study should be run in the same gel for comparison. (3) Most importantly, since individual fragments cannot be assigned to specific genes, it does not permit formal genotyping.

Paternity determination is important both for the management of captive colonies and for the testing of certain sociobiological hypotheses. For example, in one study of ring-tailed lemurs (*Lemur catta*) in a semi-free-ranging colony, fingerprinting analysis was used to investigate the role of female selection to avoid inbreeding. For this study it was important to demonstrate the degree of genetic similarity in all possible male-female pairs and the identities of all pairs that reproduce. The parentage information obtained revealed that females always mated with males likely to share 25% or fewer genes, or with the least-related male. There was no evidence of any female reproducing with either a son or a matrilineal nephew. This behavior is viewed as the trigger for the evolution of male dispersal. In the wild, ring-tailed lemurs live in groups that include several males and several females. Males migrate annually between groups, while females tend to remain in the group where they were born (philopatric). There is intense competition for estrous females. In the study of the ring-tailed lemurs, introduced males which were less related to the resident females were able to impregnate a large number of females even though they remained bottom-ranked in the male hierarchy. It seems that the avoidance of inbreeding overrides the dominance relations among males to influence male mating success.

Microsatellites. The microsatellites, or short tandem repeat loci, are a series of repeated motifs of a two to six base pair sequence which are scattered throughout the nuclear genome. The alleles differ by the number of motif copies. They are inherited in a mendelian fashion, which permits unambiguous parentage exclusion, as well as making more accurate assessments about the population structure and other parameters such as population subdivision and levels of gene flow. Most individuals are heterozygous, and unique allele combinations are common, allowing distinctive profiles to be built for all individuals. Microsatellites are studied by targeting the specific section of the DNA where they are located. With the development of the polymerase chain reaction (PCR) technique, it is possible to make multiple copies of specific sections of DNA. One advantage of microsatellites is the ability to make multiple copies of the targeted sequence, making it possible to use small amounts of DNA for study. Such DNA may be obtained from saliva, semen, hair, bone, tooth, or fecal material. This is particularly critical in primatological studies where it is necessary to collect genetic material noninvasively from the animals without disturbing them or disrupting the habituation process. Trapping may result in mortality, which is certainly a major concern for studies on endangered species.

Several studies have used microstallites to test different hypotheses about the evolution of social structure in primates. A study of chimpanzees (*Pan troglodytes*) in the Gombe National Park in Tanzania has shown that males tend to share a higher number of alleles per locus than females, indicating that males are in fact more related to one another than are females. The kin selection theory predicts that the degree of relatedness among males, who are philopatric, should be substantially different from that of females, who usually disperse at adolescence; and in fact, that seems to be the case. It is believed that closely related males form a kin group that cooperates to defend a territory, increase access to females, and consequently increase their reproductive success. Nonetheless, in a different study on west African chimpanzees from the Taï Forest in the Ivory Coast, it was shown that females also seek to mate outside their social group. Of 21 mother-infant pairs studied, the microsatellite study showed that at least 7 infants must have been sired by males from other communities. In this case, it seems that furtive extragroup mating may be the only way for females to exercise mate choice, without losing the protection provided by their male social partners. This is not what the kin selection theory would predict.

Another study that uses microsatellite markers to assess levels of similarity involves the toque macaques (*Macaca sinica*) from Sri Lanka. These animals typically live in multimale or multifemale groups; but unlike the chimpanzees, the females are philopatric, while the males always migrate out of the group. Paternity analysis in this group revealed that the offspring produced by a female usually consists of half-siblings because few males father more than one offspring with a particular female. Furthermore, it was found that the social unit of macaques does not correspond to the reproductive unit and that fertilizations by nonresident males were indeed common.

Mitochondrial DNA. The mitochondrial DNA is a circular molecule which in primates is about 16,500 nucleotides in length. This piece of DNA resides in the cell's mitochondria. It has several genes, which are mostly involved in the electronic transport and oxidative phosphorylation of the mitochondrion. This is a fast-evolving molecule, and most importantly, for genetic marker purposes, it is transmitted predominantly through the maternal line. This allows for construction of a much clearer picture of the evolutionary relationships among maternal groups, without the complications resulting from a recombination of genomes, as with the nuclear genes. Mitochondrial DNA studies are performed by sequencing specific segments of the molecule and then directly comparing the similarities and differences among the individual DNA samples studied. Mitochondrial DNA has been most useful in discerning patterns of subdivision and geographic structure among different populations, as well as helping to determine the evolutionary relationships between different species.

Although mitochondrial DNA is most commonly used to determine patterns of interpopulation variation, sometimes it has been used to test certain socioecological hypotheses within a single population. In a study on social relationships among chimpanzees from the Kibale Forest in Uganda, analysis of mitochondrial DNA showed that although males in one community may be more closely related to each other than to members of other communities, coalition partnerships formed between pairs that are not maternal brothers. This is inconsistent with some behavioral observations that suggest that bonds that develop through the juvenile and adolescent years between siblings should endure later in life. It seems that chimpanzee males in this community prefer to form bonds with other individuals with whom they share complementary goals and abilities, rather than with their close relatives as would be predicted by kin selection theory.

Mitochondrial DNA has proven particularly useful in determining levels of subdivision within species and geographic affinities between such groupings. By comparing different mitochondrial DNA sequences from several individuals, it is possible to obtain a picture of how distinct different populations arose from one another, and how genetically related they are to one another. For example, an analysis of how the mitochondrial DNA variation is partitioned among different populations of the common chimpanzee proved to support the hypothesis that there are at least three distinct subspecies distributed across equatorial Africa. This study suggests that the westernmost group is distinct enough to be given full species status. Furthermore, in a recent study it was shown that chimpanzee populations from Nigeria are more closely related to the western group than to the geographically closer central subspecies. This suggests that there are at least two major groups of common chimpanzees and that the geographic split occurs somewhere in Cameroon.

The use of molecular markers in primatological studies has allowed clarification of some fundamental questions regarding social structure, and evolutionary relationships among these animals. This information has important implications for conservation efforts in that it allows for the development of more informed management plans. For example, genetic information can help to establish captive breeding programs that more accurately reflect the natural reproductive patterns of the animals involved, or it can help define the boundaries of real social and reproductive units in the wild, which can then be translated into the design of more effective natural areas of protection.

For background information *see* DEOXYRIBONUCLEIC ACID (DNA); ELECTROPHORESIS; GENETICS; MITOCHONDRIA; PHYSICAL ANTHROPOLOGY; RESTRICTION ENZYME; SOCIOBIOLOGY in the McGraw-Hill Encyclopedia of Science & Technology.

Juan Carlos Morales

Bibliography. P. Gagneux, C. Boesch, and D. S. Woodruff, Female reproductive strategies, paternity and community structure in wild West African chimpanzees, *Anim. Behav.*, 57:19–32, 1999; M. K. Gonder et al., A new West African chimpanzee subspecies?, *Nature*, 388:337, 1997; B. Keane, W. P. J. Dittus, and D. J. Melnick, Paternity assessment in wild groups of toque macaques *Macaca sinica* at Polonnaruwa, Sri Lanka using molecular markers, *Mol. Ecol.*, 6:267–282, 1997; P. A. Morin et al., Kin selection, social structure, gene flow, and the evolution of chimpanzees, *Science*, 265:1193–1201, 1994; M. E. Pereira and M. L. Weiss, Female mate choice, male migration, and the threat of infanticide in ring-tailed lemurs, *Behav. Ecol. Sociobiol.*, 28:141–152, 1991.

Prospecting

Electromagnetic geophysical prospecting is performed to minimize the number of expensive drill holes in minerals exploration. In environmental studies, electromagnetic systems are useful in providing information between monitor wells, or in areas where drilling may be environmentally dangerous.

Electromagnetic systems with one or two frequencies have been used extensively in prospecting and are adequate in simple geology with resistive host rocks, but for complex geology and conductive host rocks broadband systems become necessary. Earth resistivity values obtained with electromagnetic systems are influenced by water salinity, mineralization content, porosity, and changes in structure. Various rock types have a corresponding difference in resistivity, allowing electromagnetic methods to accurately map subsurface geology. Developments since 1980 have seen the evolution of new time- and frequency-domain electromagnetic systems that gather large amounts of data in a short amount of time, and provide information on depth, orientation, and size of both conductive and resistive features beneath the surface. Fast, multichannel geophysical systems are a direct result of the development of the personal computer.

Controlled source audio-frequency magnetotellurics. Controlled source audio-frequency magnetotellurics (CSAMT) is a relatively new, broadband, high-resolution, frequency-domain, electromagnetic sounding, and profiling system. CSAMT is used for mapping subsurface geology and structure, and in

exploration for massive sulfides, geothermal sources, hydrocarbons, and potable water. Recently CSAMT has been used for environmental and engineering applications such as mapping acid mine drainage, detecting leaks in waste containment ponds, tracing fluid flow for in-situ leaching operations, and determining subsurface structure for foundation studies.

CSAMT uses a fixed grounded dipole or horizontal loop as an artificial signal source. It is similar to the natural source magnetotelluric (MT) and audio-frequency magnetotelluric (AMT) methods which use natural electromagnetic fields generated by lightning and currents in the magnetosphere as the signal source. The artificial source for CSAMT provides a stable signal, resulting in higher precision and faster measurements than are obtainable with natural source measurements in the same frequency band. Placement of the transmitter dipole can complicate interpretation and put logistical restrictions on the survey. However, in most practical field situations, these drawbacks are not serious, and the method has proven particularly effective in mapping the subsurface in the range of 20–2000 m (70–6500 ft).

The grounded wire or loop used as a transmitting antenna for CSAMT typically has dimensions ≥1 km (≥3300 ft), and is placed at a large distance from the receiver (for example, ≥5 km or 3 mi). To determine the resistivity of the ground, the receiver measures the electric field (E-field) with a grounded dipole oriented parallel to the transmitter wire, and the perpendicular magnetic field (H-field) is measured with a ferrite or Mu-metal cored magnetic field sensor. The frequency range for typical surveys varies from 0.125 Hz to 8 kHz, with data gathered in binary steps (1, 2, 4, 8, 16 Hz, and so on). Resistivity values are calculated from the measured parameters for each frequency using the frequency (f) and the ratio of the orthogonal E- and H-fields.

Depth of exploration is proportional to the square root of the ratio of the resistivity of the ground and the frequency of the transmitted signal, and is independent of the array geometry. Inversion programs are used to calculate changes of resistivity with depth and to provide sections that map geology and structure.

Transient electromagnetics. The transient electromagnetic (TEM) technique, which is sometimes called time-domain EM (TDEM) or pulse EM (PEM), is a broadband time-domain system which is used for vertical depth sounding, profiling, and downhole measurements. In addition to base metal, hydrocarbon, and geothermal exploration, TEM is used in mapping structure and lithology, searching for sources of ground water and ground-water contamination, mapping buried waste, detecting unexploded ordinance, and for other environmental and engineering applications.

Basic TEM geophysical survey equipment consists of a high-current transmitter that drives a large loop placed on the ground and a magnetic field sensor placed inside or outside the loop, or down a drill hole, depending upon the application. Subsurface

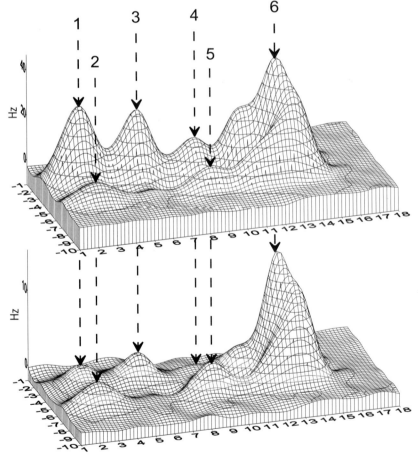

Key:
1. wood boxes, one with ferrous metals
2. wood box, mixed metals
3. wood box, nonferrous metals
4. 55-gal drum, concrete
5. 55-gal drum, foam
6. combined anomaly from dense pack metal and two filing cabinets

Fig. 1. The upper plot is a plan view of the average decay magnitudes between 0.2563 and 0.8045 ms. The lower plot shows the plan view for the average magnitudes between 0.845 and 2.539 ms. For comparison, the vertical scales have been adjusted so that the largest anomaly (6) is approximately the same in each plot. The relative differences in magnitude between the two plots provide information concerning the source of the anomalies.

information is obtained by monitoring the Earth's response to a magnetic pulse that is generated by an abrupt turn-off of current in the transmitter loop. Receiver measurements are made during the transmitter off time when only the decaying secondary fields are present. Typical time intervals measured on the decay waveforms for mining applications can vary from tens of microseconds to hundreds of milliseconds. For shallow engineering and environmental applications, time windows can vary from fractions of microseconds to 1 or 2 ms.

Resistivity calculations are a complex combination of the current in and the enclosed area of the transmitter loop, the effective area of the receiver antenna, and the received voltage at a specific time during the signal decay.

The depth of exploration in a vertical sounding configuration is proportional to the square root of the product of the resistivity of the ground and the window time on the decay curve. The depth of exploration can vary from 1 m to over 1000 m (3 ft to over 3300 ft), depending upon transmitter loop size, available power from the transmitter, and ambient noise levels. A typical guideline for maximum depth of exploration is two times the dimension of the transmitter loop. For example, for a square loop 100 m (330 ft) on a side, the maximum depth to sound would be 200 m (660 ft) under normal circumstances. For small transmitter loops, say 20 m (66 ft) on a side, the maximum depth of exploration is approximately four to five times the loop size.

Environmental and engineering applications usually require TEM systems that provide transmitter turn-off times and waveform sampling rates on the order of 1 μs in order to obtain the necessary shallow resolution.

TEM vertical sounding arrays produce essentially the same type of data as the CSAMT method, especially for a layered earth environment. However, due to the need for a large transmitter loop to explore at great depths, the effect of lateral changes in resistivity is smoothed with TEM.

New developments. Some of the important recent advances in the evolution of TEM and CSAMT exploration are the development of sophisticated computer-controlled transmitter and receiver systems, three-axis sensors, and multidimensional modeling and inversion. High-accuracy analog-to-digital converters have expanded the dynamic range of receivers, providing improved low-noise data acquisition. Low-cost memory permits recording and storage of continuous waveforms for more advanced processing in the office. Fast microprocessors and integrated circuits are being used to increase sample rates, provide higher-density data, and permit high-resolution shallow data acquisition.

A three-axis TEM downhole probe has been developed which is mainly used to locate conductive (ore) bodies that were missed by the drill hole. Before the three-axis probe was developed, measurements had to be made from four different transmitter loops on the surface to locate an off-hole body. With

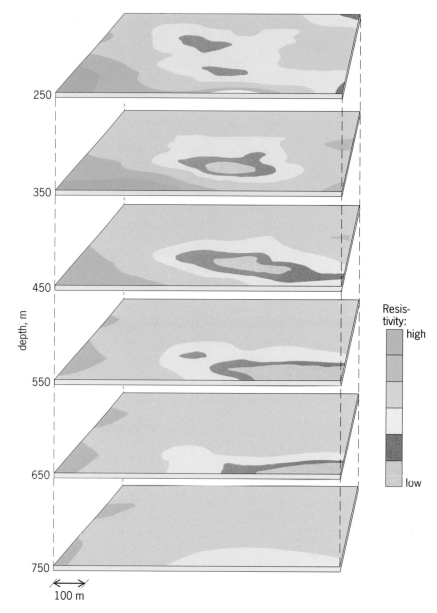

Fig. 2. Controlled source audio-frequency magnetotellurics has plan-view slices at constant depths showing downward migration of the leachate solution.

a three-axis receiver system, measurements need be made only from one surface transmitter loop. Consequently, downhole surveys are run more efficiently, and three-axis downhole TEM measurements are becoming a worldwide standard.

Very fast sampling TEM equipment is being used for detecting buried metallic waste and mapping nearsurface structure. Research into the location of unexploded ordinance is being carried out using three-axis fast sampling TEM systems. It may be possible in the near future to determine depth of burial as well as type and orientation of unexploded ordinance.

Field examples. In addition to standard mineral exploration, TEM has been used successfully to find buried metallic waste (**Fig. 1**). The eddy currents set up in metallic objects take substantially longer to decay than the earth or rock response. Therefore, a TEM system can be used as a deep-sounding metal detector by examining the data acquired after the background earth response has decayed into noise.

CSAMT has been used for a combined mining and environmental application (**Fig. 2**). These data are from a copper recovery project in a working mine in the southwestern United States. The target was a large volume of leachate solution. The location and approximate depth of the solution were unknown. CSAMT was used since the receiver dipole size (which determines lateral resolution) has no effect on the depth of investigation. Most other electrical methods require changes in transmitter sizes and separations in order to increase depth, but CSAMT requires only changes in transmitted frequency. Despite the extensive depth, CSAMT accurately located the conductive leachate solution (low resistivity), avoiding an environmental problem and permitting economic recovery of the copper-rich solution.

For background information *see* GEOCHEMICAL PROSPECTING; GEOELECTRICITY; GEOPHYSICAL EXPLORATION; PROSPECTING; ROCK, ELECTRICAL PROPERTIES OF in the McGraw-Hill Encyclopedia of Science & Technology.   Kenneth L. Zonge

Bibliography. M. N. Nabighian (ed.), *Electromagnetic Methods in Applied Geophysics: Applications*, Society of Exploration Geophysicists, 1991; R. Van Blaricom (ed.), *Practical Geophysics II for the Exploration Geologist*, Northwest Mining Association, 1992.

Pulsar

Since the discovery of pulsars in the 1960s and their subsequent identification as rapidly rotating neutron stars, pulsars have provided a unique insight into the nature of physics at high energies and in extreme conditions.

Origin and properties. A neutron star is formed in a supernova explosion, which results when a massive star runs out of fuel at the end of its life. A neutron star is the remnant of such an explosion and is extremely dense, weighing as much as 3×10^{33} grams (6×10^{30} lb, 1.5 times as much as the Sun) but having only a 10-km (6-mi) radius (about the size of Manhattan). The combination of high mass and small size results in an extremely large gravitational field, estimated to be about 10^{11} times that on Earth.

A newly formed neutron star can be sent rapidly spinning in the supernova explosion, and such a star can have a magnetic field many orders of magnitude larger than those found on Earth. In some cases, the spinning, highly magnetized neutron star generates enough electric potential to accelerate charges from the surface of the star, resulting in a beam of nonthermal radio emission which rotates with the star. An observer sees this rotating beam as a series of radio pulses as the beam sweeps across the line of sight, similar to the rotating beacon of a lighthouse.

Such an object is called a pulsar.

The Crab pulsar, located in the Crab supernova remnant which was formed in the supernova explosion seen in 1054 by Chinese astronomers, is the youngest known pulsar and is considered to be the prototypical young pulsar, with a spin period of 33 ms. More typical pulsars have much longer spin periods (about 1 s). However, there is a class of old, recycled pulsars which have obtained very fast rotation rates through the transfer of angular momentum from stellar companions throughout their lifetimes. These pulsars usually have spin periods of a few milliseconds, so the name millisecond pulsars is applied to this class of objects. The fastest millisecond pulsar known has a spin period of 1.6 ms, corresponding to 642 rotations per second.

Most pulsars that exhibit detectable radio emission are not detectable in other radiation wavebands, since the radiation that is produced falls off in brightness steeply with increasing radiation frequency. However, in some cases (such as the Crab pulsar), the pulsar can be detected in multiple wavelengths. In fact, a relatively new class of pulsars has been found, called anomalous x-ray pulsars (AXPs), which show only x-ray emission and no detectable radio emission. These pulsars are characterized by long spin periods and very large magnetic fields.

Physics in extreme conditions. As a pulsar spins, it loses energy through electromagnetic radiation and a plasma wind. Thus, although the spin period of the pulsar is very steady, it does spin down over a long period of time as it loses energy. By invoking a simple dipolar model of the magnetic field and by making some other assumptions, an observer can convert a measured pulse period and period derivative (rate of change of period) for a pulsar into physical parameters, such as age of the pulsar, surface magnetic field strength, and energy loss rate. For typical pulsars, a value of 10^{12} gauss (10^8 tesla) is not uncommon for the surface magnetic field strength. More indirect means can be used to probe the interior structure of neutron stars, which are thought to have densities in excess of 10^{14} grams per cubic centimeter.

These kinds of magnitudes indicate the value of studying such systems: nothing approaching these conditions can be produced in terrestrial physics laboratories, and it is only through studying these kinds of systems that some theoretical models in physics can be tested. A prime example of this advantage was the confirmation of general relativity as the correct gravitational theory through the use of radio-pulse measurements of a binary-pulsar system.

Parkes Multibeam Pulsar Survey. A number of searches for new pulsars have been undertaken at a variety of observatories using different instruments and techniques. By 1997, thirty years after the discovery of the first pulsar, about 750 pulsars were known and had been cataloged. In mid-1997, an international collaboration involving research groups in the United Kingdom, Australia, United States, and Italy undertook a new high-frequency (1400-MHz)

Fig. 1. The 64-m (210-ft) radio telescope in Parkes, Australia. The Parkes Multibeam Pulsar Survey is being conducted with this telescope using the multibeam receiver, located in the focus cabin of the telescope.

survey of the southern Galactic plane using a new instrument mounted on the 64-m (210-ft) radio telescope in Parkes, Australia (**Fig. 1**). This survey was designed to search the range from -100 to $+50°$ in galactic longitude within $5°$ of the Galactic plane.

The new instrument which has motivated this survey is a multibeam receiver and is capable of observing 13 distinct parts of the sky at once, thereby increasing surveying capacity by a factor of 13. This is equivalent to having 13 separate telescopes the size of the Parkes telescope for use in the pulsar search effort. This new survey, called the Parkes Multibeam Pulsar Survey (PM Survey), is about seven times more sensitive than previous surveys conducted at this radio frequency.

The high frequency of the Parkes Multibeam Pulsar Survey also has an important advantage over previous searches at more traditional lower radio frequencies (400 MHz), where pulsars are typically much brighter. In the Galactic plane, radio-wave propagation effects such as dispersive pulse delays and multipath radio scattering of pulses severely limit sensitivity to pulsed emission at low frequencies. These effects are worse for more distant pulsars, since there is then a great deal of interstellar dispersive and scattering plasma between the observer and the pulsar. The effect of the plasma is a frequency-dependent pulse delay. This delay depends on the integrated electron density along the line of sight, which is called the dispersion measure. Thus, the Parkes Multibeam Pulsar Survey is the first large-scale one to be sensitive to distant pulsars in the Galactic plane, where there are large dispersion measures (**Fig. 2**).

In early 2000, with 75% of the survey completed, the Parkes Multibeam Pulsar Survey had already discovered over 500 new pulsars, making it by far the most successful pulsar survey ever conducted (**Fig. 3**). The survey is expected to double the known population of radio pulsars by the time it is completed.

The information from the survey is made available soon after a pulsar is found and its spin parameters are determined. This information, along with the details and current status of the Parkes Multibeam Pulsar Survey, is available on the World Wide Web.

Prospects. The Parkes Multibeam Pulsar Survey not only provides a significant source of information for statistical studies of the pulsar population, but also has discovered a number of interesting individual pulsar systems, including several unusual and interesting binary systems, a large number of young pulsars, and two pulsars that have magnetic field strengths larger than any previously known radio pulsar. These kinds of pulsar systems are interesting objects to study in their own right.

For instance, one pulsar with a record-breaking magnetic field also has a very long spin period (4 s). This combination of properties suggests that it might somehow be related to the anomalous x-ray pulsars, which have similar spin periods to this pulsar but emit only x-rays and no detectable radio emission. The detection of radio emission from this pulsar has been used to rule out a recently proposed model of the pulsar emission mechanism which predicted

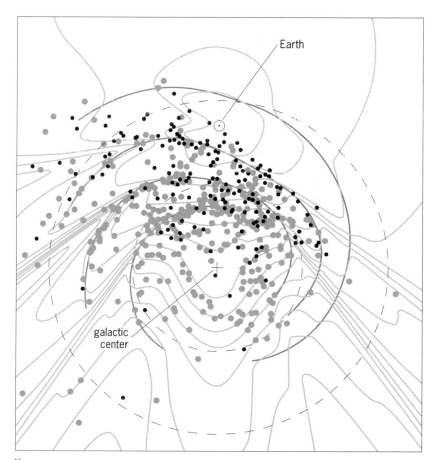

Key:

- newly detected pulsars   — contours of constant dispersion measure
- redetected pulsars   — spiral arms

Fig. 2. Projection onto the Galactic plane of the distribution of newly discovered pulsars from the Parkes Multibeam Pulsar Survey and previously known pulsars redetected in the survey. Contours of constant dispersion measure (the integrated plasma density along the line of sight) and the location of Galactic spiral arms in the Milky Way Galaxy are shown.

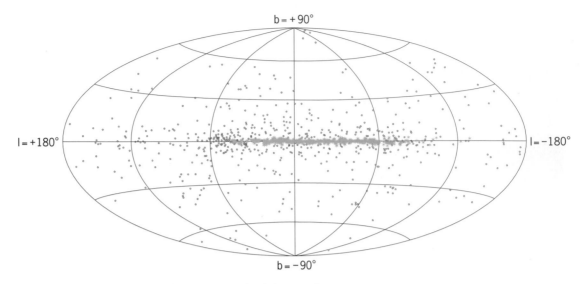

b = +90°

l = +180°   l = −180°

b = −90°

Key: · Parkes Multibeam Pulsar Survey   · previously known pulsars

Fig. 3. Distribution in galactic coordinates of new pulsars from the Parkes Multibeam Pulsar Survey and all previously known pulsars.

that radio emission should be suppressed in such a high-magnetic-field pulsar.

Followup studies of all these new discoveries are under way, and investigation into areas such as the pulsar spin properties of the sample, their spatial distribution in the Milky Way Galaxy, their polarized emission properties, and the interstellar environments in which these pulsars lie promises to provide an array of important scientific results as the Parkes survey progresses.

For background information *see* CRAB NEBULA; NEUTRON STAR; PULSAR; RADIO ASTRONOMY; RADIO TELESCOPE in the McGraw-Hill Encyclopedia of Science & Technology.   Fronefield Crawford III

Bibliography. F. Camilo et al., The Parkes Multibeam Pulsar Survey, *Proceedings of IAU Colloquium 177: Pulsar Astronomy—2000 and Beyond*, ASP Conference Series, 202, 3, 2000; A. G. Lyne et al., The Parkes Multibeam Pulsar Survey: PSR J1811−1736—A Pulsar in a Highly Eccentric Binary System, *Mon. Notices Roy. Astron. Soc.*, 312:698, 2000; A. G. Lyne and F. Graham-Smith, *Pulsar Astronomy*, Cambridge University Press, New York, 1998; R. N. Manchester and J. H. Taylor, *Pulsars*, W. H. Freeman, San Francisco, 1977.

Quantum teleportation

To be able to travel from one place to another instantly and over arbitrary distances, or at least to move objects this way, is an ancient dream. The concept of teleportation is frequently utilized in the literature of science fiction to overcome limitations imposed on space travel by the laws of physics.

In the standard science fiction approach, the sender, Alice, scans the object to be teleported in order to read out all the information needed to describe it. She then sends that information to the receiver, Bob, who uses this information to reconstitute the object, not necessarily from the same material as that of the original. However, according to quantum mechanics, it is impossible to succeed in this way. If only one individual object is at hand, it is impossible to determine its quantum state by measurement. The quantum states represent all that can be known about the object, that is, all possible, in general probabilistic, predictions that can be made about future observations of the object.

Quantum entanglement. In fact, it is quantum mechanics that comes to the rescue and makes teleportation possible using a very deep feature of the theory, quantum entanglement. Entangled quantum states were introduced into the discussion of the foundations of quantum mechanics by Albert Einstein, Boris Podolsky, and Nathan Rosen in 1935. In the same year, Erwin Schrödinger introduced the notion of entanglement, which he called *the* essence of quantum mechanics.

In order to discuss entanglement, one specific case will be considered, and the possible experimental results will be examined (**Fig. 1**). There are many possible sources that can create many different sorts of entangled states. The source under consideration will be assumed to be the one used in the first teleportation experiment, which produced photons in a singlet polarization state. This means experimentally the following: Each one of the photons on its own is completely unpolarized. Therefore, neither photon is polarized initially, but as soon as one photon is measured, it randomly assumes one polarization and the other photon is instantly projected into the orthogonal polarization state, no matter how far the two are separated. The fact that these correlations

Fig. 1. Principle of quantum entanglement for two photons emitted by a source. Each photon travels to its own two-channel polarizer, each of which can be rotated around the respective beam direction. Independent of the orientation of the polarizer, each detector (H or V) has the same probability of registering a photon. If the two polarizers are oriented parallel, the two photons will always be registered in different detectors; that is, if one photon is registered in its H detector, the other is registered in its V detector, and vice versa.

cannot be understood through individual, albeit unknown, properties that each photon carries locally is the essence of Bell's theorem, and gives rise to the concept of nonlocality of quantum mechanics. From an information-theoretic point of view, the interesting feature of entanglement is that neither of the two photons carries any information on its own. All information is stored in joint properties. If one photon is measured, it assumes randomly a property and then, by necessity, the corresponding property of its partner is defined.

Concept of teleportation. It was first realized by Charles H. Bennett and his colleagues that entanglement can be utilized to make teleportation possible (**Fig. 2**). Alice, who is in possession of the teleportee photon in a particular quantum state, and Bob initially share an ancillary pair of entangled photons, say in the singlet state described above. Alice then subjects her teleportee photon and her member of the ancillary pair to a Bell measurement. A Bell measurement is designed in such a way that it projects the two photons into an entangled state even if they were previously unentangled. This is a very tricky procedure both conceptually and experimentally. Conceptually, it means that the measurement must be performed in such a way that it is not possible, even in principle, to determine from the measurement result which photon was the teleportee and which was the ancillary. They both have to lose their individ-

uality. The result of the measurement must reveal only how the two photons relate to each other. A Bell measurement has four possible results if the objects considered are defined in a two-dimensional Hilbert space just as is done to describe the photon's polarization. One of the four states is the singlet state discussed above. The other three states also define specific relations between the two photons, though different ones than those for the singlet state.

Alice therefore now knows how the teleportee photon relates to her ancillary one, and since she knows in which state the two ancillaries were produced and hence how these two relate to each other, she finally knows precisely how the teleportee relates to Bob's photon. More formally speaking, as a result of Alice's measurement Bob's photon is projected into a state which is uniquely related to the original state; the specific relationship is expressed by which of the four Bell states Alice obtained. Alice therefore informs Bob of her measurement result via a classical communication channel, and he, by applying a simple transformation on his photon, changes it into the original state.

In one of the four cases, Alice obtains the information that her two photons have been projected into the singlet state, the same state in which the ancillaries were produced. Then, she knows that Bob's photon is instantly projected into the original state; the transformation that Bob has to apply is a unitary transformation, that is, one that makes no change to his photon. That Bob's photon instantly becomes an exact replica of the original seems to violate relativity. Yet, while Alice knows instantly that Bob's photon, no matter how far away, is already an exact replica, she has to inform Bob of the Bell measurement result such that he can actually make use of the information it carries.

The result of the Bell measurement is not related at all to any properties that the original photon carries. Thus, that measurement does not reveal any information about its state. Therefore, the operation that Bob has to apply is also completely independent of any properties of the original photon. The reason that quantum measurement succeeds is that entanglement makes it possible to completely transfer the information an object carries without reading out this information.

Experimental realization. The experiment therefore faces a number of challenges: (1) how to produce the entangled photons, and (2) how to perform a Bell measurement for independent photons. In the first experimental realization, the entangled photons were produced in the process of spontaneous parametric downconversion. This is a second-order nonlinear process where a suitable crystal, in the experiment beta barium borate (BBO), is pumped with a beam of ultraviolet radiation. A photon from that beam has a very small probability to decay spontaneously into two photons which then are polarization-entangled in just the way necessary for

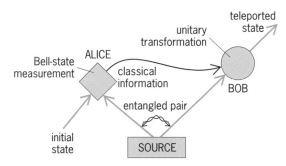

Fig. 2. Quantum teleportation procedure. Alice has an original particle in the initial state, and Alice and Bob also share an entangled pair. Alice then performs a Bell measurement and transmits the result of that measurement in the form of two classical bits to Bob who, by a simple unitary transformation, can turn his ancillary photon into an exact replica of the original. (*After D. Bouwmeester et al., Experimental quantum teleportation, Nature, 390:575–579, 1997*)

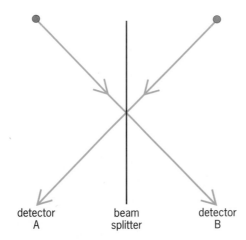

Fig. 3. Bell analysis using a 50/50 beam splitter.

the experiment. The more tricky part is the Bell measurement because, in essence, it requires that the two photons are registered such that all information about which was the teleportee photon and which the ancillary is irrevocably erased. This is a nontrivial requirement since the two photons are coming from different directions, they might arrive at different times, and so forth.

In the experiment, the Bell measurement was performed using a semireflecting mirror (**Fig. 3**), which acted as a 50/50 beam splitter. Two photons were incident onto the beam splitter, one from each side, and each one had the same probability of 50% to be either reflected or transmitted. If each of the two detectors in the outgoing beam registered a photon in coincidence, then no information existed as to which incoming photon was registered in which detector, and the two were projected into the entangled singlet state. Narrow-bandwidth filters in front of the detectors further served to erase any time information which could also serve to identify the photons.

In this experiment, only one of the four possible Bell states could be identified, the singlet state. This certainly reduced the efficiency of the procedure, though in those cases in which the two detectors at the Bell-state analyzer registered, teleportation worked with a fidelity escaping all possible classical explanation.

In another experiment, it was even possible to teleport a photon that was still entangled to another one. This is a rather curious situation because then the teleported photon does not yet carry any information. Its state will be determined by the measurement that Alice decides to perform on its twin brother. What all these experiments reveal is really that the quantum state is just a representation of the information that has been acquired. In the case of entanglement, it is only information on how objects relate to each other without any information on their individual properties. And in the case of teleportation, what happens is that Alice's observation changes the quantum state that Bob observes. In other words, what can be said about the situation

changes due to an observation by Alice. This gives very strong support to the Copenhagen interpretation of quantum mechanics.

Another experiment has demonstrated that it is possible to transfer the polarization state of one photon to another photon using a theoretical analogy to quantum teleportation, even though these two photons were entangled from the beginning and thus not independent. More recently, the teleportation of continuous variables has been demonstrated, instead of the discrete ones discussed above.

Prospects. While presently the teleportation distance is of the order of 1 m (3 ft), it should certainly be possible to extend the distance for photons to the order of a few tens of kilometers using optical fiber. It should also be possible to extend these procedures to more massive objects, in particular to atoms, for which entanglement has been shown to exist, and maybe someday to more massive bodies like macromolecules. There is a question as to the size of the largest bodies for which quantum entanglement can be implemented. This points to the experimental challenge as to the size of the largest bodies for which quantum phenomena can be seen in the future.

A possible future application of quantum teleportation and entanglement swapping that is discussed very intensely today is the transfer of information between future hypothetical quantum computers.

For background information *see* HIDDEN VARIABLES; NONLINEAR OPTICS; NONRELATIVISTIC QUANTUM THEORY; OPTICAL MATERIALS; QUANTUM MECHANICS; QUANTUM THEORY OF MEASUREMENT in the McGraw-Hill Encyclopedia of Science & Technology.

Anton Zeilinger

Bibliography. C. H. Bennett et al., Teleporting an unknown quantum state via dual classical and Einstein-Podolsky-Rosen channels, *Phys. Rev. Lett.*, 70:1895–1899, 1993; D. Bouwmeester et al., Experimental quantum teleportation, *Nature*, 390:575–579, 1997; D. Bouwmeester, A. K. Ekert, and A. Zeilinger, *The Physics of Quantum Information, Quantum Cryptography, Quantum Teleportation, Quantum Computation*, Springer-Verlag, 2000; C. Macchiavello, G. M. Palma, and A. Zeilinger, *Quantum Computation and Quantum Information Theory*, World Scientific, 2000; A. Zeilinger, Quantum teleportation, *Sci. Amer.*, 282(4):50–59, April 2000.

Radar interferometry

Imaging radar interferometry (IRI), a relatively new microwave remote sensing technology, is a method of combining imagery collected by radar systems on board airplane or satellite platforms to map the elevations, movements, and changes of the Earth's surface. This article focuses on how IRI is employed to measure movements of the Earth's surface using data from satellite-borne radar. These movements are detected by examining the difference between imagery collected at one time, the reference time, over a given area and imagery collected at another time, the repeat time, over the same area. This is called repeat-pass IRI. Movements of the Earth's surface detectable with IRI can be due to natural phenomena, including earthquakes, volcanoes, glaciers, landslides, and salt diapirism; or anthropogenic phenomena, including ground-water and petroleum extraction, watering of farms, or underground explosions. Locations in southern and central California and Nevada where these movements have been studied are plotted in **Fig. 1**. It is interesting to note that changes in the Earth's surface that are detectable using IRI can be due to fires, floods, forestry operations, moisture changes, vegetation growth, and ground shaking.

The first study (A. K. Gabriel and others) that demonstrated how IRI could be used to measure movements of the Earth's surface was published in 1989. Imagery was collected by an L-band radar system aboard the *Seasat* satellite (**Table 1**) to detect swelling of the ground resulting from selective watering of agricultural fields in California's Imperial Valley. However, until the publication in 1993 of the spectacular interferometric maps of ground movements caused by the 1992 Landers, CA, earthquake (D. Massonnet and others; H. A. Zebker and others) [**Fig. 2**] and ice movements within the Rutford Ice Stream, Antarctica (R. M. Goldstein and others), the method's usefulness as a geodetic tool had gone unrecognized. Since that time, a multitude of workers have used data from the *European Remote Sensing Satellite (ERS)*, *Japanese Earth Resource Satellite (JERS)*, Radarsat, and the space shuttle's SIR-C/X-SAR radar imaging systems (Table 1) to study earthquakes, volcanoes, glaciers, landslides, ground subsidence, and plate boundary deformation worldwide (Fig. 1).

Imaging the Earth. As a satellite platform orbits the Earth, the imaging radar system on board maps out a swath on the ground by transmitting and receiving pulses of microwave electromagnetic energy (**Fig. 3**). The radar's antenna is pointed to the side at the "look angle," and the width of the signal's beam is determined by the antenna's dimensions and the frequency of the transmitted signal. The mapping is repeated after a number of days called the repetition period (Table 1). After the signal data are col-

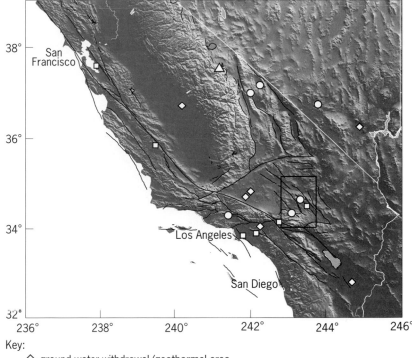

Key:
◇ ground-water withdrawal/geothermal area
○ earthquake
△ volcano
□ interseismic/postseismic deformation

Fig. 1. Locations and types of published IRI earth movement studies in southern and central California and Nevada. The black lines are faults in California. The box contains the area shown in Fig. 2.

lected by the radar system, the data are transmitted to Earth and received at a number of strategically located ground receiving stations (GRS). If a satellite-borne radar system does not have an on-board tape recorder, signal data can be received by a ground station only if the satellite is within a radial distance of the station. Ground receiving station coverage of the continents and Poles is excellent, but data cannot be received over large portions of the Pacific and Indian oceans. After reception at a ground station, the signal data are computer-processed into high-resolution imagery. The high-resolution imagery is a two-dimensional array of complex numbers. Each

TABLE 1. Civilian synthetic aperture radar (SAR) satellites used for IRI studies

Satellite	Agency and country	Launch year	Frequency band (GHz)	Altitude, km	Repetition period, days	Incidence angle	Swath width, km	Resolution, m
Seasat	NASA/U.S.	1978	L (1.3)	800	3	23°	100	23
ERS-1	ESA	1991	C (5.3)	785	3, 35,168	23°	100	25
JERS-1	NASDA/Japan	1992	L (1.2)	565	44	35°	75	30
SIR-C	NASA/U.S.	1994	X (9.7)	225	Variable	15–55°	15–90	10–200
	DASA/Germany		C (5.2)					
	ASI/Italy		L (1.3)					
ERS-2	ESA	1995	C (5.3)	785	35	23°	100	25
Radarsat	Canada	1995	C (5.3)	792	24	20–50°	50–500	28

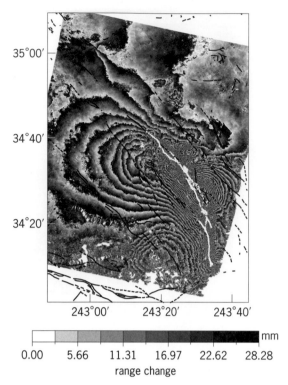

35°00'

34°40'

34°20'

243°00'   243°20'   243°40'

| 0.00 | 5.66 | 11.31 | 16.97 | 22.62 | 28.28 | mm |

range change

Fig. 2. Interferogram spanning the Landers, CA, earthquake in June 28, 1992. The images combined to form this interferogram were taken on April 24 and August 7, 1992. Black lines trace faults. White lines trace the earthquake rupture. Note that coherence is lost near the earthquake rupture.

element of the array contains an estimate of the amplitude and phase of the radar signal reflected from a patch of ground corresponding to a pixel in the image.

Imaging radar interferometer. An interferometer measures the difference in the lengths of the two round-trip paths traveled by a sinusoidal signal from two sensors, separated by a known distance, called the interferometer baseline, to a target. In this simple case, the two sensors are separated only in space. For measuring movements of the Earth's surface, the imaging radar interferometer is composed of two sensors separated in both space and time (the radar antenna on a single satellite passing over the Earth twice), and the satellite is far enough from the Earth that the paths traveled by the signals at the two times of imaging are considered parallel to each other. The difference in path length is proportional to the difference between the phases of the signals reflected off a patch on the ground and received at the radar antenna at the two times of imaging. After removing the difference in path length due to the spatial separation of the satellite positions during its two passes, the difference in path length, or range change, is equal to the distance that the ground moved in the direction toward or away from the satellite: the satellite line of sight (LOS) [Fig. 3]. In Fig. 2, a "wrapped" radar interferogram, formed by combining imagery collected by the *ERS-1*, maps the movements of patches on

the ground in the line-of-sight direction associated with the 1992 Landers earthquake. Each cycle, or fringe, represents approximately 2.8 cm (1.1 in.) of motion.

Radar phase. The measured phase of a periodic signal can take on values only in the range $[0, 2\pi]$. Thus, the phase measurements in a radar interferogram are "wrapped" into 2π increments. Each 2π increment corresponds to one-half of a radar signal wavelength (Table 1) of range change. The phase measurements in interferograms are sometimes left wrapped and sometimes unwrapped (the appropriate multiples of 2π are added to the phase measurements) and converted to absolute range change. Because using a computer algorithm to add the appropriate number of 2π increments to each phase measurement sometimes results in a loss of signal over an area that has visually interpretable fringes, leaving the phase wrapped can be advantageous.

Because randomly oriented scatterers within a patch of ground have reflected the signal detected by the radar, the phase of the detected signal has both a random part and a deterministic part. The random part is incoherent, while the deterministic part is coherent. The IRI method utilizes the phase-coherent part of the radar's signal. If the random part of the phase in the image collected during the reference pass of the satellite is different from that of the corresponding phase in the image collected during the repeat pass of the satellite, the coherence of the phase difference in the interferogram is lost. When coherence is lost in a region in an interferogram, the phase cannot be measured. In

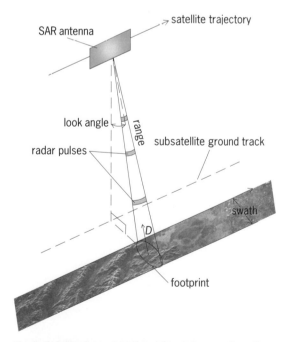

Fig. 3. Satellite-borne imaging radar system configuration. *D* indicates movement of a patch on the Earth in the direction of the radar line of sight.

TABLE 2. Natural and anthropogenic phenomena resulting in ground movements measurable with IRI

Phenomenon	Width, m	Range change, m	Displacement gradient	Measurable with IRI?; limiting factors
Earthquake coseismic	6000–100,000	0.1–1	10^{-4}–10^{-6}	Yes
Earthquake postseismic	11,000	0.05	10^{-6}	Yes
1-year interseismic	5000–100,000	0.001–0.01	10^{-6}–10^{-8}	Sometimes; atmospheric noise
Fault rupture	0.1–10	0.01–10	10^{2}–10^{-3}	Sometimes; large displacement gradient
Rutford Ice Stream (Antarctica)	10,000	5	10^{-4}	Yes
Deflation of Mount Etna (Italy)	60,000	0.1	10^{-6}	Yes
Catastrophic volcanic eruption	50–50,000	10–1000	10^{1}–10^{-4}	Sometimes; large displacement gradient
Pumping in East Mesa geothermal field (California)	6500–16,000	0.056	10^{-6}–10^{-5}	Yes
Tidal loading	400,000–7,000,000	0.03–0.2	10^{-7}–10^{-9}	Sometimes; small displacement gradient
1-year postglacial rebound	100,000–5,000,000	0.002–0.02	10^{-6}–10^{-10}	No; small displacement gradient

Fig. 2, for example, coherence is lost in some areas near the earthquake rupture, imparting noise to the image.

Limitations and measurement error. The measurement of seismic, volcanic, and glacial displacement (movement of the Earth's surface) signals using IRI is well documented in the scientific literature since their displacement gradients and spatial scales fall well within the limits of the method (**Table 2**). Representative phenomena include the coseismic and postseismic phases of the 1992 Landers earthquake cycle, aftershocks of the Landers earthquake, the deflation of Mount Etna, and flow within the Rutford Ice Stream. The displacements associated with catastrophic volcanic eruption, near-fault fault rupture, the interseismic phase of the earthquake cycle, postglacial rebound, and tidal loading lie near or beyond the boundaries of the method's applicability. The range of spatial and temporal scales over which the IRI method can be applied is dependent on the parameters of the radar imaging system (Table 1). In all cases, atmospheric noise and phase noise levels constrain the smallest line-of-sight displacement signal that can be measured. Atmospheric and phase noise levels are typically 5 cm (2 in.) and a few millimeters, respectively.

The amount of time that an interferogram may span while retaining phase coherence is controlled by the characteristics of the surface (for example, vegetated or barren). Over time, the movement of scatterers or a change in the dielectric properties within a patch of ground can change the incoherent part of the radar's signal, causing the phase of the signals returned from that patch to be uncorrelated with the phase of previously returned signals. If this happens, the interferometric phase cannot be recovered. Phase decorrelation can be linear with time or can be seasonally dependent. In spite of this effect, interferograms spanning as much as 7 years have been computed for dry desert locations.

The spatial dimensions of detectable displacement signals are limited by four parameters: the pixel size (Table 1, Resolution), the swath width (Fig. 3), and the upper and lower limits of the amount of displacement gradient. The pixel size and swath width are physical limitations on the spatial wavelength of the displacement signal that can be measured. Displacement signals with spatial wavelengths smaller than an image pixel or much larger than the size of an image scene cannot be detected with IRI alone. The displacement gradient limitations are dictated by the criteria of one interferometric fringe per pixel and one fringe per scene for steep and shallow displacement gradients respectively. For the *ERS* systems with each fringe representing 2.8 cm (1.1 in.) of line-of-sight displacement, the resolution is 30 m (98.4 ft) and the swath width is 100 km (62 mi), giving approximate bounds of 10^{-3} on the steepest displacement gradient and 10^{-7} on the shallowest displacement gradient detectable.

For background information *see* IMAGE PROCESSING; INTERFEROMETRY; MICROWAVE; RADAR; REMOTE SENSING; SATELLITE (SPACECRAFT); TOPOGRAPHIC SURVEYING AND MAPPING in the McGraw-Hill Encyclopedia of Science & Technology.

Evelyn J. Price; J. Bernard Minster

Bibliography. A. K. Gabriel, R. M. Goldstein, and H. A. Zebker, Mapping small elevation changes over large areas: Differential radar interferometry, *J. Geophys. Res.*, 94(7):9183–9191, 1989; R. M. Goldstein et al., Satellite radar interferometry for monitoring ice sheet motion: Application to an Antarctic ice stream, *Science*, 262:1525–1530, 1993; D. Massonnet et al., The displacement field of the Landers earthquake mapped by radar interferometry, *Nature*, 364:138–142, July 8, 1993; H. A. Zebker et al., On the derivation of coseismic displacement fields using differential radar interferometry: The Landers earthquake, *J. Geophys. Res.*, 99(B10): 19,617–19,643, 1994.

Radio broadcasting

Audio program broadcasting, traditionally an analog service using either amplitude or frequency modulation (AM or FM), is rapidly evolving to digital methods. Digital audio broadcasting (DAB) promises to bring to listeners an audio signal with vastly improved characteristics, accompanied by additional digital data-based services not available from the analog signals now in use. This article discusses the in-band/on-channel approach to implementing terrestrial digital audio broadcasting, and the first global satellite digital broadcasting system.

In-Band/On-Channel Digital Audio Broadcasting

In-band/on-channel is the preferred approach for implementation of terrestrial digital audio broadcasting services in the United States, given the lack of available spectrum in a new band of frequencies (that is, frequencies not already allocated to the terrestrial radio broadcasting service). This section provides

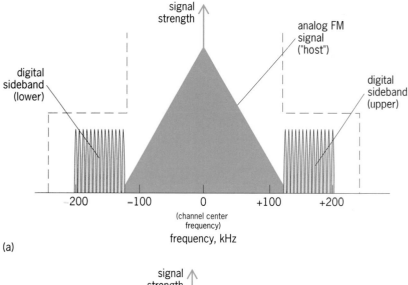

(a)

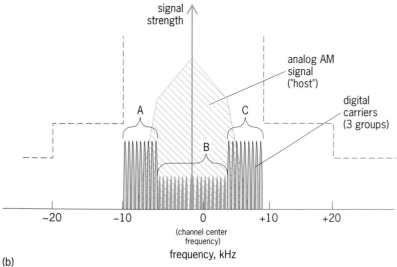

(b)

Fig. 1. Proposed in-band/on-channel (IBOC) signals. (*a*) FM band. (*b*) AM band.

background information on this approach and discusses systems under development.

Currently, the predominant form of digital audio broadcasting being implemented around the world is based on the Eureka-147 standard. Since each Eureka carrier is approximately 1.5 MHz wide (accommodating multiple audio programs or other data services on each carrier), it is not possible to incorporate the Eureka carriers into the existing AM and FM broadcasting bands (from 535 to 1705 kHz, and 88 to 108 MHz, respectively); instead, new spectrum must be allocated for their use. Hence Eureka is sometimes called a "new-band" service.

In 1992 the International Telecommunication Union Radiocommunication Sector (ITU-R) instituted worldwide allocations for digital audio broadcasting services, which were primarily in the L-band (1452–1492 MHz) and the S-band (2310–2360 MHz in the United States, and 2535–2655 MHz in parts of Asia and Europe). Many countries have made use of these allocations to initiate digital audio broadcasting service; in the United States, two satellite digital audio radio service (SDARS) providers have each been granted licenses for 12.5-MHz portions of the U.S. S-band digital audio broadcasting allocation (25 MHz total bandwidth), and expect to begin transmissions to subscribers in 2000 or 2001.

Since there are no frequencies available in the United States for the implementation of a new-band terrestrial digital audio broadcasting service, the broadcasting industry is pursuing the development of digital audio broadcasting systems which are designed to be used in the existing broadcast bands and are compatible with (that is, do not cause unacceptable interference to, and do not receive unacceptable interference from) the analog signals currently in use. These systems are referred to as in-band/on-channel (IBOC) and are being designed and tested for both the AM and FM bands by a number of system developers (proponents).

An IBOC system is designed to support concurrent use of a radio station's existing analog signal and a new, digital signal. This enables an orderly transition from analog to digital service without rendering existing receivers obsolete, giving listeners time to obtain new receivers capable of working with the IBOC digital signal. Some IBOC proponents envision a second transition, after there is sufficient market penetration of IBOC digital receivers, from the initial hybrid IBOC approach (which utilizes analog and digital signals) to an all-digital IBOC signal which would entirely fill the signal mask with digital carriers, eliminating the analog carrier entirely and resulting in further benefits to the service, especially an increased data capacity and a greater coverage area. Those proponents would deploy IBOC receivers which accommodate both hybrid and all-digital signals from the start, so that listeners would need to upgrade their equipment only once to take full advantage of present and future IBOC technology.

Designing a viable IBOC system has proven to be a formidable challenge. The approach has typically been to take advantage of the unused portion of the spectrum for the AM or FM service in the immediate vicinity of the analog carrier (as defined by the service frequency allocation mask), or to implement frequency reuse by including an additional carrier (or carriers) in quadrature to the existing analog carrier (**Fig. 1**). In either case, the analog signals are in proximity to the digital signals, and great care must be exercised to prevent unwanted interference between them.

First-generation systems. A series of laboratory and field tests were conducted by the Electronic Industries Association (EIA) and the National Radio Systems Committee (NRSC, cosponsored by the EIA and the National Association of Broadcasters, NAB) during 1994–1996 on a number of digital audio broadcasting systems (**Table 1**). Of those systems participating, four were of the IBOC type (three FM, one AM). The characteristics of these systems, and those of next generation systems, are somewhat similar but differ in many respects as well (**Tables 2 and 3**).

In these tests, all four of the first-generation IBOC systems were shown to be unsuitable for deployment as viable digital audio broadcasting systems for various reasons. In spite of this overall result, all four systems demonstrated excellent audio quality in an unimpaired environment, and a posttest evaluation done by one of the proponents on their IBOC systems, as well as the corresponding test data, concluded that the IBOC concept was valid.

TABLE 1. Systems participating in EIA/NRSC tests*

System	Type/Band	Tests performed in: Laboratory	Field
Eureka-147	New-band terrestrial/ L-band	4	4
VOA/JPL	Satellite/S-band	4	4
AT&T/Lucent	IBAC/FM-band	4	4
AT&T/Lucent/ Amati	IBOC/FM-band†	4	
USADR FM-1	IBOC/FM-band	4	
USADR FM-2	IBOC/FM-band	4	
USADR AM	IBOC/AM band	4	

* IBAC = in-band/adjacent-channel. IBOC = in-band/on-channel. USADR = USA Digital Radio, Inc.
† This system was tested in two modes of operation: double sideband (DSB, which utilized both upper and lower digital sidebands) and lower sideband (LSB).

Next-generation systems. A number of technical papers released in 1997 described new techniques for IBOC signal processing and "breakthroughs" which the proponents felt would greatly improve upon the performance of the first-generation systems.

Improved perceptual audio coding algorithms. Advances made in audio coding technology allow for a reduction in the bit rate necessary to achieve the desired sound quality, resulting in reduced bandwidth requirements for the digital sidebands, which in turn reduces interference between these sidebands and the IBOC analog "host" (Fig. 1) as

TABLE 2. Comparison of FM IBOC system parameters

Parameter	First-generation systems				Next-generation systems[1]		
	AT&T/Amati (DSB)	AT&T/Amati (LSB)	USA Digital Radio-FM1	USA Digital Radio-FM2	USA Digital Radio	Digital Radio Express	Lucent Digital Radio
Diversity	None	None	None	None	Time and frequency	Time and frequency	Time and frequency
Simulcast with analog?	No	No	No	No	Yes	Optional	Optional
Audio coding rate, kilobits per second	160	128	128–256 (variable)	128–256 (variable)	96	128	128
Audio coding technique	PAC	PAC	Musicam	Musicam	MPEG2-AAC	MPEG2-AAC	PAC
Channel coding	Reed-Solomon	Reed-Solomon	Concatenated code (variable rate)	Concatenated code (variable rate)	Complementary Punctured Code (CPC)	Concatenated (Trellis outer, block inner)	Concatenated (Trellis outer, block inner)
Modulation technique	DMT[3]	DMT	Multicarrier/ CDM	Multicarrier/CDM (with frequency slide)	OFDM[2] (each QPSK)	OFDM (each carrier 8PSK)	OFDM (each carrier QPSK)
Radio-frequency bandwidth[4]	150 kHz	75 kHz	200 kHz	400 kHz	140 kHz	136 kHz	146 kHz
Data capacity,[5] kilobits per second	<15	<15	<64	<64	32–104	≈48	50–100

[1] Systems under development in early 2000; some parameters are estimated or may change.
[2] OFDM = orthogonal frequency-division multiplexing.
[3] DMT = Discrete Multitone, a form of orthogonal frequency-division multiplexing.
[4] Bandwidth of digital signal components only, not including bandwidth of accompanying analog signal.
[5] Actual data capacity used is flexible; use of higher data rates may involve reducing bit rate available to digital audio or increasing interference to analog portion of signal.

TABLE 3. Comparison of AM IBOC system parameters

Parameter	1st-generation system	Next-generation systems*	
	USA Digital Radio	USA Digital Radio	Lucent Digital Radio
Diversity	None	Time and frequency	Time and frequency
Simulcast with analog?	No	Yes	Optional
Audio coding rate, kilobits per second	96	48/32/16	48/32/20
Audio coding technique	Musicam	MPEG2-AAC	PAC
Channel coding	Rate 3/4 forward error-correcting code (FEC)	Under development	Concatenated (Trellis outer, block inner)
Modulation technique		OFDM† (each carrier 32-QAM)	OFDM† (carriers 16- and 32-QAM)
Radio-frequency bandwidth	40 kHz	20 kHz	20 kHz
Data capacity	None	Up to 16 kilobits per second	Under development

*Systems under development in early 2000; some parameters are estimated or may change. Information regarding Digital Radio Express's AM IBOC system was not available.
† OFDM = orthogonal frequency-division multiplexing.

well as with adjacent IBOC and analog broadcast signals.

Diversity techniques. Signal structures incorporating time and frequency diversity are used, making these new systems more robust in the presence of channel impairments such as multipath fading, as well as in the presence of adjacent and cochannel interference (due to nearby radio signals assigned to the same or adjacent frequencies). Time diversity involves sending two copies of the same signal at different times, and can be implemented in a number of ways. Using this technique, a brief channel impairment (for example, signal obstruction as the receiver passes under a bridge) will affect one copy but not the other, and the receiver is designed to recognize this and use only the unaffected version. With frequency diversity, the digital audio signal is distributed across the allocated radio frequency band in a redundant fashion so that interference affecting only part of the band (for example, an adjacent channel interferer located in the upper portion only) can be removed and a usable signal can be extracted from the noninterfered part.

Back-up channels. Next-generation IBOC systems incorporate a back-up main audio channel, which alleviates two significant problems encountered in the first-generation systems: excessively long acquisition times, and a tendency to exhibit a "cliff effect" failure at the edge of coverage (whereby the audio signal almost instantly goes from high-quality digital audio to muting). Two types of back-up channels are being proposed: a digital, low-bit-rate version of the full-bit-rate main channel audio signal (with noticeably reduced quality), and the existing, analog main channel audio signal, used as a back-up to the IBOC digital signal.

Also in 1997, another IBOC system proponent emerged with an FM IBOC system in hardware prototype form, and plans for development of an AM IBOC system. As a consequence of these developments, the NRSC's Digital Audio Broadcasting Subcommit-

tee prepared a generic test plan for use by IBOC system developers to support a thorough evaluation by the NRSC of next-generation IBOC technology.

System evaluation and regulation. Two important tasks will need to follow the successful completion of IBOC system development before these systems can be deployed. First, systems need to be independently evaluated to demonstrate that they are significantly better than existing analog systems, and that they can be integrated into the existing broadcast environment without undue interference to existing signals. In addition, the regulatory framework under which IBOC technology can be introduced needs to be established through the rulemaking process of the Federal Communications Commission (FCC). This process was initiated in October 1998 by the submission to the FCC of a Petition for Rulemaking by one of the proponents, and progressed with the October 1999 release (by the FCC) of a Notice of Proposed Rulemaking (NPRM).   David H. Layer

Global Satellite Digital Broadcasting

On October 19, 1999, it became possible, throughout Africa and even beyond, to receive more than 25 high-quality multilingual music, news, and educational programs through a new portable radio. This event concluded 10 years of effort by WorldSpace Corporation to create the first digital direct audio and multimedia broadcasting service.

The first major building block for this digital radio system was put in place on October 28, 1998, with the successful launch of the system's first geostationary satellite, AfriStar, which was followed by the second, AsiaStar, in March 2000. When the full system is in operation, it will provide instant access to large geographical areas in three continents through three such satellites, located roughly equidistant around the world at the 21,105, and 265°E longitude geostationary orbital locations. The total target audience of the three satellites is over 4.6 billion people in Africa, Asia, and Central and South America. These

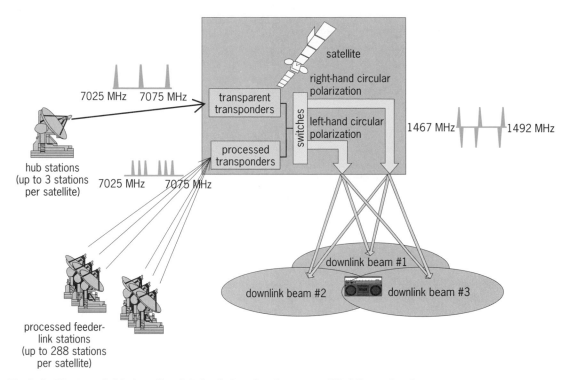

Fig. 2. Architecture of global satellite digital radio broadcasting system. (*WorldSpace Corp.*)

satellites broadcast enough power in the 1467–1492 MHz range (that is, the L-band) that receivers need only a small patch antenna about the size of an ordinary saucer. No dish is necessary. So long as a direct line of sight is maintained with the satellite, the built-in patch antenna is sufficient to support excellent reception and complete portability.

Each of the three regions is served through one geostationary satellite. The three satellites share a common system architecture (**Fig. 2**). The three downlink beams direct the satellite's power to the target areas, while the uplink is a global beam. This architecture enables uplinking programs from almost one-third of the Earth around the target areas. For downlinking in Africa, as an example, the programs can be beamed up to the satellite from anywhere in Europe, western Asia and, of course, Africa itself.

This system offers broadcasters two alternatives for uplinking their signals to the satellites. The first is the traditional broadcast architecture using "bent-pipe" or transparent transponders. These require all programs in a given beam to be transmitted from one "hub" or transparent feeder-link station (TFLS). The second alternative has been especially developed to enable the transmission of programs from anywhere in the global uplink beam, thus eliminating or reducing considerably the often extremely high back-haul communications costs from the broadcaster to a remote hub station in developing countries, especially across international borders. This mode is labeled "processed" since it utilizes a custom-designed processor on board the satellite in order to integrate in-

coming programs and to convert them into a single time-division multiplex (TDM) carrier for downlink broadcast. The uplink stations used in this mode are called processed feeder-link stations (PFLSs).

At the transparent feeder-link station, the incoming programs are multiplexed to form a time-division multiplex carrier with a capacity of 1536 kilobits per second (kbit/s) of digitally encoded information. One satellite can have a maximum of three transparent feeder-link stations, one for each beam. Each processed feeder-link station, however, converts only its own broadcast channels to the 16-kbit/s prime-rate channels (PRCs) and directly transmits them to the satellite in a frequency-division-multiple-access (FDMA) mode along with other processed feeder-link stations in the beam or region. Each satellite can have as many processed feeder-link stations as needed, with a theoretical maximum of 288, equal to the total number of prime-rate channels in one satellite.

Satellites. The three satellites are identical in design. Alcatel Space Industries, France, is the prime contractor for in-orbit delivery of these satellites, which are based on the Matra Marconi Space 2000+ platform. Each satellite has six transponders, two per beam. Each beam transmits a minimum of 20 kilowatts of effective radiated power [that is, 43 decibels above 1 watt (dBW)] in each of the two TDM carriers, one transparent and one processed. The satellite has adequate redundancy, fuel, and reliability to guarantee performance over 12 years.

Each satellite has its own operational and control network, managed from its own dedicated Regional

Operations Center (ROC). Three discrete networks provide for the management for the three satellites. For highest reliability, each satellite has two fully redundant Telemetry, Command, and Ranging (TCR) stations. The three Regional Operations Centers have mutual backup capability in case any one of them is lost due to fire or other disabling events.

L-band digital radios. The user radios for this system follow the traditional heterodyne principle. Their design maximizes reliability and minimizes manufacturing costs for a consumer product that is to be distributed and serviced worldwide. The use of custom application-specific integrated circuit (ASIC) chipsets contributes to the high reliability, low cost, and low power consumption. Batteries, alternating-current power supplies, simple solar power adapters, or equivalent sources can power the radios. Currently, the radios are manufactured by four companies, but they all meet a common overall specification. Through their built-in microcontrollers, they provide the listener the ability to select any of the broadcast channels in any of the time-division multiplex carriers within reach, depending on location with respect to one or more beams. In addition to built-in speakers, each radio has an external audio jack and a data port. The port can provide up to 128 kbit/s of data from any of the selected broadcast channels.

Broadcast and business networks. The system provides access to the satellites through an integrated broadcast and business network. Such networks are configured to evolve with the use of the system.

The broadcast and business network for Africa is expected to have one hub and 13 processed uplinks in operation. The Johannesburg transparent feeder-link station, with access to the transparent transponders for all the three beams, provides an effective means of beaming "global" programming throughout the continent. The Johannesburg transparent feeder-link station and the London processed feeder-link station also provide facilities for the real-time synthesis of music and information with "live voices," distributed through the Internet.

In an intercontinental system, the most crucial element is to have real-time information about the status of all broadcasts, radio features, and other system information. The first such Quality Management Network, in Africa, overlays the Satellite Operation Network and the broadcast and business networks. In addition to the traditional crewless Communication System Monitoring (CSM) station at Libreville, Gabon, this network will use silence detectors, round-the-clock staffing by technicians at feeder-link stations, and centralized remote monitoring systems. The Satellite Operation Network and the Quality Management Network integrate at the Regional Operations Center to provide full-time surveillance of the complete system. Status, health, and quality information for every service is planned to be provided on a real-time basis to customer service centers in major markets.

Services. Each user radio has access to a minimum of two time-division multiplex carriers, each with 1536 kbit/s of information. This information can be

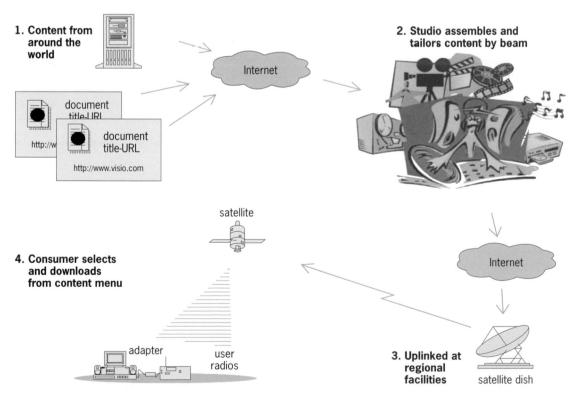

Fig. 3. System architecture of multimedia service using the global satellite digital radio broadcasting system. (*WorldSpace Corp.*)

TABLE 4. Capacity of global satellite digital broadcasting channels

Bit rate, kilobits per second	Quality	Maximum number of channels per beam
16	AM-low (small amount of data)	192
32	AM-high (stock exchange data)	96
48	FM-stereo (typical FM station)	64
64	FM-high-fidelity (good music quality; hotels, offices, airlines, and so on)	48
96	Near compact disk (CD) [excellent music quality]	32
128	CD (optimum music quality; multimedia with video clips)	24

used in any combination of multiples of 16 kbit/s, with the maximum bit rate in a broadcast channel of 128 kbit/s (**Table 4**). Any broadcast channel can carry either audio or data programs.

Audio programs are encoded with MPEG 2.5 Layer 3, now in extensive use in MP3 players. Encoding at 32kbit/s is adequate for news and talk programs, while encoding at 64kbit/s and higher provides excellent quality. The overall system design allows the broadcasters to match the bit rates to their needs.

Data information transmitted on any of the broadcast channels can be directed to a data port, which can be connected through a simple adapter to any personal computer or data reception device. Such data services have attracted the interest of banks and grocery chains, and could be used in weather alerts and other similar applications.

A multimedia service expected to be introduced during 2000 (**Fig. 3**) will provide access to user-selected content from around the world through direct downloads to the computer, connected through a special adapter to the receiver data port. A modern personal computer with sufficiently large hard-disk storage capacity will play high-quality video clips as called upon by the user. Users will be able to download up to 20 gigabytes a month.

System performance. After the launch of the first satellite, detailed system tests were carried out throughout Africa and neighboring areas to validate the performance at all levels. These checks confirmed the soundness of the overall system design and technologies adopted: on-board processing high-power satellites, ASIC chips for radios, and MPEG 2.5 Layer 3 voice encoding. After minor adjustments mainly at the software levels, all tests met or exceeded the requirements. The radios functioned well beyond the specified beam boundaries. (The specified and actual beam boundaries are shown in **Fig. 4a**.) This was analyzed to be a result of higher power from the satellite than specified and the need for less than the planned system margin

as long as the line of sight to the satellite was maintained.

Implementation plans and prospects. The launch of AfriStar and the evaluation of the system in Africa have prepared the way for speedy implementation of the rest of the system. The AsiaStar satellite was successfully launched on March 21, 2000, and accepted in orbit on July 20, 2000. As in the case of AfriStar, it is expected that AsiaStar's performance will go well beyond the inner boundaries of the coverage area shown in Fig. *4b*.

Launch of the third satellite, planned over Central and South America, is expected in the summer of 2001.

The satellites have a design life of 12 years and can be expected to last a few years longer. The overall system design provides sufficient flexibility to allow newer and wider-band services with changes only in the feeder-link stations and possibly radios.

In terms of overall system capabilities, the next major step is full mobile capability with the current satellites. Tests have demonstrated that the radios work satisfactorily even from fast-moving vehicles as long as the line of sight is maintained. Urban environments, however, do have obstructions to the line of

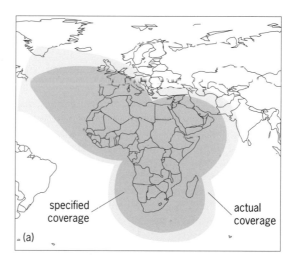

specified coverage   actual coverage

(a)

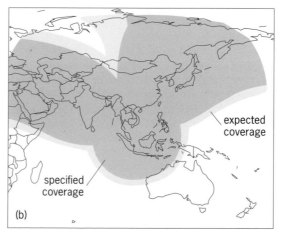

expected coverage

specified coverage

(b)

Fig. 4. Coverage areas of the (a) AfriStar and (b) AsiaStar satellites.

sight to the geostationary orbit. In order to counter this, a terrestrial retransmission technology will be field-tested in 2000, after which automobile radios could be introduced progressively in selected urban areas.

For background information *see* COMMUNICATIONS SATELLITE; DATA COMPRESSION; MODULATION; RADIO BROADCASTING; RADIO SPECTRUM ALLOCATIONS in the McGraw-Hill Encyclopedia of Science & Technology.   D. K. Sachdev

Bibliography. J. Campanella, An onboard processing digital satellite-to-radio broadcast system, *Pacific Telecommunication Conference*, Hawaii, January 1999; J. Gatski, Digital radio—today and tomorrow, *Audio*, pp. 32–37, January 1998; ITU-R Recommendation BO. 1130-1: *Systems Selection for Digital Sound Broadcasting to Vehicular, Portable and Fixed Receivers for Broadcasting Service Satellite (Sound) in the Bands in the Frequency Range 1400–2700 MHz*, Annex 3 on Digital System D; R. K. Jurgen, Broadcasting with digital audio, *IEEE Spectrum*, pp. 52–59, March 1996; B. W. Kroger and P. J. Peyla, Compatibility of FM hybrid in-band on-channel (IBOC) system for digital audio broadcasting, *IEEE Trans. Broadcast.*, 43:421–430, 1997; I. G. Masters, The future of radio, *Stereo Rev.*, pp. 83–86, October 1997; D. K. Sachdev, The WorldSpace System: Architecture, plans and technologies, *NAB, Broadcast Engineering Conference*, 1997.

Radioactive beams

In several nuclear physics laboratories, a new capability exists to produce beams of radioactive (unstable) nuclei and, before these nuclei spontaneously decay, use them to gain insight into the reactions on and structure of nuclei never before accessible. Radioactive beams are particularly useful to study stellar explosions such as novae, supernovae, and x-ray bursts. These explosions are some of the most catastrophic events in the universe, generating enormous amounts of energy while synthesizing the elements that make up lifeforms and the world. These spectacular explosions involve, and in some cases are driven by, reactions where the atomic nuclei of hydrogen (protons) and helium (alpha particles) fuse with (are captured by) radioactive isotopes of heavier elements to form new elements. The capability to produce beams of radioactive nuclei is now allowing the first direct measurements of these reactions, providing crucial information needed to theoretically model cataclysmic stellar events and to understand the origin of many chemical elements.

Nuclear reactions in stars. Stars are born when gas and dust in space condenses under its own gravity to a large body with a central density and temperature sufficiently high to ignite fusion reactions between atomic nuclei. The carbon-nitrogen-oxygen (CNO) cycle is a catalytic sequence of nuclear reactions that generates energy, making massive stars shine and balancing the crushing inward pressure of gravity.

Carbon, nitrogen, and oxygen "seed" nuclei capture four protons (the fuel) and eject an alpha particle, liberating energy in the process (**Fig. 1***a*). Typical temperatures and densities at the core of a massive star where these nuclear reactions occur may be approximately 10^7 kelvins and 100 grams per cubic centimeter, respectively. Under these conditions, the rates of such nuclear fusion reactions (which have been measured in the laboratory) are extremely slow. Some CNO cycle reactions transform catalytic seed nuclei into radioactive isotopes of different elements, which then spontaneously decay to a stable nucleus in typically a few to a few hundred seconds, well before they will undergo any additional fusion reactions.

Stellar explosions. During stellar explosions such as novae or x-ray bursts, a different sequence of nuclear reactions occurs. Nova explosions are thought to occur in binary star systems (two stars orbiting each other) when one star of the pair—a cold compact white dwarf star—is able to gravitationally pull material (mainly hydrogen) off the surface of its close binary companion in a phenomenon known as accretion. This situation is not uncommon: there are

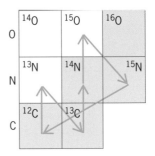

(a)

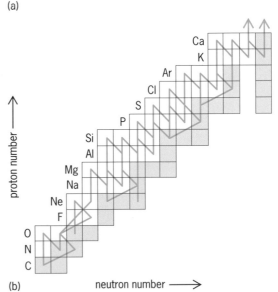

(b)

Fig. 1. Sequences of nuclear reactions occurring in stars. The shaded boxes represent individual stable nuclei, the white boxes radioactive nuclei. The arrows represent nuclear reactions leading to transforming one nucleus to another. (*a*) Carbon-nitrogen-oxygen (CNO) cycle, occurring in nonexploding stars. (*b*) Reactions on radioactive isotopes occurring in stellar explosions.

approximately 40 novae in the Milky-Way Galaxy each year. After approximately 10,000 years, enough hydrogen has collected, or accreted, on the white dwarf surface to raise the temperatures and densities to 10^8 kelvins and 100–10,000 grams per cubic centimeter, respectively. These conditions are sufficient to ignite nuclear fusion reactions between the accreted hydrogen and the carbon and oxygen (or in some cases oxygen, neon, and magnesium) heavy nuclei which make up the white dwarf. The fusion reactions generate energy, which raises the temperature of the accreted layer, which exponentially increases the rates of all the fusion reactions. This becomes a runaway thermonuclear explosion where the temperatures may reach $3–4 \times 10^8$ kelvins and the energy generated by the nuclear reactions causes ejection of a sizable fraction of the accreted layer off the surface of the white dwarf. The energy released in these enormous thermonuclear explosions can be up to 10^{31}–10^{38} joules, in a thousand seconds—10^{24} times the energy released in powerful thermonuclear explosions on Earth.

Since nuclear fusion reaction rates increase exponentially with increasing temperature, they occur approximately 10^{16} times faster in stellar explosions than in a normal star. This is so fast that protons can be captured by radioactive isotopes before they have a chance to spontaneously decay. Sequences of nuclear reactions occurring in novae are therefore different from those in ordinary stars (Fig. 1b). Heavier nuclei, perhaps as high as mass 40 (calcium) and beyond, can be assembled in novae, ejected into space, and eventually incorporated into new stars and planets; even human bodies are made up of this "stardust." The high rate of nuclear reactions in novae also means energy is generated faster, influencing many aspects of the explosion. A similar situation is thought to occur in x-ray bursts, where the accretion from a companion star onto the surface of a neutron star occurs. Here, the temperatures can peak at more than 10^9 kelvins, the densities may reach as high as 10^6 grams per cubic centimeter, and isotopes up to mass 100 (tin) and beyond may be synthesized.

Measurements. Until recently, direct measurement of the fusion reactions occurring in stellar explosions was impossible. This is because beams of radioactive nuclei were not available, and targets of these nuclei would spontaneously decay before a measurement could be made. Computer models of nuclear burning in stellar explosions therefore had to rely on theoretical estimates of many crucial reaction rates. In some cases, these estimates have been shown to be incorrect by many orders of magnitude. Because of these uncertainties, critical comparisons of theory to astrophysical observations to determine the temperatures, densities, and duration of these events, as well as the origin of the elements in the world, were difficult to make.

The recent availability of beams of radioactive nuclei in nuclear physics laboratories is enabling experimental determinations of the nuclear reactions

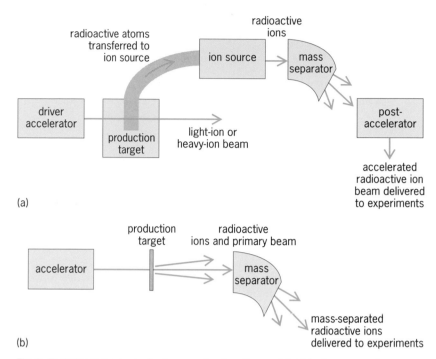

(a)

(b)

Fig. 2. Techniques for producing beams of radioactive nuclei. (a) Isotope separator on-line (ISOL) technique. (b) Projectile fragmentation technique.

that drive stellar explosions. One approach to radioactive beam production, pioneered at CERN (Switzerland), is the isotope separator on-line (ISOL) technique, used at Louvain-la-Neuve (Belgium) and at Oak Ridge National Laboratory (United States) [**Fig. 2a**]. One accelerator bombards a target with a beam of stable nuclei, and a small number of the radioactive atoms of interest are produced through nuclear reactions. These atoms are transported, by various techniques, including thermal diffusion, to an ion source where they are ionized (removing or adding electrons to give atoms an electrical charge) and extracted. The radioactive ions are then mass-separated from other ions and accelerated to energies needed for nuclear physics experiments by a second accelerator. The ISOL technique can produce very high beam qualities, purities, and intensities; the disadvantages are that only a few radioactive beam species can be generated from each combination of production target and primary beam, and that beams with short lifetimes (less than 1 s) are difficult to produce.

To measure the fusion rate between radioactive heavy ions and hydrogen nuclei, a number of techniques can be used once a radioactive beam is produced. First, a beam of radioactive nuclei at a specific energy is directed at a thin (gas or foil) target containing hydrogen or helium. A direct measurement technique then involves counting the products of the fusion reaction (nuclei and protons) in sophisticated detection systems (**Fig. 3**). One effective system consists of a mass separator followed by charged particle detectors. By varying the energy of the radioactive beam, the probability of

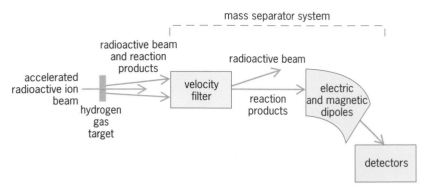

Fig. 3. Technique to measure a thermonuclear fusion reaction occurring in stellar explosions. A radioactive beam bombards a target with hydrogen (protons), and the products of a fusion reaction (as well as unreacted beam particles) enter a mass separator. The products of the thermonuclear reaction are steered onto a detector for counting, while the unreacted beam particles are deflected away.

fusion as a function of energy is determined. Combined with a calculation of the relative energy distribution of the particles at a given temperature in a star, the fusion rate is determined as a function of temperature. Indirect techniques are also used to determine reaction rates, such as measuring the scattering of the heavy-ion radioactive beam off protons or alphas to discover resonances that may enhance the fusion reaction. Reactions that have been studied with ISOL beams include the fusion of the unstable ^{13}N, ^{17}F, ^{18}F, and ^{19}Ne nuclei with protons and ^{18}Ne with alphas. These reactions are all important for understanding element production in nova explosions.

A complementary radioactive beam production technique is projectile fragmentation, used at Michigan State University (United States), RIKEN (Japan), GANIL (France), and GSI (Germany) [Fig. 2b]. When a high-energy beam of stable heavy ions passes through a thin target, the beam particles (projectiles) can break up into fragments—some of which are the radioactive isotope of interest. The desired fragments are then mass-separated from other ions and steered toward a target to undergo the reaction of interest. The projectile fragmentation technique can produce beams of very short lifetimes (10^{-6} s or less), and the same setup can be used to produce many different beam species; the disadvantages are that high beam quality, purity, and intensity are difficult to obtain. Reactions studied with projectile fragmentation beams include the fusion of ^{7}Be and ^{13}N with protons, both by measuring the time-reversed reactions (for example, ^{8}Be breaking up to a ^{7}Be plus a proton). Both ISOL and projectile fragmentation techniques have also been used to measure the properties (masses, spins, parities, energy levels, and decay properties) of nuclei that are important in astrophysics calculations. Other techniques for producing radioactive beams have been used at Notre Dame University and Argonne National Laboratory in the United States. Additionally, a number of facilities are currently under construction worldwide or planned. All together, these measurements are enabling nuclear physicists to directly measure some of the nuclear reactions that power cataclysmic stellar explosions.

For background information *see* CARBON-NITROGEN-OXYGEN CYCLES; CATACLYSMIC VARIABLE; NOVA; NUCLEAR REACTION; NUCLEAR STRUCTURE; NUCLEOSYNTHESIS; STELLAR EVOLUTION in the McGraw-Hill Encyclopedia of Science & Technology.
                                                    Michael S. Smith

Bibliography. D. Arnett, *Supernovae and Nucleosynthesis*, Princeton University Press, 1996; D. D. Clayton, *Principles of Stellar Evolution and Nucleosynthesis*, University of Chicago Press, 1983; C. E. Rolfs and W. S. Rodney, *Cauldrons in the Cosmos: Nuclear Astrophysics*, University of Chicago Press, 1988.

Renewable resources

Over the past century, petroleum-based products gradually replaced similar products that were once made from plants. However, now a wide variety of fuels, chemicals, lubricants, adhesives, plastics, and other materials derived from renewable plant resources are being substituted for petroleum-based products. Economic, technical, environmental, social, and political forces are driving this transition.

Plant resource. In the United States the plant resource is huge. The nation exports enough unprocessed corn grain, approximately 50 million tons/yr (45 million metric tons/yr), to meet a very large fraction of the domestic need for chemicals and plastics. Waste biomass (plant material) amounts to at least 300 million tons/yr (272 million metric tons/yr)—more than enough to meet the needs for organic chemicals and plastics and to contribute significantly to liquid fuel needs of approximately 150 billion gallons/yr (568 billion liters/yr).

Plant material is inexpensive. For example, corn grain at $2.75/bushel ($0.08/liter) and crude oil at $18/barrel ($0.11/liter) are roughly equivalent in cost per unit weight, both costing about $110/ton ($121/metric ton). Many crops and residues, such as forage grasses, hays, and rice straw (referred to collectively as cellulosic materials), are in fact much less expensive than oil—they are available in very large quantities for less than $40/ton ($44/metric ton; see **illus.**). Moreover, plants are a widely produced renewable resource, while oil is a nonrenewable

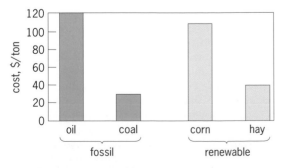

Cost of various raw materials.

resource whose production is much more concentrated geographically and whose price must eventually rise to reflect increasing demand and declining supply. Many experts involved in monitoring and measuring oil reserves predict that the era of inexpensive oil may be ending soon. Thus, the long-term availability and prices of plant raw materials may be more stable and predictable than that of petroleum.

Through long experience, chemical engineers have learned that the cost of producing commodity goods depends on two primary factors: the cost of the raw material from which the commodities are produced, and the cost of the processing required to convert the raw materials into the desired commodities. With plant raw material costs already low and trending lower, the key technical issue is to significantly reduce the costs and economic risks of processing plant material into useful products.

Biomass processing. Plant material processing can be divided into two broad areas. The first area is the conversion of cellulosic materials, which are composed primarily of the structural compounds cellulose, hemicellulose, and lignin, as well as a wide variety of less abundant compounds, including protein. The second area is the conversion of grains and oilseeds, which are composed mostly of starches, oils, and protein. The properties of these major constituents strongly influence their processing.

Cellulosics. For cellulosic materials, three major issues affect conversion costs: (1) the resistance of cellulosic materials to biological conversion, (2) the cost of the enzymes (cellulases) which break cellulosic materials down into sugars, and (3) the variety of sugars that are produced during the breakdown. Sugars are versatile, reactive compounds that can be converted biologically to a wide variety of products. For example, considerable progress has been made in genetically engineering microorganisms to ferment both the five- and six-carbon sugars in cellulosic materials to ethanol. Similar approaches should apply to other commodity bioproducts.

A number of advances have been made in reducing the costs and increasing the effectiveness of cellulases (although an order-of-magnitude cost reduction in enzyme cost is probably still needed for economic viability in fuel ethanol production). Some of the required cellulase cost reduction will certainly come through research advances, but much of it is likely to occur through large-scale, integrated production in biorefineries, described below. One promising approach to lower-cost and more effective cellulases is to genetically engineer a single microbe to produce the necessary enzymes and to simultaneously ferment the resulting sugars to the required products. This approach reduces the inhibition caused by buildup of sugars, increases overall reaction rates, and reduces the capital investment required.

Less progress is apparent in cost-effective technologies to reduce the resistance of cellulosic materials to biological attack. However, liquid-ammonia-based treatments and liquid-hot-water processes offer some exciting potential that has been at least partially realized. Technological "end runs" around treatments that reduce the resistance of cellulosics, followed by bioconversion, may be possible, for example, by first gasifying plant biomass and then fermenting the resulting gas mixture.

Starches, oils, and protein. Conversion of starch crops to chemicals is significantly more advanced than is the conversion of cellulosic materials. For example, processes to convert sugars derived from corn starch to valuable aromatic compounds—such as shikimic acid, vitamins, flavoring agents, monomers for polymer production, organic acids, and road de-icing salts—have been announced or are being developed. Most of these processes are biologically based. They rely on either enzymes or microorganisms, whether genetically engineered or not. However, advances are continuing in nonbiological catalytic conversion of plant-derived sugars and organic acids. Compared to the progress in producing desired chemicals, progress in methods to separate chemical mixtures resulting from plant material processing has been slower.

Commercial-scale production of chemicals and chemical intermediates from plant material is growing rapidly. The progress of the nascent industry is symbolized by recent actions of two chemical giants, Dow Chemical and DuPont, Inc. Dow Chemical recently entered into a joint venture with Cargill, a very large grain trading company, to produce lactic acid from corn starch as a monomer for polymer production. DuPont is developing new biological routes to textile fibers by fermentation of corn starch, and recently divested itself of its petroleum production operations as both a symbolic and actual move toward a future based more on renewable plant materials. The most recent DuPont annual report highlights the company's emphasis on sustainability, of which renewable raw materials is one aspect.

The New Uses Council® promotes new products and industries based on agricultural commodities. On its web site, for oilseeds it appears that much of the research and technology for producing specialty oils and lubricants is privately held and that only the properties of the products themselves are disclosed. Industrial chemical production from plant proteins is much less developed than for either oils or starches. Some work has been done on new adhesives from plant proteins, and at least one group is interested in producing transgenic proteins in oilseeds that might be recovered as part of the oilseed refining process.

Genetic engineering. Not only can microbial and enzymatic biotechnology be used in the processing of plant materials, but one of the most interesting and potentially powerful technologies driving chemical production from renewable resources is the ability to genetically modify the plant raw material itself. Plants can be bred or genetically engineered to be easier to process, for instance, by reducing the lignin content of cellulosic materials. Also, the plants themselves can be genetically modified to produce valuable compounds that might be recovered during processing. This approach has been demonstrated for production of biodegradable plastics called polyhydroxyalkonates. Genetic modification of oilseeds to produce improved industrial chemicals, including polymer resins and other products, is also being pursued.

As a further example, a technically very challenging approach to making low-cost cellulases is to genetically engineer plants themselves to produce the required cellulases. The cellulases are then released as active enzymes in the processing facility. The potential of plant biotechnology, as well as microbial biotechnology, to reduce the costs of chemical production from plant material has scarcely been tapped. The possibility of modifying the raw material itself, either to add valuable compounds to it or to make it easier to process, does not exist for petroleum, and is a major advantage of plant raw materials for chemical production.

Biorefineries. Powerful economic forces will probably dictate that chemicals and other plant-derived products will be produced in large, integrated processing facilities called biorefineries. Indeed, prototype biorefineries already exist as corn wet mills, oilseed processing plants, and pulp and paper mills. Corn wet millers, for instance, are continually adding new products to their line.

Further development of biorefineries will reduce the costs of chemicals from plant material by reducing capital costs, making more complete use of raw material, and permitting incremental investments in new facilities rather than investing in completely new processing facilities. Biorefineries will yield a variety of products that will tend to increase over time. Processing costs will be gradually reduced.

Many biorefinery products such as liquid fuels, organic chemicals, and materials can also be produced by petroleum refineries. However, biorefineries can manufacture products that oil refineries cannot, including foods, feeds, and biochemicals. These additional capabilities will give biorefineries a potential competitive edge and enhanced financial stability. However, a great deal of technology and product development remains to be done before biorefineries and their products achieve their full scale and economic potential.

Various impacts. With some caveats, environmental groups tend to strongly favor plant-derived fuels and chemicals over petroleum-derived counterparts. The bulk of the evidence indicates that such chemicals and fuels will tend to be produced by less polluting technologies, will be less likely to accumulate in the biosphere, will tend to have more favorable life-cycle energy costs, and also will have near-zero net carbon dioxide emissions. Extensive planting of grasses to support large-scale chemical and fuel production will help build soil quality, reduce erosion, and minimize contamination of surface and ground waters by fertilizers and pesticides. Producing chemicals, fuels, plastics, and other products from plant materials will help strengthen rural economies and diminish the steady decline in net farm income.

Environmental and farm groups strongly supported bills recently introduced in the U.S. Congress to advance the sustainable production of chemicals and fuels from plant material. Research described in these proposals would focus on overcoming the resistance of cellulosic materials. Many legislators believe that plant biomass can become the "new petroleum" and thereby provide the United States and the world with the benefits of a renewable, widespread, and environmentally compatible source of chemicals and fuels. These bills also envision product diversification research to catalyze the development of biorefineries, and provide for research to reduce separation costs and to discover new separation approaches. Finally, these bills would support environmental and life-cycle analyses to guide the development of chemicals and fuels from plant material.

A recent report of the National Research Council begins its Executive Summary with these words: "Biological sciences are likely to make the same impact on the formation of new industries in the next century as the physical and chemical sciences have had on industrial development throughout the century now coming to a close. The biological sciences, when combined with recent and future advances in process engineering, can become the foundation for producing a wide variety of industrial products from renewable plant resources."

For background information *see* AGRICULTURAL SOIL AND CROP PRACTICES; ALCOHOL FUEL; BIOMASS; CELLULOSE; COAL; CONSERVATION OF RESOURCES; CORN; ENERGY SOURCES; GENETIC ENGINEERING; HEMICELLULOSE; LIGNIN; PETROLEUM; RENEWABLE RESOURCES; STARCH in the McGraw-Hill Encyclopedia of Science & Technology.   Bruce E. Dale

Bibliography. R. G. Lugar and R. J. Woolsey, The new petroleum, *Foreign Affairs*, pp. 88–102, January–February 1999; D. Morris and I. Ahmed, *The Carbohydrate Economy: Making Chemicals and Industrial Materials from Plant Matter*, Institute for Local Self Reliance, Minneapolis, August 1992; National Research Council, Board on Biology, Committee on Biobased Industrial Products, *Biobased Industrial Products: Priorities for Research and Commercialization*, August 3, 1999; Special issue, *Biotechnol. Prog.*, 15(5):775–883, September–October 1999.

Risk-based environmental restoration

The use of terms such as risk assessment, risk-based corrective action (RBCA), and risk-based environmental restoration has been on the rise in the environmental cleanup industry. For example, over 40 states have adopted, or are considering adoption of, RBCA procedures for dealing with contaminated sites based on standardized risk management approaches developed by the American Society of Testing and Materials (ASTM). Many contaminated sites, including most sites associated with leaking underground storage tanks, are now managed using risk-based environmental restoration.

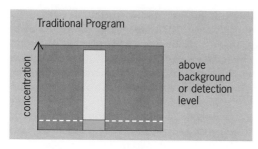
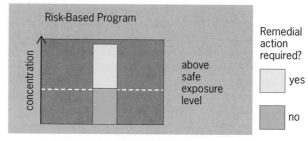

Fig. 1. Definition of contamination under a traditional cleanup program and a risk-based program.

Risk-based approaches. Since the late 1980s, two new concepts about contaminated sites have emerged: (1) removing contaminants from the subsurface is much more difficult than first thought, and (2) contaminants remaining in the subsurface are not a major environmental threat at many sites. For example, the Environmental Protection Agency (EPA) conducted detailed reviews of ongoing ground-water remediation systems. It concluded that several factors, particularly residual source materials called nonaqueous phase liquids (NAPLs), precluded restoration of ground water at 24 sites. A subsequent study conducted by the National Research Council (NRC) in 1994 concluded that ground-water pump-and-treat methods could require extremely long operating periods (in some cases, centuries) to restore ground water to drinking-water standards at many sites. Other studies performed in California and Texas in 1995 and 1997 have shown that many sites contaminated with spilled gasoline pose extremely little or no risk to human health and the environment, leading environmental regulators to change policies and stop requiring expensive cleanup systems at most of these sites.

New paradigm. In partial response to these studies, a new paradigm called risk-based environmental restoration has been gaining acceptance as an appropriate remediation strategy. In this approach, the cleanup actions are targeted toward the hazard and not the chemical (**Fig. 1**). Contaminated sites are first characterized in terms of sources, transport mechanisms, and receptors to permit a calculation of the risk posed by site contaminants (**Fig. 2**). Cleanup measures are then applied as needed to prevent human or environmental exposure to harmful levels of site contaminants.

Concerns and response actions. An environmental release of contaminants can pose a variety of hazards, depending on the location, magnitude, and nature of the release. Key types of environmental hazards include human health and ecological hazards (posed by the toxicity of chemicals to human or ecological receptors); nonbiological resource impacts (destruction of a natural resource, such as water resources belonging to a state); esthetic impacts (causing a nonhazardous but unsightly or nuisance problem); and safety impacts (from dangerous conditions caused by having contaminants in subsurface utilities, such as explosive gases).

The goal of risk-based environmental restoration is to assess each of these concerns and define appropriate cleanup actions on a site-specific basis. Currently, human health concerns are the central focus of many state and federal risk-based cleanup rules, as there are established procedures for calculating the potential risk to human health. Such procedures are now being developed to perform ecological risk assessments, where the risk posed by contaminants to plants, animals, and the ecosystem can be calculated. Evaluation of nonbiological resource impacts, esthetic impacts, and safety impacts is also part of most risk-based approaches, but usually involves a qualitative assessment rather than the formal calculation procedures that typify human health risk assessments.

Human health risk procedures. Under a risk-based approach, an exposure assessment is always conducted to determine whether the release could result in human exposure in excess of safe levels. The environmental engineer or scientist must address various exposure scenarios, hypothetical mechanisms whereby chemicals on affected soil or ground water could move to a point of human intake. For many contaminated sites, the ground-water pathway that leads to potential ingestion will be important. Other pathways that are typically reviewed include inhalation of vapor and particulates, dermal contact with soil, ingestion of soil and dust, leaching from soils to ground water, and discharge to surface water.

Basic steps. Risk-based environmental restoration can be distilled to four steps shared by most risk-based regulatory programs.

Step 1: Site assessment. Collect site information to characterize soil and ground-water impacts and identify potential receptors. Key data should include site soil and ground-water conditions, location of actual and potential receptors, and concentrations of

Fig. 2. Exposure pathways.

chemicals of concern in various media (such as soil and ground water).

Step 2: Exposure assessment. Conduct an exposure pathway screening analysis to identify those exposure conditions which could apply to the site (commonly based on the presence or absence of source media or receptor, and the presence or absence of chemicals above the threshold screening level).

Step 3: Risk/cleanup standard calculation. Calculate potential exposure conditions and compare to protective criteria. The calculations are based on the following procedure: (a) An environmental model is used to project how much contaminant levels decline between the source and the receptor in a particular media (such as ground water). (b) A list of accepted exposure factors (such as the amount of ground water that people drink every day or the amount of air that they breathe) is used to estimate how much of the contaminant actually is consumed by the receptor. (c) Toxicological factors from EPA databases are used to determine how much risk (such as cancer risk or the risk of damaging various organs) is associated with consuming a certain amount of chemical (**Fig. 3**). When the calculations are run in the forward mode (left to right), the actual risk to human health is generated and compared to acceptable levels defined by regulatory agencies [for example, a common acceptable risk level used by many regulators for carcinogenic chemicals is 1 excess cancer death per 100,000 (or 1,000,000) exposed persons]. When the calculation is run in the backward mode, site-specific cleanup levels for soil and ground water that will protect human health are calculated (Fig. 3).

Software is available to make these calculations easier by combining fate and transport models, standard risk assessment exposure factors, chemical or toxicological databases, and regulatory-agency-mandated target risks in one integrated package (for example, the RBCA Tool Kit). These tools allow users to easily calculate the risks associated with a particular site (the forward calculation) and to calculate cleanup standards for the source zone at a site that will be protective of human health and the environment (the backward calculation).

Step 4: Response action. Develop a cleanup strategy to minimize risk by preventing exposure to harmful levels of chemicals. Appropriate measures may involve (a) removal or treatment of affected media, (b) containment measures to prevent exposure to soil or ground water left in place, or (c) institutional controls, such as deed recordation, to limit future uses of the property as needed to prevent unsafe exposure conditions (for example, limit a property to commercial or industrial uses with no ground-water extraction). Each of these measures may successfully achieve the risk protection criteria. Consequently, the choice among these options is not a risk-based decision but a function of technical and economic considerations as well as land-use plans. The final response action should serve to achieve the applicable protective standards while preserving the active and productive use of the property.

Outlook. Risk-based management is becoming an accepted method under many regulatory programs for responding to chemical releases to the environment. With this approach, various impacts caused by site contaminants are assessed. To evaluate the potential risk to human health, which is the most common type of risk assessment, a calculation is conducted using environmental models, accepted exposure factors, and toxicological data. These calculations can be performed either in a forward mode to yield the risk the site poses to receptors, or in a backward mode where safe cleanup standards are determined. At sites where excess risk is predicted to occur, risk-based management approaches allow

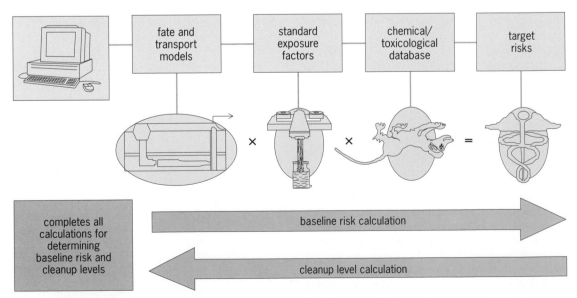

Fig. 3. Forward baseline risk calculation and backward cleanup level calculation. (*From J. A. Connor et al., Guidance Manual for RBCA Tool Kit for Chemical Releases, Groundwater Services, Inc., 1998*)

more flexibility in response actions by allowing containment and institutional controls in addition to standard removal or treatment alternatives.

For background information *see* DECISION THEORY; ENVIRONMENTAL ENGINEERING; ENVIRONMENTAL TOXICOLOGY; LAND RECLAMATION; INDUSTRIAL HEALTH AND SAFETY; RISK ANALYSIS in the McGraw-Hill Encyclopedia of Science & Technology.

Charles J. Newell; John A. Connor

Bibliography. American Society for Testing and Materials, *Standard Provisional Guide for Risk-Based Corrective Action*, ASTM PS 104–98, 1998; R. Begley, Risk-based remediation guidelines take hold, *Environ. Sci. Technol.*, 30(10):438–441, 1996; J. A. Connor and R. L. Bowers, Guidelines for Risk-Based Corrective Action Modeling for Chemical Release Sites, *NGWA Petroleum Hydrocarbons Conference*, Houston, November 1998; National Research Council, *Alternatives for Ground Water Cleanup*, 1994.

Salmon

Salmon are large, predatory fish belonging to the genera *Oncorhynchus* and *Salmo*. The defining characteristic of salmon is their anadromous lifestyle: they spawn in fresh water, migrate to the ocean during development, and at maturity return to fresh water. Upon their return, salmon exhibit high site fidelity, spawning at or very near their natal breeding grounds, although a small fraction of individuals do stray to other areas. This general strategy proved to be enormously successful, with prodigious numbers of salmon traversing many river systems prior to human interference. However, as human-induced threats have continued to increase, in many cases salmon distribution and population sizes have decreased. Recognizing salmon's importance as an economic commodity, cultural symbol, and ecological indicator, scientists and managers have bolstered their efforts to identify threats, develop mitigation strategies, and ultimately recover these dwindling stocks.

General biology. Despite variation within and among species, all salmon share the same basic life cycle. In late summer or fall, eggs are deposited and fertilized in fresh-water gravel beds, usually in running water but in some cases along lake shores. In late winter or spring, individuals hatch as 20–30-mm-long (1–2-in.) alevins, which are nourished by an attached yolk sac. Alevins typically remain in the protected gravel bed until they deplete their yolk supply, at which point they emerge from the gravel as fry. Subsequent fry dispersal patterns depend largely on innate responses to gravity, light, and water flow direction. Although some species differ, fry generally form loose aggregate groups that move rapidly downstream, either at night or under the cover of the stream bank. In some species and locations, fry may enter the ocean as soon as 1 week after hatching. In others, fry remain in fresh water for up to 3 years as camouflaged parr that prey on stream invertebrates;

these parr eventually migrate to coastal estuaries during an identifiable smolt stage, characterized by physiological, morphological, and behavioral preparation for salt-water residence. From estuaries, juvenile salmon enter the ocean and experience rapid growth. Marine-phase salmon then embark on a long migratory journey during which they become sexually mature. Upon reaching maturity, at ages ranging 1–7 years depending on the species, adults relocate to the originating river mouth and migrate upstream to the spawning grounds. Timing is often coordinated seasonally, resulting in distinct runs that recur annually. This upstream migration can take days or weeks, depending on the distance traveled; salmon spawning grounds can be found at distances exceeding 3200 river-kilometers (2000 river-miles) from the ocean, and at elevations exceeding 1200 m (4000 ft) above sea level.

Species diversity. The genus *Salmo* contains the Atlantic salmon (*S. salmo*), a species that occurs throughout the North Atlantic Ocean and spawns in eastern North America and western Europe. Unlike Pacific salmon species, the Atlantic salmon can complete more than one migratory cycle and are thus iteroparous (they can breed multiple times). Halfway around the world, the genus *Oncorhynchus* includes seven semelparous (one-time breeding) salmon species that occur naturally in the North Pacific Ocean and spawn in western North America and coastal Asia. Two of these species, masu (*O. masou*) and amago (*O. rhodurus*), occur only in Asia, whereas the remaining five species are also found in North America:

Chinook or king salmon (*O. tshawytscha*) can exceed 46 kg (100 lb) at maturity, and often spawn in tributaries located a considerable distance from the ocean.

Sockeye or red salmon (*O. nerka*) are generally smaller, and are uniquely adapted to rearing in interior lakes rather than in streams or rivers.

Chum or dog salmon (*O. keta*) have the broadest geographic distribution, ranging from the south coast of Korea to the central coast of California.

Coho or silver salmon (*O. kisutch*) are relatively widespread across both the Asian and western North American coasts, but are the rarest salmon throughout much of their range.

Pink or humpback salmon (*O. gorbuscha*) are the smallest of the salmon, typically weighing less than 2.5 kg (5 lb), but are also the most abundant.

Within these species, different local populations exhibit very different behavioral and phenological traits. This has led scientists to subdivide each species into multiple populations referred to as evolutionarily significant units (ESUs), each of which harbors enough genetic uniqueness to warrant its own management and conservation agenda.

Causes of endangerment. Many salmon ESUs have experienced dramatic declines during the past century. In the western United States, salmon have been extirpated from 40% of their original range. In many basins where salmon still endure, the migratory runs are much smaller than historic levels. For example, annual returns of chinook salmon to the Snake River system (Washington, Oregon, and Idaho) fell from roughly 1.5 million fish in the 1800s to fewer than 2000 in the mid-1990s. In the North Atlantic, the total number of Atlantic salmon dwindled from 800,000 in the mid-1970s to fewer than 100,000 in the late 1990s. As a result of these declines, the new millennium begins with more than two dozen ESUs listed as either endangered or threatened under the Endangered Species Act.

Climatic cycles and trends operating on moderately long time scales have been implicated as an important influence on salmon productivity. By causing variation in ocean currents, which determine the location and extent of coastal upwelling, climate changes can drastically affect marine productivity. This in turn shifts the carrying capacity (the maximum number of individuals the environment can support) for salmon and other marine residents. However, little is known about how climatic variability superimposes upon anthropogenic alterations of both fresh-water and marine systems. At least over shorter time scales, it is clear that humans have had a considerable impact on salmon populations. The primary anthropogenic threats to salmon persistence are often referred to as the "four H's," in reference to habitat degradation, harvest of fish, hatchery releases, and hydropower projects.

Habitat degradation. Habitat degradation results from widespread human activities such as logging, mining, grazing, and road development. These alter critical hydrologic attributes, including sediment delivery, stream morphology, flow rates, water temperature, and water quality. Such changes can reduce adult fecundity, directly increase mortality of immature salmon by creating lethal physical conditions, and indirectly increase mortality by disorienting fish and facilitating increased predation.

Harvesting. Harvest depletes populations via direct removal of adult salmon either from rivers or from the open ocean; this not only reduces the population size but also decreases phenotypic diversity. Since virtually all members of a stock enter into the river basin during a relatively short period of time, coordinated harvesting operations located along mainstem rivers can rapidly devastate entire stocks. Marine fishing operations many not be as efficient but are more difficult to monitor. In addition, the migration routes of many salmon carry them through the waters of multiple countries, sparking controversy over international fishing rights.

Hatchery release. Hatchery-released salmon, although arguably important in augmenting overall population numbers, can have detrimental ecological and genetic impacts on wild salmon. Artificially grown salmon differ from wild salmon in size and behavior, and when released into rivers they can outcompete wild fish, introduce parasites into the wild, attract predators, and stimulate abnormal timing of downstream migration. In an evolutionary context, hatchery rearing may select for traits that correspond to lower fitness in the wild; for example, whereas wild fish escape predation by retreating to cover when a shadow looms above, hatchery feeding practices tend to favor salmon that more readily ascend to the surface. Subsequent interbreeding between hatchery and wild fish, a common phenomenon, will continuously introduce less-fit phenotypes into the wild population.

Hydropower projects. Hydropower projects, namely dams, pose difficult obstacles for migrating salmon. Some structures, such as Grand Coulee Dam on the Columbia River, completely block off large areas of historic salmon habitat. More commonly, dams are passable but nevertheless result in loss of some fraction of the migrating run. The effect of dams is probably greatest on juveniles, which not only are injured by turbines and spillways during actual dam passage but also can experience higher mortality in the warm, low-flow, predator-rich reservoirs impounded above each dam.

Approaches to recovery. There is considerable disagreement over the most efficient means of recovering and conserving salmon stocks. Since recovery efforts will be expensive, scientists are currently trying to identify which suite of remedial actions will achieve the greatest recovery at the lowest cost. Nevertheless, it is clear that addressing any one of the "four H's" will benefit salmon populations to some degree.

Habitat-based threats can be mitigated both by protecting remaining high-quality spawning areas and by actively restoring degraded areas. Effective restoration will require a complex set of activities that vary depending on local watershed conditions. Examples of restoration activities include revegetating stream banks, reducing sources of water pollution, and buffering streams from erosion.

The impacts of harvest can be controlled by restricting or even banning the allowable catch of salmon. Although enforcing catch limits in the open ocean requires international coordination, this can be achieved through pacts such as the 1999 Pacific Salmon Treaty Agreement between the United States and Canada. Meanwhile, fishing effort along internal waters can be managed by local and federal agencies.

Even without closing down hatcheries, the impacts of hatcheries can be reduced by improving their practices. For example, hatchery releases can be better timed to minimize interbreeding and detrimental ecological interactions between wild and nonwild fish. Methods of selecting fish to stock hatchery programs can also be improved in order to reduce the genetic differences between wild and nonwild fish.

The most aggressive measure for abating dam passage mortality is breaching existing dams; however, this represents an expensive alternative. A more conservative approach is to invest money into research and development of technologies for allowing safe fish passage. These include fish ladder systems for up-migrating adults, and barge programs for down-migrating juveniles. The effectiveness (and possible side effects) of these technologies are not well understood, but efforts are under way to make necessary hydropower projects more salmon friendly.

For background information *see* CONSERVATION OF RESOURCES; ENDANGERED SPECIES; FISHERY CONSERVATION; MARINE FISHERIES; SALMONIFORMES in the McGraw-Hill Encyclopedia of Science & Technology.   Jim Regetz

Bibliography. Committee on Protection and Management of Pacific Northwest Anadromous Fish, *Upstream: Salmon and Society in the Pacific Northwest*, National Academy Press, Washington, DC, 1996; C. Groot and L. Margolis (eds.), *Pacific Salmon Life Histories*, UBC Press, Vancouver, BC, 1991; J. Lichatowich, *Salmon Without Rivers: A History of the Pacific Salmon Crisis*, Island Press, Washington, DC, 1999; D. Mills, *Ecology and Management of Atlantic Salmon*, Chapman and Hall, New York, 1989.

Scenario-based design

Scenario-based design is a family of techniques in which the use of a future system is concretely described at an early point in the development process. Narrative descriptions of envisioned usage episodes are then employed in a variety of ways to guide the development of the system. Scenario-based design changes the focus of design work from defining system operations (that is, functional specification) to describing how people will use a system to accomplish work tasks and other activities.

Origins. During the early years of the Cold War, strategic planners came to rely on scenarios to anticipate and analyze future contingencies. The situations with which they were concerned were complex and unfamiliar. Scenarios facilitated vivid and broad-scope analyses that encouraged consideration of contextual details and temporal dynamics that were sometimes overlooked in more formal contingency planning. The linear structure of time facilitated comprehension and integration of the many interacting elements in a problem situation, while emphasizing to analysts that circumstances are constantly changing. Scenarios were found to stimulate imagination, helping analysts generate new contingencies and relationships. Finally, scenarios reduced the perceived costs of considering more alternatives. The "accidental war scenario," in which a mistaken launch of a single tactical nuclear missile somewhere in Europe triggers a cascade of events, culminating in all-out global war, was discovered through scenario analysis and became a touchstone of strategic planning for a generation. Prior to the late 1940s, no planner had ever considered such escalating contingencies (or cataclysmic outcomes).

Beginning in the 1970s, scenario-based methods were widely adopted and developed in corporate strategic management. Scenario analysis was credited with Royal Dutch Shell's success during the mid-1970s oil crisis. Since 1980, scenario-based techniques have developed in key areas of computer system and software design, including requirements engineering, human-computer interaction, and object-oriented software design. These separate lines of methodological development have begun to converge around the proposal that various scenario-based practices can be mutually leveraged throughout the system development process.

Requirements engineering. Requirements engineering is the process of identifying and articulating needs for new technology and applications. It involves a wide range of activities, including interviews with potential customers and future users of new systems, observations of workplace activity that new systems are intended to support, and participatory workshops involving direct collaboration among various stakeholder constituencies (users, their managers and coworkers, system developers, documentation designers, and user interface specialists).

Several kinds of scenarios are used in the requirements process. Routine work-flow scenarios describe typical episodes of the human activity that the new system must support. By describing work practices vividly, scenarios help to keep developers focused on the user's needs. Problem scenarios describe episodes of breakdown in work flow, including difficulties in usability and threats to safety. They concretize outcomes that the new system must avoid. Envisionment scenarios describe possible alterations of extant situations. They can be taken as initial design proposals, sometimes called paper prototypes, and at the same time be used instrumentally to evoke further requirements and analysis from users and developers. They encourage "what if" reasoning.

As an example, a problem scenario might describe obstacles that a person using the telephone encounters in organizing a community meeting. A related envisionment scenario might describe how such a task might be carried out using a community network. For example:

Harry is worried about local power line plans; he goes to Virtual Town Hall to organize a community meeting. He fills out a meeting form with "power line" as topic, "Thurs 7–9" as date/time, a paragraph describing his concerns, and his name as contact. He searches the town database for the current power line plan, adds graphical annotations, and attaches the document. A room at the high school is available, and Harry reserves it. He sends out the meeting notice, classifying it as "general interest."

Scenarios help to integrate the requirements engineering process by providing a single type of representation to evoke, codify, and analyze various sources of requirements information. The trade-offs implicit in the scenarios can be articulated as an a priori design rationale, guiding design work rather than merely describing its outcomes. For example, the Virtual Town Hall may strengthen direct democracy, but will increase administrative email traffic.

Such an explicit design rationale can help to clarify the root concepts for the system early in the development process, promoting more elegant design solutions. The accessibility of scenarios to nontechnologists facilitates greater participation by users. Scenarios can be created by the users themselves, or created by designers and shared with users to identify and prioritize requirements.

The flexibility of scenarios facilitates management of emergent requirements—the new design goals that often become apparent during system development. Requirements scenarios can be modified continuously to provide an overall view of the most current understanding of the goals for the system.

Human-computer interaction. Human-computer interaction involves the design and evaluation of systems as they are experienced and used by people. It includes understanding and modeling the perception, cognition, behavior, and social interaction of work activity, and developing user interface displays and interaction devices, and associated documentation and training to support human characteristics and preferences.

Human-computer interaction forces a strongly task-oriented perspective on defining systems and their uses. Human-computer interaction designers use scenario walkthroughs to develop transparent and consistent rubrics for the appearance and behavior of displays and controls, sometimes called user interface metaphors. Scenario walkthroughs are used to ensure that the information displayed by the system in any given state suggests appropriate actions and interpretations to users, and that error recognition, diagnosis, and recovery information is available, accurate, and easy to employ. Training, online help, and other system documentation now typically present information in a task context, that is, as a scenario description.

In the system development process, human-computer interaction closely couples design and evaluation. Envisionment scenarios can be detailed in terms of specific goals for user performance and experience—for example, how quickly on average users will be able to perform routine tasks, like scheduling a community meeting, with what error rates, and with what levels of satisfaction. Such explicit usability goals can become part of the design scenarios for the system, and subsequently can be assessed with test subjects.

Such evaluation work goes on throughout the development process. Early in development, the performance and experience of subjects in test scenarios can be used as formative evaluation to refine the original goals for the system. Later in the development process, similar scenarios can be used as summative evaluation to verify that development goals were met.

Object-oriented software engineering. Scenario-based approaches to requirements engineering and human-computer interaction were dramatically integrated in the 1990s by scenario-based approaches to software development. The key bridging insight is that the people and things described in requirements scenarios, and the user interface display objects and controls of human-computer interaction scenarios, can correspond to the same software objects. This insight derives from the distinction between software models and views in object-oriented software: Software models describe underlying functionality, views describe the presentation of the functionality.

Scenario-based approaches to object-oriented software engineering suggest taking the nouns and verbs of an envisionment scenario as a first-approximation object model: The nouns are the objects, the verbs are the methods (capabilities) of the objects. In the community meeting example, the Virtual Town Hall, the database, the meeting, the notice, and the room would be part of the initial object model. A form can be filled out; a plan can be searched for, copied, and annotated; a room can be reserved; a notice can be sent.

Scenarios are then run as simulations on such object models, successively elaborating the models in terms of what each object is responsible for (what data it holds, what methods it uses) and how objects collaborate (share data to enable one another's methods). For example, running the community meeting scenario against the initial object model suggests that the meeting object creates the form to gather user data, that it works with the room to schedule itself, that it holds its own topic, date/time, and location, and that it creates the notice.

A stronger scenario-based software development method is use cases. A use case is a set of system event traces that accomplish a particular scenario goal within a given system model. A simple example is the "Get Cash" use case in an automatic teller machine (ATM). The set of event traces gives the software designer a precise way of verifying how the use case scenario has been implemented in the software.

System life cycle. Scenario-based practices currently span most of the software development life cycle: requirements development and analysis, envisionment and design development, user interface design and prototyping, software development and implementation, documentation and training development, and formative and summative evaluation.

Surveys of contemporary development methods indicate that the use of scenarios is pervasive but not systematic. Developers say they would like more comprehensive methods and better tool support. An underlying tension in this is that a key property of scenarios as planning and design tools is that they seem quite concrete to the analyst or designer, while actually leaving most details unfixed. This has the effect of engaging greater imagination and critical reflection in system development work. However, the tension between the benefits of roughness and the need for explicit engineering methods will have to be resolved during the coming years.

For background information *see* HUMAN-COMPUTER INTERACTION; INFORMATION SYSTEMS ENGINEERING; OBJECT-ORIENTED PROGRAMMING;

SOFTWARE ENGINEERING; SYSTEMS ENGINEERING in the McGraw-Hill Encyclopedia of Science & Technology.   John M. Carroll

Bibliography. J. M. Carroll, *Making Use: Scenario-Based Design of Human-Computer Interactions*, MIT Press, Cambridge, MA, 2000; J. M. Carroll (ed.), *Scenario-Based Design: Envisioning Work and Technology in System Development*, John Wiley, New York, 1995; I. Jacobson et al., *Object-Oriented Software Engineering: A Use Case Driven Approach*, Addison-Wesley, Reading, MA, 1992; M. Jarke, X. T. Bui, and J. M. Carroll, Scenario management: An interdisciplinary approach, *Requirements Eng.*, 3(3–4):155–173, 1998.

Seasonal affective disorder

Seasonal affective disorder (SAD), or winter depression, was first described in a 1984 National Institute of Mental Health (NIMH) study. Researchers at NIMH and, soon after, at other research centers (including Fairbanks, New York, and Basel) cataloged for the first time a syndrome of annually repeating depressive symptoms that were refractive to bright artificial light exposure.

Many worked to describe the unique features of the illness and estimate its prevalence in the general population. It has been estimated that upward of 5% of Americans may suffer from this disorder. Although variations in the pattern are seen from individual to individual, a working definition of the syndrome includes the following: (1) recurrent major depressive episodes start around the same time each year (such as October–November) and end around the same time each year (such as April–May); (2) full remission of symptoms is experienced during the unaffected period of the year (for example, May–August); (3) over the lifetime course of the illness, there are relatively more seasonal depressive episodes than nonseasonal episodes; and (4) seasonal depressive episodes occur in at least two consecutive years.

People suffering from seasonal affective disorder often exhibit atypical vegetative symptoms of depression such as increased sleep length, weight gain, and craving for carbohydrates, and many others suffer subsyndromal winter doldrums (short of major depression), also responsive to light.

Light therapy. As opposed to antidepressant drug therapies, which can take 2 weeks or longer to produce effects, light therapy made a noticeable difference in patients' symptoms within days. However, this striking effect was, from the researcher's point of view, a mixed blessing. There was concern that the obvious administration of bright light in a disorder which was, by definition, a consequent of the darker days of fall and winter led to a large placebo response that would not be sustainable over time. Indeed, the validation of the disorder itself would be hampered by lack of an adequately plausible control for research studies.

The early years of research into seasonal affective disorder centered on the issues of placebo controls. The issue of time of day that patients were exposed to bright light had important implications both theoretically and in the pursuit of an adequate control. A number of researchers believed that seasonal depression was correlated with, if not caused by, a circadian phase shift. The body's internal circadian clock, located in the hypothalamus, relies on adequate, timed light exposure to maintain synchrony with the solar cycle as time of year and geographic locations vary. As the morning light levels dim in fall and winter, the signal to the brain may be inadequate to maintain normal entrainment of the internal clock and the body rhythms it drives, such as temperature and hormone secretion. According to the hypothesis, people slip out of synchronization with their environment, and the result is depressed mood as well as the atypical depressive symptoms of increased carbohydrate intake and lengthened sleep period.

According to one theory, bright light administration should be most effective for a majority of patients, if taken in the morning upon waking. The light would provide the missing signal the brain needs to entrain proper circadian phase, and the patient would regain equilibrium with the environment.

Another group of researchers, at the NIMH, argued for a photic response model, in which it was overall number of photons received by the eye, and not time of day, that was significant. By this model, morning and evening light should be equally efficacious.

Currently, the weight of evidence seems to be on the side of the phase-shift hypothesis. Morning light of appropriate intensity, duration, and timing shifts circadian rhythms earlier, as measured by changes in the secretory cycle of the hormone melatonin sampled from blood plasma or saliva. At the same time, morning light is significantly more effective than evening light (which can be seen as a placebo control) for most seasonal affective disorder patients, suggesting that a circadian phase delay is implicated in the etiology. Early morning treatments such as bright 10,000 lux for 30 min upon waking, or, as M. Terman has discovered, low-illumination naturalistic dawn simulation in the bedroom during sleep, are effective and safe treatments for this disorder. Because of the novelty of these approaches, many doctors are still inexperienced in their administration, but guidelines are available. Professional consensus advises patients with clinical depression not to self-treat.

Therapeutic application. A practical development under investigation is the precise timing of light exposure to maximize the antidepressant effect of seasonal affective disorder. The most effective time for morning light exposure appears to be about 8 h after the onset of melatonin secretion, a circadian clock marker. Two approaches can be used to estimate this internal phase: (1) sampling melatonin from the saliva in the evening, when secretion begins (however, this requires a laboratory assay not yet readily available to physicians), and (2) analyzing the baseline sleep pattern (melatonin onset occurs on average about 5.9 h before the midpoint of sleep).

With the beneficial effect for seasonal affective disorder established, researchers are investigating new applications of light therapy, such as for non-seasonal depression, premenstrual depression, and depression during pregnancy. There are preliminary indications of success, although the adequate dose of light may be greater than for seasonal affective disorder. In cases where neither mode of treatment supports a full recovery, the adjunctive use of light and medications (both serotonin and norepinephrine reuptake inhibitors) is under study, but there is a precaution that photosensitizing drugs be avoided.

An alternate nonpharmacologic intervention, negative air ionization delivered at high intensity, has been shown effective for seasonal affective disorder in a placebo-controlled trial. Exposure to these ions is imperceptible, and a current trial is evaluating their administration during sleep.

The application of light therapy for circadian sleep disorders (delayed and advanced sleep phase syndromes), in which depression is often absent, holds promise as a means to relieve reliance on benzodiazepine sleeping pills. Artificial bright light exposure in the morning upon awakening, as well as bedroom dawn simulation, may also be effective for relief of mild insomnia at bedtime and oversleeping the alarm clock.

For background information *see* AFFECTIVE DISORDERS; BIOLOGICAL CLOCKS; LIGHT; SLEEP AND DREAMING in the McGraw-Hill Encyclopedia of Science & Technology.   Brian P. Rafferty; Michael Terman

Bibliography. *Arch. Gen. Psychiatry*, vol. 55, no. 10, October 1998; A. J. Lewy et al., The phase shift hypothesis for bright light's therapeutic mechanism of action: Theoretical considerations and experimental evidence, *Psychopharmacol. Bull.*, 23:349–353, 1987; N. Rosen et al., Prevalence of seasonal affective disorder at four latitudes, *Psychiatry Res.*, 31:131–144, 1990; N. E. Rosenthal et al., Seasonal affective disorder: A description of the syndrome and preliminary findings with light therapy, *Arch. Gen. Psychiatry*, 41:72–80, 1984; M. Terman, Light on sleep, in W. J. Schwartz (ed.), *Sleep Science: Integrating Basic Research and Clinical Practice*, Karger, Basel, 1997; M. Terman et al., Seasonal affective disorder and its treatments, *J. Pract. Psychiatry Behav. Health*, 5: 287–303, 1998.

Seismic tomography

The relative motion of lithospheric plates at the surface of the Earth is directly related to natural hazards such as earthquakes and volcanoes, and it can cause long-term variations in climate. Plate tectonics is the surface expression of slow, large-scale deformation of rock in the deep interior the Earth. On a time scale of millions of years, the mantle silicates (for example, olivine, pyroxene, garnet, and perovskite) form a strong "taffy" that flows in a process known as mantle convection. Mantle convection is the major mechanism by which Earth loses the heat produced by its accretion about 4.5 billion years ago, its subsequent differentiation (for example, the segregation of the metallic core), and the decay of radioisotopes such as uranium and potassium. On short time scales, however, mantle material behaves as a solid. This behavior allows the propagation of longitudinal (*P*) and transverse (*S*) seismic waves, which speed up in "cold" downwellings and slow down in "hot" upwellings so that recordings of these waves can be used for the mapping of mantle flow.

In the past half century, the scale of mantle convection, which relates critically to compositional stratification and the thermal and chemical evolution of the planet, has been a big puzzle. A major challenge has been to evaluate and reconcile the range of observations and constraints provided by different scientific disciplines. Earth's heat budget (the balance between heat production and heat loss) and the geochemical analysis of ocean floor basalts suggest that distinct mantle reservoirs have retained their identity for 2 billion years or more. One reservoir boundary is typically placed at 660 km (410 mi) depth, that is, between the upper and lower mantle. Seismic imaging and computational geodynamics indicate, however, that this interface is not an effective barrier to mantle flow, and suggest that convective circulation occurs at a larger scale. This article highlights the recent developments in seismic imaging that changed views on mantle convection.

Computational advances. Since the pioneering studies in the mid-1970s, advances in technology (faster computers, increased mass storage), inverse theory, and data quality and volume have vastly improved the tomographic imaging of Earth's deep interior structure. In a parallel development, understanding of the images has improved dramatically because spectacular advances in computational geodynamics facilitated the integration of the geological constraints on past plate motion at Earth's surface and the results of experimental and theoretical mineral physics with the snapshots of convection provided by seismic imaging.

Different inversion strategies. For the imaging of global structure, two methods have become popular, each with advantages and disadvantages. The first represents lateral variations in seismic properties by superposition of global basis functions, such as spherical harmonics. This class of tomography is attractive for imaging structure at a long wavelength λ, because the number of model parameters (which scales as l^2, with harmonic degree l inversely proportional to wavelength $\lambda = 2\pi r/l$, with r radius) is then small enough to resolve the coefficients by direct inversion of carefully processed waveform data.

For structure at length scales of several hundred kilometers or less, such as slabs of subducted lithosphere in the upper mantle, a large number of global basis functions would be required, which prohibits direct inversion. Moreover, the coefficients can no longer be determined accurately owing to uneven data coverage on the relevant length scales, and artifacts are introduced in regions of poor coverage. It then becomes attractive to represent wavespeed variations by local basis functions, such as nonoverlapping constant-slowness volumes (for example, tetrahedrons, voronoi cells, rectangular blocks) or cubic splines or wavelets that interpolate between grid values. In this class of tomography, the large number of model parameters necessitates the use of iterative solvers such as least squares (LSQR) or Simultaneous Iterative Inversion Technique (SIRT), with solution selection and resolution assessment less elegant than for direct inversions, but regularization (damping) can be used to avoid artifacts in regions of limited data coverage. During the 1990s, the cell size used in regular grid inversions decreased from about $6° \times 6°$ to 2×2.

Flexible parametrization. Spatial variation in data coverage owing to an uneven source and receiver distribution remains a major problem in travel-time tomography. Global basis functions offer no flexibility for regionalization, but a local basis can be adapted to lateral variations in data coverage. Small blocks can be used in densely sampled regions without unnecessary overparametrization of poorly sampled regions. Ideally, such irregular grids reflect the spatial variation of resolution, but since this is difficult to quantify they have been designed on the basis of sampling or regional interest.

Better data. The success of any tomographic study depends critically on data quality. Most shear-wave studies have been based on waveform data that were carefully selected and processed by individual investigators, but for global P-wave inversions such data sets have only now begun to be constructed. With almost 15 million entries, the largest single data source available for tomography consists of the travel-time residuals processed and published by the International Seismological Centre (ISC). This data set is noisy, but its size and redundancy allow the extraction of structural signal. Many researchers have processed the ISC data prior to inversion. Using nonlinear procedures for earthquake relocation and seismic phase reidentification, Engdahl and coworkers improved hypocenter parameters and travel-time residuals for a large range of seismic phases. The agreement between images based either on arrival times inferred from careful waveform processing or on the routinely processed travel times demonstrates the value of this data processing.

Mantle structure from seismic imaging. Long-wavelength models continue to be improved, with current expansions up to $l = 24$, but many early results have proved to be robust. Such models do not, however, resolve trajectories of mantle flow in sufficient detail to determine unequivocally whether or not convection is stratified at 660 km (410 mi). Indeed, they have been used to argue either way. In the 1990s, travel-time tomography with local basis functions mapped upper-mantle slabs in more detail and made several seminal contributions to the understanding of mantle convection.

First, regional studies demonstrated that some slabs of subducted lithosphere penetrate into the lower mantle while others are trapped in the upper mantle. Slab deflection may occur beneath Banda, Izu Bonin, and the southern Kurile island arcs, and beneath the Tyrrhenian Sea; deep slabs, sometimes severely deformed in the transition zone, have been detected beneath the Mariana, Tonga-Kermadec, Sunda, and the northern Kurile arcs, the Philippines, the Aegean Sea, and Central and South America. Differences in subduction style can be caused by interplay between relative plate motion (lateral trench migration) and the deformation of slabs when they encounter resistance (for example, higher viscosity or a depressed phase boundary). Experimental and numerical fluid dynamical experiments support this view, but selective weakening of the descending plate by grain-size reduction upon phase transformation may also contribute. The complexity caused by interaction of downwellings with the upper-mantle transition zone may persist to near 1000 km (621 mi) depth, but the significance of this depth is not yet established and slabs can sink to even larger depth.

Second, independent P and S studies have begun to agree on structure as small as several hundred kilometers—a development that increased the credibility of this class of imaging and may prove to be a milestone of tomography. They revealed a relatively simple pattern of narrow high-wavespeed structures in the lower mantle beneath plate boundaries with a long history of subduction and indicated that these deep structures often connect to seismogenic slabs in the upper mantle. These structures disintegrate in the bottom 1000 km (621 mi) of the mantle, but some fragments seem to connect to heterogeneity near the base of the mantle, for instance beneath eastern Asia and central America. The correlation between the P and S images persists to large depth but may break down near the base of the mantle.

Third, despite theoretical and practical difficulties in the mapping of seismically slow anomalies, several studies now suggest that mantle upwellings are continuous over a large depth range, supporting the view that plumes originate (at a boundary layer) below the 660-km (410-mi) discontinuity. Image resolution—in particular in radial direction—continues to form a formidable obstacle, however.

Mantle convection. The above observations render untenable the conventional views of either convective stratification at 660 km (410 mi) or undisturbed whole-mantle flow. The 660-km discontinuity distorts mantle flow, occasionally resulting in local and transient layering, but many slabs penetrate to at least 1700 km (1056 mi) depth in the mantle. The change in structure and heterogeneity spectrum between 1700 and 2300 km (1056 and 1429 mi) depth may be real, but its origin is not yet known. It may point to stratification of some sort in the deep mantle, but it may also reflect changes in plate motion in the distant past. An alternative explanation for the slablike lower-mantle structures and their apparent continuity to upper-mantle subduction zones is that they are due to thermal coupling and coincidental alignment of structures in separately convecting upper and lower mantles. However, this is contestable: It would be very fortuitous indeed if slowly changing structures in the sluggish lower mantle align with rapidly changing structures in the less viscous upper mantle. Thermal coupling can work, but it is too slow to explain the large depth of slab penetration beneath young convergent margins, and is inconsistent with the constant dip angle inferred for several slabs. Moreover, if only heat is exchanged, thousands of kilometers of subducted lithosphere must have accumulated in the upper mantle beneath margins with a long subduction record, for which there is no observational evidence.

The geophysical evidence against rigorous stratification at 660 km (410 mi) depth is strong, and if isolated and seismically visible "reservoirs" exist they are likely to reside at a greater depth. A mantle convection scenario that can be considered is one in which—apart from the upper and lower boundary layers (lithosphere and D″, respectively)—three domains are identified. In this view, recycling of slab material involves the top 2000 km (1243 mi) or so of the mantle, which has a relatively uniform major element composition, and represents the depleted and outgassed source of mid-ocean ridge basalts. The upper-mantle transition zone (400–1000 km or 249–621 mi depth) divides this depleted part into a well-mixed, low-viscosity domain and a deeper one with high viscosity and slower transients, and mantle flow across it is distorted by viscosity stratification, effects of phase transformations in the mantle silicates, and the direct influence of relative motion of plate boundaries at the Earth's surface. The bottom 1000 km of the mantle, undegassed and enriched in heat-producing elements, is not yet mixed with the overlying mantle. For long-term survival, this layer must have a slightly higher intrinsic density. The interface between the depleted and enriched mantle domains would be close to isopycnic (that is, compositional and thermal effects on buoyancy are in balance), and significant dynamic topography can develop with some slabs penetrating to near the core mantle boundary (CMB); this resembles the "penetrative" convection proposed previously for stratification at 660 km depth. The anomalous deep mantle "layer"—if it indeed exists—could represent differences in composition or phase chemistry (for example, mantle silicates versus compounding oxides); or in an evolutionary sense, it may not yet have been churned by subduction. Slabs may lose their excess negative buoyancy well before reaching the very base of the mantle, and since the time for effects of plate motion to diffuse to large depths is large, few slabs may have had sufficient time and negative buoyancy to reach the CMB.

Future research. Seismic tomography has not solved the debate about the scale of mantle convection by demonstrating the deep penetration of many slabs, but it has moved research away from conventional, but inadequate, end-member convection models. Many issues regarding mantle convection remain. Seismic imaging will continue to play a central role in constraining the pattern of convective flow, but several issues must be sorted out. However dramatic the "red-and-blue" images, actual understanding of them is unsatisfactory. Better constraints are needed on the amplitude of the changes in P and S wavespeed, and their ratio $\delta lnV_S/\delta lnV_P$, and integration of them with results from experimental and theoretical mineral physics to quantify changes in temperature, phase, and bulk composition. The trajectories of mantle convection can be delineated in even more detail. Outstanding issues include the ultimate fate of the slabs that penetrate across the upper-mantle transition zone, and in particular the source region and morphology of the return flow (plumes?). The latter requires a significant effort to improve data coverage beneath regions far away from seismically active plate boundaries. Seismic anisotropy can also be used as a tool for delineating flow trajectories. Continued imaging of mantle structure beneath convergent margins and better integration with the record of plate motions through computational geodynamic modeling will further the understanding of subduction and its partnership with mantle convection.

For background information *see* EARTH, CONVECTION IN; EARTH INTERIOR; LITHOSPHERE; SEISMOLOGY; SUBDUCTION ZONES; TECTONOPHYSICS in the McGraw-Hill Encyclopedia of Science & Technology.

Rob D. van der Hilst

Bibliography. F. Albarède and R. D. van der Hilst, New mantle convection model may reconcile conflicting evidence, *EOS Trans. Amer. Geophys. Union*, 45:535–539, 1999; H. Bijwaard, W. Spakman, and E. R. Engdahl, Closing the gap between regional and global travel time tomography, *J. Geophys. Res.*, 103:30055–30078, 1998; L. Boschi and A. M. Dziewonski, High- and low resolution images of Earth's mantle: Implication of different approaches to tomographic modeling, *J. Geophys. Res.*, 104: 25567–25594, 1999; G. F. Davies, Penetration of plates and plumes through the mantle transition zone, *Earth Planet. Sci. Lett.*, 133:507–516, 1995; S. P. Grand, R. D. van der Hilst, and S. Widiyantoro, Global seismic tomography: A snapshot of convection in the Earth, *Geol. Soc. Amer. Today*, 7(4): 1–7, 1997; H. Kárason and R. D. van der Hilst, Improving the tomographic imaging of the lowermost mantle by incorporation of differential times of refracted and diffracted core phases (PKP, P_{diff}), *J. Geophys. Res.*, 2000; H. Kárason and R. D. van der Hilst, New constraints on 3D variations in mantle P wavespeed, *EOS Trans. Amer. Geophys. Union*, 80: F731, 1999; L. H. Kellogg, B. H. Hager, and R. D. van der Hilst, Compositional stratification in the deep mantle, *Science*, 283:1881–1884, 1999; C. Lithgow-Bertelloni and M. Richards, The dynamics of Cenozoic and Mesozoic plate motions, *Rev. Geophys.*, 36, 27–78, 1998; J.-P. Montagner, Can seismic tomography tell us anything about convection in the mantle?, *Rev. Geophys.*, 32:115–137, 1994; J.-P. Montagner, Where can seismic anisotropy be

detected in Earth's mantle? In boundary layers ....,
Pure Appl. Geophys., 151:223–156, 1998; M.
Ritzwoller and E. M. Lavely, 3-dimensional models
of Earth's mantle, *Rev. Geophys.*, 33:1–66, 1995; B.
Romanowicz, Seismic tomography of Earth's man-
tle, *Annu, Rev. Earth Planet. Sci.*, 19:77–99, 1991;
W.-J. Su, R. L. Woodward, and A. M. Dziewonski,
Degree 12 model of shear velocity heterogeneity in
the mantle, *J. Geophys. Res.*, 99:6945–6981, 1994;
R. D. van der Hilst, S. Widiyantoro, and E. R.
Engdahl, Evidence for deep mantle circulation from
global tomography, *Nature*, 386:578–584, 1997; S.
Zhong and M. Gurnis, Mantle convection with plates
and mobile, faulted plate margins, *Science*, 267:838–
843, 1995.

Shark

There are approximately 250 modern species of
sharks and 350 species of their close relatives, the
skates and rays. Collectively these elasmobranchs
(fishes whose gill openings are exposed instead of
being covered by an opercle as in most other fishes)
are distantly related to the chimaeras (holocepha-
lans), and they are classified with them in the class
Chondrichthyes (jawed fishes with a layer of prismatic calcification lining the cartilaginous internal
skeleton, and small skin denticles instead of large
bones in the skin). Although chondrichthyans lack
features of modern bony fishes, discovery of bone
tissue in some fossil sharks suggests evolution from
bony ancestors.

The oldest fossils attributed to chondrichthyans
are isolated skin denticles from the Harding Sandstone of Colorado (late Ordovician, 450 million years
ago). The earliest shark teeth are from the Early
Devonian of Spain (*Leonodus*, approximately
400 Ma). The oldest skeletal fossils (from the mid-
Devonian, for example, *Pucapampella*, approximately 375 Ma, from Bolivia and South Africa)
reveal features previously known only in bony fish
(osteichthyans), thus narrowing the evolutionary
gap between them and chondrichthyans.

Many different kinds of sharks existed by the Late
Devonian, including distant relatives of chimaeras.
A great evolutionary radiation, ultimately involving
more than 20 extinct families of sharks and a dozen
or so families of chimaeralike fish, began in the
Devonian and persisted through the Mississippian
and Pennsylvanian. Many families disappeared in the
Pennsylvanian and Permian, although only a few
were affected by the Permian mass extinction (approximately 250 Ma), and one or two stragglers existed into the Triassic (such as the last xenacanths
and edestids).

These early sharks were anatomically and ecologically far more diverse than those of today.
Cladoselachian sharks (for example, *Cladoselache*,
Late Devonian) were relatively unspecialized except
for stiff, hydrofoillike paired fins and a deeply forked
tail, and were probably fast-swimming predators.
Xenacanth sharks (including *Leonodus*, Devonian;

Orthacanthus, Permian) were eellike and had teeth
with sharp, bifurcated cusps. Almost all xenacanths
lived in fresh-water environments, including
swamps, lagoons, and rivers, and were probably ambush predators. Stethacanthid sharks (Devonian-
Pennsylvanian) had a spine-brush complex behind
the head. Presence of this complex was sex-linked
in some forms (such as *Falcatus*). Edestid and euge-
niodontid sharks (Mississippian-Triassic) had stiff
paired fins like those of cladoselachians, and also
possessed spirals of teeth which grew progressively
larger in the middle of the lower jaw (such as
Edestus).

The subsequent history of sharks during the Mesozoic Era (Triassic, Jurassic, and Cretaceous, 250–
65 Ma) is reminiscent of that of dinosaurs and mammals on land. Hybodont sharks were dominant
throughout much of the Mesozoic, but their origins
can be traced back to the Late Pennsylvanian (*Hamil-
tonichthys*, from Kansas). They were abundant (judging from numbers of fossilized teeth) and also ecologically diverse and widespread, with fresh-water
forms as small as 15 cm (6 in.) long and marine
forms over 4 m (13 ft) long. Contemporary with
Jurassic marine hybodonts were early relatives of
modern sharks. At first these were small [mostly
under 1 m (3 ft) long] and uncommon, but they
rapidly increased in numbers and diversity. For example, in the marine fossil beds of Holzmaden, Germany
(Early Jurassic, 200 Ma), there are large specimens of
Hybodus, but fossil relatives of modern sharks and
rays are extremely rare. Conversely, at nearby
Solnhofen (Late Jurassic, 150 Ma), shark fossils include early representatives of modern hexanchoids,
horn sharks, nurse and carpet sharks, dogfish, angel sharks, and primitive rays, but only one specimen of a hybodont shark. Hybodonts survived into
the Early Cretaceous worldwide and were particularly successful in fresh-water habitats, with distinctive endemic faunas in Europe and North America,
southeast Asia, and perhaps western Gondwana
(South America and Africa). In the Late Cretaceous,
hybodonts were largely replaced by modern sharks
and rays, with one notable exception; the small hybodont *Lonchidion* persisted until almost the end of
the Cretaceous in North America, in fresh-water habitats which few other chondrichthyans were able to
colonize. Apparently no hybodonts survived beyond
the end of the Cretaceous (65 Ma).

Modern sharks (and rays) are distinguishable
anatomically from hybodonts and other extinct
sharks by the presence of heavily calcified vertebrae
and specialized features in the teeth, skin denticles,
and fin spines. These modern attributes were probably not all acquired at once, but the early fossil record
is fragmentary and no clear picture has yet emerged
(isolated teeth, denticles, and fin spines of modern
type are known from the Mississippian and Pennsylvanian, but the earliest shark vertebrae are Triassic).
More complete skeletal remains of generalized modern sharks are known from the Early Jurassic (such
as *Palaeospinax*). The earliest fossils referable to an
extant shark family are hexanchoid teeth, also of

Early Jurassic age. By the Early Cretaceous, many modern families of sharks and rays were present.

There are two hypotheses regarding the evolution of modern sharks and rays: Either rays evolved from within the sharks, and are therefore more closely related to some sharks than to others; or modern sharks and rays share a common ancestor and are therefore of equal antiquity. The first hypothesis is supported by phylogenetic analyses of morphological features, and suggests that the closest relatives of rays are saw sharks, angel sharks, squaleans (*Squalus*), bramble sharks, hexanchoids, frilled shark (*Chlamydoselachus*), and (more distantly) the galean sharks (including port jackson, carpet, dogfish, bull, tiger, mako, and white sharks). The second hypothesis is more in accordance with stratigraphic data; the earliest ray fossils are Early Jurassic (200 Ma, about the same age as the oldest hexanchoid fossils), whereas the oldest known angel sharks are Late Jurassic (150 Ma) and the oldest known saw sharks, bramble sharks, and squaleans are Late Cretaceous (approximately 75 Ma). Phylogenetic analyses placing rays within squalean sharks require rays to have lost essentially all the basal characters used in the analyses, and imply that the stratigraphic range of modern sharks (mostly documented from isolated teeth) is seriously underrepresented in the Triassic and Jurassic.

For background information *see* ELASMOBRANCHII in the McGraw-Hill Encyclopedia of Science & Technology.			John G. Maisey

Bibliography. II. Cappctta, C. Duffin, and J. Zidek, Chondrichthyes, in M. J. Benton (ed.), *The Fossil Record 2*, Chapman and Hall, London, 1993; P. Janvier, *Early Vertebrates*, Oxford University Press, 1996; J. A. Long, *The Rise of Fishes*, University of New South Wales Press, Sydney, 1995; J. G. Maisey, *Discovering Fossil Fishes*, Henry Holt, New York, 1996.

Ship structural design

With the widespread availability of inexpensive and powerful computers, the field of ship design is undergoing changes as radical as the transitions from wood construction to steel and from sail power to mechanical propulsion. While some of the tools made possible by computers, such as structural analysis using finite element methods, have been available for over three decades, only recently has technology been able to provide the capabilities to understand and manage the complex interaction between a ship and its environment.

Design considerations. Ships are among the largest and most complicated structures built. In addition to having a hull form that allows for movement through water with minimum resistance, a ship must have an interior arrangement that maximizes the volume available for whatever cargo the ship is intended to carry, with features to load and discharge the cargo in minimum time. This may involve large openings in the deck characteristic of container ships, or an intricate arrangement of cargo and ballast tanks for a ship designed to carry liquid chemicals in bulk. Large ships are comparable in size to the tallest buildings (see **table**), and they must be designed for 20 or more years of service in a corrosive saltwater environment with waves that may approach 30 m (100 ft) in height during a storm. The designer's goal is to minimize the amount of steel in the ship to reduce cost and weight, while providing enough steel in the right configuration to avoid fractures from high stresses and metal fatigue.

Structural design. In principle, the design of structural components is the same for ships as for any other structure. In its simplest form, the required structural properties are a function of the maximum expected load on the component, the minimum specified strength of the material, and appropriate factors of safety. Designers use various references and analytical tools to determine the characteristics of a ship and the details of the structure, often relying on experience with prior designs. The basic approach has not changed significantly in the past 50 years, although the degree of sophistication certainly has, as more research is completed, analytical capabilities increase, and experience is gained from new designs. For new designs that are similar to existing ships, as is usually the case, new features and modifications often can be addressed through analysis of the local structure affected by the changes, or through extrapolation of existing criteria. However, if the design is significantly beyond practical experience, a more basic first-principles approach must be used. Such an approach still requires the designer to establish the hull form and general arrangement of the ship, as well as estimates of the distribution of mass and structural configuration for the preliminary design.

Loads on structures. The commonly recognized standard for commercial ship design assumes a service life of 20 years. Design service life determines

Characteristics of typical large tanker designs over the past 50 years						
Year built	Length, m (ft)	Breadth, m (ft)	Draft, m (ft)	Cargo capacity, long tons*	Deck/bottom plating thickness, mm (in.)	Material yield strength, N/mm^2 (ksi)
1950	190 (625)	26 (84)	10 (33)	28,000	29 (1.12)	235 (34.0)
2000	320 (1050)	58 (190)	22 (72)	300,000	20 (0.79)	315 (45.5)

*1 long ton = 2240 lb = 1.016 metric tons.

the number of waves encountered, maximum wave height, assumed amount of corrosion, and other factors important to ship design. Published data and computer programs provide designers with the environmental criteria appropriate for design, such as seasonally and geographically adjusted wave height, period, and sea spectral data. There are several computer programs available to predict and analyze the motions and accelerations of the preliminary ship design in the ocean environment. The accelerations and wave profiles are used to determine static and dynamic (including inertial) loads on different areas of the ship's structure from cargo, liquids in tanks including the effects of sloshing, and wave impacts on the sides and bottom structure. The loads are expressed as pressures, forces, and bending moments, both globally and locally. This process must be repeated for all anticipated loading conditions for the ship, from full load to ballast conditions, for various ship speeds, and for different headings and wave conditions, because the response of the ship depends on those variables. In general, the conditions that produce the maximum load for one part of the structure are different from the conditions that affect the design of other parts. In addition, the individual components of the load from bending, wave pressures, cargo loads, and so forth that act on a point on the structure at any given time are usually not in phase with each other. Therefore it is very difficult to resolve the magnitude and direction of the maximum force on any point for purposes of design. To simplify the calculation, the designer may approximate the maximum load by maximizing a dominant load component and adding the other load components that are simultaneously associated with it. For example, the critical design condition for floors and girders in the double bottom of a tanker may be shear forces when the ship is heading directly into the waves at full-load draft with the double bottom tank and cargo tank over it both empty.

Stress analysis. Once the critical loading patterns for a design are known, the adequacy of the structure can be evaluated by typical analysis techniques, which can be as simple as beam approximations or as complicated as finite element analysis. This approach, which is commonly referred to as working stress analysis, has its roots in classical strength-of-materials theory, and has been the traditional analysis philosophy for ships up to the present time. In recent years the approach has become more sophisticated with the application of computers, which have enabled designers to make refinements based on analysis. Those changes in ship structural design have led designers to routinely consider additional modes of failure beyond the traditional tensile yield and ultimate stress criteria, such as buckling of large panels and fatigue cracking of structural details.

Stress analysis also involves factors of safety to account for uncertainties and variabilities in design, construction, and operation. Limits of accuracy in design analysis, variations in the quality of workman-ship during construction, and differences in how ships are loaded, operated, and maintained are accounted for in a general way by factors of safety. These are also used to provide design margins for random variables, such as maximum wave height and mechanical properties of mass-produced steel products. In the working stress approach, factors of safety are applied to the loads, the material properties, or both, to account for the degree of uncertainty between what is assumed during design and what may actually occur when the ship is in service. Factors of safety may be adjusted based on service experience or design and analysis methods. In general, factors of safety are lower for highly detailed and advanced analyses, where uncertainties are less than for simple analyses with more assumptions and approximations.

Design standards. Just as there are safety codes for the design and construction of buildings, there are internationally recognized standards for ships. Classification societies such as the American Bureau of Shipping and Lloyd's Register of Shipping have existed for well over a century to develop, publish, and apply safety standards for ships. The societies are nongovernmental organizations that began as national associations to provide independent technical expertise in ship design and construction to protect the interests, usually financial, of ship owners and ship insurers. Modern classification societies now compete internationally, and they use their extensive analytical capabilities and experience in reviewing designs, monitoring construction, and inspecting ships in service to continually refine and update their standards. The standards, known as Rules, were initially simple formulas and tables for individual structural components which, when assembled, produced a sturdy and seaworthy ship. There were few requirements that applied to the ship as an integrated structure. Changes to the Rules were brought about by gradual changes in the size and complexity of the structures and through feedback from ships in service. Components that failed had to be made stronger.

In the 1970s and 1980s a number of things happened that rendered the old approach obsolete: Computers enabled designers to perform detailed calculations by finite element analysis and to rapidly evaluate design alternatives and new concepts. In response, designers started to base designs on analysis rather than experience. At the same time, several external factors influenced ship design: market forces created a boom in ship construction, economies of scale led to a rapid and unprecedented increase in the size of ships, shipyards introduced widespread use of high-tensile steel to reduce weight and costs, traditional long-term ship owners were replaced by corporations with little ship experience, and ships came to be viewed as assets rather than investments. In addition, stress analysis was used to justify additional decreases in steel to reduce weight and cost, and the potential impact of the various changes in design on inspection and maintenance was not appreciated.

In the 1980s, unexpected problems began to appear in ships as a result of the changes in design technology. Fatigue and buckling are failure modes that are relatively insensitive to changes in the tensile strength of steel. Extensive use of high-strength steel and stress analysis contributed to fatigue cracks and panel buckling because of higher stresses in the structure. Damages to ship hulls from heavy seas and the number of major fractures in relatively young ships increased. Classification societies recognized the need to place their Rules on a more rational scientific basis and embarked on major research and development programs to improve the design technology of modern ships. In 1993 the first Rules based on dynamic loads and a consistent philosophy of rational design were published. The Rules are substantially more complex than the traditional prescriptive Rules, and computer software is required to efficiently apply the Rules to new designs. The benefit of this approach is that it leads to a redistribution of steel in the structure so that a stronger and more robust ship can be designed without an appreciable increase in steel weight.

Advanced design concepts. Modern design codes for many civil engineering structures are based on rational methods using safety factors that give appropriate consideration to observed statistical distributions of the design factors. Under the general heading of reliability-based codes and design procedures, there are various approaches that differ in the degree of complexity and the required input information. Two approaches now being investigated for ships are the safety index concept, which is a probabilistic analog of the factor of safety; and load and resistance factor design (LRFD), in which the logarithms of the variables related to load and strength are considered to follow the normal distribution. LRFD was adopted by the American Petroleum Institute in 1989 as a recommended practice for design of fixed offshore platforms.

The dynamic load component approach, which is now part of the Rules, is an intermediate step between traditional prescriptive Rules and what would be considered reliability-based Rules. The formulations of load components can serve as a basis for developing partial safety factors for purposes of design. Research is being conducted into evaluating the reliability of individual structural components to determine where further improvements in the Rules can be made.

For background information *see* FINITE ELEMENT METHOD; MERCHANT SHIP; SHIP DESIGN; STRUCTURAL DESIGN in the McGraw-Hill Encyclopedia of Science & Technology.   Jack Spencer

Bibliography. H. H. Chen et al., New approach for the design and evaluation of double hull tanker structures, *Trans. SNAME*, 101:215–245, 1993; Y. N. Chen and A. Thayamballi, Consideration of global climatology and loading characteristics in fatigue damage assessment of ship structures, *Symposium on Marine Structural Inspection, Maintenance, and Monitoring*, SNAME, pp. VI.D, 1–13, March 1991; C. Guedes Soares et al., Reliability based ship structural design, *Trans. SNAME*, 104:357–389, 1996; E. V. Lewis (ed.), *Principles of Naval Architecture*, Society of Naval Architecture and Marine Engineers (SNAME), 1988; A. Mansour et al., *Assessment of Reliability of Ship Structures*, Ship Structure Committee, 1997.

Single-atom laser

A laser that uses a single atom as its gain medium was first realized in 1994. This laser uses a low-density beam of barium atoms traversing a small optical resonator with highly reflective mirrors. Light emission and amplification are achieved via quantized Rabi oscillation.

Every laser consists of two essential components: an optical resonator (also called a cavity), typically formed by two mirrors facing each other; and a gain medium between the mirrors, which generates and amplifies the light. For laser oscillation to occur, the laser gain—the increase in the intensity of light as it passes through the laser medium—must be greater than the loss caused by imperfections in the laser mirrors and other factors.

Comparison with conventional lasers. Appreciation of the single-atom laser requires an understanding of how a conventional laser operates. Conventional lasers, in which light is amplified by the process of stimulated emission, require a very large number of atoms in the laser medium to provide enough gain to exceed the loss. For example, a helium-neon laser emitting a 1 milliwatt beam may contain 10^{16} neon atoms and about 10 times as many helium atoms. Light amplification, due to the neon atoms (active atoms), reaches equilibrium when there are roughly 10^9 photons in the laser cavity. Therefore, tens of millions of atoms are needed to maintain each photon in the resonator. In general, conventional lasers require at least 100,000 active atoms per photon stored in the resonator. The active atoms alternate between two of the energy states. Light amplification can occur only when the number of the active atoms in the higher-energy, or excited, state exceeds the number in the lower-energy state. This condition is called population inversion.

Quantized Rabi oscillation. The single-atom laser uses an alternative method of light amplification based on a process called quantized Rabi oscillation. Rabi oscillation is the periodic exchange of energy between atoms and a single electromagnetic field mode. When an atom interacts with only a small number of photons, the Rabi oscillations are quantized—that is, they occur at discrete frequencies determined by the number of photons.

One consequence of quantized Rabi oscillation is that an excited atom can be induced to emit a photon simply by placing it in a very small cavity. If the cavity is resonant—that is, if its dimensions are adjusted so that the photons emitted by the atom can build up inside the cavity—a strong coupling may occur which causes the atom to emit a photon much more quickly than it would in free space. This process is called vacuum Rabi oscillation because there are initially no photons in the cavity.

Micromaser and microlaser. A single-atom maser, or micromaser, utilizing the quantized Rabi oscillation was demonstrated in 1984. In this experiment, a beam of Rydberg atoms—atoms in which the outermost electrons are excited to large, circular orbits—flowed one by one into a resonant, superconducting microwave cavity. As the atoms passed through the cavity, they emitted photons at an increased rate, consistent with a theory based on quantized Rabi oscillations.

The single-atom laser, or microlaser, is the optical version of the micromaser. Excited two-level barium atoms from an oven stream into a small resonator one by one and emit photons at a wavelength of 791 nanometers (at the upper end of the range of visible wavelengths). The first photon is emitted by vacuum Rabi oscillation, and further amplification occurs through the quantized Rabi oscillation process. As the number of photons in the cavity grows, the probability that a subsequent atom will emit another photon increases, up to some level. The photon buildup continues until the rate of loss from transmission, absorption, and scattering at the mirrors equals the rate of photon emission from the barium atoms. When the average number of atoms in the cavity was 0.4, the atoms emitted about 10^6 photons per second, enough to maintain one photon in the cavity at all times; when the average atom number was increased to 0.7, the output of the laser rose by a factor of 7. This clearly shows a thresholdlike behavior, indicative of laser action.

Prospects. The single-atom laser is a new experimental tool for studying quantum atom-field interactions and laser oscillation. It is a simple system, consisting of a two-level atom and a single-mode cavity, so that rigorous comparison with theory can be made. Due to the quantized Rabi emission process, the single-atom laser is expected to exhibit unusual nonclassical behavior (behavior that can be explained only by quantum-mechanical theory). In contrast to the linear increase in output as the pump rate is increased above threshold in a conventional laser, the single-atom laser is expected to show a second threshold as the number of intracavity atoms is increased to much greater than one.

The emission spectrum of the light emitted by the single-atom laser will also display unconventional features, which may have an impact on the theory of laser spectral lineshapes. The single-atom laser is predicted to be a source of nonclassical light (light with uniquely quantum-mechanical properties). In particular, the photon number distribution in the cavity is expected to exhibit sub-Poisson statistics; that is, the fluctuation in the number of photons in the cavity will be less than for any classical light source, including conventional lasers, a phenomenon called photon antibunching.

Experiments are under way to study the unique, nonclassical features of the single-atom laser. These experiments will measure the second-order intensity correlation function, $g^{(2)}(\tau)$, by studying the emitted photons as a function of time, and the distribution of photons in the cavity. Measuring $g^{(2)}(\tau)$ will allow researchers to study photon bunching and antibunching (features of nonclassical light), while measurement of the intracavity photon distribution will provide a direct measurement of cavity photon statistics.

Another feature to be studied is the operation of the microlaser in the mesoscopic regime, where the number of intracavity atoms exceeds one but is still well below a macroscopic quantity. One of the motivations of microlaser- micromaser research is to investigate the quantum theory of the laser. In a microlaser in which one or a small number of atoms interacts with a single cavity mode in a controlled fashion, it should be possible to observe effects that are averaged out in conventional lasers. A classical field, the type generated in a conventional laser, is reached only if a sufficient amount of randomness is introduced into the system. By altering the randomness of the microlaser, it should be possible to demonstrate the transition between microlaser behavior and that of a conventional laser, and examine how it occurs. In these experiments, the amount of randomness or noise to the system will be gradually increased, either by varying the pump excitation process or the atom-cavity interaction. For example, the flow of excited atoms into the cavity may be modified to increase the variability of times for different atoms to flow through the cavity mode. Similarly, the degree of coupling variation may be modified by allowing different atoms to travel through different parts of the cavity mode. The various atoms will then experience different atom-cavity coupling strengths. In each case, the flux of atoms entering the cavity can also be varied. By studying the increase in photon emission as the pump rate is increased, the transition between microlaser behavior and classical laser behavior can be studied. Measurement of photon statistics and laser linewidth will be used to study the evolution from nonclassical to classical laser behavior.

For background information *see* LASER; MASER; QUANTUM MECHANICS; RYDBERG ATOM; SQUEEZED QUANTUM STATES in the McGraw-Hill Encyclopedia of Science & Technology.

Chung-Chieh Yu; Chris Fang-Yen; Abdulaziz Aljalal; Ramachandra Dasari; Kyungwon An; Michael S. Feld

Bibliography. K. An et al., Microlaser: A laser with one atom in an optical resonator, *Phys. Rev. Lett.*, 73:3375–3378, 1994; M. S. Feld and K. An, The single-atom laser, *Sci. Amer.*, 279(1):56–63, July 1998; D. Meschede, H. Walther, and G. Muller, One-atom maser, *Phys. Rev. Lett.*, 54:551–554, 1985.

Sleep

There are two main states of sleep: REM (rapid eye movement) sleep, typically associated with a higher level of brain neuronal activity, and nonREM sleep, typically associated with synchronized and slower neuronal activity, especially in the cortex. A study of sleep includes records of the electroencephalogram (EEG, a measure of "brain waves") which provides an assessment of brain activity by using sensors (electrodes) placed on the scalp to detect small (microvolt) signals produced by the synchronous activity of cortical neurons. In addition, eye movements are recorded with the electrooculogram (EOG), and muscle tone with the electromyogram (EMG). This ensemble of records is known as a polysomnogram. It enables researchers to describe and to quantify the stages of sleep.

Stages. As sleep onset approaches, the low-amplitude, fast-frequency EEG of alert wakefulness yields to stage 1 sleep, a brief transitional phase between wakefulness and true sleep. This is followed by stage 2 sleep, during which episodic bursts of rhythmic, 14–16-Hz waveforms occur in the EEG. These are known as sleep spindles. During stage 2, the EEG frequencies slow still further, and this process continues with stages 3 and 4, which are defined by the presence of high-amplitude, slow (0.5–4 Hz) waves, called delta waves. The low-voltage, fast-frequency EEG pattern of REM sleep is in marked contrast to delta-wave sleep, and resembles the EEG pattern of wakefulness. REM sleep is also characterized by the presence of bursts of rapid eye movements and by loss of muscle tone. Excluding REM sleep, the other sleep stages are often grouped together and called nonREM sleep, and stages 3 and 4 are often termed deep slow-wave sleep.

There is a typical and predictable progression from one sleep state to another during the night. As the night begins, there is a stepwise descent from wakefulness to stage 1 through to stage 4 sleep, followed by a more abrupt ascent back toward stage 1. However, in place of stage 1, the first REM sleep episode usually occurs at this transition point, about 70–90 min after sleep onset. After the first REM sleep episode, the sleep cycle repeats with the appearance of nonREM sleep; and then, about 90 min after the start of the first REM period, another REM sleep episode occurs. This rhythmic cycling persists throughout the night.

Neuronal changes. The high-voltage, synchronized, slow-wave activity in the cortex during most of non-REM sleep contrasts sharply with the low-voltage, fast-frequency pattern, called desynchronized or activated EEG, that is a characteristic of wakefulness and REM sleep.

A major advance of recent years has been learning which neurotransmitters (chemicals used by neurons in communication) are important in EEG activation. It is now known that groups of neurons, using acetylcholine as the neurotransmitter, ascend from specific brainstem areas to innervate thalamic nuclei important in EEG desynchronization and synchronization. The thalamus is a midbrain structure ideally placed to modulate information that passes to the cortex from other parts of the brain. In addition to these brainstem systems, there is another cholinergic activating input both to the thalamus and directly to the cortex that arises from a localized area of the

basal forebrain, called the nucleus basalis of Meynert. Other brainstem neuronal projections, using different neurotransmitters, also play a role in exciting thalamic and cortical cells during EEG desynchronized states.

Thus, neurons in both the thalamus and cortex are activated during wakefulness and REM sleep. This activation occurs because the state-specific release of neurotransmitters onto these neurons changes their electrical discharge rate by changing permeability to certain ions and hence altering the voltage difference between inside and outside the cell membrane (that is, the membrane potential). NonREM sleep begins as excitatory influences from the brainstem and basal forebrain structures are reduced. Studies indicate that the rhythmic, synchronized waves of nonREM sleep arise as a result of interactions between thalamic neurons and other neurons that project from the thalamus to the cortex. Neurons that project back from the cortex to the thalamus complete a neuronal loop with thalamic neurons, and this loop oscillates. This oscillation is reflected in synchronized changes in the cortical neurons' dendrites (cell branches that receive input). This synchronization is responsible for the EEG waves of nonREM sleep, including the spindles of stage 2 sleep and the delta waves of deep slow-wave sleep. The different frequencies that are seen on the EEG are due to the different degrees of membrane polarization of neurons in the circuit, as excitatory input continues to decline as sleep deepens.

Need for sleep. It is not known why sleep is needed. Many theories have been posited and some evidence has been gathered for all of them, but at present none is entirely convincing or complete. Two things are certain, however: humans spend about a third of their lives in sleep, and they cannot do without it for any length of time. Hence sleep must play a vital biological role. The need for sleep depends on the time of day (circadian factors) and the time awake. The need for sleep grows stronger the longer one stays awake, as homeostatic mechanisms come into play to increase the pressure for sleep. A possible answer to the puzzle of the functions of sleep will come from understanding this homeostatic control of sleep.

A current hypothesis is that the purine nucleoside adenosine may act as an endogenous sleep factor and mediate the sleepiness that follows prolonged wakefulness. Adenosine is linked to energy metabolism as a component of high-energy phosphates; levels of adenosine may therefore increase in certain specific areas of the brain during wakefulness as a result of increased metabolism during wakefulness. Pharmacological experiments first suggested that adenosine might be an important mediator of sleep because it could promote sleep and decrease wakefulness. Support was also provided by the nearly ubiquitous use of caffeine to promote wakefulness: the pharmacological effect of caffeine at levels achieved in the brain after normal consumption is the blockade of the adenosine receptor. In recent experiments, it was found that perfusing adenosine directly into cholinergic basal forebrain and brainstem areas produced an increase in sleep. Furthermore, extracellular concentrations of adenosine in the basal forebrain cholinergic region were higher during spontaneous wakefulness when compared with nonREM sleep in freely behaving animals. Perhaps most convincing, progressive increases in adenosine occur in the basal forebrain during artificially prolonged wakefulness, followed by a slow decline during recovery sleep. Mimicking this basal forebrain rise in adenosine through pharmacological means leads to a sleep pattern identical with that seen following prolonged wakefulness.

Disorders. Sleep medicine includes study and treatment not only of those primary sleep disorders related to pathology of the mechanisms of sleep and arousal, but also of those secondary disorders caused by other medical conditions affecting sleep. For example, breathing abnormalities can disturb sleep, and sleep apnea remains by far the most important presenting complaint at sleep disorder centers. Apnea during sleep is a pause in breathing which lasts for more than 10 s and which typically interrupts sleep. It can be caused by collapse of the upper airways, referred to as obstructive apnea, or there can be a failure of breathing commands from the brain, described as central apnea. Other examples of secondary sleep disorders are those insomnias associated with mood or generalized anxiety disorders, or caused as a side effect of medication.

In a recent Gallup survey, 9% of American adults reported chronic insomnia and an additional 27% reported transient insomnia during the preceding 12 months. Thus, a remarkably high 36% of the surveyed population exhibit some form of insomnia. If minor sleep problems are excluded, there is little variation among western countries, and overall, about 20% of the general population appears to be affected by severe insomnia. If insomnias are classified as transient or chronic, however, national differences emerge. The prevalence of chronic insomnia in the United States (9%) can be compared with 19% in France (the highest) and 7% in Spain (the lowest). Even if national differences are noted in the prevalence of insomnia, all studies agree that problems with sleeping are more prevalent in women and in the elderly. However, few of those with chronic insomnia actually seek help for the condition, though sleep medicine clinics are now widespread and anyone suspecting the presence of a sleep disorder should consult a physician for referral.

The current classification of sleep disorders as recognized by the American Academy of Sleep Medicine is as follows:

DYSSOMNIAS

A. *Intrinsic Sleep Disorders*
  1. Psychophysiological insomnia
  2. Sleep state misperception
  3. Idiopathic insomnia
  4. Narcolepsy
  5. Recurrent hypersomnia
  6. Idiopathic hypersomnia
  7. Posttraumatic hypersomnia
  8. Obstructive sleep apnea syndrome
  9. Central sleep apnea syndrome
  10. Central alveolar hypoventilation syndrome
  11. Periodic limb movement disorder
  12. Restless legs syndrome
B. *Extrinsic Sleep Disorders*
  1. Inadequate sleep hygiene
  2. Environmental sleep disorder
  3. Altitude insomnia
  4. Adjustment sleep disorder
  5. Insufficient sleep syndrome
  6. Limit-setting sleep disorder
  7. Sleep-onset association disorder
  8. Food allergy insomnia
  9. Nocturnal eating (drinking) syndrome
  10. Hypnotic-dependent sleep disorder
  11. Stimulant-dependent sleep disorder
  12. Alcohol-dependent sleep disorder
  13. Toxin-induced sleep disorder
C. *Circadian Rhythm Sleep Disorders*
  1. Time zone change (jet lag) syndrome
  2. Shift work sleep disorder
  3. Irregular sleep-wake pattern
  4. Delayed sleep phase syndrome
  5. Advanced sleep phase syndrome
  6. Non-24-hour sleep-wake disorder

PARASOMNIAS

A. *Arousal Disorders*
  1. Confusional arousals
  2. Sleepwalking
  3. Sleep terrors
B. *Sleep-Wake Transition Disorders*
  1. Rhythmic movement disorder
  2. Sleep starts
  3. Sleep talking
  4. Nocturnal leg cramps
C. *Parasomnias Usually Associated with REM Sleep*
  1. Nightmares
  2. Sleep paralysis
  3. Impaired sleep-related penile erections
  4. Sleep-related painful erections
  5. REM sleep-related sinus arrest
  6. REM sleep behavior disorder
D. *Other Parasomnias*
  1. Sleep bruxism
  2. Sleep enuresis
  3. Sleep-related abnormal swallowing syndrome
  4. Nocturnal paroxysmal dystonia
  5. Sudden unexplained nocturnal death syndrome
  6. Primary snoring
  7. Infant sleep apnea
  8. Congenital central hypoventilation syndrome
  9. Sudden infant death syndrome
  10. Benign neonatal sleep myoclonus

Dyssomnias include those disorders that cause either a difficulty in getting to sleep or staying asleep, or excessive daytime sleepiness. Examples include insomnia and narcolepsy, which is characterized primarily by bouts of sleep during the day and sudden muscle atonia as the signs of REM sleep intrude into wakefulness. Parasomnias have been defined to include all those disorders that are manifested as undesirable intrusions of behavior, or abnormal autonomic nervous system function, occurring primarily during sleep. An example is the presence of muscle tone during REM sleep, which is manifested as REM sleep behavior disorder, in which a patient acts out his dreams because of this muscle activity.

For background information *see* BIOLOGICAL CLOCKS; BRAIN; ELECTROENCEPHALOGRAPHY; PURINE; SLEEP AND DREAMING; SLEEP DISORDERS in the McGraw-Hill Encyclopedia of Science & Technology.   Christopher M. Sinton; Robert W. McCarley

Bibliography. T. Porkka-Heiskanen et al., Adenosine: A mediator of the sleep-inducing effects of prolonged wakefulness, *Science*, 276:1265–1268, 1997; T. Roth and S. Ancoli-Israel, Daytime consequences and correlates of insomnia in the United States: Results of the 1991 National Sleep Foundation survey, *Sleep*, 22(suppl. 2):S347–S353, 1999; M. Steriade, R. Curró Dossi, and A. Nuñez, Network modulation of a slow intrinsic oscillation of cat thalamocortical neurons implicated in sleep delta waves: Cortically induced synchronization and brainstem cholinergic suppression, *J. Neurosci.*, 11:3200–3217, 1991; M. von Krosigk, T. Bal, and D. A. McCormick, Cellular mechanisms of a synchronized oscillation in the thalamus, *Science*, 261:361–364, 1993.

Snake

Snakes are fascinating animals. These elongate, limbless reptiles may possess deadly venom, can reach enormous sizes, live in almost every imaginable habitat, and are vital components of numerous mythologies. In the science of vertebrate evolution, an enduring enigma has been the how, where, when, and why of snake evolution, and the identity of the likely lizard candidate for closest snake relative. The one aspect of snake evolution commonly agreed upon is that snakes are derived from within lizards (snakes and lizards constitute the order Squamata). The problem has centered on the absence of complete snake fossils, and the characters that such fossils would bring to investigations of snake and lizard phylogeny. While whole body fossils of lizards are known from 135-million-year-old rocks, similarly complete fossils of early snakes were known only from 80-million-year-old rocks (such as *Dinilysia patagonica*).

Pachyrhachis. Three fossils previously thought to be ancient aquatic varanoid lizards have recently been reinterpreted as marine snakes from the Upper Cretaceous [97 million years ago (Ma)] oceans of southern Europe and the Middle East. The most widely known of these fossil snakes, *Pachyrhachis*

problematicus, with rear legs, shows important features that are transitional between snakes and lizards. The snake is known from two largely complete, articulated specimens, found at Ein Jabrud, north of Jerusalem (**Fig. 1a** and *b*). A third specimen, *Haasiophis terrasanctus*, from the same quarry is currently being described, as are new specimens of legged snakes from slightly younger rocks in Lebanon (*Podophis*). *Pachyrhachis* has a small, lightly built skull and a long body with thickened ribs and vertebrae that exhibit most of the derived features of modern snakes. However, it also possesses lizard characters (such as a tall coronoid bone) and several features that are shared with mosasauroids (for example, a ball-and-socket intramandibular joint). The neck of *Pachyrhachis* is long and slender, as is the long, laterally compressed trunk. The forelimbs and shoulder girdle are absent, while the pelvis and hindlimb are well formed but greatly reduced in size (Fig. 1c).

Pachyrhachis was probably a slow-swimming ambush predator that inhabited shallow reefs and lagoons—a niche very similar to that occupied by many modern sea snakes which forage for prey by inserting their small heads and slender necks into cracks and crevices on the reefs. The pachyostosis (bony thickening of vertebrae and ribs) exhibited by *Pachyrhachis* is an adaptation for diving and aquatic locomotion. Similar features are present in other well-known Cenomanian snakes: *Pachyophis*, *Haasiophis*, *Podophis*, *Similiophis*, and *Mesophis*. Unfortunately, only a small number of isolated vertebrae are known for fossil snakes older (125–98 Ma) than *Pachyrhachis* and are therefore phylogenetically and paleoecologically uninformative.

However, using character data from *Pachyrhachis*, *Pachyophis*, and a large number of fossil and modern snakes and lizards, several recent studies have produced well-supported hypotheses of squamate phylogeny. These studies independently find the nearest relatives of snakes to be a diverse group of Upper Cretaceous seagoing lizards known as mosasauroids (dolichosaurs, adriosaurs, aigialosaurs, and mosasaurs). Dolichosaurs and adriosaurs were small lizards (0.5–1 m) with small heads and long necks, bodies, and tails; and small but well-developed limbs. They appear in the fossil record at the same time as *Pachyrhachis* (**Fig. 2a**). Aigialosaurs and mosasaurs achieved large body size (1–10 m) and had large heads, short necks, and long tails. Mosasaurs had limbs that were modified into large paddles (Fig. 2b); aigialosaurs had limbs resembling those of typical terrestrial lizards.

Fossil evidence. The hypothesis that mosasauroids might be the closest lizard relative of snakes is in direct conflict with the long-held idea that snakes evolved from a small, fossorial (burrowing) lizard ancestor. The identity of which burrowing lizard (amphisbaenids, dibamids, pygopodids, and burrowing scincids) this might be has remained as unresolved and controversial as the recent suggestion of an aquatic ancestry. The burrowing hypothesis is also

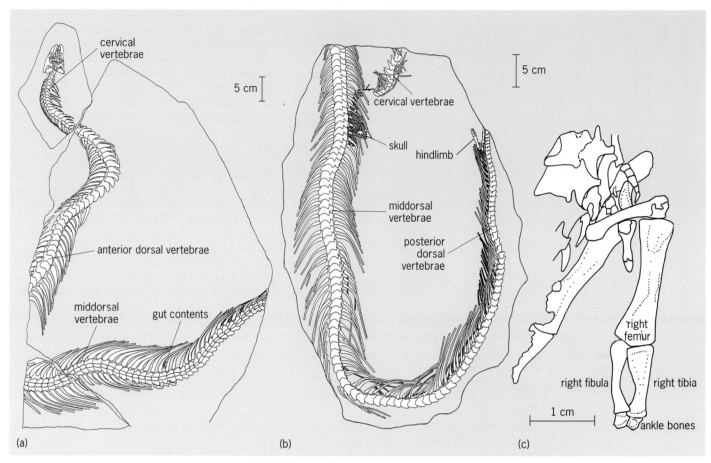

Fig. 1. *Pachyrhachis problematicus.* (*a*) Holotype specimen. (*b*) Paratype specimen; note hindlimb. (*c*) Detail of hindlimb as preserved on paratype.

linked to the habits and morphology of scolecophidians, *Anomochilus*, uropeltids, cylindrophids, and aniliids—all small, highly fossorial snakes—that are held to be the most primitive living snakes. More advanced snakes are supposed to be secondarily surface-living, and therefore it has been concluded by some that fossoriality is primitive for snakes.

Recent phylogenetic hypotheses contradict the fossorial origin view by making two major revisions (**Fig. 3**): (1) *Pachyrhachis* is a basal snake (more primitive than modern fossorial snakes); (2) mosasauroids are the closest relatives of snakes among lizards, not burrowing lizards (snakes and mosasauroids are referred to as the Pythonomorpha).

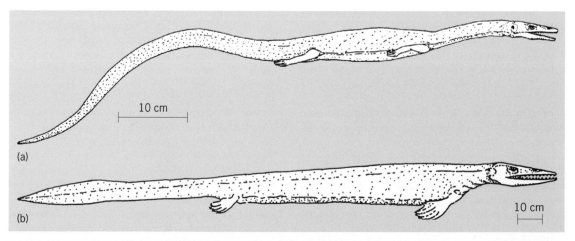

Fig. 2. **Dolichosaurs and mosasaurs.** (*a*) Typical dolichosaur, with small head, long neck, small limbs, and long tail. (*b*) Typical mosasaur, with large head, short neck, large paddlelike limbs, and long tail.

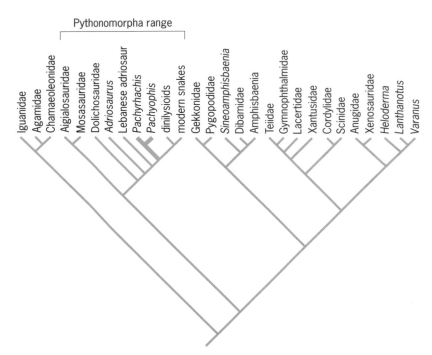

Fig. 3. Squamate phylogeny including *Pachyrhachis* and *Pachyophis* (thick line denotes this clade). Pythonomorpha indicates the group formed by snakes and mosasauroids. The phylogeny is a composite derived from cladograms published independently and collectively by M. W. Caldwell, M. S. Y. Lee, and J. S. Scanlon.

Thus, fossoriality cannot be primitive for snakes, but must have evolved within snakes, in taxa more derived than *Pachyrhachis*, and the macrostomatan condition in snakes (wide distension of the jaws, mobility of various skull bones, and the ability to swallow large prey) is primitive for snakes as well. Interestingly, a similar form of skull bone mobility, related to feeding mechanics, is present in all mosasauroids.

Two possible scenarios for snake origins can be derived from a snake-mosasauroid grouping in which *Pachyrhachis* is a primitive snake: (1) Marine adaptations, primitive for pythonomorphs, are retained in mosasauroids and *Pachyrhachis*. More derived snakes revert to terrestriality but retain the anatomical specializations inherited from aquatic ancestors. This scenario predicts that most basal pythonomorphs found in the future, including snakes more primitive than *Pachyrhachis*, will be aquatic. This hypothesis appears to be supported by the fact that many poorly known taxa such as dolichosaurs and other basal snakes are indeed aquatic. (2) Pythonomorphs were primitively terrestrial, with convergent marine adaptations occurring in mosasauroids and *Pachyrhachis*. This scenario is supported by the following observations: Mosasauroids are more lizard-like in general body form, with paddlelike limbs in mosasaurs, and presumably used hydrodynamic methods to maintain depth (hydrofoils such as paddles and active swimming). *Pachyrhachis*, however, is elongate and almost limbless, and used hydrostatic methods (pachyostosis) to maintain depth. This scenario would be unequivocally supported only by the

discovery of primitive relatives of mosasauroids, or snakes more primitive than *Pachyrhachis*, that show terrestrial habits. While a terrestrial origin for snakes cannot yet be excluded, what seems unlikely is that the origin of snakes was initiated around burrowing adaptations.

The study of snake evolution remains a provocative and intriguing area of research, with new data and ideas leading to some progress in the understanding of snake origins and relationships.

For background information *see* SQUAMATA in the McGraw-Hill Encyclopedia of Science & Technology.
Michael W. Caldwell

Bibliography. M. W. Caldwell and M. S. Y. Lee, A snake with legs from the marine Cretaceous of the Middle East, *Nature*, 386:705–709, 1997; R. L. Carroll, *Vertebrate Paleontology and Evolution*, W. H. Freeman, New York, 1988; M. S. Y. Lee, G. L. Bell, and M. W. Caldwell, The origins of snake feeding, *Nature*, 400:655–659, 1999; G. Underwood, A contribution to the classification of snakes, *Publ. Brit. Mus. (Nat. Hist.)*, 653:1–179, 1967.

Solid-state devices

Solid-state devices operate by controlling the electrical, optical, magnetic, mechanical, or thermal properties of a well-organized solid thin-film structure. They are used in industries such as entertainment, education, transportation, communication, military, environment, and health care. The advancement of solid-state devices has been phenomenal, with new products being introduced on a regular basis. **Table 1** lists some of the major application areas of solid-state devices. The computer industry is the main driving force for the advancement of these devices.

Since solid-state devices are composed of multilayer thin films, the device structure, material properties, and manufacturing processes are basic factors that influence the device performance. Examples of silicon-based transistors will be discussed in this article.

Structures. The transistor is a three-terminal device generally used as a switch or amplifier. The most common silicon-based transistors are the metal-oxide-semiconductor field-effect transistor (MOSFET), bipolar junction transistor (BJT), and thin-film transistor (TFT) [see **illus.**]. The first two are the most important single-crystal silicon-based devices used in very large scale integrated circuits (VLSICs) for logic and memory functions. The third is the key element in the active matrix liquid crystal display (AMLCD). MOSFET and TFT are insulated-gate field-effect transistors (FETs). They are operated on the same principle; that is, the current flows between drain and source, which is controlled by the voltage at the gate electrode. The BJT is operated on the principle of regulating the current between collector and emitter by the base current.

TABLE 1. Solid-state-device application areas

Application areas	Devices
Very large scale integrated circuits	Metal-oxide-semiconductor transistor, bipolar transistor, capacitor, resistor
Flat-panel displays	Thin-film transistor, capacitor, field-emission diode (FED), light-emitting diode (IED), microelectromechanical system (MEMS)
Storages	Magnetoresistive (MR) or giant magnetoresistive (GMR) recording head, laser diode
Photovoltaic	*p-n* junction cell, diode
Sensors and imagers	Charge-coupled device (CCD), photodiode, phototransistor, capacitor, resistor

These basic transistor structures can be modified to carry out specific applications or to match certain process limitations. For example, the silicon dioxide (SiO_2) gate dielectric of a MOSFET can be replaced by a stacked dielectric/metal/dielectric structure to form a floating-gate transistor. The new transistor is a nonvolatile memory device that stores charges in the dielectric for a long period of time. In another case, an electron-trapping silicon nitride (Si_3N_4) film can be added to the gate silicon dioxide layer to form another type of memory device. In contrast, the TFT structure can be changed dramatically. For example, the bottom gate structure can be changed to the top gate structure, or the top channel protection layer can be eliminated. The TFT manufacturing process can be simplified by these changes, but the transistor characteristics are deteriorated at the same time. In another case, the drain region can be purposely offset from the gate to create a high-voltage TFT.

Device characteristics. The basic requirement for a solid-state device is to perform within the specifications for a long period of time with minimum deterioration of characteristics.

For the MOSFET and TFT, a high speed (that is, field-effect mobility), a large on-current, and a small leakage current are essential properties. Other transitional properties, such as the threshold voltage, the subthreshold slope, and the transconductance, should be tightly controlled. Most of these characteristics are controlled by the semiconductor-gate dielectric interface properties, such as the interface density of states. It is imperative to optimize the physical and chemical properties of this interface, for example, with proper thin-film materials or adequate process conditions, to achieve the low interface density of states. For the bipolar transistor, the emitter current gain is an important parameter to look for. Since it is a junction device, the transistor performance is controlled by qualities of the junctions and the bulk silicon substrate material.

The device's long-term reliability can be examined with accelerated tests. For example, shifts of the FET characteristics are often measured after it has been stressed with a high voltage at a high temperature for a period of time. This kind of accelerated test is used to predict the life expectancy of the device under the normal operation condition. The test data can also be used to analyze the device failure mechanism. Similar types of tests are used to screen products in quality control.

Materials. Three types of materials are used in solid-state devices: semiconductors, dielectrics, and conductors. The composition, bond structure, morphology, and electrical properties are commonly examined. Since the majority of materials used in

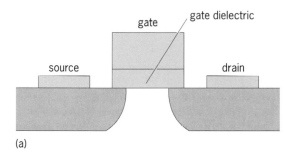

(a)

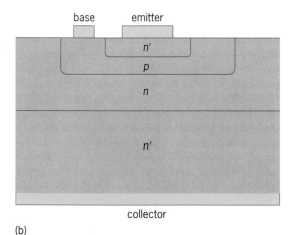

(b)

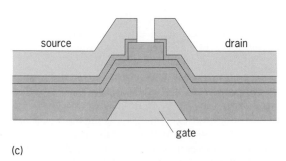

(c)

Various silicon-based transistor structures. (*a*) MOSFET. (*b*) Bipolar function transistor. (*c*) Thin-film transistor.

advanced solid-state devices are in thin-film form, both their bulk and interfacial properties are critical to the device performance. A high-quality thin film could be unintentionally damaged by a harsh process condition or by contamination from impurities.

Semiconductors. An important property of the semiconductor material is the bandgap (E_g) between the conduction and the valence bands. The material's electrical and optical properties deteriorate with the existence of energy levels within the bandgap, such as gap states. For example, single-crystalline silicon ($E_g = 1.1$ eV) has a highly ordered, long-range structure with almost no gap states. All types of defects, such as point (for example, vacancies), one-dimensional (for example, dislocations), and two-dimensional (for example, stacking faults), can contribute to gap states. These defects are caused by factors such as segregation of impurities or local strains. In contrast, the hydrogenated amorphous silicon (a-Si:H, $E_g = 1.1$ eV) does not have a long-range order and is full of tail and deep states due to the existence of a large number of dangling bonds. The defects of the polycrystalline silicon (polysilicon) exist at grain boundaries and within grains.

Semiconductors are often doped with impurities (dopants) at various energy levels. There are two types of dopants. The *n*-type dopant, such as phosphorus or arsenic atoms in silicon, typically has an ionization energy above the semiconductor's gap center. The *p*-type dopant, such as the boron atom in silicon, typically has an ionization energy below the gap center. The semiconductor's electron and hole drift mobilities, as well as resistivity, change with the type and concentration of the dopant. The device-active area, such as the channel region of a MOSFET, commonly is lightly doped, while the nonactive areas, such as ohmic contacts, isolation regions, and the conductive polysilicon gate, usually are heavily doped. For bipolar transistors, device active areas, such as emitter and collector, are heavily doped.

Dielectrics. Dielectrics are used as part of the device or in the periphery area. The former includes applications such as the gate dielectric of a MOSFET or the insulating layer of a capacitor. The latter includes applications such as the intermetal insulating layer, the device isolation layer, or the passivation layer. The most common dielectric materials in very large scale integration (VLSI) are silicon dioxide, silicon nitride (Si_3N_4), phosphorus-doped SiO_2 (PSG), boron-doped SiO_2 (BSG), and boron phosphorus-doped SiO_2 (BPSG). Other organic or inorganic dielectric materials, such as polyimide, spin-on glass (SOG), tantalum oxide (Ta_2O_5), and ferroelectrics, have also been used in certain manufacturing processes or special products.

The dielectric thin film should have a low leakage current ($I_{leakage}$, for example, $<10^{-13}$ A) and a large breakdown voltage (V_{BD}, for example, $>10^6$ V/cm). Silicon dioxide can satisfy these requirements and is widely used in current devices. Other properties, such as the charge trapping capability, the dielectric constant (k), and morphology, are important. For most insulating applications, the dielectric film should not trap or retain electrons. However, for the nonvolatile memory devices, the gate dielectric film should trap and retain electrons for a long period of time. The silicon nitride film is an ideal material for this kind of device. For future generation devices, dielectrics with extreme dielectric constants, such as $k < 3$ or > 10, are required in specific device areas.

Conductors. Conductors are used to transmit electrical signals between devices or for the circuit's inputs and outputs. Electric conductivity is a significant property. In the design of advanced integrated circuits (ICs) or flat-panel displays, the general trend is to shrink the solid-state-device geometry and, at the same time, to increase the die casting size. Therefore, signal delay through the interconnect line often becomes the bottleneck of the whole circuit. Currently, aluminum (conductivity ~2.7 $\mu\Omega\cdot$cm) is most widely used interconnecting material in VLSI. Copper (conductivity ~1.7 $\mu\Omega\cdot$cm) gradually becomes popular for the high-density integrated circuit. Other properties, such as hillocks formation, electromigration, adhesion, chemical inertness, and process capability, are critical to the yield and reliability of devices.

Although a high conductivity is desirable, other properties are also important for certain applications. Low-conductive refractory metals, silicides, and metal compounds are used locally to enhance the interconnecting function. For example, titanium or tantalum has been used as a barrier layer between aluminum and heavily doped silicon to prevent aluminum from spiking into silicon. The same conductors are used as an adhesion layer for copper or as a barrier layer at the contact area of two metals. Tungsten is used as the plug metal to fill high-aperture-ratio connection holes (vias). Metal silicides are often formed on polysilicon for the MOSFET gate application. They are also used to form ohmic contacts. Transparent conductors, such as indium tin oxide (ITO), are commonly used in optical devices, because they can conduct current and, at the same time, transmit more than 80% of light in the visible wavelength range.

Fabrication processes. The majority of solid-state devices are fabricated by thin-film technology, comprising five basic processes: deposition, thermal process, doping, etching, and lithography.

Deposition. Thin films can be deposited by physical vapor deposition (PVD) or chemical vapor deposition (CVD). PVD transfers the material from the target to the substrate surface using a physical means such as thermal evaporation, electron beam, laser beam, or sputtering. Sputtering is the most popular PVD method in production because it can supply a uniform film over a large area with a high throughput. Sputtering is carried out by bombarding the target with high-energy ions that are generated from a direct-current (dc) or radio-frequency (rf) plasma.

The PVD setup is simple, requiring only a target and an energy source, under vacuum. Properties of the PVD film, such as composition and morphology, can be tightly controlled under proper process conditions. For most applications, PVD is used to deposit conducting films, such as aluminum, copper, titanium, cobalt, and chromium, that have properties the same as, or similar to, those of the targets. The deposited films can also be different from the target materials. For example, tantalum oxide can be deposited from a tantalum target using a reactive sputtering process with the argon-oxygen mixture. A three- or four-component film can be deposited from several targets using the co-sputtering process. The PVD film usually has a large number of dangling bonds and a high defect density, which makes it improper for semiconductor or dielectric applications in the critical device area.

CVD is a method of forming a film by carrying out chemical reactions on the substrate surface. Reactive gases are introduced into a heated chamber, where they are dissociated, adsorbed, and reacted. Reaction products are accumulated on the surface, and by-products are desorbed. CVD can be carried out at atmosphere pressure (APCVD) or low pressure (LPCVD), such as under vacuum. The required temperature of a CVD process is dependent on the feed gas. For example, silicon dioxide can be deposited at a temperature lower than $450°C$ ($842°F$) if silicon hydride (SiH_4) and oxygen (O_2) are used, or at $900°C$ ($1652°F$) if tetraethylorthosilane and oxygen are used. The reaction temperature can be lowered by generating plasma-phase reactions in a LPCVD reactor, that is, plasma-enhanced chemical vapor deposition (PECVD). For example, silicon dioxide can be deposited below $300°C$ ($572°F$) using PECVD. This is a nonequilibrium thermodynamic process, and the reaction products are nonstoichiometric. PECVD films have characteristics different from those deposited by APCVD or LPCVD. CVD methods can be used to deposit dielectric, semiconductor, and conductor films. In VLSI production, CVD is exclusively used to deposit dielectrics, such as SiO_2, Si_3N_4, phosphorus-doped SiO_2, and boron-doped SiO_2; and metals, such as tungsten.

Thermal. A thermal process is a high-temperature treatment step that creates new device functions or improves material properties. In VLSI manufacturing, the following operations are done by thermal annealing: diffusion, thermal oxide growth, dopant activation, crystal damage repair, doped glass (PSG, BSG, and BPSG) reflow, silicide formation, metal and compound anneal, and dangling-bond passivation. The two types of thermal processes are conventional furnace annealing and rapid thermal annealing (RTA). The conventional furnace annealing is carried out in a horizontal or vertical quartz tube which is surrounded by heating elements. A large number of substrates can be processed in one batch. Temperature, time, and gas are the major process parameters. The tube temperature is gradually ramped up and down, preventing thermal shock to the substrate.

The type of gas used in the process is dependent on the applications. For example, oxygen-containing gases are used in oxidation, glass reflow, and the drive-in step of a diffusion process. Doping gases, such as phosphine, borane, or diborane, and hydrogen are used in the doping process. Forming gas (a mixture of hydrogen and nitrogen) is used to lower the resistivity of the deposited aluminum film. Hydrogen is used to passivate dangling bonds in polysilicon. Inert gases, such as argon and nitrogen, are used in nonreaction processes.

The RTA reactor is composed of a rectangular quartz reactor and a high-temperature source (such as a lamp). Only one substrate is processed each time. The substrate temperature is usually raised at a high rate, for example, greater than $120°C/min$ ($248°F/min$), by heat radiation from the lamp. Therefore, it is a dynamic process. In addition to temperature and residence time, the temperature ramp-up and ramp-down rates are important process parameters. The major advantage of the RTA process is its low thermal budget and high temperature. RTA is especially effective in growing very thin oxide and nitride films, preparing shallow dopant profiles, and forming thin silicides. The RTA process generates thermal shock to exposed films and substrates. Therefore, it is applicable to selected materials and device structures.

Doping. The doping process creates a certain dopant concentration profile in a semiconductor. Doping is one of the most important steps in preparing basic devices, such as ohmic contacts, isolations, threshold adjustment, conductive polysilicon, collectors, and resistors. The two common doping processes are diffusion and ion implantation. Diffusion is a thermal process. The dopant is driven into the unmasked semiconductor material at a high temperature by a concentration gradient. The dopant is introduced into the reactor from gas, liquid, or solid sources. For the silicon substrate, the common gas-phase sources are phosphine (PH_3), diborane (B_2H_6), boron chloride (BCl_3), boron bromide (BBr_3), and arsine (AsH_3). Liquid dopants, such as phosphorus oxychloride ($POCl_3$), phosphorus tribromide (PBr_3), trimethylborate [$(CH_3O)_3B$], and antimony chloride (Sb_3Cl_5), are introduced by evaporating the liquid or by bubbling with a carrier gas, such as oxygen. The solid dopant can be supplied as solid disks or solidified spin-coated films. In the former case, a solid compound, such as boron nitride (BN), ammonium dihydrogen phosphate ($NH_4H_2PO_4$), or arsenic oxide (As_2O_5), is loaded adjacent to the substrate. During high-temperature annealing, the dopant is vaporized in the oxide form, transported to the silicon surface, and diffused from the oxide film into silicon. In the latter case, a liquid organic compound is spun on the substrate surface. During high-temperature annealing, it is converted into a dopant oxide film from which the dopant is subsequently diffused into silicon. Two types of dopant profiles can be formed from a diffusion process. The constant source process, which comes from the gas-phase dopant source, supplies a complementary error function (cerf) concentration profile. This kind of profile is good for heavily doped shallow junctions such as emitter, source, and drain. The limited source process, which usually comes from the solid or liquid dopant source, supplies a gaussian concentration profile. This kind of profile is suitable for deep, low-concentration regions, such as the base.

The principle of ion implantation is similar to that of a mass spectroscope: the dopant-containing gas is ionized, the dopant ion is separated from other ions with the assistance of a magnetic field, and the selected ion is subsequently accelerated and impinged into a semiconductor. The energetic ions are brought to rest by the combination of electronic and nuclear stopping mechanisms. A thermal annealing step is required to repair the damaged crystal structure and, at the same time, to activate the dopant. There are two main process parameters for ion implantation: current and energy. The former in combination with time determines the total dopant dosage. The latter controls the depth and profile of the dopant. Doping by ion implantation differs from that by diffusion in significant ways. First, ion implantation does not require a high temperature and can be finished in a short period of time. This is especially important in preparing advanced devices that contain small-geometry, shallow junctions. Second, the diffusion-generated dopant profile has a smooth concentration distribution, with the highest concentration located at the surface. The implantation-generated profile has a sharp concentration drop around the highest concentration area that is away from the surface. This allows the preparation of some unique device structures such as silicon implanted with oxygen (SIMOX). SIMOX is a type of silicon-on-insulator (SOI) structure that is critical for the next-generation high-speed and radiation-immune integrated circuits.

There are other nonconventional doping methods, such as non-mass-separation ion shower and PECVD heavily doped negative (n^+) film. They are less effective than ion implantation and are mainly used in preparing TFTs.

Etching. Etching is a process of removing a material at selected locations. Since almost every film in a solid-state device needs to be etched at a certain stage, a large number of chemicals are used in the etch area. Key requirements in an etching process are high etch rate, large etch selectivity between two different films, controlled wall profile, minimal undercut of mask, and reduced process-induced damage to films and devices. The microloading effect, which is caused by the variation of the local etch rate corresponding to different mask densities, should also be avoided. The two common etching methods are wet and dry. The wet process is carried out by immersing the substrate in a solution that dissolves the selected film. It requires a very simple equipment setup and can achieve an extremely high selectivity. However, it is difficult to supply a vertical wall profile with negligible undercut of the mask.

Therefore, the wet etch method is used in preparing devices with minimum dimension larger than 2 micrometers. The dry process is carried out by exposing the substrate in a plasma environment. The process involves complicated plasma-phase reactions, ion bombardment, and surface reactions. The equipment is expensive and the process is complicated. However, the wall profile, vertical or sloped, can be tightly controlled and the undercut of the mask can be minimized. The chemical consumption of a dry process is very little because it is a vacuum technology. Therefore, dry etching is exclusively used in preparing small-geometry VLSI devices. Dry etching is also used in manufacture of large-area TFT arrays because it can avoid residue formation that is a serious problem for some wet etching processes.

Lithography. Lithography is a process of defining a pattern on a substrate. It is the most frequently used process in the manufacture of solid-state devices. For example, an advanced CMOS process requires more than 20 lithography steps. Each etching step needs a lithography process to define the mask pattern. A lithography process includes three major components: photoresist, mask, and aligner.

The substrate is coated with a photoresist layer that is subsequently aligned to a mask and exposed to a light source using an aligner. The pattern is delineated after the exposed photoresist is soaked in a developing solution. The resolution is influenced by all three components. The photoresist is a mixture of a base polymer, a photosensitizer, and solvents. The two types of photoresists are positive and negative. When exposed to a certain light source, the positive photoresist changes characteristics (for example, due to the formation of new carboxylic bonds) from insoluble to soluble in a developer, such as an alkaline solution. The negative photoresist changes characteristics (for example, due to the formation of a crosslinked polymer network) from solvent-soluble to insoluble.

The mask is composed of an opaque pattern on a transparent substrate. The pattern on a mask can be the same size or up to ten times larger than the actual pattern size to be defined on the substrate.

The aligner is used to transfer the pattern from the mask to the substrate. It contains a light source, a projection system, and a substrate loading station. For current VLSI manufacturing, an optical aligner containing an ultraviolet light source (wavelength > 365 nanometers) is widely used. Shorter-wavelength light sources (for example, <351 nm) are necessary to define very small geometry patterns. Other types of energetic beams, such as e-beam, ion-beam, and x-ray, are also available for extremely small devices. According to the design of the light projection method and the loading station, the aligner can be classified as contact, proximity, or projection type. The common requirements for a mask aligner are resolution, alignment accuracy, and throughput. The projection aligner is exclusively used in contemporary VLSI fabrication because it satisfies the resolution and alignment requirements. It generates few defects because the mask is not in contact with the substrate. However, the system is complicated and expensive. For the high-resolution operation, the exposure field is small. A stepper that repeatedly steps and exposes the same pattern on the substrate has to be used. The process time is long and the throughput is low.

Advanced topics. The general trend in solid-state-device fabrication is toward higher speed, lower power consumption, and multiple functions. For VLSICs, this means shrinking the transistor geometry, using the multilevel interconnection structure, and combining logic and memory functions in one chip. For TFTs, this means increasing the size and density of the TFT array as well as integrating the driver and array transistors into the same manufacturing process. All of these require new thin film materials, process technology, and device design.

There are two critical dielectric material issues that must be solved before the next-generation VLSIC can be successfully manufactured. The high-k material (for example, $k > 10$) is aimed at replacing the thin-gate silicon dioxide dielectric (that is, <2 nm) that is required for the <100-nm MOSFET. It is also necessary for the ever-shrinking storage capacitors. In addition to the high dielectric constant, the new film should have a low leakage current and a low interface state on silicon. The low-k material (for example, $k < 2.5$) has to be used as the intermetal insulator. The parasitic capacitance between two conductors are reduced with the decrease of the insulator's dielectric constant. The signal delay in the very small pitch interconnection design becomes very large if silicon dioxide is used. A new low-k dielectric that is stable and compatible with other process technologies needs to be developed.

There are many new processes that have been developed for future-generation VLSICs (**Table 2**). CMP, which is applicable to metals and dielectrics, is complementary to many existing planarization methods. There are many studies on the slurry chemistry and the end-point detection of the CMP process. The total device isolation has been studied for decades. In addition to wafer bonding and silicon-on-sapphire (SOS), the SIMOX product has recently been introduced into the market. Many process issues, including the cost and material damages, still need to be

solved. Copper in combination with the low-k dielectric material can solve the signal delay problem for the high-density circuit. However, copper still has the fundamental dry-etching problem that will restrict its application to very high density integrated circuit design.

For background information *see* CONDUCTOR (ELECTRICITY); DIELECTRIC MATERIALS; ELECTRONIC DISPLAY; INTEGRATED CIRCUITS; SEMICONDUCTOR; SOLID-STATE CHEMISTRY; SOLID-STATE PHYSICS; TRANSISTOR; VAPOR DEPOSITION in the McGraw-Hill Encyclopedia of Science & Technology.   Yue Kuo

Bibliography. D. Christiansen (ed.), *Electronics Engineers' Handbook*, 4th ed., McGraw-Hill, 1996; A. A. R. Elshabini-Riad and F. D. Barlow, *Thin Film Technology Handbook (Electronic Packaging and Interconnection)*, McGraw-Hill, 1997; T. L. Floyd, *Electronic Devices*, 5th ed., Prentice Hall, 1998; T. L. Floyd, *Electronic Devices: Electron Flow Version*, 3d ed., Prentice Hall, 1998; B. G. Streetman and S. Banerjee, *Solid State Electronic Devices*, 5th ed., Prentice Hall, 1999.

Space flight

In 1999 there was extraordinary activity in the exploration, utilization, and commercialization of space, as well as new developments that will increasingly characterize and dominate human activities outside the Earth's boundaries (**Table 1**).

United States accomplishments included the first crewed visit and service mission to the International Space Station (ISS), the launch of the x-ray observatory *Chandra*, the first woman commanding a space shuttle mission, the first global three-dimensional topographic map of Mars, the first evidence of a planet orbiting a pair of stars, the first optical image of a gamma-ray burst, discoveries by the Hubble Space Telescope, and its highly successful repair and refurbishment by a shuttle mission.

As in 1998, not only were there more commercial satellites on orbit than military satellites, but there were also far more commercial space launches. Over the last 6 years, the number of worldwide commercial launches increased by an average of 47%, while overall launches have remained steady, numbering between 70 and 93 per year. In 1999, out of 70 successful launches worldwide (1998: 77), 54 (77%) were commercial launches (carrying 120 commercial payloads), compared to 41 (53%) in 1998 (**Table 2**). In the civil science satellite area, worldwide launches totaled about 26, as compared to some 19 in the preceding year.

Russia's Earth-orbiting space station *Mir* was left without a crew for the first time in 10 years. The International Space Station was visited by the first service mission in preparation for the arrival of the first "permanent occupancy" crew in 2000, while major elements of the station began accumulating at NASA's launch facilities in Florida awaiting their turn in the progressing assembly schedule. NASA's Mars

TABLE 2. Advanced process technology for VLSI manufacturing		
Areas	Technology	Examples
Planarization	Chemical-mechanical polishing (CMP)	Damascene, dual Damascene
Isolation	Silicon-on-insulator	Silicon implanted with oxygen
Metalization	Copper	Electroplating, plasma etching

TABLE 1. Significant space events in 1999

Mission designation	Date	Country	Event
Mars Polar Lander	January 3	United States	First attempt to land near Mars's south pole. Arrived December 3, after September 23 loss of *Mars Climate Orbiter*, but was also lost. Given up by NASA early in 2000.
STARDUST	February 7	United States	NASA's comet probe, launched on a Delta-2 rocket. Currently on its way to Comet Wild-2, where it is to arrive in 2004.
Soyuz TM-29/Mir 27	February 20	Russia	Launch of *Mir 27* crew of three, including French researcher Jean-Pierre Haignère and Slovak Ivan Bella; left *Mir* on August 27 unoccupied for first time in 10 years.
WIRE	March 4	United States	*Wide-Field Infrared Explorer*, launched on a Pegasus XL; lost after Earth orbit insertion due to excessive tumbling.
Landsat 7	April 15	United States	Launch of new Earth observation satellite as a major part of NASA's Mission to Planet Earth program. Carries Enhanced Thematic Mapper (ETM) Plus.
STS 96 (*Discovery*)	May 27	United States	First human visit to the new International Space Station (ISS) and the first supply and service mission, a pathfinder for future heavy logistics flights to ISS.
QuikScat	June 20	United States	NASA's *Quick Scatterometer* spacecraft; measures wind speeds and directions over the world's oceans from space.
FUSE	June 24	United States	NASA's *Far-Ultraviolet Spectroscopic Explorer*; determines relationships between interstellar medium and star formation, mass created during big bang, etc.
Progress M-42	July 16	Russia	Second crewless resupply mission to *Mir* of 1999; brought equipment and propellants to prepare *Mir* for an extended period of unoccupied dormancy.
STS 93 (*Columbia*)	July 23	United States	Launch of the *Advanced X-ray Facility* (*AXAF*), now called *Chandra X-ray Observatory*, third in NASA's series of Great Observatories.
IKONOS	September 24	United States	First of a new generation of nonmilitary Earth-imaging satellites to provide high-resolution images with detail at the 1-m (3.3-ft) level for commercial use.
Shenzhou	November 19	China	Crewless 14-orbit test flight and recovery, on an uprated CZ-2F, of China's human space flight Project 921, using a modified Russian Soyuz spacecraft.
XMM	December 10	Europe	*X-Ray Multi-Mission Observatory*, Europe's equivalent of Chandra and Hubble, launched on the first operational flight of Europe's Ariane 5 heavy lifter.
Terra	December 18	United States	Flagship of NASA's new-millennium Earth Observation System, for new research into the interactions of Earth's land, ocean, air, ice, and life as a whole system.
STS 103 (*Discovery*)	December 20	United States	Third maintenance and repair mission to Hubble Space Telescope, rescuing it after loss of four gyroscopes, by major overhaul with new systems.

exploration program suffered the loss of two successive automated probes, the *Mars Climate Orbiter* and the *Mars Polar Lander*.

Four flights from the two major space-faring nations (down from 7 in 1998) carried 22 humans into space (17 less than in 1998), including 5 women (6 in 1998), bringing the total number of people launched into space since 1958 (counting repeaters) to 834, including 84 women, or 400 individuals (35 female).

United States Space Activities

The four reusable shuttle vehicles of the U.S. Space Transportation System (STS) continued carrying people and payloads to and from Earth orbit for science,

technology, operational research, systems maintenance, and station logistics, accomplishing several important missions. After having moved into actual orbital assembly in the preceding year, the International Space Station program accomplished further development steps.

Space shuttle. During 1999, NASA successfully completed three space shuttle missions, three less than in 1998, bringing the total number of shuttles launched since program inception to 96.

STS 96. This May 27–June 6 mission involved the first crew visit to the International Space Station. *Discovery* was docked to the Unity/Zarya complex from May 29 to June 3 (**Fig. 1**). The crew of seven represented three station partners—the United States,

TABLE 2. Space launches and attempts in 1999		
Country	Number of launches*	Number of attempts
United States (NASA, Department of Defense, commercial)	29	(33)
Russia	26	(28)
Europe (European Space Agency, Arianespace)	10	(10)
People's Republic of China	4	(4)
Japan	—	(1)
India	1	(1)
Brazil	—	(1)
Total	70	(78)

*Successful launches to Earth orbit and beyond.

Canada, and Russia—and included three women. *Discovery* also released the student satellite *STARSHINE* on June 5.

STS 93. The July 23–27 flight of *Columbia* featured the launch of the *Chandra X-ray Observatory*. The crew of five, under NASA's first woman commander, Eileen M. Collins, included French mission specialist Michel Tognini. The observatory was successfully deployed 7 h 16 min after launch and subsequently boosted itself to a final orbit of 86,992 by 6034 mi (139,188 by 9655 km), with a period of 63 h 28 min. Secondary objectives included firing of *Columbia*'s jet thrusters at various times during the flight to help an Air Force satellite gather data on the characteristics of jet plumes in space; operation of the Southwest Ultraviolet Imaging System (SWUIS) from a side hatch window, collecting data on ultraviolet light originating from a variety of planetary bodies; and assessment of the Treadmill Vibration Isolation and Stabilization system (TVIS), an exercise system planned for the Space Station.

STS 103. The December 19–27 flight of *Discovery* performed the third maintenance-repair mission to the Hubble Space Telescope. The mission, originally planned for mid-2000, became necessary when the telescope had to be put in "safe" (dormant) mode on November 13 with only two of its six gyroscopes still functioning. Telescope capture on December 21 was followed by berthing in the shuttle cargo bay and 3 days of extravehicular activity to replace and install new equipment before the restored telescope was released on December 25.

International Space Station. When completed, the International Space Station will have a mass of about 1,040,000 lb (470 metric tons). It will be 356 ft (108 m) across and 290 ft (88 m) long, with almost an acre (0.4 hectare) of solar panels to provide up to 110 kilowatts of power to six state-of-the-art laboratories. Led by the United States, the station draws upon the scientific and technological resources of 16 nations: Canada, Japan, Russia, the 11 nations of the European Space Agency (ESA), and Brazil.

Launches and assembly of station elements in orbit began in 1999. This second phase of the Space Station program covers station assembly up to initiation of orbital research capability with a permanent crew. It will be followed, in 2001 and later, by Phase 3, which includes further expansion and completion with the addition of more laboratory and habitation facilities, structural trusses, and solar power arrays. As currently planned, the station will require a total of 45 assembly flights, with 33 to be launched by the U.S. shuttle and 12 on Russian boosters. Interspersed among these missions will be logistics missions by the shuttle (for a total of 37 shuttle flights), Russian *Soyuz* flights to launch crews, and multiple *Progress* tanker flights for refueling the growing structure in orbit.

Accomplishments during 1999 included the first crewed logistics-supply flight of a space shuttle to the early assembly in orbit in May and June; testing of hardware and software for station elements to be launched in 2000 and 2001; successful implementation of a newly developed Multi-Element Integrated Test (MEIT), which functionally connects the first

 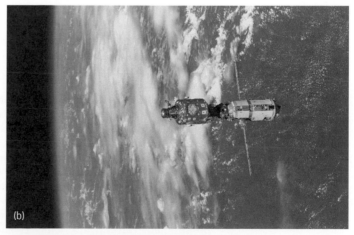

Fig. 1. Visit of the space shuttle *Discovery* to the International Space Station (mission STS 96). (*a*) Astronaut Tamara Jernigan handles the United States–built crane which was later installed on the station during the May 30, 1999, space walk. (*b*) The station moves away from *Discovery* on June 3, with the United States–built node Unity (left) and the Russian-built Zarya/FGB module (right). (*NASA*)

several U.S. elements of the station on the ground in a series of integrated tests; the completion of the Mission Control Center and the Payload Operations Integration Center; and delivery of the U.S. laboratory module Destiny and the airlock module to the launch site in Florida in preparation for MEIT, along with other components. Interface testing between the U.S. Mission Control Center in Houston and the Russian Mission Control Center in Moscow was successfully completed.

Logistics. STS 96, the second space shuttle mission to the station, was the first supply flight, regarded as a pathfinder for future heavy logistics missions to the new orbiting base. After docking on May 29, mission specialists Tamara E. Jernigan and Daniel T. Barry began a spacewalk to transfer two cranes (one Russian, one U.S.-made) from the shuttle's cargo bay to the station's outside (Fig. 1*a*), installed two portable foot restraints, and attached three bags with tools and handrails for future assembly operations. After the shuttle's hatch to the station's mating adapter PMA-2 was opened for leak and pressurization tests, Jernigan and Valery Tokarev opened the entrance to the node Unity, followed by three more hatches through PMA-1 into FGB/Zarya. The other crew members followed and began transferring supplies, equipment, and water. They also replaced 18 recharge controller units for the six Zarya batteries, installed mufflers over noisy FGB fans, and replaced a power distribution unit and transceiver of the node communication system. At work conclusion the crew had transferred 3567 lb (1618 kg) of material to the station.

ICM. Work was also progressing on an Interim Control Module (ICM), built by the Naval Research Laboratory for NASA, which would provide a limited U.S. on-orbit attitude control and reboost capability as a contingency against shortfalls in the Russian contributions.

Propulsion module. Additional contingency plans for ensuring U.S. flexibility include the development of a propulsion module for the Space Station and modifications to the shuttle fleet for enhanced reboosting of the station. Preliminary designs for the propulsion module were completed during 1999.

Advanced transportation systems activities. There is a 3-year-old NASA-industry cooperative effort to develop a reusable space launch vehicle to eventually take over launchings for a fraction of the current cost of space transportation with turnaround rates considerably lower than those of the space shuttle. This work is continuing at Lockheed Martin with the development of the X-33 as a technology demonstrator for a single-stage-to-orbit reusable launch vehicle. During 1999, most manufacturing for the X-33 was completed, and assembly was getting under way for a rollout of the demonstrator vehicle. However, structural weaknesses in the advanced solid-graphite composite liquid-hydrogen tank, which resulted in structural failure of the tank's outer skin during a pressure test with cryogenic loading on November 3, caused

a major setback for the program, delaying it by perhaps several years.

The smaller air-launched X-34, being built by Orbital Sciences Corp., will test reusable launch vehicle technologies. X-34 flights began on June 29 with the first of several captive-carry flights of the vehicle under the belly of an L1011 aircraft. During 1999, rocket engine tests continued on the 60,000-lb (267-kilonewton) thrust liquid-oxygen (LOX)/kerosine Fastrac engine for the X-34, and the 500,000-lb (2.2-meganewton) XRS-2200 LOX/liquid hydrogen linear aerospike engine for the X-33.

NASA is also developing the X-43 as part of the Hyper-X program which bridges aircraft-type vehicles and space launch vehicles. Its goal is to demonstrate hydrogen-powered, air-breathing propulsion systems that could ultimately be applied in vehicles from hypersonic (speeds higher than five times the speed of sound) aircraft to reusable space launchers. In 1999, the first of three experimental vehicles arrived at NASA's Dryden Flight Research Center in California to prepare for flight in mid-2000. The 12-ft-long (3.6-m), unpiloted, non-rocket-propelled X-43 vehicles are powered by supersonic combustion ramjets (scramjets) after acceleration by a Pegasus booster rocket air-launched from a B-52 airplane. *See* HYPERSONIC FLIGHT.

NASA is also developing a crew return vehicle to eventually take over the emergency lifeboat function for the Space Station from the currently chosen Russian Soyuz three-seater capsules. In 1999, NASA continued with full-scale flight testing of the X-38 prototype test vehicle by dropping it from a B-52 at 23,000 ft (7000 m) altitude, in order to study the latter stages of the crew return vehicle's mission, when it transitions from subsonic lifting body flight to descent and landing under a large parafoil.

Space sciences and astronomy. In 1999, the United States launched 11 civil science spacecraft, up three from the previous year. Since 1995, NASA has markedly increased the number of civil satellites it develops and launches, following the switch in development strategy, shortly after the loss in August 1993 of the *Mars Observer*, from large, expensive satellites to smaller and more numerous ones.

Hubble Space Telescope. Nine years after it was placed in orbit, the Hubble Space Telescope continues to probe far beyond the solar system. One of the space telescope's most important projects is to determine more accurately the expansion rate of the universe. The new estimate of the age of the cosmos is 12–13.5 billion years, and the reduction in uncertainty also supported the view that the universe will not collapse due to gravity but will continue to expand indefinitely.

Among the images from the Hubble are supermassive star clouds in the center of the Milky Way Galaxy, pictures of differing evolutionary paths of galaxies obtained by peering deep inside the centers of star clusters and galaxies to resolve structures, bulges and bars of bright stars, the unusual bipolar shape of the

Butterfly (or Papillon) Nebula in the Large Magellanic Cloud (**Fig. 2**), and a dying star in the process of turning from a normal red giant into a planetary nebula.

When problems with the telescope's attitude control gyroscopes left only two of the six gyroscopes functioning, temporarily disabling the facility, NASA quickly prepared an emergency space shuttle repair and servicing mission by dividing the regular maintenance and service mission scheduled for mid-2000 in two flights and launching the first one, STS 103, in December. The highly successful mission, during which the crew installed 13 electronic systems and new protective blankets for the telescope, left it with a major increase in computer and data storage capability, new battery components, an upgraded guidance system, and six new attitude gyroscopes, laying the foundation for significant increases in observing capability.

Chandra. After several postponements during its development, testing, assembly, and shipping, NASA's third "Great Observatory" (after *Compton* and Hubble), the *Chandra X-ray Observatory* was carried to orbit on July 23 by the space shuttle *Columbia.* Named in honor of the late astrophysicist Subrahmanyan Chandrasekhar, Chandra was formerly known as the *Advanced X-ray Astronomy Facility (AXAF).* With a total launch mass of 12,930 lb (5870 kg), it is the largest satellite ever deployed by the space shuttle and the world's most powerful x-ray telescope. It uses a high-resolution camera, high-resolution mirrors, and a charge-coupled-detector (CCD) imaging spectrometer to observe, via x-rays, some of the most violent phenomena in the universe which cannot be seen by the Hubble's visual-range telescope. After barely 2 months in space, Chandra had already delivered an image of the Crab Nebula (**Fig. 3**), revealing a brilliant ring, never seen before, around the nebula's heart. Chandra also found long-sought "power lines" in the Crab, which connect the powerful spinning collapsed star with the luminous gas remnants around it.

SOHO. In November, NASA engineers struggled to regain control of the European-U.S. *Solar and Heliospheric Observatory (SOHO)* after briefly losing contact with it due to a software error. A software patch returned the probe to normal operations.

By imaging strong ultraviolet reflections of sunspots on the far side of the Sun in the solar atmosphere, *SOHO* opened a way for scientists to study the side that is out of view from Earth. Results from *SOHO* also indicate that the waves in the Sun's atmosphere are produced by vibrating solar magnetic field lines. In November, *SOHO* tracked, along with NASA's *Transition Region and Coronal Explorer (TRACE),* a pass (transit) of the planet Mercury in front of the Sun for its entire duration of 51 min. The data will allow improved measuring of the Sun's outer atmosphere, or corona. *See* SUN; TRANSIT (ASTRONOMY).

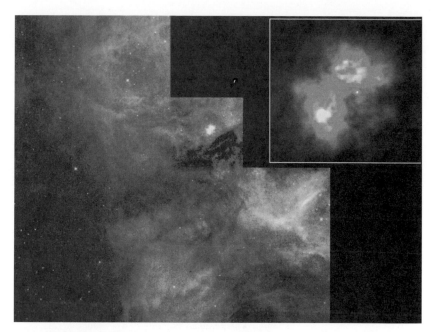

Fig. 2. Hubble Space Telescope view of N159, a maelstrom of glowing gases and dark dusk, 170,000 light-years away in the Large Magellanic Cloud, with the Butterfly (or Papillon) Nebula buried in its center. The inset shows details of the structure of the nebula, less than 2 light-years in size. (*M. Heydari-Malayeri, Paris Observatory, and NASA/ESA*)

Galileo. Galileo in 1999 continued to return data on Jupiter and its satellites, with several encounters with Jupiter's moons: one with Europa, four with Callisto, and two with Io. The first Io encounter, on October 11 (**Fig. 4**), was at 380 mi (612 km); and on November 25, the probe flew by Io at the extremely short range of 187 mi (300 km), and survived the intense radiation there. The probe found sulfuric acid on the frozen surface of Europa, beneath which

Fig. 3. Center of the Crab Nebula in x-ray light, imaged by the *Chandra X-ray Observatory* on September 29, 1999. Visible are rings of high-energy particles that are being flung outward near the speed of light from the center, and powerful jets emerging from the poles. (*NASA/Chandra X-ray Observatory/Smithsonian Astrophysical Observatory*)

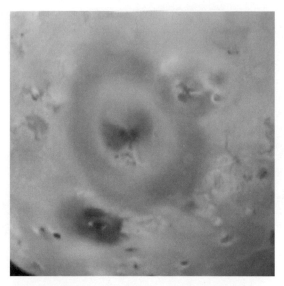

Fig. 4. Composite image of Jupiter's satellite Io, taken on October 11, 1999, at a range of 11,000 mi (17,000 km), showing brightly glowing lava from the volcano Pele. The image is centered on the large ring of sulfur that was deposited by Pele's plume and reaches more than 800 mi (1300 km) in diameter. (*NASA*)

may lie a liquid ocean. This theory is supported by patterns of arc-shaped cracks in the surface, called cycloids, that are probably caused by tidal forces.

Cassini. NASA's *Cassini* spacecraft flew by Venus on June 24 and then made a close approach of Earth of 727 mi (1163 km) on August 17, on its last of three inner-planet flybys designed to accelerate the scientific probe toward its 4-year mission at Saturn, beginning in 2004. *Cassini* had also flown past Venus in April 1998. The spacecraft remains in excellent health.

DS-1. NASA's *Deep Space 1* (*DS-1*) technology test satellite on July 29 undertook the closest encounter with an asteroid ever attempted when it flew within 10 mi (16 km) of the asteroid 1992 KD, newly named Braille. To alter its trajectory toward the rendezvous, *DS-1* performed a 6-week burn of its low-thrust xenon ion engine in March and April. *DS-1* relied on its experimental autonomous navigation system, AutoNav, to guide itself past the asteroid. This system determines position by optically sighting on asteroids and stars, calculating the future trajectory, and devising and executing engine firings to meet the desired trajectory conditions. The spacecraft was launched on October 24, 1998, into a stretched-out elliptical orbit around the Sun. Its mission is to test several advanced technologies for future interplanetary science missions, particularly the ion engine which uses electric power to accelerate ionized xenon fuel to over 18 mi/s (30 km/s) for high-efficiency low-thrust (0.02 lbf, 9.4 grams) power. Other advanced technologies on board are testing power generation with concentrator solar arrays and Ka-band communications.

Lunar Prospector. By deliberately crashing the *Lunar Prospector* spacecraft into the Moon at the end of its low-budget research mission in circumlunar orbit,

NASA had hoped to get evidence of hidden water ice on the Moon. The controlled crash into a shadowed crater near the lunar south pole did not produce any ultraviolet spectral lines of hydroxyl (OH) molecules in the cloud kicked up by the impact, which would have been a water "signature."

QuickSCAT. NASA's *Quick Scatterometer* (*QuickSCAT*) mission to measure wind speed and direction over the world's oceans from space was launched on a Titan 2 on June 20. The 1914-lb (870-kg) spacecraft, which replaced a critical NASA "SeaWinds" radar lost when Japan's *ADEOS* satellite failed in 1997, was placed in a Sun-synchronous orbit of 98° inclination and 499 mi (803 km) altitude. In September the radar tracked an Antarctic iceberg, measuring 24×48 mi (38×77 km), which could have threatened international shipping.

ACE and Wind. The two NASA spacecraft *ACE* (*Advanced Composition Explorer*) and *Wind* during May found that the density of the solar wind dropped by more than 98%, making it possible to observe electrons flowing directly from the Sun's corona to Earth. The severe change in the solar wind also changed the shape of the magnetosphere and produced an unusual auroral display at the North Pole.

Stardust. NASA's comet probe *Stardust* was launched on February 3 on a Delta 2 to begin its mission to intercept a comet and return close-up imagery and a soil sample to Earth. On its trajectory to its rendezvous with Comet Wild-2 in 2004, the spacecraft went suddenly into a safing mode on March 18, but controllers quickly restored normal operation.

WIRE. The *Wide-Field Infrared Explorer* (*WIRE*) was launched on March 4 on a Pegasus XL air-launched booster to conduct extragalactic science surveys in the deep infrared. After deployment, the spacecraft was observed to be initially tumbling at 60 revolutions per minute, a rate higher than expected. After significant recovery efforts, *WIRE* was declared a loss on March 8.

FUSE. NASA's *Far Ultraviolet Spectroscopic Explorer* (*FUSE*) was launched on June 24 from Cape Canaveral, FL, on a Delta 2 Med-Lite vehicle. The 3000-lb (1360-kg) spacecraft was placed into the targeted 480-mi (768-km) orbit inclined 25° to the Equator, despite a misalignment of 5.3° during its installation on top of the Delta booster. The spacecraft's mission is to characterize relationships between the interstellar medium and star formation and determine how much mass in the universe was created during the big bang.

NEAR. Almost 3 years after its liftoff in February 1996, the *Near Earth Asteroid Rendezvous* (*NEAR*) spacecraft fired its engine on January 3 to gain a second chance to meet and orbit the asteroid 433 Eros after a failure of the first of several rendezvous maneuvers on December 20, 1998, changed plans. Instead of meeting its rendezvous with Eros in January 1999, *NEAR* was set to fulfill its research mission in mid-February 2000.

Mars exploration. In 1999 Mars continued to be the focus of interest, even if partly for spectacular failure. *Mars Global Surveyor* continued to produce the highest-resolution images of Mars to date, after concluding aerobraking into an operational orbit using atmospheric drag. However, the *Mars Climate Orbiter* suffered a stunning failure, followed by the disappearance of *Mars Polar Lander*. As investigations into the basic designs of low-cost robotic Mars missions are continuing, new missions are anticipated for 2001 and beyond.

Mars Global Surveyor was the first of a planned series of Surveyor-type Mars explorers. After its arrival at Mars on September 11, 1997, it started a long series of aerobrake passes around the planet. After reaching its operational orbit early in 1999, it began its mapping mission on March 9. On March 28, the 5-ft (1.5-m) high-gain antenna was successfully deployed. Since then, *Mars Global Surveyor* has been transmitting a steady stream of high-resolution images of Mars. They show a world constantly reshaped by forces of nature, including shifting sand dunes, monster dust devils, wind storms, frosts, and polar ice caps that grow and retreat with the seasons (**Fig. 5**). In August, the Mars Orbiter Camera captured images of the shadow of the Martian satellite Phobos on the planet's surface.

In September, NASA's *Mars Climate Orbiter* prepared to enter orbit around Mars to study the planet's climate and atmospheric circulation, and to serve as a communications relay for the *Mars Polar Lander*. On September 23, however, the spacecraft failed to enter orbit due to a mix-up in measurement units between two separate operations teams at Lockheed Martin and NASA's Jet Propulsion Laboratory. The numerical values used for trajectory modeling had been calculated in English units by spacecraft engineers and were mistakenly assumed, by spacecraft navigators calculating attitude control maneuvers, to be in metric units. As a result, the spacecraft began its planned orbit insertion burn at about 37 mi (60 km) altitude, about 15.5 mi (25 km) lower than the minimum altitude for survival of the spacecraft, and thus was destroyed by atmospheric friction.

After this loss, NASA's quickly established Mishap Investigation Board had about 2 months to investigate the cause of the failure and ensure that the *Mars Polar Lander* would not suffer a similar fate. Contact with *Mars Polar Lander* was lost as expected on December 3 after the spacecraft had turned its antenna away from Earth by 75° and shut off its transmitter in the process of assuming its proper entry attitude. Contact with the lander was never regained, and at the end of 1999 it remained unknown whether it had entered the Martian atmosphere and landed as planned at the so-called Mars Layered Deposits near the south pole. It is also not known whether its two *Deep Space 2* (*DS-2*) penetrator microprobes separated from the spacecraft before atmospheric entry and impacted on the surface.

Pioneer 10. Launched in 1972, *Pioneer 10*, the longest-lived interplanetary explorer, continues its voyage as contact with it is still maintained by NASA's Deep Space Network. Currently at a distance of 7 bil-

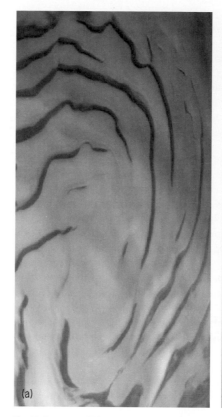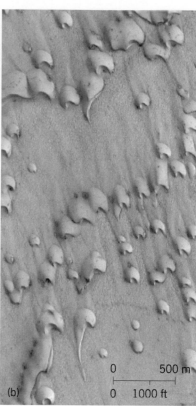

Fig. 5. Images of Mars from the *Mars Global Surveyor*'s Mars Orbiter Camera. (*a*) Wide-angle view of the north polar ice cap taken in May 1999. (*b*) Sand dunes in Chasma Boreale, a giant trough that nearly divides the north polar ice cap in two, in early (local) spring (September 1998). Dark sand is still mostly covered by frost left over from the northern winter season. Shapes of the dunes indicate wind transport. (*NASA/JPL/Malin Space Science Systems*)

lion miles (11 billion kilometers) from Earth, *Pioneer 10* is passing through the transitional region between the farthest traces of the Sun's atmosphere, the heliosphere, and free intergalactic space. Signals transmitted by the spacecraft need 10 h 10 min to reach the Earth.

Earth science. Earth science advanced in 1999, with launches of major observation systems. These civilian Earth-observing missions, coordinated by NASA's Earth Science Enterprise, began new initiatives of a complex program that includes science and applications research, in cooperation with domestic and international partners.

Landsat 7. The 4662-lb (2100-kg) *Landsat 7* Earth-imaging satellite was successfully launched on April 15 on a Delta 2 into a 438-mi (750-km) Sun-synchronous polar orbit. Mostly distinguished by its Enhanced Thematic Mapper Plus (ETM Plus), it is a considerable improvement over *Landsat 6*, which suffered a failed launch in 1993. Expectations are that *Landsat 7*'s Earth observations will once again, as with the Landsats in the past, become the foundation for both terrestrial research and application activities.

Terra. As the first in a new spacecraft series—the Earth Observation System (EOS) satellites—the 10,506-lb (4765-kg) *Terra* was launched on December 18 on an Atlas/Centaur. Formerly called

EOS-AM-1, *Terra* achieved a 437-mi (705-km) circular, Sun-synchronous orbit, similar to *Landsat 7*. The spacecraft has five closely coupled science instruments for integrated studies of the Earth, from the top of its atmosphere down through its cloud layers to the surface of its seas and lands. Two smaller satellites in the series, *EOS-PM* and *EOS-Chemistry*, are in advanced stages of development. Altogether, the EOS program will eventually comprise 25 spacecraft.

ACRIMSAT. The *Active Cavity Radiometer Irradiance Monitor Satellite* (*ACRIMSAT*) was launched on December 20 on an Orbital Science Taurus rocket. The 115-kg (253-lb) satellite is currently circling Earth in a polar orbit at an altitude of 425 mi (680 km). The instrument is designed to measure small, sustained changes in the total solar irradiance of as little as 0.5% per century, which could be the primary causal factor for significant climate change on time scales of many decades.

Department of Defense activities. U.S. military space organizations continued their efforts to make space a routine part of military operations. Military launch attempts from Cape Canaveral (FL) and Vandenberg (CA) in 1999 totaled seven payloads with two failures. Of particular importance was the launch of the 6000-lb (2720-kg) Advanced Research and Global Observation Satellite (Argos), the Air Force's largest and most capable research and development satellite, on a Delta 2 on February 23. Argos carries nine payload experiments for 30 research objectives.

Commercial space activities. A strong, ongoing demand for satellites, launch vehicles, and ground equipment driven by the expansion of the telecommunications industry continued to support the infrastructure segment of the space industry. The development of LEO satellite constellations, which require a large number of small satellites in orbit, has begun to dramatically expand the requirements for satellite launches. While two satellite mobile-phone projects, Iridium LLC and ICO Global Communications Ltd., had to file for bankruptcy protection late in 1999, other projects, such as Globalstar and Orbcomm, have been more successful.

The *Ikonos-1* satellite was lost on April 27 due to failed separation of the Athena-2's payload shroud. The second launch of the solid-propellant vehicle, on September 24, was successful, however, and *Ikonos-2* became the first nonmilitary satellite to provide high-resolution images with detail at the 1-m (3.3-ft) level to the commercial market.

The first demonstration flight of the commercial Sea Launch rocket was successful on March 27, with the launch of a 10,300-lb (4700-kg) test dummy into geosynchronous transfer orbit. It was followed by the success of the first commercial flight on October 10, which launched the *DirecTV-1R* satellite for U.S.-wide digital television services. Sea Launch Co. was formed in 1995 by companies in the United States, Russia, Norway, and Ukraine. The Sea Launch system consists of a floating mission control center and rocket-assembly factory (Commander), a self-propelled launch platform (Odyssey), and a Russian Zenit-3SL rocket.

Of the 33 total launch attempts by the United States in 1999 (versus 36 in 1998), 25 were on commercial expendable launchers (plus 3 space shuttles and 5 launches of the military Titan 2 and 4), with only two failures, including 10 Delta-2 vehicles, 5 Atlas 2A's, and 3 Pegasus XL's, 2 Athenas, 1 Taurus, and 2 sea-launched Zenits. There were 70 U.S. commercial payloads, with 41 launched on U.S. carriers and 29 on foreign launchers (China, 2; Russia, 25; Europe, 2). The second launch of the powerful Delta 3 with nine strap-on boosters, carrying the *Orion 3* communications satellite, failed on May 5 by placing the satellite in the wrong orbit.

Russian Space Activities

Despite the unabated slump in national economy and continuing political uncertainties, Russia in 1999 showed no slack in its space operations from 1998. Its total of 26 successful launches (out of 28 attempts) exceeded the previous year's 24 (out of 25 attempts): 12 Soyuz-U (one crewed), 9 Protons (two failures), Zenit-2, 2 Molniyas, 1 Tsiklon-2, 2 Kosmos-3M, and 1 Dniepr.

In its partnership with the United States in the development of the International Space Station, integration and checkout testing continued on the Russian-built and -owned Service Module Zvezda (Star), the long-awaited third building-block of the station. In May, Zvezda was transported to the Baikonur launch complex in Kazakhstan.

Space station Mir. By the end of 1999, Russia's seventh space station, in operation since February 20, 1986, had circled the Earth approximately 79,255 times. However, the station was abandoned in August when its owner, RSC-Energia, was unable to fund continued crewed operation. Counting from its last brief period of nonoccupancy (September 1989) to the departure of the last crew in 1999, *Mir* had been inhabited continuously for 3643 days (10 years). It has been visited 38 times, including 9 times by a U.S. space shuttle. To resupply the occupants, the Space Station was visited in 1999 by two automated *Progress* cargo ships, bringing the total of *Progress* ships launched to *Mir* and the two preceding stations, *Salyut-7* and *Salyut-6*, to 85, with no failure (except for the collision of one of the drones with the station in 1997).

Soyuz TM-29 was launched on February 20 with the *Mir 27* crew, Viktor Afanasyev, Jean-Pierre Haignère (France), and Ivan Bella (Slovakia). The mission was the sixth joint French-Russian *Mir* expedition and the seventh joint orbital flight by the two countries. Gennady Padalka (from the *Mir 26* crew, launched in 1998) and Bella returned to Earth in *Soyuz TM-28* on February 28, while *Mir 26* cosmonaut Sergei Avdeev continued on with Afanasyev and Haignère.

On July 18, the *Progress M-42* cargo drone docked to deliver, among other things, a backup computer intended to provide motion control redundancy during the forthcoming period of at least 6 months of crewless operation of *Mir*. After installing the new systems and preparing *Mir* for its untended dormancy, Avdeyev, Afanasyev, and Haignère returned to Earth in *Soyuz TM-29* on August 27. Avdeyev had spent 389 days on *Mir* and a record total of 742 days in space.

Commercial space activities. The Russian space program's efforts to enter the commercial market continued to progress in 1999, but also suffered a severe setback with the loss of two Proton launchers. Between 1985 and 1999, 137 Proton and 358 Soyuz rockets were launched, with nine failures of the Proton and nine of the Soyuz. Of the nine Protons launched in 1999, seven were for commercial customers. After the second Proton crash, on October 27, no further Protons could be launched in 1999 due to a temporary embargo on launches imposed by Kazakhstan and the need for a thorough investigation.

Of the three launches of the Russian-Ukrainian Zenit-2 rocket, two were conducted from the new ocean-based Sea Launch facility Odyssey. After its failure in 1998, the Zenit thus made a comeback of considerable commercial importance. The satellite navigation system GLONASS, Russia's equivalent of the Global Positioning System, requires 24 satellites for the full system, but there were only 15 in the constellation by late 1999.

European Space Activities

Arianespace continued to operate a successful series of nine Ariane 4 launches, one less than in 1998, carrying 10 commercial satellites for customers such as India, Korea, France, and the United Kingdom. At year's end, the Ariane 4 had flown 122 times, with seven failures, from its Kourou, French Guyana, spaceport.

The first commercial launch of the Ariane 5 heavy-lift booster took place at Kourou or December 10. However, it carried a government payload, the *X-ray Multimirror (XMM) Observatory* of the European Space Agency. The largest European science satellite ever built, the *XMM* was deployed to an initial orbit of 71,216 by 531 mi (113,946 by 850 km), inclined at 40° to the Equator. Later, the spacecraft used its hydrazine thrusters to boost its perigee (low point) to 4375 mi (7000 km). The telescope, Europe's equivalent of NASA's *Chandra X-ray Observatory*, has a length of nearly 36 ft (11 m) with a mass of almost 8800 lb (4 metric tons). *XMM* carries three advanced telescopes, each housing 58 high-precision, wafer-thin concentric mirrors designed to detect millions of hitherto invisible x-ray sources. The observatory's three scientific instruments—a photon-imaging camera, reflection-grating spectrometer, and optical telescope—will allow *XMM* not only to image super-hot x-ray sources but also to distinguish their "color" (temperature).

Asian Space Activities

India, China, and Japan have space programs capable of their own launch and satellite development activities, and South Korea inaugurated its space program in 1999.

Japan. Japan progressed with its satellite production, acquisition, and launch programs. The country's National Space Development Agency (NASDA) has recently taken a step toward competing in the commercial launch market by developing the H-2A vehicle, an uprated and more cost-effective version of the costly H-2 that began operations in 1994.

Japan's space plans encompass missions to the Moon and to Mars. Its Institute of Space and Astronautical Science (ISAS), which is collaborating with NASDA on the crewless lunar exploration mission Selene, in 1998 launched its *Nozomi* spacecraft, to Mars. Due to a thruster malfunction, the arrival date of the probe at Mars has slipped from October 1999 to December 2003 or January 2004.

Japan is participating in the International Space Station program, with the development of the Japanese Experiment Module (JEM), now called Kibo (Hope), along with its ancillary remote manipulator system and porchlike exposed facility. Its intentions to develop the H-2A as a routine supplier vehicle of the station, by means of its H-2 transfer vehicle (HTV), which will carry about 13,000 lb (6 metric tons) of provisions, were dealt another severe blow in 1999 when the H-2 launcher, on its seventh flight since 1994, suffered its second straight malfunction (against five successes) on November 15. As a consequence, plans to begin flying the H-2-derived H-2A in 2000 were delayed for an indefinite period, and the decision was made to terminate the H-2 launch program. Lost with the H-2 was the 6400-lb (2900-kg). *Multifunctional Transport Satellite (MTSAT)*, Japan's first wide-area augmentation satellite for meteorology and global positioning in support of airline operations.

China. The People's Republic's space program showed a strong comeback in 1999 from its previous years' commercial launcher setbacks. There were four successful missions of the Long March (Chang Zheng, CZ) rocket, including three commercial launches. These comprised one CZ-2C with two *Iridium* communications satellites and two improved CZ-4B's, one carrying a *Fengyun-1* meteorological satellite and a *Shijian-5* science satellite piggy-backed to it into polar orbit, the other with the two Brazilian satellites, *CBERS-1* for imaging and *SACI-1* for science research. The fourth launch, on November 19 on an uprated CZ-2F booster, was a crewless test flight of China's human space flight program, designated Project 921 and announced in 1998. The 16,000-lb (7200-kg) spacecraft named Shenzhou, a modified version of the Russian Soyuz vehicle, orbited the Earth 14 times during a 21-h flight that ended with the descent module's parachute landing and successful recovery on the plains of Inner Mongolia. The first crewed flight is now expected for the near future.

India. The Indian Space Research Organization (ISRO) has intensified its development programs for satellites and launch vehicles. ISRO plans in 1999 included 15 satellite missions and 10 indigenous launch vehicle missions through 2003. India's indigenously developed Polar Satellite Launch Vehicle (PSLV), which evolved from the earlier SLV-3 and Augmented SLV series, on May 26 launched the *IRS-P4* (*Oceansat-1*) as its primary payload, along with two microsatellites from Germany (*Tubsat-C*) and South Korea (*Kitsat-3*), on its first commercial launch. The PSLV, a four-stage rocket with a unique combination of solid and liquid propellant stages, stands 144 ft (44 m) tall; it can put a payload of up to 2650 lb (1200-kg) in polar Sun-synchronous orbit. Its first launch, in 1993, was a failure, but the following flights were generally successful. The 1999 launch was the fifth flight and the second for the upgraded version, which has four of its six solid-propellant strap-ons ignited on the ground (instead of two) and two in the air.

The next step for India is attaining geostationary capability for large communications payloads. This is the purpose of the Delta 2–class Geostationary Satellite Launch Vehicle (GSLV), which uses the same first and second stages as the PSLV, but with four liquid propellant boosters instead of the six solid strap-ons, and a single cryogenic stage replacing the third and fourth PSLV stages. ISRO developed the cryogenic engine, with a first test fire in early 1998 of a pressure-fed version; the flight version is to use turbopumps.

South Korea. After North Korea's failed first space mission in 1998, South Korea announced a 5-year initiative to design, build, and launch a commercial space cargo rocket, and to use the launcher to create a commercial launch business for the country.

For background information *see* ASTEROID; COMMUNICATIONS SATELLITE; INFRARED ASTRONOMY; JUPITER; MARS; MILITARY SATELLITES; MOON; REMOTE SENSING; SATELLITE ASTRONOMY; SOLAR WIND; SPACE FLIGHT; SPACE PROBE; SPACE SHUTTLE; SPACE STATION; SPACE TECHNOLOGY; SUN; ULTRAVIOLET ASTRONOMY; X-RAY ASTRONOMY in the McGraw-Hill Encyclopedia of Science & Technology.

Jesco von Puttkamer

Bibliography. European Space Agency, *Press Releases '99*; *Jane's Space Directory, 1999–2000*; NASA Public Affairs Office, *News Releases '99*; *State of the Space Industry—1999*, Space Publications LLC; *United States Space Directory—1999*, Space Publications LLC.

Space technology

The National Aeronautics and Space Administration (NASA) and other organizations are pursuing ideas that are not merely refinements of existing technology, but possible breakthroughs that will result in more efficient rockets, unlimited power production, and greatly reduced cost. Other ideas, like inventions of the past, such as the transistor, may lead to unexpected results.

Tethers. In 1996 a Tethered Satellite System (TSS-1R, with R standing for reflight) flew on the space shuttle. Its purpose was to demonstrate tether dynamics and power generation. The principle for producing power is the same as for a terrestrial generator. In a generator a conductive wire rotates through a magnetic field. This produces a force which pushes the electrons along the wire, into a load (say a light bulb, which lights up), and then back to the generator, completing the circuit. The Sun emits electrons in what is called the solar wind. The Earth's magnetic field lines trap these electrons. The TSS-1R had a satellite on the end of a 19.6-km (12.2-mi) conductive tether. The tether moved through the magnetic field lines and produced the same force as does a generator. In order for the electricity to flow through the tether, there had to be a complete circuit. Therefore, at the other end of the tether there was an electron gun shooting electrons into space. The solar wind's electrons struck the tether. The magnetic field moved the electrons down the tether to the gun, which then shot them back into space. The predictions were that, under ideal situations, 0.5 ampere of electric current would be produced. In actuality, the tether was not deployed to its greatest length, and yet TSS-1R still generated a full 1.0 A. Using a tether would therefore seem to be one way for spacecraft to generate electricity simply and efficiently.

The same principle can be used in reverse. If electricity is sent into a generator, it produces a magnetic field. This pushes against the magnetic field that is around the generator, and the generator turns, becoming a motor. Similarly, if a tethered spacecraft sends electricity through the tether, a magnetic field is produced. This pushes against the magnetic field of the Earth, and the spacecraft moves. This increases or decreases the velocity of the spacecraft. NASA has announced a Propulsive Small Expendable Deployer System (ProSEDS) being produced under the Future-X program. This is a propellant-free propulsion system that should reduce the cost of space exploration (see **illus.**)

ProSEDS can be used to decrease the velocity of a spacecraft, a process known as braking. ProSEDS will be attached to the second stage of a Delta II rocket. Stage two normally returns to Earth after about 6 months because atmospheric drag brakes the spacecraft. ProSEDs will try to produce an addition orbital decay of 5 km (3 mi) a day. Further research and the development of a fully operational unit could change the deorbit of the Delta stage from 6 months to 14 days.

Tether propulsion could benefit a wide variety of spacecraft, including the Space Station. Current plans are for NASA to reboost the station several times a year with conventional propellants. These would be brought up on the shuttle, which would be expensive. This cost could be eliminated by using a tether system weighing approximately 200 kg (440 lb) with a tether 10 km (6.2 mi) in length.

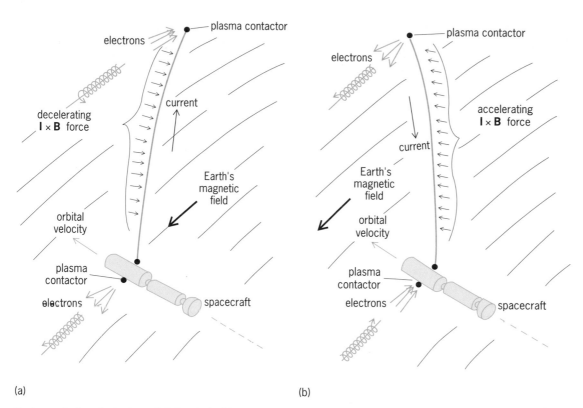

Deployment of an electrodynamic tether in the (*a*) power generation and (*b*) propulsion modes.

Flywheels. Flywheels store mechanical energy using a spinning wheel. When connected to a generator, the spinning flywheel produces electricity. Thus, the flywheel can be used to store electricity like a battery. NASA is developing a flywheel energy storage (FES) system for the Space Station. The station's solar arrays will provide power for it by converting sunlight into electricity, part of which will be used to charge batteries in the station. When the station enters the shadow of the Earth, the batteries will supply power to the station through the battery charge discharge unit. The flywheel energy storage system would replace the batteries and the battery charge/discharge unit. The flywheels will store more energy than the batteries, thus allowing extra electrical capacity for experiments. They also last longer, and therefore should save considerable expense over the life of the station. Testing at Johnson Space Center is scheduled to start in 2001, with a planned launch to the Space Station in 2004.

Magnetic levitation. Magnetic levitation (maglev) is currently used to propel high-speed trains and roller coasters. A linear induction motor levitates the vehicle above a track, which greatly reduces friction. NASA is investigating the use of maglev to accelerate spacecraft up to 1000 km/h (600 mi/h). Once it reaches that speed, the spacecraft would ignite its rockets and lift off. In 1999 at Marshall Space Flight Center in Huntsville, AL, NASA had a 15-m (50-ft) maglev track installed that levitated a 13-kg (30-lb) spacecraft. A 122-m (400-ft) track is being planned which will be used to determine how to control a

rocket moving on it at high speeds, and how to move it using as little energy as possible. By accelerating the rocket with maglev, the total propellant needed to get a spacecraft into orbit could be reduced by as much as 20%.

Air-breathing rockets. In 1996 Marshall Space Flight Center began testing air breathing rockets, otherwise known as rocket-based, combined cycle engines. A normal rocket engine burns fuel and oxidizer to produce thrust. The air-breathing rocket augments the oxidizer with air from the atmosphere. This increases the performance by about 15% over a normal rocket engine. When the rocket reaches Mach 2—twice the speed of sound—the oxidizer is shut off because enough oxygen in the air is going through the engine. At about Mach 10 the rocket is at high altitude where there is not enough oxygen in the air to burn. The oxidizer is turned back on, and the vehicle accelerates into Earth orbit. These engines could produce spacecraft that are completely reusable, could take off and land at airport runways, and would have turnaround times as low as a few days. General Applied Sciences Laboratory (Long Island, NY) is currently testing this type of engine.

NASA Breakthrough Propulsion Physics Program. In 1996 NASA tasked Marshall Space Flight Center to propose a plan for developing radical new propulsion methods. This is called the Breakthrough Propulsion Physics Program (BPPP), and its purpose is to look for fundamental breakthroughs in physics that will lead to totally new types of space transportation. Other programs are refining existing technologies to make a better rocket; the task of the Breakthrough Propulsion Physics Program is to innovate.

To do this, Marshall Space Flight Center set a goal that, using current technology, was clearly impossible: practical travel to the stars. By setting such a goal, they eliminated the tendency to extrapolate using existing solutions.

The objective of the program is to produce, within the next few years, credible, affordable, and measurable progress toward this goal. Marshall Space Flight Center has requested proposals for research, and a few examples of submitted proposals follow. Although some of these may appear to be in the realm of science fiction, Marshall Space Flight Center will examine them carefully, select a few, and pay for the research.

Mass variation. Some researchers in general relativity have shown that inertia (a property of matter by which it remains at rest or in motion in a straight line at a constant speed unless a force is applied) has both an acceleration-dependent term and a time-dependent transient term. The latter predicts that an object with a time-varying energy density will have a variation in rest mass. In other words, its rest mass and real mass will be different. An experiment using vibrating capacitors appeared to show this difference in mass, but the vibrations may have led to false readings. The proposal would eliminate the vibration problem by using rotation of a four-capacitor array charging and discharging in a certain sequence. If the mass variation is real, a force would be produced. This force could be used for propulsion utilizing no propellant.

High-temperature superconductors. High-temperature superconductors may be able to change gravity. The proposal is to try to construct an experiment to prove that a superconductor pumped with radio frequencies can modify gravity. If the theory is proved correct, this could lead to another propulsion system that uses no propellant.

Vacuum energy density. There is a prediction in the field of quantum electrodynamics that there is a near-infinite vacuum energy density. That is, in a vacuum the energy available may be very great because of the variations in the electromagnetic fields in empty space. Surfaces have been shown to change the energy density of the vacuum. Two conducting plates placed very close together are forced together, presumably by the vacuum fluctuations. This is called the Casimir effect. One of the proposals is to investigate the use of surfaces other than parallel plates to alter the vacuum energy. A rectangular cavity, for instance, should produce forces inward or outward, depending on the ratio of the sides. This will test the quantum electrodynamics predictions, and could lead to another propulsion system or virtually limitless energy production.

For background information *see* FLYWHEEL; GENERATOR; MAGNETIC LEVITATION; MOTOR; ROCKET PROPULSION; SPACECRAFT PROPULSION in the McGraw-Hill Encyclopedia of Science & Technology.

Jeffrey C. Mitchell

Bibliography. L. Johnson and M. Hermann, International Space Station Electrodynamic Tether Reboost Study, *NASA Tech. Mem.*, TM-1998-208538, July 1998; M. G. Millis, NASA Propulsion Physics Program, NASA TM-1998-208400, 1998, in *Missions to the Outer Solar System and Beyond*, 2d IAA Symposium on Realistic Near-Term Advanced Scientific Space Mission, Aosta, Italy, June 29–July 1, 1998, ed. by Genta, pp. 103–110, International Academy of Astronautics.

Stable isotope

Stable isotope analysis is a rapidly expanding field for investigation of ancient foodwebs and ecosystems. Since the first such anthropological study over 20 years ago, which charted expansion of maize agriculture using radioactive carbon ($^{13}C/^{12}C$) in human bone collagen, the toolkit has expanded to include nitrogen ($^{15}N/^{14}N$) isotopes in organic residues, and carbon and oxygen ($^{18}O/^{16}O$) isotopes in calcified tissue minerals. The tissues reflect the isotope composition of the food that was eaten. The theoretical basis has been validated in numerous field observations and laboratory feeding studies. The advantage of these kinds of tracers over other forms of archeological evidence is that quantitative information can be obtained about what was actually eaten, rather than what was discarded. Furthermore, both individual and group choices can be investigated, allowing comparisons to be made along the lines of age, gender, and status. Only dietary studies based on bones and teeth will be described here. The basis for use of these tools is outlined, along with some applications which illustrate the principles, advantages, and constraints of the techniques.

Stable light isotopes. Naturally occurring stable isotopes of an element differ in nuclear mass, leading to small differences in thermodynamic and kinetic properties, which for light elements (less than atomic mass 40) lead to partitioning of isotopes during chemical and physical processes. This results in changes in their relative abundances, or fractionation, and provides a natural tracer for the elements of life as they cycle through physico- and biochemical pathways in food webs and animal tissues. The differences are predictable but small, and by convention isotope ratios are expressed in the delta (δ) notation in parts per thousand (‰) relative to a standard (R = isotopic ratio):

$$\delta X(‰) = (R_{sample} - R_{ref})/R_{ref} \times 1000$$

PDB (Peedee Belemnite, a marine carbonate) is the standard used for $^{18}O/^{16}O$ and $^{13}C/^{12}C$, and atmospheric N_2 (AIR standard) for $^{15}N/^{14}N$. Negative values denote that the sample has lower abundances of the heavier isotope than does the standard.

Isotope pathways in ecosystems. The isotopic composition of food is reflected in all tissues of an animal, but since bones and teeth generally survive longest, they are the standard archives for isotope signatures.

Proteins in bone and tooth dentin provide the source for organic $\delta^{13}C$ and $\delta^{15}N$ values, while inorganic $\delta^{13}C$ and $\delta^{18}O$ values are determined from carbonate substituted within the calcium phosphate apatitic structure, or $\delta^{18}O$ alone from apatitic phosphate. Alteration of the original signature during fossilization is an important constraint for application of isotope tools, which must always be carefully evaluated.

Carbon isotopes are the most widely applied isotope tools for probing diet. At the base of the terrestrial food chain, two dominant photosynthetic pathways among terrestrial plants, C_3 and C_4 (after the number of carbon atoms in the first product), differ in the degree of discrimination against heavier ^{13}C. The C_3 plants, including all trees, woody shrubs, herbs, and temperate or shade-loving grasses, have distinctively lower $\delta^{13}C$ values compared to C_4 subtropical and tropical grasses and, more rarely, arid-adapted shrubs. Marine ecosystems are higher in ^{13}C than terrestrial C_3 ecosystems. Encoding in the bone collagen and mineral of consumers occurs with different positive offsets for each tissue, some of which may vary according to biosynthetic pathways and dietary quality. Variability in $\delta^{15}N$ exists between ecosystems, related to local soil conditions and environment. Stepwise trophic enrichment occurs in animals due to excretion of ^{15}N-depleted urea. Marine foods are higher in ^{15}N compared to most terrestrial foods, except in the case of plants and animals from arid areas with low mean annual rainfall, which are anomalously high in ^{15}N. In contrast, $\delta^{18}O$ is controlled less by food than by isotope effects in the water cycle, which vary greatly across the globe and in plants and animals.

C_4 agriculture. In piecing together subsistence patterns of prehistoric people, one pervasive problem is that a large element of the puzzle, the plants, is usually missing. This is a real problem for studies of crop domestication. Therefore, isotopic differences between C_3 and C_4 plants can be useful for tracking expansion of nonindigenous C_4 crops into new habitats. This principle was used to track expansion of C_4 maize into the North American woodlands where indigenous plants were all C_3. Previously, appearance of settlements and earthworks among the Hopewell people before A.D. 400 was believed to be based on arrival of maize agriculture. However, human bone collagen $\delta^{13}C$ values showed consistent C_3-based diets until about 800, then there was a dramatic switch to high maize diets by 1000 (**Fig. 1**) Subsequent studies have further explored the expansion of maize into new habitats, including equatorial forests of South America, and the expansion of other crops, such as sorghum (C_4) and rice (C_3).

Dependence on marine foods. Isotopic studies have successfully addressed questions about the extent to which coastal communities relied upon marine foods, or more precisely, marine protein, using the differences between marine and terrestrial $\delta^{13}C$ and $\delta^{15}N$. The first study to use this principle showed that Mesolithic people in Denmark relied heavily on marine resources, but surprisingly, Neolithic, Bronze

Age, and Iron Age people largely ignored them. Locally fish did not become important again until Medieval times (Fig. 1). Heavy reliance on marine foods was also revealed for coastal hunter-gatherers on the western Cape coast of South Africa, particularly between 2000 and 3000 years ago; it seems that women ate slightly less of these resources than men. In contrast, values for skeletons buried just 60 km (37 mi) into the interior indicated little marine food. These observations suggested two discrete subsistence patterns and challenged models which proposed that the coast and inland regions were parts of the same transhumance pattern.

In regions where some of the plant cover is C_4, it is more difficult to differentiate between marine and terrestrial diets, but here nitrogen isotopes can prove useful. Complications introduced by aridity and trophic level mean that this tool must be carefully applied. Bone collagen $\delta^{15}N$ of skeletons from sites along the southern Cape coast of South Africa, where vegetation is a mix of C_3 and C_4 plants, showed that exploitation of marine foods was highly variable for the region as a whole. However, some consistent differences existed between skeletons from sites as little as 15 km apart, suggesting economic differences and territorial boundaries between adjacent groups (Fig. 1).

Several isotopic indicators were used to reconstruct diets of the prehistoric islanders of the Marianas Archipelago in the western Pacific. Collagen $\delta^{13}C$ and $\delta^{15}N$ values showed a pattern of 20-50% marine protein consumption, but apatite $\delta^{13}C$ values pointed to an unexpected ^{13}C-enriched, protein-poor food source. This latter source was almost certainly

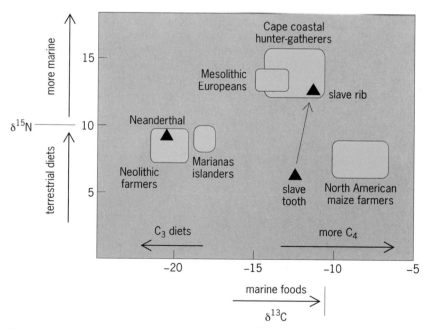

Fig. 1. Typical stable carbon and nitrogen isotopes ratios for bone collagen, portrayed as boxes, from groups with different diets. Individual values are shown for the Cape of Good Hope slave woman, and the Neanderthal individual from Marillac, France. Arrows indicate ranges for terrestrial and marine diets in $\delta^{15}N$ and $\delta^{13}C$, and for C_3 and C_4 signatures in $\delta^{13}C$. The Hopewell people are represented by a broader group labeled "North American maize farmers."

sugarcane (a C_4 grass), but nobody had suspected that it formed an important dietary resource. Current understanding is that proteins in food are preferentially routed into structural proteins like collagen, with the result that high protein foods, like marine foods, are overestimated from collagen $\delta^{13}C$ measurements. Apatite $\delta^{13}C$, however, reflects composition of the entire diet.

Life histories. A promising new approach takes advantage of the different formation and remodeling rates in various skeletal elements to determine the dietary life histories of individuals. Bone is constantly remodeled, so isotope composition reflects long-term dietary averages, while tooth enamel (and to a lesser extent, dentin) reflects conditions at the time of formation. Analyses of tooth dentin and enamel of an early eighteenth-century slave woman from the Cape of Good Hope showed that she had spent her formative years in warmer climes where C_4 foods were eaten. Her bones told a different story: they reflected more C_3 and marine foods and fewer C_4 plants, which indeed do not occur in this winter rainfall region. The isotopic variability showed that she was a first-generation slave. In the same region, dietary shifts occurring from childhood to capture and enslavement have been similarly tracked among a group of skeletons of shipwrecked slaves. Despite relatively poor preservation of bone material at a site in highland Guatemala, combined $\delta^{13}C$, $\delta^{18}O$, and $\delta^{15}N$ in adult tooth enamel and dentin allowed reconstruction of culturally diverse patterns of introduction of solid foods and weaning.

Hominid diets. Collagen is a stable protein, but it degrades on geological time scales. Under favorable circumstances, it can be recovered from late Pleis-

tocene material. The $\delta^{15}N$ in a 40,000-year-old Neanderthal from France indicated a surprisingly high trophic level diet (a diet with a high proportion of animal foods), and combined collagen and enamel isotope analyses of Neanderthals hold promise for probing the diet and lifestyles of these enigmatic hominids. Discovery of the relative inertness of enamel has also created a powerful new tool for addressing questions about the diets, habits, and environments of hominids in earlier periods. Isotope studies have been valuable in research on the South African early hominid localities, which are cave sites that have acted as natural traps and that lack good contextual evidence. The robust australopithecines (*Paranthropus robustus*) found in the site of Swartkrans, between 1 and 2 millions years ago, were believed to be vegetarians concentrating on tough fruits and roots, because their massive facial architecture seemed adapted for heavy processing of foods. However, $\delta^{13}C$ in their enamel showed about 25% C_4 foods (**Fig. 2**), which can be explained in only two ways: either they ate C_4 grasses, or they ate animals which ate the grasses. The second explanation is more likely because there is no sign of scratches by grass phytoliths (microscopic plant silica bodies, often showing distinctive shapes; especially common in grasses) on their teeth. *Paranthropus* is believed to have been an omnivore rather than a dedicated vegetarian. The $\delta^{13}C$ values from early specimens of the human genus, *Homo*, occurring at the same time as *Paranthropus*, show that they also consumed about 25% C_4-based foods, as did an earlier, 3-million-year-old hominid, *Australopithecus africanus*, from the site of Makapansgat Limeworks in South Africa. At Makapansgat, the C_4 contribution was more variable, but also more surprising because it was apparently a dense woodland with fewer C_4 plants. Even at this early stage, hominids presumably regularly left the safety of the trees to forage in the open patches of grass. This behavior sets them apart from close relatives like chimpanzees.

Future directions. Stable-light-isotope approaches present fresh ways for unlocking the secrets of past human and hominid behaviors. New directions will likely take several directions. Attention to variation within individuals promises to provide details of complete dietary life histories of ordinary people, from the cradle to the grave. A fundamental problem for constructing quantitative interpretations of paleodiet from isotopic analyses is the current poor understanding of the biochemical pathways and fate of dietary macronutrients during conversion to body tissues. Controlled feeding studies of rodents showed that dietary protein is routed to bone collagen, and documented $\delta^{13}C$ diet-tissue differences for collagen and apatites. The extent to which these patterns can be generalized to larger animals and humans is uncertain, and requires further experimental work.

For background information *see* APATITE; ECOSYSTEM; ISOTOPE; PALEOBOTANY; RADIOCARBON DATING in the McGraw–Hill Encyclopedia of Science & Technology.   Julia Lee-Thorp

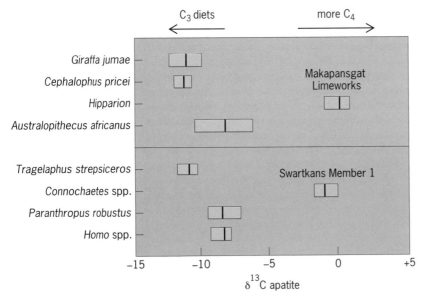

Fig. 2. $\delta^{13}C$ values for hominids (*Australopithecus africanus*, *Paranthropus robustus*, and *Hano* spp.) from Makapansgat and Swartkrans, in South Africa, shown as boxes incorporating means and standard deviations, along with some typical animal values for comparison. *Giraffa jumae* (giraffe), *C. pricei* (duiker), and *T. strepsiceros* (greater kudu) are browsers, while *Hipparion* (three-toed horse) and *Connochaetes* spp. (wildebeest) are grazers. Values for the animals provide a comparative range for that habitat, and can also provide more detailed glimpses of the environment.

Bibliography. H. P. Schwarcz and M. J. Schoeninger, Stable isotope analyses in human nutritional ecology, *J. World Prehist.*, 34:283–321, 1991; J. C. Sealy, R. Armstrong, and C. Schrire, Beyond lifetime averages: Tracing life histories through isotopic analysis of different calcified tissues from archaeological human skeletons, *Antiquity*, 69:290–300, 1995; J. Sealy and S. Pfeiffer, Diet, body size and landscape use among Holocene people in the Southern Cape, South Africa, *Curr. Anthropol.*, in press; M. Sponheimer and J. A. Lee-Thorp, Isotopic evidence for the diet of an early hominid, *Australopithecus africanus, Science*, 283:368–370, 1990.

Sun

The *Transition Region and Coronal Explorer (TRACE)* explores the dynamics and evolution of the solar atmosphere from the photosphere to the corona with high temporal and spatial resolution. The *TRACE* Observatory produces images of the Sun in the ultraviolet and extreme ultraviolet regions of the electromagnetic spectrum, corresponding to a temperature range from 5×10^3 to 2.5×10^6 K. Flare plasma at 2×10^7 K is also imaged when present.

TRACE is the first solar-observing satellite in the Small Explorer series. Launched April 2, 1998, into a polar, Sun-synchronous orbit ranging in altitude from 600 to 650 km (373 to 404 mi) at an inclination of 97.8°, it can observe the Sun continuously for 9 months of the year. The orbit produces 3-month-long eclipse seasons, during which the spacecraft passes briefly into the Earth's shadow every 90 min. The estimate after orbital insertion was that *TRACE* would stay in its Sun-synchronous orbit for at least 5 years.

Scientific objectives. The *TRACE* Observatory is designed to explore quantitatively the connections between fine-scale magnetic fields at the solar surface and the associated plasma structures in the solar outer atmosphere. The structure and dynamics of the solar corona are intimately connected with the emergence at the solar surface of strong magnetic fields generated inside the Sun. Three-dimensional regions of hot magnetized plasma are formed above the surface (**Fig. 1**).

One of the fundamental problems in coronal physics is to explain how the coronal gas is heated to temperatures of several million kelvins, and to understand the conditions under which stored energy is released rapidly in the corona to produce flares, mass ejections, and other transient phenomena. Because these phenomena connect the 5800 K photosphere with the million kelvin corona, *TRACE* uses multiple ultraviolet and normal-incidence extreme ultraviolet channels to collect images of atmospheric plasmas at temperatures from 10^4 to 10^7 K (see **table**).

Many of the physical processes in the solar atmosphere, such as plasma confinement, reconnection, wave propagation, and plasma heating, are encountered in space physics and much of astrophysics as

Fig. 1. *TRACE* image of active region on the solar surface, taken on May 19, 1998, at a wavelength of 17.3 nm, which covers the Fe IX and Fe X emission lines.

well, making *TRACE* a pathfinder for the understanding of these processes throughout the universe.

Instrumentation. The *TRACE* telescope is a Cassegrain design with a 30-cm (12-in.) aperture and a square field of view of 8.5×8.5 arcminutes, somewhat more than one-fourth the diameter of the Sun. Larger views are obtained by repointing the telescope to build up a mosaic image (**Fig. 2**). The

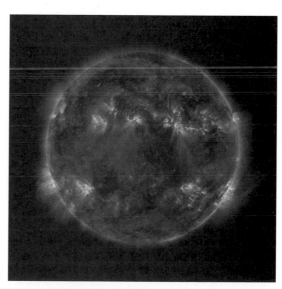

Fig. 2. *TRACE* full-Sun mosaic image taken on October 10, 1998, at a wavelength of 17.3 nm.

TRACE temperature coverage		
Wavelength, nm	Emission	Temperature, K
17.3	Fe IX and Fe X lines	$0.8–2.0 \times 10^6$
19.5	Fe XII line	$0.9–2.1 \times 10^6$
19.5	Fe XXIV line	$10–25 \times 10^6$
28.4	Fe XV line	$1.5–4.0 \times 10^6$
121.6	Lyman-alpha line	$10–30 \times 10^3$
155.0	C IV line	$0.6–2.5 \times 10^5$
160	Ultraviolet continuum	$4–10 \times 10^3$
170	Continuum	$4–10 \times 10^3$
500	White light	$4–6 \times 10^3$

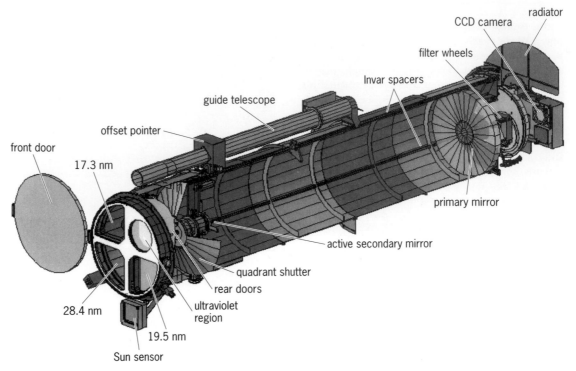

Fig. 3. Cutaway view of the *TRACE* instrument. Wavelengths of the four quadrants are indicated.

telescope is divided into four quadrants, each having a special coating to make it reflective in a specific wavelength band; the primary and secondary mirrors have matching coatings. A large aperture wheel rotates to expose one of the four channels at a time, with the image from each channel ending on a single electronic array detector in the focal plane common to all four channels (**Fig. 3**). The resolution of the telescope is limited to 1 arcsecond (with 0.5-arcsecond pixels) by the charge-coupled-device (CCD) detector.

The data rate from *TRACE* to the ground reaches 700 megabytes per day. With image compression, this provides more than one million images per year. *TRACE* has an open data policy, and the original data may be obtained without proprietary restriction on the World Wide Web.

Results. In addition to the inherent usefulness of the data obtained on-orbit by *TRACE*, coordinated observing programs using data from other satellites and from ground-based observatories are extending the range of scientific programs that can be carried out. The initial results from *TRACE*, described below, include both types of studies.

Chromosphere-corona transition region. Although the prevailing view of the solar atmosphere is no longer based on simple plane-parallel models, the nature of the connection between the bright coronal structures and the solar surface magnetic fields is still uncertain. The raggedness of the interface between the high- and low-temperature portions of the solar atmosphere is quite clear in the *TRACE* data (**Fig. 4**). Cool material extends upward to heights of 10,000 km (6000 mi), and hot loops extend downward to heights of perhaps 2000 km (1200 mi). However, these hot and cool features are intermingled, rather than connected to each other.

Comparison of the hot coronal structures with high-resolution ground-based data indicates that although there is a general agreement between the location of the hot loops and the location of enhanced magnetic fields on the solar surface, there is very poor agreement between the two at the highest resolution limits. These results seem to indicate that there is some as-yet undetermined magnetic

Fig. 4. Corona-chromosphere interface, as seen by *TRACE* at a wavelength of 17.3 nm.

complexity in the chromosphere, and they may also indicate that coronal heating takes place at surfaces separating magnetic flux bundles, rather than within the bundles themselves.

Coronal fine structure. The *TRACE* coronal observations strongly support the fundamental view that in a hot magnetized plasma, energy transport is efficient along the magnetic field direction but is strongly inhibited in the direction perpendicular to the field. Regions that are spatially close to each other may therefore be largely decoupled, while distant regions may be closely linked. This is illustrated in Fig. 1, showing long thin threads of hot plasma that are fairly uniform along their length but exhibit a large contrast with neighboring locations. The overall structure of the hot corona is largely determined by the magnetic field, but comparison of the observations with models of the coronal field based on surface field measurements shows that the coronal structure is often more sheared than expected, indicating that there are strong electric currents flowing through these regions.

Cool material at coronal heights. One surprising observation in the new *TRACE* data is the large amount of cool material at coronal heights. The extreme-ultraviolet wavelengths observed by *TRACE* are relatively easily absorbed by cool material. A structure having 10^{18} atoms per square centimeter of material at normal solar composition along the line of sight will absorb more than half of the extreme-ultraviolet radiation. The cool material must be located between the extreme-ultraviolet source and the Earth, so that the observation of dark linear absorption features, as seen in Figs. 1, 2, and 4, indicates the presence of cool, dense material at coronal heights. This material is also seen at the limb, lying well above the photospheric surface and often oriented horizontally. This indicates that the material is being supported by horizontal magnetic fields. Time sequences of images at high cadence show that this material is constantly in motion, at several kilometers per second, flowing in all directions. Often, adjacent field lines show cool material flowing in opposite directions, and there are many examples of flows stopping and changing directions. These flows are not to be confused with so-called surges, which are more rapid and are generally short-lived transient phenomena.

Flows in hot coronal structures. Beginning in the 1970s, it became clear that the inner corona could not be modeled as a plane parallel atmosphere with inhomogeneities, as had been done for the previous century. Instead, the closed loop, consisting of hot plasma enclosed by a magnetic flux bundle emerging at one location on the solar surface and returning at a distant location, became the fundamental building block of a topologically complex atmosphere. Because cross-field energy transport is inefficient in a hot plasma, these loops represent relatively isolated mini-atmospheres, with a temperature and density structure determined by local conditions.

The loop atmospheres have typically been divided into two classes: quasi-static loops and flare loops. The former class are those that show slow variations compared to the equilibration time scales, and the latter include rapid brightenings that range from nanoflare to full-flare levels. The *TRACE* observations show not only that coronal loops are far thinner than had previously been thought, but also that the assumption of hydrostatic equilibrium is not generally valid. A significant fraction of the observed loops exhibit continual outflows of hot material. The flows begin at the loop footpoints with low velocity and accelerate steadily outward, reaching several hundred kilometers per second at heights of order 100,000 km (60,000 mi).

Flares. The combination of high spatial resolution, extended temperature range, and high temporal cadence of the *TRACE* data provides extremely useful flare data.

Ultraviolet observations in cool chromospheric lines such as the Lyman-alpha (121.6 nanometers) show the initial footpoint brightenings in flares at a very early stage, coinciding with the hard x ray emisison observed in other instruments such as the *Yohkoh* spacecraft. These brightenings occur at the time of initial energy release in the flare, before chromospheric material evaporates into the corona and before any substantial amounts of hot plasma appear in x-rays.

The *TRACE* extreme-ultraviolet observations confirm the so-called standard model of flares, in which a closed magnetic structure opens outward, usually accompanied by the ejection of a cool, dense filament. An initial energy release from a location high in the corona results in energy flows down the legs of the magnetic structure, heating the chromosphere and filling the corona with the heated material. The decay phase of the flare consists of the formation of higher loops, representing the successive reclosing of the magnetic field lines opened in the initial eruption, with the lower-lying inner loops closing first.

The observations also indicate that a complex magnetic topology is an essential part of the process. Energy release appears along separatrix surfaces, which represent the boundaries between magnetic field regions having different connectivity. A quadrupolar field configuration may be necessary for the eruption to occur. The opening outward of overlying field lines is present in many of the models, and such field-line motions are often observed in *TRACE*, some tens of minutes before the flare brightenings or filament eruptions are seen.

For background information *see* SUN; ULTRAVIOLET ASTRONOMY in the McGraw-Hill Encyclopedia of Science & Technology.   Leon Golub

Bibliography. L. Golub and J. M. Pasachoff, *The Solar Corona*, Cambridge University Press, 1997; L. Golub and J. M. Pasachoff, *The Sun*, Harvard University Press, 2001; B. N. Handy et al., *The Transition Region and Coronal Explorer*, *Solar Phys.*, 187:229–260, 1999; A. M. Title, The million-degree solar corona, *Sky Telesc.*, 98(4):56–57, October 1999.

Superconductivity

The high-temperature superconducting compound $YBa_2Cu_3O_x$ (YBCO) has attracted great attention ever since its discovery in 1987. The interest in this material lies not only in fundamental studies of superconducting mechanisms but also in many important engineering applications. Wireless telecommunications has been a growing field of application, particularly in the development of radio-frequency devices using high-temperature superconductors.

Cellular telecommunications. The Federal Communication Commission (FCC) defines cellular as: "A high capacity land mobile system in which assigned spectrum is divided into discrete channels which are assigned in groups to geographic cells covering a cellular geographic service area. The discrete channels are capable of being reused in different cells within the service area." Each coverage area (cell) is a circle with a radio base station at the center, and together these cells completely cover the service area. Each cell can have 99 channels that are available to users. A typical wireless telephone call proceeds in the following steps:

1. Power up: A mobile set measures signals from base stations in its area, "hand-shakes" with the one with the strongest signal, and remains in its "ready" state.

2. Outgoing call: A user enters the number to be called and hits "send." The user's mobile set sends information to the base station, and requests a voice channel. The mobile switching center assigns voice channels. The mobile set tunes to the assigned channel and is connected through the mobile switching center.

3. Incoming call: The called mobile set receives pages from all base stations, acknowledges the page to the local base station, tunes to the assigned channel, and is connected via the mobile switching center. Its user then receives a ringing alert.

Cellular telecommunications are growing rapidly in North America, Europe, and Asia. However, today's best conventional radio filtering techniques, including cavity preselectors, interdigital or combline passband, cavity notch or passband, and especially ceramic and ferrite loaded filters, do not perform well enough to provide the level of filtering that will be required by dense, heavily used radio-frequency communication systems. As channels are placed more closely together, present-generation radio-frequency equipment loses its ability to discriminate between channels. As a result of the poor performance of conventional filters, the systems often experience failure, which is characterized by (1) poor voice quality (static, "foreign" conversations, and inaudible conversations); (2) lack of a signal (the user is outside the covered area); (3) "blocked" calls (the system is busy, and the customer is unable to initiate a call); and (4) "dropped" calls (the connection is lost in midconversation).

YBCO thin-film devices. Therefore, more selective filters with lower insertion losses for dense radio

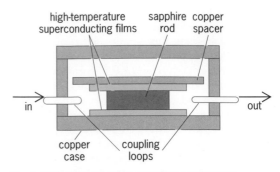

Fig. 1. Dielectric resonator using high-temperature superconducting thin films.

networks must be designed to satisfy the rapidly increasing demand in telecommunications. High-temperature superconducting YBCO compounds offer promise in this regard by virtue of the extremely low surface resistance that these materials exhibit at cellular frequencies. Low surface resistance means low losses when the electromagnetic waves containing communication information propagate through the surface of the component materials. One of the basic components in a radio-frequency device in a wireless system is a microwave resonator. A typical high-temperature superconducting resonator incorporates two parallel superconducting YBCO thin films separated by a dielectric substrate in the form of a sapphire disk (**Fig. 1**). The electromagnetic fields decay exponentially along the radial direction away from the surface of the disk. In all cases, the overall Q of the resonator is determined by the combination of the contributions, neglecting radiative losses, from the conductor and from dielectric losses.

Thin films can be fabricated by using various synthesis techniques such as molecular beam epitaxy, sputtering, and chemical vapor deposition. High-quality YBCO thin films exhibit excellent microwave properties at cellular frequencies, and ultrahigh Q resonators using these films have been developed for telecommunications. The Q value reaches 10^6 for high-temperature superconducting/dielectric cavity resonators and 7500 for a high-temperature superconducting microstripline resonator at a temperature of 77 K ($-196°C$ or $321°F$) and a frequency of 5 GHz. The YBCO thin film also exhibits an extremely low surface resistance of 400 $\mu\Omega$ ($\pm200~\mu\Omega$) at 77 K and 10 GHz. With such a high Q value, radio-frequency devices can provide excellent performance at cellular frequencies. For comparison, the cavity quality Q of a conventional filter made of copper is only 2000–3000. However, radio-frequency components made of thin films require complex synthesis systems, making them expensive and thus less attractive to industry.

Growth of single-domain YBCO. Recently a new way of making radio-frequency component materials has emerged. Instead of using thin films as the key components, single-domain YBCO has been processed with similar radio-frequency properties. Single-domain materials have several advantages. The

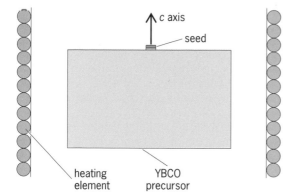

Fig. 2. Concept of seeded melt growth.

the cup. The *c*-axis-oriented domain structure was confirmed by x-ray diffraction, which indicated that the seeded melt growth YBCO displays excellent crystallinity.

The surface resistance of the single-domain YBCO has been measured by the dielectric resonator method and found to reach 530 $\mu\Omega$ at 77 K and 2.82 GHz, which is comparable to surface resistances of thin films. **Figure 4** shows the assembled cavity resonator and the radio-frequency characterization system. A special coupling connector is made by extending the center conductor of an SMA connector as a coupling probe. The cavity is designed to resonate at 18.4 GHz. Measurements of the cavity parameters are made using a network analyzer.

crystal can be manufactured into a three-dimensional component, the component does not require any substrate, and it is much more economical. A crystal growth method called seeded melt growth has been developed to grow large single-domain YBCO (**Fig. 2**). The precursor powders ($YBa_2Cu_3O_x$ and Y_2BaCuO_5 powders in a certain proportion) are pressed into a green pellet, and a seed single crystal is placed on the top of this pellet. NdBaCuO and SmBaCuO single crystals have been widely used as seeds. These crystals have considerably higher melting points than that of YBCO. The precursor is then heated to a temperature above 1050°C (1922°F) but below the melting point of the seed crystal. In this way, it is ensured that the precursors have partially melted while the seed remains solid. After the $YBa_2Cu_3O_x$ is thoroughly melted (note that Y_2BaCuO_5 remains in the solid phase, which "holds" the partially melted precursors in an upward position), the temperature is lowered at an extremely slow rate of 0.2–1°/h. Near the crystallization temperature, the YBCO crystal starts to form, but it prefers to grow on the bottom surface of the seed in the liquid. Since the seed is a single crystal, the newly grown crystal from the liquid will follow the crystal orientation of the seed and eventually grow into the entire body of the precursor. When the process is completed, a single-domain YBCO crystal is fully grown with a given crystal orientation with respect to the crystal surface. Usually, the *c* axis of the single domain is normal to the top surface of the sample.

Resonators using single-domain YBCO. Using seeded melt growth, it is easy to grow high-performance radio-frequency components. A very simple millimeter-wave resonator consists of a cavity formed from a cup-shaped base and a flat cover plate (**Fig. 3**). This resonator can serve as a key component in a radio-frequency filter for wireless telecommunications. To grow a single-domain YBCO crystal with a cup geometry, the seeded melt growth process must be slightly modified. The seed crystal is placed on the bottom of the cup, which is a preshaped precursor (Fig. 3*a*). Crystal growth takes place near the seed first and propagates through the entire body of the cup. Figure 3*b* shows the products: the cover and

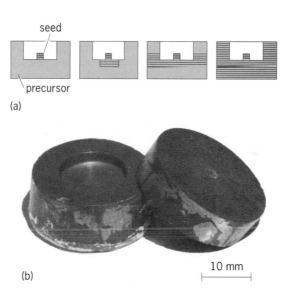

Fig. 3. Simple millimeter-wave resonator (cavity cup geometry) made of single-domain YBCO. (*a*) Successive stages of net-shape-processing of the cup. (*b*) Finished single-domain YBCO components (cavity and cup) processed by seeded melt growth.

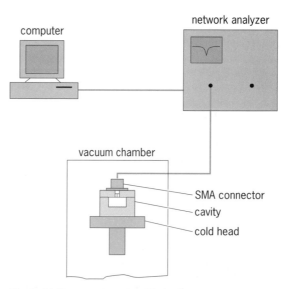

Fig. 4. Cavity resonator assembly for Q-factor characterization.

The cavity is placed in specially built closed-cycle refrigerator, and the cavity Q at resonant frequency is recorded as a function of temperature. The measured Q of the cavity has reached 10,200 at 35 K (−238°C or −397°F), a value that is much higher than that of its copper counterparts. This Q value is expected to increase significantly as the microstructure of the crystal is further optimized. The Q value may vary significantly, depending upon the design and resonant mode for the same type of material.

High-temperature superconductors thus exhibit excellent properties for radio-frequency device development. The current research has already shown great promise for practical applications in wireless communications. With the radio-frequency properties further improved by melt processing, it is certain that high-temperature superconductors will play a key role in many critical areas, particularly in the electronics industry.

For background information *see* CAVITY RESONATOR; CRYSTAL GROWTH; MOBILE RADIO; Q (ELECTRICITY); SUPERCONDUCTING DEVICES; SUPERCONDUCTIVITY in the McGraw-Hill Encyclopedia of Science & Technology.   Donglu Shi

Bibliography. A. Lauder, K. E. Myers, and D. W. Face, Thin film high-temperature superconductors for advanced communications and electronics, *Adv. Mater.*, 10:1249–1254, 1998; K. E. Myers, High temperature superconducting materials for microwave engineers, *Microwave Prod. Dig.*, November 1998; J. M. Phillips, High-temperature superconducting thin films, in D. Shi (ed.), *High Temperature Superconducting Materials Science and Engineering*, pp. 305–343, Pergamon Press, Oxford, U.K., 1995; J. C. Phillips, *Physics of High-T_c Superconductors*, Academic Press, Boston, 1989; D. Qu et al., Net shape processing of single domain YBCO for a novel high-Q millimeter wave resonator, *Physica C*, 315:36–44, 1999.

Supersonic dislocations

The existence of dislocations was postulated almost 100 years ago to explain permanent plastic deformation and nonlinear behavior in materials under large loads. The importance of dislocations for the scientific understanding and development of materials was recognized during the 1930s. Today, it is well known that dislocations are line defects in the crystalline order of materials and act as a vehicle of translation within the material, like a wave in the carpet helps to move it across the floor. Dislocations are the main carriers of plastic deformation in metals or semiconductor crystals, but they are also formed when parts of the Earth's crust move against each other. Dislocation motion governs the forming of almost all engineering parts, ranging from wire drawing to the forming of aircraft bodies. Understanding the dynamics of dislocation motion is therefore the key to the explanation of many different materials processes and phenomena ranging from the deep drawing of metal cans to the brittle or ductile response of materials, and reaches geological dimensions with the description of fault propagation during earthquakes. The recent finding of dislocation motion at supersonic velocities is of outstanding importance in this respect, since it was believed until then that dislocations cannot surmount the barrier at the shear wave velocity.

Mathematically, dislocations can be described as singularities in the elastic continuum, like electrons can be described as singular points in the electrodynamic space. From this analogy, it is possible to transfer many results of classical electrodynamics into the theory of dislocations. In particular, it can be shown that both particles approach a limiting velocity, following Einstein's special relativity theory. The limiting velocity corresponds to the speed of light for electrons and the velocity of acoustic shear waves in case of dislocations.

At the beginning of the twentieth century, theoreticians such as A. Sommerfeld found valid solutions for the motion of the particles above the limiting velocity. This seems at first somewhat paradoxical because the particle is then moving faster than the information that it is coming. Correspondingly, theory predicts that a dislocation moving at supersonic velocities should be followed by a Mach cone like a supersonically moving airplane. The crucial question is whether dislocations or electrons can ever surmount the limiting velocity to reach these supersonic states. At this point, Sommerfeld's electrons and dislocations differ in one important aspect. The physical space of the electrons is linear. The linear theory is therefore a mathematical abstraction of reality. In contrast, dislocations move in an elastic medium which is only approximately linear, since the atomic forces have nonlinear components. These nonlinearities can often be neglected, but nevertheless make linear theory an approximation to reality.

One way to test the linear elastic relativistic theory of dislocations is to use atomistic computer simulations where all the nonlinearities of the atomic interaction can be taken into account—albeit in an approximate manner. Attempts to accelerate dislocations beyond the limiting velocity in atomistic simulations were unsuccessful, until they were directly nucleated as supersonic dislocations in a stress concentration. The stress concentration (**Fig. 1**) is

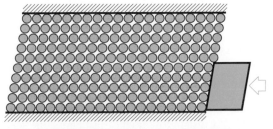

Fig. 1. Geometry used to study supersonic dislocations. The supersonic dislocations are injected into a prestrained thin strip of tungsten crystal by pressing the edge of a rigid body into the material.

induced by slowly pressing the edge of a rigid body into a tungsten crystal.

Even though this method has been shown to work for different materials in different crystallographic orientations, it is not entirely clear why it works. For example, it is unclear whether a strong stress gradient is sufficient or whether the nonlinearity of the atomic interaction is a necessary ingredient to a successful creation of these supersonic dislocations.

Once the dislocations have reached the supersonic stage, atomistic simulation methods can be used to study them in detail. The first simulations yielded some surprising results, which cannot be explained by classical linear dislocation theory. For example, the core structure of a subsonic dislocation (**Fig. 2***a*) and the core structure of a dislocation moving faster than the shear wave velocity (Fig. 2*b*) differ substantially. The subsonic dislocation is characterized by a core width of about two atom spacings, while the core of the supersonic dislocation is several times larger.

Similarly, the radiation of the supersonic dislocation does not correspond to the radiation expected from linear elasticity theory. Following the linear theory, a dislocation in an isotropic material such as tungsten should send out a symmetric Mach cone. Figure 2*b-d* displays the kinetic energy of the atoms around the dislocation core and clearly shows increasingly complex and interesting radiation patterns with increasing dislocation velocity. The obvious asymmetry between the radiation above and below the glide plane is a very clear indication for the importance of the nonlinearity of the atomic interaction in the dislocation core region. The presence of the radiative field at all dislocation velocities above the shear wave velocity indicates that the dislocation consumes energy while traveling. Linear elastic theory predicts that supersonic dislocation motion should be radiation-free at some particular velocities. Consequently, nonlinearities must account for the need to constantly drive the supersonic dislocation with high shear stresses to keep it in the supersonic regime.

At first glance, the required high shear stresses seem to limit the practical importance of supersonic dislocations motion. However, low-temperature deformation of metals such as iron, molybdenum, or tungsten can produce the high background stresses required for continuous long-distance propagation at supersonic speed. Materials with crystal structures of lower symmetry and a limited number of slip systems such as intermetallic alloys or semiconductor crystals often reach such stress levels.

In addition to the motion of individual dislocations, deformation at low temperatures and in low-symmetry crystal structures is produced via mechanical twinning. The kinetics of mechanical twinning is poorly understood, and textbooks usually describe mechanical twinning simply as a cooperative process. However, twinning can also be described as the motion of partial dislocations on subsequent glide planes, and the apparently cooperative behavior could be explained by the supersonic motion of these partial dislocations. Such mechanical twinning by the motion of supersonic partial dislocations is displayed for a twin at the tip of a moving crack in

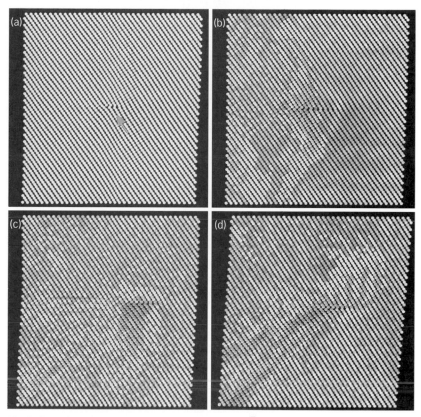

Fig. 2. Snapshots of the atomic configuration of small regions around dislocations in tungsten. (*a*) Stationary dislocation. Viewing along the direction indicated by the arrow clearly displays an extra plane of atoms above the glide plane of the dislocation, the characteristic of an edge dislocation. The dislocation core does not significantly change when the dislocation is moving subsonically. (*b-d*) Same dislocation at several supersonic velocities. The blue color indicates the magnitude of the instantaneous kinetic energy of the atoms. The dislocation is moving at approximately (*b*) 1.3, (*c*) 1.4, and (*d*) 2.3 times the shear wave velocity. Linear elastic theory would predict vanishing radiation for the dislocation in *c*. The dislocation in *d* is moving faster than all wave speeds and therefore has a radiative field which possesses both shear wave and longitudinal wave character.

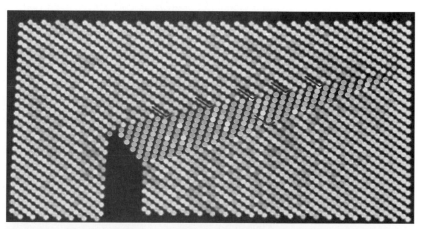

Fig. 3. Snapshots of the atomic configuration of a twin attached to the tip of a moving crack in tungsten. The light blue color indicates the magnitude of the momentary kinetic energy of the atoms. The partial dislocations, indicated in dark blue, move away from the crack tip at approximately 1.5 times the shear wave velocity until they are blocked at the rigid border of the model used for these simulations. When they are expelled from the dislocation pile-up formed at this border, they fall back into the fracture surface at a velocity exceeding five times the shear wave velocity.

Fig. 3. The stress concentration at the crack tip injects the partial dislocations at a velocity of approximately 1.5 times the shear wave velocity.

Atomistic simulations of supersonic dislocation motion clearly show that dislocations have new and unexpected properties in the hitherto unexplored supersonic space. A better understanding of their motion may hold the key to a better understanding of low-temperature forming processes and mechanical twinning as well as the propagation of geological faults. Future studies will concentrate on the materials-specific aspects of supersonic dislocation motion and on the experimental characterization of these dislocations.

For background information *see* CRYSTAL DEFECTS; CRYSTAL STRUCTURE; FAULT AND FAULT STRUCTURES; FORGING; METAL, MECHANICAL PROPERTIES OF; METAL FORMING; PLASTIC DEFORMATION OF METAL; SHOCK WAVE; SIMULATION; STRESS AND STRAIN in the McGraw-Hill Encyclopedia of Science & Technology.

Peter Gumbsch

Bibliography. P. Gumbsch and H. Gao, *J. Computer Aided Mater. Des.*, 6:137, 1999; P. Gumbsch and H. Gao, *Science*, 283:965, 1999; J. Weertman and J. R. Weertman, in F. R. N. Nabarro (ed.), *Dislocations in Solids*, vol. 3:1, North-Holland, Amsterdam, 1980.

Synthetic chromosome

A chromosome is a single deoxyribonucleic acid (DNA) molecule with its associated protein components. In the case of many viruses, most bacteria, and eukaryotic organelles, this DNA molecule is circular; but in the case of most eukaryotic organisms with cell nuclei and large genomes, the genome is partitioned between a number of linear DNA molecules. In simple eukaryotes such as *Saccharomyces cerevisiae* (baker's yeast), the relatively small size of the genome (more than 12 million nucleotide base pairs) has made the analysis of these chromosomes rather easy at the DNA level. Much progress is being made in understanding the proteins involved in chromosomal processes such as DNA replication, recombination, localization within the nucleus, and segregation of the replicated chromosomes to the daughter cells with high accuracy. This last function is arguably the most fundamental role of the chromosome.

Eukaryotic chromosomes. The chromosomes of *S. cerevisiae* have provided a powerful model for the study of eukaryotic chromosomes. Because of the small size of the genome and the power of yeast genetics, it has been possible to define and isolate the three DNA components which are required for a minimal chromosome. These are the telomeres, centromeres, and origins of replication. Telomeres are specific simple DNA sequences. They cap the ends of the linear DNA molecules and provide both a means of protecting and replicating the chromosome termini and a means of ensuring that these natural ends, unlike chromosome breaks, do not signal DNA damage to the cells. This would otherwise cause a checkpoint arrest of the cell cycle. Centromeres in *S. cerevisiae* comprise a short (125 bp) region of DNA with two domains separated by an adenine-thymine (AT) rich region. A number of proteins are known that bind to this region, which is centerd on a region of chromatin containing a specific centromeric histone-like protein in a nonnucleosomal configuration. Origins of replication in the yeast again consist of relatively short regions of DNA which bind the proteinaceous origin recognition complex. Assembly of these three components has been used extensively to produce yeast artificial chromosomes (YACs), which were important in the early stages of the Human Genome Project. *See* BACTERIAL GENETICS.

Telomeres and centromeres. Telomeres in mammalian cells have the same basic architecture as in yeast, and this conservation has led to rapid progress in the area of telomere biology. One aspect is that cloned vertebrate telomeric DNA is available and has been used to manipulate chromosomes by telomere-induced fragmention in vivo. This represents one route toward generating synthetic chromosomes for mammalian cells in which an existing chromosome is manipulated, for example by homologous recombination, to give a smaller desired product (**illus.** *a*).

In contrast to the telomere, there is little detectable conservation of nucleotide sequence or organization at mammalian centromeres. As a consequence, the nature of the mammalian centromere has been disputed, with three basic views proposed. The simplest was that there was a short underlying DNA sequence akin to the 125 bp needed in yeast and sufficient for both meiotic and mitotic centromere function, but it had simply not been found as it was buried in the repeated sequences associated with mammalian centromeres. A contrasting view was that the repeated sequences themselves were the important features, with their sequence differences between species explained on the basis that the repetitive DNA set up a heterochromatic chromatin structure required for kinetochore formation. A third view is that formation of a functional centromere is an epigenetic, chromatin structure–based phenomenon that might not be dependent on the underlying DNA sequences. If the centromere was epigenetically determined—and experiments in *Drosophila* and observations in human marker chromosomes support this idea—there might be an insurmountable barrier to formation of a functional centromere taking the approach used in yeast of introducing naked DNA into cells. Experiments in *S. pombe* suggested that such a barrier existed even with the relatively small centromeres of this organism, and it was possible that with larger centromeres of higher eukaryotes this might be more of a barrier. This has turned out not to be the case. *See* DEOXYRIBONUCLEIC ACID (DNA).

Centromeres. Two recent approaches to creating chromosomes for mammalian cells have been based on the use of a human repetitive DNA sequence

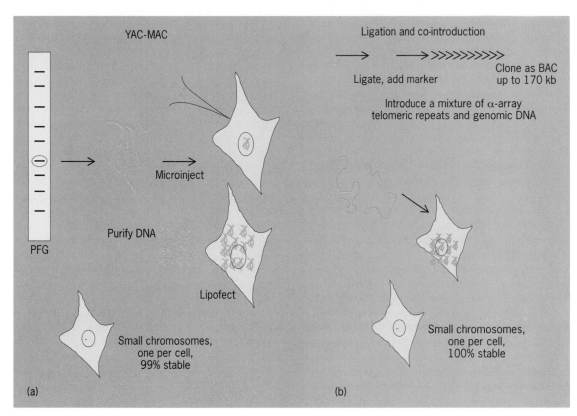

Two approaches to creating chromosomes for mammalian cells. (*a*) Modified yeast artificial chromosomes (YAC) to create mammalian artificial chromosomes. (*b*) Ligation and co-introduction of telomeric repeats and genomic DNA to give rise to artificial chromosomes.

family, alpha satellite, as a source of centromere function. This tandemly repeated sequence is found at the centromere on all human chromosomes and is tightly associated with the kinetochore, the assemblage of proteins to which microtubules attach. Although related sequences are found in similar locations in other primate chromosomes, there is little sequence homology with other sequences at the centromeres of other mammalian chromosomes. Nevertheless, when combined with telomeres and selectable markers either by a combination of in vivo and in vitro ligation (B) or by using a modified YAC (illus. *a*), this class of DNA can give rise to chromosomes. When introduced into cells by processes such as electroporation (application of a pulse of electricity) or by uptake mediated by lipids (lipofection), artificial chromosomes are formed in a high proportion of the cells taking up the DNA.

Both of these approaches generate broadly similar chromosomes (mammalian artificial chromosomes, or MACs), which are larger than the size of the input DNA molecules apparently as a result of the formation of multimers of the incoming DNA. These chromosomes can be detected by fluorescent in situ hybridization with DNA probes unique to the synthetic chromosome. In some cases, the chromosomes have been shown not to contain host cell DNA and to be linear molecules that are presumed to be capped by functional telomeres. The nature of the DNA acting as an origin of replication is unclear. The evidence

that these constructs have formed functional centromeres (with active kinetochores) comes from immunocytochemistry showing that characteristic proteins such as CENPA, C, and E are present; and from observations that the chromosomes are attached to the spindle at anaphase and, critically, that the chromosomes replicate and are segregated accurately at cell division in the absence of a genetic selection for maintenance. Since these chromosomes are present in one to two copies per cell, even a small percentage loss per cell division would rapidly result in a cell population lacking the chromosomes.

So far, these types of chromosomes have been produced only in a limited range of cell types, and the host cell requirements for MAC formation are unclear. Alternative methods such as the chromosome engineering approaches first described do not produce completely synthetic chromosomes, and transfer preformed chromosomes from cell to cell rather than introducing DNA. In this case, the chromosome is not being reformed and the range of host cells seems wider. *See* GENETICS.

Applications. Potential uses of mammalian artificial chromosomes fall into two categories. First, they can be used as an experimental platform to study parameters of chromosomes and chromosome function. As an example, these chromosomes could be used as part of an assay for aneuploidy inducing mutations in genes such as the spindle checkpoint genes. Aneuploidy is a feature of many tumors and is the major single cause of perinatal mortality in humans. Systems made by creating cells or animals with supernumerary chromosomes marked with genes encoding fluorescent proteins would also make it possible to monitor the effect of different DNA sequences on the karyotypic stability of such chromosomes in a number of different background situations.

The second major area of use is in biotechnology and gene therapy applications. Because these DNA molecules form chromosomes in cells, they should have the capacity to act as vectors for the maintenance of very large fragments of DNA. It is generally apparent that correct gene expression, such as is needed for gene therapy applications, results from the committee action of many regulatory elements often spaced widely in and around the gene in question. The capacity to carry large DNA fragments will be important in biotechnology applications, because it opens up the possibility of encoding multiple genes in a pathway on a single-vector system. Finally, there may be safety advantages, because these chromosomes can be constructed entirely of human DNA sequences, their lack of integration into an existing chromosome will result in freedom from disruption of a functional gene (insertional mutagenesis), and the chromosomes can be removed from cells when needed.

For background information *see* BACTERIAL GENETICS; CHROMOSOME; DEOXYRIBONUCLEIC ACID (DNA); GENE; HUMAN GENETICS; MOLECULAR BIOLOGY; RECOMBINANT GENETICS in the McGraw-Hill Encyclopedia of Science & Technology.   Havard Cooke

Bibliography. C. J. Farr et al., Generation of a human x-derived minichromosome using telomere-associated chromosome fragmentation, *EMBO J.*, 14: 5444–5454, 1995; J. J. Harrington et al., Formation of de novo centromeres and construction of first-generation human artificial microchromosomes, *Nat. Genet.*, 15:345–355, 1997; M. Ikeno et al., Construction of YAC-based mammalian artificial chromosomes, *Nat. Biotech.*, 16:431–439, 1998; H. F. Willard, Human artificial chromosomes coming into focus, *Nat. Biotech.*, 16:415–416, 1998.

Systematics

A firm understanding of phylogenetic relationships is central to elucidating many evolutionary questions. However, assessing relationships in many groups requires the compilation and phylogenetic analysis of data sets of molecular and nonmolecular traits for numerous taxa. This is particularly true for many large groups of organisms (such as fungi, bacteria, insects, and green plants) for which relationships have remained obscure despite decades of study using traditional methods. The need for phylogenetic analysis of large data sets is not restricted to higher taxonomic groups, but may involve any portion of the taxonomic hierarchy, extending to the population level, or even to the level of strains of bacteria or viruses.

Large data sets. Although the phylogenetic analysis of large data sets involving hundreds of taxa often is central to understanding relationships within many groups, the feasibility of such analysis has been debated. Large data sets are problematic in parsimony analyses because of the enormous number of trees possible for a large number of taxa: The number of potential solutions increases superexponentially as taxa are added. For large data sets involving hundreds of taxa, the number of possible trees likely exceeds the number of atoms in the universe.

Early simulation studies also suggested that the phylogenetic analysis of large data sets was impractical. For example, in some instances (involving extreme branch-length heterogeneity), the correct reconstruction of phylogeny for only four taxa requires over 10,000 base pairs of sequence data. Such problems and complexity with only four taxa prompted some workers to propose that large phylogenetic problems be broken into a series of smaller problems, with one extreme view being to break large data sets into a large number of four-taxon problems.

Another problem posed by large data sets involves the assessment of support for individual clades. Two commonly used procedures for estimating branch support are the bootstrap and the Bremer support or decay index.

Early parsimony analyses of large data sets seemed to bear out, in part, the dire predictions of computational difficulty. For example, parsimony searches of large data sets of 500 *rbcL* sequences and 228 18S ribosomal deoxyribonucleic acid (rDNA) sequences were never completed (even after investments of several years of computer time)—they were simply terminated. Significantly, empirical and simulation studies suggest that large data sets are much more tractable than previously thought. Three general approaches (not mutually exclusive) are used to analyze large data sets encompassing hundreds of taxa: (1) the addition of taxa and characters (a total evidence approach); (2) the use of fast or quick searches such as the fast bootstrap and parsimony jackknife; and (3) the application of computer programs such as NONA and the RATCHET to facilitate faster searches.

Addition of taxa and characters. Both simulation and empirical studies indicate that adding taxa and increasing the number of characters (base pairs in most cases, although any characters may be used) in phylogenetic analyses not only may increase the accuracy of the estimated trees but also may reduce the computational difficulty. These results are in contrast to earlier suggestions that large data sets may be extremely complex and difficult to analyze. These studies suggest that adding taxa, while perhaps counterintuitive, makes phylogenetic analyses more straightforward, apparently because the addition of taxa breaks up long branches and disperses homoplasy (such as parallel changes—for example, an indepedent change from guanine to adenine at a given nucleotide position in two unrelated organisms).

The addition of characters requires combining multiple data sets (usually multiple gene sequences) for the same suite of taxa—a total evidence approach. Significantly, empirical studies demonstrate that the time needed for parsimony analysis actually decreases with the addition of characters and taxa. In addition to shorter run times, combined data sets show tremendous improvements in internal support (that is, higher bootstrap or jackknife values) for clades, as well as increased resolution. The explanation for these results seems to be that each data set contains a certain amount of "true" signal, as well as false signal or "noise" (homoplasy). As data sets are combined (total evidence), the true signal is reinforced and becomes much stronger than the confounding homoplasy.

Quick searches. A significant problem with the analysis of large data sets is the difficulty in assessing internal support (or confidence) for clades. Large data sets are not amenable to standard approaches such as the bootstrap and the decay or Bremer support analysis. However, computer programs that conduct fast bootstrap and fast jackknife analyses are now available, and they were designed with large data sets in mind.

Several studies illustrate the value of conducting relatively quick searches and saving only those clades above a minimum threshhold of internal support. For example, the parsimony jackknife method is well suited for the quick analysis of large data sets and has been applied to a data set of 2538 *rbcL* sequences (this required only 360 hours); analysis of a 567-taxon, three-gene data set was completed in only 60.63 hours. Below a minimal threshhold (such as a bootstrap or jackknife value of 50%), confidence in a clade is low or nonexistent. Well-supported clades appear relatively quickly in the analysis of big data sets; continued computer analysis involving poorly supported branches does not suddenly result in strongly supported clades. Lengthy parsimony analyses may, in fact, be a waste of time.

Parsimony analysis. The numerous improvements and new options available (in PAUP* 4.0) have been a great asset to those interested in analyzing large data sets. One obvious improvement is the faster speed with which PAUP* 4.0 conducts heuristic parsimony searches compared to previous versions. Perhaps one of the most important developments in the analysis of large data sets is a new computer program that greatly enhances the ability to find shorter trees using parsimony. A new method called the RATCHET has been developed which is applied using the programs DADA and NONA. When applied to large data sets, the RATCHET quickly found trees shorter than those recovered by PAUP* 4.0. Hence, phylogenetic analysis of large data sets via parsimony has benefited greatly from recent developments in software; continued developments in this area are anticipated, making the analysis of large data sets ever more straightforward.

Total evidence. Systematists have been increasingly aware that reliance on a single data set may result in insufficient resolution or an erroneous picture of phylogenetic relationships. It is now common practice to use multiple data sets (both molecular and nonmolecular) for phylogenetic inference. This aspect of systematics has been facilitated by automated DNA sequencing, which has made the rapid acquisition of multiple molecular data sets relatively straightforward.

Although multiple data sets are needed for estimating phylogenetic relationships reliably, different genes may possess different histories. Consequently, incorporating multiple data sets into phylogenetic studies is not a casual undertaking. Essential tasks in the analysis of multiple data sets include assessing congruence between different phylogenetic trees and data sets to determine if they are providing conflicting results. In this way the investigator can ascertain whether multiple data sets should or should not be combined into a single data matrix prior to phylogeny reconstruction.

Three alternatives have been proposed for handling multiple data sets in phylogenetic analyses: the combined approach, the consensus approach, and the conditional combination approach. In the combined approach, all available data should be combined into a single matrix before phylogenetic analyses. Because the phylogenetic information from all characters is considered simultaneously in such analyses, this method has also been referred to as the total evidence approach. In contrast, others argue that multiple data sets should be analyzed separately (never combined) and the different phylogenetic estimates compared. The consensus approach seeks similarities between independent analyses for phylogenetic corroboration. Conditional combination involves combining data (total evidence) except in those instances in which significant heterogeneity exists between data sets and the heterogeneity appears to be attributable to different branching histories.

There has been considerable debate regarding the advantages and limitations of the combined, consensus, and conditional combination approaches. The conditional combination method seems to be a very reasonable approach. That is, employ total evidence unless there is evidence that the individual data sets are in conflict or incongruent (produce very different trees). A number of congruence tests are available; these represent a means for exploring data, providing the information needed to make informed, justifiable decisions regarding whether or not multiple data matrices should be combined. In some cases, however, it may be appropriate to combine data immediately. For example, because the chloroplast and mitochondrial genomes are each uniparentally inherited as a unit and not subject to recombination, multiple chloroplast DNA or multiple mitochondrial DNA sequences can each be readily combined.

Several authors have stressed that statistical tests for congruence may not provide a definitive answer as to whether it is appropriate to combine data. That is, even if congruence tests reveal some low level of heterogeneity between different data sets, the investigator may be justified in combining those data sets. Furthermore, while incongruence among data sets does present problems for phylogenetic inference, incongruence can also provide important insights into evolutionary (including molecular evolutionary) processes. For example, at lower taxonomic levels (such as the species or population levels) incongruence between a chloroplast and nuclear-gene phylogeny may be indicative of past hybridization or introgression, and hence may provide an important window into past evolutionary events.

Douglas E. Soltis; Pamela S. Soltis

Supertree reconstruction. In attempting to resolve the evolutionary relationships among all the species within a large group (such as all mammals), most systematists would agree that the most desirable solution is to collect the same set of data for all the species in question. However, this is often too expensive, not possible (for example, molecular data for fossil species), or has not yet been achieved. A secondary strategy relies on the fact that at least some phylogenetic information is available for many species. So long as there is some overlap among all the species in these disparate pieces of information, they can be combined to produce a larger, more comprehensive phylogeny. The information can take the form either of primary data ("total evidence") or phylogenetic hypotheses ("supertree reconstruction"). Supertree reconstruction resembles consensus techniques in that it combines phylogenetic trees. However, unlike most consensus techniques, it is able to combine "source trees" with different sets of species. Thus, the supertree can be much larger than any single source tree and often allows novel statements about relationships to be made.

Building supertrees. Supertree algorithms can be classified as either direct or indirect. Strict supertree construction is analogous to consensus techniques in that source trees are combined directly. However, it requires that the source trees do not conflict with one another (they are compatible), and therefore this method cannot be applied universally to all sets of source trees. Other direct techniques have been proposed that do not possess this limitation (such as a modified version of the semistrict consensus algorithm), but these have not gained wide acceptance.

By contrast, the indirect method of matrix representation with parsimony analysis (MRP) is more popular because it can combine any set of source trees. MRP uses additive binary coding to represent the nodes on a source tree as a series of binary matrix elements. Each node is described by one element. Species that are descended from a given node are scored as 1, otherwise 0, except for species that are not present on that particular tree, which are coded as missing. The various matrix representations (one for each source tree) are combined into a single matrix that is then analyzed by a parsimony criterion to produce a single supertree (multiple equally most

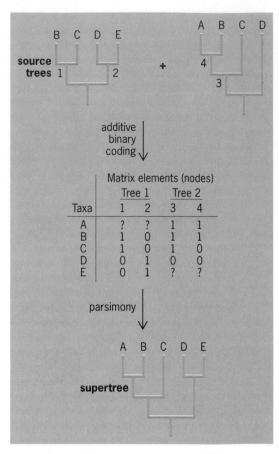

Fig. 1. General methodology to produce an MRP supertree, including the coding procedure. Note that the supertree makes the novel statement not found in either source tree that A is more closely related to B and C than it is to E.

parsimonious solutions are summarized using strict consensus; **Fig. 1**).

Unlike direct methods, MRP also allows the relative strength of the different sets of relationships on the supertree to be estimated using many of the standard parsimony-based techniques. One exception is the widely used bootstrap, which requires the characters to be independent of one another. This is not true of the elements produced through matrix representation: for any given source tree, the elements derived from it must support one another, and so are nonindependent.

Issues and solutions. A perceived limitation of supertrees is that they discard information. Different source trees or nodes within a single tree may not be equally well supported, and such information is not retained, as it is when the primary data are combined. In addition, secondary signals exist within data sets that may interact when these data sets are combined to yield a novel solution (signal enhancement). However, combining data requires that the data types are compatible. This is not always the case. For instance, most morphological data need to be analyzed using parsimony, whereas many types of molecular data can be analyzed only by using distance methods. By combining trees, supertrees can combine phylogenetic hypotheses derived from incompatible data. For indirect methods at least, some of the information regarding differential support both between and within source trees can also be incorporated by weighting the matrix elements in proportion to the robustness of the nodes they indicate. For a given source tree, matrix elements can be weighted either identically according to a support measure for the entire tree (such as a consistency index), or individually according to a support measure for the node they represent (such as bootstrap frequencies or Bremer decay indices). Computer simulations suggest that this procedure does improve accuracy.

MRP is essentially a parsimony analysis. Although MRP analyses run faster than conventional parsimony analyses (because the amount of homoplasy or noise in the matrix is decreased), they will still run into analogous computational limitations with large numbers of species. There are simply too many possible combinations of species for all to be searched. For example, with more than 20 species, heuristic search strategies must be employed rather than the more desirable branch-and-bound methods that guarantee an optimal solution. For even larger data sets (say, more than 100 species), even standard heuristic search strategies may be too slow. Fortunately, the recent development of several methodological shortcuts allows the construction of very large supertrees. The basic strategy involves compartmentalizing the single very large problem into a nested series of smaller ones that are computationally easier to solve. In the first step, the entire matrix is analyzed using a fast approximate search strategy that can also identify strongly supported clades. The resampling technique of parsimony jackknifing, whereby only a certain proportion of the characters are included at random and analyzed for a large number of replicates, is a good candidate strategy although the higher than usual proportion of missing data in the MRP matrix may preclude using the jackknife. Each well-supported clade is then resolved individually using a full parsimony analysis. The topologies of these resolved clades are then held constant and joined together to form a giant constraint tree. Searching only for solutions that do not conflict with this constraint tree eliminates many alternative topologies, thereby making it possible to analyze the entire matrix at once to determine the specific relationships of all the included species (**Fig. 2**).

Utility. To date, supertrees have been published for all extant species of the mammalian orders Primates and Carnivora, and many more are under construction. The two mammalian supertrees represent the first complete species-level phylogenies for either order, and have been used extensively to examine various macroevolutionary questions. For example, it has been determined that certain groups within each order have significantly higher net speciation rates than the remaining groups (by having more species than expected given their time of origin). This makes it possible to examine for ecological

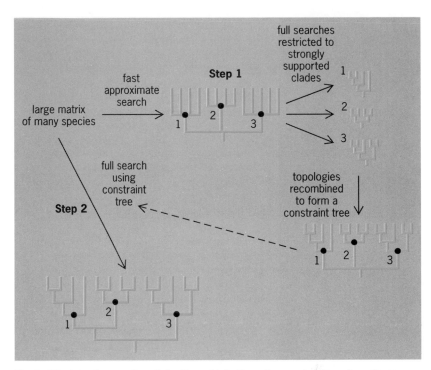

Fig. 2. Principle of compartmentalization, which allows the construction of very large supertrees. Step 1 determines the topologies of smaller, strongly supported clades, which are combined to form a constraint tree that restricts the search space for the overall matrix in Step 2.

correlates (such as body size or habitat) that might explain these results. Conversely, identifying groups with significantly lower net speciation rates has important conservation implications by identifying possible common features that might put members of these groups at a greater risk of extinction.

For background information *see* PHYLOGENY; TAXONOMIC CATEGORIES in the McGraw-Hill Encyclopedia of Science & Technology.

Olaf R. P. Bininda-Emonds

Bibliography. B. R. Baum, Combining trees as a way of combining data sets for phylogenetic inference, and the desirability of combining gene trees, *Taxon*, 41:3–10, 1992; B. R. Baum and M. A. Ragan, Reply to A. G. Rodrigo's "A comment on Baum's method for combining phylogenetic trees," *Taxon*, 42:637–640, 1993; O. R. P. Bininda-Emonds et al., Building large trees by combining phylogenetic information: A complete phylogeny of the extant Carnivora (Mammalia), *Biol. Rev.*, 74:143–175, 1999; J. S. Farris et al., Parsimony jackknifing outperforms neighbor-joining, *Cladistics*, 12:99–124, 1996; A. D. Gordon, Consensus supertrees: The synthesis of rooted trees containing overlapping sets of labeled leaves, *J. Classif.*, 3:31–39, 1986; B. D. Mishler, Cladistic analysis of molecular and morphological data, *Amer. J. Phys. Anthropol.*, 94:143–156, 1994; D. M. Hillis, Inferring complex phylogenies, *Nature*, 383:130, 1996; P. Huelsenbeck, J. J. Bull, and C. W. Cunningham, Combining data in phylogenetic analysis, *Trends Ecol. Evol.*, 11:152–158, 1996; A. Purvis, A modification to Baum and Ragan's method for combining phylogenetic trees, *Syst. Biol.*, 44:251–255, 1995; M. A. Ragan, Phylogenetic inference based on matrix representation of trees, *Mol. Phylogenet. Evol.*, 1:53–58, 1992; A. G. Rodrigo, A comment on Baum's method for combining phylogenetic trees, *Taxon*, 42:631–636, 1993; A. G. Rodrigo, On combining cladograms, *Taxon*, 45:267–274, 1996; F. Ronquist, Matrix representation of trees, redundancy, and weighting, *Syst. Biol.*, 45:247–253, 1996; M. J. Sanderson et al., Phylogenetic supertrees: Assembling the trees of life, *Trends Ecol. Evol.*, 13:105–109, 1998; D. E. Soltis et al., Inferring complex phylogenies using parsimony: An empirical approach using three large DNA sets for angiosperms, *Syst. Biol.*, 47:32–42, 1998; D. E. Soltis, P. S. Soltis, and J. J. Doyle (eds.), *Molecular Systematics of Plants*, II: *DNA Sequencing*, pp. 297–348, 1998; M. Steel, The complexity of reconstructing trees from qualitative characters and subtrees, *J. Classif.*, 9:91–116, 1992; D. L. Swofford, PAUP*: Phylogenetic analysis using parsimony, version 4.0, 1998; D. M. Williams, Combining trees and combining data, *Taxon*, 43:449–453, 1994.

Thermodynamics (biology)

The principles of classical equilibrium thermodynamics are adequate to describe the thermal characteristics of the molecules that constitute living matter. Analysis of thermal behavior under particular physical conditions has enabled researchers to understand, for instance, the native folding or unfolding of monomeric (having a single polypeptide chain) and polymeric (made of repeating subunits) proteins and nucleic acids, and the catalytic properties of enzymes. This has resulted in the development of various routine tests, for example, enzyme and immunological assays using thermistors (resistive electrical circuit elements used to measure temperature). However, the living matter composed of these molecules is not at equilibrium, and the processes involved in maintaining that state are irreversible in nature. Most scientists recognize that thermodynamic insight into these processes requires application of theoretical principles of irreversible thermodynamics, developed principally by I. Prigogine, for a living system in an open environment. The exceptions include a rigorous analysis of microbial growth that was based entirely on classical thermodynamics and gave apparently sensible results for the special case of microorganisms growing in a vessel closed to the environment. Whatever the form of the analysis, it is obvious that organisms require energy to live and grow and, for the most part, they produce heat. This is truly the subject of thermodynamics applied to the field of bioenergetics.

Thermodynamic background. The metabolic process for maintaining life in animals can be regarded as the continuous flux of electrons from the chemical bonds of substrates to oxygen in the mitochondria.

Within these organelles, this flux is used to maintain the proton flux, the energy of which is harnessed to the synthesis of adenosine triphosphate (ATP). During growth, some of the electrons are conserved in the accumulation and structuring of biomass, but the vast majority are lost as water. In thermodynamic terms, the high-quality, useful energy (Gibbs energy) in the chemical bonds of the substrates is used mainly to produce ATP for the coupled energetic demands of ATP hydrolysis in (1) synthesizing biomass; (2) maintaining the physiological state of the cell as a diffusion nonequilibrium; (3) performing the internal work concerned with the functions of the cytoplasm; and (4) in whole animals, accomplishing the external work done by muscle. In the energy transformation to synthesize ATP, the quality of the energy is reduced but the energy is not destroyed; and from the second law of thermodynamics, this is the reason why entropy is always generated within the organism. It was Erwin Schrödinger who recognized that this is contrary to the organism's need to maintain a high level of organization. Therefore, internal entropy production must be transferred to the environment either as secreted molecules of higher net entropy than the substrates (Schrödinger's negative entropy, or negentropy) or as heat.

Thus, Gibbs energy is the driving force for the redox reactions that sustain life and growth. A small part of it is dissipated entropically as biomass, and in cultured animal cells some of the entropy produced is secreted as macromolecules; but in general, the majority of it is exported as heat, acting to dissipate the Gibbs energy from substrates. This is a far cry from the notion in classical thermodynamics that entropy is simply a mathematical expression. Put simply, these considerations mean that the growth of organisms and cells can be measured directly from the rate of heat production using a calorimeter, a technique first exploited in biology by Antoine Lavoisier in 1783 and still a powerful tool.

Mayer's enthalpy balance method. The physician Julius Mayer conducted experiments over 150 years ago using a machine driven by a horse to deduce a value for the mechanical equivalent of heat. He presented his theory of the conservation of energy—the first law of thermodynamics. He then developed a physiological theory of combustion in which there is a general balance between the amount of matter consumed and the evolution of heat, so as to occasion growth and the renewal of worn-out parts. In this way, he introduced the concept of the enthalpy balance method in terms of receipts and expenditure. Mayer's method was subsequently applied to animals. A dog lived for 45 days in a respiration calorimeter, producing 72,588 kilojoules (18.7 W) of heat energy while utilizing 72,827 kJ of (net) chemical energy from nutrients, calculated from the dog's respiratory metabolism and fecal and nitrogenous excretion. The enthalpy balance approach now has been extended to tissues, especially striated muscle, and to cells originating in the body but adapted to grow in culture, as well as to plants and microorganisms.

In the early twentieth century, A. V. Hill showed unequivocally that Gibbs energy was the driving force for metabolism in striated muscle, and not the conversion of the energy stored in a temperature gradient into a form of work (Carnot engine). In later studies, it was discovered that, after quantifying the thermal contribution of all the metabolic reactions with the observed heat production, there was still some "unexplained" heat (for instance, 21% of the total in frog sartorius muscle). This was found to be due to the change in entropy associated with the movement of calcium (Ca^{2+}) ions during the contraction/relaxation cycle of the muscle. In this respect, it has been shown that the majority of the heat produced by isolated neurons is also due to changes in entropy caused by the ion movements that generate the action potential in nerve conduction. Thus, not all the heat produced in animal tissues and cells is derived from chemical reactions.

Biotechnological exploitation. The possibility of monitoring the growth of microorganisms in industrial applications by measuring their rate of heat production has been known for some time. More recently, however, it has become clear that the complex metabolism of animal cells in batch culture can be recorded on-line by circulating them between the fully aerated culture vessel (bioreactor) and a flow microcalorimeter. The heat flow rate was made specific to volume fraction of viable cells (biomass) by estimating the capacitance of the cell suspension with the probe of an on-line dielectric spectrometer. The specific rate acted as the on-line biosensor of metabolic activity. After measuring the concentrations of the major materials, a simplified equation for the growth reaction was constructed for Chinese hamster ovary cells genetically engineered to secrete interferon-γ (IFN-γ):

Glucose + glutamine + O_2 $\longrightarrow$

biomass + IFN-γ + lactate + CO_2 + H_2O + heat

Using Hess's law, the molar reaction enthalpy was obtained and the reaction validated by the enthalpy balance method. Stoichiometric calculations showed that the cells demanded glucose and glutamine in the ratio of 2.7:1 rather than 5.5:1 as supplied in the commercial medium. This information acted as the trigger to modify the medium according to cellular requirements. It resulted in the doubling of the specific growth rate and a 26% increase in the specific IFN-γ rate. The theoretical assertion that the specific heat flow rate is a function of the metabolic activity was validated from the experimental evidence by constructing stoichiometric plots of the data for the substrates and products against the specific heat flow rate (flux) to show the monotonic increasing relationship (**Fig. 1**).

The classical way to improve the yield of secreted

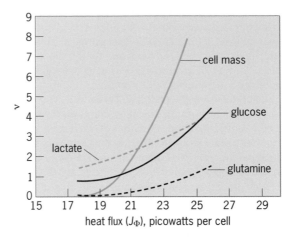

Fig. 1. Curves showing that heat flux is a function of metabolic activity with respect to the exact proportion (stoichiometric number, ν) of the molecules of glucose, glutamine, and lactate in the stoichiometric reaction in the text.

protein is to feed fresh medium to the culture when there is a decrease in metabolic activity. This can be detected by the heat flux probe, but first it was necessary to demonstrate that the response is strictly proportional to the different levels of metabolic activity by use of continuous cultures that give a set of steady states. This is the first demonstration of metabolic steady states in animal cells (**Fig. 2**). It was now possible to program software that activates a pump to deliver fresh medium to the cells when the heat flux probe indicates a noticeable decrease in metabolic activity—a fed-batch culture.

The ability of heat measurements to detect metabolic activity has been noted in the pharmaceutical industry in which animal cells cultured in 384- or even 1538-well microtiter plates are insulted by computer-synthesized compounds to discover their potential as drugs. The challenge lies in multiplexing the detectors as thin-film, thermopile transducers or fabricating multiple integrated circuit (IC) calorimeters to match the number of microtiter wells in

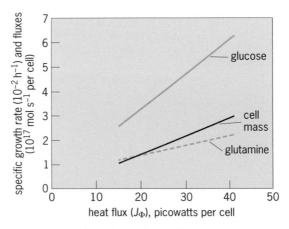

Fig. 2. Curves demonstrating that cell growth is directly related to metabolic activity (heat flux) in terms of glucose and glutamine metabolism.

robotic technology. The closest approach so far utilized infrared thermography on microtiter plates containing C3H10T1/2 fat cells that produce considerable heat. However, the detection limit is more than three orders of magnitude less sensitive than CT (conventional thermopile) calorimetry.

Calorimetric-respirometric (CR) ratio. A. L. Lavoisier stated that respiration is a slow combustion. It has been shown that the oxidation of all carbon compounds produces approximately the same amount of heat per amount of oxygen (CR ratio). As seen in the reaction above, animal cells excrete noncombusted lactate under aerobic conditions, and this gives a more exothermic CR ratio. Lactate is a waste product from particular biomass building blocks that cells synthesize because they are not available in the culture medium. Therefore, the CR ratio is used on-line to indicate the relative proportion of metabolic activity that can be ascribed to biomass accretion.

For background information *see* BIOLOGICAL OXIDATION; CHEMICAL THERMODYNAMICS; ENTHALPY; ENTROPY; GIBBS FUNCTION in the McGraw-Hill Encyclopedia of Science & Technology.   Richard Kemp

Bibliography. L. Garby and P. S. Larsen, *Bioenergetics: Its Thermodynamic Foundations*, Cambridge University Press, Cambridge, 1995; F. M. Harold, *The Vital Force: A Study of Bioenergetics*, Freeman, New York, 1985; R. B. Kemp, *Handbook of Thermal Analysis and Calorimetry*, vol. 4: *From Macromolecules to Man*, Elsevier, Amsterdam, 1999; M. P. Murphy and L. A. J. O'Neill (eds.), *What Is Life? The Next Fifty Years*, Cambridge University Press, Cambridge, 1995.

Time synchronization

The Global Positioning System (GPS) is a space-based source for accurate and reliable positioning, navigation, and timing data available anywhere on Earth, 24 h a day, 7 days a week. The use of GPS timing has rapidly increased, and it is currently part of the critical infrastructure of the United States. In particular, GPS timing is increasingly used as the primary reference timing source for network synchronization in industries such as telecommunications and power distribution. This has been the trend internationally as well.

Since the 1960s, the telecommunications indus-

TABLE 1. Detrimental effects due to loss of timing (GPS) signal	
Service type	Detrimental effect
Voice	Noise
Fax	Loss of picture content
Data	Need for retransmission, leading to reduced throughput
Video	Occurrences of freeze frames
Encryption	Need for retransmission of encryption key

try has moved from analog transmission to a fully synchronized all-digital network. A key element has been synchronous optical network (SONET) technology. Synchronization can be defined as an arrangement for operating digital switching and transmission systems at a common clock rate. Along with the benefits of digital architecture, including more efficient use of network bandwidth, come higher sensitivities to out-of-synchronization events (slips).

The telecommunications industry has partitioned its network into two subnetworks: transmission and signaling (**Fig. 1**). The transmission network carries the payload or services provided by the carrier, such as data, voice, and other content. The signaling network carries all the information needed to establish dialed connections within the public switched network, that is the "phone system." The signaling network is encrypted since it carries all of the call set-up and billing information.

Synchronization is vital for the throughput capacity and service reliability of telecommunications systems. For example, when the clocks of the transmit and receive switches are not synchronized, a slip occurs and data are lost due to the misaligned clocks. The amount of data lost depends on the degree to which the two clocks are not in synchronization. The detrimental effects of slips depend on the services affected (**Table 1**). Encryption is the service most sensitive to slips.

The divestiture of the Bell System changed the overall industry from one major provider to a number of carriers offering a variety of telecommunications services—all requiring accurate synchronized timing that can be successfully distributed over many networks. With multiple carriers there are multiple interfaces between carriers. The need for a standardized system to define the relationship of the various timing references in an increasingly diverse and complex architecture is recognized and accepted.

Network synchronization standards. Telecommunications distribution lines run at 1.544 megabits per second (Mbps), referred to as T1, the basic transmission unit in North America, or at multiples of this rate. A T1 line provides 24 multiplexed voice channels. Each voice channel undergoes 8000 samples per second. The samples represent 256 voltage levels (8 bits). The 8-bits-per-channel samples are combined with 8 bits each from the 23 other channels and packed into a 193-bit block that includes one additional synchronization bit. Within the United States, the T1 standards committee develops

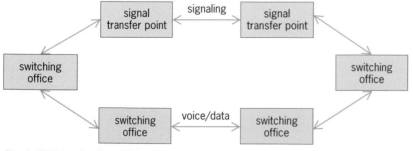

Fig. 1. Telephone network signaling. One call, whether voice or data, uses both the transmission and signaling networks.

interconnection standards for the national telecommunications systems. It comprises representatives of exchange and interexchange carriers, manufacturers, and general-interest groups. The American National Standards Institute (ANSI) accredits these standards.

Technical subcommittee T1X1.3 is responsible for synchronization interface standards. The latest published standard is *Synchronization Interface Standards for Digital Networks* (ANSI T1.101–1999). This standard specifies that network nodes shall be traceable to a primary reference standard, and it prescribes interface specifications and defines the components and relationships of a synchronization network.

The ANSI standard describes a hierarchy of stratified clocks (**Table 2**). Only stratum 1 clocks are

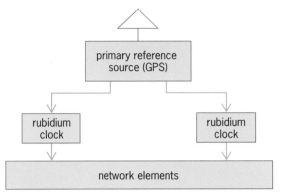

Fig. 2. Intraoffice distribution of timing signals.

TABLE 2. ANSI standard hierarchy of stratified clocks			
Stratum	Accuracy	Holdover stability	Technology
1	1.0×10^{-11}	Not applicable	GPS, cesium clock, LORAN-C
2	1.6×10^{-8}	1.0×10^{-10} per day	Rubidium clock
3E	4.6×10^{-6}	1.0×10^{-8} per day	Quartz clock
3	4.6×10^{-6}	3.7×10^{-7} per day	Quartz clock
4E	3.2×10^{-5}	Not required	Quartz clock
4	3.2×10^{-5}	Not required	Quartz clock

completely autonomous. All lower-level clocks must be dependent upon a higher-stratum clock for their timing reference and ultimately must be traceable to a stratum 1 clock as the primary reference source for timing synchronization. A network must derive its timing from a stratum 1 primary reference source, whether this source is part of its internal network or is obtained from a connection to another carrier's network.

GPS in telecommunications services. Telecommunications services are limited by the amount of throughput capacity that the physical system can reliably support. The more accurate the timing is, the more efficiently the physical system can support data and other transmissions. GPS enables increased throughput by providing a reliable, extremely accurate, and cost-effective timing source. Though cesium clocks present an alternative technology as a primary reference source, GPS is much cheaper to install and maintain. Therefore, more GPS-based primary reference sources can be used throughout any given network, thereby improving its overall quality. When primary timing is distributed throughout the network, any breaks within the system can be almost instantaneously rerouted. For example, service can be more easily restored after breakage due to severe weather, backhoes, or natural disasters by using multiple GPS timing sources. These advantages and the long-term commitment by the U.S. government to

support GPS have made it the system of choice for network timing and have led to the deployment of large numbers of GPS units within telecommunications industry synchronization networks.

GPS service is typically provided within telecommunications central offices where a GPS signal is received and in turn used to correct local rubidium clocks or, in some cases, high-performance quartz oscillators (**Fig. 2**). These disciplined oscillators provide the timing signals to drive the telecommunications network elements. They also provide buffering and isolation between the GPS constellation and the operating telephone network. In the event of a GPS signal degradation or interruption, these oscillators are capable of maintaining the synchronization quality of the telephone network at the ANSI standard and the related interface standard specified by the International Telecommunications Union—Standards Sector (ITU-T) of less than 1 part in 10^{11} frequency drift for a period of several weeks.

Impact of SONET. Before SONET ring technology was deployed, most networks were arranged in a star configuration. Connecting the star topology to the primary reference source was fairly straightforward (**Fig. 3a**).

SONET ring topology was widely deployed because it can provide almost instant circuit restoration in the event of a cable failure. However, it is very sensitive to missynchronization. With a SONET ring the payload is sent in both directions, clockwise and counterclockwise, around the ring (Fig. 3b). When the ring is broken, due to a cable cut or equipment failure, all nodes on the ring instantly look in the opposite direction for payload data. The synchronization signals, however, are sent in only one direction around the ring. This is done to avoid the possibility of sending a synchronization signal in one direction and having it returned from the other direction, thereby creating a timing loop—an insidious condition that unfortunately does not create alarms and is therefore very difficult to locate. SONET ring engineering must be done carefully to avoid such situations.

GPS is one solution to this problem. Installation of GPS at each node provides primary reference source–quality synchronization at every node on the ring. Not only does this practice resolve any timing-loop issues, but it also improves the quality of the

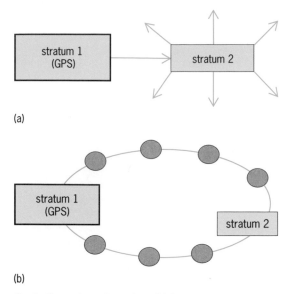

(a)

(b)

Fig. 3. Network configurations. (*a*) Star configuration and tie into synchronization timing source. (*b*) SONET ring configuration. Payload signals are sent in both directions; synchronization signals are sent in only one direction.

network. It is feasible due to the low cost of GPS. However, not all network operators implement this GPS deployment plan as of this time.

Effects of potential GPS failure. In principle, having one GPS satellite in view for part of the day is sufficient to derive network timing from the GPS signal that is accurate enough to meet standards. Some older equipment requires visibility of more than one GPS satellite and is particularly vulnerable to GPS outages. However, even if GPS service was not available, the networks would continue for some time. Although the possibility of a total GPS constellation failure rendering no satellites visible is virtually nil, such a failure will be discussed to illustrate the potential effects of a complete outage.

Wireline network. A partial GPS constellation failure would not be noticeable on a wireline network. However, should the highly unlikely situation of a total GPS constellation failure occur, the network would slowly degrade, with the consequences becoming noticeable in a week to one month's time. After that time, slips would start occurring and increase in frequency. Eventually there would be geographic blackouts until the entire network failed due to failure of the signaling network. As synchronization degraded, the different systems and technologies would be affected in varying degrees. Voice communications is very tolerant of the loss of or degradation of synchronization, whereas the encrypted signaling network is very sensitive to timing errors. While technically it is still possible for the network to carry voice communications over the payload transmission network, no calls would be established due to failure of the encrypted signaling network that could no longer instruct the switches in how to set up the calls. Services that are more demanding of precise synchronization than voice would not be possible as the synchronization degrades.

Wireless networks. There are several types of wireless telephony services. The most common is personal cellular phone service, using either the CDMA (code-division multiple access) or the GSM/TDMA (Global System for Mobile Communications/time-division multiple access) formats. There are also broadband wireless services and miscellaneous services.

The CDMA cellular phone system uses the GPS time scale. GPS receivers with inexpensive quartz oscillators are deployed at most nodes in the systems. In the extremely hypothetical event of a serious GPS failure (for example, no GPS constellation), it would be 1–3 days before this system experienced serious problems. CDMA systems are the most vulnerable to those GPS failures that prevent timing synchronization based upon GPS.

GSM/TDMA cellular phone systems use quartz-based oscillators and are dependent upon wireline carriers for access to a primary reference source signal. They would be fairly tolerant of GPS failures and would probably work as long as the wireline network was operational. So, as with the landline system, in a matter of weeks to one month, these systems would experience service degradations.

A broadband wireless system provides point-to-point high-capacity connections and services. It too would probably maintain service as long as the wireline network was operational.

Paging networks would fail quickly. Voice-over-data networks, asynchronous transfer mode (ATM), and so forth will have to be tested to determine their susceptibility to timing outages. Customer-provided networks or private networks would probably be an order of magnitude worse than the carriers to which they were connected.

For background information *see* ATOMIC CLOCK; DATA COMMUNICATIONS; ELECTRICAL COMMUNICATIONS; INTEGRATED SERVICES DIGITAL NETWORK (ISDN); LOCAL-AREA NETWORKS; MOBILE RADIO; PULSE MODULATION; SATELLITE NAVIGATION SYSTEMS; TELEPHONE SERVICE in the McGraw-Hill Encyclopedia of Science & Technology.   Ed Butterline; Sally L. Frodge

Bibliography. E. Butterline and S. Frodge, *Telecommunications Synchronization and GPS*, Institute of Navigation GPS 1999 Proceedings, 1999; R. DiEsposti et al., *Benefits and Issues on the Integration of GPS with a Wireless Communications Link*, 29th PTTI Proceedings, 1997; H. Lee, *Development of an Accurate Transmission Line Fault Locator Using the GPS Satellites*, BC Hydro and Power Authority, 26th PTTI Proceedings, 1994; K. Martin, *GPS Timing in Electric Power Systems*, Institute of Navigation GPS 1999 Proceedings, Bonneville Power Authority, 1999; D. Mills, *Internet Timekeeping Around the Globe*, 29th PTTI Proceedings, 1997.

Tissue engineering

The loss or failure of an organ is one of the most devastating and costly problems in health care. The current options for treatment include transplanting organs from one individual to another, performing surgical reconstruction, or using mechanical devices such as kidney dialyzers. While there have been major advances in the development of drugs, surgical procedures, and medical equipment designed to improve the care of these patients, these options remain imperfect and often impair the quality of life. Patients with diabetes endure several insulin shots each day, and often their blood sugar is not controlled well enough to prevent devastating complications of the disease. Patients with failing kidneys are put on dialysis, which is fraught with pitfalls and complications, including infections and eventual fatal renal failure. Transplantation is limited by donor shortage; many patients die while on the waiting list for a heart or liver transplant. In the pediatric patient population, where congenital diseases are a leading cause of organ failure, the shortage of donors is particularly severe. Fortunately, a new alternative to therapy emerging: the fabrication of new organs and functional tissue using the techniques of a new scientific discipline, tissue engineering.

General description. Tissue engineering is the creation of tissue or organs to replace lost form or function. Although there are different approaches to the creation of new tissue, most investigators use cells combined with matrices. The process begins with the in vitro culture of isolated cells. These cells are then seeded onto a matrix consisting of polymers or collagen, the protein that forms scaffolding in normal human tissue. The matrix provides mechanical support for the cells and guides their structural development. Once the cells are seeded onto the polymer, the matrix-cell construct is implanted into the host. The location of implantation depends upon what type of tissue is being engineered. The construct can be implanted as a closed system (**Fig. 1**), isolated from the host tissue, or as an open system (**Fig. 2**), integrated into the host.

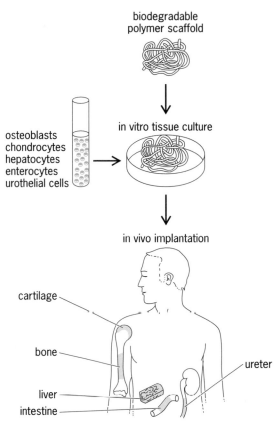

Fig. 2. Schematic illustration of the tissue engineering approach to fabrication of functional living tissues. Tissue-specific cells are seeded on highly porous three-dimensional biodegradable polymer scaffolds and, after varying conditioning periods in culture, are implanted. Vascularization, organization, and remodeling occur as the implants become incorporated into the body. The polymer matrix degrades at a controlled rate, leaving permanent new tissue without foreign-body elements. (*After R. Langer and J. P. Vacanti, Tissue engineering, Science, 260:920–926, 1993; copyright 1996 by the American Association for the Advancement of Science*)

In open systems, where the transplanted cells are in direct contact with the recipient, the transplanted elements become incorporated into the host. The matrix degrades over time, leaving only the new tissue in place in the host. Key issues in this process include the type of matrix used and the cells chosen for implantation.

Matrices. The matrix used in tissue engineering creates and maintains a space for the formation of the tissue and guides its structural development. Important characteristics of the matrix include mechanical strength, biodegradability, and high surface-to-volume ratio. The surface-to-volume ratio ensures the adequate delivery of nutrients to cells as they grow and proliferate on the matrix. In addition, biocompatibility in the host and cell adhesiveness are necessary in order to ensure survival of the mammalian cells on the matrix. The polymers are porous, allowing diffusion of oxygen and nutrients to the implanted cells. Synthetic materials such as lactic-polyglycolic acid or polyacrylonitrile–polyvinyl chloride and natural materials such as collagen, hydroxyapatite, or alginate are in use, often in combination. Most of the early experiments in tissue engineering

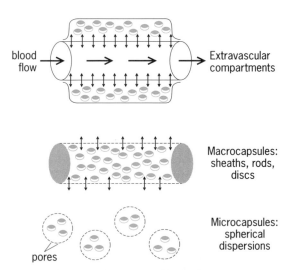

Fig. 1. Configurations of implantable closed-system devices for cell transplantation. (*After R. Langer and J. P. Vacanti, Tissue engineering, Science, 260:920–926, 1993; copyright 1996 by the American Association for the Advancement of Science*)

used polyglycolic acid polymers (a material also used in surgical practice as dissolvable sutures). The polymers can be fabricated into specific shapes, designed for use in tissue-engineered heart valves, blood vessels, or cartilage and bone tissue. The shapes can be simple, such as a tube for the manufacture of intestine or blood vessels, or more complex such as the shape used to engineer a nose or ear. The use of natural materials in combination with synthetic polymers has been investigated. Coating the polyglycolic acid polymers with collagen has been shown to increase cell adhesiveness. The incorporation of specific growth factors into the polymer has been investigated. It has been shown that epidermal growth factor, in a slow-release form, increases vascularization and engraftment of liver cells in animal models.

Cells. The cell type chosen for use in tissue engineering is critical. In laboratory studies, progenitor cells from syngenic (genetically identical) animals are harvested from the tissue of interest and seeded onto the polymer scaffold. This construct is then implanted into an animal of the same syngenic strain. In clinical practice, the cells are generally derived from the patient or from close relatives. A reliable source of cells for a wide variety of clinical applications would be useful. For example, human stem cells could potentially be isolated and manipulated to differentiate into the appropriate cell type.

Applications. Scientific experimentation using the general concept of tissue engineering was attempted as far back as 1933, when investigators encased mouse tumor cells in a polymer membrane and inserted them in the abdominal cavity of a pig. During the next several years there were major advancements in cell biology and polymer chemistry, setting the stage for the field of tissue engineering. In 1975 a publication reported the use of pancreatic islet cells in semipermeable membranes for glucose control in diabetics. In the past two decades, the field of tissue engineering has greatly expanded to include virtually every tissue in the human body.

Skin. Tissue-engineered skin substitutes are used in clinical practice. The source of cells is fibroblasts and keratinocytes isolated from human foreskin obtained from circumcised newborns. These cells have enormous proliferative potential and are readily available. The cells are seeded onto a collagen scaffold, which serves as a neo-dermis. The end result is a skin construct made up of the two layers that constitute human skin, the dermis and the epidermis. Clinical studies done on patients with skin loss from burns, diabetic ulcers, or dermatologic surgery have demonstrated the usefulness of these products.

Pancreas. The implantation of pancreatic islet cells to cure diabetes mellitus is an example of a closed system in tissue engineering. Pancreatic islet cells produce insulin, which is lacking in diabetics. The cells are implanted into the diabetic host within a chamber with a semipermeable membrane. Glucose diffuses freely through the membrane, and the islet cells respond by secreting insulin, which also diffuses through the membrane and into the bloodstream. The exclusion of larger entities such as antibodies and complement factors protects the transplant from destruction by the host's immune system.

The examples described above are in either clinical practice or trials. Their development and success is encouraging with regards to the application of tissue engineering to other areas of the human body. One ultimate goal of tissue engineering is the manufacture of internal organs, complete with a blood supply and the ability to perform functions specific to that organ. The creation of internal organs such as liver, intestine, heart, kidney, and many others is under active laboratory investigation.

Liver. Each year 26,000 people die of end-stage liver disease in the United States at a cost of $9 billion. A major goal in tissue engineering is to provide replacement liver tissue for patients with hepatic failure. It has been shown that hepatocytes survive on biodegradable polymer scaffolds in vitro and in vivo. The hepatocytes are seeded onto polymer scaffolds and subsequently implanted into vascularized tissue beds such as the mesentery or omentum. The implanted cells tend to reorganize into structures resembling those found in normal liver tissue. This process involves various methods of hepatotrophic stimulation. For example, co-transplantation of the hepatocytes with cells that secrete known liver mitogens improves growth and survival of the liver cells.

A problem in designing functional internal organs is the need for a blood supply for nutrient and gas exchange. One approach under investigation uses devices with a branching vascular network consisting of endothelial and smooth muscle cells. The hepatocytes could then be seeded on this structure, growing around the preformed blood vessels. The use of bioreactors is another possible solution. The bioreactor provides controlled flow and mixing under in vitro conditions so that the tissue can develop form and function prior to implantation.

Outlook. The field of tissue engineering provides a possible solution for many difficult and costly health problems. The Food and Drug Administration has approved the use of tissue-engineered skin; other fabricated ectodermal structures such as cartilage and bone are not far behind. The fabrication of whole internal organs remains a challenge, but the technologies described above and new technologies provide promise for the future.

For background information *see* BIOMEDICAL ENGINEERING; CELL ORGANIZATION; LIVER; PANCREAS; SKIN in the McGraw-Hill Encyclopedia of Science & Technology.   Antonia E. Stephen; Joseph P. Vacanti

Bibliography. R. P. Lanza, R. Langer, and W. L. Chick (eds.), *Principles of Tissue Engineering*, Academic Press, 1997.

Transcranial magnetic stimulation

Transcranial magnetic stimulation (TMS) is a relatively new neurophysiologic technique that allows the safe, noninvasive, and relatively painless stimulation of the human brain if appropriate guidelines are followed. Transcranial magnetic stimulation can be used to complement other methods to study the pathways between the brain and the spinal cord and between different brain structures, and to map cortical brain functions. In addition, transcranial magnetic stimulation provides a unique methodology to determine the true functional significance of the results of neuroimaging studies and the causal relationship between focal brain activity and behavior. Modulation of brain activity by repetitive transcranial magnetic stimulation can transiently change brain function and may, in the future, be developed into a therapeutic tool for a variety of neurological and psychiatric illnesses.

The machine. The principles that underlie transcranial magnetic stimulation were discovered by Michael Faraday in 1831. A pulse of current flowing through a coil of wire generates a magnetic field. The rate of change of this magnetic field determines the induction of a secondary current in any nearby conductor. In transcranial magnetic stimulation, the stimulating coil is held over a subject's head. As a brief pulse of current is passed through the coil, a magnetic field is generated that passes through the subject's scalp and skull without attenuation (only decaying by the square of the distance). This time-varying magnetic field induces a current in the subject's brain that depolarizes neurons and generates effects depending on the brain area targeted.

Therefore, in transcranial magnetic stimulation, neural elements are not primarily affected by the exposure to a magnetic field, but by the current induced in the brain (electrodeless, noninvasive electric stimulation).

In the early 1980s researchers developed the first compact magnetic coil stimulator (see **illus.**). Soon thereafter, transcranial magnetic stimulation devices became commercially available. The design of magnetic stimulators is relatively simple, comprising a main unit and a stimulating coil. The main unit is composed of a charging system, one or more energy storage capacitors, a discharge switch, and circuits for pulse shaping, energy recovery, and control functions. Different charging systems are possible; the simplest design uses stepup transformers operating at a line frequency of 50–60 Hz. Energy storage capacitors can also be of different types. The essential factors in the effectiveness of a magnetic stimulator are the speed of the magnetic field rise time and the maximization of the peak coil energy. Therefore, large energy storage capacitors and very efficient energy transfer from the capacitor to the coil are important. Typically, energy storage capacity is around 2000 joules; 500 joules are transferred from the capacitors into the stimulating coil in less than

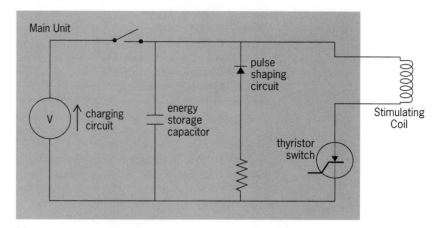

(a)

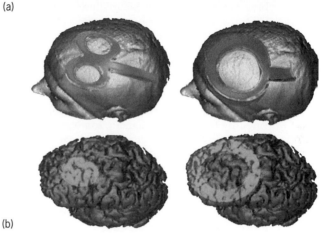

(b)

Principles of transcranial magnetic stimulation. (a) Simplified schematic diagram of a standard (single-pulse) magnetic stimulator (*modified from A. Pascual-Leone, D. Bartres-Faz, and J. P. Keenan, Transcranial magnetic stimulation: Studying the brain-behavior relationship by induction of "virtual lesions," Phil. Trans. Roy. Soc. London B, 354:1229–1238, 1999*). (b) Placement of the focal figure-eight (butterfly) and the circular coil, along with the approximate areas of stimulation in the brain.

100 microseconds via a thyristor, an electronic device that is capable of switching large currents in a few microseconds. The peak discharge current needs to be several thousand amperes in order to induce currents in the brain of sufficient magnitude to depolarize neural elements (approximately 10 mA/cm^2).

During transcranial brain stimulation, only the stimulating coil needs to come in close contact with the subject. Stimulating coils consist of one or more well-insulated coils of copper wire frequently housed in a molded plastic cover. Stimulating coils are available in a variety of shapes and sizes. The geometry of the coil determines the focality of brain stimulation (see illus.). A figure-of-eight coil (also called a butterfly or double coil) is constructed with two windings placed side by side, and provides the most focal means of brain stimulation with transcranial magnetic stimulation available to date. Current knowledge suggests, largely based on mathematical modeling, that the most focal forms of transcranial magnetic stimulation currently available affect an area of 0.5×0.5 cm at the level of the brain cortex. Stimulation is restricted to rather superficial layers in the convexity of the brain (cortex or gray-white matter junction), and direct effect onto deep brain structures is not possible. Digitization of the subject's head and registration of the transcranial magnetic stimulation sites onto the magnetic resonance image (MRI) of the head permits anatomical specificity of the transcranial magnetic stimulation effects by identifying the actual brain target in each subject. The use of optical digitization and frameless stereotactic systems represents a further improvement by providing on-line information about the brain area targeted by a given coil position on the scalp.

Mechanism. The precise mechanisms underlying the brain effects of transcranial magnetic stimulation still have many unknowns. Currents induced in the brain by transcranial magnetic stimulation flow parallel to the plane of the stimulation coil (approximately parallel to the brain's cortical surface when the stimulation coil is held tangentially to the scalp). Therefore, in contrast to electrical cortical stimulation, transcranial magnetic stimulation preferentially activates neural elements oriented horizontally to the brain surface. Exactly what neural elements are activated by transcranial magnetic stimulation remains unclear, and may in fact be variable across different brain areas and different subjects. The combination of transcranial magnetic stimulation with other neuroimaging and neurophysiologic techniques provides an enhanced understanding of the mechanisms of action of transcranial magnetic stimulation and a novel approach to the study of functional connectivity between different areas in the human brain.

Safety concerns. Transcranial magnetic stimulation, especially repetitive transcranial magnetic stimulation (rTMS), remains an experimental technique, side effects are possible, and strict safety and ethical guidelines need to be followed. There are relative and absolute contraindications to transcranial magnetic stimulation. Examples include metal anywhere in the head (excluding the mouth), cardiac pacemakers and implanted medication pumps, intracranial or intracardiac electrodes, raised intracranial pressure, pregnancy, a history of seizures, a family history of epilepsy, and medications that might increase the risk of seizures. The main safety concern when using transcranial magnetic stimulation is its potential to induce a seizure, even in subjects without any predisposing illness. This risk is low (in the order of 1 in 1000 studies or less) and essentially limited to the application of repetitive transcranial magnetic stimulation. Safety guidelines that advise on the appropriate repetitive transcranial magnetic stimulation parameters to minimize the risk of a seizure were developed; no seizures have been induced by repetitive transcranial magnetic stimulation since then. Approximately 10–20% of subjects studied with transcranial magnetic stimulation develop a muscle tension headache or a neck ache. These are generally mild discomforts that respond promptly to an aspirin, acetaminophen, or other common analgesics. Repetitive transcranial magnetic stimulation can also cause ringing in the ears or even transient hearing loss if the subjects do not wear earplugs during the studies. Furthermore, transcranial magnetic stimulation rarely causes mild and very transient memory problems and other cognitive deficits. Finally, it is important to realize that transcranial magnetic stimulation has been studied only for approximately 15 years, and the data in humans are still sparse. Although animal studies have not shown any risks of brain damage or long-term injury to the brain or its functions after transcranial magnetic stimulation, caution is still imperative.

Applications. In clinical neurophysiology, transcranial magnetic stimulation is primarily used to study the integrity of the motor fibers that connect the brain with the spinal cord (central motor pathways). Transcranial magnetic stimulation is applied to the motor cortex, and motor evoked potentials (MEPs) are recorded using electromyography and surface electrodes tapped over the belly and tendon of the target muscles. Frequently, in order to fully interpret the results, motor cortex transcranial magnetic stimulation has to be combined with peripheral nerve, nerve plexus, or spinal root stimulation. Studies can provide important diagnostic and prognostic insights in patients with motor-neuron disease (for example, Lou Gehrig's disease), multiple sclerosis, strokes, or spinal cord lesions. The specific sites of stimulation, the recorded muscles, the maneuvers used for facilitation of the motor evoked potentials, and the evaluation of the different response parameters have to be tailored to the specific questions asked. The development of special techniques offers the opportunity of widening the clinical uses of transcranial magnetic stimulation. For example, paired-pulse transcranial magnetic stimulation can be used to study intracortical excitability and provide insight into the pathophysiology of movement disorders such as Parkinson's disease or the mechanisms of action of different medications. Repetitive transcranial magnetic stimulation can be used in the study of higher cortical functions, particularly for the noninvasive determination of the language-dominant hemisphere. Finally, the integration of transcranial magnetic stimulation with image-guided frameless stereotactic techniques can be used for noninvasive cortical mapping, and thus can aid in the presurgical evaluation of neurosurgical patients.

In addition to such clinical applications, transcranial magnetic stimulation provides a unique tool for the study of causal relationships between brain activity and behavior. Delivered appropriately in time and space, transcranial magnetic stimulation can transiently block the function of neuronal networks, allowing for the creation of a time-dependent virtual lesion in an otherwise healthy brain. This type of transcranial magnetic stimulation was used in the study of the visual cortex. When applied to the occipital lobe at appropriate intensity, transcranial magnetic stimulation blocks the detection of visual stimuli presented approximately 100 milliseconds earlier. Recently, researchers showed the utility of this application in a study demonstrating that congenitally and early Braille subjects need the visual cortex for tactile Braille reading.

Finally, recent studies have shown that repetitive transcranial magnetic stimulation may be used to modulate the level of excitability of a given cortical area beyond the duration of the stimulation itself. Remarkably, depending on the stimulation frequency and intensity, it seems possible to potentiate or depress cortical excitability. The possibility of enhancing behavior by applying repetitive transcranial magnetic stimulation at parameters that may potentiate cortical excitability is intriguing and could have a profound impact on neurorehabilitation and skill acquisition. The modulation of cortical excitability beyond the duration of the repetitive transcranial magnetic stimulation train itself raises the possibility of exploring potential therapeutic uses. A variety of neuropsychiatric conditions are associated with disturbed cortical activity as documented by neuroimaging and neurophysiologic studies. Forced normalization of such disturbed cortical excitability might lead to a symptomatic improvement.

For background information *see* BRAIN; MAGNETIC FIELD; MOTOR SYSTEMS; NEUROBIOLOGY in the McGraw-Hill Encyclopedia of Science & Technology.   Fumiko Maeda; Alvaro Pascual-Leone

Bibliography. A. T. Barker, R. Jalinous, and I. L. Freeston, Non-invasive magnetic stimulation of the human motor cortex, *Lancet*, 1:1106–1107, 1985; M. Hallett, Transcranial magnetic stimulation: A tool for mapping the central nervous system, *Electroencephalogr. Clin. Neurophysiol. Suppl.*, 46:43–51, 1996; J. C. Rothwell, Techniques and mechanisms of action of transcranial stimulation of the human motor cortex, *J. Neurosci. Meth.*, 74:113–122, 1997; P. M. Rossini and S. Rossi, Clinical applications of motor evoked potentials, *Electroencephalogr. Clin. Neurophysiol.*, 106:180–194, 1998; A. Pascual-Leone, D. Bartres-Faz, and J. P. Keenan, Transcranial magnetic stimulation: Studying the brain-behavior relationship by induction of "virtual lesions," *Phil. Trans. Roy. Soc. London B*, 354:1229–1238, 1999; E. M. Wassermann, Risk and safety of repetitive transcranial magnetic stimulation: Report and suggested guidelines from the International Workshop on the Safety of Repetitive Transcranial Magnetic Stimulation, June 5–7, 1996, *Electroencephalogr. Clin. Neurophysiol.*, 108:1–16, 1998.

Transcription

The growth and specialization of every living cell is governed by a complex program of differential gene expression. One fundamental way to regulate gene expression is through the control of transcription, the enzymatic process in which ribonucleic acid (RNA) is synthesized by copying from the deoxyribonucleic acid (DNA) template. Transcription of a given gene may be regulated at one or more steps (initiation, elongation, and termination) catalyzed by an enzyme, RNA polymerase. The initiation step is the most common mechanism for turning genes on or off, and has been studied intensely. In prokaryotes, transcription is carried out by a single RNA polymerase enzyme, comprising four protein subunits plus a regulatory protein called sigma factor. The sigma factor recognizes a DNA sequence known as the promoter located adjacent to the protein-encoding portion of the gene.

In eukaryotes, the RNA polymerase and the regulatory DNA sequences are significantly more complex. There are three distinct RNA polymerases: RNA polymerase I (Pol I) and III (Pol III) specialize in transcribing genes that encode RNAs with high demand, those of ribosomal RNAs and small RNAs including transfer RNAs, respectively. RNA polymerase II (Pol II) transcribes as many as 100,000 different genes in mammals to produce messenger RNAs which generally encode proteins. The three RNA polymerases consist of at least a dozen subunits, some of which are common to all three enzymes. The two largest subunits of each enzyme share structural similarities with those of the bacterial RNA polymerase and specify the basic copying function. In addition to the 12-subunit RNA polymerase, accurate initiation of transcription requires a large complement of general transcription factors unique to each enzyme.

Regulatory regions. Promoters serve as the docking site for the transcription machinery. In general, promoters lie adjacent to or upstream of the first nucleotide transcribed by RNA polymerase (known as the initiation site). In prokaryotes, a typical promoter contains two canonical DNA sequences (sequences that are very similar in the promoters of different genes), known as the −35 and −10 boxes (positioned 35 and 10 nucleotides, respectively, upstream of the initiation site) that are recognized by the sigma subunit of the RNA polymerase.

In eukaryotes, the promoter structure is more complex (**Fig. 1**). Many promoters transcribed by Pol II contain a sequence rich in adenosine (A) and thymidine (T) residues, termed the TATA box, located about 25–30 nucleotides upstream of the transcriptional initiation site. The TATA box is bound by the general transcription factor TFIID, which in turn recruits other general transcription factors and Pol II. In addition to the core promoter region, most genes have one or more regulatory regions farther upstream of the promoter (termed the regulatory promoter region) or many kilobases upstream or downstream from the promoter (enhancer regions). Enhancer regions are able to regulate transcription over a very long distance on the DNA in an orientation-independent manner. Both the regulatory promoter and enhancer regions are composed of specifically arranged binding sites for DNA-binding regulatory transcription factors (activators and repressors). Combinations of these factors bind to the specific target DNA in response to extracellular and intracellular signals and modulate the level of transcription of the linked gene. A typical organism may express hundreds of different DNA-binding regulatory transcription factors. Many display a modular structure, consisting of a DNA-binding domain separated from at least one effector domain that

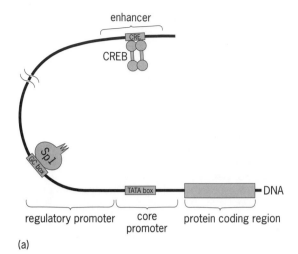

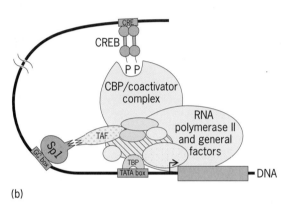

(a)

(b)

Fig. 1. Interaction between activators and specific coactivators recruits RNA polymerase II to the core promoter and results in transcription of a gene. (*a*) Transcriptional control regions can be divided into the core promoter which lies adjacent to the transcription initiation site, the regulatory promoter, and the more distant enhancer region. The core promoters of many protein-encoding genes contain a TATA box which functions as a binding site for the general transcription factor TFIID composed of TBP and multiple TAFs. Sequence-specific DNA-binding transcription factors such as Sp1 and CREB bind to recognition sequences (GC box and CRE, respectively) in the regulatory promoter or more distant enhancer. (*b*) Coactivator complexes are recruited to the gene through interactions with the activation domains of Sp1 and CREB. In many cases, this is regulated in response to extra- and intracellular signaling. For example, phosphorylation of the activation domain of CREB (indicated by P) is necessary for association with the CBP coactivator. The coactivator complexes in turn specify recruitment of general transcription factors and RNA polymerase II that results in transcription initiation (indicated by arrow).

can either stimulate (activation domain) or repress (repression domain) transcription. Most DNA-binding regulatory transcription factors do not contact the subunits of Pol II directly; instead, they recruit an equally complex array of cofactors that mediate the function of the activation/repression domains.

Coactivators and corepressors. Transcriptional cofactors were discovered through a combination of in vitro transcription assays using defined components and through genetic analyses in yeast. For example, a transcription reaction reconstituted with purified general transcription factors and Pol II di-

rected a low basal level of transcription from a TATA box–containing template DNA. Addition of a DNA-binding regulatory transcription factor such as Specificity protein 1 (Sp1) resulted in a marked increase in RNA synthesis when general transcription factor TFIID was present in the reaction, but not with the TATA box–binding protein (TBP; the primary DNA-binding component of TFIID) alone. This experiment led to the discovery of a dozen or more TBP-associated factors (TAFs) that together with TBP constitute TFIID. The activation domains of Specificity protein 1 and other DNA-binding regulatory transcription factors stimulate transcription by interacting with a subset of TAFs, which are referred to as coactivators. In addition to TFIID, a number of different protein complexes containing coactivators have been identified. The coactivators generally function by serving as a bridge between the DNA-binding transcription factors and the components of the general transcription machinery.

The cyclic AMP–responsive element binding protein (CREB) is a DNA-binding transcription factor that becomes modified in response to an extracellular signal. Specifically, CREB is phosphorylated by a protein kinase that is activated by the binding of cyclic AMP. The phosphorylated CREB binds to a specific DNA sequence present in many target genes and activates transcription. Recent research shows that after CREB binds to DNA it recruits a transcriptional coactivator called CREB-binding protein (CBP) through a phosphorylated domain of CREB. CBP in turn interacts with the components of the Pol II general transcription machinery, facilitating the initiation of transcription. CBP also possesses an intrinsic enzymatic activity that plays a role in its coactivation function. Many unrelated DNA-binding transcription factors, including the nuclear receptors for steroid and nonsteroidal hormones, have been shown to activate transcription by associating with the CBP coactivator.

Factors that assist in the function of repressor proteins have also been identified and have been termed corepressors. How the coactivators and corepressors function has been the subject of intense investigation during the past decade. These cofactors may function in one of two ways: they serve as bridging factors or chaperones to facilitate protein-protein interactions between DNA-binding regulatory transcription factors and the components of the general transcription machinery; or they are effective through intrinsic enzymatic activities that modify chromatin, resulting in activation or repression of the linked target gene.

Regulation by chromatin. Eukaryotic genomes require significant compaction in order to fit into the nucleus. The human genome, for example, contains nearly 2 m (6 ft) of DNA which must fit into a nucleus of approximately 6-micrometer diameter. This extraordinary degree of packing is achieved by wrapping the chromosomal DNA around a core of proteins (histones) to form repeating structures known as nucleosomes. Further stacking of the nucleosomes

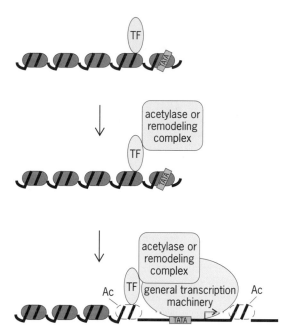

Fig. 2. Transcriptional activators counter chromatin-mediated repression by recruiting enzymes that remodel the local chromatin structure. In eukaryotic cells, DNA is packaged into a regular array of histone/DNA cores known as nucleosomes (shaded in gray). They prevent the general transcription machinery from accessing the core promoter region of the gene (TATA box). Many transcriptional activators (TF) are able to bind to their target DNA sequences in the context of chromatin, and through protein-protein interactions they recruit coactivator complexes that alter or remodel the local nucleosomes, allowing general transcription factors and RNA polymerase II to reach the core promoter and initiate transcription (indicated by arrow). Remodeling complexes fall into two broad classes: ATP-dependent remodeling enzymes which mobilize the nucleosomes, allowing them to slide along the DNA; and acetyltransferases which add acetyl groups (Ac) to histones, loosening contacts between nucleosomes.

gives rise to a fiber that is assembled into a higher-order structure known as the chromatin fiber. Any biochemical process involving DNA, such as transcription, replication, recombination, and repair, must contend with the compacted DNA within chromatin. Nucleosomes block the binding of the general transcription machinery to promoter DNA, preventing a gene from being transcribed (**Fig. 2**). The accessibility of promoter DNA to RNA polymerase can be modulated by multiprotein complexes that either remodel nucleosomes using the energy derived from the hydrolysis of adenosine triphosphate (ATP), or covalently modify the nucleosomes themselves. These complexes are recruited to the nucleosomal DNA by recognizing certain DNA structures, or perhaps more commonly by interacting with DNA-binding transcription factors that can bind to target sites in the context of chromatin.

Several coactivators, including CREB-binding protein, possess a histone acetyltransferase (HAT) activity, which adds acetyl groups to lysine residues in the tails of histones. This covalent modification decreases the interactions between nucleosomes within the chromatin fiber, resulting in greater access of transcription factors to the DNA. Thus, DNA-binding transcription factors can activate transcription by interacting with a coactivator that acetylates histones to facilitate recruitment of the transcription machinery. Consequently, a number of corepressor proteins act as histone deacetylases, removing the acetyl groups and allowing recompaction of the chromatin. It should be noted that acetylases and deacetylases may also modify proteins other than the histones to regulate transcripton. Acetylases and deacetylases are commonly found as part of multiprotein coactivator and corepressor complexes, respectively. Recruitment of such complexes is determined by specific interactions between the DNA-binding regulatory factors and the components of the cofactor complex.

Transcription and disease. Mutations in transcription factors or in gene regulatory sequences are responsible for a large number of human diseases. Those involved in developmental abnormalities and cancer are most clearly understood. The transcriptional coactivator CREB-binding protein and the closely related p300 protein provide a convenient illustration of how different mutations in one or two transcription factors can result in a variety of human diseases. Inactivation of one of the two copies of the CBP gene results in Rubenstein-Taybi syndrome, a congenital disorder involving mental retardation and cranial and digital malformations. Patients with the syndrome also show a predisposition to cancer, and mutations in p300 are associated with colorectal cancer. These loss-of-function mutations are thought to disturb the relative levels of CBP and p300 protein in a cell, resulting in abnormal expression of genes that depend on the coactivator function of CBP/p300. Several acute myeloid leukemias contain chromosomal rearrangements in which CBP or p300 have been fused to various chromatin-associated proteins. The resulting CBP and p300 fusion proteins represent gain-of-function mutants which inappropriately modify the chromatin structure of genes involved in differentiation or cell cycle control, resulting in deregulated growth of myelomonocytic cells.

Summary. Recent advances in understanding transcriptional regulation in eukaryotes have led to identification and characterization of many coactivators and corepressors that mediate the activation and repression functions of the DNA-binding transcription factors. These cofactors exist as multiprotein complexes that associate with both the DNA-binding regulatory factors and general transcription machinery. The discovery of chromatin remodeling complexes has heightened awareness to the active and important role that chromatin plays in the differential expression of genes. Transcription is without doubt one of the most important biological processes, holding the key to the development of all organisms, as well as the cause of many genetic disorders such as cancer. Future research will undoubtedly uncover new and unexpected mechanisms underlying transcriptional regulation.

For background information *see* DEOXYRIBONU-CLEIC ACID; GENE; MOLECULAR BIOLOGY; NUCLEIC

ACID; NUCLEOPROTEIN in the McGraw-Hill Encyclopedia of Science & Technology.

Naoko Tanese; Angus Wilson

Bibliography. E. M. Blackwood and J. T. Kadonaga, Going the distance: A current view of enhancer action, *Science*, 281(5373):61–63, 1998; G. A. Blobel, CREB-binding protein and p300: Molecular integrators of hematopoietic transcription, *Blood*, 95(3):745–755, 2000; B. D. Strahl and C. D. Allis, The language of covalent histone modifications, *Nature*, 403(6765):41–45, 2000; R. Tjian, Molecular machines that control genes, *Sci. Amer.*, 272(2):54–61, 1995.

Transit (astronomy)

The term "transit" is used in several ways in astronomy. A hundred years ago its most common usage referred to the image of a star, planet, or other celestial body traversing the cross-hairs of a telescope that was fixed to move only in a north-south direction, and was essential to the determination of time and celestial coordinates. A second common usage of transit refers to a satellite passing in front of its parent planet as seen from the Earth. It was suggested as early as Galileo that the timing of such transits across the face of Jupiter by its four largest satellites would provide a solution to the age-old problem of navigation at sea—a solution which, however, never proved satisfactory. A third usage of transit refers to the passing of either Mercury or Venus in front of the Sun as seen from Earth. It is this phenomenon that will be examined in this article.

Among the planets, only Mercury and Venus are seen to transit across the Sun's face. This is because their orbits around the Sun are smaller than Earth's, and so these planets are sometimes located between the Earth and the Sun. Since Mercury orbits the Sun every 88 days and Venus every 225 days, such transits might be expected to be quite frequent, but in fact they are relatively rare, particularly in the case of Venus. This is mainly because the planes of these planetary orbits are tilted with respect to the plane of Earth's orbit, by $7°$ in the case of Mercury and over $3°$ in the case of Venus. The disk of the Sun, by contrast, extends only a quarter of a degree above and below Earth's orbital plane, and so for the most part the planets pass above or below the disk of the Sun as seen from Earth. There is thus an additional requirement for a transit: the Earth-Sun line must be close to the line of intersection of the Earth's and the planet's orbital planes (the line of nodes). When this happens, the planet will lie close to Earth's orbital plane while passing between it and the Sun, and will be seen projected against the disk of the Sun. (Obviously, any given transit will be invisible to people for whom it is night at the time; also, since transits can take up to about 7 h to complete, it is possible to see the start but not the finish of a transit, and vice versa, depending on whether the transit is in progress at local sunset or sunrise.)

Transits of Mercury and Venus in the neighborhood of the present time are as follows:

Mercury	*Venus*
1973, Nov. 10	1761, June 6
1986, Nov. 13	1769, June 3
1993, Nov. 6	1874, Dec. 9
1999, Nov. 15	1882, Dec. 6
2003, May 7	2004, June 8
2006, Nov. 8	2012, June 6
2016, May 9	2117, Dec. 11
2019, Nov. 11	2125, Dec. 8

Intervals between transits of Mercury vary between 3.5 years and 13 years, while transits of Venus come in pairs separated by 8 years, with intervals between pairs alternating between 113.5 and 129.5 years. Mercury transits fall in either May or November, while Venus transits occur in either June or December, reflecting the necessity for Earth to be near one node or $180°$ away (6 months of orbital motion) at the other in the case of each planet in order for a transit to occur. These relations do not hold over much longer time spans covering many millennia, when, for instance, transits of Venus no longer come in pairs.

Transits of Venus. The German astronomer Johannes Kepler was the first to predict a transit (of Venus, in 1631), and the English astronomer Jeremiah Horrocks was the first astronomer known to have actually observed a transit of Venus (in 1639). It was another English astronomer, Edmond Halley, who, beginning in 1676, drew attention to the possibility of using transits of Venus to greatly improve knowledge of the scale of the solar system. It was possible in Halley's day to find the relative locations of the planets expressed in terms of Earth's distance from the Sun, but what this Earth-Sun distance actually was in absolute units like today's kilometers or miles was only very poorly known. As history would show, much more than just knowledge of the solar system's scale hinged on calibrating the Earth-Sun distance. This is the first rung in a long ladder of astronomical methods for distance determination; without it astronomers would not have been able to determine the distances of stars, and this knowledge, in turn, leads to methods for calibrating the Earth's location in the Milky Way Galaxy, to finding the distances of external galaxies, and finally to the scale of the universe itself. Moreover, without knowledge of stellar distances it would not have been possible to determine the masses, sizes, energy output, and other attributes of stars, which in turn lead to the study of their lifetimes and evolution, including that of the Sun. In short, a great deal of astronomy and astrophysics hinges on knowing the Earth-Sun distance, and Halley was quite right in urging later astronomers (he never lived to see a transit of Venus himself) to make every effort to observe such transits and so improve greatly the knowledge of the Earth-Sun distance.

Determining Earth-Sun distance. The principle of determining Earth-Sun distance using Venus transits is quite simple. It is a two-stage process, requiring first setting up a scale map of the solar system and then determining the scale of the map by measuring the distance between any two objects on it. In this case the two objects are Earth and Venus.

The scale map is set up by using Kepler's third law of planetary motion: If a planet has an average distance d from the Sun, and takes a time P to revolve once around the Sun, then P^2 is proportional to d^3. P can be determined by observing a planet's position in the sky night by night. Venus, for example, takes 225 days to circle the Sun, the Earth 365 days. Since this is a scale map, a unit can be chosen for distance, in this case the Earth-Sun distance called the astronomical unit (AU). Going back to Kepler's third law

$$(225/365)^2 = (d/1)^3$$

gives where d is Venus's distance from the Sun, and Earth's distance from the Sun is, by definition, unity. This leads to $d = 0.72$ AU. So at the time of a transit of Venus, when Earth, Venus, and the Sun are lined up, the distance between Earth and Venus must be $1 - 0.72 = 0.28$ AU.

The second part of the process deals with finding the distance between Earth and Venus during the transit in everyday units such as miles or kilometers. If there are two observers of the transit, A and B, as widely separated on Earth as possible (especially north-south), then, as the **illustration** shows, the transit path as seen by each observer will be slightly different. By measuring the difference between the two paths, it is possible to determine the angle AVB, and then, if the distance between A and B is known, the distance between Earth and Venus can be calculated. It was Halley's insight that the difference between the transit paths could best be determined by timing the durations of the two observed transits; the French astronomer Joseph-Nicolas Delisle later pointed out that determining the difference in starting or ending times of the two tracks could also be used. The actual angular difference between the two paths is less than 1/50 of the angular diameter of the Sun. This explains why transits of Mercury cannot

be used to determine Earth-Sun distance using this method. During transit, Mercury is more than twice as far from Earth than is Venus, making the difference in the two observed paths too small to be useful.

Progress. The leading scientific nations of the eighteenth century, particularly Britain and France, sent out expeditions to the most remote parts of the world to observe the 1761 and 1769 transits of Venus and thereby determine the distance of the Earth from the Sun. Various factors degraded their results, notably the "black drop" problem. This was caused by the dense atmosphere of Venus, which made Venus appear to be attached to the edge of the Sun by an extended ligament even when the disk was clearly within that of the Sun. This confused the observers' timings considerably. In addition, methods then in use to determine latitude and longitude, and thus the baseline AB distance, were still primitive and faulty.

The 1874 and 1882 transits of Venus were widely observed, and now photographs could be taken of Venus on the Sun's disk, giving much more precise measurements. This, coupled with greatly improved knowledge of observers' latitudes and longitudes, led to much better results, especially when the eighteenth-century data were reanalyzed and combined with the nineteenth-century work. The Earth-Sun distance of $149,590,000 \pm 310,000$ km that was derived from these four Venus transits would not be surpassed in accuracy until the development of radar astronomy led to the astonishing value of $149,597,870.691 \pm 0.030$ km.

The next transit of Venus will be on June 8, 2004, and it is to be expected that the novelty of this event, which has not been seen for nearly 122 years, will attract many observers. It will best be seen from northern latitudes starting at approximately 05:13 a.m. Greenwich Mean Time and concluding at about 11:25 a.m. The best earth-bound sites for observing the entire transit will be eastern Europe, the Middle East, and India. North America is not well placed for this transit, although Newfoundland will see roughly the last half starting at local sunrise. Boston will see the final two hours or so, Chicago the final hour, but nothing of the transit will be seen from the west

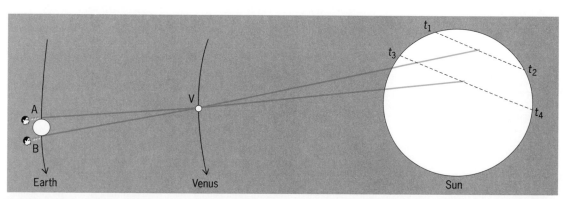

Transit of Venus across the Sun as seen by two terrestrial observers, A and B. Each observer sees Venus projected against a different part of the Sun's disk, and this difference in position of the two tracks allows the determination of the angle AVB. This, together with the baseline between A and B, yields the distance of Venus from the Earth. Observer B sees the transit along the upper line starting at t_1 and ending at t_2. Observer A sees Venus transiting along the lower line starting at t_3 and ending at t_4.

coast. However, appropriate spacecraft will likely be used to observe the spectacle, making it available to interested persons worldwide.

For background information *see* ASTRONOMICAL UNIT; KEPLER'S LAWS; PLANET; RADAR ASTRONOMY; TRANSIT (ASTRONOMY) in the McGraw-Hill Encyclopedia of Science & Technology.   J. Donald Fernie

Bibliography. S. J. Dick, W. Orchiston, and T. Love, Simon Newcomb, William Harkness and the nineteenth-century American transit of Venus expeditions, *J. Hist. Astron.*, 29:221–255, 1998; E. Maor, *June 8, 2004: Venus in Transit*, Princeton University Press, 2000; H. Woolf, *The Transits of Venus: A Study in Eighteenth Century Science*, Princeton University Press, 1959.

Tumor suppressor gene

Mutations in the gene for the tumor suppressor protein p53 are found in approximately 50–60% of all human cancers and thus constitute the most frequent alteration in a single cancer-associated gene. The prevalence of p53 mutations in human cancer has spurred research worldwide to decipher p53 functions. It is now clear that the major function of p53 is to preserve the integrity of the genome of a cell under various conditions of cellular stress, en-

dowing p53 with the title "guardian of the genome," coined by David Lane, one of the discoverers of p53 in 1979.

Multifunctionality of p53. p53 is a truly multifunctional protein. It consists of several domains, which exhibit a number of biochemical activities and interact with a large variety of cellular and viral proteins (**Fig. 1**). The p53 core domain (amino acids 100–300) harbors at least three biochemical activities. (1) It mediates sequence-specific deoxyribonucleic acid (DNA) binding to p53 consensus DNA sequences. Together with the bipartite N-terminal transactivation domain, this function renders p53 a sequence-specific transactivator. (2) The p53 core domain also recognizes complex non-B DNA structures, in both a sequence-specific and non-sequence-specific fashion. (3) In addition, the p53 core domain exhibits an intrinsic 3′–5′ exonuclease (removes nucleotides from the ends of DNA) activity.

As the p53 core domain is the major target for mutational inactivation of the p53 gene (Fig. 1), its multiple activities obviously are relevant for the tumor suppressor function of p53. The C-terminal domain of p53 (amino acids 320–293), separated from the core domain by a flexible hinge region, harbors the p53 nuclear localization signals, an oligomerization domain, and a basic domain, which is able to bind non-sequence-specifically to DNA and

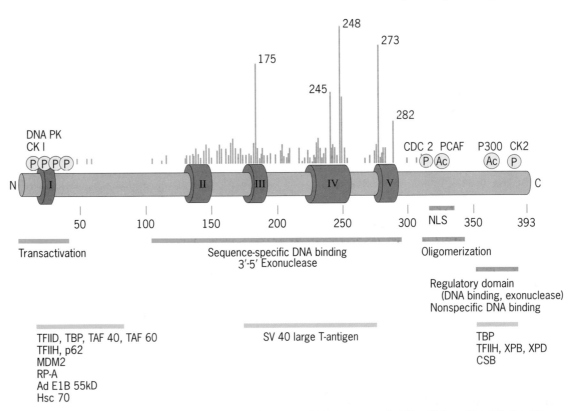

Fig. 1. p53 landmarks. Roman numerals represent the five regions that are conserved within p53 from all vertebrates. Known phosphorylation (P) and acetylation (Ac) sites are indicated. The vertical bars, clustered in the center of the p53 molecule, indicate amino acid residues mutated in human tumors (hot spots are identified by amino acid number). Below the molecule, horizontal bars indicate the current information concerning various domains of p53 for biological activities, p53 DNA interactions, and p53-protein complex formation. CK 2 is casein kinase 2; CSB, Cockayne's syndrome B protein; DNA PK, DNA-dependent protein kinase; NLS, main nuclear localization signal; RP-A, replication protein A; SV 40, Simian Virus 40; TAF, transcription-activating factor; TBP, TATA-Box binding protein; TF, transcription factor; XPB, xeroderma pigmentosum B protein; XPD, xeroderma pigmentosum D protein.

ribonucleic acid (RNA), and to exert an RNA and DNA reannealing activity. The basic C-terminal end also is the major regulatory domain of p53, affecting both p53 sequence-specific DNA binding and p53 exonuclease activity.

All major domains of p53, but especially the p53 N- and C-termini, are targeted by cellular and viral proteins. These proteins either are partners of p53 in various p53 functions or regulate, that is, inactivate, p53 functions. The physiologically most relevant cellular protein in this respect is the MDM2 protein, which binds to the p53 N-terminus and inhibits the transactivation function of p53, and it also targets p53 to proteasomal degradation. As the *mdm2* gene is a transcriptional target for the p53 protein, MDM2 and p53 are connected via a negative autoregulatory feedback loop.

Genomic integrity. The best-analyzed tumor suppressor function of p53 is that of a sequence-specific transactivator of cellular genes, which are involved in cell-cycle checkpoint control or apoptosis. In the absence of cellular stress, p53 is a latent protein that is rapidly turned over and is present in normal cells only in small copy numbers of 1000–10,000 molecules. The high turnover is due to the interaction of p53 with the MDM2 protein. Various cellular stress signals, most importantly DNA damage, activate different signaling cascades, which lead to phosphorylation of p53 at N-terminal and C-terminal phosphorylation sites. Phosphorylation of p53 first disrupts the p53-MDM2 interaction, resulting in metabolic stabilization of p53. Second, phosphorylation activates the sequence-specific transactivator function of p53, leading to the upregulation of genes encoding cell-cycle inhibitors, like p21^{waf1} or 14.3.3σ, which induce growth arrest in the G1 or G2 phase, respectively, or of repair associated genes, like *gadd45*. The p53-induced growth arrest allows time to repair the inflicted DNA damage before it can be fixed as a mutation during the next round of DNA replication. p53 also activates a number of genes involved in apoptosis, like the *bax*, *fas-R*, and several redox-related *PIG* genes. However, induction of apoptosis by p53 is complex and involves nontranscriptional pathways, too.

p53 interacts with a variety of repair-associated proteins, and accumulating evidence strongly suggests that p53 is directly involved in repair processes and in the control of their fidelity. p53 also is involved in the fidelity control of homologous DNA recombination, and has been described as "sensing" DNA damage by recognizing DNA mismatches leading to DNA bulges. The idea of a direct involvement of p53 in repair processes is strongly supported by the discovery that p53 exhibits an intrinsic 3′-5′ exonuclease activity. Exonucleases are required for nearly all processes of DNA metabolism, such as DNA replication, long-patch DNA repair, postreplicative mismatch repair, and DNA recombination. p53 exonuclease activity thus strongly expands p53's possibilities as a guardian of the genome. *See* CELL CYCLE (CANCER).

Dual role model. Comparative analysis of the sequence-specific DNA binding and the 3′-5′ exonuclease activities of p53 revealed that these activities are regulated in an opposing manner. As sequence-specific DNA binding is a hallmark of an activated p53, the implication is that the nonactivated (latent) p53 will perform exonuclease activity. The exonuclease activity of noninduced p53 could be involved in a variety of possible functions of p53, which all contribute to avoid mutations in the genome. The postulate thus is that the basic function of p53 is its direct involvement in the repair of endogenous DNA damage and the prevention of mutational events resulting from such damage. Superimposed are the up-to-now better-characterized functions of p53 as a superior control element in integrating cellular stress signals, followed by the induction of either growth arrest or apoptosis (**Fig. 2**). The basic function of p53 to directly engage in repair processes must not be restricted to its noninduced state, but could also be exerted by a subclass of p53 after induction. Thereby, p53 would be able to exert its full range of biochemical activities acquired for maintaining the integrity of the cell's genome.

Mutant p53. More than 80% of all mutations in the p53 gene are missense point mutations in the coding region of the p53 core domain, leading to the expression of a full-length p53 protein with an amino acid exchange. Such a mutational spectrum is quite unusual for a tumor suppressor, as most tumor suppressors are inactivated by gene truncation or deletion or by promoter inactivation. The unusual mutational spectrum implies a selection advantage for tumor cells expressing such a mutant p53, and thus that mutant p53 exerts oncogenic properties. The oncogenic properties of mutant p53 are not yet understood at the molecular level. However, evidence obtained from the analyses of tumor banks strongly supports the concept that at least certain point mutations within the p53 gene not only serve to eliminate the tumor suppressor functions of p53 but enhance the aggressiveness of the respective tumors, leading to a poorer prognosis for tumor patients. In this regard, it is an important characteristic of at least most epithelial cancers that mutations in the p53 gene are late events during their development, often associated with the onset of invasiveness. p53 mutations thus are associated with tumor progression rather than with tumor initiation. The genetic instability of tumor cells expressing mutant p53 will allow the selection of more aggressive tumor cell variants and of tumor cells resisting tumor therapy. In addition, mutant p53 is suspected to actively suppress the responsiveness of tumor cells to various anticancer treatments.

Prognosis and therapy. The large number of tumors containing p53 mutations render p53 a prominent target for applied tumor research. In contrast to wild-type p53, which is usually a stable protein, mutant p53 accumulates in tumor cells. Detection of enhanced levels of p53 in tumor tissue is indicative for the expression of a mutant p53, and is already

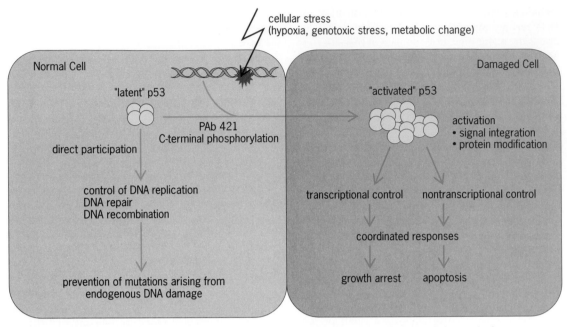

Fig. 2. Dual role of p53 as guardian of the genome. The current view of p53 as a superior control element in the responses to various types of cellular stress is depicted on the right. The left provides an extension of this model, according to which a noninduced p53 actively participates in the prevention of mutations arising from endogenous DNA damage. Note that functions of a noninduced p53 can also operate under conditions of cellular stress, if one assumes that after cellular stress different functional subclasses can exist within the same cell.

commonly used in tumor diagnosis. The value of mutant p53 as a diagnostic and prognostic marker will be enhanced by sequence analyses, allowing the classification of the aggressiveness of the respective mutant p53 as derived from the analyses of tumor banks.

The most challenging aspect of applied p53 research is the development of therapy regimens based on the p53 status of the tumor cells.

Gene therapy approaches. Wild-type p53 is able to induce apoptosis under appropriate conditions, whereas mutant p53 has lost this activity and even seems to actively block at least certain apoptotic pathways. Therefore, gene replacement, that is, introduction of wild-type p53 into tumors by various vector systems, is one of the aims of a p53-based gene therapy. In addition to the problems common to all gene therapy approaches, such as tumor-specific delivery of the therapeutic gene and its high-level expression in tumor cells only, several p53-specific problems should be resolved: the transduced wild-type p53 should not hetero-oligomerize with the endogenous mutant p53, because this would result in its inactivation; and it should specifically induce apoptosis rather than growth arrest. Both problems can be overcome by genetically modifying the wild-type p53 to create a "super p53," which is more potent in induction of apoptosis than wild-type p53, and that contains a "foreign" oligomerization domain preventing hetero-oligomerization.

A completely different gene therapy approach exploits the fact that certain viruses have to eliminate p53 function for their replicative growth. In the *Onyx* adenovirus the gene encoding the E1B 55kd protein is deleted. This protein binds and inactivates p53 (Fig. 1). Because the *Onyx* virus cannot inacti-

vate p53, it can only poorly replicate in cells expressing wild-type p53, but does well in cells expressing no p53 or functionally inactivated p53. High-titer injection of the *Onyx* virus into tumor tissue thus will specifically destroy the tumor cells.

Conventional approaches. Development of low-molecular-weight compounds to be used as drugs in p53-based therapies is a promising alternative to p53-based gene therapy. One possibility is the restoration of the wild-type transactivator function of mutant p53 by drugs directly binding to the mutant p53. Although possible, and demonstrated to work in vitro with tumor cells, the challenge will be to develop a drug that specifically reactivates mutant p53 without activating wild-type p53 in healthy tissues. Conversely, inactivation of the oncogenic properties of mutant p53 will possibly render otherwise resistant tumors amenable to conventional tumor therapy. A prerequisite, however, will be the identification of the oncogenic functions of mutant p53 at the molecular level. Finally, recent evidence has shown that inhibition of the transactivation function of wild-type p53 in healthy tissue by a systemically applicable compound prevents radiation-induced apoptosis in tissues surrounding the tumor, and thereby allows the use of very high doses of radiation in tumor therapy. Obviously, treatment with this compound does not abolish p53-mediated protection of the healthy tissue from radiation-induced DNA damage, supporting the concept of an active involvement of wild-type p53 in repair processes in the absence of p53 transcriptional activation (Fig. 2).

Like no other tumor-associated protein so far, p53 has stimulated both basic and clinically oriented molecular tumor research. Although current understanding of the molecular functions of p53 is still far ahead of its translation into p53-based therapies, this avenue of p53 research is picking up momentum. Given the importance of p53 in tumor treatment, any successful p53-based tumor therapy should provide a major breakthrough in the fight against cancer.

For background information *see* CANCER (MEDICINE); CELL CYCLE; GENETICS; MUTATION in the McGraw-Hill Encyclopedia of Science & Technology.

Wolfgang Deppert

Bibliography. Compilation of review articles on p53, *Cell. Mol. Life Sci.*, vol. 55, 1999; *Reviews: p53, Oncogene*, vol. 18, no. 53, 1999.

Turbulence modeling

The need for turbulence modeling was first made explicit by Osborne Reynolds's paper in 1895 on the consequences of averaging the Navier-Stokes equations. The nonlinear convective transport terms in those equations (which can be written in the form $\rho \mathbf{v} \cdot \nabla \mathbf{v}$, where ρ is the fluid density, $\mathbf{v}$ is the fluid velocity vector, and ∇ is the gradient operator, provided ρ is constant) led to the appearance of time-averaged products of fluctuating velocities—now known as Reynolds stresses—which were solely responsible, in mathematical terms, for the fact that turbulent and laminar flows differed so starkly in their behavior. But the Reynolds stresses are unknown quantities with regard to the Navier-Stokes equations, and thus a method has to be provided for their approximation: that is the task of turbulence modeling. Some of the pioneers in fluid mechanics—G. I. Taylor, L. Prandtl, A. N. Kolmogorov, and Th. von Karman—made notable investigations in the field of turbulence modeling, but it was only with the appearance of general methods of computational fluid dynamics for solving the Reynolds-averaged Navier-Stokes (RANS) equations in the 1960s that turbulence modeling became a major subject in its own right.

Eddy viscosity models. The widening horizons that the computational methods brought into view underlined the fact that any useful model had to provide a reasonably general route for determining the local average time and length scales of turbulence, which implied developing transport partial differential equations for these or related quantities. Thus, from the 1970s onward, there has been an emphasis on models requiring the solution of at least two such equations. The earliest models adopted the idea that turbulent mixing, analogous to molecular mixing, was governed by an effective viscosity, v_t, which was not a property of the fluid but a consequence of the local state of turbulence. The effective viscosity follows Eq. (1), where V' and l are local turbulent

$$v_t \propto V'l \qquad (1)$$

velocity and length scales. The scalar property v_t relates the Reynolds stresses to the local time-mean velocity gradients. An equivalent, more widely used form is Eq. (2), where k is the kinetic energy of the

$$v_t = c_\mu k^2 / \varepsilon \qquad (2)$$

turbulence, ε is the viscous dissipation rate of this kinetic energy and, outside the viscous sublayer, c_μ is supposedly constant. (The viscous sublayer is a very thin region next to a wall, typically only 1% of the boundary layer thickness, where turbulent mixing is impeded and transport occurs partly or, in the limit as the wall is approached, entirely by viscous diffusion.) In fact, the transport equation solved for k is close to the exact form first obtained by Reynolds, while that for ε is almost entirely empirical. Such two-equation eddy viscosity models are currently used for well over 90% of industrial applications of computational fluid dynamics.

Second-moment closure. However, the reliability of the eddy viscosity models is low in flows affected by force fields or where the velocity-gradient field is complex—as it usually is in flows requiring computational fluid dynamics analysis. Potentially, the most reliable route forward is to provide transport equations for the Reynolds stresses themselves, thus abandoning the eddy viscosity notion. This level of approximation, known formally as second-moment closure, typically requires between 50% and 200% more computing time than an eddy viscosity model, depending on the flow in question. It is, however, a particularly attractive approach because the influential stress-generation terms, including any due to gravitational or Coriolis forces, can be handled without approximation. Moreover, it is a level where the modeling that is still required for other processes in the stress-transport equations can be rationally developed.

Early models of this type from the 1970s suffered from two main shortcomings: They employed the same equation for ε as eddy viscosity models, and they introduced wall-proximity corrections (designed to mimic the blocking effect of a wall on velocity fluctuations normal to that surface) that were valid only for infinite plane surfaces. Those shortcomings still afflict most commercial software, though at the research level a new generation of models has achieved notable successes even for singular test cases such as J. O. Hinze's partially roughened rectangular channel in **Fig. 1** The figure shows a half cross section of the channel through which fluid flows. Because of the anisotropy of the resultant Reynolds stress field in the plane of the cross section, secondary motions are induced, leading to a marked upward displacement of the measured axial velocity contours. The second-moment closure leads to a very close agreement with experimental observations. By contrast, any eddy viscosity model (whose constitutive stress-strain relation implies isotropic stresses in components where the strain is zero) would lead to no secondary motion at all.

Nonlinear eddy viscosity model. By assuming that the stress transport processes are proportional to those for turbulence energy, and with the help of

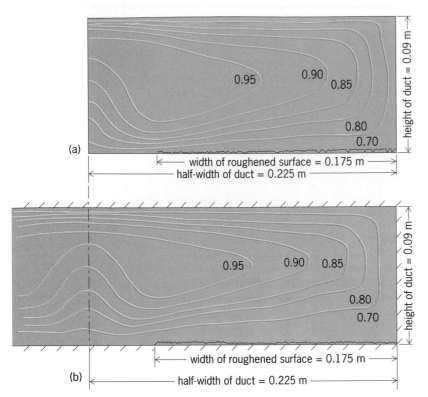

(a)

width of roughened surface = 0.175 m
half-width of duct = 0.225 m
height of duct = 0.09 m

(b)

width of roughened surface = 0.175 m
half-width of duct = 0.225 m
height of duct = 0.09 m

Fig. 1. Measurement and modeling of flow through a partially roughened duct, showing effect of turbulence-induced secondary flow on axial velocity contours. A half cross section of the duct is shown, and contours are labeled with the local streamwise velocity divided by its maximum value. (a) Predictions of the model. (b) Experimental values. (*After B. E. Launder and S.-P. Li, On the elimination of wall-topography parameters from second-moment closure, Phys. Fluids, 6:999–1006, 1994*)

Mathematica (or some similar symbolic computing system), the erstwhile transport equations can be simplified to explicit algebraic equations in a form equivalent to a nonlinear eddy viscosity model. The best models of this type achieve in many cases accuracies not far short of second-moment closures for computing times only 15% longer than an equivalent linear eddy viscosity model.

Fig. 2. Example of Rayleigh-Bénard convection using transient RANS modeling, Instantaneous trajectories of massless particles in three vertical planes are shown. (*After S. Kenjeres and K. Hanjalic, Transient analysis of Rayleigh-Bénard convection with a RANS model, Int. J. Heat Fluid Flow, 20:329–340, 1999*)

Large-eddy simulation. As computing power continually advances while costs fall, there is an increasing use of large-eddy simulation to resolve difficult problems, especially where the ensemble-averaged flow is time-dependent (for example, in an internal combustion engine or the flow over the rotating blade of a moving helicopter). In large-eddy simulation, a large proportion of the turbulence is resolved directly by way of a three-dimensional time-dependent numerical solution, and a model is employed only to account for turbulence with scales too fine to be resolved. This relatively fine-scale turbulence experiences less extreme states than the turbulent field taken as a whole, and is usually approximated by an algebraic sub-grid-scale model similar to Eq. (1), where the length scale is taken proportional to the local internodal spacing. A more refined approach, in which the turbulence spectrum resolved by the large-eddy simulation is extrapolated to higher wave numbers to determine the sub-grid-scale viscosity, is gaining popularity. However, despite the appealing simplicity of the notion of an isotropic eddy viscosity in modeling the sub-grid-scale stresses, there is a growing belief that it must be abandoned. In other words, the anisotropy of the turbulent stresses is thought to persist into the fine scales.

TRANS modeling. An alternative though superficially similar approach is to solve the RANS equations in a time-dependent mode, a strategy sometimes known as TRANS (transient RANS) modeling. The distinction between large-eddy simulation and TRANS may be recognized by considering the consequences of an indefinite grid refinement: The former then reverts to a direct numerical simulation, with the sub-grid-scale viscosity reducing to the molecular value; the latter, however, should experience no change in the modeled stresses. The TRANS strategy has recently been applied to Rayleigh-Bénard convection, where fluid in a rectangular container is heated from below with buoyantly driven turbulent convection ensuing (**Fig. 2**). A time average of the resultant simulation led to much closer agreement with exact direct numerical simulation results than a conventional RANS treatment, while computational cost would have been at least an order of magnitude less than for a large-eddy simulation treatment. *See* DIRECT NUMERICAL SIMULATION.

Modeling heat and species transfer. While this discussion has focused on the problem of momentum exchange by turbulence, analogous modeling problems arise if heat or species transfer by turbulent mixing is the subject of interest. As would be anticipated, there are also precisely analogous modeling strategies. Of course, even where the only goal is to determine the distribution of some scalar quantity, the velocity field (and thus the Reynolds stresses) must still be determined since the flow field transports the scalar. While usually the same level of modeling is adopted for the turbulent heat or species flux and the Reynolds stresses, there are also many examples when, for particular reasons, either a more or a less elaborate model has been adopted for the scalar flux than for the Reynolds stresses.

Prospects. Turbulence modeling remains an intensely active field of research. Important problem areas include the development of accurate but economical strategies for the very thin near-wall sublayer, where molecular and turbulent transport effects are simultaneously important; the handling of two-phase flows where a range of different approaches is required depending on the nature and relative concentration of the separate phases; turbulent combustion employing Monte Carlo methods or transport equations for probability-density functions; and an intimidating range of problems associated with air and water movement in the natural environment where, because of the large scales involved, buoyant effects are dominant.

For background information *see* COMPUTATIONAL FLUID DYNAMICS; CONVECTION (HEAT); FLUID-FLOW PRINCIPLES; NAVIER-STOKES EQUATIONS; TURBULENT FLOW; VISCOSITY in the McGraw-Hill Encyclopedia of Science & Technology.   Brian E. Launder

Bibliography. T. B. Gatski, M. Y. Hussaini, and J. L. Lumley (eds.), *Simulation and Modeling of Turbulent Flows*, Oxford, 1996; M. Hallbäck et al. (eds.), *Turbulence and Transition Modelling*, Kluwer, Dordrecht, 1996; M. D. Salas, J. N. Hefner, and L. Sakell (eds.), *Modeling Complex Turbulent Flows*, Kluwer, Dordrecht, 1999.

Ultracold molecules

The field of ultracold atoms (that is, atoms cooled to temperatures below 1 millikelvin) has grown tremendously over the past 15 years. Cold neutral atoms have seen important applications in atomic clocks, quantum electrodynamics, and tests of fundamental symmetries. Magnetic trapping and evaporative cooling, along with the study of ultracold atomic collisions, have led to the creation of atomic Bose-Einstein condensates, atom lasers, and degenerate atomic Fermi gases. Similarly, the creation of ultracold molecules should open up new areas of physics and chemistry. *See* BOSE-EINSTEIN CONDENSATION.

Motivation. A key motivation behind cooling molecules is simply to slow them down. As a gas of molecules is cooled, their average velocity is decreased and the spread in molecular velocities narrows. Thus, cooling allows longer measurements (because the molecules move out of the measuring apparatus more slowly) and reduces the Doppler blur due to the velocity spread. Both of these effects lead to more sensitive measurements and improved molecular spectroscopy.

These improvements are important not only for studying molecular physics but also for studying fundamental physics. The internal structure of certain molecules provides an ideal laboratory for sensitive measurements of fundamental physical quantities. For example, highly polar molecules are used in searches for the electron's electric dipole moment, a currently undetected physical quantity of great consequence. The ability to produce large numbers of ultracold molecules could improve such measurements.

Ultracold molecules have large de Broglie wavelengths, and hence their interactions are quantum-mechanical. Like atoms, molecules can collide elastically and inelastically. In addition, colliding molecules can undergo chemical reactions. Studies of collisions between ultracold molecules may make it possible to examine chemistry in a new regime.

Comparison with cold atoms. The most commonly used technique to cool neutral atoms is laser cooling. In this method, atoms are cooled by resonantly scattering laser light. Each scattered photon gives the atom a momentum kick and slows the atom. However, the momentum kick of a single photon is small, and thousands of photons must be scattered in order to slow an atom from room temperature to ultracold temperatures.

Certain atoms have a very simple internal structure, and it is easy to scatter a large number of photons off them in a controlled fashion. Each time such an atom absorbs and emits a photon, it returns to the same internal state it started in, and is ready to repeat the process. However, the internal structure of molecules is much more complex. Unlike atoms, molecules can rotate and vibrate, greatly complicating their level structure. After a molecule scatters a photon, it will often (and randomly) wind up in a state which cannot absorb light from the original laser. So, to efficiently laser-cool molecules, many different laser frequencies are needed simultaneously. So far, this requirement has proved prohibitively difficult to fulfill.

Evaporative cooling. Another powerful technique for cooling atoms is evaporative cooling inside a magnetic trap. This is the technique used to produce Bose condensates and the coldest temperatures ever obtained, and it should be directly applicable to molecules.

The idea is simple. Using magnetic fields, a cloud of atoms is confined and levitated in a vacuum. This breaks the thermal connection between the atoms and the environment. The atoms can then cool themselves through evaporation, the same process that cools a cup of hot coffee. In evaporation, the highest-energy atoms escape. The remaining (lower-energy) atoms rethermalize via elastic collisions to a reduced temperature. But unlike a cup of coffee, the energy threshold of a magnetic trap can be continuously tuned to optimize the evaporation process. With this tuning, evaporative cooling has been successfully used to cool trapped atoms into the nanokelvin range.

Evaporative cooling is general, as it requires only collisions between the trapped particles. Magnetic trapping of molecules requires only that they be magnetic. Fortunately, many molecules (especially radicals) have this property. The trick with trapping is to get the molecules into the magnetic trap in the first place. Magnetic traps are conservative potentials; if

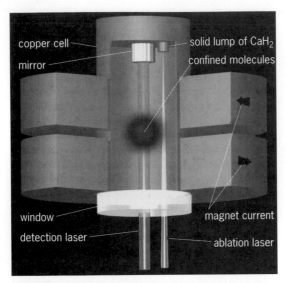

Fig. 1. Buffer-gas loading apparatus for magnetic trapping of molecules. (*After J. D. Weinstein et al., Magnetic trapping of calcium monohydride molecules at millikelvin temperatures, Nature, 395:148–150, 1998*)

a molecule is dropped in, it will simply bounce out. The trapping process is further complicated because magnetic traps are also very shallow potentials. Thus, to be confined in the trap, the molecule must first be reduced to a low energy. For these reasons, efficient trapping requires cooling.

Buffer-gas loading. One effective technique to cool molecules uses a buffer gas. A kind of cryogenic refrigerator, called a dilution refrigerator, can cool macroscopic objects to a few millikelvins. If molecules could be cooled to this temperature, they could easily be magnetically trapped. Unfortunately, the cold walls of a dilution refrigerator cannot be used directly to cool molecules because they would be adsorbed; they would freeze onto the surface of their container. However, helium-3 (a naturally occurring isotope) remains a gas down to temperatures of about 250 mK. Helium gas can thus be used as a thermal link between the molecules and the refrigerator, and can cool molecules down to 250 mK.

Buffer-gas cooling can be used to trap molecules. In this technique, a magnetic trap is filled with a cold buffer gas, and hot molecules are then introduced. The molecules fall into the trap, undergo elastic collisions with the helium buffer gas, and cool to a temperature beneath the trap depth. They are now confined. The helium buffer gas could then be removed, breaking the thermal connection between the trapped molecules and the dilution refrigerator. The molecules could then be further cooled via evaporation.

The buffer-gas loading technique has been successfully used with helium-3 buffer gas to trap both atoms and molecules. For the molecule-trapping experiment, calcium monohydride (CaH) was trapped. This compound was produced, thermalized, and trapped within a copper cell (cooled by a dilution

refrigerator) inside the bore of a superconducting magnet (**Fig. 1**). The CaH was created via laser ablation of a solid sample of calcium dihydride (CaH$_2$) near the edge of the trap potential; a focused, high-intensity pulsed laser blasted CaH molecules out of the CaH$_2$. The hot molecules diffused through the helium gas, and elastic collisions between the CaH and the helium gas thermalized the molecules to the temperature of the helium. They were confined by the magnetic fields and trapped. In these preliminary experiments, 10^{11} molecules were trapped at a temperature of 400 mK. While these molecules may still be warm by laser cooling standards, it should be possible to evaporatively cool them.

Photoassociation. A very different approach to producing cold molecules is through molecular photoassociation. This technique circumvents the entire problem of directly cooling molecules. In ultracold photoassociation, the atomic constituents of the target molecule are cooled, and ultracold molecules are built directly out of the ultracold atoms.

Simple atom-atom collisions alone cannot form a molecule, even if the reaction is energetically favorable. A third body is needed to remove the excess energy and make the reaction possible. This catalyst can be as simple as a third atom or as ethereal as a photon. In photoassociation, the latter is used to actively form molecules out of individual atoms.

The reaction is driven by using a laser to excite two adjacent atoms into an excited state of a bound molecule. The excited molecule will eventually give up its extra energy by emitting another photon, a process which will (randomly) produce either two unbound atoms or the desired bound molecule (**Fig. 2**).

Greater efficiency and control over the reaction can be achieved by using a second laser to actively drive the excited molecule into its ground state. Using stimulated emission rather than spontaneous emission would make it possible not only to increase the likelihood of producing a molecule but also to use the second laser frequency to select its specific rotational and vibrational state.

Photoassociation experiments have been conducted with all of the alkali atoms as well as atomic hydrogen. Photoassociated ultracold potassium and cesium dimers (K$_2$ and Cs$_2$) have been observed. In these experiments, molecules are produced at a rate of a few thousand per second at temperatures of

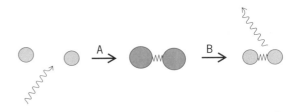

Fig. 2. Steps in the photoassociation process. In process A, two unbound atoms are driven to form an excited molecule by a laser photon. In process B, the excited molecule releases its internal energy in a second photon, producing a stable molecule.

hundreds of microkelvins. Much higher production rates are expected.

If photoassociation is done inside a trapping potential, the ultracold molecules produced will be trapped. In preliminary experiments, dozens of ultracold molecules were trapped. It is expected that with improved production rates this initial trapping number will be greatly increased.

Photoassociation of ultracold atoms is important not only as a source of ultracold molecules but also as a valuable spectroscopic tool. Photoassociation spectra provide extremely precise measurements of the interatomic interaction of the molecule's constituent atoms. These have been a vital tool in understanding ultracold atomic collisions.

Molecular beam deceleration. There has also been progress in the slowing of molecular beams, the traditional tool of molecular physics. A molecular expansion cools molecules by allowing a gas of molecules to expand out of a nozzle into vacuum. This produces a beam of molecules which are cool with respect to each other but which all have a very high forward velocity. Because of their peculiar "monochromatic" velocity distribution, specialized methods can be used to decelerate these high-velocity molecules.

Electric fields have been used to slow down a pulsed beam of molecules. Much as magnetic fields can be used to push molecules, so can electric fields. A pulse of carbon monoxide molecules was decelerated by a series of 63 pulsed electric fields. This slowed the beam from 225 to 98 m/s (738 to 322 ft/s). In other work, a molecular beam was slowed mechanically. The nozzle emitting the molecules was simply moved in the direction opposite to the molecular flow. While these methods do not narrow the velocity distribution of the molecules, they do reduce their average velocity and hence provide longer interaction times and the potential for more sensitive measurements. As these methods are improved, it should be possible to catch a slow packet of molecules with a trap.

For background information *see* CRYOGENICS; LASER; LASER COOLING; LOW-TEMPERATURE PHYSICS; MOLECULAR BEAMS; PARTICLE TRAP in the McGraw-Hill Encyclopedia of Science & Technology.

Jonathan David Weinstein; John M. Doyle

Bibliography. H. L. Bethlem, G. Berden, and G. Meijer, Decelerating neutral dipolar molecules, *Phys. Rev. Lett.*, 83:1558–1561, 1999; A. Fioretti et al., Formation of cold Cs$_2$ molecules through photoassociation, *Phys. Rev. Lett.*, 80:4402–4405, 1998; W. C. Stwalley and He Wang, Photoassociation of ultracold atoms: A new spectroscopic technique, *J. Mol. Spectros.*, 195:194–228, 1999; T. Takekoshi, B. M. Patterson, and R. J. Knize, Observation of optically trapped cold cesium molecules, *Phys. Rev. Lett.*, 81:5105–5108, 1998; J. D. Weinstein et al., Magnetic trapping of calcium monohydride molecules at millikelvin temperatures, *Nature*, 395:148–150, 1998.

Underwater acoustic pollution

The ocean is hardly the "silent world" described by Jacques Cousteau. It is a noisy place where wind chop, crashing surf, earthquakes, breaking ice, and calling animals generate an undulating background of diverse sounds. The marine environment is a dense particulate-filled medium that inhibits the conduction of light but at the same time enables sound to travel much farther and faster than it does in the terrestrial world. As a result, marine mammals rely on sound for most aspects of their life history. Toothed whales use high-frequency biosonar to locate prey and to learn about their environment. Baleen whales use low-frequency sounds for long-distance communication and possibly navigation. Sound plays an important role in the mating behavior of most whale and many seal species. It has been suggested that most marine mammals may use passive listening to aid in location of prey, avoidance of predators, and navigation during migration. Given the importance of sound to marine mammals, it is likely that they are sensitive to anthropogenic noise.

Humans have always relied on the oceans for transportation and commerce, but over the last century use of the ocean has skyrocketed and there has been an unprecedented increase in the amount of noise added to the ocean's natural background. Human-generated underwater noise originates from ship traffic, offshore industrial activities, and to a lesser extent ocean sensing. Ship traffic alone has increased the ambient noise level 10 times over the period between 1950 and 1975. Additional industrial activities include use of air guns in seismic exploration, explosives in construction work, and equipment in offshore drilling.

Another source of anthropogenic noise that potentially impacts marine mammals comes from the use of acoustics for oceanographic research and defense purposes. For example, geophysical surveys use air guns and sonic generators to study the geology of the offshore marine environment and to create detailed maps of the sea floor. Sound is used as a probe to study ocean currents and temperature. A number of the world's navies use high-frequency tactical sonar, and they are developing low-frequency sonar for use in antisubmarine warfare.

The potential impacts of noise on marine mammals can be physiological or behavioral. These effects depend on distance from, and amplitude and frequency of, the sound source. Physiological damage is associated with extremely loud sources and explosions. Explosions are the acoustic pollutant of greatest concern, since they produce a shock wave, which propagates differently than other acoustic sources and can cause considerable physical and acoustic trauma, such as ruptured lungs or permanent damage to the hearing system. Underwater detonations are typically associated with marine construction, demolition, and military operations. The U.S. Navy ran into serious environmental resistance

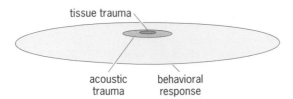

Fig. 1. Zones of impact for an extremely loud sound or blast. Notice that the area of physiological harm is very small relative to the area of behavioral response.

as it planned to detonate explosives (under congressional direction) near a new class of destroyer in order to test its ability to withstand a near miss.

Auditory damage is still possible when an animal is outside shock-wave range. Damage can be permanent or temporary. It is common to have a temporary threshold shift (TTS) with decreased hearing sensitivity when an animal is exposed to loud sounds. Depending on the duration and intensity of the sound, this change can last for a few hours to a few days. Repeated exposures to sounds that cause TTS can result in permanent hearing loss. These permanent physiological effects are more dangerous to animals, but the potential numbers of animals exposed is often very small due to the limited geographic range over which high-amplitude sounds travel (**Fig. 1**).

Farther from loud sound sources where physiological impacts are no longer of concern, there are still potential behavioral effects. These effects are considerably lower-risk, but they may impact a greater number of individuals due to the greater geographic range of exposure. Behaviorial impacts do not damage the animal physically but in some way change its behavior or prevent it from receiving important information about its environment. If a sea lion misses the vocalizations of an approaching killer whale due to sound masking, it could be eaten. It is more likely that animals bothered by anthropogenic noise would just leave the area. This may be a concern if the animal leaves a "critical habitat." Behavioral changes can result from any sound introduced in the environment that the animal is capable of hearing. Given the tremendous distances that sound can travel in the ocean, these effects can occur at considerable range from the sound source.

To better understand the impact of anthropogenic sound on marine mammals, several levels of research are necessary. The first is simply evaluating the ability of animals to hear noises of concern. The most traditional way of doing this involves training animals to respond to tone tests, much the way that human hearing tests are performed. A new method measures the invoked auditory nerve stem response. This involves playing tones to animals and using electrodes to monitor whether nerves in the auditory complex fire in response. This technique has the advantage that it can be performed on untrained animals. Finally, comparative morphology can be used to examine the internal ear anatomy of postmortem animals. This is also useful in studying whether an animal has

suffered from repeated exposure that damaged its hearing or if it was exposed to an extremely loud sound (explosions) that caused immediate and permanent damage. In reference to masking, studies are limited to trained animals or animals being studied through evoked auditory potential. Animals involved in masking studies can also be used to study what levels of sound induce TTS.

Another level is in the field. The most obvious questions addressed here concern the role of sounds in marine mammals' natural history. What types of sound do these animals produce? What are the functions of their sounds? What types of sounds do their predators and prey make?

Probably the most direct research into the impacts of noise on marine mammals concerns study of wild animals' response to real anthropogenic noise sources or "playbacks"—an experimental paradigm where sounds of interest are played through an underwater speaker to subject animals. This work began in the 1980s when playback experiments were used to project recordings of air guns and drilling noises to bowhead whales in the Bering Sea and to gray whales migrating along the California coast. Gray whales were observed to make slight but definite course changes around the speaker, avoiding the "120 dB region," or the area around the source where noise levels exceed 120 decibels (re 1 micropascal at 1 m). Even more interesting was the result observed during the same study when researchers broadcast the sounds of killer whales, which prey on gray whales. Whales immediately dived and hid among the kelp beds to escape. Obviously the killer whale sounds were far more disturbing to the gray whales than certain anthropogenic noises.

Although high-amplitude low-frequency sound sources have been used in oceanographic research for some time, it was not until the Heard Island Feasibility Test that concern was raised about the potential deleterious effects of a loud low-frequency sound source on ocean fauna, particularly marine mammals. A research project that followed on the success of the Heard Island study was the Acoustic Thermometry of the Ocean Climate (ATOC) experiment. This project tested whether changes in the speed of sound measured over long distances (3000–5000 km or 1800–3000 mi) could be used to measure integrated ocean temperatures. A Marine Mammal Research Program was initiated to determine if the loud sounds required for this project could harm or disrupt marine mammals. This program examined whether the behavior and habitat use of marine mammals in Hawaii and California changed in response to transmissions of the ATOC sound source. In Hawaii, playback experiments were conducted with humpback whales during their breeding season. In California a full operational ATOC sound source was installed on the Pioneer Seamount 100 km (60 mi) off San Francisco; in a sense, this was the largest playback experiment ever performed. Aerial surveys were conducted to monitor the distribution of cetaceans and pinnipeds in the immediate vicinity of the

ATOC loudspeaker. The majority of marine mammals did not appear to avoid the sound source. Humpback and sperm whales were exceptions, showing some avoidance of the area in the transmitter's immediate vicinity. These results suggest that while ATOC did not cause significant levels of displacement, some species were aware of it.

One problem with playbacks is that, due to ocean variability, sound fields are uneven. It is very difficult to assess the effects of the sound on animals when the sound frequency and intensity to which the animal is actually exposed cannot be measured. To overcome this issue, custom recording devices were built that could be attached to the backs of deep-diving elephant seals. Seals carrying these recorders along with instruments for monitoring their dive behavior were then released near the ATOC source to see if their behavior changed in response to ATOC operations (**Fig. 2**). Elephant seals exposed to sounds 20–30 decibels above ambient levels showed only slight alterations in behavior. No dramatic responses, such as escape dives or retreats to the surface, were observed.

Acoustic pollution is one of a number of human-generated impacts on the marine environment. Marine mammals might accommodate to any specific insult. However, the cumulative impact of a variety of stresses is both insidious and difficult to measure, let alone manage. In the United States, the Marine Mammal Protection Act makes it illegal to harass or otherwise harm marine mammals. The problem is defining when a marine mammal has been harassed. As a result, there is a poor link between the laws governing how marine mammals are managed and the true biological issues underlying the laws. Research is needed to help identify the relevant biological issues as they relate to the health and stability of the populations so that the appropriate legal framework necessary for sensible management can be developed. Do these disturbances result in changes in the population? Do they cause the animals to avoid important habitats? How often short-term or acute effects can occur must be considered. It is important to determine which behaviors should be observed and whether short-term changes are indicative of long-term effects where animals begin to avoid critical habitats. The technology to measure very specific changes in marine mammal behavior is increasing. However, there is insufficient perspective to know how useful these measures will be in assessing impacts to critical activities such as feeding or reproduction. It is therefore important to understand not only the sounds that marine mammals respond to but also the factors that define the habitats critical for feeding and reproduction. Damage to these habitats by acoustic pollution or any other pollutant will likely result in a decline in the marine mammal populations that utilize them.

For background information *see* ACOUSTIC NOISE; ACOUSTICS; EAR; HEARING; LOUDNESS; MASKING OF SOUND; NOISE MEASUREMENT; PHYSIOLOGICAL ACOUSTICS; PSYCHOACOUSTICS; SOUND; WAVE MO-

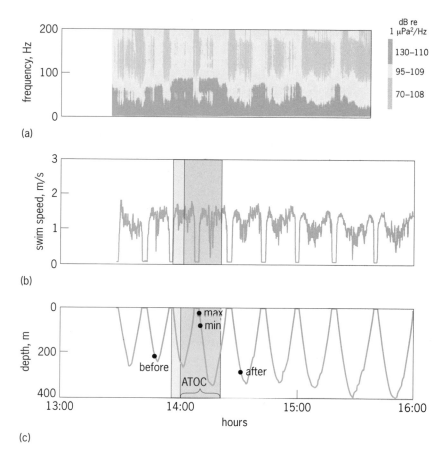

Fig. 2. Data obtained from an elephant seal released near the ATOC sound source. (*a*) Spectrogram acquired from the acoustic data logger. (*b*) Animal swim speed. (*c*) Animal diving pattern. The shaded area shows when the ATOC source was on: the lighter area is the 5-min ramp-up period, and the darker area indicates when the source reached full power operating for 20 min. "Before" (102 dB) and "after" (103 dB) represents the sound pressure level measured prior to and after turn-on of the source. The maximum sound pressure level measured when the source was on was 132 dB re 1 μPa, and the minimum was 119 dB re 1 μPa.

TION in the McGraw-Hill Encyclopedia of Science & Technology.   Daniel P. Costa; Sean A. Hayes

Bibliography. W. Burgess et al., An intelligent acoustic recording tag first results from free-ranging northern elephant seals, *Deep Sea Res. II*, 45:1327–1351, 1998; D. P. Costa, The secret life of marine mammals: New tools for the study of their biology and ecology, *Oceanography*, 6(3):120–128, 1993; J. Gordon and A. Moscrop, Underwater noise pollution and its significance for whales and dolphins, in M. P. Simmonds and J. D. Hutchinson, (eds.), *The Conservation of Whales and Dolphins: Science and Practice*, John Wiley, New York, 1996; *Low-Frequency Sound and Marine Mammals: Current Knowledge and Research Needs*, National Research Council, Washington, DC, 1994; W. J. Richardson et al., *Marine Mammals and Noise*, Academic Press, San Diego, 1995.

Vaccine

Despite the large degree of success of many vaccines, humans are still plagued by diseases such as AIDS, chronic hepatitis, and cancer. Together these three diseases are responsible for over 530,000 deaths per year in the United States, 94% of this number being attributed to cancer alone. Without an effective vaccine, education is one of the few ways available for controlling disease. For example, education about high-risk behavior has helped bring the 78,000 reported cases of AIDS in the United States in 1993 down to 43,000 reported cases in 1999. Alterations in diet and lifestyle and having regular checkups can aid in lowering the reported cases of certain cancers. Nevertheless, the development of an effective vaccine would be the optimal solution to lowering incidence of AIDS and cancer. Increasing knowledge of the human immune system, together with understanding of the mechanism by which vaccines provide immunity and how pathogens infect and evade the host defenses, allows for a focused approach on the development of effective vaccines. In the search for a vaccine, the cost of manufacture, ease of delivery and transport, and effectiveness at directing the immune response toward the pathogen with little negative impact on the host are taken into account. The effectiveness of a vaccine depends on the type of vaccine as well as the characteristics of the target pathogen. A large variety of vaccine strategies are available, and new delivery systems are being developed. Since different pathogens exhibit a variety of mechanisms for evading the human immune response, defining the immune response that would be most effective against a particular pathogen is also an important step in vaccine development.

Immune system. Vaccines function by attempting to create immunologic memory of the pathogen before the individual encounters it naturally. If an individual has been vaccinated, a natural encounter with the pathogen triggers the immune system to respond. Since the immune system has encountered the pathogen before, in the form of the vaccination, the response is quick and strong and the pathogen is eliminated before it has a chance to cause disease. There are two major arms of the acquired immune system that can mediate eradication of the pathogen. The cellular arm consists primarily of cytotoxic T lymphocytes that attack pathogens replicating within host cells. The humoral arm is made up of B lymphocytes which secrete antibody molecules that bind pathogens outside host cells and act to neutralize infection or promote killing of the pathogen by other components of the immune system.

In vaccine development, the form of vaccine used depends on the type of immune response that is desired. Pathogens that replicate within host cells are not likely to be affected by circulating antibody because the antibody is unable to enter the cells. The cytotoxic T lymphocyte response represents a primary component in fighting these intracellular pathogens. Cytotoxic T lymphocytes are able to recognize pieces of the intracellular pathogen, termed antigens, on the surface of the infected cell. The infected cell, in order to warn the immune system of infection, presents these antigens on the surface using a protein complex referred to as major histocompatibility complex (MHC) class I molecules. These antigens are presented to the MHC class I pathway to activate the cytotoxic T lymphocytes via another component of the immune system, referred to as the antigen-presenting cell. After the cytotoxic T lymphocyte recognizes the antigen, it is then considered primed and immunologic memory has been established; however, no killing occurs at this point. The killing of the infected cell begins after subsequent encounters with antigen that activate the T cell to secrete cytotoxins. Once the infected cell or tumor cell is killed, the pathogen and/or tumor cell die as well (**Fig. 1**).

Many pathogens do not replicate within the cell, and even those that do are at one point, usually during transmission, outside the host cell. Organisms outside the host cell are not effectively killed by cytotoxic T lymphocytes, and the humoral immune response is normally the most important in fighting these pathogens. Antibodies are proteins secreted by B cells that specifically bind antigens expressed on extracellular pathogens and function in various ways to eliminate infection. An antibody response is generated by the B cell after antigen has bound its cell surface receptor, which is also an antibody. Pathogens can also be engulfed by other specialized antigen-presenting cells such as macrophages or dendritic cells. Once bound or engulfed, the antigen is pulled into the cell, processed, and presented

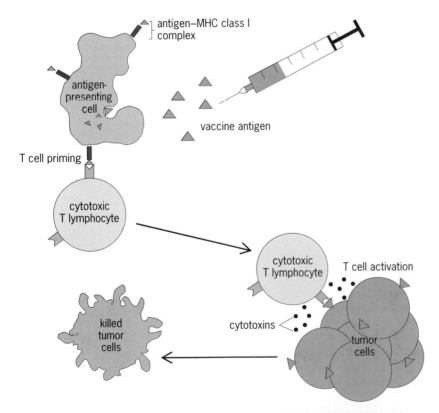

Fig. 1. Killing of tumor cells by cytotoxic T lymphocytes. Vaccine antigen is taken up by the antigen-presenting cell and enters the MHC class I processing and presentation pathway. An antigen-specific cytotoxic T lymphocyte recognizes the processed antigen–MHC class I complex on the surface of the antigen-presenting cell and is then primed. Upon a second encounter with antigen, such as antigen depicted here on the surface of tumor cells, the cytotoxic T lymphocyte is activated to release cytotoxins that then destroy the tumor cells.

on the surface using the MHC class II complex. A group of helper T cells recognize this antigen in the context of MHC class II and respond by secreting cytokines (proteins that regulate the intensity and duration of an immune response). These cytokines activate the B cell to become either a plasma cell or a memory B cell. The plasma cell begins to secrete large quantities of antibody that are highly specific for the antigen on the pathogen. The memory B cell remains in the body awaiting a second encounter with antigen, at which point it can begin secreting antibody.

Once antibodies are secreted into the circulation, they can act on invading pathogens in a variety of ways. (1) These antibodies can opsonize the pathogen by coating the outer surface of the pathogen, allowing immune cells to recognize, engulf, and kill the pathogen. (2) Antibodies can neutralize infection by binding surface molecules that normally aid the pathogen in adhering to and entering the host cell. If these molecules are bound by antibody, the pathogen may not be able to infect a cell and therefore dies. (3) Antibody can activate the complement cascade, a series of proteins that cause lysis of the cell membrane of pathogens when antibody is bound. (4) Antibody may also participate in a process referred to as antibody-dependent cell-mediated cytotoxicity (ADCC) in which antibody bound to the surface of a pathogen recruits effector cells to kill the pathogen. Various immune cells can serve as effector cells in ADCC, including natural killer cells, macrophages, and polymorphonuclear cells or neutrophils. These effector cells have receptors on the surface which bind the Fc component of the antibody molecule. Once the Fc receptor is bound, the effector cell is activated to secrete cytotoxins and the tumor cell or pathogen is killed (**Fig. 2**).

Though cancer is rarely thought to be caused by a pathogen, cancerous cells often express modified or novel antigens similar to a pathogen that are seen by the immune system as foreign. The antigens are processed within the cell and presented on the surface by MHC class I molecules. The immune system can respond to cancer cells similarly to an intracellular pathogen infected cell, and therefore the cytotoxic T lymphocyte response plays a large role in eliminating cancer cells. The humoral response, however, can also play an important role in fighting cancer. Though the HIV and hepatitis viruses replicate within the host cell, from the time of transmission of the virus to the time of infection of the host cell, the pathogen is outside the cell and vulnerable to antibody-mediated mechanisms of pathogen neutralization and killing. Antibody binding to gp120, the viral protein which mediates adsorption and entry of the human immunodeficiency virus (HIV) into the host cell, can interrupt viral entry into the cell. Hepatitis B virus can be stopped by neutralizing antibody to the hepatitis B surface antigen. In fact, the cytotoxic T lymphocyte response may not always be desired. Too many killed host cells can result in organ failure, as has been proposed when a strong cytotoxic T lymphocyte response is directed against the liver of a

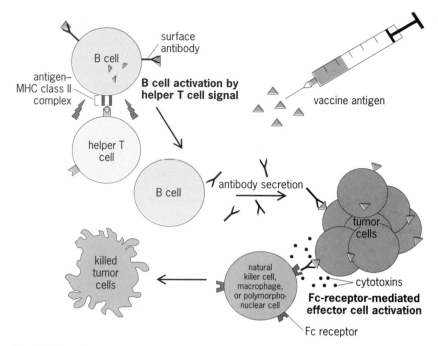

Fig. 2. Killing of tumor cells by antibody-dependent cell-mediated toxicity. Vaccine antigen is taken up by the antigen-presenting cell, which is represented here by a B cell. The surface antibody on the B cell binds the antigen and pulls it into the cell, where it enters the MHC class II processing and presentation pathway. A helper T cell then recognizes the processed antigen–MHC class II complex on the surface of the antigen-presenting cell (B cell) and releases a signal to activate the B cell. The B cell goes on to secrete antibody specific for the vaccine antigen. Antibody bound to the surface of tumor cells can bind an effector cell (such as a natural killer cell, a macrophage, or a polymorphonuclear cell) via Fc receptors on the effector cell surface. This antibody-Fc receptor interaction activates the effector cell to secrete cytotoxins that destroy the tumor cells.

hepatitis-virus-infected individual. In cancer elimination, a cytotoxic T lymphocyte response is highly desired; however, antibody can also mediate cancer cell killing via ADCC.

Current developments. Since memory has to be established before destruction of the pathogen by the cellular or humoral arm of the immune response can occur, the process may take long enough to allow a strong pathogen to establish itself within the host and cause disease. This is where vaccination comes into play. Vaccination provides a safe means of exposure to antigens so that the immune system can generate a memory response long before a natural encounter with the pathogen occurs. In a vaccinated individual, once a pathogen enters the body, the T cells are seeing antigen for the second time and immediately begin killing the infected cell. This eliminates the time span required to generate a memory response and reduces the chances that a pathogen will have enough time to cause disease before it is destroyed.

Subunit vaccines using components of the pathogen as antigen have been genetically engineered. Live vector vaccines are made up of a live bacterium or virus that has been modified so it cannot cause disease, but contains pathogen proteins or genes encoding these proteins which can then be expressed in the host. A more recently described vaccination strategy, termed genetic immunization or DNA (deoxyribonucleic acid) vaccines, utilizes nucleic acids which encode the antigens of the pathogen as a means of inducing an immune response. Prime-boost strategies have been used where a live vector or DNA vaccine is used to prime the immune response, and boosters are given with a subunit vaccine. Based on their composition, recombinant subunit vaccines predominantly invoke humoral immune responses and antibody-based mechanisms of immunity (Fig. 2). Unless modified to access MHC class I pathways, subunit vaccines induce little to no cytotoxic T lymphocyte responses. Live-vector-based vaccines can induce both humoral and cell-mediated responses. They have been used primarily to induce cytotoxic T lymphocyte responses, as the level of the antibody response when compared to recombinant subunit approaches is reduced. DNA vaccines can also generate antibody and cytotoxic T lymphocyte responses; the level of each of these immune responses is dependent on the nature of the vaccine and the expression of the gene encoding the vaccine antigen in particular cell types. Each of these strategies has advantages and disadvantages that become considerations in developing a particular vaccine preparation.

HIV and AIDS. A number of different HIV vaccine strategies have been examined, and some have been evaluated in human clinical trials. The first human clinical trial on an HIV vaccine occurred in 1987 and employed a recombinant subunit approach. Since that time, a number of approaches have been tested. The most promising strategies include livevector, DNA, and recombinant subunit approaches either alone or in combination. The goal of these approaches is to induce both antibody and cytotoxic T lymphocyte responses specific for various HIV antigens. Some of these approaches are in their last stage of human testing. However, it remains to be determined whether there will be an effective HIV vaccine that prevents AIDS in the near future.

Hepatitis. A number of viruses have been identified that cause hepatitis, a disease affecting the liver in humans. They include hepatitis A, B, C, D, E, and G viruses. Hepatitis A and E viruses cause an acute, self-limiting infection that is transmitted by the oral-fecal route and includes contaminated food and water. Rarely is infection by hepatitis A and E viruses life-threatening; these pathogens have not been associated with chronic hepatitis, liver disease, or liver cancer. A vaccine for hepatitis A virus is available. However, it is hepatitis B and C viruses that have been responsible for most cases of chronic viral hepatitis and liver disease. Both of these viruses have been associated with primary hepatocellular carcinoma, a form of liver cancer. These pathogens are transmitted by contaminated blood proteins, intravenous drug use, and unprotected sexual activities. The first subunit vaccine for hepatitis B virus employed the hepatitis B surface antigen and was licensed for use in 1981. An improved recombinant hepatitis B surface antigen subunit vaccine was developed, and mandated vaccination of newborns has decreased the incidence of hepatitis B virus infection in developed countries. With this vaccine, it appears that antibodies to hepatitis B surface antigen are primarily responsible for protection from infection and disease. Hepatitis B surface antigen vaccination has also resulted in hepatitis C virus infection becoming the number one causative agent of chronic viral hepatitis. Unfortunately, hepatitis C virus presents vaccine developers with similar problems observed in HIV vaccine development and testing. Many of the approaches utilized in an attempt to develop vaccines against HIV are also being used in hepatitis C virus vaccine development. These include recombinant subunit, live-vector, and DNA vaccination approaches. There are presently no vaccines available for hepatitis C virus, and the evaluation of vaccine strategies is in the early stages of human testing.

Cancer. In many kinds of cancer, vaccines may be an appropriate form of therapy. These include viral induced cancers where the viral antigen is expressed on the cancer cell and represents a tumor-specific target antigen for vaccination. This viral encoded tumor antigen is seen by the host as foreign. Other forms of cancer include tumors that are not sensitive to chemotherapy and radiation therapy and are difficult to completely remove by surgery. These latter types of cancer can overexpress certain antigens, referred to as tumor-associated antigens, on their cancer cells. Tumor-associated antigens may also be expressed on normal host cells, but at lower levels. Because of the expression on normal host cells, tumor-associated antigens may not be recognized by the immune system as foreign. Vaccination strategies attempt to induce immune responses against either tumor-specific or tumor-associated antigens after the tumor cells are already present. This approach has been termed therapeutic vaccination. It differs from the situation with pathogens where vaccination occurs before exposure; this approach is termed prophylactic vaccination. Yet, in instances where a pathogen causes a chronic infection or disease because the immune system has not been adequately activated, or has been activated to inappropriate antigens or the pathogen, therapeutic vaccination represents a modality for treating chronic infection. In cancer, when a risk factor such as infection with a certain type of virus has been identified, prophylactic vaccination could be used to prevent rather than treat the cancer. There are presently a number of latter-stage human clinical trials that are evaluating therapeutic vaccine strategies against several different types of cancer.

Summary. Vaccines and vaccine strategies have come a long way since they were first developed. They have been successful in preventing a number of infectious diseases that cause morbidity and mortality in humans and animals alike. Some of these vaccines have even been responsible for the eradication of certain diseases. However, when it comes to certain viruses and forms of cancer that can evade the host immune responses, the success of vaccines has been limited. Understanding continues to increase about what components of the acquired immune response are important for immunity and how pathogens and cancer cells can evade the immune response. Undoubtedly, the development and testing of new vaccination strategies that can target specific immunity and address issues related to evasion will continue to be active areas of research. Vaccines may not be applicable to every disease condition, but they will still play a major role in disease prevention and treatment in the future.

For background information *see* ACQUIRED IMMUNE DEFICIENCY SYNDROME; ANTIBODY; ANTIGEN; ANTIGEN-ANTIBODY REACTION; CANCER (MEDICINE); CELLULAR IMMUNOLOGY; HEPATITIS; IMMUNOLOGY; VACCINATION in the McGraw-Hill Encyclopedia of Science & Technology.

A. M. Watts; M. H. Shearer; R. K. Bright; R. C. Kennedy

Bibliography. C. A. Janeway et al., *Immunobiology: The Immune System in Health and Disease*, 4th ed., Garland Publishing, London, 1998; S. A. Plotkin and E. A. Mortimer, Jr., *Vaccine*, 2d ed., W. B. Saunders, 1994; D. B. Weiner and R. C. Kennedy, Genetic vaccines, *Sci. Amer.*, 281:50–57, 1999.

Very Large Telescope

The Very Large Telescope (VLT) will be a ground-based, optical and infrared telescope, operated by the European Southern Observatory (ESO), with the greatest collecting area and the highest angular resolving power of any such instrument in the world. It will be equipped with advanced imaging and spectroscopic instruments.

Initiatives aiming at the realization of a large European telescope started in the late 1970s. The basic design of the Very Large Telescope was thoroughly discussed among European astronomers in the early 1980s. Based on a detailed concept and an associated financial plan for the construction and the subsequent operation of the Very Large Telescope, the ESO Council approved the project in 1987.

Fig. 1. Paranal platform with components of the Very Large Telescope. The Control Building is in the foreground. The railway tracks on which the 1.8-m (6-ft) telescopes for the VLT Interferometer will move and the individual observing stations are visible.

The Very Large Telescope forms a part of an integrated capability. While the most visible components are installed at Paranal Observatory (**Fig. 1**) in northern Chile, many related activities take place at the ESO Headquarters in Garching, Germany. Thus, while the actual observations are made at Paranal, the preparation of blocks of observing time, subsequent data handling and archiving, and continued development of improved instrumentation and initiation of new programs take place at the ESO Headquarters.

The Very Large Telescope consists of a large number of components. Chief among these are the four unit telescopes (**Fig. 2**), each of which is equipped with an 8.2-m (27-ft) monolithic Zerodur mirror. These telescopes are housed in specially designed enclosures which contribute to the optimization of observing conditions and protect them from adverse environmental influences. Unit telescope 1 (Antu, the Sun, in the Mapuche language of the indigenous people) saw "first light" in May 1998, followed by unit telescope 2 (Kueyen, the Moon) in March 1999, and unit telescope 3 (Melipal, the Southern Cross) in January 2000. The fourth unit telescope (Yepun, Sirius) is scheduled to see first light at the end of 2000.

Some of the main scientific tasks are vested in the Very Large Telescope Interferometer which, in addition to the unit telescopes, includes a number of smaller movable telescopes which can be placed at various positions on the observatory platform in order to form different interferometric configurations (**Fig. 3**).

The location of the observatory in a very remote area has necessitated the construction of a complete infrastructure at Paranal. This includes the auxiliary buildings (maintenance, staff quarters, and so forth) as well as the interconnection of these (roads, electrical cabling, and water). Paranal is connected to the other ESO installations, in particular the headquarters in Garching, by means of a permanent satellite link for data transmission and communications.

The main advantages of the Very Large Telescope are the size of its optical surface (more than 200 m² or 2000 ft², more than any other telescope in the world); the very high angular resolution achievable, in particular with the Very Large Telescope Interferometer (about 0.001 arcsecond at a wavelength of 1 μm); as well as the excellent observing conditions at Paranal (the large number of clear nights, very good seeing conditions, and low atmospheric water vapor content). A main design goal for the Very Large Telescope has been to take the fullest advantage of all of these features.

Main elements. The main mirrors (M1, M2, and M3) of each unit telescope have been manufactured to extremely tight specifications. Together they ensure the excellent optical characteristics of the Very Large Telescope in terms of available field of view and angular resolution. This capability is supported by the incorporation of an advanced active optics system that controls the shape of the 8.2-m (27-ft) primary mirror and the positioning of the 1.1-m (3.6-ft) secondary mirror.

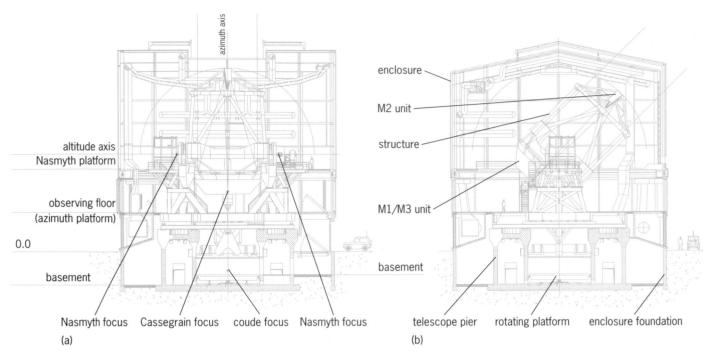

Fig. 2. Sectional views of one unit telescope of the Very Large Telescope, showing the main components. (*a*) Front view. (*b*) Side view.

In addition, adaptive optics at the Nasmyth and coudé foci will significantly improve the image quality, first at near- and mid-infrared wavelengths, and later, as more advanced technologies become available, at progressively shorter wavelengths. In support of this capability, and to enable adaptive-optics-supported observations over a large part of the sky, one of the unit telescopes will be equipped with a sodium-laser guide-star facility.

Optics. Each of the 8.2-m (25-ft) telescopes has four foci; two Nasmyth foci, one Cassegrain focus, and one coudé focus (Fig. 2). The Cassegrain focus is located behind the prime mirror (M1) and within the cell that actively supports it. The Nasmyth foci

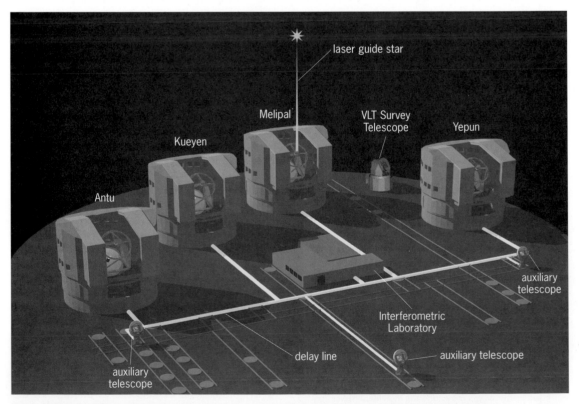

Fig. 3. Unit and auxiliary telescopes of the Very Large Telescope and their linkage in the VLT Interferometer.

are located on observing platforms on either side of the horizontal axis of the telescope structure and are able to carry very heavy instruments. The coudé focus is obtained by transferring one of the Nasmyth foci to a location in the telescope basement by means of a relay system consisting of a train of mirrors. From the coudé focus the light can be sent to the interferometric focus.

Great Technological advances in manufacturing the four 8.2-m (27-ft) Zerodur blanks and in the subsequent polishing process have ensured that the performance of these mirrors is well within the strict specifications established by the ESO. The secondary (M2) mirrors of beryllium are of extremely light-weight design, so that it is possible to control and change their position at high frequency, for instance during infrared observations. The elliptical tertiary (M3) mirror of Zerodur is exceedingly flat, and is used to divert light to the Nasmyth and coudé foci.

Both the Cassegrain and Nasmyth foci are equipped with adapter-rotators, which form the mechanical interface between the telescope and the astronomical instruments. The adapters have various supporting functions, including accurate guiding during the observations. The rotators are necessary, because the focal fields will rotate during observations due to the altitude-azimuth mounting of the telescope.

Main mirror cell and tertiary tower. The main mirror cell, a welded metal structure that is attached to the bottom end of the telescope tube, supports the 8.2-m (27-ft) primary mirror. The mirror is held in place by axial and lateral supports. Some of these supports are computer-controlled (that is, by active optics), and together they ensure that the large, flexible mirror retains its optimal shape under the changing gravitational forces that it experiences during the motion of the telescope.

The cell structure is a complex mechanical system, which has been manufactured in an innovative way, ensuring a very high stiffness-to-weight ratio. The Cassegrain focus is located inside the cell.

The tertiary mirror assembly is on a tower approximately 2.5 m (8.2 ft) above the primary mirror. Like the main mirror cell, the tertiary tower contains a number of electromechanical systems that ensure optical alignment during operation of the telescope. A mechanism at the top of the tower is used to move the mirror away from the optical path when the instrument at the Cassegrain focus is used.

Secondary mirror unit. The secondary mirror unit is a fairly complex, opto-mechanical system consisting of the light mirror of beryllium and its support. It allows the mirror to move in different directions with a total of $5°$ of freedom for focusing, centering, and pointing. In this respect, the unit forms an integral part of the active optics system and is therefore crucial for the optimization of the astronomical observations.

The mirror assembly includes a chopping system, allowing rapid oscillations. This enables the telescope to point at two adjacent sky fields in quick succession, a capability that is of particular importance for infrared observations.

Main structure. The unit-telescope main structure provides a stable mounting for the optical components and the focal instruments. It is a classical altitude azimuth mount, which stands about 20 m (65 ft) tall and has a total weight of 430 metric tons (474 short tons). It allows the optics to point to specified celestial objects and to track them during their diurnal motion by rotating the telescope about two axes.

The structure has two components, the fork and the tube. The fork is supported by hydrostatic pads moving on two concentric tracks fixed to the telescope foundations, whereby the structure rotates around a vertical axis. The tube is supported on two bearings at the telescope centerpiece which allow it to point from zenith to the horizon.

On either side of the structure are the two Nasmyth platforms that provide access to and support the large Nasmyth instruments. Within these is a coudé tube that protects the light beam deflected toward the coudé focus (when in use).

Instrumentation. The Very Large Telescope will be equipped with a number of advanced, innovative astronomical instruments with which observations can be performed in a large number of domains and modes. Most of these instruments will remain fixed at a particular telescope focus, thus avoiding time-consuming instrumental exchanges and guaranteeing long-term stability and efficient calibration.

The spectral region of observation ranges from the ultraviolet (300 nm) to the mid-infrared (25 μm). The achievable spectral resolutions range from low (a few 100) to very high (100,000 or more).

Interferometry. From the outset, the Very Large Telescope was conceived as an array which would make it possible to observe in the interferometric mode. The Very Large Telescope Interferometer (Fig. 3) will consist of the four 8.2-m (27-ft) unit telescopes and several smaller 1.8-m (6-ft) auxiliary telescopes, which will move on tracks (Fig. 1). They can be placed at 30 different stations, thus ensuring the most complete possible interferometric images. The scientific goals include the search for extrasolar planets, the study of star formation and early stellar evolution, the monitoring of stellar surface structures, and investigations of the central 0.1 parsec of the Milky Way Galaxy as well as active galactic nuclei elsewhere.

The various subsystems needed to implement the interferometer include the unit-telescope coudé trains, which will direct the beams from the telescopes toward the delay lines in the interferometric tunnels. The auxiliary telescopes will be equipped in a similar way. The delay lines will equalize the optical path length differences and transfer the images from the telescopes to the interferometric laboratory. The stability requirements are extremely critical but technically feasible.

The interferometer will be equipped with three focal instruments at the Interferometric Laboratory. They will operate in different modes, including high-resolution imaging and spectroscopy as well as astrometry with microarcsecond precision.

For background information *see* ADAPTIVE OPTICS; ASTROMETRY; ASTRONOMICAL OBSERVATORY; ASTRONOMICAL SPECTROSCOPY; INTERFEROMETRY; OPTICAL TELESCOPE; TELESCOPE in the McGraw-Hill Encyclopedia of Science & Technology.

Michael Naumann; Richard West

Bibliography. *ESO Annual Report*, pp. 34–46, 1998; *ESO Messenger*, published quarterly.

Volcano

Progress in the science of volcanology tends to be episodic and governed by accidents of nature—the volcanic eruptions themselves. Although recent years have not been marked by events as dramatic as those of Mount St. Helens in 1980 or Pinatubo in 1991, for the first time several submarine eruptions have been monitored. Further, ongoing eruptions at Kilauea since 1983 and Montserrat since 1994 have provided unprecedented opportunity to monitor eruptive processes and the underground movement of magma. In addition to this progress based upon direct observation, numerical and analog experiments have led to breakthroughs in understanding the mechanisms of explosive eruptions. Finally, recent symposia on the nature of ocean island volcanism and long lava flows have resulted in advanced understanding of those phenomena.

Ocean island volcanism. Several features at Hawaii and other ocean island volcanoes have led to the recognition of new types of hazards that had not been anticipated. Sector collapse has now been identified at most ocean islands, involving landslides of hundreds to thousands of square kilometers. These failures may be catastrophic or gradual, as at Kilauea currently, where the Global Positioning System (GPS) and other geodetic techniques have documented that its south flank is moving seaward about 10 cm (4 in.) per year. These giant landslides are direct hazards, and they may cause tsunamis that overwhelm nearby coastal areas. Although the principal hazard at ocean islands was long thought to be property damage by lava flows, large explosive eruptions have now been documented on Kilauea, Iceland, the Canary Islands, and the Galápagos.

Ocean island volcanoes provide the most comprehensive evidence for the composition of the Earth's mantle and indirect evidence of its dynamics (**Fig. 1**). The prevailing theory is that ocean island basalts originate from mantle plumes that in turn derive from oceanic lithosphere that subducted over a billion years ago. Although this theory was proposed nearly 20 years ago, new trace-element studies along with oxygen and osmium isotopic data are providing confirming evidence. Details are being worked out on the types and amount of ancient sediments, gabbro, and subduction-zone processing involved. In addition to these details, a question remains as to where the ancient lithosphere resides—at the 660-km (410-mi) seismic discontinuity or at the base of the mantle. Another paradox is that helium isotopic studies indicate a significant lower-mantle contribution to ocean island basalts, in addition to the ancient subducted lithosphere. Recent studies of the distribution of ocean island volcanoes and seamounts on the Pacific plate have renewed questions about the fixity of hot spots by demonstrating relative movements between at least some chains (especially Marquesas, Pitcairn, Society, and Macdonald). This suggests that models of absolute plate motion that depend on the alignments and ages of all ocean island chains may be incorrect, because the sources of some intraplate volcanoes apparently wander. Alternatively, they could indicate that intraplate deformation simply blurs the record by displacing the site of active volcanism in the vicinity of fixed hot spots. The issue is controversial.

Submarine eruptions. Although the majority of the world's volcanoes are submarine, there has been no direct observation of a deep submarine eruption. However, rapid responses to several recent submarine eruptions have permitted volcanologists to inspect the immediate aftereffects of submarine volcanism. One submarine eruption was from Loihi seamount off Hawaii in 1996. The eruption was first revealed by an earthquake swarm recorded by land-based instruments. Sonobuoys, ocean-bottom seismometers, and water-sampling devices were deployed as soon as possible to measure the effects of the eruption. Inspection from deep submersibles revealed that a new pit crater had collapsed, and the eruption produced glassy breccias from a separate vent. The composition of the glasses revealed that Loihi's magmatic system is evolving historically just as it had prehistorically. New age-dating techniques involving short-lived isotopes in the actinide decay chain were used to constrain the eruption time to within a few weeks. Even more should be learned from the next eruption, because real-time monitoring instruments are now deployed on the sea floor at Loihi.

Since 1993, the U.S. Navy Sound Surveillance System has detected three eruptions in real time along the Juan de Fuca and Gorda ridges off the west coast of the United States. Each of these eruptions has produced lava flows and intense hot-spring activity. The

Fig. 1. Fire fountaining from a vent on the flank of Cerro Azul Volcano in the Galápagos Islands during the September 1998 eruption. Vent height is approximately 100 m (330 ft). (*Courtesy of Rachel Ellisor*)

most recent of these submarine eruptions was in 1998 at Axial seamount, a hot-spot volcano on the Juan de Fuca Ridge. This eruption represents a breakthrough in submarine research, because for the first time monitoring instruments were in place at a submarine eruptive site. In addition to the eruption of lava flows, the eruption was accompanied by major dike intrusion along 50–60 km (31–37 mi) of the rift. The documentation of the eruption was unequivocal, because lava enveloped some of the instruments previously deployed on the sea floor. It was discovered that the volcano behaves similarly to subaerial volcanoes, with catastrophic deflation during effusion of the magma and dike emplacement. In this case, the caldera dropped over 3 m (10 ft). The New Millennium Observatory has recently been deployed on Axial seamount, and is providing real-time monitoring of the volcano.

Emplacement of lava flows. The emplacement of long (tens to hundreds of kilometers) lava flows has been enigmatic: their dimensions seemed to require enormous emplacement rates, which in turn dictate turbulent flow and rapid cooling. Recent field studies on active flows suggest instead that sheetlike lavas are emplaced as laminar flows that develop an upper crust and then inflate from within. Thus, the crust insulates the flow interior, requiring smaller eruption rates to attain great length. This style of flow is thermally efficient, and such a mechanism may also be typical of submarine sheet flows by minimizing the cooling effects of water. Field and modeling studies of tube-fed flows have shown that they are also more thermally efficient than had been supposed and can attain great lengths. Moreover, field evidence has shown that tube-fed flows can erode into their bases. This insight will have important consequences in modeling efforts and interpretation of ancient and planetary lavas.

The implications of these findings are exceedingly important to studies of flood basalts. Eruption rates of the Roza member of the Columbia River Basalts are now estimated to be on order of 1000–10,000 m³/s (35,000–35,000 ft³/s), similar to rates of a historical eruption in Iceland but much higher than those of recent Hawaiian eruptions. At these rates, emplacement of the Roza member would have taken more than 14 years. This interpretation is not universally accepted: other evidence suggests that the flows were channelized, cooled quickly, and emplaced over the course of weeks to months.

The morphological distinction between pahoehoe and aa lava flows (both have the same composition but vary in appearance) continues to be an important topic of lava flow research. Case studies demonstrate that the principal control must be differences in the rheological properties of the magma, especially changes that accompany cooling, effervescence, and partial crystallization: aa has a higher density of microlites and fewer, more deformed vesicles than pahoehoe lavas, even when they are products of the same eruption (**Fig. 2**). The rheological transformation in turn must be due to the compositions of the magma and the thermal evolution during eruption and flow.

Explosive eruptions and pyroclastic flows. Explosive eruptions present the greatest volcanic hazards, owing to their sudden nature and widespread effects. After the explosive mixture of gas, ash, and pumice exits the vent, the mixture can be less dense than the atmosphere and rise as a buoyant plume, or if it is denser, it will flow across the ground in pyroclastic flows. Because of their potentially huge size, high temperature, and velocity, pyroclastic flows are extremely hazardous and are the focus of intensive research. Such was the case at Mount Pinatubo, and an important volume (C. G. Newhall and R. S. Punongbayan, eds.) was published based on the unprecedented observations and measurements made there during the 1991 eruption and afterward. Scaled analog experiments and numerical modeling of pyroclastic flows have increased the understanding of the mechanisms of magma fragmentation, flow, deposition, and the effects of topographic barriers. It is still not fully understood whether the flows travel as dilute, inflated turbulent clouds or as fluidized, denser masses. Whether the flows stop and deposit their load en masse or progressively aggradate also remains controversial, as the field evidence and modeling constraints are equivocal. Buoyant plumes are becoming better understood and were the subject of a major treatise (R. S. J. Sparks and others) that

Fig. 2. Lava flow in the Galápagos Islands, with aa lava in the background and pahoehoe lava in the foreground. The hammer suggests scale. (*Courtesy of Rachel Ellisor*)

provides a state-of-the-art theoretical analysis of these plumes and deposition from them. These predictive models will surely result in better preparedness and reduction of hazards from pyroclastic fallout. This is especially important for air travel above volcanic regions.

Volcano deformation. Technological advances are likely to lead to major advance in the understanding of volcano deformation. In particular, after pioneering studies at Kilauea and Etna, GPS instruments are being deployed on many of the world's restless volcanoes. GPS instruments are capable of measuring movements of less than a centimeter both vertically and horizontally. Basaltic shield volcanoes are shown to inflate slowly and steadily over years as magma intrudes and fills a shallow magma chamber. During eruptions, volcanoes can deflate catastrophically as the magma pressure inside the volcano decreases over the course of hours. Results from stratovolcanoes and silicic calderas are not nearly so clear, possibly due to more active hydrothermal systems and deeper magma chambers. Costs of monitoring instruments are decreasing, so continuous real-time arrays are becoming viable. Time-series data are important, especially when combined with seismic monitoring, because they can capture intrusion events which will lead to better understanding of the mechanics of magma intrusion.

For background information *see* ASH; BASALT; BRECCIA; CALDERA; LANDSLIDE; LAVA; LITHOSPHERE; MAGMA; PUMICE; PYROCLASTIC ROCKS; SEISMOLOGY; VOLCANO; VOLCANOLOGY in the McGraw-Hill Encyclopedia of Science & Technology.

Dennis J. Geist; Rachel Ellisor

Bibliography. K. Cashman, H. Pinkerton, and J. Stephenson, Special section on long lava flows, *J. Geophys. Res.*, 103:27281–27566, 1998; C. G. Newhall and R. S. Punongbayan, *Fire and Mud: Eruptions and Lahars of Mount Pinatubo, Philippines*, University of Washington Press, Seattle, 1996; R. S. J. Sparks et al., *Volcanic Plumes*, Wiley, New York, 1997.

Waterjet

Although propelling a ship with a waterjet can be considered a more modern method than with a conventional propeller, the idea behind it is an old one. In 1631 David Ramsey was awarded an English patent for his idea of propelling a ship with the working principle of modern waterjet propulsion systems. In 1687, Isaac Newton in his *Philosophiae naturalis principia mathematica* formulated the laws of science that are applicable to Ramsey's idea.

Layout and basic principle. The waterjet can be divided into three major sections: the inlet duct; the pump unit consisting of impeller, stator, and nozzle; and the steering assembly (**Fig. 1**). The inlet duct guides the water toward the pump unit and transfers the speed or kinetic energy of the water flow into pressure or potential energy in front of the pump face. The impeller, driven by the prime mover, increases this available potential energy with the pressure increase resulting from the pump head. After the water flow has passed the stator blades, which take out the rotation caused by the rotating impeller, the water jets out to atmospheric conditions through the nozzle. The potential energy that was available in the form of pressure is transformed in the nozzle to kinetic energy.

With the steering assembly, this kinetic energy can be used for steering and reversing the ship. The steering and reversing section is not always required; a jet without a steering assembly is referred to as a booster jet.

Laws of science. Newton's second law defines the relation between a force exercised on a mass and the resulting acceleration: Force = mass × acceleration. The water flowing through the jet can be identified as the mass, while the acceleration is determined by the difference between the speed with which the water enters the propulsion system at the start of the inlet duct and the higher speed with which it exits at the nozzle. The force that is required to accomplish the acceleration is put into the system by the impeller that is driven by a prime mover such as a diesel engine, gas turbine, or electric engine.

Newton's third law says that every action results in an opposite and equal reaction. In other words, the force or action used for the acceleration of the water will result in an equal and opposite reaction force that is transferred via the waterjet construction to the ship. It is this force that propels the ship forward. A waterjet propulsion system can be classified as a reaction propeller and can be placed in the same category as jet and rocket engines, with the difference being the fluid that is used.

Waterjet size selection. Selecting the optimum waterjet size for a ship's design conditions is an iterative process with the objective of finding the jet size that gives the optimum efficiency with minimum weight and dimensions at an acceptable cavitation load of the impeller. Cavitation can occur when the pressure of the fluid is at any point reduced to the vapor pressure and vapor bubbles are formed. If these vapor bubbles come into an area of higher pressure and implode near the impeller surface, the energy released from these implosions will cause erosion damage of the impeller surface. The first step in the waterjet size selection process is calculating the initial pressure available in the inlet duct from the inlet duct efficiency, the ship's speed, and the ship's length. This pressure is referred to as the net positive suction head available or [NPSH(A)]. Due to its dependence on the usually fixed design parameters such as the ship's speed and length, it is a fixed value and therefore the starting point of the selection process.

The optimum waterjet size can now be selected by comparing the requirements for the net positive suction head of various waterjet sizes [NPSH(R)] with the NPSH(A). If for instance the NPSH(R) of a random selected waterjet size is too high, that is, the

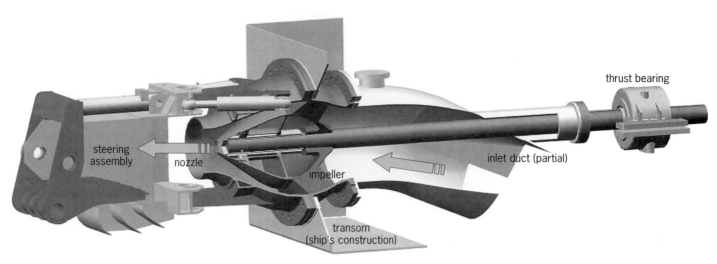

Fig. 1. The waterjet.

particular waterjet size requires that a higher initial NPSH be available, a larger waterjet with a lower NPSH(R) has to be selected.

The NPSH(R) of a pump and its size are related through the power density (ratio of input power to impeller surface). A jet with a high power density will turn at a relatively high speed and will cause a relatively large decrease of the NPSH(A); in other words, it requires a high initial net positive suction head. If the size of the waterjet is increased, the impeller surface will increase and through that the power density, and thus the requirement for the net positive suction head is lowered. For the optimum waterjet size, the NPSH(R) and the NPSH(A) are in balance and match the operating conditions of the ship.

Steering and reversing. Through a waterjet built into today's common ferry flows an average 19 m^3/s (5000 gallons/s) of water, jetting out of the nozzle with a speed of about 30 m/s (98 ft/s). This massive beam of water can be used for steering and reversing the vessel. To accomplish this, a steering assembly is mounted behind the nozzle. This steering assembly can be rotated sideways with the use of hydraulic cylinders (**Fig. 2a**). By doing so, the beam of water is bent off, resulting in a reaction force that is transferred to the ship via the waterjet construction. For reversing, a reversing plate is mounted inside the steering assembly. When the reversing plate is moved into an upright position, the beam of water is reversed and flows out the bottom of the steering assembly in the opposite direction (Fig. 2b).

Advantages of waterjet propulsion. There are several advantages of waterjet propulsion compared to a conventional propeller, with the most important being the higher efficiency for speeds above approximately 30 knots (55 km/h) and the high possible power densities for the impeller [up to 10,000 kW/m^2 ≈ 8400 kW/yd^2; 1 m^2 (≈1.2 yd^2) driven by 5000 kW has a power density of 5000 kW/m^2 (≈4200 kW/yd^2)]. Furthermore, appendices such as rudders (steering is integrated in the waterjet itself) and shaft struts are not required. Due to their

absence and thus the clean hull, the resistance of the ship can be significantly lower, especially at the high speeds common for waterjet-propelled vessels. Another reason for choosing a waterjet can be shallow-water operation. Unlike a conventional propeller mounted on a shaft protruding under a ship's base, the waterjet installation is located entirely above the baseline and forms an integral part of the aftship (**Fig. 3**).

Applications. The waterjet-driven vessels of today are primarily used for fast transportation. With speeds of 35–45 knots (65–83 km/h), they are gradually replacing some of the slower conventional propeller-driven ferries. Ships with speeds of 60–75 knots (110–140 km/h) are expected in the near future, and will possibly offer an alternative for

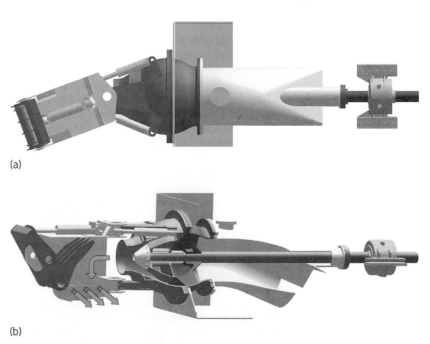

(a)

(b)

Fig. 2. Steering assembly that can be rotated sideways with the use of hydraulic cylinders. (a) Steering. (b) Reversing.

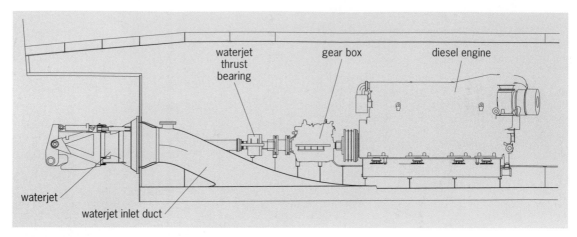

Fig. 3. Installation of a waterjet in a ship's hull.

commuter traffic in areas where highways are congested. Furthermore, fast cargo transport over the oceans will probably narrow the gap between airfreight and the conventional container vessel. With the increase in speed and the development of fast cargo transportation, the gas turbine will strengthen its current modest position in the fast ferry industry. Fast container vessels equipped with five waterjets, each driven by a 50-MW gas turbine, are under development and will probably enter service by 2005. The waterjet industry is still very much in development.

Research and development. With the anticipation of ship speeds rising to 75 knots (140 km/h) in the near future and with the possible next step to 100 knots (185 km/h) or more, the flow phenomena in the inlet duct are increasingly important. The inlet duct plays a vital role for the waterjet, and it has to ensure that the velocity distribution of the flow field in front of the pump face is as uniform as possible. Advanced computational fluid dynamics (CFD) software is used to model the flow through the inlet and to predict when unwanted effects such as flow separation and cavitation occur. Other research and development efforts are focused on the optimization of the inlet duct efficiency and the reduction of the weight of the entire waterjet installation with the use of advanced materials. However, reliability remains an important issue, and given the hostile sea environment and the usually high power densities, today's waterjets are still almost entirely constructed from stainless steel plates with parts such as impellers cast from duplex, an austenitic-ferritic steel ($\sim$22% chromium, $\sim$5% nickel), whose high mechanical strength and resistance to corrosion cracking in seawater, general corrosion, and pitting and crevice corrosion make it a good material for this environment.

For background information *see* BOAT PROPULSION; CAVITATION; COMPUTATIONAL FLUID DYNAMICS; FERRY; JET PROPULSION; MARINE ENGINE; PROPELLER (MARINE CRAFT); PROPULSION; SHIP POWERING AND STEERING in the McGraw-Hill Encyclopedia of Science & Technology.   Johan Huber

Bibliography. J. S. Carlton, *Marine Propellers and Propulsion*, Butterworth-Heinemann, 1994; *5th International Conference on Fast Sea Transportation—Fast '99*, Seattle, August 31–September 2, 1999; *International Conference on Waterjet Propulsion—Latest Developments*, Amsterdam, October 22–23, 1998; *16th Fast Ferry International Conference*, Nice, France, February 2000.

Wavelets

Wavelet transforms are a relatively new mathematical tool, extensively used for signal analysis because of their capability to extract from a signal information localized in time and frequency (or space and scale). They offer a powerful technique for studying unsteady or chaotic phenomena. Indeed, wavelet decomposition has been widely applied to the analysis of data taken in turbulent flows, with the aim of clarifying aspects correlated to the presence and influence of organized vortical structures (often called coherent structures) which, in fully turbulent conditions, cannot be analyzed in detail by numerical simulation or flow visualization. This topic is relevant for the so-called shear flows, such as jets and wakes, where coherent structures are directly responsible for mixing, advection, momentum, and mass transfer, and therefore are very important for many practical applications such as combustion, turbulence control and drag reduction, and noise emission and control. The wavelet transform has been applied also to image processing, and promising results have been achieved in the analysis of images obtained by optical measurements in fluid dynamic experiments. Since their introduction in the early 1980s by researchers working on seismic data, wavelet transforms have been used in a variety of fields (for example, in computer graphics, optics, structural vibrations, medicine, and bioengineering). Much research is in progress so that the limits of application of this powerful technique cannot be precisely defined yet.

Application in flow experiments. The physical interpretation of data obtained in fluid dynamic experiments is an objective which, unfortunately, can rarely be pursued by the direct analysis of the sequentially sampled signals, and is often a challenging task. It suffices to think of chaotic phenomena or turbulent flows to understand that the extraction of global deterministic properties may be quite difficult and sometimes impossible. It is therefore necessary to perform appropriate data manipulations, the procedure called signal analysis, in order to obtain as much physical information as possible. From a practical viewpoint, such manipulations are usually carried out by projecting the measured data, for example, a velocity time series, onto suitable basis functions. Given a time signal $f(t)$, the decomposition is given by Eq. (1), where the quantities w_i, given by Eq. (2), are the coefficients and the Ψ_i, are basis

$$f(t) = \sum_i w_i \Psi_i(t) \qquad (1)$$

$$w_i = \int f(t) * \Psi_i(t)\, dt \qquad (2)$$

functions. One of the most widely used methods for turbulence data analysis is the Fourier transform, which uses trigonometric basis functions, infinitely or widely extended in time. The main limitation of this decomposition is that even if details in the frequency domain are correctly retrieved, information on the time (or spatial) location of a particular frequency within the signal is completely lost. This follows directly from the uncertainty principle: good localization in frequency determines a loss of localization in the physical space, and vice versa. The limits of the Fourier decomposition might be overcome by the use of the wavelet transform where the basis function used is derived from translation (by a factor b) and dilatation (by a factor a) of an elementary function Ψ (the so-called mother wavelet), which is localized both in the physical space and in the frequency domain up to the uncertainty principle. The wavelet transform of a signal $f(t)$ is therefore given by Eq. (3).

$$w_{ab} = \int f(t) * \Psi[(t - b)/a]\, dt \qquad (3)$$

The wavelet adapts the width of its time slice according to the frequency components to be extracted, acting as a microscope which decomposes separately different frequencies: low frequencies (or large scales) are analyzed with coarse resolution, large frequencies (small scales) with finer resolution. The choice of the best wavelet basis is dictated mainly by the physical problem or the application to be studied. For example, the use of complex wavelets is usually dictated by the smoothness of the mother wavelet shape, or by the possibility of gaining additional information from the analysis of the phase of the complex wavelet coefficients, or by the redundancy of the coefficients obtained, which might be useful for image-compression algorithms. How-

ever, the latter property could be a problem when large amounts of data must be analyzed, so that, in these cases, orthonormal real wavelets are usually preferred. Whatever the type of wavelet adopted (complex, continuous, orthonormal, discrete, or in the form of packets), the possibility of a multiresolution analysis renders the wavelet transform very attractive for an application to the analysis of fluid dynamic data and in particular for chaotic or turbulent signals.

Turbulence and coherent structures. In a three-dimensional fully developed turbulent flow, the three velocity components associated to a generic fluid particle fluctuate randomly in time and space. A turbulent flow is also characterized by a cascade mechanism which brings energy from the large eddies to smaller and smaller ones down to the dissipative length scales, where energy is irreversibly dissipated into heat. Even if both the chaotic nature and the energy fragmentation of the process are correctly retrieved by the Fourier analysis, other important, and sometimes surprising, physical information is obtained by the application of the wavelet decomposition.

Of practical interest is the study of turbulence generated by jets issuing in still fluid or by the wake forming behind a body immersed within a fluid in relative motion. When a jet or a wake is in turbulent conditions, the vortical structures, clearly visualized in laminar conditions, are no longer observed and the flow appears as fully chaotic. An example of a velocity signal taken in a turbulent jet flow is shown in **Fig. 1a**. As expected, the velocity fluctuates randomly, and no deterministic contribution seems to be present. In Fig. 1b, the same velocity signal is examined with the wavelet transform. Here the local energy (squared wavelet coefficients) is shown. The presence of dark and light regions in the figure indicates that, even for fixed frequencies, the energy strongly fluctuates. This behavior, which is completely missed by the Fourier analysis, suggests that the chaotic nature of the flow is in some sense only apparent: localized deterministic objects are embedded within the fully chaotic background and induce localized but strong energy bursts at random temporal locations. This picture was confirmed by numerical simulations, which have shown that such objects are strong vortices whose shapes are statistically the same once the flow conditions are fixed. These structures are not space-filling but appear intermittently in time and space and significantly affect the vorticity (strictly correlated to the velocity gradients) and kinetic energy statistics, causing them to be strongly nongaussian. This behavior, except for the topological properties of the structures, characterizes any kind of turbulent flow, and jets and wakes in particular.

The wavelet transform may be used as a basis for constructing statistical procedures aimed at the extraction of averaged features. Such information is important for practical applications, since it elucidates global characteristics of the flow which do not

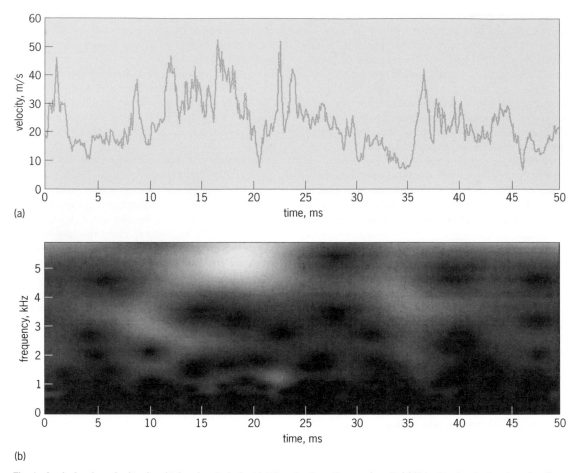

(a)

(b)

Fig. 1. Analysis of a velocity signal taken in a turbulent jet flow far from the nozzle exit. (*a*) Velocity signal, showing chaotic behavior with no periodic oscillations. (*b*) Local energy map, showing squared wavelet coefficients obtained by the wavelet transform of the signal. Lighter regions are high-energy regions localized in time and frequency.

depend significantly upon the initial conditions and therefore can be extended to broad classes of phenomena. As an example, for the case of shear flows, it has been found that the contribution of the localized bursts to the overall energy content of the flow is significant, indicating that the vortical structures, even if appearing randomly within the fluid, are capable of strongly influencing global physical properties.

By tracking the energy bursts and performing proper conditional statistics, it is also possible to retrieve the averaged time signature that coherent structures induce on the velocity signals during their passage through the probe used for the velocity measurements. This information is useful in understanding which types of structures are encountered (ring vortices, filaments, vorticity sheets, and so forth). Results obtained in experiments demonstrated that the averaged shape strongly depends on the turbulence generator, such as a jet, a wake, a grid, or a boundary layer. This dependence is indicated in **Fig. 2**, where examples of averaged signatures obtained in different flow conditions are shown. The time axis is normalized with respect to the dissipative time scale (usually named the Kolmogorov length or time scale) proper to each flow condition, whereas the velocity amplitudes are arbitrar-

ily rescaled in order for different plots to be better compared to each other. From the physical viewpoint, the differences among the three plots are important since they limit the application of the concept of universality, which is commonly associated to turbulence when its Fourier counterpart is considered.

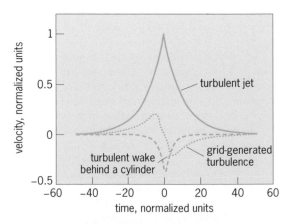

Fig. 2. Averaged time signatures of the velocity segments associated with the energy bursts obtained by the wavelet analysis of the velocity time series. The cases of various turbulence generators are shown.

An interesting application concerns the analysis of the destabilization mechanisms which characterize the spatial evolution of shear flows during the transition to turbulence. The most surprising result (**Fig. 3**) is that the destabilization processes usually observed in laminar conditions (where flow visualizations or numerical simulations successfully apply) may be extended to fully turbulent flows, provided the unsteady and intermittent nature of coherent structures is accounted for. In this sense, a new form of universality is recovered.

Image processing. Wavelet analysis has been applied in image processing mainly for data filtering and image compression. The first application derives directly from the selectivity properties of wavelets, which permit elimination of undesired noise effects usually encountered in particular locations within an image. This procedure is performed by eliminating or interpolating the wavelet coefficients corresponding to the location and the size of the noise disturbance. The second aspect is related to the fact that the manipulation of digital images in their raw form might be very expensive in terms of computer memory storage. The wavelet transform is then used as a method for reducing the amount of data associated to the image. Indeed, redundant information might be eliminated with special wavelet algorithms with no loss of quality in the resulting reconstructed image.

An example of the wavelet decomposition of an image obtained in a wake flow is shown in **Fig. 4**. A planar flow visualization was obtained in a jet flow issuing into a cross stream by positioning a laser sheet close to the nozzle exit and mixing the jet flow with fluorescein, a laser-sensitive dye. The lighter regions of Fig. 4 therefore correspond to the jet flow whereas the dark regions denote external flow belonging to the cross-stream. The acquired digitized picture (Fig. 4a) was decomposed by adopting a continuous complex mother wavelet of Mexican hat type (Fig. 4b–d). This choice was dictated by the simplicity and smoothness of the mother wavelet type as well as by the need for redundant coefficients which, for the case examined here, where the number of data samples is not sufficiently large, might help to obtain good resolution even at the coarsest scales. The image was transformed using the two-dimensional counterpart of the decomposition given in Eq. (3), so that the resulting coefficients are also bidimensional functions of the space. In connection with the selectivity properties of the wavelet transform, the two-dimensional maps of the wavelet coefficients permit the extraction of physical information regarding the contribution of structures of different size at the different scales and frequencies considered.

Prospects. The application of wavelet analysis to data obtained in real turbulent flows (both time series and two-dimensional images) offers numerous possibilities for the understanding of physical properties underlying the chaotic nature of turbulence, in particular for extracting new features regarding the role played by coherent structures. When

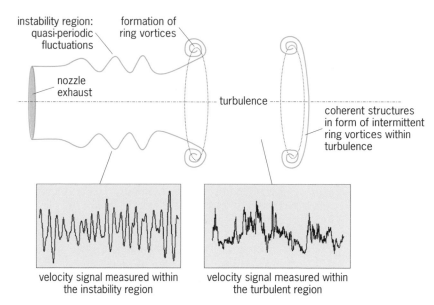

velocity signal measured within the instability region   velocity signal measured within the turbulent region

Fig. 3. Transitional features observed in a turbulent jet by the application of wavelet analysis. This behavior in turbulent conditions unexpectedly resembles that observed in the transition of laminar jets, but instantaneous visualizations of the jet flow in such conditions fail to reveal any of the transitional stages shown here.

a flow is fully turbulent, these vortices appear rarely within the fully chaotic background but, due to their high degree of energy, strongly influence the overall properties of the turbulent flow, and therefore are quite important. The use of wavelets has helped to show that any shear flow is characterized by the presence of organized structures whose topological

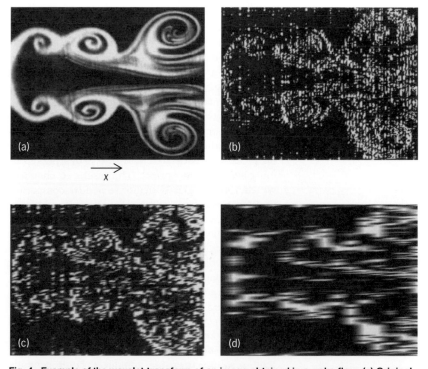

Fig. 4. Example of the wavelet transform of an image obtained in a wake flow. (a) Original image, which was treated by a wavelet transform along the x axis. (b–d) Wavelet coefficients with decreasing resolution. By changing the resolution, the peak values of the coefficients (lighter regions) are associated with different regions. The wavelet transform therefore gives useful information on the localization (both in space and in terms of resolution) of particular events associated with the visualized fluid dynamic phenomenon.

properties are strongly influenced by the turbulence generator even if their temporal or spatial statistics might appear universal.

As a conclusion, wavelets may be considered as the correct glasses to be used to observe detailed features of turbulence. Future applications should help researchers not only to enlarge the physical knowledge of chaotic phenomena but also to discover new strategies for theoretical modeling of turbulence, which remains a challenging task.

For background information *see* CHAOS; FLUID FLOW; FOURIER SERIES AND TRANSFORMS; IMAGE PROCESSING; JET FLOW; LAMINAR FLOW; TURBULENT FLOW; VORTEX; WAKE FLOW; WAVELETS in the McGraw-Hill Encyclopedia of Science & Technology.

Roberto Camussi

Bibliography. J Morlet, Sampling theory and wave propagation, *Proc. 51st Annu. Meet. Soc. Explor. Geophys.*, Los Angeles, 1980; M. Farge, Wavelet transforms and their application to turbulence, *Annu. Rev Fluid Mech.*, 24:395–457, 1992.

Weathering of silicate minerals

Igneous and sedimentary silicate rocks constitute more than 80% of the Earth's surface, so chemical weathering of silicate minerals has profound implications on the physical environment. Chemical weathering is driven by the differences in the thermodynamic conditions that existed at the time of mineral formation and the thermodynamics of ambient conditions at the Earth's surface. The solid-state characteristics of silicate mineral phases, generally established at high temperatures or pressures, continue to be reflected during weathering through mineral compositions, crystallographic structures, and the petrographic fabric and textures of silicate minerals—all factors which influence rates of rock decomposition. In turn, ambient processes most influencing silicate weathering are associated with the flow and chemistry of water at the Earth's surface. The term "weathering" implies a strong dependency on processes associated with the hydrosphere, atmosphere, and biosphere. The results of chemical weathering are clearly demonstrated by comparing the effect of increasing time on plagioclase feldspar grain morphologies shown in **Fig. 1**.

Some of the oldest direct applications of weathering to practical issues were related to economic geology, in particular to laterites and the formation of bauxite deposits and in the supergene enrichment of metal deposits. Charles Darwin, writing in 1876, attributed extensive laterization observed in Brazil to submarine processes, while A. Brognniart, his contemporary, attributed feldspathic decomposition in granite and the origin of kaolin clay to electric currents resulting from the contact of heterogeneous rock types. However, other researchers, such as M. J. Fournet and C. F. Hart writing as early as 1833, more correctly attributed observed chemical weathering to "the efficacy of water containing carbonic

acid" in promoting the decomposition of igneous rocks.

Most recent advances in quantifying rates of silicate weathering, both experimentally and in field situations, have been driven by an increasing awareness of its importance in a number of environmental issues. These advances have paralleled the development of other branches of chemistry and physics. For example, the development of fundamental theories based on statistical and quantum mechanics has permitted insights into the often complex chemical reactions involving natural minerals and water. The development of new analytical instrumentation has permitted direct characterization of the nature of the physical and chemical mineral-solution interface. Some of the useful techniques applied to mineral weathering include Auger electron and x-ray photoelectron spectroscopy, x-ray absorption spectroscopy, and tunneling and atomic force microscopy. Recognition must also be made of the exponential increase in computation power and speed without which data reduction and interpretation of complex natural processes would not be possible.

Neutralization of acid precipitation. Acidification of soils, rivers, and lakes is a major environmental concern in many parts of the increasingly industrialized world. Areas at particular risk are upland watersheds where silicate bedrock, such as granites and schists, are resistant to chemical weathering and are overlain

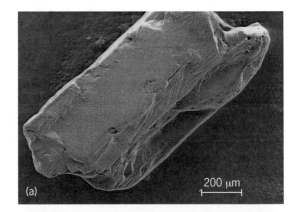

Fig. 1. Comparison of surface morphologies of plagioclase feldspar grains weathered in granitic soils. Soil ages are (*a*) 10,000 years and (*b*) 600,000 years. The more highly weathered grain shows preferential dissolution along defect structures.

by thin organic layers. Although atmospheric deposition of hydrogen and sulfur is the most recognized factor in watershed acidification, land-use practices such as conifer reforestation also create acidification problems. Chemical hydrolysis of silicates during weathering is the only process by which acidity can be neutralized over the long time in such enviroments. A reasonable environmental objective is to decrease atmospheric emissions to a level where the input of acidity is equal to or less than the rate of silicate weathering in sensitive watersheds. The principal question is the feedback between the two processes. Recent advances in characterizing silicate mineral dissolution as a ligand exchange reaction indicate that rates of silicate reaction vary exponentially with the concentration of protons adsorbed. Additional complexities recently documented included the role of aluminum, which is mobilized under acidic conditions and is involved both in competing surface exchange reactions and in controlling in the saturation state of coexisting aqueous solutions.

Nutrient cycles. Chemical weathering of silicate rocks contributes many inorganic nutrients utilized by vegetation. Nutrients such as potassium, magnesium, calcium, and boron are contributed directly to soils by the weathering of primary rock-forming silicates such as feldspars, amphiboles, and micas. Other nutrients such as phosphorus and sulfur are contributed from minerals such as apatite and pyrite, which occur as accessory phases and as inclusions in silicate rocks. Increases in soil fertility during initial silicate weathering can be related both to release of these inorganic nutrients and to the increase in secondary clay content which increases water retention. However, the end products of extensive weathering found in the older soils are ultimately depleted of these inorganic nutrients, producing soils with low fertility and permeability.

The extent and rate to which silicate weathering contributes these elements in terms of open and closed nutrient cycles is an area of active research. Many tropical ecosystems are underlain by very thick, highly weathered regoliths that contain a minimum of primary silicates. Under such closed system conditions, macronutrients are not contributed from silicates weathering, but are recycled through the soil by shallow rooting systems. In more temperate enviroments, nutrient cycling occurs in an open system. The regolith is a thinner and deeper rooting system that extracts a far greater nutrient input from weathering of primary silicates. Common organic compounds such as citrate and acetate produced by organisms can accelerate silicate dissolution by complexing ligands at the silicate surface. Also, microbes present on silicate substrates enhance weathering reactions.

Recent advances in understanding silicate weathering rates have utilized the concept of soil sequences in which weathering characteristics can be defined in terms of a single variable. Thus, a lithosequence is a series of soils developed on different par-

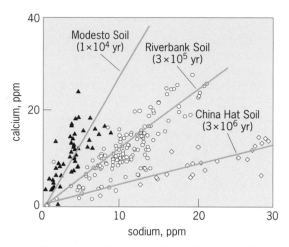

Fig. 2. Decreases in the concentrations of calcium relative to sodium in soil pore waters from soils of increasing age in chronosequence developed on glacial outwash from the Sierra Nevada of California.

ent rocks, a climosequence comprises soils affected principally by differences in precipitation and temperature, and a chronosequence includes groups of soils that are exposed to different durations of weathering. An example of calcium compared with sodium concentrations in soil pore waters from a chronosequence developed on alluvial outwash from successive glaciation of the Sierra Nevada of California is plotted in **Fig. 2**. With increasing age, the pore waters become progressively depleted in calcium as the more weatherable calcium-containing silicates are removed. This decrease in calcium occurs in parallel with a decrease in soil organic carbon, indicating diminished biological productivity in successively older soils. The extent of such calcium deficiencies is becoming widely recognized, particularly in forested regimes impacted by acid precipitation and timber harvesting.

Global carbon dioxide cycle. Climate, principally temperature and precipitation, is proposed as a linkage by which the rates of surficial weathering of silicates closely balance rates of long-term atmospheric carbon dioxide (CO_2) production. This CO_2 buffering has promoted stable climatic conditions that have permitted the continuation of life on Earth. Increases in atmospheric CO_2, such as during periods of increased volcanic activity, increase temperatures due to the greenhouse effect, which increases silicate weathering, and in turn, draws down CO_2. In contrast, diminished atmospheric CO_2 decreases temperature and suppresses silicate weathering, which leads to a subsequent buildup of CO_2. Much of the alkalinity produced by consumption of CO_2 during these reactions is ultimately sequestered over geologic time in marine carbonates.

This linkage between climate, surficial silicate weathering, and atmospheric CO_2 is not universally accepted. Other recent explanations include low-temperature sea-floor basalt alteration and the influence of tectonics rather than climate on silicate weathering rates. An important issue is the

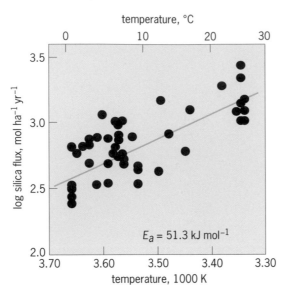

Fig. 3. Average annual dissolved silica fluxes from a global distribution of small watersheds underlain by granitic silicate rocks. Data are plotted against the inverse of absolute temperature. The Arrhenius activation energy for silicate weathering (kJ · mol⁻¹) corresponds to the slope of the linear regression fit to the data.

quantitative impact of temperature and precipitation on chemical weathering of silicate rocks. Such effects have been investigated both experimentally and in the natural environment. The effects of temperature on weathering rates are experimentally established for silicate minerals such as feldspars and quartz with average experimental activation energies of 50–80 kilojoules (19 kcal). These activation energies predict that a temperature increase from 0 to 25°C (32 to 77°F) would increase the weathering rate by an order of magnitude, an effect that should be observable in the natural environment. Direct observations of temperature impacts on natural weathering processes have proven elusive. The most relevant study to the climate issue would be of a natural weathering system that has undergone sustained temperature change. However, long-term data required for such a study are not available, and surrogate weathering studies comparing spatially separated climatic regimes are employed. The utility of such comparisons depends on the ability to separate the effect of temperature from other variables influencing chemical weathering, including precipitation, geomorphology, vegetation, and lithology. This ability decreases as the scale of the weathering process increases. This explains why recent comparisons of solute concentrations and fluxes in large-scale river systems most often fail to detect a temperature effect. In such systems, solute concentrations are dominated by rapid weathering of nonsilicate minerals, including evaporites and carbonates.

Although limited in number, recent comparisons of smaller-scale weathering environments have been more successful in documenting temperature impacts due to an increased ability to separate out other weathering variables. The results of one such investi-

gation summarized the annual silica discharge fluxes from a global distribution of small watersheds underlain by granitic rocks (**Fig. 3**). The average annual air temperatures varied from 0°C (32°F) for high-altitude alpine catchments to 27°C (81°F) for mountainous tropical watersheds. The temperature-dependent slope corresponds to Arrhenius activation energy of 51 kJ/mol (12 kcal/mol), which is equivalent to that for the experimental silicate dissolution. This correspondence demonstrates a potentially strong feedback between silicate weathering, climate, and CO_2 drawdown.

For background information *see* ACID RAIN; AMPHIBOLE; ANALYTICAL CHEMISTRY; APATITE; CLIMATOLOGY; FELDSPAR; MICA; PYRITE; QUARTZ; REGOLITH; SILICATE MINERALS; SOIL; WEATHERING PROCESSES in the McGraw-Hill Encyclopedia of Science & Technology.

Art White

Bibliography. S. W. Bailey et al., Calcium inputs and transport in a base-poor ecosystem as interpreted by Sr isotopes, *Water Resources Res.*, 32:707–719, 1996; P. C. Bennett, F. K. Hiebert, and W. J. Choi, Microbial colonization and weathering of silicates in a petroleum-contaminated groundwater, *Chem. Geol.*, 132:45–53, 1996; O. P. Bricker and K. C. Rice, Acidic deposition in streams, *J. Environ. Sci. Technol.*, 23:379–385, 1990; C. P. Burnham, Pedogical processes and nutrient supply from parent material in tropical soils, in J. Protor (ed.), *Mineral Nutrients in Tropical Forest and Savanna Ecosystems*, Blackwell Scientific, London, 1989; J. O. Drever, The effect of land plants on the weathering rates of silicate minerals, *Geochimica Cosmochimica Acta*, 58:2325–2332, 1994; W. F. Ruddiman, *Tectonic Uplift and Climate Change*, Plenum Press, New York, 1997; R. E. Stauffer, Granite weathering and the sensitivity of alpine lakes to acid deposition, *Limnol. Oceanog.*, 35:1112–1134, 1990; A. F. White et al., The effect of temperature on experimental and natural weathering rates of granitoid rocks, *Geochimica Cosmochimica Acta*, 63:3277–3291, 1999; A. F. White and A. E. Blum, Effects of climate on chemical weathering in watersheds, *Geochimica Cosmochimica Acta*, 59:1729–1747, 1995; A. F. White and S. L. Brantley, Chemical Weathering Rates of Silicate Minerals, *Reviews in Mineralogy*, Mineralogical Society of America, Washington, DC, 1995.

Wetting (physical chemistry)

Wetting and dewetting phenomena occur if a liquid is in contact with another phase, typically a solid substrate. If the substrate exerts an attractive force on the liquid molecules, the surface is lyophilic and the liquid attains a relatively large contact area with the substrate surface; this is the case of wetting. Dewetting corresponds to the situation in which the substrate is lyophobic and exerts a repulsive force onto the liquid; the liquid retracts from the surface, and there is relatively little contact area between liquid and substrate.

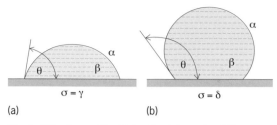

Fig. 1. Side views of liquid droplets (a) on a lyophilic substrate and (b) on a lyophobic substrate. The two phases in contact with the substrate σ are denoted α and β. Both surfaces are laterally homogeneous and characterized by a uniform value of the contact angle θ. For the lyophilic substrate $\sigma = \gamma$, the contact angle $\theta = \theta_\gamma$ is smaller than $90°$. For the lyophobic substrate $\sigma = \delta$, the angle $\theta = \theta_\delta$ is larger than $90°$.

The difference between wetting and dewetting can be directly observed for the macroscopic bodies encountered in everyday life. For instance, human skin is usually water-repellent, or hydrophobic. Water is repelled (dewets) from the feathers of water birds and the leaves of plants. An example of wetting is the thin tear film which covers the human eye. Such films are stabilized by surface-active molecules which reduce their surface tensions and prevent their dewetting.

In general, a liquid droplet on a solid substrate is bounded by two types of interfaces, the liquid surface (or liquid-vapor interface) and the substrate surface. These two surfaces meet along the contact line which represents the edge or boundary of the liquid surface. The corresponding angle at which these two surfaces intersect is known as the contact angle and is denoted by θ (**Fig. 1**).

The shape of a macroscopic droplet is strongly affected by gravity, which becomes important as soon as the linear dimension of the droplet exceeds the capillary length of the liquid. For water, the latter length scale is about 4 mm. Large droplets are flattened out by gravity and assume the shape of a puddle with a thickness on the order of the capillary length.

Small droplets with a size below the capillary length are not affected by gravity. Such droplets can attain the ideal shapes shown in Fig. 1. These shapes are given by segments of spherical caps and are characterized by a constant value of the contact angle. This value satisfies the classical Young equation, which follows from the force balance of the different interfacial tensions along the contact line. A lyophilic surface and a lyophobic surface correspond to a contact angle which is smaller and larger than $90°$, respectively.

The two substrate surfaces shown in Fig. 1 are laterally homogeneous; that is, the whole substrate is either lyophilic or lyophobic. This implies that the contact angle has the same value along the whole surface. To a certain extent, this value depends on external control parameters such as the temperature or the composition of the liquid, and thus may be changed by varying these control parameters.

For a laterally homogeneous surface, complete and

partial wetting correspond to a vanishing contact angle $\theta = 0$ and to a small but positive contact angle $\theta > 0$, respectively. Likewise, complete and partial dewetting occurs if the contact angle is given by $\theta = 180°$ and $\theta < 180°$, respectively. In some systems, the interface between a liquid and its vapor can undergo a transition from partial wetting to complete wetting as an external control parameter is varied; this process corresponds to the usual wetting transition which was discovered about two decades ago.

Liquids on structured and imprinted surfaces undergo a novel type of wetting (or dewetting) transition not related to small changes of the contact angle close to $\theta = 0$ (or to $\theta = 180°$). These morphological wetting transitions occur since these surfaces contain both lyophilic and lyophobic domains characterized by small and large contact angles, respectively.

Structured and imprinted surfaces. The structured and imprinted surfaces considered here consist of different surface regions or domains. For simplicity, the focus will be on two types of domains, lyophilic and lyophobic. These surface domains may have different shapes, and may form regular or irregular patterns.

Several experimental methods are available by which surface patterns can be created with domain sizes in the micrometer range. Three examples are elastomer stamps which can create patterns of hydrophobic alkanethiol on metal surfaces; vapor deposition through grids which cover part of the surface; and photolithography of amphiphilic monolayers which contain photosensitive molecular groups.

Some regular domain patterns are shown in **Fig. 2**, where the lyophilic and lyophobic domains are gray and white, respectively. If a liquid condenses on such a surface, it will start to wet the lyophilic regions. In this way, the two-dimensional domain pattern acts as a template for the three-dimensional morphology of the wetting liquid which can form droplets, channels, or thin layers.

It is obvious that the underlying pattern of surface domains determines the wetting morphology to some extent since it provides certain constraints. It turns out, however, that one surface pattern may lead to several distinct morphologies. Thus, as a control parameter, such as the volume of the condensed liquid, is varied, the system may undergo a morphological transition at which the shape of the wetting liquid undergoes a pronounced change.

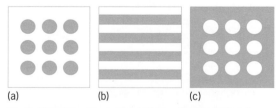

Fig. 2. Top views of regular patterns of surface domains. The gray and the white surface regions are lyophilic and lyophobic, respectively. (a) A regular array of lyophilic domains within a lyophobic matrix. (b) A surface covered by lyophilic and lyophobic stripes. (c) A regular array of lyophobic domains within a lyophilic matrix.

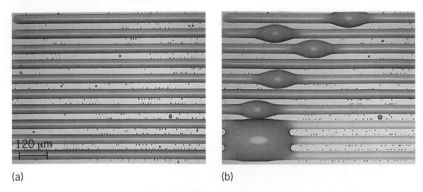

(a)   (b)

Fig. 3. Channel transition of water channels on a striped surface. (a) **If the amount of water per channel is below the critical volume, the channels are thin and homogeneous and their shape is given by cylindrical segments.** (b) **If the water volume exceeds the critical value, each channel develops a single bulge. In this example, the width of both the hydrophilic and the hydrophobic stripes is 30 micrometers.**

Channel transition. One example of a morphological wetting transition which has been studied in some detail is the transition of water channels on hydrophilic surface stripes as shown in **Fig. 3**. The two micrographs show the state of the water channels before and after the transition, respectively.

In the experiment, a hydrophobic surface with hydrophilic surface stripes is in contact with slightly supersaturated water vapor. The water starts to condense on the hydrophilic stripes and first forms many little droplets. As more water is deposited onto the stripes, these droplets coalesce until the hydrophilic stripes are completely covered by water, and the contact lines of these channels are located at the surface domain boundaries, that is, at the boundaries of the stripes. In this way, a thin microchannel is formed having the shape of a cylindrical segment with constant cross section and small contact angle. If water is added to these channels, the contact angle grows continuously until the water volume reaches a critical value at which the channel morphology undergoes an abrupt change, and each channel develops a single bulge as shown in Fig. 3b.

If two or several neighboring microchannels undergo such a transition, the resulting bulges may touch each other (or the neighboring channel) and coalesce. As a result, one has liquid bridges which connect neighboring channels. A bridge between three channels is visible in the left bottom corner of Fig. 3b. The presence or absence of such bridges is mainly controlled by the width of the hydrophobic surface regions which separate the hydrophilic stripes.

This channel transition is rather different from the classical Rayleigh-Plateau instability of a free-standing liquid cylinder, characterized by the decay of this cylinder into a periodic array of many droplets. In contrast, the morphological channel transition leads to a new stable state with a single bulge of the channel. Furthermore, while the free-standing cylinder will always undergo a Rayleigh-Plateau instability, the homogeneous channel turns out to be stable as long as its volume is sufficiently small.

The channel transition has been studied both theoretically and experimentally (**Fig. 4**). Direct inspection shows that the agreement between theory and experiment is rather good. In the experiments, the striped surface domains were created by thermal vapor deposition of magnesium fluoride (MgF_2) onto a hydrophobic silicone rubber or thiolated gold substrate through appropriate masks. The resulting stripes have a width of 30 micrometers. The hydrophilic MgF_2 stripes had a contact angle $\theta = \theta_\gamma$ of about 5°. Both the silicone rubber and the thiolated gold had a contact angle $\theta = \theta_\delta$ of about 108°. The projected shape of the channel was studied by optical microscopy, the shape of the contact line by surface plasmons. As shown in Fig. 4, the contact line was found to detach from the hydrophilic stripe and to make an excursion across the hydrophobic surface domain.

The theoretical shapes have been determined by minimization of the interfacial free energies of the water channel. In principle, the free energy contains additional line tension contributions arising from the contact line, but these are relatively small and can be neglected for wetting structures on the micrometer scale. Therefore, the only parameters which enter the calculation are the two contact angles $\theta = \theta_\gamma$ and $\theta = \theta_\delta$ of the hydrophilic and hydrophobic domains, the geometry of the surface domains, and the total amount of condensed water. Thus, the theory does not contain any fitting parameter. In contrast to the experimental observations, the theoretical

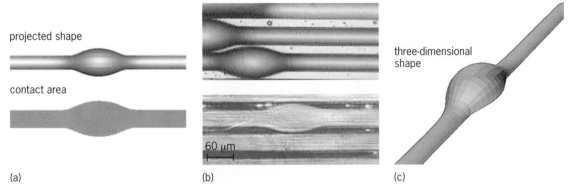

projected shape

contact area

three-dimensional shape

(a)   (b)   (c)

Fig. 4. Channel state with one bulge, with comparison of (a) **theory and** (b) **experiment for the projected shape of the channel and for the shape of the contact line.** (c) **Full three-dimensional shape as determined theoretically.**

calculations also provide the full three-dimensional shape of the bulge state.

Morphological wetting transitions. The channel transition provides one example of a morphological wetting transition. From a theoretical point of view, however, it is quite obvious that such transitions represent a generic feature for wetting (and dewetting) of structured surfaces. In general, the two phases which are in contact with the structured surface need not be a liquid and a vapor phase as implicitly assumed in the previous discussion. All that is required are two phases, say α and β, in contact with a structured surface, and a wettability contrast for one of these phases, say β, provided by the two types of surface domains.

The two phases can both be liquidlike arising, for example, from phase separation within a multicomponent mixture. The $(\alpha\beta)$ interface between the two fluid phases is characterized by an isotropic interfacial tension and will assume a shape which is characterized by constant mean curvature as follows from the Laplace equation. A similar shape problem is encountered for soap bubbles which also have a surface of constant mean curvature. From a mathematical point of view, the main difference between the shape of soap bubbles and the wetting morphologies considered here arises from the constraint on the contact line since this line is attracted toward the domain boundaries within the substrate surface.

If the contact line were forced to sit on top of such a domain boundary, that is, for a hard constraint, differential geometry provides a few general theorems which ensure the existence of a constant mean curvature surface as long as the mean curvature is sufficiently small. In addition, there are also some theorems about the possible existence of two different shapes with the same constant mean curvature; these two shapes are known as the small and the large solution in the mathematical literature. As the volume of the wetting liquid is changed, a bifurcation between these two types of shapes will be found. The channel transition provides one example for such a bifurcation; additional examples which have been studied include an array of circular domains, which may be lyophilic or lyophobic, ring channels on annular domains, and capillary condensation within pores bounded by structured surfaces.

Morphological wetting transitions will also occur if the wetting phase β is a solid. In this case, the $(\alpha\beta)$ interface has an anisotropic tension and may be affected by elastic strains. Thus, the corresponding shapes are more difficult to calculate, but this does not change the presence and the overall character of the transition. One model system for which such a transition has been explicitly determined is the simple cubic lattice gas which is also known as the Kossel crystal. Another process which involves morphological wetting transtions is surface melting adjacent to a structured substrate.

The presence of these morphological transitions is not restricted to structures in the micrometer range. First of all, such transitions also occur on larger length scales, as recently demonstrated for soldering processes on metal stripes which had a width in the millimeter range. Second, they should also occur on smaller length scales, that is, for surface domains in the nanometer range. In the latter case, the wetting morphologies will also be affected by the energetics of the contact line.

Nanodomains and contact line tension. Several experimental tools have been developed in order to create surface domains which have a linear dimension between a few and a hundred nanometers. These methods include lithography with colloid monolayers, atomic beams modulated by light masks, and microphase separation in diblock copolymer films. Using such methods, it is possible, at least in principle, to perform systematic wetting studies in which the size of the underlying domain pattern is varied over a wide range of length scales.

A wetting liquid in contact with a substrate surface containing nanodomains should exhibit new morphologies and new morphological transitions which are strongly affected by the contact line tension. The latter quantity, which can be positive or negative, was already introduced by J. W. Gibbs, but its sign and its magnitude is still a matter of intense debate. Indeed, the contact line is often affected by impurities and defects whose size cannot be controlled in the experiments.

In contrast, using structured or imprinted surfaces, the linear dimension of the wetting structures may be varied in a controlled and systematic manner. If the wettability contrast is sufficiently large, the contact line is effectively pinned to the domain boundary within the substrate surface. Therefore, the size of the surface domains now represents an effective control parameter. In particular, the morphological wetting transitions occur at certain critical sizes at which the line tension starts to dominate the shape.

Microbridges and microchips. Several well-established technologies use wetting and dewetting phenomena at laterally structured surfaces; two examples are flatbed printing and soldering processes. The morphological transitions discussed here have been frequently observed in the context of these technologies. Thus, these transitions may be studied on the millimeter scale as has been demonstrated for soldering channels on annular metal stripes.

On the micrometer scale, morphological wetting transitions are expected to lead to new applications. Some applications could be based on the construction of bridges arising from the channel transition on neighboring surface stripes. Such a bridge can be stable as in Fig. 3b or may spread over the whole hydrophobic surface domain, depending on the width of the latter domain and on the wettability contrast.

Unstable bridges could be used, for example, for the construction of fluid microchips or microreactors. There is the case of a wettability pattern where pairs (or multiplets) of hydrophilic stripes have a smaller hydrophobic separation. First, the different channels on the stripe pairs (or multiplets) are filled with different reactants. Second, by moving the system through the channel transition, the formation of liquid bridges can be induced by simply increasing the volume of the channels. In this way, small amounts of reactants could be prepared in a well-mixed state without external stirring.

Stable bridges can be placed at controlled positions by using striped surface domains with a nonuniform width or with corners. In this way, two-dimensional networks of microchannels can be created. After a certain pattern of liquid channels and bridges is made, it can be stabilized by freezing, polymerization, or sol-gel reactions. In this way, both rigid and soft structures can be produced with a large variety of morphologies between two and three dimensions.

For background information *see* FLUIDS; INTEGRATED CIRCUITS; INTERFACE OF PHASES; NANOSTRUCTURES; PHASE TRANSITIONS; PRINTED CIRCUIT; SOLDERING; SURFACE TENSION; VAPOR DEPOSITION in the McGraw-Hill Encyclopedia of Science & Technology.

Reinhard Lipowsky

Bibliography. H. Gau et al., *Science*, 283:46–49, 1999; P. Lenz and R. Lipowsky, *Phys. Rev. Lett.*, 80: 1920–1923, 1998; R. Lipowsky, P. Lenz, and P. Swain, *Colloids Surf. A*, 161:3–22, 2000.

X-ray crystallography

To understand the properties of materials, structural information on an atomic level is essential. If crystals of sufficient size (>50 micrometers) and quality can be grown, single-crystal x-ray diffraction techniques can be applied to obtain this information.

Several thousand crystal structures are determined using these very powerful methods each year. Even smaller crystals (down to about 5 μm on an edge) can be studied if a high-intensity synchrotron x-ray source is used. However, many materials of industrial or scientific importance are polycrystalline (crystallite size <5 μm), and only powder diffraction data can be measured. Although such data are necessarily inferior to single-crystal diffraction data, structure determination is still possible in simple cases.

Considerable effort has been expended recently to extend the range of structural complexity that can be addressed when only powder diffraction data are available. This surge in activity can be attributed to the high interest in the structures of polycrystalline materials in many different fields, and to significant technological advances that open up new possibilities. The special characteristics of synchrotron x-ray sources and the increase in available computer power have been particularly important in the realization of some of these new methods.

Powder diffraction. A typical polycrystalline sample used to collect a powder diffraction pattern contains millions of crystallites, so the diffraction pattern is simply a superposition of millions of single-crystal diffraction patterns. Unfortunately, the crystallites (and therefore their diffraction patterns) are present in all possible orientations. This means that reflections with the same or similar diffraction angle, which are well separated in the single-crystal pattern, are superimposed in the powder pattern (**Fig. 1**). Only the sum of the intensities of these overlapping reflections can be measured, so the information content of the data is reduced. If there are too many

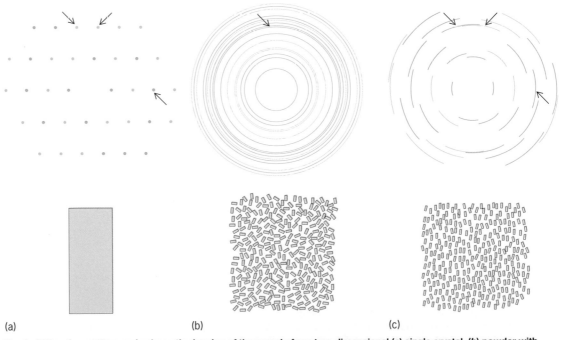

(a) (b) (c)

Fig. 1. Diffraction pattern and schematic drawing of the sample for a two-dimensional (*a*) single crystal, (*b*) powder with randomly oriented crystallites, and (*c*) textured powder. A graded scale has been used to represent the reflection intensities. The arrows highlight three reflections with similar diffraction angles (2θ) that are separate in the single-crystal pattern but overlap in the normal powder pattern. In the textured powder pattern, these reflections can be separated if the pattern is measured appropriately. The diffraction angle increases radially from the center of each diffraction pattern.

of these overlapping reflections, conventional single-crystal approaches to structure solution, which rely heavily on the accuracy of the individual reflection intensities, will fail.

Synchrotron radiation. The steady increase in the number and complexity of crystal structures solved from powder diffraction data during the 1990s is due in part to the increased availability of synchrotron radiation sources with dedicated powder diffraction beamlines. By taking advantage of the high collimation and high intensity of a synchrotron x-ray beam, powder diffraction data with a resolution considerably higher than that possible from laboratory sources can be collected. The peaks in the powder diffraction pattern become extremely sharp, so the overlap of reflections with similar diffraction angles (or interplanar d-spacing) is minimized (though it cannot be eliminated entirely). Not only does this facilitate the determination of the unit cell dimensions (derived from the positions of the peaks) and the space-group symmetry (deduced from systematically absent reflections), but also it allows more accurate intensities to be extracted for the individual reflections. With such improved data, more complex structures can be solved from powder diffraction data using conventional crystallographic techniques.

Despite this improvement in data quality, the structural complexity that can be handled still falls well below that which can be tackled with single-crystal data. To improve the situation, either supplementary data (for example, chemical information about the material) or a way of unraveling the intensities of the reflections that are still involved in overlap is needed. One way of improving the estimation of the relative intensities of overlapping reflections is to measure data from a powder sample in which a preferred orientation of the crystallites (texture) has been introduced intentionally to produce a sample in which not all crystallite orientations are equally represented.

Texture method. Powder diffractionists need to ensure that the crystallites in a sample are randomly oriented, because a preferred orientation of the crystallites can result in a misleading distortion of the intensities in the diffraction pattern. In principle, however, more information about the relative intensities of individual reflections can be obtained from a textured sample if it is measured appropriately.

The advantages of using a textured sample rather than one with randomly oriented crystallites is illustrated in Fig. 1. For simplicity, a two-dimensional case is shown, but the extension to three dimensions is straightforward. For the single crystal, all reflections are separated in space, and their individual intensities can be measured unambiguously (Fig. 1a). For the ideal powder sample, all orientations occur with the same frequency, so rings (spheres in three dimensions) of constant intensity are generated for each reflection (Fig. 1b). The diffraction pattern can be measured along any radial direction (that is, with the sample in any orientation). For a textured sample, the crystallites are oriented preferentially, so not all crys-

tallite orientations occur with the same frequency, and an intensity fluctuation is observed along the rings (spheres; Fig. 1c). By measuring diffraction patterns along different radial directions (that is, with the sample in different orientations), at least some of the overlapping reflections can be deconvoluted.

To describe the systematic intensity fluctuations caused by the preferred orientation of the crystallites, the texture of the sample must be determined. This is done by measuring the variation in the diffracted intensity as a function of the sample orientation (tilt and rotation) for a single (nonoverlapping) reflection. The resulting pole figure is a measure of the number of crystallites in diffraction condition at each sample orientation. With a few such pole figures, the orientation distribution of the crystallites can be determined. Using this information, sample orientations that yield maximum contrast for overlapping reflections are selected, and full diffraction patterns are collected at these orientations. By combining the texture information with the full diffraction pattern data, a set of single-crystal-like reflection intensities can be extracted.

Experimental setup. Test calculations on simulated data show that the method described above works extremely well. However, the realization of the theory as a practical technique requires the unique characteristics of a synchrotron beam. On a conventional laboratory diffractometer with a divergent x-ray beam, tilting the flat-plate specimen, which is necessary for the measurement, leads to a violation of the parafocusing condition (parts of the sample are moved off the focusing circle), and this defocusing results in severe peak broadening and a corresponding increase in reflection overlap. With a parallel synchrotron beam, however, no focusing is required, and by using a crystal analyzer in front of the detector to act as a very fine receiving slit, all sample orientations can be measured with the same high resolution (**Fig. 2**).

The high intensity of the synchrotron beam is

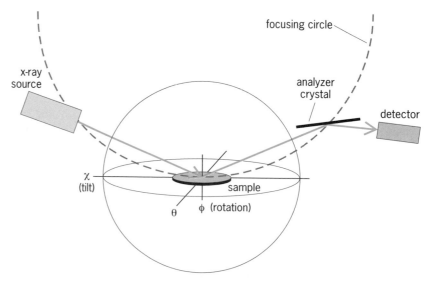

Fig. 2. Experimental setup used for data collection.

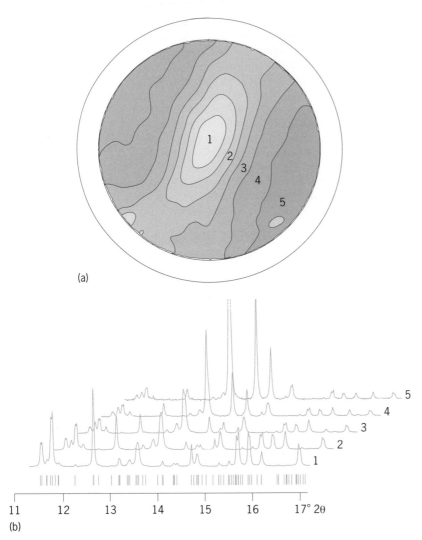

(a)

(b)

11   12   13   14   15   16   17° 2θ

Fig. 3. Portions of the data collected for the determination of the structure of UTD-1. (*a*) Pole figure for the 102 reflection. The rotation angle ϕ is plotted counterclockwise around the circle (0° at the right), and the tilt angle χ increases radially from the center (0° at the center and 90° at the outermost circle). Intensities are inversely proportional to the intensity of the blue color. Sample tilt and rotation angles selected for the collection of full diffraction patterns are indicated as 1–5. (*b*) Small sections of the full diffraction patterns collected at the sample orientations are indicated. The positions of the symmetry-allowed reflections (in terms of the diffraction angle 2θ) are indicated with tick marks above the 2θ axis.

Sample preparation. Needlelike crystallites (about $0.5 \times 0.5 \times 40 \ \mu m^3$) were mixed with a small amount of polystyrene solution, and then a thin layer of the sticky mixture was smeared on a glass slide and allowed to dry. Additional layers were applied in the same manner until the sample was thick enough (about 0.6 mm). This produced a relatively robust sample with most of the needles aligned approximately along the smear direction.

Data collection. Pole-figure data for seven single reflections and full diffraction patterns at five sample orientations were measured. As an example, the pole figure for the 102 reflection is shown in **Fig. 3**a. The numbered points indicated on the pole figure correspond to the five sample orientations selected for the measurement of full diffraction patterns. The intensity differences in those diffraction patterns are readily apparent in the small sections shown in Fig. 3b.

Data analysis. The texture was determined from the pole-figure data, and then a single set of reflection intensities was extracted from the five diffraction patterns using the texture information to quantify the correlation between the patterns. Conventional crystallographic methods were applied to this single-crystal-like dataset, and the complete 4-connected zeolite framework structure and the organocobalt complex within the framework channels (69 symmetry-independent nonhydrogen atoms) could be found without difficulty.

This exploitation of preferred orientation to facilitate the determination of crystal structures of polycrystalline materials can be applied to any class of compounds. The only requirement is that a textured sample can be prepared. Then, in principle, crystal structures as complex as those routinely solved by single-crystal methods can be determined.

For background information *see* CRYSTAL STRUCTURES; CRYSTALLOGRAPHY; SYNCHROTRON RADIATION; X-RAY CRYSTALLOGRAPHY; X-RAY DIFFRACTION; X-RAY POWDER METHODS; ZEOLITES in the McGraw-Hill Encyclopedia of Science & Technology.

Thomas Wessels; Lynne B. McCusker

Bibliography. R. J. Cernik and P. Barnes, Industrial aspects of synchrotron x-ray powder diffraction, *Radiation Phys. Chem.*, 45:445–457, 1995; K. D. M. Harris and M. Tremayne, Crystal structure determination from powder diffraction data, *Chem. Mater.*, 8:2554–2570, 1996; T. Wessels et al., An ordered form of the extra-large-pore zeolite UTD-1: Synthesis and structure analysis from powder diffraction data, *J. Amer. Chem. Soc.*, 121:6242–6247, 1999; T. Wessels, Ch. Baerlocher, and L. B. McCusker, Single-crystal-like diffraction data from polycrystalline materials, *Science*, 284:477–479, 1999.

essential in order to obtain sensible counting statistics at all tilt and diffraction angles. Even so, with this reflection geometry setup, data collection requires about 3 days of synchrotron beam time. Attempts to reduce the data collection time by as much as an order of magnitude by changing to a transmission geometry and a two-dimensional detector system are in progress.

Application. The texture method has been used to determine a number of complex structures that could not be solved from the intensities extracted from a conventional powder diffraction pattern collected on an untextured sample. To illustrate the full procedure of the texture approach, its application to the structure solution of the zeolite UTD-1 ($[Si_{64}O_{128}] \cdot 2(Cp^*)_2CoF_{0.75}OH_{0.25}$), the first extra-large-pore high-silica molecular sieve, is described below.

Yeast functional analysis

Analysis of the genome of *Saccharomyces cerevisiae* (brewer's and baker's yeast) has provided an opportunity for developing new tools for the functional analysis of eukaryotic genomes. One of the most powerful approaches is the generation of specific deletion mutants. Phenotypic analysis of the mutant strain may well reveal the function of the missing protein. To date, classic processes for systematic disruption require several steps: cloning of the gene into a plasmid, construction of a restriction map, and replacement or elimination of the coding region of the gene. The procedure is time-consuming and has not been carried out in a systematic way.

Using a polymerase chain reaction (PCR)-mediated strategy for construction of a gene replacement cassette, a new and efficient approach to gene deletion in yeast has been developed. The PCR gene targeting method exploits the extremely precise mitotic recombination system of *S. cerevisiae*—each gene locus can be replaced by simple integrative transformation—and the construction of a gene replacement cassette containing a marker (*kanMX*) which confers geneticin resistance to *S. cerevisiae*. Transformants are thus selected on the basis of the marker.

Several research groups are using this approach to delete yeast genes systematically and then examine the resulting strains under several different conditions. For example, the European Functional Analysis Network (EUROFAN) program has undertaken the creation of an information and material resource consisting of a collection of specific deletant strains, plasmids containing the individual genes, and disruption cassettes available to the scientific community for the manipulation of genes in any *S. cerevisiae* strain. In order to generate deletion mutants and to carry out analysis of their phenotypes, a set of new techniques, including mass-murder analysis, transposon mutagenesis, and microarray technology, has been developed.

PCR gene targeting. Deoxyribonucleic acid (DNA) molecules consisting of a marker cassette flanked by short or long homology regions to the target locus can be generated by PCR in order to construct disruption cassettes. In short flanking homology PCR (SFH-PCR), a pair of long chimeric oligonucleotide primers (about 55 base pairs) showing homology with both the gene of interest and the marker gene is used (**Fig. 1***a*). To gain greater flexibility in marker choice, the marker-specific sequence can be replaced by sequences that are homologous to the multiple cloning site of the plasmid used as a template carrying the marker gene. The resulting PCR product contains the marker module flanked by at least 30 base pairs, the minimal length for targeting in *S. cerevisiae*. As an alternative, the LFH-PCR technique—the addition of long flanking homology regions of several hundred base pairs to the marker module—leads to improved transformation efficiencies and avoids the effect of strain polymorphism (Fig. 1*b*). This latter protocol uses dual-step PCR. In the first PCR, two pairs of primers and *S. cerevisiae* genomic DNA are used to amplify the promoter and the terminator regions of the target gene. The inner primers also carry 5′-extensions (20–25 bases) derived from

the marker module in order to generate, at one end of each fragment, short overlapping homologies to the selection marker. In the second PCR, with marker DNA as template, the two PCR fragments serve as long primers to produce the open reading frame (ORF) targeting cassette.

Selectable marker. Deletions are created either by replacement of the target gene with suitable auxotrophic (requiring a specific growth substance in addition to the minimal requirements for normal metabolism and reproduction) markers or with a dominant kanamycin resistance marker. After deletion of the gene, the selectable marker remains integrated in the genome and can no longer be used in the modified strain. This is undesirable, especially if the goal is to delete a second open reading frame. The *URA3* marker offers an advantage in that the Ura$^+$ transformants are able to lose the gene at low frequency by recombination events. The deleted Ura$^-$ strain could be selected for its ability to grow on 5-fluoroorotic acid (the so-called pop-out method). The selection marker, *kanMX*, is a hybrid gene expressing a bacterial aminoglysoside

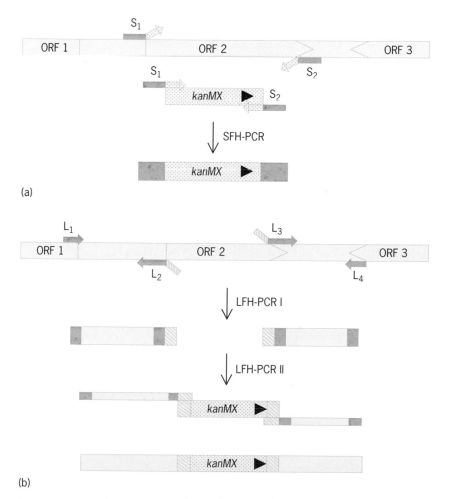

Fig. 1. Two analytic techniques. (*a*) Short flanking homology–PCR technique. The disruption cassette generated consists of a marker DNA flanked by small homology regions to the target gene. (*b*) Long flanking homology–PCR technique. The disruption cassette generated consists of a marker DNA flanked by long homology regions to the target gene. (*After A. Wach et al., Guidelines for EUROFAN B0 Program*)

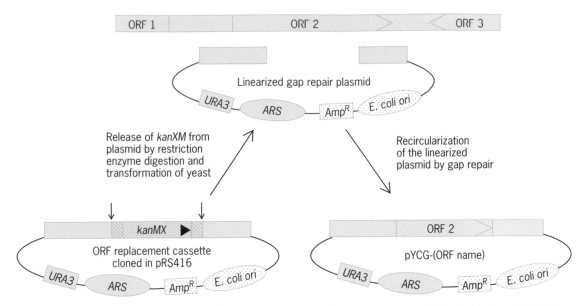

Fig. 2. Schematic view of the construction of the cognate gene clone by gap repair in yeast. (*After A. Wach et al., Guidelines for EUROFAN B0 Program*)

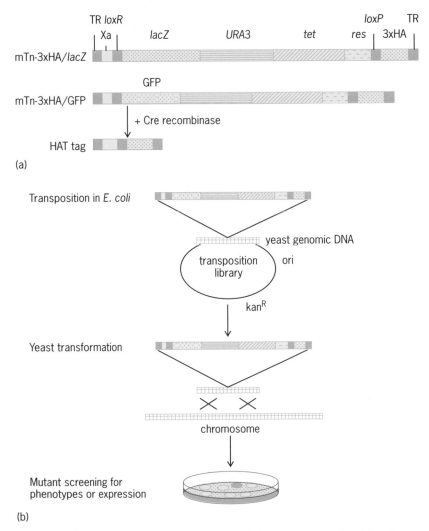

Fig. 3. Transposon mutagenesis. (*a*) Structure of mTns transposons, and excision after Cre expression. (*b*) Construction of the library insertion mutant.

phosphotransferase under control of a strong fungal promoter (the TEF gene of *Ashbya gossypii*). *Saccharomyces cerevisiae*, as well as other yeasts and certain filamentous fungi, acquires resistance to the drug geneticin (G418) when transformed with the *kanMX* module. Use of this marker does not depend on the presence of auxotrophic markers in the host strain, and because it lacks homology to yeast DNA, false-positive transformants are eliminated. The *kanMX* gene has the additional advantage of rendering *Escherichia coli* resistant to kanamycin. Also, it is possible to remove the kanamycin resistance gene from the genome by the introduction of directed repeats of *loxP* recombination sites flanking the *kanMX* deletion cassette.

Construction of deletant strains. Polymerase chain reaction products are used for the transformation of *S. cerevisiae* cells. Directed gene alterations can be obtained in both haploid and diploid strains. The proper genetic structure of the transformants is verified at the molecular level. Essential genes can be collected in the form of heterozygous diploid strains and, for their study, the corresponding open reading frames can be fused to regulated promoters (such as *GAL1*). Regulated expression makes it possible to conditionally switch off the expression of the essential gene under investigation (for example, by changing the carbon source). Deletion cassettes containing long flanking regions can be cloned in both replicative plasmids in *E. coli* for future gene disruptions and also in *E. coli–S. cerevisiae* shuttle vectors that contain the *URA3* gene as a yeast selectable marker for gap-repair cloning of the gene.

The mass-murder strategy allows the simultaneous deletion of several open reading frames. It is also based on the transformation of yeast by PCR products containing a selection gene and homologous target regions (target sequence homolog). Yeast genomic fragments, which serve as targets for recombination, are cloned in yeast split-marker vectors. Yeast is co-transformed with a plasmid pair containing the chosen combination of target sequence homolog which flanks the desired deletion.

Gap repair. Functional complementation of the lethality or of the phenotype observed in a deletant mutant is a final demonstration that the absence of the protein encoded by the gene studied is indeed the cause of the observed phenomenon. The gap-repair technique can be used to clone the cognate (of the same lineage) gene onto replicative plasmids (**Fig. 2**). The marker, but not the flanking homology regions, has been removed from the plasmid containing the disruption cassette. When such a linear DNA fragment is introduced into *S. cerevisiae*, the gapped plasmid can be repaired to a circle by copying the chromosome. The plasmid can be rescued in *E. coli* by transformation with total yeast DNA. It can be used to transform the yeast deleted for this gene to perform transcomplementation. In vivo gap-repair cloning of genes is preferred over PCR amplification of genes because of the error rate of PCR polymerase.

Transposon mutagenesis. Transposon mutagenesis, a method developed for research in bacterial genetics, can now be used in many species. Successive generations of transposons have been developed for yeast. The set of mTn's (mini Tn3 derivatives) contains terminal repeats (TR) and the *res* site of Tn3, the tetracycline gene (*tet*) for selection in *E. coli*, and the yeast auxotrophic marker *URA3*. mTn's also contain the coding region for reporter proteins, either β-galactosidase (*LacZ*) or the *Aequorea victoria* green fluorescent protein (GFP). At one end of each transposon, the *lox* site (recombination site) is adjacent to a coding region for the cleavage site of Factor Xa protease. At the other end, *lox* is adjacent to a sequence encoding three copies of the hemagglutinin epitope (HA). In-frame fusions between the yeast coding region and the reporter protein can be identified by β-galactosidase activity or fluorescence. The transposon creates insertion mutations in the target gene, allowing phenotypic analysis, and can be reduced by the *cre-lox* site-specific recombination to a smaller element that leaves an epitope tag inserted in the encoded protein (**Fig. 3**).

The advantage of this system is that in a single mutagenesis it is possible to generate null mutations, conditional alleles, epitope-tagged alleles, mutations in different domains of a protein, and report fusion, affording much information about a gene and its encoded protein. *See* GREEN FLUORESCENT PROTEIN.

Microarray technology. Functional analysis of genes can be carried out without the construction of deletion strains. Microarrays of DNA consist of microscopic spots, each of which contains identical single-stranded polymeric molecules of deoxyribonucleotides (usually oligonucleotides or complementary DNAs) attached to a solid support such as a membrane, a polymer, or glass. DNA microarrays containing almost all yeast open reading frames are now available. Gene expression can be monitored for a large number of genes under different growth conditions by isolation of the poly messenger ribonucleic acids (mRNA's) of the culture labeled fluorescently by reverse transcription. The labeled products can then be used to probe DNA microarrays. Moreover, the expression of many genes can be monitored in strains deleted for a given gene.

All the experimental approaches described here make it clear that the scientific community dedicated to research into yeast is building up an integrative view of the workings of this relatively simple eukaryotic model. The results obtained with *S. cerevisiae* and other yeast species should be directly applicable to understanding the functioning of the genomes of higher organisms.

For background information *see* DEOXYRIBONUCLEIC ACID (DNA); GENE; GENETIC ENGINEERING; GENETIC MAPPING; MOLECULAR BIOLOGY; NUCLEIC ACID; YEAST in the McGraw-Hill Encyclopedia of Science & Technology.

M. Carmen López; Encarnación Fermiñán;
Manuel Sánchez; Angel Domínguez

Bibliography. A. J. P. Brown and M. F. Tuite (eds.), *Yeast Gene Analysis*, Academic Press, London, 1998; P. Ross-Macdonald et al., A multipurpose transposon system for analyzing protein production, localization, and function in *Saccharomyces cerevisiae*, *Proc. Nat. Acad. Sci. USA*, 94:190–195, 1997; A. Wach et al., New heterologous modules for classical or PCR-based gene disruptions in *S. cerevisiae*, *Yeast*, 10:1793–1808, 1994.

Contributors

The affiliation of each Yearbook contributor is given, followed by the title of his or her article. An article title with the notation "in part" indicates that the author independently prepared a section of an article; "coauthored" indicates that two or more authors jointly prepared an article or section.

A

Acuña, Dr. Mario H. *Laboratory for Extraterrestrial Physics, NASA Goddard Space Flight Center, Greenbelt, Maryland.* MARS'S MAGNETIC LINEATIONS.

Agarwal, Dr. Ramesh. *National Institute for Aviation Research, Wichita State University, Wichita, Kansas.* COMPUTATIONAL FLUID DYNAMICS.

Alexander, Rebecca W. *Skaggs Institute of Chemical Biology, Scripps Research Institute, Beckman Center, La Jolla, California.* MULTIFUNCTIONAL PROTEINS.

Allen, Prof. David. *Department of Chemical Engineering, University of Texas, Austin.* AIR QUALITY.

An, Kyungwon. *Center for Macroscopic Quantum-Field Lasers, Korea Advanced Institute of Science and Technology, Taejon.* SINGLE-ATOM LASER—coauthored.

Anderson, Dr. John D., Jr. *Silver Spring, Maryland.* HYPERSONIC FLIGHT.

Angers, Dr. Denis A. *Soils and Crops Research and Development Research Centre, Agriculture and Agri-Food, Sainte-Foy, Quebec, Canada.* CARBON SEQUESTRATION—coauthored.

Anjalal, Abdulaziz. *G. R. Harrison Spectroscopy Laboratory, Massachusetts Institute of Technology, Cambridge.* SINGLE-ATOM LASER—coauthored.

Arnold, Dr. Frederick, P., Jr. *Advanced Research Systems, University of Chicago, Illinois.* COMPLEX ORGANIC COMPOUNDS.

B

Ball, Prof. Kenneth S. *Department of Mechanical Engineering, University of Texas, Austin.* MOLTEN GLASS JETS—coauthored.

Banfield, Prof. Jillian. *Department of Geology and Geophysics, University of Wisconsin, Madison.* GEOMICROBIOLOGY—coauthored.

Bañuelos, Dr. G. S. *Plant/Soil Scientist, U.S. Department of Agriculture, Agricultural Research Service—Water Management Research Laboratory, Fresno, California.* PHYTOREMEDIATION.

Barker, Dr. James. *Department of Earth Sciences, University of Waterloo, Ontario, Canada.* GROUND-WATER CLEANUP.

Barker, Dr. William W. *Department of Geology and Geophysics, University of Wisconsin, Madison.* GEOMICROBIOLOGY—coauthored.

Battino, Prof. Rubin. *Department of Chemistry, Wright State University, Dayton, Ohio.* Gas solubility.

Baudry, Dr. Michel. *Neuroscience Program, University of Southern California, Los Angeles.* MEMORY—COAUTHORED.

Bélanger, Dr. Gilles. *Soils and Crops Research and Development Research Centre, Agriculture and Agri-Food, Sainte-Foy, Quebec, Canada.* CARBON SEQUESTRATION—coauthored.

Bergman, Prof. Theodore L. *Department of Mechanical Engineering, University of Connecticut, Storrs.* MOLTEN GLASS JETS—coauthored.

Bi, Dr. Xiaoning. *University of California, Irvine.* MEMORY—coauthored.

Bininda-Emonds, Dr. Olaf. *Section of Evolution and Ecology, University of California, Davis.* SYSTEMATICS—in part.

Blaxter, Dr. Mark *Institute of Cell, Animal and Population Biology, University of Edinburgh, United Kingdom.* NEMATODA.

Bolduc, Dr. Chantal. *University of British Columbia, Vancouver, British Columbia, Canada.* HAIR LOSS—coauthored.

Boyce, Dr. Brendan F. *Department of Pathology and Laboratory Medicine, University of Rochester Medical Center, Rochester, New York.* BONE—coauthored.

Brenan, Prof. James N. *Assistant Professor, Department of Geology, University of Toronto, Earth Sciences Centre, Toronto, Ontario, Canada.* BASALT.

Brierley, Dr. Corale L. *Principal, Brierley Consultancy LLC, Highlands Ranch, Colorado.* BIOMINING.

Bright, R. K. *Earle A. Chiles Research Institute, Franz Cancer Center, Portland, Oregon.* VACCINE—coauthored.

Brocks, Dr. Jochen. *Australian Geological Survey Organisation, Canberra.* MOLECULAR FOSSILS.

Buseck, Dr. Peter R. *Departments of Geology and Chemistry/Biochemistry, Arizona State University, Tempe.* BACTERIAL MAGNETIC MINERIALS—coauthored.

Butterline, Ed. *Symmetricom, San Jose, California.* TIME SYNCHRONIZATION—coauthored.

C

Caldwell, Dr. Michael W. *Research Scientist, Paleobiology, Research Division, Canadian Museum of Nature, and Adjunct Research Professor, Earth Sciences Department, Carleton University, Ottawa, Ontario, Canada.* SNAKE.

Camussi, Dr. Roberto. *Dipartimento di Ingegneria Meccanica e Industriale, University of Rome, Italy.* WAVELETS.

Carroll, Prof. John M. *Professor of Computer Science, Education, and Psychology, and Director of the Center for Human-Computer Interaction, Virginia Tech, Blacksburg.* SCENARIO-BASED DESIGN.

Casazza, John A. *Springfield, Virginia.* ELECTRIC UTILITY RESTRUCTURING.

Chapman, Dr. C. Richard. *Professor, Department of Anesthesiology, University of Washington, Seattle.* PAIN.

Chen, Prof. Hao. *School of Information Management and Systems, University of California, Berkeley.* ELECTRONIC MAIL—coauthored.

Chen, Dr. Walter Y. *Scenix Semiconductor, Inc., Mountain View, California.* ASYMMETRICAL DIGITAL SUBSCRIBER LINE.

Cleveland, Dr. Robin. *Department of Aerospace and Mechanical Engineering, Boston University, Massachusetts.* MICROSCOPIC MICROPHONES.

Connor, Dr. John A. *Groundwater Services, Inc., Houston, Texas.* RISK-BASED ENVIRONMENTAL RESTORATION—coauthored.

Cooke, Dr. Howard. *MRC Human Genetics Unit, Western General Hospital, Crewe Road, Edinburgh, United Kingdom.* SYNTHETIC CHROMOSOME.

Cooper, Dr. Roger A. *Institute of Geological and Nuclear Sciences, Lower Hutt, New Zealand.* GRAPTOLITES.

Costa, Dr. Daniel P. *Department of Biology and Institute of Marine Science, University of California, Santa Cruz.* UNDERWATER ACOUSTIC POLLUTION—coauthored.

Crane, Peter R. *Royal Botanical Gardens, Kew, Richmond, Surrey, United Kingdom.* ANGIOSPERMS—coauthored.

Crawford, Dr. Fronefield, III. *Massachusetts Institute of Technology, Cambridge.* PULSAR.

Creager, Prof. Stephen E. *Department of Chemistry, Clemson University, Clemson, South Carolina.* MOLECULAR WIRES.

Cummings, Prof. Peter T. *Distinguished Professor of Chemical Engineering, Chemistry and Computer Sciences, University of Tennessee, Knoxville, and Distinguished Scientist, Chemical Technology Divison, Oak Ridge National Laboratory, Oak Ridge, Tennessee.* MOLECULAR SIMULATION.

D

Dale, Dr. Bruce E. *Professor and Chair, Department of Chemical Engineering, Michigan State University, East Lansing.* RENEWABLE RESOURCES.

Dasari, Ramachandra. *G. R. Harrison Spectroscopy Laboratory, Massachusetts Institute of Technology, Cambridge.* SINGLE-ATOM LASER—coauthored.

De Boeck, Dr. Jo. *IMEC, Leuven, Belgium.* MAGNETIC RANDOM ACCESS MEMORIES.

Decareau, Dr. Robert V. *Microwave Consulting Services, Amherst, New Hampshire.* MICROWAVE TECHNOLOGY.

Delwiche, Prof. Charles F. *Assistant Professor, Cell Biology and Molecular Genetics, University of Maryland, College Park.* HORIZONTAL GENE TRANSFER—in part.

Deppert, Prof. Dr. Wolfgang. *Heinrich-Pette-Institut für Experimentelle Virologie und Immunologie an der Universität Hamburg, Germany.* TUMOR SUPPRESSOR GENE.

deYoung, Prof. Brad. *Department of Physics and Physical Oceanography, Memorial University, St. John's, Newfoundland, Canada.* OCEAN PHYSICAL-BIOLOGICAL MODELS—coauthored.

Dickens, Dr. Gerard. *James Cook University, School of Earth Sciences, Townsville, Queensland, Australia.* LATEST PALEOCENE THERMAL MAXIMUM.

Domínquez, Angel. *Departamento de Microbiología y Genética, Instituto de Microbiología Bioquímica, Universidad de Salamanca, Spain.* YEAST FUNCTIONAL ANALYSIS—coauthored.

Doyle, Dr. John M. *Physics Department, Harvard University, Cambridge, Massachusetts.* ULTRACOLD MOLECULES—coauthored.

E

Ehrfeld, Dr. Wolfgang. *Institut für Mikrotechnik Mainz, Mainz, Germany.* CHEMICAL MICROREACTORS—coauthored.

Ellison, Rachel. *Department of Geology and Geological Engineering, University of Idaho, Moscow, Idaho.* VOLCANO—coauthored.

Entry, Dr. James A. *U.S. Department of Agriculture—Agricultural Research Services, Kimberly, Idaho.* FUNGI—coauthored.

Erickson, Dr. Lori A. *Resident in Pathology, Department of Laboratory Medicine and Pathology, Mayo Clinic, Rochester, Minnesota.* CELL CYCLE (CANCER)—coauthored.

F

Fagan, Dr. William F. *Department of Biology, Arizona State University, Tempe.* BIODIVERSITY.

Fahnline, Dr. John B. *Research Associate, Applied Research Laboratory, Pennsylvania State University, University Park.* ACOUSTIC EQUIVALENT SOURCE METHOD—coauthored.

Fang-Yen, Chris. *G. R. Harrison Spectroscopy Laboratory, Massachusetts Institute of Technology, Cambridge.* Single-atom laser—coauthored.

Farkas, Dr. Daniel F. *Department of Food Science and Technology, Oregon State University, Corvallis.* High-pressure food processing.

Feld, Prof. Michael S. *G. R. Harrison Spectroscopy Laboratory, Massachusetts Institute of Technology, Cambridge.* Single-atom laser—coauthored.

Fermiñán, Encarnación. *Departamento de Microbiología y Genética, Instituto de Microbiología Bioquímica, Universidad de Salamanca, Spain.* Yeast functional analysis—coauthored.

Fernie, Dr. Donald. *Professor Emeritus of Astronomy, University of Toronto, and David Dunlap Observatory, Richmond Hill, Ontario, Canada.* Transit (astronomy).

Fleming, Dr. Robert J. *Associate Professor, Department of Biology, University of Rochester, New York.* Notch signaling.

Fogel, Dr. David B. *Natural Selection, Inc., La Jolla, California.* Evolutionary computation.

Follett, Dr. Ronald F. *U.S. Department of Agriculture—Agricultural Research Service, Fort Collins, Colorado.* Carbon sequestration—in part.

Forman, Dr. Barry. *Assistant Professor, Molecular Medicine, City of Hope National Medical Center and Beckman Research Institute, Gonda Diabetes Research Center, Department of Molecular Medicine, Duarte, California.* Nuclear hormone receptors.

Fowler, Dr. Frank W. *Department of Chemistry, State University of New York, Stony Brook.* Macromolecules.

Franklin, Dr. Stanley P. *Math Sciences Department, University of Memphis, Tennessee.* Consciousness.

Friis, Dr. Else Marie. *Professor and Head of Department, Department of Paleobotany, Swedish Museum of Natural History, Stockholm, Sweden.* Angiosperms—coauthored.

Fritschel, Dr. Peter. *Massachusetts Institute of Technology, Cambridge.* Gravitational radiation.

Frodge, Sally L. *U.S. Department of Transportation, Washington, DC.* Time synchronization.—coauthored.

Fujita, Dr. Etsuko. *Brookhaven National Laboratory, Chemistry Department, Upton, New York.* Carbon dioxide reduction.

G

Gage, Dr. Fred H. *Professor, Salk Institute, Laboratory of Genetics, La Jolla, California.* Neurogenesis—coauthored.

Garey, Dr. James R. *Department of Biology, University of South Florida, Tampa.* Invertebrate evolution.

Gaub, Prof. Hermann. *Lehrstuhl für Angewandte Physik, Ludwig-Maximilians-Universität München.* Chemical bond—coauthored.

Geist, Dr. Dennis J. *Department of Geology and Geological Engineering, University of Idaho, Moscow, Idaho.* Volcano—coauthored.

Getz, Dr. Godfrey S. *Professor and Chairman, Department of Pathology, University of Chicago, Illinois.* Lipoprotein.

Golub, Dr. Leon. *Harvard-Smithsonian Center for Astrophysics, Cambridge, Massachusetts.* Sun.

Grandbois, Dr. Michel. *Assistant Professor, Department of Physics and Astronomy, University of Missouri-Columbia, Missouri.* Chemical bond—coauthored.

Grantz, Dr. David A. *Director, Kearney Agricultural Center, University of California, Parlier.* Air pollution—in part.

Greenspan, Prof. Ehud. *Professor-in-Residence, Department of Nuclear Engineering, University of California, Berkeley.* Nuclear reactor—in part.

Greytak, Prof. Thomas J. *Associate Department Head for Education, Department of Physics, Massachusetts Institute of Technology, Cambridge.* Bose-Einstein condensation—coauthored.

Gruen, Prof. Armin. *Institute of Geodesy and Photogrammetry, Eidgenössische Technische Hochschule (ETH), Zurich.* Photogrammetry.

Gumbsch, Dr. Peter. *Max-Planck-Institut für Metallforschung, Stuttgart, Germany.* Supersonic dislocations.

H

Haggerty, Dr. Stephen E. *Department of Geosciences, University of Massachusetts, Amherst.* Diamond.

Hale, Dr. Rick. *Assistant Professor, Aerospace Technology, University of Kansas, Lawrence.* Composite structures.

Hamielec, Prof. Archie E. *Department of Chemical Engineering, McMaster University, Hamilton, Ontario, Canada.* Metallocene catalysts—coauthored.

Harris, Dr. Ruth A. *U.S. Geological Survey, Menlo Park, California.* Earthquake.

Hayes, Sean A. *Department of Biology and Institute of Marine Science, University of California, Santa Cruz.* Underwater acoustic pollution—coauthored.

Heer, Daniel. *Lucent Technologies, Bell Labs Innovations, North Andover, Massachusetts.* Electronic security.

Hendrikse, Dr. Jan. *Toronto, Ontario, Canada.* MOSFET sensors.

Hershkovitz, Dr. Israel. *Department of Anatomy and Anthropology, Sackler Faculty of Medicine, Tel Aviv University, Tel Aviv, Israel.* Paleopathology—coauthored.

Hu, Dr. Jianying. *Lucent Technologies Bell Labs, Murray Hill, New Jersey.* Electronic mail—coauthored.

Huber, John. *Lips Jets BV, Drunen, The Netherlands.* Waterjets.

Hyde, Prof. Kevin D. *Director, Centre for Research in Fungal Diversity, Department of Ecology and Biodiversity, University of Hong Kong.* Fungal diversity.

I

Itano, Dr. Wayne M. *National Institute of Standards and Technology, Boulder, Colorado.* CRYSTALLINE PLASMA.

Izpisúa Belmonte, Dr. Juan Carlos. *Associate Professor, Salk Institute for Biological Studies, Gene Expression Laboratory, La Jolla, California.* ASYMMETRY—coauthored.

J

Jones, Dr. Gareth E. *Professor of Cell Biology, Randall Institute, King's College, London, United Kingdom.* CELL MOTILITY.

Juric, Prof. Damir. *Assistant Professor, George W. Woodruff School of Mechanical Engineering, Georgia Institute of Technology, Atlanta.* BOILING.

K

Kadak, Prof. Andrew C. *Department of Nuclear Engineering, Massachusetts Institute of Technology, Cambridge.* NUCLEAR REACTOR—in part.

Kan, Amy T. *Department of Environmental Science and Engineering, Rice University, Houston, Texas.* ECOLOGICAL AND HUMAN HEALTH—coauthored.

Kellogg, Prof. Louise. *Professor and Vice-Chair, Department of Geology, University of California, Davis.* EARTH MANTLE.

Kemp, Prof. Richard B. *Institute of Biological Sciences, University of Wales, Penglais, Aberystwyth, United Kingdom.* THERMODYNAMICS (BIOLOGY).

Kennedy, Dr. Ronald C. *Department of Microbiology and Immunology, University of Oklahoma Health Sciences Center, Oklahoma City.* VACCINE—coauthored.

Kiesewalter, Dr. Stefan. *Institut für Mikrotechnik Mainz, Wissenschaftlich-technische Koordination, Mainz, Germany.* CHEMICAL MICROREACTORS—coauthored.

Kleppner, Prof. Daniel. *Department of Physics, Massachusetts Institute of Technology, Cambridge.* BOSE-EINSTEIN CONDENSATION—coauthored.

Kletz, Dr. Trevor A. *Process Safety Consultant, Cheadle, Cheshire, United Kingdom.* CHEMICAL PROCESS SAFETY.

Koopmann, Dr. Gary H. *Distinguished Professor of Mechanical Engineering, Pennsylvania State University, University Park.* ACOUSTIC EQUIVALENT SOURCE METHOD—coauthored.

Kuo, Prof. Yue. *Dow Professor of Chemical Engineering and Electrical Engineering, Department of Chemical Engineering, Texas A&M University, College Station.* SOLID-STATE DEVICES.

L

Lal, Prof. Rattan. *Ohio State University, School of Natural Resources, Columbus.* AIR POLLUTION—in part.

Launder, Prof. Brian E. *Department of Mechanical Engineering, Thermodynamics and Fluid Mechanics Division, University of Manchester Institute of Technology, Manchester, United Kingdom.* TURBULENCE MODELING.

Layer, David. *National Associations of Broadcasters, Washington, DC.* RADIO BROADCASTING—in part.

Ledbetter, Tim. *Pacific Northwest National Laboratory, Richland, Washington.* MINING POLLUTION.

Lee-Thorp, Dr. Julia. *Department of Archaeology, University of Cape Town, Rondebosch, South Africa.* STABLE ISOTOPE.

Leibovitch, Dr. Evan. *Starnix, Brampton, Ontario, Canada.* OPEN SOURCE SOFTWARE.

Lele, Prof. Sanjiva K. *Department of Aeronautics and Astronautics and Mechanical Engineering, Stanford University, California.* COMPUTATIONAL AEROACOUSTICS.

Lerner, Dr. Richard A. *Skaggs Institute for Chemical Biology, and Department of Molecular Biology, Scripps Research Institute, La Jolla, California.* CATALYTIC ANTIBODIES—coauthored.

Letcher, Prof. Trevor M. *Department of Chemistry and Applied Chemistry, University of Natal, Dalbridge, South Africa.* CHEMICAL SEPARATION; ENVIRONMENTAL POLLUTION.

Levin, Dr. Richard I. *Associate Dean, Professor, and Director, Laboratory for Cardiovascular Research, and Director, Training Program in Cardiology, New York University School of Medicine, New York.* ATHEROSCLEROSIS.

Levine, Prof. William S. *Department of Electrical Engineering, University of Maryland, College Park.* HYBRID CONTROL.

Lipowsky, Prof. Dr. Reinhard. *Managing Director, Abteilung Theorie, Max-Planck-Institut of Colloids and Interfaces, Golm, Germany.* WETTING (CHEMISTRY).

Lloyd, Dr. Ricardo V. *Professor of Pathology, Department of Laboratory Medicine and Pathology, Mayo Clinic, Rochester, Minnesota.* CELL CYCLE (CANCER)—coauthored.

Loague, Prof. Keith. *Department of Geological and Environmental Sciences, Stanford University, Stanford, California.* NONPOINT SOURCE POLLUTION.

López Cuesta, Dr. M. Carmen. *Departamento de Microbiología y Genética, Instituto de Microbiología Bioquímica, Universidad de Salamanca, Spain.* YEAST FUNCTIONAL ANALYSIS—coauthored.

Lopresti, Dr. Daniel. *Bell Laboratories, Lucent Technologies, Inc., Murray Hill, New Jersey.* INFORMATION RETRIEVAL—coauthored.

M

McCarley, Dr. Robert W. *Department of Psychiatry, Harvard Medical School, and Brockton VA Medical Center, Brockton, Massachusetts.* SLEEP—coauthored.

McCusker, Dr. Lynne B. *Laboratorium für Kristallographie, Eidgenössische Technische Hochschule (ETH), Zürich, Switzerland.* X-RAY CRYSTALLOGRAPHY—coauthored.

McGeer, Tad. *Insitu Group, Bingen, Washington.* AUTONOMOUS AIRCRAFT—coauthored.

McKinney, Dr. Frank K. *Department of Geology, Appalachian State University, Boone, North Carolina.* BRYOZOA (PALEO-ECOLOGY).

Maeda, Dr. Fumiko. *Laboratory for Magnetic Brain Stimulation, Department of Neurology, Beth Israel Deaconess Medical Center, Harvard Medical School, Boston, Massachusetts.* TRANSCRANIAL MAGNETIC STIMULATION—coauthored.

Maher, Dr. Barbara A. *Centre for Environmental Magnetism and Palaeomagnetism, School of Environmental Sciences, University of East Anglia, Norwich, United Kingdom.* LOESS.

Maisey, Dr. John G. *Axelrod Research Chair, Division of Paleontology, American Museum of Natural History, New York.* SHARK.

Martin, Prof. Dr. W. *Institut für Botanik III, Heinrich-Heine Universität Düsseldorf, Germany.* HORIZONTAL GENE TRANSFER—in part.

Massare, Dr. Judy A. *Department of Earth Sciences, SUNY College at Brockport, New York.* MARINE REPTILES.

Michalopoulos, Dr. George K. *Professor and Chairman, Department of Pathology, University of Pittsburgh School of Medicine, Pittsburgh, Pennsylvania.* LIVER REGENERATION.

Miller, Dr. James S. *Associate Curator and Head, Applied Research Department, Missouri Botanical Garden, St. Louis.* BIOPROSPECTING.

Mitchell, Jeffrey C. *Orlando, Florida.* SPACE TECHNOLOGY.

Moon, Dr. Randall T. *Investigator, Howard Hughes Medical Institute, Department of Pharmacology, University of Washington, Seattle.* CANCER—coauthored.

Moore, Ellen. *Department of Environmental Science and Engineering, Rice University, Houston, Texas.* ECOLOGICAL AND HUMAN HEALTH—coauthored.

Moore, Dr. Patrick. *Selsey, Sussex, United Kingdom.* ASTRO-NOMICAL CATALOGS.

Morales, Dr. Juan Carlos. *Center for Environmental Research and Conservation, Columbia University, New York.* PRIMATE BEHAVIOR.

Morison, Dr. James. *Polar Science Center, Applied Physics Laboratory, University of Washington, Seattle.* ARCTIC OSCILLATION.

N

Naumann, Dr. Michael. *European Southern Observatory, Garching bei München.* VERY LARGE TELESCOPE—coauthored.

Nellessen, Prof. Paula Donnelly. *Department of Biology, Albuquerque Technical-Vocational Institute, Albuquerque, New Mexico.* FUNGI—coauthored.

Nelson, Dr. Stanley F. *Assistant Professor of Pediatrics, UCLA Medical Center, Los Angeles, California.* DEOXYRIBONUCLEIC ACID (DNA) MICOARRAYS.

Newell, Dr. Charles J. *Groundwater Services, Inc., Houston, Texas.* RISK-BASED ENVIRONMENTAL RESTORATION—coauthored.

Noble, Alan. *Felton, North Somerset, United Kingdom.* BALLOON.

O–P

O'Craven, Dr. Kathy M. *Center for Ophthalmic Research, Brigham and Women's Hospital, Boston, Masschusetts.* ATTENTION—coauthored.

O'Toole, Dr. George. *Assistant Professor, Department of Microbiology, Dartmouth Medical School, Hanover, New Hampshire.* BIOFILM.

Pascual-Leone, Dr. Alvaro. *Laboratory for Magnetic Brain Stimulation, Department of Neurology, Beth Israel Deaconess Medical Center, Harvard Medical School, Boston, Massachusetts.* TRANSCRANIAL MAGNETIC STIMULATION—coauthored.

Patzkowsky, Prof. Mark E. *Assistant Professor, Department of Geosciences, Pennsylvania State University, University Park.* BACKGROUND EXTINCTION.

Pedersen, Prof. Kaj Raunsgaard. *Department of Geology, University of Aarhus, Denmark.* ANGIOSPERMS—coauthored.

Peterson, Dr. Michael P. *Editor, Cartographic Perspectives; Chair, International Cartographic Association Commission on Maps and the Internet; and Professor, Department of Geography/Geology, University of Nebraska, Omaha.* CARTOGRAPHIC ANIMATION.

Poole, Dr. R. Keith. *Professor, Department of Microbiology and Immunology, Queen's University, Kingston, Ontario, Canada.* DRUG EFFLUX PUMPS.

Pósfai, Dr. Mihály. *Department of Earth and Environmental Sciences, University of Veszprém, Veszprém, Hungary.* BACTERIAL MAGNETIC MINERALS—coauthored.

Powell, Prof. Thomas M. *Department of Integrative Biology, University of California, Berkeley.* OCEAN PHYSICAL-BIOLOGICAL MODELS—coauthored.

Presley, Dr. John F. *Cell Biology and Metabolism Branch, National Institute of Child Health and Human Development, Bethesda, Maryland.* GREEN FLUORESCENT PROTEIN.

Price, Dr. Evelyn J. *Berkeley Seismological Lab, University of California, Berkeley.* RADAR INTERFEROMETRY.

Q–R

Quéré, Dr. David. *Physique de la Matière Condensée, Collège de France, Paris.* FLUID COATING.

Rafferty, Brian P. *New York, New York.* SEASONAL AFFECTIVE DISORDER—coauthored.

Reeder, Dr. Jean D. *U.S. Department of Agriculture—Agricultural Research Service, Crops Research Laboratory, Fort Collins, Colorado.* CARBON SEQUESTRATION—coauthored.

Regetz, Dr. Jim. *Department of Ecology and Evolutionary Biology, Princeton University, Princeton, New Jersey.* SALMON.

Reicosky, Dr. Donald C. *Soil Scientist, U.S. Department of Agriculture—Agricultural Research Service, North Central Soil Conservation Research Laboratory, Morris, Minnesota.* CARBON SEQUESTRATION—in part.

Retallack, Dr. Gregory J. *Department of Geological Sciences, University of Oregon, Eugene.* PALEOSOLS.

Richardson, Dr. Michael K. *Senior Lecturer in Anatomy and Developmental Biology, Department of Anatomy and Development Biology, St. George's Hospital Medical School, Cranmer Terrace, London, United Kingdom.* DEVELOPMENTAL SEQUENCES.

Rietmeijer, Dr. Frans J. M. *Institute of Meteoritics, Department of Earth and Planetary Sciences, University of New Mexico.* INTERPLANETARY DUST PARTICLES.

Rothschild, Dr. Bruce M. *Arthritis Center of Northeast Ohio, Northeastern Ohio Universities College of Medicine, and Carnegie Museum of Natural History, Youngstown, Ohio.* PALEOPATHOLOGY—coauthored.

Rowen, Alan. *New York, New York.* MARINE ENGINE.

Ruiz-Trillo, Dr. Iñaki. *Departament de Genètica, Facultat de Biologia, Universitat de Barcelona, Spain.* ACOELA.

Ryan, Dr. Aimee. *University of California, Michael G. Rosenfeld Lab, La Jolla, California.* ASYMMETRY—coauthored.

S

Sachdev, D. K. *Senior Vice President, Engineering and Operations, WorldSpace Corp., Washington, DC.* RADIO BROADCASTING—in part.

Sánchez, Manuel. *Departamento de Microbiología y Genética, Instituto de Microbiología Bioquímica, Universidad de Salamanca, Spain.* YEAST FUNCTIONAL ANALYSIS—coauthored.

Santos, Dr. Fabrício R. *Departamento de Biologia Geral, ICB/UNFMG, Belo Horizonte, Brazil.* HUMAN MIGRATIONS—coauthored.

Scardovelli, Dr. Ruben. *DIENCA, Lab. di Montecuccolino, Bologna, Italy.* DIRECT NUMERICAL SIMULATION—coauthored.

Schimmel, Dr. Paul. *Skaggs Institute of Chemical Biology, Scripps Research Institute, Beckman Center, La Jolla, California.* MULTIFUNCTIONAL PROTEINS.

Schiraldi, Prof. Alberto. *Dipartimento di Scienze e Tecnologie Alimentari e Microbiologiche, Università degli Studi de Milano, Milan, Italy.* FOOD SCIENCE.

Schuman, Dr. Gerald E. *U.S. Department of Agriculture—Agricultural Research Service, High Plains Grassland Research Station, Cheyenne, Wyoming.* CARBON SEQUESTRATION—coauthored.

Schwarz, Dr. Joshua. *Physicist, National Institute of Standards and Technology, Gaithersburg, Maryland.* GRAVITATIONAL CONSTANT.

Seidel, Dr. George E., Jr. *Animal Reproduction and Biotechnology Laboratory, Colorado State University, Fort Collins,* CLONING (GENETICS).

Shabat, Doron. *Skaggs Institute for Chemical Biology, and Department of Molecular Biology, Scripps Research Institute, La Jolla, California.* CATALYTIC ANTIBODIES—coauthored.

Shapiro, Dr. Jerry. *University of British Columbia, Vancouver, British Columbia, Canada.* HAIR LOSS—coauthored.

Shearer, M. H. *Department of Microbiology and Immunology, University of Oklahoma Health Sciences Center, Oklahoma City.* VACCINE—coauthored.

Shedlock, Dr. Kaye M. *U.S. Department of the Interior, U.S. Geological Survey, Geological Hazards, Denver Federal Center, Denver, Colorado.* INTRAPLATE EARTHQUAKES.

Shi, Dr. Donglu. *Department of Materials Science and Engineering, University of Cincinnati, Ohio.* SUPERCONDUCTIVITY.

Shihabuddin, Dr. Lamya S. *Postdoctoral Fellow, Salk Institute, Laboratory of Genetics, La Jolla, California.* NEUROGENESIS—coauthored.

Sinton, Dr. Christopher M. *Department of Psychiatry, Harvard Medical School, and Brockton VA Medical Center, Brockton, Massachusetts.* SLEEP—coauthored.

Sitomer, James. *Draper Laboratories, Cambridge, Massachusetts.* GUIDANCE SYSTEMS.

Smith, Dr. Michael S. *Leader, Nuclear Astrophysics Research Group, Physics Division, Oak Ridge National Laboratory, Oak Ridge, Tennessee.* RADIOACTIVE BEAMS.

Soares, Dr. Joao B. P. *Institute for Polymer Research, Department of Chemical Engineering, University of Waterloo, Ontario, Canada.* METALLOCENE CATALYSTS—coauthored.

Soini, Dr. Ylermi. *Department of Pathology, University of Oulu, Kajaanintie, Finland.* APOPTOSIS.

Solounias, Dr. Nikos. *Department of Anatomy, New York College of Osteopathic Medicine, Old Westbury, New York.* GIRAFFE.

Soltis, Dr. Douglas E. *Department of Botany, Washington State University, Pullman.* SYSTEMATICS—coauthored.

Soltis, Dr. Pamela S. *Department of Botany, Washington State University, Pullman.* SYSTEMATICS—coauthored.

Song, Prof. Pill-Soon. *Dow Chemical Professor, Department of Chemistry, University of Nebraska, Lincoln.* PHOTOTAXIS.

Spencer, Dr. Jack. *Vice President, American Bureau of Shipping, Houston, Texas.* SHIP DESIGN.

Sproat, Dr. Richard. *Human-Computer Interface Research, AT&T Labs—Research, Shannon Laboratory, Florham Park, New Jersey.* ELECTRONIC MAIL—coauthored.

Stephen, Dr. Antonia E. *Research Fellow, Laboratory of Tissue Engineering and Organ Fabrication, Massachusetts General Hospital, Boston.* TISSUE ENGINEERING—coauthored.

T

Tanese, Dr. Naoko. *Department of Microbiology, New York University School of Medicine, New York.* TRANSCRIPTION—coauthored.

Tanimoto, Prof. Toshiro. *Professor of Geophysics, Department of Geological Sciences, University of California, Santa Barbara.* EARTH OSCILLATION.

Terman, Dr. Michael. *Director, New York Psychiatric Institute, Clinical Chronobiology Program, College of Physicians and Surgeons of Columbia University, New York.* SEASONAL AFFECTIVE DISORDER—coauthored.

Thomson, Prof. Keith S. *Director, Oxford University Museum of Natural History, Parks Road, Oxford, England.* COELACANTHS.

Thorpe, Dr. Chris. *Associate, Howard Hughes Medical Institute, Department of Pharmacology, University of Washington, Seattle.* CANCER—coauthored.

Tomson, Dr. Mason B. *Professor, Department of Environmental Science and Engineering, Rice University, Houston, Texas.* ECOLOGICAL AND HUMAN HEALTH—coauthored.

Tyler-Smith, Dr. Chris. *Department of Biochemistry, University of Oxford, South Parks, Oxford, United Kingdom.* HUMAN MIGRATIONS—coauthored.

V

Vacanti, Dr. Joseph P. *John Homans Professor of Surgery, Director, Laboratory of Tissue Engineering and Organ Fabrication, Massachusetts General Hospital, Boston.* TISSUE ENGINEERING—coauthored.

Vagner, Dr. Juris. *Department of Aeronautics and Astronautics, University of Washington, Seattle.* AUTONOMOUS AIRCRAFT—coauthored.

Vander Heuvel, Dr. John P. *Center for Molecular Toxicology, Pennylvania State University, University Park.* NUCLEAR RECEPTOR.

van der Hilst, Prof. Rob. *Associate Professor of Geophysics, Department of Earth Atmospheric and Planetary Sciences, Massachusetts Institute of Technology, Cambridge.* SEISMIC TOMOGRAPHY.

Vignona, Laine. *Department of Environmental Science and Engineering, Rice University, Houston, Texas.* ECOLOGICAL AND HUMAN HEALTH—coauthored.

Vincent, Prof. Colin A. *School of Chemistry, University of St. Andrews, St. Andrews, Fife, Scotland.* LITHIUM BATTERIES.

von Puttkamer, Dr. Jesco. *Office of Space Flight, NASA Headquarters, Washington, DC.* SPACE FLIGHT.

Vorder Bruegge, Dr. Richard W. *Special Photographic Unit, Federal Bureau of Investigation, Washington, DC.* DIGITAL IMAGING (FORENSICS).

W

Waggoner, Dr. Ben. *Department of Biology, University of Central Arkansas, Conway.* EVOLUTION.

Wagner, Dr. Frederic H. *Ecology Center, Utah State University, Logan.* INTRASPECIFIC VARIATION.

Watts, A. M. *Department of Microbiology and Immunology, University of Oklahoma Health Sciences Center, Oklahoma City.* VACCINE—coauthored.

Weinstein, Dr. Jonathan David. *Physics Department, Harvard University, Cambridge, Massachusetts.* ULTRACOLD MOLECULES—coauthored.

Weir, Prof. Ron D. *Department of Chemistry and Chemical Engineering, Royal Military College of Canada, Kingston, Ontario, Canada.* ADVANCED MATERIALS.

Wessel, Dr. Thomas. *Laboratorium für Kristallographie, Eidgenössische Technische Hochschule (ETH), Zürich, Switzerland.* X-RAY CRYSTALLOGRAPHY—coauthored.

West, Dr. Richard. *European Southern Observatory, Garching bei München.* VERY LARGE TELESCOPE—coauthored.

Westermarck, Dr. Jukka. *European Molecular Biology Laboratory, Heidelberg, Germany.* ENZYME.

White, Dr. Arthur F. *Research Hydrologist, National Research Program, U.S. Geological Survey, Menlo Park.* WEATHERING OF SILICATE MINERALS.

White, Dr. Morris F. *Howard Hughes Medical Institute, Joslin Diabetes Center, Boston, Massachusetts.* INSULIN.

Widder, Dr. Edith A. *Senior Scientist, Harbor Branch Oceanographic Institution, Fort Pierce, Florida.* BIOLUMINESCENCE.

Wildman, Dr. Howard G. *Biotic Resources, ExGenix Operations Pty. Ltd., Victoria, Australia.* FUNGI (MEDICINE).

Wilfong, Dr. Gordon. *Bell Laboratories, Lucent Technologies, Inc., Murray Hill, New Jersey.* INFORMATION RETRIEVAL—coauthored.

Wilson, Dr. Angus C. *Department of Microbiology, New York University School of Medicine, New York.* TRANSCRIPTION—coauthored.

Wolfe, Dr. Jeremy M. *Associate Professor of Ophthalmology, Harvard Medical School, Center for Ophthalmic Research, Brigham and Women's Hospital, Boston, Massachusetts.* ATTENTION—coauthored.

X–Y

Xing, Lianping. *Department of Pathology and Laboratory Medicine, University of Rochester Medical Center, Rochester, New York.* BONE—coauthored.

Yost, Dr. William A. *Director and Professor of Hearing Sciences, Parmly Hearing Institute, Loyola University, Chicago, Illinois.* PRECEDENCE EFFECT (HEARING).

Yu, Chung-Chieh. *G.R. Harrison Spectroscopy Laboratory, Massachusetts Institute of Technology, Cambridge.* SINGLE-ATOM LASER—coauthored.

Z

Zaleski, Stephane. *DIENCA, Lab. di Montecuccolino, Bologna, Italy.* DIRECT NUMERICAL SIMULATION—coauthored.

Zeilinger, Prof. Anton. *Institut für Experimentalphysik, University of Vienna, Austria.* QUANTUM TELEPORTATION.

Zonge, Dr. Kenneth L. *Zonge Engineering and Research Organization, Inc., Tucson, Arizona.* PROSPECTING.

Asterisks indicate page references to article titles.

A

ABC (ATP-binding cassette family), 131
Absolute zero, 64
Acanthocephala, 217
Accidents (chemical process safety), 95
ACE (Advanced Composition Explorer), 362
Achiral cyclopentadienyl catalysts, 243
Acid mine drainage, 173
Acid precipitation:
   nonpoint source pollution, 273
   silicate minerals, weathering of, 422–423
Acidianus brierleyi, 55
Acoela, 1–3*
   molecular systematics, 2
   phylogenetic analysis, 2–3
Aconitase, 265
Acoustic arrays, 248
Acoustic equivalent source methods, 3–6*
   boundary methods, 3–4
   demonstration problem, 5–6
   inverse source methods, 4
   quiet machinery, design of, 4–5
Acoustic feedback, 110
Acoustic Thermometry of the Ocean Climate (ATOC), 406–407
Acoustics:
   acoustic equivalent source methods, 3–6*
   computational aeroacoustics, 107–111*
   precedence effect, 308
   underwater acoustic pollution, 405–407*
ACRIMSAT (Active Cavity Radiometer Irradiance Monitor Satellite), 364
Acritarchs, 154
Actins, 87, 88

Activation energy, 271
Active Cavity Radiometer Irradiance Monitor Satellite (ACRIMSAT), 364
ADCC (antibody-dependent cell-mediated cytotoxicity), 409
Adenosine, 348
Adenosine diphosphate (ADP), 103
Adenosine triphosphate (ATP), 103
   drug efflux pumps, 131
   thermodynamics (biology), 384
   transcription, 395
ADEOS satellite, 362
ADEPT *see* Antibody-directed enzyme prodrug therapy
ADP (adenosine diphosphate), 103
Adrenal hormones, 270
Adriosaurs, 350
ADSL *see* Asymmetrical digital subscriber line
Advanced Composition Explorer (ACE), 362
Advanced Encryption Standard (AES), 148
Advanced materials, 6–8*
   applications, 6
   thermodynamics, 6–7
   transition-metal chalcogenides, 7–8
   transition-metal silicides (ceramics), 7
Advanced Research and Global Observation Satellite (ARGOS), 364
Aequorea victoria:
   green fluorescent protein (GFP), 182, 183
   yeast functional analysis, 433
Aequorin, 183
Aeroacoustics *see* Computational aeroacoustics
Aerobic respiration, evolution of, 154
Aerosondes, 36–38

AES (Advanced Encryption Standard), 148
Afanasyev, Viktor, 364, 365
Afar rift, 134
Africa:
   global satellite digital broadcasting, 326, 327
   sharks, 343
AfriStar satellite, 324, 326
Aftershocks (earthquakes), 137
Aggregate interplanetary dust particles, 209, 210
Agriculture:
   air pollution, 12–14
   carbon sequestration, 75–76
   nonpoint source pollution, 273, 274
   stable isotope, 369
AIDS, 408, 410
Aigialosaurs, 350
Air bags, automobile, 246
Air-breathing engines, 203
Air-breathing rockets, 367
Air pollution, 8–14*
   agriculture, 12–13
   atmospheric pool, 9–10
   biogenetic hydrocarbon emissions, 14
   biotic pool, 11
   carbon, 8–9
   carbon emission, 11–12
   crops, effects on, 12–14
   nonpoint source pollution, 273
   soil carbon pool, 10–11
   uptake of pollutants, 14
Air quality, 15–17*
   ozone, 15–16
   particulate matter, 16–17
Air-traffic control, 45
Alagille syndrome, 276
Alcatel Space Industries, 325
Aleut-Eskimos, 198–199
Alkylaluminums, 245
Allelic frequency, 214